THIRTEENTH APOSTLE

AMASA MASON LYMAN

THIRTEENTH APOSTLE

The Diaries of Amasa M. Lyman | 1832–1877

Scott H. Partridge, editor

Signature Books | 2016 | Salt Lake City

SIGNATURE LEGACY SERIES

design by Jason Francis

frontispiece: Lyman as a missionary in New Hampshire, from Orson F. Whitney's 1892 *History of Utah*, 1:301

 Printed on acid-free paper and composed, printed, and bound in the USA. www.signaturebooks.com

21 20 19 18 17 16 6 5 4 3 2 1

LIBRARY OF CONGRESS CATALOGING-IN-PUBLICATION DATA

Names: Lyman, Amasa M. (Amasa Mason), 1813–1877, author. | Partridge, Scott H., editor.
Title: Thirteenth Apostle : The Diaries of Amasa M. Lyman, 1832–1877 / edited by Scott H. Partridge.
Description: Salt Lake City : Signature Books, 2016. | Includes bibliographical references and index.
Identifiers: LCCN 2016012293 | ISBN 9781560852360 (alk. paper)
Subjects: LCSH: Lyman, Amasa M. (Amasa Mason), 1813-1877—Diaries. | Mormon Church—Apostles—Diaries. | Mormon missionaries—Diaries.
Classification: LCC BX8695.L92 A3 2016 | DDC 289.3092—dc23 LC record available at http://lccn.loc.gov/2016012293

CONTENTS

Publisher's note

As we began preparing this volume for publication—proofing the typescript against the original diaries, fact-checking, and typesetting through chapter 3—all in collaboration with the compiler and editor Scott Partridge, we were shocked to learn in September 2015 that Scott had suddenly died at age eighty-five. A few days later, he was buried at the San Joaquin National Cemetery in California in an achingly beautiful setting and a send-off that was touching. We heard from his widow Nadine and sons Brad and Stephen, both at the time and afterward, that they were committed to seeing this project through to the end since it had meant so much to Scott.

It is hard to imagine the amount of time the compiler and editor devoted to the diaries, sitting in isolation in the Church History Library archives transcribing endless diaries using the permitted pencil and legal pad. Someone with less experience with such documents would not be able to decipher the handwriting or understand the context, so we are beneficiaries of his unwavering commitment and knowledge. The first sign of his persistence was convincing the archivists that he, as a descendant of the controversial apostle, should be allowed to see what was at the time considered sensitive material.

To illustrate how times change, midway through the project the church decided to make the Amasa Lyman Collection available to researchers as part of its limited edition of seventy-eight DVDs entitled *Selected Collections*, after which Scott was able to work from his home in Patterson to finish the transcription. By the time Signature Books was ready to devote resources to the project, the LDS Church History Library had posted scans of the diaries online as part of its expanded public resources.

Continuing with the pre-press preparation of the manuscript following Scott's death, several people in the office devoted months to continuing where he left off, to guarantee that the quality of the manuscript remained consistent throughout. From inside the office, John

Hatch proofed the entire transcript against the online scans. He and Ron Priddis picked up with the annotation where Scott had left off, while from outside the office we enlisted the help of copy editor Bryan Buchanan in proofing the galleys, including double-checking against the online scans when necessary. We think the resulting product would have made Scott proud.

There is one thing that would have disappointed him, since he envisioned a volume that would have included some of Lyman's correspondence and sermons, as well as diaries. As we discussed ways to keep the page count down, it became inevitable that the letters and speeches would have to wait for another day. We are pleased, however, that even though the book approaches 1,000 pages we were able to retain Scott's plan of presenting the diaries in full. Readers will find that, through both the suspenseful parts and mundane records of day-to-day routines, the life and reflections of Scott's ancestor are remarkably fascinating—especially the overall arc of the subject's life from Mormon apostle to séance-enthusiast.

It was a pleasure to work with Scott over the brief time we were acquainted with him. He submitted his manuscript years prior to publication, with the intent that it would be included in our former Significant Mormon Diaries series—something we feel guilty about because he waited patiently as we published other volumes in the series that had already been scheduled to appear ahead of his, while he warned us more than once that we shouldn't put it off too long due to his steadily increasing age. Now we reassure ourselves that he was at least able to see three chapters completed, and the beginnings of the fourth chapter, which he was doing the final corrections to, and that he could see his manuscript would materialize in book form and provide fodder for future generations of Mormon scholars. His introduction, penned long before his death, gives an idea of his generosity of spirit, in how he saw Amasa Lyman as a talented individual, ultimately flawed like the rest of us, doing what he believed to be right, despite what anyone else thought.

Introduction

In October 1862 a large portly man made his way down a wide street in Salt Lake City. Those who passed instantly recognized him, tipped their hats, and offered a hello. The fall weather was pleasant and the day clear for the large crowds gathered at the annual state fair just a few blocks away. But that was not this man's destination. Instead, he stopped in front of the stately Beehive House, turned and went into the side office. He had an audience with the president of the LDS Church, Brigham Young.

Amasa Mason Lyman was forty-nine and had returned a few weeks earlier from a two-year mission to the British Isles. After taking a steamboat to New York and a train through the Midwest, he had ridden a horse across the plains from Nebraska to Utah, the third and final time he would undertake that kind of journey. As he and President Young sat and spoke to each other, their statements of goodwill and outward affection masked the underlying complication in their relationship. Young got to the point: he told Lyman that the time had come for him to settle down, build a permanent home, and care for his large family.

The news came as a shock to Lyman, who reflected that he had been away on various missions for the church for thirty years, and that his health had become unpredictable. He was growing tired, he said. "Altho the reward of the just is slow, it is nevertheless sure," he wrote in his diary.[1] Little could either man predict that within five years, Lyman would be back facing Young, defending himself against a charge of heresy. For his independence in theological matters, he would be removed from the Quorum of the Twelve, and a few years after that he would be formally cut off from the church.

Before his 1870 excommunication, Lyman was many things in the church: one of the early converts, one of the earliest members of the Quorum of Twelve Apostles, a convincing speaker and successful missionary,

1. Diary entry for May 21, 1863, herein.

a pioneer organizer of major settlements, and an advocate of polygamy after Joseph Smith introduced the topic to him. Lyman's extensive journals stretch across a forty-five-year ministry, through his precipitous fall from prominence, and provide a rare insider's look at how Mormonism was advanced through the Southern States, to the West Coast, and across the ocean to the British Isles.

His experiences ranged from unique to widely shared, but he fundamentally defined himself as a missionary, whatever his calling or assignment. His first mission was to win hearts and convert people to the faith. After that, he went throughout the United States collecting funds for the temple, then for the western migration. He went to the gold fields of California to collect tithing. He selected the location and built up the colony of San Bernardino in southern California. He was sent to preach through the vast Utah settlements. He was relied on during the Utah War to reconnoiter the Colorado River. Finally there was his foreign mission, including trips through Ireland, Scotland, Wales, and the Scandinavian countries prior to his last assignment to retire in Fillmore and help build up the onetime territorial capital.

It is little wonder that Lyman's excommunication has puzzled scholars and descendants. His diaries reveal a serious-minded, deeply committed, kind-hearted, empathetic man with a wry sense of humor, whose beliefs and experiences—extensions of what he had been taught as a Mormon convert—came into conflict with the church when he took some of the concepts of Mormon theology to their ultimate conclusion. How unfortunate that the same stubbornness that attracted him to the church is what later caused him to break with his associates. A summary of his life's work may help readers understand the arc of his life as they peruse his diaries, beginning with his birth on a plot of land belonging to his mother's parents in New Hampshire on March 30, 1813. His father, Roswell, left in search of work, possibly to labor on the Erie Canal, and was never heard from again.[2] His mother, Martha, re-married the widower Isaiah Emerson in 1822, and the nine-year-old Amasa struggled to get along with his step-father. It was decided that the boy should live with his grandfather, Perez Mason, until 1824

2. Sheriff, *Artificial River*.

when the old man died and Lyman was shuffled off to live with Uncle Parley Mason.[3]

Two of Mormonism's most prolific missionaries visited the Mason household in 1832: Lyman E. Johnson and Orson Pratt, and they impressed Amasa so much he wanted to be baptized.[4] Not so his uncle, who stated that if the young man joined the Mormons, he would have to leave the house. So at age of nineteen, Amasa made the decision to cast his lot with the missionaries, who said they were building a religious community in Kirtland, Ohio. Having made up his mind, Lyman walked for thirty days across seven hundred miles to the shores of Lake Erie. There he met the man behind the new religion, and before long Lyman found himself seated with the weight of Joseph Smith's hands on his head as he was ordained an elder in the church. For the next thirty-five years of his life, he would engage in an uninterrupted tack of church service stemming from that ordination.

Lyman's first assignment was to search out sympathetic souls in central Ohio and northern Virginia (now West Virginia). For the first time in his life, he picked up a pen and recorded his daily activities in a small diary. He typically did this at the end of the day over candlelight. He returned in February 1833 to Kirtland when rumors were circulating that church members in Missouri were being driven from their homes. Even so, he was told he was needed in upstate New York, and off he went. Returning in 1834, he found Joseph Smith wanted to do something to aid the members in Missouri and raised what he called the Camp of Israel, a militia to rescue what he called Zion.

For Lyman, the experience was one of unfortunate sickness, a manifestation of what became a lifelong malady involving fatigue, fever, and pain that he referred to as the ague (flu) but was probably malaria. When a diplomatic resolution was found to the conflict in Missouri, Lyman trudged back to Ohio with the rest of the men, stopping occasionally to speak to people about their faith. In Kirtland he took advantage of his break in church assignments to marry Maria Louisa Tanner on June 10, 1835. He loved his bride and admired her family, all stalwarts in the church and demonstrating the kind of family cohesion he lacked in his

3. Hefner, "Apostasy of Amasa Mason Lyman," 7.
4. Marquardt and Shepard, *Lost Apostles*, 45.

own family, something he would write about often in his diary. After his excommunication three decades later, Maria Louisa would be the only wife (he had eight) who would stand by him without wavering.

In the spring of 1836, he participated in the religious ceremonies in the new Kirtland temple and "became connected with the Quorum of High Priests."[5] He was called again to mission labors, but returned to be by Maria's side toward the end of 1836 when she gave birth to their girl Matilda. The next eight years saw Lyman survive several highs and lows in church history. For instance, the LDS bank in Ohio collapsed and precipitated a backlash that forced the church out of its Kirtland headquarters. Lyman followed the trail of refugees to Missouri and enjoyed a brief reprieve there before, within two years, he would find himself imprisoned, chained alongside Joseph Smith, about to be expelled from the state. At first he found temporary employment but discovered he was not very good at menial tasks. It foreshadowed his lifelong challenge in providing for his family when most men did so through manual labor and his talents lay elsewhere. Even in places like San Bernardino, where he lived longer than a few months, he was an administrator. He could convert people and manage them, however fleeting the temporal compensation was for that.

On October 11, 1838, during the Mormon War, Lyman ended up in a cell in Richmond, Missouri, with six other high church leaders. When Joseph Smith was transferred to Liberty Jail about thirty miles away, Lyman was released. He caught up with his family in Illinois and enjoyed another stint of relative peace despite a series of short mission assignments. His relationship with Joseph Smith grew stronger. Based on their mutual respect, it made sense that Lyman was ordained to the prestigious position of apostle on August 20, 1842, and given a place in the Quorum of the Twelve. However, it signaled future difficulties when Orson Pratt, who had been removed from the quorum,[6] was restored within months and Lyman had to sit out for a while as an apostle in name only, without any specific responsibilities or authority. He was a third wheel: the thirteenth apostle.

Perhaps in compensation for his temporary demotion, Smith introduced Lyman to the concept of polygamy, saying his public denials

5. Lyman, "Autobiography, 1856."
6. Bergera, *Conflict in the Quorum*, 27.

were a ruse to keep reporters at bay. It was a special obligation for all the elders, Smith said, and Lyman should think about entering into the practice. After Smith's death, Lyman complied by marrying a second wife on September 6, 1844, the seventeen-year-old Caroline Ely Partridge. At thirty-one, Lyman was almost twice as old. Within the month he married Caroline's sister, Eliza Maria Partridge, who had previously been married to Joseph Smith. Eventually Lyman would come to have eight wives and father thirty-seven children.

The fall of Nauvoo brought an end to the short-lived era of relative stability in Illinois. Lyman worked to exhaustion through 1845 in helping to finish the temple and then in preparing to travel west. He married two more plural wives in January 1846: Paulina Eliza Phelps and Priscilla Turley. Paulina was seventeen years old and Priscilla was sixteen. Both young women were stalwarts in the church with parents who were equally strong in the faith. Priscilla's family had come from Canada, and her father, Theodore Turley, had allegedly offered his daughter to Joseph Smith as a wife. If so, it indicated that part of Lyman's allure may have been his status in the church.[7] Lyman was part of the sub-rosa church organization called the Council of Fifty that oversaw the migration west to what is now Florence, a suburb of Omaha, Nebraska; the pioneers called it Winter Quarters.

The trek there in the middle of winter was hard-going. The snow was deep, the winds cold. The Mississippi River was frozen over in some areas and full of treacherous ice chunks in others. Lyman had difficulty putting together enough provisions but managed to be ready when the first company crossed the river on February 1, 1846, his wives (he now had six) all traveling in the group. The landscape was not any better in Iowa. The roads were muddy and a gloomy overcast sky emptied itself periodically on the travelers. Lyman had an infected tooth and was bedridden part of the time.

After several months of struggle, the emigrants staggered into the main camp at Winter Quarters, too exhausted to follow Brigham Young's urging to prepare to push farther west. The vanguard company the next year would not leave until April 1847, and the pioneering group would include Lyman. They crossed Nebraska and Wyoming on their

7. Lyman, *Amasa Mason Lyman*, 90.

way to the Great Basin. In Wyoming, Young sent Lyman on a detour to Pueblo, Colorado, to gather Mormon members of the US Army who had been left their due to sickness and converts from Mississippi who had encountered them. Lyman and a small group of men picked their way through 250 miles of dangerous Indian territory to find the dispirited group, whose members said they were wary of continuing on, and direct them toward the Salt Lake Valley. Many of them became friends for life.

When they reached the valley, it was a few days behind the July 24, 1847, arrival of Brigham Young's company. Lyman helped scout the valley for water and other resources before turning around and heading back with Young to Nebraska to organize subsequent companies of immigrants, leaving the rest of the pioneers behind to survive the winter. When the group reached Winter Quarters, they organized a First Presidency with Brigham Young at the head, and Lyman was sent to the Southern states to organize church members into emigrant parties. He found enough members willing to go to fill several wagon trains, and he directed one of them as far as Winter Quarters. A curiosity about the Southern members was that they brought their slaves with them. Lyman had now traveled more than 3,000 miles from Illinois to Utah and back again, through the South, to Winter Quarters. He had developed a greater understanding of Southern plantation culture and made more lifelong friends. Now he would make a second trip in less than a year to the Great Salt Lake, this time with his family.

Lyman and George A. Smith were assigned as co-captains of one of the companies that left alongside wagon trains led by Brigham Young and Heber C. Kimball in May 1848. The trip was largely uneventful until Lyman experienced another sick spell and had to be relieved by Smith, who merged his group with one led by Willard Richards. A relief column met the two trains at Fort Bridger and helped them into the valley, where Lyman and his three wives found a small single-room cabin with a leaky roof to stay in. It may be that the discomfort of their accommodations played a role in Lyman accepting a call almost immediately to join Porter Rockwell to California. While Lyman was away, his wives joined with some of the Mississippi converts in settling an area about ten miles south in what they called Cottonwood, although the women would have to rely partly on the charity of their neighbors to survive.

Lyman's mission was perilous and arduous. It reflected Brigham Young's ambivalence about the gold fields, which he knew could be exploited for the benefit of the church or ignored because they were the devil's playground. Lyman's immediate assignment was to collect tithing from LDS prospectors and send what he could to church headquarters. He was accompanied on the West Coast by apostle Charles C. Rich, and this began a lifelong association as the two worked their way into the campgrounds and hearts of the LDS men. After collecting all they could, Lyman started back with a company of thirty-four well-armed men on August 17, 1850.

Lyman found his family impoverished, but decided there was not much he could do about it, as part of the pattern whereby he would visit occasionally but not linger. If he was not sent abroad, he would travel through the Mormon corridor on his own initiative, speaking and visiting with the Saints in their communities. When Brigham Young decided that another colony was needed at the southern end of the string of settlements, he called Lyman and Rich to make it happen. Accordingly, the apostles gathered provisions and a few family members on March 11, 1851, and started south for the staging ground where Young wanted to visit the twenty-five families he had called and give them a cheerful word and a good send off. He was met by an unprecedented 437 persons with 150 wagons, all ready to go. His displeasure was pronounced. For a moment, he was speechless, but later he raged that he "was sick at the sight of so many Saints running … after the god of this world (gold)."[8] How Lyman and Rich had let this get out of control was beyond him, and the awkwardness of it created a permanent psychological fissure, the president taking it personally that so many members would rather live among non-Mormons than to abide his leadership.

The 600-mile journey from central Utah to San Bernardino was one of the most difficult ever attempted by nineteenth-century pioneers. The path was uncertain, the water scarce, the feed equally unpredictable. The environment was inhabited by hostile Indians. It included a fifty-mile stretch that lacked any water at all. Over the next five years, Lyman would master the trail as he followed it to and from southern California. The

8. Historian's office, "History of the Church," Mar. 20, 1851.

initial scouting expedition was the most suspenseful. They reached the Cajon Pass in June 1851 and camped on the edge of the Santa Clara Valley while awaiting confirmation of where their permanent location would be. While they waited, they held a conference, organized an ecclesiastical structure, set up a school, and celebrated a wedding. The good times were overshadowed by the scarcity of provisions. Lyman and Rich knew they had to act quickly to negotiate with land owners. Then remembering their previous success in northern California, they went to the gold fields to collect funds from LDS people toward purchase of suitable property.

Young wanted the colonists to find unimproved land that would not cost anything. The problem was that so little good land was left, Lyman and Rich felt compelled to seek out the Californios and finally to buy the Rancho San Bernardino, stirring Young's suspicion that they lacked financial acumen. It was, in fact, difficult for Lyman and Rich to come up with the money: the down payment of $25,000 for the Lugo Brothers and a loan at 2 percent per month for the remaining balance of $52,000. What is more, the ranch contained less than half the acreage promised and unsettled water rights. There were also competing land-grant claims that took months to unravel. Young offered little support, which made it all the more impressive that the two apostles were able to successfully plant the colony and see it thrive.

The colonists erected an outdoor pavilion for meetings, a fort to protect them from unfriendly natives, and a lumber mill in the adjacent mountains with a road through the forests to the mill. The need for lumber was so great that the mill grew into a satellite town. In the valley, people planted gardens outside the fort and cultivated the land for grain. Surveyors were laying out the streets and lots for the future city. On September 4, 1852, the colony held a Harvest Feast. Lyman returned to meet with Young in Salt Lake City and to fill a preaching assignment, and while there he married his eighth and final wife, another Partridge sister, Lydia. He grew accustomed, while in San Bernardino, to also head west through the villages of El Monte and Los Angeles to San Pedro, where he would conduct business or board a ship to San Francisco.

In 1853 the colony attract dissidents from Utah as well as freighters, mail carriers, and stockmen who brought a free-wheeling atmosphere to the town. Lyman welcomed anyone who contributed to the local economy, but over time rebellion against his and Young's theocratic pronouncements stirred up factions that opposed Lyman and Rich. The apostles continued to build the city by renegotiating the terms of the loan. One can imagine the shock in 1856 when President Young told them they were both needed in Europe, then as they began closing their business affairs the Utah War intervened. Lyman took one son with him to hurry back to lend their support to Utah in April 1857. As US troops marched across the plains from the northeast, rumors were circulating that there would be soldiers invading by water from the southwest, and Lyman's knowledge of the southern Utah terrain made him the choice, along with seven others, to reconnoiter the Colorado River. After finding nothing, he returned to Fillmore, the territorial seat, as the conflict lumbered to a negotiated peace. It was not until April 1860 that Lyman finally received a letter confirming his appointment as president of the European Mission. As such, he and Charles C. Rich were to preside over all the missions outside of the Americas—in effect, over the whole global church. They were specifically asked to collect contributions for church headquarters and to facilitate emigration.

They began their journey on May 1, 1860. The trip was transacted with relative ease as they took a steamboat from Omaha east to Chicago and a train from there past Niagara Falls to New York City. It was a far cry from the hellish walk across Iowa fourteen years earlier. After a few days, they boarded a ship and arrived in Liverpool on July 27, and being there in person, the two were able to resolve the primary problems facing the mission. For instance, there was an excess of tithing funds in the hands of the missionaries, beyond what they needed. Second, the mission had a specific calling of full-time pastor for large congregations, for which the pastors were well paid. Lyman and Rich restructured their callings to include proselytizing during the week to utilize their talents. Lyman's other responsibilities included editing the *Millennial Star*, for which he wrote weekly articles, and serving as ultimate authority for church activities in Europe. Despite their progress, Young came to doubt their ability to stem the flow of money and dispatched George Q. Cannon to oversee the funds. Lyman and Rich were to focus on preaching, Young wrote. This may have stung, but it also freed Lyman so he could travel extensively and visit far-flung areas and meet the converts.

When reading the journals for 1860–62, it is difficult not to conclude that Lyman's time in Europe was the happiest of his life. He assumed, perhaps naïvely, that his family would be cared for in Utah, while for the time being he had few temporal concerns himself as he ordered suits custom made and sat for portraits. He spent much of his time preparing and delivering sermons that he polished like a politician giving a stump speech, repeating the same address at different locations. He was expanding his theological worldview too, as the sermon that was so controversial indicated. In addition to that, he went sightseeing whenever possible to become familiar with the culture, and he engaged in a regimen of self-improvement by performing written drills in his diaries for penmanship and spelling. He missed his family, but he seemed intrigued by the teeming metropolises of the world of which he felt a part.

While visiting the Saints in Scotland in March 1862, he delivered his famous discourse entitled "The Nature and Mission of Jesus." He intended it as a definitive statement of the Mormon view of the relationship between God and man. As strange as it appears today to Mormon ears, it reflected the optimism of the founder's theological underpinnings. What was controversial was that he said Jesus was not so much a God-Savior as an older-brother exemplar. Believers, he asserted, did not need a savior; people were capable of improving themselves through decency and good works. He must have been fairly satisfied with his speech because he had it published in the *Millennial Star*.

When Lyman and Rich were released from their mission and sailed for home in May, Rich went to Washington to do some lobbying and Lyman visited relatives and friends in Massachusetts, New Hampshire, Ohio, and Vermont. He marveled at the now-abandoned and derelict temple in Kirtland. Traveling by rail and steamboat to Nebraska, he purchased an ox team to pull him to Salt Lake City. Meeting with Brigham Young, he heard at long last that he could settle down and care for his family. This would be a new lifestyle for him, and he took several months arranging to sell or trade his land in Salt Lake City and Farmington, while he otherwise traveled from place to place to see his family and friends, spoke in the Old Tabernacle, attended theatrical presentations, and was a featured speaker at general conference.

His eight wives and twenty-seven children were situated in Parowan,

Minersville, Beaver, Farmington, and Salt Lake City. It would not be hyperbolic to say that he probably would not have recognized many of his children. And as enjoyable as it was to spend time again with them, Fillmore was hardly the retirement spot he had envisioned. He preferred Salt Lake City with its theatre and mercantile shops. By the end of general conference, April 1863, he finally headed to the middle of the state and arrived exhausted, his boys setting up a tent for him to live in while he sketched out a homestead and arranged for multiple houses for his wives. Even then, minor church assignments beckoned.

He remained an active preacher who visited wards and counseled with local leadership. An admirer of Abraham Lincoln, he spoke at a memorial service in May 1865 after the president was murdered. What weighed on his mind more than national politics, though, was how he would support his family. He embarked on a few ventures, including sheep herding and milling, that were moderately successful. If he thought the church would help him, his drift toward theological heterodoxy complicated that assumption. Someone must have placed Lyman's 1862 Dundee sermon into Brigham Young's hands, but even if not, Young would have probably heard of Lyman's views eventually. It was beyond belief to Young that one of the apostles would deny the blood of Christ. While the president had people scouring the territory looking for heretical beliefs, the greatest heresy of all was lurking in the mind of someone in his inner circle.

From Lyman's perspective, it was odd to be meeting with fellow apostles on January 27, 1867, to defend himself for his theological views. He had known most of these men for three decades. His initial reaction was defensive, but he broke down and admitted his folly, saying through his tears that he would write a retraction for the *Deseret News*. After doing so, he became angry as he thought about what he considered to be his shabby treatment, and determined to double down by delivering a sermon with the same explicit assumption about Jesus. It was a defiant stand, for which he knew there would be repercussions. He was not the only church apostle to cross swords with Young. On this occasion, however, the church president's reaction was swift and harsh. On April 29, 1867, Lyman was dropped from the quorum and banned from exercising any priesthood authority. At the October general conference, the action against him was presented to the congregation and received unanimous approval.

After that, only Lyman's first wife, Maria Louisa, stayed with him. The three Partridge sisters, Caroline, Eliza, and Lydia, immediately left. They were encouraged to do so by Brigham Young, who directed the bishop to provide them with assistance. Cornelia had died in 1864 after a long illness, but Dionetia, Paulina, and Priscilla would distance themselves over the next several years as their husband's interests diverged from their own. Most of Amasa's children remained loyal for a while. His daughter Maria left her husband William Clayton because he sided with the apostles against her father.

There is an unexpected gap in the diaries from January 1864 to August 1868 depriving us of Lyman's immediate reaction to these events. It makes for a jarring narrative break, jumping from Lyman's preaching, traveling, and participating in prayer circles in 1864 to shucking corn, working on a mill, harvesting fruit, and reading to his children in 1868. As he returned to church attendance as a regular congregant, his ward grew comfortable enough to periodically ask him to speak, and he responded by keeping the topics tame. Impressed, Brigham Young gave him a spot in the exclusive School of the Prophets. It seemed Lyman was on his way back to full fellowship until he received a visit from an old friend that changed everything.

He wrote in his diary without fanfare that in August 1869, William S. Godbe, a former missionary with Lyman in Britain, had stopped by. Godbe was already leading what was known as the New Movement, a splinter group that was in opposition to Young's hold on territorial politics. They published a magazine with articles contributed by some of the most literate people in the territory, and they resisted the economic hegemony and spiritual oppression they felt they were living under. Within two months of the visit, Godbe and colleagues such as Elias Harrison were excommunicated. Their reaction was to create their own denomination, the New Church of Zion. All they needed was a church president.

Lyman made the announcement to a stunned and subdued family on May 8, 1870, that he had accepted the leadership of the new church. Some of the family, especially his oldest son, Francis M. Lyman, were devastated. Within days, Amasa was formally excommunicated from the

Church of Jesus Christ of Latter-day Saints. For Francis, to see his father removed from the Quorum of the Twelve had been one thing, but to see him excommunicated and appointed head of a rival church was even more difficult—but he did not sever his relationship. Four of Amasa's children chose to align themselves completely with their father: Agnes, Love, Maria, and Lorenzo. The four formally resigned from the LDS Church and became involved in their father's spiritualism.

The Zion Church sponsored the spiritualist circles that regularly received messages from spirits beyond the veil.[9] In the rest of the country, it was a fad, but not in Utah. Mormons who chafed under Young's autocratic rule may have considered the New Church of Zion otherwise acceptable, if it had not been for the strange turn the church took. Brigham Young advised the Saints to let the movement run its course, "not to … wish them evil," nor "to speak, or write about them" either.[10] Lorenzo Lyman confirmed that he was "not … badly treated" by people in the community, but there was a persistent undercurrent of "silent contempt" for spiritualists.[11]

Amasa had shown a passing interest in spirit communication as early as 1853 while in San Bernardino, and again while on his mission to the United Kingdom. In 1870 it was different, in that he began to record daily séances and visits from deceased Mormon leaders Joseph Smith, Hyrum Smith, Heber C. Kimball, and Newel K. Whitney; western figures Kit Carson and Chief Wakara; and family members including his father and grandfather. His interest in seeing spirits waned over time, but he still participated in séances fairly regularly to his death.

The New Church of Zion burned bright and fast, so that within months of organizing, it declined from hundreds to "a loose confederation of liberal thinkers."[12] That is not to say that the reform movement died. It continued to push against authoritarianism. While Young called for vigilance, Lyman actively promoted free thinking and proselyted among his old friends and acquaintances, attending public and private meetings to further the cause of the New Movement. He wrote often in his journal

9. Cf. diary entry for Sep. 22, 1870, herein.

10. "Minutes of the School of the Prophets," Apr. 23, 1870.

11. Lorenzo Lyman to Amasa M. Lyman, Sep. 9, 1870, Amasa Lyman Collection, CHL.

12. Walker, *Wayward Saints*, 209.

about sermons he delivered to members of the New Zion church and Mormon dissidents. He even became unhappy when denied the use of LDS chapels to deliver his sermons and began expressing contempt for the narrow-mindedness he perceived in Latter-day Saints, branding them with the label he had once used to describe opponents of the faith.

His frustration may have emanated from the sting of trying to provide for his family. A lifelong missionary, church administrator, and leader of people, he was left with few ideas on how to earn money as a common laborer. His property boasted apple and peach orchards, and he owned part interest in a mill. He had sheep. In Salt Lake City, he purchased a house because of the demands on him as president of the new church, and he worked for a time at the Godbeite *Salt Lake Tribune*. He became an insurance representative for California Mutual Life. As the influence of the New Movement waned, he moved back to Fillmore in 1873.

In his twilight years he learned how to farm. At sixty he was irrigating orchards, storing fresh apples underground during the winter months, and cutting and drying fruit to sell. Much of the rural economy was based on barter, so he traded fruit for work on his home and other services. He quickly grew restless, his diary entries becoming terse. He devoted more space to telling what books he read than to farming. In 1875 he recorded a seventy-five-day stint of nothing but reading history books and tracts on spiritualism.

He decided to build a new house for him and Maria Louisa to live in during their declining years and wanted it to be first-class with a fence to keep livestock out of his orchards. The house would never be finished. Despite the increased time he was expending on manual labor, he was still round in the middle. In all the years he had spent walking, riding a horse, and driving a carriage or wagon on church errands, he had never been thin. However, in an era when many Americans had not traveled more than 100 miles from home, he had seen the easternmost and westernmost coasts. Occasionally he was slowed down by his sickness and a chronic pain. Now old age was setting in. He was becoming weaker. "The heat and labor were more than I could endure,"[13] he wrote in June 1873. Over the next year, he developed a lung infection, broke a foot, sprained

13. Diary entry for June 7, 1878, herein.

his wrist, and became reacquainted with an old pain in his side. He was on the scaffolding of his new house when it collapsed. He fell several feet, breaking his leg, and was bedridden for six weeks.

Continuing his interest in spiritualism, he joined the national Free Religion Association and the National Liberal League. He did so despite the cool treatment he received from former friends and neighbors. In his mind, people should have allowed him the same courtesy to believe what he wanted that he extended to them. There is no evidence that he regretted any of his life decisions. In the early days of 1877, he concluded that he should write an autobiography and defense of his beliefs, for which he purchased a large quantity of good writing paper. He obtained a number of new books. Not that he had become a recluse; he often still lectured at public halls and attended musical performances. On January 29 he scribbled in his diary his oft-written line, "Not feeling well." The next day he was "much worse" and "confined to my bed." After recording on February 2 that he was "very weak," he wrote the last three words in his diary the following day: "Same as yesterday." On February 4, 1877, with his wife Louisa and son Francis by his side, he slipped away forever.

The cause of death was "pleurisy [pneumonia] and lung fever."[14] The church-owned *Deseret News* waited three weeks to report it with a tiny notice in the back of the newspaper. The *Salt Lake Tribune*, by contrast, published an initial notice, a longer obituary, and finally a report on the memorial service.[15] He was buried in Fillmore dressed in the black suit and black boots of a businessman or minister rather than the traditional white clothing associated with a Mormon burial. When his son Francis was ordained an LDS apostle three years later, his prominence, and the sands of time, created enough space that he thought his father's legacy could be reassessed. He pled with some persuasion in 1890 that his father should be returned to church membership, his apostolic status retroactively restored. Lorenzo Snow concurred, but other church leaders disagreed. It took the passing of Wilford Woodruff and George Q. Cannon over the next two decades for the apostles to finally agree that Amasa should be reinstated.

14. "Died," *Deseret News*, Feb. 21, 1877.

15. "Death of Amasa Lyman," Feb. 7, 1877; "Amasa M. Lyman," Feb. 25, 1877; "Amasa M. Lyman," Feb. 27, 1877, *Salt Lake Tribune*.

On January 12, 1909, Francis stood waist deep in water in the font of the Salt Lake Temple as proxy for his father's re-baptism, John Henry Smith the officiator. Having been interested in the state of a person's soul after death and the possibility of communication with the dead, this vicarious act was an appropriate way to conclude his life story. He was confirmed by LDS President Joseph F. Smith, a nephew of church founder Joseph Smith. Finally, priesthood blessings were re-conferred upon the departed by Smith, accompanied by John R. Winder and Anthon H. Lund. After the ceremonies were completed, Francis could barely contain his joy as he related to his niece Lucretia Ranney his delight that Joseph F. Smith had performed the final ordinances. Joseph F. was the one who had replaced Amasa, the thirteenth apostle, in the Quorum of Twelve in 1867.[16]

16. *AML*, 493–94.

Editorial procedures

The documents

The diaries are part of the Amasa Mason Lyman Collection at the Church History Library in Salt Lake City.[1] Beginning in 1832, after embarking on a mission two years after the church's founding, Lyman kept track of his daily activities. He continued to do so until the day before his death in 1877. The record fills forty-three volumes that were typically notebooks of varying sizes.

After he died, the diaries passed to his oldest son, Francis M. Lyman, who, despite his father's excommunication and Francis's own appointment to the LDS Quorum of the Twelve, thought his father's legacy in helping establish the church in its founding decade was important. He therefore made the notebooks available to the church, as indicated by the 1884 notation by the Church Historian and recorder, Wilford Woodruff, that he "saw Amasa M Lymans Journals which He had written for many years."[2] Sometime thereafter, the diaries were donated to the staff of the Church Historian's Office.

Lyman saw his diary as having several purposes: to keep track of his travels, to provide documentation for ecclesiastical matters, and to record family information. Sometimes he wrote every day, sometimes weekly, and other times he reminisced about what had occurred several months previous. There are financial notations, poetry, and exercises in grammar and penmanship, as well as blank pages. Some entries were squeezed into the margins or entered later and out of order.

Rarely did he disclose intimate details about his personal life. He was less guarded after he was removed from the Quorum of the Twelve Apostles, but not gossipy. As strange as it might seem today, when diaries are

1. MS 829, Church History Library (CHL), Church of Jesus Christ of Latter-day Saints (LDS).

2. Kenney, *Wilford Woodruff's Journal*, 8:241.

assumed to be a record of personal thoughts and feelings, in Lyman's time it was common to devote more space to trivial details about the weather than about the birth of a child, for instance. Diarists relied on their journals to retrace their steps when they traveled that way a second time, in remembering people's names and where they stayed. The official church records were often drawn from its leaders' diaries. Lyman's letters, also available at the Church History Library, reveal the subject's warmer side.

The older Lyman became, the more likely he was to grab an older notebook and make a few brief entries and then move on to a fresh journal. Where the entries from an 1855 diary end, they are followed by his daily writings for 1876. I have put the entries into their proper chronological order and indicated where source notebooks change. Readers will also notice that some entries refer to Lyman in third-person. When people traveled together in those days, they would compare notes and often copy from each other, as several of Lyman's diaries indicate.[3] There are also portions that appear to have been kept by clerks, that are not in Lyman's hand, such as the trail journal from Iowa to Salt Lake City in 1847 that was recorded by Albert Carrington on Lyman's behalf.

Lyman might keep records for a time on loose sheets and small daybooks and polish the writing later, as his May 1860 entries are a good example of. After he was called on a mission to Liverpool, he wrote daily entries in pencil in a small pocketbook while on the trail from Salt Lake City to the East Coast. He later copied his entries into a larger notebook, perhaps on the ship while sailing to Liverpool, and worked on the wording. There are strikeouts and extra-linear additions. Finally, his more formal journal was meticulously prepared, written in ink, most likely when he was back home in Utah and wanted a more permanent keepsake.

Aside from the degree of care Lyman devoted to penmanship, depending on whether he was writing as he traveled or polishing the wording after the fact, his handwriting and vocabulary changed over time. One can even see him experimenting with writing that is more expressive and high-minded, while practicing his spelling and handwriting. The fact that he read widely must have also contributed to his vocabulary and narrative style. In any case, there is an apparent evolution in his

3. George Q. Cannon copied from other diaries as a Hawaiian missionary. See Orton, ed., *Journals of George Q. Cannon*, xxiii.

writing skills. His early journals are hard to read, with sloppy penmanship. They lack consistent punctuation or spelling. For instance, within a few pages he might refer to a span of horses as a *teem*, *teeam*, or *team*. But his later journals are neat and legible, have more consistent spelling, and have a more adult style of expression.

The editing

This volume seeks to accommodate specialists and lay readers alike—those who will read it cover-to-cover and those who will use the index for specific details. I have included all the diary entries that were available to me,[4] but not the random math notations, financial records, and doodles which he often made at the front or back of a notebook. Nor have I included the newspaper clippings he sometimes added. Where he practiced his handwriting, I included just enough to give a flavor of it.

I standardized dates (month, day, year; day of the week), adapting what Lyman sometimes wrote in an abbreviated form in the margin or above the line. Early on, he rarely separated out entries and instead kept a running narrative that mentioned the passing of time as part of the story. Rather than reduce that to a staccato repetition of dates, with awkward transitions, I kept the rambling entries intact, creating breaks where it seemed natural, such as at the end of a thought or sentence.

A good deal of silent editing was unavoidable, as follows (all other edits noted in the body of the text or annotation):

1. Missing periods added.
2. Errant commas deleted.
3. Capitalization added at the beginning of sentences and to proper nouns.
4. Paragraph breaks added to lengthy entries.
5. Periods deleted after brackets for expanded initials (B[righam] Young).
6. Duplicate words deleted ("the the").

I used [plain brackets] to clarify or provide context where needed, and for punctuation [?] beyond what is mentioned above. I added people's

4. A note in the CHL catalog states that portions of the collection remain closed to research. In some instances, I was not able to see the originals for volumes that subsequently appeared in the church's *Selected Collections* DVDs in slightly redacted form; they remain redacted in the current presentation.

[first names] on first mention in an entry. Some dates and proper names were underlined in pencil, perhaps by a later editor, and I retained the <u>underlining</u> to give a sense of what the actual diary looks like.[5] I also took that approach to ~~strikethroughs~~ and [illegible] words. And if misspelled words were understandable, I left them as is; if not, I corrected errant letters within br[a]ckets or followed a misspelled word with the proper or modern spaelieng [spelling] in brackets. If Lyman left a space to fill in, I added [blank].

The footnotes are meant to provide context; explanations of archaic words, customs, and technologies; and clarifications of what comes later in the diaries, for instance; as well as information about source documents. I have drawn on primary and secondary sources for the annotation, and listed the sources in the bibliography. Information about people appears in two places: the biographical register for individuals mentioned frequently and in the footnotes for people who were representative of the cultural environment in which Lyman existed.

5. For information on how the Journal History was created, including underlines in source documents, see Bergera, "Commencement of Great Things," 23–39. Family members may have also marked the diaries when preparing eulogies or short biographies.

1 Countering the Pharisees of Babylon, 1832–1844

At age nineteen Amasa Lyman left his home in New Hampshire to join the Latter-day Saints in Ohio on a journey of 700 miles. After thirty days on the road, he arrived in Hiram, where he was welcomed by the John Johnson family. In July 1832, Joseph Smith arrived and called Lyman to be a missionary, and also ordained him as an elder. Like many early converts, he began keeping a journal for the first time as a missionary, including in it details of preaching and traveling throughout small towns along the Ohio River, mostly in Ohio and Virginia, then in western New York and Pennsylvania and eventually as far as New Hampshire, where he visited his family. He would be called back to Kirtland for Zion's Camp before resuming his missionary work. His diary is sporadic and makes only brief mention of some major events, with large gaps during the times he was not acting as a missionary.

August 23, 1832; Thursday. A brief sketch of the travils of Amasa M. Lyman from the time of his calling to the ministry[1] which was August the 23rd 1832 at which time I was ordained with Bro Z[erubbabel] Snow and on the next day we left the place where we there were which was in Portage Co[unty] Ohio[2] and traveled southward to the town of Shalersville where we [c]alled on a brother who was sick with a dissease.

1. The two missionaries were ordained and set apart by Joseph Smith and Oliver Cowdery and traveled "without purse or scrip." The first page of Lyman's diary contains ink blotches that partially obscure some words such as "calling."

2. Portage County is in the northeastern part of the state and is derived from the old Portage Trail, running between the Cuyahoga and Tuscarawas Rivers.

His health was prayed for and laid hands on him in the name of Christ and the dissease was immediately rebuked. Their the Lord began to manifest himself unto us which gave us reason to rejoise and on the 25th we left and went south as far as the town of Talmage wher there was two brethren where we arived about 3 in the afternoon. We gave out an apointment for a meeting on the sabath but there was no people that did attend and on sabath evening we meet for a prayer meeting and as brother Snow opened the meeting the Devil came in and seized a woman and held her. We prayed and commanded him to depart in the name of Jesus and she was set at liberty and went forward and was baptized and confirmed and was blessed with the comforter[3] and from thence we journeyed as far as Chipeway & from ther[e] on the 28th as far as Green Tow[nship] where we held one meeting and af[ter] left this place. On the 29th & on the 30th we arrived in Millersburg where on the 31st we held one meeting and journeyed about 19 m^ile^s to a small town by the name Keene where we held a meeting the same day and were atacked ^by^ one of the teachers of Babylon ^who^[4] sought by sarcasm and black guard[5] to bring the work of the Lord into disrepute but the Lord did not suffer us to be confounded.

September 1, 1832; Saturday. Traviled south as far as Jefferson. We held one meeting and went to Dresden ^Muckingham County^[6] and

3. Lyman later recorded details of this incident in his personal writings: "We sang and prayed, and Brother Snow proceeded to make some remarks, but in an instance a chilling sensation pervaded my entire body, and a cry of alarm from the bed attracted the attention of all. On stepping to the bedside we discovered that Miss Smith's face and her entire form were distorted in the most shocking manner, her eyes were glaring wildly, but apparently sightless, her respiration was very difficult and her limbs were rigid as iron; the common restoratives were used without effect, we laid our hands upon her and rebuked the devil when she was instantly relieved, but in another moment she was bound as before. We kneeled down by her bed and prayed, when she was again released, and asked for baptism, stating that she had been acting against her convictions of right in some conversations we had held with her during the day. We repaired to the water, and there under the mantle of night introduced the first souls in the church as the fruits of our labors." Lyman, *Amasa Mason Lyman, Pioneer,* 28.

4. A small piece of the page is missing and the words "by" and "who" were written in by a different hand. The derogatory "teachers of Babylon" drew from the mystical description of Babylon in Rev. 17:3–8, portraying the ancient empire as the source of all evil.

5. "Black guard" was "a vulgar term applied to a mean fellow who uses abusive, scurrilous language, or treats others with foul abuse." Webster, *American Dictionary,* 1828.

6. Dresden is a village located in Muskingum County along the Muskingum River. The words "Muckingham County" were written above Dresden in pencil.

held one meeting and on the 3rd left this place and and journeyed 7 mi[le]s beyond Zanesville ^Muckingham^ and on the 6th we went to Dover held one meeting & on the 7th held one meeting in the same place and the day following we resumed our journey and went as far as Grand Fork where we held one meeting on the 16th & ~~there a~~ we held ^a^ meeting in Windsor[7] and the same day administered the Lords supper to the Church & we taried in this place until the 20th when we went to Virginia Cabell County.[8]

I would here remark that on the 15th Broth S^eymour M^ Brunson arived where we were much to our joy and satisfaction of his brethren and to the confounding of his enimeis in Virginia. We held one meeting & taried until the 26th then recrossed the Ohio riv[er into Ohio] and meet brothers Seymour & John [Philemon] at [Wm Topins?] and held meeting with them and then returned to Virginia in company with brother Brunson on the 27th.[9] I returned to Windsor [Ohio] and held a meeting on the 28th with brother John at Thomas Nance. On the 29th attended a meeting at the same place and brothers [Zerubbabel] Snow & Brunson was present brother Brunson preached. We taried in Windsor until the 4th of Oct had a Church meeting but owing to some illegal procedings in members the difficulty was not settled. The 5th brother Seymour preached the vision[10] it was received by all save one of the members of

7. Not to be confused with the existing town of Windsor, Ohio, farther north. It can be difficult to trace Lyman's exact locale because towns across state borders, and occasionally within the same state, shared the same name. For clarity, when Lyman crosses borders, I have added the state name in brackets after the first town he visited in that state. The duplicate names have confused some previous biographers who identified Lyman as being in some distant town when he was almost certainly in a similarly named, less distant one.

8. The county is on the far western edge of present-day West Virginia.

9. Prior to the Civil War, western Virginians were economically aligned with Ohio and Pennsylvania. In fact, they chafed against the influence of slave owners in the Virginia legislature. After the state seceded in 1861, the non-slave portion broke off to form West Virginia, which was admitted into the Union in June 1863. McPherson, *Battle Cry of Freedom*, 297–98.

10. This is Joseph Smith's and Sidney Rigdon's vision on February 16, 1832, in which they saw the three levels of heaven, now LDS D&C 76. It corresponded to the theological speculations of Emanuel Swedenborg, Alexander Campbell, and others at the time but departed so far from traditional beliefs about heaven and hell that some LDS members struggled to reconcile it with their prior convictions. Godfrey, et al, *Joseph Smith Papers*, Documents Series, 2:179–82.

the church who after apostatized here. I would remark that I Amas[a] & Zarubable [Snow] laboured with our hands in assisting brother Seymour to prepare an house for his family and this day held a meeting on Sand Fork [Virginia] where the people did not behave decent but we found two that after obeyed the truth.

October 3, 1832; Wednesday. Zarubable [Snow] and I held a meeting on Bullskin Creek [Ohio] then returned to Virginia.

October 12, 1832; Friday. We held a meeting on a stream called [Mudr] in Cabell Co [Virginia] and from this to the 13th we spent the time in private meetings with the people and on the 19th we held a meeting near a stream called Guyandotte.

October 23, 1832; Tuesday. We returned to Windsor [Ohio] & on the 28th I and brother John Fisher held a meeting in the church.

November 4, 1832; Sunday. Brothers Seymour [Brunson] Zerubabel [Snow] and John Philemon and myself meet for the purpos of settling some business which was ocasioned by the transgress^ions^ of Jane Fuller. Lane and Perlina were expelled and sister Harriet Brun^son^ was received as a member of the Church.

November 8, 1832; Thursday. Brother and I went to Sandfork [Virginia] held one meeting.

November 10, 1832; Saturday. Brother [John] Philemon and myself went to V.A. held one meeting on the 11th and on this day Bro Luke [Johnson arrived] at Guyandotte.

November 13, 1832; Tuesday. We returned to Widsor ^Ohio^ and on the 18th attended a meeting at Brother Seymours [Brunson] and brother Zerubbabel [Snow] preached and on the 20th held a meeting with the brethren and on 23rd held a conference B Luke [Johnson] president and Zerubbabel clerk and on the 24th went to VA with brother L[uke].

November 25, 1832; Sunday. Held one meeting. Dec the 2 attended meeting, Brother Seymour Brunson and we held a meeting at the same place and on the 8th we left this place anon.[11]

December 10, 1832; Monday. Arived at Mr. Hunts in Racoon Township [Pennsylvania], and on the 11th traviled 11 hrs. and held one meeting on the 12th and on the 13th traviled 5 hrs and held meeting and

11. Quickly or immediately; without intermission, according to Webster, *American Dictionary.*

on the 15th returned to the Hunts. On the 16th held one meeting and on the 17th went on to Oak Hill held two meetings.

December 18, 1832; Tuesday. Held one meeting and on the ~~19th held one meeting~~ went to Jackson [Virginia] held one meeting on the 20th and left the place.

December 22, 1832; Saturday. Held a meeting on Hales Creek [Ohio] at Mr. [Merrit] Prices. On the 23rd held a meeting in Bloom Township [in] Sioto Co.

December 23, 1832; Sunday. Held a meeting at Mrs. [illegible].

December 24, 1832; Monday. We held a meeting at Mr Citingman.

December 28, 1832; Friday. Held a meeting at Mr. Bees and baptized Sister Hannah Price and on the 30th we held one meeting at the same place and baptized Merit Price and held a meeting at Mr. Smiths the same day. On the 31st went to Mr. Wellses.

January 1, 1833; Tuesday. Held a meeting, at the above named place then returned to Bloom. Spen[t] the time in privat discourse with the people until the 5th then held a meeting ~~a~~ at Mr [Merrit] Prices baptized himself and wife the same evening. Held a meeting at Mr. Smiths.

January 6, 1833; Sunday. We preached in the Methodist house to a large congregation and the Lord blessed us with his spirit in declaring his word in plainness to the people but it was in a measure cast by unbelief.

January 7, 1833; Monday. Held meeting in Whelersburg. Had a large concourse of peo[ple]. We were blessed with liberty in declareing the word held 5 mee^tings^ in this vicinity.

January 13, 1833; Sunday. Preached at Bloom from this to the 26th held 8 meetings baptized 2.

January 27, 1833; Sunday. Held a meeting and baptized one person from this to the 5th of Feb. Held 5 meetings in company with brother H[azen] Oldrage [Aldrich] and on the 5th returne^d^ to Guyandott [Virginia] held one meeting attended to some business then returned to Mrs McDaids.

February 13, 1833; Wednesday. Held a meeting at this house and on the 15th held a meeting with brother [Zerubbabel] Snow and [John] Fisher we were opposed by one of the teachers of babylon.

February 17, 1833; Sunday. Held a meeting at J. Stephen^son^.

February 18, 1833; Monday. Held a meeting at G Pickerells.

February 19, 1833; Tuesday. We started for the northern part of Ohio where we arived the 8th of March and held 6 meetings on the way here brother [Zerubbabel] Snow and I was parted for a season.

March 21, 1833; Thursday. I started for the east in company with brother Wm Cahoo^n^ traveled east as far as Madison where on the 22d we held a meeting. Here cleansed our feet against ^those who had rejected us.^[12]

March 23, 1833; Saturday. We [went] east as far as Springfield, P.A. ^Penn^ where there was a Church of about one hundred members. Some were in a state of desponden^cy^ becaus their Heavenly Father had chastened them when they [were] lead by a dillucive spirit. We held three meetings with them laid before them the blessing in being chasened when wrong, they began in a measure to see and give heed.

March 27, 1833; Wednesday. We traviled about 5 hrs to the south and [blank] held one ^meeting.^

March 28, 1833; Thursday. Spent the day in private conversa^tion.^

March 29, 1833; Friday. Held one meeting and the Lord blesed us with his spirit that we spake with tongues[13] and prop^hesyed^ and from this to the 31st taried in Conneaut [Ohio] on which day we held a meeting and the Lord blessed us in declareing the word in plainness to the cleansing of our garments from their blood and left that place and went to Girard [Pennsylvania] here brother J[ohn] Boyington had baptize^d^ about 50 diciples. Attended a meeting with them and same evening there was 5 baptised. On the 2nd attended a meeting brother O[rson] Hide preach and on the 3d we left this place and journeyed south as far as McKean and on the 4th left this place went as far as Coneauttee [Creek]. Here they rejected our testimony but here the word of the Lord was verified unto us as unto the prophet in days of old for the Lord opened the heart a woman likened to the widdow of Sarephath.[14] She invited us to

12. Ritually shaking the dust from one's feet is mentioned in the New Testament (Matt. 10:14-15; Acts 13:51), and it became a way for LDS missionaries to express their contempt for people who rejected their message. LDS D&C 24:15 expands the meaning to include "cleansing your feet by the wayside."

13. Early Mormons engaged in the charismatic practice of speaking in tongues. Over time the practice faded, and today the gift is considered to be the less miraculous ability of missionaries to master foreign languages over time.

14. In I Kings 17, the prophet Elijah is said to have met the poor widow Zarephath and to have asked her to bring him water and bread. On the brink of starvation

hold a meeting abou[t] 4 m[ile]s from where we then were in Cassawaga [Cussewago] Township where we held one meeting an[d] the[y] opened their doors for more preaching.

April 5, 1833; Friday. We cleansed our feet against the inhabitants of Conneauttee [Creek] that who rejected our testimony concerning the Gospel of Chris^t.^

April 6, 1833; Saturday. We returned to Conneauttee [Creek] and the same evening at one Mrs. Waldo^s^ here one of the pharisees of Babylon required a sign that he might know the truth of the Gospel of Christ by having a blind man restored to sight who was at that [time] cursing and swearing.

April 7, 1833; Sunday. Attended a meeting with breth^ren^ O[rson] Pratt and L[uke] Johnson. On the evening of the same day we held a meeting at the corners in McKean.[15] They were a stiffnecked and a hard hearted people desireing us to depart out of there coast but after meeting were requested to hold a meeting in the school house near Mrs. Sterates and also a woman requested us to go and see her son who was sick. We complyed with her reque^st^ we found him a low state of mind we laid before him the gospel and the blessings thereof. While here application of was made for preaching. This being granted we repaired to Mr Wilcocks and on the 9th we cleansed our feet against a man who rejected our testimony and desired us to depart out of their coast. On the evening of the same day held a meeting in the neighbourhood near Mr Sterats. Had a very attentive congregation and we were blessed with the spirit. On the 10th returned to the widow Daniels where we saw a man with whom we had some conversation concerning the things of the kingdom. He appeared to be enquiring after the truth, on the evening of the same day held a meeting and spake of the gathering of Israel. On the 11th Preached 4 m[iles] from Conneauttee [Creek] and returned to Mr. Galoways where we arrived about 7 oclock in the evening amid all the appearance ^of a^ blackening tempest that gathered around us, but the Lord held the fierceness of the tempest in his own hand until we found

herself, she nevertheless does so and finds that her containers of oil and grain are miraculously replenished.

15. In 1861 the small business district in McKean Township, then called McKean Corners, became a separate jurisdiction called Middleboro. *History of Erie County*, 1:781–82.

shelter under the hospitable roof of our friend and on the 12th, returned to to Mckean. On the 13th went to Mr. Thurlows and a Mr. Harisons.

April 14, 1833; Sunday. Held a meeting near Mr Ster^ats^ where some men of the baser sort made some disturbance from thence repared to the corners preached to a large congregation. Two priests present that night. Lodged with Mr Brown.

April 15, 1833; Monday. Went to Mr. [William] Staffords where we had an interview with a teacher of the Methodist society in the which I saw the extent of the blindness that covereth the minds of men unenlightened by the gospel and on the 16th returned to Mr. Ds. In the evening preached in Mr F[isk]s neighbourhood. Here we had another evidence of the depravity of the teachers of Babylon. This night lodged with B Colm and on the 17th taught him the gospel and went to Mr. Harisons and on the 18th we returned to Mr Colms in the evening preached to Mr. Harisons. Here met with some opposition from one of the wise men of Babylon his remarks had the desired effect on the minds of the unwarry to set them against the work.

April 19, 1833; Friday. Preached to Wm Staffords.

April 20, 1833; Saturday. Went to our appointment.

April 21, 1833; Sunday. Preached go a large concourse of people. The same day returned to Mr. G[aloway]s taried all night.

April 22, 1833; Monday. Journeyed east as far as Harper Creek [Harborcreek] taried all night and preached to the people.

April 23, 1833; Tuesday. Arived in Westfield [New York] taried until the 28th preached to the people in that place and they we[n]t forward in to the waters of baptism to the number of 15. They were confirmed and spake with tongues some of them the same day.

April 29, 1833; Monday. Went to the lake [Erie] & baptized three in the evening held a council and on the 30th went to Fayette.[16]

16. There is some confusion over whether this Fayette is the one in the Finger Lakes region, well known to Mormons as the home of the Whitmer family and scene of important founding events in the history of the church. Edward Leo Lyman, in his biography, suggested that Lyman and his companions made use of the Erie Canal for the 150-mile journey. However, a note in the the Journal History, relying on the diary of missionary Evan Greene, identified Fayette as a town in Chautauqua County in the westernmost part of the state. *AML*, 13; Journal History, Apr. 16, 1833.

May 1, 1833; Wednesday. I journeyed south as far as Perysberg to brother [Freeman] Nickersons.[17]

May 3, 1833; Friday. Held a meeting with brother Z[erubabbel] Snow & H[orace] Cowen and baptized 5. Their is a prospect that some more will obey the Lord. On the sabbath of the 5th preached in a barn with brother Z[erubabbel] preached the same day in Villanova.

May 6, 1833; Monday. Preached in the same town.

May 7, 1833; Tuesday. Returned to brother [Freeman] N[ickerson's] held a meeting and expounded the laws of the Church.

May 8, 1833; Wednesday. Brothers [Zerubbabel] Snow, [Horace] Cowen & [William] Cahoon & myself went to Leon held a meeting and gave out an apointment for the next sabbath. Here we parted with brothers Snow & Cowen [and] went to the village of Rutlodge [Rutledge, Chautauqua County]. Left [with] an appointment for the 11th taried in the vicinity until the 11th fulfilled our appointment for that day.

May 12, 1833; Sunday. Preached in Leon meeting house.

May 13, 1833; Monday. Returned to Perysberg. On our way thither we waded through the two or three m[iles] this day attended meeting with brothers [Zerubbabel] Snow & [Horace] Cowen and [blank] were baptized.[18]

May 14, 1833; Tuesday. Went to Lodi with brothers [Zerubbabel] Snow & [Horace] Cowen. Brother S[now] preached to the people here we left the brethren and returned to Perysberg and on the 15th preached in Vallanova in the evening went to brother Carpen^ters^.

May 16, 1833; Thursday. Preached in the block school house held a meeting in the evening of the same day.

May 17, 1833; Friday. Went to Fayette held two meetings. Here we found brothers E[van M.] Green & [William] H[arrison] Sagers.[19]

May 18, 1833; Saturday. In company with the above named brethren came to Perysberg held two meetings and on the 20th, held one meeting

17. The towns Lyman repeatedly visited, such as Leon, Villenova, and Perrysburg, were located in about a forty-mile radius of southwestern New York state near Lake Erie and the Pennsylvania border.

18. Evan M. Greene recorded that between May and the end of June, nineteen people were baptized in the Villenova area. Greene diary, vol. 1, undated list at back of diary.

19. Evan M. Greene and William Harrison Sagers had arrived from Kirtland with John Boynton.

and on the 21st preached in hanover and on the 22nd came to Perysberg. Gave out three appointments and on the 2nd preached to brother [Freeman] N[ickerson].

May 24, 1833; Friday. Preached in the town of Villanova and on the 25th preached in the McBride settlement[20] and on Sabbath the 26th preached in a barn to a large congregation preached again the same day and also on the 27th preached at brother C[arpenter's].

May 28, 1833; Tuesday. Preached in Villanova, the people made some disturbance.

May 29, 1833; Wednesday. Preached at Mr. Richardsons.

May 30, 1833; Thursday. Preached in the McBride settle^ment.^

June 2, 1833; Sunday. Preached in the block school ^house.^

June 5, 1833; Wednesday. Preached in the McBride settlement and also on the 6th preached at brother [Freeman] N[ickerson] and baptized two persons.

June 7, 1833; Friday. Went to my appointment where I found brothers E[van M.] Green & A[fred] Fisk.

June 9, 1833; Sunday. Preached at brother [Freeman] N[ickerson] and baptized 7 and on monday the 10th preached to Mr. Richardsons & on the 11th preached near Mr. Riters in Villano^va.^

June 12, 1833; Wednesday. Preached near Mr. Alleons this in company with brothers E[van M.] Green & [William] H[arrison] Sayers and on the day of 13th met brother [William] Cahoon in Villanov^a^ preached & baptized 4 persons.

June 14, 1833; Friday. Preached in the McBride Settlement and on the day ensuing came to brother [Freeman] N[ickerson] where we saw brother cutler.

June 16, 1833; Sunday. Preached & baptized 4 persons from thence went to Fayette.

June 18, 1833; Tuesday. Went and bathed in Lake Erie.

June 20, 1833; Thursday. Held a meeting in the Church.

June 21, 1833; Friday. Returned to Villanova here found brother H[arpin] Riggs.

---

20. This is the Reuben McBride family farm near Villenova Township. The family became prominent church members and would eventually travel west to Utah under Brigham Young.

June 23, 1833; Sunday. Went to Conawango held a meeting and returned to Perys^be[rg].

June 24, 1833; Monday. Laboured with Wm Nickols.

June 25, 1833; Tuesday. Held a meeting at brother [Reuben] McBrides for the purpose of organizing this branch of the Churc^h^. Brother J[ohn] Boyington presided over the meeting. Ordained two deacons also baptized two in the evening repared to Brother [Freeman] N[ickerson's].

June 26, 1833; Wednesday. Went to Villanova where we took leave of brothers J[ohn] Boyington & E[van M.] Green who journeyed to the east.

June 29, 1833; Saturday. Preached & baptized one per^son.^

~~*June 30, 1833; Sunday*. Went to Persyberg and on the 1st preached twice two times.~~

June 30, 1833; Sunday. Preached two times, was blessed.

July 1, 1833; Monday. Returned to Persyberg.

July 2, 1833; Tuesday. Preached in Villanova.

July 4, 1833; Thursday. Preached & baptized two persons.

July 7, 1833; Sunday. Preached to brother [Reuben] McBride.

July 9, 1833; Tuesday. I started to the west in company with brother McNickers reached Westfield [New York] on the 11th held a meeting with the brethren.

July 12, 1833; Friday. Preached in Portland and on the 13th returned to Westfield and on the 14th preached in brother L[orenzo] Barn[es home].

July 17, 1833; Wednesday. Preached in Portland & on the 18th returned to Westfield. Held a meeting with the brethren.

July 21, 1833; Sunday. Preached in brother L[orenzo] Barn[es home].

July 25, 1833; Thursday. Held a meeting with brother G Bishop.

July 28, 1833; Sunday. Preached in Portland returned to Westfield had a meeting.

July 30, 1833; Tuesday. Wrote a Leter to [acquaintances in] Virginia.

July 31, 1833; Wednesday. Copied my journal.[21]

August 1, 1833; Thursday. Preached in Portland went to Perysberg visited the brethr^en^ taried ~~until the~~ and baptized ^one.^

21. Instead of writing daily, Lyman appears to have set aside a time each week to record in his journal. He likely worked from memory.

August 9, 1833; Friday. Returned to Westfield on the 10th preached to brother L[orenzo] Barn[es].

August 12, 1833; Monday. Preached in Mayville the 13th [then] returned to Westfield where I taried until the 20th held three meetings with br[other]s E Piring & L[orenzo] Barn[e]s and on the 20th went to Harmony[22] in company with brother H Kig.[23]

August 21, 1833; Wednesday. Came to Jamestown on the 22nd preached and baptized ^one.^

August 24, 1833; Saturday. Went to Caroll and on the 25th returned to Jamestown preac^hed^ & returned to Caroll and held a meeting on the 27th returned to Jamestown held two meeting ^&^ returned to Perysberg.

August 31, 1833; Saturday. Preached in Chery creek.

September 1, 1833; Sunday. Laboured with some refractory[24] members who in consequence of disobedience were cut off in meeting held for that purpose on the 2nd to the number of three the same evening held a meeting with the brethren.

September 3, 1833; Tuesday. Brother Wm C[ahoon] left me and and departed for the land of Kirtland [Ohio] & I continued my labour in the regions round about until the 16th when I took my journey to the west. The 19th arived in Gerrard [Girard, Pennsylvania] where I meet brother Z[ebedee] Coltrin with whom I laboured in the congregations of the saints and of the wicked until the 24th of Oct. dureing which time the power of God was displayed in healing the sick through our ministry.

October 25, 1833; Friday. Started for the east. Went as as far as Villanova. Taried in the region until Dec. the 3rd when I journeyed to the west as far as Elk Creek [Pennsylvania] where I found brother O[rson] Pratt & L[uke] Johns^on.^ There I received a mission to go to the east and with them I returned to the east in which time in company with Johnson held several meetings while on our journey.

December 30, 1833; Monday. Arived in Genaseo [New York][25] here

---

22. Harmony, New York, a small town near Lake Erie, is in the same general area of the other towns Lyman visited.

23. Lyman wrote "Kig" at the end of a line where the name trails off and becomes illegible.

24. "Obstinate in opposition or disobedience," according to Webster, *American Dictionary*.

25. Geneseo is west of the Finger Lakes, the farthest east Lyman had yet traveled.

we met brothers O[rson] P[ratt] & J[ohn] M[urdock] and with them atended to dealings with some refractory members in the Church many of whom were cut off from the [church] even to the number of about 20.[26]

January 1, 1834; Wednesday.[27] Visited the breth[ren] and sist[ers] [in New York] according to apointment.

January 2, 1834; Thursday. Four H[igh] P[riests] and 3 Elders present in Church meeting & about one half of the Church. After the meeting was opened we explained the vision & shewed the reason why E[zra] Landen was expelled and the following persons requested their names to be taken from the Church records & manifested a bad spirit.[28] Viz: Lester More[,] Daniel C. More[,] Lettetia Bosley[,] Rodman Clark[,] Aaron Rolly Kelly. The Church were called on to lift their hand against them & they were declareed to be no more members of the church of Christ.[29] We appointed another Church meeting the Monday following then closed Amen.

---

26. About the first of December, Lyman returned to Ohio. While on the way, he met with Lyman Johnson, Orson Pratt, and John Murdock in a branch of the church in Erie County and was ordained to the high priesthood on December 11 by Johnson and Pratt. Soon thereafter he accompanied Orson Hyde to visit Jedediah M. Grant's family. Grant's sister Theda remembered how dramatically that visit changed the family's lives:

> When I was twelve years of age, two Mormon missionaries came to my father's farm near Erie, Pennsylvania. They were Amasa Lyman and Orson Hyde. My father was deeply interested in this new religion and invited these missionaries to hold cottage meetings in our home. My mother lay sick with rheumatism and could hardly stand to have any one touch her.
>
> I remember how tall Elder [Amasa] Lyman looked as he stood by the side of Mother's bed telling us of the gifts and blessings of the restored gospel and that these blessings follow the believer, in this day, as they did in the days of the Savior. My Mother asked why she could not be blessed as she had perfect faith that God could heal her. The elders placed their hands on her head and prayed for her recovery. Later that evening my mother got up, dressed herself, went out of doors and climbed the stairs, which were on the outside of the house and, with my help, prepared a bed in which the elders slept that night. (Reminiscence of Theda Grant Reeves, as told to Joseph Hyrum Grant Jr., Nov. 26, 1904, Lathrop, Mo., typescript in possession of Alvin G. Pack, Salt Lake City.)

27. This portion of Lyman's diary was recorded as one long narrative weeks after the fact, probably in two or three separate sittings. I have broken up passages where Lyman wrote down a date.

28. Ezra Landen was a high priest in Geneseo, who was excommunicated on December 31, 1833, over his refusal to accept the vision of the three degrees of glory (D&C 76). See Shepard and Marquardt, *Lost Apostles*, 70.

29. The church was officially named the Church of Christ in 1830 and became

January 3, 1834; Friday. Visited the members of the Church & preached to the world in the evening.

January 5, 1834; Sunday. Brothers Orson [Pratt] and John [Murdock] preached to the Church.

January 6, 1834; Monday. Met in Church meeting present 4 High P[riest]s E[lders] 4 & about half of the Church. ~~that~~ The first motion was that we received Brother Joseph Smith Jr as a Servant of God, a Prophet a Seer a Revelator & a Translator to bring forth the misteries of the Kingdom to build up the Church of Christ in these last days & receive all the Rev. that came through him as being the word of the Lord and will abide the order of the Church of Christ. The vote was unanimous by the uplifted hands one member excepted. We then proceded to cut off the following persons Viz: Hannah More[,] Albert More[,] John Bosley[,] Ruby Landen[,] John Heth. The brethren and sisters renewed their covinent. The H[igh] P[riests] & E[lders] were to ^visit &^ deal with them and warn them to apear at the Church meeting on Saturday next and instructed the Church in various things even so Amen.

January 7, 1834; Tuesday. Visited the members acording to apointment.

January 8, 1834; Wednesday. Went to Genesee.

January 9, 1834; Thursday. Attended a prayer meeting. Taught them all to pray. Held other meetings and held two Church meetings and 10 members were expelled and on Friday the 24th I left Geneseea and came to Menden. Held 2 meetings in company with broth. L[uke] Johnson an from this place journeyed to the east as far as the town of Lyons where I arived on the 29th in company with broth. [Alvah L.] Tipetts, and on the evening of the 30th held a meeting. We found the brethren here in a low state of mind in consequence of not haveing been taught the principles of the doctrine of the Kingdom. I was some what astonished to learn that they had not observed the ordinances of the house of God in any respect.[30] On the evening of the 31st held a meeting and the word of the

---

the Church of the Latter Day Saints in May 1834, then the Church of Jesus Christ of Latter-day Saints in 1838.

30. His reference to "ordinanaces of the house of God" implied the Lord's Supper, healing blessings, and priesthood ordinations, all of which were performed in homes. It would be two years before the first Mormon temple would be completed in Kirtland.

Lord by the power of the spirit found its way to the hearts of some, and Sunday the 2nd of Feb, held meeting. The same evening held a meeting & on the evening of the 3rd held a meeting at brother Fosters and the brethren renewed their covenents one with the other and the Lord and union prevail^ed.^

February 5, 1834; Wednesday. An[d] on the 5th advised a concourse of people on the occasion of a funerel. The people were very indifferent. On the evening of the same day held a meeting and on the 7th journeyed as far as Waterloo an on the 8th arived in Spafford and on the 9th preached to the brethren in that place, and on the evening of the 10th held a meeting, on the evening of the 11th also an on the 12th.

February 12, 1834; Wednesday. Journeyed to the east as far as Fabuz [Fabius, New York] to brother [Samuel] Newcombs. Preached at the corners and on the 13th arived in Edingburg,[31] and on the 16th attended in the first part of the day and then journeyed to the east, and on the 17th arived in Bolton Waren County[32] where we found some brethren who were under ^severe^ embarassment because of division both in official and private [among the] members and on the 19th called a meeting of the official members of this branch of the Church.

February 20, 1834; Thursday. On the 20th we journeyed a[s] far as Whitehall and from thence to Castleton [Vermont] and on the 21st taried with my uncle in that place.[33]

February 22, 1834; Saturday. And ^on^ the 22nd journeyed as far as Royalton[34] and from this place I journeyed to my native place in Lyman, N[ew] H[ampshire,][35] at which place I arived on the 25th and on the 26th

31. Lyman has likely confused some dates because Edinburg is about 150 miles from Spafford. The Erie Canal was not in service in the winter and passage was difficult.

32. Warren County is in the far northeast section of New York state.

33. Lyman had a number of uncles. It is not clear from the records who was living in Vermont in 1834.

34. South Royalton is known today as the site of the Joseph Smith birthplace memorial, but Lyman gives no indication he was aware at the time of the town's significance. The details of Smith's early life became intertwined with the Mormon narrative only after the official history was published in 1842. See "History of Joseph Smith," *Times and Seasons*, Apr. 1, 1842.

35. Lyman, Grafton County, New Hampshire, was named after General Phineas Lyman, a veteran of the Seven Years War and distant relative of Amasa Lyman; both descended from Richard Lyman Jr., who was born in 1617 in England and emigrated to Connecticut, where he died in 1662.

went to Littleton and held one meeting & on the 27th journeyed to the north and on the 2nd of March preached to the brethren in Charleston [Vermont] and on the 3rd came to S.t. Johnsbury ~~I~~ where I taried until the evening of the 4th and on the 5th returned to Bath [New Hampshire] where I taried until the 10th when, I, in company with brother H[azen] Aldrich started for Bolton [New York]. Arived in Benson [Vermont] on the 14th and met with brother Lyman Johnson [with] whom on the 15th ~~wha~~ we held a meeting, and another on the 16th.[36]

March 17, 1834; Monday. On the 17th brothers O[rson Pratt] and L[yman Johnson] left for N[ew] H[ampshire]. [I] taried in Benson [Vermont] preparing to go up to Zion.[37] A part of two days, choped wood with brother [Daniel] C[arter][38] and Saturday, the 22nd, went to visit brother L. On the 23rd preached twice in the evening of the same day. Had a meeting at brother [Harlow] R[edfield]'s and on the 24th journeyed to the north and on the 25th arived in Charlotte and on this day wrote a letter to my mother and on the 26th crossed the lake [Champlain] ~~to~~ and went to the town of Lewis [New York] where I found a band of brethren desiring to serve the Lord but labouring under some disadvantages for a want of understanding. Taried in this place and taught them until the 7th of April and received of them $16½ to help me to go to Zion & also $2 for papers and [$]4 for revelations.

April 7, 1834; Monday. The 7th started for Bolton where I arived on the 8th with brother A[lvah L.] Tippets. On the evening of the 10th held meeting at brother [John] Taners[39] in Bolton and instructed the Church in company with brother H[azen] A[ldrich] and L[yman] Johnson until the 15th when brothers A[ldrich] and J[ohnson] left for the west.

36. The intent of Amasa's visit to New Hampshire was to deliver the gospel message to his mother and other relatives. In spite of his sincerity and zeal, neither his mother nor any other family member joined the faith.

37. While visiting Missouri in 1831, Joseph Smith declared via revelation that Jackson County was to be "the land of promise & the place for the City of Zion" (Godfrey, et al, *Joseph Smith Papers*, Documents Series, 2:5–12).

38. Daniel and Clarissa Carter were converted to Mormonism by cousin Jared Carter in Benson in 1832.

39. It was during this visit to the home of John Tanner that Amasa met his future wife, Maria Tanner. She and her father and several other family members had joined the church three years earlier.

April 12, 1834; Saturday.[40] I taried until the 12th then started for Kirtland [Ohio] where we arived on the 6th of May after a journey of 17 days. Taried in Kirtland three days and then took our journey for the land of Missouri[41] or the land of captivity of our brethren in tribulation where we arrived about the 18th of June after a tedious yet a prosperous journey although after our arival the destroyer rode through the camp to whose fury some fell victims and went to rest in the paridise of God. Viz[42]

1. John Carter ... H. P.
2. Seth Hitchcock ... Teacher
3. Erastus R. Rudd ... Elder
4. Eber Wilcox
5. Edward Ives
6. Betsy Parish[43]
7. Jesse B. Lawson
8. A[lgernon] S. Gilbert ... H. P. ^and agent^
9. Alfred Fisk, Elder
10. Noah Johnson
11. Sylvester Wilkinson ... Elder
12. Elias Strong ... Elder
13. Robert McChord
14. Jesse Smith ... Elder
15. Sister English

---

40. Lyman's brief record of his travels back to Kirtland and participation in Zion's Camp may have been written as late as mid-July 1834.

41. By 1834 well over 1,000 Mormons had colonized Jackson County. Cultural tensions were inevitable since the Saints were largely from New England and the other settlers were mostly Southerners. Mormons announced that God had sent them there, then William W. Phelps invited "Free People of Color" to join the Mormons. Long-time Missourians were incensed, and violent skirmishes ensued until a state militia compelled the Mormons to leave.

Joseph Smith responded with his own militia, the "camp of Israel," organized in Ohio, but from the outset the militia's journey was ill-fated. Arguments were frequent, travel was hampered by illness and by the number of participants. Lyman described it as a "tedious yet a prosperous" march, capturing the attitude of most of the volunteers. Once they arrived, the militia was disbanded, to the dismay of those who wanted to fight. See Launius, *Zion's Camp*.

42. The camp was afflicted with cholera, causing severe dehydration and in some cases death within a few hours.

43. Zion's Camp included some eleven women who cooked and laundered clothes and a baggage train of twenty-five wagons. Radke-Moss, "We Also Marched."

16. Phebe Murdock
17. Seth W. Engles
18. Timothy Bancroft

After our arival in the vicinity of our brethren [in Missouri] and administering for a season to the wants of the afflicted I commenced labouring for brother [Edmund] Durfy on the 7th of July and in counsil held on the 12th I received a mission to go with brother Lyman Wight to visit the brethren who were driven out from their inheritancy and learn the strength of the Lords house in this land and on Monday the 14th began to make preparation for fulfilling the mission by filling up my journal.

July 15, 1834; Tuesday. The 15th attended to preserving the property of our brethren who were disceased.

July 16, 1834; Wednesday. The 16th attended to like business from this time to the 3d of August. Attended to the business of my mission agreeable to appointment in numbering the Saints dureing which time I attended 6 meetings in company with brother Z[ebedee] Coltrin and I[saac] Morley & on the 27th of July I preached at brother D[avid W.] Pattens. Spoke from the 50th Psalm, ["]Out of Zion the perfection of beauty God hath shined.["][44]

July 31, 1834; Thursday. I here make a few remarks more full than foregoing. On the 31st of July the Grand Counsil was called acording to the law by which s[ai]d Counsil was established in consequence of the absence of two of the members of the counsil [and] brother Z[ebedee] Coltrin and myself wer chosen pro tem to fill their places. The first matter laid before us for our consideration [was] the propensity of chosing certain men to instruct the Saints in the time of their Captivity. Two spoke upon the case four wer chosen. The next case was that of brother S[amuel] Brown in which case brothers Z[ebedee] Coltrin and S[imeon] Carter wer elected to speak in behalf of the Church and in behalf of the accused brother O[rson] Pratt and myself. After examining the testimony and investigating the case it was decided that he Brown should make certain confessions and give up his licence and retain a standing in the Church as a private member until he should shew

44. Ps. 50:2.

himself worthy to receive authority to go forth and preach the gospel to the nations of the earth.[45]

August 5, 1834; Tuesday. From this time until the 5th I was with the brethren in the Hewlet branch.[46] Attended a meeting with brother L[eonard] Rich and in said branch laid hands on some sick folks who were blessed of the Lord and on the 6th met in counsil and again chosen in place of W[illia]m McLellin and was chosen to speak in behalf of the Church in the ~~caseo~~ case of the Hewlet branch concerning certain principals which the s[ai]d branch inculcated. After receiving the testimony it was decided that the Hewlet branch did not receive the word of the Lord through the gifts as they professed and brother Simeon Carter and myself were appointed to go to the s[ai]d branch and apprize them of the Decision of the counsil and instruct them in the things of the kingdom.

August 6, 1834; Wednesday. According to the foregoing appointment we went to visit the said branch of the Church the most of whom wer found willing to receive and conceded to the decision of the presidents.

August 8, 1834; Friday. On the 8th I was attacked with the fever and a voilent pain in my head from which I was delivered by the power of God. In ~~af~~ a few days I was attacked with the ague and fever with which I was afflicted until the 2ond of November when it left me and returned no more.[47] I continued with the brethren in Clay County until the 21st of Dec.[48]

---

45. Brown's support for speaking in tongues cost him his priesthood license. Vogel and Dunn, "The Tongue of Angels."

46. The Hulet Settlement was west of Liberty, Missouri, in Clay County.

47. This was probably malaria. Lyman was afflicted with it, off and on, for the rest of his life. He expressed gratitude to Elias Higbee's wife for caring for him.

48. Here Lyman takes a nearly year-long break from his diary. In the interim he returned to Kirtland to be ordained a Seventy by Joseph Smith, Oliver Cowdery, and Sidney Rigdon and to ask Maria Tanner to marry him, writing her the following letter:

> Dear Sister: Kirtland, Ohio. May 31, 1835
>
> While the mantle of night is spread around The works of nature, I take my pen that through Its silent language I might communicate to you Some of the feelings of my heart. Having been a wanderer, and desiring to Enjoy the blessings that would result from the society of a companion who would participate with Me in the changing scenes of life, if you desire Or feel willing to converse with me on the subject Of matrimony, please write your answer below. It is with the belief that I would be happy In your company that I write you. Receive this from your friend, A. Lyman. To Miss L. M. Tanner. Please answer this tomorrow.

Maria preserved the letter for years, eventually giving it to her son, Francis. She must have responded positively because ten days later, on June 10, 1835, she and Amasa

July 5, 1835; Sunday.[49] Had an interesting ^meeting for^ intstructing the saints. The Lord blessed us greatly.

July 6, 1835; Monday. Visited Fish Lake situated in Freedom [New York].

July 7, 1835; Tuesday. At the Lewises [home] preached to a small but attentive congregation some of them were desirous to hear further concerning the great work of the Lord. No [converts] were made. Left [after making] another apointment.

July 8, 1835; Wednesday. Passed through Ellicottville the County seat of Cattaraugus, Co. In this place I expected to preach but I not finding the apointment I passed on. Put up for the night with Sister [Marcia] Allen in Mansfield.

July 9, 1835; Thursday. Preached to a small congregation and left an apointment. The people were disposed to hear concerning the work of the Lord.

July 10, 1835; Friday. Had an attentive congregation of people after meeting they desired us to call and preach on our return. We left an apointment. It was cheering to my hear[t] to se[e] the clouds of prejudice give way before the mild rays of everlasting truth to se[e] the word of truth find sway to their hearts that they would hear more of the worke of the Lord.

July 11, 1835; Saturday. This day heard from Kirtland and learned concerning the tra[n]slating of certain egyptian records.[50]

---

were married by Elder Seymour Brunson. They took a five-day honeymoon, then Amasa resumed his missionary labors for another six months while Maria continued to live with her parents. His preaching in the east resulted in "liberal additions to the Church," he wrote. The missionaries traveled through the panhandle area of Pennsylvania to Allegheny County, New York, "over 2,000 miles of travel" and the delivery of "nearly 200 sermons." *Millennial Star*, 27:503.

49. Lyman departed from the reminiscent style and began making daily entries again, on June 15, but since they are non-narrative lists of towns and distances traveled, they are omitted here. On July 5 he started interspersing his lists with brief notes and then lengthier entries.

50. Joseph Smith said the Egyptian papyri he purchased in Kirtland from Michael Chandler, a traveling antiquities dealer, were the writings of Abraham. They were published as such, in Smith's own translation narrative, in the *Times and Seasons* and then canonized as part of the Pearl of Great Price in 1880. In 2014 the LDS Church published an essay acknowledging that the translation may not be literal, while at the same time reinforcing the church's belief in the divinity of the narrative's message (LDS.org., "Translation and Historicity"; Ritner, *The Joseph Smith Papyri*).

July 12, 1835; Sunday. This day ^at 4 oclock^ preached to a large congrega^tion^ who heard[51] attentively the word of the Lord. In the former part of this day I attended a meeting of the presbyterian order and heard from one who stood as their teacher. The things which he taught and while he said much concerning the blessings of heaven but gave us no understanding of the way or principle upon which we were to come to the enjoyment of the blessings of the way of Life and salvation. Which caused me to say in my hea[r]t how long shall error reign how long shall superstition spread its mantle of impenitra[b]le darkness over the minds of men.

July 13, 1835; Monday. This day took leave of brother Z[erubbabel] Snow in the village of Lodi in Perrysburg, where he was to preach at 5 oclock.

July 15, 1835; Wednesday. Had no meeting this day acording to apointment because of the rain.

July 16, 1835; Thursday. The people listened attentively. Left another apointment for the next week.

July 17, 1835; Friday. Preached to an attentive congregation.

July 21, 1835; Tuesday. This day preached to an attentive audience. Taried all night with a Mr Blaredell who appeared disposed to receive light. We conversed freely and may the Lord bless his word to the children of men.

July 22, 1835; Wednesday. This day passed through the village of Waverly where I had an apontment at 5 oc[loc]k but no persons attended.

July 23, 1835; Thursday. Attended meeting with brother Z[erubbabel] Snow, the people listened attentively and desired to hear again. The Lord bless them.

July 25, 1835; Saturday. Were opposed by one of the priests of Babylon.

July 27, 1835; Monday. This day meet with Elders L[yman] Shirman and J[azemiah] B. Smith from Kirtland. In meeting this day we were opposed by ~~a baptised Elder H Licter~~ universal preacher Wm Todd,[52] while enquiring for [appointments] we came to Mr Brown whom we found s[u]plicating the throne of god but he would not give us entertainment.

July 28, 1835; Tuesday. Visited Mr Delapps. They were believing in the word of the Lord.

51. Lyman writes *He* here, failing to finish his thought.

52. Universalists, who believed in universal salvation, were among the largest congregations in the United States at the time.

July 30, 1835; Thursday. This day met with Elder J[ohn D.] Parker from Kirtland.

August 4, 1835; Tuesday. On the evening of the same day had some conversation with a Mr Harper.

August 9, 1835; Sunday. One [meeting] in Ashford & one in east Otto. The people listened attentively and desired more instruction.

August 10, 1835; Monday. Taried all night with Mr Fay. This day passed some fields of corn that were destroyed by the frost, so he that causes the sun to rise on the evil and the good suffers the hopes of husbandman to be blasted. But is this all while the vegitable world suffers from the chilling blast sweeps over the plain[?] Whats the sound that salutes my ear, as borne as it were upon the wings of the wind as destroyer in the ^land^ to whose withering touch thousands and tens of thousands fall victims on the right hand and on the left, wher to day we behold stately Kingdoms that aford us fair specimen of the pompous grandure of the earth. To morrow nought but a scene of desolation meets the eye of the beholder who then cannot say with the preacher that all is as a thing of nought and all is vanity.[53]

August 13, 1835; Thursday. This day wrote a letter to Kirtland. In the evening it rained.

August 14, 1835; Friday. This day wrote to [acquaintances in] Illinois.

August 16, 1835; Sunday. One [meeting] in Lava & one in Orrangeville.

August 17, 1835; Monday. The people listened attentively and may the Lord bless them.

August 20, 1835; Thursday. This day it rained. Had but few hearers. Left another appoint^ment.^

August 27, 1835; Thursday. This day attended an apointment at Mr. Delapps but had no congregation.

August 28, 1835; Friday. Taried all night with Mr. Benidict. Conversed with them about the great work of the Lord and may the Lord bless them.

September 4, 1835; Friday. This day had an interview with two of the preachers of the gentiles whose names were Pratt & Cook.

---

53. This entry is part of Lyman's efforts to expand his vocabulary. He never mastered some words but his vocabulary improved.

September 6, 1835; Sunday. This day it rained by reason of which I disapointed one apointment.

September 8, 1835; Tuesday. Had an attentive congregation may the Lord bless the word.

September 9, 1835; Wednesday. This day attended the funerel of a child the son of a Mr. Whitny. The people listined attentively, may the Lord bless to them this dispensation of his providence.

September 12, 1835; Saturday. This day attended a conference of Elders before whom Elder D. Hix was tried for not keeping the Word of Wisdom[54] and was restored to fellowship by covinanting to keep and teach the same.

September 13, 1835; Sunday. This day I attended two meetings in Rushford and one person was baptized. After meeting walked to Freedom.

September 20, 1835; Sunday. This day I had the pleasure of the company of Elder P[arley] P. Pratt.

September 22, 1835; Tuesday. Had an attentive congregation.

September 28, 1835; Monday. This day was opposed by one of the priests of that god without body or parts who withstood the truth as did Jannes and Jambres but his folly was manifest as theirs also was.[55]

April 7, 1836; Thursday. This day left Kirtland on a mission to the east in company with Brother Nathan Tanner. We traveled 123 m[ile]s. I put up with Sister Foster, were kindly treated. On the 9th arived in Springfield PA.[56] With pleasur I reflect upon priviliges we enjoy. While leaveing my home an old lady stood in her door and blessed us as we went along.

April 13, 1836; Wednesday. In Springfield held a 2 meetings and on the 13th arived in Westfield [New York] the distance of ~~a~~ 52 m[ile]s.

April 15, 1836; Friday. Arived [in] Persia. Taried all night with Mr. [Harvey] Redfield wer kindly treated.

April 16, 1836; Saturday. Came to Otto 7 m[ile]s. Here I taryed with

54. The Word of Wisdom (D&C 89) is the divinely ascribed prohibition against alcohol, coffee, tea, and tobacco. Adherence to it fluctuated until the twentieth century when it became a symbol of Latter-day Saint identity. Today observance is required for entry into an LDS temple. Dirkmaat, et al., *Joseph Smith Papers*, Documents Series, 3:11–24; Peterson, "Word of Wisdom."

55. Jannes and Jambres were Pharaoh's magicians who competed with Moses and Aaron. Exod. 7:11–12, 2; Tim. 3:8.

56. This is now North Springfield in northwest Pennsylvania, near Lake Erie, not Springfield Township outside of Philadelphia.

brother H[arvey] Redfield an held 3 meetings. The Lord blesed us with his spirit in declaring his word. The people were cut to the heart. After meeting walked 6 m[ile]s and put with Mr. Mallup and on Monday the 18th came to Franklinville. Stayed with Mr. Simonds.

April 19, 1836; Tuesday. On Tuesdsay 19th came to Farmersville, 12 m[ile]s. On this day attended a Conference at brothers J. S. Hackes house. Here parted with the brethren R[euben] Hadlock, H[arvey] Redfield and C[hapman] Duncan.

April 20, 1836; Wednesday. On the 20th held one meeting at Mr. Coaldrakes and journeyed to brother Eatons,[57] 6 m[ile]s to the town of Rushford.

April 21, 1836; Thursday. On the 21st went to Mrs. Whites. Taried all night.

April 22, 1836; Friday. On the 22nd went to Mr Hammonds. Taried all night.

April 23, 1836; Saturday. 23d. Came to brother Kendals. Held 2 meetings and one on the 24th. Wedding Mr. L. Eaton & S Brunson.

April 25, 1836; Monday. 25th came to Portage to Elder [blank]. On the 26th came to Castile and on the 26th returned to brother + held one meeting.[58]

April 28, 1836; Thursday. On the 28th visited brother [Hiram] Kellogg. It was a fine pleasant day. 4 years ago this day I was baptized by Elder L[yman] Johnson. On the 29th went to Grove and on the 30th returned to brother [blank]. Held one meeting. On this day visited a young lady who had been bourne by sickness for more than one year and prayed for her and she received strength to obey the Lord.

April[:] traviled 305 m[ile]s; Held 13 meetings and one &; was not disturbed and attended one.[59]

May 1,1836; Sunday. Baptized Sister Rebeckah Gilman, and preached twice at brother Markses. This day we were called to ^administer to^ three sick persons, traviled 3 m[ile]s.

57. Probably Frazier Eaton, an 1835 convert from Rushfield who donated $700 to the Kirtland temple and reportedly apostatized when he was not able to get a seat at the dedication. Journal History, Nov. 15, 1864, 5.

58. Lyman appears to be recording about once a week rather than daily, which could explain why he has forgotten a few names.

59. This summary in the center of the page was accompanied by the Hebrew word for nineteen, probably learned at the School of the Prophets in Kirtland.

May 2, 1836; Monday. Traviled 12 m[ile]s and on the 3[rd] traviled 5 m[ile]s. Held one meeting an baptized 2, and on the 4th administered to one sick person and went to Carlisle, 12 m[ile]s and on the 5th held one meeting. Left brother [Nathan] T[anner].

May 6, 1836; Friday. On the 6th returned to Oakhill, 7 m[ile]s, on the 7th went to Sunday 5 m[ile]s and held one meeting and on 8th had a meeting and baptized one person and returned to Oakhill 5 m[ile]s.

May 9, 1836; Monday. On the 9th preached at brother D. Bennetts and on the 10th went to the town of Springwater with Wm N. Olney, 25 m[ile]s. On the 11th held one meeting.

May 12, 1836; Thursday. On the 12th parted with brother Nathan Tanner in the town Liman. On the 14th arived in the town of Scipio from Springwater 80 m[ile]s.[60]

May 15, 1836; Sunday. On the 15th preached in the baptist house in Scipio. On the morning of the 17th arived in Homer ^30 m[ile]s^. Preached twice. On the 23d arived in the town of Fredingburg, 160 m[ile]s. Taried with the widdow Heart.

May 24, 1836; Tuesday. The 24th held one meeting and the 26th arived in Bolton 25 m[ile]s and on the ~~26~~ 27th held one meeting. On the 29th held 2 meetings. Elder H[arrison] Burges[s] attended with me.[61]

June 2, 1836; Thursday. The 2d held one meeting an the 4th held one meeting. This day meet with brother brother [Nathan] Tanner on the 5th held 2 meetings.

June 10, 1836; Friday. On the 10th held one meeting on the 11[th] preached in Waringsbury [and] on the 12th held 2 meetings in Bolton.

June 16, 1836; Thursday. On the 16th baptized one person [and] on the 17th 36 m[ile]s [to] Saratoga. 18th 7 m[ile]s [and] on the 19th held one meeting [and] on the 20th read the life of Elias Smith.[62]

---

60. Traveling from Springwater to Scipio brought them within ten miles of Palmyra, where Joseph Smith lived until January 1831.

61. Here Lyman added a series of dashes across the page to separate the May and June entries.

62. Elias Smith was a Christian Connection minister. It should be noted that Lyman largely abandons his narrative style at this point and begins putting the date on the left, followed by the distance traveled and how many meetings he scheduled, with the exception of the June 29, 1836, entry that simply says "went fishing." That was followed by several blank pages and then dates and expenses, including food received such

January 17, 1841; Sunday.[63] This day held meeting at the house of Jos Smith Jnr. Lyman Wight addressed a large congregation from the 8 Chap of John. Followed by remarks by Jos & Hyrum and myself. In the afternoon sat in Quorum of High Priests & was ricd [received] a member of that body. Returned home at night.[64]

January 18, 1841; Monday. This day Br A[aron] F[arr] and myself drove 20 miles in a cutter. Held a meeting in a schoolhouse in the village in Van Buren Co. [Iowa].[65] Br Lyman [Wight] addressed a small congregation of [illegible] who payed good attention. He read 35th Psalm and made some very appropriate remarks and I also in conclusion made some remarks appointed a meeting on the Wednesday 2 weeks following.

January 19, 1841; Tuesday. This day traveled up the Des Moines River on the ice 24 miles and held a meeting by candle light in the village of Rising Sun [Iowa]. Had an attentive audience. Brother Lyman [Wight] addressed them on the fall of Adam and on the first principals of the Gospel. He had great liberty. The congregation was however disturbed by some person stoning the house. [Next two pages illegible.]

In the evening at which time Br. Lyman addressed a small congregation from the 21st Chapt. of Isaiah. He had liberty & the people paid good attention. I made a few remarks in conclusion & left an appointment for Saturday following 2 weeks.

January 22, 1841; Friday. After breakfast we left the house of our friend Esqr Guthrie who accompanied us to Nauvoo [Illinois]. From there [to the Smith's] house where I stayed all night. Found my wife & child laboring under a severe cold.

January 23, 1841; Saturday. This day crossed the Mississippi [River] in company with Brother Lyman [Wight] to Brother Jos[eph] Smith Jun.

---

as a bushel of corn or side of beef. Lyman resumes a short narrative record on May 11, 1842, in another book. For clarity, I have kept the entries in chronological order.

63. The four-and-a-half year gap in Lyman's diary neglected several important events in Mormonism and in Lyman's own life. For instance, the church collapsed in Ohio with the failure of the Kirtland Anti-Banking Safety Society. Loyal members moved to Missouri, where tensions led to the Mormon War of 1838. Lyman was imprisoned alongside Joseph Smith before he moved to Nauvoo, Illinois.

64. Several lines, written in pencil, are smudged beyond recognition. Two pages are almost entirely illegible.

65. Many of Lyman's excursions took him to the small towns throughout eastern Iowa, just north of Nauvoo.

January 24, 1841; Sunday. Went to Augusta [Iowa] and attended meeting had an attentive congregation.

January 25, 1841; Monday. On the 25th went to Flint Creek,[66] held 2 meetings in company with brother Frederick Kesler. Taried all night with brother Harell.

January 26, 1841; Tuesday. The 26th went to Virginia Grove held meeting at Mr [William] Duncans. At night the 27th went to Mr Smiths and ~~had~~ held meeting. On the 28th returned to Augusta. Held meeting with brother [Lyman] Wight. 3 came forward for baptism.

January 29, 1841; Friday. Went to West Point. Brother [Lyman] Wight addressed an attentive congregation. Taried with Dr Burke.

January 30, 1841; Saturday. The 30th went to home and on the 31st attended a meeting in Nauvoo.

February 1, 1841; Monday. Attended the municipal election in Nauvoo [and] on the 2nd went to brother Clarks held meeting. On the 3d went to Farmington.

February 4, 1841; Thursday. On the 4th went to Pitsburg. Held a meeting at Mr. Persons.

February 5, 1841; Friday. On the 5th & 6th was detained in Vanburen as a witness. On the 7th preached in Vanburen to an attentive people and gave out an apointment for the night at Mr Wm Duncans. Had an attentive people.

February 8, 1841; Monday. The 8th taried with Wm Duncan [and] on the 9th went to brother Burks [and] on the 10th taried with brother Burks.

February 11, 1841; Thursday. On the 11th went home. On the [illegible] went to Nauvoo from thence to West Point in company with brother [George L.] Miller. Preached at night. On the 13th went to Augusta. 14th preached 2 times.

February 15, 1841; Monday. Went to Burlington.

February 16, 1841; Tuesday. Returned ~~home~~ to Montrose. 17th was at home. 18th attended a meeting at Nashville. 19th preached at Montrose. 20th went to West Point. Attended the celebration of the birth of Washington and the 21st preached at Augusta at night.

66. Flint Creek was a small settlement on the river of the same name.

February 22, 1841; Monday. On the 22d went to Thomas Downing [in] Henry County. 23 went to brothers Charles Barney preached at night on the 24th went to Newlondon. Had an interview with priest of the Campbellite order.[67]

February 25, 1841; Thursday. Went to Augusta. Preached at night.

February 26, 1841; Friday. Went to West Point. Preached on the Book of Mormon. 27th ~~ret~~ returned to Augusta. 28th brother [Lyman] Wight preached 2 were baptized. Preached again at night.

March 1, 1841; Monday. Returned home [and] on the 2ond went to Nauvoo. Taried until the 5th. Returned home.

March 6, 1841; Saturday. Taried at home. 7th went to Montrose. Monday the 8th attended the election and went to Nauvoo[,] taried until the 10th. Returned home and went to Nauvoo. Taried until the 13th. Went to Augusta. Taried until the 15th. Held 2 meetings [and] went to West Point. ~~Brother~~ Preached at night.

March 16, 1841; Tuesday. Went to Farmington. Brother S preached. Taried with a Mr Death.[68]

March 17, 1841; Wednesday. Went to Van Buren. Preached at night. Preached the 18th, went to the [village of Rising] Sun. Preached at night.

March 19, 1841; Friday. Went to West Point. Preached on the 20th. 21st returned to Montrose. Preached. 22ond went to Nauvoo.[69]

May 11, 1842; Wednesday. Left Nauvoo for the south.[70] Took passage on board the Steamer Rappids. On the 12th arived in St. Louis [Missouri] [and] reshiped on board the Alex Scotte.[71] On the night of

---

67. The Campbellites, or Disciples of Christ, of Ohio counted among their number a charismatic preacher named Sidney Rigdon, who split with Alexander Campbell in 1830 to join the Mormons.

68. One hopes Lyman is making a wry joke by writing "Mr Death," but who this might be is unclear.

69. The 1841 diary ended here, followed by a blank page, then new entries in pen beginning with "Nauvoo Sept 10th 1842" written at the top. The May–June 1842 entries were kept in a different book.

70. Once more the gap in Lyman's diary signaled the end of one mission and the start of another. He would now travel south to Kentucky and Tennessee before returning to Nauvoo.

71. The *Alexander Scott* was a large and famous paddle steamer in operation on the Mississippi River from 1842 to 1854. For a time it counted among its crew a young Samuel Clemens. "Mark Twain," *Chicago Tribune*, July 4, 1875.

the 13th arived at Millers Point KY. On the 14th started for Dresden[,] Weakley County, Tennessee. On Sunday the 15th preached at night.

May 17, 1842; Tuesday. Preached 2 m[ile]s from town. On the night of the 18th preached in Dresden. Taried until the 23rd when I attended a funerel with the masonick brethren.[72] Taried in the vicinity [and] preached as often as there was opportunity until the first of June.

June 4, 1842; Saturday. From this time until the 4th held meetings as opportunity presented when brother [Lyman] Wight came subsequent to which time we laboured together.

June 12, 1842; Sunday. On the 12th we preached in the Courthouse in Dresden. Taried with Capt Davis [and still] taried in Dresden until the 17th. Brother [Lyman] Wight went to KY. I preached in the Courthouse once on Sunday the 19th we held meeting at [Jesse and Amelia] Berrys on the Monday folowing went to Gibson County to the branch of the Church there. Held one meeting instructed them an[d] silenced two of their Elders for teaching delusions and returned to Dresden. On the 23rd this night brother [David] C[rider] held a meeting at Mr. [John] Bowerses.

June 24, 1842; Friday. Went to brother McIntosh, taried until [blank].[73]

> Question[:][74] When storms of winds are past & gone/ Shall sudden calm appear/ I have often seen in ashes deep/ Lay hidden cowls of fire/ With confidence mark well your ^mind^/ You shall in this a question find/ Sweet is the question mark it well/ Heart upon heart & so farewell/
>
> Answer[:] To answer this I want not long/ Night shades the deeds of many a ^wrong^/ Maria Louisa Lyman
>
> Home[:] 1. Torn from our friends and captiv ^led^/ Mid armed legions bound in chains/ That peace for which our fathers bled/ Is gone

72. Lyman drew a mallet at the end of this line, a Masonic symbol.

73. The next page is empty. Lyman thereafter returned to using his diary for monetary notations. After several more pages, he began practicing his handwriting, carefully recording the names and birthdates of his family. The next pages included the alphabet, recorded in a neat pen.

74. As part of his efforts to improve his grammar and handwriting, Lyman wrote poems in his diary. I have replaced the line breaks with slashes to conserve space.

and dire confusion reign/ 2. Zion our peacef[ul] happy home/ Where oft we joined in praised pray,/ A desolation has become./ And grief and sorrow linger there./[75]

Honour[:] Amasa Lyman/ and his wife and child/ were you beyond the rolling/ sea love would find wings/ to fly to you had I the/ wings of Noah's dove/ how soon I would fly to/ the Artemitia

September 10, 1842; Saturday.[76] Left on a mission in company with brothers [Heber C.] Kimball[,] [Brigham] Young[,] and [George A.] Smith. Went to Lima [Illinois,] had meeting on the sabath [and] found fifty labourers for the ministry. Baptized 13. On the 12th left for Quincy. In the after part of the day it rained. We were some wet but through the merciy of God we sustained no injury. Put up with brother U[riah] B Powel for the night in the morn^ing^ found brother Holister. Breakfasted with brother P then went to brother Crandalls. At night had meeting in the Courthouse. Brother George preached [and] on the night of the 14th I preached to an attentive people. Taried with sister Pinkam morning of the 15th quite cold.

November 2, 1843; Thursday.[77] Left Nauvoo for Indiana on board the steamer Iowa. My wife had the ague. Went to brother H[arvey] Redfields whose family we joined well on the 10th. Traviled down the Mississippi to the mouth of the Ohio [River] then up the same to Lawrenceberg [Indiana] ^on the 10th.^ From thence we traveled by land to

75. Following the poems, Lyman wrote out the alphabet, some Hebrew characters, and his children's names.

76. Lyman was ordained an apostle on Aug. 20, 1842, at age twenty-nine. This started his vacillating position in the church hierarchy for the next three years, initially replacing Orson Pratt in the Quorum of Twelve Apostles but becoming the thirteenth apostle when Pratt was reinstated in January the next year. Lyman was temporarily made the fourth member of the First Presidency, reinforcing his status as an elite leader without a clear role, until he was admitted into the quorum again in 1845. *AML*, 62–64, 66–67; Bergera, *Conflict in the Quorum*, 27–35.

77. The journal jumps ahead more than a year, at first in pencil, as if Lyman is taking notes, then repeated in pen with more details. Lyman may have already secretly taken his first plural wife, Dioneta Walker Whitney, as historian Edward Leo Lyman argues, saying it likely took place in July 1843. Another researcher, George D. Smith, suggests that it probably happened later in 1845. Regardless, Lyman had a private interview with Joseph Smith on polygamy and married six women from 1844 to 1846. *AML*, 72; Smith, *Nauvoo Polygamy*, 606, 646n231.

Trenton, Franklin County. Taried with brother Scouts until the 14th. Held 4 meetings then went to Fayette County my family were sick all the time, some of them.

November 16, 1843; Thursday. On the 16th brother [William] Martindale left for Washington [Township] Warren County.[78] Myself went to stop with brother Budd for a time the wether from the first of our journey was for the most part wet and cold the clouds commenced to break with some tokens of pleasant wether.[79]

November 17, 1843; Friday. The weather cool and pleasant without rain. 19th held 4 meetings one in Alquina one at brother [William] Steels had attentive audience. On Monday the 20th it rained. 21st visited brother Golden the weather fine. 22ond fine weather taried at home. On the 23d cloudy in the morn^ing^ with indication of rain.

January 4, 1844; Thursday. On the 4th of Jan 1844 settled in Alquina.

January 7, 1844; Sunday. On the 7th went to Union County. Preached at brother R[obert] Richeys on Thursday night of the 11th preached to br [William] Steels the weather warm with rain and of mud there is no lack. This week my wife had a very serious unwelcome visit from the ague and fever.

April 11, 1844; Thursday.[80] Left St. Louis's on board the steam boat Mandan. On the 16th landed the pass at Fushes[?].

The truth is a treasure whose possessor is ever richly compensated for whatever of sacifise its acquisition may require. It is truth that stays the heart amid all the conflicting scenes of human life.

It is truth that lights the bon fire of hope beyond the confines of the tomb. With our path illumed and our hearts cheered by the ^brightning^ prospects the its sacred light reveals we can smile defrance to the raging storm and welcome as heavans richest boom the change that awaits all liveing and shall release our tired tired spirits from the restraints of dul mortality and bid us welcome ^to^ the purer joys of imortality and eternal life.[81]

---

78. Not to be confused with Washington City in Daviess County, Indiana.

79. The entry continues several pages later. Pages likely fell out of the diary and were reinserted in the wrong order.

80. This entry, written in pencil, appears in a later diary after several blank pages.

81. Lyman wrote this as part of his efforts to practice grammar and handwriting. It appears a few pages after the April 11, 1844 entry and is followed by more blank pages.

June 4, 1844; Tuesday.[82] Started on a journey to the east.[83] Traviled to Brookville in company with brother [George] Dikes[84] and passage on board the canal boat Patriot.[85] Arrived in Cincinnati [Ohio] on the 5th. Found the brethren well lodged with broth. Perly. On the 6th spent the day with Sister Evens. Lodged with brother Baker on the 7th was introduced to Sister Maryweather from whom I received a present of a book for a journal. To day went to the Rolling mill and nail factory and the water works.[86] The weather was very warm in the afternoon cloods with some rain called on Sister Evans. At evening went to sister Maryweathers with sisters E and G. Lodged at bro Bakers.

June 8, 1844; Saturday. Weather fine. Spent some time in reading on the 9th preached at 11 oclock at the engine house[87] at 3 oclock attended a church meeting at Father Hewetts. At candle light preached at the hall. Lodged at brother Bakers. The weather is though rather warm and sultry.

June 10, 1844; Monday. The 10th in the morning parted with brother J Youngs. Spent sometime about the leavy in the after noon received a visit from a Mr Price who says that he was called when Joseph Smith was and informed us that Smith has not the authority of the priesthood as he is not Michael that shall stand up for his people and also that all the

---

82. The remaining 1844 entries and those in the next chapter for 1845–46 are from a new diary.

83. Lyman was to meet with George J. Adams to campaign for Joseph Smith's US presidential candidacy, spearheaded by the newly formed Council of Fifty in Nauvoo. Rogers, *Council of Fifty*, 5–7.

84. George P. Dykes and Amasa Lyman led the campaign delegation in Indiana. *Times and Seasons*, Apr. 15, 1844.

85. The Whitewater Canal, begun in 1837 in Brookville, was dug adjacent to the Whitewater River for forty miles to the confluence with the Ohio River at Lawrenceburg, Indiana. Fox, *Memoirs of Wayne County*, 1:123–24.

86. The water works were built in 1821 at what is now Sawyer Point. They provided residents with culinary water through wooden pipes, the water pumped out of the river by horse-powered treadmills until 1824 when the horses were replaced by a steam engine. Mike Boyer, "Acclaimed City Water Works System Fueled Growth," *Cincinnati Enquirer*, Mar. 18, 2012.

87. The "engines" were water pumps that volunteers transported to fires on horse-drawn wagons; they were stored in engine houses, or garages constructed for fire-fighting equipment. Where Lyman attended a lecture in an engine house on Fifth Street, the garage had presumably been converted into a multi-purpose civic building. Goss, *Cincinnati*, 2:59–65; "Lectures," *Western Midnight Cry*, June 22, 1844.

athority of the clergy from the English Church down to the prophet at Nauvoo is of human origin.

As I was about to retire the alarm of fire called our attention. We repaired to the vicinity of the fire when we learned that the fire comenced in a large steem mill near the river which was burnt to the ground. Returned to my lodgings. A pleasant night.

June 11, 1844; Tuesday. This Morning the 11th quite cool. Was down to the levy [levee][88] this morning went over the [Mill Creek] river the to brother Scofield. In the evening went to brother Perleys and on my return to my lodgeing heard a Millerite preach.[89]

June 12, 1844; Wednesday. Weather still cool. Spent this morning in reading went the Foundary[90] of brother Baker dined with Sister Meryweather after which I went to the meeting to brother Cakes on 4th st on Thursday.

June 13, 1844; Thursday. The 13th took some medicine was not about much through the day. Was quite ill through the night.

June 14, 1844; Friday. Rained some. Walked about some. Healthe improved some at night went to the museum. There I saw some of the wonders of nature and some of the depravity of fallen humanity was manifest in the tragical scene of the death of Mrs Cowen and her two children by the hand of the husband and father.[91] The sad fruits of je^al^ousy. Oh! thou bane of domestic felicity from thy carroding curse may this heart be ever free.

To day for the first time saw the Prophet[,] a paper printed in the City of N.Y. by the saints.[92] Was holy gratified that so much is doing for

88. The levee was the commercial dock and environs, known for the freedmen who lived and worked there. Buchanan, *Black Life on the Mississippi*, 47–49.

89. Millerites were the followers of William Miller, who believed the Second Coming of Christ would occur in 1843–44, thereafter continuing in their faith and offering various justifications for why the earth had been granted a reprieve.

90. That is, a foundry for purifying and casting metals.

91. In October 1835, John Cowan killed his wife, Mary, and two children with an axe, for which he was hanged. Before he died, he said he regretted killing his children. *Murder Will Out*, 11–12.

92. *The Prophet*, a four-page LDS newspaper, was founded in New York City in May 1844 as part of Joseph Smith's candidacy for the highest federal office. The paper ran for one year before its editors, George T. Leach and A. E. Wright, were excommunicated for sympathizing with Sidney Rigdon after Smith's death. Crawley, *Descriptive Bibliography of the Mormon Church*, 1:254–57.

the truth and may it spread and gloryously triumph in the omnipotence of its own strength.

June 15, 1844; Saturday. Weather still warm and pleasant. My health still improving. Wa[t]ching still ^for^ brother George [Adams] who has not yet come. Sunday the 16th preached at the hall at 11 oclock. Rained some. Lodged at Mr Painters.

June 17, 1844; Monday. Wa[t]ched [for] the friends from the west. On the 18th meet with brother H. Lamaw, weather still warm still looking for brother [George] A[dams].

June 19, 1844; Wednesday. Went to the levy. No news from the west. Weather very warm and sultry. Lodged at brothers Baker the last night my health as useal returned and wrote a leter to brother Taylor.

June 20, 1844; Thursday. Saw brother [Milo] Andros and Fretwell. Returned to Sisters Evanses and read an exposition of Farier [Charles Fourier] system of assosiation. Friday 21st spent the day mostly in reading. At night heard a lecture on association by Mr Whittley. Lodged at Mr Painters.

June 22, 1844; Saturday. Spent the day in anxious expectation for coming friends but saw none. Sunday the 23rd preached at the hall twice.

June 24, 1844; Monday. Went to Newport in Kentucky. Spent the day with brother Crookfield. Gave out an apointment for meeting on Tuesday 25th. At 5 oclock repaired to the Court house at the time for meeting and to my surprise no ladies and some half dozen men and two pigs were all that turned out from the great town of Newport. It tells for the place. Returned to the city [and] lodged at Mr Painters.

June 25, 1844; Tuesday. Spent the day in reading in evening there was some rain. Thursday 27th warm with rain.

June 28, 1844; Friday. Weather still warm. On Saturday the 29th heard from Nauvoo by the S[team] B[oat] Godess of Liberty.[93] On Sunday the 30th preached at the hall in the morn^ing^. At evening at Newport Kentucky.

July 1, 1844; Monday. Spent the day in reading. Weather continues

93. What Lyman had not yet heard was that Joseph Smith and his brother Hyrum were murdered the day before in Carthage, Illinois. The only telegraph line in the country stretched from Washington, DC, to Baltimore, so elsewhere the news still traveled by horse or steamboat.

very warm with some indications of rain this [evening]. Visited sister Carter. Lodged at Mr Painters. Tuesday the 2ond weather still warm.

July 3, 1844; Wednesday. Heard the report of the murder brothers Joseph and Hyrum Smith. Anxiously waited through the day for correct information on the matter.

July 4, 1844; Thursday. No information yet great preparation had been made to celebrate the birth of American ^liberty^ which might hither have been turned into its funeral.

July 5, 1844; Friday. On Friday the 5th remained in suspence. On Saturday the 6th the news was confirmed.[94] On Sunday the 7th preached at the hall. In the evening of [which] meet with brothers [Henry J.] Adams and [Thomas] Lyne from Nauvoo.

July 8, 1844; Monday. Spent the day with the brethren. Tuesday the 9th meet brothers Bear and Snow.

July 10, 1844; Wednesday. Weather warm meet with the brethren on wednesday 10th at night heard a funeral discourse on the death of Joseph & Hyrum Smith by Elder H Adams to a large congregation. On the morning of the 11th brothers Adams and Lyne started for the east.

July 12, 1844; Friday. At 4, oclock started for Trenton [Ohio] where I meet with brothers W & W[illard] Snow from Alquina [Indiana].[95] Found the friends well. Crossed the river and went to brothers Chappelows. Lodged at brother Millers. Brother Willard left for Mt Carmel [Ohio] on the evening of the 13th. Lodged with brother Chappelow.

July 14, 1844; Sunday. Wether still warm and dry. Preached at the schoolhouse in the evening it rained. On Monday the 15th went to brother Belks where I met my wife and children. They were well. Remained one day and on the 17th went to Hagerstown [Indiana] on the 18th went to Washington [Ohio]. Preached at night.

July 19, 1844; Friday. Went to Alquina on the 20th and 21st. Held meeting on the 22ond. Went to Trenton on the 23d went to Cincinnati where I remained until Thursday the 25th. On this day took passage on

94. In a day of instant alerts on portable devices, we can only imagine the anguish Lyman must have felt while he waited ten days for confirmation of the initial reports of the death of his friend and mentor.

95. Lyman is traveling back to Illinois by way of northern Kentucky, southern Indiana, and Ohio.

board the S[team] B[oat] Virginian for St. Louis [Missouri] where we arived in safety. From thence to Nauvoo where I arived on the 1st day of August and on the 7th the brethren of the twelve arived and called a special conference on Tuesday the 13th.[96]

96. The entry was apparently written in one sitting, likely after Lyman had arrived back in Nauvoo.

2 The Long Road to the Great Basin, 1845–1847

This portion of Amasa Lyman's diary covers his last days in Nauvoo and journey from Winter Quarters to the Great Basin. Reflecting the challenges and chaos of the times, the narrative shows little regard for careful chronological order. Lyman would begin making entries in one diary book, finish them in another, and return to the first book to make more entries years later. This was also the first time he kept entries as a husband and church leader instead of as a missionary. The trail notes were kept by Albert Carrington, who acted as a secretary for the whole pioneer company, and are included because they are part of the Lyman Collection at the LDS Church History Library and record his activities, along with the others of the company.

January 24, 1845; Friday. Opened the [Nauvoo] Library. Weather cool, and pleasant. Saturday 25th went to the hall in the morning. In the afternoon went to the Temple [and] saw some of the Twelve. Conversed [with] them. Weather fine and warm this evening. Saw Sister [Sarah?] Pratt. Went to brother [John] Taylors [and] saw brother O[rson] Hyde.

January 26, 1845; Sunday. Attended meeting at the Masonick Hall. This day heard of the repeal of the Charter of our city.[1] In the evening meet in the Quorum. Monday 27th went to the hall. The weather was

1. The Nauvoo Charter granted wide latitude to the Mormons, but by 1845 the political winds had shifted enough in Illinois to allow for its repeal. The state government of Illinois intended to step in and regulate the Mormons. Leonard, *Nauvoo*, 284–86, 465–68. A copy of the charter is in Dinger, *Nauvoo City and High Council*, 567–73.

cold. In the evening preached at the concert hall on the subject of our temperal interests.[2] The weather still cold cool and pleasant.

January 28, 1845; Tuesday. Went to bro Collages blessed his child in the evening went to the Temple and procured a subscription for the cuting of the stone for my house. At night attended the trades meeting at Mr Galeys room. Brother [John] Taylor presided. The subject of our temperal interest was freely discussed and my self and Br Taylor wer apointed a committe to select twelve men to present [for consideration] to the next meeting to be accepted as counsil of the [trade] assosiation.

January 29, 1845; Wednesday. The weather fine and pleasant. Went to the temple. Counciled with the (12). This day bought and concecrated a bottle of oil.[3]

January 30, 1845; Thursday. Weather fine went to Lima [Illinois] in company with bro Collage, arived at Father [Isaac] Morl[e]ys about 4 oclock found the friends well enjoying peace and [experiences] from in the faith [in the] past [and] patiently looking forward to the time of reward when the just shall be crowned. In the journey of to day saw bro Miles from N. H.

January 31, 1845; Friday. The weather still cool and fine. Stayed with Sister [Cornelia] Levit.[4] On this morning went to bro Edwin Whitings. In the evening went to a blessing meeting at the house of sister Buchannon.

February 2, 1845; Sunday. Weather fine. Preached in the morning and in the evening to a large audience. Monday 3d came home to Nauvoo found the family well. Went to the Election this day. The weather turned cold.

---

2. The Nauvoo Concert Hall was finished just two days before. "The ceiling was arched and had sounding jars … [that] had cost nearly one thousand dollars." The purpose of the clay "acoustic jars" was to absorb sound and reduce the echo. Journal History, Jan. 24, 1845.

3. Another entry dated Jan. 29 appears later in Lyman's journal surrounded by blank pages. The CHL catalogues it as an 1845 entry; however, it does not seem to fit the entries for 1845. It reads: "Left the stage 18 m[ile]s from Hollys Springs [Iowa] with br Thomas. Traviled 20 m[ile]s arived at Br Dunbars. 9 oclock br Flanigan went on the stage to Pontotoc."

4. If this is Cornelia Eliza Leavitt, Amasa Lyman had married her as a plural wife just a few months prior in Nov. 1844. She was the niece of future LDS president Lorenzo Snow and daughter of Enoch and Leonora Snow Leavitt.

February 4, 1845; Tuesday. Meeting Counsil ^50^.[5] In the evening went [to] the trades meeting where a committee of 12 were apointed to manage the affairs of the trades union and bro [John] Taylor and G[eorge] A Smith and my self wer apointed to preside as a court of final appeal in all matters of difference. Stayed at bro [George] Millers over night.

February 5, 1845; Wednesday. Weather still fine and pleasant but cool. Thursday 6th went with my wife to bro [David] Yearsleys where the patriarch was present and Mother [Lucy Mack] Smith and ^a^ number of the wi[d]ows of the Smith family wer present. Had a pleasant and agreeable time together. Parted in peace with the blessing of God attending us to our homes an[d] the widows and Children of the martyred saints may the sun of prosperity and peace continuously shine.[6]

February 7, 1845; Friday. Attended [to my duties] at the Library and also meet at bro [John] Taylors in company with the 12 liveing constitution 10 of whom were present.[7]

February 8, 1845; Saturday. Went to the Temple and called at bro Chases in the evening. Bro Snow came in and we drew the plan of a house. Weather warm and pleasant. Sunday the 9th went to the seve[n]ties meeting in the morning and obtained a subscription for the hawling of the stone for my seller [cellar] and obtained a liberal one from the High Priests at their meeting the same day.

February 10, 1845; Monday. Laid off the ground for my house. Tuesday the 11th the brethren turned out and dug out my celler and my well. This day a Mr [John C.] Elliot was arested on the charge of murder in the case of the assasination of Josep[h] and Hyrum Smith.[8]

February 12, 1845; Wednesday. Stoned up my well. This day [John C.] Elliot was examined and commited to jail. This day sister [Laura]

---

5. The Council of Fifty was a political body formed by Joseph Smith in March 1844 to aid his campaign for US president and help explore settlements in Texas and the West. See Rogers, *Council of Fifty*.

6. The legacy of Joseph Smith remained so embedded in Mormonism that tensions inevitably developed between the family and his primary successor, Brigham Young. This meeting with Lucy ended peacefully, but she would continue to champion her youngest son, William, as a successor until his excommunication in Oct. 1845. Shepard and Marquardt, *Lost Apostles*, 213–35.

7. This was the council of the trades association that oversaw mercantile development, although without yet a written charter.

8. Elliott, the deputy sheriff of Hancock County, Illinois, was never brought to trial.

Knap[p] came to Nauvoo and buryed her husband [Silas]. Taried with us all night.

February 13, 1845; Thursday. Obtained some help on my house this day [until] it stormed so as to hinder the mason from work. Friday 14th attended at the Library hall and in the evening went to the [Masonic] Lodge and engaged br E Hargroves to work for me in the Lodge[9] and then returned home. This day heard of the arest of some [Mormon] men for stealing who wer sen[t] to Quincy Jail to await their trial in the spring. They who dance should pay the fidler.[10]

February 15, 1845; Saturday. On Saturday the 15th procured a rope for my well from br [Howard] Egan. On Sunday the 16th preached at the Masonick Hall. On Monday the 17th went to br[11] Horners. On Tuesday the 18th went after lime[stone] to br Holdens. In the after noon went to the meeting of the liveing constitution. In the evening attended the trades meeting and preached.

February 19, 1845; Wednesday. Attended to the work on my house. Thursday the 20th it stormed much every way to the discomfiture of the wolf hunters.[12] Went to br W[illard] Richards from there to the Temple.

February 21, 1845; Friday. Worked on my house this night rained. On Saturday the 22ond went to the High Counsil. On Sunday the 23d spent with bro [Orson] Pratt. On Monday the 24th went to Macidonia[,] weather fine.[13]

February 25, 1845; Tuesday. Transacted some buisness and in the evening attended meeting in the school house and preached to a large audience and taried all night with sister Morse. On the morning of the 26th left

9. The building that housed the Masonic Lodge also contained city offices and a public auditorium, so Lyman, although a founding member of the lodge, sometimes attended general civic meetings there. Hogan, *Founding Minutes of the Nauvoo Lodge*.

10. In November 1844, Brigham Young warned that "Elders who go borrowing horses or money, and running away with it" would "not have as much leni[enc]y as heretofore," which when quoted in the Feb. 5, 1845, edition of the *Quincy Whig* appeared to be a concession that those who had been arrested were guilty. "October Conference Minutes," *Times and Seasons*, Nov. 1, 1844.

11. Lyman repeats "to br" at the bottom of one page and at the top of the next.

12. Mormons feared that a county wolf hunt involving local militia was a cover for hunting "Mormons and Jack-Mormons," the latter being LDS sympathizers. *Times and Seasons*, Jan. 15, 1845.

13. Macedonia (Webster, Illinois) was twenty miles southeast of Nauvoo, not to be confused with the larger Illinois town of the same name but 500 miles distant.

for Nauvoo in company with some brethren who came supposeing that we were in danger from the mob but through the mercy of God we were all safe and well. Their visit was made in company with brothers B[righam] Young[,] H[eber] C. Kimball[,] O[rson] Pratt[,] E[dwin] D Woolley[,] Wm Clayton[,] George Grant[,] J[ohn] K[ay,] J[ohn] L. Smith.

February 26, 1845; Wednesday. It snowed. Arived at home found all well. On the 27th was in cou[n]sil and received an apointment to go and visit the company that were with bro [James] Emett in company with br D[aniel] Spencer and Moses Smith to advise and counsil them in matters of salvation in their present circumstances.[14]

February 28, 1845; Friday. On Friday the 28th started on our journey by the way of Camp Creek to get a horse for bro [Moses] Smith[,] bro [Daniel] Spencer[,] and my self. Taried over night with Cp L[ibbeus] T Coons. We were awaked in the morning by the padering [pattering] of the rain of the cabin roof.

March 1, 1845; Saturday. In the morning it hailed considerably which caused us still to tax the hospitality of br [Libbeus T.] Coons until the storm was past. Our time passed off quite pleasantly in the discussion of incidents of our past history which was a feast to our memories as we [~~illegible~~] were partners in the Zion Camp. At 10 oclock started for Ft. Madison [Iowa]. When we arived at at Apanuse [Appanoose, Illinois] there was so many teams there that we could not cross [the Mississippi River]. We then went to Nauvoo but did not succeed in crossing that day. Taried at home over night. In the night the wind changed from south to the north and it was colder in the morning but quite cloudy. Waited all the day for the wind to fall. Went home at night.

March 3, 1845; Monday. Crossed the [Mississippi] river. Passed through West Point the County seet of Lee County [Iowa] situated on a beautiful prarie in the midst of a well settled country. From thence we traviled in a northern direction to Scunk river which we found skirted with oak and hickary and some wallnut. We crossed the river at the town of Loeb. They have co[nstructed] rope ferry [and] two mills[,] one

14. This was an assignment from the Council of Fifty to bring James Emmett home to Nauvoo. Emmett had initially obtained permission to lead a company to the Dakotas, but Brigham Young suspected he was disloyal and demanded that he return. Rogers, *Council of Fifty*, 77–85.

sawing and one for grinding[,] two stores[,] two publick houses[,] one distillery[,] one blacksmith[,] two coopers[,] two doctors[,] no lawyers or preachers. From thence traviled nor[th]west 7 hr put up with Mr Henderson from N.Y. in Henry Co.

March 4, 1845; Tuesday. ~~Thursday the~~ Tuesday the 4th left Mr. Hendersons traviled northwest. Crossed Big Creek passed Mount Pleasant a fine town the County seat of Henry with 4 stor[e]s 3 taverns 2 blacksmiths from thence traviled northerly course 18 m[ile]s put up with a being having the human form though a disgrace to the race haveing a frame house and barn no chairs and worse than all he lacked the quality [of] humanity. His name was Custard a sweet name given to bitter thing in this instance. In the morning Wednesday the 5th left this desert so destitute of human kindness traviled north to Washington County seat of that County with 3 stor[e]s 1 tavern and jail, 2 blacksmith[s].

Passed through town 3/4ths of a mile. Breakfasted with Mr Dawson continued our journey to English river put up with Mr Wason who owns a mill at this point they have a good framed bridge that speak well for the citizens of the place. This ^day^ traviled 25, m[ile]s [and] were 20 m[ile]s from Iowa City. This day found a bee tree that furnished us with some honey. Found good entertainment with friend W. Crossed Crooked Creek.

March 6, 1845; Thursday. Traviled 30 m[ile]s crossed 2 bear creeks put up with Mr Taylor where we meet with brs Thomas and Francis Edwards. This day passed a beautiful praire the most of it in the new purchase.[15]

March 7, 1845; Friday. Crossed honey Wallnut and Richland creek. The timber [is] principaly walnut oak hickory and lym[e] praire undulating and beautiful.

March 8, 1845; Saturday. Arived at the tent of brother [Moses] Smith found the family well.

March 9, 1845; Sunday. Went to the camp of the breth found them in health generaly discharged the duties of our mission.[16] On Monday the 10th returned to br [Moses] Smith house. Family had gone to the settlement.

---

15. In 1845, Isaac Galland, who had sold land to Mormons in Illinois in 1839, was relieved of his remaining, disputed holdings through a sheriff's sale in Iowa. Flanders, *Nauvoo*, 29.

16. Lyman and his companions met with James Emmett, whose group was camped eight miles northwest of what is now Marshalltown, Iowa, 100 miles west of Iowa City. Hartley, "Mormons and Early Iowa History," 229.

March 11, 1845; Tuesday. Returned to the settlement put up with Mr Trotter after a ride of 32 m[ile]s without dinner. This day wrote a letter to br [Lyman] Hinman and sent it by the hand of Thomas Edewards seignor.

March 12, 1845; Wednesday. Traviled down the Iowa River 28 m[ile]s over a fine country. Put up with Mr James Duglas, to whom Simpson Emet was in debt when he left and did not pay him.

March 13, 1845; Thursday. Traviled down the Iowa River to Iowa City the seat of government which from its location would indicate the motives of interest or advantage influenced the commissioners in its location rather than beauty. Its publick buildings are the state house a fine stone building 5 churches 1 court house ^and jail^ 3 taverns 6 stores from thence we traviled south 27 m[ile]s which made in all 38 m[iles] crossed this day Deer Creek[,] Old Mans creek[,] English River at Mc Clares Mills ~~then~~ 15 m[ile]s south of the City [we] crossed Goose and Long Creek and whisky run. Put up with a Mr Grouble 6 m[ile]s east of Washington.

March 14, 1845; Friday. Traviled south 31 m[ile]s crossed Crooked Creek at Ricks Mill from thence passed a beautiful prarie of 15 m[ile]s. Came to New London a small town with one tavern 2 stores 2 black smiths from thence we traviled East 6 m[ile]s and put up with Mr Wood.

March 15, 1845; Saturday. Passed Augusta to Fort Madison from thence to Nauvoo. The distance of 30 m[ile]s. Found the people well at home. On the 16th there was meeting at the stand where I gave a statement of my mission to the wilderness to see the company with brs [James] Emet & [John] Butler.[17]

March 17, 1845; Monday. On Monday the 17th went to bro J[ohn] Higbees the weather turned quite cold [with] the wind from the north. Tuesday the 18th attended the counsil all day ^Wednesday the 19th^ spent the day about town. Thursday the 20th was in counsil at night. On Friday the 21st attended at the Library all day at counsil at night. On Saturday the 22ond was in counsil all day the weather fine and pleasant. The counsil adjourned until ~~Saturday the 5th of April~~ Tuesday next.

March 23, 1845; Sunday. Sunday the 23d went to the meeting of the High priests on Monday night of the 24th attended the meeting of the

17. James Emmett continued on with a group of around 100 to Vermillion, South Dakota, and later went to Salt Lake but then continued on to California, where he died in 1852. Bennett, "James Emmett at the Vermillion," 217–33.

Bishops wher brs J[ohn] Higbee and J[oseph] B. Nobles and Chandler Rodgers wer ordained bishops and Tuesday the 25th sat in counsil all day counsil ajournned until Saturday the 5th of April. On the 26th & 27th was bussy about my home.

March 28, 1845; Friday. On Friday the 28th in the evening attended a party at the mansion [house]. On Saturday the 29th went to Laharp with my wife. On Sunday the 30th preached 3 times on Monday the 31st returned to Nauvoo. On Tuesday the 1st of April was confied to my bed with cold. On Wednesday the 2ond left my bed attended to business until conference which commenced on Sunday the 6th which held until Tuesday the 8th. On Monday the 7th at a meeting of the stockholders of the Nauvoo House As[sociation] when myself and br G[eorge] A. Smith were appointed trustees in the association.

April 9, 1845; Wednesday. On Wednesday the 9th was in counsil all the day. At night attended the concert. On Thursday the 10th commenced business with the trustees. On Friday the 12th met in counsil at night attended the ~~attended the [illegible] of the Carthage Murder~~ concert at the hall.

April 13, 1845; Saturday. Attended the election of the trustees of the town of Nauvoo. At night attended a party of the old police. On Sunday the 14th attended a meeting at the stand. At night went to the Mansion in company with the twelve and others to see the United States Marshall who had some civil process to serve on br [Brigham] Young and others. The weather very warm and dry on Monday ^the 14th^ went to the office and commenced the business of the Nauvoo House br [George] Miller was there in the morning.

April 15, 1845; Tuesday. On Tuesday the 15th met in council in the afternoon. Wednesday the 16th attended at our office weather still dry. On Thursday the 17th was in council in relation to the company that ~~are~~ were with Lyman Wight and wrote an epistle to them by the hand of brother Samuel Bent.[18] At night met at br W[illard] Richards for prayers and council. Weather still hot and dry on Fridy the 18th.[19]

---

18. Lyman Wight, another claimant to Joseph Smith's prophetic title, led a group to Texas until the Pedernales River flooded the settlement. After a few other attempts at creating a permanent colony, Wight joined the Reorganized Church under Joseph Smith III. See Johnson, *Polygamy on the Pedernales*.

19. The diary ends abruptly, followed by several blank pages. At the end of this diary,

April 24, 1845; Thursday.[20] Visited Mr Randall Fredrick W. Marshall and Lady[,] the Scottish Giant & Giantess.[21]

April 26, 1845; Saturday. Attended at the trustees office. The 30th of Apr 30th.[22]

May 24, 1845; Saturday. This morning the capstone of the temple was laid. Present of the twelve[:] B[righam] Young[,] H[eber] C. Kimball[,] J[ohn] E Page[,] W[illard] Richards[,] O[rson] Hyde[,] O[rson] Pratt[,] G[eorge] A Smith[,] J Taylor [and] A[masa] Lyman were present with the Bishops and others of the authorities of the Church. The work was done in the name of the Lord and sealed with a shout of hosanah. The people were then dismissed from their labours to rest and hallow the day.

At 10 oclock attended the funerel of the wife of Br Wm Smith at the stand. Sermon by Elder O Pratt.[23]

May 26, 1845; Monday. Meet in council at Br G[eorge] Millers with Br Wm Smith. Tuesday the 27th it rained. Wednesday the 28th had settlement with Br Foster and had fifty cents in advance.

May 29, 1845; Thursday. The weather cool and pleasant called at the hall where Mr [Selah] Vancyckles [Van Sickle] was painting this day Mrs. Lyman.[24] Went over the river to bro W[illard] Snows.

May 30, 1845; Friday. Met in counsil with the twelve. Present B[righam] Young J[ohn] Taylor O[rson] Hyde O[rson] Pratt A[masa] Lyman G[eorge] A Smith B[ishop] G[eorge] Miller C[harles] C. Rich.

May 31, 1845; Saturday. Went to the temple and to Br [John] Higbees. Had B[righam] Youngs horse and buggy. Sunday June the 1st the weather fine and pleasant. Had meeting at the stand. Preaching by Elders

---

several pages have been cut out. It is impossible to know who removed them and when.

20. This begins a new diary book, with "Memorandum bought April 21st 1845 Amasa Lyman" written at the top.

21. Randall Marshall, "the Scotch Giant," was 7'6" and weighed 432 pounds. His wife was 6'5". They traveled with P. T. Barnum for a while. Barnum sued them for leaving, but the Marshalls prevailed. "Grand Olympic and U.S. Circus," *Sangamo Journal*, Apr. 15, 1847; Walker and Coffin, *Western Law Journal*, 4:557.

22. This is the complete entry, followed by a blank page, then financial purchases.

23. Caroline Smith was told she had "dropsy," a catch-all diagnosis for swelling. Before her death she was "tapped" (meaning drained) of more than fifty-three gallons of fluid. Walker, *William B. Smith*, 221.

24. Selah Van Sickle also painted Brigham Young and other portraits for the Nauvoo temple in 1845. Major, "Artworks in the Celestial Room of the First Nauvoo Temple," 60–64.

[Heber C.] Kimball[,] [John] Taylor[,] and Young. On Monday the 2ond meet in counsil at Bishop [George] Millers. Was in bed part of the day my health being poor this day.

June 3, 1845; Tuesday. My health remained poor. My health continued poor until Sunday the 8th.[25]

June 9, 1845; Monday. Was in counsil at the Temple on the subject of building the tabernacle.[26] Was engaged about the M[ansion] H[ouse] until Sunday the 15 when we called upon the people to ~~maintain~~ redeem their pl[e]dge made to build the house.

June 16, 1845; Monday. By Single dollars mostly we gathered over $200 an[d] we loaned $175 to Bishop N[ewel] K. Whitney. On Tuesday the 17th continued to receive some money about 60 or 70 dollars. Continued to recieve money through the week. The weather was wet Sunday 22ond.[27]

Youths ^are fleeting^ fondest hopes ^bought^ hovered. However bright they seem they live but for the moment then vanish like a dream. But if its joy unceasing that you desire to know from truths eternal fountain that joy forever flows. This forest land is pleasing.[28]

1) This forest land is pleasing. It is pleasing sure to me. Such were the scenes of childhood that once delighted me.

2) But youthful scenes have passed ^away^ and others now are here. Burdened with cares when on[c]e they ^come^ to mark the passing years.

3) While now on life's tempestuous sea my fragile bake is tossed around the tempest rages high and yet it harms me not.

4) While perched upon the mountain ^wave^ by howling tempests river still bright gleams hopes becon ^free^ that lights my native heavan.

5) ^When dark the tempest pierce the gale^ by hells dark powers driven. Tis then though feeble I am strong my trust is all in heavan.[29]

April 8, 1847; Thursday.[30] Prest. Amasa Lyman Journal of his trip as

---

25. The second line is written with different ink, perhaps indicating that Lyman's illness was so severe, he could not finish the entry.

26. This was intended to be a tent to protect the congregation from the weather. Watson, "The Nauvoo Tabernacle," 416–21.

27. The rest of the page is blank and the next page has more financial notations.

28. This paragraph is not part of an entry but is Lyman's practice at penmanship. The rest of the page is blank, then on the next page he continues his practice.

29. In Lyman's 1844–46 diary is a short notation about the future site of the Salt Lake Temple, showing that he would grab old journals to make brief notes without regard to chronology. The rest of the diary consists of financial records.

30. Lyman did not document the year 1846, which was spent crossing Iowa

Pioneer from April 8th 1847 to April 11th.[31] A Lyman left the camp of Winter Quarters, Omahau nation with his company of pioneers, April 18th/47 about 3.P.M. just as P[arley] P Pratt arrived from England. Traveled 7 miles & camped ^A Lyman went [back] to [the] city^. Country very broken; all quiet and safe.

In company, waggons & teams as follows: A Lyman 1 waggon, 3 horses, 1 rading mare, A Lyman[,] Albert Carrington & Sterling Driggs with it. Barnabas L Adams, 1 waggon, 2 horses, with Roswel C Stevens. A[lbert] W Collins[32] furnished 1 waggon, 2 mules, John Gleason & Charles Burk with it. Joseph Matthews 1 waggon, 2 mules, 1 riding mare, Gilbard Summe is with him. James M. Flake furnished 1 waggon, 2 mules, & 1 cow, with a black man named Green [Flake].[33] Fielding Garr[34] furnished 1 waggon[,] Norman Taylor 1 horse, A[lexander] P Chesley 1 mare & go with said waggon. Daniel Thomas[35] furnished 1 baggage waggon 3 mules & 1 horse. John Thomas driver.[36] John Brown in company with 2 waggons, 4 mules, 4 oxen, 2 cows, with Matthew Ivory. David Powel, & 2 black boys[37] named Oscar [Crosby] & Hark [Lay].[38]

Territory to the Indian lands west of the Missouri River. The city of Omaha would emerge after the Omaha Tribe relinquished the area by treaty eight years later. Lyman built a log cabin for two of his seven wives and got others established with relatives prior to his departure with the western expedition in 1847.

31. This entry begins Albert Carrington's record of Lyman's trail experiences. The journal was kept in a larger notebook with wide pages. Carrington's handwriting is small and cramped, and as the record goes on, he squeezes as much writing as possible onto the page. This portion of the diary appears after Lyman's own June 1847 entries. I have arranged the entries chronologically.

32. Collins did not travel with the company in spite of having provided a wagon; he went west with the Edward Hunter–Jacob Foutz Company.

33. James M. Flake stayed in Mississippi and sent his slave Green on ahead to prepare things for him. Slaves often took their owners' surnames. While all the other men in the company are listed by full names, the black members of the camp are listed by their first names only and called "boys" in the narrative.

34. Garr traveled with the Jedediah M. Grant–Willard Snow Company in 1847.

35. Daniel Thomas traveled west with the Hunter–Foutz company.

36. John Thomas was soon reassigned to the Hunter–Foutz company.

37. It is unclear when Green Flake, Hark Lay, and Oscar Crosby obtained their freedom, but Brigham Young showed some reluctance to sell slaves to other owners or break up slave families. Green Flake was called "saucy" and "disafected" by William Crosby, his Utah owner after James M. Flake died. See William Crosby to Brigham Young, Mar. 1851, Brigham Young Office Files, CHL, and Brigham Young to William Crosby, Mar. 12, 1851, Brigham Young Office Files, CHL; Turner, *Brigham Young*, 218–29; Reeve, *Religion of a Different Color*, 148–61.

38. Readers can find the complete company information at the CHL's "Mormon

April 9, 1847; Friday. G[eorge] A Smith's team came up April 9th[,] himself soon after, ½ past 2.P.M. April 9th at 3.P.M. A[masa] Lyman ^A Lyman rtnd about 2.P.M.^ & company started, traveled 12 miles & camped at ¼ past 8.P.M. in the open prairie, Rodney Badger, one of our company, came up with us just before we camped. O[rson] Pratt[,] E[zra] T Benson[,] & Wilford Woodruff with their companies camped with us. Chesley Gleason, [Barnabas] Adams & Summe stood guard; country [an] open broken prarie; all quiet and safe.

April 10, 1847; Saturday. Started at 6.A.M. & traveled steadily til 3.P.M. reached the Elk Horn [River][39] & camped; distance 20 miles; guard, J[oseph] Matthews, [John] Brown,[40] [Matthew] Ivory, [Rodney] Badger, [Roswell] Stevens, [David] Powel & [Charles] Burke; [Orson] Pratt, [Ezra T.] Benson & [Wilford] Woodruff crossed [the Elk Horn River] with their companies; country open, broken prarie, a view of the Platte river & bottom from the Elk Horn Bluffs, bottom very wide & level,[41] with but little timber on the banks; all quiet & safe. 6 waggons to go on [ahead] & 13 men. 1 baggage waggon & driver. Distance traveled 39 miles.

April 11, 1847; Sunday. A[masa] Lyman and company commenced ~~the~~ crossing the [Elk] Horn [River] soon after breakfast about ½ 7.A.M. on a raft & all crossed just as B[righam] Young & H[eber] C Kimball came up about 10 A.M. all the waggons were crossed & went down the Horn ½ mile & formed a line. G[eorge] A Smith on the extreme ~~right~~ ^left all quiet.^

April 12, 1847; Monday. ^John Thomas went with the bagg[ag]e waggon.^ After early breakfast A[masa] Lyman, with the 12 & ^R[oswel]l Stevens &^ some others started back to Winter Quarters; most of the teams started on at the same time & 4 of A Lyman's waggons. We traveled 11 miles up the Platte [River],[42] the bottom very wide & level & camped without much order, there being no one appointed to form the

---

Pioneer Overland Travel" webpage, http://history.lds.org/overlandtravels.

39. West of Omaha, the Elk Horn River flows south into the Platte River.

40. There are three Browns in the company: John, George Washington, and Nathaniel; John was the more prominent of the three.

41. The *bottom* Carrington refers to throughout the trail journal is the passageway the pioneers travel on between the river to one side and the rising bluffs to the other. He kept detailed notations of the land in anticipation of future overland travel.

42. The pioneer company followed the Platte River west across Nebraska until the fork, from which they followed the North Platte River into Wyoming.

line. ^Col [Stephen] Markham afterward came up & formed a line the same afternoon.^ Weather cool, cloudy, & windy; the Platte is very wide, with low sandy banks & shallow, swift current, the bottom on each side is very wide & level & the bluffs rise low & sloping from the edge of ^the^ bottom. Col S Markham called the men together about sundown, gave them some good counsel, about keeping the commandments & to be careful, watchful & prayerful, & do as they were told by the 12 even to the smallest particular.

It was voted to abide the counsel of Col Markham, H[enry] G. Sherwood & Tho[ma]s Grover until the 12 returned. Jackson Redding [Return Jackson Redden], Barnabas Adams, Tarleton Lewis, & J[ames] Case were appointed to start in the morning & hunt a ford or crossing on the [Elk] Horn higher up to sorten the distance from Winter Quarters & strike the Platte higher up & avoid some sloughs on the East ^of^ the Horn & in the Platte bottom. All quiet and safe.

April 13, 1847; Tuesday. ^Elder [John] Taylor returned to Winter Quarters from England.^ Redding, [Barnabas] Adams, [Tarlton] Lewis & [James] Case started after breakfast to hunt the Fords. [Sterling] Driggs waded on to the island for game, got nothing. The road committee returned & reported unfavorably. Weather, light clouds, but pleasant. All quiet.

April 14, 1847; Wednesday. Cloudy, commenced showering soon after 7 A.M. quit showering about 11 A.M. cool. All quiet.

April 15, 1847; Thursday. Clear & pleasant, about 3.P.M A[masa] Lyman, with the 12 ^& R[oswell] C Stephens with a cow furnished by A[lbert] W Collins,^ & 4 waggons that stayed at the Horn came up. G[eorge] A Smith & waggon came up about ½ past 5 P.M., company called together & addressed by B[righam] Young. Guard set. All quiet.

April 16, 1847; Friday. After breakfast the camp was called together & formed in a double ring, no. of men 143,[43] women 3; ^children 2. Lorenzo Young being the only man who took his family.^ Business open by prayer by B[righam] Young; remarks by G[eorge] A Smith, H[eber] C Kimball, Bishops [Newel K.] Whitney & [Joseph B.] Noble. Commenced organizing by appointing Cols [Stephen] Markham & [Albert]

43. This count did not include the three black slaves.

Rockwood Captains of hundreds or of 72 & 71; Tarleton Lewis, Addison Everett, Br. [James] Case & John Pack captains of 50s; Charles Shumway, B[arnaba]s Adams, John Brown, Howard Egan, Seth Taft & the 12 who are along (8) ^captains of ten^; Col Markham was appointed Captain of a standing guard & he picked out 50 men, 12 at a time, ~~to be relieved every 2 hours~~ ^stand ½ the night.^

The leather boat came up on the 15th & was in the ring. A[masa] Lyman, myself [Albert Carrington], Adams &c sent letters back to our families. No. of waggons 72, besides the boat. At 2 P.M. started & traveled up the Platte 4 miles & camped in line at 4; distance 4 miles. Weather cool & cloudy. The road keeps up the bank of the Platte. Instruments brought by [John] Taylor & [Parley] Pratt [from England], 1 artificial horizon, 2 septants, 2 circles of reflection, 2 barometers, 1 telescope, several thermometers.[44] ^A Lyman went ahead & looked out a campground. Cool & cloudy.^

April 17, 1847; Saturday. Started sun after 8 A.M. traveled up the Platte 7 miles & camped about 11. Thermometer, an hour by sun, stood at 26°, wind very high & cold, some cloudy. At 5.P.M. the camp were called together & formed in tens. President B[righam] Young proposed that we organize as a military body. B Young was elected Lieu[tenant] General, S[tephen] Markham Col, John Pack 1st major, Shadrac Roundy 2nd [major]. Prest Young then told every man who walked to camp [with] a gun ^loaded^ & the teamsters to have theirs where they could find their hands on them easily; teams to travel by 10s & ^not^ separate.[45] No man to go out ^of their 10^ unless sent. Thomas Tanner was appointed captain of the cannon with 8 men. Tho[ma]s Bullock clerk of the company. A[masa] Lyman with his waggon & B[arnabas] L Adams with his were formed into the line next to H[eber] C Kimball.

In Forming into 10s E[zra] T Benson was captain of the 2nd 10, with waggons & men as follows: Doct [Willard] Richards, Thos Bull[o]ck & George Brown with 2 waggons[;] Amasa Lyman, Albert Carrington, Sterling Driggs, Barnabas L Adams & Roswell C Stevens

44. The company kept records of temperature, longitude, latitude, and surrounding landmarks to aid future treks.

45. Overland travelers were more likely to die from cholera, drowning, and accidental gun wounds than by Native American attacks. See Smith, *Intimate Chronicle*, 300n41.

with 2 waggons. E T Benson & Thos Grover with 1 waggon (5 waggons & 10 men) all quiet. List of the men belonging to the standing guard, drawn from A Lyman's company.[:] B L Adams captain of 10, M[atthew] Ivory, D[avid] Powel, J[oseph] Matthews, A[lexander] P Chesley, G[ilbard] Summe, R[odney] Badger, C[harles] Burke. A trading waggon from the Pawnees belonging to Benway [Charles Benoit] camped just below our line; they had a Spaniard, whom they had rescued from the Pawnees; ~~5 trading waggons.~~

April 18, 1847; Sunday. Wind high & very cool from the south east, cloudy; towards evening wind high but milder & but a little cloudy. 6 waggons ^belonging to Sarpee [Peter Sarpy]^ came down from Pawnee with peltry, feed, cotton, wood & corn. A tree was fell[ed] on an ox, [which was] hurt some, but he walked off in a short time. Ellis Eames went back in company with the trading teams; he got disheartened, being sick.[46] Thermometer at 5.2 M, air 53 5/10 mercury 52 9/10.[47] Barometer 28 8/100. Captains of tens Wilford Woodruff ^1st^, E[zra] T Benson ^2nd^, P[hineas] H Young ^3rd^, [Luke] Johnson ^4th^, S[tephen] H Goddard ^5th^, C[harles] Shumway ^6th^, [James] Case ^7th^, S Taft 8, H[oward] Egan 9, A[ppleton] M Harmon 10, John Higby 11, L[evi] Jackman 12, J[ohn] Brown 13, J[oseph] Matthews 14. E T Benson called his 10 together, & gave instructions as follows, at ½ past 8 the bugle to sound & ^all^ to attend prayers & all to be in bed & the fires put out by 9; at 5.A.M. the bugle to sound & all to rise in their beds & attend prayers & every one be ready to start at 7; every man who does not drive a team to walk beside his waggon with a loaded gun[,] lock[ed,] leathered & caps ready. The sound of the bugle at other hours to be an alarm. E T Benson resigned & Tho[ma]s Grover was elected captain of the 2nd 10.[48] Camp to form in a ring with the off fore wheel against the right hind one of the lead way. Gun, tongues out. All quiet.

April 19, 1847; Monday. Warm & pleasant; started at ½ past 7 A.M.

---

46. William Clayton recorded that Eames was coughing blood; in spite of his serious illness, Heber C. Kimball said if he left the camp he would be spiritually lost. Smith, *Intimate Chronicle*, 299; Bagley, *Pioneer Camp of the Saints*, 124n40.

47. The air thermometer measured the height of a column of water based on the expansion or contraction of oxygen rather than of mercury.

48. Benson's "resignation" is not discussed in the other trail journals and may have been temporary.

& traveled till 2. P.M. 12 miles. Road dry & level up the Platte bottom. Camp formed on the bank of the river; soon after we camped O[rrin] P Rockwell, J[ackson] Redding, J[esse] C Little & Tho[ma]s Brown came up. Horsestock ~~(we of men in the 144)~~. After resting & bathing, traveled 8 m[ile]s. Road as usual, waether quite warm but some cloudy; camped in a semicircle on the Platte. Platte as usual very wide, pm 1 to 2½ m[ile]s & studded with Isleands; tho bottom on the South side appears narrow at this point, & all our route to day & the bluffs rise bold from its edge, like those on the Missouri [River]. Along the route from the road ^to^ the bluffs the bottom will average 10 m[ile]s. Received vial of gun cotton as a present from Tho[ma]s L Kane by the hands of Elder J C Little ^of Peterburo, N.H.^ Saw 1 indian at a distance on a horse or ferry. Latitude 41° 27' 5". All quiet. Took a glass of brandy with the 12 & a few others, at the invitation of O. P. Rockwell, which he received as a present from Tho[ma]s L. Kane.

April 20, 1847; Tuesday. Started ¼ to 8, traveled 2 or 3 m[ile]s & crossed ~~a~~ Shell Creek, 4 or 5 yds wide, rested at noon, Latitude 41° 25'2", camped in a semicircle on the bank of the Platte ^at ¼ past 4^ with browse plenty & handy, distance 18 m[ile]s. The fishing party who went ahead in the morning had caught some fine buffalo & [at] camp (213), A[masa] Lyman gave a large buffalo for his mess [food rations]. Road dry & very level, face of the country & river as yesterday. Weather warm, a fine breeze & some cloudy. A[masa] L[yman] visited a village of Prairie dogs, J[oseph] Matthews shot one. Found the skeleton of an elk with a very large pair of antlers.

April 21, 1847; Wednesday. Started soon after the ox teams, which all started together (21) met a few Pawnees towards noon, who were very friendly; [we] past their village & a trading ^house^ something like a mile off on our left; stopped to rest on the Loop Fork,[49] [when] several Pawnees came up from their village; some presents were made ^to^ the chief by the brethren, ^he appeared dissatisfied;^ A[masa] Lyman presented a hand of Tobacco.

Weather in the morning, cloudy, sprinkled a little, about 3 P.M. it commenced thundering & lightening & rained quite hard for an hour

49. The Loup Fork is south of present-day Columbus, about 75 miles west of Winter Quarters. It runs parallel to the Platte for several miles.

or more, the wind then became quite high & continued so sometime. Camped on the Loup Fork about 5, all safe. Distance 22 m[ile]s. Thermometer 51°, Barometer 28½ at ½ past 5 A. M. The Loup Fork & its scenery is precisely like the Platte, only the stream is much smaller. A very strong guard was put out on [account] of our nearness to the Pawnees, A Lyman was one. The first ½ of the night not disturbed by Indians.

April 22, 1847; Thursday. Traveled about 1¾ m[ile]s & crossed Looking Glass Creek, about 6 yds wide, at a good ford. At noon reached Beaver Creek ^12 or 14 yds wide^ & rested & ^crossed at a good ford.^ Latitude at this place, 41° 25' 13" meridian observation by Prof O[rson] Pratt,[50] camped on Plum Creek at the missionary station. Feed good hay put up by the settler last summer & corn fodder. Weather, clear & warm, with a pleasant breeze. Distance 18 m[ile]s.

This missionary station was for the Pawnees & was under the superintendance of ^the^ Rev J[ohn] Dunbar.[51] It's beautifuly located for this prarie country on Plum Creek about 1 mile above its entrance into the Loup; on the second bottom. The view on the North & West is bounded, at a distance of ½ to 1 mile by a low range [of] hills, through which Plum Creek comes from the North, fringed on its banks by cotton wood, Elm, Coppernut, burn oak, ash & willow.

To the South & East the view is open, commanding the Gov[ernmen]t [Indian] Station, the Loup & its Islands & bottoms for some distance & the dividing ridge between it & the Platte. The Station had 2, 1 story & ½ hewed ^double^ loghouses, quite well finished & 4 other log dwellings, with several out houses & yards, & some 80 acres of ground fenced & broken & cultivated with corn. The only furniture left was the castiron of a premium no 5 [skillet] & a rotary cooking stove. The missionaries left this station last summer for fear of the Sioux. The Government Station was situation[ed] about ½ mile below the M[issionary] Station, on the opposite side of the creek; it apparently consisted of some 6 or 7 buildings, on 3 sides of a small square with the South side open & picketed & a blacksmith shop about 200 yds lower down. 1 log stable, near the picketing was all the building left by the Sioux, when they

50. Pratt was an autodidact and occasional teacher.

51. Dunbar and fellow preachers Samuel Parker and Samuel Ellis nevertheless abandoned the station the previous year. Jensen, "The Pawnee Mission," 301–10.

farmed last summer. Laying about the ruins were some 17 plow irons, several waggon tires, waggon ropes, bands & other irons, & some waggon wheels, with several flat & square bars of rolled iron, & some slab iron &c. Quite a surface of ground had been broken about the station in different patches, & some of it cultivated with corn.

April 23, 1847; Friday. Started at ¼ past 12. M [noon] ^having occupied most of the forenoon in company with several of the Breth[re]n in looking for a ford below the mouth of P[lum] Creek^ & crossed the creek at a ford with quite steep banks, rolled on & crossed in about 4 m[ile]s ^at a ford about [blank] yds wide^ & stopped on the Loup, where Bishop [George] Miller crossed last summer, distance 6 m[ile]s. Prof O[rson] Pratt crossed with his carriage with the aid of several men; Elder [Wilford] Woodruff then drove in with 2 yoke of cattle before his horses & [took] several men with a drag of rope & crossed, Br J[ohn] Pack also crossed with his waggon. The Prest then ordered the rest to go up about ½ miles further & form^ed^ for camping, which was done about 1 hour by sun P.M. The Fording [across the river] was very bad owing to the quick sand & consumed much time & labor, even to get over the 3 waggons.

Our camp was within ½ mile of the ^ruins of the^ Pawnee village, it was partialy burned last summer by the Sioux. When they burnt the Govt Station, the Pawnees were away at the time. Whe~~y~~^n^ they returned they rebuilt the burnt portion & built several other lodges; they were burned out again by the Sioux last winter & only ~~one~~ 2 lodges ~~is~~ ^are^ now entire, apparently their council lodge, with a diameter of about 50 ft in the clear inside. The lodges were built circular, & probably average about 39 ft in diameter & with their stables occupied some 10 acres of ground. Their corn was put in holes dug in the ground like this[52] & lined with bark or puncheon,[53] or matting. A horse belonging to Prest [Brigham] Young died last night, cause unkown as there were many opinions probably choked to death by his chain halter ^weather very pleasant^.

April 24, 1847; Saturday. The site of the ruins of the Pawnee Town has been a noted place for many years & at the ^time^ [it] was burned, there were about 6000 inhabitants, being one grand band of divisions of

52. To represent the holes, Carrington drew something that looks like a glass beaker with a narrower top than bottom.

53. *Puncheon* was flat lumber typically used for flooring.

the Pawnee Nation, which has been for many years & is yet the terror of all the Western Tribes.[54] The Site is very beautiful, being on the North side of the Loup, where the 1st bluff rises abruptly from the waters edge, some fifty ft & forms a ^very level^ second bottom, bounded on the West by Willow Creek at the distance of about 1 mile. On the North at the same distance by a range of gradual rising hills, which form a ridge at the height of the general elevation & the country laying North, & running round to ^the^ South East & sloping down to the river bottom at a distance of about 2 miles. Facing South & looking to the East & West in command in the foreground; & a view of the Loup & its islands for some 8 or 10 miles & ^& in the distance^ & the low ground between the Loup & Platte; & the timber of the Platte island; ~~& its water is several places~~ at an apparent distance opposite of a bout 15 m[ile]s.

The ruins occupy a space of from 15 to 20 acres ^some [others] think 40 [acres]^ the number of lodges from appearances was above 200, with only 2 entire, they ^were^ all built circular, with an entrance way of from 5 to 10 ft long, 4 or 5 ft wide & 6 ft high; their average diameter in the clear was about 10 ft, varying from 20 to 60 ft, height from 12 to 20 ft with a hole in the top from 2 to 3 ft across for the escape of the smoke & covered with earth to some depth. In building they threw out the earth level to the depth of about 1½ ft, they then placed from in the ground a circle of strong forks at equal distances & laid strong poles in them, then small poles were placed around with their tops resting on the horiz[on]tal ones, & secured in their places by raw hide ropes. [f]or their relative position see figure.[55] The next row of forks & poles were disposed of as the first, except they were placed more upright, & were of course longer & fewer in number. The 3[rd] course of covering poles were sustained at their extreme ends by being firmly lashed together with raw hide ropes a& conveying to a center at the top to form ~~form~~ the circular outlet for the smoke, were quite strong, the whole was then covered with grass & earth ~~a circular seat ^of earthen^ wall (except at the entrance) round the outer edge, ^at the surface level^ about 1½ ft high & 2 or so wide~~.

54. Between around 1820 and 1860, when the Pawnee were decimated by disease, their many settlements along the Platte and Loup Rivers vanished.

55. Carrington drew a small image of a lean-to that resembled the side view of a soccer goal, the net drawn back tight.

Interspersed were their horse pens built of small poles from 10 to 15 ft set in the ^ground^ uprightly & close together & bound at the ^height^ of about 5 or 6 ft by horizontal poles lashed on with raw hide; also the holes for secur~~e~~^ing^ their corn. They had partialy fortified their ^town^ by a low embankment of earth & sod. As you go N[orth] from the ruins across the level plain & rise [to] the gradualy sloping hills, you pass several graves of their braves, & some in the higher ground; they were buried in as upright ^sitting^ pos~~ition~~^ture^ facing the East, the ~~aportune~~ ^opening^ being covered with poles & matting, & a ^circular^ mound of Earth & sod to the height of from 5 to 6 ft raised upon [the] N[orth].

The view from this height, varies ~~only~~ from that ~~of~~ ^from^ the Town, ~~only~~ in looking ^S[outh]^ & to the right & left facing S[outh] in commanding a more extensive prospect of the Loup & Platte, & the low prairie between them, to appearance as far as the eye can extend up & down, the 2 ruins seem to run nearly paralell. As you turn & face the North, you see an open, rolling prairie, as a very uniform elevation with neither trees or shrub, except on & near the margins of the small creeks emptying into the Loupe. Around the common burying ground were laying numerous human bones & skulls, dug up by the wolves, & bea[s]ts.

^Weather very pleasant.^ ~~24th~~ Between 8 & 9 A.M. movements were made to cross the Loupe, the route across the river was staked off & the ^teams^ waggons commenced fording[,] some ^un^loaded, others ½ so but the majority with their loads, all doubling teams, meantime the boat was busily used for carrying over goods from the bank opposite the camp ground. As the teams passed & repassed, keeping the same track, the ford kept improving, the the quicksand packing, until the last waggons with full loads passed over more easily than the first ones did empty. Every^thing^ was got over safe & sound by about 6 P.M. for which we all felt to thank ^the^ Lord. We then rolled 4 m[ile]s & camped on the Loup, the prairie haveing been [previously] burned, the [new] grass looked quite green. Weather very pleasant. The 2 rafts that the council decided last night to build were built this forenoon in good style & season, S[tarling] Driggs assisted; a man crossed on one of them & left in on a sand bar, the other was let go adrift about 3 P.M. showing that our raft men were correct in their judgement, which were that a raft could not be managed to advantage in crossing ^goods over so strong & boiling a current.

April 25, 1847; Sunday. Another very pleasant day, but more wind. Brs [Alexander] Chisley, [Norman] Taylor, [Joseph] Matthews, & a black boy,[56] started for the Pawnee ruins for raw ^hides^ from the horse pens to make ropes of. Brs [Sterling] Driggs, [Roswell] Stephens, & [Albert] Carrington went to washing, finished about 11 A.M. rested & read awhile, & about 2 P.M. Brs [Amasa] Lyman, Carrington & Driggs took good wash & swim in the Loup just below the camp. Between 4 & 5 ^P.M.^ Brethren were called together, & addressed briefly by G[eorge] A. Smith, Prest [Brigham] Young & several of the brethren, GA Smith advised the men not to hunt game they did not need nor shoot ducks & geese & let them go down stream.[57] Prest Young said he was perfectly satisfied with the camp & with our movements, & he had never been in company with so many men under like circumstances whose house was [composed of] so much union & harmony. Also remarked that wherever you find a man fond of binding up ^men^ with covenants to ~~them~~ ^him^ you may mark it that [that] man & the ones bound with ~~them~~ ^him^ will sooner or later be bound to be burned & he wanted the ^camp^ to learn wisdom all its time & treasure up knowledge.

Br Chesley upon his return in crossing the river rode into some quicksand holes & his mare after flounc^e^ing about for some time finaly turned over on her back & him under the water all over, when he had to let go the rifle he had to extricate himself after doing ^which^ he hunted some time for the rifle but the quicksand & the deep & varied channel just below prevented him from finding it. The rifle was worth some 10 or 12 dollars & belonged to Rodney Badger. ^We saw^ Antelope to day across the Loup.

April 26, 1847; Monday. We were all roused to arise by the sound of the bugle just before day break; the alarm was caused by the guard firing upon some Indians who had crept upon the ^line^ within 2 rods, they ran & the guard counted 6. Their moccasin tracks were plain to be seen

56. None of the other trail diaries mention which of the black men this might have been.

57. Thomas Bullock recorded that a wolf walked within fifty rods of the meeting without disturbing anyone, which Bullock thought affirmed Smith's teaching. Bagley, *Pioneer Camp of the Saints*, 132.

when day broke. No damage done. Started at ½ to 8 A.M. Stopped to rest at ¼ to 12 M [noon].

The ruins of an old Pawnee town could be easily seen from this ^point^ at a distance of about 4 m[ile]s NW across the Loup. Started at ½ past 1. Crossed a great number of Indian trails all converging to & divergeing from the old ruins. Passed a little in our right, the ruins of another old Indian village located like the others, at a point where the bluffs rise bold to the second bottom; there had been 10 or more lodges some quite large & the [g]round around had been cultivated to some little extent, & the old vegetation appeared very rank. Rolled on & stopped at ¼ past 4 on the steep banks of a small creek, rising in the divid^e^ing ridge & emptying into the Loup. The camp was formed under the high bank directly on the margin of the creek, at the distance of ½ to 1 mile from the Loup. ^The ~~bottom~~ bed of this little creek is rocky (limestone).^ Buffalo, grass, & Artimesia (or wild sage) occured occasionaly in patches to day, & near our camp there was considerable buffalo dung.

No road this day, only as we made it. If a person does not consider timber an essential, in beautiful scenery, then the scenery to day all of our route was very beautiful, as we passed up ^on^ the edge of the second bottom of the Loup, commanding a view of the level bottoms of the Loup & its ^dividing^ ridges. Weather as usual very pleasant. ^Time 7 hours.^[58] Distancd 19 m[ile]s. J[esse] Little's & Doct [Willard] Richard's horses strolled of to a distance back of the camp & after dark (by moonlight) a great deal of search was made for them, but unsuccesfuly.

April 27, 1847; Tuesday. Started at 8, at the same time Brs [Orrin Porter] Rockwell, [Joseph] Matthews, Thos Brown, John Eldredge, started to look for the 2 missing horses, rolled on & turned our [wagons] to rest at 2 on some good grass, 5 or 6 inches high, started at ½ past 3 & rolled on till ½ past 5, & camped by a creek with sandy bed, about 2 yds wide, & emptying into the Platte; time of travel 7 hours, distance 18 m[ile]s. We have made our own roads for the last 2 days, seeing no other waggon tracks. Buffalo dung & bones were quite plenty on our route. Some antelope were seen, & Brs J[ohn] Brown & [Roswell] Stevens shot one. Passed a village of prairie dogs, & with ^them^ in one of

58. This insertion was written in blue ink, contrasting the black of the rest of the journal.

their holes was a rattlesnake, in another an owl. Buffalo & muskete grass quite plenty, which with other kinds of grass made the prairie look quite green. Most of the ~~day~~ ^route^ there has not been a tree or bush in sight, general course ~~WSW~~ ^SW by S^ (to strike the Platte), over a surface whose general elevation was quite level, but more or less uneven from the effect of the wind on the light sandy soil. Owing to the great proportion of sand in the loam, & probably to dry seasons & but little dew the grass is disposed to grow in bunches.

The teams suffered this day from want of water, there being none from creek to creek. Weather some cloudy but pleasant & warm, about 5 the wind blew quite strong a few minutes & it sprinkled a little. The Brethren who went for the horses returned just before dark, & reported that they found where the Indians had tied 1 horse all night & soon struck the trail of both horses, going back, which they followed to within a short distance of Sioux day camp ground where all at once [they were] at their horses, but failing & being told to put out, they returned towards the timber a short distance off on the Loup, & ^as^ they went they fired 6 times at the Brethren, but without effect, the Brethren did not fire, but returned ~~& came back~~ ^these Indians the Br knew to be Pawnees.^ Soon after the camp formed[,] a horse of Lewis Barney's was shot in the foreleg just below the body, & the bone broken very badly. It was done accidentally, on [account] of some rifles being laid in a waggon loaded & capped & one of the brethren in pulling out his coat raised the hammer so high that the gun went off. ~~Our hunters ^saw^ some 7 or 8 buffalo.~~ Came in vision of the Platte about ½ past 4.

April 28, 1847; Wednesday. The horse that was accidentaly shot last night, was shot this morning to put him out of his misery. The 4 horses dead & missing were all lost through carelessness. ^(Distance from Winter Quarters to head of Grand Island 252 miles.)^[59] Crossed the small creek before us, ford quite muddy. Traveled 6 hours, distance 15 m[ile]s up the Platte, as we supposed opposite Grand Isleand; over a country very level even for this level region, soil as usual, vegetation to[o], no timber except on the Island. Weather cloudy, some cooler, & quite a breeze all day. A[masa] Lyman shot a wild goose. Camped in a circle, waggon

59. Grand Island, named by French traders, sits between the Platte and Wood Rivers. It was settled by German immigrants in 1857.

tongues[60] out. A few antelope were seen to day & a few deer upon the Island. Our horses, for a few feeds have had 1 qt of corn pr head at [and] a few, 2 a day, & seem to ~~do~~ hold their own. Struck an old trading trail, with now & then a waggon track to be seen.

April 29, 1847; Thursday. Weather pleasant, cloudy & some cool in the evening. Crossed a creek about 8 yds wide at a good ford, supposed to be the Wood River of [Samuel] Mitchel's map,[61] scattering & timbered with cottonwood, elm, white ash, willow, plum trees, &c., the latter in blossom. Time of travel 7 hrs, distance 18 m[ile]s. Feed rushes[62] on the island, cotton briars, grass, & corn. A few deer, 20 or 30 antelope, & many geese seeing 2 of the latter killed. A Beautiful section of level land with a quick soil lies between Wood River & the Platte with plenty of timber if used carefuly. Grass not sufficient to sustain teams without they lay still.

April 30, 1847; Friday. [Traveled] up the Platte following the old trail. Watered at 12 in a small creak a point in the trail where the next company should stop over night. Rolled on till 5 & some teams being faint, we camped without wood or water, except a little we dug for, distance to the Platte over 1 mile & no wood is here on this bank & the ground between buggy. [Sterling] Driggs shot a goose, P[hineas] H Young took it to dress for the feathers. Trail time 7 hrs, gait quite slow, distance 17 m[ile]s. Weather smoky, wind very high & cold from the N[orth]. Thermometer at sun down 41c. My fingers are so cold I can't hardly write. Slept warm. G[rasses] & soil as usual, no timber, except on the Island.

May 1, 1847; Saturday. Thermometer at sunrise 30° Weather cloudy & very cool, with high wind. Travel time 9 hrs, distance 18 m[ile]s. Teams traveled together, some ox teams very weak, from want of feed. Camped about 2 miles above the head of Grand Island, on one ^of^ the ravines which make down from the bluffs, with a few trees on it, & water in the holes. The road most of the day was quite uneven on account of occasionaly ravines making down from the bluffs, & the ^wallow holes^ [~~illegible~~] of the buffalo, ~~where they licked up the saltiest deposits~~ that occurs very frequently & has for some 40 m[ile]s also from the prairie dog holes, which cover a surface of 1000s of acres, with the vegetation

60. The tongue was the wooden part to which the horses were hitched.
61. Samuel Mitchell was an American mapmaker and geographer.
62. Grass-like plants.

so closely eaten by ^[prairie] dogs^ in many places that five will not run. No timber, except on the Islands, & ^a few trees on the^ creeks & ravines. We saw buffalo to day about 10.AM for the first time, 3 or 4 at first, then quite a herd along the face of the bluffs about 4 miles off & a little ahead, past noon we halted a little, & several of the brethren took horses & large pistols & started for them, we had a fine view of the chase from our line, A[masa] Lyman & John Brown, singled out & killed a very fine cow, J[oseph] Matthews killed a fine calf & altogether there were killed 7 calves, 4 cows, & 1 bull, we had a fine lot of good meat for supper, better than beef.

May 2, 1847; Sunday. Thermometer at sunrise 20°, most of the brethren busy taking care of their buffalo meat. Weather clear & pleasant in the morning, but soon clouded up & became cool again. We started about 4 P.M. & rolled 3 m[ile]s to get better feed, camped by a prairie run, close by [the] Platte; no wood but small willows. Our goose ^came^ back, looking pretty blue, [Phineas] Young pretending he had forgot who he got it off. Ice froze last night in the water bucket ¼ inch thick. Latitude at our Saturday night camp by meridian observation, by Prof O[rson] Pratt, 40° 41' 42", our camp being about 2 m[ile]s above the Island & almost opposite as near as we could tell, where [John C] Fremont took an observation, at a distance across the river of about of between 2 & 3 m[ile]s makeing the observations [that] in amount agree, counting out the N[orth] & S[outh] distance between them. The Saline Efflor-essence of Fremont[63] that occurs so frequently, as far as one can judge are the Lord's salt dishes for his cattle, & as far as we can analize them, with the tongue, they contain salt, a small proportion of saltpeter & d[itt]o of sulphur; the 2 latter we are not positive about, they have the appearance of scattered ashes, being a thin whitish excretion on the surface.

May 3, 1847; Monday. Weather cloudy, but little wind, & warmer. After breakfast several men went out to the bluffs to still hunt buffalo, among them A[masa] Lyman & S[tarling] Driggs. In the afternoon wind higher & quite cool. The hunters returned with 2 antelope, S Driggs shot one of them. A small party went up the river to explore the route, they

63. John C. Frémont wrote that "the ground was covered in many places with an efflorescence [coating] of salt, and the plants were not numerous," to which "a rapid evaporation in the great heat of the sun probably contributes, as the soil is entirely unprotected by timber." Jackson and Spence, *Expeditions of John Charles Frémont*, 1:184, 188.

went 10 or 11 m[ile]s & one of the party saw some Indians, & they all returned. A party was sent out to notify the hunters of the nearness of Indians. We lay by to day to rest our teams & let them feed, as our corn was getting scarce. The hunters of the hunters [the search party] came in about dusk & brought 2 calves ~~dead~~ they had killed. About 9 A.M. the cannon was fired, to let the Indians know we had one. S Driggs accidently lost R[oswell] C Steven's pistol.

May 4, 1847; Tuesday. About 4 A.M. cannon fired again. The sun rose clear & pleasant. We crossed the little riv[er] before us easily, at its outlet, Platte here, about 2 m[ile]s wide, well named, Nebraska, a shallow water.[64] Some timber on the head of the river we crossed, & a few trees occasionaly on the bank of Platte, timber on its islands getting scarcer. Towards noon, 3 trading waggons called a halt opposite us, on the Oregon route;[65] one of their men waded over, in deepist water, knee deep, his name was Charles Beaumont; 9 men in the company, with peltry, 16 days from Fort Laramie.[66] We came over for sugar & coffee, we improved the short ^time^ he would wait & handed him 51 letters for Winter Quarters & presented him with about ½ bushel of bread & flour, an article he said he had not eaten for 3 years, he was very friendly & said he wanted no money for taking our letters. Brs J[ohn] Brown & [Thomas] Woolsey went over to see their leader, we went in about 3 m[ile]s & turned out to wait for them. Grass poor, prairie recently burned by the Indians. J Brown & co returned & reported pretty good feed, & a good hard road, (Oregon route[)].

The camp was called together, report heard, remarks made & in view of all we knew it was voted that we keep up the N[orth] side of the Platte, till we get to Larimie. Traveled 11 m[ile]s & camped near Platte, by a clear prairie run & in pretty good feed, not burnt. Camp was called together in the morning [and] laws read, & a volunteer to aid the

---

64. The Indians called the river Nebraska (flat water), and the French translated it to La Riviere Platte (flat river). Carrington would have seen it referred to as the Nebraska in Frémont's writings (Ibid., 1:188).

65. Mormons traveled on the opposite side of the river most of the journey to avoid contact with Missourians, although the north side of the Platte had once been used by trappers and missionaries. Kimball, *Heber C. Kimball*, 156.

66. Fort Laramie in eastern Wyoming was an essential stopping point for supplies before crossing the North Platte and the Sweetwater River on the way to South Pass.

standing guard, A[lbert] Carrington volunteered. No fresh sign of Indians in our neighborhood, except the burning of prairie grass on our right, near & among the Bluffs opposite & ahead & back, probably burning for buffalo range.

May 5, 1847; Wednesday. Sun rose clear & warm, wind S[outh]. Buffalo feeding round in sight just outside our stock. Crossed the run before us at a good ford & kept up the Platte between the old [north-side] trail & the river, over fresh burnt prairie wind very high from the S[outh], severe on teams & men, some of the road softish, better to have kept the old trail, about noon took on the old trail, & rested a little, feed poor; the men horseback chased some buffalo, killed 5 calves & 1 cow, & took 1 calf alive. A[masa] Lyman killed 1 calf, J[oseph] Matthews the cow & about 4 P.M. came to ^a^ wall of fire reaching from the River to the bluff, we quartered back about 1 mile & camped on the Platte, found a good patch of feed. Distance 14 miles.

May 6, 1847; Thursday. Quite pleasant; started ½ past 5 A.M. in order to pass the fire ahead, which was well damped down by the night & a shower about 3 A.M. Passed the fire & a strip of old grass & turned [animals] out to feed. R[oswell] C Stevens killed an antelope. The calf that ^was^ taken alive got kicked by a horse mule, last night, & killed; just before we turned out at noon a very young ~~calf followed~~ ^calf followed Luke Johnson into the camp, they put him in a waggon. About starting time Prest [Brigham] Young^ & a few other men rode out to prevent our cows from mixing with the buffalo, ~~& a few others rode ^out to keep over^~~ the prest lost his spy glass. Went to look at a poor old buffalo cow, who soon lay down while we were all looking at her. Camped in a semi circle on the bank of Platte, distance 20 m[ile]s, feed poor, teams failing. No timber on either bank of Platte yesterday nor today, quite a breeze from the W[est].

May 7, 1847; Friday. A[lbert] Carrington stood [guard] from ½ past 12 to ½ past 4. [He was the] 6th [of] 10 standing guards. Wind very high from the N[orth] waiting for an axle to be fixed, & our teams to fill themselves; buffalo all round; fuel last night & this morning a little wood & buffalo dung. Camp called together to see about team for the cannonage. Br E[rastus] Snow received quite a chastisement from the

Prest [Brigham Young] for neglecting the cows yesterday.[67] Started at ¼ to 11 & traveled till 3, distance 8 m[ile]s. Buffalo in great abundances & passing to & from the river & playing, old & young. Camped in ring on the Platte, feed tolerable good. Camp inspected military fashion. O[rrin] P Rockwell found B Young's spy glass. Very cloudy & quite cool towards evening sprinkled a little. ~~8th clear & pleasant.~~ A[masa] Lyman killed a pole cat.

May 8, 1847; Saturday. Sun rose clear, no wind, weather quite warm; road over level ground, but rough from the multitude of trails running across our track from the bluffs to the river, made by the buffalo passing to & fro, & shallow basin like places, they make in pasturing & wallowing; halted about noon to rest; the whole bottom has the appearance of an old fed out pasteur, only the dung is almost as thick as it usualy is about a barnyard; the grass is so closely fed out that the weeds are quite thick. The herds of buffalo this for^e^noon have been ~~immense~~ countless, almost extending on both bottoms from the river to the bluffs in such numbers that the ground on the opposite side appears black & width on both sides about 4 m[ile]s length about 8 [miles]; as we passed up the river near the bank the buffalo would beat back & as we halted, in front of us the line of buffalo reaching from the river to the bluffs, looked like a solid dark wall, depth back unknown; feed poor; O[rrin] P Rockwell killed a cow.

While nooning [William] Smoot's 2 horses went out to see the buffalo, a few 100 yds off & commenced running with them & [Thomas] Grover & J[ohn] Brown had quite a race on their horses to head them & get them back. Rolled on & camped in a semicircle on the bank of the Platte, just below where the bluff cuts off the bottom for a short distance. A[masa] Lyman went ahead about 4 m[ile]s to look out feed &c to lay by over Sunday. ^Here^ found a better place than this. Distance 11 m[ile]s.

May 9, 1847; Sunday. Rolled on 4 m[ile]s to find better feed, passed the point of bluff by ta[c]king down the bank & keeping up the sandy beach ^& bottom^ ~~for 2 miles~~ & came out in the bottom again very

67. Young had to chase after the cattle which caused him to lose his forty-dollar spyglass. Kenney, *Wilford Woodruff's Journal*, 3:170. Snow wrote, "In attempting to exhonorate myself from blame I drew from him a severer chastisement; it is the first I have had since I have been in this church, which is nearly fifteen years and I hope it may last me fifteen years to come." Erastus Snow, Journals, May 7, 1847, in CHL.

easily but in case the water should be high, the hills ~~ar~~ are easily passed over. Camp~~ed~~ called together at 3 PM. W[ilford] Woodruff made a few remarks, felt well; O[rson] Pratt also felt well, but thought it uncertain ^whether^ we could return [to Winter Quarters] ^on acc[ount] of the distance^ this fall. A[masa] Lyman spoke upon the principle of learning all the time to be patient in the school we are in, which would be better to us than gold or silver. Camped in a semicircle on the bank of Platte, bottom narrower about 1 mile wide here, soil more sandy. Some of the boys had quite a play with the horns & tail of a young bull, ~~quite~~ ^some^ poor. Several buffalo lay along our route on the 8th dead, probably from starvation generaly.

May 10, 1847; Monday. A board was put up on a post with a letter in it for the next company, writing on the board ~~"look in this." Cool, wind NW~~ on side, "look in this & you will find a letter," on the other "316 m[ile]s from Winter Quarters, westward bound, pioneers. Cool, wind N ~~W~~ E. Rolled over a better soil & [recent] growth of grass not burned; crossed a clear, gravely run 6 yds wide. [Orrin Porter] Rockwell & J[ohn] Brown chased a wild horse; a good many buffalo, feeding at the foot of the bluffs. Joseph Hancock killed a 3 yrs old cow, meat good.

Nooned, clear & warm; better grass, Bottom widening again, from 1 to 3 m[ile]s, soil quick & good, well watered; ^rolled on^ [and] crossed another narrow run; a deer killed; the bluffs are low ranges of hills generaly, in many places on their sides & tops perfectly naked, & ~~are~~ cut up into holes & ditches &c by the effect of wind & rain on the higher evil[68]; 2 gorges in the ridge, for the passage of the runs we crossed. Camped in a semicircle on the bank, opposite an island with plenty of cottonwood groves; grass better, water & wood plenty. A[masa] Lyman shot a hen, meat tough. Some cloudy, but little wind. Distance 10 m[ile]s.

May 11, 1847; Tuesday. Sun rose clear, no wind, air cool, a few higher clouds, blacksmithing going on. Horn sounded at 4 AM. Started at ¼ to 10, rolled on with the bluffs, about ½ mile on our right, & [the] long island in the river, with several small & a few large Cotton Wood trees & several small cedar on it. The bottom on the S[outh] side appears very narrow & the bluffs accending to Freemont, from 2 to 500

68. The word is clearly *evil,* but it seems likely Carrington meant *level.*

ft high, elevation very sudden for sand & clay much cut up into points [peaks] & ravines, ^but opposite our camp they begin to slope and become smoother.^ At ½ 12 watered. Passed over a ^low^ spur of the bluffs a short distance, bottom widened again directly to [and] from 1 to 1½ m[ile]s, crossed a gravely run about 5 yds wide; [rolled] on ½ mile & camped in a circle about ¾ m[ile]s from the river. Feed middleing. Distance 9 m[ile]s. Warm through the day, cloudy, breeze from the South. But few buffalo seen. ~~13th~~ Latitude ½ mile W[est] of camp, by N[orth], observation by Prof O[rson] Pratt, 41° 7' 44".

May 12, 1847; Wednesday. Horn [bugle] at 4[a.m.]. Quite cool, wind SE. Crossed a small run, nooned, A[lbert] C[arrington] & several others went back into the bluffs to hunt, several buffalo about quite thin ^in flesh^ yet. J[oseph] Matthews killed a 13yr old buffalo heifer. A vertical section of the hill country taken anywhere, within the distance we went back, (between 1 & 2 m[ile]s) & as much farther as we could see, would present the same view as from the bottom. An isometric sketch[69] of the hill country would present innumerable peaks & knobs, more or less rounded, with deep circular holes, ~~&~~ ^with^ ragged edges in many of them, & between basins of all sizes, from a few yds across to ½ a mile, & ravines shallow & deep, long & short, & all over the surface, rough & smooth, run buffalo trails, & scattered very thickely, buffalo bones & dung.

Soil light colored more, as deep as any of the ravines will show, stained in places by iron rust. Grass scanty, in many places none, from the effect of buffalo pawing ~~&~~ rubbing & wallowing & the force of the wind on the light soil when the grass roots are thus torn up. Distance 12 m[ile]s. Clear & warm in the P.M. camped in a circle near the mouth of a small run; & about 1 mile from where some Indians probably Sioux had camped & left some week or 10 days ago; they had killed several buffalo & left their old moccasins. A[masa] L[yman] ~~kept~~ ^rode in^ his waggon, being unwell.

May 13, 1847; Thursday. Quite cold, ^cloudy^ wind NE & high; crossed a small run; rolled on & cross^ed^ a small clear shallow quicksand sand bottom stream, about 10 rods wide & camped in a semicircle on its bank & near its outlet, supposed by G[eorge] A Smith to be the Rawhide

69. That is, a drawing that gives three-dimensional depth.

of ^*^[70] the traders; it is probably of some considerable length as it makes quite a passage through the bluffs, & affords considerable water; it is the first stream ^of any size^ we have crossed since Wood River. Distance 11 m[ile]s.

May 14, 1847; Friday. Cloudy & cool, wind SE, commenced lightening early & about 9 rained quite hard for some time, cloudy, cool & showering through the day; our course wound round through the hills, to avoid a point in the bluffs where they come to the water quite bold for about ½ mile ^& about 1½ m[ile]s above our company^; came on to the edge of the bottom again & nooned. J[ohn] Higbee killed an antelope. This point of bluffs is directly opposite the commencement of the high ground between the N[orth] & S[outh] Fork, it commands a good view of the head of the level ground between the 2 forks, with an occasional glimpse of the water of the S[outh] Fork, the course of the N[orth] Fork for a long distance, studded with small islands, with not a tree & hardly a bush in sight in any direction; you can also see, looking S[outh] of E[ast], the point of junction of the 2 Forks, at a distance according to [John C.] Fremont of 18½ miles, from the point of high ground between them; the average breadth of the level land between the Forks is some 4 m[ile]s length 18½.

The average width of the N[orth] Fork so far is about ¾ miles, very shallow, with quick sand bottom. Since the junction, the bluffs in both sides, have taken a lower elevation, probably about 150 ft, smoother & more grass upon them, & opposite our resting place all three of the ranges take about the same elevation, the middle rather the lowest, & as far back as one can see to the N, NE & NW, the hills look ^like^ billows on the ocean in a high storm. Bluffs this day composed mainly of sand, still grass grows on them, sufficient to sustain cattle.

J[ohn] Brown killed an antelope, also P[hineas] H Young 1, J Higbee a badger, Luke Johnson & E[ric] Glines a bull, meat brought in next morning, O[rrin] P Rockwell shot a bull & A[masa] Lyman, J Brown, [Roswell] Stevens &c, pursued in some distance into the bluffs, & killed it, but as it was late & they far off, only a little of the meat was brought in. Camped in the form of a letter S owing to a mistake, about ¼ mile

70. The asterisk has a top-of-the-page notation, "Junction Bluff Creek."

from the river & from a low spur of the bluffs making to the water. Feed good. Distance 8½ m[ile]s, road winding, to get through the hills, & sandy. In the first watch an object supposed to be an Indian creeping on the horses was fired upon by R[odney] Badger, & it made off, without saying good by.

May 15, 1847; Saturday. Cool & cloudy, wind N.W. began to rain, about breakfast time, quite hard, wind pretty high, started while showering & wound through the low hills, about 1 mile very easily, with the exception of the sand, came on to a narrow & wet bottom, sandy by the edge, & grass good, stopped to feed showering all the time; PM a little showery, rolled on & camped in a circle about ½ mile from the Fork. O[rrin] P Rockwell killed a bull. Distance 7 m[ile]s; bottom wetish, feed good.

May 16, 1847; Sunday. Cloudy & very cool, wind N.N.W. in the PM some warmer & not so cloudy. Camp called together, for meeting, Cols [Stephen] Markham & [Albert] Rockwood gave some good advice, & Elder H[eber] C Kimball some good teaching, partly as follows, ["]not a man of us will fall if we go straight &c learn by precept also by example, that ye may profit by the experience of others ye[a], do not God's servants bless? Cultivate a spirit of blessing &c, I shall not kill game on the sabbath, unless it is necessary; if a man was wrong, do not follow his example, but that of the good; we shall recieve more glory for faithfuly performing this mission, than for any other we have ever engaged in; have no malice; I believe angels go before us day to day, angels were seen by the brethren in going to Jackson [County, Missouri], in Zion's Camp, in 1834; 9 of that camp are in this [camp].["]

E[ric] Glines killed a bull, & an [pregnant] antelope with 2 young in it. The small runs we crossed spring some mile or 2 in the bluffs, & one more numerous than heretofore, bluffs not quite so sandy. The county for ^some^ distance back in the bottom & on the bluffs is so closely pastured that there is no appearance of fire having run over it for years; a few wells dry, water tastes of iron rust. Buffalo plenty all the time.

May 17, 1847; Monday. Very cool, some cloudy, wind W.N.W.; A[ppleton] M Harmon put another wheel to his roadometer, gaged for 10 m[ile]s; rolled on & passed a low spur of the bluffs, for about 2 m[ile]s, road when [it] is struck [in the river] the bottom was made along the edge of the bluffs; bottom for some 10 m[ile]s will average about 3 m[ile]s in width, quite wet, near the bluffs, crossed several small runs & some sloughy places, & a good length of wet ground, & camped in a circle; within about 1 mile of the river. We passed a point where the bluffs come to the water's edge on the other side for the first time, & continue so, about 1 mile then a space of very narrow bottom, then the bluffs again come down quite bold, for about 1½ m[ile]s, with small cedar trees scattered ~~en~~ ^over^ the sides & in the hollows. The road to all appearance would have been better if we had kept up on the river bank from the hills we crossed. 3 bulls & 2 antelopes were killed & brought in. A[masa] L[yman] killed 1 of the [ante]lopes; quite warm from 10. A.M. 3 or 4 wells [to]day about 4 ft deep. Distance 12¾=[71]

May 18, 1847; Tuesday. Cloudy & warm, wind E.S.E. Captains of 10 called together, Prest. [Brigham] Young made remarks of which the following is the purport as reported to me; the hunters do not start out soon enough, but lay around until the teams start & then have to go farther for game & hinder the camp in going so far into the hills to haul meat; the horsemen were blamed for not takeing more care to look [for] the best route, many for turning up their noses at fore quarters of meat, & the whole for being indolent & they had better put their horses into the teams.[72] [The] route quartered [where] the bank ^gave the appearance of rock, in the cedar bluffs on the S side for the first time^ came in just below the cedar bluffs opposite, 3 deer drinking & walking about in the river water [in a] very shallow ~~a~~ bed[,] good to judge by their motions, ~~moved~~ crossed a run ^rattlesnake creek^[73] about 1 rod wide, ~~passed on~~ emptying just at the commencement of the cedar bluffs opposite, more old grass than usual, nooned, cloudy & report of thunder from WSW, sprinkled a little occasionaly.

Camped in a circle on the W[est] bank of a clear run about 2 or 3 yds wide, (Eagle Creek) & about ½ mile above its outlet; through the night, rained quite moderately most of the time, wind N[orth,] feed poor.

---

71. Carrington added an equal sign followed by "18th" to indicate the start of the next-day's entry. I have retained my date formatting for clarity and readability.

72. Young was angry that meat was wasted; he ordered that no more game be shot until needed. Amasa Lyman was one of the men chastised for failing to watch for a better path, which may explain some of Carrington's frustration at the route they take. Smith, *Intimate Chronicle*, 316; Kenney, *Wilford Woodruff's Journal*, 3:178.

73. Young named it "Rattle Snake Creek" after John Higbee shot a large rattlesnake there. Bagley, *Pioneer Camp of the Saints*, 158.

Camp called, & ordered to drive in all cattle & horses near them, when they went to gather them in ^penaltys be sent for them^ to stop in the road to water, under penalty of traveling in the rear of the cannon the rest of the day. Distance 15¾ m[ile]s.

May 19, 1847; Wednesday. Started at 5 to find better feed, crossed a small run & turned out to feed, grass tolerable, bottom narrow & wetish, started about 8, began to rain quite steady & tolerably fast. Wind E[ast], soon crossed another run about 1 rod wide & began to rise [to] the sand bluffs which come to the water for ¾ mile, road up & through quite sandy, hard pulling, passed on to the bottom across a small run & stopped at 11 on account of its still raining; the route would probably have been better over the bluffs if we had passed up the run further & wound among the hills where they are not so sandy or keeping h[e]r[e] up the river under the bluffs; started at 3 still raining at times quite hard, rolled on 2 m[ile]s & camped in a semicircle on the river bank. Wind N.N.E. Feed middling. Distance 8 m[ile]s rained till nearly dark.

May 20, 1847; Thursday. Cloudy & coolish, wind N.N.W. bluffs as usual sometimes, pretty well tumbled & sharpened up, at others smoother, at times sand predominates, then clay, now & then an appearance of rock in the face of the bluffs on the S[outh] side; started at 8 stopped at ¼ 11 ^past^ at a point within ½ mile of the river, where a low spur of hills runs down from the bluffs, average width of bottom 2 m[ile]s, soil good, road good, the hills & bluffs have come to the water on the S[outh] side almost the whole distance, ~~e~~ with a good many small cedar trees growing on them; 1 cedar tree on the N[orth] side, with a young ^dead^ indian wrapped in a hide with his wooden ~~boal~~ bowl & spoon & a small bag, ~~lash[?] on~~ ^tied in^ its branches; passed just before we stopped, a large patch of pigweed.

Horizontal strata in the bluffs on both sides, apparently of limestone, mostly on the S[outh] side; crossed a run soon after starting; feed good; cool; several ^very^ small Islands, scattered along, but hardly any of them support even bushes, until we get to this point where some of them have small cedar trees; while moving, A[masa] Lyman & 3 others crossed over, in the boat to the mouth ^of^ a short dry hollow opposite & found the Oregon road to come down the hollow^*^[74] & take the S[outh] bank of

74. The asterisked notation says "ash hollow, trees small."

the Fork, ash in the hollow, & mountain cherry bushes; the strata of rock proved to be limestone; rolled on about 2 m[ile]s & crossed a swift, quick sand bottom creek from 10 to 11 rods wide, passed on, bottom, grass, soil &c as in the A.M.

Came to a point where a low range of hills came to the river, & just at the point, a run about 4 yds wide emptied into the river, rolled on ½ mile, between the low hills & run, & camped at 6 in an oval, by the run & within ½ mile of the river. Distance 15¾ m[ile]s. So far since the Oregon road came over, the bottom is a mere stripe, the ledgey bluffs rising just back of the bank; on this side with the exception of the 2 spans of very low hills the bottom is about 2 m[ile]s wide & good for grass; by our camp, the low hills come near the run, which is about parallel with the river, flat bottom of ½ mile & more between the 2, the hills reach back some distance to the main bluffs; opposite bluffs quite bold & ledgey;[75] through the day this side only 1 place where the strata show ^the gorge of the creek^; few buffalo seen; pigweed plenty; 1 pole cat seen & 1 prairie hen [grouse].

May 21, 1847; Friday. Pleasant, cloudy at sunrise, no wind, breaking away started at 8; stopped at ½ past 11^in middle of bottom^; a board of distances was put up at the camp ground; hills retreated, width of bottom from 2 to 4 m[ile]s, soil good, clayey, quite wet in places from the rain of 19th. S[outh] side, no bottom, distance for A.M. 7¾; 3 or 4 deer seen; air pure & good; feed good; started at ¼ to 2, & kept up near the center of the bottom, road heavy from the late rain, bore to the W.N.W & crossed a very low range of hills, which had swept round & come to the river, passed through a very rich pigweed patch & kept on near the base of the low hills on our right, & the river 1 mile or more on our left, at ½ past 5 line stopped, in view of our front horseman just ahead among whom were 2 mounted Sioux, soon turned a little towards the river & camped in a circle about 1 mile off, a few buffalo seen on the other side, P.M. distance 7¾ = 15½.

The bluffs on the S[outh] side keep their rocky ledge, up to a dry hollow of some apparent length, whose mouth is about ½ mile higher up than our camp, they then keep on at a lower elevation & are much

75. Below this underlined portion is a + symbol and the notation, Castle Bluffs 8 m[ile]s above Ash Hollow.

smoother & without rock of any consequence, showing a few small ash trees in the hollow; very little bottom on the S[outh] side; hills low on the N[orth], bottom wide, grass good & plenty ^old grass very thick [and] waist high;^ between our camp & the river & up as far as one can see, there is very heavy cut of old grass of a good kind resembling timothy or red top. ~~22nd~~ The route would have been nearer & probably much better to have struck from our camp to the low hill we crossed. ~~22nd~~ A ^piece of^ petrified bone of a very large animal [we] picked up on the low hills. We crossed by the roadside in a dry gravel channel, made by the rain water of the hill country.[76]

May 22, 1847; Saturday. A little cloudy; pleasant breezes; started ¼ past 8, rolled on, road good, crossed a clear run ^about 11^ 3 or 4 rods wide emptying in just about the cedar bush bank opposite; stopped to noon at ½ past 11; a few scattering pine trees, small, on the ridge opposite; an occasional narrow strip of bottom on S[outh] side, hills smoother; N[orth] side bottom averages about 1 mile; occasional appearance of rock both sides, 2 buffalo seen on S[outh] side, soil gravely, a weed called by the boys "old man" quite plenty also a weed some call rag weed, prickly pear occasion^a^ly; feed rather short & scattering; points in the Oregon road visible occasionaly; 7¼ m[ile]s; started again about 2 & came 4¼ m[ile]s then wound away & over the bluffs 3 m[ile]s onto the bottom 1 mile & camped in a circle within about ½ mile of river, distance 15½ m[ile]s, first 4¼ miles over a dry hard bottom, & across several dry beds of runs in high water; from the ridge of bluffs [where] the road crossed we could see chimney rock, & view the very curious & broken ground all round us & excpecialy on our right & ahead, crossed the gravely bed of a run, some 8 rods wide, 3 times, in the hills, hauling through the beds of the runs very heavy.

Old Man weed very plenty, smells & tastes some like wormwood; a few small cedar trees in the bluffs a young grey eagle brought into camp, also another petrified mammoth bone, portion of the main ^or thigh^ bone of the hind leg, diameter 5 inches[,] circum[ference] 15 d[itt]o.

A thunder storm passed round us & dropped a few sprinkles.

76. The vanguard company was about fifty miles from what is now called the Agate Fossil Beds where in 1904 scientists would discover prehistoric giant boars and dwarf rhinoceroses.

The bluffs opposite our camp on the N[orth] are named by the Prest [Brigham Young] Bluff Ruins. They present an appearance of ruined castles with their turrets, towers, terraces & walls much dilapidated; it has been caused probably by the breaking down of the horizontal strata of limestone which is quite thin, & the washing away of the marbly foundation of the strata by rain, sun & wind, constantly operating; a marbly clay appears to be the main body ^of^ the hills & bluffs, many foreign specimens of rock a^re^ strewn all over the beds of the many runs & on the tops & sides of the highest hills & bluffs in many places, such as granite of several varieties, quartz, green stone &c & a great amount of flint of various shapes & sizes.

May 23, 1847; Sunday. Some cloudy quite warm, Br [Nathaniel] Fairbanks [was] bit in the ancle by a rattlesnake, made quite sick.[77] About noon, camp assembled & meeting was began by singing prayer by Prest [Brigham] Young, singing, a few remarks by E[rastus] Snow, the Prest then spoke for some time, & advanced the following ideas in his remarks, "the fruits of ~~this~~ our works in this mission, will be tasted by us in this world & in that to come & eternaly for good or evil, according to our works. I feel highly pleased with this camp & its movements, all goes well &c. No underhanded work in the gospel, all is plain, & all things belong to the upright and honorable. No man has disobeyed my counsel that I know of. I will do the scolding ^to this camp^ no other man shall, our mission will soon be looked upon as among the first works of the church. A place must be prepared for giving endowments & teaching revealed principles that have not been taught publickly. We built the temple & fin[ished it] in spite of the opposition of wicked men.["][78] About 5 wind blew very hard, about 7 began to rain hard, continued to rain till towards 10, wind high through the night. Latitude, M[eridian] observation, 41°, 33' 03". Barometric [pressure] higher up bluff above the surface of the river 235.

May 24, 1847; Monday. Very cloudy, wind cold, a few flakes of snow

77. Charles Harper saw this as karma, noting that Fairbanks had been teasing a different snake a few minutes before (Harper, Diary, May 23, 1847). Luke Johnson, who had some medical training, applied a cornmeal tobacco paste to the wound, which caused Fairbanks to vomit. Bagley, *Pioneer Camp of the Saints*, 164; Smith, *Intimate Chronicle*, 321.

78. Carrington would pause and write a close-quote mark, only to immediately write an open-quote mark indicating that Young was still speaking. I have removed these.

flying, wind last night & this morning N.N.W.; started 20 minutes past 8. Stopped to rest 35 minutes past 12, road hard & good, bottom more rolling than usual; a curious shaped & low portion of bluff, nearly opposite on S[outh] side, looking like a fortified round tower with a detached funnel; still cloudy & very cool; 10 m[ile]s. 2 Sioux came to us while we were resting. Started ¼ to 3 ^rolled 6½ m[ile]s^ & camped in a circle within ¼ m[il]e of river, road good, feed poor, clouds breaking away, wind fell; bottom wide & not so rolling; just as we formed camp, 35 Dacutahs [Dakotah Indians], men women & children, mounted crossed the Fork to visit us, they were very friendly, clean, well dressed, well formed, good size & well behaved. A[lbert] C[arrington] went out to them to read 2 letters in French, given them as recommends, one to O wash to cha ou le belle journie,[79] signed P D Papin, the other to brave Bear,[80] not signed, both good.

May 25, 1847; Tuesday. Quite a frost, clear, mild & pleasant. The Dacotahs came down from their sleeping place, ½ m[il]e above & remained about our camp until we started, behaved perfectly well, we gave them some bread last night & this morning; traveled 12 m[ile]s; road dry & generaly very level, but rough from inequalities, course nearly through the center of a wide bottom & camped in a circle, about 4 m[ile]s E.N.E. from Chimney Rock on the S[outh] side; by Barometric calculation by Prof O[rson] Pratt, at our last night's camp, higher above ocean. 337 ft & 686 ft above the junction, being a rise from that point of 5 ft 6 ⅓ inches to the mile. Latitude by H[orizontal] observation 41° 41' 46".[81] O[rrin] P Rockwell killed 2 antelopes, A[masa] L[yman] 2 hares. But little air, quite warm. Grass middleing, principle grass, ["]buffalo grass," widest place in bottom about 6 m[ile]s.[82] Several wells dug.

May 26, 1847; Wednesday. Some cloudy, warm, a fine breeze from the W[est], started at 8, stopped at 12. 7¼ m[ile]s, started ½ past 2, camped

79. Meaning "O Chief Wash te cha, regarding a pleasant journey."

80. Pierre D. Papin was appointed director of Fort John by the American Fur Company in 1845. Brave Bear was James Bordeaux, a fur trader renowned for his good relations with the Sioux. Bagley, *Pioneer Camp of the Saints*, 177n11.

81. Pratt had eight instruments for estimating the camp location: two artificial horizons, two barometers, a reflection circle, two sextants, and a telescope. Kimball, *Historic Resource Study*, 50.

82. A drawing of Chimney Rock breaks the line here, flanked by the words "Chimney Rock no rock, all marly clay."

at 5 in a circle, near the river; grass pretty good; road level, bottom wide & dry, the road would be better if it kept the bank, on account of grass & driftwood & water at all times; 4 antelopes killed; sprinkled a little about sunset. 5 m[ile]s = 12 [total]. Our camp is nearly opposite Terrace Bluffs, of marly clay, constantly wasting, & in plain view of Chimney Rock.

May 27, 1847; Thursday. Cloudy, but very pleasant, with a fine breeze, started at 8, stopped at 12, route close by the river, grass good; road fine; nearly opposite Scotts Bluffs on the S[outh] side. From Ash Hollow to Chimney Rock by our road 72½ m[ile]s. Width of river opposite our lasts night's camp 792 yds; 8 m[ile]s. 2 [ante]lopes killed, A[masa] L[yman] killed 1; started about 2, & camped in a circle about 5 near the river, & just above the most Northern point of Scott's Bluffs, 5¾ [miles] = 13¾ [miles total for the day], grass &c as in A.M. Stopped this early on account of grass just ahead looking short.

Bottom still very wide. About 6 began to rain quite fast, wind high from N.N.E., a few bushes on the opposite bank. Scotts Bluffs & those above & below are of the prevailing marly clay formation & cut up into all manner of curious & fantastic shapes by the action of the elements & fast wearing away. Rained slowly till about 9 in the evening. Since we left bluff ruins, after you leave the river bank from ½ to 1½ m[ile]s, the bottom is very dry till you reach the low range of hills from 3 to 4 m[ile]s then dry for about the ^same^ distance to the main bluffs, so that the best grass is confined to the strip of bottom along the river.

May 28, 1847; Friday. Cool & cloudy, quite misty about 7, wind E.N.E. River takes a sudden bend from Scotts Bluffs to the N.W. or at most N[orth] for a short distance; laid by till about 11 for fear of rain, started & soon came to where the bottom was narrow & quite sandy & continued so for about 3 m[ile]s with a small clear run close on our left, then about 4 m[ile]s of good hard road along a wide bottom again, then instead of keeping on the edge of dry bottom, the road pilot struck across the wetish bottom lying near the river & we had 4½ m[ile]s of first wetish, then sandy, then tolerable road & camped in a circle near the river with plenty of driftwood, but poor grass, the new being mixed up with the old; cool and cloudy. 11½ m[ile]s, a few scattering cotton wood trees & small willows on the small islands & the S[outh] ~~side~~ bank misted & sprinkled in the night.

May 29, 1847; Saturday. Cool & cloudy, began to sprinkle & mist quite steady about 5; the Prest ^last evening^ made some remarks against so much levity, card playing, dancing &c as there was going on. Wind N.E. slacked up misting about 10, wind E. At ¼ to 12 the Prest [Brigham Young] lectured the camp very sharply & very well upon the subject of levity, such as dancing, fiddling, card playing, much trials, loud laughing & talking, contention &c showing what such a spirit would lead to, & that he did not wish to go any farther with such a spirit in the camp &c, then called the 12 together, then the high priests (18) including 4 bishops, then the seventies (76), then the elders (8) left those who did not belong to the church, 2 sick in waggons, 2 away hunting; the Prest then called upon them by quorums & they all covenanted with uplifted hand to return to the Lord with renewed prupose of heart, & leave off those practices that tend to evil. Good remarks by Elders [Heber C.] Kimball, [Orson] Pratt & [Wilford] Woodruff.[83]

Started ½ past 1, stopped ½ past 5, & camped in a circle near a spring run about 5 yds wide, & just above a point where the river runs from the south to N[orth] across the bottom about 2 m[ile]s. Several trees on the islands, ~~& S bank~~. Road good, grass good, sand rock showed in the bluff for the first time close by the road & about 2 m[ile]s below our camp; just below us the N[orth] Fork runs a serpentine course to & fro across the bottom for the first time. The Oregon road just below Scotts Bluffs turns behind the [river] to avoid the Bluff, & comes on to the river after 2 d[ay]s travel just below the large trees on the islands. ^Iris said that the Black Hills could be seen from Scotts Bluffs on a clear day.^ At a point about 10 mile or more below our camp, it crosses horse creek, which empties above Scotts Bluffs on the S[outh] side. Road [taken on the] 28th would have been nearer & better to have continued on the dry hard bottom. The grass on the hard bottom is thin & short, but good where the bottom is wetish, which is the case very frequently, in patches of some length & breadth, lying near the river & always to be command[ed] for camping purposes, as to grass, driftwood & water.

Elder Kimball remarked that not ^one^ of us or of our families would

83. Young's rebuke became an important memory for camp members, who saw in its effects a secular journey transformed into a spiritual one. William Clayton recorded Young's complete remarks in Smith, *Intimate Chronicle*, 324–33.

die till our return, if we would abide counsel as given. Elder Woodruff ~~counseled~~ ^motioned that^ all ~~to~~ burn up their cards, gammon boards & dice for they were useless lumber. ^M[ile]s 8½.^

May 30, 1847; Sunday. Rain 30th. Peppergrass on the hills. Appointed as a day for fasting [and] prayer; warmer, but still cool & cloudy, wind E. About 9 the camp assembled for prayer meeting, Bishop T[arlton] Lewis presiding, praying, singing & remarks, confessing &c by the brethren, all good, meeting closed ½ past 10, [and] about 12, the brethren assembled to partake of the sacrament. Bishop Lewis presiding. At the same time, the 12 & 9 others, with their clothing repaired to a bason in the hills, & stationed O[rrin] P Rockwell & A[lbert] Carrington on the look out while the rest clothed [in temple robes], & went through the usual signs & prayed, the Prest [Brigham Young] being mouth. Soon after they dressed it began to sprinkle about ½ past 1 & then to rain just as we got back to camp.[84]

The low range of hills ~~of hills~~ that has continued so long, begins just below the sand stone Bluffs to take a higher elevation, & becomes more broken as you rise on the ridge & look at the land extended back at the same elevation broken barren & rolling for 4 or 5 miles then there is a breadth of lower ground, still rolling & barren for from 5 to 10 miles extending to the main bluffs; an immense quantity of pebble stone is scattered promiscuously over this barren & broken region.

About ^4^ the Prest [Young] invited the 12 & Brs Carrington, [Charles] Shumway & [Erastus] Snow to take a walk, we ascended the ridge & then proceeded to the top of a high peak about 2½ m[ile]s from camp, we then had a fine view of the main ridge of bluffs on either side ^of the river^ from 20 to 30 m[ile]s apart & of this intervening level, rolling & tumbled up surface & the course of the river up & down for a long distance ~~with~~ also the towering Black Hills, between the points WNW. & SW. ^air line [as the crow flies] 40 m[ile]s^ & Chimney Rock to the S.E. Br G[eorge] A Smith offered up a very appropriate prayer & we got back to camp about dusk in season to have a look at a very fine

84. This was considered the high point of the overland experience to many of the pioneers. The Council of Fifty was invited to participate in the prayer circle, but Thomas Bullock missed the call and wrote that "I have been deprived of one of my greatest & sacred privileges." Rogers, *Council of Fifty*, 131–33.

specimen of lunar rainbow, which occured soon after, about 7. It has been a day of much joy & satisfaction to us, peace, quiet & harmony prevailing in the camp & ^our^ stock full fed & well rested, & we all felt well & thankful for the sudden change for the better since our covenant.

May 31, 1847; Monday. Clear & pleasant breeze from the W.N.W. Started about 8, turned off our course a little to find grass, stopped [at] ½ past 12, distance 9¼ m[ile]s, grass thin; course very direct ^road good^ bottom varying much in breadth owing to the windings of the river, generaly very dry, with scanty grass, ridge quite broken, many of the peaks barren from sand, others covered with gravel & pebble stones. Distance across bottom & river from ridge to ridge 5 or 6 m[ile]s on an average. Started ¼ to 3 [then] stopped [and] ^camped^ ½ to 7 in 2 parallel lines on the gravely bank of a swift run from 20 to 30 ft wide, & about 1 mile above its outlet. Course quite direct road quite sandy, & grass thin, passed several good sized cotton trees, & stumps & trunks on the islands & banks, accompanied by long fringes of willow & many cotton bushes; 1 deer killed by J[ohn] Higby, dis[tance] 7¼ [miles]. ~~June 1st clear & pleasant.~~ Latitude by H[orizontal] observation, 43 04' 44". Much the most bottom on N[orth] side, quite a frost.

June 1, 1847; Tuesday. Clear & pleasant; started soon after breakfast, crossed the small run before & soon came to good hard ground; bottom from 2 to 4 m[ile]s wide, quite dry & hard, with thin grass[,] trees, green & dead, more numerous & large, & small pine or cedar trees, or both, quite plenty in the bluffs on both sides of river, little or no bottom on S[outh] side, just before we stopped ¼ past 12, passed 5 old sod chimneys near the S[outh] bank;[85] grass thin, 4½ m[ile]s; after nooning ^Latitude 42° 09' 24"^ traveled 7½ m[ile]s, road generaly quite sandy, grass scattering, & camped in a semicircle on the river bank about opposite Fort St. John,[86] on ^W side [of]^ Larimies Fork, & 1½ ^to 2^ m[ile]s from our camp, channel much narrower ^108 yds wide^ above Larimies Fork, & deep & currents strong. Our camp fires to night presented quite a cheerful & old fashioned appearance, wood being plenty.

85. Settlers built sod houses as temporary structures until they could build more permanent homes.

86. The fort was founded by John Baptiste Richard as a trading post. Bagley, *Pioneer Camp of the Saints*, 175n6.

Cloudy, sprinkled a few drops just after dark. Soon after we camped 2 of the brethren that had come up from Pueblo[87] 2 weeks last Sunday ^16th^ came over in our boat, they were pleased to see us & we them, they were 15 d[a]ys coming from Pueblo, did not hurry & laid by some, distance 250 m[ile]s. The Crows [Indian tribe] had been down just before they came to [on] the first & stole 25 horses from the post in daylight.

June 2, 1847; Wednesday. The 12, A[lbert] C[arrington] & several others crossed the N[orth] Fork walked 2[00] or 300 yds to the ruins of Fort Platte Co tradeing post, the outer & inner walls are pretty much intact, built of large sun dried brick about 15 ft high, 2½ ft thick, & enclosing a parallellogram 144 ft by 103 ft, with 2 large gate ways 1 for stock &c the other the main entrance, opening into the hollow square around which the buildings are ranged against the walls, with a wall between it & the space allotted to stock.

We next went to Fort St. John & were politely received by Mr [James] Beaudeaux & Co 17 in all. Walls &c at Fort Platte, the enclosure 168 ft by 116, the main building 2 stories high & forming part of the wall with a smallish double planked door, opening through an entranceway into the hollow square is open court, round, which are ranged mostly against the walls, the store room blacksmith stoneware rooms cook rooms &c, stableing &c along the east wall with a waggon entrance & strong door in the middle. On the S[outh] side, the main entrance [has] folding doors high & wide, double ash plank thickly studded with spikes over the main entraince, is raised a square tower of light frame work weather boarded with a flag staff near up from it.

Several squaws & young children about, prob^ab^ly belonging to the traders. We chartered their flat board & took a ride down the rapid currents of Larimies Fork, 3 or 4 m[ile]s in its windings to the mouth about ½ mile below our camp, then towed up & crossed over to camp[,] some cloudy. Mr Baudeaux said the first post was established here in 1833 & that it was 300 m[ile]s from here to Bridgers Fort,[88] or Black's Fork of Green River & where the Oregon & California roads fork. 2

87. Sick detachments of the Mormon Battalion and Mormon immigrants from Mississippi wintered in Pueblo, Colorado, in 1846–47.

88. Fort Bridger was one of the final stopping points for Mormons before the last push to the Salt Lake Valley. It was named after the well-known mountain man Jim Bridger.

flanking projections of square towers [are] seen up above the walls & roofes, 1 in the SE & [one] in the NE corner. They send their peltry[89] from this post to Ft Pierre [South Dakota] 400 m[ile]s overland on [to] the Missouri [River], where the steamboats take it. Latitude M[eridian] observation by O Pratt 42° 12' 13" at Ft St John, width of larimie Fork or same place 41 yds. Some cloudy & quite warm.

June 3, 1847; Thursday.[90] Pleasant, with a strong wind from ESE, commenced ferrying over the N[orth] Fork about 5. Kept busy until ½ past 1 when a severe hail & rain storm began to pour on us, accompanied with heavy lightning & thunder, lasted 1 hour. A[masa] Lyman started about 11 for Pueblo [Colorado] to counsel the movements of men & things there. In company [Roswell] Stevens, [Thomas] Woolsy & [John] Tippetts of the Mormon Battalion.[91] Sprinkling occasionaly. A[lbert] C[arrington] sent a letter to his wife, for A. Lyman, to be forwarded the first chance. Rained a good deal through the night.

Pioneer Journal of Amasa M. Lyman Kept by Albert Carrington 1847[92]

June 4, 1847; Friday. Green River and some men bound for California and some Frenchmen and their families going to Fort John passed through the Bluffs and camped on Horse Creek.[93] Good grass, timber, some trees ^and^ willows. Killed a deer.

June 5, 1847; Saturday. Weather cloudy wind from the north [blank]. Soil clay and some sand[,] the principle grass the baffaloe in the vicinity of streams quantities of sage few buffalo and antelopes a pack of wolves [illegible].[94]

89. That is, animal pelts.

90. On this day Lyman was called away to lead the group of ninety-three Latter-day Saints from Mississippi who had wintered in Pueblo with the Mormon Battalion's sick detachment. Carrington continues the journal another nineteen pages. I have not included it because Lyman is no longer part of the company. Readers can find the rest on the *Selected Collections* DVDs and online as the Amasa Lyman Journals, vol. 8, CHL website.

91. The Mormon Battalion (aka Iowa Volunteers) was sent to help in the Mexican-American War in exchange for President James K. Polk's support for the Mormon migration to the West. Three sick detachments of over 250 soldiers wintered in Pueblo alongside the Mississippi Saints.

92. This incomplete portion was kept in a different diary than the main trail journal, but in spite of the title, it was kept by Lyman and not Albert Carrington.

93. Some previous pages may be missing, explaining this abrupt first sentence.

94. The next three lines are written in faded pencil.

Encamped on a creek [illegible] of fine timber on grass clay soil. In the afternoon we encountered a severe storm of hail that [blank] and poured down upon us in one unbroken avalanche for twenty minutes it was with difficulty that we could keep our horses in camp by a small branch without wood. Rained some through the night yet from the wet we received no harm.

June 6, 1847; Sunday. Morning very cloudy a dense fog hovered over the entire country that rendered the objects invisible, but as the sun arose ~~arose~~ it became plain about eleven oclock. Stop[p]ed at the first water dried our skins and blankets. This morning some baffaloe and plenty of [them] in sight. The prarie is broad swells with gentle ascent and decent. The country appears one broad desolate waste with not one shrub to break the monotony of the scene. Camped on a small creeke without wood.

June 7, 1847; Monday. Wind easterly weather fine traveled 3 m[ile]s. Found timber in on the creek on which we camped there ~~missed~~. Lost the trail and traveled on around by a small salt lake about one mile in diameter the water is to[o] salt[y] to drink. It was quite shallow and clear about one mile south was another lake some less in size and fresh water. This afternoon the land is covered with the prickly pair. Towards night found some grass and the soil became sandy like land on the plattowe [and] lack of moskitoes.

Camped on a stream grass good and plenty of dear the river one ½ mile wide.

June 8, 1847; Tuesday. Crossed the stream in the morning without trouble found the trail leading from the village of the Indians up to S[outh] F[ork]. Rains in the afternoon threatened and we backed up for it but it rained all around us but we were not wet the bottom of an average width of one mile that portion near the river affords good grass.

June 9, 1847; Wednesday. Traviled a short distance and killed a pelican for breakfast. We measured it 7 ft from tip to tip of his wings[,] was fat. Passed on up the river found the trail of the company from Purbelow [Pueblo] where they had crossed south fork. We recrossed the river on their trail an[d] followed on directly down the river at dark. Crossed ^the^ Creek Laprele and camped.

June 10, 1847; Thursday. Weather fine passed over to Crow Creek passed up the creek and camped above where we missed the trail on the 7th.

June 11, 1847; Friday. Started before the sun was up. Traviled 10 m[ile]s breakfasted by a small lake from which saw some Buffaloe and some of our brethren in chase traviled on and found brother Smithson[95] who had killed a Buffaloe. We next met br [Nelson] Higins [and] came to the camp on Bear Creek. Found the Brethren in good health and spirits.

June 12, 1847; Saturday. Passed on camped on a spring branch of Horse Creek.

June 13, 1847; Sunday Went to Horse Creek held meeting delivered the instruction from the Council to the brethren which they received with apparent satisfaction and manifested a willingness to abide in the same as formerly.

June 14, 1847; Monday. Traveled to and camped on Bear Creek this morning. Bro Thomas Williams and others left for Ft. John in search of some stolen animals and found them in possession of some Frenchmen who were unwilling to give them up.

June 15, 1847; Tuesday. Left Bear Creek for the Fort with about 20 men to recover the stolen property a part of which we recovered.[96]

95. The Mississippi contingent of some ninety-four was made up almost entirely of twelve families, including fourteen Smithsons. This would have been Allen (29) or William (41).

96. Following this entry Lyman wrote the dates for June 16–24 but without adding any content. Because he had been sent to Pueblo, he would not be in the July 24 company as it entered the Salt Lake Valley for the first time. In addition to Brigham Young's company of nearly 150 and Lyman's Pueblo company, more than 1,500 pioneers would continue to arrive between Sept.–Oct. 1847 and would stay through the winter while Young, Lyman, and other leaders returned to Winter Quarters to prepare more emigrants for the 1848 trek. Lyman would cross the plains two more times to help guide immigrating Mormons.

3 The Deep South and California Gold Fields, 1847–1852

After returning to Winter Quarters in the fall of 1847, Lyman received an assignment to help lead the Mississippi members west. His account reads like a missionary journal, and it was a mission of sorts even though his assignment was to canvass the state and round up the members to lead them to Utah. He was in charge of one of several wagon trains as far as Council Bluffs, Iowa. When he became sick, his leadership was relinquished to someone else; but all arrived in the Great Basin and he was given another adventurous assignment, this time to tour the gold fields in California and collect tithing from the many LDS prospectors and inn keepers in San Francisco, Sacramento, San Jose, Placerville, and elsewhere, then to establish a Mormon colony near Los Angeles. It was a busy time for him, but he was in his mid-thirties and full of vigor, at least when he was not sick.

Amasa Lyman's Book[1]

Farewell, Fare the[e] well my friend as eaver, Friendships ties we ne'er can seaver [sever], They've bound us strong & close together, Will they disolve? No, neaver, neaver. Sketches & dates of a mission of Elder Amasa Lyman to the State of Miss[issippi] in the year of A. D. 1848.

December 28, 1847; Tuesday. Tuesday morning the 28th of Dec ^1847^. One day after the special Conference at C[ouncil] Bluffs [Iowa],

1. This is written on the first recto of the diary, followed on this page and the next by two undated sentences.

I left for the South, In company with Bros [Ezra T.] Benson[,] [Erastus] Snow[,] & [William I.] Appleby who were going on a Mission to the East. We came on to Bro Wm Snows & stayed over night.[2]

December 29, 1847; Wednesday. Wednesday the 29th[3] left Bro Snow in Bro John Scotts carriage & traveled some 25 miles & stayed with Bro Preston Thomas, who accompanys me south.

December 30, 1847; Thursday. We traveled 25 miles & stayed at Mr Walden's. ~~Friday 30th traveled 25 miles to Mr Bushes on the Sations bottana~~.

January 1, 1848; Saturday. Came 25 miles to Bro Lakes.

January 2, 1848; Sunday. The first day of ^January 1848.^ Started early, the weather was beautiful—the New year came in mild & pleasantly. The King of day illuminated our paths & the Heavens smiled on our heads. We reached Savannah [Missouri] at sundown a distance of 26 miles.

January 3, 1848; Monday. Myself & Elders [Ezra T.] Benson[,] [Erastus] Snow[,] & [William I.] Appleby, took a faster conveyance as our business urged us on, leaving Bros [Preston] Thomas[,] [James H.] Flanigan[,] & [John] Scott to come together.

January 4, 1848; Tuesday. ~~Tuesday~~ ^Mon.^ We took the stage at Liberty[4] for Hanibal on the Mississippi River, thinking that the River was open & that we could get a boat for St. Louis. We reached Hanable on the 6th & finding the river closed hired a hack to carry us through to St. Louis. We all arrived safe on the 12th after a long, coald, muddy & circuitous rout[e] of 15 days. We found a welcome & warm reception amongst the Saints in St. Louis.

---

2. William Snow lived in Council Point, Iowa, several miles below Council Bluffs, and worked the Mormon ferry there until he himself led an emigrating company west in 1850. See, e.g., Mays, "Picturing History: Council Point, Iowa," *Deseret News*, Nov. 23, 2011; Platt, "Early Branches of the Church of Jesus Christ of Latter-day Saints, 1830–1850," 13.

3. Lyman is a day behind in numbering, although someone has penciled in corrections for the next few days.

4. Lyman explained elsewhere that he felt compelled to use an alias after he realized the hotel owner in Liberty, Missouri, was someone who had helped guard Joseph Smith when the Mormon leader was incarcerated there. Lyman went by his middle name and called himself Esquire Mason. *AML*, 152.

We got the Epistle of the Twelve Printed at the Republican office[5]—I preached to the Saints, & gave such instruction & council as I deemed necessary—explained my mission & after attending to all our business—& a few days refreshment cha[ng]ing of linens & procuring some mea^ns^ to defray expenses, we resolved to prossicute our journey.

January 20, 1848; Thursday. We took passage on the Steamer Kit Carson for Memphis [Tennessee], the fair being $9.00. We arrived on the 24th & stoped 2 miles out of town at Mr. Moreheads[,] Bro [Preston] Thomas & friends[, for] 2 days.[6]

January 26, 1848; Wednesday. We secured our passage in the stage to Aberdeen in Mississippi the central point of our mission[7]—the fair was 11.00 eleven dollars each—the distance was 150 miles. We arrived in Aberdeen on Wednesday the 2nd day of Feb. On the rout[e] we called at Bro Dunbars who lives between Holly Springs & Pantotoc. He assisted us in our journey.

February 3, 1848; Thursday. We arrived at Bro [William] Crosbys who was glad enough to see us & bade us welcome to his hospitalities—The brethren in this neighborhood are prepairing to move to the Church in the West.[8]

We found the country quite broken from Memphis out, tremendious bad roads—a poor soil, mostly of red clay, with a thin surface of black dirt—as a general heavy timbered—after we had traveled 100 miles we found plenty of pine timber. The principle product of the land is cotton, this & negroes ocupied the attention of the planters.[9]

5. The epistle admonished church members to "gather yourselves together speedily" at Council Bluffs, the staging area for the exodus. To those in "England, Scotland, Ireland, Wales, & adjacent islands and countries we say emigrate as speedily as possible … to New Orleans & from thence direct to Council Bluffs." The epistle was set and printed at the *Daily Missouri Republican*, which itself ran the full text of the announcement on Jan. 19, 1848. "General Epistle from the Council of Twelve Apostles to the Church … scattered throughout the earth," Dec. 23, 1847, Brigham Young Office Files, CHL; Crawley, *Descriptive Bibliography of the Mormon Church*, 2:29–30.

6. Joseph Morehead Jr. (1773–1828) was Preston Thomas's father-in-law and uncle.

7. All the subsequent towns Lyman lists until his return to Council Bluffs are in Mississippi. Aberdeen is midway between Tupelo and Columbus.

8. Crosby was president of the Buttahatchie Branch near Caledonia, twenty miles from Aberdeen.

9. Having been raised in the North, Lyman may have been surprised by what he found in the South. For instance, the branch president in Buttahatchie was a wealthy plantation owner with plenty of slaves. Alexis de Tocqueville noticed how abruptly

February 6, 1848; Sunday. I preached to the Saints at Bro [William] Crosbys school house.

February 7, 1848; Monday. I preached in the evening at Mother [Sarah] Crosbys. The effect of the whole was good.

February 8, 1848; Tuesday. Bro [Preston] Thomas & myself started for Noxabee to acomplish if possible the object of our mission—Bro [William] Crosby ^& Bro [John] Brown^[10] furnished us with horses to ride & chainge to bear our expenses & started at 10 o clock.

We reached Columbus a distance of 30 miles & stayed all night. They had a meeting in Columbus to night to take into consideration something about the "Telegraph." Bro. Thomas found some oald acquaintances [a] Mr. Bluitt.

February 9, 1848; Wednesday. We traveled 25 miles to Colonol Harless where we received kind treatment.

February 10, 1848; Thursday. Before starting we explained to Mr. Harless the object of our mission, he gave us $5.00 & invited us to call on our return. We passed through Macon & stoped for the night with Mr. Chaimbors whose wife & daughter belong to the Church they were rather coald & distant

February 11, 1848; Friday. ~~To night~~ We stoped at Mr Griffens. From thence we came through Summerville continued on & stayed with John Lamphy for the night; he & his wife were glad to see us & made many enquireys of us.

February 12, 1848; Saturday. We took an ~~early~~ late start. I promised to call on our return—We passed through Philadelphia[11] & travled some 35 miles & stayed with Mr. Steel, where we met with good treatment.

February 13, 1848; Sunday. We left Mr. Steels after late breakfast & called to see Mr Joseph Morrow with whom we had some business—to day we traveled 28 miles & stayed all night in Hillsboro the county town of Scott County—we met with no incouragement here.

---

things could change when traveling through the different sections of the country, where one might find on "the right bank of the Ohio" no slaves and on "the left bank the scene changes so suddenly that you think yourself on the other side of the world." Pierson, *Tocqueville in America*, 582.

10. John Brown was married to William Crosby's sister Elizabeth.

11. Philadelphia, Mississippi, is about halfway between Aberdeen and Jackson.

February 14, 1848; Monday. We travled over a poor sandy—long leaf pine country, found bad roads & travled 31 miles & stopt with Mr Bott fo[u]r miles from Brandon, the County town of Rankin County.

February 15, 1848; Tuesday. We left Mr. Botts' & passed through Brandon—crossed Pearl River & passed through Jackson the Capital of the State of Mississippi & stoped for the night with Milighan.[12]

February 16, 1848; Wednesday. We started early & traveled at pritty fast rate all day as we wanted to get Bro [Hamilton] Jetts. We found a poor sandy country today & after a heard [hard] days ride we arrived at Bro Jetts at dark. He was not at home—had gone to Red River.[13]

February 17, 1848; Thursday. We remained with the breathren who were very glad to see us & here from the Church.

February 18, 1848; Friday. We visited Bro [John] Knights family & returned again to Bro Jetts. He came home to night.

February 19, 1848; Saturday. We again visited Bro Knights in company with Bro Jett. In the afternoon we returned to bro J.s & stayed over night.

February 20, 1848; Sunday. We bade farewell with Bro J[ett]s family—on leaving he gave us one & a ½ [English gold] sover[eig]ns—& seemed disposed to assist the Church in this time of poverty, but he is imbarrest with depts & has a large istate on red River to manage—to day traveled some 25 miles & arrived late in the evening at Bro Blacks—Here we found some good Mormons firm in the faith but not able to do much for the Church.

February 21, 1848; Monday. We left Bro Blacks after early dinner. He give us $3.00.

February 22, 1848; Tuesday. We started & had only mounted our horses when it commenced raining—It commenced thundering & lightning so we were detained some 3 hours—we passed through Jackson

12. The entries here are so similar to Preston Thomas's diary, Lyman probably copied this portion of his narrative from his companion. For instance, Thomas recorded on this date that he "left Mr. Bott's early, passed through Branded, crossed Pearl River, passed through Jackson, travelled 26 miles and stayed for the night with Mr. Miligan."

13. Hamilton Jett lived sixty miles south of Jackson in Monticello on a slave plantation and worked another piece of land near the Red River, 160 miles west in Louisiana. The February 18–19 entries refer to his brother-in-law John Knight Jr., who was married to Jett's sister Mary Amanda Jett (1828–1902). Hamilton's own spouse, Louisa H. Knight (1815–1891), was his brother-in-law's sister. She was Hamilton's fourth wife, the previous three having died.

where they were firing cannon selebrating Washingtons berthday—The legislation [legislature] was in session. We crossed Pearl River & passed through Branden & stopt with Mr Bott.

February 23, 1848; Wednesday. We started after Breckfast. The morning was fine & clear, but about noon it clouded up & commenced raining & continued till we arrived at Hilsborough. We stoped with Mr. Eastland for the night, we stayed with him on our way down.

February 24, 1848; Thursday. Left Hilsborro. On our way up we called at Mr Joseph Morrow's with whome we had business—from there we continued on to Bro Steels & stayed with him all night. We had first rate fair with Mr. Steel—who is a fine man.

February 25, 1848; Friday. We left Mr Steels—after some 8 miles we came to a large creek called Kentucky which was much swollen with late rain—the bridge was ^partly^ carried away & it was with difficulty we got over at all. We came on through Philadelphia to the house of Mr. [John] Lamphy whose wife is the sister of Mr. [James] Flake, an acquaintance of Bro [Preston] Thomas—they used us well.[14]

February 26, 1848; Saturday. Before we started Mr. [John] Lamphy gave us $2.00 in specie [coins] & a 5 dollar note on the Memphis bank which is broken. It is not worth 40 c[en]ts on the dollar. He also gave us a 10 doller note on the bank of Mobeal [Mobile].[15] With many kind expressions they bade us fare well. (The $10.00 was to be taken to Bro. [James M.] Flake[.)] We came on & stayed all night & stayed with Mr. Harless—he was not at home.

February 27, 1848; Sunday. We travled all day through the mud a distance of 25 miles to Columbus put up our horses at the tavern & spent the night with Major [Thomas] Bluett[16] in fulfillment of our promise

14. James Flake is the person whose slave, Green Flake, traveled west with Brigham Young in 1847. Where Lyman and his companion say the Lamphys made good use of them, the missionaries were probably put to work in exchange for compensation (see next entry).

15. Until the Civil War (1861–65), there was no national currency. Banks issued their own notes, and their value depended on the bank's solvency.

16. Thomas Garton Blewett was a veteran of the War of 1812. His elegant new house (see next entry) took up a full city block and has been preserved as a museum. It was inherited by his daughter Regina and son-in-law James Harrison, who became a member of the Confederate Congress. See "Collection Overview," Harrison Papers.

when we passed down—he gave us a hearty welcome & invited us to attend church with him after supper. We did so & herd quite a discourse on the progress & prosperity of the Church, his text was from the Song of Solomon. Major B & family belongs to the baptis[t] Church.

February 28, 1848; Monday. This morning Major B[luett] invited Bro [Amasa] Lyman[17] to pray in his family—he made an able prayer indeed every word was watched as was afterwards acknowledged—we passed through ~~the~~ ^an^ ordeal of the most scrutinizing ^gase [gaze] &^ kind. For Mormons were quite [a] curiosity—this morning we were shown the garden by Mrs. Bluett which is truly splendid. We procured cuttings of figgs & Pomegran^ats^ which we propose taking to the City of the Great Salt Lake if we can preserve them.

After our stroal through the garden, we were shown a large new building which Mr B was building for a family residence—we were conducted through several of its apartments & from the top of which we had a fine view of the City of Columbus. On the observatory we were joined by Mrs [Regina] Harreson, who followed us up for the express purpose of becoming acquainted with Mormons. She is a woman of splendid accomplishments. She asked us a thousand ^& one^ questions & expressed a desire to learn of our doctrine. We promist to send them some books explaining our doctrine when an opportunity offered.

Major B. invited us to stop & preach, but time would not permit us to do so at present—He then invited us to call & preach if we ever passed through the country again; & if any of our Elders passed tell them to stop & preach.

This will be a good place for an Elder to come & if any of our Elders passed this way tell them to call & preach for them. This is a good place for an Elder to pull in & make a beginning, as through Major B's influence the truth may be brought before the people under favor^able^ circumstances. After tarying a few hours with them we Bade them farewell. They expressed many kind wishes for us.

From thence we continued our journey to Bro Crosby's & arrived at night fall—wearied with a long [journey] of near 500 miles through mud & water.

---

17. Lyman is copying from Preston Thomas's diary again.

February 29, 1848; Tuesday.[18] Morning we met Bro J[ames] Flanigan who [had] accompanied us from Councel Bluffs—he remain^ed^ in Bro [William] Crosbys neighborhood till we returned. In all our journeying in the Southern country we found a general spirit of enquiry after Mormonism. The feald is open for a rich harvest—through the labors of faithful & prudent ministers of the word of Truth. We remained in the neighborhood of Bro Crosbys some 8 or 10 days, nothing of note transpired during this time.

March 6, 1848; Monday. Sister Mary C. Parchman presented me with a very handsome brush, made of the fethers of the Pea Bird's tail to be presented to Sister [Maria Louisa] Lyman.[19] Sister P. is a good woman but her Husband does not belong to the Church & drinks very hard—She wants to gather herself & children with the Saints but fears that her husband will never take her.

March 8, 1848; Wednesday. Bro [James] Flanigan took Brother P[reston] Thomas 17 miles on the rout[e] to his Uncles—at 10 o clock it commenced raining & continued till the next morning. Bro Flanigan came back by watter & was completely drenched with rain.

March 10, 1848; Friday. We left Bro [William] Crosbys place on horses furnished by Mr. [William] Lay[20] & Bro. [Francis M.] McKowen, by swimming one creek we got to Cotten Gin on the Thom Bigby [Tombigbee] River, we crossed it & traveled through the bottom which was very wet & muddy to ^32 miles^ to Oakalona [Okolona][21] a small country town of some 100 inhabitants, a place wich will be famous in History for its depravity & meanness, the disorder & unmannerly conduct of its inhabitants. S^h^ortly after we entered the Hotell our attention was attracted by a fight wich broke out amongst a drunken rabble in the street. The first site we got of the row was a man thrashing another with a cheair

18. Lyman's date is correct because it was a leap year.

19. Amasa had seven wives in 1848, but Maria Louisa was his first. Polygamy would not be made public for another four years, so we can assume that if he intended to give the gift to another wife, he kept the beneficiary a secret.

20. Even though William H. Lay never joined the LDS Church, he emigrated with his Mormon friends; he was one of those who sent a slave ahead to Utah in 1847 under John Brown's supervision to build houses and plant crops in advance of his arrival. See Thiriot, "Hark (Lay) Wales: A Slave in Zion," *Keepapitchinin*; Lythgoe, "Negro Slavery in Utah," 40-54.

21. Okolona is twenty miles south of Tupelo.

over the head with all his might. This scene continued till in the night. The Landlord tried to excu^se^ his town & appologise for the outbreak by saying that such rows were of a rear [rare] occurence.

Next an elderly gentleman intro^duced^ himself to us as an Alabamian. After a short conversation with him he expressed his sentiments on religion by stating that the dead ought to be forgotten as soon as they die & should never be called to mind by likenesses, & when this closed another man entered somewhat advanced in years—He broched a conversation on morrals & politics. His oppinion was that the religious bigotry of the times in prohibiting the sail of liquors caused these outbrakes, that those who used liquors would have them anyhow & he was one of them. He cursed the preachers off as the most ungreatful & most damnable class of scoundrels in the world. That they were daily abusing their best friend the Deavil!!! That if it were not for him they could not get their living. Next he followed on politics, & uttered his imprecations against the [President James K.] Polk party—he stated the Press was ulogizing John Quincy Adams as a venerable statesman, he ~~stated~~ ^said^ it ought to read a damned Yankee Scoundrell—a damned Abolitionist trying to raise the negroes to cut their master's throats, after he himself had enriched himself by the slave trade.[22]

The next scene was introduced by music from the violin, by a fellow who could play only 3 or 4 tunes & these he sawed away at till he crucified them—Then followed a scene of imbicility in an other part of the house. The principle actor of wich was an old foolish woman who by her whims & foolish oddities amused her auditors in such a stile as to cause roars of laughture at short intervalls.

Time had passed away & 9 o clock had arived—the Land Lord by ~~his~~ ^our^ request conducted us to our sleeping appartment. But the prospect for sleeping was indeed poor. Soone after the drunken anti Morrelist anti religionist, anti Polk & Adams man entered our room as a partner for the night. By the by he was afflicted with the rheumatism & at short intervals would brake out in awfull groanings & cursings, first he would curse the

22. John Quincy Adams's single term as US president ended in 1829, but in 1830 he was elected to the House of Representatives and became a leading Congressional opponent of slavery. He died Feb. 23, 1848. Nagel, *John Quincy Adams*.

pains then in his leg & then himself, this together with his breath wich was equal to a small stillhouse was our prospect for sleeping.

A little time had elapsed & we had gotten into a doze, when we were arroused by an uproar & outcry wich could not have been far surpassed if the reigons of the dammed had all been turned loose to try themselves— The facts of this last act are as follows, to carry on the sport some fellows streached a roap across the road near where a liceum[23] was going on & then went off some distance & rused a sham fight with tremendious hollowing cries of distress &c. The crowd all rushed from the House & one after another as fast as they came to the roap went heels over head on the groun^d^ till the number had incresed to quite a pile—by this time they began to discover their mistake & soone concluded to adjourn for the night. This ended the picture for the night with the exception of the frequent groanings & curs^ings^ of our partner in the room.

In all this we had a fare picture of the degredation, the disorder & unmannerly conduct of of the People of Oakalona. In fact after the usual exceptions there could nothing be seen that indicated gen[i]us, science, art, religion, goodness, greatness, or even ~~with~~ good manners & Cevility. Thus we spent the night of the 10th.

March 11, 1848; Saturday. From thence we came to Pantotoc rested a short time[,] got the news[,] found a favorable impression left on the minds of the people by Bro [James] Flanigan's preaching—they wanted us to stop & preach for them. We came on 6 miles & staye^d^ with a Mr. Dunken over night.

March 12, 1848; Sunday. We traveled some 32 miles to Bro Dunbars—here we found Bro [Preston] Thomas who had come on a head of us.

March 13, 1848; Monday. We rested at Bro. Dunbars & found his feelings & those of his family somewhat chainged & disturbed occasioned by the reports of some apostates[,] a Mr Nowlen.

March 14, 1848; Tuesday. Bro. [James] Flanigan carried Bro [Preston] Thomas to Holly Springs on horseback—on his way home [blank].

March 15, 1848; Wednesday. Bro. [James] Flanigan & I left Bro Dunbars for Purdy intending to meet the emigrating breathren[24]—Bro.

23. A lecture or theater performance.

24. Lyman is going to lead 13 families, 90–100 individuals in all, including about 35 slaves, north through Tennessee and Kentucky to the Ohio River where they will take

Dunbar came with us some 20 miles—he gave some 75 dollars for the aid of the cause. He gave Bro. [Preston] Thomas $10.00 & to Bro Flanigan 5.00 & to me he gave 30.00 besides when we went down 20.00 making in all 65.00.[25]

March 16, 1848; Thursday. Last night we stayed with a Mr. Childers an odd Baptist Preacher—he treated us kindly—from his house we traveled across a slope of uneaven country, much of the bottom some mirey, we found heavy timber on the bottom of Beack C[ree]k[,] black & white gum on the ri[d]ges [from] Pine—the land very poor which is fit for cultivation. The buildings miserably poor. We traveled some 40 miles to day it was near 9 oclock before we got a place to stay all night.

March 17, 1848; Friday. We rode into Purdy & found by inquiry that the breathren had not yet come up—we found ourselves in Genoa. We turned down to meet the company travled on slo[w]ley some 5 miles & put up for the night. We found a young man by the name of Halleday who had married the man's daugh^ter^. He was a Mormon but the people knew knothing of it &c &c.

March 18, 1848; Saturday. We traveled on some 3 miles & met the breath[ren]. After a little rest & the usual salutations we joined the camp & traveled on west through Purdy some 7 miles & camped; the breathren had but got there tents pitched when it commenced Raining & continued till morning. This was the first rain for 10 days & for the time of year the weather has been remarkably fine. There has been no snow & little or no frost in Miss[issippi] on all our journey. So mild is the climate.

March 19, 1848; Sunday. The weather cleared of[f] fine & clear luckily for the breathren their tents & waggon covers kept the Rain out, indeed after a whole nights rain I saw not an unpleasant countenence. I herd not a word of dissatisfaction [instead] a spirit of union seemed to prevade the whole Company which consisted of some 70 or 80 persons, about one ½ blacks[,] 11 waggons. To day the wheeling was quite heard [hard]. We travled some 17 miles—we pass^ed^ through a small town called Jacks Creek—it consisted of one store & post office.

---

passage on the Mississippi River to St. Louis, purchase supplies there, and continue on to the Missouri River to Council Bluffs. For the number of slaves, see the entry for March 19 below; also Goodridge, *William Brockman Bankhead.*

25. Lyman aligned the numbers and added them up on the right side of the page.

March 20, 1848; Monday. The brethren concluded to rest their teams & not travel.

March 21, 1848; Tuesday. The state of the weather was such that we could not travel, on the evening of the 20th it commenced raining & continued a heavy rain till 12 o clock the next day; during our detaintion I took the opportunity of instructing the brethren in many things.

March 22, 1848; Wednesday. We traveled but 9 miles & camped on account of high watter.

March 23, 1848; Thursday. We got an early start & passed through Lexington [Tennessee] & traveled 18 miles. Joyous spring[,] with all her lovelyness & [s]weet fragrance, her new dressed & s[w]eet flowers adorn the walks—the fields & the gardens—the fruit trees & the forrest trees. The people where we stoped last night invited us to preach for them. Accordingly Bro [William] Crosby & I preached to them—they listened with great attention.

March 24, 1848; Friday. We travled some 12 miles—we passed through Huntingdon. We stoped at 3 o clock on account [of] some sickness.

March 25, 1848; Saturday. We moved on some 18 miles[26] & stoped on account of high watter. I find Ken[tucky] & Tenn[essee] to be the best Peach country I ever was in. They look lovely all covered with blossoms.

March 26, 1848; Sunday. We travled through Paris the County Seat of Henry County.

March 27, 1848; Monday. We travled 18 miles.

March 28, 1848; Tuesday. We travled some 18 miles. We passed through Mayfield [Kentucky] at 3 o clock & I imagined from the degrees of curiosity & amusement manifested that they took us to be Gen[era]l Scott & his army returning from the war!!![27] To night Bro [William] Crosby counted out [donated] to ~~Bro. Lyman~~ the mission & the call of the council of the Church of $1000.00 ~~Bro. John Brown gave to the mission 200.00.~~ Crosby gave Bro [James] Flanigan 50.00. ~~Elizabeth Crosby gave 50.00.~~ Bro Crosby & his wife are noble soulid people. The secret acts of men, if noble are far the noblest of their lives.

26. This looks as if Lyman originally wrote *12 miles* then corrected it to *18*.

27. That is, General Winfield Scott of the Mexican-American War. The treaty of Feb. 1848 transferred fifty-five percent of Mexican territory, including the Great Basin, to the US.

March 29, 1848; Wednesday. We travled 18 miles to night. The Breathren sent money by us to procure their outfit[s] [teams].

March 30, 1848; Thursday. We travled 15 miles to the Ohio River. The river was so hig[h], ^& the ferry boat so broken^ that the brethren were to be detained some time before they could cross.

Bro [Francis M.] McKowen gave me 5.00. Bro ^John^ Brown donated to the call [of] the mission $200.00 & sent for his outfit 72.75

Bro Wm Crosby sends for his outfit 300.00. Elizabeth Crosby donated to the mission 50.00[,] [to] her outfit 100.00

John H. Bankhead donated to the mission 20.00 & sends for his outfit 202.00.

Frances McKowen donated to the mission 15.00 & sends for his outfit 145.00

March 31, 1848; Friday. We attempted to cross the Ohio River but the wind was so high that we failed.

April 1, 1848; Saturday. We crossed early in the morning by paying each ferrage .75. At 3 o clock P.M. we got on the Steamer S. Right for Cairo [Illinois]. They charged us 3.00

April 2, 1848; Sunday. We shiped on the Independence for St. Louis [Missouri], "charge" each 5.00

April 3, 1848; Monday. We arrived in St. Louis at 12 oclock the whole passage including frate & storage 20.00. We found that Bro. [Preston] Thomas had passed up to the Bluffs [Council Bluffs]. To day I purchased some cloathing to the amount [of] 17.25.

April 4, 1848; Tuesday. I purchased a trunk set at $12.00.

April 6, 1848; Thursday. I made a bill [order] with Beach & Eddy [store] in articles of Cloathing 64.31. I purchased ~~some~~ ^a^ gun[,] blanket & leger[?]

April 7, 1848; Friday. Bro. [Ezra T.] Benson arived from the east.

April 9, 1848; Sunday. Bro. [Ezra T.] Benson & I preached to the Saints in St. Louis.

April 10, 1848; Monday. Bro E[rastus] Snow arived from the east—We done up all our business.

April 11, 1848; Tuesday. We left St. Louis on the steamer Mandan for C[ouncil] Bluffs—This boat was chartered by Beach & Eddy to take up a stock of goods ^&c^. On the 11th Bro [William] Crosby arrived in St. Louis. At 9 oclock P.M. the boat shoved out from port.

April, 12, 1848; Wednesday. We reached St. Charles.[28]

April 13, 1848; Thursday. The boat ran upon a rock & was injered so much that she had to go back to the stocks.

April 14, 1848; Friday. We made New Port [Portland].

April 15, 1848; Saturday. The boat lay on a bar all day.

April 16, 1848; Sunday. The Capt told us he would have [to] discharge the whole cargo & go back to the stocks with his boat.

April 17, 1848; Monday. The Company of Saints no [numbering] 100 all got themselves & effects on shore & struck up their tents on the bank of the Mo [Missouri] river to wate the return of the Boat. I went back on the boat to see that the contract [for passage] was fulfilled.

April 19, 1848; Wednesday. The boat reached St. Louis. I remained in St. Louis 8 days waiting on the boat.

April 23, 1848; Sunday. I preached twice to the people in St. Louis.

April 26, 1848; Wednesday. The Mandan being repaired we left St. Louis again for the Bluffs.

April 28, 1848; Friday. We reached Portland & commenced loding up again.

April 29, 1848; Saturday. We were all loadend [&] ready to go on.

April 30, 1848; Sunday. In the morning we were again under way & proceeded on to St. Joseph without much difficulty & arived there on the 5th of May. There the boat took in a lott of flour for the bluffs from Beach & Eddys.

May 6, 1848; Saturday. We left St. Joseph & proceeded on with no particular difficulty.

May 8, 1848; Monday. We reached Fort Kearney at 3 o clock P.M. While there we had a tremendious hail storm.

May 9, 1848; Tuesday. We reached Winter Quarter at dark. We found our friends all rejoiced to see us—I found on ariving at my Little

---

28. The steamboat traveled north for fifteen miles, veered west at the confluence of the Missouri River, and traveled thirty miles to its first stop, St. Charles, the onetime French-speaking capital of Missouri.

Cottage that my family were all well but that one of my little daughters had died during my absence.[29]

May 10, 1848; Wednesday. Bro [James] Flanigan & I purchast a stock of Flour for our Miss[issippi] brethren, the no. of 132 lbs at $5.75 cts amounting to 759.00.

May 11, 1848; Thursday. I spent the day in straightening up my business—reporting & learning the course to pursue in relation to moving to the [Salt Lake] Valley. In the course of a few days I found it to [be] advisable for me to moove to the valley. Consequently commenced arra[ng]ing my business to that end.

May 23, 1848; Tuesday. Bro. [William] Crosby's company arived in fine spirits, all ready to take right hold of the work & move right on to the valley.[30]

May 26, 1848; Friday. Bro. [James] Flanigan Left on a mission to the east.

April 12, 1849; Thursday.[31] Started our packs and animals in [the] charge of Clark Covil and others who went as far as the north canyon [now Bountiful] and camped my self and brother [Orrin Porter] Rockwell. Taried in the City until the 13th Fr^i^day when we left and traviled as far north as J. P. Barnards with whom we taried all night. On Saturday the 14th traveled to Ogdens fork of the Weber where we found our company makeing a raft for crossing as the stream was to high to ford. The raft being completed we crossed our packs on Sunday the 15th. We crossed our animals and got some of our animals that had run away. On Monday the 16th traviled to Boxelder.

April 17, 1849; Tuesday. Traviled to Bear river and crossed 80 m[ile]s from the City. On Wednesday 18th built bridge and crossed the Maladd

29. This was four-year-old Ruth Adelia Lyman.

30. Lyman's company no sooner left Winter Quarters on June 30 than it was combined with Willard Richards's due to Lyman's illness. He was so sick, he was unable to speak at times. He was often susceptible to illness and more willing than able to complete some assignments, a recurring trait of his.

31. A year has passed since Lyman set out for Salt Lake City. He has received his new assignment to minister to the church in California, where he will spend most of his time in San Francisco and circling around the Mormon Island region. Mormon Island was a dry spot between the American River and a canal alongside the river. Lyman will head north to the Oregon Trail, west to the Raft River to a cutoff that takes travelers south, then west along the Humboldt River to the Sierra Nevadas. *AML*, 168–96.

[River in Idaho, went] 23 m[ile]s [farther] and camped at [the] warm springs[,] water [a] little brackish [and] no timber but plenty of sage.[32] On Thursday the 19th traviled 25 m[ile]s and overtook the camps that preceded us. Camped on short feed the packs still in advance one day. Friday the 20th traviled 20 m[ile]s camped by the spring at the foot of the mountains.

April 21, 1849; Saturday. Traveled 25 m[ile]s camped on short feed. Sunday 22ond traviled 20 m[ile]s saw some Indians[,] camped on good feed weather fine and warm.

April 23, 1849; Monday. Traviled 25 m[ile]s camped on goose creek [Utah] the creek high[,] feed short[,] the pack party still in advance of us. This days travil hilly and rough today saw some antilope and wild geese.

April 24, 1849; Tuesday. Traviled 20 m[ile]s camped at the Beaver Spring. Feed torerable good, the pack party in advance of us 2 days by their letter ~~this~~ found this morning.

April 25, 1849; Wednesday. Traviled 30 m[ile]s camp on a slew [swamp]. Good water and feed no wood. On Thursday 26th traviled 15 m[ile]s camped on a smal creek running into Marys river [Humboldt] good feed and sage.[33]

April 27, 1849; Friday. Traviled 15 m[ile]s camped on slew running into Marys river big sugee [flood]. Today crossed 2 mirey slews.

April 28, 1849; Saturday. Traviled to Marys river ^8 m[ile]s^ which was so high we had to raft it then crossed 4 mirey slews camped at the bluffs.

April 29, 1849; Sunday. Traviled 30 m[ile]s camped on a slew. Monday 30th traviled 30 m[ile]s camped in the canyon.

May 1, 1849; Tuesday. Traviled 30 m[ile]s camped on the river. Wednesday 2ond traviled down the river 30 m[ile]s. This day crossed the river.

May 3, 1849; Thursday. Traviled 25 m[ile]s camped mostly salaratus land. Friday 4th traviled 30 m[ile]s this day found letter of the 2ond[,] the pack party 2 days in advance.

---

32. They are connecting with the Oregon Trail near today's Lava Hot Springs on the Portneuf River, a onetime winter camp grounds for the Shoshone Indians.

33. Peter Ogden named it Mary's River, but John C. Frémont's designation was in honor of Alexander von Humboldt, the German explorer.

May 5. 1849; Saturday. Traviled 25 m[ile]s on the river feed good. Some little complaint of ill health in camp to day.

May 6, 1849; Sunday. Traviled 22 m[ile]s. D[aniel] P. Clark quite sick camped by ford. Monday 7th traviled 25 m[ile]s camped on short feed. Clarks health improveing.

May 8, 1849; Tuesday. Traviled 18 m[ile]s on river pour feed. Wednesday 9th traviled 12 m[ile]s and breakfasted then traviled to the slew which made 30 m[ile]s. Tolerable feed and brakish water. Thursday 10th traviled 25 m[ile]s camped at the sink[,][34] tolerable feed bad water.

May 11, 1849; Friday. Traviled 32 m[ile]s to the salmon trout. D[aniel] P. Clark sick. Started at 2 oclock A.M. Saturday 12th laid by. [blank] Clarks health improving. This night Indians troublesome.

May 13, 1849; Sunday. Traviled 17 m[ile]s. We had barely left camp when it was filled with Indians. Monday 14th traviled 15 m[ile]s. Tuesday 15th traviled 25 m[ile]s. Wednesday 16th traviled 30 m[ile]s camped at the mouth of the canyon. ~~Thursday 15th traviled 16 m[ile]s crossed the mountains.~~

May 17, 1849; Thursday. Traviled 6 m[ile]s [today and] 20 m[ile]s [on] Friday 18th, crossed the ridge 20 m[ile]s [on] Saturday 19th[,] the last ridge. Stormed camped with no feed.

May 20, 1849; Sunday. Traviled 18 m[ile]s Monday 21st[,] 8 m[ile]s Tuesday 22ond[,] 5 m[ile]s Wednesday 23rd[,] 12 m[ile]s Thursday 24th[,] 20 m[ile]s Friday 25th[,] 25 m[ile]s [and] camped near Hensley's in the digens [diggings].

January 1, 1850; Tuesday.[35] This day was in San Francisco[,] morning cloudy. Called on Mr [George] Wi[n]ner this morning, learned he was not going to the States.[36] Lodged at Bro [Seth] Lincolns.[37]

34. The Humboldt sink is a dry lake bed the river disappears into.

35. Lyman is writing in a small calendar book with pre-printed dates and limited space. At the bottom of each entry, he tells where he lodged that night.

36. California would not become a state until September 1850; settlers in the territories referred to the eastern part of the country as "the states." George and Hanna Winner were Mormon converts from Toms River, New Jersey, whose son born in 1840 was named after the Book of Mormon character Moroni.

37. Seth Lincoln was the branch president of Mormon Island and lived in a house he and Addison Pratt had built together. The two had recently returned from a mission to Tahiti. Cowan and Homer, *California Saints*, 19.

January 2, 1850; Wednesday. To day called on Br [Quartus S.] Sparks. The weather rainy & unpleasant. Lodged at Br. [Seth] L[incoln]'s.

January 3, 1850; Thursday. Weather pleasant and suny rained in the evening had this evening a conversation with Br. [Morgan] Bates[38] on the principles of the Gospel. Lodged at Br. [Elijah Ward] Pells.[39]

January 4, 1850; Friday. Weather fine. S^p^ent this day on the beach, the scene was grand. This night had lengthy conversation with Mr. [Morgan] Bates. Lodged at Br [Elijah Ward] P[ell]s.

January 5, 1850; Saturday. To day went to the Mission of Dolorus met there General [John] Wilson.[40] Lodged with Br [Quartus] Sparks.

January 6, 1850; Sunday. Returned to Br. [Elijah Ward] P[ell]s. Here meet with Br [Morgan] Bates. Lodged with Br Pells.

January 7, 1850; Monday. Monday returned to San Francisco called on br [George] Win[n]er lodged with br [Seth] Lincolns.

January 8, 1850; Tuesday. This morning called on Mr [Samuel] Branan left with him a leter for Mr [William] Squire.[41] Lodged at Br [Seth] Lincolns.

January 9, 1850; Wednesday. This day baptized Morgan Bates in the waters of the Pacifick. Lodged at br [Seth] Lincolns.

January 10, 1850; Thursday. Called on General [John] Wilson at the Ward House completed our address to the Governor.[42] This day commenced writing to Br [Orson] Hyde [of the LDS Quorum of the Twelve]. Lodged at br [Elijah Ward] Pells.

January 11, 1850; Friday. This day continued my leter [to Elder Hyde]. Lodged at br [Elijah Ward] Pells.

January 12, 1850; Saturday. To day closed my leter to bro [Orson]

---

38. Bates left a newspaper career in the east (a young Horace Greeley was an employee of his), but would put his talent to use as the *Alta California*'s editor.

39. Pells was another Mormon who came to California on the *Brooklyn*.

40. Wilson had served in the War of 1812 and Black Hawk War in Missouri but not as a general. In 1850 he was a federal Indian agent.

41. He probably means William Squire Clark, who built the first wharf in San Francisco. A Mormon by that name, William Squire, had served in the Mormon Battalion but had returned to Utah, revisiting California only briefly in 1847.

42. Wilson was sent by President Zachary Taylor to Salt Lake City and San Francisco to consult with leaders on whether they might agree to a single slave-free state. Young agreed, but when snow delayed Wilson's progress he arrived too late in Sacramento to meet with the delegates to the constitutional convention.

Hyde. Today meet with General [John] Wilson. Lodged at br [Elijah Ward] P[ell]s.

January 13, 1850; Sunday. Wrote a leter to br [Wilford] Woodruff [of the Quorum of the Twelve]. At night had an interview with br. [Morgan] Bates. Lodged at br [Elijah Ward] P[ell]s.

January 14, 1850; Monday. This morning went to the beech to see a drowned man. Sent my leters to Washington[,] to Boston[,] & Iowa.[43] Lodged at br [Seth] Lincolns.

January 15, 1850; Tuesday. To day the mail steamer California sailed. Parted with my friend George E. Tyler wh[o] left for the states. Lodged at br [Seth] Lincolns.

January 16, 1850; Wednesday. Visited br. [Elijah Ward] Pells. Lodged with br. P.

January 17, 1850; Thursday. This morning received of br Peech $25.00 & also a dress coat from br Light. Lodged at br. [Seth] Lincolns.

January 18, 1850; Friday. To day called on br. Haden an[d] Mrs Lawwin an[d] got some books.

January 19, 1850; Saturday. To day traviled to Sacramento City on the Senitor [to] meet on board Mr. [John S.] Fowler.[44] Arivid [arrived] in the night [and] traviled to the City Hotell in a boat.[45] Lodged at City Hotell.

January 20, 1850; Sunday. Remained at the Hotell the water receding slowly. Lodged at Hotel.

January 21, 1850; Monday. To day visited Captain [Jesse D.] Hunter[46] who with his family were liveing on raised floors above the water. The Capt agreed to accompany me to San Diego. Lodged at Hotell.

January 22, 1850; Tuesday. Left the City in a boat. Traviled to the [John Sutter's] Fort then walked to camp of D[aniel] P. Clark & Dr [Darwin] Richardson & M[arcus] L[afayette] Shepherd.[47] Lodged at camp.

43. The letters were sent to John M. Bernhisel (Washington, DC), Wilford Woodruff (Boston), and Orson Hyde (Council Bluffs).

44. John S. Fowler, a church member, owned City Hotel in Sacramento. The *Senator* plied the river from San Francisco to Sacramento and back every other day, along with sixteen other steamships. "History of Steam Navigation in the United States," 22.

45. They called this the Great Flood of 1850. See, e.g., "The Flood at Sacramento," *Daily Alta California*, Jan. 16, 1850.

46. Hunter was given the rank of captain as a member of the Mormon Battalion.

47. Among these LDS prospectors, Shepherd was connected by marriage to one of Lyman's brothers-in-law.

January 23, 1850; Wednesday. Visited Dr. [William] McIntire.[48] Lodged at the Doc[tors].

January 24, 1850; Thursday. This day lodged at do[ctor William McIntyre's].

January 25, 1850; Friday. Visited ~~Br. Rosecrance~~ camp. Lodged at camp.

January 26, 1850; Saturday. Visited Br [Charles W.] Roserance. Lodged at his house.

January 27, 1850; Sunday. Went to the Hotell. Lodged at Hotell.

January 28, 1850; Monday. Remained at the Hotell. Lodged at the same.

January 29, 1850; Tuesday. Traviled to the City of [San] Francisco on the McKim. Lodged on board.

January 30, 1850; Wednesday. Went [to] the Missions Deloras. Lodged with br [Quartus S.] Sparks.

January 31, 1850; Thursday. Returned to [San] Francisco. Lodged at br [Seth] Lincolns.

February 1, 1850; Friday. Went to Pell hom[e]. Lodged with br [Elijah Ward] Pell.

February 2, 1850 Saturday. Went to the mission. Lodged with Br [Charles] Crisman.[49]

February 3, 1850; Sunday. Returned to [San] Francisco today [to] meet with Mr. [Samuel] Brannan. Lodged at br. [Seth] Lincoln.

February 4, 1850; Monday. Remained at home was not well. Lodged at br [Seth] Lincolns.

February 5, 1850; Tuesday. Went to the shiping office. Lodged at Br [Seth] Lincolns.

February 6, 1850; Wednesday. Went to Br [Elijah Ward] Pells. Meet with Br [Morgan] Bates. Lodged at br. Pells.

February 7, 1850; Thursday. Secured our pasage on board the T O Brown.[50]

---

48. William L. McIntyre had been the assistant surgeon for the Mormon Battalion.

49. Crisman was living at Mission Dolores at the time, but he was best known for having established the first grist mill in the Salt Lake Valley.

50. This was a coastal passenger ship known as a barque, a large ship with three or more masts.

February 8, 1850; Friday. Lodged at Br [Seth] Lincolns. Went on Board Ship to sail to San Padro [Pedro] with bros. [Jesse D.] Hunter, [Charles] Chrisman, [Robert] Clift.

February 9, 1850; Saturday. On board ship set sail to San Pedro.[51]

February 10, 1850; Sunday. Ship anchored at Santa Cruz.

February 11, 1850; Monday. Started to go on shore at Santa Cruz. Could not on account of the surf.

February 12, 1850; Tuesday. Weighed anchor [and] started to Monterey. Went ashore & was shaved.[52]

February 13, 1850; Wednesday. Went ashore at Monterey again.

February 14, 1850; Thursday. Remained on board. Saw the St. Marys man [of] war frigate come into port.[53]

February 15, 1850; Friday. Set sail did not get out [of port] far.

February 16, 1850; Saturday. A light wind not making much headway.

February 17, 1850; Sunday. Light wind and not making much headway.

February 18, 1850; Monday. Still at sea.[54]

February 19, 1850; Tuesday. Still at sea.

February 20, 1850; Wednesday. Arived at San Ped^ro^[,] here meet with news of br [Charles C.] Rich and company. Taried over night.

February 21, 1850; Thursday. To day went to Los Angeles. There we meet some 80 of the brethren from the [Salt] Lake.[55] Taried over night.

February 22, 1850; Friday. Parted with brs. [Jesse D.] Hunter[,] [Charles] Crismon & [Robert] Clift and returned to San Pedro. Remained there until the [blank].[56]

March 2, 1850; Saturday. Shiped for San Francisco on the Brig Placair [captained by a] Capt Picket. Raised our anchor and put to sea with 50 passengers[,] nearly all seasick.

---

51. San Pedro was the major port serving southern California at the time. Twenty-five miles south of Los Angeles, it contributed to the inland town's transformation from a ranch town of 1,600 inhabitants in 1850 to an urban center of 6,000 in 1870.

52. A mission town and former Mexican capital of Alta California, Monterey was among the most civilized coastal settlements at the time.

53. The USS *St. Mary's* patrolled the west coast for over fifty years.

54. This and the next entry were written in a hasty scrawl.

55. Brigham Young called gold missionaries to California in October 1849. Their assignment was to raise funds to bring back for the church's benefit. Campbell, *Establishing Zion*, 49–51.

56. This is followed by several blank pages. The month of March had several other blank pages as well.

March 13, 1850; Wednesday. Arived in San Fra[n]cisco [and] found br [Charles C.] Rich had gone to the mines. Taried for his return here. Meet br A[d]dison Pratt.

March 17, 1850; Sunday. To day had meeting at br [Barton] Moureys. Lodged with br [Seth] Lincoln.

March 24, 1850; Sunday. To day had meeting [blank].

April 1, 1850; Monday. To day shiped for the City of Sacrimento on the Steamer Eldorado with the brethren for the mines. At Benecia[57] meet with Br C[harles] C. Rich who returned with me on board. Lodged ~~at the City Hotell~~.

April 2, 1850; Tuesday. To day arivied in the City. Lodged at the City Hotell.

April 3, 1850; Wednesday. To day went to the country with br [Charles W.] Rosecrans. Taried with him all night. Here parted with the mining company.

April 4, 1850; Thursday. To day visited br [Jeremiah] Root here met with P[earson B.] Reading[58] who had rebroken his arm[,] another reward of drunkness. What folly[!] Lodged at [Charles] Rosecrans.

April 5, 1850; Friday. Shiped for San Francisco on the Steamer Senate. On board met with Sister [Fanny] Corwin.[59] Lodged on board. Fare $30.00.

April 6, 1850; Saturday. Landed from the steamer. ~~Lodged at Br Lincolns.~~ Lodged at bro [Barton] Mowrys.

April 7, 1850; Sunday. Preached at br [Barton] Mowrys. At the close of the meeting [I] meet Br [Jesse D.] Hunter from below. Lodged at Br [Seth] Lincolns.

April 8, 1850; Monday. To day meet [with] Bros [Charles] Crismon & [Jesse D.] Hunter and settled on arrangements for purchase of the Ranch of Chino.[60]

---

57. A port town at the mouth of the Sacramento River, founded by former Mexican General Mariano Vallejo in 1847, Benicia would become California's state capital in 1853.

58. Reading had found gold on his property in 1848, shortly after the discovery at Sutter's Mill.

59. Sam Brannan's mother-in-law.

60. Lyman agreed to purchase the ranch from Isaac Williams without seeing the land. A year later Williams would renege on his offer, and Lyman would be forced to admit that the land lacked enough timber and water for use as a colony, although not before hundreds of Mormons had arrived and camped there. *AML*, 181–82.

April 9, 1850; Tuesday. Spent the day with the brethren. [I] parted with br [Jesse D.] Hunter who went to Sacramento. Lodged at Br [Barton] Mowrys.

April 10, 1850; Wednesday. Wrote an epistle to the Saints in the Society I[s]lands [Tahiti]. Lodged at br [Barton] Mowrys. Selected a site for a Chapel on the land of br [Seth] Lincoln.

April 11, 1850; Thursday. Wrote Br [James] Flanigan to Liverpool. Meet with br [Moses] Meder.[61] Lodged as usueal.

April 12, 1850; Friday. Spent the day in instructing & blessing bros [Addison] Pratt & [John] Brown at Br Lights.

April 13, 1850; Saturday. To day visited br John Rolins.[62] Lodged at br [Barton] Mowrys.

April 14, 1850; Sunday. To day dined with D[aniel] P [Clark] & P Jones.[63] Lodged at br [Barton] Mowrys.

April 15, 1850; Monday. To day went to the Mission Dolorus. Lodged at Br C[harles] Crismonds. Ordained G[eorge] W. Sirrine to the office of Elder.

April 16, 1850; Tuesday. To day returned to the City of San Francisco. Lodged with br [Barton] Mowrys. Meet with br [Morgan] Bates whom we ordained an Elder.

April 17, 1850; Wednesday. Spent the day in preparing to leave. Lodged as usueal.

April 18, 1850; Thursday. To day apointed Brs G[eorge] W. Sirrine & E[lijah] W. Pell agents to procure means for building a chapel. Lodged at br [Barton] M[owrey]s.

April 19, 1850; Friday. Parted with the brethren in [San] Francisco and went to the Mission to Br [Charles] Crismons.

April 20, 1850; Saturday. Remained at br [Charles] Crismons makeing some preparation for our journey to day. The Steamer sailed with br [Seth] Lincoln & family.

April 21, 1850; Sunday. Left the mission.[64] Traviled 35 m[ile]s [and] camped on oat fields under an oak.

---

61. Moses A. Meder was prominent in cattle and lumber in the Santa Cruz area.

62. John Roylance, aka. "Rollins," a former Mormon Battalion soldier, was at Sutter's Mill when gold was discovered.

63. Elbert P. Jones was the first editor of Sam Brannan's *California Star* and otherwise an attorney and store owner.

64. As historian Leo Lyman observed, the next few months saw Lyman and Rich

April 22, 1850; Monday. Traviled to Pueblo [de San José]. Dined at Mr Edys[,][65] thence to br [John] Horners where we lodged. [Traveled] 30 m[ile]s.

April 23, 1850; Tuesday. Went to br [Daniel] Starks. At night [I] meet the brethren of [the] neighbourhood at br Marshalls. Left the[m] in [the] charge of br [Daniel] Baldwin[66] [who] instructed them in relation to their tithing. Lodged at Br [John] H[orners].

April 24, 1850; Wednesday. This morning called on br Mail who let me have a horse in exchange for the one I started with which was to weak for the journey. Camped near Sulivans Ranche. [Traveled] 15 m[ile]s.

April 25, 1850; Thursday. Traviled ~~15 m[ile]s~~ ^45 m[ile]s^ camped near Graysons Ferry [on the far side of the Central Valley].

April 26, 1850; Friday. Traviled up the river 12 m[ile]s. Crossed at Hardins Ferry [and] camped on the plain. [Traveled] 30 m[ile]s.

April 27, 1850; Saturday. Traviled to the trading post of the Salt Lake Company. [Traveled] 36 m[ile]s [today].

April 28, 1850; Sunday. Taried at trading post. Br [Howard] Egan returned in evening.

April 29, 1850 Monday. Went to Maraposa [Mariposa] [with] br [Howard] Egan in company. Found the brethren all generally well. [Traveled] 30 m[ile]s [today].

April 30, 1850; Tuesday. Taried with the[67] brethren. At night taught them[,] all [are] in good spirits.

May 1, 1850; Wednesday. Taried with the brethren. Settled some arrangements for gathering tithing.

May 2, 1850; Thursday. Returned to Salt Lake Trading post[,] meet with Capt [Jefferson] Hunt.

May 3, 1850; Friday. In the evening crossed the Mersede [Merced River] and camped on dry creek [after traveling] 12 m[ile]s. Paid cash for fery $1.25.

May 4, 1850; Saturday. Crossed the Toulumne [Tuolumne River]. Traviled 30 m[ile]s [and] camped. At night [a] horse run off. Cash paid $4.50.

---

traveling around the bay and through central California collecting large sums of gold in tithing, a dangerous undertaking. *AML*, 183.

65. William H. Eddy was a survivor of the Donner Party tragedy.

66. Baldwin was the LDS branch president.

67. The phrase "with the" is repeated.

May 5, 1850; Sunday. Laid by to recover our animals. Capt [Jefferson] Hunt returned with animals about noon [and] br [Howard] Egan returned at night.

May 6, 1850; Monday. Traviled to Mormon Gulch[68] and dined. Saw the brethren there [and] parted with brs [Jefferson] Hunt and [Howard] Egan. Crossed Stanislaus [River] camped. [Spent] $8.55 [on supplies].

May 7, 1850; Tuesday. Traviled to the Calivarus [Calaveras]. Stoped at br [William] Athurtons place who was not at home [but] found there brs [James R.] Allread & Rusel[l]. Heard of fire [brigade] in San Francisco.[69]

May 8, 1850; Wednesday. Waited for the return of br [William] Athurton. Night came but burought not with it our absent friend.

May 9, 1850; Thursday. ~~Still waited for the return of br Athurton.~~ To day brs [Charles C.] Rich & [James] Rollins left for the north And I still remained.

May 10, 1850; Friday. Still awaited the return of br [William] Athurton.

May 11, 1850; Saturday. Still awaited the return of br [William] Athurton.

May 12, 1850; Sunday. Past the day in reading. Nothing of interest ocuring.

May 13, 1850; Monday. Still taried for the return of br [William] Athurton.

May 14, 1850; Tuesday. To day br [William] Athurton arived.

May 15, 1850; Wednesday. Left Calivarus [Calaveras]. Crossed the Macullume [and] camped at Jacksons creek.

May 16, 1850; Thursday. Traviled to the Macaurini [and] camped at coats ferry.

May 17, 1850; Friday. Visited br John Rhoads [in Sloughhouse,] traviled to br [Asahel] Lathrops [in El Dorado].[70]

---

68. This was located at what became Tuttletown, about sixty miles east of Stockton.

69. As San Francisco was beset by fires in 1849–51, people organized private fire brigades, usually funded by insurance companies, and eventually (but not yet) established publicly financed fire departments.

70. Asahel A. Lathrop was known for running the Mormon Tavern about five miles from Mormon Island.

May 18, 1850; Saturday. Visited br [Jefferson] Edmunds[71] with ^br^ [Charles C.] Rich. Meet br O[rrin] P. [Rockwell] [and] returned to br [Asahel] L[athrop's].

May 19, 1850; Sunday. To day started on our journey. Went [to] br [Jefferson] Edmunds [and] taried over night.

May 20, 1850; Monday. Went to green spring saw M[y]r[on] Tanner. Crossed the river at Coloma [and] traviled to Greenwood Valey. There meet with the brethren last from the Lake [Salt Lake City].

May 21, 1850; Tuesday. Taried with the breth who [then] paid tithing and their dues the most of them.

May 22, 1850; Wednesday. Traviled to Capt [Jesse D.] Hunter's [and] taried over night.

May 23, 1850; Thursday. To day called and dined with br [Samuel] McMurt[re]y[,] then went to br [William] Leffingwells [and] taried over night.

May 24, 1850; Friday. To day crossed the south fork at Salmon Falls. Dined with br A[rieh] C. Brower.[72] Traviled to Cock Spring [and] put up with br H[enry] Jacobs.

May 25, 1850; Saturday. Dined with br [Jeremiah] Root. Lodged in Sacrimento City at City Hotell.

May 26, 1850; Sunday. Waited for the return of br [John S.] Fowler but he did not come [so] in the evening [I] returned to br [Jeremiah] Roots [and] lodged there.

May 27, 1850; Monday. Crossed the American Fork. Went to br ~~Jas Harmonds in the~~ [William] McIntires lod[g]ed there. ~~In the morning we visited br Harmonds lodged at br Rosencrans.~~

May 28, 1850; Tuesday. This morning visited br Ja[me]s Harmon. In the evening went to br [Charles W] Rosecrans.

May 29, 1850; Wednesday. To day visited [battalion member] br Anthony Blackburn [and] taried over night.

May 30, 1850; Thursday. Went to Sacrimento [and] heard of the death of br. J[ames] M. Flake which was caused by falling from his mule

71. Edmunds and partner Orrin Porter Rockwell owned the Deer Creek saloon twelve miles east of Mormon Island. A famous gunslinger, Porter was operating under a pseudonym, James B. Brown, to avoid attention and keep an eye out for trouble.

72. Brower owned a hotel called Brower House six miles north of Mormon Island at Salmon Falls. He would soon return to Salt Lake City and become a *Deseret News* printer.

[on] May 22nd. [He] died [on the] 23rd 2½ oclock A.M.[73] Lodged at br [Jeremiah] Roots.

May 31, 1850; Friday. Traviled to Mormon Tavern [and] there meet with Capt [Jefferson] Hunt and O[rrin] P. [Rockwell].

June 1, 1850; Saturday. ~~To day br [Charles C.] Rich went~~ To day went to Hang Town [Placerville][74] [and] meet with breth. from the south.

June 2, 1850; Sunday. To day returned to br [Jefferson] Edmunds [and] deposited there br [James M.] Flakes gun and coat. Left his mules with br [William] Beers.

June 3, 1850; Monday. Returned to the Mormon Tavern. Meet with br [Charles C.] Rich.

June 4, 1850; Tuesday. To day meet with Capt [Jefferson] Hunt [and] spent the day at his place.

June 5, 1850; Wednesday. To day Capt [Jefferson Hunt] and br [Daniel P.] Clark left and br [Charles C.] Rich and my self taried.

June 6, 1850; Thursday. To day traviled to br [Arieh C.] Browers and dined then went to br [William] Lefingwells where we taried over night.

June 7, 1850; Friday. To day traviled to green woods valey.[75] Taried with the brethren [and] colected some tithing.

June 8, 1850; Saturday. To day traviled to and crossed the middle fork at the bridge above the Spanish Barr, thence the camp of the California company. David Smith.

June 9, 1850; Sunday. To day visited George Boyds camp where we meet with br Morris who deposited with me 178 dollars for P[arley] P. Pratt. Br Boyd returned in the evening.

June 10, 1850; Monday. To day left br [George] Boyds traviled to Br [Samuel] McMurtrys.

June 11, 1850; Tuesday. Went to br [Jesse D.] Hunters [then] in the evening went to br [James] Harmon's on foot.[76]

---

73. Keeping in mind that Lyman and Flake had known each other since at least 1848 in Mississippi, the news must have been painful to receive.

74. Hangtown was what people called Dry Diggins, now Placerville, a settlement known for its enthusiastic support of capital punishment.

75. John Greenwood operated a trading post there, 20 miles north of Placerville.

76. This implies that they usually rode horses, which is confirmed by other entries as well. Alongside the horses, they had pack mules. See the entries for Apr. 24; May 4; June 2, 14; July 6, 25, 27.

June 12, 1850; Wednesday. Remained with br [James] H[armon's]. It rained some today.

June 13, 1850; Thursday. Today returned to br [Jesse D.] Hunters where we lodged.

June 14, 1850; Friday. To day returned to br [Asahel] Lathrops. Turned out our mules.

June 15, 1850; Saturday. Went to br [Jefferson] Edmunds where we meet the grand daughter of Father Bosley married to a D P Crafton.

June 16, 1850; Sunday. Remained with br [Jefferson] Edmunds. My health not very good.

June 17, 1850; Monday. Still remained at br [Jefferson] Edmunds. Today heard of the late fire in San Francisco which ocured on Friday the 14th.[77]

June 18, 1850; Tuesday. Still at br [Jefferson] E[dmund]s. To day meet brs [John] Stodard and [William] Beers. My health still poor from the effect of dispepsy.

June 19, 1850; Wednesday. To day went to br L[athrop's and] meet with br [Anthony] Blackburn.

June 20, 1850; Thursday. To day meet with brs [Jesse D.] Hunter and [Jefferson] Hunt and [Howard] Egan and [Joseph] Cain.

June 21, 1850; Friday. To day left with br [John] Stodard three parcels of gold belonging to brs [Jonathan] Crosby[,] [James H.] Rollins[,] and [Daniel P.] Clark. Left with br [Jeremiah] Root with whom we lodged.

June 22, 1850; Saturday. Went to Sacrimento to C[ity] meet with br [Thomas] Blackburn[78] from Salt Lake from whom we learned that they had some trouble with the Indians [Battle of Fort Utah] of whom some 32 were killed.

June 23, 1850; Sunday. This morning took passage for [San] Francisco on the steamer Hartford. Br [Charles C.] Rich returned yesterday to br [Asahel] Lathrops to see br Green and get some news.

June 24, 1850; Monday. Went to the mission Doloras with br

77. In this conflagration, one of the "great fires of 1849–1851," the city lost 300 buildings.

78. Thomas and his brother Abner were trying to establish a trading post near Lake Tahoe, although they would soon give it up and be robbed by Indians on their return to Salt Lake City.

[Barton] Mowry. Visited br [Quartus S.] Sparks whom we found quite sick. [We] returned in the evening.

June 25, 1850; Tuesday. Visited br [Elijah Ward] Pells with whom I taried all night ~~in~~ [blank]. To day received a present of a writing desk from br [Morgan] Bates.

June 26, 1850; Wednesday. This morning heard that br [Charles C.] Rich had arived in San Francisco and meet him there.

June 27, 1850; Thursday. To day settled the tithing accounts and found myself poor in funds but tithing sufficient to pay the church's debts.

June 28, 1850; Friday. Spent the day in Francisco and we visited Samuel Brannan who made me a present of some $500.00. [I] made an arange[me]nt for the books in his possession.

June 29, 1850; Saturday. Went to the mission. Dined with br [Charles] Crismon then visited br [Quartus S.] Sparks whom we found much improved in health.

June 30, 1850; Sunday. This morning returned to Francisco. Br J. Lewis this morning made me a present of a saddle. Dined with D[aniel] P Jones [and] in the evening meet br [Morgan] Bates.

July 1, 1850; Monday. Remained in the city [and] made some purchases of goods for home. Dined with Mr [Samuel] Brannan. To day heard of gold digins on the east side of the Sire Navada Mts.

July 2, 1850; Tuesday. To day went to the Mission Doloras and lodged with br [Charles] Crismand.

July 3, 1850; Wednesday. To day br [Charles C.] Rich started for Santa Cruz [but] the stage being full coul[d] not get a pasage had to wait.

July 4, 1850; Thursday. To day went to Pueblo St Joe [San José], in the stage. Lodged at the City Hotell.

July 5, 1850; Friday. Went to br [John] Horner on foot.

July 6, 1850; Saturday. Visited br Mails settled for the horse [but] learned the animal I left ~~need~~ there was stolen.

July 7, 1850; Sunday. Returned to Puebloe [San José and] lodged at City Hotell.

July 8, 1850; Monday. Remained in town.

July 9, 1850; Tuesday. Returned to [Mission] Dolorus by the stage. Found that br [Charles C.] Rich had returned the day previous. Lodged at the Bullshead. Brs [Charles] Crisman & Lewis paid some tithing.

July 10, 1850; Wednesday. Returned to the City of San Francisco [to] meet with br [Charles C.] Rich.

July 11, 1850; Thursday. Spent the day in trading [for goods to travel] for home.

July 12, 1850; Friday. To day commenced packing our freight for the journey to the [Salt] Lake.

July 13, 1850; Saturday. To day finished packing.

July 14, 1850; Sunday. To day dined with Mr E P Jones who made me a present of three hundred dollars. Also visited br [Elisha] Hyatt who paid 200 dollars tithing.

July 15, 1850; Monday. Shiped on board the Steamer Hartford for Sacramento City. [We] were delayed by accident until 2 oclock in the morning.

July 16, 1850; Tuesday. Traviled slowly up the river to Sacremento where we meet brs [Jesse D.] Hunter & [Abner] Blackburn who were ready to go below.

July 17, 1850; Wednesday. To day meet br Hyrum Clark from Salt Lake with the mail. Lodged with br H[enry] Jacobs.

July 18, 1850; Thursday. Visited the camps of the Saints on their way to the Society Islands whom we found in good health and good spirits.[79]

July 19, 1850; Friday. Commenced writing leters to the [First] Presidency and others. Lodged at camp.

July 20, 1850; Saturday. Continued our labour of writing and counciling the brethren and cisters.

July 21, 1850; Sunday. Had meeting and continued our writing. Lodged at camp.

July 22, 1850; Monday. Finished writing & closed up the mail and started [it] for the [Great Salt] Lake by brs Barnard and Foot. Lodged at br A[sahel] L[athrop].

July 23, 1850; Tuesday. Went to br John Rhodes on the Macausine [Moccasin Creek] whom we did not see as he was not at home. We however taried until morning.

July 24, 1850; Wednesday. Traviled to Brighton.[80] Stoped with br

79. Among other missionaries, Addison Pratt was on his way back to Tahiti, this time accompanied by his wife Louisa.

80. Brighton was on the eastern outskirts of Sacramento.

[Jeremiah] Root [and] visited the camp of the [Mormon] Island Mission. Lodged with br Root.

July 25, 1850; Thursday. This morning br A[benezer] Hanks loosed our mules and they left immediately and all our search for them proved vain. We walked to S[acramento] City.

July 26, 1850; Friday. Closed our business with the mission brethren & returned to br [Jeremiah] Roots where we lodged.

July 27, 1850; Saturday. Started for br [Asahel] Lathrops. Soon after starting we found our mules, tied up by ^a^ Mr Bowles who found them fast in the brush by their halters. Lodged at Lathrops.

July 28, 1850; Sunday. Met with br [Samuel] McMurtry and family at Salmon Falls on his way to the [Tahitian] Islands. Lodged at br [William] Leffingwells.

July 29, 1850; Monday. Traviled to Murderers bar[81] from thence to Greenwood valy. Lodged at br [David] Seelys camp. Visited br Hazen Kimball who was very sick.

July 30, 1850; Tuesday. Traviled to and lodged at the camp of br Joseph Cain where we had a talk with brethren at night.

July 31, 1850; Wednesday. Taried with the brethren. Br [George] Boyd returned in the evening. To day saw some experiments with a submarine dress in the river.[82]

August 1, 1850; Thursday. This morning returned to greenwood and dined with br [Benjamin] Crow then parted with br [Charles C.] Rich. Traviled to and lodged in Coloma.

August 2, 1850; Friday. Returned to br A[sahel] H Lathrops. Meet br [James H.] Rollins and [Daniel P.] Clark from Carson river.

August 3, 1850; Saturday. Went to Sacramento. Bought some stores for the journey home.

August 4, 1850; Sunday. To day returned to br [Jeremiah] Roots where we lodged.

August 5, 1850; Monday. Returned to [Asahel] Lathrops.

August 6, 1850; Tuesday. Prepared goods for packing over the mountains.

81. This was a sand bar in the middle of the American River where four prospectors from Oregon were killed by Indians. Their associates from Oregon killed over 30 Indians in retaliation.

82. Miners were experimenting with diving bells and waterproof suits to prospect under water. Holliday, *The World Rushed In*, 357.

August 7, 1850; Wednesday. Remained at [Asahel] L[athrop's] preparing to move.

August 8, 1850; Thursday. Went to town for the balance of goods.

August 9, 1850; Friday. Returned to [Asahel] Lathrop's.

August 10, 1850; Saturday. Continued our preparations for the journey.

August 11, 1850; Sunday. In company with br [Daniel P.] Clark went to Mr Martins near the Murderers Barr.

August 12, 1850; Monday. Went br [James] Harmond. Lodged at br [William] McIntyres.[83]

March 10, 1851; Monday. Left town [Salt Lake City] with two wagons, on Tuesday the 11th arived at Cotenwood [Holladay].[84]

March 12, 1851; Wednesday. Left Cotenwood with five wagons. Traviled 5 m[ile]s camped on dry Cotenwood [Creek].

March 13, 1851; Thursday. Remained on dry creek. To day br [William] Crosby rolled into camp.

March 14, 1851; Friday. Traviled to the Hot Spring south 6 m[ile]s. Weather cool but pleasant. This evening visited Jordan [River] which at this point assumes the appearance and character of a mountain torrent rushing wildly down its narrow chanel.

March 15, 1851; Saturday. Br Richardson went to Salt Lake City for the mail. In the evening bro Shepherd and [Sidney] Tanner came into camp and in the evening the Widow Tanners teems.

March 16, 1851; Sunday. Weather pleasant all well in camp.

March 17, 1851; Monday. Traviled round the mountain into Utah [County] 10 m[ile]s. Camped on dry Creek [Lehi]. Br [Charles C.] Rich taried with us. Over night [we] lost one yoke of oxen.

March 18, 1851; Tuesday. Traviled 8 m[ile]s and camped on Battle Creek [Pleasant Grove].

---

83. Lyman stops writing in his calendar here and resumes in a notebook allowing for a running narrative with the next entry, seven months later. I will break up the storyline by day as much as possible. The entries were sometimes recorded by a different individual, probably a clerk, based on the handwriting.

84. When Lyman returned to Salt Lake City in Nov. 1850, he was called to colonize Rancho del Chino in southern California. Some of the Mississippi Saints joined him, who had settled in Cottonwood (aka Holladay's Settlement) on the eastern side of the Salt Lake Valley. Lyman will also collect a few relatives and missionaries destined for the Iron Mission at Fort Louisa (Parowan) or foreign destinations. The final wagon train had over 400 people in eight companies.

March 19, 1851; Wednesday. Remained and hunted the lost stock. Found the lost oxen but lost 2 mules.

March 20, 1851; Thursday. Traviled to and camped on the Provo [River].

March 21, 1851; Friday. It snowed. Spent the day in gathering stock of which we found all but one cow. In the evening the weath[er] was pleasant.

March 22, 1851; Saturday. Left camp on the Provo [River]. Traviled to Hoble Creek. I then proceded to Potetenete [and] lodged with Br Steward.

March 23, 1851; Sunday. The camp and traviled to Petetenete [Payson] where all the camp were collected for California and Little Salt Lake [Parowan]. ~~Sunday~~ ^Sunday^ 23d held meeting in the fort at Payson and in the evening commenced the organization by electing Andrew Little Capt of the entire camps and also Joseph Matthews and David Seely Capts of fiftys who proceeded to the organization of the camp in companys of ten.

March 24, 1851; Monday. Completed the work of organization when ten companies of tens ~~wit~~ were reported[,] five of whom const[i]tuted the first division of the camp and moved on 6 m[ile]s to ~~Petetenete~~ to sumit creek [Santaquin].

March 25, 1851; Tuesday. Traviled 12 m[ile]s to willow creek [Mona]. This night the snow fell 2 inches deep [and] in the night one cow left the herd and returned to sumit creek.

March 26, 1851; Wednesday. Myself and br [Daniel P.] Clark returned as far as Springville where we found my cow and calf. Were kindly entertained by br A[aron] Johnson.

March 27, 1851; Thursday. Returned as far as Spring Creek[,] camped with Capt [Jefferson] Hunt.

March 28, 1851; Friday. Left the cow with Capt [Jefferson] Hunt and traviled to our camp on the Severe [River].[85] This night it snowed.

March 29, 1851; Saturday. Crossed the river and camped on the south side of the river.

March 30, 1851; Sunday. This day laid over at the Severe. Very windy.

March 31, 1851; Monday. Bro P[arley] P. Pratt[86] and C[harles] C.

85. Their camp was midway between today's towns of Mona and Scipio.

86. Pratt was traveling to California on a mission to Chile. He was not part of the San Bernardino group per se, although his authority as a senior apostle was recognized.

Rich with all the company camped then trav[eled] to [Ciam?] grove at the south end of Rabbit Valley. Water southeast of grove 1½ miles.

April 1, 1851; Tuesday. Bro P[arley] P. Pratt [and] C[harles] C. Rich with Capt [David] Seely & D Luns left us[,] and [our company of] 10s remained through the day.

April 2, 1851; Wednesday. Bro W[illiam] Crosby elected capt of our camp[,] company 2 [of] 10s. Camp rolled on to Cedar Springs say 10 m[ile]s on a[nd] camped.

April 3, 1851; Thursday. Camp laid over. Good feed. Capt [Andrew] Lytle & co. came up this evening. Heavy rain & hail through the night.

April 4, 1851; Friday. Camp rolled on to Cotton wood Creek 10 miles. Road muddy. A[ndrew] Lytles Co. remained.

April 5, 1851; Saturday. Our camp remained on Cottonwood [Creek]. All well & cattle on good feed. Capt [Jefferson] Hunt & son came up with us and camped. Some rain through the night.

April 6, 1851; Sunday. Camp remained over this day. Weather cold, rain and snow occasionally through the day & previous night.

April 7, 1851; Monday. Pleasant. Rolled on to Millard Creek say 8 m[ile]s. Found Walker and his band were encamped up the creek some 3 m[ile]s.[87] He appears quite civil. Camp gave them some mush & milk &c. Some letters were sent by him to Salt Lake. A[masa] L[yman] [also wrote letters] to B[righam] Y[oung]. Feed down the creek.

April 8, 1851; Tuesday. Cool but pleasant, all well. Rolled to next creek ^2nd willow^ 9 m[ile]s & camped. Good feed up the creek.

April 9, 1851; Wednesday. Camp rested till ½ past 1 oc[lock]. Then rolled on 4 m[ile]s and ^camped^ at Rocky point without water.

April 10, 1851; Thursday. Pleasant, started early. Road good for 4 miles then hilly on ^Sevier^ mts 5 m[ile]s down river to creek, 3 m[iles] [illegible] up the creek ¼ m[iles].

April 11, 1851; Friday. All well, pleasant. Camp went on 5 m[ile]s u[p] [a] small cottonwood creek and camped. A[masa] L[yman] & Capt [William] Crosby remained to find some lost horses. Found them and came on.

April 12, 1851; Saturday. Pleasant. Camp staid here through the day.

87. In two years Chief Wakara would lead the Timpanogos tribe in war against the Mormons, without peace until his death in 1855. Wimmer, "The Walker War Reconsidered."

Sidney Tanners & 2 10s made [it with] Capt [Andrew] Lytle [to] come up with us. A new camp[,] leaving bal[ance] of their division behind.

April 13, 1851; Sunday. All well[,] warm[,] and pleasa[nt]. Both divisions drove up [with] the teams and we selectid our out[fits] and rolled on say 5 m[ile]s and camped on the bluff of Big Hollow. Capt [Jefferson] H[unt], A[masa] L[yman] & [Daniel] C[lark went with William] Crosby [and] searched up the hollow for water [and] found none, drove stock South Ea[st] 2 m[ile]s to water. Bro [Robert] Eggburt & Cunningham joined us from Last Div[ision].

April 14, 1851; Monday. All well, and pleasant. Camp rolled on to Beaver some 12 m[ile]s. Food poor some trout caught by the boys.

April 15, 1851; Tuesday. Warm. Laid still on Beaver until 2 OC[lock] then rolled up the mountain say 6 m[ile]s and camped. Guarded ^my^ cattle this night.

April 16, 1851; Wednesday. Very warm this morning. Cattle & horses troublesome to find. Started ¼ p[ast] 9 & rolled to first creek in s[ight]. Pro[bab]ly say 30 m[ile]s. Road very bad over Mts[,] rocky &c. Afternoon windy and cold [with] rain (feed late).

April 17, 1851; Thursday. Camp did not travel. A[masa] L[yman] & others went up to fort [Parowan]. G[eorge] A. Smith come back to camp with them. Capt [Andrew] Lyttle & [Joseph] Matthews, with their Div[isions], came up and camped.

April 18, 1851; Friday. Pleasant & warm in morn[ing]. Camp mooved about 9 OC[lock] and went to summit creek 7 m[ile]s south of fort there we find Capt [David] Seely & his Division. They have lost 1 ox[en] by the Indians.

April 19, 1851; Saturday. Cold, both rain & snow through the night and frequent flurry of snow in the forenoon. G[eorge] A. Smith visited camp. Nothing important done this day. Afternoon pleasant but windy.

April 20, 1851; Sunday. Pleasant in the morning—but cool and windy in the afternoon. Meeting was called in the caral. G[eorge] A. Smith addressed the congregation[,] it being composed of the whole camp and most of the brethren from the city. (His remarks were good and aplicable to the Saints generally.[)] Also Bro [Parley P.] Pratt, [Amasa] Lyman & [Charles C.] Rich gave a short lecture. Bros L[yman] & Rich required each individual name that was willing to abide their council in California and yoke themselves up with them in the cause and building up ^of^ the Kingdom of God.

April 21, 1851; Monday.[88] Cool and cloudy this morn[ing]. A drive was made of the stock and Bros [Parley P.] Pratt & [Charles C.] Rich with their company rolled on[,] except Bro Harris & family ^who stayed back to find cattle^. Returns ^were^ made out to send to G.S.L.C. [Great Salt Lake City]. 2 births in camp Sisters Morse & Eggbert[89] [are doing] all right.

April 22, 1851; Tuesday. Cloudy. Made an early drive and Learned [that] most of the stock was on hand. Some of our te[a]m [went] North [illegible] & others went to canyan to make tar. Others in camp making coal & black smithing, afternoon some snow and rain. G[eorge] A. S[mith] visited camp.

April 23, 1851; Wednesday. Pleasant at 9 OC[lock] drove up the cattle and separated those belonging to our division but not without considerable difficulty. Camp rolled [out] about 12 oc[lock], and went on say 5 m[ile]s & camped at [blank] springs. Good feed in the bottoms &c. A[masa] Lyman remained back to find his cow [but] did not find her. Camp called together at night to make arrangements about guard. All covenanted to do their duty. Capt [Jefferson] Hunt exhorted them to faithfulness to God and themselves & A. L[yman] Capt [William] Crosby told them which would be required of them.

April 24, 1851; Thursday. Cloudy. Camp started about ½ past 9. Went on to Little Muddy or Cottonwood and camped about 12 oc[lock] Trav[eled] 7 [miles]. Feed tollerable. Showery through the fore part of the day. Mr. Hyde came from [the] back train with one yoke [of] oxen for (A. Lyman also his lost cow).

April 25, 1851; Friday. Warm & cloudy. Showery through the day—camp rolled some 9 m[ile]s and camped near Iron springs or creek. Feed short. Capt [Sidney] Tanner came into camp this morning for Bro Cunningham to return and visit Bro. [Truman] Swarnout & wife who was sick. 1 Pahute [Indian] in camp.

---

88. The next two entries were written in pencil, then traced over in pen.

89. The two mothers were Seviah Cunningham Egbert and Nancy Lucinda Pratt Morse. Egbert gave birth to John Charles Egbert the day before. She was traveling with her husband, Robert, and their two-year-old. Morse, a plural wife of Justus Morse, gave birth to Henry Morse. Most of the colonists were traveling as families.

April 26, 1851; Saturday. Verry warm. Rolled on to Willow or Mountain Springs 11½ miles. Feed and water scarce. Stock very uneasy.

April 27, 1851; Sunday. Camp rolled early this morning. Yoked up as soon as light and mooved on to Canyon Creek 10½ m[ile]s. Plenty wood & water, feed up the creek 1½ m[ile]s.

April 28, 1851; Monday. All well[,] pleasant & warm. Went on to Divide Springs 10½ m[ile]s, ½ [off] the road[,] hilly & rocky. Camped early. Men packing wood & making coal pit. Prepare[d] black smith shop. Good place for fort. Some 500 acres good land.

April 29, 1851; Tuesday. Pleasant, & all well, camp busily engaged in cutting & welding tin &c. Cattle doing well, & excellent feed, a fine place for a small settlement.

April 30, 1851; Wednesday. Some cloudy & cool in morning[,] but pleasant through the day. The day ocupied in setting tire & blacksmithing.

May 1, 1851; Thursday. Pleasant. The day ocupied as yesterday—Capt [Andrew] Lytle &c came up to day.

May 2, 1851; Friday. The camp started about 10 oc[lock] and ^went^ some 8 m[ile]s to springs south side of divide. Some rain & thunder. Road Hilly and some Rocks.

May 3, 1851; Saturday. Pleasant. Camp started about ½ past 10 and traveled on to [a] spring at head of S[an]t[a] Clara [River].[90] Pres [Amasa] Lyman went back to Divide Springs to find a cow that was left yesterday. Found her and returned, Road hilly & Rocky.

May 4, 1851; Sunday. Very warm, camp laid still to day. Meeting call[ed] about 3 oc[lock]. Pres [Amasa] Lyman[,] Capts [Jefferson] Hunt & [William] Crosby ocupied the meeting in telling the camp their duty and the necessity of doing the same it being necessary for our salvation. Found Bro [Parley P.] Pratt: camped here 29 Apr. and a note saying look out for Indians.

May 5, 1851; Monday. (Warm) Camp Rolled this morning down St Clarra some 12 miles & camped, very little feed. The road has been very hilly[,] rocky and sandy—Capt [William] Crosby's large carriage badly broken. ^Crossed creek some 10 times.^

90. The pioneer wagon trail bypassed present-day St. George (founded 1861) because the Virgin River Narrows were impassable. Instead, the trail swept in a large arc to the southwest from Parowan through what are now Veyo and Gunlock to the Muddy River in Nevada. See Lyman and Reese, *The Arduous Road.*

May 6, 1851; Tuesday. ^Morning^ Warm. Cattle restless and hungry. Men fixing carriage. Camp started about 10 oc[lock]. Rolled to where road leaves river & camped[,] not much feed. Road brushy[,] hilly & heavy sand. Crossed River some 5 or 6 times – crossings steep and deep.

May 7, 1851; Wednesday. Bros [Amasa] Lyman, [William] Crosby and others went back to hunt cow of Bro [William] Crosby's. Left yesterday, found where she had been killed with two yearlings by the Indians. Camp started ½ past 7. Trav[eled] some 8 m[ile]s up a canyon from St. Clarra and camped without water, road very rocky and hilly. Casteels Pahute ran off with his horse—some feed.

May 8, 1851; Thursday. Started early and trav[eled] on to Rio Virgin say 6 m[ile]s. Watered at Old Beaver dam some 4 m[ile] back. Road Rocky & some sand.

May 9, 1851; Friday. All well. Started about ½ past 9 and trav[eled] some 10 or 12 miles. Crossed River 8 times[,] Road very sandy. Feed rather short—salt[y] grass & some game. 9 head cattle during this night left at Beaver dam and 3 lost[,] 1 Hugheses[,] 1 [Robert] Smith[,][91] 1 Casteels.

May 10, 1851; Saturday. Sent out our cattle with a guard of 6 men. Indian shot 3 with arrows but none dangerous[ly], found a line here from Genl. [Charles C.] Rich saying all well and no difficulty with Indians. Left the same for Capt [Andrew] Lytle ann[ouncing] we were all well, tha[t] no cattle killed &c. Camp trav[eled] from about 2 m[ile]s when an alarm was raised, Indians drawing off some cattle but was false. We trav[eled] some 5 m[ile]s and camped about 1 oc[lock]. Good feed &c.

May 11, 1851; Sunday. Pleasant and warm. The camp did not move until 2 oc[lock] then rolled some 5 m[ile]s and camped. Road sandy.

May 12, 1851; Monday. Camp started at 10 and went some 6 miles and camped[,] very sandy. Road grass salt & water brackish.

May 13, 1851; Tuesday. Warm & strong south wind through the day, dust very bad, camp started ½ past 9. Trav[eled] some 8 m[ile]s & camped in good feed about 1 oc[lock]. Near 3 oc[lock], 3 Pahutes made their appearance on the other side of river [and] wished to come in camp. They

91. Robert Marion Smith, one of the captains, was traveling with his wife Rebecca Crosby Smith and fourteen black slaves. California authorities would eventually learn of the slaves at San Bernardino and take them into custody, the Smiths becoming the object of a high-profile legal case in which their slaves were freed. Lapp, *Blacks in Gold Rush California*, 119–21.

came over & stayed through the night, are very peacible. Capt [Jefferson] Hunt with several others went down the river to look out road to Muddy [River, Nevada]. Returned & reported favorably. Found a line from Genl [Charles C.] Rich some 3 m[ile]s back where old road leaves the river.

May 14, 1851; Wednesday. Some cloudy with strong southw[est] wind through the day. Camp rolled on say nine miles ^crossed river^ 5 times ^making [a total of] 21 times^. Road very sandy and many quick sand holes which made the road bad. Left a line this morn[ing] for Capt. [Andrew] Lytle. Feed first rate. Pahutes plenty. Camped on the Muddy [River] near the mouth.

May 15, 1851; Thursday. Windy in morn[ing], wind n[orth] e[ast]. Camp started ½ past 9. Trav[eled] some 6 m[ile]s ^up Muddy [River]^ and camped. Sandy & dusty & hard trav[e]ling. Feed plenty. Indian wheat turning yellow, but in small patches.

May 16, 1851; Friday. Warm. Camp started about 10 oc[lock] only expecting some 6 m[ile]s to Old Road, but in this was mistaken, we found it to be 12 or 15 m[ile]s, both sandy and mountainous passing up & down dry canyans, did not get into camp till about 9 oc[lock]. 2½ m[ile]s below old crossing. Casteel left one ox. Indians drove off 1 horse for [Daniel] Baldwin while on the road.

May 17, 1851; Saturday. Cool this morning. Several Indians in camp, Baldwin about to shoot one Indian[,] scared. Camp started about 10, rolled up 2½ [miles to] old crossing & camped, feed tolerable. Iron spring Indian[s] came back & followed us up to the last crossing of Muddy [River].

May 18, 1851; Sunday. Camp stayed here until about 3 oc[lock], then rolled out for the desert. Capt [Jefferson] Hunts ten & Capt [Alfred] Bibees having started 1 hour in advance leaving Capt. [Robert] Smiths and Capt [Daniel P.] Clarks line in the rear, we trav[eled] to ½ way [to Las Vegas Springs] by 2 & [and were camped by] ½ past 3 oc[lock] ^in morn[ing]^. Casteel left 1 waggon at Muddy (Old [crossing]).

May 19, 1851; Monday. We started as yesterday (Capt [Robert] Smith being in rear) about ½ past 6 and trav[eled] on to the Vegas,[92] Capt [Jefferson] Hunt arived about ½ past 3, [Alfred] Bybee 4½, [Daniel

92. John C. Frémont stopped by in the 1840s and left nothing behind. The first structure built there would be the Mormon fort of 1855, erected four years after the San Bernardino pioneers passed through. The Spanish words *las vegas* mean "the meadows."

P.] Clark 5½[,] Smith say 7 oc[lock]. Some cattle gave out & all verry tired. The Vegas is a beautiful spring branch of good water capable of carrying a mill or 2 & good grass & land for tillage. Enough for at least 50 inhabitants (with plenty of meskeet for fire wood, but no building timber[)]. P.S. One yoke Bro [Amasa] L[yman']s oxen gave out, no cattle left on this desert. The weather has been remarkably cool and well adapted to our ca[u]se, the road being gravelly & sharp on cattle feet.

May 20, 1851; Tuesday. Camp remained on the Vegas, our cattle are in fine feed, the day occupied in shoeing cattle[,] washing & wresting themselves &c &c. Warm in fore noon, cloudy & some rain in afternoon with cool wind.

May 21, 1851; Wednesday. Pleasant & warm the day occupied in sho[e]ing cattle & fixing wagons.

May 22, 1851; Thursday. Clear & warm. Very warm about 9 oc[lock]. Some of Capt [Andrew] Lytle's co[mpany] were discovered coming towards us, and about twelve oc[lock] Capt Lytle with the horse & mule team came up, we had previously driven up our cattle and were ready to roll out of the way our camp accordingly rolled up the creek 4½ m[ile]s & camped. V[e]r[y] good feed, Capt Lytle['s] co[mpany] had ^lost some horses & cattle & killed 2 or 3 Indians.^[93]

May 23, 1851; Friday. Camp remained here through the day & shod some cattle. Verry warm through this day. Capt. Joseph Mathews came up from his camp to go [ahead of the wagon trains] with A[masa] Lyman & Capt [Jefferson] Hunt to [Isaac] Williamses [Chino] Ranch but it was postponed to a future day.

May 24. 1851; Saturday. Very warm in fore noon. A[masa] Lyman, [William] Crosby, [Jefferson] Hunt and most of the men in this train went back to last train. A meeting was held in which A L[yman] gave them a severe lecture on their conduct in killing Indians & abusing them as it seems they have done—also for playing cards and the General spirit of recklessness which was manifested by individuals. Pleasant breeze in afternoon. Sister Tabin sick.

May 25, 1851; Sunday. Pleasant wind from the south through the

---

93. Men in the rear train mistakenly thought Indians had stolen some cattle, and although they were rebuked, they were not otherwise held accountable for their murder.

day. Camp still remain. Sister Tabin quite sick and was deliv[ere]d of a daughter between 11 & 12 at night.

May 26, 1851; Monday. Warm day & cool night. Camp all remained till near 3 oc[lock] when Capt [Jefferson] Hunt & Bibees ten rolled on leaving us to start on the morrow. 1 cow of A[masa] Lymans missing.

May 27, 1851; Tuesday. Cool this morning, cattle very restless through the night, drove up the cattle early & rolled on, road very rocky and hard on cattles feet. Trav[eled] some 13 or 14 m[ile]s and came up with other 2 tens about sun set and camped.

May 28, 1851; Wednesday. Cool in morning. Our part of the camp laid here to day, found good feed and plenty of water 1½ m[ile]s north near the highest Rocky point in a hollow which we named Ash Hollow[,] [and] w ^Capt. [Jefferson] H[unt] & [William] Crosby went on the road[:] up hill and rocky nearly all the way.^

May 29, 1851; Thursday. We started from here this morning, tollerable early and went on to M[oun]t[ain] springs some ten miles, here we stoped, our cattle got a little water and some grass which we found in the canyan west of the springs, we stayed here some three or four hours then drove up and started on near sundown and trav[e]l[ed] till ¼ to 12 then stoped till morning.

May 30, 1851; Friday. (Very cool.) We left at sun Rise and traveled on to Stump Springs where we arrived at 8 oc[lock] making in distance from spring 22 m[ile]s. Here we found the other company again, the water is tollerable scarce, but plenty if rightly managed for all the stock. Drove the cattle 3 or 3½ m[ile]s n[orth] of west to find feed. Poor[,] some water at lower end of this grass hollow. Capt [William] Crosby & [Jefferson] Hunt—&c went on at 10 oc[lock]. The road from M[oun]t[ain] Spring to this place is good and nearly all down hill we kept our cattle in this hollow through the day & night [and] dug a large hole for a reservoy to water out of next day.

May 31, 1851; Saturday. Cool, the guard that was with the cattle found in the morming that many of the cattle were missing. The[y] accordingly started [with] what they had up to camp and then commenced a search for the ballance. Found all but 18 head in the course of the day, Br [Amasa] L[yman] & D[aniel] P. C[lark] staid to search for them and the camp rolled on and trav[eled] 6 m[ile]s on [and] camped on some feed at [the] left of the road [where] there is plenty of feed for 1 or 2 m[ile]s in extent here. A L[yman] and D. P. C[lark] returned to us at 10 ^oc[lock] no cattle^.

June 1, 1851; Sunday. Cool, camp left at sun rise found we had not been on the best of the feed as it was dark when we arrived here. ^Saw other company at Stump Springs.^ Bro A. L[yman] & Dan C[lark] started back again in search [of cattle]. Camp rolled on to archelete or Resting Spring. The road is very Rocky with two heavy hills to go up and down. We arrived at these springs about 3 oc[lock]. Our cattle were glad to find rest as they much needed it. Capt [Jefferson] Hunt ^and comp[any] were here.^

June 2, 1851; Monday. We laid still and wrested ourselves, the back train commenced rolling in about 1 oc[lock] and continued coming till near midnight. Capt [Jefferson] Hunt [William] Crosby & co[mpany] rolled on this morning.

June 3, 1851; Tuesday. Laid still to day, good feed. Bros [Amasa] Lyman and [Joseph] Matthews making arrangements to go to settlements. The amt. of provisions and groceries wanted by the camp assessed, calculating to buy them at Francisco, Bro L[yman] & M[athew] started after dark.[94]

June 4, 1851; Wednesday. This morning Capt. Smith & co[mpany] rolled out about 9 oc[lock]. Rolled down on to the Amayashe or Lye Creek and ~~camped~~ bated our teams 1 or 2 hours then went on to spring making about 7 m[ile]s (feed salt grass & tooly[])—met 2 men from Salt Springs.

June 5, 1851; Thursday. Left this morning for salt spring[95] where we arrived about sun set. Road Rough and very sandy. Company bought some sugar [and] coffe[e] tobac[co] &c of Gold Diggers. Left here about 12 oc[lock] at night for the desert.

June 6, 1851; Friday. Camp trav[e]l[ed] some her[e] 8 m[ile]s and stoped till sun Rise then went on slowly through the day. Weather

94. Apparently Lyman and Rich hurried on to catch a ship to San Francisco. Lyman will soon start a new diary, while the person who seems to have been helping with the trail journal (see the third-person entries for Apr. 20, 23, 24; May 3, 4, 7, 23, 24, 26) will continue making notations for two more months.

95. Salt Spring is about 100 miles southwest of Las Vegas, 30 miles north of what is now Baker, California.

warm. Cattle suffering for water. Found 1 waggon of Sis Flakes and one of Genl [Charles C.] Richs company. Ma[jority of] herd [has] been left. Trav[eled] on through the night (all night) several cattle gave out before morning.

June 7, 1851; Saturday. In the morning we found ourselves opposite the dry Lake. Here we rested an hour then trav[eled] on to Bitter Spring where we arrived say 9 oc[lock] in morn[ing].

June 8, 1851; Sunday. Laid over til sun down then rolled out for Mohave leaving 1 of A[masa] L[yman's] waggons [and] 1 of Bro Turleys an[d] trav[eled] most of the nigh[t][,] some cattle gave out and was left.

June 9, 1851; Monday. Morn[ing] found us without 3 m[ile]s of the top of the Ridge. Road sandy and heavy. Rolling trav[eled] on over the Ridge down to mouth of canyon. Here we stopped till eve then rolled on and arrived at Mohove [River] about 3 oc[lock] next morn[ing].

June 10, 1851; Tuesday. Laid over. [William] Crosby & [Jefferson] Hunt left here.

June 15, 1851; Sunday.[96] [William] Crosby & ten [Daniel P.] Clark & ten & part of [Robert] Smiths ten rolled out and trav[eled] on slowly until the R[obert] S[mith company can catch up,] when we Clark ten arrived at the mouth of the Cahoon Pays [Cajon Pass, California] where we found all the head camps. Crosby having arrived some 3 days before us.

August 9, 1851; Saturday.[97] Bro [Charles C.] Rich and Hopkins left for San Pedro and the brig Freemont.[98]

August 10, 1851; Sunday. Attended meeting with P[arley] P. Pratt and on Monday 11th went to Sacrimento.

August 12; 1851; Tuesday. Went by stage to Salmon Falls.

August 13, 1851; Wednesday. Returned to Sacramento City.

August 14, 1851; Thursday. Taried.

August 15, 1851; Friday. Returned to San Francisco.

December 11, 1851; Thursday. Left San Bernardino for San Francisco. Traveled to Chino where we lodged. Here we had an interview with Capt Walker just arived from New Mexico.[99]

---

96. Entries for June 11–14 repeat that they "laid over."

97. Lyman begins his new journal here, introduced by "Amasa Lyman/ Los Angeles County/ Cal/ July 31st, 1851" in ink. The first several pages contain financial notations.

98. Lyman was with them, on his way north to secure loans for the colony.

99. Joseph Reddeford Walker was an explorer and mountain guide. The *Los*

December 12, 1851; Friday. Traviled to Los Angeles put up with [Mormon-friendly attorney and politician] Mr. [Lewis C.] Granger.

December 13, 1851; Saturday. This morning had an interview with [and] lodged with Br Granger.

December 14, 1851; Sunday. Sunday 14th went to San Pedro paid Mr Stephens 5 dollars for storage & [illegible].[100] Arived at dark and shiped on board the Steamer Sea Bird[,] arived at Santa Barbary at 5 oclock Monday Morning.

December 15, 1851; Monday. Laid land by to discharge freight. Weather fine and pleasant.

December 16, 1851; Tuesday. Laid by at San Lewis Obispo.

December 17, 1851; Wednesday. Morning arived at Monterey. Laid by for freight and passengers arived in San Francisco.

December 18, 1851; Thursday. Taried with br [George] Win[n]ers preached at br Thomas at night.

December 19, 1851; Friday. It rained remained in the City.

December 20, 1851; Saturday. Morning started for San Jose in the Steamer Union the weather is pleasant and fine in the evening arived at br Horners.

December 21, 1851; Sunday. Had meetings at br Starks and returned to br [John] Horners.

December 22, 1851; Monday. It rained and we taried at br H[orner]s taried in the settlements until Friday the 26th when we started for San Fr[ancisco] at 12 oclock on the Steamer [blank]. Lodged at br [George] W[inner]s taried until Monday the 29th then went to Sacramento in company with br Wood.

December 30, 1851; Tuesday. Went to [Charles W] Rosecrans.

December 31, 1851; Wednesday. Went to the Widow Harmonds.

January 1, 1852; Thursday. Went to Sacramento.

January 2, 1852; Friday. Went to Salmon Falls.

January 4, 1852; Sunday. Went to deer Creek and returned to the falls and received of br E[benezer] Hanks one thousand dollars and 5 dollars for the general [fund].

Angeles Star announced his recent return from the Southwest: "Captain Joe Walker, the renowned mountaineer, has arrived from New Mexico with a company of twelve men." Gilbert, *Westering Man*, 240.

100. Lyman switches to pencil, with smudged portions throughout.

January 5, 1852; Monday. Went to Sacramento[,] received of Orin Smith 13.50 for Wm. Aldrich.

January 6, 1852; Tuesday. Went to San Francisco.

November 16, 1852; Tuesday.[101] Left San Bernardino came about 14 miles and camped in the Cajon pass.

November 17, 1852; Wednesday. [Traveled] about 10 or 12 miles and camped on the top of the hill.

November 18, 1852; Thursday. Came to the [illegible] about noon. Stopped & got some breakfast & started & came 5 or 6 miles & camped on the Mohave [River]. Cloudy & cold.

November 19, 1852; Friday. Started and traveled all day & camped on the Mohave had hard work to keep warm.

November 20, 1852; Saturday. Came 16 or 17 miles & camped at the ~~first~~ last camping on the Mohave warm and pleasant.

November 21, 1852; Sunday. Left the Mohave come within a mile & a half of the bitter springs and camped for the night.

November 22, 1852; Monday. Came to the salt spring.

November 23, 1852; Tuesday. Came to the [blank] ranch and found [Henry G.] Sherwoods Co[mpany]. The missionary brethren came at night[,] got letters from home.

November 24, 1852; Wednesday. Laid bye the weather very cold. [I] wrote to San Bernardino.

November 25, 1852; Thursday. Came past resting springs & camped. 10 miles before we got to the stump springs.

101. The November 1852 entries appear in a diary catalogued as CHL vol. 32, in the middle of entries from 1869.

4 Colonizing San Bernardino, 1853–1855

After he arrived in southern California, Lyman's diary reflected the worries of establishing a colony. He was preoccupied with debt, mills, the weather—any of which could make or break their success. He was anxious about the mail and concerned about the three wives and children he left behind in Utah. While on a journey back to Utah in 1853, he married his eighth and final wife, Lydia Partridge, sister of two of his previous wives, Caroline and Eliza.

Exacerbating the challenge of establishing a foothold in southern California was Brigham Young's indecisiveness about the venture. Although he wanted to see the settlement succeed, he resented the liberties the colonists took due to their distance from Utah. Many of the colonists were strong-willed, a few had gold fever; others were unhappy with Young's iron hand, as the church president rightly sensed. The success of the colony should have cemented the relationship between Lyman and Young, showing that Lyman could be relied on to carry out Young's vision. Instead, it frayed their relations and set the stage for permanent future damage.

April 20, 1853; Wednesday.[1] To day started for San Bernardino[,] the weather fine and warm. Traviled ten m[ile]s to Cottenwood [Utah]. Stoped with br Nathan Tanners family whom we ~~fou~~ found well. Left

1. Lyman had traveled back to Utah to consult with Young and was now returning to San Bernardino. The entries for the first two months were recorded in the same book as the 1848 notations from Mississippi.

Caroline [who is] sick.[2] The prest [Brigham Young] started for Iron C[ount]y to day.

April 21, 1853; Thursday. Today traviled to Battle Creek [Pleasant Grove]. Stoped with br. Samuel White[,] [a battalion veteran]. The prest [Brigham Young] not up yet. The weather cloudy with light rain in the evening.

April 22, 1853; Friday. Snowing this morning with north wind. Dined with br [Sterling] Driggs and then went to Provo atended a meeting. At 4 oclock taried with br Wall.

April 23, 1853; Saturday. To day traviled to Springville and preached at 2 oclock. At 6 oclock a general meeting convened for the settlement of some differences which were all amicably settled.

April 24, 1853; Sunday. Traviled to the Spanish Fork settlement where we held meeting then went to Payson where we stayed over night and held a meeting.

April 25, 1853; Monday. Traviled to Nephi[,] lodged with br Barker. Light rain through the night.

April 26, 1853; Tuesday. To day left Nephi with our party for home. The prest [Brigham Young] left with his train for Manti. My wife [Caroline] went with them. The weather pleasant and warm. Camped at Severe bridge[3] the night cool with indications of rain.

April 27, 1853; Wednesday. This morning weather pleasant and clear. Traviled 24 m[ile]s and nooned at Cedar Springs. In the evening went to the west part of Filmore and camped. Took super and breakfast with br [Henry] Sta^n^dage.[4]

April 28, 1853; Thursday. Weather fine. Traviled to and nooned on Corn Creek [Kanosh]. From Corn Creek traviled to and camped on Pine Creek.[5] Wind from the south and very high all night.

April 29, 1853; Friday. Traviled until 10 oclock then laid by for the wind to lull. In the evening we traviled to and camped on Beaver. Wind still high ~~in~~ [and] dureing the night light fall of snow.

---

2. Caroline Lyman had given birth to daughter Martha on April 1, 1853.

3. The bridge was constructed in 1852 by Timothy Foote near Yuba Lake. See Journal History, Nov. 18, 1852, CHL.

4. Henry Standage was captain of Fort Fillmore during the Wakara War beginning in 1853. Wimmer, "The Walker War Reconsidered," 113–18.

5. This is south of Cove Fort, not the Pine Creek west of Fillmore.

April 30, 1853; Saturday. To day traviled to Parowan. This evening weather more pleasant. Held meeting in council house.

May 1, 1853; Sunday. Weather warm & pleasant. This morning wrote a leter to my family. Traviled to Coal Creek [Cedar City]. Held meeting. In the evening we were kindly received by the Saints.

May 2, 1853; Monday. Traviled to Wilow Creek found good grass. While here a company of four wagons ca[m]e allong on there way to the land of gold. Later part of the night cool.

May 3, 1853; Tuesday. Started halfpast (5)[6] oclock. Traviled to grass valy in the top of the rim ^of the basin^ where we stoped for breakfast. The wind rising[,] gras[s] good. Arived here at (9 oclock) to this point from Parowan [is] (69 m[iles]). From this point traviled down the Sa^n^ta Clarra [River] [for] 17 m[ile]s where we meet br Ja[me]s Brown and party of six men on their way to the [Salt] Lake by whom we received leters from San Bernardino and sent some to the Lake [Salt Lake]. The night not cold.

May 4, 1853; Wednesday. Started at (5 oclock) [and] traviled 10 m[ile]s. Stoped for breakfast grass ^plenty^ but not good. Traviled 32 m[ile]s ~~(Thursday 5th)~~ passed the [town of] Beaver dam[7] and camped on the sand ridge. Arived at this point (at 9 oclock ¾).

May 5, 1853; Thursday. Weather pleasan[t]. Breakfasted and started at (6 oclock) traviled 32 m[ile]s. To day saw several Indians [and] gave them some bread and they left us to pursue our way in quiet. Camped at half past (6 oclock).

May 6, 1853; Friday. Breakfasted and started at (7 oclock). At (12 oclock) had risen [on] the Bluff from the Rio Virgin. Traviled (16 m[ile]s) and nooned. Traviled 12 m[ile]s. Camped on the Mud[d]y [River] at (8 oclock) no Indians to trouble us.

May 7, 1853; Saturday. Started at (6 oclock) traviled (55 m[ile]s). Camped on the Vagus [Las Vegas Springs] [at] half past 12 oclock and early and wayworn we saught our beds with the comfort of sup[p]er.

May 8, 1853; Sunday. Started at (11 oclock A.M) traviled 18 m[ile]s. Camped at Cotenwood Springs at (7 oclock pm).

6. The parentheses around the hour of the day are in the original, here as elsewhere in the diary.

7. This is now the area known as the Arizona Strip.

May 9, 1853; Monday. Breakfasted and started at (6 oclock AM). Traviled to the Stump Springs [near Pahrump] where we found a [new] camp of emigrants on their way to Cal. Arived here at (2 oclock pm) stoped for diner stoped until half past (5 oclock pm) then traviled (6 m[ile]s) and camped.

May 10, 1853; Tuesday. Started at half past (4 oclock AM) traviled to resting spring (19 m[ile]s). Arived here at half past (11 oclock AM) stoped for diner half past (3 oclock PM). Started and went to Maryoshe arived here at (8 oclock PM).

May 11, 1853; Wednesday. Started at (5 oclock AM) traviled to Salt Springs. Arived here at (10 oclock AM) [and] here we meet Brothers Alexander Williams & Wm Perkins and company on their way to the [Salt] Lake. Started at half past (3 oclock PM) camped at half past (11 oclock PM) in the canon between Salt and Bit[t]er Springs.

May 12, 1853; Thursday. Started at (5 oclock AM) reached Bit[t]er Springs at (8 oclock AM). B[r]eakfasted and left at (11 oclock) ^AM^ and reached the Mohave at (8 oclock PM). Br [Charles C.] Rich arived at ~~(12 oclock)~~ midnight.

May 13, 1853; Friday. Started at (9 oclock AM) weather coole wind high feed good water plenty traviled 30 m[ile]s.

May 14, 1853; Saturday. Started at half past (5 oclock AM). ~~T~~ Crossed the Mohave and traviled 10 m[ile]s and camped in the Cedars.

May 15, 1853; Sunday. Started at (5 oclock AM) and traviled to the first water in the ca[n]yone [Cajon Pass] where we stoped for breakfast. We arived at San Bernardino about (6 oclock PM) found our families and friends well and our selves glad that the journey was acomplished.[8]

June 20, 1853; Monday. Visited br [George K.] Win[n]ers. In the evening went up the mountain to br [Justus] Morses sawmill [with] br [Charles C.] Rich & [Richard R.] Hopkins in company.[9]

June 21, 1853; Tuesday. Returned to the valy.

June 22, 1853; Wednesday. Weather fine. This morning purchased a mule of S. Stodard for 90 dollars. To day settled with br Sidn[e]y Tanner

---

8. Below this last entry, Lyman wrote "1853," left several blank pages, and skipped a month before writing in a new diary. He switched to pencil, which is sometimes faint, although the handwriting is more legible than previously.

9. The lumber mill was so important that it evolved into a small satellite settlement.

for hawling and selling my flower [flour]. This evening with the council and the school commisioners determined the salery of the school teachers for the last year to ~~be divided~~ be $1200 which was satisfactory.

June 23, 1853; Thursday. Weather still warm. Br [Richard R.] Hopkins sick. Paid Sidney Tanner 101.00 and took his receipt for $153.25.

June 24, 1853; Friday. Weather still warm. To day paid $35.00 to br J. R. Cade for harness and [$]90.00 to A[rvin] Stodard for a mule.

June 25, 1853; Saturday. Weather warm. This morning concluded a trade with [Justus] Morse &c for an interest of 2 fifths in the lumber and shingle mill at between 10 and 11 hundred dollars. This after noon sold the personal property of David Cade deceased.[10]

June 26, 1853; Sunday. Weather ~~th~~ warm. My health beter than yesterday. Preached today to rather a sparse congregation.

June 27, 1853; Monday. The morning clouday. Recieved of br Wm Mathews $90.00 dollars. This evening recieved of Br Wm Mathews $10.00.

June 28, 1853; Tuesday. Weather warm. Po[l]ls opened for the election in the school house.[11] Recieved a visit from Mr Domingus[12] from the co[a]st. Dureing the day 175 votes were polled. All this day we were anoyed by the Spaniard [Dominguez] who wanted the house. This evening ~~the~~ Dr [Ira] Burrus gave some medicine to my son Marion[13] who was threatened with the inflamation of the brain.

June 29, 1853; Wednesday. This morning Marions health some improved. The anoyence of the Spaniard still continued but after some exchange of propositions he left without comeing to any definite conclusion.

June 30, 1853; Thursday. To day went with brs [Charles C.] Rich and [George W.] Sirrine to survey for mill race[14] to the flouring mill.[15] To day

10. Cade's horse fell on him. He was in a coma-like state for ten days, then died. Lyman, *San Bernardino*, 97.

11. In April the Mormon population voted to create its own county. Now the settlers were voting for temporary county officers. Ibid., 90–91.

12. Manuel Domínguez was a prominent landowner and former mayor of Pueblo de Los Angeles, the judge who ruled on the ownership of Rancho de San Bernardino in 1842. "San Bernardino City," *Daily Alta California*, Mar. 22, 1886.

13. This is future LDS apostle Francis Marion Lyman.

14. A mill race is the channel or sluice the water travels through to power the mill wheel.

15. The gristmill for flour was two miles from the fort at Lytle (Warm) Creek. Brown and Boyd, *History of San Bernardino and Riverside Counties*, 81–82.

paid one thousand and seventy five dollars to Mr [Ezra] Chase[16] for his intrest in the sawmill built by [Justus] Morse, Bingham and Co.

July 1, 1853; Friday. Cloudy and cool. This morning paid Thomas Bingham $15 dollars for care to D[avid] Cade dureing his illness from the avails of Cades estate also paid [William] Mathews $3 dollars from the same. $21 dollars and seventeen cents of money belonging to the estate of David Cade remaining in hand for which he has credit on our Books.

July 2, 1853; Saturday. Cloudy. This morning spent the day with my son who was sick.

July 3, 1853; Sunday. Br [Charles C.] Rich preached. I remained with my sick son whose symtoms were changeing for the beter.

July 4, 1853; Monday. This morning received of Jefferson Hunt by br. [Charles] Rich $75.00 dollars for wheat and barley belonging to the estate of Nathaniel Farebanks ^dead^. Marion ~~apea~~ apears beter this morning. This evening a balloon was sent up from this place.

July 5, 1853; Tuesday. To day collected moneys from Daniel Starks $500.00,[17] from H[orace] A. Skiner $500.00, from Sidney Tanner $100.00, from S Shepherd $400.00.

July 6, 1853; Wednesday. To day brs [Charles C.] Rich and [Richard R.] Hopkins started for San Francisco. Marions health improveing. This evening engaged br Samuel Rolf to make a bill of lumber and timber for the store house.[18]

July 7, 1853; Thursday. Weather very warm. Marion still improveming. To day br [Archibald] Sulivan was grinding [with] rather discourageing news from the mountain sawmill [that] the water [feeding the mill race was] failing.

July 8, 1853; Friday. Still warm[,] Marion still improveing.[19] To day br [Isaac] Grundy enquired if we had employed br [Archibald] Sulivan[20]

---

16. Ezra Chase and family recently arrived from the gold fields in Eldorado County in northern California.

17. Daniel Stark and the others listed here were investing in the gristmill.

18. Samuel Rolfe was a member of the LDS stake presidency. The 300-square-foot granary next to the mill was the storehouse. Lech, *Pioneers of Riverside County*, 69.

19. Lyman's brief references to Francis Marion's illness do not betray how worried Amasa and Maria were that their son might die. According to Edward Leo Lyman, this was the beginning of Amasa's acceptance of spiritualism (*AML*, 205–07); cf. entry for Aug. 14, 1853, below.

20. Isaac Grundy was a slave overseer on his parents' plantation in Kentucky before

to tend the mill and when told we had[,] he remarked that he would bring over some acounts he had engaged [for] some help to work with saw mill next week.

July 9, 1853; Saturday. Weather still warm. This morning rode into the wheat field to witness the operation of the thresher cleaner and reaper and notice the general condition of the crop which is extensively injured by the rust.[21] On my return had an interview with br [Isaac] Grundy who gave some acounts in favour of the mill. This evening atempted to send up the balloon but failed.

July 10, 1853; Sunday. To day weather very warm. Had a pleasant meeting. This evening the mail came in which brought some newss from Salt Lake bearing date of the 13th of May. My family there were well except C[arolyn] E. L[yman], the leters informed us of the death by drowning of [sheriff] Rodney Badger in a generous atempt to save a drowning family of whom he saved the mother and three children. But in atemp^t^ing the rescue of the 4th himself and ^the^ child ~~the child~~ were drowned.[22]

July 11, 1853; Monday. To day another mail arived by the return of Judge [Daniel M.] Thomas but little additional news ~~ot~~. To day was called on by br [Archibald] Sulivan for some help on the mill race and in the evening br J[ohn] Brown called on me for the thousand dollars borowed from him last year to purchase sacking for grain which was lost by G[eorge] Garner, this call at this time is a specimin of some mens generosity which acomodates you to day [but] aparently to distress you worse tomorow. But this [debt] is but one of the social evils that afflict the world.

July 12, 1853; Tuesday. To day visited br G[eorge] Garner who promised to asist me in raising the money for [John] Brown.

July 13, 1853; Wednesday. To day purchased of John Roubidoux one pair of mules for 300 dollars in cash. This evening gave to George Garner

---

learning of Mormonism. Archibald Sullivan converted to Mormonism while recovering from an illness on his way to the gold fields.

21. The settlers had a horse-drawn combine that harvested stalks of grain, separated the grain from the straw, and "cleaned" (winnowed/sifted) the grain to remove impurities and reduce the threat of fungal infection. See Collins, "At the End of the Trail," 76.

22. Badger, the sheriff who attempted to rescue a family when its wagon became stuck in the Weber River, is considered the first Utah police officer to have died in the line of duty.

my receipt for 542 dollars it being in part payment of the money lost by him last year.

July 14, 1853; Thursday. This morning took up John Browns note of one thousand dollars my self paying 199 dollars. When about to go to bed I received on express from Capt [Christopher S.] Lovell at Jurupa[23] asking for asistance to arest a band of robers who had made an atack of on a party of Mexicans who had been fighting them for two days. At the sound of the horn the people came to gather when we raised some 30 men to start the next morning to put them selves under the command of Capt Lovell for the performance of the required services. Prest D[avid] Seely and Sherif [Robert] Clift were of the party.

July 15, 1853; Friday. This morning at a litle past 9 oclock the volunteers of last night were ready and left the fort[24] for Jurupa. The weather cloudy and cooler than usuall. To day made some inefectual efforts to raise some help to work on the saw mill in the Mill Creek Kanyon.[25]

July 16, 1853; Saturday. To day my health was quite poor. Keept my bed most of the day[,] as yet have had no authetic authentic news from the volunteers.

July 17, 1853; Sunday. To day my health quite poor but I preached. To day the volunteers returned from their bloodless trip it proveing to have originated in fears instead of facts.

July 18, 1853; Monday. This morning Br [George W.] Sirrine with five [hired] hands started for the Mill Creek sawmill. This evening called the people together and elected thre[e] deligates to H[enry] G. Shirwood[,] Q[uartus] S. Sparks and Isaac Williams of Chino to attend the destrict convention to be held at Los A[n]g[e]les on the 21st for the nomination of a candidate for Senator.

---

23. Near today's Riverside, the Rancho Jurupa was established by Louis Rubidoux, a French-speaking fur trapper from Missouri. Christopher S. Lovell, who had served under Winfield Scott in the Battle for Mexico City, was under orders to secure the Cajon Pass by establishing a post at Jurupa. Frazer, "Lovell's Report on the Cahuilla Indians, 1854."

24. The colonists' first construction project was the stockade occupying eight acres and surrounded by a twelve-foot fence, situated where the county courthouse now stands. They lived in the stockade, or fort, for the first year. Shaw, *San Bernardino*, 11, 53.

25. Mill Creek Canyon, directly east of San Bernardino, includes the 18-mile creek that originates in the 11,500-foot San Gorgonio Mountains and empties into the Santa Ana River.

July 19, 1853; Tuesday. To day purchased adobies for the store[26] and engaged brs [Robert] Egbert & Stow to work on the Millcreek Sawmill. Also engaged br Ja[me]s Baily to make the adobies for the Domingues house.[27] This evening had an interview with Dr [Ira] Burus at br Wm Stouts.

July 20, 1853; Wednesday. To day completed the purchase of adobies for the store and engaged br J[ames] Baily to make the adobies for the ~~Domigiez~~ Dominguez house.

July 21, 1853; Thursday. To day Sherif [Robert] Clift went in search of the murderer but did not find him.

July 22, 1853; Friday. Weather still warm. Juan Antonio[28] came to get grinding [wheat] done prepareitory to their feast.

July 23, 1853; Saturday. Weather warm. This evening a Spaniard was arested and tried before justice [John] Brown ~~for~~ on the charge of stealing a horse.

July 24, 1853; Sunday. Had a pleasant meeting in the evening went with Dr. [Ira] Burrus to visit Mr. [James] Waters.[29]

July 25, 1853; Monday. Visit[ed] the flouring mill and received of A[rchibald] Sullivan $168.40 cts of mill money.

July 26, 1853; Tuesday. This morning let Br Ja[me]s Baily have thirty dollars in cash to aply on adobies. Also one plank 16 ft [long]. Traviled up to the mill on the mountain where we arived about 4 oclock. Brs W[ellington] and D[avid] Seelys were along. Found the water very low. Br [Henry G.] Shirwood and company were surveying. Taried all night with br [Justus] Morse.

July 27, 1853; Wednesday. Visited br [Charles] Crismonds mill and made some arangements for lumber. After diner came down the mountain [and] on ariveing learned that Mr. Van Norden[30] had died of consumption and that Mr. [James] Waters was sick again.

---

26. This store, constructed of adobe bricks and located in the stockade, should not be confused with the wooden storehouse for grain located in the canyon. The retail store was owned by Lyman, Rich, and stake clerk Richard Hopkins. Lyman, *San Bernardino*, 92–93.

27. James Bailey was the son of a prominent miner and land owner in the Placerville area. The large adobe Dominguez home in Compton, west of San Bernardino, has been preserved as a museum.

28. Juan Antonio was the Cahuilla Indian chief who had made regular raids against Mexican ranchers. For some reason, he was friendly toward Americans.

29. James Waters was a onetime mountain man who decided to purchase a lot in San Bernardino and raise cattle while serving as a justice of the peace.

30. Lyman wrote that "Brother Vanorder" had traveled from Iowa in search of

July 28, 1853; Thursday.[31] Taried about the fort and commenced writeing to the [Salt] Lake.

July 30, 1853; Saturday. To day received leters by mail from Prest [Brigham] Young and others and my family. In the afternoon rebuilt the Bridge near the Blacksmith shop.

July 31, 1853; Sunday. Atended meeting. Br [Benjamin F.] Grouard preached. This evening finished up my mailmat[t]er for Salt Lake.

August 1, 1853; Monday. Went to the Saw mill on Mill Creek. Arived at dark found the men prospering in the work.

August 2, 1853; Tuesday. To day taried at the mill.

August 3, 1853; Wednesday. Remained at the mill.

August 4, 1853; Thursday. We started the mill. It worked well.

August 5, 1853; Friday. We spent the morning in improveing about the mill. Continued all day.

August 6, 1853; Saturday. Returned to the fort received leters from Brs [Charles C.] Rich and [Richard R.] Hopkins wishing a cariage to be sent to the coast for them. Commenced getting up a team but did not succeed. This evening visited br Hopkins children who were mending slowly.

August 7, 1853; Sunday. Had meeting. Br [Quartus S.] Sparks preached on the resurection. [F]rom news of this morning I delayed starting the cariage until Monday morning. [T]he news aluded to was brought by Saumeul Hoffman.

August 8, 1853; Monday. This morning started my cariage for Br [Charles C.] Rich & [Richard R.] Hopkins whom he met at Cocomingo [Rancho Cucamonga] and returned in the evening.

August 9, 1853; Tuesday. To[day] passed the day with Br [Charles C.] Rich and to day commenced the store.

August 10, 1853; Wednesday. This morning received of Bishop [William] Crosby 78 dolars in tithing funds and took up Theodore Thorps note by paying the balance due which was 350 dollars. In the evening visited Bro. Jones.

August 11, 1853; Thursday. Paid cash $2.50 cts for labour on the store.

August 12, 1853; Friday. My health quite poor this ^evening^ witnessed a surgical operation on the person of br Marshal Hunt who lost

gold, joined the church, and died of consumption. Lyman to Brigham Young and the Council of the Twelve, July 29, 1853, in Brigham Young Office Files, CHL.

31. Lyman wrote both "Thursday 28th" and "Friday 29th" to cover both days.

his left leg below the nee by geting into the threshing machine.[32] The operation was painful and severe.

August 13, 1853; Saturday. My health quite poor started our teams for the co[a]st for goods. Ten in number.

August 14, 1853; Sunday. To day br [Charles C.] Rich preached. [M]y health still poor. Preached to day on the subject of spiritual communication.

August 15, 1853; Monday. To day went to the grist mill with Brs [Charles] Rich[,] [George] Sirrine & [Isaac] Grundy to efect a settlement. Br G in the evening[,] Br Rich in company. Mr. Alexa[n]der & [Daniel] Clark started to visit the mountain mills. Weather extreamly hot. Called this evening to see Br Marshal Hunt who seemed more than usueualy free from pain. Dr. [Ira] Burrus expressed to me some doubts as to his recovery.

August 16, 1853; Tuesday. To day the mountain party returned. To night had a meeting with Br. J[ohn] Brown. To night it rained some.

August 17, 1853; Wednesday. This morning paid of my money 1.50 cts for pork for G [Joseph Jasper?] Wilson also 1.50cts worth of paper soap & salt.

August 18, 1853; Thursday. To day witnessed the dressing of the limb of Marshal Hunt when the Drs co[n]cluded to try to save him without amputation. In the evening 7 of our teems returned from the coast without accident. Raised the roof on the store.

August 19, 1853; Friday. Continued the work on the store.

August 20, 1853; Saturday. Continued our work on the store.

August 21, 1853; Sunday. Held meeting br [Charles C.] Rich preached. Spent the evening in visiting the sick. This is the day beyond which the Dutch Dr said br [Marshall] Hunt could not live but still he lives.

August 22, 1853; Monday. To day wrote to my family at Salt Lake. To day received 11.50 for beef. To day br D Dixon hawled timber for hog lot.

August 23, 1853; Tuesday. This morning started the teams to San Pedro sent money to San Francisco for mill irons[33] for br [David] Seely.

32. Jefferson Hunt's oldest son, Marshall, survived but needed a wooden leg after the operation. Lyman, *San Bernardino*, 98–99.

33. The saw-mill irons were the circular and upright saws, gears, shafts, gudgeons, and related parts, according to the 1859 Tredwell & Pell catalogue, "with full description, of agricultural and horticultural implements and machinery."

To day hireed of J. Cade 1060.00 dollars at 2 percent per month also engaged 8000 lbs flour to Isaac Williams at 8 dollars per hundred [pounds].

August 24, 1853; Wednesday. Prosicuted the work on the store[,] in the evening commenced opening our goods.

August 25, 1853; Thursday. Continued opening our goods some of which we found slightly damaged by wetting. Worked late to night.

August 26, 1853; Friday. To day bought one yoke of catle of bishop [William] Crosby continued to put up our goods. In the eveing ~~Matulda~~ Matilda[34] was taken sick.

August 27, 1853; Saturday. Continued buisness in the store after night. The teams arived from the coast with the remnent of our goods. This ~~Sunday~~ morning the mail was opened received leters from Salt Lake bringing news of the death of Father John Burk.[35]

August 28, 1853; Sunday. To day held meeting preached on the evils of recklessness. Matildas health improveing.

August 29, 1853; Monday. To[day] opened our store had a good run of trade.

August 30, 1853; Tuesday. ~~Mon.~~ To day visisted the flouring mill[,] trade good.

August 31, 1853; Wednesday. This evening wrote leters to the [Salt] Lake by a party of Mexicans goeing to New Mexico.

September 1, 1853; Thursday. This ^morning^ closed and sent off our leters.

September 2, 1853; Friday. This morning for Los Angles camped between the point and [Mission] San Gabriel.

September 3, 1853; Saturday. Went to [Manuel] Dominguez aranged our business and went to Los Angles and commenced our trade.

September 4, 1853; Sunday. Loaded our teems and started for home stayed at the Monte with Mr [Ira] Thompson.[36]

September 5, 1853; Monday. Traviled to Kokomungo [Rancho

---

34. A daughter of Amasa and Maria Lyman, Matilda fully recovered.

35. Burk and Lyman had crossed the plains together in 1848. Burk settled in Ogden in 1850 and was buried there.

36. El Monte is fifteen miles west of San Bernardino, built around the Willow Grove Hotel and stage depot, founded by Ira W. Thompson, a New Englander who came west for gold rush and made it as far as southern California.

Cucamonga] stoped and ate some fruit arived home at 11, oclock broke the cariage near home.

September 6, 1853; Tuesday. To day some tickets arived here from Los Angles. At night had a general meeting of the voters heard a statement of his views from J[ames] P McFarland.[37]

September 7, 1853; Wednesday. To day held a general election.

September 8, 1853; Thursday. To day the returns came in from the diferent precinks.

September 9, 1853; Friday. To day had an interview with br [Henry] Shirwood and traviled over the ground for the city and in the evening received a communication from Mag[istrate] J[ustus] McInstry on the subject of the settlement by our people of the Galipagus Isleands the communication we refered to the Presidency at the Salt Lake for their action.[38]

September 10, 1853; Saturday. To day received from Bishop Nathan Teny the grape the products of our vineyard. In quality they were unsurpassed by any in the country.

September 11, 1853; Sunday. To day had meeting.

September 12, 1853; Monday. This evening paid H. E. Parish five hundred dollars.

September 13, 1853; Tuesday. Sent some money by S[amuel] Shepherd to Burton [in] San Pedro.

September 14, 1853; Wednesday. To day went to the flouring mill. To day stoped grinding to repair.

September 15, 1853; Thursday. To day took some hogs to the mill.

September 16, 1853; Friday. To day br [Henry G.] Shirwood commenced surveying the city we located the publick square also engaged to deliver some barly to Lieutenant [George] Stoneman of the U.S.A. E[n]gaged in surveying rail road.[39]

---

37. James Porter McFarland was a candidate for a seat, which he won, in the state senate.

38. Justus McKintry was in the army quartermaster corps. Eight years later, at the start of the Civil War, he was court martialed in St. Louis for embezzlement. The dubious letter promised to put the men in touch with "a gentleman distinguished in political circles ... for many years at the head of the armies of Equador." Justus McKintry to Lyman and Rich, Aug. 31, 1853, Brigham Young Office Files, CHL.

39. George Stoneman Jr. was a professional soldier who served as the Mormon Battalion's quartermaster and would eventually become governor of California. With the Army Corps of Topographical Engineers in 1853, he was exploring a railroad route to the sea.

September 17, 1853; Saturday. Was at the flouring mill.

September 18, 1853; Sunday. This morning br [Richard R.] Hopkins started for Los Angles to day br Hosea Stout[40] spoke to the people.

September 19, 1853; Monday. Bought some barley of Marion Perkins and the Mrs. [Perkins]. [Amasa] Lyman[,] [William] Crosby & Flake started for Mr [James H.] Rollands.

September 20, 1853; Tuesday. Spent the day at the flouring mill in the evening returned to the fort spent some ~~f~~ time with the surveying party.

September 21, 1853; Wednesday. To day changed the location of the publick square and in the evening br [Charles C.] Rich went to Mill Creek mill and was acompanyed by br H[osea] Stout the weather very hot.

September 22, 1853; Thursday. To day started the flouring mill found it to work well.

September 23, 1853; Friday. To day went to [Clark S.] Traheas to eat fruit. This morning broak my cariage and took my lumber wagon.

September 24, 1853; Saturday. To day attended a party at the School house.[41] [C]hildren of both schools.[42] [A]ll went off well.

September 25, 1853; Sunday. To day br [Charles C.] Rich preached.

September 26, 1853; Monday. To day determined the location of the knew [new] mill race.

September 27, 1853; Tuesday. To day br Dixon returned from the coast. To day sold two mares to H. M. Taneer f[or] 40 bushels of wheat.

September 28, 1853; Wednesday. To day went to the flouring mill. To day br J[oseph] Wilson came down from Mill Creek mill and reported the presence in the country of some of the Utah Indians.

September 29, 1853; Thursday. To day the Mill race broke so that the mill stoped.

September 30, 1853; Friday. To [day] employed some 12 hands to repair the race but made a failure.

October 1, 1853; Saturday. To day brock [broke] the ground[stone] on the new race.

---

40. Hosea Stout was the Utah territorial attorney general; he had been the church's police chief at Winter Quarters, Nebraska.

41. He repeated "at the school."

42. There was a small schoolhouse inside the fort where Olive Tenney taught forty children and a log-cabin school outside the fort where Lydia Van Leuven taught the children of lapsed Mormons. See Atchley, "Program Will Trace History of Mission School."

October 2, 1853; Sunday. To day br Harvey Green preached to the people.

October 3, 1853; Monday. Finished surveying the mill race to day. A heavy fire broake out in the wheat field but was extinguished.

October 4, 1853; Tuesday. Went to the flouring mill with brs [Charles C.] Rich[,] [Harvey] Green & [Hosea] Stout and then went over the city grant. Returned and had a meeting of the High Council and the Bishops & their councils to deliberate on the subject of the price of city lots.

October 5, 1853; Wednesday. This morning commenced prepareing our financial report for the conference.

October 6, 1853; Thursday. This morning our conference was opened and continued in session untill Sunday the 9th when it was ajourned untill the 6th of April next.

October 10, 1853; Monday. Resumed our work on the mill race in which labour we engaged some Indians.

October 11, 1853; Tuesday. Continued our work on mill race and our preperations for the departure of br [Richard R.] Hopkins to San Francisco to purchase goods. The weather some cloudy with indications of rain.

October 12, 1853; Wednesday. Cloudy this morning. Br [Richard R.] H[opkins] defers starting from this [place] until Sunday morning next on account of [the] steamer.

October 13, 1853; Thursday. To day the people turned out en mass to help on the mill race. To day an express reached us from Lieutenant [George] Stoneman informing us that he wanted 25000 lbs of barley 8 thousand lbs delivered on the Mohave, where he expected to be by the 16th. Also heard news that determined us to start the party for [San] Francisco tomorow. This evening the men promised to work to morow.

October 14, 1853; Friday. This morning Brs [Richard R.] Hopkins[,] [Quartus S.] Sparks, [Charles W.] Wandell & Farnsworth & [John C.] Cor[e]y started for [San] Francisco. The breth[ren] worked again on the [mill] race.

October 15, 1853; Saturday. To day we sent off our teams with 8 thousand lbs of barley to be delivered on the Mohave for the party surveying Railroad. A portion of the people spent the day in a social dance. This evening had an offer of some goods brought here to sell from Los Angles.

October 16, 1853; Sunday. To day had a pleasant meeting[,] in the evening met with and advised the company who were goeing to Salt Lake not to go at present.

October 17, 1853; Monday. To day bought a lot of goods of Mr Goodman from Los Angles to the amount of eleven hundred dollars.

October 18, 1853; Tuesday. To day had a conversation with councilor [Jonathan] Scott[43] in relation to land titles.

October 19, 1853; Wednesday. To day Br [Nathan] Tiney commenced my ditch on ~~any~~ ^my^ lots. Went this morning to look at some farming land on the Sant Anna.

October 20, 1853; Thursday. To day setled with br [Nathan] Teny for work on my ditch paid him $9.05 cts. To day visited br [Daniel] Starks family himself being absent.

October 21, 1853; Friday. To ^day^ delivered 6 [blank] barley on lieutenant [George] Stonemans order.

October 22, 1853; Saturday. To day sent to San Bernardino for barley.

October 23, 1853; Sunday. To day br [Benjamin F.] Grouard preached. In the evening held a school meeting and engaged brs ~~Gres G~~ Harvey Green and W[ashington] H. Cook to teach. This evening determined to send Brs A[ddison] Pratt & [Benjamin] Grouird to the society islands.[44]

October 24, 1853; Monday. To day we prosecuted over work on the mill race.

October 25, 1853; Tuesday. To day the mail arived from Salt Lake. This evening br Ja[me]s Lewis arived from [San] Francisco. He brought us leter from Brs [John M.] Horner[,] [Richard R.] Hopkins and others.

October 26, 1853; Wednesday. To day went to see some oxen belonging to br D Dixon but did not purchase.

October 27, 1853; Thursday. To day the people some of them turned out to work on the [mill] race. To day dined with br [Daniel] Starks with my own and br [Charles C.] Rich's families. In the evening visited the grist mill.

---

43. Jonathan R. Scott was a law partner with Benjamin Hayes and Lewis Granger, also a member of the Los Angeles City Council and a justice of the peace.

44. Pratt and Grouard had already served in Tahiti, but in 1852 the French had banned Mormons from preaching if they lacked the means to support themselves. It was determined that Grouard's native wife, Nahina, should return. The two men put her on a ship but stayed behind in San Bernardino themselves. See "Historical Note," Addison Pratt Family Papers.

October 28, 1853; Friday. To day the wind was very high[,] the work on the mill race still progressing. To day br J[oseph] Mathews brought my lumber from Mill Creek for the hawling of which I was to pay him out of the store.

October 29, 1853; Saturday. The work still progressing slowly on the mill.

October 30, 1853; Sunday. The people were adressed to day by brs. A[dison] Pratt & Ja[me]s Lewis. In the evening three strangers were baptized.

October 31, 1853; Monday. This morning commenced writeing to the president [Brigham Young] & council [of Twelve]. To day we raised and paid out the sum of $1600.00 in the evening [and] past [it] to the hand of Adison Pratt the subsc[r]iption money for the mission to the amount of $144.00.

November 1, 1853; Tuesday. To day turned the water to the [gristmill on] but in consequence of the breaking of the gate stem the water broke the race. This evening finished writing to the presidency and wrote to my family.

November 2, 1853; Wednesday. To day closed up our mail mater for the [Salt] Lake and put our help to repairein[g] the break of yesterday. ~~(Thursday ^3d^) to~~ This evening br [Richard R.] Hopkins returned from San Francisco.

November 3, 1853; Thursday. To day our teams arived from San Pedro all sound except one of br Richs wagons broak. This evening recieved of Lieutenant [George] Stoneman for barley & beef one thousand and fifty five dollars & sixty five cents.[45] This morning Brs ^H[osea]^ Stout[,] [Washington] Cook & [Harvey] Green started for Salt Lake [and] one load of goods arived by M[arcus] L. Shepherd.[46] Repairs on the mill progressing slowly this evening some persons in town connected with the railroad survey.

November 4, 1853; Friday. Continued our repairs on the mill.

November 5, 1853; Saturday. To[day] myself & br [Charles C.] Rich spent the day at the mill.

45. Lyman wrote an X to indicate that he had received the money. Often he used the front and back pages of his diary to track expenses.

46. Marcus "Lafeyette" Shepherd had marched to California with the Mormon Battalion and then stayed to work in the gold fields, becoming a successful freighter in San Bernardino. He later moved his office to Beaver, Utah. Lyman, *Overland Journey from Utah to California*, 163.

November 6, 1853; Sunday. Had meeting. Several strangers present.

November 7, 1853; Monday. To day made some improvements on the mill race. This evening started the mill.[47] Weather showery through the day.

November 9, 1853; Wednesday. ~~(Tuesday ^8th^)~~[48] To day went with Br [Charles C.] Rich to look to some trespass that had been commited on our timber. Found it to have been taken by br John Haris[49] who in his eagerness to posess himself of it had forgotten to ask for it. This evening visited the mill ^flour^ which was running well the works gave promise of durability. To day we started five teems for San Pedro.

November 10, 1853; Thursday. The surveying party in town in charge of Lieutenant Parks.[50] In the evening went with br [Charles C.] Rich to visit br Ervin Stoddard who was very sick ~~wt~~ with the bloody flux [dysentery].

November 11, 1853; Friday. This morning visited the grist mill. This evening meet and prayed for Br E[rvin] Stoddard.

November 12, 1853; Saturday. Went to brs [Orlando H.] Carters and de[l]ivered 9000 lbs barley to Lieutenant Parks and received of him four hundred and nineteen dollars & ~~min~~ 40 cts and received also for br [Thomas] Tompkins $12.28.

November 13, 1853; Sunday. Held meeting. [I]n the evening br [George] Chorpenning the mail contractor arived from San Francisco.

November 14, 1853; Monday. To day wrote leters to Salt Lake. This evening our teams returned from the coast.

November 15, 1853; Tuesday. To day weather cloudy and dark. This morning the mail started for Salt Lake the party consisted of four men[:] Ja[me]s Williams[,] Charles Crandall[,] George McDougal and Mr Moris. [T]his evening br Newell arived who had been detained by the sickness of his horse.[51]

---

47. This seems to be the beginning date for the flour mill. The settlers are shipping lumber to San Pedro to sell and probably will add ground barley and wheat to their offerings.

48. There is no entry for Nov. 8. Lyman continued to write the wrong date for the next three days, then scratched them out and corrected them.

49. John Harris converted to Mormonism when he and his wife were immigrating to Oregon and encountered Mormons on the trail.

50. Lt. John G. Parke was a US army engineer.

51. The federal government had just issued the first mail contract for southern California to a Dr. Copeland, who subcontracted with Jefferson Hunt. The men listed

November 16, 1853; Wednesday. To day we wrote to brs John Horner and also remited to him one thousand dollars started four teams to the coast. This evening Capt [Jefferson] Hunt [~~illegible~~] & br [Alden] Jackson returned from Los Angles where they had been to ajust the division of the ~~Los Angl~~ Los Angeles county debt and asertained that the amount to be paid by San Bernardino County was something less than four thousand dollars.

November 17, 1853; Thursday. This morning it commenced to rain. [T]his evening the High Council meet to consider the mater of puting in with all commity to locate ~~locate~~ a field for wheat.

November 18, 1853; Friday. This morning weather windy and dry favourable for building. This evening the field commite reported good land and plenty of it for wheat we then apointed a committee to ascertain who wanted land in the new field. The committee were J. D. Holliday[,] M[arcus] L Shepherd[,] PJ Mese Wm J Cox.

November 19, 1853; Saturday. Weather still pleasant this evening ~~put~~ put up the Joise on the office for the uper floor also to day the High council meet to Adjust a difficulty between David Seely and Charles Crissmond.

November 20, 1853; Sunday. To day held meeting. Published the arangement to commence the [sabbath] schooll.

November 21, 1853; Monday. To day there occured a small break in the mill race to repair[,] [for] which we had to turn off the water. This evening the men trespassing on us at yucaipa wer in the store.

November 22, 1853; Tuesday. This evening our teams returned from San Pedro also br Harvey Green returned being unable to proceede to Salt Lake as also bro W[ashington] M Cook. At night opened our goods.

November 23, 1853; Wednesday. To day dined with Sister Mary B. Carter. This evening this visited the Grist mill it was doeing well. Made arangements to go to Los Angeles.

November 24, 1853; Thursday. This morning started for Los Angelos by the way of Cheno put up with Col. [Isaac] Williams. The weather in the morning warm[,] in the evening cool.

November 25, 1853; Friday. To day went to town where we arived at 4 oclock. Took sup[p]er at the Bella Uneion.[52] To night it rained.

---

here were the carriers. Holladay, "Pioneer Mail Carrier." George Chorpenning, mentioned in the Nov. 13 entry, carried the mail from Salt Lake City to Sacramento.

52. The Bella Union in Los Angeles was "upscale," with "a saloon and a french

November 26, 1853; Saturday. This morning still ra[i]ny. Wrote to J[ohn] M. Horner and Alexander & Banning.[53] This evening completed our small purchase and about 4 oclock left for home. About sundown it commenced to rain. We put up at the Monte glad to find a shelter from the rain.

November 27, 1853; Sunday. Started for home where we arived about 9 oclock found my sick children geting beter.

November 28, 1853; Monday. This morning visited the Grist Mill then visited Sister [Keziah] Boyle who was very sick. This evening visted the Indians who was shot by the Sheriff [Robert Clift]. This evening the Indian died. An inquest was held over his body by Coroner [William] Cox and the verdict rendered was that he came to his death by a shot from the Sheriff on the discharge of his duty. This evening heard a report from the field ~~comt~~ commity on the quantity of land in the contemplated field.

November 29, 1853; Tuesday. This morning Sister [Keziah] Boyle died. To day we went with Mr. Ja[me]s Waters to see the sheep belonging to Col. [Isaac] Williams returned at night weary. Had a meeting and defered the laying out of the land in the new field until Thursday.

November 30, 1853; Wednesday. To day we visited the Grist mill [and] mad[e] an arangement to send some suplies to Brauns Guthery [Guthrie] & co. To day Sister [Keziah] Boyle was buried.

December 1, 1853; Thursday. To day visited the new wheat field [and] commenced the new dam on the creek.

December 2, 1853; Friday. This morning went to the Grist Mill. Br [Sterling] Driggs went to measure our wheat land in the field this morning started our teams [fifty miles south to] Temecula.

December 3, 1853; Saturday. Weather pleasant. To day went with brs [Charles C.] Rich & Hurley to explore City Creek Kanyon.

December 4, 1853; Sunday. To day preached a funereal sermon. To day Judge [Daniel M.] Thomas released Mr. Carlisle on a writ of Habeas Corpus.

---

restaurant," even though it was only a single-level adobe structure built by Isaac Williams in 1835 as his home. In the 1840s it served as Mexican Governor Pio Pico's capitol.

53. The most important freight company in Southern California, run by George C. Alexander and Phineas Banning. Lyman, *San Bernardino*, 160; *Los Angeles Star*, Apr. 22, 1854.

December 5, 1853; Monday. To day br Whitlock agreed to go to work at his trade for one dollar and fifty cents per day and [Amasa] Lyman[,] [Charles C.] Rich & [Richard R.] Hopkins were to furnish stock as needed. This morning Col Noris with his party left to prosicute their business of surveying.

December 6, 1853; Tuesday. To day prosicuted our improvements on the mill race. To day Mr. Carlisle went to Yucaipa[,] [10 miles to the east].

December 7, 1853; Wednesday. To day received of C[harles] C. Rich [blank] 20.50 for an intrest in the mill hogs. This evening attended a meeting of the Teachers of the Sabath school association at the residence of Br Qartus Sparks who with Daniel M. Thomas & J[ohn] D. Holladay were elected superintendents of the school. J[ohn] P. Lee[54] was chosen clerk of the association to keep the record of the same that a history of their ~~doe~~ doeings might be preserved.

December 8, 1853; Thursday. To day the mail arived from G. Salt Lake City brought by [freighter] Mr [John Henry] Ki^n^keade. Received leters from my family there and one from Br Blair general news good.

December 9, 1853; Friday. Some indications of rain. Started for Millcreek Mill where we arived in the evening found the men repaireing the mil[l].

December 10, 1853; Saturday. Rainy. This morning finished the repairs on the mill and sawed some. In the evening stayed over night on acount of the rain that was incesant.

December 11, 1853; Sunday. This morning no rain the mountains covered with snow. Started for home and arived there in the.[55] No meeting[,] had an interview with Mr [Lewis C.] Granger.

December 12, 1853; Monday. To day had a talk with Squire Granger in relation to the Title of our land. This evening had a talk with br [Edward] Davis in relation to running our flouring mill. Defered the conclusion until morning.

December 13, 1853; Tuesday. This morning we concluded an arangement with br [Edward] Davis and his sons to run the mill[,] the father at $100 dollars per month the eldest son at $50.00 the youngest at $30.00.

54. John Percival Lee was one of the Southern Saints from Tennessee. In two years he will become the San Bernardino librarian.

55. Lyman failed to finish this sentence. It occurred at the end of the page.

This morning made a contract with Mr Hyrum Williams[56] to deliver two thousand dollars worth of lumber ~~at the~~ in this city at seventy dollars per thousand ft for which he paid one thousand dollars in cash and gave his note for one thousand dollars worth of corn at 4 cts per pound. The weather rainy.

December 14, 1853; Wednesday. This morning some indications of rain. Started two teems for the coast and visited the Grist Mill.

December 15, 1853; Thursday. To day visited the Grist Mill saw the movement of the machinery for cleaning wheat. To day offered some men 1.50 per day but they would not work.

December 16, 1853; Friday. This morning started our teams for Temecula.

December 17, 1853; Saturday. To day visited the Grist Mill and engaged br Whiticer [Thomas Whittaker][57] to do some work for me. To day received some leters by the Los Angles mail from Salt Lake written in August. This is the way we get news [four months later] from our friends. Some letters came of brs J[ohn] M Horner in San Jose.

December 18, 1853; Sunday. To day had meeting in the evening I maried Mr Ja[me]s Baily and Miss Imogene Winers. This evening the sabath school was a organized.

December 19, 1853; Monday. ~~To day visisted the Grist Mill.~~ To day our teems arived from San Pedro.

December 20, 1853; Tuesday. To day started one team to hawling corn from Jurupa.[58] Received a leter from br Stephen Markham intrducing Col. [William] Hollister[59] to our aquaintence.

December 21, 1853; Wednesday. To day it rained all day. This evening our teams returned from Jurupa.

December 22, 1853; Thursday. To day our teams went to Jurupa for corn. To day killed my ox weather fine.[60]

---

56. Hiram Williams was the brother of Isaac Williams, owner of the Chino Ranch.

57. Thomas William Whitaker was a carpenter and former missionary to Tahiti.

58. Rancho Jurupa was twenty miles southeast of San Bernardino.

59. William Welles Hollister was at that time approaching San Bernardino with 10,000 merino sheep he was herding across country from Ohio. He would eventually purchase a successful ranch near San Jose.

60. This is the last daily entry in this diary book. The remaining pages contain financial notations, blank pages, and copied correspondence.

December 23, 1853; Friday. To day our teams returned from Jurupa[,] weather continues fine. This evening br Ebenezer Hanks arived from the mineing country and brought a leter from Thomas S. Williams.

December 24, 1853; Saturday. The mor[n]ing pleasant [blank].[61]

January 17, 1854; Tuesday. This morning started for San Francisco in company with br David Seeley & Qartus Sparks.[62] Traviled to the Monte where we arived at (9 oclock[)] put up at the Monte house.

January 18, 1854; Wednesday. ~~Tuesday~~ To day called at Los Angles transacted some buisness then continued our way to San Pedro where we arived (by 7 oclock) in the midst of a severe storm of rain and wind. But the rigour of the storm was soon forgoten as we were refreshed by the kind hospitality of Messers Alexander & Banning. We learned that the steamers Goliah & Southerner were both below[,] the former expected up tomorow.

January 19, 1854; Thursday. This morning the weather fair the storm has pass[ed]. Settled with br [Marcus L.] Shepherd at 9 dollars each of which I received thirty four dollars and fifty cts for which he should have credit.

January 20, 1854; Friday. Passed the day in waiting the return of the Steamer. In the evening there was a large addition to the numbers allready waiting mostly Spanish & French [travelers]. Night came but no boat and now for sleeping the only room offering any comfort for the ladies is ours so down we piled and passed the night and yet no boat.

January 21, 1854; Saturday. This morning the Southerner arived about 11 oclock and left at 6 oclock when commenced my sea sickness which did not cease while on board nor yet when we came on shore in [San] Francisco where we arived on (Tuesday 24th).[63]

January 24, 1854; Tuesday. At 12 oclock still sick we here met with br A[lden] A M Jackson who took us to the Temperence House[64] Keept by Mr. Hillman. Here we stayed until ~~Wednesday~~.

61. The entry ends abruptly, followed by three blank pages before the diary resumes on Jan. 17, 1854.

62. Lyman was seeking funds to pay the colony's loan, but even as he sailed, there was an economic contraction in California. Lyman, *San Bernardino*, 120–21.

63. While Lyman was away, Charles Rich became ill and Richard Hopkins became the de facto colony leader. Hopkins to Brigham Young and Council of Twelve, Feb. 6, 1854, in Brigham Young Office Files, CHL.

64. Isaac Hillman's Temperance House had sixty rooms and dining space for 200

January 25, 1854; Wednesday. When I traviled out in the City and found Brother [Harley] Mowrys an[d] was invited to stop with him which I did[,] remained in the City until (Sunday the 29th). My health slowly improveing. To day meet with and preached to the Saints.

January 30, 1854; Monday. Went to Benecia with Capt [Jefferson] Hunt. Spent the day [there and] in the evening went to Sacrimento.

January 31, 1854; Tuesday. ~~(Wednesday Feb 1st)~~ Taried at Sacrimento for the stage[,] lodged with Daniel P. Baldwin.

February 1, 1854; Wednesday. Went by stage to see br E[benezer] Hanks at Salmon Falls from whom I received eleven hundred dollars and on 2ond Thursday returned to [San] Francisco by stage and steamer. Taried here until (Sunday the 5th).

February 5, 1854; Sunday. Whe[n] [blank] There was meeting. Brs [Henry G.] Sherwood & [Quartus S.] Sparks preached. Passed the time in the City until (Saturday the 11th) when I shiped on board the Southerner in company with br [Addison] Pratt and d[a]ughter[,] Brs [Benjamin F.] Grouard[,] Sherwood & [the] mail. As we came on board[,] from [an] accident one of the boilers became useless the repaire of which detained us all night dureing which time a severe storm raged out side.

February 12, 1854; Sunday. We are still delayed. To day it rained so that we did not attend meeting. At 10 oclock we were under way.

February 13, 1854; Monday. About noon arived at Monterey. Discharged some freight [and] left here at sunset.

February 14, 1854; Tuesday. Stoped at San Luis Obispo left here at 10 oclock.

February 15, 1854; Wednesday. Arived at Sato Barbary [Santa Barbara] and discharged freight.

February 16, 1854; Thursday. Landed at San Pedro & traviled to the Monte. To night some rain.

February 17, 1854; Friday. Reached home about 9 oclock. This evening it rained came home with br Woodwards Sun [son].

February 18, 1854; Saturday. This morning visited br [Charles C.] Rich whom I found very low. Administered [a blessing] to him and from

---

guests. It was part of a growing national movement to cater to teetotalers. Walters, *American Reformers,* 141.

this moment he continued to improve. The general health of the people was beter than when I left for the North.

February 19, 1854; Sunday. To day held meeting and informed the people of my success above.

February 20, 1854; Monday. To day the Circuit Court commenced its session Judge Haze [Benjamin Hayes] presiding.

February 21, 1854; Tuesday. To day visited the Gr[i]st Mill this evening court ajourned until the next term.

February 22, 1854; Wednesday. This morning myself and br [Richard R.] Hopkins started for Chino[,] lodged with Col [Isaac] W[illia]ms.

February 23, 1854; Thursday. Traviled to Los Angles dined with Mr Rowland[65] lodged with Mr Lewis [C.] Granger made some arangements for the payment of our debts.

February 24, 1854; Friday. To day started for home stayed at the Monte with Mr John Crandall.

February 25. 1854; Saturday. Traviled home where we arived about dark found br [Charles C.] Rich much improved in health.

February 26, 1854; Sunday. To day held meeting and made the last calls previous to making our settlement [of debt].

February 27, 1854; Monday. To day collected money for the impending payment to the amount of $18000.

February 28, 1854; Tuesday. This morning started for Los Angles with br [Charles] Riches team driven by br [Hiram] Blackwell. Brs [Andrew] Lytle & [James H.] Rollins were our company. We called on Lewis Roubidoux of whom we loned[66] three thousand dollars at two per cent per month. Lodged at Chino.

March 1, 1854; Wednesday. To day traviled to Los Angles deposited our moneys at Messers Foster & Wadham and lodged our party in their stores lodged ~~our~~ myself & br [Richard R.] Hopkins with Mr [Lewis] Granger br [George] Sparks whom we expected from above had not arived which delayed the consumation of our business until (Monday the 6th.)

---

65. Probably John A. Rowland, who built one of the first grist mills in the Los Angeles area. He was a major landowner and cattle rancher. His son William married Manuelita Williams, a daughter of Isaac Williams.

66. Lyman's wording implied that they loaned money; in fact, they borrowed $3,000 from Louis Rubidoux. He would later turn against Lyman and Rich and demand payment. Lyman, *San Bernardino*, 189.

March 5, 1854; Sunday. Received a leter from br [George] Sparks informeing me that on acount of the steamer starting before his money became due he was obliged to wait untill he returned Monday. We saw the parties interested and effected a settlement by paying on thre[e] of the four notes the [sum][67] of $6586 and on the [other] $3220. Took up the old notes save one and the mortgage and gave Lyman[,] [Charles C.] Rich & [Richard R.] Hopkins notes for the balance of $29998 to be paid on or before the first day of July, at interest of two percent per month. This evening started for home. Lodged at the Monte.

March 7, 1854; Tuesday. Reached home before dark found that br [Charles] Rich had still improved dureing the week. We improved our ways by building three bridges. ^Saturday 11th wrote to B[righam] Young & Council.^

March 12, 1854; Sunday. The health of br [Charles] Rich still improveing. To day preached to the people.

March 13, 1854; Monday. The weather is pleasant. To day br [Charles] Rich rod[e] out for the first [time].

March 14, 1854; Tuesday. To day went to see br Robert Smith. Not finding him at home I went to Bishop [Nathan C.] Tenneys saw our vineyard and our fruit orchard both which promise well.

March 15, 1854; Wednesday. To day it rained. Today bought of Joseph Hyde 2 mules at $250.

March 16, 1854; Thursday. The weather fine & warm. Some mules in town for sale at $70 dollars and under rather dull sale. To day employed one hand on the mill race also Br [Charles C.] Rich [employed] one hand & single teem. To day had my mules shod to send to the [Salt] Lake and turned out with the stock of Mr. [James] Waters.

March 17, 1854; Friday. This morning some signs of rain which were early verified by its raineing. To day purchased some goods to send to Salt Lake. To day some portion of a surveying party came into town.

March 18, 1854; Saturday. This morning rainy as yesterday.

March 19, 1854; Sunday. To day held meeting but little rain. Some strangers in to hear [blank].[68]

---

67. The pencil is smudged here but Lyman's intent can be inferred.

68. The rest of the line is blank. Since it was Sunday, the visitors were likely attending the worship service.

March 20, 1854; Monday. This morning the weather fine and clear the mud gradualy disppearing much to our comfort & conveneience. To day Messers Fraser & Bancan left with their stock. Also we received an invitation from Chino to furnish a party of men to folow and punish some horse thieves.

March 21, 1854; Tuesday. This morning the weather fair and pleasant. To day continued our work on the ~~stred~~ street at night. Had a talk at br [Charles C.] Richs with br [Jonathan] Newman & son in relation to some wheat taken from our mill by the latter. Agreed to meet again tomorow night for the ajustment of the mater. This evening brs [Sterling] Driggs & [Daniel P.] Clark found our beef & killed it.

March 22, 1854; Wednesday. This morning the weather still pleasant and warm. To day packed some goods for the [Salt] Lake. In the evening had another interview with [Jonathan] Newman[,] [Nathan] Heart[69] & others in relation to the stolen wheat. Agreed to visit the mill in the morning to assertain what the parties might know as to the location of the wheat in the mill.

March 23, 1854; Thursday. This morning the parties interested in the wheat meet and settled. Nathan Heart gave his Due bill for the value of the wheat to be paid in wheat or cash. This evening we finished packing for the [Salt] Lake and finished writing Capt Waters. Started this evening to night it rained.

March 24, 1854; Friday. This morning the rain mostly ceased we loaded our wagons and brother [Hiram] Blackwell started with br [Sterling] Driggs to acompany him as far as the top of the Mountain. This evening it rained.

March 25, 1854; Saturday. This morning weather cloudy with some rain. Made out a bill of lumber to send to the Mountain Mill.

March 26, 1854; Sunday. This morning brs [Sterling] Driggs & [Hiram] Blackwell returned from the Cahoon in search of runaway stock. Some indications of rain. To day had meeting br [Charles C.] Rich was in attendance although not able to preach to us.

March 27, 1854; Monday. This [day] rather cloudy betokening rain.

69. Nathan Hart was fourteen when he accompanied his nineteen-year-old brother James on the march of the Mormon Battalion, making Nathan about twenty-one here.

This after noon visited the school with br [Theodore] Turley to give some advise. This evening received some news from San Francisco and the Sandwich Isleands by the arrival of br [Ed] Den[n]is from the later place.[70] The cause of truth is still onward.

March 28, 1854; Tuesday. This morning cloudy with indications of rain. To day visited the building grounds of br [Charles C.] Rich. To day met & conversed with Br [Ed] Den[n]is & [Stephen] Franklin.

March 29, 1854; Wednesday. To day visited the party that were take-ing out the creek for irigation at the point where brs J[ohn] & Wm Lewis had their dam.[71] To day br [Charles C.] Rich went on a visit for the first time since his sickness. This evening some rain.

March 30, 1854; Thursday.[72] To day begins the forty-~~first~~ ^second^ year of my life. Forty one [two][73] years ago in the Township of Lyman State of Newhampshire and County of Grafton, at a quiet & rather unpretending farming establishment[,] the property of my maternal grandfather[,] there wa[s] as I have been informed a gathering together of a Circle of friends to exchange congratulations on the advent of a stranger who about that time made his apearance which ~~circu~~ circum-stance was received [or accompanied by] a declaration of his intentions to become for an indefinite length of time an inhabitant of this sphere although the apearances of the stranger were not the most promising inheriting as he did all the weakness and ~~infant~~ dependence of infant mortality born to no patrimony but poverty. No home but the wide World[,] through its broad fields and ever varying vicesitudes has lain my devious way[,] until through the blessing of Heaven on my exertions I am what I am. When my children and ^others^ read this let them "take courage as the ceaseless struggle of virtue results in victory.["]

March 31, 1854; Friday. Weather clear and plesant. Br [Charles]

70. Edward Dennis and Hawaiian wife, Hakuole, brought an interest in spiritualism to the colony and would soon join other dissenters two miles from the fort. See, e.g., Remy and Brenchley, *A Journey to Great Salt Lake City*, 2:457–62

71. Brothers John and William Lewis put together a steam-generated saw mill in Twin Creek Canyon (now Waterman Canyon, five miles from Mill Creek), with a boiler they confiscated from an abandoned gold mine.

72. The month (March) is penciled in next to the date, likely by a later clerk at the historian's office. There is a line down the left side of the page meant to highlight the entry, also likely added by a later clerk.

73. Lyman drew an arrow from here to his previous correction, "forty-second."

Rich rode out again to day asisted Bishop [William] Crosby in planing a house for his residence.

April 1, 1854; Saturday. This morning weather fine becoming gradualy warmer. To day secured a lot of fenceing and brought it on to the ground for incloseing the new office.[74]

April 2, 1854; Sunday. To day held meeting. Br [Charles C.] Rich was in attendance and made some remarks. Weather warm. There has been a commet visible here for several nights. Of the history character destination and purposes of ^aerial^ traviler we have as yet had no acount.[75]

April 3, 1854; Monday. To day the mechanicks turned ^out^ to work on the office. To day the County Court was in session.

April 4, 1854; Tuesday. To day the mail came in from Los Angles from the states and England. Continued our labours on the office.

April 5, 1854; Wednesday. Weather fine[,] work on the office progressing slowly. To day visited the wheat field near the mountain road[,] the wheat looked quite promiseing. Our recent visitor the comet still with us varying with the exhibition of his luminous train our useualy bright [sky] on star light nights. This evening ajourned our work on the office until after conference.

April 6, 1854; Thursday. Weather pleasant and warm. [Church] conference was opened at (10) oclock for particulars. Read minutes at a little past the midle of the day ajourned until tomorow 10 oclock. At night the wind was high from the north. In the morning we found ourselves powdered without the agency of the barber.

April 7, 1854; Friday. ~~Saturday~~ Our conference continued with increaseing interest. The house was crowded the weather was fine and warm.

April 8, 1854; Saturday. We were deprived of the servises of our clerk to day in consequence of his being employed in takeing depositions in cases pending in law betw[e]en some of the old sitizens of the country. The conference was well attended some were baptized as was the case yesterday.[76] Sister [Caroline] Jackson added to our musick that of her own both vocal & instrumental.

---

74. Also known as the Council House, it accommodated postal and city offices. Lyman, *San Bernardino*, 133.

75. Known as the Great Comet of 1854, it was visible for a month.

76. These may have been rebaptisms, common in the mid-nineteenth century.

April 9, 1854; Sunday. The weather fine our meeting was largely attended. Several strangers were present. With the conclusion of the evening servises the conference was ajourned until the 6th of Sept next. A good feeling pervaded the people as they parted to resume their various avocations in life[,] that this feeling may long continue is my prayr.

April 10, 1854; Monday. To day resumed our work on the office. To night the mail arived from Salt Lake by Br [Leonard S.] Conger bringing the news of the Death of br Willard Richards who died on the 13th March[77] and also ~~the~~ Clarisa the wife of Father John Smith.[78]

April 11, 1854; Tuesday. To day continued our work on the office. To day miself and br [Charles C.] Rich and families visited br [George W.] Sirrine. To night closed up my mail mat[t]er for the [Salt] Lake. Prospects good that we shall have our council room soon in which to meet and transact our buisness.

April 12, 1854; Wednesday. To day the mail by Mr Holiday started for S[alt] L[ake] the party numbered 4 men. To day the joiners left the office and the masons commenced theirs [work].

April 13, 1854; Thursday. To day went to look out the way for bringing the water into the City in company with brs [Charles] Rich[,] [Richard R.] Hopkins[,] [James] Rollins & [William] Cox. [We] found the chance good. This evening br [Charles] Rich tried the galvanick battery for the improvement of his health.[79] Wind high to day work on the office slowly progressing.

April 14, 1854; Friday. Weather pleasant this morning. To day went with Br [Samuel] Rolf to determine by the level the practicability of bringing the water into the City where it was needed. The result more than answered our expectations. This evening some of the masons Dunkerley & [Richard] Varley[80] were drunk another evidence of the still remaining weaknesses of humanity.

---

77. Richards was a close confidant of Joseph Smith. Richards died at forty-nine of dropsy. *Deseret News*, Mar. 16, 1854.

78. Clarissa Loomis Lyman Smith, mother of apostle George A. Smith, was Amasa's second cousin. *Deseret News*, Mar. 2, 1854.

79. Electrical currents were thought to stimulate cells, also small magnets worn as necklaces. "The Execution of Kobler," *Columbia Democrat*, Jan. 11, 1840; *Frank Leslie's Illustrated Newspaper*, Mar. 5, 1881.

80. Richard M. J. Varley (1822–1887), an English convert, was a brickmason and San Bernardino police officer.

April 15, 1854; Saturday.[81] This morning about 9 oclock was felt the shock of an Earthquake by some of our citizens. This evening Father [Samuel] Gould arived from Parowan [Utah] with some emigrants. The[y] came in on foot haveing left their wagon on the way their stock was very poor. This evening finds the work on the office not complete.

April 16, 1854; Sunday. Weather fine this morning. Yesterday the first lumber from Br [David] Seelys mill came into town it looked well and speaks well for the mill and affords another evidence of the continual development of the resources of our country.[82] To day had a pleasant meeting. This evening held our meeting in the new office and considered the expediency of building a schoolhouse[,] the maner of building and plan of the house refered to the Commissioners and a committy of their [choosing for] apointment. This evening advised with Br [Theodore] Turley in relation [to] the mater of proveing what he supposed to be a silver mine in the mountains of Millcreek.

April 17, 1854; Monday. This morning paid Lewis Jacobs[83] $28 dollars in cash made an apointment to visit the Mountain Mill to morow. Assisted brs [Samuel] Rolf and [William] Cox to survey the water ditch which part of the work we completed before night. This evening brs [Charles] Rich & [Richard R.] Hopkins returned from their fishing excursion to the mountain. This evening in settlement with Thos Williams we were charged with forty two days work done in about one month.

April 18, 1854; Tuesday. This morning settled with br Whitlock and sold him our stock which left him in debt to us a small amount we then started up the mountain where we arived before night found br [Justus] Morse engaged in repaireing the Mill which repairs we completed next day. This evening it rained some.

April 19, 1854; Wednesday. To day it rained. Started the mill, it run well for some little time when it became loose again.

April 20, 1854; Thursday. Still ra[i]ny. To day visited the folks at the Steem Mill[,] dined at br Lewises. In the evening it rained hard and continued through the night.

81. Lyman wrote this date vertically in the margin.

82. Brothers David and Wellington Seeley had a mill near the Lewises' in what is now Waterman Canyon. Robinson and Harris, *San Bernardino Mountain Trails*, 34–35.

83. Lewis Jacobs was a Jewish miner and the first merchant in San Bernardino to build a store outside the fort. Cataldo, *Images of America: San Bernardino California*, 22.

April 21, 1854; Friday. This morning still raining. Made out some bills for lumber and left with br [Justus] Morse. Selected 8 joists and put them up together with some inch lumber. About one oclock started for home on the way we tiped the cariage over onto the mules which new maneuver they bore very quietly. In this operation we had no breaks reached home about 5 oclock without rain although the signs of recent rains were spread over the face of the land. Found on our return the Losangles [Los Angeles] mail had arived by which we received leters and papers from Capt [Jefferson] Hunt our representitive in the Legislature among other thing[s] informing us of the passage of a bill for the incorporation of the City of San Bernardino a copy of which he promised to send us by the next mail.

Heard this evening that dureing our abcence that br Josiah Hendricks had received a lengthy revelation its object & purport I have not yet learned. Tonight there was more rain. Learned that the water ditch was completed and its cristal bounty was already makeing glad the City of the Saints. Our gardens & grain fields ar[e] clad in their richest robes of green in acknowledgement of the blessing of the recent rains.

April 22, 1854; Saturday. This morning myself and Br [Charles C.] Rich had an interview with br [Josiah] Hendricks on the subject of his revelation. A little friendly reasoning and kind admonition soon satisfied him that he had been deceived and he seemed much pleased that he was corected. To day borowed of br [Quartus S.] Sparks a table for our office until we could get one made.[84] Brought and deposited in the office some of my books. Dureing the day we had a succession of showers atended with some thunder. This evening two of the Filibusters who were with Col [William] Walker called on us for employment. One of them a printer seemed somewhat anxious to start a paper here.[85] To day we apointed br Wm Cox water master to take the supervision of the water ditch to see to its building & preservation & the distribution of the water to the citizens.

84. When the town was incorporated on April 1, Lyman was listed as mayor even though the first election would not be held until June 5. Lyman was anxious to move into the nearly completed Council House.

85. William Walker hired mercenaries disguised as colonists ("filibusterers") to overthrow central American governments and establish a Southern slave culture there. He toppled the Nicaraguan government and ruled there for a year but was executed in Honduras in 1860.

April 23, 1854; Sunday. To day weather rather cool had meeting in the morning in the evening meet for prayers in our new uper room.[86]

April 24, 1854; Monday. To day entered into partnership with Brs [Charles C.] Rich[,] [Richard R.] Hopkins & [James H.] Rollins under the [name] of Lyman Rich Hopkins & Co. To day a Mr Allen from Marysvill called on us for a chance to settle with us and to purchase land. This evening br [Thomas W.] Whitaker helped me to make out some bills of lumber for my hous[e].

April 25, 1854; Tuesday. This [morning] about 7 oclock my wife Maria was delivered of a fine daughter[87] all geting along well. This evening meet with Br Chapman Duncan who was here enroute for Parowan Utah. To night with Br [Thomas] Whitiker and [Fred] Parris made some changes in the plan of my house.[88] This morning sent a leter to br Benj Matthews informing him that my self and br [Charles C.] Rich accepted his proposition to sell his intrest in the Millcreek Mill for two hundred and twenty-seven dollars on Ranch acount.

April 26, 1854; Wednesday. This morning went to br Robert Smiths to hire his colored wooman to work for us.[89] Then went with br [Charles C.] Rich and others on a fishing excursion on the creek west of Cahoon [Cajon]. Stayed over night camped west of the creek by the first spring. This evening fished with indiferent luck returned to camp with fish sufficient for sup[p]er & breakfast for our party. The night was pleasant but cool. The stars in rich profusion with smiling fasces looked out upon the rude scene of our rest.

April 27, 1854; Thursday. This morning early we were astir and returned to our fishing t[h]o our success was no better than yesterday. A little past noon we started for home where we arived about 3 oclock the most tangible evidences left with us of our trip was our pa^i^ns and weariness of body.

86. Lyman and Rich were later criticized for holding "secret meetings" in the Council House's upper room. The meetings were, in fact, temple-like sessions called prayer circles. Lyman, *San Bernardino*, 177; Quinn, "Latter-day Prayer Circles"; also entries for May 14; July 16, 30, 1854, below.

87. Love Josephine Lyman.

88. Lyman's house was built inside the stockade with separate living quarters for each of his five wives.

89. This was probably thirty-five-year-old Biddy Mason, whose owner, Robert Smith, would be paid for her labor.

April 28, 1854; Friday. To day Brs Cory & Brown commenced hanging the [wall] paper in the council house. To day visited the gristmill. To day moved the post office into the new office. This evening Matilda[90] was taken suddenly ill while at the Drs office and stayed over night at br [Quartus S.] Sparks as she was not able to get home.

April 29, 1854; Saturday. To day wrote a leter to my family at the [Salt] Lake also settled with the miller. To day Br Cory finished papering our uper room. In the afternoon it rained. Matilda continued very ill. To day payed some men who had been [going] to work for us at the Mountain Mill.

April 30, 1854; Sunday. Today the California and Salt Lake mails came to hand[,] by both of which we received leters one from Prest B[righam] Young. To day the weather rainy between the showers brought Matilda home ~~a~~ in an aparent state of insensibility[,] at night she became more quiet and sleept. Weather still cool and damp. To night answered the Prests leter. In the morning closed up my leter to my family at the Lake.

May 1, 1854; Monday. Weather pleasant. This morning Brs [Charles C.] Rich[,] [Richard R.] Hopkins & [James H.] Rollins started in the stage for San Pedro enroute for San Francisco. This morning received a petition from Colo. [Alden] Jackson to the secretary of the Treasury for the apointment of inspector of customs at the Cahoon [Cajon] and Sangorgona [San Gorgonio] passes[91] to which I procured the requisite signitures and returned the same by the hand of Br [Richard R.] Hopkins. This done I went to the Grist Mill with Br [George W.] Sirrine had some talk with Br [Edward] Davis in which he said that if we thought his proposition for running the mill too high he would take less. Matildas health still improveing.

May 2, 1854; Tuesday. To day in company with Brs Sidney Tanner & David Frederick went to Mill Creek Mill to see the condition of the mill and engaged br Frederick to saw for $3.00 per thousand and his wife to cook for the mill hands at one bit[92] per hand per day and they have their

90. Amasa's and Maria's daughter Matilda would recover.

91. San Gorgonio Pass cuts between the San Bernardino Mountains on the north and the San Jacinto Mountains to the south. It is one of the steepest passes in the U.S.

92. A bit was a Spanish silver coin worth about 12½ cents.

provision found [funded]. Also engaged the Bishops hands at 30 ft of lumber per hand per day.

May 3, 1854; Wednesday. To day returned home. On our return visited and dineed with Sister [Olive] Tenny and looked at the fruit trees and vineyard both of which looked well. Found Matilda still improveing in health. To night received leters from Salt Lake beareing date of April 1st informing me of a draft of 625.55 to be paid on sight.

May 4, 1854; Thursday. To day had an interview with br J. Ralting.

May 5, 1854; Friday. To day advised with Br Wm Mathews in relation to the application of labour on the San Bernardino road. In the evening engaged br Arvin Stoddard to finish the survey of the City at one dollar and twenty five cents per lot. Indications of rain to night.

May 6, 1854; Saturday. This morning raineing very little. To day [for] the picknick went to City Creek the weather became fair and pleasant. To day a Mexican under the direction of Mr. Butts came to file a declaration of his intentions to become an American citizen. His name was Jose Valenzualaz.

May 7, 1854; Sunday. To day had meeting. In the evening meet for prayers.

May 8, 1854; Monday. To day in company with br [Thomas] Whitiker went to the Mountain Mill which we found doeing very well.

May 9, 1854, Tuesday. To day selected some lumber weather pleasant loaded the teem for home.

May 10, 1854; Wednesday. To day returned home without any accident where we arived about 3 oclock. To night the mail from [San] Francisco arived by which we received leters from brs [Charles C.] Rich & [Richard R.] Hopkins bearing date of May 4th. [Also had mail from] San Pedro and some packiges of papers from the states.

May 11, 1854; Thursday. To day passed the time in the City. This morning Mr. Arington, merchant from [San] Francisco called at the office. Him and lady were here on a visit. Weather cloudy with signs of rain which fell through the night in small quantity.

May 12, 1854; Friday. Passed the day in the City. In the [evening] received a load of lumber by br Buten. Payed some attention to the work on the Road.

May 13, 1854; Saturday. This morning wrote a leter to Brs [Charles

C.] Rich & [Richard R.] Hopkins by br Hazen Kimble [Kimball]. Went to the Flowering [flour] Mill and advised with Br [George W.] Sirrine in relation to the repaireing of the road at that point. My health quite poor.

May 14, 1854; Sunday. Today held meeting some strangers present. My health still poor not able to meet with the prayr circle. Passed a sick and restless night.

May 15, 1854; Monday. This day was the time for the cessions of the District Court but haveing no clerk they done no buisness and by consent of parties removed certain cases on the docket to Losangles [Los Angeles]. My health still bad at night found some rest though very broken.

May 16, 1854; Tuesday. This morning my health somewhat improved was out a little thoug[h] very weak. To day visited Dr [Ira] Burows who was very sick this evening. Find my health slowly improveing[,] the Dr no beter but rather sinking under the influence of dissease though unable to render the so much needed relief. He has our constant prayrs and best wishes for his recovery.

May 17, 1854; Wednesday. To day my health still improveing dined at bro [Stephen] Franklins. This evening large number of stranger Indians in town wishing as useual to eat the bread of idleness but we concluded not to feed them unless they would go to work which they were not willing to do.

May 18, 1854; Thursday. My health still poor no news from above.

May 19, 1854; Friday. To day received a load of lumber from the mountain. Some rain this evening.

May 20, 1854; Saturday. To day the weather some more pleasant than useual. To day the mail arived from Los Angles but no leters for me but a present from Dr. [John M.] Bernhisel of the report of Capt Stansbury of the exploration of the Salt Lake & Utah [Lake].[93]

May 21, 1854; Sunday. Weather fine. Held a meeting my health still pour. Meet in the [prayer] Circle this evening had a pleasant time.

May 22, 1854; Monday. To day sent bill of lumber to Mill Creek Mill and four teams on the mountain for lumber.

May 23, 1854; Tuesday. My health still poor. This evening the teems

93. As early as April 1849, Captain Stansbury and the topographical engineers were sent to the Great Basin. They completed their exploration in 1851. Stansbury, *Exploration and Survey of the Valley of the Great Salt Lake of Utah.*

returned from the mountain. To day received 2 quarters of Beef one from br [Edward] Davis one from br [Alfred] Bybee.

May 24, 1854; Wednesday. To day went with br Joseph Mathews to examine the road, he was to work as supervisor.

May 25, 1854; Thursday. To day the mail came in by the stage from San Pedro. Got leters from Bro [Charles C.] Rich & party learned that [they] intended to start home on Saturday next. This evening bought a cariage of br [Joseph] Kelting. Capt [Jefferson] Hunt arived in stage.

May 26, 1854; Friday. To day wrote leters one to Prest Young one to my family sent out in the mail. My health still faileing.

May 27, 1854; Saturday. To day visited the wheat field near the Mountain found it lookeing fine. This evening received a load of lumber by br Mesick my health no beteter. To day received by Capt [Jefferson] Hunt a leter from Dr Mcintire expressive of his wishes to come here in the fall.

May 28, 1854; Sunday. To day held meeting my health still poor. This evening meet in the [prayer] circle.

May 29, 1854; Monday. To day Colo [Isaac] W[illia]ms came to town and Wm Leete started three teeams for the coast for goods. Weather warm.

May 30, 1854; Tuesday. To day sent br [Thomas] Whitiker to do some work on the Grist Mill. My health some what beter. To day settled our acount of lumber with Mr [Hyrum] Williams found acording to the receipts 712 ft yet due him although there was 1000 ft hawled from the mill and not acounted for by Joseph Wilson and the hawling payed for in lumber by br [Sidney] Tanner.

May 31, 1854; Wednesday. To day went to see where Br J Clift had commenced makeing adobies in the street and advised him to desist which he said he would do. This evening Br [Thomas] Whitaker commenced working on my house.

June 1, 1854; Thursday. To [day] gave licence to a pedler for one month.

June 2, 1854; Friday. To day the brethren arived from San Francisco in good health and spirits. My health still poor. Today received a leter from br N[athan] Tanner who was in Francisco.

June 3, 1854; Saturday. To day our teams returned from San Pedro. To day 2 men were bound to keep the peace before Justice [Andrew] Lytle. Probabily now there will be peace. The weather very cool for the season.

June 4, 1854; Sunday. Br [Charles C.] Rich preached. In the evening meet in the [prayer] circle.

June 5, 1854; Monday. To day there was an election for City officers the folowing was the result for Mayor A[masa] Lyman[;] for council C[harles] C Rich[,] G[eorge] W. Sirrine[,] Daniel Starks[,] Wm. J. Cox ~~for attorney~~ Q[uartus] S Sparks[;] for marshall J. D. Holliday[;] assessor T[heodore] Turley[;] for Treasurer J[ames] H. Rollins[;] atarney A[lden] A. M. Jackson. To day purchased some articles of groceries to the amount of thre[e] dollars and sixty cts for br Ellis Eames. On the road this day Br [James] Baily commenc[ed] makeing my adobies for my house.

June 6, 1854; Tuesday. The weather dull and cloudy. Emigrants still comeing in.

June 7, 1854; Wednesday. This morning cool and clouday. Our streets to day presented some cases of drunkeness mostly[94] among the new comers some enquire^ing^ for labour at high prices.

June 8, 1854; Thursday. To day received some 16 hundred ft of lumber by brs [Norman] Taylor[95] & [John] Holliday.

June 9, 1854; Friday. To day Br P[arley] P Pratt arived with an company of missionaries for the Pacifick Isleands[,] himself to establish a gathering point in California. Weather very warm.

June 10, 1854; Saturday. Received some lumber and in the evening located some City lots for Capt Ja[me]s Waters. To night the city councilors were sworne into office.

June 11, 1854; Sunday. To day held meeting. [We] were addressed by br P[arley] P. Pratt. In the evening had a meeting and agreed to hire a man to guard the barley field for fifty dollars per month.

June 12, 1854; Monday. To day Br P[arley] P. Pratt left for San Francisco to prepare the way for the missionaries awaiting here the results of his efforts. To night it commenced raining.

June 13, 1854; Tuesday. This morning still raining. In the afternoon myself and Br [Charles C.] Rich & [Edward] Patridge went to Bishop [Nathan] Tennys. In the evening the rain mostly ceased.

June 14, 1854; Wednesday. This ~~m~~ morning went and examined the

94. The word "mostly" was repeated here.

95. Norman Taylor was a teamster who drove one of the first wagons into the Salt Lake Valley with Brigham Young in 1847.

wheat in the field which they were harvesting and also the vineyard and fruit trees which under the labour and care of Br [Nathan] Teny are looking well. As we were about leaveing to return home [the Cahuilla Indian chief] Wan [Juan] Antonio came haveing heard as he said that Christians were to be made there that day but for want of an interpreter we could not say much to him more than to have him wait a little time until the return of Br [Parley P.] Pratt from the north. In the evening Br Wm Hyde arived from Australia haveing in charge a company of Saints.

June 15, 1854; Thursday. To day succeded in procureing the teems for the coast to bring the Brethren up who were in waiting there. On Monday the 12th Truman Swarthout commenced to work for 20 dollars per month.

June 16, 1854; Friday. To day Br [Charles C.] Rich started for Losangles [Los Angeles]. To day the boys commenced hawling sand for the house. H~~e~~ad a long conversation with br E[llis] Eames.

June 17, 1854; Saturday. To day the mail ar[ri]ved from Losangles [Los Angeles]. To day had a talk with some of the natives on the subject of our religion. They manifested some intrest in the mater but it was like the sunlight strugling through the murkey clouds that spell the comeing or departure of the storm so dense and black the da[r]kness that is broodeing over them. But the spirit of the Lord is at work.

June 18, 1854; Sunday. Held meeting [and] were adressed this morning by Elder Wm Hyde from Australia where he has been on a mission. He was acompanyed by a small company of Saints for this place. ~~in~~ This evening a portion of the stranger [foreign] Saints arived in good spirits and were received at Bishop [William] Crosbys.[96] Br [Charles C.] Rich returned this evening.

June 19, 1854; Monday. To day the proprietor of the Los Angles Star Mr. [James S.] Waite was in town. To day Began hawling the adobes for my house. To day my self and br [Charles C.] Rich were called on by the Assesor and responded to his call. We found him scroupulously careful of the Countys intrests and as regardless of individuals.

96. See the entry for June 22 below referencing William Hyde's sixty-eight Australian immigrants. Crosby's log cabin outside the fort was the colony's first hotel, called by non-Mormons "the bishop's tavern." Palmer, "Historians Make Room for a Landmark Hotel."

June 20, 1854; Tuesday. To day the Editor of the [Los Angeles] Star was her[e]. The weather warm. Br Case came to Town to get some relief in takeing care of a sick man an emigrant. This after noon the City council was in cession to concider the intrest of the City.

June 21, 1854; Wednesday. To day an emigrant Died her[e] by the name of [blank] and was prepared for buriel. By the charity of the citizens we succeeded in procureing houses for all of the new arivals of Saints.

June 22, 1854; Thursday. To day agreed with br Edward Davis to run our flouring mill. At night had a meeting for the benifit of the Australian Brethren and also raised a subscription of grain to pay for guarding the Barley Field. The weather very warm.

June 23, 1854; Friday. To day the weather was very warm. A Mr. Jackson[97] got his leg brooke by the falling of his horse. Mr Wm Crow arived from Scarimento.

June 24, 1854; Saturday. To day the mail from San Pedro brought us leters from San Francisco by which we learned of the purchase of a vesel for the isleand trade.[98] Also a leter from P[arley] P. Pratt stateing that he had engaged the passage of the brethren on the Southerner for ten & twenty dollars to leave San Pedro on the 7th of July.

June 25, 1854; Sunday. To day held meeting. This evening had a talk with the members of the Isleand mission.

June 26, 1854; Monday. To day an election was held to elect a board of supervisors of the water for the Township. Received some money on Ranch Acct.

June 27, 1854; Tuesday. To day received some stakes from the mountain for surveying. To day a fire ocured in the wheat field on the south side of the Santa Anna which resulted in the destruction of some 3 + [or] 4 hundred Acres of grain. So much for the reckless gratification of one mans wants regardles of the intrests of others. The fire is said to have got out from a camp fire of John Ward who is said to have declined helping to extinguish it. This is the last feature in this picture of reckless selfishness. When will men cease to do evil against themselves[?]

97. Lyman's lack of familiarity makes it unlikely this is Alden Jackson.

98. Missionary Nathan Tanner was commissioned to purchase a ship for transporting Polynesian immigrants to San Bernardino, but he could not make the *Rosalind*, a fixer-upper, seaworthy. Woods, "The Palawai Pioneers on the Island of Lanai," 9–11; see also the entry for July 28 below.

June 28, 1854; Wednesday. Weather warm. Today continued to receive money on Rancho Acount.

June 29, 1854; Thursday. To day commenced to write to Prest [Brigham] Young. This morning Br [Charles C.] Rich started for Los Angles Via Chino to try to effect some thing in the mater of our Debts there.

June 30, 1854; Friday. To day Messers Douglass & Reed were here from Los Angelos County. This Morning star a messinger to le[t] Brother [Charles C.] Rich know of his mule at San Gabriel which he secured.

July 1, 1854; Saturday. To day closed up my leters for Salt Lake. To day received some funds for Ra[n]cho [San Bernardino].

July 2, 1854; Sunday. To day held meeting. This morning Br [Charles C.] Rich returned from Losangles [Los Angeles] haveing put off our debts a short time. At night had a meeting of the People to consider the mater of the ~~maner~~ plan we should adopt to pay for the place. The mater was agitated but we came to no definite conclusion.

July 3, 1854; Monday. To day passed the time mostly in writeing and discussing the maner of paying our debts.

July 4, 1854 Tuesday. This morning Br [Charles C.] Rich & myself sent our teams to cary the Missionaries to San Pedro. To day there were some men here from Jurupa who were drunk and with drunkenness were disturbeing the quiet of our streets and insulting our citizens. In the evening at half past 7 oclock my wife Cornelia was delivered of a son,[99] and thus closed our celibration of our nations birth and ^that^ of my son.

July 5, 1854; Wednesday. To day decided upon the plan for surveying the farming Lands and agreed to start on tomorow for Chino to see Col [Isaac] Williams in relation [to] a proposition for the building of some fence to inclose his place for which he proposed to help in ~~our~~ the payment of our debts.

July 6, 1854; Thursday. To day in company with Br [Charles C.] Rich & [Richard R.] Hopkins went to Chino to see Colo [Isaac] Williams in relation to building his fence which we agreed to do to the amount of 30 Miles for the consideration of $36000 dollars to us paid as shown per contract. At night the weather was cool.

July 7, 1854; Friday. This morning Br [Charles C.] Rich[,] [Richard

99. Henry Elias Lyman.

R.] Hopkins & Colo [Isaac] Williams went to see together the place of Begining the fence. On their return the contract was drawn and mutualy signed by the parties. [Amasa] Lyman & Rich of the first & Isaac Williams of second part and at 2 o'clock started for home where we arived about 9 oclock.

July 8, 1854; Saturday. To day atended the Buriel of Br [Nathan] Tenny's Child.[100] To night had a meeting of some of the brethren to concider the mater of the payment for the place.

July 9, 1854; Sunday. To day held meeting and apointed the Board of Teachers to obtain subscriptions [of stock] for the payment for the Rancho.

July 10, 1854; Monday. To day were engaged in geting subscriptions of stock to aply in payment for the Ranch. We found on the subscr[i]ption of available property and cash to amount to $23,000.

July 11, 1854; Tuesday. To day the weather very warm. Sent a messenger to Colo [Isaac] Williams with [a message] to let him know that we could not fulfill the contract [to build the fence].[101]

July 12, 1854; Wednesday. To day aproved some ordinences passed by the City Council. The weather to day was extreamely hot.

July 13, 1854; Thursday. To day the weather still hot. Recieved some money on acount of titheing from Bishop [William] Crosby. To day an inquest was held by Coroner [William] Cox over the body of an Indian who was shot by a Spaniard while in the act of stealing his[,] the Spaniards[,] horses.

July 14, 1854; Friday. Weather warm some sickness from the extreeme heat. This evening went to the warm Creek to Bathe. After my return went with Dr. [Ira] Burows to visit Br. [Quartus S.] Sparks son who was sick But was some beter.

July 15, 1854; Saturday. To day a party of Indians were here to enquire into the circumstances of the death of the Indian killed by the Spaniard a few days since. To day Br [James H.] Rollins started for Losangelos on Buisness. This evening br [William] Hyde returned from the mountain where he had been for the benifit of his health.

---

100. Phoebe Relief Tenney was apparently a stillborn child or died soon after birth.

101. In spite of their overwhelming need for funds, Lyman and Rich came to believe the fence would divert workers away from caring for San Bernardino. Lyman, *San Bernardino*, 139–40.

July 16, 1854; Sunday. To day held meeting were adressed by Br [William] Hyde in an interesting maner. In the evening meet in the circle for prayr.

July 17, 1854; Monday. To day went to the mountains. Arived at the residence of br [Justus] Morse at dark where I taried.

July 18, 1854; Tuesday. To day selected Lumber such as I could find for my house. About noon started for the City where I arived about 5 oclock, found Br H[iram] Blackwell from Salt Lake with leters from my family who were well. Father John Smith[102] died the night before br Blackwell left. Found Jose Maria Lugo here after money. We promised him some in two weeks.

July 19, 1854; Wednesday. To day went to the Grist Mill which had received some damage from the water turned on as supposed by the boys who were Batheing in the race.

July 20, 1854; Thursday. To day received from Br George Win[n]er some specimens of Q[u]artz with Gold in it.

July 21, 1854; Friday. To day had a consultation with Br [Lysander] Woodworth in relation to the plan of my house in which he proposed some alterations. This evening learned that two men had gone to search for gold so strong its Magick.

July 22, 1854; Saturday. To day the weather warm. Br [David] Fredrick came down from Mill Creek Mill.

July 23, 1854; Sunday. To day the weather warm held meeting. In the evening meet in the [prayer] circle.

July 24, 1854; Monday. To day had some men Cleaning out the mill race in which we got alon[g] very very well.

July 25, 1854; Tuesday. To day went to the mill where br Summie was engaged in makeing a Been [bin] for grain received on Ranch ac[coun]t.

July 26, 1854; Wednesday. To day wrote leters to my family and to the President [Brigham Young] and visited the mill.

July 27, 1854; Thursday. To day the mail started for Salt Lake. Br Wm Hyde was of the party [to Utah] in rather poor health. To day received some wheat on Rancho Ac[coun]t. ~~This evening~~

July 28, 1854; Friday. To day the mail came in by which I received a

102. John Smith was the younger brother of Joseph Smith Sr., uncle to Joseph Jr., founder of Mormonism, and father to apostle George A. Smith.

leter from Br Nathan Tanner stateing that he had paid for the vesel and was goeing on her to the Isleands. We received a copy of the Southern Californian.

July 29, 1854; Saturday. To day built a dam to turn more water to the Grist Mill. Sent for a smut machine[103] to San Francisco. Received leter from [attorneys Jonathan] Scott & [Lewis] Granger stateing that our note to Jose Maria [Lugo] must be paid to B[enjamin] D[avis] Wilson.[104]

July 30, 1854; Sunday. To day held meeting. In the evening meet in the circle for prayrs.

July 31, 1854; Monday. To day started to Losangles [Los Angeles] to settle some buisness connected with the Ranch in company with Brs [Andrew] Lytle & [James] Rollins. Traviled as far a[s] Cucamongo.

August 1, 1854; Tuesday. To day traviled to Los Angelos had an interview with Messes Scott & Granger. In the evening lodged with Mr Granger.

August 2, 1854; Wednesday. Made some arangements with Mrsers Scott & Granger. In the evening started for home[,] stayed at the Monty [El Monte] at J Crandalls.

August 3, 1854; Thursday. Came home where we arived at night. Some signs of rain.

August 4, 1854; Friday. To day went to the Grist Mill with Br [Charles] Rich.

August 5, 1854; Saturday. To day went in company with Brs [Charles] Rich & [William] Crosby to visit Dr [Ira] Burows farm and eat of his mellons of which he had some fine specimins. Had a very pleasant out[ing].

August 6, 1854; Sunday. To day held meeting Br [Charles] Rich preached. In the evening meet in the [prayer] circle.

August 7, 1854; Monday. To day the Board of Equilization[105] were in

---

103. To remove the smut fungus, the grain was run through a vertical centrifuge that scoured and separated the heavy seeds from the powdery black spores.

104. Benjamin Davis Wilson was a fur trapper who liked the San Bernardino area. He married the well-do-do daughter of José Antonio Yorba, purchased Rancho Jurupa, and became mayor of Los Angeles.

105. Daniel Thomas was a judge for the Court of Sessions, where he heard felony cases, while the board of equalization considered tax matters. Lyman was no doubt confused about the court's name.

cession judge [Daniel N.] Thomas presiding. Went to the mill to arange for makeing a been [bin] for Barley.

August 8, 1854; Tuesday. To day the Court still in cession. Went to the Flowering [flour] Mill and commenced a been [bin] for Barley. Had 2 hands cleaning Ranch wheat.

August 9, 1854; Wednesday. To day had some hands cleaning wheat and also Building [the] Barley Been [bin]. In the evening went to look at some five Acre lots and determin[e] their price.

August 10, 1854; Thursday. To day sold some farming land to Br [Theodore] Thorp also repaired the mill dam which broak again at night.

August 11, 1854; Friday. To day repaired the dam. To night the Carier arived with the mail from Salt Lake. They were traviling 16 days and brought news that Bros [William] Hyde & [Leonard S.] Conger were atacked at resting springs by the Indians. 2 men were wounded lost one mule 2 wounded and part of the mail lost. Our leters [from Salt Lake] wer dated 18 & 19 of July.

August 12, 1854; Saturday. To day in company with Br [Charles] Rich went to the Grist Mill to make terms with the miller but he had left home. At night the City Council meet.

August 13, 1854; Sunday. Held meeting [and] in the evening meet in the [prayer] circle. This night my teeth began to ache and continued all night.

August 14, 1854; Monday. To day the mail arived which brought us news from Brs [John M.] Horner & [Quartus S.] Sparks. Br H[orner] had purchsed our smut mill and forwarded the same. Visited the Flowering [flour] Mill.

August 15, 1854; Tuesday. This morning Brs [Charles] Rich & [James] Rollins started for Los Angelos on Business. My health is very poor.

August 16, 1854; Wednesday. Received a leter from Messers Scott & Granger. My health still poor.

August 17, 1854; Thursday.[106] My health still poor. Kept my Bed until Sunday night when it commenced to rain. I still remained in bed until Tuesday the 22ond when I left my bed tho not my room. The weather became fair. I suffered some loss in adobies.

August 24, 1854; Thursday. My heal health still improveing. To day

106. Lyman recorded the correct day as Thursday but misdated it as the 16th.

we made out some Deeds for lots of Land. To day bought two mules of Josiah Hendricks for two hundred dollars on Ranch Acount.

August 25, 1854; Friday. To day comenced writing for the Salt Lake mail [pick-up]. Sold to the mail contractor one mule at one hundred dollars this after noon. Had two hands on the mill Race.

August 26, 1854; Saturday. To day finished writing for the mail. In the evening attended a meeting of the Teachers. Their reports as far as made were Generaly favourable as to the condition in [which] they found the Brethen. I gave them some instruction.

August 27, 1854; Sunday. To Day maried Mr Leonard Buterfield to Miss Susanah Bates. Held meeting [and] Br [Charles C.] Rich preached [but] the congregation rather thin. In the evening meet in the [prayer] circle. Matildas health very poor was up with her most of the night.

August 28, 1854; Monday. To day Br [Charles] Rich started for Los Angelas in company with Capt [Jefferson] Hunt on buisness. Engaged Brother Woodworth to lay out the foundation of my house.

August 29, 1854; Tuesday. To day with Woodworth laid the foundation of my house. Received a visit from Br John Brown who wanted some money. Made things easy with him and he went home.

August 30, 1854; Wednesday. To day engaged some help on my house.

August 31, 1854; Thursday. To day commenced to lay up my house. In the evening Br [Charles] Rich came home from Los Angelos from which place he brought the mail.

September 1, 1854; Friday. To day work progressed slowly on my house. This evening I agreed to start to San Francisco next Tuesday to procure means to pay our Debts.

September 2, 1854; Saturday. To day continued the work on my house. In the evening attended a meeting of the City Council.

September 3, 1854; Sunday. To day held meeting. In the evening meet in the circle. Two of my children were taken sick now to night. To night had a meeting of a portion of the Voters to concider the maters conected with the elections.[107]

September 4, 1854; Monday. Passed the day in geting ready to go above [north].

107. Lyman put a diagonal line across the mid-point of this sentence, suggesting that he changed his mind, maybe because of his sick children.

September 5, 1854; Tuesday.[108] Left San Bernardino for San Francisco where I arived on Monday the 11th about 9 oclock. Found Br [Parley P.] Pratt and family well. Here I met Brs Nathan Tanner and Edward Partridge and Br George Canon who was engaged in waiting for Br Pratt. While here Br [John M] Horner called in [and] made an apointment for tomorow.

September 12, 1854; Tuesday. Visited Miss Livingston & [John D.] Holladay who promised to render me all the asistance in their power in my Business. Also meet Br [John M.] Horner who also promised the same. To day examined som[e] water rams[109] and a Smut Mill such as we had purchased.

September 13, 1854; Wednesday. To day visited Br [John M.] Horner at his office an[d] visited Mr. Duncans Sales Rooms in company with Brs [Parley P.] Pratt & [Walter] Dodge[110] and [Nathan] Tanner and sisters Pratt[,] [Ellen] Dodge & Evins.

September 14, 1854; Thursday. To day called on Mrs Livingston & [John D.] Holladay but received small encouragement in money maters. In the evening meet a party of Gentlemen who were interested in navigating the Colorado River as high as the Reo Virgin thus opening a way for the introduction of goods to Utah by the Gulf of Cal[ifornia]. Thus to bring the benifit of commerse into close proximity with our settlement near Santa Clara, it wa[s] agreed to present the mater to General Wool[111] and ask for his cooperation in effecting the exploreing of the river above Fort Yuma. That it may succeed and at the (expence of Uncle [Sam]) is our wish.

September 15, 1854; Friday.[112] To day visited the Surveyor. Wrote some for home.

September 16, 1854; Saturday. This afternoon was introduced to General [John E.] Wool of the United States Army who said that he

---

108. He switched diaries here for his journey to San Francisco.

109. A ram is a valve that builds up enough pressure to force water uphill.

110. Horticulturalist Walter E. Dodge would soon introduce figs, pears, and wine grapes to southern Utah. Lancaster, "Dixie Wine," 24–25, 35–36, 67.

111. General John E. Wool was commander of the US Army on the Pacific Coast. Steamboat traffic to Utah would prove elusive.

112. Lyman mislabeled the day as "Thursday" and then continued writing one day off until Sept. 23 when he wrote two entries for the date as both 22 and 23.

should order the exploration of the Colorado River to its highest navigable point[,] in which if they succeed it will probably open a shorter way than the present for goods by the Gulf of California.

September 17, 1854; Sunday. Started on the Steamer Uneion for Uneion City in company with Brs [John] Horner & [Quartus S.] Sparks & [Joseph] Cain. Taried all night on the boat.

September 18, 1854; Monday. Attended meeting in the morning at the Hotell. Br [Quartus S.] Sparks preached in the evening I preached at the school House to an attentive audience lodged with Br [John] Horner. Ate some ripe fruit from his orchard.

September 19, 1854; Tuesday. Started early in the stage for Uneion City. From thence went on the boat to San Francisco where I arived about sun down. To night met Br [Charles] Wandall.[113] Lodged at Sister Evins House she being absent.

September 20, 1854; Wednesday. Spent the day in an unavailing search for Judge S[c]ott.

September 21, 1854; Thursday. Learned where the Judge had his office but could not see him.

September 22, 1854; Friday. Visited Mr. Wood of Adamson Co. but did not effect any thing but some talk.

September 23, 1854; Saturday. Was introduced to a b[r]oaker but this don[e] no good.

Past the day in writing to Br [Charles C.] Rich and seeing Br [George Q.] Canon & Dew[e]y. [I] start for the south [with] some encouragement in money matters.

September 24, 1854; Sunday. Had meting at Br [Parley P.] Pratts [and] in the evening visited Br Jon[e]s and wife [where] with some Welsh friends [we] had a pleasant time.

Sepember 25, 1854; Monday. To day waited on the moneid men but did not effect anything this evening. Called on Mr Donihue & ordered the castings for our mill. (On Saturday the 23d received from Major Chorpenning the sum of three hundred dollars for Lyman & Rich [company].[)]

September 26, 1854; Tuesday. Had an interview with Mr Wheeler [of

113. Charles W. Wandall, president of the Australian mission, 1851–53, would join the Reorganized LDS Church and die in Australia on a mission for them.

Norris & Co. Shipwrights] who promised to let me have the money. Not being able to find Judge Scott we did not conclude the mater. This evening made an engagement with Br Bates who works at the Alta Office also received the Deseret News as late as the (17th) of August.

September 27, 1854; Wednesday. To day concluded an arangement with Norris & Co for the money we wanted. In the evening had an interview with br Madre & Br Morgan Bates.

September 28, 1854; Thursday. Went with Br [Quartus S.] Sparks to examine some plaineing machienery in view of purchaseing. Called on Mr Wheeler with our deed of the rancho.

September 29, 1854; Friday. Received on [Uriah] Tylers Draft [$]201.45 and paid out of the same on Bloomer and Lougee Bill [$]132.40.

September 30, 1854; Saturday. ~~(30th) (1st)~~ Started for home on the Goliah. In our starting we had the company of the Yankee Blade[,] the Carter[,] and the Sonora[;] of them al[l] we lost sight in the fog.

October 1, 1854; Sunday. ~~(31st)~~ The weather fog[g]y passed quietly along our way under the prudent care of Capt Haly a little sick.

October 2, 1854; Monday. Still fog[g]y. In the morning found the Yankee Blade a wreck just above point conception spent the day in rescueing her passangers. In the night went to Santa Barbary and left the passengers for that place.[114]

October 3, 1854; Tuesday. ~~(2ond)~~ Arived in San Pedro about (12) oclock took stage for Losangles [Los Angeles] where we arived at dark and lodged at the Bella Uneion.

October 4, 1854; Wednesday. ~~(3rd)~~ Started for home traviled very slow in conceqence of the weak state of our team. Arived at home about 1 oclock on [Thursday].

October 5, 1854; Thursday. ~~(4th)~~ Found my family well and my house progressing finely some indications of rain.

October 6, 1854; Friday. This morning Br [James H.] Rollins['s] daughter Nancy Died from an effetion [infection] of the brain. Still some

114. The *Yankee Blade* was overtaken by thieves looking for gold bullion, causing the ship to crash; the survivors were rescued by the *Goliah*. Point Conception is a headland (sea cliff) seventy miles west of Santa Barbara. Spearman, "The Wreck of the Yankee Blade."

signs of rain. To day the Lawyer from San Francisco arived to settle the mater of a loan of money to pay for the Rancho.

October 7, 1854; Saturday. To day mad[e] and exicuted the writings pertaining to the aforementioned loane.

October 8, 1854; Sunday. Held a meeting and concluded our conf^e^rence and adjourned to (April) 6th 1855.

October 9, 1854; Monday. Started for Los Angelos in company with Br J[ames] H. Rollins[,] stoped over night at Monte.

October 10, 1854; Tuesday. Reached town but were unable to do any buisness in concequence of the absence of parties interested for whom we sent.

October 11, 1854; Wednesday. The [steamer] Southerner arived but brought no news for us. Passed the day in ineffectual atempts to raise money for the Drafts which we were to receive on the loan. Buisness moves rather slow.[115]

October 12, 1854; Thursday. Waited all the day for the arival of Mr [Diego] Sepulveda[116] but he did not come. In the evening sent the Notary Publick to him with a power of Atorney for him to sign in favour of [the one in] San Franc[isc]o. To night made a call on Capt [Jesse D.] Hunter.[117]

October 13, 1854; Friday. [Diego] Sepulveda arived and in the afternoon we finished up our buisness and started for home. Put up at the Monte.

October 14, 1854; Saturday. Started for home where arived at dark, found the people well. The General [Charles Rich] geting ready to start for the [Salt] Lake.

October 15, 1854; Sunday. Held a meeting. Had a full house in [the meeting]. Visited Br [Charles] Rich.

October 16, 1854; Monday. Passed the day at home. Br [Charles] Rich still geting ready to leave. To day Mr. [Isaac] Slover was brought home Dead from wounds received from a Grisley Bear.[118]

---

115. Lyman secured a new loan of $20,000 to pay off the original loan for the rancho, buying time but otherwise not solving the problem. Lyman, *San Bernardino*, 140–41.

116. Sepulveda, nephew of the original owner of Rancho San Bernardino, Antonio Maria Lugo, was a well-connected rancher. The original debt had transferred to Sepulveda.

117. Jesse D. Hunter was a Mormon Battalion veteran and successful Los Angeles brick merchant.

118. Slover was a mountain man from Kentucky who presumably shot the bear and followed it into the brush to confirm the kill, when it fatally mauled him.

October 17, 1854; Tuesday. To day Br [Charles] Rich expressed his wish to withdraw from the firm of Lyman Rich Hopkins & Co.[119]

October 18, 1854; Wednesday. To day Br [Charles] Rich started for the [Salt] Lake his wagons having started the day before. Was busy sorting and takeing acount of my lumber.

October 19, 1854; Thursday. Past the day at home about my house. In the afternoon went to the Mountain Mill. Some light showers in the valy.

October 20, 1854; Friday. ~~Saturday~~ Selected some lumber at our mill and returned home much fatigued. Weather fine.

October 21, 1854; Saturday. Went with Br Varley to see some land. Let him have a lot of eight Acres. In the evening went to Br [Marcus L.] Shepherds in the botom.

October 22, 1854; Sunday. Held meeting [and] Br [Benjamin F.] Grouard preached in the morning. In the evening meet in the [prayer] Circle and agreed to send a party to look for a chance to procure gold by diging to enable us to meet our indebtedness on the ranch, the exploration to be under the supervision of brs [Theodore] Turley & D[avid] Seely. This morning Marion Perkins and John Mathews started for the Mohave to bring in the Generals [Charles Rich's] mule.

October 23, 1854; Monday. Spent the day in the City. To day the first case arising under the city ordinances was tried by Justice [Alden] Jackson. The offence drunkness fine $50.00 fifty dollars and costs. To day sold lot to Judge Pinnock for one hundred and fifty dollars (the No. 17 of the five acre survey). Some indications of rain.

October 24, 1854; Tuesday. Went to the mill and determined the extent of the mill reservation and located some of the Brethren who were e[n]camped there. Returned home. Dined with [blacksmith] Br [Clark S.] Fabun.

October 25, 1854; Wednesday. Spent the day in selecting lumber about my house. To day got a new promise from Nathan Hart that he would pay for the wheat that was taken from our mill.

October 26, 1854; Thursday. To day Charles Allen & Jasper Wilson were commited by Justice [Alden] Jackson for steeling a barell of pork

119. Rich was going to Salt Lake for an unspecified amount of time and could not contribute to the day-to-day management of the company.

from the store of Mr. [Louis] Glaser. To day borowed some lumber from A[ndrew] J Workman and from D[aniel] P. Clark.

October 27, 1854; Friday. Was engaged on my house puting in floor timbers and in lifting them hurt my side. Dureing the day mail came in from the states via Los Angelos. Paid Br. [Uriah] Tyler fifty dollars in cash and received of Wm Crosby fifty one dollars.

October 28, 1854; Saturday. Spent the day about my house. Br [Richard R.] Hopkins returned this evening. At night received a note from His Honour Judge [Benjamin] Hays of Losangles [Los Angeles] (per hand of Mr. [Truman] Swarthout) in which he wished us to cooperate with them in secureing the murderers of Mr. [James] Ellington. We sent some fifteen men under the direction of the Sheriff ^[Robert] Clift^ & the Marshall [John D.] Holliday.[120]

October 29, 1854; Sunday. Weather fine. The sheriff and party started this morning. To day held meeting[,] in the evening meet in the [prayer] circle.

October 30, 1854; Monday. Had a severe north wind blowing all day rendering it very unpleasant to atend to out door buisness. At night meet with the company who were goeing to look for gold. The wind somewhat abated.

October 31, 1854; Tuesday. Received some money in small amounts. In the evening Received a leter of introduction purporting to come from Br J[ohn] M Horner introduceing Mr Conroy as a Lawyer and School Teacher. His apearance was rather suspicious and the leter was signed John A. Horner.[121]

November 1, 1854; Wednesday. To day Brs B[enjamin] F. Mathews & H[iram] H. Blackwell started on their mission in the south.[122] To day the [gold] prospecting company left on their erand and may God spead and protect them. ~~This evening~~

120. Felipe Alvitre was arrested and convicted for the murder of Ellington, an El Monte farmer. Within four months of the original crime, Alvitre was publicly hanged—twice because the rope snapped the first time. Guinn, *History of California*, 188–89; Moore, "Felipe Alvitre is Hanged Twice."

121. Horner's middle name was Meirs.

122. Blackwell and Matthews were called on missions to the southern states to organize more emigrating companies.

November 2, 1854; Thursday. Commenced laying the cloth on my House Roof. Received some lumber from the mountain.

November 3, 1854; Friday. Passed the day about my house. In the evening Br [James H.] Rollins returned from Los Angelos and after night his old house was discovered to be on fire or some goods inside. The fire was soon extinguished the damage but small. To day commenced painting my House Roof.

November 4, 1854; Saturday. Remained at home weather stil dry.

November 5, 1854; Sunday. Held meeting some strangers were present. Some high wind. To day the [prayer] circle did not meet.

November 6, 1854; Monday. This morning went with Br [Richard R.] Hopkins to replace the stakes removed from the corners of some[123] of the lots near the Publick Square.

November 7, 1854; Tuesday. ~~Monday~~ Went to the Grist Mill to arange for the cleaning of some wheat.

November 8, 1854; Wednesday. Worked on my house and wrote to S[alt] Lake.

November 9, 1854; Thursday. Went with Capt [Jefferson] Hunt & Edwin Dayly [Daley] to look at some land in the five acre survey and let them have some fourteen lots. Returned in the evening and attended to some Buisness in the Office in relation to the money loned of Pioche Bayerque & Co[124] of San Francisco. Weather still fine work progressing slow[ly] on my House.

November 10, 1854; Friday. Friday passed the day in the city [and] about my house. Finished covering the Roof and commenced raising the coridor.

November 11, 1854; Saturday. Passed the day in work on my House. This evening engaged Br Lowe to work on my House.

November 12, 1854; Sunday. Held meeting. In the evening meetin [we held] the [prayer] Circle. In later part of the night James Williams returned and brought news of the mail.

November 13, 1854; Monday. To day several trials were had before Justice [Alden] Jackson[,] one for a violation of the city ordinance in

123. This starts a new page. Lyman repeated "of some."

124. French emigrant Francois Pioche and business partner Jules Bayerque opened a store for miners before turning to banking. Dalin and Fracchia, "Forgotten Financier."

relation to Drunkeness. He was fined fifty dollars and costs. In the evening the mail arived from Salt Lake I received one leter from my family and one from Br [Charles C.] Rich [who was] on the Desart near Mudy [River] all well.

November 14, 1854; Tuesday. Passed the day about Home the weather still dry. To day concluded a trade with Hyrum Williams for his goods and the rent of his store.

November 15, 1854; Wednesday. Passed the day about my house.

November 16, 1854; Thursday.[125] Passed the day at home. The weather fine and some of the emigrants arived and we raised five hundred dollars for Mr Jas Waters.

November 17, 1854; Friday. Friday the wind high from the north. To day payed to order of John Brown[126] two hundred ^and sixteen^ dollars twelve and a half cts thus completeing the payment of the Last thousand dollars received of him.

November 18, 1854; Saturday. We[n]t to dine with the w[idow Elizabeth] Tanner and in the evening meet with the City Council. There were not enough present to do any Buisness [so] we agreed to meet on Monday morning.

November 19, 1854; Sunday. Held meeting. In the evening meet in the [prayer] circle. This evening Sister [Mary Jane] Sparks returned home. The mail arived from Los Angelos. Some indications of rain.

November 20, 1854; Monday. To day we recei[ve]d a visit from Senitor [William M.] Gwin.[127] Went with him to visit the warm spring. To day engaged some teams to deliver some wheat to Mr Daltons[128] also to day Br [Andrew] Lytle agreed to aid me in Building a City Prison.

November 21, 1854; Tuesday. This morning Senator [William M.] Gwin left on his return to Francisco. At ^evening^ heard the report from

---

125. Lyman returned to his previous diary book so that the rest of the entries for November follow the Sept. 4 entry.

126. John Brown (not to be confused with the Mormon pioneer of 1847) was a former mountain man who joined the LDS Church; as one of the settlers' creditors, he grew increasingly impatient. Beattie and Beattie, *Heritage of the Valley*, 215; Lyman, *San Bernardino*, 317–20.

127. Gwin was a Democrat seeking re-election as he traveled through the state. According to Beattie and Beattie, he was respectfully received "with the courtesy due so high an official," *Heritage of the Valley*, 353.

128. This is likely Henry Dalton, owner of Rancho Azusa near Chino.

the party who had been searching for gold of which they found no large amount. Weather still fine with good prospects.

November 22, 1854; Wednesday. Spent the day about my house and dined at Br [Stephen] Franklins and called on br [Theodore] Turley who was badly poisoned by By quick silver [mercury] in his bread. His eye and face were badly swollen. At night the owners of the lumber mills in the mountain meet at the office and and agreed to sell lumber at $40.00 dollars per thousand except Br A[ndrew] J. Cox who said that he should sell twenty-five.

November 23, 1854; Thursday. Went with Capt Jas Waters and let him have some 13 five acre lots. To day began setting my fence in front of my House.

November 24, 1854; Friday. Passed the day in the City. To day the mill stoped [working] by failing of the Bridgetree [beam supporting the shaft]. In the afternoon the wind came down from the north.

November 25, 1854; Saturday. To day four men were fined by Justice [Alden] Jackson for Riotous conduct in the street one 25 the other three 30 dollars each. This evening commenced to lay out a ditch for the water in front of my House.

November 26, 1854; Sunday. Held meeting the weather still fine. This evening my health rather poor did not meet with the [prayer] circle.

November 27, 1854; Monday. Weather still fine passed the day at home.

November 28, 1854; Tuesday. To day went to the Grist Mill and in the after noon located the City Lockup. At night meet with some of the mill owners and apointed A[ndrew] J. Cox & Thomas Bingham a committee to engage a man or men to work the Mountain Road.

November 29, 1854; Wednesday. Went with Br [Robert] Smith and look at some land on the other side of the river. Returned in the evening.

November 30, 1854; Thursday. To day the stage arived from the coast and brought Mr [George W.] Sirrine and news of the mail. Tomorow some signs of rain.

December 1, 1854; Friday. In the morning borowed 1000 ft of lumber of Charles Chapman to be repaid in lumber. Then went to look at some five acre lots with Brs Philips & Jones.

December 2, 1854; Saturday. To day was engaged in makeing out our communication for S[alt] Lake. It rained most of the day. In the evening the stage came in and brought in the mail contractor Major [George] Chorponing.

December 3, 1854; Sunday. No rains to ~~day. Past the day about my hous in the~~ to day had no meeting on acount of the dampness of the ground.

December 4, 1854; Monday. To day passed the day about the house. At night finished my writeing for the mail.

December 5, 1854; Tuesday. To day the mail started for the [Salt] Lake, no rain to day.

December 6, 1854; Wednesday. Spent the day on my House. Weather quite cool.

December 7, 1854; Thursday. To day worked on my House. In the evening had an interview with some of the Brethren from Coal Creek [Cedar City, Utah]. They talked going to Yucypa in view of settling some ten families.

December 8, 1854; Friday. Passed the day at home weather still fine. To day finished cl[e]aning for delivery the wheat on the Dalton contract.

December 9, 1854; Saturday. Past the day at home. The wind high in the evening.

December 10, 1854; Sunday. Held meeting. Some of the emigrants from Coal Creek were there.

December 11, 1854; Monday. Received an order from Cheno for a load of flower [flour]. To day made an arangemen[t] to go with Br [George W.] Sirrine to look at some land.

December 12, 1854; Tuesday. Went to the mill and saw Br [George W.] Sirrine and looked at the land returned home very weary.

December 13, 1854; Wednesday. To day Brs Hopkins & Mathews started to see Mr McClanihan. to get the money for the wheat.

December 14, 1854; Thursday. Went with some of Coal Creek Brethren to see some land. To night the mail arived also Br [Theodore] Thorp. Some signs of rain.

December 15, 1854; Friday. To day went to let Br [Jacob] Casteel have lots [acres of land]. My health not good.

December 16, 1854; Saturday. Remained at home.

December 17, 1854; Sunday. Held meeting weather fine ~~on~~.

December 18, 1854; Monday.[129] Br [Richard R.] Hopkins started for

129. This entry appears after the entry dated the 19th, Lyman having realized his

Los Angelos in company with Capt [Jefferson] Hunt who was starting for the [state] Legislature.

December 19, 1854; Tuesday. To day in consequence of his drunken and boistrous conduct to his family and others I discharged Br [Edward] Davis from the mill.

December 20, 1854; Wednesday. Had a labour with Br [Edward] Davis who confessed that he had done wrong but was sory and would do beter on which condition he was forgiven. Brs J[oseph] Tanner was present and also A[ndrew] Lytle Wm Mathews also his son William.

December 21, 1854; Thursday. Br [Richard R.] Hopkins still away.

December 22, 1854; Friday. To day Br [Richard R.] H[opkins] returned haveing done the Buisness that called him away ~~and~~.

December 23, 1854; Saturday. To day passed the day about my House.

December 24, 1854; Sunday. Held meeting. In the evening went with Br [Richard R.] Hopkins to see Cister [Agnes] Flake in relation to her makeing a will.

December 25, 1854; Monday. To day went with Br [William] Crosby to locate his farm. Returned and dined with Br [Theodore] Turley. To day Messers [Lewis] Granger[,] Osborn and others from Losagles [Los Angeles] came to town.

December 26, 1854; Tuesday. Passed the day in Town.

December 27, 1854; Wednesday. To day the Losangles [Los Angeles] party started for home. To day killed my hogs.

December 28, 1854; Thursday. Passed the day about home.

December 29, 1854; Friday. To day the mail came in from the coast brought leters from [John M.] Horner & [Quartus S.] Sparks.

December 30, 1854; Saturday. Past the day about my House.

December 31, 1854; Sunday. Held meeting some strangers present.

January 1, 1855; Monday. Had a fine rain. The work on my house still progressing slowly. Made out some Bills of finishings for the House to send up the country by Br [Theodore] Thorp.

January 2, 1855; Tuesday. To day the stage left for San Pedro by it Br [Theodore] Thorp by whom I sent three hundred dollars to get some things for me.

---

failure to include an entry for the 18th and corrected it.

January 3, 1855; Wednesday. To day Br [James H.] Rollins started to town with two teames with Flour and Lumber. To day the County Court was in session.

January 4, 1855; Thursday. It stormed. Passed the day at home.

January 5, 1855; Friday. Wrote Leters for the [Salt] Lake [mail and] received mail from the north.

January 6, 1855; Saturday. The mail defers starting until Monday.

January 7, 1855; Sunday. Held meeting were adresed by br [Benjamin F.] Grouard [and] in the evening br Noris was Baptized.

January 8, 1855; Monday. To day the mail started. In the evening meet with the City Council.

January 9, 1855; Tuesday. Looked [at] land.

January 10, 1855; Wednesday. The same [as above].

January 11, 1855; Thursday. Let Br [Horace A.] Skin[n]er and [wife Laura Ann] Farnsworth [Skinner] have some land. To day Br [William] Crosby agreed to buy ~~TS~~ Thomas Bingham's interest in the Mountain Saw Mill for the sum of three thousand dollars.

January 12, 1855; Friday. To day went [to] see some lots for Br [Ellis] Eames.

January 13, 1855; Saturday. Went to see some land with Br Sidney Tanner.

January 14, 1855; Sunday. Held meeting. In the evening went to see Sister Rich who was sick.[130] The weather warm and pleasant.

January 15, 1855; Monday. Went to the mill to let some people have some land, at night meet with the City Council.

January 16, 1855; Tuesday. Started for Ucypa [Yucaipa] in company with Brs [Richard R.] Hopkins[,] [James H.] Rollins & [Alden] Jackson stayed at Br [James S.] Browns over night. Had a talk with the Indians and gave them the possession of the place where [illegible] had lived who is to leave within the next 8 days with this they seemed well pleased.

January 17, 1855; Wednesday. Returned home on our way stoped at San Bernardino. In the evening returned home.[131]

130. This is in reference to one of the three (of six) wives Charles Rich brought with him to San Bernardino: Mary Ann, Amelia, and Harriet. Arrington, *Charles C. Rich*, 158.

131. The town was being laid out and houses built beyond the fort, whereas Lyman's house, which was being enlarged, was within the stockade.

January 18, 1855; Thursday. Made some efforts to raise some money But did not succeed.

January 19, 1855; Friday. Passed the day about Home. Weather warm and dry.

January 20, 1855; Saturday. To day the Election came off to fill the vacencies in the City Council. Sidney Tanner and Marcus L. Shepperd were elected councilmen. T B Noris atorney. Gilbard Summe pound keeper. This evening the mail came in from the coast.

January 21, 1855; Sunday. Held meeting in the course of the day shereff [Robert] Clift & Marshall Holiday & party returned with the horse theif they went after.

January 22, 1855; Monday. To day received of Br William Baxter the sum of one thousand dollars at 12 per cent per anum for 6 mont[h]s. Also engaged Br [S]parks to work on my house.

January 23, 1855; Tuesday. Went to where the boys were surveying land for the Tanners. To night I received 150 dollars From Eliza Tanner.

January 24, 1855; Wednesday. Had a well dug found water in ten ft. this evening some wind today a young man by the name of Singleton ^shot^ himself accidentaly and died of the wound about 9 oclock, P.M.

January 25, 1855; Thursday. This morning about 4 oclock Sister Agnes Flake died in the 36 year of her age. She had her reason till the last she fell asleep in peace and has gone to meet her departed husband [James].[132]

January 26, 1855; Friday. To day we buried Sister [Agnes] Flake. In the ^evening^ the stage came with the mail from the north ~~from the~~.

January 27, 1855; Saturday. To day went to the mill and got some 300 ft of lumber in the evening the City Council meet and done some buisness.

January 28, 1855; Sunday. To day held meeting weather fine some baptisms to day this evening some indications of rain.

January 29, 1855; Monday. Went to Mr. [Louis] Rubidoux of whom we borowed 1000 dollars for one month at three percent per month this evening the mail from Salt Lake arived and some 15 men for the States among whom was Br [William H.] Hooper of the firm of [John M.] Horner & Co. I received leters from my family and from Br [Charles C.] Rich who were all well at date.

---

132. When Flake died of tuberculosis, the Lymans took in three of her children. Lyman, *San Bernardino*, 305–06.

January 30, 1855; Tuesday. This morning br [Richard R.] Hopkins started for Los Angles in the stage. To day had a conversation with Br George Sirrine in relation to some thing that transpired on Sunday with which he was not pleased. Before leaveing he became satisfied to some extent.

January 31, 1855; Wednesday. Went to Br [Silas] Har[r]ises to get some [soil] turning done. In the evening Bishop [William] Crosby returned from the mountain.

February 1, 1855; Thursday. To day we had some rain went with Br [Sidney] Tanner to look at some land.

February 2, 1855; Friday. To day wrote some for the [Salt] Lake [mail].

February, 3, 1855; Saturday. Continued my writeing but the stage did not arive this evening. Br [Richard R.] Hopkins ariveed and brought the word that the steamer had not arived at San Pedro.

February 4, 1855; Sunday. To day held meeting told the people to bring in there [live]stock subscribed on Ranch acount.

February 5, 1855; Monday. Waited for the [mail] stage but it did not arive. To day the Court of sessions was in Cesion.

February 6, 1855; Tuesday. Court still in Cession. To day the mail arived.

February 7, 1855; Wednesday. To day we had some rain. Made some arangements to go to Town engaged a brand[ing iron] to be made for the Ranch [live]stock. To day the mail started for the [Salt] Lake.

February 8, 1855; Thursday. Started for Los Angelos with Br [James H.] Rollins lodged at the Monte.

February 9, 1855; Friday. Went to Town and attended to buisness in the evening returned to Monte.

February 10, 1855; Saturday. Returned home found all well.

February 11, 1855; Sunday. Held meeting weather cool.

February 12, 1855; Monday. To ^day^ the Probate Court was in Cession to atend to buisness conected with the Estate of Agnes Flake.[133]

133. Flake's death threw into question the ownership of her slaves, including her favorite, Lizzy (Freeman, *Life and Times of William Jordan Flake*, 14–24). She requested that another be sent from Utah during her illness, but Brigham Young intervened to prevent that (Amasa Lyman to Brigham Young, July 2, 1854, Brigham Young Collections, CHL). Her slaves were technically freed when they entered California, but they would not have known it (Scholten, "A Look into Black History in San Bernardino").

February 13, 1855; Tuesday. Received some [live]stock on Ranch Ac[coun]t.

February 14, 1855; Wednesday. Continued to receive [live]stock as above. This evening the Bishop came down from the mountain mill which was doeing very well.

February 15, 1855; Thursday. Sent the ranch [live]stock to Brother Robert M. Smith to herd[,] [in] number 26 head[;] to receive 4 head more 2 cows and 2 year olds.

February 16, 1855; Friday. Went to the mountain mill which we found doeing very well although the water was failing some from the dry winds.

February 17, 1855; Saturday. Returned home the wind was very high.

February 18, 1855; Sunday. Held meeting weather pleasant. In the evening the stage arived with the mail from the north. I received a leter from Edward Partridge on the Sandwich Isleands. Br [David] Seely returned from the north.

February 19, 1855; Monday. Today the Destrict Court was in Cession[,] Judge Haze presiding. To day some rain.

February 20, 1855; Tuesday. Court still in Cession. Heavy rain all day and very cold.

February 21, 1855; Wednesday. Heavy rain. To day the Court ajourned paid [Louis] Roubidoux one hundred & fifty dollars.

February 22, 1855; Thursday. To day went with Brs [William] Mathews & [William] Cox to select a place for bringing the water into the City. Had some rain. Dureing the day received some locust trees from the nursery of Br [Alden] Jackson.

February 23, 1855; Friday. Some rain went to the mill. In the evening ^had call from^ Brs [Benjamin F.] Johnson[,] Cairn [Thomas Karren][,] and [James] Lawson on their way to S[alt] Lake.[134]

February 24, 1855; Saturday. This evening went to Grist Mill still raineing some.

February 25, 1855; Sunday. Held meeting [and] were adressed in the morning by Brother [Benjamin] Johnson. In conclusion I made some remarks on the subject of a [prospecting] party[']s going to the mines to raise some gold to help us to pay our debts against the Rancho. At night

134. They were returning from a two-year mission to the Sandwich Islands. Journal History, Mar. 7, 1855.

had a meeting at which over fifty men promised or gave their names to go and get all they could and have it aplied in payment of the debt less the expences of their outfit and liveing if the same is furnished by Lyman & Rich [Company].

February 26, 1855; Monday. We prosicuted our arangements for mines. Increaseing signs of rain. This evening the mail from Salt Lake arived I received leters from my family[,] Br [Charles C.] Rich & Prest [Brigham] Young. News good in the main.

February 27, 1855; Tuesday. Still signs of rain. Went to the mill to secure the killing of some pork and the makeing of a cloth house [tent] for the mineing expedition.

February 28, 1855; Wednesday. Still some indications of rain. Passed the day at home.

March 1, 1855; Thursday. To day went to the mill where our pork was killed for the mines.

March 2, 1855; Friday. Commenced writeing for the [Salt] Lake [mail]. Weather fine.

March 3, 1855; Saturday. Closed up my communications to the [Salt] Lake.

March 4, 1855; Sunday. Held meeting Messers [Lewis] Granger[,] [Myron] Norton & Washburn~~n~~ were present.

March 5, 1855; Monday. Continued our exertions to get our party off for the mines the men mostly reported themselves deficient in outfit of every kind.

March 6, 1855; Tuesday. Still makeing preparation for the mineing party. To day Col Noris came in from his surveying on his way to San Francisco.

March 7, 1855; Wednesday. To ^day^ the party for the mines got ready to leave and one of the wagons started.

March 8, 1855; Thursday. To day the company started for the mines. Gave some citizens a caution in relation to some rabid dogs.

March 9, 1855; Friday. The northern mail came in not much news. I received a leter from Br Nathan Tanner.

March 10, 1855; Saturday. To day it rained all day. Filled small bill at the store for Col [Henry] Washington.[135]

135. Washington was a US deputy surveyor.

March 11, 1855; Sunday. Had no meeting to day as it rained all day. At night had an interview with Dr [Ira] Burrus & Br N[athan] C Tenney.

March 12, 1855; Monday. To^day^ still rainy. In the evening Mr [Jonathan] Scott & [Abel] Sterns[136] arived from Los Angles.

March 13, 1855; Tuesday. Still raineing was in the rain the most of the day. At night the rain ceased until morning.

March 14, 1855; Wednesday. To day still raineing. Sterling [Driggs] went to cary Judge Scott out of Town.

March 15, 1855; Thursday. Some little rain several Houses damaged by the water.

March 16, 1855; Friday. The weather fine. This morning Jas. Grible left ~~prision~~ prison and promised to keep the peace.

March 17, 1855; Saturday. Weather fine and pleasant.

March 18, 1855; Sunday. Held meeting in the school house. This evening Mr [Phineas] Baning from Losangles [Los Angeles] arived to advise with me about takeing goods to Salt Lake.

March 19, 1855; Monday. The weather pleasant commenced clearing my ground for a fruit garden.

March 20, 1855; Tuesday. Weather fine.

March 21, 1855; Wednesday. To day Br Baldwin started up the mountain to put up our circular saw. Some hands were repareing the road.

March 22, 1855; Thursday. To day Brs Noris went to Town Los Angeles, Br M[arcus] L. Shepherd started for the mines, with a party of eight. Weather still warm.

March 23, 1855; Friday. Weather fine. Bishop [William] Crosby went to the mountain. In the everning I atended a meeting of the teachers and gave them some instruction for the conference.

March 24, 1855; Saturday. Weather fine mail arr[i]ved from the coast.

March 25, 1855; Sunday. Held meeting. In the ^evening^ the mail from Salt Lake arived with news from General [Charles C.] Rich and a circular from the Presidency.[137]

March 26, 1855; Monday. To day I plowed my garden. This evening

---

136. Abel Stearns, originally from Massachusetts but a citizen of Mexico, was a wealthy cattle rancher and flour mill owner.

137. The circular came from Rich's lobbying in Salt Lake City. "Owing to the scarcity of money" in the colony, the church would contribute $38,000 to the remaining balance. Journal History, Mar. 8, 1855; Clark, *Messages of the First Presidency*, 2:157–58.

Bishop [William] Crosby came down from the mountain with lumber some indications of rain.

March 27, 1855; Tuesday. Weather fine. Stage left for the Coast. To day demolished the old office.

March 28, 1855; Wednesday. Went to the mountain mill in company with Br [Richard R.] Hopkins.

March 29, 1855; Thursday. Started for home but broak our wagon and brought no lumber. Found when I got home that the old bowry was removed.

March 30, 1855; Friday. Cloudy with rain on the mountains. To day Brs [Andrew] Lytle & [William] Cox returned from the mines with the report of their failure to get gold as they hoped when they started.

March 31, 1855; Saturday. Still signs of rain. To day prepared my ground for planting in my garden.

April 1, 1855; Sunday. Held meeting.

April 2, 1855; Monday. Weather still pleasant. This evening the mail from the north arived.

April 3, 1855; Tuesday. Remained at home my health poor wrote for the [Salt] Lake.

April 4, 1855; Wednesday. To day the mail started for the [Salt] Lake wind high from the north.

April 5, 1855; Thursday. To day I exchanged car[ri]ages with Col [Alden] Jackson weather still fine.

April 6, 1855; Friday. Comenced the cession of our confrence small audience in atendance.

April 7, 1855; Saturday. Continued our conference with increaseing numbers and interest weather fine.

April 8, 1855; Sunday. Our place of meeting full to overflowing. In the evening administered the sacrament[138] and ajourned to Sept 6th. Weather still fine.

April 9, 1855; Monday. Made some preperations for sending some goods to the [Salt] Lake country. This morning received two hundred dollars from Br [Thomas] Tompkins on Ranch acount. This morning Br [Willard] Whipple started for San Jose[,] by him I sent 40 dollars to

138. The eucharist was administered erratically in the early church years.

bring on his return Sister Cook[139] from the Hospital. The money was furnished by her sister Tanner.

April 10, 1855; Tuesday. Secured a wagon for the trip to the [Salt] Lake for the use of one here.

April 11, 1855; Wednesday. To day Col Noris came to town for some suplies. Talked with Br [Thomas W.] Whitett [Whitaker] about buying his lot and [blank].

April 12, 1855; Thursday. Engaged 2 teems to go up the mountain for lumber.

April 13, 1855; Friday. The teems went up the mountain Bro [Thomas] Whitaker with them.

April 14, 1855; Saturday. Teems returned from the mountain with lumber.

April 15, 1855; Sunday. Did not atend meeting. In the evening the people were adressed by Mr. Calwell a Methodist preacher.

April 16, 1855; Monday. Heavy rain. To day settled with Br Thomas Bingham prepareitory to his starting to the [Salt] Lake.

April 17, 1855; Tuesday. To day our wagons started for the [Salt] Lake some showery in the mountains.

April 18, 1855; Wednesday. To day Br [James H.] Rollins started on his journey on horse Back.

April 19, 1855; Thursday. Weather fine passed the day at home.

April 20, 1855; Friday. To day Br Hendricks returned from the Cajone. Br [Isaac] Goodwin laid some stone for me. Col [Henry] Washington came in from the plains for some hands.

April 21, 1855; Saturday. Had an election for super[v]isors for our County there was some opposition from a faction headed by V[alentine] J. Hering[,] F[rederick] M. Van Luven & B[enjamin] F Grouard. The faction candidates received[:] Grouard 13[,] Van Leuven 19 votes. [Our candidates received:] [William] Crosby 100 [Daniel] Starks 89.[140]

April 22, 1855; Sunday. Held meeting br [Benjamin F.] Grouard made some ^remarks^ reflecting blame on the community as being the

139. Probably Mary Ann Cook, wife of John Cook and daughter of Theodore Turley.

140. Grouard seems to have realized too late that his decision to run for office would be unwelcome. He and the other opposition candidates were excommunicated after showing what Henry Boyle called "a regular mob spirit" in their challenge of church-approved candidates. Lyman, *San Bernardino*, 152–56.

cause of his misfortune and also declared his intentions to go to the state of N. H. to outstrip the influence of his evil Genuse [genius].[141]

April 23, 1855; Monday. To day Br [Richard R.] Hopkins started for Los Angeles on buisness and caried down Leut Parks. To day received $50.00 for Ranch barley. In the evening the northern mail arived with leters and papers containing the news of the Death of the Czar of Rus[s]ia.[142]

April 24, 1855; Tuesday. Weather fine passed the day at home received a load of lumber By Br Rawlin of eight hundred ft.

April 25, 1855; Wednesday. To day Sheriff [Robert] Clift went to Mill Creek to make some arests.

April 26, 1855; Thursday. To day the mail from Salt Lake arived bringing papers and leters news generally good. Br [Charles C.] Rich starts for this place on the first of May.

April 27, 1855; Friday. To ^day^ wrote to Br B[enjamin] F. Mathews in the south[ern states].

April 28, 1855; Saturday. Weather fine.

April 29, 1855; Sunday. Held meeting at which Brs B[enjamin] F Grouard [and] F[rederick] M Van Luven were disfellowshiped for pursueing a f[r]actious course of conduct.[143]

April 30, 1855; Monday. To day gave leters of recomendation to Mr [William] Sanford[,] [a freighter] who was goeing to Salt Lake to sell goods.

May 1, 1855; Tuesday. Started with Br J[oseph] Mathews for the coast went to the Monte[,] there we met the people we owe goeing after. Staid at Mr Crandalls.[144]

May 2, 1855; Wednesday. Returned home found all as well as when I left.

May 3, 1855; Thursday. Wrote some leters for the [Salt] Lake to day Br [Walter] Dodge arived with his family received $100 dollars titheing from Br Willard Whipple.[145]

---

141. Grouard was originally from New Hampshire and determined he could be more successful in his home state.

142. Nicholas I died of pneumonia during the Crimean War on Mar. 2.

143. A year later a notice in the *Deseret News* would tell of additional excommunications of high-profile settlers Nathan Hart and Robert Smith. Journal History, Mar. 16, 1856.

144. Probably Lucien D. Crandall, a grocer.

145. Several families from San Francisco arrived in San Bernardino in April–May

May 4, 1855; Friday. To day went to look at some lots with Br Dodge who succeeded in pleaseing himself.

May 5, 1855; Saturday. Remited some money to Francisco and Los Angelos by Mrs Noris & Rockefel[le]r.

May 6, 1855; Sunday. Held meeting weather fine.

May 7, 1855; Monday. ~~To held~~ The City election was held at which the regular nomination was sustained. Some indications of rain.

May 8, 1855; Tuesday. Went to look out some roads some rain on the mountain received my freight from the coast.

May 9, 1855; Wednesday. To day joined in matrimony Mr. B[enjamin] F Dewy & Miss Alvira Smithson.

May 10, 1855; Thursday. Remained at home. Weather warm some signs of rain.

May 11, 1855; Friday. To day called on the school which is doeing very well.

May 12, 1855; Saturday. Weather fine. This evening meet with the common Council.

May 13, 1855; Sunday. To day held meeting had a full house and an attentive one weather fine.

May 14, 1855; Monday. Received the mail from the north. To day advised with Brs [Willard] Whipple[,] [Walter] Dodge and [George] Warren in relation to their goeing into trade.

May 15, 1855; Tuesday. My health quite poor. ~~Received some money for land from Daniel Taft.~~

May 16, 1855; Wednesday. Received some money from Daniel Taft on Ranch Act $90.00.

May 17, 1855; Thursday. Brs [Nathan] Tanner[,] [Chauncy] West & [Redick] Allread arived her[e] on their way to Salt Lake.

May 18, 1855; Friday. To day took a ride with Bros [Nathan] Tanner & [Chauncy] West. My health not good[;] had an interview with Col [Isaac] Williams from Cheno.

May 19, 1855; Saturday. My health poor kept my bed most of the day.

May 20, 1855; Sunday. Held meeting. My health very poor. To day

---

1855 en route to Salt Lake City. They included the Brimhalls, Dodges, Smiths, Warrens, Wilkinses, and Whipples. Journal History, Apr. 30, 1855.

the factionists held meeting at the house of Charles Chapman the meeting was addresed by Mr. [Frederick M.] Van Luven.

May 21, 1855; Monday. The company from Santa Clara arived in good health and spirits.

May 22, 1855; Tuesday. Visited the camp of the Brethren [from San Francisco] who concluded to change their locality.

May 23, 1855; Wednesday. Had an interview with Br [William] Walice who concluded to stop here and help us. This evening Brs [Jefferson] Hunt & [Theodore] Thorpe arived by the stage from the north.

May 24, 1855; Thursday. Went to City Creek with a party of the Brethren [and] returned in the evening. My health poor weather warm.

May 25, 1855; Friday. Worked on the road to day Judge [Benjamin] Hay[e]s and party arived from Losangles [Los Angeles].[146]

May 26, 1855; Saturday. The Destrict Court was in cession Judge [Benjamin] Hayse presiding. Weather warm.

May 27, 1855; Sunday. Held meeting. We were adressed by the returning missionaries Brs [Reuben] McBride[,] [Chauncy W.] West & [Nathan] Tanner & also Capt [Jefferson] Hunt. The weather warm the congregation large.

May 28, 1855; Monday. Received of Wm Wallace four thousand dollars & of Br [Walter] Dodge eleven hundred. To day had a labour with Br Noris who promised reformation.

May 29, 1855; Tuesday. This morning Br [Richard R.] Hopkins started for Losangles [Los Angeles] & Br [Willard] Whipple for San Francisco. My health very poor.

May 30, 1855; Wednesday. My health very poor weather very warm.

May 31, 1855; Thursday. My health still poor weather very hot. Party starting on their journey for the [Salt] Lake.

June 1, 1855; Friday. To day weather hot. My health poor.

June 2, 1855; Saturday. Went to the cayone and returned.

June 3, 1855; Sunday. Held meeting. My health very poor.

June 4, 1855; Monday. Weather some cooler. Had an interview with Mr. [Lewis] Granger.

June 5, 1855; Tuesday. To day General [Charles C.] Rich came in from Salt Lake[,] with him came his eldest son [Joseph Rich].

146. Two blank pages follow before the diary resumes.

June 6, 1855; Wednesday. Went to meet Br [George Q.] Cannon at the Cahoon [Cajon Pass].

June 7, 1855; Thursday. Passed the day with Br [Charles C.] Rich.

June 8, 1855; Friday. To day keept to my bed from the effects of illness until the 13th.

June 10, 1855; Sunday. ~~Held meeting Br Rich preached My health not good.~~

June 11, 1855; Monday. ~~Passed the day in town My health poor.~~

June 23, 1855; Saturday.[147] Saturday on which day our special Confrence convened. The first buisness of which was to concider and act upoon the case of Prest David Seely who was droped from his presidency for his abus[e] to Br Lewis Jacobs. Then presented to the conference the subject of the payment of Ranch Debts which the people all agreed to help pay.

June 24, 1855; Sunday. Continued our Conference. To day the conference voted to make a last strong effort to meet the Debt on The Ranch and 80 of the Brethren volunteered to help raise the money.

June 25, 1855; Monday. Concluded and ajourned our conference.

June 26, 1855; Tuesday. In the afternoon meet set apart and blesed the brethren for their mission.

June 27, 1855; Wednesday. Wrote our circular to the Saints and inhabitents of this state asking their cooperation in paying for San Bernardino.[148]

June 28, 1855; Thursday. This morning Br [Richard R.] Hopkins started for Los Angeles to procure the printing of our circular and attend to other Buisness.[149]

---

147. The entries for the 10th and 11th have a large X drawn through them and a note that says, "From the 13th to the (23d)," indicating that Lyman's health was poor and he stopped recording until June 23.

148. This plea from Lyman and Rich was sent throughout the state and published in newspapers inviting anyone interested to invest in San Bernardino, candidly admitting that the colony needed funds. Lyman and Rich to "Saints and All Friendly to the Cause of Truth in the State of California," July 1, 1855, Amasa Lyman Papers, box 4, fd 22, CHL; "Mormon Missionaries," *Los Angeles Star*, Aug. 4, 1855.

149. Here the entries for 1855 end. The remainder of the entries are for 1876, with financial notations in the back for 1854–55.

5 "To Save the Effusion of Blood," 1855–1858

Lyman would not be able to rest or find peace when Brigham Young called him home in October 1855 to conduct a preaching tour throughout the territory. During this era of the Mormon Reformation, the Mountain Meadows Massacre, and the Utah War, Lyman kept his diary sporadically and never stepped back far enough, despite being caught in the weeds of these events, to offer a broad view. For instance, he was in southern Utah a few months after the brutal mass murder of 120 emigrants in 1857 but wrote nothing about it, focusing instead on his own travels and the people he met. Yet the sketchy documentation he does offer during this period speaks volumes about the nature of travel in those days, the kinds of relationships that existed between Mormons and non-Mormons—including Indians, what people's concerns were, and what the state of his family, church, and the nation were at the time. The diary ends abruptly in May 1858, but he picked it up again two years later in preparation for his mission to England.

October 25, 1855; Thursday.[1] Started for Salt Lake [at] 5½ oclock traviled as far as the Cajon Pass and camped [at] 10½ oclock. Weather fine and pleasant.[2]

---

1. A note on the first page of this diary states in pencil that it was "perused by Andrew Jenson in Aug 1915."

2. Lyman kept a list of financial transactions between June and Oct. 1855 but nothing more. For example, "Monday 20th paid for bord $15. [On the] 21st Received of Wm Crosby $30. Loaned Dr. Andrew $20." These financial notes have been omitted from the current presentation.

October 26, 1855; Friday. Waited in Camp for the remainder of our company. In the after noon Mr Davenports & Family came into camp. After night the returned missionaries came in[3] and about midnight General [Charles C.] Rich came into camp. The weather cool. Marion[4] came from home to night.

October 27, 1855; Saturday. Traviled to the foot of the mountain where we arived about 9 oclock. Had some grass for our stock. This evening General J[efferson] Hunt was with us.

October 28, 1855; Sunday. To day passed over the mountain which we accomplished by 10 oclock and here parted with our friends and passed on to the Mohave [River] where we arived about 4½ oclock. This evening meet party from Salt Lake City traviling. Very dusty.

October 29, 1855; Monday. This morning started at 7 oclock.[5] Traviled 25 m[ile]s and camped by 3 oclock. Good water & grass, this morning the horse belonging to Br [William] Fotheringham[6] ran away on the way back to the ^mountain^. We left Br F. in pursuit.

October 30, 1855; Tuesday. This morning left camp at 7 oclock[,] traviled and camped below the round mountain at 2 oclock. Br [William] F[otheringham] returned last night at 9 oclock haveing folowed his horse to the ~~f~~ top of the mountain. This morning we past Mr [Benjamin F.] Grouard who came up in the night.

October 31, 1855; Wednesday. Started from camp at 2 oclock and traviled to lower water on the River and stoped at 3 oclock. Stayed until 5, and left and traviled out on the plain some 8 or 10 m[ile]s. Camped on good grass.

November 1, 1855; Thursday. Left camp at 6½ oclock reached the Biter ~~sp i^i^ n~~ Springs at 5 oclock found the water scarce. To day meet several droves of stock looking rather poor.

November 2, 1855; Friday. Started at 7½ oclock A.M. Reached the

---

3. The missionaries returning from Australia (Elder Frost), the East Indies (Findlay, Fotheringham), and the Sandwich Islands (Allred, Keeler) joined Lyman's wagon train back to Salt Lake City. "Arrivals," *Deseret News Weekly*, Dec. 5, 1855.

4. Francis Marion Lyman, Amasa Lyman's oldest son.

5. Lyman expected to make the journey between Salt Lake and San Bernardino many more times, and so he likely underlined how long it took to travel from one stop to another for future reference.

6. Fotheringham was returning from a mission to India that also took him to Singapore, Hong Kong, and the Pacific islands. Fotheringham, *William Fotheringham*.

Salt Springs[7] at 6½ oclock. To day encountered a severe storm of wind that made us nearly Blind. At this place we fed and tied up our stock.

November 3, 1855; Saturday. Started at 1½ oclock. Reached ^Maryoshe^ by 9½ oclock.

November 4, 1855; Sunday. Left camp at 8 oclock. Reached the Resting Spring at 2 oclock.

November 5, 1855; Monday. Started 7½ oclock. Reached the stump springs after dark the Spanish Mares belonging to Br Maxwell went back on the road. No grass at this camping. Fed our stock Grain.

November 6, 1855; Tuesday. This morning some 3 men went in pursuit of the stock with which they returned about 11 oclock. A part of our camp started at the useual time of starting and arived at Cottenwood springs about 10 oclock P.M. That portion of the camp that remained with me started at 11½ oclock A.M. After traviling some 12 m[ile]s one of the mules that belonged to Br [Charles C.] Rich was taken sick and had to be taken from the team. The hindrance caused us to camp at Mountain Springs where we arived at 9 oclock P.M.

November 7, 1855; Wednesday. Resumed our journey at 6¼ oclock and reached Cottenwood Springs at 7½ oclock, found the advance of our party all well with plenty of feed and water. We concluded to wait until tomorow to have the advantage of the Grass for our stock.

November 8, 1855; Thursday. Started 8½ oclock. As we were leaveing camp we meet Br Sloan on his way to uper California where his Daughter Mrs. Warner lives. The old man had one man and a woman with him. As we neared the Los Vages we meet some 5 Wagons on their way to California. We arived at Fort 3 oclock. Found Elder [William] Bringhurst and Company all well. We received a kind welcome from the members of the mission.[8]

This Mission we found in a Prosperous condition. The fort in process of erection is a fine structure encloseing an area of some 150 ft square

7. The trail from California to Utah skirted the southern edge of Death Valley where Bitter Springs, Salt Spring, and Resting Springs were vital watering holes, each about forty miles from one another. They were formerly stops along the Old Spanish Trail. In what is now Nevada, the path detoured to Stump Spring, Mountain Springs, and Cottonwood Spring along a route explored in 1844 by John C. Frémont.

8. Bringhurst and twenty-nine others had been called to establish the fort at Las Vegas Springs. Discovery of lead in the nearby mountains created confusion and turmoil in the colony and eventually the abandonment of the fort. Today it is a Nevada state park.

designed when finished to furnish some 28 tenaments. The walls are of Adobies on a foundation of rock and when completed will be 14 ft high with 2 entrances, the site is well selected to answer the purposes of its Location. The natives were very friendly and working for food and clothing. We gave our stock in charge of some of the Red Brothers who keep them safely through the night and returned them to us in the morning.

November 9, 1855; Friday. Remained with the brethren and went with Br B[ringhurst] to look at the wheat and corn which was very fine. ~~(Saturday 10th)~~ In the evening had a meeting with the members of the mission who were there and some of the Lamanites [Book of Mormon term for Indians], we had a pleasant time.

November 10, 1855; Saturday. ~~From our~~ Started on our journey and af^ter^ haveing traviled some few ~~ms~~ m[i]l[e]s from the Fort I received by the hand of a carier a leter from my sister Mrs. Ruth E. Goo[d]all in the State of V. T. from whom I had not heard for some 20 years,[9] also one from Brother W[eeden] V. Hakes informeing me of the Death of his Daughter Sister [Susan Hakes] Fabun. We traviled into the Desert and camped until after midnight when we resumed our journey.

November 11, 1855; Sunday. Traviled as far as the Mudy [River] where we were meet by a larg party of the natives of whom some hundred and fifty had been Baptized and apeared very friendly. We engaged the Indians to herd and wa[t]ch our stock all of which they performed Faithfully to our satisfaction. We left them feeling well.

November 12, 1855; Monday. Started for the Rio Virgin where we arived and camped about 8 oclock. Here again the Indians Guarded our stock for us for less than they would have expected of us if they had rendered us no service.

November 13, 1855; Tuesday. Started at <u>9 oclock</u>. Camped again at <u>1 oclock</u>. Again employed the natives to Guard the stock. This evening wrote some for home. While eating diner a party of five men passed from Salt Lake 2 weeks since, and before I had completed my leters [the carrier] E[dward] Hope returned on his way to San Bernardino haveing left Br [Leonard S.] Conger [to] pursue his way alone. I sent my communication for home by him. Some slight rain this evening weather cool.

9. This was the start of a twenty-two-year correspondence between the siblings that Lyman cherished.

November 14, 1855; Wednesday. This morning the Indians returned our stock to us and we started from camp at 8½ oclock. Camped again at 12½ oclock with high winds. Again gave our stock in charge to the Indians. Just at dark Br David Savage and party with the mail came into camp. With them were some five or six Utah Indians on their way to the Mudy to trade for women and children. This evening it snowed on the mountain ajacent to the river.

November 15, 1855; Thursday. This morning our stock came in looking very well. We parted with the mail party and resumed our journey at 8 oclock. Camped at Beever Dam[10] at 2 oclock wind high. To night had but one Indian.

November 16, 1855; Friday. Started before the sun was up and reached the Santa Clara [River] [at] 6½ oclock. To night herded our own stock had good feed.

November 17, 1855; Saturday. Started 8½ oclock and camped at the head of the Santa Clara [River] at 5 oclock. To night had the Indians to herd our stock. To night Br [Benjamin R.] Hultz[11] cattle ran away to the Mountain Meadow. Had the Indian Chief Jim with us to night.

November 18, 1855; Sunday. Started 8 oclock. Traviled 8 m[ile]s and meet Brother [Benjamin] Hultz with his cattle. Camped at the meadow at 2 oclock some snow on the hills good feed. To night Br Hultz came into camp.

November 19, 1855; Monday. This morning started at 8 oclock on the new road which we found to be much beter than the old one.[12] Camped at 3 oclock some snow through the day. At evening the clouds broak away. We had good feed at this place.

November 20, 1855; Tuesday. This morning started at 8 oclock. Traveled until 11 oclock when we arived at Coal Creek [Cedar City][13] where

10. Beaver Dam is immediately west of the Virgin River Gorge, where Old Highway 91 runs south from Shivwits on the Paiute Reservation west of what is now St. George to meet up with today's I-15 near Mesquite, Nevada.

11. Benjamin R. Hulse was a missionary at the Las Vegas Fort under William Bringhurst.

12. The new road was funded by Congress to get mail to southern California. Lyman, *Overland Journey from Utah to California*, 5.

13. At the time, Fort Cedar was a small settlement in the Iron Mission. Isaac Haight and others built a blast furnace there in 1851 on the Little Muddy Creek, renaming it Coal Creek. The iron works operated on and off again for seven years.

we were meet and welcomed by Br [Isaac] Hayte [Haight] and the brethren of [this] place and our selves and stock were kindly cared for with hay and grain. This evening held meeting and preached to the people Lodged at Br Haytes.

November 21, 1855; Wednesday. This morning left Coal creek for Parowan where we arived [at] 3 oclock. Stoped with Br H[orace] M. Alexanders whom with his family we found well as was the people. This evening meet with Brs [George B.] Wallace and [Joseph B.] Nobles[14] who were on a mission from Salt Lake through the Southern settlement.

November 22, 1855; Thursday. Passed the day in the city. Preached to the people. At 6 oclock some indications of a storm.

November 23, 1855; Friday. This morning it snowed on acount of which we defered starteing until we learned that the Prest [Brigham Young] would start one week from Monday next for Fillmore.[15] On heareing of which we started on our journey at 2 oclock it was still storming. Traviled as far as Buck Horn Springs[16] where we arived after dark where we camped with some of our party who had preceded us a few hours. At night the storm abated.

November 24, 1855; Saturday. This morning resumed our journey. Traviled as far as the Beaver [River] which we crossed. Passed on some five or six m[ile]s and camped. Some snow on the ground. To day meet 2 parties of gold hunters on their way to California to find the realiz^e^ation of their[17] Golden Dreams. They were traviling on foot with their beds and provisions packed on some poor Horses.

November 25, 1855; Sunday. To day traviled to and camped in the Can^y^on east of Dog Valey[18] where we found Messers [John B.] Guard [Gard] and Williams who had preceded us from Parowan. They passed on to Corn Creek [Kanosh]. We had good grass our stock done well.

November 26, 1855; Monday. Traviled to Fillmore where we were

14. Wallace and Noble were on a three-month "home mission" to southern Utah, Wallace having previously been in the presidency of the British Mission and Noble a member of the original First Quorum of Seventy.

15. Fillmore was so named to flatter US President Millard Fillmore and served as the capital of the territory for five years, 1851–56. Lyman records passing state legislators on their way to meetings in, for instance, the entry for Nov. 30, 1855.

16. Buckhorn Springs was a small watering hole between Panguitch and Beaver.

17. There is a page break and Lyman repeated the phrase "of their."

18. Dog Valley is six miles north of Cove Fort.

well received by the brethren to whom we preached at night Lodged with Br [John A.] Ray Prest of the place.

November 27, 1855; Tuesday. Traviled and camped within 3 m[ile]s of the Severe River where we meet Br J[acob] H[amblin] missionary to the Indians on his way to Coal Creek with some goods for that place.

November 28, 1855; Wednesday. Traviled to Nephi City[19] on Salt Creek where we arived about 7 oclock. To day 2 of my mules failed and we had to drop them from the team. We stoped with sister [Martha] Haywood[20] who entertained us kindly as also did Br [John] Wo[o]lf[, also] our stock.

November 29, 1855; Thursday. This morning started on our journey. I here left off two of mules from my cariage. Traviled to day to Palmyra[21] where we were all kindly cared for by br [Stephen] Markham and the Saints under his care. To night spoke to the people who all appeared well satisfied Lodged with Br. M[arkham].

November 30, 1855; Friday. To day traviled to and stoped in the settlement called Lake City [American Fork] under the charge of Br [Leonard E.] Harrington by whom I was kindly entertained. In the evening spoke to the people. In course of the night there was a high wind from the south folowed with a change of the wind to the north. To day meet Father [Isaac] Morley and wife on their way to Fillmore. Made no call at Provo.

December 1, 1855; Saturday. Breakfasted early and was on our way to the City [of Salt Lake] the ~~the~~ termination of our journey where we arived without accident about 5½ oclock. Found my family all well and we all felt to thank God that we had been preserved to meet again. Found Presidents [Brigham] Young and [Heber C.] Kimball in rather poor health.

December 2, 1855; Sunday. This morning went to visit President [Brigham] Young whom I found feeble but improveing. Attended meeting heard Br [Hugh] Findley give a naration of some of the incidents of his mission in Hindostan.[22] In the afternoon I spoke to the people.

---

19. Nephi was settled in 1851 and named after a Book of Mormon prophet.

20. Martha Spence Heywood, a plural wife of Joseph L Heywood, was a school teacher in Nephi.

21. Palmyra was named after Joseph Smith's hometown in upstate New York.

22. Hindostan referred to northern India (now also Bangladesh and Pakistan). Hugh Findlay and William Willes traveled there in 1851 but struggled to gain converts.

Subsequent to the meeting I meet with the prayr circle ^over^ ~~at~~ the Prests Office, at which time the Prest gave me instruction to remain and preach to the people for a time and then to travil south as far as Fillmore for the same purpose.

December 3, 1855; Monday. This morning meet with Br [Heber C.] Kimball as he was starting for Fillmore in rather feeble tho slowly improveing Health. The weather pleasant and warm.

December 4, 1855; Tuesday. To day was called to attend the funerel of the Son of Bishop N[athaniel] H. Felt[23] who was absent on a mission to East. Spake to those present on the ocasion. Here meet with Bishop J[oseph] L. Heywood with [whom] I last meet in Uper California and other old Friends.

December 5, 1855; Wednesday. To day paid the Tything Office one thousand dollars in cash to the Cr[edit] of Lyman and Rich, also delivered to Bishop [Edward] Hunter one mule valued at Eighty dollars to the Cr of Charles Crismon.

December 6, 1855; Thursday. Passed the day at home with my family. In the evening rode in my cariage with some of the family as far as Br J[ohn] Steels. The weather Cloudy with indications of storm. Made some preparation for sending my team north for some hay.

December 7, 1855; Friday. This morning the promised storm was on us. The snow fell freely and in a short time our city and surrounding country had doned the robes of winter. To night attended a weding party at Br S[eth] M. Blairs.[24] Some snow falling. Returned home at 10½ oclock at which time it was clear and starlight.

December 8, 1855; Saturday. This morning the weather clear sent my team to Br E[zra] T. Clarks for some hay. Made some calls on some sisters whose husbands were absent on missions.

December 9, 1855; Sunday. Spake to the People in the tabernacle. This evening my team returned with Hay.[25]

---

23. Nine-year-old Nathaniel died the day before while his father, Nathaniel H. Felt, was in New York City co-editing *The Mormon* periodical and Washington, DC, meeting with politicians, including President Franklin Pierce.

24. Seth Blair married Sarah Maria East in mid-November.

25. The discourse hinted at Lyman's evolving beliefs about Jesus, in that he suggested that Christ was a man who became perfect by following the word of God. "He was, simply, a holy man. How came he to be holy? Just as you and I … [by] being guided

December 10, 1855; Monday. To day sent my team and cariage to cary an old lady to the grave yard. Made some few buisness calls in the city.

December 11, 1855] Tuesday. Spent the day in writeing for the south. Some snow falling through the day [but] rather warm.

December 12, 1855; Wednesday. To day visited Br Sars and left with him some Rose cutings from the South. Returned and wrote some and in the evening visited Bishop Thomas Callister. This evening received a call from Br [John] Lyon the poet.[26]

December 13, 1855; Thursday. To day visited some of the Governors family[27] on the hill in the evening finished writeing for the south.

December 14, 1855; Friday. To day remained at home on acount of the weather. Paid Br Glover $20.00.

December 15, 1855; Saturday. Started on my northern tour and traviled as far as the City of Farmington. Put up with Br D[aniel] P. Clark. To night it stormed severely from the north.

December 16, 1855; Sunday. This morning spoke to the people who all listened attentively. At night stoped with Brother J[ohn] Gleasons.

December 17, 1855; Monday. To day traviled as far as the residence of Bishop William Kay[28] by whom we were kindly entertained. This evening it stormed severely but ceased with the seting of the sun. Made an apointment [to speak] for the next Thursday night at the Fort in Kays ward [Kaysville].

December 18, 1855; Tuesday. Started and traviled as far as Binghams Fort [Ogden] and put up with Sister Burk.[29] Spoke to the people this evening at their school room wich was filled to over flowing with an attentive audience.

---

by holy influences" Lyman's theology would lead to his separation from mainstream Mormonism beginning in 1867. *Journal of Discourses*, 3:166

26. Scottish emigrant John Lyon had a collection of verse, *The Harp of Zion: A Collection of Poems &c.*, published by the church in Liverpool in 1853 "for the benefit of the Perpetual Emigrating Fund."

27. Brigham Young was the territorial governor until the Utah War (1857–58) when non-Mormon Alfred Cumming was appointed to the office by President James Buchanan.

28. William Kay, an English emigrant, was the first bishop of Fort Kay, the original name of Kaysville due to the six-foot-high protective wall around the town.

29. Lydia and Charles Burk helped settle Bingham's Fort in 1851, three miles north of Ogden on what is now 2nd Street. Lydia was a daughter of Sidney Tanner.

December 19, 1855; Wednesday. Returned to Ogden City and stoped with Brs Jas. & Alexander Brown. To night spoke to the people of the city who crowded the meeting place altho it rained considerably.

December 20, 1855; Thursday. To day returned to Kays Fort put up with Br R[eddick] N. Allred. To night spoke to the people acording to the previous apointment. Had an attentive audience discourse reported by Br [William W.] Burton.

December 21, 1855; Friday. Returned to Farmington [and] stoped. Br A Burk myself stayed with Br [Daniel P.] Clark. This evening had an interview with Br Thos Grover with whom I had not meet before since [18]49. To night wind high.

December 22, 1855; Saturday. Returned home on our way called on and dined with the family of Br [Charles C.] Rich at his farm. Reached home at dark found all well. Weather very cool.

December 23, 1855; Sunday. Attended meeting at the Tabernacle. Heard a discourse from Br [Gilbert] Clements. At night attended meeting at the schoolroom in the 12th Ward heard a discours from Br. H[enry] Heriman [of the First Seven Presidents of Seventy]. Spoke to the people after him.

December 24, 1855; Monday. Passed the day at home writeing for the southern mail. In the evening made a call on Bishop [Thomas] Callister.

December 25, 1855; Tuesday. To day spoke to the people at the 14th Ward. Did not attend the festivities of the evening on acount of indisposition.

December 26, 1855; Wednesday. This morning remained in bed the most of the day. In the evening received a call from Brs Johnson and N[athan] Tanner.

December 27, 1855; Thursday. Went to dine with a part of the Governors family.[30] Had an interview with Br [William W.] Willis[31] and a very pleasant visit. Taried until evening then came home.

---

30. Governor Young was spending the holidays in Fillmore, 150 miles to the south, after opening the 1855–56 session of the legislature on December 11. On the 25th he and others were celebrating Christmas Day in the new capitol building. For his return to Salt Lake City, see the entry for Jan. 20, 1856.

31. William W. Willis was a former member of the Mormon Battalion and one of the settlers in the Iron Mission, where he would become mayor of Cedar City. He also helped colonize the town of Beaver.

December 28, 1855; Friday. Visited Brother Nathan Tanner. Taried until evening and returned home.

December 29, 1855; Saturday. Spent the day in writing. In the evening made a call on Sister Rich.

December 30, 1855; Sunday. Attended meeting in the Tabernacle spoke briefly to the people while the sacriment was passing. When the meeting was ajourned at night spoke to the people in the school house.

December 31,1855; Monday. To day received leters from San Bernardino by the mail which arived on the 30th. News rather cheereing than otherwise.

January 1, 1856; Tuesday. Spoke to the people of the 14th Ward at their school rooms. In the evening wrote for the mail.

January 2, 1856; Wednesday. Closed up and dispached my mail mater to the south and east. Sent the historical picture of the [First] Prest Council and Twelve [Apostles] to my sister in the state of Vermont town of Holland.[32] In the evening called on Br [Thomas] Calister to get him to do some work prepareitory to starting on my mission south.

January 3, 1856; Thursday. Closed my preparation for journey [south through Utah]. The weather pleasant and warm.

January 4, 1856; Friday.[33] This morning my wives Paulina [Eliza Phelps Lyman] & Lydia [Partridge Lyman and] I started for the southern settlements. Traviled as far as the Cottenwood stoped with Brother Nathan Tanner.

January 5, 1856; Saturday. Weather pleasant traviled far as the city of Lehi in Utah Valey. Called on Br John Brown[34] whom with family we found well.

January 6, 1856; Sunday. To day preached to the people of Lehigh [Lehi] who listened attentively. Their meeting house like their salvation is yet unfinished but is ready to receive the roof. In the afternoon went to Mountainsville [Alpine]. Took Paulina [Eliza] to her fathers. To night

32. This may have been the sheet of portraits that was printed in *Route from Liverpool to Great Salt Lake Valley* in 1853.

33. In accordance with instructions from President Young, Lyman began an extended tour of southern Utah, meeting with church members and speaking in their meeting halls.

34. Lyman's longtime friend and pioneer from Mississippi, not the southern California settler.

spoke to the people in their school house which was filled to overflowing. Stayed over night with Father[-in-law] Phelps.

January 7, 1856, Monday. Returned to Lehi and left Paulina with her father. Took in Lydia also Br John Brown and wife and traviled as far as Pleasant Grove. Stoped with Br Shadrick Driggs.[35] Br. Brown and wife stoping [with] Br. S[amuel] White.

January 8, 1856; Tuesday. This morning called with Mrs. [Lydia] Lyman to see sister MaryAnn Pratt. Then went some around the town to see the improvements. Meet with Bishop Henson Walker, then dined with Br [Samuel] White. At night spoke to the people in their school house their meeting house not being yet finished but enclosed. Lodged with the bishop by whom we were very kindly entertained.

January 9, 1856; Wednesday. This morning continued our journey to the city of Provo. Whe arived in the evening stoped with Br Harvey Redfield. This evening it rained.

January 10, 1856; Thursday. This morning made a call on the sisters Smiths, wives of Br G[eorge] A. who was away to Filmore in the Legislature.[36] The weather still mild. At night spake to the people in one of their publick halls. To night lodged with Br Jones and Br [John] B[rown] and wife with the Peter Roberts.

January 11, 1856; Friday. Went to Springville stoped with Br Wm Millers. At night spoke to the people in their school house which was crowded to overflowing.

January 12, 1856; Saturday. Traviled as far as the city of Palmira stoped with Br ~~Sthep~~ Stephen Markeham weather still mild.

January 13, 1856; Sunday. To day spoke to the people in their school house. Lodged with [the teacher,] Br [Silas] Hilman. To night folowed Br [John] B[rown] in an adress to the people.

January 14, 1856; Monday. Journeyed as far as Payson put up with Father Mik^s^ell [John A. Mikesell]. To night spoke to the people in their school house.

---

35. Shadrach F. Driggs was a wagon-maker from Connecticut who did wagon repairs in Pleasant Grove and brought culinary water to the fort through wooden pipes. Driggs, *Driggs Family History.*

36. The apostle/legislator had two wives in Provo who lived in the same house: Hannah Maria Libby Smith and Lucy Meserve Smith.

January 15, 1856; Tuesday. To [day went to] Nephi City on Salt Creek. Stoped with Br [George] Barber[37] weather cool and frosty.

January 16, 1856; Wednesday. To day caled on sister [Martha] Heywood with whom we dined. To night spoke to the people. Weather cold Lodged at Br [John] B[rown]s.

January 17, 1856; Thursday. Returned to Payson. Stoped with Elder Jas Pace [and] spoke to the people again. While here had some shoes put on my mules for which the Bishop settled.[38]

January 18, 1856; Friday. Returned to the uper settlement on the Spanish Fork. Put up with the Bishop Wm Pace spoke to the people in the afternoon. Br [John] Brown addressed them again at night.

January 19, 1856; Saturday. Returned to Spr^i^ngville stoped with Sister Huntington.[39] Myself and wife lodged with Br [William] Millers, to night Bishop [Aaron] Johnson returned from Filmore.[40]

January 20, 1856; Sunday. Spoke again to the people, this morning saw the governor [Brigham Young] on his return home. In the afternoon Br [John] B[rown] addressed the people. To night visited the Bishop & family. Lodged with Br [William] Miller.

January 21, 1856; Monday. Returned to Lehi stoped with Br [John] Brown. To night had an interview with Br Parker[,] J[ohn] D. who was returning from the Legislature.

January 22, 1856; Tuesday. Went to Mountainville [Alpine] at night spoke to the people. Lodged with Bishop [Isaac] Houston. Found [wife] Paulina and [son] Roswell M. [Lyman] well.[41]

January 23, 1856; Wednesday. Went to Lehigh stoped with Bishop [David] Evens. At night preached a funeral sermon called for by the death of Br McGraw. The weather slightly stormy.

January 24, 1856; Thursday. To day had some shoes put on my mules

---

37. George Barber, from England, helped settle Beaver, Utah, with two wives and children, then opened a farm-tool store in Smithfield in northern Utah.

38. That is, probably paid for in trade.

39. Mary or Hannah, two wives of Oliver B. Huntington.

40. Aaron Johnson was William Miller's father-in-law and bishop of Springville. Both were justices of the county court, and Johnson was one of the fourteen members of the upper house of Utah's legislature.

41. Amasa's child was Mason R. His deceased father was Roswell M., so Amasa has confused their names here. In any case, his son was destined to die at age fifteen. The mother, Paulina Eliza Phelps Lyman, was the sixth of Amasa's eight wives.

for which Br John Murdock settled. To day visited at Br Murdock and stayed over night.

January 25, 1856; Friday. Returned to Br N[athan] Tanners stayed over night. Br [John] Brown acompanyed us.

January 26, 1856; Saturday. This morning reached home. Found all well my self somewhat the worse for so much preaching and traviling in the cold. In the afternoon attended a mass meeting convened in the Tabernacle to consider the mater of geting up an express weekly or daily [mail service] from M[iss]o[uri] to Cal[ifornia]. Meeting ajourned to Saturday next.[42]

January 27, 1856; Sunday. My health poor keept to my bed most of the day.

January 28, 1856; Monday. Sometime to day the California mail arived.

January 29, 1856; Tuesday. This morning received my leters by the mail giveing me information of the sic[k]ness of my daughter Maria Louisa and also of the loss by fire of our saw mill in the mountain and also of the sale to Br. E[benezer] Hanks of one third of the rancho of San Bernardino.[43] Wrote some for the mail.

January 30, 1856; Wednesday. To day had an interview with the Prest [Brigham Young] in relation to our buisness in Cal[ifornia]. He said he wished me to get through it and then go to Europe and travil through that country.[44]

January 31, 1856; Thursday. To day wrote for the mail and dispatched the same.

February 1, 1856; Friday. To day had an interview with Br Truman O. Angel. Called on Br. E[zra] T. Benson. My health quite poor weather more mild.

---

42. Many attempts to set up an express mail service that could deliver letters and news in a few days from the midwest to the west coast were made in the 1850s. The famed Pony Express lasted only two years, from 1860–61, until the telegraph offered competition. Utah's first telegraph line stretched from Salt Lake City to Omaha. *Deseret News*, Feb. 2, 1856.

43. Hanks sold his personal property in California to become a member of the Lyman & Rich Co. by investing $26,000. His support delayed the ranch's default. Lyman, *San Bernardino*, 174.

44. Lyman will depart for England in 1860 with his frequent partner, Charles C. Rich.

February 2, 1856; Saturday. From this [date] to the (Tuesday the 5th) remained mostly at home.

February 5, 1856; Tuesday. To day spent the day with Prest [Brigham] Young went with him through his houses.[45] At night meet with the Regency.[46]

February 6, 1856; Wednesday. To day attended a social party of the members of the Mormon Battallion.

February 7, 1856; Thursday. Attended fast meeting in the 14th Ward spoke to the people.

February 9, 1856; Saturday.[47] Remained at home [due to] my health [being] poor.

February 10, 1856; Sunday. Attended meeting in the Tabernacle heard Br Orson Pratt preach.[48]

February 11, 1856; Monday. Passed the day with Br B[righam] Youngs family on the [nearby] Hill.

February 12, 1856; Tuesday. Visited sister Mary Fredrick, in company with Eliza [Partridge] Lyman. In the evening spoke to the Seventies in the Hall.[49]

February 13, 1856; Wednesday. Visited to Bro Nathan Tanners in company with Br [Reddick] Allread and wife. At night went to the theater.

February 14, 1856; Thursday. Spent the day at home had company.

February 15, 1856; Friday. To day spent the day at the Seventys Hall.

February 16, 1856; Saturday. Started north went as far as Centerville. Taried with Sister Emiline Rich.[50]

---

45. The Beehive House, the most famous home associated with Young, was built in 1854. The Lion House was under construction but would be finished later in 1856. Young would also build homes near the mouth of Emigration Canyon and in southern Utah.

46. The regents of the University of Deseret discussed producing a children's reader in the Deseret Alphabet, a phonetic-based approach to language created by George D. Watt. Journal History, Feb. 4, 1856; Alder et al, "Creating a New Alphabet for Zion," 275–86.

47. Lyman wrote in the date for Feb. 8 without recording an entry.

48. Pratt extolled the virtues of science as a way to understand God and obtain salvation. *Journal of Discourses*, 3:291–98.

49. The old Seventies Hall was a small adobe building south of Temple Square.

50. Emeline Grover Rich married Charles C. Rich in secret in Nauvoo, Illinois, in Feb. 1846, just before the departure across Iowa. The town of Centerville Lyman mentions is about ten miles north of Salt Lake City.

February 17, 1856; Sunday. Spoke to the people in the morning and evening and lodged with Br J[ohn] D. Parker.[51]

February 18, 1856; Monday. To day went to Br [Perrigrine] Sessions. Spoke to the people of the City Bountiful in the night lodged with Br S[essions].

February 19, 1856; Tuesday. Returned home found all well weather still moderate.

February 20, 1856; Wednesday. To day engaged a man to prune my fruit trees. Called on Prest [Brigham] Young. This morning wind from the south in the night it snowed.

February 21, 1856; Thursday. Passed the day mostly at home. Wind from the north at night some frost.

February 22, 1856; Friday. To day attended court. This evening meet with the Philosophical Association[52] weather still open.

February 23, 1856; Saturday. Attended court again.[53]

February 24, 1856; Sunday. Attended meeting in the Tabernacle Br [Joseph G.] Hovey preached and was folowed by the Prest [Brigham Young] who curst the enemies of Zion in our midst and all the people said Amen.[54] This week passed without incident. Passed some time with the Presidency and Historian in reviseing portions of Church history.[55]

---

51. John D. Parker had been an Iowa sheriff and bodyguard of Joseph Smith. He married two daughters of another famous lawman, Shadrach Roundy. In Centerville, Parker was a tax collector and probate judge.

52. Lyman meant the "Polysophical Association," a group that discussed arts and other humanities and sponsored performances.

53. This bizarre case grabbed the attention of church leaders, who attended the trial and heard Margaret Williams testify that a man approached her about plural marriage, then introduced her to another man who asked her to be a plural wife without a ceremony. After they had engaged in intercourse three times, the man alternated between threatening to murder her and paying her to be quiet. It appears that the jury could not decide on a verdict and the two men and one woman were all let go. "Minutes of the Testimony of Margaret Williams," Feb. 22, 1856, in Brigham Young Office Files, CHL.

54. This was one of Young's most fiery sermons. A week later he would tell Mormons that their sermons should be so—"like peals of thunder." The rhetoric is said to have contributed to the Mormon Reformation, the Santa Clara ambush, the Utah War, and the Mountain Meadows Massacre. Van Wagoner, *Complete Discourses of Brigham Young*, 2:1052–58.

55. The history, begun under Smith's direction in 1839 and continued by church historians Willard Richards and George A. Smith, was published serially in the *Times*

March 2, 1856; Sunday.[56] Preached in the morning to the people in the Tabernacle. Prest ~~Grant~~ [Brigham] ^Young^ and [Jedediah M.] Grant folowed.

March 3, 1856; Monday. Meet with the Presidency to revise History. I continued from day to day until [blank].

March 7, 1856; Friday. When I called on the President and heard some news from the seat of Indian war[57] no fighting weather mild.[58]

September 2, 1856; Tuesday.[59] Tuesday evening parted with my family in S. L. City and traviled to Cotten wood and put up with Br Nathan Tanner.

September 3, 1856; Wednesday. Traviled [to] Pleasant Grove put up with Br S[aul] White.

September 4, 1856; Thursday. Dined with Br. Driggs and then went to Provo. Put up with Br Bullock. Tonight it rained. Br [John] B[rown] came home about 9 oclock.

September 5, 1856; Friday. Traviled to Spanish Fork stoped with Bishop John Butler. In the evening was present at the mariage of his Daughter.

September 6, 1856; Saturday. Spent the day with the Bishop [John Butler].

September 7, 1856; Sunday. Spoke to the people in the morning and in the evening went to Payson and preached to the people. Stoped at Br Tanners.

September 8, 1856; Monday. Traviled to Nephi lodged with Bishop [Jacob G.] Bigler and spoke to the people. Br [George B.] Wallace came up this evening. The wind was high to day and cold.

September 9, 1856; Tuesday. Traviled to the Severe [River] where we camped. The weather was cold.

---

and Seasons to 1846 and restarted later in the *Deseret News*. Vogel, *History of Joseph Smith*, 1:ix–xxii; Park, "Developing a Historical Conscience," 115–34.

56. Lyman did not record any dates or entries from Feb. 25–Mar. 1.

57. The Tintic War of Feb. 1856 started when hungry natives stole some cattle in Utah County and reportedly killed a few Mormons. A posse was led by the collaborative sub-chief Tintic and an unknown number of Indians were killed. Journal History, Feb. 23–26.

58. Four blank pages separate the Mar. 7 entry from the next entries in Sept. 1856.

59. Lyman and Rich were told by Brigham Young to return to San Bernardino and conclude their affairs so they could leave for missions in Europe (see the entry for Apr. 19, 1857, below), signaling the end of their involvement in southern California. Lyman, *San Bernardino*, 371–75

September 10, 1856; Wednesday. Traviled to Fillmore stoped with the widow [Abigail] Owens. Preached to the people.

September 11, 1856; Thursday. Dined with Br [Noah W.] Bartholomew and traviled to Corn Creek [Kanosh] and camped. Had some of the natives in camp.

September 12, 1856; Friday. Traviled to Cove Creek and camped at 4 oclock.

September 13, 1856; Saturday. Traviled to Beaver and camped at 5 oclock. Had some natives in camp. Weather warm did not call at the settlement.

September 14, 1856; Sunday. Traviled to Parowan and preached to the people. They let me have some Oats and Flour.

September 15, 1856; Monday. Went to Ceader City. Preached [and] taried with Br [Isaac] Hayte.

September 16, 1856; Tuesday. Traviled to Mountain Meadow found our company there.

September 17, 1856; Wednesday. Traviled to the foot of the Santa Clara [River and] had the natives to watch our stock.[60]

September 18, 1856; Thursday. Traviled as far as the Beaver Dam and turned out. Had no Indians in camp. To day had some Missionary Berries [strawberries].

September 19, 1856; Friday. Traviled down the river as far as the Muskeete [Mesquite] Grove where we meet the mail on its way north and also Br [William P.] Jones from the lead mine beyond the Los Vegas on his return to S L City for materials for a furnace.

September 20, 1856; Saturday. Traviled to within 4 m[ile]s of the foot of the big hill where we found the company that had left us at the Grove.

September 21, 1856; Sunday. Came to the Mudy [River] had a fine rain. In the night had the natives to guard our stock they stole from some of our party some blankets ^as^ useual to keep their hand in.

September 22, 1856; Monday. Started for Los Vegas where we arived on Tuesday evening. From the recent rains there was heavy mud on the desert.

September 23, 1856; Tuesday. Arived at the Fort found President

60. Five months later, as part of the rising tensions in Utah territory, four men would be ambushed near this spot on the Santa Clara, with John Tobin suffering massive wounds. Parshall, "Pursue, Retake & Punish."

[William] Bringhurst and company well and feeling well. They received us kindly and ministered to our wants.

September 24, 1856; Wednesday. Taried at the Fort and in the evening spoke to the people who were pleased.

September 25, 1856; Thursday. Left our warm hearted friends at Los Vegas and traviled to the Cottenwood Springs and camped, had the natives with us whom we employed to watch our stock.

September 26, 1856; Friday. Traviled to the Lead Mines.[61] Found the brethren all well and in good spirits.[62]

April 18, 1857; Saturday. Started for S Lake the Sheriff and party of some 25 men acompanying us.[63] Camped in the Cahoon [Cajon Pass] our heavy wagons haveing preceded us some two days with Br [Charles C.] Riches family.

April 19, 1857; Sunday. Traviled up the can[y]on at the uper water. Parted with Br E[benezer] Hanks whom we blest before parting, for the acomplishment of his labours as our general agent in California while we are absent on our mission to Europe. As we passed the sumit of the mountain Br [Norman] Taylor and Stoe came to us with one of the Gener[al's] mules that had strayed. Went to the River Mohave and camped 1½ m[ile]s from the uper crossing where we found those who had preceded us all well.

April 20, 1857; Monday. To day did not move camp. In the morning brs [William] Mathews and [Sidney] Tanner came into camp they haveing camped back ½ mile. Dureing the day one of Br [Charles C.] Riches

61. The lead mines were in the Spring Mountains, about sixty miles west of Las Vegas.

62. "The end of this Book" is written below this entry. It was not the end of the book. He later recorded entries from 1872 in the same diary; the next chronological entry comes from a different diary in which he began making entries seven months later.

63. The sheriff and twenty-five men rode alongside the wagons to protect the emigrants from disgruntled settlers who felt they were being abandoned. Lyman listed the emigrants under the line, "Memorandum of company that traviled to Utah with Elders Lyman & Rich starting from the 15th to the 18th of April 1857," as "Amasa Lyman & Son Marion, C. C. Rich & Family, Sidney Tanner, Wm Mathews & son Cuningham, Wm P. Smith, John Henry Rollins & Hanah Rollins & children ^2^, Lydia Taylor & 2 children, Elinor Morse & child, Joseph Ridges wife & child, F A Hamond & family, H Murphy, David Williams, William Bringhurst & family, Br Hawke & son, Miles Henderson & son, Phebe Woodworth, John Woodworth, Timothy Covert, Dick A. Blackman, Sister Westover, Saul Smith & wife, John Tate, a boy from India, Charles Hardy from Australia traviled with us as far as Biter Springs where he left & returned to Cal[ifornia], Joseph Hunt, John King, David Savage, Jessie Bishop, Wm Bateman."

mules got injured so as to be unfit for the journey[;] he was force[d] to replace him by purchaseing one from Br Norman Taylor.

April 21, 1857; Tuesday. This morning one of my mules had gone back on acount of which we still remained in camp my son [Francis] Marion goeing back for the mule. This morning our visiting party left us to return [to San Bernardino]. Among them were my wife Maria and daughter Matilda and husband[,] [son] Amasa and Daughter Josephine. We said our adieus and sat down to write the same. The only death reported in camp was that of a shanghigh cock [rooster] belonging Br [Charles C.] Rich cause of death unknown. This evening Marion returned with the mule.

April 22, 1857; Wednesday. This morning left camp at 8 oclock traviled 18 m[ile]s. Camped at 5½ oclock with the old settlers the Hunts. Some grass and good water, to day we were joined by Bro [William] Bringhurst[,] [Francis A.] Hamond[64] and [David] Savage. Our co is now full numbering 28 effective men.

April 23, 1857; Thursday. Left camp at 7½ oclock traviled 16 m[ile]s and camped at 4 oclock on twenty m[ile]s. Weather very warm slightly relieved by a pleasant wind. Feed and water plenty.

April 24, 1857; Friday. Laid by on acount of some stock that ran away. In the evening the boys returned with the stock.

April 25, 1857; Saturday. This morning some stock gone. We moved our wagons 4 m[ile]s. Br [William] Mathews and son [Cunningham] went in search of the missing stock. Camped at 12 oclock good water and feed. Just at dark Br Mathews returned with the stray stock. The wind high and very cold.

April 26, 1857; Sunday. Left camp at 7½ oclock traviled 12 m[ile]s. Camped at the lower camp on the Mohave at 2 oclock had some Indians with us from the Colorado [River]. The weather cool and pleasant.

April 27, 1857 Monday. Left camp at 10 oclock, passed over the sumit towards Biter Springs and camped at 1 oclock in the morning.

April 28, 1857; Tuesday. Started about 6 oclock and arrived at the

64. Francis A. Hammond was a whaling-ship boatswain (senior crewman) until he broke his back and was put ashore in the Sandwich Islands in 1844. Three years after recovering, he sailed to San Francisco, converted to Mormonism, and returned to Hawaii as a missionary. He went on to become a stake president in southeast Utah.

springs at 10 oclock where we meet a party from Salt Creek who were fleeing from the Phantom of their own discontent (a wearysome and fruitless journey in evry thing but their disappointment). Remained here through the day and improved the watering places. The weather rather warm altho coller [cooler] at night.

April 29, 1857; Wednesday. Left camp at 3½ oclock, traviled until 12 oclock and camped. Feed our stock and tied [them] up until morning.

April 30, 1857; Thursday. Started at 6 oclock and traviled about 10 m[ile]s to the parting of the roads. There parted with Br [Charles C.] Rich and party who were goeing the old road by Salt Springs and we went to Kingston Spring[65] where we arrived with our wagons at 10 oclock. Watered and feed and tied up for the night the water tolerable good, feed none.

May 1, 1857; Friday. Remained at the spring and drove our stock to the grass about 2 miles. Dureing the day some Indians were seen on the hills. Tied up [our stock] at night.

May 2, 1857; Saturday. At one oclock evening we left the spring and traviled until 9 oclock when we halted an[d] feed then traviled all night.

May 3, 1857; Sunday. Stoped at 5 oclock in the morning. Fed and breakfasted and traviled on. Arrived at the Mountain Springs, 5½ oclock. There we were met by a party of the Lamanites one of whom had a package of leters for Br [Charles] Rich which he delivered to me after which we regaled the party on a kettle of mush[66] which the[y] disposed of in a summary way. Tied up our stock at night and feed [them] grain as there was no grass.

May 4, 1857; Monday. This morning left camp at <u>8 oclock</u> arrived at the Cotonwood Spring 4½ oclock. Found plenty of feed and water, employed the natives to herd our stock.

May 5, 1857; Tuesday. To day laid by to rest our stock the weather cool and pleasant. The chief and family with us. In the evening Jim came to us from the Mountain Springs but brought no news of Br [Charles] Rich for whom he had a leter.

---

65. Kingston Peak is twenty miles west of the current Nevada/California border. The spring is just east of the peak.

66. The mush was prepared by boiling cornmeal in a kettle. It was then often poured it into a pan to dry, cut into squares, fried, and sweetened with molasses.

May 6, 1857; Wednesday. Still waiting for the party behind. Wind high and weather cool. Had the chief Brigham with us.

May 7, 1857; Thursday. Still remained in camp, wind still high. In the evening at 3 oclock Br [Charles] Rich and party came in and brought in two disabled wagons one minus a wheel, one [minus] an axeltree and sister [Lydia] Taylor was verry sick. Aside from this the party were in good health. They left one animal belonging to John Woodworth.

May 8, 1857; Friday. To day repaired the wagons and nursed the sick wooman. The wind had lulled the weather pleasant the sick somewhat improved.

May 9, 1857; Saturday. Left camp at 7½ oclock. Reached Los Vegas at 7 oclock found the fort a desolation a sad monument of the foly of poor short sighted selfish man who can sacrifice the interests of a kingdom and people on the alter of personal selfishness.[67]

May 10, 1857; Sunday. Laid by and repaired wagons and shod some stock the wind was high.

May 11, 1857; Monday. In the morning the ox teams started and a little later the general [Charles C. Rich] with his mules and at 2½ oclock we folowed them. Halted for sup[p]er before dark and then traviled on until 2 oclock [in the] morning when we came to the camp of Br Rich and party. About this time they learned that some Indians had shot one ox belonging to Br [Ebenezer] Hanks. They [Rich's party] took up their teams and traviled with us.

May 12, 1857; Tuesday. This morning halted at 7 oclock for breakfast. Traviled on arrived at Mudy [River] at 5 oclock. Found a large party of natives awaiting our arrival. The last night we traviled all night not sleeping any.

May 13, 1857; Wednesday. Left the Mudy [River] and traviled to the high ground and camped had good grass. After we had camped Br Joseph Hyde and party came ~~to~~ in on their way to California. They had 2 wagons and 7 men.

May 14, 1857; Thursday. Left camp and traviled to the Rio Virgin,

---

67. Brigham Young appointed Nathaniel Jones to oversee the lead mines. Jones and William Bringhurst, the mission president, quarreled over them, so Young released Bringhurst only to hear from his successor that the fort was in shambles. Young closed the mission. Woods, *A Gamble in the Desert*, 157–69.

camped about 1 oclock. Had the Chief Sosho and band with us. They herded our stock for us and returned them to us in the morning.

May 15, 1857; Friday. Traviled about 12 m[ile]s and camped at 3 oclock with the Chief Isaac and his band with whom we had a friendly talk and had them to heard our stock.

May 16, 1857; Saturday. Left camp at 7 oclock. ~~Arrived at Cotton-wood or Beaver dam at ha~~ Camped at 3 oclock distance 12 miles. ~~At this point~~

May 17, 1857; Sunday.[68] Bro [Amasa] Lyman left us to visit the settlements on the Rio Virgin & Santa Clara [Rivers]. Left camp at 7¼ Oclock. Camped at the Beaver-dam at 4½ O clock. Found good water. The water of the Rio Virgin up which we have been traveling for the last four days modestly rivals in its aromatic taste the water of the far famed Bitter Springs.

Left the camp in company with Br David Savage and an Indian guide for the purpose of visiting the mission on the Santa Clara and the Rio Virgin. We left camp at 5 oclock in the morning and at 10 oclock we were at the Cottenwood Spring or the Beaver Dam so called. At this point we left the California Road and folowing an Indian trail commenced our journey over the high mountain between the point where we left the Rio Virgin and the Santa Clarra. We rode on quietly for a few miles and passed over a small ridge when we began to congratulate ourselves on the ease with[69] which we were geting along when upon asking our guid the direction of the trail we were informed by him that its cours lay up the face of the highest and most forbiding mountain in sight. The forbiding aspect of the rocky aclivity seemed to bid defiance to human prowes and promised to furnish a task for the agile mountain goat. Dreading the toil but more the idea of defeat we began the ascent which at length we overcame by walking mostly on o[u]r hands and feet our mules climbing over the jaged rocks like mountain sheep.[70]

68. This entry is taken from three separate portions of the diary. The first sentence from May 16 was circled in pencil with an arrow drawn to the next entry. The remainder of the first paragraph, under the date May 17, was copied from someone else's diary, which is why Lyman is referred to in third-person. The subsequent paragraphs appeared after the June 8 entry and continued for seven pages.

69. "With" was written three times.

70. The Castle Cliffs portion of the Old Spanish Trail, thirteen miles north of

The sumit gained from our lofty pearch we could see that by a diferent rout the sumit could be gained with comparitive ease. We traviled on until we were ~~sourour~~ surrounded by the darkness of night and how far from our destination we knew not but for some Hours we traviled over low hills and then down a smo[o]th gravel wash. When we again interogated our guide as to the cours of our trail he pointed abruptly to the left when our attention was called to a rocky mountain that stretched its jaged sumit skyward beyond where the eye could reach in the doubtful light [that] surrounded us. To climb this ruged ascent in our jaded condition seemed an Herculion Task. But after our guide had provided himself with a torch aided by its fitful glare we commenced our perilous ascent but soon came to an ascent so abrupt that Br S[avage]'s mule fell down and but for the timely aid of her master would have rolled to the botom of the Hill.

We then returned to the Base of the mountain to spend the cheerless night in waiting for the returning light of Day without water[,] Blankets or Bread to cheer or refresh us. In our excessive weariness we sank down upon the arid bosom of our Mother (Earth) and were in a few moments oblivious to all around us until the return of Day awaked us to conciousness and we arose from our rude bed and prepared to resume our toilsome way when by another route we succeeded in gaining the sumit.

From this point we could see that the sumit gained by so much toil could have been reached with ease had we traviled down to wash a short distance. The R[o]cky precipice terminated in a Gentle ascent up which we could [have] rode our mules with ease thus showing to us that the old way is not always the best.

May 18, 1857; Monday.[71] Left camp at 7½ Oclock. Camped in the cannon [canyon] at 6 Oclock. Cloudy all day a little rain in the night. Distance traveled 13 miles. Last night Sister [Mary Jane] Hammond presented her lord a daughter [Mary Morsalle Hammond].

This morning we arrived at the Fort on Santa Clara [Fort Clara]

Beaver Dam, was 3,000 feet higher in elevation. Beaver Dam is in Mohave County, Arizona. Castle Cliffs is in Washington County, Utah.

71. The May 18–21 entries are written in two separate parts of the diary from the perspective of the main company and of Lyman himself. On May 24, when he rejoined the group, he resumed making daily entries.

just as its inmates were arising from sleep. We were kindly received and entertained by Elder Samuel Knight who had charge of the post in the absence of Br [Jacob] Hamblin.[72] The brethren at this place have built a stone fort one hundred feet sq[u]are inside of which are the rude cabins in which its ocupants reside. At present they have some land in cultivation with and for the natives with whom there seems to exist a good feeling at present. We taried here through the day. In the evening ~~we we we~~ Br Hamlin returned. We spoke to the people.

May 19, 1857; Tuesday. Left camp at 7 Oclock. Camped on the Santa Clara[73] [River at] 12½ Oclock. Here we met Armstrong & Park. Traveled 3 miles to the ca[nyon]. Distance 14 miles.

This morning we traviled over a succesion of low ridges a distance called 10 m[ile]s which brought us to the point on the Rio Virgin where the mission for raiseing cotton have located their farm for this purpose.[74] We found this mission consisting of some fifty familys under the Presidency of Elder Robert Coving who informed me that he thought they could get in their present locality 1000 acres of good land. They reported haveing found a good [cattle] heard[ing] ground in the vicinity with plenty of grass and water and wood. At night I preached to the people.

May 20, 1857; Wednesday. Left camp at 8 Oclock. Halted at noon and partook of some slight refreshemnts. Camped at 6 Oclock at last crossing of Santa Clara. Distance traveled 17 miles.

This morning we started for Harmony where we arived about Sun set. Put up with the Sister L[avina] Lees, Br [John D.] Lee being absent from Home.[75]

May 21, 1857; Thursday. Left camp at 8 Oclock. Halted at noon. Camped at 6 Oclock on the Mountain Meadows. Distance traveled 14

---

72. Hamblin and Knight had both been called as missionaries to the Indians. Hamblin was thirty-eight years old, Knight twenty-four.

73. "Santa Clara" is written over another word in heavy ink, making the first word illegible.

74. The cotton mission was led by Robert Covington and Samuel Adair on the assumption that the dire national situation prior to the Civil War would create more demand for cotton. The settlers toiled unprofitably into the early twentieth century before abandoning the enterprise. Brooks, "The Cotton Mission."

75. John D. Lee had fourteen living wives, of which Lavina Young Lee was the eleventh.

miles. This evening at 6¼ Oclock Brother Cha[rle]s Richs little daughter Tunis died after an illness of about six hours.[76]

This morning we spoke to the people of Harmony and then we traviled on to Cedar City whose inhabitants we found hapy and well. Here we waited until Saturday when our [wagon] train came in all well.

May 22, 1857; Friday. Some of the brethren were busy all the morning making a coffin for the child. Left camp at eleven Oclock. Halted at Painter creek to dine. Camped at 5 Oclock distance traviled 12 miles.

May 23, 1857; Saturday. To day we arrived in Cedar City where we taried until Tuesday.

May 24, 1857; Sunday.[77] To day we preached to the people who seemed to enjoy the spirit of their faith.

May 25, 1857; Monday. Laid by for repairs of some of Br [Charles C.] Riches wagons.

May 26, 1857; Tuesday. Traviled to and camped on Sumit Creek.[78] Br [Charles C.] Rich and myself went to Parowan and preached to the people.

May 27, 1857; Wednesday. We travilled to and camped on Little Creek and Br [Charles C.] Rich and myself preached to people of Read Creek.

May 28, 1857; Thursday. Traviled over the Divide and camped in the Canyon. Had good grass but no water only what we caried along in our wagons.

May 29, 1857; Friday. We passed the settlement on Beaver to whom we preached and while here the mail from Cal[ifornia] arrived. We traviled to and camped on Indian Creek.

May 30, 1857; Saturday. This morning I left the camp and traviled with the mail party to Salt Lake where we arrived on the 3d of June and found my family all well.

June 7, 1857; Sunday. To day atended meeting at the Bowry.

June 8, 1857; Monday. To day Br [Charles C.] Rich and family arrived in the City and on Friday the 12th my son [Francis M.] came as also Brs [William] Mathews and [Sidney] Tanner with the organ.[79]

---

76. Tunis Harriett Rich, daughter of Harriett and Charles Rich, was about to turn two years old when she died of an unspecified illness.

77. Lyman stopped copying from the main wagon train and returned to his own narrative at this point.

78. Summit Creek lies between Cedar and Parowan Valleys.

79. Lyman was accompanied from California by Joseph R. Ridges, who was

July 1, 1857; Wednesday.[80] I have spent the most of my time in the city makeing a visit to Farmington to my farm. I have my teems engaged in hawling wood. To day I am writeing. To night the mail arived from Cal[ifornia].

July 2, 1857; Thursday. This [day] received my leters from the office. Visited Capt Hooper on buisness. This morning had a pleasant rain.[81]

January 11, 1858; Monday. Left Cedar City this morning at 11½ A. M. on an exploring expedition south, accompanied by brn Jas. Lewis, W[illiam] H. Dame, Silas S. Smith,[82] from Parowan—J[ohn] M. Higbee, Nephi Johnson, J. S. Walker, Atha Carter and W[illiam] H. Shearman from Cedar, with two four horse wagons and a horse for each man to ride. Reached Painter Creek about 8½ P.M, after a very cold ride. Staid all night with Sis [Jane] Hultz. Distance 25–6 m[ile]s.[83]

January 12, 1858; Tuesday. Left camp 9¼ A.M. Camped at the forks of the Santa Clara at 6½ P.M.[84] Pretty good feed across the creek. Weather moderate and clear. Dis[tan]ce 26 miles.

January 13, 1858; Wednesday. Left camp at 9¼ A.M. Morning cloudy and cold. Reached the log house at the first camping place on the Clara at 1 P.M. Dist[an]ce 10 m[ile]s. Brs [John M.] Higbee[85] and [James]

---

returning from a mission in Australia. Ridges was hauling equipment for the tabernacle organ that Ridges himself would build.

80. Lyman wrote "From the 8th of June until the present" between the entries.

81. There are blank lines here, after which Lyman resumed his diary six months later, during which the Utah War began and the massacre at Mountain Meadows was carried out. In Aug. 1857, Brigham Young wrote to William Crosby in San Bernardino and ordered all Mormons to "gather ^up^ ~~here~~ to these valleys" (Young to Crosby, Aug. 4, 1857, in Brigham Young Office Files, CHL). Word was sent to all outlying settlements to sell their property and return to the Wasatch Front. Lyman went south to help arrivals on their way (MacKinnon, *At Sword's Point*; Walker, Turley, and Leonard, *Massacre at Mountain Meadows*).

82. Smith had just arrived from the Sandwich Islands, where he had been mission president.

83. The handwriting, spelling, and dating in this part of the journal depart from Lyman's characteristic style, which means that he likely kept loose sheets or separate diary books for his rough drafts and had someone help him copy those entries into his bound diaries.

84. The river divides into three forks in the Pine Valley Mountains about fifteen miles southeast of Mountain Meadows.

85. John M. Higbee was one of a handful of men indicted as a co-conspirator in the 1857 Mountain Meadows Massacre and excommunicated for his participation. He was a counselor to Isaac Haight, president of the Iron Mission in Cedar City.

Lewis, who had been round by Harmony, ar[rive]d in the course of the afternoon in company with Jacob Hamblin, bringing a quantity of fresh beef. Toward evening it commenced snowing, and fell about 3½ inches deep on the bottom and from 6 to 10 in the mountain.

January 14, 1858; Thursday. Staid in camp all day on ac[coun]t of the snow and various things which had to be done. Capt [Daniel] Stark's train, consisting of 16 wagons arrived about 2 P.M.[86] Weather clear & moderate.

January 15, 1858; Friday. Left camp at 9½ A.M. Mor[nin]g clear and very cold—the snow remains on the ground. I remained behind with Brn [William H.] Dame, [James] Lewis, [John M.] Higbee & Nephi Johnson to hunt two animals which were missing. Bro S[ilas] S. Smith and [William H.] Shearman accompanied the wagons which reached the summit at 1 P.M. & Beaver Dam at 5½ P.M. Snow on the mountain from 6 to 8 inches deep. Br. Dame and myself reached camp at 7 PM after a hard ride. The rest of the camp arrived about ½ an hour afterwards. Plenty of the natives for company at our camp. Clear, but cool; though moderate compared with the last three days.

January 16, 1858; Saturday. Left camp at 10½ A.M. Mor[nin]g clear and pleasant. Struck the virgin in 3 m[ile]s and found a comp[an]y of 3 wagons camped about a mile below the hill. Farther on met Fayette [Marcus de Lafayette] Shepard's train of 6 wagons. Sister Sargeant and family from San Francisco were along. Crossed the river 4 times & camped on the bluff just below the peach orchard at 4 P.M., distance to day 15 m[ile]s. Afternoon cloudy & cold.

January 17, 1858; Sunday. Br Jacob Hamblin from the Clara Fort joined us this morning.[87] Morning clear & beautiful. Sun rose brightly the atmosphere is warm & pleasant and all around is calm & delightful. Heavy dew last night & frost. Our animals have strayed off this morning so that we are detained in camp. Found the animals about 11 A.M. and left camp at 11¾ A.M. Travelled 12 miles and camped at 6½ P.M. with Prest Wm Cox's company of 10 wagons. Road heavy sand.

January 18, 1858; Monday. Mor[nin]g clear and pleasant. Left camp

86. This is one of several wagon companies that traveled from San Bernardino to Salt Lake City. Some of the groups had several dozen people, while others had only one or two families.

87. This line is written vertically in the margin of the diary as an afterthought.

at 9¾ a.m. Left 1½ bush[el]s of grain with the Indian Chief Tosho to keep for us till we returned. This was done not only, on our own present accommodation, but also, in order to prove Tosho & find out whether he can be trusted. Proceeded down the Virgin 6 miles & then commenced the ascent of the hill, the summit of which, we gained without doubling teams by the aid of the natives, who, for the small remuneration of a crackers, packed the heaviest part of our loads up the hill. Reached the Muddy at 7¾ P.M. where we found about 40 waons camped. Distance to day 26 miles. Road very good after we gained the top of the hill. Night air quite chilly—but moderate.

January 19, 1858; Tuesday. Mor[nin]g clear, warm & pleasant. Heavy dew last night with light frost. Remained in camp to day, as another company was expected to come in through the course of the day, but did not arrive.

January 20, 1858; Wednesday. Morning cloudy but not very cold. Left camp at 8½ a.m. Travelled 27½ m[ile]s and stopped about 4 P.M. to wait on some bunch grass to the right of the road, within sight of the dry lake and about 4 miles southwest of it. Met one of the Parowan teams returning, bringing a family. Wrote to the President [Brigham Young] from this place. Harnessed up and proceeded on our journey about 8 P.M. Met the mail at 8¾ P.M. Stopped ½ an hour [a]go to get the news. Reached the Vegas Fort about 3. a.m. where found some 60 wagons camped, including Captain Lytle['s], Case['s,] and Clark's Companies.

January 21, 1858; Thursday. Mor[nin]g cloudy but warm. Remained in camp to day to recruit our animals. Preached about 12 m., and again in the evening, but was cut short by the rain as I had to speak out of doors.

January 22, 1858; Friday. Morning clear & pleasant. Left 5 of our party here to remain until we returned viz—Brns [James] Lewis, [John M.] Higbee, S[ilas] S. Smith, Walker and Miller. Were accompanied from this place by br. Robert Clift of San Bernardino. Left camp at 9½ A.M. About 12 o'clock we had quite a heavy & cold storm of rain. Camped by the first water on Cottonwood Creek at 3½ P.M. Towards night commenced to rain again. Made our beds under the wagon, & by the aid of the wagons & some saddle blankets managed to keep the rain out, but got our bed wet by a canteen leaking through the wagon bed above us. Distance to day 18 miles = poor feed.

January 23, 1858; Saturday. Morning cold. Still threatens to rain. The horses had wandered off in the night about two miles toward Williams Camp. Left camp at 8½ A.M. Reached Mountain Springs at 12½ P.M. where we staid till 4 P.M. to feed ourselves and animals. Had quite a sharp but brief snow storm. Snow through the Kanyon about 3 inches deep. Proceeded to the junction of the roads where we saw a fire which we supposed to belong to a camp at Stump Springs, so we took the road towards it for 3 miles when we discovered it to be an Indian fire off the road. Turned back to the Kingston road, and camped in the wash about 200 ft from the junction. Distance to day 18 m[ile]s on our course. 24 miles in all. No feed. Beautiful moonlight night—not so cold as usual.

January 24, 1858; Sunday. Left camp at 7¾ A.M. Found a little water—enough for our horses—in holes at the dry lake 15 or 16 miles from the junction of the roads. Stopped about 1½ P.M. to feed our animals. Found considerable water in the rocks to the right of the road going down the wash to Savage's Spring. Arrived at the point of the Mountain—½ a mile from Savage's Spring at 8. P.M. where we found George Crisman camped with several wagons. Also Joseph Smith from the S[andwich] Islands.[88] Camped here for the night.

January 25, 1858; Monday. Warm, pleasant day. Sent the animals over to Kingston Spring to water, & then moved camp down to Savage's Spring.

January 26, 1858; Tuesday. Beautiful day. No mail yet. After supper sent out the old Indian who has been staying with us since our arrival here—to watch the horses, but he soon returned, reporting Br [Robert] Clift's horse which was the finest in the band, missing, and that he had seen Indian tracks following the trail of the horse. Bro N[ephi] Johnson, R. Clift, A[rthur] Clarke immediately started in pursuit on horseback but could not find anything of the horse although they rode about 15 miles on the trail and must have come very close upon the Indians as they heard them whistle. They returned about daylight next morning.

January 27, 1858; Wednesday. Mor[nin]g clear and warm. Bros [William H.] Dame, [Nephi] Johnson and [Arthur] Clarke started back to Cedar City with the wagon. Selected Brs [Robert] Clift and [William

88. This is future LDS president Joseph F. Smith, nephew of the founding prophet. He was called to serve in Hawaii at age fifteen and was returning home at sixteen. Ricks, *"My Candid Opinion,"* vii–xvi.

H.] Shearman to accompany me to meet my family. Took three animals, packing our blankets, a little road feed, and a few crackers on one—and riding the other two, and proceeded towards the Mohave, not expecting, however, to have to go farther than Bitter Spring at most. Reached the forks of the road at dusk. Rested an hour or so & then went on up the Kanyon where we camped for the night.

January 28, 1858; Thursday. Left camp about 7½ a.m. Day clear and pleasant. Found water at the dry lake for our animals. Reached Bitter Spring about 11 a. m. Rested here till 4 P.M. Fed our animals most all the grain we had left, and eat a crackers or two ourselves. Camped about 5 miles from the summit where we found a little hay some one had left which furnished a scanty supper for our horses.

January 29, 1858; Friday. Left camp about sunrise. Crossed the summit and after passing through the Kanyon perceived the gentile ox wagon, that started from Kingston 2 days before, about 6 miles ahead of us. Met Freeman & Seth Tanner and Wm Flake with our team and a drove [herd] of horses & mules accompanied by two Indians Jim & Bill from Tejas [Texas] to help drive the stock—about 8 miles from the Mohave they stopped and got a good dinner for us which was very acceptable after living on about 2 crackers a day. Let our animals feed on the sand grass, which is good and abundant here, and then gave them a good feed of barley. About two miles farther on, met br [Elisha] Hyate [Hyatt] with two wagons. Reached the Mohave shortly after sundown. Day very warm.

January 30, 1858; Saturday. Mor[nin]g warm and pleasant. The camel train and about 75 dragoons & 6 govt. wagons passed this morning.[89] After we had saddled up and started found the mail boys camped about 300 yds below us. They ar[rive]d on the Mohave about 4 a.m. While here "Tobin" came up and appeared very friendly. Got a cup of coffee with the boys, and left camp about 11. a.m. Passed a portion of the troops. Halted at the fish pond to water and rest our animals & got a lunch for ourselves.

---

89. In 1857 the US Congress commissioned the exploration of possible land routes and waterways through the Southwest under Edward Beale, who traveled with thirteen surveyors, twenty-five camels, a mule train, and members of the 1st Cavalry Regiment of Dragoons from San Francisco. The path they explored became Route 66.

Proceeded to the Point of the Mountain 2 miles beyond the Sugar Loaf[90] where I found my family camped—8 wagons in all.[91]

January 31, 1858; Sunday. Clear and pleasant. Left camp about 9½ a.m. Passed Major [George] Blake and his Com[pany] and camped at the Sugar Loaf. He informed us that the expedition to explore the Colorado had been perfectly successful, that there were three steamers on the river, that another of 5 feet draught was to be placed on it in a short time, that they had ascended within 70 m[ile]s of the mouth of the Virgin & that they expect to be able to reach its mouth with vessels of that draught. He also hinted that 3000 men w[ould] be sent up that way.[92] Camped, about an hour after sundown, at the last camping place on the Mohave, about 200 yds below where we camped on the night before last.

February 1, 1858; Monday. Morning cool and rather cloudy, but became warm & clear about 9. a.m. Some of the mules missing to day. Br Sam[ue]l White went after them. Were detained here in consequence.

February 2, 1858; Tuesday. Day quite warm and clear. Br [Samuel] White did not return till evening when he brought his 4 missing mules who had gone back about 25 miles, but when we drove up the stock in the evening, found that 4 others were gone. Hunted for them about two hours but could not find them.

February 3, 1858; Wednesday. [Francis] Marion [Lyman] and Joel White went after the missing mules. Returned about noon in company with br [Nathan] Tinney [Tenney] bringing two of the mules. Two others went after the balance. Day warm & pleasant.

February 4, 1858; Thursday. Weather clear & warm. The brn returned about 10 P.M. ^last night^ with the missing mules. Br [Nathan] Tinneys wagon in company with Sis [Louisa Barnes] Pratt's, [Margaret Ann] Bell's, [Ann] Taylor's &c arrived this evening. They are nearing the last of the San Bernardino emigration.

February 5, 1858; Friday. Left camp about 1 P.M. Stopped to get supper and feed the animals at the dry lake about 10 m[ile]s from the

90. Sugarloaf Mountain is a nearly 10,000-ft. peak in the San Bernardino range.

91. This is Lyman's destination. Having located his family, he will now begin backtracking across the desert to the east.

92. With over 2,000 troops bivouacked near Fort Bridger in Wyoming, awaiting orders from US President James Buchanan to begin their offensive, the possibility of another army entering the territory from the south was a real concern.

Mohave. Went on a mile [to] the other side [of] the summit and camped about 1 a.m. Weather clear and warm.

February 6, 1858; Saturday. Left camp at sunrise. Day warm & pleasant. Reached Bitter Springs at 1 P.M. Found some dry grass a short distance below the spring and to the right of it. Remained here all night.

February 7, 1858; Sunday. Morning cold, but day quite warm. Left camp at 10½ a.m. Stopped to feed and get supper about 4 m[ile]s beyond the mouth of the Kanyon. Camped for the night at 2 a.m. 2 m[ile]s this side of the Point of the Mountain—15 m[ile]s from Kingston. Night windy, dusty and very disgagreeable.

February 8, 1858; Monday. Left camp a 7½ a.m. Reached Kingston at 2 P.M. Camped on the point opposite Savage's Spring about sundown. Day clear but windy and disagreeable.

February 9, 1858; Tuesday. Left camp at 12m. Stopped to feed and get supper about 5 m[ile]s from the summit. Camped for the night at 2. a.m. on this edge of the dry lake. Night pleasant and tolerably warm.

February 10, 1858; Wednesday. Left camp at 7. a.m. Stopped to feed and get breakfast [on] the other side the lake. Reached mountain springs at 8. P.M. Day warm and pleasant.

February 11, 1858; Thursday. Left camp at 9½ a.m. Reached William's camp at 3 p.m. Day warm & pleasant with the exception of the wind which almost always blows down this Kanyon.

February 12, 1858; Friday. Lay in camp to day. This morning John Mayfield, Geo Clark, and Joseph Tanner arrived with a light wagon and five animals. Day windy & cold.[93]

February 13, 1858; Saturday.[94] Travilled as far as Los Vegas where we found Brs Seth and Freeman Tanner, Br [William] Crosby and family with whom we staid till morning.

February 14, 1858; Sunday. Repaired our wagon and travelled on to the Muddy where we arrived at 3 o'clock on the morning of the 15th.

---

93. This last sentence was written vertically in the margin of the page.

94. Lyman breaks off from the main body of immigrants to travel faster to Salt Lake, accompanied by US diplomat Thomas L. Kane, who would mediate between the federal troops and Brigham Young. See Grow and Walker, *The Prophet and the Reformer*, 233–37. I have omitted a seven-page account of the main group's progress in favor of Lyman's own record that was nevertheless entered into the diary in someone else's hand.

February 15, 1858; Monday. Slept here till daylight, and then proceeded to the Rio Virgin and camped some miles up the river.

February 16, 1858; Tuesday. Proceeded to the Beaver Dam, where we found Capt[ai]n [Jefferson] Hunt. Took supper with him at dark and went on to the mouth of the Kanyon ~~on~~ ^leading to^ the divide where we camped.

February 17, 1858; Wednesday. Travelled on to the Camp Springs[95] where we took breakfast. Proceeded then to the foot of the Santa Clara, at which point I left the party and travelled to Fort Clara, where I slept at Bishop [William] Crosby's. Then preached to the people.

February 18, 1858; Thursday. Went to the cotton farm – from thence to Harmony where I arrived about 2. A.M. of the 19th. Slept an hour or two at John D. Lee's.[96]

February 19, 1858; Friday. Travelled on to Cedar, here I remained till the morning of the 20th.

February 20, 1858; Saturday. Started for Salt Lake City. Our company was composed of Col. [Thomas] Kane, myself, Joseph Mathews and E[dward] L. Mills. We travelled to, and lodged at, Beaver.

February 21, 1858; Sunday. Travelled to Fillmore, where we slept for a couple of hours on the morning of the 22nd.

February 22, 1858; Monday. ~~Sunday~~ Proceeded to Salt Creek [Nephi] where we arrived about 1.a.m of the 23rd.

February 23, 1858; Tuesday. ~~Monday~~ Travelled to Payson where we arrived about sundown. Lodged with bishop Charles Hancock.

February 24, 1858; Wednesday. Travelled on to ~~Lake City~~ ^American Fork City^ where we lodged with bishop L[eonard] E. Harrington.

February 25, 1858; Thursday. Reached Salt Lake City ~~when~~ about 4 P.M. This evening had an interview with the Governor [Brigham Young], Col. [Thomas L.] Kane was present and had a kindly greeting with his old friends of '46 at which time he visited us at Council Bluffs [Iowa].

I remained with my family until the 8th of March on which day I

---

95. Camp Springs was located two miles west of the Paiute village of Shivwits.

96. It seems impossible that Lyman would not have asked Lee about the Mountain Meadows Massacre, which had occurred five months prior and for which Lee would be tried and executed.

left for the south having in company, Brs [Cunningham] Mathews and [Edward] Mills, and Sister Leona Morley. Reached Lehi to day.[97]

March 9, 1858; Tuesday. Reached & staid at Payson.

March 10, 1858; Wednesday. " " " Salt Creek.

March 11, 1858; Thursday. " " " Cedar Springs.

March 12, 1858; Friday. " " " Fillmore.

March 13, 1858; Saturday. Reached and staid at Beaver were I was detained by the stormy weather until Friday the 19th.

March 19, 1858; Friday.[98] On the evening of this day I reached Parowan, where I found part of my family. Here I remained until Monday morning the 20th.

March 22, 1858; Monday. When [today] I reached Cedar [City]. From this time until the ~~first of~~ last of March was occupied in preparing for the exploring expedition to the Colorado.

March 31, 1858; Wednesday. Br Bennett brought his carriage and took me to Harmony where I remained over night and preached to the people. Brs W[illiam] S. Warren[,] David Holladay[,] and Norman Taylor accompanied me here.

April 2, 1858; Friday. Preached to the people of Washington, and ^solemnized two marriages^. In the afternoon of the same day went in company with Prest [Harrison] Pierce and br Glade to Heberville,[99] where br. Joseph Horn was opening a farm under the direction of the Presidency. From thence to Fort Clara where lodged at Bishop [William] Crosby's.

April 3, 1858; Saturday. Preached to the inhabitants of the Fort; and in the afternoon bid adieu to our friends at Fort Clara and joined the balance of ~~the~~ party at the foot of the river.[100]

97. Brigham Young sent Lyman and eighteen mounted men back to southern Utah to see if it was, in fact, possible for troops to steam up the Colorado River. They left on Mar. 8, 1858

98. There are no entries for several days. Lyman will begin recording consistently again on Apr. 2.

99. Heberville was south of Fort Clara. The settlers raised cotton there until the flood of 1861 took out the village and its rock dam. Washington is east of Fort Clara. Harrison Pearce was one of the Mississippi converts.

100. Lyman listed the "names of the party" as: Amasa Lyman, Robt Clift, Spanish Interpreter, Ira Hatch, Guide & Piede Interpreter, Freeman Tanner, John ^D.^ Holladay, David ^H.^ Holladay, [Francis] Marion Lyman, Henry G. Boyle, Walter C. Dodge, Wm.

April 4, 1858; Sunday. Left the Clara about 8. a.m. Nooned about 3 miles beyond the summit. After we started again, one of the mules kicked his pack off, in consequence of a want of proper arrangements & scattered a sack of crackers over and along the road. Reached the Beaver Dam about 5 P.M. and found one of my pack mules, having on all my clothing, ammunition &c was missing. Marion [Lyman] and Harvey Clark went back after it. Sent our animals out to the grass about 1½ miles distant, but they were so restless we had to bring them in and tie them up.

April 5, 1858; Monday. Sent the stock to the grass again for two or three hours. Marion [Lyman] & Harvey [Clark] arrived with the missing mule and all the things safe, about 10 a.m. Packed up and moved down to the peach orchard at 12m. arriving there about 4 P.M. Called the members of the company together and organized them by dividing into two messes—appointing br Freeman Tanner Capt[ai]n of Mess A and Br. John D. Holladay Capt[ai]n of Mess B and Robert Clift Captain of the whole company. Very little feed here & the mules inclined to stray so we tied up to night. Called the camp together and had prayers.

April 6, 1858; Tuesday. Left camp at 6 a.m. C[unningham] Mathews mule ran off about 3 miles. Reached "Isaac's" camp at 9½ a.m. Stopped here for the day as there is good feed on the hills. Br [Robert] Clift complained here of severe pain in his leg & foot, & of being very unwell. He was in bed most of the day and has considerable fever.

In the evening gave the br[ethre]n my views and advice with respect to the course I wished them to pursue, both with regard to their intercourse with each other, and the various duties which will develop upon them in the course of our trip. Weather rather cool but pleasant.

April 7, 1858; Wednesday. Left camp at 7½ a.m. Went down the Virgin about 4 miles & then turned to the right and took Walker's trail over the hills—a rough road but somewhat shorter. Ascended the big hill near when the old /[18]49 road takes up it. About 10 miles from where we left the Virgin found excellent grass and halted to feed for 2½ hours. Reached the Muddy about sunset, where we found br. David Savage's company camped. Dr. McIntyre was along. Preached to the people in the evening.

April 8, 1858; Thursday. Remained in camp all day. Wind blowing

---

S. Warren, Marcus L. Shepherd, Cunningham Mathews, Edward L. Mills, Henry Jennings, Fred L. Perris, Taylor Crosby, Norman Taylor, Harvey Clark, Wm H. Shearman.

a perfect gale all day—covering everything with sand and dirt. Very unpleasant. Towards evening had a slight sprinkling of rain. Read the President's circular to the camp.[101]

April 9, 1858; Friday. Left camp at 7½ a.m. Reached the halfway stopping place at 2½ P.M. Let our animals get dinner and started on at 4½ ^P.M.^ The main part of the [wagon] train reached the Vegas at 10. P.M. But myself and a few others arrived there at 11¼ P.M. Found br[e-thre]n [Benjamin R.] Hultz, Oscar Hamblin & Sidney Burton there as missionaries. Br [Robert] Clift's leg and foot have continued very bad but tonight he was much worse then usual. High fever and general weakness. Day cool and pleasant for travelling.

April 10, 1858; Saturday. Remained in camp. Br [Robert] Clift continues very sick. Did the best we could to relieve him. Occupied the day, which was warm and pleasant, in regulating our packs and preparing for the desert between here and [eighty miles southeast to] the Colorado.

April 11, 1858; Sunday. Concluded to wait another day for br [Robert] Clift as he thinks he will be able to accompany us tomorrow. The wagons with which we have been travelling thus far left this morning a 7½ a.m. for San Bernardino. Preached to our little company a 11. a.m. Day very warm, otherwise pleasant.

April 12, 1858; Monday. Left the Vegas a 7.20 m a.m. and reached Resting Springs in 9 miles at 10-10 m a.m. Rested here till 12m. Our course from this place lay up a long, rough, rocky & uneven slope to the mouth of a Kanyon or pass, which by our observation we made at the Fort Vegas bears "southeast" (Magnetic) from the latter place. Stopped in the Kanyon to let the stock feed on a little dry grass we found, at 4 P.M. Distance this afternoon 12 miles.

Left camp at 6 P.M. Continued through the Kanyon and down a long wash and slope across a dry lake—a level stretch of 4 or 5 miles—and up the opposite slope, which was not quite so rough as the one we ascended this morning. Stopped at 11. P.M. in a barren desolate place, as

101. On April 6, US President James Buchanan issued a proclamation that said Mormons were "under the influence of leaders to whom they seem to have surrendered their judgment." However, "to save the effusion of blood," he offered "a free and full pardon to all who will submit themselves to the just authority of the Federal Government." Buchanan, "Proclamation."

br [Robert] Clift's leg was so bad he could not ride any farther that night. Distance since supper 17 m[ile]s. Day warm & pleasant.

April 13, 1858; Tuesday. Left camp at 5 a.m. Reached the holes where Ira [Hatch] expected to find water in about 7 miles at 7. a.m. Were much disappointed at first in not finding more than enough water to wet our lips—but by hunting round a little in the neighboring ravines we found as much as we needed for our own use—but not sufficient to water the stock. Were detained here an hour filling our canteens kegs &c &c when we proceeded over a very rough road for about 7 miles when we halted at 10½ a.m.to get breakfast. Coming down one of the Kanyons this morning, br. [William] Shearman's best mule got one of the prickly pear burrs on ~~his~~ one side of his mouth and in his efforts to knock it off stuck it in more deeply. We had to throw him before we could get it off and in the operation he got stifled [suffocated], in consequence of which he had to be turned loose.

Resumed our journey at 12m. and reached the Colorado at 3 P.M. Distance 12 m[ile]s. The whole country over which we passed between the Vegas & Colorado is barren and desolate in the extreme, without a single spring, and scarcely any grass, but abounding in cactus & prickly pear bushes which are very annoying, and indeed dangerous to the animals. The country all around the Colorado on both sides presents the same barren, rocky, mountainous desert aspect, and there is no feed but brush and a little scattering dry bunch and salt grass, and that very scarce.

This river is rightly named for it is very red and muddy. A few hundred yards above where we struck the river, on the same side, the rocky bluffs rise perpendicularly from the shore to the height of several hundred feet—rendering it impossible to get down to the water if approached from that quarter. The opposite shore is not so bold. The water here is shallow on this side, but swift and deep near the opposite shore. Day has been very warm.

April 14, 1858; Wednesday. Moved down the river about two miles to a place where there is a little grass. The river here is about 250 yards wide and runs quite swiftly in the channel. Piede [Paiute] Jim swam over & back, with the assistance of a dry stick to buoy him up.

April 15, 1858; Thursday. Left camp at 8¼ a.m. In a few miles below this place the country on each side of the river begins to widen out into long gradual slopes up to the mountains, assuming the appearance, to a great extent, of the country in the vicinity of the Virgin. Our route to day lay over the bluffs and along the edges and tops of precipices bordering on the river. A very rough rocky and hilly road. Camped at 1½ P.M. at a place where there was tolerable good bunch grass. Distance 15 miles. Day very disagreeable. Very high wind and plenty of dust. One of the three Indians who have accompanied from the Vegas sent down to the Hyatt wickyups [wigwams] about three miles below and brought up about a dozen of the Hyatts [Mojave Indians], who staid at our camp all night.

April 16, 1858; Friday. Immediately after breakfast, Oat-sen-a-wantz,[102] the principal chief, arrived accompanied by ~~about~~ several of his minor chiefs and some 15 or 20 warriors, making 35 in all who were present with us. They are a fine looking race of men and will compare very advantageously with the Piede tribes[103] in size as well as in many other respects. The old chief was so considerate as to remain with his party some distance from our camp, when he learned we were at breakfast until we had done. And in their deportment in camp, and obedience to their chief they set an example which many of our own people might imitate with advantage.

We had quite a long "talk," & he expressed a desire to cultivate friendly relations & intercourse with us, and also said he intended to pay us a visit in the settlements. Gave him flour and meat to make their breakfast and then gave the chief the few presents we had brought for him, consisting of a blanket, shirt, knife and a piece of tobacco. He gave everything away, not keeping even a pipe full of tobacco for himself. The blanket he cut up into breech cloths and together with the tobacco divided out according to age and rank—the shirt he gave to one, and the butcher knife to another. He, himself had one, only a hickory shirt and a plaid breech cloak.

Left camp at [blank] and proceeded by a tolerably good road, 12 miles down the river where we camped on good grass at [blank]. The banks of the river here on this side are so steep that the stock had to be

102. Little is known about Oat-sen-a-wantz, apart from rare contact with white travelers. A few months after their encounter with Lyman and his company, the Mohave would attack immigrant trains, leaving settlers and natives alike dead. *AML*, 266–67.

103. Piedes was the regional name for the southern Paiute tribes in Arizona and Utah.

driven a short distance below to get down to water. Our course to day lay on this side of a quite large island [Cottonwood Island] in the river, about 10 m[ile]s long. Weather quite sultry. At night had a little rain—thundering & storming heavily to all appearance in the mountains to the W. and NW. of us. Very glad to see it rain in the mountains as it will probably be a benefit to us in crossing the deserts.

April 17, 1858; Saturday. Morning rather cloudy, and cool enough to be pleasant. Quite a number of the Hyatts remained in our camp last night. Left camp at 7½. a.m. For the next 3 or 4 miles the road is pretty good—the next 9 or 10 miles over a very mountainous, rough, rocky road, through narrow defiles, down the sides of sharp, craggy rocked hills, and along the sides of precipices where a single misstep would precipitate an animal down a hundred feet or more. Noticed one place in particular, about 10 m[ile]s from our camp this morning, which affords excellent facilities for commanding the river, as the channel is, at this point, on this (west) side of the stream, and the adjacent rocks & ravines afford protection and shelter for a great number of men.

Saw a few of the squaws as we came down the river to day. Also learned from br [Ira] Hatch that the Hyatts are at war with the Apaches and that Oat-sen-a-wantz and his party were out on a war excursion when they arrived at our camp. Stopped about 12½ P.M. to noon. Proceeded again at 2½ P.M. Went 12 or 13 miles farther over a pretty good ^road^ with the exception of a very short distance and camped at sundown on good grass, close by one of the Hyatt wickiups and wheat fields. Oat-sen-a-wantz sent us word that some of his men intended to stampede our mules if they had an opportunity, and that we had better tie them up. He also sent his low chief Totab, and two others to stay at our camp all night and see that no mischief was done us.

We hobbled nearly all the mules, and having made every precaution in our power, all but the guard went to bed. About 9. p.m. the animals took a sudden fright and came very near running over the packs and our beds. They came within a foot of my bed and ^had^ I awakened a second later, would undoubtedly have run over me, and Marion who was sleeping with me. They did not run many yards, however, before we succeeded in stopping them.

April 18, 1858; Sunday. Left camp about 7½ a.m. and proceeded down the river to the place where we were to meet Oat-sen-a-wantz and his chiefs, and where they have their villages on both sides of the river. The road from the Mohave, made by the government troops, intersects the river at this place. The country on each side of the river continues to open out wider & wider into long gradual slopes from 8 to 12 miles long on each side of the stream; but the tillable land is confined to the immediate river bottom, which in the widest place we can see for some miles down, does not exceed a mile or mile and a half in width. The bottom is here quite picturesque & beautiful and contained a considerable number of good sized cottonwood trees. The water is also much better than higher up, and is almost clear.

Soon after we stopped, Oat-sen-a-wantz made his appearance attended by a large con course of his people both male and female. As we did not yet know what kind of a reception we should meet with, we made every preparation for either a hostile or peaceful one. I soon found, however, by their appearing accompanied by their women and without their arms, that they were peacefully disposed.

I concluded to stop all day with them, and have more talk with the chief and ascertain further their feelings towards us. We accordingly moved down into the bottom, where we were soon surrounded by about 250 of the natives—of both sexes—who had assembled prepared to have a gala day, devoted to mirth and enjoyment. They mingled with us freely and with confidence—seemed to enjoy themselves very well, and for Indians behaved themselves remarkably well. They begged but little, compared with the Piedes & then principally for tobacco. They all appeared to be in good healthy condition, with but a very few exceptions, and [to] judge from their appearance they must have plenty to eat. Notwithstanding they mixed with us so freely, and had abundance of opportunities to steal, yet they took but one or two small articles, and that was discountenanced by their chief.

Some of their women are well made and possessed of tolerable good looking features—and, in their antique dresses of bark and wool, reaching from their waist to their knees, they made quite a picturesque, and tasty appearance. The most of them, however, are corrupted & polluted by the little intercourse they have had with the Americans and one or two are afflicted with venereal disease, which if not checked, and unless a course is taken to prevent it, will no doubt soon spread among the rest of the tribe. They judged us, at first, by what they had seen and known of the Americans who have visited them, and offered to let us have their women to use, in consideration of blankets, tobacco, etc.; but when we told them that we did not come for such purpose—that we did not want it, and that it was wrong, they seemed much pleased and their confidence was increased. Oat-sen-a-wantz renewed his expressions of friendship and desires to have some of our people come and live with them, & assured me he would protect them.

The day has been exceedingly disagreeable, on account of the high winds and cloud of dust blowing all the time. We could not eat while the crowd was in camp as we had not sufficient to feed them all—but when they were nearly all gone we had supper, and fed the chief, and the few others who remained. Called them all together and had prayers.

April 19, 1858; Monday. Left camp at 7 a.m. accompanied by a guide to show us the nearest way over to Kingston Springs. Followed the road made by the troops, which makes up the slope almost due west from the river. About 22-3 miles bro[ugh]t us to a good spring in a Kanyon, with pretty good grass. Camped here about 2½ P.M. Day cool and pleasant.

April 20, 1858; Tuesday. Left camp at 7½ a.m. Proceeded up the Kanyon for 1½ or 2 miles, keeping to the right hand, and then over a very rough rock and steep hill. Crossed a quite extensive plain covered with good grass—then ascended a long slope and crossed the range of mountains lying west of us—a little to the right of the highest ridge. Descended a steep hill and a long wash for some distance, and then turned to the right up a ravine and in ½ a mile came to a small spring on the left hand of the ravine, which, by dipping all night, afforded a few gallons apiece for our animals. Good feed—but the stock were too dry to eat much. Day tolerable cool. Named this <u>Pleasant Spring</u>.

April 21, 1858; Wednesday. Left camp at 8 a.m. Proceeded down a long wash and slope across the valley, where we passed close to one of the surveyor's stakes. Up the opposite slope to the mountain lying a little N. of W from our last night camp & passing up a long wash between a range of reddish hills on our left and a pile of dark looking hills to our right, making a straight line for the large dark mountain which we could see beyond the first range, [we] reached the top of the first range of mountains through the Kanyon and then descended by a steep hill down the Kanyon for about 2 miles then turned to the left over the low foot hills for about 2½ miles where we came to a spring in a small ravine or gully to our right—just about opposite the highest point of the mountain that rises to our right. ^Named this water Saline Spring.^ And lying S.W. from the point of the same mountain where it makes down towards the large dry lake which lies about 10 miles to the N.E. of us, and which extends, apparently, 25 miles or more to the N. The feed here is splendid, and has been of the same kind from about 5 miles the other side [of] the hill. Distance to day 25 miles. Succeeded in gitting all the water our animals wanted to drink at this spring, by dipping and watering them in a bucket.

April 22, 1858; Thursday. Concluded to lay by here to day.

April 23, 1858; Friday. Left camp at 7½ a.m. Proceeded up the large wash and through the low pass a little N. of W. from our last night camp—then turned to the right travelling N. along the base of the mountains for 7 or 8 miles when we came to a spring on the hill side at the foot of the big mountain—on the S. side of it. The Indians have had a small corn patch here. Water is plenty at present—though the stream from the spring is small—and sinks a few rods from the source, but the Indians say there is water here all the year round, and by digging a large hole to hold the water so that it would not spread and sink so soon, a large number of stock might be watered here. ^Found some wild flax growing on our way today.^ Feed is scarce in the immediate vicinity of the spring. Kingston Springs according to the Indians is about 18 miles W. of this place. Concluded to call this Corn Springs[,] the adjacent valley Corn Spring Valley. Found considerable good feed on the hills near by.

April 24, 1858; Saturday. Left camp at 7½ a.m. Went down the wash, to avoid the rough road over the mountain, then turned to the right doubling the point of the mountain, crossed a good many of the foot hills, and then right down another long wash to the dry lake lying at the foot of the Lead Mine Mountain. Crossed the lake and camped by a sulfur spring, about 300 yds from the Sand Bluffs which the Indians have dug out. The water has a very peculiar and exceedingly disagreeable taste—but in the absence of better it is very welcome. We watered our stock, and then cleaned out the hole, which is about 6 or 7 feet long, 2 to 3 wide, and the water, in the deepest place, about 4½ feet deep. Found it to be a living spring, and the water ran in fast enough to enable us to water all the stock again, about 9 P.M. It is situated about 20 miles from the lead mines, and about 8 or 9 miles E of the Kingston Spring road. There is some bunch grass about here. Enough to bait on. ^N.N.E. (magnetic) from the W. point of Corn Spring Mountain.^ Our Indian guide left us this morning to return to the Colorado. We gave him a shirt and provisions to last him back. We came to the conclusion to leave this place at 2. a.m. tomorrow. Day has been very warm. ^Distance to day 20 m[ile]s.^

April 25, 1858; Sunday. The guard drove up the animals about 2. a.m. and either while we were getting breakfast or watering the mules, through negligence in not properly guarding the animals, several of them strayed off and took the back track. Taylor Crosby, Norman Taylor & Harvey Clark went after them and brought all back but br [Robert] Clift's pack mule. One of the mules kicked br H. Clark on the leg, between the hip and the knee. It was a severe blow, and knocked him down—causing him to vomit freely. N. Taylor and T. Crosby assisted him to camp. His leg is swelled very badly and so sore he can scarcely move it. Made a bed for him and applied wet cold cloths. Br Clift went after his missing mule, and has not at this hour (about 10 a.m.) returned. Br [Henry] Boyle[104] has gone out to meet him with some water.

Morning is very hot. Br Boyle returned in about an hour having overtaken br Clift and left him the canteen. Br. Clift returned about 3 p.m. with the missing mule, having been gone about 10 hours. Concluded to leave Br[ethre]n Clift, Freeman Tanner and H. G. Boyle with H. Clark to bring him on so soon as he should be able to ride, or some other conveyance should come for him—and proceed with the balance of the party, as there was but little feed there, and that not of the best kind.

Wrote a note and sent it by "Mexican" to br [Benjamin R.] Hultz, to request him to send his wagon up to the lead mines and farther if necessary, to meet the br[ethre]n & carry H. Clark to the Vegas. Got supper and left camp at sundown for the lead mines leaving Piede Jim with the br[ethre]n at camp, so that they could send word to me if anything

104. Henry G. Boyle and others of the Mormon Battalion had explored a route from Los Angeles to Salt Lake City. They were the first to plot the southwestern trail since the Spanish explorers.

unexpected should occur. In the night Ira [Hatch] missed the trail and in consequence, the latter part of the distance was very rough, but after ascending and descending a good many sheer and rocky hills we reached the lead mines in safety about 2 a.m of the 26th. Remained here till morning did not find water enough here to give our stock any and but very little feed. The night was very pleasant for travelling being cool and yet mild and having the light of the moon all the way.

April 26, 1858; Monday. Left our camp about 7. a.m. Reached Cottonwood Springs about 11. a.m. and camped by a spring ~~½ miles~~ ^200 yds^ to the left of the road, and between it and the road that comes down from Williams camp. Day very warm.

April 27, 1858; Tuesday. Remained in camp to wait for the balance of the party. Drove the stock up to William's Camp after breakfast where there is excellent feed. Day cloudy and cool—a few drops of rain fell in camp—considerable must have fallen in the mountains to all appearances. Piede Jim arrived about noon bringing word that br [Robert] Clift and his party were at the lead mines this morning—that br. Harvey [Clark] much better, and able to ride with tolerable ease—and that the Indians crept into their camp the night we left them at the spring and while they were asleep and stole br. Clift's roan mule. They arrived in camp about dark.

April 28, 1858; Wednesday. Left camp about 7½. a.m. Met br [Jacob] Hamblin about 5 m[ile]s from the Vegas Spring with the wagon, accompanied by two other brethren on their way to the lead mines, for br Harvey [Clark] they turned back with us. Reached the fort and camped about 1 p.m. Day cool and pleasant for travelling but too windy and dusty to be agreeable in camp.

April 29, 1858; Thursday. Left the fort at 6½ a.m. Morning very cold—appeared to be storming in the mountains around us. Reached the grass—halfway about 1.P.M. stopped an hour and a half. Had quite a smart shower of rain along in the afternoon. Reached the Muddy about 9.P.M. in company with two others—the packs and the balance of the company having got there an hour before us. Ira [Hatch] and Br [Henry G.] Boyle went up to the wickyups and got an Indian to herd o[u]r animals.

April 30, 1858; Friday. Beautiful, pleasant morning. Left the Muddy at 2½ p.m. Reached the gap on the bench by the old road and camped at sunset. Piede Caster Thomas went with us to guard our stock. Was quite cold, and had a smart shower ^of rain.^

May 1, 1858; Saturday. Left camp at 6½ a.m. Stopped at Isaac's camp to noon. Sent brn H[enry] G. Boyle and Taylor Crosby on to the fort in advance to let them know the day we should arrive there. Went on to the Peach Orchard and camped about 6 P.M. Day warm.

May 2, 1858; Sunday. Left camp at 7 a.m. Stopped two hours at the Beaver Dam, and then went on to the Santa Clara. The packs and most of the [wagon] train arrived there about 8 P.M. Myself and br [William] Warren got to camp about an hour afterwards. The night was quite dark and F[red] Perris'[105] pack mule strayed away from the [wagon] train & could not be found—Turned the mules out by themselves—hobbled—as we could not find them to get them all together and could not see to find feed. Day was very warm. Evening mild and pleasant.

May 3, 1858; Monday. Gathered our mules together—F[red] Perris having found his about a mile back towards the spring & left camp about 7½ a.m. Reached Clara Fort about 11 a.m. where we rested etc. 2½ P.M. Partook of an excellent dinner which had been prepared for us by the citizens. Proceeded to the "she-spitz" or Land Rock Springs distance 5 miles, where there is good feed. Camped here for the night. Day warm & pleasant.

May 4, 1858; Tuesday. After breakfast we proceeded to the Cotton Farm on the Rio Virgin. Stopped for 3 hours, and took dinner with the President [of the Washington branch]—Br Robert Covington. Went on to br Charles Crisman's about 6 miles farther up the river and camped. Took supper with him & his family.

May 5, 1858; Wednesday. Part of us took breakfast with br Ezra Chase, and the balance with br. [Charles] Crisman. Had to hunt a couple of hours for our animals as the Indians who herded them went to sleep and let them stray off. Succeeded in finding them all, and left camp about 9 a.m. Travelled to within 7 miles of Harmony and camped on Ash Creek. The early part of the morning was clear and pleasant, but

105. Frederick T. Perris was a young British surveyor who apprenticed with an architect in Australia prior to his family's immigration to America. In time he become the chief engineer for the Atchison, Topeka and Santa Fe Railway and oversaw construction of the railroad through the Cajon Pass into San Bernardino.

it clouded up. The wind commenced blowing hard & cold, and a little rain fell on us—a good deal apparently in the mountains. The wind blew directly in our faces, which made it very disagreeable causing our eyes to smart and our heads to ache. Br John Holliday went on to the fort this evening to tell them we were coming, and to have breakfast prepared for us in the morning.

May 6, 1858; Thursday. Left camp by day break. Morning cold, windy and drizzly. Reached Harmony about 7.a.m. The weather continued to grow more stormy & we concluded to accept br John D. Lee's invitation to stay with him till tomorrow. Preached to the people in the school house at 11 a.m.

May 7, 1858; Friday. Morning cold, windy and cloudy. Left the fort about 9.a.m. Soon after we left it commenced to rain and continued to do so nearly all the way to Cedar City—where we arrived about 1 P.M.[106]

106. This entry is followed by a few blank lines; the next entry in this diary book is for Dec. 1862.

6 Mementos of the Old World, 1860

Lyman was finally set apart for a mission to Europe after years of having been promised an assignment there by Brigham Young. He was accompanied by his usual mission companion, apostle Charles C. Rich, and son Francis M. Lyman. He recorded the now-familiar journey of once again crossing the plains, but this time, indicating the passage of time, they were able to travel by rail from Detroit to upstate New York and across a suspension bridge to Niagra Falls, then on through New England to New York City. Lyman would also visit relatives in Massachusetts, New Hampshire, and Vermont prior to setting out across the ocean on a steamship. In England he begins writing editorials for the *Millennial Star* and conducting day-to-day mission business, as well as traveling through Britain and Scandinavia—getting a glimpse of Queen Victoria and Prince Albert on one occasion and visiting areas of Scottish history from the time of William Wallace and Robert Burns. Portions of the diary are so similar to Rich's that one has to assume they relied on one another for details.

April 30, 1860; Monday.[1] Previous to starting on my mission for

1. The entries for Apr. 30–May 19 appear in three separate volumes held at the CHL. Lyman initially wrote in pencil in a small daybook catalogued as vol. 18, then copied these entries into another notebook, vol. 19. Finally, he would carefully recopy these entries in pen into a larger notebook, catalogued as vol. 17, along with his missionary certificate and a letter from the First Presidency. He drew a large letter *X* through the original entries in vol. 18 to indicate they had been copied. The careful handwriting and pristine care of the copied journal suggests that he saw his mission to England worthy of remembrance. I have used vol. 17 because of the added details, removed strikeouts, and correction of some spelling errors.

Europe I received the following documents which are here inserted in full.[2]

May 1, 1860; Tuesday. About 5 P.M. I started on my mission to England in company with Bro. C[harles] C. Rich and Elders F[rancis] M. Lyman, Joseph Rich, John Tobin, and John Brown. The party of brethren with whom we travelled were, David Savage, Richard Johnson, Henry Harrison Noyes and Samuel White; also Elders W[illiam] H. Dame and Reuben [A.] McBride.[3]

As we passed out of the city the streets were enlivened by the presence of Sunday May parties of our children who were paying their annual tribute of admiration to the floral beauties of the opening Spring. In consequence of our late hour of starting we only travelled a few miles and camped [east of Sugar House on Parley's Creek] near the residence of Bro. Ira Eldredge with whom myself and Bro Rich lodged for the night. We were kindly entertained and passed the night very pleasantly.

May 2, 1860; Wednesday.[4] This morning some of our mules were not at hand in consequence of which Bros [Henry] Noyes, [Reuben] McBride and [Samuel] White taried to recover the missing stock. We travelled to day to what is called Parley's Park.[5] Camped for the night at half past five o'clock near the crossing of East Canyon Creek. The locality of our camp was on the north-east quarter of the beautiful park sacred to the memory and housing the name of the lamented Parley [Pratt][6] and in sight of bro Samuel Snider's lumber mill and bucket factory.[7] As we were about retiring to rest the parties with the missing stock came into

2. The three documents are his Elder's Certificate signifying that he is a missionary, a letter of appointment to Lyman and Rich from the First Presidency outlining expectations for immigration and finances, and the blessing Lyman received from Brigham Young setting him apart for the mission.

3. Some of these men were on their way to overseas missions, while others had been assigned to a church mule train to purchase and haul farm machinery from the Midwest to Utah Territory.

4. In the left margin next to this entry, Lyman wrote in faint pencil "Note to be added."

5. Parley's Park City, later just Park City, was named after apostle Parley P. Pratt. It was primarily an area where the three or four families lived and grazed cattle.

6. Pratt was murdered by Hector McLean, whose wife he had taken as a plural wife of his own. Givens and Grow, *Parley P. Pratt*, 373–91.

7. Samuel Comstock Snyder was the first settler in Parley's Park, where he and his family endured extreme weather and Indian raids to run a sawmill and later a gristmill.

camp. At this point we received an addition to our party of two men—Alexander Dempster an attaché of the army and George W. Kelly who said he was a discharged soldier; there was also in our company John Eldridge from Filmore going to the States on his own account. Our road today was rather rough. It can be much improved in its condition and by changeing its location in some places. Weather fine.

May 3, 1860; Thursday. Left camp at forty five minutes past eight o'clock A.M. and travelled to and up Chalk Creek one mile above the coal mine. Camped at half past five P.M. Road up the creek rough. We went into the mine and saw the several veins which have been opened. The coal appears to be in large quantity and of good quality. The industry and perserverance of Bro. [John] Sprig[g]s[8] in opening the mine is certainly commendable. There is on Chalk Creek some very good land and a fair chance for its improvement. The grass was rich and plentiful.

May 4, 1860; Friday. This morning Bro [John] S[priggs] brought us some specimens of coal which we carried for comparison in the East. Left camp at 9 O'clock and fifteen minutes. Some clouds and wind from the west. Continued our travel up the creek, and made noon halt at ten minutes past 12 O'clock. Travelled from this point four hours and camped on Bear River in a sheltered position by the timber while it was storming on the mountains. During the night the weather became clear and the change was attended with frost. At this point we were reminded of New England by the drumming of a pheasant or partridge.

May 5, 1860; Saturday. Left camp at half past seven and at two o'clock we reached the mail station on the old road. We learned that the ox-train had passed this point about 10 O'clock; and that Bishop [Edwin D.] Woolley and party passed on by the old road. We followed the ox-train down the Muddy [Creek] about three miles when they left the river and passed in an easterly direction over some high land where there was no former trail. This portion of our travel was heavy. From the summit of high land we discovered the ox-train in the distance; we overtook them and camped with them at twenty minutes past seven P.M. We found

8. The territorial legislature offered a $1,000 incentive in 1854 to anyone who could establish a workable coal mine within forty miles of Salt Lake City. John Spriggs and William Kimball applied but were rejected because the mine, at what became Coalville, was forty-five miles away and the coal was of inferior quality. Bancroft, *History of Utah*, 736–37.

Capt. [Joseph W.] Young and Company in good health and spirits.[9] From this point we sent an express to intercept Bishop Woolley and party at the Lower Crossing of the Muddy. Took supper with Capt. Young. The Capt. seemed to be quite at home in his business, and is doubtless a good man for the work assigned him.

May 6, 1860; Sunday. This morning there were some indications of a storm. Travelled to a point on the Muddy where the ox-train had halted for breakfast. We taried there untill 10 O'clock then passed on to the Lower Crossing of the Muddy where we arrived at dark. During or morning halt a large band of Indians came down to the river near us and camped, being weather wise, under a sheltering bluff. In passing the high ground to-day we met a snow storm, and at our camp sight found our express men had not seen the bishop [Edwin D. Woolley] as he had not passed that way. Feed not plentiful. Weather cold.

May 7, 1860; Monday. This morning I received $1100 from Capt. Young and receipted for the same to Joseph W. Young. Gave some counsel to the brethren of the missionaries, and received into our Company Elder James Brown the 3rd, Walter M. Gibson and Samuel Lorenzo Adams; then parted with the ox-train, left camp at half past nine o'clock, travelled to Ham's Fork and crossed on the bridge built by the government.[10] Camped at half past three, wind high from the north with some snow. The country to-day was covered with cattle. After coming into camp we experienced a severe snow squall after which the weather became clear and we proceeded to organize the camp by electing James Brown Captain and John Tobin Sergeant of the Guard, with W[illiam] H. Dame to act as chaplain.

May 8, 1860; Tuesday. This morning weather clear and cool. We left camp at seven o'clock and arrived at the ferry on Green River at half past twelve, where we were detained two hours. We learned here that [Edwin

9. A nephew of Brigham Young was leading a church wagon train like the one Lyman and the missionaries were traveling in. It was headed in the opposite direction and was loaded down with supplies and immigrants. Over the next eight years, the church would send some forty trains of about fifty wagons each on this freight haul. Arrington, *Great Basin Kingdom*, 205–08.

10. Ham's Fork is a tributary of the Green River and flows about fifty miles shy of today's Rock Springs, Wyoming, past the town of Granger. The bridge was located near the confluence of Ham's Fork and Black's Fork.

D.] Woolley and party had preceded us some two and a half hours. Drove some ten miles and camped at 15 minutes past 5 P.M. Some Indians came into our camp. Weather not so cold as yesterday. At dark our stock had all left us, and for a time we were uncertain of their recovery, but at length we succeeded and had them again in our possession, and were thus relieved from the torture of uncertainty. Weather cool and wind high.

May 9, 1860; Wednesday. Weather pleasant. Left camp at 5 A.M., traveled one hour and then turned our stock out on thin but good grass. After grazing our stock for a time we passed on and made noon halt at Crossing of Big Sandy. From this point on travelled to Little Sandy where we stopped for supper at half past two, and then travelled untill dark and made dry camp.

May 10, 1860; Thursday. Left camp at ½ past 4 A.M. and on passing a high ground we, for the first time, saw the Bishop's [Edwin D. Woolley] company in the distance, encamped to the right of our road. We halted on Pacific Creek for our breakfast at ½ past 6: some small grass. As we stopped the wind arose much to our annoyance. During our halt, Bishop W[ooolley] and party passed us. We were again under way at ½ past 8 O'clock. At ½ past 3 we camped on Willow Creek. This evening passed over a deep drift of snow: the grass but slightly grown. Had some little rain: the wind high. We were joined during the evening by Bishop Wooley's company, composed of 14 men, 6 women and 12 children. They came into our organization for the journey, the names of the men were as follows: E. D. Woolley, Samuel Woolley, Joseph Price, John Cutler, Don C. Babbit, Samuel H. B. Smith, Joseph F. Smith, George Beebe, Alfred Beebe, P[hilip] H. Buzzard, F. H. Buzzard, Wm. Capener, Nephi Johnson, Mr. Davies.

May 11, 1860; Friday. Camp called at 4 A.M. Started at 6. Passed over the Rocky Ridge and moved on the Sweet Water [River] one mile east of the Mail Station.[11] Grass better than last night. Arrived here at 15 minutes to 11 o'clock, & at fifteen minutes past 1 were again on the way. Travelled to the 5th crossing of Sweet Water, grass poor, arrived at 3 P.M. Were visited by some Shoshone Indians whose encampment was

11. This is about eighty miles north of today's I-80. The trail took a northeastern jog to cross Ham's Fork and then the Green River and then to follow the Sweet Water River to the North Platte and Fort Caspar.

a short distance below us on the river. The wind rose in the evening and continued high through the night. The Indians returned to their lodges and promised to come in the morning to trade.

May 12, 1860; Saturday. Camp called at 4 A.M. The wind had subsided. The Indians returned and have for trade some buffalo meat and some revolvers. We trade with them while our men are recovering some of our stocks which had strayed. Myself and Bro. [Charles C.] Rich took breakfast with Bro. George Beebe. The missing stock came in and we were on the move when we learned that one of the party who had been in quest of the missing stock had not returned. We waited his return untill 15 minutes to 9 O'clock when we moved on and nooned at the fourth crossing of the river at twenty minutes past 12. From thence passed on and camped for the night in a small cave in the Rattle Snake Hill at twenty minutes past 4. From shelter of our position we were relieved from the wind which was very high. Here Bro. [David] Savage opened a fine spring in the base of the hill.

May 13, 1860; Sunday. This morning we gathered our stock for a march when it began to snow so violently that we were under the necessity of remaining untill one o'clock when the storm subsided and we traveled till night and then turned our stock on the hills. The weather during the night became clear, but remains cold.

May 14, 1860; Monday. This morning left camp at 6 o'clock and traveled to a point opposite the Independence Rock[12] where we halted at twenty minutes to 11. Grass thin and short. Halted for 2½ hours, then forded and left the Sweet Water, passed over to Greasewood Creek and camped at ½ past 4 o'clock. Wind somewhat high and cool: drove our stock one mile from camp for grass. During the night weather became mild and pleasant.

May 15, 1860; Tuesday. This morning left camp at half past 6 A.M. and as we came in sight of Prospect Hill[13] we met a party under the direction of Capt. [William F.] Reynolds making a topographical examination

---

12. A landmark on the Oregon and Mormon Trails (it was said you had to reach it by July 4 to avoid snow in the Rockies), Independence Rock is halfway across Wyoming on the Sweetwater River. See Kimball, *Historic Sites and Markers*, 84.

13. Prospect Hill is thirteen miles east of Independence Rock. It was called Prospect Hill because this was the first place emigrants could get a glimpse of the mountains and gauge the weather conditions.

and survey of the country on the head waters of the tributaries of the Missouri and Colorado.[14] They were escorted by troops. Made noon halt at ten minutes to eleven. Resumed our travel and camped for the night on the Platte River, about five miles above the bridge at twenty minutes past four: the weather somewhat cool. Bands of deer and antelope in sight, from our camp, on the opposite side of the river. During the day there was an accidental discharge of a rifle in the wagon of P[hilip] H. Buzzard. To night felt slightly indisposed from cold contracted on the journey. The weather during the night was quite cool from our proximity to the river and the snow-clad hills.

May 16, 1860; Wednesday. Raised camp at 20 minutes to 7 A.M. Traveled over a high ridge to the river at the upper Bridge, thence down the north side of the river over a very sandy road. Halted below Bridge at 20 minutes to 11. During this morning Bro. Samuel White fell in attempting to get on his wagon and was slightly injured by the wheel passing over his leg. Our noon halt was at a point where Capt. Jas. Brown crossed with his detachment of the Mormon Battallion in 1847. This detachment I piloted from the head of Crow Creek to Great Salt Lake.

At this stage of our journey we have a few cases of sickness. We were on the move at one o'clock and made camp for the night twenty minutes to four o'clock. While camping this evening the mail coach passed us on the other side of the river; and also a train of five wagons the weather was warm and pleasant, grass plentiful and good. At this point caught some fish.

May 17, 1860; Thursday. Weather fine and warm we were on move at twenty minutes past six oclock, when some distance on the way we learned that a two mule team and two men were on the campground. We halted for them a short distance below Deer Creek Ferry [Glenrock, Wyoming] at half past ten, were again on the move, made halt and fed at one oclock and camped for night at five oclock. Pleasant camp and good feed.

May 18, 1860; Friday. Weather pleasant. Capt. [Walter M.] Gibson rather ill this morning, and were on the move at fifteen minutes past 6 oclock Traviled over a high broaken and rough country made a halt

14. Lieutenant William F. Raynolds explored the upper western United States from 1859–60 with specialists from the US Army Corps of Topographical Engineers, accompanied by thirty infantry. During the Civil War, he would become a brigadier general.

at half past 10 oclock, during which the men [Alexander] Demster and [George W.] Kelley were arested on charges of robery and desertion, by Sargent [John] Mix and party from Fort Laramie. This afternoon the wind was high rendering our travil unpleasant. To night fuel scarce but feed plenty wind high during night.

May 19, 1860; Saturday. This morning wind had subsided. The Sergeant and prisoners breakfasted with us, after which he hired some animals of our party on which to take our prisoners and left us. We were on the move at seven and made noon halt at 12 oclock on Deep Creek. Grass good wind high. At 3 oclock were again on the way. Camped for the night at Box Elder Spring. At five oclock several of our party are out hunting, they have returned without game.[15]

May 20, 1860; Sunday.[16] This morning moved at seven oclock. Our road today was very hilly this morning ~~meet~~ ^we met^ a large drove of horses bound for California. They belonged to Mesers Gales ^&^ Parker.[17] Made noon halt at Cottenwood Springs at 12 ~~oclock~~. The high wind makeing it rather uncomfortable. At ten minutes to 3 ~~oclock~~ we were again underway; camped for ^the^ night on the river, some three m[ile]s above at 5 oclock wind very high. [Had] the sunset when the weather became calm and pleasant.

May 21, 1860; Monday. This day ^we^ laid by. ^I^ wrote leters home and one to President [Brigham] Young. ^We^ built a raft, crossed to the fort, and obtained both leters and papers by the mail. In the evening ^we^ held a meeting. ^We^ saw in the papers of the day a manifesto from Joseph Smith son of the prophet.[18]

May 22, 1860; Tuesday. Struck camp at half past 6 ~~oclock~~. This

15. In the middle of the May 16 entry, Lyman abruptly switched from black ink to blue and began to show signs of impatience, reverting to poor spelling and less punctuation. The May 19 entry is the last in his otherwise carefully manicured vol. 17.

16. For May 20–Aug. 7, Lyman reverts to a daybook and crosses out entries as he copies them into his diary. The diary has its own additional improvements, as well.

17. "G. H. Gale and Mr. Parker" from Kalamazoo, Michigan, intended to drive 100 horses to Sacramento, accompanied by 42 men. Near Carson City they were attacked by Indians and lost three horses. *Sonoma County Journal*, July 6, 1860.

18. After Joseph Smith III was installed as president of the Reorganized LDS Church in Amboy, Illinois, in April 1860, he delivered a speech that was labeled a manifesto. The event was attended by his mother, Emma Hale Smith Bidamon, and other prior church dignitaries. Scherer, *The Era of Reorganization*, 92–100.

morning we received an addition to our company of two men, one woman and a child. Their names were Murry and wife and child, and Thomas Collins. Made noon halt twenty to 12 oclock. Camped for night at 6 oclock, had wood and grass, we^a^ther to day very warm. In the evening we met a train bound for Cal[ifornia], they had fine horses. At this point we caught some fish.

May 23, 1860; Wednesday. ~~This morning had~~ Heavy fog and dew. Our sick ^are^ improv~~e~~ing. As we are prepar~~e~~ing to start, an emigrant train is passing to the west with ox teams. Twenty minutes to 7 oclock were ready to move. Made noon halt at twenty minutes to 1 oclock. During our ^noon^ halt ^we^ were passed by a train of horses. Weather very warm. We traveled two hours and camped ^at 5:20^ twenty minutes past 5 oclock. Grass good but no wood and but few chips. No dew to night. Our camp ~~to night~~ is a little below Scotts Bluff [Nebraska Territory].

May 24, 1860; Thursday. Moved camp ^at^ twenty minutes to 6 ~~oclock, made noon~~ halted at half past 11 ~~oclock~~. Grass poor, wind high. Half past three were ready to move then waited one hour for [Philip H.] Buzzard. ^At 6^ camped for the night at fifteen minutes to 6 oclock. A train from the east ~~were~~ camped in sight. Wind was high dureing the night.

May 25, 1860; Friday. Struck camp at 6 ~~oclock~~. During our morning drive we saw four trains enroute for Cal^ifornia.^ Made our noon halt at ^10:30^ ~~half past 10 oclock~~. Wind very high. On starting this morning six of the wagons of the party fell back ~~and have not yet arived~~ but came ~~in~~ in course of an hour. At 1 ~~oclock~~ we were on the move. To day we have observed some ten [wagon] trains moving ~~east~~ ^west^ and one east; wind not so high ~~as in the morning~~. Camp rather bare of feed, but prolifick in grumbling. Camped at ~~fifteen minutes to~~ 5 ~~oclock~~. At this point ^I^ turned over the responsibility of the management of the camp to the owners of stock; the Capt [James Brown] resigned and Bishop [Edwin D.] Woolley justified himself as usual.

May 26, 1860; Saturday. This morning the camp voted to retain Capt. [James] Brown in his former position as captain of the company. ^At 7^ we moved from camp; ~~at fifteen minutes to 7 oclock~~. Made halt at spring creek at ^10:00^. ~~Twenty five minutes to 11 oclock~~ Grass good. ~~At this point~~ A company from Iowa nooned ~~and~~ sharing the grass with us. ~~Fifteen minutes to~~ ^At^ 1 ~~oclock~~ we were on the road and camped for the night at ^4:40^ ~~twenty minutes to 5 oclock as we camp~~ An emigrant train is passing, they camped in sight on the river above ^us^. Two of their men are in our camp for trade. This evening wind blowing from the East.

May 27, 1860; Sunday. Were on the move at half past 6 ~~oclock~~. ~~This morning~~ Mrs. Alfred Beebe was reported sick. ^We^ made halt at half past 10 ~~oclock~~, wind high from the south, grass good and abundant, chips ~~not plenty~~ ^few^. At ^1:20^ ~~twenty five minutes past one oclock~~ ^we^ were on the way; the sick were reported better. Camped for night at ^5:40^ ~~twenty minutes to 6 oclock~~. Wind still high, ~~dureing the night~~ some thunder and rain.

May 28, 1860; Monday. ^We^ struck camp at ~~fifteen minutes to~~ 6 ~~oclock~~, traveled for two hours then ~~in~~ laid by to await a favourable change in the we^a^ther. At ~~half past~~ 11^:30^ ~~oclock~~ we were again underway travel~~ed~~^ing^ until 2 ~~oclock~~. The rain continuing, we camped on the bed of a small creek in a sheltered position. The storm ~~continued to~~ rage^ing^ with unabated fury. The road was thronged with emigrants, mostly for Cal^ifornia^. The wind was high dur~~e~~ing the night.

May 29, 1860; Tuesday. Struck camp at 7; ~~fifteen minutes to 7 oclock~~ ^At^ north bluff fork made noon halt ~~fifteen minutes past 12 oclock~~. ~~at this point~~ We ~~meet~~ ^met^ a party from Iowa and Wisconsin, enroute for Cal[ifornia]. Br [Nephi] Johnson's team had to stop in the sand hills but came up dureing our halt. ~~Which~~ This is said to be the place where A[lmon] W. Babbitt was killed by the Indians.[19] This evening we past two parties ~~of emigrants~~ for Cal. ^At 6 we^ Camped a few miles above the mouth of the South Fork of the Platte ~~at twenty minutes to 6 oclock~~. ~~The weather here became mild~~ The wind subsiding we had a quiet night.

May 30, 1860; Wednesday. ~~This morning the weather~~ Bright and clear, though rather cool. Were up and away at ^6^ ~~fifteen minutes past 6 oclock~~. ~~Soon after we started we~~ Passed a camp of Pike's Peakers[20] ~~they were~~ fording the ^shallow^ River. ~~From their camp the ford was shalow~~ ^We^ made noon halt at a spring ~~on South side of road at twenty five minutes to~~ at 12 oclock. Grass good and abundant. ^We^ passed

19. Babbitt was killed by natives at Ash Hollow in western Nebraska in 1856 while traveling to Salt Lake City from Florence, Nebraska.

20. Gold was discovered between Denver and Pike's Peak in 1858, and those who rushed in to profit from the discovery were called Pike's Peakers, the equivalent of California's Forty-Niners. Denver was founded by the gold-seekers.

the mouth of South Platte, several trains ~~were~~ ^being^ in sight on the opposite side of the river. Weather warm ~~dureing our halt~~. 4 men passed with a hand-cart bound for Pike's Peak. They stated their rate of travel to be from 25 to 30 miles per day. They appeared healthy and strong. As I write another train ~~are~~ ^is^ coming up. At ~~fifteen minutes to~~ 3 ~~oclock~~ we were moveing on and camped at the west foot of Sand Bluff. ^At 5^ ~~twenty five minutes past 5 oclock~~ an eastern train ^was^ in camp [with the] east foot [of Sand Bluff] in sight. From the junction of the North and South Platte[21] the desert appearance of the country has been varied by the presence of timber, principally on the isleands ~~which is undoubtedly the cause of its preservation~~ and thus preserved from the fires that an^n^ually spread ~~more or less~~ over the extensive bottom lands ~~of these Rivers~~. ~~Weather pleasant this evening.~~

May 31, 1860; Thursday. This morning our stock was reported to have stampeded but was soon recovered. ~~This morning some~~ Storm clouds in the south with ~~some~~ lightning last evening. ~~Some~~ Buffalo were seen ~~by some of our party this~~ producing ~~its~~ ^the^ usual excitement ~~but~~. We ate none of their [the animals'] meat for the good reason that it was not caught.[22] We were under way at ~~fifteen minutes to~~ 6 ~~oclock~~, made halt at 11 ~~oclock~~. Camped for ^the^ night on Buffalo Creek at ~~half past~~ 8 ~~oclock~~, ~~at this point~~ saw some game.

June 1, 1860; Friday. This morning some buffalo ^came^ near camp while ^we were^ breakfasting. [Alfred] Beebe and [Philip H.] Buzzard, who had fallen behind yesterday, came ^at 9^ into camp ~~fifteen minutes to 9 oclock~~. ~~Were on the way traviling~~ down the creek. ^We^ halted ^at 9:30^ ~~half past 9 oclock~~. Remained until one oclock. Camped for night beside ^a^ dry slough at ^5 P.M.^ ~~fifteen minutes to 5 oclock~~ A large emigrant train camped on the river ^was^ in sight. To day the wind has been high, rendering our travel unpleasant. We obtained water by digging, but it was strongly impregnated with sulpheur ~~but~~ ^but^ clear and cool. At this point we arranged to part company with those who could not travel so fast, as the return teams were disposed to travil [faster for] the remainder of the journey.

21. At the present town of North Platte, Nebraska, 100 miles shy of Fort Kearny, the two forks of the river converge.

22. It was an unsuccessful hunt, in other words.

June 2, 1860; Saturday. At ~~fifteen past~~ 6^:15^ ~~oclock~~ ^we^ were on the move ~~traviled to~~ and made noon halt ^at 11:20^ on Wood River at Dr. He^n^ry's Ranch ~~twenty minutes past 11 oclock~~. ^We^ passed ~~on~~ from this ^place^ and camped for night at ^5:30^ ~~ten minutes past 5 oclock~~. To day I called on Joel H. Johnson.[23] Weather warm.

June 3, 1860; Sunday. We struck camp a ^5:30 A.M.^ ~~half past 5 oclock~~ ^and^ made noon halt on the river at ^11:30^ ~~at half past 11 oclock~~. This morning I me~~e~~t Joseph E. Johnson.[24] Our traviling party was reduced by the stop^p^ing of [Philip H.] Buzzard, [Alfred] Beebe, and [Nephi] Johnson. ^We^ camped for night below ^the^ mouth of [the] slough on the river ^5:20^ ~~at twenty minutes past 5 oclock~~. Went to is~~le~~and for wood. To day ^we^ met John Lewis returning from the States with one wagon and team and a flock of sheep. With him was his br inlaw Charles Crismond Junior.

June 4, 1860; Monday. At ^5:15^ ~~fifteen minutes past 5 oclock~~ ^we^ were under way & made noon halt on Prairie creek at ¼ to 10 oclock, then traviled to and crossed the Loup Fork ~~and~~ camp~~ed~~^ing^ for the night a short distance below Columbus. At ^5:20^ ~~twenty minutes pat 5 oclock~~ ^At this point^[25] ^We^ Learned to day that a train of some 30 Mormon wagons had passed Columbus on their way to Utah Via Genoa.[26]

June 5, 1860; Tuesday. Started at ^5:15^ ~~fifteen minutes past 5 oclock~~ and made noon halt at ^9:40^ ~~twenty to ten oclock here~~. ^We^ met Reuben Strong, an adherent of Joseph Smith Junior [III]: he was on his way to Pike's Peak. ^We moved out at 12:30.^ at half past 12 oclock. ~~were on the way~~ Had some rain in the evening^:^ camped for the night at the Widow Haga's Rancho, and lodged in the house no rain dureing the

23. Johnson was a prominent Latter-day Saint who acted as an Indian missionary, penned hymns, and founded Enoch, Utah.

24. Joseph E. Johnson served as postmaster of Kanesville, Iowa, across the Missouri River from Omaha, then as editor of the newspaper in Wood River, but would shortly give that up to move to Utah.

25. This phrase was added later and circled in pencil with an arrow indicating where it should be inserted.

26. Columbus is about eighty miles west of Winter Quarters/Omaha where the Loup River feeds into the Platte, and Genoa is twenty miles beyond Columbus. The wagon train was Warren Walling's company of 190 Mormon emigrants who left Omaha on May 30 and would arrive in Salt Lake City on Aug. 9.

night. Mr Haga the husband of the widow perished in a storm of snow near this place some three years ~~prevously~~ ^ago^.

June 6, 1860; Wednesday. The weather bright and clear. ~~This morning~~ ^We^ moved camp at 6 oclock; roads rather slippery from ~~the~~ recent rains. ^We^ made halt near Rawhide Creek at 11 oclock, the traviling heavy on the little papilion [creek]. ^We^ me~~e~~t a hand cart company with forty carts and five wagons, 255 souls, under the direction of Capt. Daniel Robinson—a company mostly English ^with^ some Welsh and Swiss.[27] In the evening some light snow about 10 oclock. Brs G[eorge] Q. Cannon[,] J[ames] D. Ross[,] John Smith and others came to our camp in good health & spirits.[28] The night was clear and bright. The company were in fine spirits, this ^act^ they evinced by songs ~~by which they~~ enlivening the passing hours, ere we retired ~~to rest~~. Br Cannon remained with us all night.

June 7, 1860; Thursday. Weather bright and clear. Called the company together and gave them such instruction as their circumstances and the prospective journey required. This done, we started for Florence[29] ~~where we~~ meet^ing^ some of our acquaintences ^and^ din~~ed~~^ing^ with br Loran Walker and Patriarch John Smith.[30] ~~And~~ At night I ~~maried~~ ^united in marriage^ a Miss [Mary Ann] Hirsher to Br Miner ^G.^ Prisbry.[31]

June 8, 1860; Friday. This morning ^we^ attended a meeting called by br [George Q.] Cannon in the Bowery.[32] Weather fine, and ~~pleasant to day~~ ^we^ received a donation ^of $57.00^ for the benifit of the missionaries. ~~The amount was fifty seven dollars.~~ To day some of [our

27. This was the ninth of ten handcart companies to walk to Utah. After the famous tragedy of the Willie and Martin Companies, when over 200 emigrants perished in the snow in Wyoming in 1856, the handcarts kept coming for four additional years. William G. Hartley, "Handcart Companies," in Powell, *Utah History Encyclopedia*, 242–43.

28. The company was not far from the Mormon community of Council Bluffs, Iowa.

29. Florence was the site of Winter Quarters, now part of Omaha.

30. Lorin Walker married into the Smith family, his wife, Lovina, being Hyrum Smith's daughter. "People of the Time," Joseph Smith Papers website.

31. Miner G. Prisbrey was a fifty-five-year-old missionary to Canada where he met his bride, Mary Ann Hershey, a seventeen-year-old. The couple would go on to have eleven children together.

32. In July 1846 the immigrants built a shelter in Council Bluffs, Iowa, that served as their meeting place until a wood-frame "tabernacle" could be built. The bowery was "on a bluff about sixty feet west of the lower bridge on Mosquito Creek … between Elder John Taylor's tent and Elder Wilford Woodruff's." It was open-sided and had leafy tree branches for a roof. Raymond, "Council Bluffs, 1846–1852."

group] prosicute their journey east. To day me~~e~~t with [Brigham Young's nephew] Brigham H. Young and Bishop E[dwin] D. Woolley who left for St. Louis this evening. This evening ~~myself~~ Br [Charles C.] Rich and [George Q.] Cannon and myself examined a man [by the name] of Richen who was charged with stealing a wagon. He plead guilty to the charge and confessed he had stolen one yoke of oxen. He was put in charge of keepers, from whom he escaped.[33]

June 9, 1860; Saturday. To day weather warm rained very little. Dined with Br [Jesse] Murphy.[34] The man Richen has been captured and is now awaiting his trial. At night went to lodge with br. Diem this evening met with Judson Stoddard.

June 10, 1860; Sunday. ~~Some rain this morning.~~ Attended a meeting of the Swiss Saints. Rain ~~continued to fall~~ ^fell^ through the day. In the evening visited br. Wm. Johnson, with whom we lodged and partook of of his good cheer with a small circle of friends.

June 11, 1860; Monday. ^We^ had ^a^ meeting in the Bowery, after which we dined with br Nathan Davis. In the evening ^we^ called on Sister West from New York. Lodged with br Wm. Piper. This evening ^I^ assisted in the organization of br John Smith's company for the plains. Weather very warm.

June 12, 1860; Tuesday. This morning ^we^ me~~e~~t with br Daniel Brown (father of Jas Brown 3rd); he came some 25 miles to se[e] us. ~~On~~ Yesterday ^I^ was presented with a coat and a pair of Gaiters [leather leggings] by br Wm. Piper. This evening the steamer Emilie came to Florence; we went on board where we meet John Robins. We took supper with br Laserty and family; the Sisters [Jane and Mary] Tulledge[35] were present. ~~Some~~ Rain. ~~dureing the night.~~

June 13, 1860; Wednesday. Rainy ~~this morning~~. Wrote letter to G[eorge] A. Smith. The rain subsided & I went to Omaha with brs

33. Charles Rich recorded that Richen returned the wagon and oxen before his escape, though as Lyman notes, he was recaptured the next day.

34. Jesse Easters Murphy was preparing to lead a company of 279 emigrants to Utah with 40 wagons, 255 cattle, and a threshing machine.

35. English emigrants Jane and Mary Elizabeth Tullidge were preparing to travel west together in the Jesse Murphy company. Both were in their twenties. Their thirty-year-old brother Edward would emigrate the next year and become a prominent LDS author and critic. Bushman, "Edward W. Tullidge and the Women of Mormondom," 15–17; see also the entry below for Dec. 7, 1860.

[William] Piper, Hate [Horton D. Haight] & Green ^and^ taried for an hour and returned to Florence.

June 14, 1860; Thursday. This morning arranged the different companies to transport some of the poor which they professed a willingness to do. Sent br [John] Tobin to Omaha to watch for a boat & give us word

June 15, 1860; Friday. To day ^I^ parted with our friends in Florence, and in company with br [George Q.] Cannon, went to Omaha, ^w^here we put up at the Fremont House but took super at the Farnam house with br John Robins and family

June 16, 1860; Saturday. This morning ^we^ took passage on the Steamer Omaha (Capt. Saltmarsh) for St. Joseph. ^We were^ Tied up at Nebraska City. At this point ^we^ me~~e~~t the Jetta and Emilie [steamers]. ^The^ weather ^is^ warm and sultry, so we were nearly boiled by morning.

June 17, 1860; Sunday. ~~The morning~~ Slightly cooler; our party all arose healthy & me~~e~~t at breakfast. To day ^we^ were on a sand bar for some ~~length of~~ time, the ~~residue~~ ^rest^ of the day ^we^ were detained in takeing in freight and consequently traviled but little.

June 18, 1860; Monday. ^We^ arrived in St. Joseph [Missouri] one short hour too late for the train; this was against us but in favour of the Hotells of which we patronized he Planters. While here met with Mr. [Archibald] Kerr who had been in Utah in the employ of Messers Livingston Kinkaid and Co.

June 19, 1860; Tuesday. Started on the morning train for Quincy [Illinois], where we arived at five oclock, ^At Palmyra we^[36] parted with Br Charles C. Rich and his son Joseph C. Rich and son in law John Tobin. Dureing the night myself and br G[eorge] Q. Cannon my son Francis M. and Elder Reuben McBride traviled to Chicago.

June 20, 1860; Wednesday. Our party breakfasted at The Massisoit House.[37] This done we went to Mr. [Peter] Schuttler's factory in which he informed us he always had on hand the materials for 1000 wagons.[38] We found Mr. S. a very pleasant gentleman. He seemed much pleased

36. This line appears later in the entry, then is circled with an arrow pointing to this spot.

37. The Massasoit House was a popular, six-story hotel that opened in 1857. It burned in the Great Chicago Fire of 1871 but reopened in 1873.

38. Mormons had often relied on wagons from Schuttler's factory in Chicago for the trek to Utah.

in showing us his factory in all its parts. At 8 oclock took [train] carrs for Detroit.

June 21, 1860; Thursday. We arived at Detroit half past 7 oclock, changed car~~r~~s, and passed on to the Falls of Niagara, where we arived at 5 oclock P.M. ^We^ had a brief and partial view of the two wonders of the world—the Bridge & Falls, we then passed on to Albany.[39]

June 22, 1860; Friday. ^We^ arived in Albany at ^4:45 a.m.^ ~~fifteen minutes before 5 oclock~~ ^and^ passed on to New York [City] where we arived at 10 oclock. We called on br [Jonah] Croxhall.[40] He was absent in Albany with Saints who were traviling under charge of br Calkin. I passed about the city with br [George Q.] Cannon. In our walk ^we^ saw some of the Japanese party on Broadway, in their apearence they much resemble the John Chinaman we had seen in California.[41]

June 23, 1860; Saturday. Spent the day mostly in the office[42] with br [George Q.] Cannon and others. This evening at five oclock br Cannon left on his labours in Florence. Before he left, he helped me to some clothing which came very timely; and may he never want. The weather quite warm.

June 24, 1860; Sunday. I held meeting in Williamsburg[43] preached two discourses and returned to the City. In the night very weary, and ~~with~~ ^having a^ cold, rested ~~but~~ poorly.

June 25, 1860; Monday. To day ^I^ commenced to write my journal. The weather opressively warm [and I] was aflicted with head ache.

June 26, 1860; Tuesday. Did not go out today. At night went to visit br [Bernard H.] Schettler. Had conversation with Dr. Berghaugsh who professed to be highly pleased with the principles ^we^ taught and asked

---

39. The 1855 suspension bridge was designed by John A. Roebling, who would go on to design the Brooklyn Bridge.

40. LDS convert Jonah Croxall arrived in the United States from England in 1857, but rather than travel immediately west he became president of the New York conference. When he continued he journey in 1861, it was likely to avoid the escalating Civil War.

41. "John Chinaman" was a catch-all name for Chinese immigrant laborers.

42. The church had an office in New York City to help immigrant-converts on their way to Utah, to assist missionaries on their way to Europe, and to print proselytizing literature.

43. Williamsburg was for many years a separate village before it was absorbed into Brooklyn in 1855. Burrows and Wallace, *Gotham*, 719.

to be remembered in our prayrs. Br [Jonah] Croxall was with me and while we were gone br Jas Brown the 3rd arived.

June 27, 1860; Wednesday. This morning my son F[rancis] M. L^yman^ and R[euben] A. McBride arived dusty and travil worn from a visit to their friends in the state of Ohio.

June 28, 1860; Thursday. This morning at 8 oclock I took the carrs for Boston [Massachusetts] with my son F[rancis] M. L[yman]. We arived in Boston at 5 oclock. Found br Thomas Hudson with whom we lodged and in the evening had an interesting visit from br Stephen Stanford the President of the Saints in Boston. Before leaveing New York I received from br [Jonah] Croxall and receipted for the same seventy six dollars and seventy five cents. Sixty in cash and the balance in Clothing for my son.

June 29, 1860; Friday. This morning went to the depot in time to learn that the morning train had gone. We returned to br [Thomas] H[udson]s and I spent the day reading Mountaineer[44] giveing news of Indian ~~news~~ war in western Utah and other news from home.

June 30, 1860; Saturday. At half past 7 oclock ^we^ took carrs for Barnet [Vermont] ~~where we~~ ariv~~ed~~^ing^ at 5 oclock. About sundown arived at the residence of my cousin Albert Mason where as travilers we called for sup[p]er which we were enjoying when my cousin came in ~~and entered into~~ and entered into conversation with us as strangers, when, however, we became known to him he acorded us a most hearty welcome.

July 1, 1860; Sunday. To day ^we^ attended a Methodist meeting and heard a Mr. Malory a coloured gentleman preach.[45] ^At^ 5 oclock P.M. I addressed a congregation of my old friends; they listened attentively and with apparent intrest. At night lodged with my cousin Philip Mason on the pre^m^ises where I was born. With these [premises] time and change had dealt rather rudely and many of the recollections of my childhood, like the years in ^which^ I knew them, had passed away.[46]

---

44. In 1859 the short-lived *Mountaineer* was founded in Salt Lake City to report the news in a way that defended the Mormon etablishment against verbal attacks from the Fort Douglas newspaper, the *Valley Tan*. The *Mountaineer* closed in 1861.

45. Mr. Mallory was not the regular pastor but filled in for a year while Amasa G. Burton was on leave from the Fairlee Methodist church. It would have been unthinkable for most white congregations at the time to have a black pastor. Hemenway, *Vermont Historical Gazetteer*, 903.

46. Someone made red marks in the left margin to highlight where genealogical information was located, either for church records or perhaps for a biography.

July 2, 1860; Monday. My cousin Philip very kindly carried us in his carriage to my cousin John Chaltern's ~~who received us kindly~~. We dined with him ~~after which~~, we ^then^ called upon and spent an hour with my Mother's only liveing sister.[47] After this[,] rode to Littleton Village where we took stage for Lancaster [New Hampshire] where we arived about 9 oclock, put up at the Lancaster House.[48]

July 3, 1860; Tuesday. This morning ^we^ took stage to Northumberland; from thence traveled by railway to North Stratford; from thence by private conveyence to Coalbrook [Colebrook] Corners.[49] There we hired another conveyance, which ^c^aried us to the residence of my sister Lucy Pillbro.[50] ^We^ took super with sister P. and at night went in company with Sister and husband [William] some 2 m[ile]s to see my mother whom I found in good health. Her age was 75 years. [My] [step]father Emerson was confined to the House with decreptitude and blindness. We passed the night ~~with~~ ^at^ mothers.

July 4, 1860; Wednesday. To day ^we^ taried with mother until 3 oclock, then bade her farewell, and returned to my sisters, where we passed the night.

July 5, 1860; Thursday. This morning br [William] Pillbro and wife [Lucy] acompanied us to North Stratford, where we arived about 11 oclock; here ^we^ said adieu to sister and ^her^ husband, and traviled by rail to Island-Pond [Vermont], from hence by stage to Charleston Holow, from thence by private conveyence to the residence of my sister Mrs Ruth Goodall in the town of Holland. My sister Ruth, whom I found sick, was the only one of my relatives who recognized me after an absence of 28 years. My brother-in-law Richard Pe^a^body Goo^d^all received me kindly. They had around them an interesting family of children. Taried with them over night.

July 6, 1860; Friday. ^We^ remained with my sister until 5 oclock P.M., when br Richard [Goodall] carried us to Derby Line, the residence

47. Lyman's aunt Lois Mason Hurlbut would die the next year in June 1861.

48. The Lancaster House opened in 1858 as a respectable alternative to the taverns one encountered on the road. Somers, *History of Lancaster*, 515–16.

49. Lyman is traveling through the northern tip of the state along the Connecticut River dividing New Hampshire from Vermont. Colebrook is ten miles from the Canadian border.

50. Lucy was Lyman's half-sister, daughter of Martha Mason and her second husband, Isaiah Emerson.

of my cousin June Mason Thompson, with whom we tar^r^ied until morning. ^Then^ my cousins carried me to the stage station, ~~some~~ ^about^ 2 miles.

July 7, 1860; Saturday. ^We^ traviled by stage to Barton [Vermont], ~~from~~ then to Barnet by rail, ~~from~~ thence to North Monroe on foot, & lodged with cousin Albert Mason, whom, with family, we found well. ^I^ had an interview with my cousin Ruth Mason and ^with^ some of my old acquaintences who called in to see me.

July 8, 1860; Sunday. To day I preached in the Monroe meeting house; in the evening went to the residence of my cousin Jedediah Buffom, with home [whom] we taried over night, ~~were~~ kindly treated.

July 9, 1860; Monday. This morning Cousin [Jedediah] B[uffum] ~~very kindly~~[51] took me to the station in Barnet in his carriage; at the station I me~~e~~t ~~with~~ two of my old schoolmates, Lyman Stanby and George Harleton. ^We^ arived in Concord by rail in the evening Called on my cousin James L. Mason whom I had not seen for 35 years; he was princip^a^l~~e~~ foreman in Mr. Abbot's ^coach^ factory with which establishment he had been connected some 25 years.[52] Taried with cousin over night.

July 10, 1860; Tuesday. ^We^ resumed our journey; ~~this morning and~~ in the town of Lowell ^we^ called on and dined with ^my^ cousin Robert ~~Hall~~ Wood and family, ^[who] gave us a drink of cider the only one we had in new england.^ His wife Martha and her sister, who lived with them, were the daughters of my uncle Joseph Mason, my mother's brother and father of James L. Mason. We arived at br Hudson's in Boston at half past 5 <u>oclock</u> in the evening I spoke to ~~some~~ ^a^ few of the Saints and a number of the neighbors listened out side altho it ~~was~~ rain~~ing~~^ed^ during the time, thus evincing the anxiety they had to bear.

July 11, 1860; Wednesday. ~~To day~~ We visited Dorchester Heights; ~~and in the evening~~ called on my cousin Mr Perez Mason, known as Father Mason, The City Missionary.[53] Was kindly received by him. At half past 5

51. These pencil strikethroughs were Lyman's attempt to condense his diary to just the facts.

52. J. Stephens Abbot apprenticed as a coach maker in Massachusetts before moving to New Hampshire to open his own factory. In 1865 he and Lewis Downing formed Abbot, Downing & Co., which became one of the most successful coach-making companies in the U.S.

53. Throughout New England, "city missionaries" were volunteers with the City

~~oclock~~ took the [train] carrs for Providence [Rhode Island] where we took steamer for New York [City]. I had lived with Cousin Perez seven years.[54]

July 12, 1860; Thursday. This morning arived in N. Y. ~~and~~ mee~~ting~~ br [Charles C.] Rich and others ~~of the brethren~~. We transacted some buisness and lodged with br Gibson in Brooklin, this was Capt. W M Gibson of Sandwich Island ~~notoriety~~ ^fame^.[55]

July 13, 1860; Friday. Wrote ~~some~~ letters home went to the city [Manhattan] at 4 ~~oclock~~ and returned to Brooklin in the evening. To day a noted pirate by the name of [Albert] Hicks was executed by hanging.[56]

July 14, 1860; Saturday. To day ^we^ parted with our friends in N. Y. and went on board of the steamer Edinburough ~~and~~ ^sailing^ at 12 oclock. ~~We sailed with fair weather.~~ ^We took^ ~~takeing~~ steerage passage[57] ~~in consequence of~~ ^having^ divided our funds with the three missionaries.

July 15, 1860; Sunday. To day our attention was atracted by some posted notices that Divine Services would be held at 10 oclock but the equivocal state of our health precluded our attendance.

July 16, 1860; Monday. To day shook out the idle canvas to the friendly breeze and our gallant ship sped bravely on her watery way.

July 17, 1860; Tuesday. Some little seasickness weather became fogy. Passengers not allowed on the uper deck.

July 18, 1860; Wednesday. Weather still fogy and we were still ^in^ close quarters; below the air was very ~~bad and~~ impure.

Mission Society, founded in Boston in 1816 to help poor and homeless people. They ran the Home for Little Wanderers, the Penitent Female Refuge, and the first American affiliates of the YMCA and YWCA.

54. Lyman lived with relatives during his teenage years after his father died. *AML*, 2–4.

55. Walter M. Gibson joined the LDS Church in 1859 after returning to the continent from the Sandwich Islands. When he traveled back to the Islands, he would be accused of impropriety and would be excommunicated, but would later serve in various high government positions in Hawaii.

56. The execution took place on Bedloe's Island (now home to the Statue of Liberty). He confessed to robbing an oyster ship and killing the captain and two crewmen. "Execution of Hicks, the Pirate," *New York Times*, July 14, 1860.

57. By the 1860s passage across the Atlantic had become more comfortable and swift, taking only a few days instead of weeks, and passengers on the iron steamer *Edinburgh* wrote a letter to the editor in praise of the crew. Still, the dangers were evident in the news later that same year that the *Edinburgh*, on a return trip, had caught fire and sunk in the middle of the ocean. "Emigrants Upon Steamships," *New York Times*, May 21, 1860; "Marine Disasters," *Seaman's Friend: The Sailor's Magazine*, 155.

July 19, 1860; Thursday. Weather cool and one sail in sight to day on our starboard quarter.[58] Stil fogy this evening.

July 20, 1860; Friday. Stil fogy; some sickness on board; we have all sails set to day. Distance from N.Y. 1405 miles at 2 oclock.

July 21, 1860; Saturday. Wind fair and some fog; our gallant ship stood proudly on her course, dashing the foam from her path as though she sought a fairer wreath with which to deck her brow, our prayr is God speed thee on thy ocean way, and his potent arm be ever around the^e^ and thy freight of souls! ~~Distance~~ ^We made^ to day 250 miles. ~~At the time of writing quite fogy.~~

July 22, 1860; Sunday. Somewhat clear; one sail in sight on larboard quarter At half past 10 oclock Divine Service was held on board in the Saloon by a clergyman from Virginia on his way to Scotland. His remarks were beautiful lucid and Rich in the spirit of true Christian charity and benevolence, offering to the mind those principles that are to the traviler ore life's desert waste a refreshing oasis. Rich in the eliments of bliss and hap^p^iness to invigorate and strengthen poor, fallen degenerate humanity in its struggle onward and upward to salvation and freedom.

July 23, 1860; Monday. To day a slight change of weather; wind more northerly Latitude at 12 oclock 57 + 14 Longitude 24 + 25. Some inquiry [by passengers] in regard to the Gospel. Distance to day 250 miles from N.Y 2167 miles.

July 24, 1860; Tuesday. Fog cleared ~~away conciderably~~. ^We^ sailed 243 m[ile]s the day passed in the usual monotinous maner.

July 25, 1860; Wednesday. Some rain this morning took in some sail. In the afternoon the monotony of our journey was broaken by the sight of Cape Clear and a small fleet of war steamers numbering eleven ~~they were~~ ^was^ near the entrance of Bantry Bay.[59] They were somewhat imposeing in their apearance mounting from 75 to 120 guns. The sun shone this evening.

July 26, 1860; Thursday. ~~This morning~~ About two ~~oclock~~ A.M. we landed about 30 passengers at Q[u]eenstown, Ireland. This caused the call for breakfast to be rather thinly attended. The weather fair and clear,

58. That is, the right-rear of the boat. The left side of a ship is the port side, the right the starboard side, and the area between the middle of the ship and the stern (or rear) is the quarter.

59. Bantry Bay is in the county of Cork in southwest Ireland.

land in sight in the distance on the Irish coast; several sails in sight; ~~evening our proximity to our destination~~ this evening in sight of Holyhead on our starboard quarter at sunset we are oposite Holyhead with the Snowdown mountain in sight.[60]

July 27, 1860; Friday. ~~This morning~~ About 7 <u>oclock</u> we landed in Liverpool and repaired immediately to [the mission office at] <u>42</u> Islington, heartily welcomed by br N[athaniel] V. Jones whom we found in good health and spirits as were those with him in the office. They professed much pleasure at our comeing.

July 28, 1860; Saturday. ~~To day~~ ^We^ called the brethren together who came with us and gave them some counsel in relation to their ministry and provided them with the means with which to reach their fields of labour as designated by us. Br Milo Andrus came in tonight.

July 29, 1860; Sunday. To day I preached to the Saints in the Assembly Room[61] morning and evening; to night br Jacob Gates came in good health and spirits. Br Milo Andrus and Wm. Gibson were with us through the day. The brethren report the work improveing where they have laboured.

July 30, 1860; Monday. This morning some of the Elders left for their fields of labour: Elders John Brown and F[rancis] M. Lyman for London and Jas S. Brown and J[oseph] C. Rich for Nottingham [blank] in the morning. In the evening br David M. Stuart [left] for Glasgow Scotland and br Wm H. Dame and R[euben] A McBride to the Liverpool Confer[ence].

July 31, 1860; Tuesday. The weather dull. To day the brethren who came with us have all gone to their labours. To day gave br Wm. H. Perks a memorandum from the Historian of the Church of works which he wanted for history.[62] This morning the manager of the Royal Bank in the city commited suicide.[63]

---

60. Holyhead is a seaport in Wales, directly west, across the water, from Dublin. Snowdon is the highest mountain in Wales.

61. The church rented what Lyman called its "assembly room" in the Music Hall on Bold Street, half a mile from the mission headquarters.

62. The Church Historian, George A. Smith, was compiling short biographies about each member of the Quorum of the Twelve Apostles and had requested information from Lyman for that purpose.

63. Jeremiah Chaffers, a parapalegic, had lost his brother several weeks before. "Royal Bank," *Bankers' Magazine*, Nov. 1860, 405.

August 1, 1860; Wednesday. I arose this morning with a severe pain in my head produced by the humidity of the atmosphere. In the evening my head somewhat relieved.

August, 2, 1860; Thursday. ~~To day~~ Wrote for the Star,[64] ~~and~~ in the evening visited the Zoological Gardens[65] saw a fine balloon ascension and some splendid fire works. To day received from br [Nathaniel V.] Jones a transfer of the buisness with the bank.

August 3, 1860; Friday. Was writing to Elias Smith of the [Deseret] News [when] in course of the forenoon Elders J[ohn] W. Coward[,] Homer Duncan[,] and Philip De La Marr came in from Utah.[66] Received the money of the office from br [Nathaniel V.] Jones.

August 4, 1860; Saturday. This morning at 7 oclock started for Birmingham where we arived at 12:20 ~~twenty minutes past 12 oclock~~. Br Charles Penrose and others awaiting our arival. Dined with Br P. after which went out in town to b[u]y a coat for which I paid £2 pounds 5 [pence]. Lodged with br [Edward] Price. Br [Homer] Duncan from Liverpool arived at br Charles Penrose's.

August 5, 1860; Sunday. Weather fine and pleasant. Attended conference in the Oddfellows Hall. Had a pleasant meeting after which ajourned. Meet again at 6 oclock to night had heavy rain lodged with br Edward Price.

August 6, 1860; Monday. Raining which disappoints the Saints in regard to their social party. Br [Nathaniel V.] J[ones] and myself returned to Liverpool.

August 7, 1860; Tuesday. Writeing in the office. Sent some leters to the states.[67]

---

64. The *Millennial Star* was started by the Twelve Apostles in 1840 and was published continually until 1970 as the longest-running publication in the church. Peter Crawley called it inestimable in providing its "continuous record of the … Church in every corner of the globe, in some instances the only such record." Crawley, *Descriptive Bibliography*, 1:108–13.

65. The Liverpool Zoological Gardens famously allowed some animals to roam free. The owner claimed the exercise made the elephants and rhinoceroses larger and more fit than "those confined in close dens." Cowlie, *Exhibiting Animals in Nineteenth-century Britain*, 35.

66. Two of these three wealthy elders, Coward and de la Mare, had contributed £1,000 each to the Deseret Manufacturing Company in Utah. Hartshorn, "Philip De La Mare," 29–30, 66–70.

67. The rest of this page is blank. The following page contains entries from 1868.

August 8, 1860; Wednesday. This morning dispersed some parcels of fruit seeds and a leter to my family in Utah. In the evening [we] were p[r]oof reading for the Star. Wrote to br C[harles] C. Rich

August 9, 1860; Thursday. To day writing ~~for~~ miscileneous corispondence for the Mission and abroad and reading proof for the Star.

August 10, 1860; Friday. Weather rainy. Engaged in the office in home and foreign buisness. Sent bills of exchange to Jonah Croxall of N.Y. on Tapscott Smith & Co.[68] [and] for Nathan Stewart Ohio. In the evening commenced writing for the paper.

August 11, 1860; Saturday. At 9 oclock left for Notingham[69] where we arived a half past 2 oclock. Called at br David Johns, at which place we meet Brs J[oseph] C. Rich and Jas Brown in good health ^and^ at fifteen minutes to 8 oclock took the train for Mansfield where we arived at 9 oclock. Called on Cister Emmy Jones.

August 12, 1860; Sunday. At half past 2 oclock preached to the Saints in Mansfield and then went to Notingham and preached half past 6 oclock to a large audience. Heavy rain to night lodged with Br [David] Jhons the [LDS] pastor.[70] While here received a leter from my son [Francis] Marion in London.

August 13, 1860; Monday. Returned to our business in Liverpool arived at 4 oclock found all well.

August 14, 1860; Tuesday. Was writing for the Star.[71]

August 15, 1860; Wednesday. Writing in the office. To [day] Br John Tobin came in from ~~Isleand~~ Ireland. Feel dull in health.

August 16, 1860; Thursday. To day Br [John] Tobin left for Scotland.

August 17, 1860; Friday. Spent the day in the office writing.

Lyman gave up transferring rough notes to a polished diary and instead started writing in another daybook that picked up where this one left off. He will no longer cross out entries as he goes.

68. Tapscott, Smith & Co. was a passenger-ship company out of Liverpool.

69. Nottingham was known at the time for its textile mills and urban slums.

70. The LDS office of pastor was an official calling in Europe that "filled a leadership layer between mission presidency and conference presidents," as explained by Hartley, "LDS Pastors and Pastorates, 1852–55," 194. David John would emigrate in 1861 to Provo, where he would become a "regional presiding bishop" and a trustee of Brigham Young Academy.

71. In this and several subsequent brief entries, Lyman left lines blank as if he intended to fill in more later. He will spend an increasing amount of time writing editorials for the *Millennial Star*.

August 18, 1860; Saturday. As on Friday in the office writing.

August 19, 1860; Sunday. In the morning Br [Nathaniel V.] Jones preached at the Assembly Room whilst I remained in the office and preached at the same place at half past 5 oclock in the evening.

August 20, 1860; Monday. Engaged in the office all day.

August 21, 1860; Tuesday. Writeing in the office through the day. In evening visited at Br [William H.] Perks had a pleasant time returned at 10 oclock.

August 22, 1860; Wednesday. Weather rainy and dark needed some artificial light in the office. Had br [Henry] Whittall[72] with us in the office still raineing.

August 23, 1860; Thursday. Engaged in writing. Weather rainy as usual.

August 24, 1860; Friday. Writeing this morning until dinner at 2 oclock. To [day] filled [out a] check in favor of J. W. Coward left in the care of Wm H. Perks our Clerk. To day sent leter to Paris to L[ouis] A Bertrand. At five oclock in company with Br. N[athaniel] V. Jones started for London where we arived between 11 & 12 oclock. Lodged with Pastor [John] Cook whom we found well[,] as [were] Elders John Brown and F[rancis] M. Lyman.

August 25, 1860; Saturday. Rainy to day remained in all day. Some of the brethren were out. Wrote some to day.

August 26, 1860; Sunday. Weather clear and bright preached three times[,] twice to large audiences.

August 27, 1860; Monday. At 6 oclock started for Liverpool where we arived between 12 & 1 oclock. Found 8 of the missionaries from the West all well.

August 28, 1860; Tuesday. Were engaged in makeing disposition of the Elders for their further journey.

August 29, 1860; Wednesday. This day about 12 oclock the brethren left for Scandinavia eight in number.[73]

---

72. Henry Whittall was assistant editor of the *Millennial Star*. He would be killed by lightning in Nebraska two years later. "Correspondence," *Latter-day Saints Millennial Star*, Aug. 23, 1862, 539.

73. The missionaries to Europe traveled through the European headquarters in Liverpool so the church's agents could book their further passage to Copenhagen and elsewhere. At the same time, Mormon emigrants traveling in the other direction were organized in Liverpool into companies presided over by church leaders and given

August 30, 1860; Thursday. Was engaged in the office.

August 31, 1860; Friday. Writing for the Star.

September 1, 1860; Saturday. At half past ~~we~~ myself and brother [Nathaniel V.] Jones accepted an invitation from Br [William H.] Perks to go in his cariage to the review of the Militia in the park of his Lordship the Earl of Derby.[74] There was a concourse of some two hundred thousand people.

September 2, 1860; Sunday. Wrote in the morning. At half past 6 oclock in the evening I preached at the Assembly Rooms.[75]

September 8, 1860; Saturday. In company with Elder N[athaniel] V. Jones I started at ten minutes past one oclock for Glasgow, Scotland, where we arived at ten oclock P.M. Found the Brs [George] Teasdale[,] [John] Tobin and [David M.] Stuart waiting for us. From the station we repared to the residence of Br. John Reede the president of the conference with whom we lodged for the remainder of the night.

This morning I received a leter from President Brigham Young: Left Brs. C[harles] C. Rich and Jacob Gates to remain in the office dureing our absence. Retired between 12 & 1 oclock. Slept well until morning.

September 9, 1860; Sunday. This morning the weather was clear and the sun looked in smileingly in upon us and we arose to take our first view of Scotland. Attended meeting at ^68^ Irongate Hall. Had full house all Saints ajourned for one hour then reassembled and spoke again to a large and attentive audience [with] some strangers in to hear. After meeting dined with Br Reed. In the evening Br [Nathaniel V.] Jones attended [the meeting]. I did not attend but remained at Bro Rs to write. Weather still fine and cleare rather rare for this country this season which has been very rainy.

September 10, 1860; Monday. This morning the weather was fine and clear. Spent the forenoon with some of the Brethren of the Priesthood

---

group discounts. Edward H. Jeter, "Immigration," in *Mormonism: A Historical Encyclopedia*, 86–87.

74. Edward Smith-Stanley, the 14th Earl of Derby, was a Conservative leader in Parliament and Prime Minister of England three times, though for less than a total of four years.

75. Lyman began to write a subsequent entry under "Monday 3d" but stopped. The rest of this diary contains expenses. The entry for Sept. 8 appears at the start of a new book, vol. 20.

namely, George Teasdale pastor of the Scotish pastorate[,] Br E. L. T. Harrison and Elder John Reed presidents of Conferences and Elders [David M.] Stuart and [John] Tobin and Robert Sands[76] and Jas Bullock.

At twenty minutes past four my self and Brs [Nathaniel V.] Jones[,] Reed and Harrison left for Ayr [Alloway] the Birth place of the Scotish poet Burns.[77] When we arived at Ayr we learned the objects of our visit were some three miles distant on the banks of the Bonie Doon,[78] the promise of a half crown[79] secured us the services of a man with horse and carriage by whom we were whirled along at a brisk rate over the even fine road, as we neared the end of our ride in the outward direction we past the cotage of his [Burns's] birth and a little farther on we past the old Kirk [church] where Tam O'Shanter saw the witches.[80] Arived at the site of the monument erected to the memory of the immortal Burns. We were introduced to the grounds by a venerable gray haired porter. The monument is situated ^on^ a gentle rounded eminence which commands a view of the banks and braes of Bonie Doon.

In the base of the monument stands a bust of the poet resting on a polished shaft ^of^ red granite. Ocupieing a central position in this department was an antique oaken table on which rested a glass enclosure in side of which were to be seen su^n^dary momentos of the Bard. The ground around the monument are tast[e]fully laid out and ornimented with a variety of flower[s], shrubery. Thus here in such close proximity with mementoes of the dead[,] Natures floral beauties meet the eye and exhale their rich oders to cheer the sences and ^thus^ admonish the thoughtful visitor that to die is to enter into peace harmony and joy beyond those of the present sin curst world.

---

76. Robert Sands would emigrate in three years and become conductor of the first Tabernacle Choir within five years.

77. Robert Burns was so revered for his "Auld Lang Syne," "Tam o' Shanter," and other poems that people on both sides of the ocean could recite them. His "Scots Wha Hae" was such a popular Scottish ballad that it was considered the unofficial national anthem. Cf. Sillito, *History's Apprentice*, 185–201.

78. "Oft hae I rov'd by bonnie Doon / To see the rose and woodbine twine," wrote Burns about the river in Ayrshire county in his poem, "The Banks O' Doon," "bonnie" meaning beautiful. The river runs through Alloway, two miles from Ayr.

79. The half-crown was valued at one-eighth a pound.

80. In Burns's poem, a drunk Tam can see through the church window "warlocks and witches in a dance."

We ascended the monument to the hight of about forty feet from which point we had a pleasant view of the surrounding scenery.[81] While contemplating it it occured to us as not strange that while viewing what we now saw the poetry in the Soul of the immortal bard was stired.

Before leaveing the grounds on which the monument is situated we were conducted by our guide to a small building in which were the artistick representations in stone of Tom O'Shanter and Souter Johnny in the art of takeing those copious draughts that prepared Tam for seeing the witches. The brief moments of our stay with the momentoes of the dead being past[,] the silver evidence of our gratitude being dropped in the waiting palm of our aged guide[,] we entered our cab and returned to the cotage which is a small unpretending building consisting of two smal apartments in one of which we were ~~told~~ shown[,] by our host of the cotage[,] the bed on which the infant Bard first opened his eyes upon the beauties of nature that subsequently seemed to evoke the native poetry of his soul. In the same was shown us the window of about 20 inches square which was all of the kind in the room where so much of briliancy was born.

In the ajoining apartment ^were^ some rude tables and chairs which in their antique apearence brought vividly to our minds the years long past in which they were made, while the numerous names traced on this antique furniture with the knives of the visitors speak equaly plain the rudeness of the present. On one of the tables we drank some ale and ate some cake for the mutual benefit of our selves and our host of the cotage. This done we were shown an apartment of modern erection in which we saw a bust of the Bard with various momentoes of ~~of~~ the age in which he lived. This done our attention was called to the register of the place in which we inscribed our names and the place of our residence. After we had left the room a member of our party called the attention of our host to our name and position in the Church. This brought the old man to the door of our cab which we had entered for another look [at us] and [he gave us a] most polite bow. He bade us adieu.

Arived at the town of Ayre the question being agitated as to where we should stay over the night. We concluded to stop at the famous ~~Sheter~~ Shanter House ~~in~~ which is in apearence verry antique with its thatched

81. The monument has a substantial rock base several stories tall, topped by a large, open-air rotunda.

roof small windows narrow stairway and low seeling. Its walls in the apartment where the refreshments were served for the visiters were decorated with various mementoes of the past such as the picture of Burns as also Tam as he was leaveing the In[n] on the ever memorable night [of] his seeing the wiches. Among the articles of furniture in our room were the identical chairs in which the quandam friends Tom O'Shanter and Souter Johnny imbibed the intoxicating draught the influence of which lead to the wiching sequel. That seems indelibly enstamped in the memory of the people and in attestation of its truth we were shown a rude wooden cup from which these ancient worshipers at the Shrine of Bachus drank their patent libations. In its appearence it is aged and by its smell its use has not been forgotten.

Our lodgeings engaged and sup[p]er ordered we went out for a short walk in the town. As we passed along our attention was ^drawn^ to what in the distence we supposed to have been the tower of a Church but as we approached it we learned it was named The Tower of Wallace.[82] Its front on the street we were traviling was decorated with a statue of the hero in the execution of which the artist may have been true to life but not to our preconceived opinion. In the improvements and embelishments of the town there is a curious mingling of the rude and refined and the ancient and modern. The former predominate in some localities, and are evinced by the thatched roof and antiquainted windows and dillapidated walls and imperfect design [that] could be supposed to have preceded [the more refined architecture]. So grotesque an assemblage of the natures elements [rock, wood, straw] that should reflect her beauties.

We returned to sup[p]er which ~~into~~ was served for us by the Bonie Lass about the house. After partakeing of our evening cheer and discussing for a brief time the antique peculeiarities of the place and country we retired to our sleeping apartment which was in keeping with the general apearance of the place. In size it was sixteen feet long by nine feet w^i^de at one end and six at the other and seven in hight. Our ^bed^ in its cleanliness reflected creditably on the character of our hostess of the Inn. In the rude wainscotting of our small apartment were several doors[,] presenting

82. The sixty-foot-high monument to William Wallace, leader of the Scottish First War of Independence, was completed in 1857. Wallace was executed by the English (hanged, beheaded, and drawn and quartered) in 1305.

in their apearence that meet the eye no indication of their presence save the small aperture for the key which had been in requisition[,] so it was left to fancy to acount for the secrets they ~~covered~~ ^concealed^. In our pilows we found two cone shaped caps in which we ensconced our heads ere we laid down to sleep. We had not long reclined on our Cleanly Bed when we became obliveous to care and thus past the night.

September 11, 1860; Tuesday. This morning the weather being clear our breakfast over we were on our way to secure passage on one of the Clyde Steamers.[83] This we acomplished we were soon gently moveing along the placid bosom of the Clyde in the contemplation of the beautiful scenery along its shores we whiled away the passing hours.

While contemplating the beautious scenery along the lovely river we were lead to the conclusion that ~~was~~ ^it^ is no marvel that the heart of the Scott warms for his native land. For we loved it for its beauties strangers as we were. About <u>12 oclock</u> we arived at the leading feature of intrest for the day the Castelated Rock of Dumbarton.[84] Its stired in us the memories of the past we looked for the youthful and agile [Edwin] Ruthven of Miss [Jane] Porters creation and his more sturdy and stalward compatriot and patron the renowned Wallace.[85] But they seemed all to have joined the march of time and had passed away and with them nearly all the ancient artificial grandure of the place.

By a somewhat circuitous route we at length reached the foot of the rock from the land side haveing left our steamer we passed to the shore in a small boat. When arived at the gate of the Fortress we were conducted within by a very civil rather military appearing man who was there as a soldier intrusting our overcoats and umbrellas to the keeping of another. We followed our guide up the ascending stair way in the rock. They are much worn by their use in the past.

When we had made the ascent we seated ourselves on the remains of an antique tower said to have been Roman in its origin. Its remains now stood some two feet above the earth around and was circular in

83. The River Clyde flows northwest through Glasgow and into an estuary called the Firth of Clyde.

84. He means Dumbarton Castle, the fifth-century fortress that sits on a hill of volcanic basalt called Dumbarton Rock.

85. Jane Porter's 1810 novel, *The Scottish Chiefs*, was popular among young adults in Lyman's day.

form and when standing at its greatest height must have commanded an extensive view of the surrounding co^u^ntry. The top of the rock is some 250 feet above the Clyde. From this the highest point of our ascent we had a fine view of the ajacent country along the Clyde. And away to the north Ben Lomond [mountain] raised his head towards the blue vault above while ne[s]tling near its base are the Lochs of Lomand and [Mount] Ben Ledi Tay, E Katrine.

In our decent from our lofty perch we were shown some remains of the ancient wall that still braves the rude touch of passing years. Contin-ueing our decent we were introduced to the Armory. We were shown a variety of antique mementoes of the past among them was the Sword of renowned Wallace the spear and battle ax of Bruce with which he fought for Scotlands liberty on the field of Banockburn.[86] We left the rock and returned by rail to Glasgow. This evening preached in the Irongate Hall to an attentive audience of the Saints. Lodged with brother Reed.

September 12, 1860; Wednesday. To day went to Paisley.[87] Had a good time with the Saints of the branch. Lodged with Br Jas Murry. While I visited the cemetary and was impressed with the fact rendered evident by what I saw that with the people it was easier to lavish wealth on the dead rather than to bless them when liveing. In this I am confident I would be joined by the spirits of the departed could they uter to us their sentiments in regard to this mater. Rained dureing the night.

September 13, 1860; Thursday. This morning returned to Glasgow. Received and read proof of the Star. Corrected and returned the same. At four oclock started for Edinburgh in company with Brs [Elias L. T.] Harison[,] [John] Tobin[,] and [David M.] Stuart. Reached the city at fifteen minutes before 6 oclock. Found Pastor [George] Teasdale[88] in waiting lodged with him.

September 14, 1860; Friday. To day wrote some leters to the States [and] received some from Liverpool. In the afternoon went out in the city

86. Robert the Bruce defeated the army of Edward II at Bannockburn in 1314, leading to independence for Scotland.

87. Directly west of Glasgow, Paisley was supported by the weaving industry at the time Lyman visited. Paisley patterns get their name from the town.

88. George Teasdale was a twenty-nine-year-old British convert who would later become a member of the church's Quorum of Twelve Apostles. Edinburgh is about fifty miles east of Glasgow.

and dureing our short ramble I was lead to conclude that extreams [of poverty and wealth] meet here as much as in any place I have visited. Here is the closest proximity to each other are huddled together the most antique evidences of the rude and barberous with those of modern civilization and refinement. Poverty was in the streets filthy and rag[g]ed. It occured to us [as] we passed along the dirty narow lanes and saw the wan and wrinkled visage of age and poverty peereing at us through broaken casements in dillapidated walls. That the squallid and antique appearence of the picture was in keeping with the rude seting that supported it.

On our return from our strol[l] we saw what apeared to us a religious assembly listening ^to^ one acting as teacher a rather sad commentary on the truthful liberality of the proud city with all its gorgeous temples dedicated to the intrests of sufering humanity. Religion is forced into the streets.

"Consistency thou art a jewel" Where art thou found? Not in the proud city. There the high ones dispise the[e] and to the ignorant thou art unknown. The heart of the arogant is not the sanctuary. Yet thy dwelling may be with the poor and with the wise and prudent. Thou art ever to be found passed the evening giveing instruction to the elders present.

Sepember 15, 1860; Saturday. This morning received leters and papers from Liverpool. Engaged in writeing until half past 12 oclock then went to Br E[lias] L. T. Harison's with whom we dined. After which we went to visit Holyrood Palace[89] to which we were refused admitence as they were prepareing for the reception of her Magisty.[90]

So makeing a virtue of necesity we concluded to while away the intervening time as best we might and await the comeing of the liveing representatives of royalty as we were denied the privilige of gazeing upon the antique mementoes of departed greatness. While awaiting her Magisty's comeing went a short distance from the palace to a small lagoon where numbers of men and boys were amuseing themselves in sailing over its placid ~~bason~~ surface a fleet of tiny ships. In sight from this point

89. Holyrood Palace is the home of the British monarch when s/he stays in Scotland.

90. Queen Victoria and Prince Albert were about to arrive at the palace. The prince would die the next year in 1861. The queen, on the other hand, would live another forty years and leave her mark in the very name of the Victorian era, which implied a time of renewed emphasis on morals.

were the ruins of the Chapel of the good St. Anthony[,][91] said to have been in former times conne[c]ted with the palace by a subteraneos passage (of this however we were not reliably informed).

The movement of troops and other preperations were indicating the aproach of royalty. All anxiety [and] expectation was [apparent, the crowd] on the[ir] tip toe[s.] The gray ones looked wise while the young were giveing free expression to their juvenile feelings. Children were asking is the Qeen comeing. At length a movement at the extremity of the congregated mass evinced the comeing of her Magisty along the road. In her advance moved lines of gaily drest soldiers in the direction of the Palace. Immediately folowing was a cariage conveying two men whose place and position were alike unknown and unn[an]ounced to our wondering selves. In the rear of the first came another plain cariage drawn by four plainly caparisoned [cloth-draped] horses. The principal seats ~~were~~ was occupied by her Magisty and on her left sat his Royal Highness the Prince Consort [Albert].

The sombre apearence of the mourning habiliments of her Magisty gave to her homely and matronly face quite a domestick apearance that spared us the embaressment of mortification in her presence and caused us to think that she would be be altogether aproachable in circumstances where she would be more the mother [and] the woman than the Q[u]een.

This passing pagentry over we repaired to the house of brother [Elias L. T.] Harison with whom we partook of some refreshments then returned to br Teasdales. Here we met with Brother [Charles] Turner[,] Traveling Elder.[92]

September 16, 1860; Monday. This morning the weather rather dark. At eleven oclock went to the meeting place of the Saints and addressed them. After services over returned to Br [George] Teasdales and remained there engaged in writing dureing the afternoon in which time Br [Nathaniel V.] Jones addressed the Saints at their hall. Some rain this

91. St. Anthony's Chapel was built about 1420, placing it a century before the palace and about a mile distant.

92. Full-time missionaries were referred to as traveling elders. They were complemented by presiding elders (the leaders of branches, districts, and conferences) and home missionaries who did part-time proselytizing in their own towns. In the British Mission, home missionaries were the most successful. See Ronald E. Bartholomew, "The Role of Local Missionaries in Nineteenth-Century England," in *Go Ye into All the World*, 447–70.

afternoon. At half past 6 oclock I repared to the hall and found it filled to overflowing with strangers whom I addressed for one hour dureing which time they listened with undivided attention. At the close a gentleman asked if he could have some questions answered at that time and place. He was told by Prest [Elias L. T.] Harison he could not. He then remarked he could find no fault with what he had heard but said he came to hear the peculiar views of the Mormons but had been entirely disappointed. We were assured by the Saints that such a meeting had never before been seen in Edinburgh by them. Rained slightly as we returned to our lodgings.

September 17, 1860; Monday. To day we visited the castle where we saw the two young princes Leopold and Arthur[93] as they in company with their conductors were looking at the wonders of this far famed locality. After a passing notice to these juvinile liveing wonders we turned our attention to the contemplation of the silent mementoes of departed greatness in the past among which was the Mons Meg a ponderous cannon of early times.[94] We then visited a small chapel some eight hundred years old. Its only decoration was the picture of the Saint for whom it was built. We then went to the crown room to see the regalia[,] the now silent yet impressive memento of Scotland's greatness long since departed. We then visited the sleeping apartment of Mary Queen of Scotts where James the first of England was born and at the age of eight days was let down a basket from a window in this apartment the distance of several hundred feet. In the evening went to Leith and dined with br John Anderson and family and then returned to the city.

September 18, 1860; Tuesday. This morning went to Holy Rood but could not get admitance and while the brethren visited Arthur's Seat [hill] I went to the residence of br [Elias L. T.] Harrison and there awaited the comeing of night and the Priesthood [brethren] who were to meet us at 8 oclock. The hour arived an so did the brethren and we had a pleasant time together instructing and being instructed. Meeting over[,] a walk of 2 miles brought me to my lodgeings at br [George] Teasdale's. Retired past midnight.

93. Princes Arthur and Leopold were born in 1850 and 1853 respectively.

94. Mons Meg is a massive cannon at Edinburgh Castle that at one time shot stone cannon balls weighing 386 pounds each and measuring 20 inches in diameter a distance of two miles from the rampart into the surrounding countryside.

September 19, 1860; Wednesday. At 10 oclock this morning took the [train] carrs for New Castle on Tyne.[95] Arived there half past 1 oclock and was met at the station by Pastor [Joseph] Stanford and conducted to his residence where we dined in the evening. Had a pleasant meeting with the Saints at their hall. Felt considerable weary in body lodged with Pastor S.

September 20, 1860; Thursday. This morning received the proof sheets of [the Star]. Corrected an[d] returned them. Wrote and posted some leters for home and at one oclock went to wall's end. Dined with br [Duncan] McAlister on Scotch Soup. After diner went to North Shields and crossed the river to South Shields. Had tea with br Story then had a pleasant meeting with the Saints some strangers in attendance. To day meet with Elder Samuel Francis[,] meeting over we returned to Newcastle.

September 21, 1860; Friday. This morning received a leter from br C[harles] C. Rich in Liverpool, stateing the arival and disposition of 14 of the missionaries. Also a leter with funds from Elder John Van Cott in Scandinavia. The Liverpool leter answered[,] [I] spent the day in journalizing and also administered to Sister [Elizabeth] Stanford who was ill.

September 22, 1860; Saturday. This morning weather rainy & dark. Sis. [Elizabeth] S[tanford] is beter. Received a call from Elders Wm Dallin and Henry Barnet. At 11 oclock took the [train] carrs for Sunderland were meet at the station by Elder Francis [M. Lyman] with whom we dined. Spent some time in writeing then took a short walk in the city. Crossed the river Weare on the bridge and recrossed by ferry. In the evening gave instruction to the ministry of the Pastorate at the residence of Elder Francis.

September 23, 1860; Sunday. This morning had meeting with the Saints who seemed to be blessed. Preached three times dined and took tea with br Stevens and family. Took super with br [Alfred] N^e^uby and family. Returned to our lodgeings with br F[rancis M. Lyman] much wearied with the labours of the day and evening. Had severe cough

September 24, 1860; Monday. This morning at fifteen minutes past 8 oclock took the [train] carrs for London where we arived 20 minutes past 6 oclock. Found Pastor [John] Cook and family well. At the time of our arival it was raining.

95. Newcastle upon Tyne was an industrial city known for ship-building and pottery factories, 120 miles south of Edinburgh near the North Sea coast. When Lyman next travels to North Shields, just east of Newcastle, it is to the coast itself.

September 25, 1860; Tuesday. In company with Elder [Nathaniel V.] Jones and Pastor [John] Cook and my son [Francis] Marion visited the Tower [of London][96] to see the mementoes of the past that were collected at that point. Among them were many things to stir the memories of the past and strongly impress us with the truth of times ceasless flight. Returned to br Cooks in the evening in conversation with friends present until the hours of rest.

September 26, 1860; Wednesday. Awoke from pleasant sleep the sun was intrudeing its golden rays into our apartment. Its smile was welcome but far more welcome the missive I found lieing on the table which [with] certain significant marks was friendships own mesenger from that holy sanctuary of the hearts warm affections Home. Morning past buisness over I wrote some leters home. At 4 oclock went to br Wests to tea. Spent the evening with our friends there. Brs [Nathaniel V.] Jones and [John] Cook were with us. Returned to our lodgeings at br Cs. It was raining retired at 11 oclock.

September 27, 1860; Thursday. This morning the rain had ceased. Spent the morning in writeing. In the evening br and Sister Staner called and spent a few hours.

September 28, 1860; Friday. The weather somewhat wet past the day in writeing and conversation with the Elders present in regard to the old and false opinions of the age in regard to religion.

September 29, 1860; Saturday. This morning rose early. Passed the day in writing. At evening went to Madam Tausauds Museum[97] where we had the pleasure of contemplating a somewhat extensive collection of the mementoes of the past. In our visit we were acompanyed by Elder F[rancis] M. Lyman and J[oseph] C. Rich.

September 30, 1860; Sunday. To day preached three times twice in St. George's Hall[98] to crowded audiences. Dined with Sister Crossweller.

96. The Tower of London on the River Thames was built in the eleventh century and has filled many roles, including as a residence and government offices and, most notoriously, a prison. The Crown Jewels of the UK are housed there.

97. Marie Tussaud, a French woman, started displaying her wax sculptures in London in 1835. Although today Madame Tussaud's is known for its wax statues of famous celebrities and politicians, many of her early sculptures were of murder victims, murderers, and the dead of the French Revolution.

98. This was a temperance hall in the heart of London on St. George's Road. The area is known as the Elephant and Castle neighborhood after a guild sign indicating

In the evening had an atack of n[e]uralga in my head.[99] After night brs [Nathaniel V.] Jones and [John] Cook returned from Brighton where they had a good day.

October 1, 1860; Monday. Returned to Liverpool found all well and remained there until Friday the 5th when in company with Elder C[harles] C. Rich I started for Hull[100] where we arived about 3 oclock. Were met at the station by Elder Wm Cromer the President of Hull Conference. Had conversation with the Saints who came ~~in~~ to see us. The journal is continued in Book B.[101]

October 6, 1860; Saturday. This morning we engaged our passage to Hamburgh [Germany] purchased return tickets good for one month. Breakfasted with Cister Wilson and dined with br John Gibson. At 7 oclock went on board of the steamer Helen McGregor.[102] Was visited on board by Pastor [Thomas] Wallace and two other brethren

October 7, 1860; Sunday. This morning were under way at half past 9 oclock, the wind and wether were favourable &c and our highland heroine bore herself bravely onward in her watery path. We had only 3 felow passengers in the cabin, besides ourselves. Weather fine throughout the day. At night became verry sick and continued until we entered the Elbe [River estuary].

October 8, 1860; Monday. This morning the [we] commenced to rise and continued all day.[103] About 9 oclock p.m. we entered the smo[o]th water of the Elbe for which we felt very thankful. To day as the wind was at its highest as br [Charles C.] Rich and myself were alone in the cabin we discovered the boat to be on fire by the falling of the fire in the

---

that this was once where knives and scissors were made. Whitney, *Life of Heber C. Kimball, an Apostle.*

99. Neuralgia is acute nerve pain, normally in the head.

100. Kingston upon Hull is a port city on the north bank of the Humber in northeast England, 130 miles east of Liverpool.

101. A day book called Book B contained Lyman's rough account of his travel to Hamburg and was written in pencil. The rest of the present diary was used to record his activities for 1863.

102. The ship's name came from the Scottish revolutionary Helen Macgregor, whose husband Rob Roy Macgregor was immortalized in Sir Walter Scott's fictionalized account, *Rob Roy.*

103. They were probably entering the mouth of the Elbe during its tidal surge, but even so, Hamburg sat about two meters higher than the mouth of the estuary seventy miles to the west. Over the course of its flow, the Elbe rises a total of 4,600 feet.

cabin where we were. We soon extinguished the fire our star of safety was in the ascendent.

October 9, 1860; Tuesday. This morning the weather pleasant and we were traveling gaily up the beatiful Elbe. The scenery that met the gaze of the traviler was most enchanting. Thus it seemed a source of sorrow that aught so beautiful [a place] should feel the blight of sin and corruption. Arived at Hamburgh did not see our friend and we understood one thing only[,] that we understood nothing.[104]

After sundary vain attempts to learn whether our friend Van Cott had been in town or not we at suggestion of the porter we went to the Hotell where we dined on Beef stake and Eggs and Coffee about which we understood nothing only that they were good. Di[n]ner over we strooled out into the city. Our ramble lead us along the water courses that for the conveinences of commerce ramify the lower parts of the city. The general appearance was rather filthy and the buildings rather time worn and dillapidated. Leaveing this for a somewhat higher part we found a change in the appearance of the improvements. They put on an appearance that reminded us of our New York.

Returned from our ramble[,] we hired a cab to take us to Altona the Railraod station. Arived at the station our man wanted some over pay[ment.] This refused[,] he wanted a little drink money. We procured our tickets and were by the porter conducted to our cariage when we supposed some mistake had been made us. The cariage was fited up much in the stile of the first days in England. Being assured we were right we were seated and were moveing along at a very safe speed for Keels [Kiel] where we arived about 10 oclock. Here we ~~came~~ went on board the mail steamer for Ko[rsø]r [Denmark] at half past 10 oclock. Were in bead and under way weather was very rough in the Big Belt or part of the Balick on which we were traviling.[105] Arived at our landing about half past five oclock A.M. While we were dressing we [were] most agreeably surprised by meeting our brother John Vancott who had been in the place awaiting

104. The following two paragraphs were written on a loose sheet and inserted into the book to summarize the trip to meet with the Scandinavian mission president in Copenhagen. Lyman thought the president would meet them in Germany and accompany them from there, but they encountered each other in Korsør, Denmark.

105. The strait between Zealand, where they were headed, and Funen on their port side, is called the Great Belt (*Storebaelt*).

our arival for two nights and one day. We started on the railraod for Copenhagen at fifteen minutes past seven oclock. Arived at the city about 11 oclock somewhat faint from our sea sickness and travel.[106]

October 10, 1860; Wednesday. This morning while dressing Br [John] Van Cott steped into our cabin. We went by railroad to Copenhagen [Denmark] where we arived about 11 oclock.

October 11, 1860; Thursday. To day rained all day remained in the [mission] office wrote some.

October 12, 1860; Friday. This day we visited the Kastellet or Fortress of the town and the galery of paintings in the Royal Palace and the Museum of ~~Thol~~ Thorvaldsen of paintings and sculpture. Visited the ~~B~~ Kings stables. At night attended meeting spoke of the [Latter-day] Saints through interpreters. The name of the palace Christiansborg.

October 13, 1860; Saturday. Visited the Kings Gardens and Palace of Rosenborg in which were the most extensive and gorgeous evidences of the luxury in which Royalty has been pampered and supported out [of] the taxes of the poor that had ever seen.

October 14, 1860; Sunday. This morning the weather rainy cool. At 10 oclock we repaired to the meeting place whereof the Saints had two meetings well attended by Saints and strangers. Spoke three quarters of an hour translation by brs. O[la] N. Lil[j]enquist[107] and Thompson. Ajourned or dismissed at fifteen minutes past 4. At night general brethren and cisters came to see us at the office.

October 15, 1860; Monday. This morning the weather dark and rainy. This morning Elder Lars Peter Eidholm came to the office and we blessed him as he was going to labor in the ministry. Visited and partook of refreshments with Brother and Cister Skoubye.

October 16, 1860; Tuesday. This morning the weather dark and rainy. Went at 11 oclock and drank chockolate with Br & Cister Rasmusen. Returned to the office where Br [Ola N.] Lingenquist and [Anthon H.] Lund[108] came[,] being prevented from goeing on their journey on account of the storm. We walked down by the water side after the wind had

106. This loose sheet was folded and "Oct" written upside down below the entry.

107. Ola Nilsson Liljenquist, a Danish tailor, immigrated to Utah in 1857 and returned to Denmark as a missionary two years later; he would come back again in 1876 as mission president.

108. Anthon Lund, 16, taught Danish to the English-speaking missionaries. In two

subsided and we found the water had been dr^i^ven from land until it was 3 ft lower then usual. At night Br Peter Wm Pauls~~on~~^en^ was baptized by Br [John] Van Cott and was confirmed and ordained an Elder under our hands.

October 17, 1860; Wednesday. This morning took passage on the steamer Princess Louisa for Christi[a]nia [Oslo]. Traviled up the North Sea, the weather was fair.

October 18, 1860; Thursday. Was very sick was in bed until after noon. We traviled until night and then cast anchor on acount of darkness.

October 19, 1860; Friday. This morning we [were] in the smo[o]th water of the Bay of Christiania about 10 oclock landed at the city of Christiania the capital of Norway. Were met at the landing by Brs [John] Dores and Hansen who conducted us to the Hotel Scandinavia, where they had engaged a suit[e] of rooms for our acomodations. The Conference of the Saints was in session at 9 oclock. We meet them at 2 oclock had with them a good time and ajourned until Sunday. Took diner with Br Halvardsen then went to our lodgengs.

October 20, 1860; Saturday. This morning the weather was dark. At half past 9 oclock we started for a ride of some twenty miles in the country in order that we might see some thing of Norwegian life. Our conveyance consisted of two low wheeled covered cariages each drawn by two small but sinewy horses, they were fine travilers and in size well adapted to the condition of the country where feed is sca[r]se and hard to produce.

The road on which we traviled lay along the valey Kanyon of a small mountain stream. It was laid on an even grade that corisponded to that of the stream. It is the best road I have ever seen over so rocky and rough a country. On either side of the way we [saw] some examples of the liveing and labors of the poor. Their houses could be seen nestleing among the undieing green of the pine clad hills and then in contrast with this others were perched on Baren Rocks. They were mostly covered with tile which were overgrown with ^the^ moss of centurys growth.

We arived at the terminus of our ride about 2 oclock. Din[n]er ordered we walked out onto the margin of the Rands fjorden (or Rands

---

years he would immigrate to Sanpete County, Utah, and in 1889 be ordained an apostle, later becoming a counselor in the First Presidency. Hatch, *Danish Apostle*, xi–xxxiv.

Lake).[109] From our rocky perch we could see in the northmost in the distance that bounded our vision the snowclad Hills were lifting their hoary summits Heaven ward, thus reminding us of our own New England while to the west were blended in harmony the green of the forest pine against the blue of the distant horizon.

While from dense forests of pine were gracefuly curling upward the white wreathes of smoke from the residences of the hardy woodmen that nestled in the midst of the surounding ocean of liveing green. In the rear of our point of observation the green hills were lifting their towering sumits far above us as if keeping their sleepless vigils over the surounding country while several hundred feet beneath us like a lovely gem reposing in the Bosom of its romantick seting of the surounding hills, was spread out in all its placid beauty ^the^ Rands Lake.

Returning to our in[n] we partook of the cheer provided by our Host which was served for us by a dark eyed damsel the daghter of the Landlord. Haveing done the needful by way of refreshing the iner man we took some notes in regard to the maner of building with small timber which thought might be applied profitably in our own mountain home. This done we plucked from the undieing evergreen around us some small mementoes ^of^ our brief visit to the mountain wilds of Norway. Our cariages ready we were seated and whirleing along at what on a rough way might have been regarded as a dangerous speed but the good state of our road and skill of our drivers rendered our ride speady and safe. Night had brought the hours of rest to a weary world ere we reached our Hotell. When arived here we partook of some light refreshments and retired to rest.

October 21, 1860; Sunday. Meet with and spoke to the Saints. Their hall was crowded to overflowing with Saints and strangers who listened with breathless attention the translation being given by br ~~Charls~~ John Dor[iu]s and also br [John] Van Cott. At 6 oclock the audience was addressed by br [Charles C.] Rich and the translation was given by br Charles Dor[iu]s. The people listened with the most intence intrest. To

109. Lyman is probably wrong about the lake being Randsfjorden, which is fifty miles from Oslo. To get there, one has to travel alongside Tyrifjorden, which matches Lyman's report of the water's edge being about twenty miles from the capital. Even so, his rhapsodizing would be applicable to most of the fjords.

day we dined with br Halvorsen. Returned to our Hotell partook of refreshments with some of the brs and retired to rest.

October 22, 1860; Monday. This morning we called on and ministered to a brother that was afflicted with lameness and then went to see the Royal Palace that has been built or completed within the last 8 years at a cost of 700,000 dollars. We dined with br Christofersen. At 6 oclock meet with the Saints had a good time. Took tea with Christensen.

October 23, 1860; Tuesday. To day we were disappointed in starting for Gotenburgh [Sweden] by the nonarival of the steamer. We dined with br Johnsen remained with them until night. The steamer arived this evening was detained by dark weather.

October 24, 1860; Wednesday. Secured our passages on the boat and went on board at 3 oclock. Had a fine passage, arived at Gotenborg. The name of our boat was ~~Excellence Toll~~ Excellensen, Toll. The principle articles of export are oats, iron and timber and some fish.

October 25, 1860; Thursday. At half past 9 oclock were meet at the landing by the brethren and conductid~~g~~ to the Hotell Gota Kallare where we engaged a good room and had some breakfast. Aranged our toilet and called on the President of the branch R[asmus] Berntson. Were entertained with wine, coffee and fruit. Was presented with a fine opera glass by Br. Berntson. Called on some of the Brethren and partook of refreshments with them and meet with the Saints and addressed them briefly. A~~n~~ most excellent spirit prevailed with them. Returned to our Hotell and took sup[p]er. Dureing the night it rained.

October 26, 1860; Friday. This morning were up early. Breakfasted and took the cars for Föreloda. Along our route we saw woomen plowing and bearing heavy burdens. The country through which we past was mostly hilly rocky and barren. The streams were swolen by late rains. The Canall was commenced in the year 1814 and was completed about 182~~3~~5. The steamer arived and we were on board half past 3 oclock and we traviled gently through a country presenting a varied scenery such as is peculiar to the country which indicated in its appearence a greater degree of fertility than that over which we traviled this morning.[110]

110. They are traveling east across the peninsula on the Göta Canal, a 400-mile waterway that cuts through the middle of the country from Göteborg to Söderköping, south of Stockholm.

The vessel was crowded with deck passengers mostly woomen engaged in service in Stockholm. We had also with us some who from position and the posession of money think it their right to prey upon the labouring poor particularly if they are woomen. As we contemplated we pitied and felt to say within or self when O Lord will the bands be broaken that are around the poor and down troden of this sin-enthralled Land when may the human mind become, as it should be[,] the truthful reflex of thy self. And man cease to prey upon man and become the minister of blessings to his race? O wrath was stired but reflection strengthened reason and we became cool.

On the boat we received kind attention and good fare (as they very properly thought we were captains). Tied up at night on acount of darkness and those who had beds occupied them. Others got along without them. The night was pleasant which much ameloriated the condition of those out side. The people of the boat were kind to the poor, and extended them what comfort they could.

October 27, 1860; Saturday. This morning were moveing early and passed into and across a small Lake. The weather was rough some sickness among the woomen. On leaveing the lake we decended to the level of the next one a distance of fifty ft. through five locks which presented us with a specimen of excellent masonry. The work was built of granite and stands very well. At this point on the canall is a large iron works their power is water from the outlet of the lake. Their was some shiping at this point and large quantities of pig iron also one large block of buildings occupied in boat building. Retired early to bed were travileing all the night the moon shone full and bright.

October 28, 1860; Sunday. Cloudy with some little rain. Our travil to day was through a somewhat extensive lake or lakes so thickly studed with rocky islets as to render the navigation by night rather dificult and dangeous. The general Barren condition of the Country was relieved by tracts of Land indicating a good degree of fertility in some cases also supporting improvements of some pretentions. Arived in Stockholm at 3 oclock meet with the Saints at 7 oclock. Took rooms at Ry[d]bergs Hotell. The Saints were much rejoiced to see and hear us, they numbered 32 members in the city. Expect additions to their numbers soon. Our rest was tolerable disturbed some by the noise in the street.

October 29, 1860; Monday. This morning ^were visited^ by Br Gustaf Ohlson (Gustavus Olsen) President of the Conf^e^rence who conducted us to an elevated position denominated the Mountain of Moses [Mosebacke neighborhood] from which we had a good view of the city and its suburbs. The view was ~~was~~ grand and comprehensive embraceing the most densely built portion of the ~~Royal~~ city. Conspicuous over all rose the Royal Palace at this time occupied by his Magisty Charles 15th. Outside were lovely suburban residences nestling among the rocks ^which^ adds a rural beauty to what would under other circumstances, be barren and forbiding. While in our morning stroll we passed the place where the iron of the whole kingdom is collected & stored for shipment to other countries.

We also visited one of the two outlets by which the waters of the lakes in the vicinity of the city in artificial chanels of solid masonry are discharged meet the water of the Baltick,[111] the chanel was covered with fish ~~traps~~ ^boxes^ aranged to be let down into he stream when filled with the finy travilers ~~they are~~ they are thus preserved alive. From our ramble we went to visit the Kings Museum of Clothing & Armour and Arms for 500 years. We sat on a chair 226 years old saw a sleigh of the same age all belingong to Gustaf Adolfas.[112] Also the skin of the Horse on which he was killed. It is 228 years old. One old fowling gun nearly 12 feet long ^and^ 250 years old. The collection we saw extends from 1400 to the present ocupant of the Sweedish Throne whose dress while a prince was shown us.

Hired a cariage and went 1 1/8 miles to the residence of Br. Olson. As we rode along we were evidently gazed at with considerable curiosity. In the course of our ride we meet the lifeguard of the King on the street. Among other mementoes of the past was the hat which Charls the 12th of Sweeden[113] wore when he was shot. The perforation of the fatal ball is visible also the boots he wore, all of which apeared in character with the wearer Rough and ready. At 7 oclock meet with the Saints blist [blessed] and bade them farewell.

---

111. The Baltic Sea is bordered by Sweden on the west, Finland to the north, the so-called Baltic countries (Estonia, Latvia, and Lithuania) on the east, and Poland to the south.

112. King Gustavus Adolphus shaped Sweden into a regional power and was killed in battle in 1632.

113. Charles XII fought against Denmark, Norway, and Russia, and died in battle in 1718.

October 30, 1860; Tuesday. This morning the wether clear, and warm health good. Walked about the city went on to the armory grounds and saw a large collection of cannon taken in war mostly by Charles 12th from Russia. Among their new guns were some brech loading guns.[114] At night went on board the steamer Svea for Malmo,[115] had good beds rested well.

October 31, 1860; Wednesday. Weather fine had a fine run down the ~~baltick~~ bay into the Baltick which was very smooth and unrufeled.

November 1, 1860; Thursday. Weather stil fine and pleasant all day.

November 2, 1860; Friday. Awaked this morning at Malmo, and took the steamer for Copenhaven where we arived about 10 oclock. Found leters from home and one from B[righam] Y[oung].

November 3, 1860; Saturday. Passed the day in the office. At 2 oclock Ate diner with br Williamson [Niels Wilhelmsen] the President of the Copenhaven Conference. From the Saints this evening ^we received^ a small present in money amounting to £5.5. May the Lord bless them.

November 4, 1860; Sunday. This morning met with the Saints at 10 oclock. Brs [Charles C.] Rich and [John] Van Cott addresed them. A good spirit prevailed. Numbers of strangers were in attendance. At 2 oclock I spoke to the people the hall was crowded and many strangers were in. Bade the Saints adieu and at 7 oclock were.[116]

November 5, 1860; Monday. This morning ere it was daylight we were awakened by the landing of the steamer at K[i]el. We repared to the station there we waited until 7 oclock. Refreshed our selves with some coffee then rolled away to Altona a distance of 14 m[ile]s (or 5.6 German m[ile]s). Arived at half past 10 oclock took a cab for Hamburgh. Took rooms in the English Hotell which we found suplied with anxious master [landlord] & polite servants and good fare. Breakfast over we went out for a stroll in the city in which we saw much that suplied food for thought.

114. A breech-loading weapon was loaded from the back, which took less time than it did to load a musket from the front.

115. Malmø, Sweden, on the southern tip of the Scandinavian peninsula, is separated from Denmark by the Øresund Strait. The completion of a main railroad line to the city in 1856 transformed it into a major manufacturing center.

116. Lyman ends the sentence abruptly. What he neglected to write was that they boarded a steamer and sailed around the northern tip of Denmark, down to Germany, to retrace their steps to Hull, England. There is a note written down the middle of the page indicating that the information he recorded pertained to November 5.

As we contemplated the beauties of some portions of the city with its artificial lakes its shaded walks we thought how beautiful must be our own dear Zion when beautified and perfected in Holiness as the home of the just and the dwelling of God. When the world[,] regenerated with its teeming millions[,] shall be the reflection of Heaven in all its excellencies and perfections as the home of the Gods and the dwelling of the saved. Such were some of our thoughts as we looked upon the Modern Babel spread out around us whose streets and avenues were teeming with an ever restless and hetrogeneous tide of humanity embraceing all the variety from the proud Lordling surrounded with all the gaudy trapings of wealth, to the squalid representative of the most abject poverty[,] want[,] and wretchedness. Such is Hamburgh.

The sensebility we caried inside our boots admonished us to return to our rooms. Had our diner after which another stroll in the city prepared us for retireing to rest. In the privacy of our room said our prayrs for the Zion of God and selves and loved ones at home and retired to rest and sleep.

November 6, 1860; Tuesday.[117] This morning some indications of rain. From the window of my room w[h]ere I am writeing I see the masons engaged in fulfilling the saying of the prophet that iron should be made to take the place of stone [Isa. 60:17]. They were takeing out the front of a building made of brick and stone to put in a front of iron. The rebuilding of portions of the city destroyed by fire gives to those districts a more modern appearence than they had formerly worn and adds much beauty to the city and causes one to think of our own loved land.

Brs [Charles C.] Rich and [John] Van Cott have just returned from their morning strool [stroll] and propose we discuss some wine thirty years of age. We did not object. The trial made [for] the wine [tasting] was port and very good. At 5 oclock went on board of the steamer Prince for Hull, at the ship side bad[e] Adieu to br Van Cott.

November 7, 1860; Wednesday. This morning found ourselves near the mouth of the Elbe. Ate Breakfast and soon became sick from the rolling of the ship. Kept our bed all day with commotion without and within. That [from] within troubled us most.

November 8, 1860; Thursday. To day chow sick but through the

117. This entry was written in two parts, out of order, brought together here.

kindness of the steward was some what relieved. Took a little refreshment. In evening rose and took the fresh air this helped me much.

November 9, 1860; Friday. This morning as we came into the Humber we were relieved from the rolling motion and our sickness entirely subsided. Landed at Hull about 11 oclock. Found Elder [William] Cromer. We are exceedingly thankful to our Father in Heaven for his kind protection that has preserved us. In the evening attended a meeting of the Saints in Hull.

November 10, 1860; Saturday. At an early hour we on the [train] carrs for Liverpool where we arived at 15 minutes past 3 oclock. Found the people in the office all well.

November 11, 1860; Sunday. This morning brs [Charles C.] Rich & [William H.] Dame were at the meeting with the Saints and I preached at half past 6 oclock eve.

November 12, 1860; Monday. To day wrote leter of instruction for the Saints. This evening br Jacob Gates came in to see us, passed the day in the office.

November 13, 1860; Tuesday. To day Pastor [William] Ba[y]lis[s] came to see us. Conversed with him in relation to the changes about to be introduced as indicated in the Presidents leter from Zion.[118]

November 14, 1860; Wednesday. To day wrote a leter to President [Brigham] Young, my health rather poor since my return to humid atmosphere of this place and the confinement of the office. Considerable private corispondence through the mission.

November 15, 1860; Thursday. Wrote to day to br G[eorge] A. Smith. Attended to some business in the office.

November 16, 1860; Friday. Passed the day in the office engaged in corispondence.

November 17, 1860; Saturday. Wrote some leters home and to my cister in N[ew] H[ampshire] and in Beaver [Utah]. This evening brother

118. Brigham Young wrote to Lyman and Rich complaining that the mission was spending too much on missionaries. A new apostle, George Q. Cannon, would soon arrive to take control of the "printing, binding, and shipping departments and of all financial affairs," while the existing brethren would continue to look after the "spiritual interests and welfare of the mission." Young did not seem to trust Lyman and Rich with finances in the wake of the San Bernardino experiment. Young to Lyman and Rich, Sept. 13, 1860, in Brigham Young office files, CHL.

Edward Edwards arived and received leter from us to br B[enjamin] Evens in Wales.

November 18, 1860; Sunday. This morning myself and Br [Charles C.] Rich went to Manchester and meet with the Saints at half past 10 oclock. Hall well filled. Meet again at half past 6 oclock hall crowded. This ^evening^ snowing some folowed by rain, lodged with elder ^James^ McGhie.[119]

November 19, 1860; Monday. This morning went [to] the house of Pastor [William] Balis and dined there after which at 5 oclock took the [train] carrs for Liverpool arived at 6. Attended a counsil meeting and instructed the priesthood present. A good spirit prevailed.

November 20, 1860; Tuesday. Was engaged in the office with corispondence. This morning I received leter in which was [a] list of drafts on br George Cannon of which I was directed to take charge by President [Brigham] Young and did so.

November 21, 1860; Wednesday. To day engaged in the office with corispondence in the mission. To day prepared a book in which to save such receipts and other information as I might find in my traviles.

November 22, 1860; Thursday. To day was engaged in corispondence and prepareing to leave for London.

November 23, 1860; Friday. Rose early was at railroad st[ation] at 9 oclock and off for London. I arived about 3 oclock found all well. Had a coalision on the way but no harm done save some slight damage to the cylinder of engine.

November 24, 1860; Saturday. To day passed the day in the office with the brethren.

November 25, 1860; Sunday. To day meet with the priesthood at 10 oclock then meet the Saints in St. George Hall at half past 2 oclock. The Saints were addressed by Elders Jacob Gates and Milo Andrus. Ajourned until half past 6 oclock when the hall was crowded. I spake to them there were some strangers present. Retired at 11 oclock.

November 26, 1860; Monday. To day remained at br. [John] Cooks and wrote some and gave some instructions to Elders who called in dureing

119. James McGhie, a Scottish convert, was one-time president of the Liverpool Conference and may have served as the president of the Manchester Conference for a time.

the day. Weather dark dull and rainy. To day received a leter from Joseph F. Smith the news is good from all parts of the mission. In the evening saw br. Ferguson and ordered a watch made.

November 27, 1860; Tuesday. Wrote in my journal until about 4 oclock then went to br [illegible] Odels. Took tea was accompanied by br [John] Cook. Returned between 8 & 9 oclock feeling beter for my walk.

November 28, 1860; Wednesday. This morning received leters from G. S. L. City and some from the south. No rain this morning. To day went to dine and spent the evening at the house of Cister Hastler and daughters in company with brothers [John S.] Gleason & [William H.] Kelsy and [John] Cook. Had a pleasant pa^s^time, returned to lodgeings about 12 oclock. Weather rainy. Found some of the priesthood in council at br Cooks and gave them some instructions.

November 29, 1860; Thursday. This morning weather dark and rainy. Passed the day in the office until evening then went to Padington to a party. Had a pleasant time.

November 30, 1860; Friday. This morning at 9 oclock left for Liverpool where I arived half past 2 oclock found all well.

December 1, 1860; Saturday. To day attended to the mission corispondence. Wrote leter of instruction to Pastors George Teasdale ~~in~~ in Scotland als[o] a leter to br C[harles] C. Rich.

December 2, 1860; Sunday. Spent the morning in writing br [Nathaniel V.] Jones. Preached at the Assembly Rooms at which place I proceded at half past 6 oclock. Weather dark and wet my health not first rate.

December 3, 1860; Monday. To day ~~To~~ wrote instructions to publish in the [Millennial] Star for the Saints and ministry ~~throut~~ throughout the mission.

December 4, 1860; Tuesday. This morning br N[athaniel] V. Jones left for Birmingham. Was engaged in the office through the day in the evening br J[ohn] W. Coward came in to remain with me a few days. Weather dull and dark as usual with rain. This [day] was engaged in home & foreign correspondence. To day lent ten shillings to br [William H.] Perks to enable him to reach his friends he promised to repay soon. He said he had a recommend from President Young but could not produce it as it was he said in the possession of Joseph W. Young Captain of the ox train over the plains from Salt Lake to Florence.

December 5, 1860; Wednesday. Was engaged in Corespondence. Weather verry dark and dull.

December 6, 1860; Thursday. This morning received leters papers from the states leter from brother G[eorge] Q. Cannon from Florence [Nebraska] 10 Nov at above date. Himself and party were well.

December 7, 1860; Friday. The weather not so dark as usual. Past some time this morning in conversation with J[ohn] W. Coward on the principles of the great work of the later days in [which] we were joined by brother Edward Tullidge. Br C. left this evening to visit his family.

December 8, 1860; Saturday. To day wrote for the Star and attended to corespondence. Brs [Edward] Sloan & [Reuben] McBride called this evening. My health not good.

December 9, 1860; Sunday. This morning wrote for the Star and at half past 6 oclock was at the Assembly Rooms and spoke to the people.

December 10, 1860; Monday. This morning brs [Charles C.] Rich and [Nathaniel V.] Jones came in. Wrote some leters in the evening we attended a meeting of the council of the local authorities.

December 11, 1860; Tuesday. This day went to see a chapel with the view of hireing it for a meeting place. Did not conclude a trade. Received and answered some leters dureing the day.

December 12, 1860; Wednesday. This morning the weather rather dull and dark. The steamer on which we expect br [George Q.] Cannon is telegraphed will be in this evening. This evening some fifteen of the brethren from Utah arived on the steamer City of Baltimore.

December 13, 1860; Thursday. This day instructed the missionaries and appointed some to their fields of labours. Loaned £2.10 to brs Jerrimy and Biwater and the same amount to George Halliday.

December 14, 1860; Friday. This morning some six of the missionaries left by the early trains for their various destinations. Walked out in the city and bought myself a carpet bag for which I pa^i^d 14s shillings. Weather to day more than usualy pleasant no rain.

December 15, 1860; Saturday. This day attended to home corespondence. Br Bently left for the Isle of Man. My health not good severe pain in my side ariseing from spinal exertion. Weather dull and dark.

December 16, 1860; Sunday. Remained in the office through the day. Preached at half past 6 oclock in the assembly rooms. An attentive audience of the Saints and strangers. Dureing the day the missionaries from Zion spoke to the people much to their edification and mutual gratification. This morning br J[ohn] L. Smith and J[esse] N. Smith and Wm Cluff[120] left here for Leeds to visit for a few days beforre leveing for the Continent.

December 17, 1860; Monday. This morning lent to br David [John] money to buy him a hat. Had a long conversation with pastor Wm Balis in reference to the condition of the mission and its prospects spiritualy and also financially. At night attended a social party of the Saints at their meeting hall. <u>Was not pleased with their dramatick representations</u>. Br [George Q.] Cannon has ~~we~~ ^not^ come we retired to sleep and await his comeing.

December 18, 1860; Tuesday. Past the day in the office attending to corispondence and prepare[ing] mater for the Star. This morning received leters and papers from Utah no news of importance.

December 19, 1860; Wednesday. This morning our streets were covered with snow some 4 inches in depth which gave our city rather a wintry aspect and much labour for the scavengers.

December 20, 1860; Thursday. To day passed the day in the office copying journal. Weather very cold.

December 21, 1860; Friday.[121] Remained in the office all day was engaged in writing.

December 22, 1860; Saturday.[122] This morning at <u>4 oclock</u> brs G[eorge] Q. Cannon and wife [Elizabeth].[123] John Kay[,][124] C. V. Sperry [and] John Needham arived comeing via Southhampton and London. Their passage was pleasant. Passed the day in the office Passed the day with the brethren in the office. Loaned C.V.S. £2.

---

120. Just off a four-year mission to the Sandwich Islands, William Cluff would serve in the Scandinavian mission for three years and then be called back to Hawaii for a second stint there.

121. This entry is written on a separate slip of paper that was inserted over the original entry for the 21st.

122. Underneath the inserted slip is an entry with the words written vertically, "this belongs to Saturday," so I have moved it to Dec. 22.

123. Cannon had a second wife, Sarah Jenne, who remained in Salt Lake City during his European mission.

124. John Moburn Kay was an English convert who immigrated to America, returned to his homeland for a three-year mission, traveled back to Utah, only to be sent overseas again for another four years as a missionary. He died en route to Utah in 1864.

December 23, 1860; Sunday. To do went to Bolton.[125] Wa[s] acompanied by br John Kay. Had a pleasant time with the Saints returned in the evening. Received some money for expences. Weather cold and stormy.

December 24, 1860; Monday. Weather still cool the earth stil retains its snowy covering.

December 25, 1860; Tuesday. This morning is merry Christmas yet we find no relaxation from buisness for pleasure. This evening brs J[esse] N. Smith ~~and Wm Cluff~~ returned from Leeds.

December 26, 1860; Wednesday. This morning Brs J[ohn] L. Smith and Wm Cluff returned from Leeds. We commenced the preperation of their papers, for their labours.

December 27, 1860; Thursday. This morning brs J[ohn] L. Smith and John Gerber started for Switzerland and J[esse] N. Smith and Wm Cluff and J. P. R. Johanson started for Denmark via London at which point they expected to procure their pasports. Wm Gibson came in this evening.

December 28, 1860; Friday. To day was buisy in our corispondence and the credentials of the Ministry. Br Gibson left for his labours in the Cheltenham district.

December 29, 1860; Saturday. To day were engaged in the office. Had a talk with br Ephraim Mantle in relation to his remaining in the office. He agreed to remain brs J. Kay and David Cannon left for their field of labours.[126]

December 30, 1860; Sunday. Remained in the office to day while Brs [Charles C.] Rich and [George Q.] Cannon attended meeting with the Saints at the Assembly Rooms.

December 31,1860; Monday. Was engaged in the office all day in the buisness of the changes and apointments for the comeing year. Said our prayrs and retired as the new year came in.

---

125. Bolton is forty miles east of Liverpool.

126. Portions of the entries for Dec. 30–31 are written at the top of the diary page, then exed out. Lyman recopied them in full under those dates on the next page.

7 "Poverty Encircles Heaven's Brightest Gems," 1861

Lyman made his 1861 diary the lengthiest of all, some entries continuing on in a reflective and often charming, if clumsy, way with sentences meant to evoke the emotions stirred up in him by his old-world surroundings. With George Q. Cannon fully in charge of administrative duties in Liverpool, Lyman and Rich were able to bring messages of comfort and inspiration to church members in the far-flung areas of the mission. Along the way, they took an interest in the culture, writing extensively about museums and parks, even the industry they could see signs of from the trains, and disclosing an inner sympathy with those who struggled financially. He often lamented the scenes he was exposed to in the industrial areas, while other people were likely to express gratitude that they were not as unfortunate. Lyman repeatedly mentioned how saddened he was to see the working poor in urban slums, especially at the time in Ireland.

January 1, 1861; Tuesday.[1] Was in the office through the day engaged in the mission business and writeing home to my family and also to br Willford Woodruff.

January 2, 1861; Wednesday. Today stil in the hurry of preperation to turn over the [mission financial] business to br [George Q.] Cannon. Attended to some corispondence.

1. Lyman's diary for Jan.–Mar. 1861 was kept in a book with pre-printed dates. He extended entries by inserting loose sheets that were not always placed at the right spot, although I have reordered them under the correct dates based on the context of each entry.

January 3, 1861; Thursday. This day closed up my private leters to Salt Lake. Attended to some of the mission corespondence preparitory to leaveing to go abroad to commence our winter labours.

January 4, 1861; Friday. To day completed the transfer of the Liverpool office and business to br. Geo Q. Cannon and made some preperation for our journey though t[h]e mission.

January 5, 1861; Saturday. This morning at half past 6 oclock started for Notingham with br ^C[harles] C.^ Rich and Cister May Ann Lyman[2] of Mansfield [and] were on the road until 5 oclock. Evening lodged with br D[avid] John found all well except br J[ames] Brown 3rd.

January 6, 1861; Sunday. This morning wer[e] at meeting with the Saints in conference at the Durham G[uild] H[all] [at City] Hall[3] had a good meeting & in the morning ajourned until half past 2 oclock at which time were again in meeting. Presented the church authorities and were addressed by Elder J[acob] Gates. Had evening meeting at 6 oclock and ajourned conference. The Good spirit did abound with us. In this Destrict there is about 111 saints[4] but poor tho rich in faith and hope.

January 7, 1861; Monday. This morning gave council to some of the Priesthood who meet us at br D[avid] Johns. Elder J[ohn] S. Gleason[5] was with us on his way to his destrict of Newcastle on Tyne. Wrote leter to Liverpool and at ten minutes to 4 oclock took train for Mansfield and with br J[ames] Brown 3d. Lodged at the house of Mrs. Mary Warren several of the Saints came in. And were instructed by us cheered us with some good singing and we parted for the night.[6]

January 8, 1861; Tuesday. This morning went to br Simon Orton's to do some writeing. The weather pleasant passed the day in writing for

2. Lyman heard of May Ann the year before and asked David John to investigate her genealogical background to see if they were related, but they were not. David John journal, Aug. 10, 16, 24, 1860, in CHL.

3. Guild Hall is the picturesque medieval structure that fronts Market Place as the foremost structure in the town hall complex. It was built in 1356 and renovated in 1640 and 1851.

4. He wrote "111 hundred," probably meaning a little over 100, not 11,100.

5. John Streator Gleason was born in New York. He became acquainted with Joseph Smith in Illinois as a captain in the Nauvoo militia. In Utah he ran a mill near Union Fort on Little Cottonwood Creek and served as a major in the territorial militia.

6. The last sentence was added to a loose sheet inserted into the diary and connected to this spot by an asterisk.

publication. At night preached to the Saints and Strangers in Mansfield. Lodged with Miss [Mary] Warren weather clear and cold.

January 9, 1861; Wednesday. This morning myself and br [James] Brown went to Sutton in Ashfield and dined with br Merit. At half past 7 oclock preached to the Saints some strangers were in attendence. The ^Saints^ here are mostly stocking weavers and very poor.

January 10, 1861; Thursday. This morning at fifteen minutes past ten oclock left Sutton for Pinxton Wharf[7] where myself and br [James] Brown dined with br John Farnsworth. Weather stil cool and smoky. At half past 7 oclock meet with Br. [Charles C.] Rich and the Saints in Lum[b]ercoats to whom we preached. Lodged with br Farnsworth with J[oseph] C. Rich.

January 11, 1861; Friday. This morning myself and br [Charles C.] Rich started for Birmingham[8] where we arrived at 3 oclock. We lodged with Br. Edward Price the weather somewhat milder sum mud in the streets.

January 12, 1861; Saturday. Spent the day in counseling the Elders present. At night wrote some for the Star. Br Milo Andrus was with us today and severall Elders.

January 13, 1861; Sunday. To day t[w]o leters received from home to attend to some meetings preached. Wrote to br [George Q.] Cannon in answer this morning br [Charles C.] Rich left early had at 2 & 6 oclock to good houses.

January 14, 1861; Monday. To day went to the pen factory of Mesers Gillott.[9] Dined with Br. C[harles] W. Penrose took tea with Cister Cutler. At 8 oclock P.M. meet with the Priesthood had good time.

January 15, 1861; Tuesday. At 7 oclock started for Cheltenham[10] where we arived about 10 oclock and called on Cister Lusty and then went to lodge with br [Frederick T.] Perris whom with his family we found well and meet a hearty welome. We lodged there weather very cold.

January 16, 1861; Wednesday. Wrote leter to G[eorge] A. S[mith]. At

7. Pinxton Wharf was the terminus of the 15-mile Cromford Canal on which Nottinghamshire coal was shipped to railroad cars on the Mansfield–Pinxton line.

8. Birmingham, in the West Midlands region, was Britain's second-largest city.

9. Joseph Gillott began making pen nibs in 1827 and became a leading manufacturer of dipping pens.

10. Cheltenham has been a health resort, drawing on mineral springs, since the early eighteenth century.

night had a pleasant meeting with the Saints after which returned to br [Frederick T.] Perris to sup[p]er and lodging.

January 17, 1861; Thursday. To day dined with br [William] Moss, and while there br. G[eorge] G. Bywater came in. We walked out in the town and in ramble saw much to admire of beauty in the buildings and grounds.

January 18, 1861; Friday. This morning left br [Frederick T.] Perris. Dined with br [William] Moss and at 3 oclock started by train for Cardiff [Wales] where we arived about 6 oclock. Called on br Wm Gwyn on the way we saw br. Wm O. Owen[11] at Newport. lodged with br G. This evening Prest Benjamin T. Evins came to Cardiff and discussed maters prepareatory to the comeing conference and determined our apointments for Wales.

January 19, 1861; Saturday. This morning br [Benjamin] Evens [LDS] p[a]st[or] of Cardiff called to see us and brought us some news from the States[,] leter and papers. War is inevitable.[12] Dined with Br Evens after which we went to see the old Castle of Cardiff a monument of Feudel power and rule.

The principal tower in its center is in ruins. The inclosure is receiveing some repairs. The elevation of earth forming the enclosure as well as the Central Mound all appear to be the work of art. Thus the miseries of servile toil is connected with its creation. It stands out to the beholder an evidence of the misdirected energies of our race. Received of Thomas Pering £10.[13]

January 20, 1861; Sunday. This day meet with the Saints in Cardiff in conference. Had good attendence morning and evening and a good spirit was with the people. Many strangers were in attendance in the evening.

January 21, 1861; Monday. This morning sat for portrait with brs [Charles C.] Rich and [William] Gwyn. Received a present of Virgils work [*The Aeneid*] from br Wm Gwyn. Went to tea, to br John Watson

11. Owen was a native of England who immigrated to Utah and returned to Wales as a missionary. He will become president of an English conference in February (see entry for Feb. 3, 1861) but leave the LDS Church in 1863 to join the RLDS. See Derry, "Autobiography of Charles Derry," 46–47, 308.

12. Lincoln's November 1860 election led to the secession of several states the next month, so Lyman saw the writing on the wall. However, the first aggressive act would not occur for four months, making his assumption three days later that hostilities had already begun a mistaken guess.

13. This paragraph was inserted on a separate sheet.

after which we attended a social ^party^ with the Saints. We [were] much interested [and] addressed the saints at the close of the entertainment.

January 22, 1861; Tuesday. This day dined with br Shepton and blest his infant son after which we walked out to the Docks. Took tea with br Glade also sup[p]er then returned to our lodgeings. To day heard news of fighting in America between the North and South. Received some calls from the brs in relation to emigration.

January 23, 1861; Wednesday. To day dined with Wm Gwyn Keeper of the Pembroke Castle Hotell. Took tea with br Wm Gibons. At 7 oclock attended meeting at the meeting Hall had some strangers in. At the conclusion gave some instruction to the priesthood.

January 24, 1861; Thursday. This morning raining. Called to see and ministered to br Richard Barrington whom we found in the last stages of consumption [tuberculosis] and very poor. We ministered to his wants. At 10 minutes past 3 oclock left for Treeforest[14] where we spoke to the Saints and strangers in the Odd Fellows Hall, lodged with br Richard Litson.

January 25, 1861; Friday. This morning it is raining which prevents us from going out to see the country and its peculiarities so curiosity must bow to necessity. From our window we see an almost constant succession of trains of coal moveing by rail from the pits to Cardiff. Dined with br Allen. Fifteen minutes to 4 oclock took train for Merthyr[15] arived at ½ past 4 oclock.

Lodged with br Wm Morgan. Weather stil rainy and dark the streams some swoolen by the constant rain. Here met with Prest [David M.] Davi[e]s with whom we had some social interchange of feelings. Engaged a pair of boots to be made. Received leters from home bringing news of the death of my son Albert by Priscilla Turley[16] and also an acount of the death of an old and valued [friend] in the person of br Sterling Driggs who came to his death while working on a threshing machiene.[17]

January 26, 1861; Saturday. This morning the sun is shining. Its

14. Treforest is about twelve miles northwest of Cardiff.

15. Merthyr Tydfil is yet twelve miles farther beyond Treforest, or twenty-four miles from Cardiff.

16. Albert, the son of Amasa's seventh wife, Priscilla, lived only a year (Oct. 5, 1859–Oct. 20, 1860).

17. This last paragraph was written on a loose sheet and labeled "Friday" to indicate that it belonged to this entry.

cheering smile is more than welcome. Spent several hours in a stroll about the iron works. We saw the iron in all it[s] conditions from the ore to rails for the road. We were accompanied by br Wm Morgan and br T[homas] Jerimy[18] and John Davies.

January 27, 1861; Sunday. This morning meet in Conference with the Saints in the White Lion hall.[19] Had good time the spirit was free had two meetings well attended. The weather was fine and bright, yet brighter far was the light of hope that beamed in the joy[-]lighted countenances of the Saints as the[y] drank truth from its fountain.

Jaunary 28, 1861; Monday. This morning received leter from my son F[rancis] M. Lyman in London. To day received of br T[homas] Jerimy the money I loaned him in Liverpool. Wrote leter to my son in London. Did not go out today.

January 29, 1861; Tuesday. This day wrote ^a^ leter to the Saints in the Welch Mission. Was not out to day but ^was^ engaged in writing all day. At night received my boots about 11 oclock.

January 30, 1861; Wednesday. To day went by rail to Abbwe & Vale.[20] While here visited the Crumlin Bridge [railway viaduct, which is] a iron structure built across or spaning Abbw Vale in length 1800 feet greatest he^i^ght 208 feet to the wheel track traversed by the carrs. It rests on 8 supports made of tubuler iron columns. Of these were combined in each of the supports extending from their respective footings to the framework of the bridge in one bearing the spur of the [b]ridge runing into the Vale. It was truly terifick and sublimely grand to ^see^ the lengthened train with its liveing freight huried along at lightning speed by the iron horse at such a fearful height.[21]

From there went on foot to Tradegar, where we arived about 2 oclock weather dark and rainy. At night had an attentive audience of Saints and strangers. Lodged with br Thomas Jones. To night it rains.

---

18. Thomas Jeremy was born in Cerbynau, Llanegwad, Carmarthenshire, South Wales. When he immigrated to Utah, he led the Welsh church services in the Salt Lake Valley. He served two missions back to Wales.

19. The church rented space at the White Lion Inn owned by the local temperance society in Merthyr Tydfil. See "Welsh Mormon History," *Family History and Genealogy*; Clarke, *Guide to Merthyr-Tydfil*, 74–75.

20. Ebbw Vale is a Welsh town (pronounced Ebbu Vale) known for its coal and iron works.

21. An inserted loose sheet provided the details for Lyman's trip to Ebbw Vale.

January 31, 1861; Thursday. This day wrote leter to [wife] Priscilla [Turley] one to br G[eorge] Q. Cannon, Liverpool. Had severe headache to day which troubled me much did not go out to day. At night had severe attack of nuralga in my head did not sleep dureing the night but suffered much.

February 1, 1861; Friday. This morning the rain had ceased but not so the pain in my head. At 12 oclock we started on foot to Abbw Valle from there by rail to Newport[22] where we arived at thre[e] oclock from thence in the company of Prest [William] Gibson and Elder [William] Owen to Alersychan. Lodged at the Tavern White Hart Inn.

February 2, 1861; Saturday. This morning the pain in my head partialy subsided passed the day with the Saints. In the evening the pain in my head became very severe. Wrote leter to Liverpool. At night turned to our lodgings at the Inn.

February 3, 1861; Sunday. To day attended Conference with the Saints in which in addition to the usual buisness Charles Astell President of the Hertford Conference[23] was cast of[f] for transgression and Wm O. Owen was appointed in his stead. Had three spirited good meetings. To night free from pain.

February 4, 1861; Monday. This morning at 12 oclock took train for Newport. Called at Br Henry Waldens weather dark and rainy. Went for lodgeings to the Cross Keys Inn on acount of the inability of the Saints to lodge us. At night had a conversation with br Nash who had ^been^ cut off from the Church 6 years ago before without cause.

February 5, 1861; Tuesday. Passed the day at Mr. [Henry] Waldens. At night had a pleasant and attentive Audience. After speaking to the people retired to our lodgeings at the inn. Stil rainy this evening took tea at the house of br John Marks. Were entertained with some singing befoe goeing to the meeting.

February 6, 1861; Wednesday. This morning stil raining and the sun is shining. At twenty three minutes past 2 oclock I took steamer for Bristol wher we landed after a run of 2 hours. We landed in the rain lodged with br Willet Harder Conference President.

---

22. Newport is a port city fifteen miles northeast of Cardiff, across the Severn Estuary from Bristol.

23. Hertford is twenty miles north of London.

February 7, 1861; Thursday. To day wrote some leters. In the evening called on and took tea with Cisters Ould[,] Mother and daughter. Stayed in the evening had a pleasant visit. Brother T. C. King was present and Br [Willet S.] Harder.

February 8, 1861; Friday. This morning received note from br Furgeson in reference to my watch. Wrote to brother [George Q.] Cannon on the subject. Wrote leter to Hon W[Illiam] H. Hooper [of Utah] in [US Congress,] Washington D. C. Raining to day which keeps us in doors. This evening br [George] Halliday[24] came in, in good health and spirits.

February 9, 1961; Saturday. This morning received leters one from Geo A. Smith with one from br [George Q.] Cannon [in] Liverpool. This morning received from br [George] Halliday the money I ~~learned~~ loaned him in Liverpool. This evening went out to tea and sup[p]er with Elder [John H.] Kelson.[25]

February 10, 1861; Sunday. This morning met with the Saints in conference preached 3 times dureing the day and night to attentive audiences. A good spirit prevailed throughout. Dined to day with br Tucker and family whose young daughter was sick but she was recovering.

February 11, 1861; Monday. This morning meet the priesthood at Br [Willet S.] Harders and gave them some instructions in reference to their ministry. At fifteen minutes after 4 oclock took train for London. Arived at br [John] Cooks about 10 oclock P.M. Found all well.

February 12, 1861; Tuesday. To day went with br [John] Cook to Poplar [neighborhood of east London] on foot. Returned in the evening by train. Dined with br Horsepool and family. To night my son [Francis] Marion came in to see me. He was well and in good spirits. He taried with me all night and left for his duties on the ^folowing^ morning.

February 13, 1861; Wednesday. This morning the weather cool with some snow. Wrote some to day to G[eorge] A. S[mith]. In the evening called on Cister Andrews.

24. George Halliday, originally from England, immigrated to Utah and was called back on a mission. He should not be confused with John Holladay of Virginia, who settled in the Holladay area of the Salt Lake Valley. After returning to Utah, George will become bishop of Santaquin. *Tullidge's Quarterly Magazine*, Jan. 1885, 431–32.

25. Kelson emigrated in 1862 and became a candy maker in Ogden and a writer. He returned to England in the 1880s as president of the Newcastle Conference. "Death Calls Pioneer Merchant and Writer," *Deseret News*, Apr. 30, 1921.

February 14, 1861; Thursday. Continued my writing. This morning br John Brown came in. Dined with br Odell in the evening had a talk with Elder Jas H. Chalmers in the presence of Elder John Brown. Br Chalmers was released from his ministry for the commission of sins which he confessed to us.[26]

February 15, 1861; Friday. This morning had news of the fall of Gaeta.[27] Had news from Liverpool. Concluded my leter to G[eorge] A. S[mith]. In the evening visited ^in company with br [Thomas C.] Stainer^[28] [and] the family of br and Sister Edinborough. Passed the time agreeably confirmed their young son who had been recently baptized. Blessed[,] another administered to the father[,] blessed the mother and taught the family together the principles of truth.

February 16, 1861; Saturday. This morning the sun is shineing some rain last night. Br John Brown is with us this morning I have cold in my head. Ordered suit of cloth[e]s and took tea with brother Ferguson and family. Had some talk with Mr [blank] a stranger said he loved some of the principles of the Saints.

February 17, 1861; Sunday. To day had a [meeting] in St. George's Hall. Spoke three times to the people who crowded the hall to over flowing and listened with aparently intense intrest to the maters that were treated upon ^from American^ Elders. Present A[masa] Lyman, T[homas] C. Stayner, J[ohn] Brown, G[eorge] J. Taylor, W[illiam] C. Stains, John Needham and F[rancis] M. Lyman.

February 18, 1861; Monday. This morning the weather was dark and dull. Received letter from br [George Q.] Cannon in Liverpool [and] answered the same. In the evening went to Poplar [neighborhood,] took tea an[d] sup[p]er with br Horsepool and family then returned by train to br [John] Cooks who was with me. Today was troubled with cough and cold in my head.

---

26. Chalmers was a conference president. According to Leonard Arrington, he was cut off for adultery and later reinstated. Arrington, *Charles C. Rich*, 237.

27. The Siege of Gaeta was part of the struggle for Italian unification under Giuseppe Garibaldi. Present-day Italy emerged from these insurrections in 1871. Gaeta is midway between Naples and Rome.

28. Thomas C. Stayner was another British expatriate who was back in England as a missionary. He had previously been a sea captain who had commanded commercial ships to Asia and the South Pacific.

February 19, 1861; Tuesday. This morning the weather somewhat brighter less clouds and smoke. To day Called on Mr. Grove and family was kindly received by them. Partook of their hospitality taught them the truth. On parting with them left our blessing received theirs. Br John Brown was with me his lodgings are with our friends.

February 20, 1861; Wednesday. This morning called on br Earl A. Taylor to get some work done. Weather smokey and damp, troubled with cough this morning then returned to br [John] Cook's.

February 21, 1861; Thursday. This day appointed br John Lindsay to travel and preach under direction of district Prest John Brown in Essex Conference. Blest and set him apart for his mission, at night received my suit of clothing.

February 22, 1861; Friday. This morning I left London at 10 oclock. Arived in Liverpool half past 2 ~~oclock~~ P.M. Was meet at train by brs [George Q.] Cannon[,] [William G.] Mills and [Edward] Sloan.[29] Found the sick recovering. Br [Charles C.] Rich had not yet arived. My health not first rate. I have much distress in my head from cold. Lodged with br [William] Perks.

February 23, 1861; Saturday. To day remained in the office with brother [George Q.] Cannon. In the afternoon br [Charles C.] Rich arived in tolerable health and spirits. The pain in my head would not allow me to do any buisness to day.

February 24, 1861; Sunday. This day meet with the Saints in the Assembly Rooms [at the Music Hall]. Spoke to them at the hours of 2 & 6 oclock. Had attentive audiences of Saints and strangers. Br [Charles C.] Rich[,] [George Q.] Cannon & [William G.] Mills were in attendance & joined in the services of the day. At night [I] felt much wearied with the labour of the day.

February 25, 1861; Monday. This day walked out in town with Elder [Edward] Sloan my health rather poor. Lodged at 42 [Islington] where repairs are stil going on. Weather rather dull.

February 26, 1861; Tuesday. Today remained in the office. This morning br John Kay came in he was in tolerable health but very hoarse from

29. Edward L. Sloan was on the staff of the *Millennial Star*. An Irish convert, he is best known for adapting the poem, "For the Strength of the Hills," to an LDS hymn and for founding the *Salt Lake Daily Herald* and, with Lula Greene, the *Woman's Exponent*.

cold and preaching. Did not go out to day had my clothing repaired by br Williams.

February 27, 1861; Wednesday. To day walked out in the city and ordered a chain for my watch. Brs [John] Kay & [Edward] Sloan were with me passed the remainder of the day in the office.

February 28, 1861; Thursday. This morning the weather clear and bright. To day in company with brs [George Q.] Cannon[,] [Charles C.] Rich & [John] Kay visited the Anatomical Museum of Dr. [blank].[30] The visit was instructive yet sad to contemplate the evidences we saw of the fruits of degeneracy and corruption of the race.

March 1, 1861; Friday. To day we have rain and sunshine wrote leter to my family in G. S. L. City. My health rather poor Sister [Elizabeth] Cannon is sick to day. The other sick are improving. At night had heavy rain. Did not feel well suffering from nervous irritibility.

March 2, 1861; Saturday. This morning the weather more clear the rain haveing ceased. My difficulty in my head geting worse passed the day in the office writing some in my journal. Rained at close of the day and through the night. Past a sleepless night on acount of pain in my head.

March 3, 1861; Sunday. This morning did not leave my ^bed^ was not able to attend the conference held in the Assembly Rooms. At evening left my bed for a few hours and made some hot aplications to my face after which I retired and had some broken sleep.

March 4, 1861; Monday. This morning somewhat beter had some ease by remaining near the fire through the day. Could not attend to any business. No rain to day.

March 5, 1861; Tuesday. This morning my health somewhat improved. It is raining this morning the air cool and damp which gives me some pain in my head altho my nervous systim is slowly assumeing a more healthy tone. Done some transcribing of my journal.

March 6. 1861; Wednesday. To day wrote some in ^my^ journal but found myself very weak. High winds with little rain. This evening meet

30. Joseph Woodhead's Liverpool Anatomy Museum was part of a trend in the 1860s–70s toward displaying cadavers in Europe and America, and many of the museums were shut down due to public indecency laws. Bates, "Indecent and Demoralising Representations."

with brs [Charles C.] Rich & [George Q.] Cannon and prayed.[31] Had a very pleasant time after which we prepared for tomorows journey.

March 7, 1861; Thursday. This morning we were on the way at fifteen minutes past 7 oclock. Arived in Carlile[32] ten minutes past 1 oclock were met here by Elder H[enry] W. Barnet. Dined with br Blain and family and took tea with Br Gibson. The Saints were rather cold yet kind to us personaly.

March 8, 1861; Friday. At half past 3 oclock were on the road for Glasgow where we arived 10 minutes to 9 oclock. Were meet and welcomed by brs [David M.] Stuart[,] [William] Reed and [William T.] Baxter. Lodged with br Reed. As we landed it was [raining] as it had been doing some through the day raining. Found br Rs family well.

March 9, 1861; Saturday. Weather fine and bright our selves refreshed by our rest. Passed the morning with the brethren who came in to see us, in the afternoon called on br [Andrew] McFarland and family and in the evening meet the priesthood and gave them instruction.

March 10, 1861; Sunday. To day meet the Glasgow Conference had a full attendence. Preached three times dureing the day and evening. Released the president of conference & apointed another elder[,] ^Robert^ Sands. Elder John Reed was released. Weather rainy was very weary. At close of the days labor walked two miles to lodgeings.

March 11, 1861; Monday. To day wrote leters to Liverpool. Dined with Brother Jas Brown and family and took tea with br Robert Patrick and family. ^My^ health not good quite hoarse from cold. Settled a diference between Presidents [David M.] Stuart[,] [William] Reed & [Robert] Patrick and some five other brethren in reference to some private meetings.

March 12, 1861; Tuesday. This morning received leters from my son [Francis] Marion and others which I answered in the morning then dined with br John Scott and family after which went to Glasgow Green where we saw the crowd amuseing themselves at the Gymnasium provided by the city. We Saw the [Admiral Horatio] Nelson Monument.[33] Weather cool and damp took supper with Br [Andrew] McFarlain.[34]

---

31. Lyman drew a large circle to indicate he'd participated in a prayer circle.

32. Carlisle is 125 miles north of Liverpool and ten miles shy of the Scottish border.

33. This is a stone obelisk built a year after Nelson's 1805 naval victory at Cape Trafalgar (Strait of Gibraltar) against Napoleon's French and Spanish fleets.

34. This last sentence was written vertically through the entry.

March 13, 1861; Wednesday. Weather clear this morning wrote leters to Elder Geo Halliday. Had news from Utah by leters to Br [Charles C.] Rich. Dined with br. McGregor and then went to visit an old cathedral the oldest portion of which was founded in 1300. Its patron was St. Mungo who lived in 600. Took supper with sister Sharis.[35]

March 14, 1861; Thursday. This morning weather somewhat clear with high wind. Wrote leters home to Parowan had a severe headache. Dined at br [Robert] Patricks then took lodgeings for the night at the Hudsons Hotell. This evening we settled with br. John Reed for our board. While there paid him £1,1,[36] and then we went to the other tavern.

March 15, 1861; Friday. This morning at 6 oclock were on the [train] carrs for Dundee[37] where we arived at 12 oclock. Meet br Charles Turner. Passed [by] as we went the famous battle grounds of Banockburn and Sterling. The speed of our travel detracted much from its interest. The weather was unusualy bright and clear. We Dined with br Mair James [James Mair] and his family.

March 16, 1861; Saturday. To day went across the bay to Newport [Newport-on-Tay] in Kingdom of Fife[38] dined with Sister Copely. Wrote leter to my wife in Beaver some little rain during the day. Returned at night and took super with br [James] Mair and spent the evening with him and family.

March 17, 1861; Sunday. To day attended Conference in the usual place of meeting. Had good meetings I spoke to the people twice in the day and evening. Was very weary weather rainy. While at meeting a young woman at the house of br Smith had a child which she hid in the cellar it was found dead.

March 18, 1861; Monday. To day we went to Arbro[a]th and Dined with br David Buyst. Weather fine and clear. This morning called on Brother [James] Cooper and also on Sister [Elizabeth] McFarland wife of Andrew McFarland President of the Branch in Dundee. Had meeting in ^the^ evening.

---

35. The last sentence was written vertically in the left-hand margin.

36. That is, one pound, one shilling.

37. Dundee is a large city that was renowned for shipbuilding.

38. Lyman uses the medieval terminology for what was a semi-autonomous region for a time. Newport-on-Tay had about 1,000 inhabitants, compared to the larger Newport city in Wales with 24,000 inhabitants.

March 19, 1861; Tuesday.[39] This morning visited the ruin of the Abbey of St. Thomas [St. Thomas Becket] founded in elven hundred and seventy eight by King Wm ^the First^ [of Scotland] renamed the Lion. The ruins were grand and impressive. We called to see Sister Jane Duncan who was in last stage of consumption she was most comforted and resigned to go. She wished to be sealed to Wm T. Baxter.

We were shown the tomb of King Wm. [in the abbey cemetery]. At the foot of the high alter and in smal apartment that had been used as a confessional was a small chest containing a variety of antique relicks among which was the thigh bone of the br[other] of king Wm [Wallace] the Giant of Scotland.[40] We ascended to some of the high portions of ruins from which we had a pleasant view of the city. From the ruins we took a brief stroal around the seaward side of the city.

On our return we called on Sister Jane Duncan who was sinking away ap^p^arently in the last stages of consumption. The feeble glimer of life's sinking flame was visible in hectic glow that [held] upon her palid cheek. She was comforted and cheered by our call. We bade her farewell and left for Dundee. Stoped with br Jas Cooper with whom we dined. Wrote leters to Elders H[enry] W. Barnet and W[illiam] T. Cromer. At night the Local Priesthood wer together and were instructed by us in the duties of their callings. Were well pleased and retired feeling well.

March 20, 1861; Wednesday. This morning some rain. Attended to some writing. Bid adieu to br [James] Cowper [Cooper] and family and then Dined with Sister [Mary] Mair after which at twenty minutes after 2 oclock we were on the [train] carrs for Edinburgh, through the Kingdom of Fife. This country is principaly devoted to mineing and agriculture its surface is varied with hill and dale.

At the Thornton Junction we were joined by President E[lias] L. T.

39. This entry is split across two diaries. The first paragraph was the last entry in Lyman's preprinted datebook. The second and third paragraphs are the first entries in a new diary book to Aug. 1861, which he abandoned until picking it up again in 1871. I have omitted three sentences in the second paragraph because of redundancy.

40. It was always said that the reliquary contained the bones of St. Columba, the Irish monk who brought Christianity to Scotland. Lyman seems to have been under the impression that the altar harbored a bone from William Wallace too, or perhaps (the handwriting is difficult) another large-framed hero. Wallace was said to have been about seven feet tall.

Harrison who had been visiting the Saints in the vicinity. We arived in Edinburgh at 6 oclock found the families of brs Harrison and [George] Teasdale well and in good spirits. Received leter from my son F[rancis] M. L[yman].

March 21, 1861; Thursday. This morning arose refeshed with our rest. Some snow had fallen during the night. Wrote leter to [Francis] Marion [Lyman] in London. Brs [Charles C.] Rich and [Elias L. T.] Harrison went to visit Arthurs Seat[41] some snow is falling as I write. The brethren have returned. In the evening went to tea with Sister [Agnes] Aird[42] some rain. This evening meet br [George] Teasdale on our return to our lodgeings.

March 22, 1861; Friday. This morning ^went^ in company with brs [Charles C.] Rich[,] [David M.] Stuart[,] [George] Teasdale & [Elias L. T.] Harrison to visit the Castle. After seeing the wonders in this place we took some refreshment and then visited the monument erected to the memory of Sir Walter Scott.[43] The structure gives evidence o[f] uncommon taste and skill in its design and execution.

From this point we visited Ca[r]lton Hill situated in the southeastern extremeity of New Town. This eminence ^is^ nearly 2 miles in circumference and 344 feet high. The principal objects of intrest on Carlton Hill are [philosopher] Dugald Stewart's monument, Royal Observatory, [Professor John] Playfair's Monument, [Admiral Horatio] Nelson's Monument, National Monument, unfini^s^hed.[44] The above were grouped together on the sumit of the hill while on ~~the~~ ^its^ southern declivity ~~of~~ there rests an humble monument of Robert Burns. From the hill we went to the residence of br Wm Jack with whom and family we passed the evening. Here we meet br Hogg Jas [James Hogg].

March 23, 1861; Saturday. This morning weather rather wet. In

41. Arthur's Seat is the main peak (824 feet) in the hills of Holyrood Park, which is a remarkably preserved piece of nature in the center of Edinburgh.

42. The next year Aird would immigrate to the U.S. According to the ship's manifest, she was a twenty-three-year-old spinster.

43. The Scott Monument was finished at 200 feet in height in 1846. It features bronze representations of characters from Scott's most famous novels, *Ivanhoe, Rob Roy,* and *Waverley.*

44. Carlton Hill is where St. Andrew's House, headquarters of the Scottish government, is located, along with historic buildings and memorials such as the National Monument, a tribute to the war dead from the Napoleonic era.

company with brs [Charles C.] Rich, [David M.] Stuart and [George] Teasdale I visited Holyrood Palace. The most interesting of the parts of the place we were allowed to see ~~were~~ was the picture Gallery. It is 150 feet in length by 24 b[r]oad its height about 20 feet. Around its walls are suspended the portraits of a hundred reputed Kings of Scotland, from the days of Fergus 1st [mythical founder of Scotland] down to the end of the Stuart Dynasty, they were painted by a Fleming named James de Witt.[45]

From this gallery we visited the apartments of the unfortunate Mary Queen of Scots & those of Lord Darnley her husband. Who is said to have procured in his own apartments to the murder of her secretary David Riccio whos Blood stains on the floor were shown us by our garulous attendant. The spot had a dark apearance but whether this was caused by the blood of the murdered man is quite doubtful.[46] From this scene of murder we went ~~visi~~ ^to^ visit the ruins of the Abbey of Holyrood, which was founded by [King] David [I of Scotland] about the year 1128. Its length within the walls 127 feet, breadth within the walls 59 feet, breadth of aisles of which there were two: 14 feet 9 inches. Height of the east end wall to the Fleur-de-lis, 70 feet, breadth 20 feet. Height of columns, 28 feet, girth of each 16 feet, breadth of middle aisle 29 feet.

From the palace ground we went to the Antiquarian Museum, in which we ~~saw~~ saw much that was interesting and instructive. After which we visited The National Picture Gallery containing many fine paintings where we were much interested for a short time[,] after which we called upon and spent the evening with br [Peter] McKomie and family then returned to our lodgeings. Bright moonlight tonight which is rather unusual with us since our stay in this country of smoke and dark weather.[47]

March 24, 1861; Sunday. This morning meet with the Saints in

---

45. The palace was completed in 1678. Six years later the government commissioned artist James De Witt to paint portraits of the kings and queens, now contained in the Queen's Gallery.

46. David Rizzio was the queen's Italian secretary and suspected paramour, whom the queen's husband, Lord Darnley, and several accomplices stabbed fifty-six times in the queen's presence, for which Lord Darnley was killed a year later, after which the queen married his suspected murderer. The blood stains may have been preserved for the sake of visitors, as at the Peterson House across from Ford's Theater in Washington, D.C., and Carthage Jail in Illinois.

47. There is a dagger here and elsewhere throughout the diary, perhaps suggesting where additional information (since lost) was to be inserted.

Conference had a good and ~~and~~ pleasant time. Spoke twice to the Saints dureing the day at the close of the services called on br [William] Reed the President of the branch and took supper after which we returned to br [Elias L. T.] Harrisons. On Saturday night attended a meeting of the Priesthood and gave them instruction in relation to their ministry. Found myself very weary after the days labours.

March 25, 1861; Monday. This morning arose refreshed and was cheered by the receipt of a leter from my family at S[alt] Lake City the news was good. After breakfast my self and brs [Charles C.] Rich and [David M.] Stuart went to Leith and called on br John Anderson and ~~wh~~ family who extended to us a warm welcome. Mrs. A. does not belong to the Church. Brs Rich and Stuart with br Anderson have gone to see the light batery of Armstrong Guns[48] that are kept here at present. The brethren returned from seeing the guns, we Dined with br Anderson and then returned to Edinburgh. At night we attended a party of Saints of the branch. Passed a few hours very pleasantly. Instructed the party and bade them Farewell.

March 26, 1861; Tuesday. This morning commenced leter to my family in G. S. L. City. Dined with br Peter McAmie and family after which returned to br [Elias L. T.] Harisons and resumed our writing. Had some talk with brs [George] Teasdale and Harrison in relation to financial maters.

March 27, 1861; Wednesday. This morning received a call from br John Hogan who had been cut off from the Church in ~~1848~~ ^1849^, I advised him to return to the Church but he thought he had beter wait a while and acting on this conclusion we parted each to pursue our devious ways to the haven of rest and the Goal of our wishes and the reward of our toil in lifes rugged way. This done the brs [Charles C.] Rich and [David M.] Stuart haveing returned from their walk we went to dine with br James Elliot and family one mile from the city on the Dalkeith Road after which we returned to business. In the evening took sup[p]er with President Wm Reeds [family].

To day had conversation with Prest Elias L. T. Harrison who confessed that he had used some £19 pounds of Church funds since forbiden to do so in November last[,] for which[,] like most delinquents are[,]

48. The Armstrong gun was a breech-loading, field-artillery cannon mounted on a two-wheeled cart, first manufactured in the 1850s in England.

he was full of unavailing sorow and said he would do so no more. As Br Rich and my self were about retireing to bed we were presented each of us with a new hat.

March 28, 1861; Thursday. This morning raining. At 8 oclock took train for Newcastle on Tyne where we arived at 3 oclock. Were met by Elders [John S.] Gleason[,] [Joseph] Stanford & [Henry W.] Barnet at the station. Dined with Sister Sutherland after which we went by train to Walls End[49] and lodged with Brother Charles Macallister. I suffered very much through the night from cough ariseing from cold did not sleep much.

March 29, 1861; Friday. My cold no beter this morning as I write I feel poorly. To day sat for my portrait the name of the artist was Weggeland,[50] my cough was very severe through the day. At night received a call from br & sister Foster.

March 30, 1861; Saturday. Arose this morning after ^a^ restless night somewhat ^weary and soar^ rainy this morning. This morning sat for the finishing of my portrait and at twenty minutes past four oclock arived in Sunderland.[51] At 5 oclock Lodged with br Benjamin ^L.^ Newton felt much oppressed with my cold. To day I am 48 years old so time is ever on the move.[52]

March 31, 1861; Sunday. This morning meet with and instructed the Local Priesthood and preached twice to the Saints in the after part of the day. Had a good attendence each time. It was raining through the day. My health is much improved.

April 1, 1861; Monday. This morning the weather dark and damp my health still improveing. Wrote leter to br [George Q.] Cannon in Liverpool. Dined with Sister Stevens after which we visited the Town Parks.[53] They were enlived by the presence of a portion of the people

49. Wallsend on Tyne is about 100 miles south of Edinburgh, immediately east of Newcastle, England. It is the site of the Roman fort that protected the terminus of Hadrian's Wall—the impressive barrier that ran from the North Sea on the east to the Solway Estuary on the west, cutting the island in half.

50. Dan A. Weggeland was a Norwegian artist and convert to Mormonism serving a mission in England. He left for New York within days of this entry, stayed a year, and continued on to Utah. His murals grace the walls of the Manti, St. George, and Salt Lake City temples. Carter, *Enduring Legacy*, 7:242–44.

51. Sunderland is another port city, twelve miles south of Wallsend.

52. The last sentence was written in the margin as an afterthought.

53. Mowbray Park opened in 1857 as one of the earliest public spaces for common

recreating themselves altho the weather was not pleasant on acount of the rain. At 5 oclock we attended a social party of the Saints[,] remained with them until 11 oclock then addressed them briefly bade them farewell and retired.

April 2, 1861; Tuesday. This morning at 25 minutes past 7 oclock were on the way to Leedes[54] where we arived at twenty minutes past 12 oclock. Were meet at the station by brs S[amuel] H. B. [Smith] & J[oseph] F. Smith. We then Dined br Wm Shires and in the evening took sup[p]er with Sister [Emma Jane] Eastham lodged with br Shires weather dark and damp.

April 3, 1861; Wednesday. This morning received leters from Liverpool. Wrote in answer to the same and in the evening meet with the Saints in their usual meeting place of meeting. Had a good time received evidences of the Saints regards[55] at the conclusion.

April 4, 1861; Thursday. This morning received leter from br D[avid] M. Stuart. It is not raining this morning. After diner we went to brother [James] Coopers & we today visited the Town Hall. It is a fine structure. The weather became dark and damp we returned ^to br Cs^ and remained there until super after which we returned to our lodgeings at br Shires.

April 5, 1861; Friday. This morning the weather dull and damp. To day we dined with br Alfred Goodier and passed the evening and took super with br Benjamin Peel and a party of friends in and out of the Church. But little rain to day we passed the time agreeably instructing our friends.

April 6, 1861; Saturday. This morning the sun is shineing brightly and like the smile of Heaven it chases away the surrounding darkness. Our health is somewhat improved. To day we visited Mr. Broubent and family he designs comeing into [word missing]. To day we dined with Sister Silverwood an[d] son they design Emigrating the present season.

April 7, 1861; Sunday. This morning at ten minutes past 9 oclock we were on the way to Bradford where we meet the Saints in conference and

---

people to stroll among richly landscaped terraces, monuments, ponds, theatrical pavilions, and art galleries.

54. Like so many other British cities, Leeds, ninety miles south of Sunderland, experienced major growth during the industrial revolution. It was famous for its woolen products, which were transported throughout the United Kingdom via canal and railroad.

55. That is, good feelings towards Lyman.

spoke to them three times dureing the day. Dined with Br Miller in the evening took sup[p]er with br Geo Curtis. Lodged with br Owen Taylor felt much wearied with the labour of the day. Retired about 12 oclock.

April 8, 1861; Monday. This morning the weather pleasant we Dined with br Joseph Smith and family and at twenty five minutes past 3 oclock were on the way for Liverpool where we arived about half past 6 oclock. Found br [George Q.] Cannon and family well and buisy with emigration the renovating of the place at 42 [Islington] and the preperations for printing in all of which they seemed to be progressing finely.

April 9, 1861; Tuesday. This morning the weather is more than usualy pleasant. I received leter from [Francis] Marion [Lyman] in London. His health good his labour increasing. Wrote leter to Marion passed the day in the office. In the evening President E[lias] H. Blackburn[56] came in from his district to prepare for the emigrating Saints in his charge. To day read the Deseret News & Mountaineer.

April 10, 1861; Wednesday. This morning received and answered leter from Elder George Halladay. Emigrants are gathering in. No rain today. This evening br C[laudius] V. Spencer came in his health is slightly improveing he appeared in good spirits and reported well of his District.

April 11, 1861; Thursday. This morning had conversation with br Claudius V. Spencer and concluded in consideration of his poor health he had beter return home. We gave him the charge of the emigrants by the [sailing ship] Manchester. The Saints very buisy in prepareing for their journey. Was out but little to day troubled with cough.

April 12, 1861; Friday. This morning received leter from Elder Jas H. Chalmers and wrote him in answer and also sent him certificate of release from his labours in the ministry to go home to Zion and in the faithfulness of the present seek to outlive the errors of the past. To day Elder Burgoyn was cut off from the Church for the crime of adultery with the privilige of rebaptism and continueing his journey to Zion as a member of the Church without any ordination. District President Wm

56. Elias H. Blackburn was one of the church's full-time emigration officers. He converted in Pennsylvania in 1845. Within only six years, he had become the first bishop of Provo. Before leaving for Europe in 1859, he had acquired five wives. "Register of Elias H. Blackburn's LDS Records under His Bishopric, 1851–59, 1882–87," Perry Special Collections.

Gibson called in today. Preperations ar going forward with the emigrants for their journey, the weather unusualy dry and pleasant.

April 13, 1861; Saturday. This morning repaired on board of the Manchester and witnessed the Saints as they gathered on board for their journey.[57] There was much bustle but general good nature & feeling prevailed. Returned after noon much wearied.

April 14, 1861; Sunday. To day went on board of the Manchester and held meeting with the Saints instructing them for their journey. Returned at half past 4 oclock and spoke to the Saints at the Assembly Rooms. Returned home very weary.

April 15, 1861; Monday. The weather pleasant to day. Br [George Q.] Cannon and others went on board the Manchester to close the buisness with the Saints previous to sailing. I commenced writing to the President B[righam] Y[oung] in Zion and to my family.

April 16, 1861; Tuesday. This morning received leters from my wife Caroline and my niece Emily Young from G.S.L. City and answered them. Felt some pain in my head was not out to day weather dry and pleasant. Continued my leter to the president and also my home corispondence.

April 17, 1861; Wednesday. To day continued my corespondence. Br John Brown from London came in and also br Joseph F. Smith from Leedes all in good health an[d] spirits. They came to prepare the way for the emigrants to go by the Underwriter.[58]

April 18, 1861; Thursday. Today closed my corispondence for Utah. The brethren are gathering in for their emigration; some four or five of the district presidents are here. Passed the day in the office.

April 19, 1861; Friday. To day was on board of the ship Underwriter which was chartered for the second company of our emigration some few of whom were coming on board. I returned to the office and at night had a meeting of the district and conferences presidents and gave them some general instructions in reference to their duties in their several positions.

All seemed strong in faith and confident in the future improvement

57. The packet boat *Manchester* left Apr. 16 and landed in New York on May 14 with 418 passengers.

58. The *Underwriter* sailed on Apr. 23, as mentioned by Lyman on that date, and arrived in New York Harbor a month later on May 21. It had 671 passengers, including future apostle Charles W. Penrose, who called the ship "an old sailing tub." *Deseret News*, Aug. 14, 1920.

in the condition of the mission. The names of the Elders present [at the mission meeting:] Wm Gibson[,] John Brown[,] Jas Brown[,] S[amuel] H. B. Smith[,] Joseph F. Smith[,] E[lias] H. Blackburn[,] D[avid] M. Stuart[,] John Kay and John Clark, (and John Cook and Wm T. Cromer released), C[harles] C. Rich[,] Geo Q. Cannon[,] A[masa] M. Lyman.

April 20, 1861; Saturday. To day was on board the Underwriter all bustle and confusion. Men wooman and children and their trailing equipage and baggage all crowded on board yet all seemed peaceable and quiet. Dined with Brother James Mair at the Waterloo House.

April 21, 1861; Sunday. This morning the weather rainy. We learned that Underwriter had moved from the dock into the river and my self and brs [Charles C.] Rich and [George Q.] Cannon went on board and held meeting with the Saints. Gave them instruction and organized them for their journey across the ocean. They were in fine spirits. At the conclusion of our meeting it was raining. Elder Milo Andrus was apointed President of the company and Elders Homer Duncan and Charles W. Penrose his councillors. They were received by the unanimous vote of the Saints. Returned to the office much wearied did not attend meeting at the assembly rooms.

April 22, 1861; Monday. To day went on board of the Underwriter and witnessed the passing of the passengers under the inspection of the officers of Government. All passed off pleasantly we again said adieu and left, weather fine and the Saints in good spirits and full of hope of a prosperous journey. Underwriter did not sail today.

April 23, 1861; Tuesday. I remained in the office all day. Br [George Q.] Cannon drew from the Bank and forwarded by Elder Milo Andrus some £2000 two thousand pounds to the emigration agents in the U.S.A. Elder Jones and Gates. The Underwriter sailed at 8 oclock P.M.

April 24, 1861; Wednesday. This morning the weather pleasant. Br Olen Hansen from Norway [arrived]. He brings good news of the prosperity of the work in Scandinavia. Walked out in town and witnessed the purchase of an American cooking stove[59] for the house at 42 [Islington]. To day the seting of the steam boiler for the printing (commenced).[60]

59. He means a coal-fired, cast-iron stove with circular slits that "ranged" across the top to focus heat on the bottoms of pots and kettles. Ellin, "At Home with the Range," 5–15.

60. Prior to this time, the *Millennial Star* had been professionally printed. Now

April 25, 1861; Thursday. To day was engaged in writing was not out to day.

April 26, 1861; Friday. To day heard of the begining of the Civil war in the states[61] and of the surrender of Fort Sumter to the Carolinians thus the words of the Prophet are being fulfilled.[62] Continued my writing for publication.

April 27, 1861; Saturday. To day stormy[. I] secured the charter of the Monarch of the Sea for residue of our emigration. The name of the captain was [William R.] Gardner the ship belongs in New York. The Civil War in America is the leading topick of conversation. Ceased storming this evening revised and turned over my writing to the printers.

April 28, 1861; Sunday. This morning myself in company [with] brs [Charles C.] Rich[,] [George Q.] Cannon and [John] Kay were on our way to Manchester at 45 minutes past 7 oclock where we held conference and returned in the evening. We had a pleasant time with the Saints. The spirit to emigrate seemes on the increase among the people as they awaken to the intrests of the work and their intrests in the same. Strangers listened with apparent intrest to our instructions and the Saints were comforted and strengthened to go forth and struggle anew with brighter hopes for their deliverence from the land of confusion and their migration to the home of the Saints and the school of the just where the Siner fears and the honest and humble learn the principles of righteousness and thus[63] work out their salvation from sin and minister to the increase of the Kingdom of peace and truth on the Earth. We felt our selves

the mission had its own steam-driven rotary press. Cannon, "George Q. Cannon and the British Mission," 100, 111nn11–12; see also the entries herein for May 8–11, 1861.

61. Fort Sumter fell on Apr. 13, but there was no telegraph cable to transmit the news. The transatlantic cable that was laid three years earlier failed after a few initial messages, and it would not be until 1866 that a permanent line be laid. Even so, Lyman was receiving war news by ship across the Atlantic before Utahns would have learned of these events.

62. On Dec. 25, 1832, in response to the tense standoff between South Carolina and the Jackson administration over federal tariffs, Joseph Smith spoke of "wars that will shortly come to pass, beginning at the rebellion of South Carolina," and that "the Southern States shall be divided against the Northern States." After the crisis passed, no one thought much about it until the Civil War began thirty years after that. Godfrey et al, *Joseph Smith Papers: Documents, Vol. 2*, 328–31.

63. The words "and thus" were repeated here.

refreshed with our warmhearted friends in Manchester. Said our adieus and returned to our home in Liverpool.

April 29, 1861; Monday. To day passed the day in reading and did not go out.

April 30, 1861; Tuesday. This morning received leters from my family in Parowan Iron County some of which I answered. To day I received one from G[eorge] A. Smith. Did not go out to day read the mountaineer and [Deseret] news.

May 1, 1861; Wednesday. Passed the day in writing for my home corispondence.

May 2, 1861; Thursday. This morning received the news of secesson of the State of Virginia. Took a walk in the city with brs [Charles C.] Rich and [George Q.] Cannon. Had some of my teeth filled by brother John Kay. Some rain to night. Dispached leters to Church Historian also to my family in the city and in the souther^n^ settlements. The weather is dark and rainy. Brother [Olen] Hansen told us this morning that several thousand labourers were turned out of employment in the town of Bolton on acount of the effects of the American war on the cotton trade. Sad times for the poor when vice and folly are fed and fateneth at the expense of toiling honesty and virtue.

May 3, 1861; Friday. Today had a pleasant walk in the city with brs [Charles C.] Rich and [George Q.] Cannon.

May 4, 1861; Saturday. Wrote some for publication [in the *Millennial Star*]. Brother [Charles C.] Rich left this morning for Birmingham.

May 5, 1861; Sunday. This morning at half past eight oclock myself and brs [George Q.] Cannon and [John] Kay were on the way for Preston[64] where we meet the Saints in Con[ference] at half past 10 oclock. The condition of Preston Conference was made by Elder Thomas Lier, the Pr^e^st. The Conference was addressed and the buisness presented by

64. The first LDS missionaries to England in July 1837 established Preston as their home base. The reason for this was that one elder had family connections there. When they converted 1,500 people their first year, Joseph Smith sent the entire Quorum of Twelve Apostles to help in the harvesting of souls. One historian wrote that "news of [the apostles'] arrival spread so rapidly that by April 12, their first Sunday in England, some five or six hundred Saints gathered in the Preston Cock Pit, historic meeting place for dissident groups. There the seven of the twelve [apostles] then present bore testimony to the work, and spoke with power." Grant, "The Church in the British Isles," 227–28; Arrington, *Brigham Young*, 81.

Elder Cannon the sacrament was also administered, then ajourned and Dined with Elder L. and family. Conference resumed its sesion at half past two oclock I spoke to the people who listened with intrest. Closed at 4 oclock took a walk in the town and at fifteen minutes past 6 oclock left for Liverpool where we arived about 9 oclock somewhat weary. This morning received leter from Elder W[alter] M. Gibson from San Bernardino he was enroute for Jappan he reported the apostates as being verry rabid in their opposition to the truth. But their hate did yield to curiosity and they invited br Gibson to lecture.

May 6, 1861; Monday. Walked out in the morning with br [John] Kay. Passed the balence of the day in the office in reading the news from the U.S.A.

May 7, 1861; Tuesday. Passed the day in the office in writing and reading. Walked out in the town during the day.

May 8, 1861; Wednesday. To day received leter from Elder Geo Halliday and answered the same. Wrote some for publication. This evening started the engine for the printing machine.

May 9, 1861; Thursday. To day passed the time in the office. To day the first printing was done with the machine it acted well and promises well for the future. Br [Charles C.] Rich returned to day from Notingham.

May 10, 1861; Friday. To day received leter from [Francis] Marion [Lyman] and answered. Elder Jabez Woodward came in this morning enroute for Utah. He has been nearly 5 years from home and family.[65] Brs [John] Kay and [William] Perks started to Grimsby [on the eastern coast] to meet the Scandinavian emigration.

In the evening Presidents John Brown and John L. Smith and Wm H. Dame came and some of the emigrating Saints all speak cheeringly of the prospects of the work in their several districts and fields of labour. Some hindrance in the printing department probably mostly from inexperience of workmen.

May 11, 1861; Saturday. This morning ~~fill~~ wrote some leters of appointment for some traviling Elders and Conference president[s]. The

65. Jabez Woodward, an English native, had spent four years helping to open the Italian mission. He was called there a year after his conversion. On his release, he and his wife immigrated to Utah, but two years later he was sent back to Europe to help open the Swiss-German mission.

printing is moveing along very well to day without hindrence. This evening had a very severe attack of Diarhea attended with severe pain.

May 12, 1861; Sunday. My health poor suffering much pain did not attend meeting to day. Weather dark and rainy in the afternoon felt somewhat beter tho quite weak.

May 13, 1861; Monday. This morning my health somewhat improved. Received a dispach from Hull informing that Elders [John] Van Cott and [William] Perkes would be with us at night of that day and the Saints that are with them and br John Kay tomorow. After night about half past 11 oclock brs V, & P. came in all well. My health rather precarious wrote and revised some to day. Had much pain in my back and head. To day W[illiam] S. Godbe arived from Utah which he left March 29th.

May 14, 1861; Tuesday. Not feeling so well as yesterday brs [George Q.] Cannon[,] [Charles C.] Rich and [John] Van Cott were on board of the Monarch of the Sea,[66] with the Saints the residue of whom arived and br [John] Kay with them about 2 oclock.[67]

May 15, 1861; Wednesday. Spent the most of the day with the Saints on board the Monarch of the Sea. They passed inspection without an exception but had to defer our meeting for the instruction of the Saints until tomorow. Returned to the office quite weary. Number of Saints on the ship were 9~~5~~4 souls the largest shipload ever sent from here. Dined with Capt [William R.] Gardner and the inspectors.

May 16, 1861; Thursday. This morning at 6 oclock went on board of the ship to hold meeting with and organize the Saints which we did by appointing Elder Jabez Woodward[,] O[len] H. Hansen and Neilsen Wilheminson to take charge of the company. Instructed the Saints blessed and bade them farewell and God speed them was our prayr. On returning to the office I found leters from Utah. One from my wife Lydia and one from br. C[alvin] C. Pendleton. News all good and reported prospect of some missionary help here this sumer. The Monarch of the Sea sailed about 10 oclock A.M. weather pleasant and warm.

May 17, 1861; Friday. To day attended to my home corispondence

66. The *Monarch of the Sea* arrived in New York on June 16, 1861, with around 1,000 passengers. To save money, the church was using sailing ships over steamers.

67. Inserted into the diary here is a loose sheet with a printed poem titled "To My Dear Papa and Mama" by Walter C. Staynor, dated Dec. 2, 1871.

~~did not go out dureing the day~~. In the evening of today Dined with Elder E[dward] L. Sloan and blessed his infant daughter. Brs [Charles C.] Rich, [George Q.] Cannon[,] [William H.] Dame[, John] Brown[,] [John L.] Smith[,] [William] Perks[,] [John C.] Graham were of the party & last not to be forgotten br [John] Kay. Br John Van Cott left today for Scandinavia via Hull & Hamburg.

May 18, 1861; Saturday. This morning went with the party of yesterday to visit the [Wavertree] Botanick garden[s] where we were interested in the contemplation of a varied collection of vegitable curiosities from the varied parts of the Earth. In the same establishment in close proximity were the production of the high Northern latitudes and those of the general tropicks [and] each in its silent but impressive [way] spoke of the history of the paternal home whether it were the brake [bracken fern] from the swamps of New England ^or^ the luxur^i^ent banannah from the Suny Isles of the Broad Pacifick.

Here the useful grass in its dress of modest unpretending green was seen in contrast with the gaudy flowers that had no acknowledged worth beyond~~d~~ the sweet oder they exhaled orr the[68] gaudy dress they wore. Fit emblem of the family of man where virtue decked in the modest aray of truth is only loved by those who know its worth.

~~From~~ ^Leaveing^ this scene of floral beauty we indulged in a stroll in the park ajoining and from thence to the zoological gardens ^partook^ a repast such as we were furnished from some provision shops on the ground eating in the open air as the eating rooms were closed. We saw here a beatiful artistick representation of the city of Pekin in China and also a limited collection of Beasts[,] Fowls[,] and Fishes. Some taste was exibited in the arangement of the grounds and their decorations. Principaly induced (sad as is the thought) by the love of money, the root of evil, thus showing that where Virtue has no charm Gold will lure. To night said adieu to brs [John] Brown and [John L.] Smith and [John] Kay who were to leave by early morning trains for their several fields of labour.

May 19, 1861; Sunday. To day the weather pleasant. Brother J[ohn] L. Smith returned this morning as he did not succeed in geting away. Brs [Charles C.] Rich[,] [George Q.] Cannon and [John] Smith were in attendance at the meeting of the Saints. I did not attend until half

68. The words "or the" were repeated.

past 6 oclock evening when I addressed them had a pleasant time. This evening br [William] Pearks treated us to some musick from his concertina [hand organ].

May 20, 1861; Monday. This morning I wrote a leter to Elder John W. Coward from whom I had heard nothing for some months. Received and answered leter from Elder Thomas Crawly[69] Ireland. Elder W[illiam] S. Godby was with us to day and started for Dublin Ireland. Weather clear and warm. This morning ordered a vest beside this was not out today was troubled much with cough.

May 21, 1861; Tuesday. To day br [Charles C.] Rich went on an excursion to Southport my health not being good did not go out done some copying from my journal. In the evening of to day Sister Elizabeth Cannon was delivered of a fine daughter.[70] Br Rich returned much pleased with his days pastime with his friend Butterworth who was with him. He is enquireing for the truth he is a merchant. My health is not improved.

May 22, 1861; Wednesday. Some rain fell to day passed the time mostly in the office. Wrote leter to my son [Francis M.] in London wrote some for publication. In the afternoon it cleared up and the rain ceased.

May 23, 1861; Thursday. Today Elder J[ohn] W. Coward called in to see us he was in tolerable health. Spent the day in writing for publication. Br [Charles C.] Rich went on board of a large war steamer called Magestick. Some rain did not go out to day did not feel well in health.

May 24, 1861; Friday. Closed up my writing and made ready for our night journry to the emerald Isle. At 8 oclock P.M. myself and br [Charles C.] Rich accompanied by br [George Q.] Cannon repaired to the dock where there were some 3 or 4 steamers up for Ireland. Of these we chose the Eblana for ~~Jones~~ ^King^stown [immediately north of Dublin] which we were informed would arive at her destination a[t] 7 next morning. These preliminaries settled we found we were not to leave the dock until 10 oclock. We parted with br Cannon and then d^i^sarmed as

69. Thomas Crawley was president of the Irish mission. British-born, he was released in 1862 and immediately re-enlisted to serve in England. After being a missionary seven years total in both Ireland and England, he left for America in 1863 on a ship that coincidentally included a young woman he had met in Ireland, and they married onboard.

70. Georgianna Hoagland Cannon died two years later of whooping cough on the Nebraska plains, traveling with her mother, Elizabeth, while her father, George Q. Cannon, remained in England.

we were resigned our selves to our fated wating with what of philosiphy we could call to our aid in which time kindly aidid us by continuing its steady flight.

At length the monotony of our waiting was broken as weel as its silence by an admonitory peel from the bell. Then came the consequent hury of those who were not yet on board and the hasty leaveing of such as were not to remain and ^then^ came the welcome orders to cast off and we were moveing slowly from our birth in the Dock into the [Mersey] River, and as we glided noiselessly ^and stelthily^ away under the cover of night silence was around ^us^ save now and then the hoarse cry of the Capt to the mate indicating that the eye of vigilent watchfulness was directing our movements. And as we glided out into the Mers[e]y a night vision of a dayling [daytime] briliancy and beauty ^was opened to our view^. In oposite directions up and down the river were to be some re-extended linnes of lights that ~~reached~~ ^extended^ as far as the eye could reach their night cheering beams but we were not only watchers of this nocturnal picture of loveliness as if to assure us that ~~the~~ with sleepless eyes ~~of~~ ^the^ heavenly watchers were keeping their vigils over us.

The stars were looking out upon the scene around us and over all this pictures embraceing [of] so many ^and^ varied features[,] the moon in all her Queenly magisty was sheding the haloe of her silvery light. So while surounded with~~ly~~ earthly beauties, and heavens star^r^y jewels were decking the curtain of night, our good ship moved bravely on in her waterry path ^while^ to her own strength and heavens protection we commeded her and ^her liveing freight and^ with a ~~brief~~ prayr for home friends and loved ones we saught freedom from earths cares in sleeps obliveon.

May 25, 1861; Saturday. This morning felt[,] soon after wakeing[,] some seasickness. Was kindly informed by the steward that we were near our landing[,] [and] by consulting my watch found that it was 8 oclock instead of 7. Our landing at Kingstown was in a small basin like bay encircled with substantial masonry forming a place of perfect security for the shiping it would acomodate. At this point took [train] carrs for Dublin a gentle warm rain was falling on the land side of our line of travil. As we past along we caught a passing glimpse of some lovely scenery, some fine incloseures rich in their embelishments of home, of which they were a part ~~in~~ clad in the verdant habiliments of spring, the tree the shrub, the flower, the earth-carpet of green all united in adding their beauties to the surounding scene ~~of loveliness~~ in the midst of which arose in artistick beauty and loveliness the temple of home ~~sacred~~ ^dedicated^ to the intrests of humanity in the ^sanctum^ sanctorum of which should ever rest the alter of peace from which should ascend the offerings of gratitude from hearts moved ~~moved~~ by truths heavenly impulse. Such purity would be in keeping with the outward beauties that meet our hasty gaze as we ~~passed~~ ^were^ huried along ~~after~~ ^by^ the iron horse.

A half hours hasty travil brought us to the City of the Irishman's pride to which his heart cherished affections fondly cling. One of the brightest embelishments of his ~~sea~~ green sea-girt isle [met our gaze] as we left the [railroad] carrs in Dublin. The rain was stil fall[ing] which caused the covered cariages to be in demand alto after some little [time] we succeeded in secureing the shelter and conveyence we saught and were whirled along at a speed which precluded any very extensive observation of what was around us. As we alighted from our cariage a representative of a class of the inhabitants of the Ancient Metropolis appeared before us and in a most piteous tone and manner with which her tatered garments were in keeping a peny draped in her waiting palm evoked a faintly ejaculated blessing and we hoped we were now free to attend to our own wants. When as we turned to do so a stil more raged and squlid victim of poverty was awaiting for us to evince our pity by another draft on our limited funds. We turned from this spectacle of wretchedness with this thought that we could not supply all the poor so we turned our attention for the moment to our own wants.

A little inquiry lead us to the humble dwelling of our friend [Robert] Brown whose beter half was as she very frankly informed us not a member of our Church, yet in the absence of her husband she most kindly offered to prepare for us our much needed breakfast or instead of this to go in search of Elder [Thomas] Crawley. The last proposition was adapted and we were left to prolong indefinitily our already protracted fast so we began to consider our circumstances. We discovered we were left in company of the children of our kind hostess. Two cher[r]y cheeked litle girls with a younger brother. From their dark sparkling eyes brightly gleamed that intilectual light that revealed the truth that the tatered habiliments of poverty often encircle heavens brightest gems. Such was the truth that revealed it self in our contemplation of the poor labourers family. From this point we went to the residence of br Hughes and family who have been for several years in the Church and spake warily of the Ministrations of our brs [Edwin] Scott and Ferguson and Lynch. Sister Hughs kindly enabled us to break our fast after which we were cheered by the comeing of Elder Crawley who had been waiting for us at the Boat Landing.

We were conducted by br C. to 29 Uper Mercer St where he had secured lodgings for us during or stay in the City. Thus removed we effected by the hire of a jaunting carr[,] mounted on which we imagined our selves from the novelty of our position the observed of all observers ~~observers~~. As we mad[e] our hasty travil to our quarters at 29 we could discover that there was an air of freedom ~~from~~ ^with^ a width of street and cleanliness which is not seen in the more crowded and dust covered and smoked b[e]rgrimed Towns and Cities of England and Wales. When we were located in or own hired room with our friend to guide us we strolled out into the city to see the sights. That ^which first^ fixed our attention was an incloseure against the side of which the street in which we were walking terminated. We were told it was not a publick ground and consequently not open for the gratification of the curious visitor.

But in order that we might get a nearer view of its beauties we crosed the street when as we aproached the fence a gentleman on the inerside with a bland smile opened the gate for our admission saying as he did so ["]I presume you wish to enter["]. To this declareation so true to the facts we could not in candor demurr so we walked in. The name of the place is Stephens Green[71] an even smo[o]th and nearly level plat of ground of one mile in circumference. It was beautifully embelished with shade trees and a profusion of Flower shrubery and cut in diferent directions with flower bordered walks. The body of the green was covered with a luxurient Carpet of rich grass supporting above beautiful groups of native trees. As we passed through this scene of loveliness the thought was suggested to us that what we were contemplating was but an important apendage to the home of the Saints in order that the Childs early association with and

71. St. Stephen's Green is a Dublin park that was accessible only to people whose property fronted it until Arthur Guinness, of Guinness beer fame, paid to have the space redesigned and opened to the public in 1877.

contemplation of natural and artistick beauty should develop~~ment~~ in the young mind a refinement of taste for the beautiful which is in harmony with ^the^ high and holy destiny of humanity. As we aproached the opposite side of the green from our enterence a gentleman opened a gate for his own egress which aforded us the same and we continued our walk.

As the street in which we were walking lay along the side of the Trinity College[72] the sound of musick attracted our attention. On instituting an enquery we learned that the university foot races with other athletic sports were ~~takeing~~ with and under the management of the college. We aproached the enterence[,] and thanks that our coat had not yet become so seedy as to preclude our admission. We entered the park when a picture of beauty was before us. The ground with its embelishments presented a ~~rich and~~ lovely picture rich in artistic and natural beauties.

The most interesting feature that became a subject of reflection and thought as we gazed upon the scene before us was the assembly of men[,] women and children as in them we ^saw^ that which would enable us to form an idea of what could be hoped from Ireland, could her people be brought within the influence of the truth and circumstances that would favor the developement under its sacred influence of the inherent Divinity of humanity ~~in~~. Then would this truth be evident that humanity when estimated by its original endowments as well as the de[s]ign or purpose of its existence is the same in all countries and clime[s] and the so called diferences that form the distinguishing characteristicks of the diferent nationalities and families of the Earth are the result of the diference of circumstances under [which] they have lived and by which they have been surounded and influenced. In the assembled thousands that constituted the picture of human beauty that was in all its fascinating charms spread out before us we were lead to say within our selves how trancendently lovely will be the scene when in Zions sacred courts the assembled hosts of her children clothed in the sacred habiliments of purity and truth shall meet to offer that adoration and worship that is not only since[re] but true and for this reason virtuous[,] holy and just, and altogether lovely.

In the assembly the principle indication of diference that meet the

72. Trinity College is today part of the University of Dublin. Its graduates include Oscar Wilde and Bram Stoker.

eye of the observer was in the age of the parties assembled for there could be seen the ~~the~~ hoary headed sire and ~~on~~ ^at^ his ~~arm~~ ^side^ the matronly form of here [her] who had braved with him thus far the dangers incident to their voy[a]ge over lifes stormy ~~tossed~~ sea, and now the smile of content rested on their time-worn features. But they have passed and in ~~the~~ their train ~~the~~ walking withe elastic tread as tho disdaining the ground on which they trod comes the youthful representatives of humanity. Their spirits were blythe and hapy as the birds that were caroling so sweetly above us in the peaceful shade of their verdant leafy clad home. Such were some of the external charms of the scene around us and the train of thought they awakened in us as we contemplated them.

The sports and exercises as we witnessed them were suggestive of the thought that in the contest for a worthless prize vigirous health as the reward of ~~healing~~ ^temporate^ exercise was forgoten and when the sports were over we returned to our lodgings wearied with our lengthened walk. This morning myself and br Rich administered and blessed the infant son of br Hughs who was sick and very ^low.^

May 26, 1861; Sunday. This morning attended meeting with the Saints of whom there were but few in Dublin. Some strangers were in attendence and listened with intrest. After meeting we visited the Phoenix Park a platt of ground containing as we were told by our friend the Carrman [coachman] some 17,000 seventeen thousand acres. It possesses much native bea^u^ty. The surface of the ground is gently undulating and covered with a luxurient carpet of green grass save such portions as taken up by roads and other small portions devoted to the cultivation of ornamental shrubery and Flowers. To all of which was added the beauty and comfort of ~~the~~ numerous groups of native trees whose inviting shades had wooed to their cooling embrace their respective contributions from the multitude who in this spot of loveliness were passing a careless hour.

One of the features of intrest in the park was the Zoological Gardens, which comprised a somewhat extensive collection of the wonders of nature from the Eagle who with his strong pinions fearlessly traverses the uper deep and with unblinking eye drinks in the golden light of the King of day withe representatives of many of the intermediate classes down to the minute shell fish that nestles in the Ocean depths of his watery home. Last but not least in the features of the scene around us to awaken thought were representatives of humanity. Among thes[e] could be seen the idle lounger, and the thoughtful student poreing over his yet unmastered leson while some were seeking to drag food from writin[g] fiction for a mind corispondingly empty and vain while the Man of business was discussing with neighbor or friend the probabilities or improbibilities of the effects of the American war on the intrests of her Magisties broad relms.

Altho not satisfied with seeing[,] yet wearied with walking we turned our steps to the city when we encountered a hasty storm of wind rain and dust. We found a temporary and partial shelter under the lee side of a jaunting carr at the request of the owner. At this point we were near the unfinished monument in process of completion to commemorate the Duke of Wellington[73] which is one of the embelishments of the park [of] which in my opinion there is no more lovely scenery around this ancient capital ^of^ L[e]inster.[74]

The storm had past and we were mounted on our jaunting carr and on our return to our evenings engagement to meet with the Saints. As we passed along we discovered a fire in the city. Had a very pleasant meeting with our friends.

May 27, 1861; Monday. To day took a walk in the city in company with Brothers [Charles C.] Rich and [Thomas] Crawly and [John] Smith. In our stroll we visited the folowing places viz: the Catholic University Church and the Irish Museum of Industry and Trinity Coledge Museum and Library rooms. And the Old House of Parliment now used as the Irish Bank and visited the Rotunda and the Catholic Cathedral. Returned to our lodgings if not laden with knowledge we were full of weariness. Sent leter to day to br [George Q.] Cannon in Liverpool.

May 28, 1861; Tuesday. This morning visited Saint Patricks Church which is undergoing extensive renovation and repairs at the expense of Mr Gueniss.[75] Our communicative guide informed us that on the site of

73. Arthur Wellesley, Duke of Wellington, defeated Napoleon at Waterloo. He died in 1852 and his monument was completed in late 1861. Over 200 feet tall, it was the largest obelisk in Europe, taller by comparison than the Statue of Liberty.

74. This is a reference to the Gaelic kingdom of Leinster, for which the historical record extends to about 450 CE, memorialized in the name of Leinster Province (one of the four provinces of the Republic of Ireland), of which Dublin is a part.

75. St. Patrick's Cathedral was built in the late 12th century and reconstructed with funds from Benjamin Guinness, uncle to Arthur Guinness.

the present church one was founded as early as four hundred and nine by St. Patrick whose fabulous well [was] said to have ~~sprung~~ gushed up in obedience to the behest of the Saint who smote the spot with his staff. The credlous believe it altogether holy.

Leaveing the church we went to the residence of br Robert Brown with whom we dined. His wife is a Catholic but she treated us very kindly. The Saints in Dublin are very poor yet kind and warm-hearted. <u>God bless them</u>. Leaveing br Brown we made a call on the family of br ~~Hughs~~ Hughs. While here a Saint came in to inquire after the work [but] her name I did not learn. She came to our little conversational meeting which we held at our lodgeings where we taught the Saints their duties in liveing their religion in their poverty.

May 29, 1861; Wednesday. This morning made our selves ready to leave Dublin and as we do so we feel that our brief stay here will yield its fruits of good to the poor Saints here and the extention of the truth to others and at 1 <u>oclock</u> we were on the way to Lurgan[76] where we arived at half past 5 <u>oclock</u>. Found the Saints of the small branch here extremely poor but hopeful of beter times. ^We^ spake to the Saints in the evening after which we found lodging at the Hotell the first that were first-rate since we left Liverpool. This because of the poverty of the Saints.

May 30, 1861; Thursday. This morning we breakfasted with ^Sister^ Thompson. Our meal was made of soda cake ^and^ pullins (a small fish taken ^in^ Lough Nea) a body of fresh water in sight from ~~on th~~ Lurgan on the north. It is said to be 30 m[ile]s in length by 12 miles in bredth. Our breakfast over we called at br Coners for our bagage and as we passed along the street we seemed to excite much inrest with the inhabitents of the little town altho through history and tradition they had been aquainted with the Dead Apostles yet liveing ones seemed to be a great curiosity. And from the groups of the curious we were pointed out with the declareation they are the Apostles (more of truth perhaps than they designed to tell).

At 27 minutes past 12 <u>oclock</u> we were on the carrs for Belfast where we arived after an hours ride over a lovely pleasant country generaly under a good condition of agriculteral improvement. So far as the appearence of

---

76. Lurgan is in the heart of the island, northwest of Dublin.

the land would indicate the fences ^however^ were much d^i^lapidated and would in America be considered quite inadiquate to the protection of the growing crops.

Arived in Belfast and put up with a widowed Sister Ann Mckay. Her family consists of a son and daughter both of whom belong to the Church. The son ^is^ a barber the daughter is engaged in a shirt manufactory. In the evening some of the Saints came in with whom we had an agreeable pasttime. Here met with a br Gilbrath from Scotland engaged as an agent for some publishers in Glasgow. Brother G, is a practical coal miner, has a br in Provo. After all our wanderings over the earth and the destitution of her children we have witnessed it has been reserved for Ireland to afford us the evidence of the most extreme poverty we have ever witnessed as the lot of suffering humanity in what is called civilized life.

May 31, 1861; Friday. This morning it was raining when we arose and continued through the day. Passed the time mostly in writing. In the evening took sup[p]er with Sister Miller whose husband does not belong to the Church. Af^ter^ this had a pleasant meeting with the Saints and strangers at the place of our lodgings. The constant rain prevented the gratification of our curiosity in sight-seeing.

June 1, 1861; Saturday. A bright morning dawns upon us and tempts us to go out. Yielding to the inducement we took the carrs and went to Holywood a small town 4 miles from Belfast on the ^shore of the^ [Belfast] Lough. Its locality is pleasant and contiguous to it are a number of fine suburban residences. On our return we called on and dined with br Diamond. In the evening went to visit Mrs. ^Sarah^ McLennon who is enquiring into the work.

June 2, 1861; Sunday. To day attended three meetings with the Saints two in their hall and one at Sister [Ann] McKays. In the evening baptism was administered. Confirmed br Baily and some time after 12 oclock retired. To day saw Mrs Steel mother of Elder John Steel of Parowan.

June 3, 1861; Monday. Between 3 & 4 oclock were up for our travil to Londonderry, were on the carrs at 6 oclock. Arived at our destination 10 minutes past 10 oclock were ^meet^ at the Station and welcomed by our friends.

As we passed along br [Charles C.] Rich was taken ill and was forced to remain at a small way station some four hours for another train. When

[we] had ariven after takeing some refreshment we went around the old city, on the wall within which it is enclosed. The length of the wall is one mile[,] its thickness 32 feet[,] and of an average height of 25 feet. It was this encloseure that was so bravely defended by the aprentices against the ^Catholick^ army of King James.[77] Its ~~inhabitants~~ number of inhabitants we did not learn but there is now more extent of city outside of the ancient wall than within it.

There were some little indication of improvement in building among which were the new bridge over the river Foyle on which the city is built and a Catholick chapel. The location of the city is some 30 miles from the Sea. At evening spoke to the few Saints and friends who came in to our lodgings to see us at the residence of brother [David] Eccles. They evinced a cordial warm spirit for the gospel and a hope that its prospects may brighten in the future.

June 4, 1861; Tuesday. This morning parted with our kind friends of the maiden city and at 7 oclock were on the way to Belfast where we arived 1¼ past 11 oclock. Dined with Sister [Ann] McKay in the evening we called on Sister Miller after which we repaired to the boat landing and there secured passage on the Steamer Blenheim for Liverpool. About 8 oclock we were under way and as we glided slowly away we were assured by ^the^ faces of our few friends lighted with the kind smile as they mixed in the assembled crowds that gathered on the shore to witness our departure from the green isle, that warm hearts were breathing inly and silent tho earnest prayrs for our prosperity. And as we witnessed the rising emotions of affectionate tenderness as we bade them adieu we felt that or stock of the eliments of social hapiness had been increased by our visit to the poor Saints of Ireland in their own emerald isle.

June 5, 1861; Wednesday. This morning about 9 oclock we arived in Liverpool after a very pleasant passage of 13 hours. Found br [George Q.] Cannon and family well as also br John Kay with whom in the afternoon I went to Southport a small town some twenty miles distant from Liverpool on the sea shore where I staid over night and at this point the Donkey seems to be in requisition for the amusement and recreation of the pleasure seekers to the exclusion of the horse.

77. The Siege of Derry conducted by King James II was in 1689. The city held out more than 100 days before James retreated.

June 6, 1861; Thursday. This morning rose early and took a walk on the promonade. The weather was fine and pleasant and at 9 oclock returned to Liverpool and past [the time] writing and perusing the news. Today Count Cammille Carvour the great Italian statesman died. His death is regarded as a great national calamity as it will highly jeopardize the yet but partialy developed independence of Italy.[78]

June 7, 1861; Friday. Weather fine this morning in the afternoon attended a party made on the occasion of the blessing of his infant daughter by br [George Q.] Cannon. Her name was Georgieanna Ho[a]gland. We had a very pleasant time with the friends who were present on the occasion. Br [Alexander] Ross came in the evening he is to be engaged in the printing department. He has been for some time past in the Essex Conference as traviling elder.

June 8, 1861; Saturday. This morning made our selves ready for our trip to Sheffield and in the evening at fifty minutes past 3 oclock myself in company with Elders [Charles C.] Rich and [George Q.] Cannon started for the City of Cutlery where we arived 17 minues past 6 oclock. Found our friends well were joined here by Elders James S. Brown and Joseph C. Rich. We lodged with Elder [John] Clark. Presidents Joseph F. and S[amuel] H. B. Smith were with us.

June 9, 1861; Sunday. This morning meet in conference with the Saints. After the buisness disposed of the Saints were addressed by President [George Q.] Cannon after which meeting ajourned until half past 2 oclock at which time they were assembled and were addressed by Elder C[harles] C. Rich, after which I spoke for a short time. We dined and took tea with br Henry Bartram. In the evening the Saints were addressed by Elder James S. Brown after which I spoke for a time and then the conference ajourned and we retired weary to our lodgings. To day Elder Edwin Scott came to see us on acount of his release from the ministry. We defered his mater until we ^could see him in Essex his home.^

June 10, 1861; Monday. To day passed the day with the Saints. ~~Dined~~ Breakfasted with br Adams and family and took tea with br Jas Hiberd.

78. Camillo Benso, the Count of Cavour, is considered the first prime minister of Italy even though he died three months into office and the country was not completely unified until the 1870s.

At 2 oclock P.M. br [George Q.] Cannon Left for Liverpool. Took tea with br Hiberts.

June 11, 1861; Tuesday. To day after dineing with br [James] Hiberd we went to visit the iron and steel manufactory of Mr. Campbell. We were shown through the works by Mr. Sykes the foreman and partner in the works. His manifestation to us of ^the^ sociability of a friend and the urbanity of the gentleman added much to the pleasure of our visit to the works. In the works we saw an Armstrong gun in process of forgeing under a hamer of the weight of 8 tons. We saw steel in the different stages of its development. We saw the makeing and trial of Railroad springs and the manufacture of files.

This done we bade to our conductor adieu and left the scene of our visit of an hour. Returned and took tea with br Hibberd after which we went to the Giants Castle Inn to see the giant Robert Hale.[79] He was indisposed and we did not see him. Returned to br [John] Clarks where we received a call from Mrs Parker who was inquiring after the truth. On takeing leave she expressed her determination to be baptized soon. Her daughter is also believeing. Weather rainy in the evening some of the elders had meeting this evening.

June 12, 1861; Wednesday. To day at fifteen minutes past 11 oclock we left our friends in Sheffield and passing over some highly cultivated farms that presented a picture of loveliness varied by beautiful lawns ^and grassy meadows^ in their summer dress of green decked with blushing flowers that reflected natures smile ~~of~~ of peace upon us as we huried along our iron way. Elder Jas S Brown accompanied us as far as Granthem where we parted and arived in London at 4 oclock.

Put up at 30 Florence Street Islington our wants were cared for by Sister White in the absence of Sister Cook the house keeper. At about 11 P.M. br ^Wm C.^ Staines came in. He was in good health and extended to us a most cordial welcome. Retired late to rest.

June 13, 1861; Thursday. This morning after breakfast we went to Regents Park some four miles by rail. Visited there the Zoological Gardens.

79. Robert Hales, born in 1820, grew to be 7'8" and 450 lbs. and was discovered by P. T. Barnum for the American Museum in New York, where he became known as the Norfolk Giant. He returned to England and died in 1863. "Our London Correspondence," *New York Times*, Dec. 20, 1863.

Saw much to interest and instruct in the varied truths and beauties of nature in the contemplation of which the mind gathers the eliments of its own development while the body becomes weary from incesant toil. In this condition we returned home. In the evening found Prest John Brown awaiting our comeing. About 11 oclock my son F[rancis] M. Lyman came in he was in good health and spirits. The Elders report the prospects of the work as steadily improveing in this district. Altho the poverty of the Saints is great, their hope is bright for a future of blessing and peace. Marion had leter from home with goo[d] news.

June 14, 1861; Friday. Commenced our ramble to day by visiting Dr. Kan's Anatomical Museum where we saw much to instruct and listened while there to a most instructive lecture on the reproduction of our race from the benefits of which woomen were excluded by the false notions of society. We hope this state of things will not always exist.

From this place we repared to the [Royal] Polytechnic Institution where we saw some most interesting illustrations of the truths of nature. In witnessing that part that had to do with electricity we wer in our reflection carried back to the time when the great American philosopher [Benjamin] Franklin first wooed the electrick spark from the storm cloud which has since become the toy and the servent of Man to pleas[e] and to enrich and instruct him in which great work before its magic influence time seems abridged[,] and distence ^which sircumscribes the Earth^ is reduced to a mere point.

Such is the March of Mind and some of its Godlike Achievements. While here we were treated with a lecture ~~of~~ ^on^ British history which was illustrated by a searies of disolving views presenting us with the nations of the East and their costumes [and] maners from the time of ancient Egypt to the present[,] closeing with Westminster Abbey by moonlight. From this feast for the mind we returned to our lodgings weary in body but not impoverished in the spirit of our minds. We saw to day glass being spun into flexible silk-like thread after which it was made into string and tied like thread, thus prepared for use. Our past^t^ime here was rich in food ~~food~~ for thought and as we contemplated we felt to hope for the time when the mighty energies of the human mind should ~~should~~ be directed to the development of ^the happiness^ of poor humanity by lighting the smile of peace over the aspect of war.

June 15, 1861; Saturday. This morning I went in company with Elders [John] Brown and [William C.] Staines and my son [Francis] Marion and br C[harles] C. Rich to visit the Crystal Pallace we traviled by rail.[80] Arived at the place[,] we commenced our examination of this miniature world. We walked and looked ourselves weary. We then sat down and looked and then resumed our journey through the world [and] thus continued until half past 4 oclock when we witnessed the astounding feats on the rope of the renowned M[onsieur] Blonden.[81] Returned about 8 oclock. This evening had an interview with Elder Edwin Scott and we came to the conclusion to change him to a new field of labour.

June 16, 1861; Sunday. This day attended meeting at St. Georges Hall. Had a pleasant time and full house and free spirit.

June 17, 1861; Monday. Passed the day in the office and in the evening went to Sister Wests and took tea and spent the evening. Had a pleasant past-time with our friends. Retired late. Brs [Charles C.] Rich[,] [John] Brown[,] [William C.] Staines[,] [George J.] Taylor[,] and [Francis M.] Lyman were in our party.

June 18, 1861; Tuesday. This morning received leters from President [Brigham] Young[,] sent to br [George Q.] Cannon and forewarded by him. The news was good and cheering containing some indications of a prolonged stay on our parts in the mission. Went with my son F[rancis] M. L[yman] to Poplar ~~Star~~ and put up with Br John Horspool. Answered br Cannons leter and returned the Presidents'. After writing took a walk. Visited the docks and in the evening preached to the Saints of the Poplar branch and some few strangers who were in attendance. Blessed the infant daughter Mary of parents who did not belong to the Church. Had a good meeting.

June 19, 1861; Wednesday. This morning the weather is bright and cloudless wrote leter to my wife in Beaver and one to C[alvin] C. Pendleton of Parowan and one to President Brigham Young. [Francis] Marion [Lyman] left me to day to attend to some apointments.

---

80. The Crystal Palace was a large iron-and-glass building in Hyde Park, built for the Great Exhibition (forerunner of the World's Fair) of 1851. It burned down in 1936. Hoppen, *Mid-Victorian Generation*, 131.

81. Charles Blondin was famous for walking across Niagara Falls on a tightrope in 1859. In 1861 he appeared for twelve shows at the Crystal Palace doing acrobatics over pitchforks and flames. Banks, *Blondin*, 79–84.

June 20, 1861; Thursday. This morning the weather is dark and cloudy with light rain. Continued my writing until 11 oclock when in company with my son I went to 30 Florence Street[82] and in the evening in company with br [Charles C.] Rich[,] [John] Brown and my son visited br Ferguson and family. Returned to our lodgings about 12 oclock.

June 21, 1861; Friday. This morning received leter from br [George Q.] Cannon Liverpool news good. This day went and dined with our friend Mr. Grove and family. Brs [Charles C.] Rich[,] [John] Brown and [Francis M.] Lyman were there. Spent the evening with our friends in agreeable and instructive conversation. Retired late and weary. To day dispached leter to my family and also to President [Brigham] Young under cover to D[avid] O. Calder[83] also to C[alvin] C. Pendleton and John Steel of Parowan.

June 22, 1861; Saturday. Was not out to day did not feel well in health. This morning parted with my son who went to his labors with the Saints. To day an awfuly distructive fire occured by which [blank].[84]

June 23, 1861; Sunday. This morning in company with President John Brown went to the town of Brighton[85] and held two meetings with the Saints and returned in the evening haveing traviled by rail 100 miles (my seat the soft side of a board) and about 6 miles on foot and preached some 2 hours. Felt somewhat weary on returning to our lodgings. On our outward travil this morning we passed the great fire of yesterday stil burning freely as was the case in the evening on our return. Its locality was near London Bridge.

June 24, 1861; Monday. Passed the most of the day in bed on acount of ill health. Took a short walk. In the evening the great fire of Saturday stil is burning. To day the body of Mr. Braidwood the Chief of the Fire Department was recovered from the ruins where he fell on Saturday. His

82. The London conference of the British Mission was headquartered at 30 Florence Street, ironically in the Islington neighborhood.

83. David O. Calder, a Scot who emigrated in 1850, was a private secretary to Brigham Young and a Utah businessman who became treasurer of ZCMI and a member of the Salt Lake Stake presidency.

84. When the Tooley Street fire broke out in a warehouse at the wharf, it burned for two weeks and spurred creation of a municipal fire department. *Reynold's Weekly Newspaper*, June 30, 1861.

85. Brighton, directly south of London on the English Channel, was a health resort and vacation spot, with several hotels already on the waterfront.

body was not burned. His death must have been instantanious from the crushing weight of the mass of masonry under which he was buried.

June 25, 1861; Tuesday. This morning received leter from my family [in] G. S. L. City writen by [wife] Lydia dated the 8 & 10th of May. Wrote some for home and in the evening visited Madam Tausauds Museum where we saw much to instruct and amuse. Brs [Charles C.] Rich[,] [William C.] Stains[,] and [George J.] Tailor were of the party.

June 26, 1861; Wednesday. To day in company with Brs [Charles C.] Rich and [William C.] Stains went to visit Hampton Court[86] and grounds. This palatial residence was founded ~~in~~ as early as fifteen hundred by Cardinal Woolsey and passed from him to Henry the 8th. In the palace in its various parts are exemplified the tast[e]s of ancient and also of more modern builders. Its extent is grand and liberal and calculated to evoke from the thoughtful visitor a corisponding freedom of fancy. Its painting[s] are rich in the perfection of their execution as well as in historick intrest from their relation to many a thrilling incident conected with the history of the past.

As we trod its spacious halls or passed its cool and shaded courts we were haunted with the reflection that in the midst of the gaudy surroudings of wealth and luxury where we wandered with the sunshine of peace in our souls, there humanity in the midst of the same surroundings of elements of comfort and hapiness had drank the biterest dregs of the cup of sorow. From this home [to] the Royal votaries of regal wealth and vanity[,] some have passed to the scaffold. From the palace we extended our rambles to the grounds.

These are laid out on a liberal scale and with a taste for the beautiful that canot fail to convey to the mind of the contemplative visitor a somewhat corect idea of the refinement of taste enjoyed by the early founder of this modelle home. Its supply of water is in its arangement tastful and in quantity abundant. Its spacious lawns of lovely green supporting as they do their varied embelishments of floral beauty and groups of native

---

86. Hampton Court Palace was where the British monarch went to get away from the city, and for a time it served as the residence of Cardinal Thomas Wolsey, the advisor to King Henry VIII who fell out of favor by objecting to the king's separation from Catherine of Aragon. The king went ahead and married Anne Boleyn, the second of his six wives.

trees constitute a picture which the Saint could only contemplate with emotions of intense pleasure as affording a prospective view of the Beauties that will crown the Earth when she as Mother-Queen shall extend her regal blessings without stint to her children immancipated from sin and corruption. While here we were shewn a grape vine that was said to be some 99 years old and that produced each year one ton of fruit. Its training is [the] most perfect known.

In the evening after our return Brother [redacted][87] called to see us. After conversing for a time he acknowledged he had been guilty of adultery with Sister [redacted] who lodged in the same house with him. Myself and br Rich concluded that in consequence of the non publicity of their wrong that they should renew their covinents by baptism without a publick excommunication. Elder Staines was present [and] we instructed him to attend to the baptism. Br [redacted] promised to refrain from this wrong in the future.

June 27, 1861; Thursday. This morning the discarded wife of br [redacted] with whom we dealt on yesterday came in to seek some comfort and counsil. She[,] as she represented to us[,] had been much abused by [redacted] from whom she sa[i]d she had contracted while his wife a loathsome disease in the treatment for which by the physicians[,] she had [been] much lacerated about the neck. She was as she said to us without money health or friends to protect her in this state of utter helplessness. She said she knew the gospel was true and she wished to be alowed to come into the Church from which [she] had been cut off. For some time we ministered to her for her health an[d] gave her a portion of our scanty means and directed brother [William C.] Stains to see that she was baptized as she wished. Her tale was one of horor. She left hopeing she had found some relief. In the evening with brs Rich and Stains visited Coloseum. [I] was much interested.[88]

June 28, 1861; Friday. To day received leters from D[avid] M. Stuart in Scotland and wrote in answer to the same and also sent leter to my family in G. S. L. City. Brs [Charles C.] Rich and [William C.] Stains

87. Portions of these diaries are restricted at the CHL. As online scans, the library has covered up some of the names with black squares.

88. Built in the late 1820s in Regent's Park, the domed London Coliseum (not to be confused with the theater of the same name) housed a famous panoramic mural of London by Edmund Parris. Timbs, *Curiosities of London*, 221.

visited the parliment in session to day. Wrote in my journal and also wrote some for br Stuart.

June 29, 1861; Saturday. This morning at half past 9 oclock myself and br [Charles C.] Rich left our friends at Florence Street and rep^a^red to the Railway station at three minutes before 11 oclock on the way to Norwich[89] where we arived about 5 oclock. Found brs [Elias H.] Blackburn and [Richard] Bently at the Chapel House[90] both were well and extended to us a cordial welcome.

June 30, 1861; Sunday. This day I stayed at our lodging to do some writing while br [Charles C.] Rich acompanied br [Elias H.] Blackburn and [Richard] Bently to the conference. Br Rich addessed the Saints and attended to the transaction of the usual buisness. In the after part of the day I spoke to the Saints at half past 2 and 6 oclock. Had a good and pleasant time.

July 1, 1861; Monday. This morning wrote to br [George Q.] Cannon at Liverpool. The weather is pleasant and clear went out for a walk in the town the population of which is about 75000 with about 55 Churches and chapels. We visited the castle situated on a high mound in the central portion of the town.[91] From this point we had a fine view of the town and its suroundings. The ^red^ tile which predominates in the covering of the roofs from the heght from which we looked down upon them gave a general read [red] apearence to the town which forcibly reminded us of some of our American Brick built cities.

The monotanous apearence of the town was pleasantly varied by the presence of a profusion of shrubery clad in its folage of lovely green that seemed to predominate as our view extended outward from our point of observation to where the scenery of the buisy town seemed to blend and loose themselves in the rural scenery that surounded it and in the distance that bounded our vision [which] seemed to mingle in harmonious greeting [of] the deep blue of the distint horizon.

89. Norwich is 100 miles northeast of London and near the sea.

90. The church had a meeting place in Norwich off of St. Paul's Square. See "Addresses," *Latter-day Saints' Millennial Star*, July 28, 1855, 480 ("Latter-day Saints' Chapel"); Feb. 18, 1865, 112 ("chapel house"). It was called the chapel house because the house served as a chapel.

91. Parts of Norwich Castle, built in the eleventh century by William the Conqueror, still stand today.

Thus affording a somewhat varied picture of what to the thoughtful visiter [is] of this seat of religion and City of Churches. Returning we dined with brother Wm Hall and ^family^ after which we attended a tea party with the Saints. ~~We~~ Were interested with musick songs and recitations after which I addressed the audience who listened with apparent intrest. We ajourned at 11 oclock.

July 2, 1861; Tuesday. This morning my health is not good the weather is dark and rainy. Some of the Saints called to see us. We passed time in giving them instructions in the principles of the gospel. Dined with br Thrower and family at the Chapel House after which we started for Lowestoft[92] where we arived between 6 & 7 oclock. After partakeing of some refreshments with brother Chenercy and family we repared to the Assembly Room a fine hall which had been procured for the occasion.

The hall was soon filled to the extent of its capacity for siting or standing. Of the 500 people present some 40 were Saints the residue were a representation of the citizens of the town embraceing several of the clergy. The assembly listened with apparent intrest and pleasure. In the conclusion the enquirer was pleased and the objecters if any were there were silent. ~~We l~~ We lodged with brother Chenereys.

July 3, 1861; Wednesday. This morning my self and br [Charles C.] Rich called by request on br Wm Reynolds an artist and sat for our likeness. In the evening returned to Norwich. The town of Lowestoft has a population of some 15000. Its principle business is fishing. It is a resort during the summer season for the pleasure seekers. Took tea with br Crampton and family and spent the evening giveing instructions to the Saints present. Retired to rest when the short hours of the morning had come.

July 4, 1861; Thursday. This morning revised the report of the conference of last Sunday and socialized some. Had some raspberry wine from the sisters ~~whose~~ to whose health and long and hapy lives we drank and as we come to chronicle the simple incident we are reminded that this is the great aniversary of American freedom which has ^had^ its brief day of life and now is in its decline fast hastning to disolution under the blighting influence of internal corruption. And the nation seems revelling

92. Lowestoft is a beach town on the North Sea, twenty-five miles southeast of Norwich. It was an important port town and later a seaside resort.

in the bloody catastophy of is own ruin. The attached address was to day given to us which I place here for preservation.[93]

Dined with br Fredrick Wiseman. Took ^tea with^ James Wood and family after which we attended a meeting of the Saints in the Emmanuel Chapel.[94] At the conclusion felt much wearied with incessant labor and loss of sleep. Dureing the later part of the day it rained freely.

July 5, 1861; Friday. This morning in company with brs [Charles C.] Rich and [Elias H.] Blackburn left Norwich by the 6 oclock train and arived in Cambridge at 10 oclock where we met brother ^Elijah^ Larkin[95] with whom we concluded to tarry until tomorow. At night a few members of the Church and some strangers came in and we taught them. Br L. was mostly away attending to his police duties among which was an inquis[i]tion about a man recently drowned. We walked out dureing the after noon to the University grounds and buildings. Saw the Cathedral founded before and finished in the reign of Henry the 8th.

July 6, 1861; Saturday. This morning at half past 6 oclock were on the way for Bedford[96] where we arived about 10 oclock. Were met at the station and conducted by br Joseph Bull to the residence of br James L. Pembroke, were our wants were cared for and br [Charles C.] Rich and myself went to bed for a few hours and were much refreshed. We dined after which we visited Mr E. Page and Co's. large manufactory.[97] [We] were very politely shown through the works by one of the proprietors who also favoured us with an illustrated Catalogue for 1861. Weather dull and showery. Dureing the evening some of the Saints from other branches of the conference came in to attend the Sabath meeting.

93. Lyman inserted a loose sheet with a poem prefaced by, "An Address to Pres[ide]nts Rich and Lyman, spoken in Norwich, July 1st, 1861, by Sarah E. Woods, Aged 7 years, written by her Father." Lyman must have been touched to save it.

94. This was the official name of the LDS meeting place. Norwich is the capital of Norfolk County.

95. Elijah Larkin was born in Cambridge, converted to Mormonism, served as branch president, and worked as a detective for the Cambridge Crown Court. Presumably comfortable in his position and needed as a branch leader, he and his family put off emigrating until mid-1863. He eventually worked for the railroad in Ogden. Brewster and Perry, "A History of the Life of Elijah Larkin."

96. Bedford is fifty miles north of London, west of Cambridge. When Lyman visited, the industrial revolution had transformed Bedford into a key engineering city.

97. E. Page and Co. was famous for manufacturing state-of-the-art farm equipment.

Showers of rain dureing the evening. I received leters from my son in London and from br [George Q.] Cannon in Liverpool. News all good.

July 7, 1861; Sunday. This morning attended Conference with the Saints. Attended to the usual buisness of the Conference administered the Sacrament and instructed the Saints and then ajourned until half past 2 oclock at which meeting and [we were] again in session. Again addressed the Saints and adjourned until half past 6 oclock then wrote leter to br [George Q.] Cannon after which meet with the Saints and addressed them for 2 hours when the conference ajourned. We took super with brother ^Thomas^ Richards after which we retired to bed weary and worn glad to find rest from our labor and toil for brief period of time.

July 8, 1861; Monday. This morning rose slightly rested but somewhat nervous from want of rest. The weather is slighty showery heavy clouds hanging around the horizon. Passed the day mostly at our lodgeings and at 4 oclock P.M. when we meet the Saints at the tea party in the Old Georges Hall their place of meeting. After tea were entertained with songs and recitations for some time after which I spoke to them for a time and then the meeting was ajourned and we learned that we had to leave by the 7¼ oclock train in the morning.

July 9, 1861; Tuesday. This morning left our friends in Bedford and arived in Luton[98] fifteen minutes past 10 oclock where we were kindly entertained by Brother Thomas Day who with his wife have for some four years have been separated from the Church because as (they say) they could not respond to the requirements of tithing as taught in years past here. Stil they evince a love for the truth and a wish to be saved.

Dined with br Day and family and in the evening took tea with the family of Elder Wm Kemp and after tea some of the Saints came in. I taught them for some hour or two and then returned to our lodgings at br Days. To day we received a leter from President H[eber] C. Kimball in which mention was made of the death of Fathers Aphek Woodruff and Isaac Chase, under date of May 15th.[99] President Young and party had

98. Luton is twenty miles south of Bedford, thirty miles north of London, its principal industry hat making.

99. Aphek Woodruff, future church president Wilford Woodruff's father, converted five years after his son. He died on May 28 at age eight-two. Alexander, *Things in Heaven and Earth.* Isaac Chase was a mill owner and father-in-law to Brigham Young. He died on May 26 at age sixty-nine. "Died," *Deseret News*, May 29, 1861.

gone on a visit to the southern settlements in Utah. The health of our families was reported to be good at date of leter from President K[emp].

July 10, 1861 Wednesday.[100] In course of the day took a brief stroll in the town. It is said to contain 15000 inhabitants. The manufacture of straw bonets is the principle trade of the place. At night we held meeting in a hall hired for the occasion. There was an audience of some 200 in attendance embracing some 25 men the residue wer woomen. They listened attentively. On retireing felt very unwell and did not sleep.

July 11, 1861; Thursday. This morning at 8 oclock left our friends in Luton and we arived in London fifteen minutes past 10 oclock. Found all well at Florence Street. My son [Francis] Marion came in this evening [feeling] well. Br Samuel L. Adams was here with President John Brown. Saw a balloon pass over the city this evening.

July 12, 1861; Friday. This morning received note from br [George Q.] Cannon stateing he would be with us on tomorow. My health so poor I was in bed almost [all] of the day took tea [dinner] with sister White & br [Thomas C.] Stayner [who] was present with br ~~John Brown~~ John Lindsey and br [Charles C.] Rich. Felt slightly beter this evening since tea.

July 13, 1861; Saturday. This morning the weather is dull and dark some pain in my head and fever. Was not abroad during the day. Br George Q. Cannon came in from Liverpool via Birmingham. He was in good health and left all so [in good health while] in Liverpool. In consultation this evening with brs [Charles C.] Rich and Cannon we [three lines blacked out].[101]

July 14, 1861; Sunday. This morning in company with Bros [Charles C.] Rich[,] [George Q.] Cannon[,] and [William C.] Staines repared to St. Georges Hall where we meet the priesthood of the London Conference and gave them some instruction at which time [five lines blacked out]. After this had two meetings at both of which I spake to the crowded audience in the hall. Returned to our lodgings weary.

July 15, 1861; Monday. This morning several of the Elders were with us viz, John Brown[,] Jas S. Brown[,] Joseph Bull[,][102] Wm Bramell[,]

100. Lyman penned a note in the margin that said, "This belongs to Wednesday 10th"

101. In this section of diary, portions of July 13–23 were redacted because of details about John Tobin's drunkenness and adultery. See entry for July 23 below for more details.

102. Joseph Bull, from Leicester, England, immigrated in 1851 to Utah to become

John Linsey[,] Edwin Scott[,] George Reynolds[103] and G[eorge] J. Taylor.[104] Elder Scott was apointed to travel and preach in the Essex Conference and Elder George J. Taylor to preside over the same. Gave instruction to the Elders after which they all went out except brs [William C.] Staines and Taylor. I past the time in reviseing Conference minutes.[105] In the evening the brethren returned from their excursions and reported themselves interested. After which listened to a chapter of the experience of br Staines related by himself induced by refference to the catechizing of the Saints in Zion.

July 16, 1861; Tuesday. Some rain to day did not go out. Passed the time at our lodgings in conversation upon the principles of the gospel with the brethren of the ministry who were here.

July 17, 1861; Wednesday. To day in company with Elders [George Q.] Cannon and [William C.] Staines and [Francis M.] Lyman I went to the Crystal Pallace. The principle feature in the day's entertainment was a musical concert in which some 4500 children participated the entire choir numbered 5000 persons. The execution of the musick was admirable and to me deeply interesting as an exemplification of what the human mind is capable of even in childhood only needing to be ever rightly directed to enable it to tread the path of virtue of truth and life in its onward journey to the boundless future of its own interminable being.

We were informed that some 40,000 people visited the palace. To day we passed our time pleasantly wishing that we had more time to spare for the study of this mineature world. For here we can see the world

---

a printer for the *Deseret News*. Four years later he was sent to San Francisco to help print the Hawaiian Book of Mormon, and then in England he helped print the *Millennial Star*. In 1877 he was recalled to the mission, this time with his wife, for the same purpose. Tullidge, *History of Salt Lake City*, 123–26.

103. George Reynolds was a British-native missionary from 1861 to 1865. In Utah he became secretary to the First Presidency, a member of the First Council of Seventy, and in 1874 the church's test case for polygamy before the U.S. Supreme Court, which he lost. He authored several church books.

104. A son of future church president John Taylor, George J. Taylor was born in Canada (his father was British) and after his mission to England opened the first bicycle shop in Utah. He also founded companies that manufactured glass, nails, and shoes. He never married. "Inventory of the George J. Taylor Papers," J. Willard Marriott Digital Library, University of Utah.

105. Since many of Lyman's records and writing, including letters and conference minutes, were printed in the *Millennial Star*, he took considerable time working on them.

represented in its general natural and its artistic beauties and productions from the polar snows of the frigid north to the perpetual sumer of the genial tropics. All may be seen here and can here be studied with intrest and profit by the contemplative student of nature and her rich and varied beauties as also the evidences that are scatered around in rich profusion of [the] march of intellect and the march of [the] mind in the development of its Godlike qualities.

This morning received leters from Elder D[avid] M. Stuart in relation to the case of Elder John Tobin which caused us to conclude to visit Scotland immediately. I also received a leter from Jesse Broadbent Holbeck, near Leeds.

July 18, 1861; Thursday. This morning br [George Q.] Cannon received a leter from Elder [David M.] Stuart in Scotland and did not answer as we were immediately goeing there ourselves. This evening br Cannon was takeing sudenly ill and continued so through the night.

July 19, 1861; Friday. This morning br [George Q.] C[annon] is some beter but not able to travil myself and brother Wm C. Staines started at 9 oclock for Glasgow where we arived about 10 oclock P.M. Found brothers [David M.] Stuart and [Robert] Sands were both away from Glasgow. Lodged with Sister Sands.

July 20, 1861; Saturday. Received leter from br [Charles C.] Rich in London stateing that br [George Q.] Cannon had not recovered so as to be able to travil but would if able start so as to reach to day. We start this morning for Kilmarnock[106] at which place myself and br [William C.] Staines awaited the comeing of br [David M.] Stuart until evening. We past the time at the residence of br Jas Robertson. At evening repared to the station. On our return to Glasgow while awaiting the comeing of our train br Stuart arived and joined our party and returned with us. On our arival in Glasgow we meet brs Rich and Cannon. Br C. health partialy recovered, myself and br Stuart lodged at the Belle Hotell 68 Irongate Street.[107]

106. Kilmarnock, twenty miles southwest of Glasgow, was a small town until industrialization swelled its population.

107. Once again we see how fortuitous it was for Mormons that they were aligned with advocates of prohibition, renting a hall from the teetotalers for church meetings, in this case Bell's Hotel and Temperance Coffee House at 68 Irongate. "Hotels," *Post Office Annual Glasgow Directiory, 1861–1862.*

July 21, 1861; Sunday. This morning meet the Saints in the Irongate Hall which was filled to the extent of its capacity. After the morning services were over ajourned until 2 oclock and were again with the Saints who were addressed by Brs [Charles C.] Rich and [George Q.] Cannon. The Saints were deeply interested and edified. In the evening met with Elder Tobin and a few others at Br [Robert] Sands and had a conversation in relation to the pending difficulties with Elder [John] Tobin. When it became apparent to us that the presence of Sister Agnes Aird[108] was necissary and we determined that brother Cannon should go to Edinburgh and learn the nature of her evidence and determine whether she should come or not, agreed to meet again on Tuesday night in the Irongate Hall.

July 22, 1861; Monday. This morning signs of rain. On arival at br [Robert] Sands found some leters from home one from Eliza at G. S. L. and one from Cornelia [in] Parowan both under date of 6th of June. Commence[d] writeing in reply to family. In the afternoon called on brother Patrick and family with whom we took tea. Returned and lodged with br Sands. it rained dureing the night. Today we heard the statement of [redacted] in relation to br [John] Tobins' conduct to her in his attempts to seduce her. She meet us at br Robert Patricks President of the branch.

July 23, 1861; Tuesday. This morning Elder John Tobin came in to the residence of Elder [Robert] Sands and confessed that he had been guilty of drunkeness and also that he had commited the crime of adultery with a [redacted]. He had scarcely concluded when [redacted] came in and told us that Elder Tobin had been drunk at her house and had commited adultery with her. With these plain statements of facts before us withe the statements of [two or more names redacted] that ^he^ had some months previously attempted their seduction the one ^[redacted]^ in Glasgow the other [redacted] in Edinburgh. For the above named conduct myself br Charles C. Rich and Geo Q. Cannon cut Elder Tobin off from the Church and also [redacted].[109]

---

108. Since Aird's name is not redacted in the diaries, it seems likely she was more a victim than a willing partipant.

109. This story concerning Charles C. Rich's son-in-law, John Tobin, can be pieced together despite redactions. It seems he invited a woman to walk with him in a park and tried to persuade her to have sex with him, and that this was not an isolated incident since he confessed to adultery with a convert and soliciting sex from a prostitute.

In the evening at fifteen minutes past 7 oclock br Cannon returned from Edinburgh. At this time the above mentioned action in the case of Elder Tobin was taken. After which we meet with the priesthood of the Glasgow Conf and instructed them in the principles of salvation and the duties of their calling. Also we made a statement of our action in the Case of Elder Tobin and [redacted]. We then called for the sense of the meeting in regard to what we had done when they voted their concurence in the same. Only brother Thomas Crawford voteing in oposition. We then blest and dismissed the priesthood.

Before closeing the meeting br T[obin] asked the privilige to speak when he stated to the meeting that we had acted to him in a most uncharitable and cruel maner in his excommunication by which he stated his wife was widowed and his child fatherless.[110] This lead us for the information meeting to make some plain statements in refference to the circumstances under which Elder Tobin became connected with the European Mission, after which the above mentioned vote was taken as expressive of the sense of the meeting.

On the day on which myself and Elder C[harles] C. Rich left Salt Lake City to go to England Elder John ^Tobin^ was drunk and could not start with us. He did not join us until the next morning and some five or six miles on the way near the residence of Feramorz Little at which point we were met ^by^ President Brigham Young. He had been informed of the drunkeness of Tobin of the day previous and said he had no use for such men as missionaries. We im^m^ediately sent for Tobin who was in advance of us on the road. He came and talked with Prest Young and beged the privilege of ^stil^ going and proveing[,] in doing so[,] that he loved the truth and the Saints whom[,] report said[,] he cursed the day before in his drunkeness. The Prest yielded to his entreaty and he came with us to England and entered upon his labours in Scotland since which time br Tobin never in one single instance has asked for

Brigham Young forbade "any Elder … baptizing him, until he makes satisfaction to the authorities … and the parties concerned." Young to Lyman, Rich, and Cannon, Aug. 25, 1861, in Brigham Young Collection, CHL; Charles C. Rich diary, July 13–23, 1861, in CHL; *Millennial Star*, Aug. 10, 1861, 23:508; Parshall, "Pursue, Retake and Punish," 81–83; *AML*, 319; Arrington, *Charles C. Rich*, 241.

110. This is a reference to Tobin's temple sealing to his wife and child, which had been rendered null and void because of his excommunication.

any information in reference to the principles of the gospel of which he was most profoundly ignorant. With all this we have borne from the time of his earliest connection with the mission under our charge hopeing he might become more wise ~~this~~ until the glareing sins confessed by himself induced our action which he has the effrontery to tell you has been cruel.

The foregoing incidents in the history of Elder Tobin had not been mentioned by us until his own misrepresentation to the Saints made an allusion to them necissary that you might know that his present [sins] are not his first or only wrongs but only a few of the many to which he seems disposed to a[d]d that of his misrepresentations.[111]

July 24, 1861; Wednesday. This morning read leters from my son in London and one from President [Brigham] Young dated June 13th. Good news from home, and a favorable report from the southern [Utah] settlements as seen in his late visit. Answered my son's leter and also wrote some in my journal. Br [John] Tobin called in but did not give me his leter of recomendation from the Presidency of the Church.[112] Some rain fell dureing the day. Br [William C.] Staines returned from his visit to Kilmarnock after makeing our arangements for our morning start for Liverpool. Myself and br [David M.] Stuart went to our lodgings at ~~the~~ Bells Hotell.

July 25, 1861; Thursday. This morning the weather is dark and rainy. At 45 minutes past 9 oclock myself and brs [Charles C.] Rich and [George Q.] Cannon were on board the carrs at the Calidonian Railway Station for Liverpool. At this point we parted with brs [David M.] Stuart[,] [William C.] Staines[,] and [Robert] Sands. We arived in Liverpool fifteen minutes past 5 oclock. On repareing to 42 [Islington] we found all well except br Wm Ajax who was very ill.[113] We learned that the late missionaries from Utah had arived. There names were as folows John D. Chase[,] Warren S. Snow[,][114] George Peacock[,] A[nne] W. Vander

111. These last two paragraphs were written on a loose sheet and inserted into the diary.

112. That is, he refused to turn over his credentials certifying him as a missionary.

113. William Ajax, a native Welshman, emigrated with his wife, Emma, in May 1862 to the Tooele area of Utah and opened a store there. William Ajax diary, CHL.

114. Warren S. Snow, the former bishop of Manti, Utah, is known for having ordered twenty-four-year-old Thomas Lewis castrated in 1857 for interfering with Snow's courting of Lewis's girlfriend. Brigham Young disapproved of the bishop's actions,

Woude[,][115] Paul O. Schettler[,] Wm Fotheringham[,] John Talbot[,] P[arley] P. Pratt [Jr], George W. Grant[,] J[acob] G. Bigler[,] D. M. Bell and wife and neice on a visit as also Sister Minie Ann Cook.[116] The above party were all in good health except Elder J. D. Chase. Br Cannon had to advance the means to pay the passage in part of the party. The party landed here in their rough mountain costume.

July 26, 1861; Friday. To day wrote and sent leters to the states one to Eliza and one to Cornelia and one to A. S. Case of Manti. Gave some general instruction to the missionaries just arived from Zion. Weather dark and rainy. Br [William] Ajax some beter. To day sent leters to President Young in relation to the excomunication of Elder John Tobin and general news.

July 27, 1861; Saturday. Passed the day with the missionaries in conversation with them. In the evening took a walk with br [George Q.] Cannon in the city. Some little rain this evening. By leters from San Bernardino under date of May 22nd learned of the death of old Sister Kade and also that up to that time Capt Wm Gibson had not left Cal[ifornia] on his mission to Japan.

July 28, 1861; Sunday. This morning elder Edward Pugh the last of the missionaries came in and reported himself. The missionaries all except br Peacock attended the meeting in the Assembly rooms. I meet with the Saints at the same place and spoke to them at half-past 6 oclock. Had an attentive audience. Returned to 42, some of the Elders were ill the result of change of diet and want of exercise in the air. This evening br John M. Kay came in he was well and reported well of the district and the movements of the work in the same.

July 29, 1861; Monday. This morning the Sick are beter. We had meeting of the missionaries and gave them their final instructions preparatory to entering upon the duties of their mission and calling after we gave them the folowing apointments. J[acob G.] Bigler to Ireland[,]

---

telling him that "the time for such measures was still in the future, and not to be implemented in the here-and-now." Peterson, "Warren Stone Snow," 113–14, 126–33.

115. Anne Vanderwood was on his way to his native Holland as one of the first full-time missionaries there, along with German expatriate Paul Schetter. Sheeres, "From the Dikes to the Desert," 116–17.

116. Minnie Ann Cook had survived the Willie Handcart Company disaster of 1856 and its sixty-eight fatalities. She will become a polygamous wife of John Riggs.

[George] Peacock to Scotland[,] [Warren S.] Snow to South District[,] [Edward] Pugh and [George W.] Grant to Cheltanham[,] [Parley P.] Pratt [Jr] to Leeds[,] [John D.] Chase to Notingham. All to labour as traviling Elders but Bigler who was apointed [to Ireland] to take charge of Ireland and Elder[s] to labour under his direction. The[y] all seemed pleased with their appointments and were buisy in geting ready to repare to their several fields of labour on tomorow.

July 30, 1861; Tuesday. This morning Elders [John D.] Chase and [Edward] Pugh left for their respective fields of labour. Others of the missionaries are prepareing to leave for their various destinations at the earliest practicable moment. The weather cloudy with light rain br [John] Kay is assisting the brethren their preperations to leave. Wrote leter to the widow [Ann] McKay and family in Belfast and sent it by the hand of br [Jacob G.] Bigler. Commenced to write to [Church] Historian [George A. Smith].

July 31, 1861; Wednesday. This morning Elders [William] Fotheringham and [John] Talbot left for South Africa and Elder [George W.] Grant for Cheltenham. I ordered a suit of sumer or light cloths. Elder P[arley] P. Pratt [Jr] left for Leeds. In the evening gave some instruction to Elders [Anne W.] Vanderwoude and [Paul A.] Shettler and gave Elder Vanderwoude the charge of the work in Holland. The bethren seemed hopeful of their mission to the Du^t^ch.

August 1, 1861; Thursday. This morning the Elders left for Holland. None of the missionaries are here except Elder [George] Peacock. The weather more than usually bright ~~this~~ walked out in town with br [George Q.] Cannon. On our return received a [social] call from Dr. Wood the Surgeon that crossed the Atlantic with the Saints on the Under Writer. He was much pleased with the people. This evening received my suit of light cloth[e]s.

August 2, 1861; Friday. This morning at 20 minutes past 7 with Brs [Charles C.] Rich and [George Q.] Cannon were on the carrs for Manchester where we arived 45 minutes past 8 oclock. Meet with Elders [John] Kay and [William H.] Dame the ~~later~~ former of whom was slightly indisposed. Breakfasted with our friends at Old Field ~~123~~ Road 123. Some rain this morning in Liverpool but not in Manchester. Heard that some of the brethren who left with the Emigration of this year were on their return. Their number is two. Went out in the town on a desultory stroll which was not a source of much infomation as we had no historical guide without which it is dificult to learn much from a single hasty visit. Several showers dureing the day. Br Kays health is improved. We retired to rest weary with our walk.

August 3, 1861; Saturday. This morning arose refreshed to be greeted with another gentle rain. Manchester the industrial metropolis of England is situated near the southern extremity of Lancashire. It comprises the boroughs of Manchester and Salford the first returning two [members], the other one member of Parliment. The Irwell, a small stream navigable for barges divides the two Boroughs, Manchester lying to the east and Salford to the west. The Y^o^rk and the Medlock ^two small streams^ fall into the Irwell within the boundaries of the borough.

It[s] population acording to the census of 1851 amounted to 401,321 persons, and the number of inhabited houses to 68,546 of which 316,213 persons and 53,204 houses belong to Manchester and 85,108 persons and 15,342 houses to Salford. The parlimentary and corporate boroughs are not so extensive. The former including the townships Newton, Harpurkey, and Bradford not included in the borough of Manchester and part of the township of Pendlebury, not included in that of Salford. The population of the corporate boroughs at the same period was 367,232 persons dwelling in 62,208 houses being for Manchester 303,382 persons and 50,731 houses and for Salford 63,850 persons and 11,477 houses. In 1856 the population of the two boroughs has computed to amount to 427,324 persons.

It has a liberal share of railroads and their conveniences for traffick and travil haveing four ~~stations~~ namely the Victoria, London-road, Oxford, and New Bailey Stations. Its omnibus[117] acomodations are good. Its oldest religious structure is the cathedral founded in <u>1422</u> by the 12<u>th</u> baron Thomas de la Warre.[118] Manchester under the name Manceniary became a Roman station within the first century of the Christian era. This shows its antiquity and of its[119] renown we may judge when we consider that in its ancient time-worn cathedral were celebrated the nuptuals of Elder J[ohn] M. Kay

117. A horse-drawn carriage that transports several passengers at once.

118. Lyman means the fifth baron, Thomas de la Warr, who enlarged the cathedral built in 1215.

119. Lyman wrote "and its and of its."

and ~~Lady~~ ^Miss^ Ellen Cockeroft.[120] For further details of the history of Manchester reference can be had to Hand Book by Joseph Perrin.[121]

In the evening visited the Zoological Gardens at Belvue. The collections of natural curiosities were comparitively meager, the development in the assembed multitude of obcenity, drunkeness, and prostitution were disgusting in the extreme. The exhibition of fire-works was an interesting reflection of human ingenuity and imitatetive skill. As we returned to our lodgings the streets were being measured from side to side by numerous unfortunate inebriates for whom the streets seemed to have too much length but were sadly deficient in width.

August 4, 1861; Sunday. This morning we meet with the Saints in the Corn Exchange. There were some 300 of the Saints present they were addressed by Elder [George Q.] Cannon who in an eloquent and persuasive maner urged the Saints to seek to so live as to enjoy the blessings of that inspiration that brings the soul into that close communion with God that affords it a knowledge of God beyond what can be learned from the writen word. After br C, I made some remarks, when the meeting ajourned until 2 oclock. When we were again in cession and the congregation was adressed by br [Charles C.] Rich for one hour on the subject of practical religion, [he] was folowed by Elder Cannon on the same [and] spoke one half an hour when I made a few suggestive remarks in relation to the origin of right and wrong[,] of good and evil[,] life and death[,] after which meeting ajourned.

August 5, 1861; Monday. This morning the weather rather dark. We received by this morning paper news of the defeat of the federal army under command of General [Irvin] McDowel by the Confederate army commanded by General [Pierre] Beauregard and General [Joseph E.] Johns[t]on [who] commanded the wings and President [Jefferson] Davis lead the centre.[122] Passed the day pr^i^ncipaly in doors some showers dureing the day. This ~~morning~~ evening received a leter from [wife] Dionetia in Beaver or Minersville all good from that quarter. Received a leter from [Francis] Marion [Lyman].

120. The Kays were married in the cathedral in 1837 before they converted to Mormonism. John will die in Wyoming in three years en route home from his mission to England.

121. The *Manchester Handbook* by Joseph Perrin was a local history published in 1857.

122. This was the First Battle of Bull Run, fought on July 21 in northern Virginia as the first major engagement of the war.

August 6, 1861; Tuesday. This morning myself and brother [Charles C.] Rich parted with br [John] Kay and [William H.] Dame and [Reuben] McBride and returned to Liverpool [who] were meet ^at^ the station by brs [George Q.] Cannon and [John D. T.] McAllister. Found all well at 42. Wrote to Mr Benjamin Sykes of the Cyclops Steel Works Sheffield, and one to [Francis] Marion [Lyman] in London, and in the evening joined ^in^ wedlock Wm Ajax and Miss Emma Jemimah Hughes, in presence of Charles C. Rich and George Q. Cannon. In the evening to[ok] a walk in the town dureing which we called a[t] Reynolds Hall of wax figures and there we saw a baby whose age was 18 months his weight 102 lbs. His name was Thomas Reid a healthy fine looking boy his mother age 21 years. Thomas was born in Ireland and he walked at 15 months old.

August 7, 1861; Wednesday. Some showers. To day was engaged in writing out a skelliton report of discourse for the press. Received leter from [Francis] Marion [Lyman] encloseing one from my Daughter Maria Louisa from Beaver. News good from all there. We dispached leter to br John Van Cott.

August 8, 1861; Thursday. To day wrote leters one to [second wife] Dionetia ^In Minersville^ one to [seventh wife] Priscilla one to Maria Louisa my daughter and two others to my family at Beaver. Weather fine and clear no rain to day.

August 9, 1861; Friday. To day wrote to President H[eber] C. Kimball and received one from my [sixth] wife Paulina in Parowan. In the evening read some in Castle's Illustrated History of England. Found it quite concise and with its illustrations very interesting for young students of History. One item that met our eye dureing our brief reading was the notice of that date of the participatory of Godfrey of Boulion in the Crusades which occured in the year 1096 of the Christian ~~Area~~ Era. With his army he folowed in ^the^ disasterous track of his enthusastic predicesor Peter the Hermet. That of Godfrey was the first diciplined movement in this war for the reclimation of the Holyland. To day myself and brs [Charles C.] Rich and [George Q.] Cannon meet[123] and prayed; had a pleasant and hapy time together.

August 10, 1861; Saturday. This morning myself and brs [Charles C.] Rich and [George Q.] Cannon were on the way to ~~by~~ Birmingham ~~the~~ at

123. Lyman drew a circle here to indicate a prayer circle.

8 oclock. Arived at 12 oclock were meet at the landing and welcomed by President W[illiam] G. Mills with whom[,] and his lady[,] we dined and lodged. In the evening made a call on br Edward Price and family whom we found well. Br Rich lodged with ~~with~~ them.

August 11, 1861; Sunday. To day meet with the Saints in conference in the Oxford Street Chapel the poor ventulation ^of which^ rendered our meeting and the service rather wearisome and unpleasant. A most excilent spirit pervaded. The Saints in whom the hope is daily brightning of a deliverence from the opression of their poverty and ^of^ their gathering to Zion. Br [William G.] Mills gave a report of the conference after which br [Charles C.] Rich presented ^the^ authorities of the Church in usual form. They were all unanimously sustained, after which he addressed the people for an hour ^on the subject of practical righteousness^ after which I spoke to them for some thirty minutes on the importance of labouring while detained here [in England] to develope that practical purity of life which would render them acceptible to God both here and in Zion after which meeting ajourned until half-past 2 oclock when the Saints were addressed by Elder [George Q.] Cannon for some half hour. I then spake to them for an hour of the importence of chooseing a correct stand point from which to contemplate and consider the purposes of God in relation to man in order to arive at correct conclusions in reference thereto as well as the record ^of^ the scriptures.

Held our evening meeting at half past 6 oclock. The audience that filled the house to overflowing were addressed by Elder Cannon on the necessity of confidence on the part of the Saints ^in^ the liveing priesthood in order for their growth in grace and the knowledge of the truth requisite to their exhaltation to ^the^ high and holy condition in which they as the constituents of Zion must be raised to become the light of the world and the perfection of beauty out of which acording to the prophet the Lord would shine or which should from its combined and accumulated excellencies reflect the perfections of our Father and our God. Adjourned half past 8 oclock and repaired weary and worn to our lodgings glad to find fresh air after breathing as we had done for hours dureing the day the fetid atmosphere of our crowded hall and found the couch greatful to us in our weariness.

August 12, 1861; Monday. In the morning passed some time in writing and reading the news, br [William G.] Mills bought a hand book of Birmingham and gave it to me. After Din[n]er about three oclock myself and brs [Charles C.] Rich[,] [George Q.] Cannon[,] [William] Mills[,] and [Samuel] Adams walked to Aston Park where some 3 or 400 hundred of the Saints had assembled for recreation and a pick-nick party.

As we entered the park we passed along a beautiful avenue formed by two parilell rowes of aged and wide spreading Maple trees. Our walk through this avenue brought us to the Aston Hall in relation to which I gleaned the folowing items of history (from an entabliture over the front entrence)[:] namely that it was founded in 1618 by Sir Thomas Holt, and completed in 1635.[124] The structure is of brick and the surface shows some signs of decay. Some tastefuly aranged beds of flowers add their beauty to the suroundings of this old ancestored home. Passing around to the rear of the building we had a fine view of the low ground decked in its probe of modest green supporting here and there over its broad bosom some aged trees that spread abroad their giant arms richly clad with their green foilage a most tempting shade to the weary pedestrian. Here in Gods first great earthly temple were the Saints assembled for their past-time.

We traviled down from the hall and joined our friends who acorded to us a hearty welcome and a share of their simple and unostentatious provision of creature comfort for the occasion. As the saints were interesting themselves in what appeared to me little more than the wild romp of wanton thoughtless child-hood this truth ~~was~~ came floating up before my mind on the curent of thought that the creations of folly and ignorance would live while the parent of their existence (ignorence) remained.

A casualty occured to mar the festivity. Br John Smith aspiring to the lofty ascended a pole (fixed in the gound) some 20 feet from which height he fell to the ground and was severly injured by the concussion. If youthful aspirations never lead him to more serious wrongs he may out-live them. On leaveing the park we call[ed on] a br Tucker and family and took tea after which brs Rich and Adams went to their lodgings at br Prices.

Myself brs Cannon and Mills remained for a few hours and then

124. Aston Hall is a classic Jacobean English mansion in Birmingham. In 1861 it was a privately owned museum and park; today it is a historic landmark owned by the city of Birmingham. Fairclough, *The Holtes and their Successors*.

returned to br Mills. Retired at one oclock much wearied with the excercises of the day. Dureing our stay in the park br Rich was ~~acked~~ ~~atack~~ attacked with something like rheumatism in his back which rendered it dificult to walk. ^He rode to his lodgeings in a cab.^

August 13, 1861; Tuesday. At 20 minutes past 6 oclock meet br [Charles C.] Rich at the railway station and started for Liverpool via ~~Birkhen~~ Birkenhead feeling that things are moveing rather prosperously in [Burmingham] the Toy-shop of England.[125] Arived in Liverpool about 11 oclock. Felt so much out of tone for want of sleep did no buisness save a little journalizing.

August 14, 1861; Wednesday. To day had some light showers. Passed the time in writeing and reading and makeing some preperation for our Continental journey. In the afternoon Elders [Elias L.] and [John C.] Graham returned from the Isle of Man. They report that a spirit of enquiry is among the people. They baptized some persons dureing their short stay, and were heard with aparent intrest in both publick and private. Not much change in the condition of br [Charles C.] Rich's health. He is stil afflicted in his back and is otherwise ill. In the evening read some sketches of the history of the Romans in England in the century previous to the comeing of Christ, 55 years [BCE].

August 15, 1861; Thursday. To day wrote leter to [sixth wife] Paulina in Parowan.[126] Commenced the labours of the day by writeing leter to my wife Paulina in Parowan Iron County Utah in answer to one received. This done I gathered together my journal which was in parts (extending from April 30th 1860 to August 14th, 1861 and turned them over to Elder E[dward] L. Sloan who [was] engaged to copy the same into a new book I had procured for that purpose. The book was a present from br [George Q.] Cannon. Aranged with br Cannon that he should secure

125. Birmingham was nicknamed the toy shop of the world (see also Jan. 23, 1862 entry) because of its intense manufacturing output. An 1850 magazine explained, "By this phrase the orator intended to express both the flimsiness and elegance of the various manufactures of the town, and the extensiveness of the markets which it supplied.... Birmingham, in this sense, still remains the toy-shop, or rather the work-shop, of the world and supplies Europe, Asia, Africa, America, Polynesia, and Australia." Hunt, *Merchants' Magazine and Commercial Review*, 678..

126. Lyman once again abruptly switched journals, leaving a few blank lines and resuming in 1871, while continuing his 1861 entries in a different book beginning with the second sentence in this entry.

for me full files of all the works that had been published in the Star office and that were not to be bound as he might think best for their preservation. Brother [Charles C.] Rich who had been ill is feeling somewhat beter in health and spirits and is preparing for our prospective journey to the Continent.

August 16, 1861; Friday. Rose early and was engaged in makeing ready for our journey. Before leaveing myself and brs [Charles C.] Rich and [George Q.] Cannon meet in[127] and prayed for our mutual protection when parted and our meeting in the future and the general peace and prosperity ^and^ increase of the Kingdom of our Father and all who labour to promote its intrests[,] from the Prest at its head to the man that stands out side and wishes it well.

Before leaveing br E[dward] L. Sloane brought in and read to me a report of a discourse delivered by myself in the assembly room. The report was the best of any which I have been favoured in the country in the preservation of sentiment and language.[128] This done we partook of some refreshment and bade ou friends of 42 adieu for a time and were away.

We were attended to [at] the exchange station (^by brothers Cannon and Sloan; and^ the point of our departure from Liverpool) at 45 minutes past 12 oclock. Were under way for Hull, via Wigin, Wakefield, Normonton Colby. Arived in Hull 20 minutes past 7 oclock. Were meet at the Station by Elders Joseph F. Smith[,] P[arley] P. Pratt [Jr] and Charles Welch and conducted to the residence of brs Wm Burley and Samuel Brooks Bank and families ^11 Caroline Street^ where we were refreshed and lodged. Dureing the evening several of the Saints (mostly sisters as the female eliment predominates here largely in the church) came in and entertained us with some songs and I then gave them some instruction in regard to the way in which they should enter upon the labour devolveing on them as Saints that in stead of looking for a sp^e^edy termination of the work they should regard theirs as a life-long labour and then to be continued in and through all the interminable ages of

127. Lyman drew another circle here indicating a prayer circle.

128. When high-ranking church leaders spoke at worship services, a clerk would often record what was said and submit the transcript to the church newspaper, a task some clerks were better at than others. Lyman thought Sloan had done well in capturing his message and tone.

an endless future. For the Souls enlightenment and exaltation in the mansions of glory in the Kingdom of our Father as the aquisition of the constituent elements of power (the knowledge of God) shall endow the enfranchised Soul with capacity to rise in the scale of intellectual being to that high and holy destiny predetermined and made attainable for mankind by the character of the Constitution of the Race. Bestowed by our great Father upon us before we came forth as the citizens of our earthly home. Our friends seemed cheered and refreshed in their spirits to go forth and struggle stil on in the great Battle of Life for their liberty from the bondage of sin and death. Our evenings interview ended we parted with our friends who left us to our much needed rest.

August 17, 1861; Saturday. To day rose somewhat refreshed and after breakfast wrote some in my journal also sent telegraphick dispatch to br [John] Van Cott informeing him of the time of our sailing from Hull. Brs [Charles C.] Rich and [Joseph F.] Smith visited the steamer and engaged our passage to Hamburgh for 30 shillings each. Wrote leter to my son [Francis] in London. Dined with br Samuel Hallett and wife. While there was forceably reminded (as we contemplated the extent of the tenements occupied by br H.) of the opression that is forced upon the poor as the consequences of the cupidity of the Master and poverty of servant whose life and comfort are bartered indirectly to fill the treasury of his exacting landlord. The poor may bee found crowded into teniments that are unhealthy for the want of ~~healthy~~ ^pure^ air in such quantities as would promote health and impart vigor~~ous health~~ to the sons of toil whose existence is the countrys greatness and wealth.

When will man misguided learn that the life is more than meat and the body more than raiment and folowing this sanitary indication build cities and private homes in a maner that their use will be calculated to promote rather than destroy human life as is now the case here in this department of life. Humanity cries for deliverence from sin and its consequences as we see them developed in the crowded city and narow and ~~illy ventilated~~ tenements of the poor which are at best but little beter than sepuchres in which (in connection with their confinement in work-shops and manufactorys) to consumate a slow but shure decline and death.

In the evening we took tea with some orphan sisters by the name of Wilkinsons. They were in mourning for their mother who had recently died. They were in hopes of going home next year if they could get some little help which they were hopeing for from Zion from their brotherin-law who was engaged with Prest ^B[righam]^ Young.[129]

After this we repaired to the residences of brs Robert Williams and Joseph Harper where we meet the Saints and a few strangers to whom we discoursed for a short time of the importance of first learning the truth of the gospel and then in the light thus developed in the soul they would be enabled to see and understand the truth and harmony of the scriptures considered in parts or collectively as a whole or a record of the revelation of the purposes ~~and~~ of God and the principles involved in their fulfillment or consumation in the redemption of the human race and their exaltation to that high position to which as the Children of God they were predestinated by being conformed to the image of his Son that he might be the first born among many brethren instead of being alone.

After this Br Rich spoke and gave his testimony of the Later-day work. We were listened to with intrest; this done we bade the Saints ^adieu^ and then under the guidence of one of the brethren we repared on board of the Hellen Mac Gregor a distance of one mile or more the time 10½ oclock. Shortly after ariving on board we were joined by br Joseph F. Smith who had brought our baggage on board. Parted with the brethren and retired to rest on the lounges as all the births were taken before our arival in Hull.

August 18, 1861; Sunday. This morning about 3 oclock we steamed out of the Humber. The weather was clear altho the wind freshened into a breeze that created some uneasyness in the character of Sea-sickness. Our breakfast was light and din[n]er was untasted by us. The wind was some help to us as the sailors shook out the idle ca[n]vass to woo the kingly embrace of the passing breeze. This aid to the iron sinews of the Scottish Heroine [*Helen Macgregor*] seemed to impart to her somewhat more of life and she speed galantly away on her ocean path with her varied freight of life which embraced man as the noblest work of God and the lower order of animal life from the grunting swine that the Jew so much dispises to see and will not eat, the cannine race was represented as also was the more useful animal. The horse we had on board, [as were]

129. Sisters Fanny, Maria, and Grace Emma Wilkinson sailed from Liverpool in 1864 on the *General McClellan* and arrived in Utah in September.

some specimins of the Bra[h]man Cattle. These difer from our cattle in ^two^ ~~to~~ points[:] they are less in size and are peculiar in their formation haveing a hump or protuberence over the shoulders something like the Dromedary tho diferently located and not so large. Their habits ^are^ much the same as our cattle. The feline tribe was represented by a young tiger, the chatering monkey was there to remind us of the suny clime of his tropical home. where springs beauty and sumer's wealth make the year one round of vernal beauty and source of perpetual wealth to meet the varied tasts and requirements of natures children.

We had on board some cases of talking birds as evidence of the avidity ~~with~~ with which men cater to the vitiated moral taste of the age when men will pay money to hear the senseless and uninstructive prattle of a bird but will not hear the truth without money or price. Such are some of the evidences of the so called consistency of the religiously enlightened generations of the present.

The day passed without incident of note save the partial unshiping of one of the [lifeboat] ships ~~Boats~~ from its davits [crane] by a sea which nearly submerged myself and br [Charles C.] Rich as we were siting on the weather side of the deck at the time and in a position that if the boat had not fallen on the outside of the ship it would have crushed us in its fall. The crew and passengers succeeded in recovering the boat and securing it on the deck until the wind subsided.

August 19, 1861; Monday. This morning on riseing about 3 oclock (my time was English) I found my face very soar and badly swollen as I suposed at the time from the exposure to the sun the day previous. The swelling was not attended with pain altho one of my eyes was nearly closed thus giveing ^me^ somewhat the appearance of a sufferer in a pugilistick encounter which caused many a bright eye to be turned upon me with that enquireing glance ~~which~~ which seemed to say what is the mater with him? At 24 minutes past 4 oclock the sun arose a most beautiful sight. Like a king he came clad in his own habiliments of golden light and seemd as he rose from his ocean rest to shake ~~from~~ the sea-spray from his vestments of light as he traviled up his pathway of increaseing glory to dispense his priceless treasures of blessings to a waiting world.

As I sat alone enjoying the quiet bliss of the hapy revery induced by the picture of golden beauty and loveliness that covered the ocean expanse that in its native grandure was spread around until at every point it meet the bending arch of heavens blue dome, [I saw] where the blue of the upper and lower deep seemed to meet in harmonious greeting. As we folowed ^in our thoughts^ the pathway as indicated of the King of day we saw that the oceans broad expanse of mountains rugged height or the deserts trackless waste ~~could~~ could ^not^ change or stop its onward journey to the west where its joyous beams imparting Heavens smile should shed the haloe of their glory on that spot.

Pardon the thought ^which^ is above all others dear to the oean tossed wanderer from his distant home ~~in~~ in the west to the enchanting locality of this day-dream of the affections my feelings wander. And who shall say that the tribute of memory is not due to the scene of loveliness ~~to which~~ to which from evry point however remote the memory, quickened by affections warming impulse seeks the richest treasures of its stores of wealth. To thee thou center of all present expectation ^and^ future joys to thee my home my feelings turn when all else is cold and drear for in thee are hearts that beat in unison with mine own and feel alike with the absent wanderer the kindling impulses of an ever growing affection rendered ever pure by the truth and inteligent by its light. In thy light is my glory; and in thine is my increase of greatness; and in thine is my glory and my life in the present and the vast and interminable future, such is the home that with all its charms for the present, and its rich promise ^of glory^ for the future that lives and nesles for securety within thine embraces at lovely Deseret. Thy Mountain fastnesses are its soroundings of strength and the light of God is thy glory and thy chief joy.

Such O! King of day and dispenser of light to the waiting world is the home that waits for me in the mountain-heights of the distant west that must in thy continuous journey drink in thy light and be gilded with the golden radience of thy beemes and quicken into increasing life under the vivifieing influence of thy Kingly smile. Then speed the[e] on in thy pathway of light[,] nor tarry in thy course when thy kindling rays shall deck with the glory of their golden light the rugged mountains towering sumits that keep a sleepless watch around my home.

If thy light has an uterence as thou lookest in upon the sacred circle of home let thy presence tell that ~~they have~~ ^thou hast^ visited the wanderer as in the silent reverrie of unbroaken thought[, be] he far away on the ocean bi[l]lows[, he] thought of home and for the moment seemed to enjoy sweet communion with its blest inmates and seemed nomore the wanderer. As from warm affections deathless fountain he quaffed the joy that feeds the soul, and for the moment lived at home, the wifes kiss of deathless trusting affection ~~is warm~~ ^seemed^ warm on the cheek, while the prattle of inocent childhood ^seemed to^ rise around his feet. All the husband and father is awakened in the soul, and affections creation of a future of ineffible glory and bliss rises before the mind in all the facinating beauty of inimitable loveliness.

Such ^is^ the home of which in deep rev^e^rry I thought as I wached with eager intrest the stately going forth of the King of day. Others of our traviling world were now astir. About 10 oclock we were in sight of land called Allego^land^ [Heligoland] when the spirits of the sick seemed to sudenly assume a state boyency which sickness had hitherto held in check until returning health awakened it to life and exercise to the joy of all.

As we neared the mouth of the Elbe all sickness was gone. We enjoyed a good din[n]er and when night had succeded to the day the moon as if to cheer us looked smileingly out upon the scene and shed the cheering light of her own silverry rays on our watterry path as we mad[e] our ^way^ steadily over the placid Bosom of the Elbe. Under these hapy circumstances we retired to rest and a short oblivion from care.

August 20, 1861; Tuesday. This morning found us at Hamburg where we were cheered by meeting our brother John Van Cott who had come the day before. We went to the English Hotell and commenced writeing my journal while brothers [Charles C.] Rich and Van Cott ~~was~~ visited some of the Saints and from them received a present of some wine of which we partook on their return. Found it very good in taste and effect. The swelling in my face to day is some increased and has some the appearance of [illegible] inflamation and is extending over my face.

While here tasted of some fine sweet plumbs. In the evening we repaired to [the] Altona [neighborhood] ^to^ the Railway Station where we waited some time for the starting of the train for Kiel. While waiting we walked out to a point of land from [which] we had a view of the Kingdom of Hanover.[130] The country so far as our view extended was low and flat

130. Hanover was once a principality of the Holy Roman Empire, its prince one of the king's electors. It was re-granted a measure of its former high status after the Napoleanic Wars, but in 1866 it became part of the Prussian Empire.

and not ^varied^ with hill and dale. The time haveing ariven, 6½ oclock we were away from Keel enjoying the luxury of our ride by ourselves.

~~The~~ The character of the country over which we passed was generaly low the soil not rich jugeing from the grass and grain on the gro^u^nd. Arived in Kiel ^10½ oclock^. As the train disgorged its liveing freight we as part of the onward moveing mass rolled along to the Steamer. Urging ourselves a little we distenced in our journey to the boat all our competitors accept one gentlemen and lady who came up with and past us in the race, we were however on board in time to secure births for sleeping. These provisions made[,] we thought of God and Home and friends and then in sweet refreshing sleep became obliveous to care or sorrow. Arived at Cosor at 5 oclock.

August 21, 1861; Wednesday. We were awakened this morning as the passengers began to rise and regulate their toilet for the day. The morning opened bright and clear. As the train did not leave for some two hours we took a stroll to slightly elivated woody ridge outside of the town. From this point we gained a view of a smal extent of the country which retaines the flat apearence of that over which we passed on yesterday evening. Refreshed with our walk we returned to the hotell and partook of some coffee and cakes after which at 7¼ oclock were underway for Copenhaven. The entire country is flat and poor there is here little or no fenceing and the cattle sheep and horses are tethered in the pasture or on the meadows after they have been mowed. The stock generaly appears small compared with the stock with which the traveler meets in England[,] Scotland[,] or Ireland. I was informed that the Kingdom of Hanover furnishes some fine stock for the English market.

Arived in Copenhaven at our destination at 4 oclock. We were meet and welcomed at the railway station by President [Peter W.] Poulsen and several of the brethren and sisisters who were aprized of our comeing. At the office found all well and a good and generous breakfast prepared by the kind fore-thought of br [John] Van Cott for our comfort. Dr Poulson said the affliction from which I was suffering was an attack of Ir^r^icipilus [erysipelas] induced by my exposure in the sun on the passage from Hull. He gave me some medicine for its removal. After takeing our refreshments myself and brs [Charles C.] Rich and Van Cott took a brief walk around the fortifications which have recently been fited and made ready for use in case of war which was regarded as probible for a time. The war clouds have passed for the present. We noticed dureing our walk some three ships of war one of which was a steamer under the Rusian flag. Their business and destination we did not learn. Returned from our walk some weary and feeling rather weak. I was forced from sensations of weariness to seek the couch for rest.

Passed some time in conversation in reference to the principles of the gospel as applied to the creation and government of the family or domestick circle with brs Rich and Van Cott. This done we retired.

August 22, 1861; Thursday. This morning opened up clear and beautiful not much improvement in my health did not feel able to attend our corespondence with Liverpool. Br [Charles C.] Rich wrote to br [George Q.] Cannon and I was in bed the most of the forenoon. As I am writing the post has arived bringing N.Y. Herald, 6th of August. At din[n]er to day my apetite a little equivocal. Some considerable indications of fever. Was directed by the Dr [Peter W. Paulsen] not to eat or drink anything sour or apply any water to my face after the usual maner of washing. Sister Christensen called to see and speak with us she is in hopes of some help from Sanpete Utah from her brother who is residing in the settlement of Ephraim.

At 2 oclock we partook of chockolate and cakes with Prest Poulson and family. His wife tho not belonging to the Church received us kindly and seemed pleased with our call. They have two interesting children son and daughter. In the evening at 5 oclock went on board the steamer ~~Diana~~ ^Dania^ for [the city of] Alborg.[131] Br Poulson and Lady came to see us off and br [Peter O.] Thompson [Thomassen]. The ship was thronged with passengers but the provident care of br [John] Van Cott had secured us some births a luxury which many of our felow passengers did not enjoy. At the time of leaveing Coppenhagen the sea was smoth but by eight oclock there was much motion we however retired to bed and in the sweet oblivion of sleep soon forgot the disquietude of the waters on whose storm-tossed bosom we passed the night safely under the protecting care of him who tempers the wind to the shorn lamb or notes the feeble sparrow's fall. His arm was around us [and] we wer safe.

---

131. Aalborg is northwest of Copenhagen, near the top of the Jutland peninsula.

August 23, 1861; Friday. Awakeing from our sleep we found the rain falling copiosly tho the wind was less than [it had been] through the night. At 7¼ oclock were mored at the landing at A^a^lborg. Here we found our friends Elders Christian Madsen[,] H[ans] C. Hansen and Lauretz P. Larsen who conducted us to the residence of br Larsen where they had provided for our entertainment. At this place meet with Elder Jessee N. Smith in good health and spirits and progressing finely in the aquirement of the language. The brethren report some ~~some~~ opposition of late in A^a^lborg. My health is improving the inflamation is subsideing from my eyes and face. Brs [Charles C.] Rich [John] Van Cott and Smith and Hansen have gone out for a walk as the rain has ceased. I did not dare venture and acordingly remained. Several of the brethren and sisters called to see us and give us a good Danish shake of the hand which by the by is no sickly affair. For with a warm heart and a stalwart frame the souls affection must of necesity find expression in the strong grasp of earnest honest friendship as it was denied the uterence of speech to us. The brethren have returned from their stroll and report the area a pleasant one but the wind was very high and detracted from the pleasure of their walk. Passed some time in peruseing the American News as given in the N. Y. Herald. The brethren have agreed to have a cariage and team at our disposal for traviling until our return to this place.

During the afternoon a sister by the name of Gertrude Syndergaard came in and requested the ministration of the Elders in laying on of hands for h^e^aling. She was afflicted with the dropsy [edema]. She is 19 years of age, her case was rather serious and of some 1½ years ~~of~~ standing. Br Rich and others administered I did not join them on acount of my health.

This evening we held a conversation with the brethren present in reference to the principles of moral virtue and purity in the people necissary to the strength and perpituity of government and the lack of which [~~illegible~~] the great cause of the calamities that are at this ~~time~~ time ovewhelming the American nation, notwithstanding ~~their~~ ^its^ wealth and other external circumstances of a propitious character that suround ~~them~~ ^it^ yet their corruptions are hastening their ruin from which diplomacy nor legislation can save them so they perish. And hapy will we be if we profit by their example and ever seek in the purity of the people for the stability and perpituity of the government of the Kingdom of God now growing ~~in~~ in Zion. This is our work ~~and our~~.

Reminded the Elders present that we were not only called to do good to others in preaching but to do good for the Kingdom by increaseing our own stock of knowledge, thereby increasing our capacity for serveing the intrests of the Kingdom.

August 24, 1861; Saturday. Awoke feeling somewhat improved in health the rain was falling copiously but soon ceased. At half past 10 oclock we were ready for our ride to Yearing [Hjørring]. We crossed the Limfjord—or Blue Bay in a small boat while our hired car^r^iage passed over in a larger one propelled with oars. As in our journey northward we had left steam behind us.

Comfortably ensconsed in our carriage we rolled away over a fine well Mackadamized [gravel] Road. The pleasure of our ride was somewhat diminished by the necesity of keeping our carriage closed on-acount of the rain which soon however ceased and we were afforded a limited view of the country over which we were passing. It was generaly flat with gentle undulations the tops of many of which are crowned with numerous Tumuli [burial mounds] the resting places of the ashes of the departed dead of ages long past. These ancient recepticles of the dead much resemble the Tumuli so common in North America, and when ~~exkavated~~ ^excavated^ disclose the same or similar ^historical^ evidences of the ~~passed~~ ^past^. The soil is poor [and the] sand predominating in its composition the crops on the ground were light.

At half-past 1 oclock we stoped at an (Gyostgivergaard [gæstgivergård] or Inn at Bronsdeslou [Brønderslev]) to feed our team and refresh ourselves. This done we were away on the road. The character of the land seemed to change and became more sandy as we aproached Yearing. The distance from Alborg which is 6¼ [46] Danish or 29 English miles. Arived in Yearing and wer made welcome by the President of the Vensyssel Conference, Jens Chr Andersen Weibye[132] with whom we had our lodgeings.

132. Weibye, a tailor by training, served a seven-year mission and was branch president in his native city of Hjørring. In 1859 he married Sisilie Marie Pedersen, a seamstress, with the mission president's approval, and in 1862 he and his wife immigrated to Utah. He would later fill two more missions back to Scandinavia. Jensen, "From Denmark to Manti: One Man's Experience."

After partaking of refreshments some of the Elders came in to see us we gave them some ~~of~~ instructions as to the importance of teaching the people whom they bring into the Church in such a way that they would not be disappointed but find in their experience the full realizeation of their hopes and an increase of knowledge which will bind them to the Truth and save them from the evil and sorrow of apostacy. The brethren of our party were there. Their names were Elder [Charles C.] Rich[,] [John] Van Cott[,] J[esse] N. Smith[,] ^and^ [Christian] Madsen. An aged brother was present a widower by the name of Sören Sörensen named by br Van Cott Father Jacob on acount of his age and patriarchal apearence.

August 25, 1861; Sunday. This morning arose and made ourselves ready for the meeting or Conference, which had been apointed at the residence of Mr John Petersen some 11 miles distant from Yearing. About 8 oclock our carriage was in readiness and ^we^ started for meeting acompanied by Sister [Sisilie Marie] Weibye. At 10 oclock arived at the place of meeting and were welcomed by Mr Petersen and his large barn was thrown open for the conference and over the platform a half circle of green interspersed with brightly blushing flowers and in the center of the arch was the ballad of a song of welcome to us composed for the occasion & expressive of their hearty good feeling ~~with~~ with which they received us.

Conference was duly opened by prayr by Elder [Jens C. A.] Weibye and Anders Christensen acting as Clerk of Conference. The Conference was then addressed by Elder [Charles C.] Rich congratulating them on the blessing of haveing the gospel through which th^e^y may know the truth in the midst of the great variety of religious opinions extant in the world. His remarks were translated by Elder Christensen after which Elder [John] Van Cott spoke briefly after which the authorities of the Church were presented to the Conference by Elder Weibye and were sustained after which Elder [Hans Chr.] Hansen spoke to the people after which the meeting ajourned until 2 oclock.

Partook of some refreshments [that] were kindly furnished[,] a liberal treat of good rich milk a luxury rarely meet with in our travils. At 2 oclock the meeting again in cession I spoke to them for half an hour on the advantages resulting from ~~adopting~~ receiveing the gospel in its true spirit and love of the truth which will lead us to entertain kind and charitable feeling[s] towards those who are around us and who difer from us in opinions and thus avoid calling into exercise and against us and the truth a rabid blind opposition by which the progress of the ~~tru~~ Saints and the work of God are often hind^e^red. My remarks were translated by Elders Christensen and Madsen.[133]

The Conference was then addressed by several members of the traviling and local ministry after which we through Elder Van Cott blesse^d^ the people and the conference then ajourned and said our adieus to the Saints and our friends assembled and returned to Yearing. While some of the Elders remained with us I improved the opportunity to impart to them some instruction ~~in~~ in relation to the principle of regeneration for the introduction of which the principle of poligimy was revealed by the application of which [we see] to the regulation of the sexual relations and associations of the race. A check will be put upon those excesses which have so largely contributed to the physical corruption of man-kind.

August 26, 1861; Monday. Rose early and took a walk to enjoy the fresh air an^d^ a pleasant view of the surounding country which seemed one extended plain slightly diversified with gentle undulations stretching its self around us until it met the bright blue of the horizen. The blue sea in the northwest was in sight from our pleasant perch on the height of Yearing.

As we contemplated the country around us clad in its robes of autumnal brown in beautiful contrast with which the white walls of farm houses scatered over its surface were seen as so many bright stars sheding their feeble light over the field of man's toil and care, for they ~~tell~~ ^told^ of the homes humble as they may be of the hardy son's of toil whose labour is ~~the~~ ^a^ country's wealth and whose brawny arms are its strength and whose children are its rising hope for a hapy and prosperous future, under the guidance of Heavens institutions for the development of the Kingdom of God to rule the world.

Returning from our stroll and partakeing of some refreshments

133. Inserted here is a loose sheet that reads: "Welcome. We are holding conference on the border of North Jutland that we may recieve good councel the work of God to forward. From the brethren Lyman, Rich, Van Cott and J N Smith, and other brethren. All are welcome. Hosanna, joy and gladness! On this joyful day for the cause of God and us shal our songs of praise and prayer ascend to thee our God. This song of welcome was composed by Elder J. C. S. Frost and was sung by him in the conference. Translated by Anthon H. Lund."

provided by our kind host [Jens] Wiebye, this done we were again seated in our carriage for a ride into the country on the road to Frederick-haven. We traviled some 16 miles and put up for the night with a brother ~~Soren Nelsen~~ ^Soren Thompsen^ some 3 miles from Frederickhaven. He is a farmer and liveing after the maner of that class in these parts. As to habits and quality of liveing they gave us some boiled barley and milk and then as the beds were ~~m~~ [a] minus they brought in some clean straw and put it down on the ground in their parlour which was with^out^ furniture or floor. A tick filled with light feathers was given us for covering with two pieces ^of cloth^ to supply the place of a sheet which as they felt fearful of the part assigned them in the ministration to our comfort directly sliped away from us like a guilty thing thus leaveing us to nestle in the straw most forcibly reminding us of the humble dwelling of our brother Jesus. The thought was soothing in its effects and we sleept soundly and well on our humble bed of straw rendered soft by warm charity that provided it. The unfurnished condition of the house of our host was not want of age as we were informed it was some 60 years of age its roof of thatch was overgrown with moss of years accumulation.

August 27, 1861; Tuesday. We arose from our sleep refreshed after partakeing breakfast of dried fish and small potatoes we were up and away. Our road to day lay through the low hills ~~hills~~ from the highest portions of which the Categat[134] was in sight to the ~~south west~~ ^east^. The country was broaken and poor. We mad[e] a call as we passed along on some of the Saints who lived by the way side one of whom was a sister who~~se name was~~ [blank] ~~aged~~ ^was^ age^d^ 80 years. She was engaged in weaveing[,] tap[ing], ^and w[h]eeling^ and seemed to be so much attached to the work that she only left it to welcome us and then immediately resumed her work at her loom all the while talking to such of our party as would understand her in the ~~wheet~~ ^sweet^ musickal voice of child-hood. The dwelling was rude made of cobble stone and covered with thatch, and wore the general appearence of squalid poverty in those things that make life hapy and desireable.

Our visit over we rolled on and some farther on we called on a Mr Jense Neilson and wife who made us welcome a[nd] gave us some

134. The Kattegat Strait lies between the Jutland peninsula to the west and Sweden to the east, separating the North Sea from the Baltic Sea.

refreshments. ^They did not belong to the Church.^ After which we passed on to the home of brother Christopher Thompsen and family. He^re^ we were made welcome. Br T. has a most interesting family of wife and seven children the eldest 16 years of age. They were all promiseing and healthy and were enjoying the kindly spirit of the gospel. Our condition as to society and their appreciation of comfort is considerably improved since last night. The people are cleanly and bright and much improved above others in their habits of liveing. We had our beds of straw on the floor in their best room. Our beds were prepared with some care and [we were] provided with some clothing. We slept comfortably and well.

August 28, 1861; Wednesday. This morning rose early and bade our friends farewell and rolled away on the road to Alborg. As we passed we made a call on a br by the name of Niels Mortensen, and with his family had some coffee and bread and butter. As we left this place we were hindered a short time by the breaking of the pole to our carriage. This repaired we rolled on to the residence of Peder Chr. Christensen a farmer belonging to the Church. Himself and wife were in the field but came and made us welcome as soon as they were aware of our comeing. Their greeting was warm and they hastened to give us substantial evidence of our welcome in the character of a pleasant repast [dinner] the leading article of which was fresh fish with corisponding viands [foods]. Closed the repast with coffee and pastry. About 8 oclock rolled away from our kind host and family for Aalborg where we arived ~~in~~ in safety at our lodgings at br [Lauritz P.] Larsens. Passed some time in conversation with the brethren present. It consisted mostly of recurences to the history of our persecutions in Missouri and my own imprisonment there with the Prophet Joseph and others. This evening learned by telegram via N. York of the battle [of Wilson's Creek on August 10] near Springfield Missouri in wh[ich] the Confederate forces und[er] generals [Benjamin] Mac~~coloch~~^Culloch^ and ~~Priche~~ ^[Sterling] Price[,]^ the federal forces under general [Nathaniel] Lyon[,] were engaged and ^the^ federals were defeated and general Lyon killed and report said that Mc~~Colough~~^Culloch and Price were killed.[135]

August 29, 1861; Thursday. This ^morning^ was gratified with the

135. General Lyon was killed but not McCulloch or Price of the Confederacy.

recipt of a leter from my [third] wife Caroline E[ly Partridge] at G. S. L. City to which I wrote an answer. Some believeing friends came in to see us to day they talke of being baptized soon. In the evening when the sober shade of twilight was spread broad over hill and dale myself and brs [John] Van Cott and [Hans Chr.] Hansen went out for a walk dureing ^which^ we visited the cemetery which is highly improved in the floral department of its embelishments. Its walks were neat and intersecting each other at right angles. Its monuments as far as we could judge (by the imperfect light of our evening call on the resting place of the ashes of the departed dead) were simple and chaste. From this rest of the ^dead^ we extended our walk through some forest ground ajacent to the town. Returned to our lodgings refreshed with our exercise taken and the sweet fresh ^pure^ air breathed dureing our stroll.

August 30, 1861; Friday. This morning we had some talk on the subject of tent makeing for the benefit of the emigrating Saints and determined it would be to their intrest as far as they could to provide themselves with tents before starting and those of a good quality so that they would have them when they reached the frontier and when they should arive in Utah. Advised them to make the tents square and suited to the center pole which would save much cloth and render them less exposed to the wind and storm.

This done I wrote a leter to br G[eorge] Q. Cannon in Liverpool and in the evening took [a] short walk of a mile to the hill that overlooks the town. From this point we had a view of Aalborg which is a small town and has the apearence of haveing been built or thrown together without design. The buildings are many of them quite a[n]tique in their apearence. The town has no buildings that put on any pretentions ^as^ to architectural beauty ^or size^ with one or two exceptions. These ~~were~~ one of them is the military hospital and ^the other^ a large steam flowering mill. The Churches[,] of which there are two[,] are rude uncomely <u>piles</u> without attraction save such as are furnished by an ignorant and blind religion. The Jews have one Synagogue. The population is 10,000 its location is in a depression ^of the high land^ of a basin like form on the shore of the Liimfjord, which connects with the North Sea within the distence of ~~60~~ ^17^ miles. The surounding country is almost as desitute of timber as are the great American Deserts. The original forest growth haveing been destroyed the lack of enterprise ^in the people^ in that direction seems to have hindered the reproduction of timber by planting to the growth of which the country is well adapted in soil and climate as indicated by the limited specimines of forest growth which we saw which stil survive the waste of the destroyers of their race to tell the history of the past when waveing forest clad in robes of green bowed their pri[n]cely heads to the influence and pow[e]r of the passing breeze. The principle article of fuel in the town is the turf or pete [moss] which is cut up with a sharp spade in size like bricks and dried when it is fit for use. The labour of its preperation affords employ for both men and women and when dry makes a very good article of fuel.

The people we find in this country by whom the lat^t^er-day work is favorably entertained are of the peasantry or working class. They are in heal^t^h hardy and in habits ^of life^ industrious and economical from training and force of circumstances. In disposition gentle and kind and hospitable to the stranger and not wanting in inteligence that under circumstances favourable to its developement and increase would not fail to produce the legitimate eliments of a nations ~~greatness~~ greatness and strength in the wise and prudent ruler and the enlightened refined and virtuous citisens which could not fail to secure to the nation that possess them the blessings of power and also of perpituity which would be by ~~its~~ ^a^ constant increase of knowledge and corisponding virtue in the people ever saved from decline and disolution and thus life and immortality would become the property of government as it becames known by men through the gospel.

In this country the labours of the field are shared by the men and women jointly[,] manifestly to the prejudice of housewifery as it would be defined by English or American notions of what it should be. This feature in the custom of the country makes a lot of woman one of toil and of ceaseless labour until death gives its welcome rest to wearied mortality and closes a life of little bliss and much labour. This town has an antiquity of 500 years under its present name.

August 31, 1861; Saturday. Passed the day in writeing and in the evening some brothers and sisters came into town in order to attend the conference which had been appointed out of town on the oposite side of the Limfjord, to prevent anoyences from the oposition. Of the above named Saints several came in to look at us and signify that we were welcome to their country and home. They were mostly aggriculterists and hardy fine representatives of their class and seemed contented and hopeful. They furnished good material for the construction of the peaceible Kingdom of God as they combining in themselves (for the age) good physical staminy and fair native talent that culture will make great.

September 1, 1861; Sunday. This morning rose early and in haste partook of some light refreshments and made our way to the ferry and by the help of the breeze we were soon at the oposite shore and a short walk brought us to a point where we were meet by a brother with a team who kindly caried us to our place of meeting at the residence of brother Peter Christen where provision had been made for conference by haveing in readiness a large tent in connection with the two rooms in the house.

At 10 oclock the conference was opened; and was translated by Elder Christensen after which the Priesthood of the Church was presented and sustained after which the time was occupied by Elder [John] Van Cott and several traveling ministry, until half past 12 oclock then ajourned until 2 oclock when the meeting was again in s^e^ssion. There were present some 400 people. I spake to them half an hour. My remarks were translated by brother Christensen after which several of the elders spoke when the conference was blessed and dismissed.

In the fore-noon a school teacher was present and at the conclusion commenced to preach but was told to desist and when I steped from the house he was runing and rolling away at full speed some of the time on his feet and then he seemed to ^have^ changed ends. For a time he went to procure warrents for the persons who had helped send him away but was told he had no busines there so he came to meeting in the afternoon and listened civily and attentively and ^seemed^ to have profited by his admonitory ^tho^ brief experience with the Saints.

Our ~~can~~ conference over we concluded to tarry with brother Christen until Monday which as we learned disappointed many of the curious who mustered at ferry on both shores to see the apostles but were as ^they^ may ~~will~~ be in more important matters disappointed. Several of the members of the ministry remained with us seemeing egar to hear from us all they could dureing our brief stay with them.

September 2, 1861; Monday. This morning the weather fair and not cold. After breakfast we said adieu to our kind hostess Sister Christen and brother Christen kindly brought us to the ferry in his waggon. At this point we bade him farewell and crosed over to our lodgings. In Aalborg found our friends well. Number of Saints and strangers called to ^see us.^ Dur~~e~~ing the evening had singing and conversation with our visitors who thronged our ^rooms^ to see us for the last time for the present. The tickets for our return were procured and births were thus secured for our return to Copenhaven.

September 3, 1861; Tuesday. Weather somewhat darkened with clouds this morning. Made ready for our departure for Copenhagen and spent the residue of the time until ^near^ 5 oclock with our friends at Aalborg when we went on board of the Steamer Dania. ~~It was~~ The weather was wet but the rain ceased soon after we started so that we were on deck. As we passed down the bay to the sea which we reached at 7¼ oclock we were as usual per[s]ecuted by the votaries of tobaco as the[y] cast out the smoke of their stink offer~~ing~~ to the verry serious defilement of the otherwise pure and healthful atmosphere around us. To this point on our journey we had smoth water, [but] the rain admonished us to seek our rooms below. During our stay at br La[r]sens in the afternoon before going on board of the boat a Sweedish sister came to see us by the name of Maria Victor who is working for 16 dollars a year. This however is only one of many similar cases in these lands. The Saints are keenly alive to the subject of emigration and will make strong efforts for next year.

Elder J[esse] N. Smith and also Elder [Hans Chr.] Hansen acompanied us. After we retired to rest we were reminded, by certain significant sounds that disturbed the quiet of our repose that some of the passengers were sick from the increased rolling of the ship.

September 4, 1861; Wednesday. This morning we rose early to seek relief from the ~~festid~~ ^feculent^ air of our close room. As we went on deck the morning seemed opening brightly as the sun arose above the banks of clouds that lay-along the horizon. About the time of rising we past the town of Helsingöer [Helsingør], the sound ajacent to ~~wher~~ ^it^ was covered with shiping awaiting wind to move them to their various destinations.

At 8 oclock landed in Copenhaven found all well at No. 14 Lorentsens Gade, and found leters and papers awaiting us. I received one from

[Francis] Marion [Lyman] in London and one from ~~him~~ my wife Elza to him of the date of July 28th Salt Lake City. Health good at home, crops light. The sale of Fort Critenden[136] was mentioned with ^that of^ other property. I also received leter from br [George Q.] Cannon in Liverpool. I wrote a leter to my son Marion in London, after which I took a walk around the Castilla [Rosenborg Castle]. Had a fine view of the shiping in the harbour and left much refreshed with the excercise.

September 5, 1861; Thursday. After writing a little, this morning myself and brothers [Charles C.] Rich, J[esse] N. Smith, and [Peter W.] Poulson visited the Museum of Northern antiquities.[137] In ^our^ walk we saw an antique tower called Axeltaarn, founded in 1270, as a defence against the pirates by whom the land was infested. The Museum was interesting but haveing no catelogue and but verry brief time, these circumstances detracted much from the intrest of our visit. Among the relixs of antiquity we were shown, a copy of the Bible, printed in 1200, its binding was very elaborate, and embellished with precious stones. And thus affording us evidence of this fact, that men will garnish the sepulchers of the righteous or embellish the record of the word of God, when they will neither respect the ministry or teachings of the one, nor the principels inculcated in the other.

~~The~~ Our contemplation of these relics of antiquity was (though brief and hurried) instructive as showing the pr^i^nciples of progressive improvement, by which men have arived at their present condition and aquirement of mechanical and other knowledge of the arts. Our hasty visit over we returned to our lodgings, weary with being so long on our feet without rest.

As we returned from the Museum we passed through the stables of his Magesty and saw the provisions that ~~royalty~~ ^his magesty^ has made for ~~its~~ ^his^ horses which far exceed in comfort what is enjoyed by thousands of his reasoning subjects. From this point in homeward stroll we visited some encloseures containing a large number of cannons of various sizes and paterns one of which was 25 feet in length and 300

136. Fort Crittenden (originally Camp Floyd) was where federal troops established a base during the Utah War. Because the troops were needed for the Civil War, the camp was evacuated in July 1861.

137. The museum, founded in 1819, was one of the first to divide artifacts by the Stone, Bronze, and Iron Ages. Marryat, *A Residence in Jutland*, 231–33.

years old. We saw many rifled but no brich loading cannon. We wished as we passed along to ^live to^ see the time when all this great outlay for war shall be directed to the promotion of the arts of peace and the din of thundering cannon be hushed into the buisy hums of peaceful industry for the best promotion of man's hapiness.

September 6, 1861; Friday. This morning the weather is dark and rainy. Passed some time in writing in my journal. At one oclock we went out to dine with brother Hager and family Our party consisted of myself Elders [Charles C.] Rich[,] [John] Van Cott[,] J[esse] N. Smith[,] and [Peter W.] Poulson and Larsen a priest.

Din[n]er over we returned to the office where we found the New York Herald ^20th of August^ giveing some of the details of the Battle of Davis [Wilson] Creek in south-western Missouri in which General [Nathaniel] Lyon fell at head of a colum [of] the Iowa troops. The Battle was represented as a hard fought one and verry destructive resulting in favour of the Confederates[,] the federalists retreating on Rollers.[138]

In the Davis Creek Battle general Ben McCulloch of Texean war celebrity and in the circles of diplomacy of Utah Peace commission memory was in command of the Confederates with general Sterling Price of mobocratick notoriety in the reign of Lilburn W. Bogs.[139] Thinking of them ~~they~~ reminds us of our [prison] chain[s]; and of the biter cup O! how biter! of which they are drinking. In all their corruptions and sorrows we can but pity poor misguided humanity. And fondly hope for a brighter ~~dawn~~ day of peace to dawn on the sin-darkened pathway of uneducated ~~humanity~~ and degenerate man.

From the Herald we learn that while the powers of Europe are giveing evidence of their progressive movements in the direction of liberty and freedom by the giveing up of the pasport system the federal

138. The *Herald* focused on the threat to Washington, DC, after the defeat in Virginia. It is possible that Lyman's familiarity with Missouri led him to focus on the detail of General Lyon's death. Meanwhile, "rollers" were horse-drawn ambulances with wooden dowels in the beds, on which field surgeons slid litters, now called stretchers. They were so much in demand, the wagon manufacturer Studebaker began mass-producing them the next year.

139. Lyman was escorted to captivity by Sterling Price during the Mormon War of 1838. Parley P. Pratt remembered Price more charitably as someone who protected Mormons from attack. Pratt, *History of the Late Persecution*, 25; Gentry and Compton, *Fire and Sword*, 401–03.

government has retrogressed in the direction of barbarism by ~~its~~ ^this^ adoption of its relic.[140] Dark are the clouds that hang around thee My Country and could tears avail to wash away thy deep, dark, and damning sins all might well wish my head ~~were~~ ^was^ a fountain to pour out its ceasless streams to cleans and save thee;.

But whence we ask ^comes^ the darkness that enshrouds thee? Truth indicates the answer in the terpitude of thy Sins that have rendered thee deaf to the admonitions of Heaven and reckless of the Blood of its Ministers and children. Thus thy sins have dreged the cup (of thy national greatness and glory) with corruption and disolution and even now they force the poisened chalice to thy lips. The wages of thy sins the legitimate harvest of that which thou has sown.

September 7, 1861; Saturday. Remained in the office engaged principaly in writeing until 7 oclock in the evening when in company with Elders [John] Van Cott and [Charles C.] Rich I crossed the sound in the Steamer Hamlet to Malmö in Sweeden where we meet the Conference President Elder Niels Rosengreen [Nils Rosengren] by whom we were conducted to the residence of brother Niels Jensen by whom we were welcomed and br R[ich] and my self were provided with lodgeings. The greeting of our friends ~~were~~ ^was^ warm altho spoken in a language we did not understand. We learned that some members of br Jensen's family had emigrated the last season. They were two ~~of his~~ daughters. The streets gave indications of recent heavy showers of rain.

September 8, 1861; Sunday. At the unusualy early hour of 8 oclock we meet the Saints in their hall which was crowded to overflowing ~~with~~ ^as well as^ some ajoining rooms. The conference was opened and then addressed by brother [Charles C.] Rich whose remarks were translated by President [Nils] Rosengreen.

Brother Riche's remarks were preceded by a partial representation of the conference by ~~the~~ a portion of the traviling ministry. From the statistical report it apeared that the entire conf[erence] numbered 6010 [members].[141] After this br [John] Van Cott addressed the meeting. The

140. The Confederate Congress passed a law requiring uniform identification of national identity and residence to thwart northern spies. Coulter, *The Confederate States of America, 1861–1865*, 7:396–97.

141. Jesse N. Smith recorded the Swedish membership at the time as 6,055. Jenson, *LDS Biographical Encyclopedia*, 1:321.

meeting was then ajourned for one hour when at 11 oclock the meeting was again in cession. I addressed the meeting for half an hour my remarks were designed to be instructive to the ministry in the nature of their duties as ministers of the gospel of peace. My remarks were translated by Prest Rosengreen after which the Priesthood of the Church was presented and sustained unanimously then ajourned for one hour. The meeting was again in cession at 2 oclock when some local business was transacted folowed by remarks from Prest Van Cott and Rosengreen after which I said some words of adieu to the Saints and blest them and the conference then ajourned. We then went to sup[p]er with brother John Anderson. Br A has two sons in the ministry the youngest is 16 years old. The members of the ministry here are all promising young men and full of the spirit of the work in which they are engaged.

September 9, 1861; Monday. This morning in company with brothers [Charles C.] Rich and [John] Van Cotts I had a pleasant stroll through the town which is located on low flat land that rises barely above the water of the sound ajacent to which it stands. It is not entirely void of beauty haveing some fine shaded walks that evince some taste in their arangement and design to minister to the comfort of the citizens. The town is encircled by a moat that connects with and is supplied ~~by the sound~~ from the sound. ~~Its~~ ^The^ population ^of the town^ is 18000. Oil is here made from the rape seed [canola oil]. At ¼ to 1 oclock we came to Copenhagen on [a] Helsing~~n~~nør [Helsingør] [ferry]. Found all well did not go out this evening.

September 10, 1861; Tuesday. To day visited the palace ~~at~~ ^and^ grounds of Fredricksborg [Frederiksberg] situated some 4 miles from this point in the suburban portion of the city. This is the point from which Nelson gained command of the city. The highest part of this ground is crowned with the splendid resivoir from which the city receives the principal parts of its water.[142] Returned from stroll weary. Sup[p]er and the couch were welcome. Under their soothing influence[,] wearied nature for the time forgot its sor^r^ows.

September 11, 1861; Wednesday. This morning I finished and sent my

142. The caves behind the palace were excavated in 1856 and found to have subterranean cisterns, which were tapped for culinary water three years later.

leter to brother [George Q.] Cannon. This engaged me with writeing in my journal while brother [Charles C.] Rich and others went out in town.

At 5 oclock went to see the Tivoli or pleasure grounds or gardens.[143] The grounds were thronged with several thousands of visiors who all were civil and courtious in their behavior. ^There were^ no noisey demonstration of feeling such as would be witnessed in similar assemblies in England or in America all were staid and sober; saw no drunkenness.

The arangement and the decorations of the grounds were tastful and as night set in the place was illuminated with some 8000 lamps (that shed their light on the surrounding scenery through the varied transparencies that were around them). To these were added some 1000 ~~jets~~ jetteaus of gass all of which gave ^to^ the place an apearence of gorgeous splendor and dazeling beauty. In the midst of all this briliant display we could not surpress the thought of the poor whose labour had made the gorgeous display around us and who were stil left in their poverty to stil toil on in the battle of life without enjoying the benefit of their own labour. We left the grounds after some hours weary.

The pyrotechnic display that we witnessed was grand and sublime; the number of visitors to the gardens to day were as reported in the paper ^~~was~~^ 10,000.

September 12, 1861; Thursday. This morning I wrote ^for^ some-time in my journal. During the day ^I^ received letters one from President Brigham Young and one from my wife—Priscilla in Minersville and in it a note from Father[-in-law] Theodore Turley. Past the residue of the day in reading mostly from the New York Herald which came to day.

September 13, 1861; Friday. To day wrote leters to my [seventh] wife Priscilla in Minersville, Beaver County, Utah, and one to [second wife] Dionetia at the same place and one to Father Theodore Turley [Priscilla's father]. And in the evening wrote one to br John Brown in London. Received and read the M[illennial] Star.

September 14, 1861; Saturday. Today attended a meeting of the Priesthood of the Copenhagen Conf. I heard their representations of the condition of their several fields of labour which shewed the work to be

143. Tivoli Gardens (Kjøbenhavns Tivoli og Vauxhall) had lavish landscaping, bandstands, restaurants, and a theater, as well as a merry-go-round and an early roller-coaster called a gravity railroad, making it a kind of amusement park.

progressive finely. I gave them some instruction in relation to the feelings and views with which they should preach the gospel to the world in order to secure its favourable consideration by those to whom it should be preached without calling out ~~unnecesary~~ opposition to the good we ~~were~~ ^are^ seeking to acomplish. Br [Charles C.] Rich addressed the meeting. Our remarks were translated by brs [Christian] Madsen and [Hans Chr.] Hansen.

On returning to the office ^I^ received leters from brothers [George Q.] Cannon and D[avid] M. Stuart. Some rain this evening. Brother Stuart writes encourageingly of the condition and prospects of the work in Scotland: And that more evidences of the corruption of Elder John Tobin had been developed since his excommunication and departure from the country. Was not out to-day except to the meeting. Passed some time in reading and studying the English language.

September 15, 1861; Sunday. This morning at 10 oclock we meet with the Saints of the Copenhagen Conference (in a hall hired for the occasion). The number of Saints in the Conference ~~was~~ ^is^ 1136 of whom some 8 or 9 hundred were in attendence at the hall ^and many strangers.^ The conference was opened by singing and prayr after which the meeting was addressed by brother [Charles C.] Rich and his remarks were translated by Elder Anders Christensen after which the meeting ajourned until 2 oclock at which time it was again in cession and the Priesthood of the Church was presented and sustained by an unanimous vote of the conference after which some local business was introduced by President Poulson and disposed of after which I addressed the meeting encourageing the Saints to cultivate the habit of thinking of the gospel as embraceing evry good that can enhance their hapiness and has only to be known and justly comprehended ~~to~~ ^and it will^ meet every requirement of humanity ~~my remarks~~ thus secureing them against discontent and its consequence apostacy. My remarks were translated by Elder Christensen after which President [John] Van Cott offered some few closeing remarks and for us blessed the congregation and thus closed our very pleasant conference with the warm hearted Saints of Copenhaven.

After we returned to our lodgings several of the sisters came in and cheered us with singing some of the songs of that Zion they hop^e^ ultimately to enjoy as their home. Our pleasant interview with our friends was at length closed ^with a prayr for our mutual blessing.^ They bade us farewell; and departed and we retired to rest.

September 16, 1861; Monday. This morning as we entered upon our writeing a brother and some sisters came in to receive the ordinance of the laying on of hands for their healing. Brothers [Charles C.] Rich[,] [John] Van Cott[,] and [Jesse N.] Smith administered to them. My attention was called to a leter from the pen of Miss Fredericka Bremer expressive of her partial feelings for a maried man. It may be found in the 16 volume No 47 of the Millennial Star under the head of varieties.[144]

At 11 oclock myself and brs Rich Van Cott and J. N. Smith visited the residence of Sister Larsen to whom we administered for her health after which we partook of some chocolate and pastry and then returned to the office and resumed our writieing. Some of the brethren called in to see us and exchange salutations.

At 7 oclock myself and brothers Rich Van Cott and Smith called on some friends by the name of Thomp^s^on who had for some cause been cut off from the church for some years. They received us kindly and expressed their wishes to soon unite with the Church again which we advised them to do. We tasted with them some excellent wine. Brother T[hompson] is engaged in a wine store.

September 17, 1861; Tuesday. This morning I commenced to write a leter to President Brigham Young in answer to his of July 26th. Passed the day in writeing did not go out. Br [Charles C.] Rich visited a picture gallery. To day received some papers from Liverpool not rich in news.

September 18, 1861; Wednesday. To day continued my leter to the Prest [Brigham Young] and was not out today. In the evening we were presented in the office with a boquet of fine flowers by Sister Emelia Frost. Gave the sisters present some advise for the regulation of their action in reference to Matrimony while goeing to and when arived in Utah to save them from doing wrong. ~~Char~~[les]

September 19, 1861; Thursday. This morning closed my leter to the President [Brigham Young] ^and^ bought a hand book of Copenhagen.

144. Fredericka Bremer was a Swedish novelist and feminist. Her short piece in the *Millennial Star* was read by Mormons as a kind of defense of polygamy. One line read, "I confess, then, that I never find a man more captivating than when he is a married man. A man is never so handsome, never so perfect in my eyes, as when he is a husband and the father of a family." *Millennial Star* 16, no. 47 (Nov. 25, 1854): 751.

At 4 oclock Dined with brother Rasmussen and family who expressed themselves much pleased to entertain us in their humble home. Brother [John] Van Cott received the New York Herald containing details of news that had been intimated by the Telegraph previously from London.

September 20, 1861; Friday. The morning opened bright and clear. Had some pain in my head produced by indigestion and want of pure air. Walked out with Brother [John] Van Cott around the South eastern portion of the city had a pleasant view of the sound and of the Island of Amager. On my return received [Millennial] Stars from Liverpool and the [Liverpool] Mercury [newspaper]. In the everning we made ourselves ready for Saturday's journey.

September 21, 1861; Saturday. This morning rose at 5 and at 7 oclock. Myself and brothers [Charles C.] Rich[, John] Van Cott[,] and J[esse] N. Smith left Copenhaven on the carrs for Kosor where we arived at half past 10 oclock and from thence we passed by steamer to the Isleand of Fyn landing at the town of Nyborg (a distance from Kossor of 18 miles) in a northern [western] direction. In makeing this crossing we passed a small island called Sprogö [Sprogø] [blank] ~~leaving it~~ which we left to our right ^hand^ as we past. We reached Nyborg at 12 oclock. After a detention of half an hour we were seated in a post cariage for the residue of our travil to Odense[145] where we arived at 4¼ oclock and were meet and welcomed by Elder ~~Renow~~ [Christian P.] Rönnow[146] President of the Conference and conducted to his residence where lodgeings were provided for our party. Here we meet with District Presidents K[nud] C. Brown.[147] Odense is the principal town on the isleand and has a population of 16 or 18000 and second to Copenhagen in Denmark proper.

September 22, 1861 Sunday. This day we meet with the Saints of the Fyen Conference[148] who number 170. We had a very pleasant meeting.

145. Odense is a large Danish city on Funen Island, known for clothing production.

146. Christian Peter Rönnow had been president of the conference for four years. In 1860, while employed by the church, he married Margrethe Kirstine Clausen Hansen, a widow with two children, and moved with her to Utah two years later. She died in childbirth that same year, upon which Christian married Laurine Emilie Hansen and had ten children together in Panaca, Nevada. Of his four polygamous wives, one left him for another man and another returned to her husband and children in Denmark.

147. A thirty-one-year-old Danish traveling missionary, Knud H. Bruun was nearly beaten to death for preaching Mormonism. He immigrated in 1877 to Utah. See Jenson, *History of the Scandinavian Mission*, 46, 151.

148. Fyn is the Danish name for what in English is Funen Island, the large

After the opening[,] the meeting was addressed by brother [Charles C.] Rich. His remarks were translated; by Elder [Knud H.] Brown [Bruun] after which President [John] Van Cott instructed the Saints. The meeting ajourned until 3 oclock when the meeting was again in cession. I spoke to the audience for nearly half an hour brother Br[uu]n translated ~~after which~~.

The priesthood of the Church was presented and sustained. In the morning Elder [Jesse N.] Smith addressed the meeting brother Van Cott then blessed the Saints and the conference ajourned. There were some baptisms dureing the day ^and^ we ministered to some sick. Our place of meeting was handsomely decorated with wreaths of ever-green; and flowers with appropriate mottoes. In the evening were treated by a Sister Sirenson to a small muskmellon that was grown in a hothouse. We ate and thought of our own mountain home.

September 23, 1861; Monday. This morning I was engaged in writing my journal. Brother [Charles C.] Rich walked ^out^ with some of the brethren and while they were out ~~the~~ rain was falling freely and continued for some hours. After din[n]er I walked with the brethren to the residence of br Niels Jorgensen and family with whom we drank some coffee after which in company with brother [John] Van Cott I took a walk in the Park of [King] Christian the Seventh in which stands his palace. The park is beautifuly embellished with forest trees and flower shrubery.

As we returned we called on a Sister Bodel Clawson who treated us to some pairs [pears] and plumbs. My health is not good, walking gives me much pain in my back attended with nerveous irritibility. In the evening I witnessed a representation of the character, customs, and costume of the inhabitints of the Island of Fan[ø] which is situated on the west of Jutland and its inhabitents are sustained by fishing.

September 24, 1861; Tuesday. This morning some rain ~~was~~ ^is^ falling. My health not very good went with brothers [Knud H.] Br[uu]n, [John] Van Cott, and [Jesse N.] Smith and had a fine and pleasant bathe. On returning to our lodgings I had no appetite for din[n]er. To day myself brothers [Charles C.] Rich, Van Cott, and Smith were each of us presented with a silk handkerchief by Sister Bodel Clawson. After din[n]er

oval-shaped isle between Jutland to the west and Zealand to the east where Copenhagen is located.

I went with a party of brethren and Sister [Margrethe Kirstine] Rönnow to visit the Chapel of Canute the Great[149] whose bones were shown to us inclosed in an antique coffin. The length of the building is 200 feet and height 75 feet. A large organ ~~was~~ ^is^ in process of building which would cost 5000 dollars. The building has an antiquity of 800 years and is in good repair.

Returned to our lodgings weary. In the evening attended a meeting of the Saints and some strangers. The meeting was addressed by severall of the native elders. Brother Smith then spoke and then brother Rich whose remarks were translated by brother [Knud H.] Brow [Bruun]. After meeting I gave the Elders who were with us some instruction ~~as to~~ in regard to their governing of themselves in their preaching, not to preach to[o] much at once and to the same audience as they might be wearied and disgusted when if more judiciously treated an increaseing intrest would be awakened in them.

September 25, 1861; Wednesday. To day in company with brothers [Charles C.] Rich, [John] Van Cott, [Jesse N.] Smith and [Christian P.] Rennow I called on a widow Hansen who did not belong to the Church. She received us kindly and entertained us with fruit and coffee. In the evening held meeting some strangers were present. I spake to the audience about 40 minutes. My remarks were translated by brother [Knud H.] Br[uu]n who then spoke until time to close the meeting after which we administered to several persons for their health and then ritired to rest.

September 26, 1861; Thursday. To day we left Odense and traviled with our party consisting of myself brothers [Charles C.] Rich, [John] Van Cott, [Knud H.] Br[uu]n, [Christian P.] Rennow and [Jesse N.] Smith to the residence of brother Hanse Andersen a farmer with whom we taried dureing the night. While here a Mrs Andersen, who came some 9 miles to see us, was baptized and confirmed.

While here we visited a tract ^of^ pine forest of some hundred acres in extent the trees of which have been planted; and are from one to 17 years of age and they showed a corisponding diference in height. As we returned to our lodgings we encountered a shower of rain which admonished us of the folly of leaveing ^as we did^ our ~~umber^r^eler~~ umbrellas.

149. Canute the Great helped his father, Sweyn, conquer England. After his father's death, Canute ruled Denmark, England, Norway, and part of Sweden.

These were sent ^to^ us by our kind hostess and reached us just as the shower was easing.

September 27, 1861; Friday. This morning at half past 7 oclock we bade our hostess and children adieu and in company of brother [Hans] Andersen we traviled away on our road to Middle Fart.[150] On our way we called on a friend by the name of Andersen who treated us to coffee, cakes and wine. We arived in Middle Fart at 2 oclock where we dined with Sister Matilda Groos[151] and a friend and family by the name of Fredrick Larsen. From this point we crossed the little belt [Strait] on to Jutland and then by hired carriage we came to Viele[152] at 8 oclock and were welcomed by President [Johannes P. R.] Joh[a]nson.

Took sup[p]er and retired to bed weary haveing traviled nearly 50 miles dureing the day. Our travil was very pleasant affording us a fine view of the country which much resembles some of the finest and best cultivated portions of the rural districts of England or Scotland.

September 28, 1861; Saturday. ~~I~~ ^We^ arose this morning refreshed by our nig^h^ts rest. When we arose we found brs [John] Van Cott and [Knud H.] Brown [Bruun] had gone out for a walk but did not return until near 10 oclock when we had our breakfast after which I past some time in writeing and then took a walk into the Beech forest that is ajacent to the town. From the sumet of the wood crowned hill we had a pleasant view of the valley above the town and also of the the bay below. The view of this valley was truly interesting to the lover of rural beauties. While I am writeing some of the traviling ministry are comeing in to attend the conference. The weather to day is pleasant and warmer than for some day p^a^st. This evening attended a meeting of the Priesthood of the conference. The meeting was addressed by brother [Charles C.] Rich his remarks were translated by Prest [Johannes P. R.] Joh[a]nson. Some local buisness was transacted and the meeting ajourned.

September 29, 1861; Sunday. This morning ^at 10 oclock^ meet the

150. Middelfart is a town on Funen Island. The name literally means "middle way," in reference to its position on the Lillebaelt Strait.

151. Esaimine Mathilde Grooss took out a Perpetual Emigration Fund loan in 1862 and traveled to Utah. She married Carl Nilsson in 1866. They divorced a few years later and she married Frederick Hansen and lived in Provo until her death in 1926.

152. Vejle is twenty miles northwest of Middelfart and forty-five miles southwest of the prominent city of Aarhus. Fredericia, which Lyman mentions, lies between Middelfart and Vejle.

Saints in conference. After the meeting was duly opened the audience was addressed by brother [Charles C.] Rich his remarks were translated by President [Knud H.] Br[uu]n. The assembly was then addressed by President [John] Van Cott after which the Priesthood of the Church was presented to the conference and was unanimously sustained. The meeting then ajourned ~~until~~ 2 oclock.

Meeting again in cession and was addressed by myself for some 45 minutes my remarks were translated by Prest Brown [Bruun]. Elder Jesse N. Smith then addressed the meeting and was folowed by Elders Br[uu]n and Johnson ^by^ whom the meeting was briefly addressed. The Saints were then blessed on our behalf by Prest Van Cott and the conference then ajourned. A good spirit prevailed with the people and some were added to the church by baptism. We administered to some persons who were sick and thus closed the labours of the day ^and^ our hapy meeting with the Saints of ~~Veile~~ ^Fredericia^ Conference. The Saints number in ~~Veile~~ ^Fredericia^ Conference 270.

Our labour done myself and brothers Rich, ^Smith^ and Johnson walked out a short distence to the sumit of a beech-clad hill. Here we reclined on a seat which had been kindly provided to refresh the weary pedestrian whose desire to see and contemplate the beauties of the surounding scenery shoul[d] induce him to make the toilsome ascent.

From our forest perch we had a beautiful open and clear view to the westward of the valley in which beneath us was reposeing the town of Veile, the houses of which with their white walls and red tile roffs appeared in beautiful contrast with the sable green of the lovely valley in which it is built and the hills ~~that~~ ^by which it is^ surounded. The town has a population of near five thousand. The flower gardens and the forests were taxed to afford their floral beauties and deathless ever-green to decorate the meeting hall for our welcome.

September 30, 1861; Monday. This morning opened with pleasant weather. We received leter and papers from Liverpool the first from Elder E[dward] L. Sloan to myself and brother [Charles C.] Rich. At 3 oclock brother [John] Van Cott left for Copenhagen, he expects to join us next Saturday. This evening myself in company with brothers Rich, [Knud H.] Br[uu]n, [Johannes P. R.] Joh[a]nson, and J[esse] N. Smith visited the family of brother Groneman.

On our way thither we passed through a beautiful pine forest on the hill from the sumit of which we had a fine view of the bay, on the placid bosom of which was resting a small quantity of ^the^ shiping that is employed in supplying the commercial wants of this portion of the country. The principle exports of which are grain and ~~stock~~ cattle. Their imports are lumber and timber from Norway and Sweeden and iron and coal from England and Sweeden. Returned to our lodgeings weary and with severe pain in my back. Retired to bed but did not rest well.

October 1, 1861; Tuesday. This morning brought forward my writeing in my journal to the present date. In the evening I went to examine a small wind-mill made and used for raiseing water on a meadow. Such mills as the one I examined could be profitably used in many parts of Utah and thereby secure the profitable cultivation of much land (that is now idle and worthless) for hay and grain.

October 2, 1861; Wednesday. This morning the weather opened bright and clear. I wrote a leter to br [George Q.] Cannon in Liverpool. After dispaching my leter passed the time in conversation with the brethren.

October 3, 1861; Thursday. At 10 oclock this morning we left Veile for Horsens a distance of 16 m[ile]s where we arived at half past 1 oclock and stoped with brother A. Nielsen by whose kind lady our wants were considered and a rich repast was provided of which we partook and then in company with brothers [Johannes P. R.] Joh[a]nson and [Jesse N.] Smith went out for a walk dureing which we visited the Caroline garden [Caroline Amalie Lund] and then we went to the Brick-yard where draining pipes and bricks were being made. The pipes by machinery and the brick by hand. Horsens is a small town situated at the inland terminus of the bay of the same name and has a population of 9000. In the evening several of the sisters came in to see us. The brethren of the priesthood exept brs [Charles C.] Rich and Smith all went to the meeting.

October 4, 1861; Friday. At half past 5 oclock myself and brother [Charles C.] Rich and [Knud H.] Br[uu]n started for Aarhuus where we arived half-past 10 oclock and were welcomed by brothers Peter C. Geertsen[153] and Wm Cluff. The country over which we passed to day ~~was~~ ^is^

153. Peter Christian Geertsen was called on a mission a year after he converted. Six years into his mission, he was called as president of the Aarhus Conference, a position he held for another three years. Geertsen, ed., "The Journal of Peter Christian

highly cultivated and pleasantly diversified with hill and dale. The soil is richer than that of north Jutland or Aalborg County and has more timber. Our observation of the country was limited by the close ~~character~~ ^cover^ of our carraige. (<u>Arhus</u>) has a population of 11,000 and 67 Saints.

In the evening took a short walk to the hill that comands a view of town and a fine view sea-ward below the blue of the distant horizon in the distence was to be seen Samsee [Samsø] a small isleand. The ocean expance was spread out beneath us in placid beauty and inviteing loveliness. The gentle zephyr that breathed its ~~gentlest~~ softest evening music over the smo[o]th unruffled bosom of the deep disturbed not its rest but ~~with~~ ^as^ ~~the~~ ^a^ blessing to the waiting marriner ~~of~~ its peaceful impulses swelled the broad-spread bosoms of his waiting sails. And as tho impelled by the breadth of heaven the noble ship arayed in the habiliments of the sea now moved majestick as a thing of life as she past outward on her ocean path. We gazed on ~~the~~ ^her^ receding ~~picture~~ ^form^ until her lines became (in the distance that parted us) more or less indistinct like the fadeing recollections of the fleeting night dream, the dear object of which has long since joined the concourse of the bright ones who have past away and the light of ~~their~~ ^whose^ smile has faded from the circle in which we still are pushing forward in the life-long struggle of the soul for its ~~own~~ immancipation from sin and that hapy release which will enable the weary and worn voygers over life's rough sea to join (in the hapy climes of uninterrupted ~~hapiness~~ ^peace^ and joy[)] the bright circle of the just and good ^who have departed^ to taste with them in a hapy reunion, sweetened by virtue and inocence made brilliantly glorious and beautiful by the light of truth and deathless by a glorious-immortality, the fullness of that perpetualy increaseing hapines for the attainment and enjoyment of which humanity is constituted.

Full of the cheering thoughts suggested by this hopeful view of our present and the future that awaits us I returned to ~~our~~ ^my^ lodgeings and past some time in teaching some of the Elders in reference to the principles of the gospel and their duties.

October 5, 1861; Saturday. This morning after breakfast walked out to the ground and building used for drilling the recruits to the d[r]aggoons

Geertsen," 178. After he immigrated to Utah, he was summoned back to Denmark as a missionary two more times, then imprisoned in Utah as a polygamist in 1889.

[cavalry] and witnessed for a time their exercise. From this point we visited the railroad building in process of erection ~~and~~ after which in company with brother Wm Cluff I went to a high point of land contiguous to the sea from which we enjoyed a pleasant land and seaward view. The others of our party brothers [Charles C.] Rich and ~~Geritson~~ ^[Knud H.] Br[uu]n^ and ~~Christophesen~~ haveing returned to our lodgings.

Rough sea to day but the wind is favourable for brother [John] Van Cott who arived at 4 oclock in good health. Left all well at Copenhaven. At night attended a meeting of the priesthood of the conference at which some local buisness was disposed of and the priesthood were instrusted by brother Rich[,] translation by brother Br[uu]n.

October 6, 1861; Sunday. To day at 10 oclock we meet with the Saints of the Aarhuus Conference in a hall hired for the occasion. Of the Saints who number in the Conference 270, some 250 were present and some strangers. After the conference was duly opened the audience was addressed by br [Charles C.] Rich. His remarks were translated by Elder P[eter] C. Geertsen after which the meeting was addressed by br [John] Van Cott who was followed by br [Sören] Christoffersen. The meeting then ajourned; previous to the ajournment the priesthood of the Church was presented and sustained by an unanimous vote.

At 2 oclock the meeting again in cession and the audience which increased beyond the morning attendence by a large number of strangers who came in to hear and to feast their eyes in seeing the wonder of liveing Apostles. I spake near half an hour my remarks were translated by brother [Knud H.] Br[uu]n the audience listened attentively altho many were standing.[154] Brothers Br[uu]n and Geertsen addressed the meeting after which brother Van Cott blest the audience on our behalf and the conference ajourned.

In the evening the rooms at our lodgeing were crowded with Saints and friends who came to see us and speak words of welcome and thanks for our brief visit from which a good influence seems to be ariseing which promises increase to the Church of such as love the truth. They cheered us with the song and we prayed with and blessed them and parted with them.

154. Lyman wrote the last ten words of this sentence twice, implying that he was copying from a rough draft.

October 7, 1861; Monday. This morning at 11 oclock myself brs [Charles C.] Rich and [John] Van Cott parted ^with^ our warmhearted friends in Aarhuus and came by steamer to Kosar and from thence to Copenhaven by rail where we arived at 4 oclock P.M. Found all well and sup[p]er awaiting us. ^Found leters from br [George Q.] Cannon and President [Brigham] Young. Good news from home of date of 15 of August.^

October 8, 1861; Tuesday. This morning I received leters from my [fourth] wife Eliza [Partridge] and my brother[-in-law] Edward Partridge. The news from home was all good and cheering. Did not go out to day ^but^ passed the time mostly in reading the English and American papers ^and^ made arangements today for some garments to be made while we are gone to Norway.

October 9, 1861; Wednesday. This morning I wrote and sent a leter to [fourth wife] Eliza in answer to hers and at half past 11 oclock myself and brothers [Charles C.] Rich and [John] Van Cott went on board of the Steamer Princess Louisa for Christiana[155] in Norway. We left the port at half past 12 oclock. The weather was fine and a smo[o]th sea. Dureing the night we came to the town of Gotenberg where we were joined by Elder [Ola N.] Liljenquist.

October 10, 1861; Thursday. This morning was detained in my room with Sea-sickness and did not rise until 2 oclock P.M. Did not take any din[n]er. At 12 oclock we arived at the landing at Christiana and were meet and welcomed by brother Charles Doreas[156] and conducted to lodgings provided for us at the residence of brother [blank].

October 11, 1861; Friday. At 10 oclock this morning we meet with the Saints in conference and heard reports from the traviling and local Priesthood. We dined with brother ~~Halstensen and family~~ Ott~~n~~ersen & family. At 3 oclock the meeting was in cession after the buisness was dispached. The meeting was then addressed by brother [Charles C.] Rich. The Saints listened with aparent intrest. His remarks were translated by Elder [Ola N.] Liljenquist. Meeting was then ajourned until Sunday

155. King Christian IV of Denmark and Norway renamed the city of Oslo after himself, as Christiana, in 1624, and it was not until 1925 that the city regained its original name. It is about 375 miles north of Copenhagen on a fjord inlet of the North Sea.

156. Carl C. N. Dorius left home in 1857 and traveled to Utah at age 27. He was asked to return as a missionary to Scandinavia, where he stayed until 1863 and then settled in Ephraim, Utah, as a farmer and bishop until his death in 1894.

13th at 10 oclock. We took sup[p]er where we dined and then returned to our lodgeings.

October 12, 1861; Saturday. To day passed the morning in writeing. A brother Jensen came in with his daughter [Dorthea] who was deaf we gave them some advise and the daughter was baptized she haveing been several years away from the Church. Went out to dine with brother [Hans] Halstensen and family.[157] Some of our party went out for a walk after diner. I remained with the family to whom I gave instruction through brother [Carl] Doreas in regard to the promotion of ^the^ health of themeslves and children. As we were leaveing our friend in the evening as we passed down the stairway brother [Charles C.] Rich made a mistep or sliped and strained his ankle so that a cariage had to be procured for conveying him to his lodgeings.

October 13, 1861; Sunday. This morning brother [Charles C.] Rich is able to walk and with us attended the conference which was in cession at 10 oclock. I spoke to the audience for near half an hour encourageing the Saints to live their religion while they are forced to remain in the land of the wicked, away from home and the Saints in Zion. My remarks were translated by brother [Ola N.] Liljenquist. Meeting ajourned until 3 oclock at which time it was again in cession and brother Rich addressed the audience and was folowed by brothers [John] Van Cott and Liljenquist. ~~After~~ Dureing the after-noon the Priesthood of the Church was presented and sustained unanimously after which the conference was ajourned. We took super with Sister Sorensen and small party of friends. We passed the eveneing pleasantly brother Rich's lameness is no worse.

October 14, 1861; Monday. This morning wrote a leter for Sister Dorthea Jensen who is deaf. Received leter from my wife Lydia in Farmington dated Sept 5th and one from br E[zra] T. Bensen in Cache Valley. Took diner with brother Ole Petersen and while here received papers from ^the^ states and Liverpool containing some stiring war news.[158] We took super with brother Raul Christensen after which br [John] Van

157. Hans Halsteensen and his wife Hilda emigrated in 1866, two years before three of his young daughters were able to travel to Utah and reunite with the family in 1868.

158. Lyman would have learned of the Union defeat at Lexington, Missouri, on September 20 and of the endorsement of the Confederacy by the *London Post* on October 5. The Mormon view was that the country was being punished for how it had treated the Latter-day Saints.

Cott and other brethren attended a meeting of the local priesthood. Myself and brother [Charles C.] Rich did not attend.

October 15, 1861; Tuesday. The weather dark and wet this morning. Brought forward my journal to date as above after which in company with brothers [John] Van Cott and [Ola N.] Liljinquist and [Carl] Dorius I went and past the day with brother Johnson and family. Instructed them in the principles of the gospel they seemed to be edified and blest. Br [Charles C.] Rich was prevented from goeing with us by his lameness and some writing he had to do.

October 16, 1861; Wednesday. To day myself brothers [Charles C.] Rich and [John] Van Cott and [Carl] Dorius and [Ola N.] Liljenquist visited and dined with brother Jorgen Larsen and family. Took super with brother Peter Christensen and family. Brother Rich went to our lodgeing before super. Past the day pleasantly in giveing instruction to the Saints who were present. They seemed Hapy and blessed by our visit and instructions to them. The city ^of Christania^ has a population of 50000 and as I was informed there were several hundreds of men and women under medical treatment in the hospital for the venerial dissease. The moon was shineing brightly as we returned to our lodgeings.

October 17, 1861; Thursday. This morning the weather is bright and clear but cool. We dined and past the aftrnoon with brother Jacobsen and family and party of friends. At night we attended ~~to~~ a meeting of the branch. Had a pleasant interview addressed the Saints briefly and bade them adieu. As we returned to our lodgeings a fire was discovered in a house opposite our lodgings. It was however soon extinguished after which we retired to rest. The weather quite cool and wintery.

October 18, 1861; Friday. To day received papers from br [George Q.] Cannon in Liverpool also leter from the same to myself and brother [Charles C.] Rich. Brother Rich received a leter from J[ohn] L. Smith in Switzerland.[159] I visited and dined with a brother B. Miller and family after which we took super with a brother Gulbrandsen and family. While we were there Brother [Carl] Dorius went to procure our tickets for our return to Gotenberg but learning the steamer did not call at that place

159. John Lyman Smith was president of the Swiss mission, 1861–64, after which he returned to Fillmore, then settled in St. George to be near the temple until his death in 1898.

he procured tickets for Copenhagen and we were by this change forced to disappoint the Saints in Gotenberg whom we had designed to visit on our return. We returned to our lodgings and made ready for our early morning start in the morrow after which amidst the prayrs and good wishes of friends we retired to secure what rest we could dureing the few hours that were remaining for this use for us.

October 19, 1861; Saturday. This morning took an early breakfast and went on board of the steamer Princess Louise which started at 6 oclock. Bade our friends adieu the remembrences of their kindness we shall ever cherish as we pray for the blessings of our Father to be ever multiplied uppon them. We had fine weather and smo[o]th water the day passed with but little sea-sickness but enough however to spoil our din[n]er. After a fast of some 15 hours we took sup[p]er and retired to bed and enjoyed a good nights sleep.

October 20, 1861; Sunday. This morning opened clear and pleasant with some head-winds. We arived in Copehagen ¼ past 3 oclock. Found all well at the [mission] office.

October 21, 1861; Monday. This morning myself and brother [Charles C.] Rich ordered us each a trunk to be completed by next Friday noon. After wich I wrote a leter to brother [George Q.] Cannon in Liverpool. My health not verry good to day.

October 22, 1861; Tuesday. To day puchased some maps of Denmark and passed the day principally in reading. Walked out in the evening was not well the night was cool and pleasant.

October 23, 1861; Wednesday. To day past the time in studying of the English language. The weather cool and damp. To day I procured a map of Norway and Sweeden. My health is slightly improved I am waiting for our mail from Gotenberg. In the evening several of the sisters and a brother Miller came in to visit with us. We enjoyed a pleasant past-time. We prayed with and for them and parted and we retired. Our package has not as yet arived from Sweeden. Some rain during the night.

October 24, 1861; Thursday. This morning our lost parcel has not yet come to hand and I proceed to write by writeing a leter to [Francis] Marion [Lyman] in London. Weather damp and cool. At length the missing or strayed parcel from Sweeden has come in and the papers from Liverpool. In the evening visited the families of brothers Petersen ^and^ Olsen.

October 25, 1861; Friday. This morning dispached a leter to [fifth wife] Cornelia and in the afternoon received one from the same. After noon our trunks were sent in to us and we packed them for the journey and at 7 oclock P.M. we parted with our friends in Copenhagen and arived in Kosor at 10 oclock and went on board the steamer immediately for Kiel where we landed at 6 oclock A.M.

October 26, 1861; Saturday. The morning opened fine and clear with considerable show of frost. At 11 oclock we were safely shiped on board the steam-ship Emerald Isle for Hull. She was not to sail until the next morning. We concluded to stay on board until time of sailing. In the afternoon brother [Charles C.] Rich went on shore with the Capt whose name was Foster. I remained on board. Brother Rich returned from his stroll in town and brought some fine rich pears. Capt returned at dusk when we had sup[p]er and enjoyed it well and retired early to rest.

October 27, 1861; Sunday. Early this morning there was some stiring on board indicating that we were on the move down [the] E[l]be [River]. The morning opened pleasantly. We enjoyed a pleasant contemplation of a scenery of unsurpassing beauty and loveliness. Spread out over a portion of the low hills of the Holstein[160] shore of the river ^on^ the Hanover side the land is so low that our view in that direction was quite limited. As our felow passengers made their appearance we found we had the company of a lady who went up to Hamburg with us in August. We enjoyed a pleasant breakfast after which for a short time a dense fog settled down around us which caused a reduction, for a time, of our speed of travil. The fog soon left us and the weather became clear and pleasant.

October 28, 1861; Monday. Had a pleasant day and good travil no sickness something rather unusual. A good degree of sociability cheered and made pleasant our traviling family over which our kind Capt Foster presided ^with^ much of the solicitude of the Father for his children.

October 29, 1861; Tuesday. This morning at [blank] landed [in Hull]. Breakfasted at the Minirvie Hotell and at half past 9 oclock were on board of the steamer for New Holland.[161] From this point by rail we

160. The German state of Holstein lies on the northern side of the Elbe, while the southern shore offers the edge of Niedersachsen (Lower Saxony).

161. The 1820 Minerva Hotel is located on a pier and is pie-shaped like the

reached Liverpool at 4 oclock.[162] Found all well at 42 [Islington] and received a hearty welcome from brother [George Q.] and Sister [Elizabeth] Cannon and all in the office. Were favored with the news in leter from Prest [Brigham] Young under date of 18th of Sept in which he released Elder John Van Cott from his mission in this country to come home at the earliest practicable date. The President refered the determination of the length of ^the^ stay of myself and brother [Charles C.] Rich to our selves and brother Cannon.

General news from home all good and cheering ^for^ the lovers of truth and the hopeful of its uiltimate triumph for the freedom of the world from the bondage of sin and corruption, the consequences of man's ignorance of the redeeming principles of truth, the light of which alone can reveal the well-spring of life and sunder the chains of darkness that hold the ignorant, the slaves of sin, and death.

October 30, 1861; Wednesday. The weather pleasant[,] past the morning in the office attended to some writing. In the evening ordered some clothing.

October 31, 1861; Thursday. To day wrote leter to [Francis] Marion [Lyman] and commenced to write to my family at Salt Lake. Weather cool.

November 1, 1861; Friday.[163] To day I wrote a leter to my [eighth] wife Lydia in the morning after which in company with brothers [Charles C.] Rich and [George Q.] Cannon I visited the exhibition of the [Liverpool] Academy of Arts.[164] Our visit proved interesting and instructive. This done I returned to the office and wrote ^a^ leter to br Edward Partridge after wich I made ready for our journey to Leeds. Some company came in to see and converse with us. Brother John M. Kay was with us on yesterday and to day he was in good health and spirits.

November 2, 1861; Saturday. This morning at 20 minutes past 6 oclock myself and brothers [Charles C.] Rich and [George Q.] Cannon

---

Flatiron Building in Manhattan. Across the Humber Estuary from Hull, people stepped out of the ferry directly onto the pier Railway Station in the town of New Holland.

162. Lyman and Rich had traveled for seventy-four days.

163. This entry begins a new diary book.

164. Since 1810 the academy had sponsored an annual salon featuring a single accomplished artist; later the show would expand to include multiple artists.

were on the rail for Leeds. In order to decend below all that we might be the beter able to appreciate the true condition of the varied classes of humanity we purchased tickets for the third class and were by an officious man in waiting directed to what he said was our cariage in which we ensconced our selves and ^were^ begining to congratulate our selves on our good fortune when an official called for our tickets and informed us that we were in the wrong cariage. We then hustled out and were conducted to another so-called cariage and we again were seated and away.

At one of the way-stations a man joined our party and by way of giving us a little encouragement ^told us^ that we should make a change that would improve our circumstances as to comfort. The change came [and] it was a change looking along the line of waiting cariages until we found one with a single passenger. Into this we made our way altho it was only high enough to allow us to sit but not to stand. We had barely seated our^selves^ when some fisher woomen came and not being content to remain in the ajoining compartment they in a most ungenteel maner strode over the partition and placed themselves with all the stink of their fish and their own want of cleanliness ~~an~~ ^on^ the seats beside us.

From the foul stench (arising from this new accession to our party) brother Rich was relieved by the temporary loss by cold of the sence of smelling. Others of us were not so favoured and stil more to excite our fears of increasing trouble an aged and wrinkled priestess of Bachus [god of wine] commenced to light her sacrificial fire[,] in ^which^ duty however she did not succeed beyond the waste of some matches as the tobaco would not burn. She at length desisted and we were left to the punishment of the presence of stinking fish and filthy woomen which was bad enough. We thought of our unpleasant circumstances and concluded that we would again travil in the <u>chattle</u> department but only when we ~~could~~ ^can^ not travil anywhere else.

We arived in Leeds some twenty minutes after 4 oclock and were meet and welcomed by the brothers [Samuel H. B. & Joseph F.] Smiths by whom we were conducted to the residence of Elder Wm Shires the traviling Elder. My cough increased from cold contracted on the <u>railway</u>. Took tea with Sister [Jane] Eastham and daughters[165] and lodged with brother Shires.

165. John and Jane Eastham had six daughters (five other children died in infancy). The two oldest, Lucy and Emma Jane, would marry and emigrate to Utah in

November 3, 1861; Sunday. To day attended meeting with the Saints in their hall. After the conference was duly opened a report of the conf was read by President S[amuel] H. B. Smith after which the priesthood of the Church was presented by brother [Charles C.] Rich and sustained. After which I addressed the audience for one hour after which the meeting ajourned until half past 2 oclock. I did not attend the meeting in the afternoon on acount of my ill health.

In my remarks of this morning I endeavored to show the Saints the necesity of cultivating liberal and generous views of the gospel and its requirements so as to feel[,] in all they do to promote its intrests[,] that they are promoting their own intrests in all that tends to the building up of the Kingdom of God, whether paid in tithing or for the expenses of the mission ^and^ that they have an intrest in all that is connected with the development of the hapiness and salvation of humanity and by this course of liveing drive from themselves the spirit of narrow selfishness which always recognizes its own but never another's welfare and intrests.

November 4, 1861; Monday. This morning my health is not good. My lungs ar[e] much distressed with cold which gives me much pain. We dined to day with sister [Jane] Eastham and at night meet with a party of the saints at their meeting hall where we were entertained with songs and recitations after which I addressed the audience impressing upon them the importence of always remembering the Lord on occasions like the present one when assembled for pleasurable recreation. As by so doing they would be preserved ^from^ excesses of folly and a forgetfulness of their high and holy calling and relationship as saints and children of our Heavenly Father. Retired feeling much distressed in my lungs, found but little rest.

November 5, 1861; Tuesday. This morning we bade our friends in Leeds adieu and at half past 9 oclock we were moveing for Liverpool where we arived about 1 oclock. Found all well at 42 my own health was not improved. On my arival found letters awaiting me from my family in Southern Utah the news was good from home. My cold which has been verry severe for several days is giveing me much distress in my ^lungs^ today.

1864; John and Jane and the other four daughters would emigrate on the *Belle Wood* in 1865 and settle in Grantsville.

November 6, 1861; Wednesday. Today my health is poor but I commenced writeing to my family but feeling bad wrote but little. Read leter from brother D[avid] M. Stuart giveing some very encouraging news of the work in Scotland. I also by request of brother [George Q.] Cannon examined some mater which had been sent in to him for publication. In the evening my lungs much distressed and breathing difficult.

Read some little in [Richard] Burton's pilgrimage to Mecca. This is my first sight of his work. The little I have read impresses me favourably of the author as a traviler and writer and leads me to expect something honest and impartial in relation to his visit to Utah and its citizen Saints who reside there.[166]

November 7, 1861; Thursday. This morning I arose feeling beter in health than for some days past. The weather cool but pleasant ^I^ resumed my writing to my family. In this I was however somewhat interrupted by reading and listening to the reading of the current news of the day as furnished by the London and other papers that reach us.

In the evening in company with Brother [Charles C.] Rich and brother and Sister [George Q. and Elizabeth] Cannon I visited brother [William] Ajax and wife [Emma]. Passed the evening with them very pleasantly and felt my health to be improveing. When we returned to the office we found some of Cobbett's grammars[167] for the purchase of which we had made arangements previously. To day myself and brother Rich received each a half dozen portraits of ourselves which were gratuitously furnished us by the photogropher brother Wm Reynolds resident of the town of Lowestoft.

November 8, 1861; Friday. To day wrote several leters to my family in Southern Utah. My health is slightly improveing altho my close application to writing has produced some headache. Weather quite pleasant all day.

---

166. Richard Francis Burton spent years learning Arabic and Muslim customs to be able to disguise himself for his three-volume *Personal Narrative of a Pilgrimage to Al Madinah and Meccah*. He similarly visited Utah and published his *City of the Saints* in 1861, one of the best accounts of Utah from the mid-century. See Brodie's introduction to the 1963 re-issue of *City of the Saints*, xxvii–xxix.

167. William Cobbett's *Grammar of the English Language* (1818) was written while he was in exile in the United States, avoiding arrest in the United Kingdom (he had been in jail before) for seditious writings against the government.

November 9, 1861; Saturday. This day tarried in the office. Through the day and in the evening in company with brother [Charles C.] Rich and [George Q.] Cannon I took a turkish bathe which relieved my cold and pain in my head. To night the tailor brought in my cloth[e]s they fited well (their cost was £7–4s).[168]

November 10, 1861; Sunday. This morning the weather was dark cold and rainy. At half past 10 oclock the conference was in cession at the Assembly Rooms [on Bold Street]. On acount of the state of my health I did not attend the morning service but there were present Presidents [George Q.] Cannon of the Mission and [John M.] Kay of the District and [Edward L.] Sloan of the Conference.

At half past 2 oclock the conference resumed its session at which myself and brother [Charles C.] Rich (together with those who were mentioned as in attendence at the morning service) were present. The priesthood of the Church was ^then^ presented by brother Rich and was unanimously sustained by the conference after which the audience was addressed by brother Rich urgeing upon the Saints the necesity of practical purity of life in order to secure to themselves the blessings of the Holy Spirit and the consequent power over or freedom from sin. Elder Cannon followed with a spirited address to the Saints calling their attention to the subject of their emigration and the cours[e] that should be pursued by them to promote its acomplishment by cultivating a living faith in God that would not only lead them to trust in the Lord but would call into exercise evry power of the soul to effect the so much desired consumation. The meeting ajouned for an intermission.

At half past 6 oclock the meeting was aga^i^n assembled. I addressed the audience for an hour and a half impressing upon them the importance of having a knowledge of the truth developed in themselves that their confidence would not stand on what others had said or might say but in their own knowledge of the truth and consequent a^p^preciation of its intrinsick and priceless value.

November 11, 1861; Monday. To day passed the time ^in^ the office in writing. During the day we received a leter from J[ohn] Van Cott in Scandinavia ^in which^ he spoke encourageingly of the prospects of the

---

168. That would be about $800 today.

work in the parts of the mission under his charge which he has visited since we parted with him in October last. This evening brothers Wm H. Dame and Reuben A. McBride went to their fields of labour.

November 12, 1861; Tuesday. Today I packed my trunk and disposed and aranged my clothing for my departure to Newcastle and from thence to London. In the evening read the American news as givein in the London times from Dr. [William] Russell.[169] Felt some pain in my head. By request of brother [George Q.] Cannon I read and examined some mater sent in for publication in the [Millennial] Star. Weather dark and damp.

November 13, 1861; Wednesday. To day I past the time in the office engaged in writing and reading. ^I^ devoted some time with brother [Henry] Whitall as he was proof-reading for the Star. This was principaly for my own improvement in the use of Language. In the evening I walked out with brothers John M. Kay and Elias [Edward] L. Sloan. While out I saw a party of Arabs and also witnessed some gymnastick performences by them peculiar to themselves and their country. The weather this evening was rainy and cool.

November 14, 1861; Thursday. Today the weather was very wet. Bother [Edward L.] Sloan brought in my journal which he had been ~~up~~ transcribing the execution of the work pleased me much. In the evening I went out in town with brother [George Q.] and Sister [Elizabeth] Cannon and brother [Charles C.] Rich. The moon light struggled feebly out through the dense clouds of mist and smoke that enveloped the town. The visits of the Q[u]een of night to our smoke-girdled town are nearly as rare as are those of her most gracious Magesty the ruler ^of^ Brittania's broad Realms.

November 15, 1861; Friday. Passed the most of the day in the office. In the evening had a walk out in town after which I had a conversation with brother Whitall in relation to the rule of action that would[,] if persisted in, secure to those acting [in] the favour of God and the approval of their own good conciences when even others looking on might suppose them to be guilty of deriliction of duty merely because they did not get up to the standerd of right ~~as~~ as developed in the feelings of

169. The Irish reporter William Howard Russell traveled to the U.S. in 1861 to cover the Civil War for the London *Times*. He had previously covered the Crimean War and the rebellion of 1857 in India.

such observers of men's actions who think their notion of right should constitute the criterion by which the actions and the motives inducing them in others should be tried and determined. When in fact the standard thus called into requisition (inste^a^d of being the ~~ro~~ truth lucidly comprehended in the ^mind^ and embraceing only just conceptions in relation to the salvation of the parties effected by its excercise) ~~it~~, is found to consist of the notions ~~of the~~ whether corect or incorrect of the parties entertaining them and not the dictations of an enlightened judgment embraceing a knowledge of the purposes of God and man's relation to the fulfillment of those purposes. An ignorence of these betray~~s~~ men into actions ~~of~~ that are foolish and wrong because they opperate against rather than in favour of man's salvation.

November 16, 1861; Saturday. This morning brothers [Charles C.] Rich and [George Q.] Cannon and myself made our selves ready for our departure from Liverpool, Brother Rich for Notingham, myself and brother Cannon for Sunderland. As we left the station at 10 minutes before 10 oclock the clouds that hung in sullen gloom round the horizon exhibited their wintry qualities in a fall of snow that like the shroud ^that^ covers the dead and all of the form that was lovely in life, so Earth seemed to have doned the habiliments of the tomb.

And as we contemplated the hoary scene around us[,] we thought of sumer and its ways departed to be renewed again when spring should awaken a smile of gladness as universal as the reign of winter. We pursued our journey without adventure of accident save some detentions by the way which delayed our arival until 8 oclock P.M. We were meet at the station and welcomed by brothers [John S.] Gleason and [Samuel] Hargraves. We lodged with brother Newton.

November 17, 1861; Sunday. This morning at 10 oclock a meeting of the local priesthood was in cession which was attended by brother [George Q.] Cannon. I did not attend. At 2 oclock the conference was duly opened after which a brief report of the condition of the district was given by president [John S.] Gleason after which brother Cannon addressed the audience[,] after which the meeting was ajourned for an intermission. At 6 oclock the meeting was again in cession[,] when I presented the priesthood of the Church they were all of them unanimously sustained. This done I addressed the audience for an hour and a half shewing them ^that^ knowledge and purity instead of ignorance and misry exalt and save men. The people listened very attentively some infidels and strangers were present for the first time and on retiring said they should call again. Thus closed our conference and weary we retired to rest.

November 18, 1861; Monday. To day myself and brothers [George Q.] Cannon, [John S.] Gleason, and [Samuel] Hargraves and [Henry W.] Barnet went to Newcastle to visit Elder Wm Dallen who was sick. He appeared cheerful and his health was recovering its usual vigor.

November 19, 1861; Tuesday. This morning brother [George Q.] Cannon started for Liverpool. I remained and passed the day with the family of brother Nuby teaching them the principles of salvation. Brother [Henry W.] Barnet and the sisters Nuby sung some songs. The wind was high through the day.

November 20, 1861; Wednesday. To day I traviled by rail to London where I arived at half past 6 oclock having been on the road 10 and a half hours. Found all well at Florence Street and leters awaiting me one from my [second] wife Dionetia and one from Mrs. Stokes.

November 21, 1861; Thursday. To day I suffered very much all day from pain in my head which prevented me from attending to any buisness. For this reason my writing was defered. Late in the evening the pain in head subsided much to my relief. In the evening read some in R[ichard] F. Burton's City of the Saints.

November 22, 1861; Friday. To day my health is somewhat beter than on yesterday. I wrote a leter to brother [George Q.] Cannon and one to Mrs. Stokes. Brothers [George E.] Grove and [Thomas C.] Stainer called in to see me and past some time with us in conversation in regard to the priciples of the Gospel as they are being revealed as the work of the last days progresses to its consumation for the establishment of God's Kingdom to save and rule the world.

The rain was falling copiously throughout the day which imparted to the city a dark and sombre appearence. Closed the day with reading some history. I received a present from br [William C.] Stains of a book entitled the Cyclopedia of London ^by [Charles] Knight~~s~~^ it being a history of that city and much of national history as well.[170]

---

170. Published in 1851, *Knight's Cyclopaedia of London* had chapters on churches, "hospitals and lunatic asylums," "learned societies," museums, parks, theaters,

November 23, 1861; Saturday. To day I wrote a leter to my [second] wife Dionitia in Minersville in Beaver County. In the evening I walked out for exercise and air. Read some in the history of Alexander the great and also some of the history of London. In the evening brother Jewry called in to see me. He is from Salt Lake and said he had heard me preach there. He gave me some money and said he should return to Zion the next season. Read some news of the American war in the Tribune. There has been no rain to day weather clear.

November 24, 1861; Sunday. Today attended meeting ^at 2½ oclock^ with brother [William C.] Staines at St. George's [Temperance] Hall. The meeting was composed of the Lambeth Branch. The sacrement was administered after which I addressed the Saints shewing them the importence of understanding the nature of the Ordinances of the Gospel in order that their observence by us should lead to our immancipation from the bondage of sin by induceing in us that purity of life that shall be free from the taint of wrong and sinful actions in which we should emulate the purity of his life who said in r^ef^erence to the sa[c]rement of the Sup[p]er "do this in rememberence of me". Meeting ajourned until 6½ <u>oclock</u> at which time the Saints were again assembled and a goodly number of strangers in attendence. I again addressed the audience who listened very attentively. The meeting closed and we returned to our lodgings weary.

November 25, 1861; Monday. To day past the morning in the [London] office after which I rode out in the city with brother [William C.] Staines. Bought a new hat returned and found that my son [Francis] had called in my abcence. Received and read the New York Herald there was not a profusion of news from America the war is progressing.

November 26, 1861; Tuesday. This morning President John Brown came in from Kent Conference. We past the early part of the day in the office [at Florence Street]. In the evening I meet with the Saints in St. George's Hall in ^which^ they were assembled for a tea meeting. Some 260 Saints were in attendence. We were entertained with songs and recitations after partakeing of the alimentry refreshments provided. Presidents Brown and [William C.] Staines were present and Father [Thomas

---

transportation, and many other topics. Knight founded the popular *Penny Magazine*, with a circulation of 200,00, that sold for a penny every Saturday as a vehicle for educating common people about natural science and engineering.

C.] Stainer and my son F[rancis] M. Lyman. There were present on this occasion some 60 children who are attending the Saints Sabbath School. Some presents as tokens of approbation we^re^ given to some of the children and more were promised.

After this I addressed the meeting impressing on them the importence of teaching their children while young to love the truth and practice it as this would excercise a ruling and life-long influence with them to preserve them in the path of inocence and virtue. I recommended the Saints to persevere in their efforts to extend and strengthen the Sabath School. After which the meeting closed and we retired much pleased ^which^ apeared to be the case with all who were in attendence. The small hours of the morning had arived ere we had found our couch and the rest so necisary to the health of wearied humanity.

November 27, 1861; Wednesday. Past the morning in the office. About mid-day myself in company with brothers [John] Brown and [William C.] Staines visited brother [George E.] Grove and family at his residence where we were joined by my Son [Francis]. After a pleasant visit we returned to our lodgings.

November 28, 1861; Thursday. To day past the morning in the office and at 12 oclock myself and brothers Brown [William C.] Staines and [Francis] Lyman went to hear the Rev C[harles] H. Spurgeon.[171] The experiment satisfied me that my previously formed opinion of the man was correct. I looked in vain for that lofty eloquence for which I had heard him praised. His discourse containing as it did the declaration of various truths was delivered in rather a drawling spiritless and uinteresting maner.

The great and only reason which he urged why the siner should turn to and love and obey the Lord Jes^us^ was that he Jesus had suffered and died for him. Never so much as once alluding to the Heavenly principles he taught by the application of which fallen humanity would be exalted to its high destiny.

Our meeting on the present occasion with this great pulpit celebrity of the age, as he has been denominated by some, was to us another practical illustration of the fact that he who is himself ignorant is but poorly

171. Spurgeon was a Baptist minister who had just moved his congregation to a large, newly built hall called the Metropolitan Tabernacle in Mar. 1861.

prepared to illumine the darkness of those in similar circumstances. In the evening we went to the St. James Hall to hear John Hyde.[172] We listened to him while he waded through a laboured discourse of 1½ hours in length. With this meeting closed the adventures of the day.

November 29, 1861; Friday. To day myself and brother [William C.] Staines and my son F. M. Lyman went to Tulse Hill to visit Sister Smith whose husband do[e]s not belong to the Church. He received and treated us kindly and invited us to repeat the visit. At 8 oclock we parted with our friends and returned to our lodgings the weath[er] dark ~~and~~ and cloudy but no rain.

November 30, 1861; Saturday. Today in company with brother [William C.] Staines I visited the South Kensington museum[173] and the great Exhibition Building in process of erection for the international exhibition of [18]62. The day past pleasantly.

December 1, 1861; Sunday. This morning in company with brother [William C.] Stains I went to Poplar we dined with brother [John] Horsepool and family and at half past 2 oclock we meet the Saints of the Poplar branch at their usual place of meeting. I addressed the audience for the space of an hour after which the meeting ajourned and we then repired to the residence of brother [John] Bowbear with whom we took tea and then we attended a meeting of the white Chappel Branch. The hall was crowded with an attentive audience I addressed them for an hour and a half after which the meeting ajourned and we returned to our lodgings somewhat weary. The weather to day has been clear and pleasant.

December 2, 1861; Monday. To day in company with brothers [John] Brown, [William C.] Stains, and [George E.] Grove I visited and spent the day with brother [James J.] Keep and family who have recently joined the Church. Brother K. has been for 17 years in government service in the Post Office Department. We passed the day very pleasantly returned

---

172. This may have been John Hyde Jr., an Englishman who converted to Mormonism in 1847 and was called on a mission to the Sandwich Islands, where he became an anti-Mormon lecturer and wrote *Mormonism: Its Leaders and Designs* (1857). Jorgensen, "John Hyde Jr., Mormon Renegade," 120–44.

173. The Victoria and Albert Museum, built in South Kensington in 1852, displayed artifacts from the Great Exhibition of 1851 and later came to emphasize decorative arts.

to our lodgings at 10 oclock P.M. I also wrote wrote to my [second] wife Caroline [in] G. S. L. City.

December 3, 1861; Tuesday. To day past the time mostly in the office until 3 oclock when in company with brothers [John] Brown ^and [William C.] Stains^ went to Sister West's to tea and remained there until 10 oclock P.M. Had an agreeable visit with our friends to whom we imparted some instructions in relation to the principles of the gospel and their application to remove the ills of life and to increase its hapiness.

December 4, 1861; Wednesday. Remained in the office throughout the day and read Ancient history the most of the day. In the evening walked out in the city for the air and exercise in company with brother [John] Brown and [William C.] Staines. The weather was very dark and smoky in the city.

December 5, 1861; Thursday. To day my son F[rancis] M. L[yman] came to the office. I received a leter from brother [George Q.] Cannon to which I wrote an answer. The weather quite clear and pleasant. Brothers ^J[ohn]^ Brown and [William C.] Staines and my son were with me to day. At night I attended a meeting of the local priesthood in Goswell Hall.[174] I addressed the priesthood who were assembled in relation to their duties as preachers of righteousness and ministers of salvation. Ajourned about 11 oclock and returned to our lodgings.

December 6, 1861; Friday. To day I wrote some leters, one to Utah to brother Isaiah M. Coombs and one to Thomas Crawley in Ireland. During the day brother Ward an optician brought some field glasses [binoculars] for me to examine with the view of selling one to me if any should suit me. I purchased one at £3, 10s. The weather to day very dark and dull some rain in the afternoon which rendered the atmosphere some what more clear than ~~in~~ earlier in the day. Not much additional news to day from the seat of war across the Atlantick. Brothers [John] Brown and [William C.] Staines and [Thomas C.] Stainer, [Francis M.] Lyman and [George] Reynolds were with me to day. At night my son left to attend to the duties of his ministry.

174. The hall on Goswell Road was three and a half miles from the mission office and held 300 people; a few years later it was rented out once a week to London spiritualists for séances. Around the corner in the middle of King Square, Barrett's Academy was availalble to the LDS Church on Sundays.

December 7, 1861; Saturday. Passed the entire day in the office I wrote a leter to brother C[harles] C. Rich enclosing one from D[avid] M. Stuart. Read in Rawlins ancient history of Egypt.[175] Brothers J[ohn] Brown and [William C.] Staines were with me to day.

December 8, 1861; Sunday. In the morning remained in the office and at half past 2 oclock myself and brother [William C.] Staines meet with the Saints of the Somerstown Branch in their hall. I addressed them for an hour and a half urging upon them the necessity of purity and consistency of life which would secure to them the enjoyment of the spirit of God. That through its influence they might be enabled to entertain just views and conceptions of the nature and objects of the great later-day work with which they had become connected by embraceing the gospel and to enhance the interests of which they were required to gather to Zion, that their accession might be an increase of the amount and also of the strength and influence of virtue.

At half-past 6 oclock ~~we~~ after taking refreshments with brother Ferguson and family we meet with Saints of the Goswell Road Branch in the Hall of the same name. I addressed them on the subject of a living ^faith^ made perfect by works of righteousness which would have the effect to place ^man^ in the relationship with the fountain of wisdom and truth that its enlightening influences would pour an incesant stream of constantly increasing knowledge upon the soul. Thus produceing that elevation of the mind that exalts man to his legitimate position as the child of God possessing[,] and reflecting in ^this^[,] ever enlarging powers [and] the truthful reflection of the divine and Heavenly parentage from whence ^he^ has descended to the Earthly sphere of his existence from which through the aid of living faith he is strugling upwards to his home in the realms of ever increasing ^glory^ the Kingdom of his Father and his God.

December 9, 1861; Monday. This morning I received a leter from brother C[harles] C. Rich. In the afternoon dined with brother [George] Triplet and family Brother T. is a cabinet maker.[176] We taried to tea and

175. Charles Rollin, seventeenth-century rector of the University of Paris, wrote the twelve-volume *Histoire Ancienne*, widely reprinted in English.

176. George Triplett and family left London in 1866 on the ship *Caroline*. Some thirty years later he was celebrated as the "oldest member of the Tabernacle Choir," *Deseret News*, Aug. 31, 1901.

then returned to our lodgings where we found brother Geo. J. Taylor awaiting our return. Elder Taylor was in good health and spirits. Brothers John Brown and Wm C. Staines were with me. To day brother Taylor went to lodge with brother Brown at the house of brother G[eorge] E. Grove. Brother Taylor remained with us [in London] several days.

December 10, 1861; Tuesday. This morning received leter from br [George Q.] Cannon in which he stated that in consequence of news from brother J[ohn] T. D. McAlister he expected that we should have his McAlister's company at Christmas as he had[,] on being permited to return home or complete his mission by coming to England[,] concluded to accept the later. I received [a] leter from brother E[dward] L. Sloan who wrote ^to^ me from the Isle of Man reporting prospects there somewhat favourable to reintroduction of the gospel to the people of that Sea-girt Isle.

About 11 <u>oclock</u> in company with brothers John Brown and Wm C. Staines I started for Woolwich[177] by Omnibus and rail we arived just as the workmen some 16000 in number were turned out for din[n]er. We were here joined by my son F[rancis] M. Lyman and Elder George J. Taylor and brother William Ramsey. The later acted as our guide and procurred our ticket of admission he having formerly held the position of foreman of some bra[n]ch of the extensive works that have been and are still caried on at this place, the world-wide celebrity of which has been somewhat increased by ^the^ manufacture of the Armstrong Cannon under the direct superintendence of the Patentee <u>Sir</u> Wm Armstrong for the government.

The Arsenal and works occupies nearly 300 acres of land and has 2 miles of railway and a like amount of tramway for trucks and one mile of canal from 30 to 50 feet in width. They have 1000 ft. of Rifle Range and one mile of Wharfs on the river supplied with 25 powerful cranes capable of lifting from 30 to 50 tons each and one capable of lifting 100 tons. All these were worked by hydraulic power. A number of steam engines of 150 horsepower each moved the vast works which present to the eye

177. Ten miles east of downtown London, Woolwich was home to the Royal Arsenal that developed and manufactured military armaments, also the Woolwich Dockyard that built some of the most impressive ships of the day. The soccer team Arsenal F.C. was formed in Woolwich in the 1880s.

of the visitor one vast and aparently inexplicable network of the most perfect machinery, the perfection of which in its own construction could not fail to excite the admiration of the beholder which is only increased as he witnesses the realy masterly maner in which this vast ^and most ingenious^ creation of human ingenuity and mechanical skill is in the intended details of its numerous parts adapted to the acomplishment of the objects of is creation.

We were shown through the works by ~~different~~ foremen of the different departments of whom the name of Jarvis will be remembered with pleasure for his kind and gentlemanly deportment and lucid explanations of the portions of the works to which his supervision extended. After visiting the varios departments of the works from the begining of the great guns to their completion and the varied projectiles used in them and the small arms we left the grounds wearied with our restless walk. We took tea with brother Ramsey after which I meet with the Saints of the Deptford Branch[178] to whom I spoke for an hour with freedom and to their aparent edification. After meeting I returned to Florence Street.

December 11, 1861; Wednesday. To day in company with brothers [John] Brown[,] [William C.] Stains and [George E.] Grove I visited the Smithfield Cattle Club.[179] The show of stock was fine as also the exhibition of farming impliments and machinery. The crowd in attendence was dense wich detracted from the pleasure of ^the^ occasion.

After leaving Smithfield we went to the residence of brother Grove where we organized the North London branch by apointing brother George E. Grove President of the Branch. The appointment was sustained by the vote of the branch after which I gave the Saints some instructions ^to^ help them in their further journey in the way of truth for the acquisition of knowledge of the truth that renders the soul free from the power and influence of sin that only holds its power over the mind because of ignorance ~~of the truth~~. Partook of some refreshments and with brother Stains returned to our lodgings much in need of rest.

December 12, 1861; Thursday. Remained in the office throughout the

178. Five miles west of Woolwich, across the Thames from the Isle of Dogs.

179. The agricultural society held annual auctions, preceded by exhibitions to allow farmers and butchers to evaluate the merchandise, and some of the cattle were featured in the newspapers and periodicals. Powell, *History of the Smithfield Club*.

day engaged in writing and reading and in conversation upon the principles of the gospel. During the day an Italian man came in and expressed a wish to join the Church. Arangements were made for his baptism at a subsequent date. The weather was warm and wet. Brs [John] Brown, [William C.] Staines, [Francis M.] Lyman, and [George J.] Taylor and [George] Reynolds were with me during the day. In the evening had an interesting conversation with Elders Brown and Staines in relation to the changes that characterize the progress of the truth in displacing the errors that have arisen out of wrong education.

December 13, 1861; Friday. To day I received a leter from brother C[harles] C. Rich and wrote him an answer. I passed the day in the office engaged in writing, reading, and conversation with the brethren who were present with me. The weather was alternately dark and clear. The brethren present to day were J[ohn] Brown[,] [William C.] Staines, [Thomas C.] Stainer, [George J.] Taylor, [Francis M.] Lyman, and Reynolds.

December 14, 1861; Saturday. This morning I received a package of leters ^from Utah containing^ one from President [Brigham] Young under date of 13th of Nov and one from my son Oscar M. Lyman in Parowan Oct 22 and one also from his Mother [Lyman's sixth wife Paulina] of same date and one from Sanpete valey. — The leter from President Young gave myself and Elder C[harles] C. Rich permission to return home next ^emigration^ season the same leter announced the release of brother John Van Cott.

I remained alone in the office through the day. In the evening brother [William C.] Staines came in and we read some history of London and enjoyed some pleasant conversation in relation to the change of habits ~~of~~ ^in^ men that must of necesity transpire as the result of their adoption to the progressive character of the work of God in which as members of the Church they have become engaged. Which work must in its onward movement impress its own character on all ~~its h~~ who devote themselves to works of righteousness for the salvation of fallen humanity. Brothers [John] Brown and [George J.] Taylor came in and for a short time ~~engaged~~ ^participated^ in the conversation after which we parted for the night and retired to rest.

The weather to day has been quite warm being the most of the day without fire in the room where we were siting. A report of the condition of the health of [Albert,] prince consort [of Queen Victoria,] apeared on the bulletin boards stating his symptoms unfavourable signed by four doctors. At 10 minutes to eleven oclock P.M. the Prince Consort died.[180] Thus we are admonished that the circles of Royalty are not exempt from the unwelcome intrusion of Death the great leviler of all human distinctions. The mourning of the people seems universal and sincere for the departed Prince Consort of their noble Q[u]een.

December 15, 1861; Sunday. This ~~morning~~ ^day^ in company with brother [William C.] Staines I meet with the Saints of the Padington Branch. I addressed them for one hour and the^n^ ajourned. We took tea with brother [blank] White. He is blind and is engaged in teaching in a phonetic school.[181] After takeing ^of^ our refreshment we hired a cab and went to Chelsea where the Saints of that branch were assembled.[182] I addressed them for more than an hour showing them the peaceful nature and object of the gospel. The Saints listened with apparent intrest. Meeting over we returned to out lodgings weary and I sufered some ^sickness^ during the night from cold contracted during the day's travils and other labours. Retired a short time before midnight ^this was^ somewhat earlier than usual. After night I walked to the Angel Inn[183] for exercise and air the distance is one mile.

December 16, 1861; Monday. To day passed the time in the office writing to my son Oscar Morris Lyman in Parowan. The weather ~~was~~ ^is^ dark cloudy and warm, the weather-wise are looking for much sickness on acount of the state of the weather. The prospects of war with America have not diminished within last few days. The message of President Lincon is generaly construed here as more favourable to war than

---

180. Prince Albert's death was blamed on typhoid. Later historians wondered if cancer or some immune-system failure could have been to blame. English, "Was Albert Killed by Crohn's Disease?" Dec. 16, 2011.

181. There was a movement at the time to teach people Pitman shorthand and to simplify English spelling according to phonetic principles. At first adults gathered in the evenings for classes, then phonetics became part of the public school curriculum in some areas. See the reports from London and Birmingham in the *Fonetic Jurnal*, Feb., Oct. 1851, 28, 157.

182. Chelsea and Paddington are neighborhoods in central London.

183. The Angel Inn, built in the seventeenth century, was less than a mile from the mission offices. It was originally a stopping place for travelers from the north who waited overnight for "fear of the thieves who infested the road beyond." Wheatley, *London Past and Present*, 1:47.

peace. A spirit of sadness settles in gloom over the great Metropolis for the death of the Prince Consort of their beloved Q[u]een. In the evening Sisters East[,] Aslam and Andrews called to inform us that they could lodge some of the visiting brethren who were expected ^to be here^ tomorow.

December 17, 1861; Tuesday. This morning received a leter from brother [William] Bramall in answer to mine of last week. This morning brother [George] Reynolds bought for me a copy of Webster's Unabridged Dictionary for which he payed £1.4. In the afternoon brothers E[lias] H. Blackburn and Richard Bently came in from Luton and in the evening myself and brothers [William C.] Stains[,] Blackburn and Bently went to tea with Sister Andrews. After this returned to the office when brother Joseph Bull came in from Norwich. We chated for a while and then retired to rest.

December 18, 1861; Wednesday. This morning in company with brother [William C.] Stains I went to see St. Paul's Cathedral.[184] The weather being somewhat clear we promised our selves before we started a pleasant view of the great metropolis from our prospective perch on some of the elevated points of the vast pile we were about to visit.

The labours of the day opened with a walk of one mile to the Angel Inn and from thence by Omnibus we reached the Cathedral. At the entrence[, ^by^] the payment of three shillings and two pence, the visitor is entitled to work his weary way to the ball[-shaped ceiling]. Our fees paid we commenced our toilsome ascent up a flight of broad gentle and easy stairs which terminated at the galery at the Base of the dome. From this point the ascent became more narrow and less light and pleasant. Our next break of our upward journey was at the whispering gallery which extends around the inside of the great Dome at a distance from the floor below which gave the labourers below (as we contemplated them from the point) a dwarfed appearence. On acount of the repairs going forward in the building the noise prevented us from hearing the promised whisper from the oposite side as entered by the servant in atendence.

After siting and resting ourselves and contemplating the great

184. The iconic St. Paul's Cathedral was completed in 1708 and has ever since been the place of royal weddings and state funerals. It was the tallest structure in London at the time.

structure from this point we continued our upward journey. Our way becoming more and more intricate and dark. One feature of the structures attracted my curiosity and that was the very light[-weight] character of the timber of which the internal framework was composed. The nicety of its mechanical ajustment suplying the ^place of the^ larger size that I have seen used in far less structures. At length after gropeing along our dark and devious way until we were able to appreciate the very great inconvenience of having to carry 230 lbs weight up such an ascent ^and^[,] acording to an English provincialism[,] we were frequently out of puff. At length the height is gained and we steped out on the gallery as an elevation above the street of some 380 feet.

After all our toil to get[,] as we had hoped to do[,] a fine view of the city[,] to our disappointment the moving world of human existence and trafick lay ~~beneath~~ ^below^ ~~our feet~~ ^us^ wraped in a sable pall of smoke ^an article of domestic ma[n]ifacture.^ In looking down upon the pigmy apearing race beneath us (whose noisy traffick sent up one continuous and unbroaken roar to our high p^e^rch) the effect on us as from our high position we gazed down on the moveing masses below was somewhat new and strange. The lesser towers of the great edifice seemed as we saw them below strugling in feeble competi^ti^on with their giant competitor to raise themselves to his lofty altitude and extended propo^r^tions.

As we gazed ~~don~~ down on the strugling mass of humanity as it rolled its ceasless waves along the streets the thought was most vividly brought to our mind who of all the thousands living ^or^ of the dead whose ashes now are resting below have been the recip^i^ents of the life imparting knowledge of God ^in this vast templar^. If we seek to the living for our answer we are told that men can be saved now without it and all that is done to honour God in this vast pile is to bestow within its courts a blind ^and^ idoletrous worship to the name of him whom they know not and the purity of whose principles they dispise and who if he were here as anciently a houseless wanderer[,] religion armed with the weapons of bigatry would stand as sentinel at the gate to prevent the teaching within its wall of that only religion so ~~humatarien~~ ^Heavenly^ in ^its^ principles and tendences that the wicked dispise it and the honest who apply it are blest and raised to their native Heaven by its halowed and exalting influence.

We descended and visited the Tombs of Wellington and Nelson[185] and then we called on Mrs [Mary] Adamson who is sister to brother Stains. She received us very kindly and treated us with wine and fruit. We took tea with her and then receiving a ticket of admission we visited a Hall where Musical entertainments were given and also a fine collection of paintings was on exhibition. From this place we returned home. Mrs Adamson gave us an invitation to call again.

December 19, 1861; Thursday. To day in company with brother [Elias H.] Blackburn[,] [John] Brown[,] [Richard] Bently[,] [William C.] Stains[,] and [Joseph] Bull[,] I visited Westminster Abbey in the morning and in the afternoon we visited the Anatomical Museum of Dr [Joseph] Khan[186] and heard a lecture on procreation and its laws in the human race. After this returned to Florence [Road]. To day received ^a^ leter from Samuel Hargraves in Sunderland the news good.

December 20, 1861; Friday. To day myself and brother [William C.] Stains visited brother [John] Horspool and family in Poplar [seven miles east of downtown London]. Dined with them and in the evening brother H. came in ^we^ had some conversation on the subject of emigration. We advised him to move if he could with the next emigration which he seemed in favor of doing.[187] At night we returned to our lodgings where we met brothers [Thomas C.] Stainer[,] [Elias H.] Blackburn and [John] Brown with whom we had some conversation after which they left to attend a meeting of the Saints. In the evening we were joined in our visit by my son [Francis] Marion who remained for the night when we left for Florence Street.

December 21, 1861; Saturday. To day I remained in the office all the day engaged in making preparation for my return to Liverpool.

December 22, 1861; Sunday. This morning at 11 oclock I meet the priesthood of the conference in the Lambeth meeting place known as

185. The Duke of Wellington Arthur Wellesley and Lord Horatio Nelson are entombed in the cathedral crypt. Nelson was placed there in a sarcophagus in 1806, Wellesley upon his death in 1852.

186. Almost immediately after opening in 1851, the museum encountered moral and legal objections and closed down under pressure twenty years later. Bates, "Dr Kahn's Museum: Obscene Anatomy in Victorian London," 618–24.

187. John Horspool, his wife Eliza, and their six children emigrated in 1862 on the sailing ship *William Tapscott.*

St. George's Hall and gave them some general instruction in relation to their duties as ministers of the gospel. After which the meeting ajourned until 2^½^ oclock at which time the Hall was filled with Saints and strangers who listened with apparent intrest while I addressed them for an hour showing the practical utility of the work of God in imparting to the gathering eliments of his growing Kingdom the principle of undieing immortality and an endless perpituity. Ajourned until half past 2 oclock at which time the hall was again crowded to the full extent of its capacity for siting or standing room. I again addressed the audience for an hour and a half after which we returned to Florence Street accompanied by my son [Francis] Marion ^and^ made the few needful prepaerations for my early morning start and then retired for a few hours of much needed rest. Brothers [John] Brown[,] [Elias H.] Blackburn[,] [William C.] Staines[,] [Joseph] Bently[,] [Joseph] Bull[,] [Thomas C.] Stainer[,] [Francis M.] Lyman and [George] Reynolds were present with us through the day.

December 23, 1861; Monday. This morning I parted with my warm-hearted friends in London and at 10 oclock was seated in the train for Liverpool. Here parted with my son [Francis] Marion and at twenty minutes past 5 oclock I arived in Liverpool and was meet at the Station by brothers [Charles C.] Rich and [George Q.] Cannon, [William] Perkes and [John D. T.] McAllister. I found all well at 42 [Islington] and engaged in preperations for Christmas festivities. I was much wearied with my journey from London as also was brother Rich who came from Birmingham.

December 24, 1861; Tuesday. To day past the time in the office exchanging congratulations with my friends. At night walked out in town in company with brothers [Charles C.] Rich, [George Q.] Cannon and [John M.] Kay. On our return we found Elder George Peacock[188] awaiting our return. Elder P. came directly from Glasgow in Scotland where has been labouring since his arival in this country. His report of the condition and prospects of the work in Scotland ^was^ of a cheering character.

December 25, 1861; Wednesday. This morning the merry Christmas

188. George Peacock was originally from England. When he was young, his parents moved to Canada and then to the U.S. where they discovered Mormonism. He became a legislator in Utah Territory, served a mission to Britain, and aided George's Q. Cannon's wife Elizabeth and children en route to Utah without their husband/father.

went around as the home circle met with a hearty exchange of mutual good wishes for the enjoyment on the part of each one of many and hapy Christmases yet to come. The labours and duties of the morning disposed of we joined the Din[n]er party composed of the brethren engaged in the buisness and Printing Offices and with them partook of a Din[n]er prepared by brother [George Q.] and Sister [Elizabeth] Cannon. The spirit of kindly friendship lent its charm to the entertainment [and] all seemed hapy.

At half past 4 oclock P.M. we joined a convivial party at the Assembly rooms where we partook of tea and were then entertained with songs, recitations, and Pantomimical representations for several hours after which we retired as the small hours of the morning admonished us that Christmas was gone[,] to swell the volume of the past[,] and that Time's ceasless flight was bringing us constantly nearer the close of the present and the opening of the coming New year.

December 26, 1861; Thursday. This morning had my teeth examined and some of them filled by brother John M. Kay. The operation gave me some pain[,] this however soon subsided and I then engaged in writing in my journal. To day Elder Joseph Bull came in for the purpose of assisting brother [George Q.] Cannon for a time in the printing in the Machine department as the machinist who has been employed is about to leave. This evening ^I^ received a present of two pairs of woolen gloves from brother Bull. They were of his Father's manifacture. I had some neuralgic pain in my head and face during the day enough to create a general uneasiness in my system.

Sister Spencer and daughter called this evening and sat for a short time. On ^their^ leaving we were invited by Sister S. to take tea with her on Saturday evening next. Read some to day on the subject of human physiology the author was Dr [Joseph] Kahn of London. The weather cool and clear for this country.

December 27, 1861; Friday. Today I remained in the office engaged in writing in my journal and in reading Scientific and Physiological works. In the evening a Miss Robinson from the Isle of Man called in. Her mother and sisters belong to the Church. Miss R. was introduced by Miss Mary Spencer. To day brother Joseph Bull has been noticing the working of the printing ^machine^ in order to be able to take charge of it when Mr Bell who is at present working shall leave which he intends doing soon.

Elder George Peacock was with us. To day the weather has been cool I have had some pain in my head and face. Had some conversation with brothers [Charles C.] Rich and [George Q.] Cannon in regard to the disposition of some of the Elders to degrade themselves and their calling by listening to and contr[a]dicting the low scurrilous things that are said by the haters of the truth thus giving to them and their slanders a noteriety that they otherwise could not gain but instead would remain measurably unknown and their influence unfelt as hindering the steady silent yet onward movement of the truth in the progressive enlightenment of the human mind.

We felt that in sted of thus degrading himself that the minister of the gospel should occupy a high position as the exponent ^and representative^ of th^os^e principles that are in their nature and the results of their practical application ^calculated^ to elevat, enoble, and render hapy those who should subject themselves to their guidance and influence. By the ministers of the gospel taking this course, slander and its propagaters fail to procure the food on which their existence depends and without which the slanderer and his lies both ^find^ a grave in an oblivion that hides them in its darkness from the sight of Earths children who only ^are^ curst by their presence.

December 28, 1861; Saturday. To day wrote leter to Samuel Hargraves President of Sunderland Conference. Past some time reading and in the evening in company with brothers [Charles C.] Rich and [John M.] Kay and [George Q.] Cannon and wife [Elizabeth] I visited Sister Spencer and daughter. On our return to the office we were cheered by the arival from America Via Scotland of Elder J[ohn] T. D. McAllaster. He came in in good health and spirits.

This evening the Pressman who had been working for brother Cannon left he will be succeeded by brother Joseph Bull. Brothers Kay and McAllaster sang some songs after which we retired to rest in the short hours of the morning. Brother Bull was suffering from cold in his head attended with severe pain.

December 29, 1861; Sunday. The health of brother [Joseph] Bull is not much improved through the night. At 2 oclock brothers [Charles C.] Rich, [George Q.] Cannon, and [John M.] Kay attended the meeting of the Saints in the Assembly Room. I did not attend the morning meeting but meet the Saints at half past 6 <u>oclock</u> ^P.M.^ and addressed them for an hour showing them the necesity ~~of~~ for the developement of knowledge in the soul in order to the existence of hope that would ~~that~~ impart constant and lasting bliss to its posesor.

The weather was very dark cool and damp. Artificial light was in requisition the most of the day on acount of the dense smoke and fog that overhung the city. The health of brother Bull is no beter. This evening brother Kay and others gave him some attentions and some simple remedies for his relief. In the morning of to day I received a leter from br [Thomas C.] Stayner. I wrote leters to brothers Stayner and W[illiam] C. Staines in London.

December 30, 1861; Monday. This morning brothers [Joseph] Bull's health is stil bad. I passed the most of the day in writing and reading and making ready for the Conference in Birmingham. Brother Bull's health is somewhat improved.

December 31, 1861; Tuesday. This morning brothers [Charles C.] Rich, [George Q.] Cannon, and myself started at 10 minutes before 8 <u>oclock</u> for Birmingham where we arived about 12 <u>oclock</u>. We soon found our selves comfortibly quartered with President W[illiam] G. Mills where we remained during the continuence of our conference. Elders from various parts arived today ^all^ in good health and spirits.

8 Proclaiming the Savior's Mission, 1862

Lyman spent his last few months in England in a flurry of activity preparing for the next wave of leadership to arrive. Little did he realize that his sermon in Dundee in March would cause a stir of such magnitude that when news of it reached Brigham Young, it would ultimately result in Lyman's excommunication, although years after the fact. In the meantime, Lyman, Charles C. Rich, and George Q. Cannon crossed the Atlantic on a steamer in just a fraction of the time it had previously taken emigrant converts. Brigham Young wanted Cannon to represent the church in Washington, DC, as a lobbyist, and there was some urgency to begin the job. Lyman, on the other hand, took a month to visit family and old friends in New England and the Midwest before making his way to the familiar staging ground in Florence, Nebraska, for the trip west on the now familiar road between Iowa and Utah. He arrived in September, pleased to be home and able to spend time with his family and friends while he awaited the next assignment from President Young.

January 7, 1862; Tuesday. ~~Thursday~~ This morning the Elders are mostly leaveing for their varied fields of labours all appearing cheerful and hapy and hopeful of an increase to the good work which is engaging them commensurate with their own growing appreciation of its principles and values.[1]

1. Lyman did not keep a journal from Jan. 1–6. Instead he pasted in dozens of pages from the *Millennial Star* giving lists of missionaries and minutes of meetings in

Brothers [Charles C.] Rich and [George Q.] Cannon and Sister [Elizabeth] Cannon ^who was with us two days^ went to Liverpool. I remained ~~for a few days~~ to attend to some business. The weather was dark and dull. Elder G[eorge] J. Taylor who has been for the present released from preaching on acount of a hemorhage of the lungs, accompanied brother Cannon to Liverpool ^to rest^ for a season ~~of rest~~. While here ~~Bywater~~ Elder [George G.] Bywater paid me one pound and five shillings money I had loaned him when the first arived in the mission.[2] The day passed away as did the most of the Elders [to their fields of labor]. In the evening I had some very pleasant and agreeable conversation with Brothers [William G.] Mills and [George] Halliday in regard to the principles of the gospel.

January 8, 1862; Wednesday. ~~Tu~~ This morning I parted with my son [Francis] Marion who went to London. I went with brother [William G.] Mills to brother [Edward] Price's where we dined, after which we went to Sutton to see Mr [Thomas S.] Edows, a lawyer in relation to some money that had been paid into court for Mrs. [Ann] Randall of Utah. I engaged him to make out such papers as were necissary to the obtaining of the money as the administrator of the estate of Mrs Randall's husband, deceased.[3] This buisness done we returned to Birmingham Brother Mills went to meeting. I passed the evening in reading [Richard F.] ^Burton's book^ [City of the Saints] and writing my journal. Brother George Halladay stayed with me tonight.

January 9, 1862; Thursday. To day I called on Mr Edows in Birmingham after which I went with brother [William G.] Mills to see brother [George] Hewetson[4] with whom I had some conversation on the subject

---

Birmingham. After the conference, he lingered in Birmingham a few days before returning to Liverpool.

2. See entry for Dec. 13, 1860.

3. Ann Burdett Randall was a British convert whose husband, Isaac Randall, had died. Living in Payson, Utah, with her second husband, Joseph Randall, likely a relative of her first husband, she was relying on the church to help her collect some 480 British pounds owed her from Isaac's estate. Lyman was ultimately unsuccessful in that effort. See entry for May 1, 1862; Brigham Young to Amasa Lyman, Nov. 13, 1861, and Brigham Young to Joseph H. Randall, Nov. 14, 1861, Brigham Young Office Files, CHL.

4. George and Mary Hewitson and two daughters emigrated in 1864 on the ship *Hudson*. George took a second wife, Mary Ann Waring, in 1869, and became an American citizen in 1877. Probably because of his polygamy, his first wife filed for divorce and left him and their children. "Third District Court," *Salt Lake Herald*, Feb. 27, 1884.

of tent makeing. Weather very rainy. Brother [George] Halliday left to day for his field in the Lands-end District.[5] In the evening brothers [William G.] Mills and [John D. T.] McAllister attended meeting in the Farm Street Chapel.[6] I did not ago out to meeting ^but^ past the evening in reading history.

January 10, 1862; Friday. To day in company with brother [William G.] Mills I visited some of the Saints at this residences viz Brothers [Thomas E.] Gange and Naper and their families. In the evening at brother Naper's brothers Jacob ^G.^ Bigler, S[amuel] L. Adams and J[ohn] D. T. McAllister joined our party. Some little rain was falling as we returned to Farm Street. While here stoping with brother N. and family I had some conversation with them in reference to the relationship of the Spirit of Man ~~and~~ ^to^ the body in which it dwells on the Earth. The conversation was called out by some references to Phrenology[7] by some of the parties.

January 11, 1862; Saturday. This morning the rain was falling copiously. After gathering together my traviling equipage and saying adieu to Sister [Louisa] Mills in company with brother [William G.] Mills[8] I repaired to the New Street Railway Station and at twenty minutes past 11 oclock was seated in a cariage to L. Pool [Liverpool] where I arived about 4 oclock and found the friends at 42 [Islington] all well. In the evening Elder J[acob] G. Bigler arived from Birmingham after a cold and unpleasant ride of some five hours.

January 12, 1862; Sunday. This morning brothers [Charles C.] Rich

---

5. Land's End is at the southwesternmost end of mainland Britain.

6. The chapel, acquired in 1860, was at the intersection of Hunter's Vale and Farm Streets in Hockley, two miles from downtown Birmingham. It replaced a former Catholic chapel the church had been renting for some three years on Villa Street, a block away.

7. Phrenology was like palm reading but involved an analysis of a person's head shape to determine their psychological makeup.

8. William G. Mills and his wife, Louisa Sleater, converted to Mormonism in England and immigrated to Utah in 1855. He soon married a plural wife, Emily Hill, who was a survivor of the Willie Handcart disaster. In 1860 William and Louisa returned to England as missionaries, and Emily divorced him for abandonment, marrying Joseph Woodmansee. Emily went on to become a prominent poet and songwriter and is still known for her "Handcart Song" ("Some must push and some must pull ..."). William left the church while on his mission and was excommunicated for adultery in 1863 "Notice," *Latter-day Saints' Millennial Star* 25, no. 20 (May 16, 1863): 314.

and [George Q.] Cannon went to St. Hellens[9] to attend meeting with the Saints there. I remained at 42 and in the evening at 6½ oclock I addressed the Saints at the Assembly rooms showing them that the gospel was and is a system of peace to prepare the way for and build up the Kingdom of God that his will might be done on Earth as in Heaven and thus extend universal peace to bless mankind.

January 13, 1862; Monday. To day I received a leter from Eliza [Maria Partridge, Lyman's fourth wife] at Salt Lake City. The news was good from health and peace prevailing with the people. I passed the day in the office engaged in reading and writing was somewhat troubled with neuralgia in my head. The weather being dark and wet did not go out to day.

January 14, 1862; Tuesday. This day wrote a leter to [my fourth wife] Eliza M[aria Partridge] at S. L. City; and one to Platt DeAlton my son at the same place. I did not go out to day.

January 15, 1862; Wednesday. To day past the morning in writing for my home corispondence. In the afternoon Sisters McManny and Spencer called to see us and taried until evening. Brother John M. Kay entertained us with some songs and recitations in some of the dialects peculiar to the diferent shires in England.

January 16, 1862; Thursday. Today I made up my home corispondence. Was in the office through the day and in the evening I had a consultation with brothers [Charles C.] Rich and [George Q.] Cannon when came to the conclusion that myself and brother ^Rich^ had beter for the remaining time that we should be in this country before returning home in the spring travil seperately as by so doing we should extend our visits more widely among the Saints during our short stay. To day a most distressing accident occured in the Hartley Colliery [coal mine] resulting in the death of 204 men & boys by which a whole village was involved in the sorrowful consequences. 3 Saints were of the number [dead]. A fund for the relief of the sufferers in the above sad catastrophe will be raised from the people.[10]

January 17, 1862; Friday. To day I wrote a leter to my son [Francis]

9. St Helens is fifteen miles east of Liverpool.

10. The Hartley Colliery was a coal mine in Northumberland. The accident spurred Parliament to require that all new mines have an escape shaft. "Dreadful Colliery Accident," *Illustrated London News*, Jan. 25, 1862; "The Hartley-Pit Tragedy," ibid, Feb. 1, 1862.

Marion in the Essex Conference and in the evening I revised the report of some teaching I gave to the general council in Birmingham which was reported by Elder E[dward] L. Sloan.

January 18, 1862; Saturday. This morning in company with brother [George Q.] Cannon I started for Norwich via Manchester, Sheffield, Worksop, Newark upon Trent, Grantham, Peterborough ^and^ Ely ariving at Norwich at ¼ to 9 oclock.[11] We were met at the station by brother Blackburn, Bently; and [William] Bramall and by them were conducted to the Chapel House where we found brother Thrower and family all well. We were kindly cared for by them.

January 19, 1862; Sunday. This morning at half past 10 oclock we meet the Saints of the Norwich Conference ^who^ had assembled in conference capacity. Some few items of buisness were disposed of after which the audience was addressed by brother [George Q.] Cannon for one hour after which I spoke to them for some thirty minutes. The meeting then ajourned until half past 2 oclock at which time the meeting was again in cession. The audience was addressed by brother Cannon who presented the priesthood of the Church who were unanimously sustained.

I again spoke to the audience for one hour, when the meeting ajourned until half past 6 oclock when the chapel was filled with Saints and strangers. I spoke to the assembly on the principles of the gospel. The audience listened with apparent intrest a good spirit pervaded the conference which was ajourned at ¼ to 9 oclock. We retired weary with the labours of the day but feeling well in health.

January 20, 1862; Monday. To day passed the time in conversation with the Saints and some strangers who had become interested in the truth and came in to see us and make some enquiries in reference to the laterday-work. In the evening attended a tea-party of the Saints and stranger-friends in the chapel. The entertainment was varied and to some intent interesting. In the conclusion of the entertainment brother [George Q.] Cannon and myself gave some instruction as to the nature and character of entertainments from which we should seek not only recreation but for the mind that should yield its fruits of knowledge to

11. They are traveling 60 miles to the east of Liverpool to Worksop, after which they will continue 130 miles southeast almost to the North Sea coast.

elevate and enlighten the soul. The party ajourned and we retired to rest as the small hours of the morning were seting in.

January 21, 1862; Tuesday. This morning I received a leter from [Francis] Marion incloseing one from his wife [Rhoda]. Today myself and brothers [George Q.] Cannon, [Elias H.] Blackburn and [Richard] Bently walked about 2 miles to visit and dine with brother Clark and family where we met Mrs Plumstead who was seeking the truth and said she should join the Church soon. Din[n]er over we returned to the Chapel House where I received a leter from Reuben McBride from Fillmore Utah and one from brother W[illiam] G. Mills in town of Birmingham.

From Norwich we went to Lowestoft[12] where the President of the branch Brother [John] Rackam had appointed a meeting for the evening. Brothers Cannon and Blackburn attended the meeting. I did not on acount of my weariness. Brother Cannon and myself had our lodgings with brother Hewit a fisherman. Brother H. and wife think of imigrating the next season. Lowestaft is situated on the east coast of England; and on the northeast of Suffolk County.

January 22, 1862; Wednesday. To day we visited the photographic gallery of brother [William] Reynolds we dined with Sister Reynolds the widowed mother of Brother Reynolds I sat for a likeness and so did brother [George Q.] Cannon.[13] We took tea with Sister R., wrote some leters and in the evening we attended meeting in the Assembly room. We had an attentive and apparently interested audience. Several ministers were among the listners. I addressed them for an hour on the principles of the Gospel. We then ajourned and retired to seek the rest we needed. We sought rest but found but little, the more we courted sleep the farther she seemed to be from us.

January 23, 1862; Thursday. This morning at ¼ past 6 oclock myself and brother [George Q.] Cannon were seated in the train him for Liverpool myself for the toyshop of the world, Birmingham. We traviled togeth[er] as far as the town Peterborough in Northhampton County and Via Norwich in Norfolk County and Ely in the County of Cambridge. We parted at Peterborough. I continued by journey via Stamford,

12. Lowestoft is a coastal town thirty miles from Norwich.
13. See his entry for July 3, 1861.

Rutland County and Leicester, County of Leicester, Burton on Trent in County of Derby, and Lamworth in Warwick County to Birmingham in the same county where I arived about 3 oclock. Found brother [William G.] Mills and family well also brother [John D.T.] Mcallister. The morning was clear the evening was dark and rainy.

January 24, 1862; Friday. This morning I wrote a leter to President ^B[righam]^ Young on business for Mrs. Ann Randall. In the afternoon I went with brother [William G.] Mills to visit brother [George] Hewitson the tent maker and purchased some cordage for the tent. The weather was very wet all the day, my walk to day was very unpleasant and wearisome.

January 25, 1862; Saturday. This morning I wrote a leter to my son [Francis] Marion in Essex. Today brother [William G.] Mills procured for me a copy of Websters Pocket pronouncing dictionary at a cost of two shillings. The weather to day has been comparitively pleasant. In the evening a Sist^er^ Mary Low called in and entertained us with a recital of her experience in becoming acquainted with the Saints and the gospel. Sister L. is a servant to the sick and her's is the experience of many who not only have to struggle with poverty; but the biter contumely of their purse proud masters in embracing the truth. The tent maker came in I gave him some instruction in reference to the makeing ^of^ my tent as the plan of its construction was new to him.

January 26, 1862; Sunday. The morning opened bright and beautiful and brothers [William G.] Mills; and [John D. T.] Mcallister were away to their morning engagements while I awaited the coming of evening for my alloted labor for the day. At half past 2 oclock I attended a meeting of Saints and strangers in the Farm Street Chapel which was filled with an attentive audience whom I addressed for an hour. Among the listeners were some Campbelites. Some of the last named denomination have recently joined the Church.

At half-past 6 oclock after a walk of 2½ miles I meet the Saints in the Oxford St. Chapel which was well filled many strangers were in attendence. I addressed them for more than an hour on the principles and ordinances of the Gospel. A fine kind of spirit seemed to brood over the people which promises well for future increas of the good work. I retired tonight weary with the labours of the day but hope that they may not be fruitless but yield a remunerative and generous harvest through the blessing of him who giveth the increase.

January 27, 1862; Monday. This morning at twenty minutes past 11 oclock I left Birmingham and arived in Liverpool about 3 oclock. Found brother [Charles C.] Rich stil afflicted with lameness in his ankle and Sister [Elizabeth] Cannon was recovering from an atack of illness under which she had been suffering for a few days. In the evening I accompanied brothers [George Q.] Cannon and [John M.] Kay to the residence of brother John Tullidge whose infant daughter we blessed. The weather was clear and pleasant thro the day. Received a leter to day from my wife Cornelia [Eliza Leavitt, fifth wife] in Parowan Utah T[erritor]y. The news was good and cheering.

January 28, 1862; Tuesday. Today I was engaged in revising some of the minutes of the Elders Council did not go out to day.

January 29, 1862; Wednesday. Today I wrote some for my home corispondence and in the evening I went with brother [John M.] Kay to Birkenhead and attended a meeting of the Saints of that branch whom I addressed for an hour on the advantages of practical religion and the saving influence which it is calculated to exert over those under its influence.

January 30, 1862; Thursday. Today I remained in the office during the forenoon. In the evening in company with Brothers [George Q.] Cannon, [John M.] Kay, [Edward L.] Sloan, [George J.] Taylor and [Henry] Whitall I visited the Free Library to make some historical researches. We were only partialy successful. Brother [Charles C.] Rich did not acompany us as he was engaged in making himself ready for his departure on the morow.

January 31, 1862; Friday. This morning brother [Charles C.] Rich left us at an early hour. I wrote a leter to Reuben McBride of Fillmore and concluded one to my wife Cornelia at Parowan. In the evening I walked out in town in company with brothers [George Q.] Cannon and [John M.] Kay and brothers [Joseph] Bull and [George J.] Taylor. Closed the labours of the day by making some preparations for our journey of the next day to Wales.

February 1, 1862; Saturday. This morning at ¼ to 8 oclock myself and brother [George Q.] Cannon were on the way for Cardiff via Birkenhead, Chester in Chester County and Shrewsbury and Ludlow [in Shropshire][,] Hereford in Hereford County and Abergaveny Monmouth County.[14] Ariving in Cardiff we were meet at the station by brothers [Thomas E.] Jeremy, [George G.] Bywater and others and were conducted to the residence of brother Samuel Lynne Evans, the President of the Cardiff Branch, with whom we found provisions made for our entertainment during our stay in Cardiff. We were considerably weary with our day's journey. Soon after our arival we were joined by brother C[harles] C. Rich from Cheltinham we also met brother George Halliday from Bristol Gloucester ^County.^

February 2, 1862; Sunday. This morning we meet with the Saints of the Cardiff Conference and others in their hall. When the meeting was opened the condition of the Cardiff Conference was presented by brother [George G.] Bywater after which the meeting was addressed by brother [Charles C.] Rich who presented the Priesthood of the Church who were sustained by the unanimous vote of the Conference after which brother [George Q.] Cannon addressed the meeting after which the meeting ajourned until 2 oclock. At which time the meeting was again ^in^ cession in the temperence Hall[15] (the use of which had been gratuitously extended to us for the occasion by its proprietor Mr [Jacob] Mathews who attended our meetings although himself an infidel).

The conference was addressed by brother Cannon after which the meeting ajourned until 6 oclock. We took tea with brother [James] Watts and family after ~~the~~ which we were again with the people in the temperence Hall. I addressed the audience of Saints and strangers who listened with apparent intrest. The audience numbered some 6 hundred persons or more. A good and kind spirit pervaded the people in attendence throughout the day.

February 3, 1862; Monday. To day past the morning in writing after which we went to the residence of brothers Parkman and Thomas with whom we dined and in the evening myself and brother [Charles C.] Rich ^and [George G.] Biwater^ called on Sister Davies with whom we took

14. These cities were stops on the Great Western Railway's southern line, made possible by a merger with the South Wales Railway in 1862.

15. The hall, which occupied nearly the entire block, was used for all sorts of alcohol-free entertainment including theater and even a circus; the reference on Feb. 3 is to a concert and pantomime performance. The hall was later converted into a nonconformist church.

our tea. At half past 7 oclock we were in attendence at the meeting Hall where we were interested by a concert and Pantomine.

February 4, 1862; Tuesday. Remained at our lodgings throughout the day during which brothers [George Q.] Cannon and [Thomas E.] Jeremy went to Swansea to attend to some business. They returned in the evening when some members of the choir came in to brother [Samuel L.] Even's and sang for our entertainment. Brothers [Charles C.] Rich, [George G.] Bywater and [George] Halliday and [John] Morgan[16] were with me during the day. The weather was very wet through the day.

February 5, 1862; Wednesday. This morning Brothers [Charles C.] Rich and [George Q.] Cannon left[,] the first for Bristol accompanied by Elder George Halliday and the lat[t]er for Liverpool. After the departure of the brothers I past some time in writing my journal after which in company with brothers [Thomas E.] Jeremy and [George G.] Bywater I went to the residence of brother James Watts ~~with~~ and family with whom we dined, after which we taried with them until evening during which time we were joined by brother David ~~Davies~~ Moris Davies.

After takeing tea with our friends we repaired to the Meeting Hall where the Saints were assembled. ^I^ addressed them for above an hour on the necesity for our understanding from reasons within our selves that we were constituted to live beyond the Grave; and thus have the consolation of a hope founded on facts in stead of the empty declarations of the ignorant which only create an illusory hope which the realities of the Death of mortality must disipate[,] leaveing the soul thus beguiled the victim of most cruel disappointments and the slave of ignorence dark as night the gloom of which a knowledge of the truth only could relieve.

February 6, 1862; Thursday. Today in company with brother [Thomas E.] Jeremy I went to the residence of brother Shipton with whom we dined and in the evening we took tea with Sister [Ann] Saunders. After which I returned to our lodgings brothers Jeremy, [George G.] Bywater, [David M.] Davies, [Samuel L.] Evens, [Edward] Pugh and [John] Morgan were with me this evening. We enjoyed some pleasant and

16. The Welsh convert John Morgan became a well-known stone mason in Utah who worked on the Salt Lake Temple for twenty years. "Life of Master Mason Finished," *Salt Lake Herald-Republican*, Apr. 26, 1911.

instructive conversation on the principles of the gospel as revealed for the exaltation and holiness of humanity.

February 7, 1862; Friday. This morning I received leter from Geo Braithwaite which I answered. The weather is bright and clear this morning. Dined to day with Mr John Gwyn and family. They do not belong to the Church but are talking of going to Utah. After diner we returned to our lodgings. Brother [Thomas E.] Jeremy was with me to diner; and in the evening he acompanied me to the residence of brother Thomas Mathews with whose family we took tea. Brother Mathews was not at home. Returned to our lodgings brother [Edward] Pugh came in and sat with us for an hour or two. During the day brothers [David M.] Davies; and [John] Morgan left us to return to their respective fields of labor.

February 8, 1862; Saturday. This morning I received a note from brother E[dward] L. Sloan with a transcript of a discourse delivered in Birmingham for revision. I attended to the revision and returned it by post immediately. We dined with our kind Host brother [Samuel L.] Evens and at a ¼ past 3 oclock in company with brothers [Thomas E.] Jeremy and [George G.] Bywater I was on the way by rail for Mountain-ash a small village [twelve miles south of Merthyr Tydfil] situated on the Taft River the principle stream of the vale of the same name.

At the station we were meet by a number of the Saints by whom we were welcomed and solicited to spend the night with them. We accepted the invitation and myself and brother Jeremy we[re] conducted to the residence of brother James Murry[17] and family with whom we lodged for the night. After our arival a brother [blank] Shepherd and his wife called in to see us and receive some counsil from us in reference to some diferences existing betwe^e^n them of a domestic nature. I gave them advise ^with^ which they seemed to be pleased and said they would ad^o^pt it and act acordingly.

February 9, 1862; Sunday. This morning ^at 10 <u>oclock</u>^ in company with the Saints from Mountain ash myself and brothers [Thomas E.] Jeremy and [George G.] Bywater were on the way to Aberdare. On our arival we were welcomed by Elder Thomas Reese President of

17. James Murray was a miner who emigrated the following year on the sailing ship *Cynosure*. His wife, Mary, gave birth to a daughter on the ship and died in Echo Canyon, a few miles short of Salt Lake City.

the Merthyr Conference and were then conducted to the residence of brother David Williams and family with whom lodgings had been kindly provided for our accomodation during our stay here.

At 11 oclock we meet the Saints in their Hall (called the Horse and Groom).[18] The place was crowded to the extent of its capacity for standing room. The meeting was opened in due form after which the Merthyr Conference was represented by President Reese after which the Priesthood of the Church was presented and unanimously sustained by the vote of the conference. I then addressed the audience for a half an hour when the meeting ajourned to assemble in the [White Lion] Temperence Hall at 2 oclock.

The audience of Saints was assembled in the Hall at the hour and many strangers were in attendence swelling the congregation to a size much beyond the morning cession. I addressed the audience for an hour or more they listened with apparent intrest a good and kind spirit prevailed. Meeting ajourned until 6 oclock when the meeting was again in cession with a large number of strangers who listened with breathless attention while I spoke to them for an hour and a half in reference to the principles of the gospel as a system of education for the salvation of universal humanity. Meeting ajourned and we retired to rest which we much needed.

February 10, 1862; Monday. To day in company with ^brothers^ [Thomas E.] Jeremy and [David M.] Davies I went to the residence of David Reese and family distant from Aberdare 2½ miles down the Taff River at the middle Dyffryn Coaliery in ^which^ brother Joshua Evens holds the position of over man and brother Reese that of fire-man. We dined with brother Reese and his family after which brothers Jeremy and Davies left[,] the former for Aberdare[,] the later for Swansea. In the evening in company with brother Rease I went to the residence of brother Joshua Evans and family with whom we took tea Mrs Evens did not belong to the Church but she received and treated us very kindly.

After tea brothers Evens and Reese acompanied me to Aberdare[19] Via Abermman. At our host's, brother David Williams, some of the

18. The Horse & Groom was a "public house" (tavern and hotel) used by several denominations for Sunday services. It was built in 1835 and closed in 1871.

19. Aberdare, similar to Merthyr Tydfil, was a booming coal-mining town when Lyman was there.

Saints had come in who cheered us with some singing after which we retired to have that rest we much needed. The weather to day has been cool but pleasant our walk was very pleasant tho wearysome. The report of our Sabbath day meetings from the strangers who were in attendence show that a good impression was made on the numerous auditory [guests] who were adressed during the day and evening.

February 11, 1862; Tuesday. Today myself and brothers [Thomas E.] Jeremy and [David] Reese dined with brother [David] Williamses family and in the evening we took tea with a Sister Thomas then made some other calls on the Saints after which we returned to brother ~~Thom~~ Williams where some of the Saints were gathered who cheered us with some music and songs. After this [we] blessed the infant daughter of brother and sister Williams and gave some instruction in reference to the principles of truth as being in some degree connected with universal human action.

February 12, 1862; Wednesday. Today in company with brothers [Thomas E.] Jeremy and [David] Reese I called upon and dined with brother Thomas Davies and family. His wife did not belong to the Church but she received and treated us very kindly. Made a brief call on the family of John Evens after which we returned to brother [David] Williams and af^ter^ a short stay we bade our kind entertainers farewell and in company with brothers Jeremy, Reese, and Williams I walked one mile to the residence of Mr Daniel Jones and family who were baptist in religion. Mr J is cousin to brother Jeremy. We were most kindly received by the family with whom we taried until half past 8 oclock P.M. when we~~re~~ were acompanied to the station by Mr Jones and two of his little daughters who seemed lo[a]th to part with their new found kinsman and the American Stranger.

Brothers Reese and ~~Jones~~ ^Williams^ had left previously, the former to go on foot across the hills to Merthyr and the later to return home to his family. The train by which we traviled was some twenty minutes behind time but when once seated in the cariage a ride of ten minutes brought us through the mountain to Merthyr Tidville where we were meet by brother Reese and conducted to his residence here [and] by the provident care and warm kindness of Sister [Elizabeth] Reese our wants were provided for. After partakeing refreshments we retired to rest somewhat ^wearied^ with the labors of the day.

February 13, 1862 Thursday. This morning I received a leter from my wife Lydia [Partridge, eighth wife] in Farmington Utah dated Dec 29th /61. The news was good and cheering.[20] Answered the same this morning. We dined at home to day and in the afternoon we called on brother John Morgan; and family with whom we took tea after which we repaired to the Meeting Hall where the Saints and strangers had meet. I addressed them for an hour on the necesity for practical purity of life to secure the blessing of salvation from sin and Death. The audience listened with the most profound attention and interest.

February 14, 1862; Friday. This morning I was cheered by receipt of a leter from my son F[rancis] M. L. in the Essex Conference. He wrote hopefully as tho through blessing[s] of the Lord on his exertions he was beginning to overcome the ^obsticles^ and master the labors of his new position all of which gives me much joy in hopes of a hapy and glorious future for my child as he will grow in purity and the love of the truth with the increase of the Kingdom of God to greatness and power.

I wrote a leter to brother W[illiam] C. Staines in London and in the evening in company with brother [David] and Sister [Elizabeth] Reese I called upon brother Owen Thomas and family with whom we took tea. After which we were joined by brother [Thomas E.] Jeremy when we called on Mr John Roberts and family who were not members of the Church. They received us kindly and ~~procured~~ secured for our entertainment the attendence of a harper who interested us with some fine music from the famous Welch harp.[21] Mr and Mrs R[oberts] are thinking very favourably of the gospel.

February 15, 1862; Saturday. This morning made myself ready for our departure and at ¼ past 3 oclock myself and brother [Thomas E.] Jeremy were on the way for ~~Blana~~ ^~~Alf~~ Bla[i]na^ via Crumlin at which station we were detained for two hours during which time we called upon brother [blank] Jones and family with whom we took some refreshment and administered to some of the family who were sick. From thence we passed on to Bla[i]na where we were met by Elders [Richard]

20. Lyman loved to hear from his family but seemed unaware of their struggles as they relied on the goodwill of neighbors and friends in his absence. They were scattered across Utah Territory, from Farmington to Parowan 250 miles away.

21. The Welsh triple harp is a large, orchestra-style harp in a wooden frame, played seated. Its distinction is that it has three parallel rows of 27–37 strings each.

Palmer and [George G.] Bywater and were conducted to the residence of brother [blank] Jones and family where provision had been made for our entertainment. We were kindly received and cared for.

February 16, 1862; Sunday. This morning at half past 10 oclock we meet with the Saints of the Conf. The meeting was duly opened after which the condition of the conference was reported by Elder [Richard] Palmer the Prst. of the same. When the Priesthood of the Church was presented by Elder [Thomas E.] Jeremy and was sustained by an unanimous vote after which the meeting ajourned until 6 oclock. Myself and brother Jeremy dined with Mr Parry and family who think of joining the Church soon. The ajournment over we were again in meeting. The hall was crowded to its utmost capacity for standing room.

I addressed the audience for an hour or more. A good spirit pervaded the assembly and under its benign influence our conference was ajourned after which myself and brother Jeremy took tea with brother and sister [blank] after which some of the Saints came in and entertained us with some fine singing after which we parted from them to climb the steep acclivity of the hill to our lodgings which when we had gained we ^found^ the couch welcome and very greatful after the labours of the day.

February 17, 1862; Monday. This morning myself and brother [George G.] Bywater came to Cardiff Via Newport and brother [Thomas E.] Jeremy went to Aberdare. I arived in Cardiff about 2 oclock. Found brother [Samuel L.] Evens and family well. I was myself suffering some from cold I had contracted during the past week. In the evening brother [John] Morgan returned from the northern portion of the conference where he had been laboring since our departure from Cardiff. He reports some baptizing in that quarter during last week. Brother [Edward] Pugh came in and a brother Tuckfield who has been for some time separated from the Church.

February 18, 1862; Tuesday. Today I passed the time at our lodgings until evening when in company with brother [George G.] Bywater I went to the residence of brother George Parkman and family with whom we took tea and after went with brother Parkman to the Temperence Hall where he was engaged as a musician.[22]

22. George Parkman would emigrate the next year on the ship *Amazon*, along with other musicians (and families) who were in a popular Welsh musical group that in

February 19, 1862; Wednesday. This morning I received a leter from brother W[illiam] C. Staines in London giving a verry encouraging account of the condition and prospects of the work in the London Conference. During the day we were joined by Elder [Thomas E.] Jeremy from the north and in the evening in company with brothers Jeremy and [George G.] Bywater I went to the residence of brother John Watts (in temperence town)[23] with whom and family we took tea after which we went to the Saints Chapel[24] where I addressed the Saints who had assembled there for one hour on the acquisition of knowledge which constitutes eternal life.

February 20, 1862; Thursday. This morning I received a package of leters containing one from my [thirty-two-year-old] son-in-law Philo Carter [husband of Matilda] and one from my [twelve-year-old] daughter Maria Louisa both from Beaver City and [Beaver] County in Utah and one from brother [George Q.] Cannon in Liverpool and one from brother D[avid] M. Stuart in Scotland incloseing one from brother ~~Alle~~ Alexander Rogers in the Kingdom of Fife. In the after-noon some brothers came in and entertained us with some music from the harp and other instruments; After which I went in company with brothers [Thomas E.] Jeremy and [George G.] Bywater to the residence of brother Charles Sheen and family with whom we took tea and sat with them for a short time and then returned to our lodgings.

February 21, 1862; Friday. This morning I received a note from Elder [Edward L.] Sloan reporter with M[illennial] S[tar] for revision for the press. This disposed of I engaged in my corrispondence comprised of some leters for home some for the mission. To day heard some of the particulars of the recent accident in the colliery near Merthyr Tidville 50 men were lost. Dureing the day I procured the adjoined account of the ~~of~~

Utah became the Ogden Brass Band. Parkman relocated to San Jose in 1870. "The Brass Band," *Ogden Daily Herald*, Mar. 13, 1886.

23. When the train from Cardiff to Swansea was constructed in the 1850s, the course of the Taff River had to be straightened so that the former riverbed became available for development. What was built there was called Temperance Town, anchored by the Temperance Hall and Temperance Hotel (also called Thomas Raper's hotel) and surrounded by other suitable establishments. Over the years, howver, it ironically came to be "the very definition of intemperance, with more illegal drinking dens, brothels and crime than anywhere else in Cardiff" (Mortimer, "City Center," *Cardiff: The Biography*).

24. By this he means the space the church rented at the temperance hall or hotel.

~~the~~ accident in the Cethen Coal-pit of Wednesday the 19th as published in ^the^ Cambria Daily Leader of the 21st.[25] Closed the day's labors by writing to brother [George Q.] Cannon in Liverpool and brother [William C.] Staines in London.

February 22, 1862; Saturday. This morning I commenced the labors of the day by writing to brother David M. Stuart in Scotland. There is some rain falling this morning which renders the street slipery and unpleasant. Having closed my corrispondence I passed the residue of the day in conversation with pa[r]ties who came in; and in reading for my own improvement. In the evening ^I^ had an interesting conversation with brother Thomas Thomas and Samuel Evens upon the ^principles of the^ gospel as applied to the actions of men in the domestic relations of life (between husbands and wives parents and children) to produce peace and thus ~~produce~~ ^develope^ hapiness in every place where they have their application to regulate the feelings and actions of man and wooman.

February 23, 1862; Sunday. The morning opened bright and clear which ^was^ much of a relief to the days of dark weather that preceded it. Several of the Brethren came in incidentaly with whom I enjoyed a pleasant pastime. At 2 oclock I meet the Saints in their hall, the sacrament was administered after which I spoke to them for more than an hour, after which the meeting ajourned to reassemble at 6 oclock in the Temperence hall.

In company with brother Jeremy I took tea with brother Thomas Thomas and family after which we repaired to the hall where I addressed the assembled audience for an hour and a half. They listened attentively. We retired to night much wearied with our labor.

February 24, 1862; Monday. This morning at 10 oclock I was on way for Birmingham where I arived about 3 oclock. Found the Saints here well I lodged brother [William G.] Mills and family. Brother [John D.T.] McAllister was with me.

February 25, 1862; Tuesday. This morning in company with brother [William G.] Mills I went to see brother [George] Hewitson and gave him some directions about my tent. After this I started for Liverpool where I arived about half past 5 oclock. Found Sister [Elizabeth] Cannon

25. Lyman inserted here the newspaper article detailing Cethin Colliery explosion in which forty-nine people died.

some beter and heard leter read from Prest Brigham Young bearing date of [blank] Jan the news was good and cheering.

February 26, 1862; Wednesday. To day received leter from my son [Francis] Marion he wrote in good spirits and reported the good work on the increase in his conference. I revised some Counsel reports for the press and wrote leter to Marion. Brother [George Q.] Cannon and others went to see and administer to brother [William] Ajax whom they found very ill and suffering most excrutiating pain in the urinary and genital organs supposed to arise from the formation of stone in the bladder. A glance at the papers show that the Hartley [mine disaster] relief Fund has reached the amount of £4000 which if honestly and judiciously applied may relieve much suffering and want.

February 27, 1862; Thursday. This morning brother [William] Ajax is reported to be beter. Sister [Elizabeth] Cannon is also improving in health. In the evening brother E[lias] H. Blackburn came preparatory to sailing on the next Saturday for New York to assist brother John Brown the business of the emigration.

February 28, 1862; Friday. This morning about 3 oclock Brother [John] Brown arived from London and with brother [Elias H.] Blackburn went to see the American Consul and took the oath of allegience to the government of the United States. I passed the day with the Brethren in giving them such advise as promotes the successful acomplishment of the mission.

March 1, 1862; Saturday. This morning we were st[ir]ring early and the brothers [John] Brown and [Elias H.] Blackburn were ready for their departure and brother [George Q.] Cannon and myself acompanied them to their vessel where we bade them adieu and wishing them a pleasant voy[a]ge and prosperous mission. We returned to still prosecute the labors that must engage us for a time ere will folow in the track of our brethren just departed.

Our brethren who have left us this morning: May the winds be ever propitious and may no danger lurk in their path and may no enemie's hand have power over them; but may their path be radient in the light of truth that will fill them with wisdom ^and^ lead them to the hapy fulfillment of their arduous labors of love for the gathering Saints who journey Zion-ward.

March 2, 1862; Sunday. This morning the weather is dry and cool. The sick about the house are stil improving. Brother [George Q.] Cannon has gone to meeting and as the walk is long I have concluded not to go until 6 oclock P.M. I received a leter this morning from Elder R[euben] A. McBride in London indicating a wish to return home the present season. Brother Cannon received a leter from Elder J[ohn] D. T. McAllister which breathed a spirit of disaffection with his present position. In the evening I went to the assembly room[26] and spoke to the Saints upon the origin of sin and the means of its surpression. The audience listened very attentively.

March 3, 1862; Monday. This morning I received a leter from brother C[harles] C. Rich intimating his intention to visit France before returning to Liverpool to which I wrote an answer. During the day I wrote leters to Elders W[illiam] H. Dame[,] Wm Gibson[,] Charles Welch and R[euben] A. McBride. During the day I was measured for some clothing. Brother [George Q.] Cannon received a note from brother John Brown from Queenstown [New Brunswick]. Himself and brother [Elias H.] B[lackburn] were well no sea-sickness weather fine.

March 4, 1862; Tuesday. This morning opened bright and clear but very cool. Sister [Elizabeth] Cannon is stil improveing. During the day I received a leter from my son [Francis] Marion in Essex. Some snow fell to day which gave the town a wintry appearence.[27]

March 5, 1862; Wednesday. To day brother James Brown came in from Notingham and brother E[dward] L. Sloan from Belfast Ireland. Past the day mostly in the office working on my journal. Wrote a leter to my son [Francis] Marion in Essex.

March 6, 1862; Thursday. This morning I made ready for my journey to Scotland and at 2 oclock myself and brother [Edward L.] Sloan were on the way and were acompanied to the Steamer by brothers [George Q.] Cannon and [James] Brown. The weather was dark and wet. We were soon sick after we were under way which detracted much from the pleasure of our journey which was protracted to some 25 hours in length

26. The assembly room was in a Methodist chapel on Oxford Street, built in 1795 by Congregationalists. The LDS Church rented space for a few years, acquired the building in 1865, and disposed of it three years later.

27. The remaining journal contains entries from 1871–72, including mention of séances Lyman attended, and can be found in chapter 11. The next entry here comes from a new diary book with entries from Mar. 5 to Aug. 29, 1862.

during ^all of^ which I was very sick and uncomfortable. Our journey was consequently rather cold and unsocial as the rain prevented us from being on deck. The wiching beauties of the scenery along the Clyde were all wraped in the Storm's shroud that hid them from the obtrusive gaze of the curious observer of Scotland's beauties and ^her^ rural charmes.

March 7, 1862; Friday. This morning we found slight relief from our sickness as ^we^ came into the Firth of the Clyde. About 10 oclock we arived at the town of Greenock where we taried until 1 oclock and ^then^ continued our ascent of the river to Glasgow. As our steamer came to her moorings we were gladened by seeing in the crowd of expectant waiters our brothers [David M.] Stuart and [Robert] Sands whose warm greeting sent a thrill of pleasure through o^u^r souls ariseing from the reflection that we were not alone nor forgoten but that other hearts beat in unison with our own and warmed alike under friendships kindling impulses and the burning glow of that comprehensive charity that grasps a world to be saved as the object of its exercise and marking the extent of its own development and ~~and~~ applications. We were conducted to the residence of brother Sands where provisions had been made for our entertainment during our stay in Glasgow. My sickness stil continued with me for several hours.

March 8, 1862; Saturday. Today I did not go out but was engaged in writing in my journal and in ~~in~~ revising some reported discourses for publication. In the evening I meet with a portion of the priesthood of the Glasgow Conference to whom I delivered a lecture (showing some of the reasons why as ministers of the gospel we should not enter into antagonistic controversy and discussion) which was reported by Elder E[dward] L. Sloan for publication. The brethren listened with much apparent intrest while I was adressing them which much enhanced the ~~intrest~~ ^pl[e]asure^ of the occasion. The weather was pleasant to day.

March 9, 1862; Sunday. This morning at 11 oclock I meet the Saints of the Glasgow Conference in the Irongate Hall. The meeting was duly opened after which the Conference ^of Glasgow^ was represented by President Robert Sands. The report was altogether of an encourageing character shewing the good work and its hapy results to be on the increase with and among the people.

The Priesthood of the Church was then presented to the ~~Church~~

Conference and was sustained by an unanimous [vote] after which I addressed the audience for one hour. My discourse was reported by brother [Edward L.] Sloan and the meeting ajourned. At 2 oclock the meeting was again in session and I addressed the audience for an hour after which our very pleasant conference ajourned. After meeting I went to Dine with brother [Robert] Patrick and family.[28] Brothers [David M.] Stuart and Sloan were with me.

March 10, 1862; Monday. This day was past mostly in reviseing and prepareing mater for the press which we dispached to Liverpool in evening mail. During the day I received a leter from brother R[euben] A. McBride in London informing me that he had co^n^cluded that time had come for him to return home the present year. In the evening I attended a very pleasant tea party of the Saints and their friends. The entertainments were varied with music and recitations.

At the close of the evening's entertainments brother [Robert] Patrick the President of the Glasgow Branch on behalf of the conference presented me with a Scotch bonnet and plaid in ~~token~~ evidence of their kind feelings. A similar present was also presented to me for brother C[harles] C. Rich. The short hours of morning had come ere we retired to rest. ^I^ felt some neuralgic pain in my head to night while at the party.

March 11, 1862; Tuesday. To ^day^ wrote in my journal and in the evening visited and took tea with brother ~~Stuart~~ ^Jas Brown^ and family. Brothers [David M.] Stuart and [Edward L.] Sloan were with me.

March 12, 1862; Wednesday. This morning I received a leter from my wife Dionetia [Walker Whitney, second wife] in the town of Minersville Beaver County.[29] Answered the same also wrote one to Priscilla [Turley, seventh wife]. In the evening took tea with bro. Peter McFarlane & family bros Stuart & Sloan were with me.

March 13, 1862; Thursday. Left br. [Robert] Sands' at 10 minutes

28. Robert Patrick, his wife Rachel, and two young children emigrated the next year to Salt Lake City where he became a successful carpenter, merchant, counselor to Bishop Orson F. Whitney, and city alderman. He traveled during the height of the US Civil War. "Early Pioneer of Salt Lake Dies," *Salt Lake Tribune*, Sep. 1, 1918.

29. The handwriting switches abruptly here. Edward Sloan probably recorded what Lyman dictated, though, because the style remains affected in Lyman's characteristic way. For the next several entries, the writing shifts between Lyman and the clerk, while Lyman recovers from his headache.

past 6 A.M. for Dundas St. Station in company with bros. [David M.] Stuart and [Edward L.] Sloan bro Sands accompanying us to the station. Left there at 40 minutes past 6 by rail for Dunfermline.[30] Bro. Stuart provided tickets.

A pleasant ride ^through the^ country ^combining^ good arable land with varied natural beauties & fringed on our left hand by a small range of hills brought us at about 8 oclock to the field or plain of Bannockburn where on the 24th of June A.D. 1314 Robert Bruce commanding the Scotch army defeated the English army of Edward Plantaganet the 2nd of the name who wore the crown of England.[31]

The contrast between the period when sound of deadly conflict of contending hosts smote the echoes of the neighboring hills and the present when the valley presents the aspect of peaceful cultivation—when the plough & spade prepare the waiting soil to receive the seed of future blessings to humanity in a harvest of earth's life sustaining productions with no other sound to disturb the slumbering echoes than the shrill whistle of the locomotive as it speeds on over its iron track with its ever varying freight of life[—]was suggestive of the march of mind in the path of progressing & ever increasing improvement. At a distance of 3 miles to the northeast lies Stirling the theatre of many stirring events in old Scottish history.

The old castle like the rest of its ancient kindred crowns the summit of a hill and doubtless was from its commanding position a place of great strength and importance in feudal ages. The departure of the train precluded us from stopping so after changing cars we rolled away over the winding [River] Forth lying like a huge serpent of beaten silver glistening in the morning sun. After crossing the river we caught a hasty glance of the ancient city of Stirling which could not be seen from the railway depot. At a distance of perhaps a mile and a half the foundation stone is laid of a monument to the heroic & patriotic Wallace on what is called the Abbey Crags.[32]

At 10 minutes to 10 reached Dunfermline and went up to see the old

30. Dunfermline is a city northwest of Edinburgh, across the Firth of Forth, famous for manufacturing damask linen and rope.

31. King Edward II is remembered for having been murdered by English nobles due to his relationship with the French nobleman Piers Gaveston, "the king's favorite."

32. The Abbey Craig is a rocky outcropping high above Stirling, about half a mile

Abbey after having a little breakfast at bro James Hoggans. The Abbey grounds were closed but we walked through the old Abbey Church and around its grounds & graveyard. The old church is a massive structure in the gothic style rendered rather remarkable in appearance on the outside by huge unshapely protecting butresses built by King David 1st[33] to preserve it from falling[,] which may be the main reason why it stands in so perfect a state of preservation. It was built by Malcom the 3rd Canmore King of Scotland & son of Duncan [I] Macbeth's victim[34] sometime about the middle or towards the latter part of the 11th century and is said to have contained the bodies of two of his sons, boys whose stone coffins are shown in the body of the old church. One of the boys died 14 years of age the other was killed in battle [as] such at least is the local tradition whether historically true or not I cannot say.

A new church built by the ~~sg~~ site of part of the old one[,] the foundation stone of which was laid on the 10th of March 1818. [It] contains to the right of the pulpit[,] as ^the^ front of part of a gallery[,] a wooden entablature bearing on the left hand corner the inscription[:] "In this church were buried King Malcom Canmore & St. Marg^ar^et his queen who died 1093. Their sons King Edward[,] King Alexander[,] & King David and their descendants Malcom 'the Maiden'[35] and King Alexander" while on the right hand corner is ^to be^ read "In this church are buried King Robert Bruce who died 1329 his queen Elizabeth[,] his nephew sir Thomas Randolph Warden of Scotland[,] Annabella Queen of Robert the 3rd and Robert Duke of Albany[,] Governor of Scotland."[36] In the center is the Arms of England surmounted by a crown with the letters

---

north of the remains of Cambuskenneth Abbey. On top of the hill stands a 220-foot tower honoring William Wallace.

33. David I was the Scottish king whose parents, Malcolm III and St. Margaret of Wessex, built the abbey. David I ruled for nearly thirty years despite being repeatedly challenged in battle by a brother's son. Margaret was canonized in 1250 by Pope Innocent IV.

34. Shakespeare's account of Macbeth assassinating King Duncan I is based on historical accounts.

35. Malcom IV was called "the maiden" because he resisted marrying and was delicate and pious. He founded the Abbey of Paisley.

36. Robert Stewart, the Duke of Albany, served under several different monarchs and was probably responsible for the murder of his nephew. When James I was imprisoned, Robert acted as de facto king of Scotland.

[blank] I A Crown R R[37] on the sides of it and the date 1610 below. The symbol probably has reference to the act of "Kirking" being performed here by James the 6th of Scotland & 1st of England on his marriage which means going to church the first time after the ceremony. The pulpit stands nearly over what was the grave of Robert Bruch [Bruce] which was discovered when making excavations to lay the foundation of the new erection.

Outside opposite the centre of the end of the new part is the grave of St. Margaret as she is called[,] a princess who exercised a powerful influence over the condition of the ~~Scott~~ Scotch in that early age through her husband Malcom Canmore. A Saxon princess herself she possessed a love for religion & education & by her winning ways & sweet beauty as well as her unaffected piety she melted down ~~the~~ ^her^ almost savage husband. ^She was the means of^ introducing agriculture on the north side of the Forth and made herself beloved by her subjects. Her grave is covered with a couple of large rocks one raised above the other the upper being the lesser containing a large amount of fossilized animals remains principally shells.

Brother John Hogan attended us in our visit to the Church and its grounds. At half past 3 oclock we were on the way for Cowden-Beath where we arived and were welcomed by Elders ^James^ Brown[,] ^Alex^ Letham & Robert Gillespie who was the President of the branch. At night held meeting in a private home and preached to a small congregation. Bro Sloan reported for me. Slept at Sister Simpson's bro Sloan with me.

March 14, 1862; Friday. After breakfasting with S[iste]r Simpson left Cowdenbeath by rail en route for Dundee being accompanied to the station by a few of the brethren. Bros [James] Brown & [Alex] Lethem rode a few miles with us on their way to fill appointments in their ministerial capacity. We reached the Firth of Tay at ½ past 12 and crossed to the other side in a steamer where we entered the cars again & reached Dundee at 5 minutes to 1 P.M. Were met by Elder W[illiam] S. Baxter and accompanied him down to the ferry where we acrossed the Firth to Newport about 2 miles to Sister Copely's. Spent the evening preparing matter for the press.

37. The clerk wrote these letters above and below the line to mimic how they appeared in the church.

March 15, 1862; Saturday. Spent the greater part of the day preparing matter for the press. Suffered so severly with neuralgia that I was unable to accompany bros [David M.] Stuart, [Edward L.] Sloan, and [William S.] Baxter to meeting at Dundee. The[y] returned about 10 o'clock & reported a good little meeting but attendance limited[,] some of the brethren being engaged at work. Wrote a letter to my son F[rancis] M. Lyman.

March 16, 1862; Sunday. Attended conference at Dundee and preached twice. In the morning on the nature of the Savior's mission to the world and in the afternoon on the nature & design of the ordinances of the gospel. Bro [Edward L.] Sloan reported both discourses.[38] Returned to Sister Copely's with the brethren.

March 17, 1862; Monday. Engaged preparing matter for the press. Wrote to Bros [George Q.] Cannon & R[euben] A. McBride.

March 18, 1862; Tuesday. Engaged preparing matter for the press in the morning. At ½ past 3 started for Dundee on our way to Arbroath. Brs [David M.] Stuart, [Edward L.] Sloan & [William S.] Baxter my companions left Dundee by rail at 5 o'clock & reached Arbroath at 5 minutes to 6. Preached in the small hall rented by the Saints on the gathering of the saints & upbuilding of the Kingdom of God. Bro Sloan reported. Slept at bro David Buist's at which place some of the Sisters came in after meeting and entertained us with some singing.

March 19, 1862; Wednesday. Passed the morning in labor of preperation of mater for the press. At noon ~~with~~ went to the residence of brother Duncan with whom we dined. And in the afternoon we made a brief visit to the Abbey of St. Thomas now in ruins. Another entertainment of singing by the sisters. Closed the day and in the small hours of the morning we sought our rest.

March 20, 1862; Thursday. This morning e^n^gaged in preparing mater for the press until brothers [David M.] Stuart & [William S.] Baxter came

38. In the morning discourse, the sermon that was responsible for Lyman's downfall proposed that, as an extension of the idea that human nature is good, there was no need for an atonement. Rather than being in a fallen state, human beings are born innocent and progress through practice to moral clarity, Lyman suggested. He was sustained in this teaching by other missionaries such as Elias Harrison, who would become part of the Godbeite movement in Utah. The Dundee sermon was published in the *Millennial Star* in April.

in. At half past 11 o'clock we started for Newport Via Dundee. Arived at our lodgings at the residence of sister Sarah Copeley at 1 oclock and resumed our labors in the preparation of mater for the press.

March 21, 1862; Friday. The morning was somewhat darkened by clouds altho[ugh] not attended with storm. Myself and brother [Edward L.] Sloan stil prosicuted our work during the morning hours before we were forced to desist to make ready for our journey to Edinburgh. At 2 o'clock myself and brothers [David M.] Stuart, [William S.] Baxter and Sloan bade our kind Sisters Copley's farewell and in a carriage traviled to Tayport where we parted with brother Baxter and proceded thence by rail to Burntisleand station then [south] across the [Firth of] Forth to Edinburgh where we arived about 10 minutes to 6 o'clock and were meet and welcomed by brother George Peacock.

We were conducted to the residence of brother John Hutchinson and family where provisions had been made for our entertainment. I received a leter this evening from my son F[rancis] M. Lyman in Essex England. Passed on our way today Kinghorn in Fife where King Alexander lost his life by falling over a high clift or pecipice.[39]

March 22, 1862; Saturday. To day ~~at~~ past the morning in preparing mater for the press and then went to brother Peter McOmie's where we dined after which I wrote to brother [George Q.] Cannon and at night I addressed priesthood of the Edinburgh Conference who were assembled at brother McOmie's. After the meeting returned to brother [John] Hutchinson's after which I wrote a leter to brother John S. Gleason in New-castle on Tyine. This evening took tea with brother Wm Reid and family.

March 23, 1862; Sunday. To day attended the meeting of the Edinburgh Conference. Preached two discourses which were reported by brother [Edward L.] Sloan. Dined with Wm Jack and family and then returned to our lodgings and brothers [David M.] Stuart and Sloan went to the evening meeting with the Saints.

March 24, 1862; Monday. To day myself and brothers [David M.] Stuart and [Edward L.] Sloan submited to a series of experiments made

---

39. King Alexander III was traveling to visit his wife, the queen, on the northern coast of the Firth of Forth when he was thrown from his horse and killed. The part about falling off a cliff is thought to be folklore.

by brother [John] Hutchinson to obtain our portraits photographicly. At night in company with brothers Stuart and Sloan I attended a social party of the Saints in the Uneion Hall. We were entertained with songs and recitations. In conclusion I addressed the meeting my remarks were reported by brother Sloan.

March 25, 1862; Tuesday. This morning the weather was dark and damp some snow was falling. Passed some time in instructing brother [John] and Sister [Elizabeth] Hutchinson in regard to the instruction of their children in such way as to promote their physical health as the sure foundation for an extensive and continuous development of the powers and abilities of the mind through all the future of their lives by ceaseless aquisitions of knowledge. This done in company with brothers [David M.] Stuart and [Edward L.] Sloan I went to the residence of brother Wm Sims where we meet brother [George] Peacock and dined after which we went to brother [Peter] McOmie's where we took tea after which myself and brother Sloan returned to our lodgings at brother Hutchinson's and after passing some time in teaching our host and then retired to rest.

March 26, 1862; Wednesday. Weather damp & foggy. Bro [David M.] Stuart & [George] Peacock called in the morning and later on in the day Elders [James] Brown & [Alex] Lethem called. Stayed a short time and after making their adieus departed for their fields of labour. Bro John Hutchinson from Leith called through the day to receive some counsel relative to his emigration. Bro Hutchinson made some further photographic experiments on me and succeeded in taking an indifferent portrait. Spent the evening with the brethren & after the departure of Bros Stuart and Peacock spent some time in instructing our host on the importance of pursuing a course to extend our lives for usefulness as long as possible upon the earth. Packed up my things to start early in the morning. Through the day wrote to Bro [George Q.] Cannon in reply to one received from him relative to matters pertaining to the mission.

March 27, 1862; Thursday. Bade good bye to our host and hostess & in company with bros [David M.] Stuart and [Edward L.] Sloan started at 15 minutes past 7 A.M. for the railway depot off Princes St. where bro [George] Peacock met us. At 8 o'clock bade good bye to bros Stuart and Peacock and started with bro. Sloan for Newcastle-on-Tyne. At 20 minutes to 11 reached Berwick-on-Tweed where we stopped 1¼ hours.

This town was often the scene of strife between the contending Scotch and English each party claiming it as of right belonging to their respective countries. It sits at the mouth of the [River] Tweed and on the dividing line between England and Scotland.[40] Left Berwick at 5 minutes to 12 noon & reached Newcastle at 3 where we were met by Bros. J[ohn] S. Gleason & Wm Dallin by whom we were conducted to 8 High Ponteland Terrace, Barrack Road, where provisions had been made for our entertainment at the residence of Sister Sutherland and her daughters. Passed the evening in conversation with the brothers presen[t:] brother H[enry] W. Barnet was present; brother Sloan was engaged in preparing mater for the press. Brothers Dallin & Barnet left us to go to their lodgings.

March 28, 1862; Friday. This morning the weather was very dark and dreary the town was almost entirely obscured from our view. Spent the early part of the day in preparing mater for the press[,] and in the afternoon in company with brothers [John S.] Gleason and [Edward L.] Sloan I went to Sunderland where we arived at 6 o'clock and went to 3 Crow-Tree Terrace to the residence of brother Robert Paton where we lodged during our stay in town. Mrs Paton did not belong to the Church yet she made us welcome and comfortable in the enjoyment of her home. She did not attend our meetings.

March 29, 1862; Saturday. To day ^I^ attended to the final reading of some mater for the press.

March 30, 1862; Sunday. To day held two meetings with the Saints[,] my remarks were reported by brother [Edward L.] Sloan. Took tea with brother Newton and family and after our return to our lodgings I held a conversation with our hostess in relation to the gospel in my views of which she professed to believe. Before leaving brother Paton presented me with a copy ^of^ Eadie's Concordence.[41]

March 31, 1862; Monday. This morning in company with brother [Edward L.] Sloan at half past 7 oclock I was on the way to Liverpool where we arived at half past 5 oclock P.M. Found all well at 42. Sister [Elizabeth] Cannon was stil away.

---

40. Today the town is about two miles south of the Scottish border and a part of Northumberland, England, about 50 miles southeast of Edinburgh.

41. John Eadie was a Scottish theologian whose *Analytical Concordance to the Holy Scriptures* was published in 1857.

April 1, 1862; Tuesday. This morning received letters from home one from my [teenage] son Platte D. Lyman[,] [son of fourth wife][,] and one from my wife Caroline [Ely Partridge, third wife]. News good from home. Passed the day in writing and reading.

April 2, 1862; Wednesday. This morning in company with brother [George Q.] Cannon I started at 10½ o'clock for Birmingham where we arived about 2 o'clock. At brother [William G.] Mills we meet with brothers [Charles C.] Rich [John D. T.] McAllister and [Samuel L.] Adams. Brother Mills was not at home on our arival. In the evening brother Mills came in and brothers Rich & Cannon went and lodged with brother [Edward] Price. I lodged with brother Mills. The weather was rainy and unpleasant.

April 3, 1862; Thursday. Today in company with brothers [Charles C.] Rich and [George Q.] Cannon I listened to the recital of sundry maters of diferences ^between brothers [William G.] Mills[,] [John D. T.] McAllister & [Samuel L.] Adams^ after which I gave the brethren some instruction and they seemed satisfied and promised to do beter in future. A good spirit seemed to [have] influenced the brethren and they professed to be pleased with our instruction and counsel. ~~and instruc~~

The names of the brethren above alluded to are W. G. Mills J. D. T. McAllister and S. L. Adams. Passed the residue of the day with brother Mills (the other brethren having gone out) in reading and in conversation.

April 4, 1862; Friday. This morning the weather opened out bright and clear and after breakfast I walked out with brother [John D. T.] McAllister. Made a brief call on brother [Edward] Price and family after which brother Price caried us to the residence of the tent maker whom we found engaged in makeing bags for the Saints who were designing to emigrate the present season. The bags were water-proofed and appeared very good. My ^tent^ was not completed from brother [George] Hewitson's. I went and called at the store ^of^ Mr Lunt after ^which^ in company with brothers [Charles C.] Rich and [Samuel L.] Adams I called on and dined with brother William Gregg and wife after wich I returned to brother [William G.] Mills.

April 5, 1862; Saturday. This morning I parted with brother [William G.] Mills and family and at ~~8 o'clock~~ half past 9 o'clock in company with brother C[harles] C. Rich I was at the Railway Station where we were meet by brother [John D. T.] McAllister with whom we parted and were off for London where we arived about halfpast 2 o'clock. On our arival at 30 Florence Sttreet we were welcomed by brother Wm C. Staines; and brother George Reynolds.

About 10 o'clock brothers [George Q.] Cannon and [Edward L.] Sloan arived from Liverpool. Brother Rich was afflicted with a severe cold and cough attended with hoarsness that nearly prevented him from talking. My own health was not good. I had a severe pain in my head attended with a generaly feverish condition of body. The weather was dark and rainy. Brothers Rich and Cannon myself and brother Staines lodged at 30 st. Florence St. and brothers Sloan and Reynolds went to lodgings with brother [George E.] Grove and family.

April 6, 1862; Sunday. To day at half past 2 o'clock we meet the Saints of the London Conference in St. Georges Hall. After the meeting was duly opened the condition of the conference was briefly stated by President [William C.] Staines after which the audience was addressed by brother [George Q.] Cannon for an hour after which the meeting was ajourned until half past 6 o'clock. At the expiration of the ajournment[,] the meeting was again in cession and the Hall was crowded to the extent of its capacity for standing room. I spake to the audience who listened attentively. The addresses of the day were reported by Elder E[dward] L. Sloan. A good spirit pervaded the meetings the Saints felt well and hopeful in regard to their emigrations.

April 7, 1862; Monday. Passed the day counselling with bros [Charles C.] Rich & [George Q.] Cannon. In the evening bro Cannon left for Nottingham. Bro Rich much afflicted with cold.

April 8, 1862; Tuesday. ~~Monday 7th~~ To day in company with brother [William C.] Staines and [Edward L.] Sloan I visited the Kensington Museum;[42] and made some enquiries in reference to some artificial globes but did not purchase. Wrote leter to brother [William] Bramall and one to [Francis] Marion [Lyman] asking him to come to London to see me during the morning of to-day. Father [Thomas C.] Stayner was with us

42. The South Kensington Museum is now known as the Victoria and Albert Museum. It was conveniently situated, four miles from the St. George Temperance Hall and about the same distance from the mission offices on Florence Street. It featured inventions in the area of applied science and technology and replaced the former Museum of Manufactures.

and brother G[eorge] E. Grove called in to see us. Received a letter from cousin G[eorge] A. Smith of Utah.

April 9, 1862; Wednesday. The weather was dark and rainy. In the afternoon in company with brothers [William C.] Staines, [Charles C.] Rich, and [Edward L.] Sloan and my son F[rancis] M. Lyman I went to the residence of Elder G[eorge] E. Grove and family with whom ^we^ took tea after which the Saints of the North London Branch (over whom brother Grove presides) were assembled and I addressed them for an hour upon the principles of the gospel. Bro Rich spoke a little. As we were returning to our lodgings the rain was falling copiously.

April 10, 1862; Thursday. The weather stil is rainy and dark. Brothers [Charles C.] Rich and [William C.] Staines have gone out in the city. I have just received a note from brother [William] Bramall. This morning perused a letter from my daughter-in law to my son [Francis] Marion. The news from Beaver was good the family was well. At night Elder [Edward L.] Sloan and my son Marion attended a meeting of the Saints in Goswell Hall.

April 11, 1862; Friday. This morning at 8 o'clock myself and brother [William C.] Staines left the London Bridge Station by Rail for Maidstone in search of brother Reuben Hedlock[43] whom we supposed to be residing there. Our search proved fruitless as if there he was undoubtedly living under an assumed name. We returned to ^London^ where we arived at 3 o'clock. In the afternoon in company with brother Staines I visited Regent Street and purchased a leather traviling bag for which I paid £2.10. Returned to my lodgings and mad[e] preparation for my morning journey to South Hampton.

April 12, 1862; Saturday. At fifty minutes past 10 o'clock myself and brother [Edward L.] Sloan had parted with our friends at 30 Florence St and were on the way for South Hampton. Our road lay through a low country comprising some finely cultivated land and some that had much the ap^p^earance of portions of the unsettled parts of the Valleys of Utah.

We were meet and welcomed by brother [William] Bramall,

43. Reuben Hedlock arrived in England in 1840 as one of the first LDS missionaries to England and the first to reach Ireland. In 1843 he was named mission president and served for three years, then disappeared, leaving his church and family and remarrying. He moved to Maidstone, the capital of the county of Kent, and lived there to his death some twenty years later.

[Eugene] Henrioid and [blank]; and conducted to the ^St. Marys^ Cottage where lodgings were provided for myself and brother Sloan. We dined with Sister [Sarah] Eldridge [and] returned to the Cottage and received Sunday calls from the brethren and Sisters who came in to see us. All seemed in good spirits some were going to emigrate the present season and others were hopeing for the next season.

In the evening in company with brothers Bramall, Sloan, and Henriod and [George] Burgon I visited the residence of brother ~~and family~~ [blank] with whom we took tea and then returned to our lodgings for the night. The weather was beautiful throughout the day but rather cool with frost at night.

April 13, 1862; Sunday. The morning opened bright and clear. Brother [Edward L.] Sloan with the brethren attended the morning-service and I remained at the Cottage engaged in writing. In the after-noon I attended two meetings one at half past 2 o'clock and the other at half past 6 o'clock. The audiences composed of Saints and strangers were large and attentive. A most excellent spirit pervaded the people and the prospects are good for increase of the numbers of such as will be saved. The day closed and I was very weary with its labors.

April 14, 1862; Monday. This morning opened bright and beautiful and at 7 o'clock myself and brother [Edward L.] Sloan were on the way for Liverpool via Reading[,] Birmingham[,] Chester and Birkenhead where we arived after 8 o'clock P.M. During the later part of the day the rain was falling profusely. At the dock we were meet by brother [George Q.] Cannon. We found all well at 42. Was much wearied with the long ride of 13 hours. Brother James S. Brown came in to day.

April 15, 1862; Tuesday. To day wrote some in my journal. Felt very seriously the effects of the long ride of the previous day. During the day brothers [William] Gibson[,] [Thomas E.] Jeremy and [John S.] Gleason came in to make preperation for their Emigrating saints.

April 16, 1862; Wednesday. To day I revised a d^i^scourse for publication and wrote a letter to my son Platt Dealton Lyman at Great Salt Lake City Utah. During the day brother C[harles] C. Rich[,] John M. Kay and J[oseph] C. Rich came in and in the evening brothers W[illiam] C. Staines from London and W[illiam] G. Mills from Birmingham arived to make preperation for the emigrating Saints from their respective districts.

April 17, 1862; Thursday. This morning I wrote a leter to my wife Caroline [Ely Partridge, third wife] at Farmington in Utah. This morning received from a nameless friend £10 for myself and my son [Francis] Marion to help us in our necesities.

April 18, 1862; Friday. To day wrote letters[,] one to G[eorge] A. S[mith] and one to my son [Francis] Marion. I paid brother W[illiam] H. Dame £3.6 for money borowed to come to the country. To day brother Richard Bently reported to me that on yesterday a brother and Sister (with two small childre^n^) disappeared from the railroad. The name of the man was [blank]. This is the result of inattention to consil given for their preservation from other and like evils: But when ^will men be wise and prudent!^

April 19, 1862; Saturday. Weather dark and cloudy the shiping of the Saints is progressing. The lost brother of yesterday is with his family with the Saints to day he suffered no loss but the cost of his ^money.^[44]

April 20, 1862; Sunday. This morning brother [George Q.] Cannon and other brethren attended meeting in the Assembly Room. At half past 6 o'clock P.M. I was at the meeting room and addressed an attentive audience of Saints and strangers. The unexpected moving of the vessell from the Dock did not allow the emigrating Saints to attend meeting as they wished to.[45]

April 21, 1862; Monday. To day in company brothers [Charles C.] Rich and [George Q.] Cannon [we] appointed Elder James S. Brown to take charge of the Saints on board the J. M. Boyd and Elders John Lindsey and Joseph C. Rich to aid him as counselors. This done myself and brothers Rich and Cannon and others went on board the Boyd and after the ship and passengers had past examination of the officers of the government we called the Saints together and instructed them in regard to the course of conduct and deportment they should adopt to secure to

---

44. Most of the emigrating saints were poor laborers who had saved for years and relied on the Perpetual Emigration Fund to travel to the United States. For many of them, this was their first time more than a few miles from home, so the railroad schedules would have been confusing.

45. The packet ship *John J. Boyd* remained in dock another three days loading 867 passengers, of which 700 were Latter-day Saints. They arrived in New York on June 1. "Departure," *Millennial Star*, May 3, 1862, 283.

them the blessings of peace in all the vicisitudes of their varying journey of toil and labour to reach their distant home.

We bade the Saints adieu and returned to the office where the following brethren (partook of refreshment furnished by brother Cannon)[:] Rich, Cannon, Gleason, Bull, Staines, J. F. Smith, S. H. B. Smith, W. H. Dame, W. G. Mills, T. E. Jeremy, Richard Bently, J. C. Graham, W. H. Perks, D. M. McAllister, G. J. Taylor.

April 22, 1862; Tuesday. This morning brothers [Charles C.] Rich and [George Q.] Cannon visited the Saints on the Boyd as they were detained in waiting for the doctor who had not yet received his papers from London. The news [is] of a great battle near Corrinth in ^Tennessee^ which the losses are reported to be near 60,000 thousand on both sides.[46]

April 23, 1862; Wednesday. This morning received and answered a letter from my son [Francis] Marion. Had some letters of release made out for several of the Elders to go home and in the evening at forty minutes past 6 o'clock in company with brother J[ohn] M. Kay I started for Manchester where I expect to pass a few days.

April 24, 1862; Thursday. The weather was fine and clear this morning. In company with brother J[ohn] M. Kay I visited Clayton a suburbon portion of the city about 4 m[ile]s from our lodgings. Called at the residence of brother Ralph Wardell who is calculating to emmigrate this season. Bro W. was away from home on some buisness in connection with his emigration but returned just as we were leaving. We returned and called in the evening on the family of brother Owens a portion of who are making ready for their journey to Zion by the Manchester. The sisters entertained us with some fine singing.

As we returned to our lodgings we passed through the [illegible] Mill Hare.[47] A noisy and confused multitude thronged the streets which rendered our passage somewhat dificult and slightly unsafe.

---

46. The fight at Corinth (Mississippi, not Tennessee) began the campaign to control the Mississippi River and key railroads. Despite Lyman's report of 60,000 killed or injured, the casualties stood at about 2,000. Confederate General Beauregard regretted that with this battle, the South had lost "the whole Mississippi Valley and probably our cause." McPherson, *Battle Cry of Freedom*, 416.

47. This may be the Hare and Hounds neighborhood that had a famous pub of that name and an adjacent dog-racing track. "How Did Our Town's Worldwide Renown Go to the Dogs?" *Manchester Evening News*, Oct. 29, 2007.

April 25, 1862; Friday. Today passed the time in the city in company with brothers [John M.] Kay and [William H.] Dame. Received letters ~~one~~ from brother W[illiam] C. Staines from London and in the evening I received a note from brother [George Q.] Cannon stateing that the papers from Mrs [Ann] Randall had arived from Utah. This morning I signed and forwarded a letter of release for Elder Samuel Hargraves. Brother J[oseph] F. Smith came in and taried with us all the night.

April 26, 1862; Saturday. The weather was dark and rainy. Passed the most of the time in the house. In the after noon had a short walk with brother [John M.] Kay. Brothers [William H.] Dame & [Joseph F.] Smith were stil with us.

April 27, 1862; Sunday. To day meet with the Saints in their hall at half past 10 o'clock. The place was well filled. I addressed them for an hour after which the meeting ajourned ~~for~~ until 6 o'clock P.M. when the Hall was again crowded by an attentive audience whom I addressed for an hour and a half apparently to their satisfaction as evinced by their attention.

This evening parted with brother [William H.] Dame. Brother [Joseph F.] Smith stil remained with us. I felt much wearied with the labours of the day. Thirty years ago today I was bapized into the Church by Elder Lyman E. Johnson in ^Calidonia County state of V.T. at Mcendues Falls in Connecticut River.[48]

April 28, 1862; Monday. This morning at five minutes past 9 o'clock I parted with brothers [John M.] Kay and [Joseph F.] Smith at the railway station and started for Liverpool where I arived near 11 o'clock and found all well at 42. I took diner with brother [George Q.] Cannon and family and then at 45 minutes past 3 o'clock I started for Birmingham. Arived at the residence of brother [William G.] Mills about the setting of the sun [and] found all well. Some brethren and sisters came in and entertained us with some singing in which brother J[ohn] D. T. McAllister participated.

April 29, 1862; Tuesday. This morning received a letter from Elder George Peacock in Scotland which I answered and also wrote one to brother [George Q.] Cannon in Liverpool. Brought forward my journal

48. McIndoe Falls, Vermont, is just west of Lyman, New Hampshire. Unless they waded out too far, Lyman was baptized in his native state, the Connecticut River forming the border with Vermont.

to date and then in company with brother W[illiam] G. Mills I visited Sutton on buisness with Mr Ed~~e~~dews [Eddowes]. Returned at 6 o'clock. The weather has been warm and dusty so as to make our traviling rather unpleasant.

This evening received of brother Samuel L. Adams fifty pounds of gold in trust for safe keeping until we should meet in Liverpool previous to the sailing of the Ship Manchester on the 5th of May next. I also received of brother Adams some parcells of pins and needles purchased by him for brother [Charles C.] Rich and myself.

April 30, 1862; Wednesday. The morning opened bright and clear brought forward my journal of the previous day. Visited brother [George] Hewetson and family and dined with them and returned to brother [William G.] Mills in the after-noon and in the evening attended a social party at the Oxford Street Chapel where we were entertained with singing and recitations. Ajourned at 11 o'clock pleased with the varied entertainment.

May 1, 1862; Thursday. This morning I received some printed proof for reading a discourse preached in Scotland. After finishing my writing I went in company with brother [William G.] Mills to see Mr Edews and asertained that I could not collect the money belonging to Mrs [Ann] Randall on acount of lack of time previous to my return home. Two years ago to day I left home on my present mission.

May 2, 1862; Friday. This morning received a note from brother [George Q.] Cannon and at twenty minutes past 11 o'clock I was on the way for Liverpool where I arived about 3 o'clock and found several of the Elders present from diferent parts of the mission making preperation for the emigration.

May 3, 1862; Saturday. The weather was warm and clear. In the evening about 5 o'clock the Saints from London arived and with them my son [Francis] Marion who had left his field of labour to return home by the last ship of the season that is up for the 13th proximo.[49] The Saints were feeling well in regard to their prospective journey.

May 4, 1862; Sunday. This morning brothers [Charles C.] Rich and

49. That is, the next month, although Lyman was mistaken because the *William Tapscott* would sail that same month, 13th *instante* (or May 14 in reality), as the last ship of the season, and his son would be on it.

[George Q.] Cannon went to the meeting while I tarried at home and had brother [William] Perks to help me prepare my Books for the journey home. In the evening weather was dark and rainy.

May 5, 1862; Monday. To day was engaged with my Son [Francis] Marion in making preparation for our home-ward journey. In the evening we [were] all electrified by the receipt of a telegram from Salt Lake City (bearing the date of 15th of April) requiring brother [George Q.] Cannon to go immediately to the city of Washington to join Senator [William H.] Hooper.[50] We telegraphed to brother ~~in Copen~~ [John] Van Cott in Copenhaven and received answer that he could not reach ^us^ until the tenth and we then determined to sail on the 14th the first chance after sending the last ship-load of Saints for the season. We desided to place Elder J[acob] G. Bigler in temporarily in charge of the mission until the return of brother Cannon who was instructed in the telegram to retain ^charge of the^ office.[51]

May 6, 1862; Tuesday. To day with brothers [Charles C.] Rich and [George Q.] Cannon [we] organised the company of Saints (on the Ship Manchester) by ap^p^ointing Elders [John] D. T. McAllister and S[amuel] L. Aadams and Mark Barns to take charge of the company to N. Y. In the morning some rain was falling. In the after part of the day the rain ceased. In the evening a company of the Elders were together at the residence of brother Cannon.

May 7, 1862; Wednesday. At 10 minutes to 8 o'clock was on the way for Birmingham via Birkenhead. Arrived at 12 o'clock dined with brother [William G.] Mills after which I went to the residence of brother Hewitson and gave some instruction in reference to my tent.

May 8, 1862; Thursday. To day left my lodgings early in the morning and took my breakfast with brother Hewitson who furnished my tent and at 5 o'clock I left for Liverpool and arived about 8 o'clock. The cost of my tent was £5.2. Some female relations of brother [George Q.] Cannon came in.

50. President Lincoln was poised to sign the Morrill Anti-bigamy Act into law. Because of the urgency, Lyman and Rich took the steamship *Kangaroo* across the Atlantic in twelve days to unsuccessfully lobby Congress to withdraw the bill and grant Utah statehood. See Bitton, *George Q. Cannon*, 117–22.

51. Cannon returned to Liverpool on July 26, 1862.

May 9, 1862; Friday. This morning brother J[acob] G. Bigler arived from Ireland and others from other parts of the mission to prepare for the emigrating Saints. Passed the day in makeing preperations for our journey and wrote letter to Mrs Ann Randall of Utah.

May 10, 1862; Saturday. To day I received some Books from the Binders and prepared them for packing for carriage to Utah and secured the passages for our party on the Cangaroo. In the evening brother [blank] returned from London where he had been on buisness.

May 11, 1862; Sunday. This morning brother [George Q.] Cannon with several of the Elders went to meeting and brother [Charles C.] Rich and myself tarried at the office. In the afternoon brother Rich attended meeting and at half past 6 o'clock I was in the Assembly room [on Bold Street] and spoke to the people in this room [in the Music Hall where] I first spoke publically in England.

May 12, 1862; Monday. Passed the most of the day in making preperation for our journey and in the evening had a meeting of the Elders who were to remain in the field while others were returning home. We blest and set apart to the Presidency of the mission brother Jacob G. Bigler and also Elders E[dward] L. Sloan and Eugene Heriod to take the Editorial Charge of the Star and brother W[illiam] H. Perkes ~~to to~~ John C. Graham to the buisness of the office. We also set-apart Elder Richard Smith (from Ireland) to the labour of the ^ministry^ under brother Bigler.

After instructing the brethren in relation to the duties devolveing upon them in our absence from them and also in their more general relations to the work of God we retired as the small hours of the morning were close upon us. We had but a few hours of feverish restless sleep.

May 13, 1862; Tuesday. This morning closed up my trunk and other packages for the ship to send in the care of my son who was going with the Saints. Disp^a^ched my luggage to the ship and sat down to write my journal. At 1 o'clock went on board of the Tapscot with brothers [Charles C.] Rich[,] [George Q.] Cannon and others to organize the Saints for their journey which we acomplished by placing elder Wm Gibson in charge as president and Elders John Clark and Francis M. Lyman as his Counsillors.

During the time of our stay on board a lad of some 14 years of age by the name of John James from Wales fell through the Hachway to the lower deck a distance of 20 feet and by the fall his thigh was broaken. He did not however leave the ship [for medical care].[52] We completed our buisness with and bade the Saints adieu and returned to the office where we passed the most of the night in completing our preparations for our journey. I bought a double barelled shot gun and a revolver for each of which I paid five pounds.

To night we had but little sleep. The council of the Elders was comprized of the following[:] A. M. Lyman, C. C. Rich, G. Q. Cannon, J. F. Smith, J. M. Kay, Wm Gibson, J. G. Bigler, W. C. Wood, W. G. Mills, F. M. Lyman, G. Haliday, J. D. Chase, W. H. Dame, [T.] Jeremy, [W.] Bramall, [E.] Henriod, [?] Delman, [W.] Staines, [W.] Snow, [G.] Taylor, D. McAllister, [W.] Perks, [E.] Sloan, [J.] Graham.[53]

May 14, 1862; Wednesday. This morning rose at 5 o'clock and made myself ready for the journey and at 11 o'clock we were on the way. Several of our brethren who remained in the field accompanied us to the side of the steamer where we bade them and England adieu. A feeling of joy thrilled through our souls ^ariseing^ from the reflection that through the mercy [of] God our feeble efforts to do good for humanity have not been nutralized or weakened by any known impropriety or wrong.

Soon after starting we passed the Tapscot and as we steamed by we were loudly cheered by the Saints among whom could be seen the venerable head of Capt [Thomas C.] Stainer on deck and beside him Capt [James B.] Bell the gentelmanly commander of the Tapscot.[54] There were some 830 Saints on the Tapscot.

The weather throughout the day was pleasant. At 6 o'clock we passed Hollyhead. There was no sickness on board today. Night settled down calmly around us and in sleep's sweet oblivion we became for a time unconcious of the pains of the present or the weariness of the past. Rate of travil 10½ knots per hour.

May 15, 1862; Thursday. Rose at half past 6 o'clock. Weather stil calm and pleasant some of the passengers were slightly disquieted by sickness.

52. He recovered and arrived in Utah in October 1862.

53. The names were written in small print on two lines. I have silently added commas.

54. They had a good voyage even though it took the sailing ship six weeks to cross the Atlantic. James Bell was said to be an able and sympathetic captain. William Gibson journal, 2:40–42, in CHL.

My own health is good. At half past 11 o'clock we were at Qeenstown ^distant from^ where we were Liverpool 240miles. Detained until 4 o'clock P.M. Some five hundred Irish emigrants came on board at this point we also received a small accession to our number of cabin pasengers. The wind through the day was variable but the sea was smoth and weather pleasant. At half past 10 P.M. past Fastnet [Rock] distant from Dunnstown sixty miles. Sailed 147 miles from Fastnet computing the distance at 12 n[oon], Lat 51–25; Long 13–35.[55]

May 29, 1862; Thursday. We arived in New York and were meet and welcomed by brothers H[orace] S. Eldridge[,] E[lias] H. Blackburn and [John] Horspool. We took lodgings at the Steven's House, the weather was warm and sultry. Two of the vessels that were freighted with Scandinavian Saints have arived. On one of them[,] [the ship] Franklin[,] there had been some sickness and 47 deaths during the voyage. The company was in the charge of Elder [Christian A.] Madsen. The above mortality was mostly confined to the children.[56]

May 30, 1862; Friday. This morning I made some arangements for leaveing in the evening for Boston. I wrote leter to my son [Francis] Marion who is a passenger on the Tapscot and left it with brother Eldridge. At 5 o'clock in company with brother W[illiam] H. Dame I took passage for Boston on the steamer Plymouth-Rock.[57]

May 31, 1862; Saturday. And by the connecting Railway we reached Boston half past 5 oclock and proceeded by rail to the small country village of Stoneham and were made welcome by Mr James Winn husband of the Sister [Sarah Dame Winn] of brother [William H.] Dame.[58] Here

---

55. Lyman's handwriting becomes shaky and almost illegible. The entry is followed by three blank pages he probably meant to fill in later but could not at the time. See Rich diary, May 24, 1862; "Arrival in New York," *Millennial Star*, June 21, 1862, 396.

56. According to passengers onboard the *Franklin*, an outbreak of measles killed forty-five children and three adults, 10 percent of the passengers. They were buried at sea. Hans Christensen autobiography, in CHL; Jens C.A. Weibye, reminiscences and journals, ca. 1862, in CHL.

57. The steamship *Plymouth Rock*, built in Detroit in 1854, was part of the Fall River Line that took passengers from New York to the train terminal in Fall River, Massachusetts, where they could board a train to Boston. "Great Lakes Maritime Database," Digital Collections, University of Michigan Library, quod.lib.umich.edu; "Fire on Board the Steamer Plymouth Rock," *New York Times*, Sep. 26, 1865.

58. Like Lyman, Dame took the opportunity to visit family before continuing on to Utah.

I meet with his other Sister [Martha Ann Dame] and Mother [Susan Horne Dame]. We were treated with the greatest kindness. After taking some refreshment I went to Boston with brother Dame and bought some articles of clothing and while in the city called on my cousin Perez Mason[59] who is a City Missionary and resided a[t] 18 Dover Place near the head of Dover [now East Berkeley] Street. In the evening returned to our friends in the country.

June 1, 1862; Sunday. This morning attended the [Methodist] Sabbath school by the request of our friend [James] Winn and addressed the school and tarried to the meeting that followed. Heard a very good discourse from a Mr Wheeler[60] who spake very kindly to us after the services and gave us an invitation to join him in the evening services but on acount of our weariness from sickness and journeying we did not attend the meeting.

June 2, 1862; Monday. Passed the day with our friends in Stoneham. Some rain fell during the day but I received no letters from New York as I had expected. In the evening received a parcel of clothing from the merchant in Boston as he promised the day before.

June 3, 1862; Tuesday. This morning at fifteen minutes to 7 o'clock I was on the way to Barnet [Vermont] after biding brother [William H.] Dame and our kind friends at Stoneham adieu. I reached Barnet between 4 & 5 o'clock P.M. I was meet and welcomed by my old friend and school mate Franklin Paddleford[61] who kindly brought me forward to my cousin Albert Mason's where I was most kindly received and my wants cared for. I slept tonight where I resided when I joined the Church in 1832 since which time I have been abroad. This is my third call since that time.

June 4, 1862; Wednesday. To day made calls on some of my old aquaintences who all received me kindly. I lodged with my cousin Philip Mason & family whose residence was on the place where I was born at which time it was the property of my grandfather Perez Mason.[62]

---

59. This would be the last time Lyman would see his favorite cousin whose death eight months later was unexpected.

60. Wheeler was chaplain of the Methodist Society through 1864. William Burnham Stevens, *History of Stoneham, Massachusetts* (Stoneham: F. Whittier, 1891), 79.

61. Benjamin Franklin Paddleford was born in 1811 in Lyman, his family having been among the original settlers. He died in Monroe, about three miles from where he was born.

62. Not to be confused with his cousin Perez above.

June 5, 1862; Thursday. To day I traviled to the town of Littleton [New Hampshire] and called on my cousin John ^M.^ Charlton[63] with whom in the afternoon I visited my Mothers Sister Lois Dodge whom I found in poor health being evidently in a decline.[64] Lodged with cousin C[harlton] with whom I passed the time very pleasantly. The weather dry and warm rain much needed for the crops.

June 6, 1862; Friday. Passed the morning with cousin [John M.] Cha^r^lton and family. After diner cousin C. took me in his carriage to Littleton Village. On our way we called on Aunt Lois Dodge and while there I received a call from two men by the name of Millin one of whom by the name of David had formerly belonged to the Church of the Saints. He gave me a warm and pressing invitation to call upon him. From the village I went to Lancaster. While at the Village waiting for the stage I saw George Puddleford the son [of] Peter Paddleford.[65] I lodged at the Lancaster House.

June 7, 1862; Saturday. This morning at half past 6 o'clock wer[e] on the stage for Northumberland where I arived about 8 o'clock and here I hired a pr^i^vate conveyance to North Stratford and another to East Columbia where I arived about 3 o'clock at the residence of Wm Pilbro where I found my Mother and Sister [Lucy] Pilbro[66] in tolerable health. Our meeting was agreeable. Passed the evening in a pleasant conversation with my mother and sister. I found my Step-Father [Isaiah] Emerson in rather beter health than when I saw him two years before.[67] The old people were now residing with my brother-^in^-law Pilbro.

June 8, 1862; Sunday. To day I attended meeting with brother and Sister Pilbro. Heard two discourses from a Mr Morrill Methodist preacher. At 5 o'clock I preached in the school house which was crowded with attentive

---

63. John M. Charlton was a prominent resident of the Littleton community. Even though he never won an election for public office, he ran several times and always had a strong showing. Jackson, *History of Littleton, New Hampshire*, 1:484, 503, 621.

64. She died three weeks later on June 29 at the age of seventy. Simeon Dodge was her third husband, the previous two husbands having died.

65. Peter Paddleford was an uncle of Lyman's old schoolmate and well-known for designing and constructing local covered bridges and mills. Child, *Gazetteer of Grafton County, N.H., 1709–1886*, 467.

66. Lucy was Lyman's half-sister. See entries for July 1–11 for more on Lyman's relatives.

67. Isaiah Emerson was eighty years old and would live two more years.

listeners anxious to hear from the stranger. In the audience was my aged mother [and] the collection of friends[,] [who] seemed well pleased.

June 9, 1862; Monday. This day I passed the time with my mother. During the day a Mr Enoch Rogers who had heard me speak the day before came in to have some conversation. He was an infidel so called. In the evening brought forward my journal. Continued my lodging at the residence of my Sister Lucy. The ^weather^ was very warm and sultry.

June 10, 1862; Tuesday. Remained with mother and during the day in company with Father [Isaiah] Emerson. I made a call on Mr Dustin with whom we spent some time in general conversation and then returned home. The weather stil warm and dry.

June 11, 1862; Wednesday. This morning in company with my brother-in-law [William] Pilbro my Sister Lucy and my Mother I went to the Town of Colebrook to visit [step-]brother David Emerson. I had with my brother and his family an agreeable and pleasant visit and taried with them over night while our party returned home. My [step-]brother David's family is composed of his wife Alvira & his eldest daughter Susan Elma the second Lucy Adilad & Isaac Allen. The weather stil remained dry.

June 12, 1862; Thursday. This morning I returned to brother [William] Pilbro's acompanyed by sister Alvira. Passed the day in conversation with ^my^ Mother & Sisters. In the evening Sister Alvira bade us farewell and returned home.

June 13, 1862; Friday. This morning at 10 oclock in company with my brother-in-law [William] Pilbro (after saying my adieus to my Mother[,] Sister Lucy and Father Emerson) I started for North Stratford where we arived about 3 o'clock. Here I parted with my kind-hearted brother Pilbro he to return home I to wait the evening train for Island-Pond [Vermont]. The hours of waiting past I was at length seated in the carrs and a short ride of less than an hour brought me to my destination for the night.

~~As~~ I alighted[,] a ready waiter conducted me and carried my little baggage to the Island-Pond House[68] where I found comfortable quarters

68. The Pond House, built in the 1850s during a boom in the population of Island Pond from 193 to over 700, was halfway between Portland, Maine, and Montreal, Quebec. The town had two hotels, several retail stores, a church, two schools, a saw mill, and several mechanic shops to service wagons. Hemenway, *Vermont Historical Gazetteer*, 1:956.

for the night. Sup[p]er dispached I retired to rest of which I felt the need after my travil through the day and thoughts that had thronged my mind on leaving my aged Mother perhaps for the last time that we might meet and part while performing life's fitful and warying journey.

June 14, 1862; Saturday. This morning opened bright and clear. I rose early to catch the morning air to sooth the slightly feverish condition of my travil wearied body before resuming my journey. Our breakfast dispached at 6 o'clock[,] the stage was at the door. It consisted of a smal spring-wagon drawn by two horses. The interior of the car^r^iage was ocupied by one passenger a fine looking soldier and a barrel of dried apples. With these animate & inanimate passengers I found a seat and we rolled away for Charlestown.

We had not gone far when on inquirey I learned that my soldier friend and fellow traveler had been in the war and had seen some warm and somewhat dangerous service from which he had for a time been relieved on acount of sickness and was now on his way to visit his anxious parents[,] wife & child[,] and ^who^ was the anxious Mother who[se] aching heart was to find its richest ^earthly^ solace in the safe and honorable return of her gallant and heroic son? Strange as it may appear She was my only [full] Sister [Ruth] whom I was in a few ^~~miles~~^ hours ^I was^ to meet for the second time in 28 years and my traviling friend and soldier was Sergent Richard P. Goo^d^all[69] my Sister's oldest son my nephew. At the village of West Charlestown I parted with my nephew who went to the Town of Holland to see his family and I to Brownington to see my Sister whom I found in somewhat beter health than when I saw her 2 years before. I was most cordialy received by sister and family who were made doubly hapy by the news of the arival of their Son in the country.

June 15, 1862; Sunday. The day opened bright and clear and was passed away in pleasant conversation with my brother-in law [Richard] and family and in anxious looking for the returning soldier but he did not come and after our store of conjectures as to the reason we retired concluding to wait his coming with all the patience we could command.

June 16, 1862; Monday. This morning renewed our watching for the

69. Goodall would be back in Maryland in time for the Battle of Antietam in September. He would also participate in the Battles of Fredericksburg and Gettysburg. He survived, was promoted, and moved his family to Missouri, where he died in 1906.

arival of the expected ones of yesterday. About 11 o'clock my nephew [Richard] and his wife [Ellen] and child [Fred] arived much to the joy of the family circle. After Din[n]er my brother-in law & his Soldier Son and wife and his oldest Daughter [Caroline] went to visit some of their family connections and I remained with my Sister whose health would not allow her to go out. The day past very pleasantly. Evening brought home our friends and after an hour of sociable interchange of feeling we retired.

June 17, 1862; Tuesday. This morning my nephew [Richard] bade his Father and family and myself adieu to return to the sanguinary field of his service to his country. We each utered the hasty farewell with a brief prayr for his safety and the Soldier was away on his path of duty and toil. About 10 o'clock my brother Richard Goodall started for the Town of Danville to attend to some business. I did not go out through the day.

June 18, 1862; Wednesday. Passed the day with My Sister and her children in reading and in conversation on a variety of subjects.

June 19, 1862; Thursday. To day wrote leter to my Mother and received from my neice Caroline a lock of hair from each of my Sisters children as a mementoe as I could not obtain their pictures. In the evening my brother-in law returned from Danville where he had been on buisness. Made my baggage ready for the morrow's travil and retired to rest and think that my brief visit to my kindred was nearly ended and for the last time with some of them.

June 20, 1862; Friday. To day after biding my Sister and family adieu[,] by stage and rail and private conveyence I reached the residence of Mr David Millin in the Town of Littleton Grafton County N. H.[,] distant from Browningston Caledonia County VT[,] the place of starting[,] about 60 m[ile]s. On my way I called upon and dined with Aunt Lois Dodge my Mother's Sister. I was kindly received by Mr M and family who had at an early day been baptized into the Church but for want of knowledge which they failed to obtain they did not grow in the truth as they should have done. They seemed much engrossed in the world and its wealth. The residence of Mr Millin was in sight of that of my old school-fellow Henry Paddleford but not being able to walk I did not visit him ~~but past the day~~.

June 21, 1862; Saturday. I passed the day with my friend ^[David] Millin^ and his family.

June 22, 1862; Sunday. This morning Mr [David] Millen carried me to the residence of my cousin John M. Charlton. On the way I called and bade Aunt Lois & husband farewell. Received their mutual blessings and passed on at cousin John's. I saw the first time my cousin Wm Charlton and wife and in the afternoon cousin John carried me to the home of cousin Albert Mason. I felt quiet unwell to day[,] after taking some mild medicine I felt beter.

June 23, 1862; Monday. This morning bade cousin Albert and family adieu and at a quarter to 10 oclock I was on the rail for the west and at 5 o'clock P.M. I was in Springfield Mass and put up at the Massasoit House[70] concluding that on acount of my health that I would not travil at night.

June 24, 1862; Tuesday. This morning at 8 o'clock I was on the way for Buffalo [New York] where I arived about 10 o'clock and put up at the Wadsworth House. My fare [food] was indiferent.

June 25, 1862; Wednesday. This morning at ¼ to 8 o'clock I left Buffalo and arived in Willoughby [Ohio] at twenty minutes past 2 o'clock and hired a conveyence to Kirtland where I meet with my brother-in law's family who were all well. I had not seen them since 1837 when Mr [Jared] Randall[71] moved myself and family to the state of M. O.

I found on looking around that something of change had marked the flight of time. The paternal dwelling as if joining in the march of progressive ^improvement^ had doned it's Robe of white and in Q[u]eenly beauty [provided] looks-out from its lovely nesting in its verdent rest. I entered the old mansion meeting with a hearty welcome from Mrs Randall and Daughter. The apartments were much the same as when in years long-past it was ~~my~~ temporaly my home.

June 26, 1862; Thursday. To day rode out with my nephew Mr Henry Randall and made a call on Mr Charles Wightman[72] an old acquaintence of mine with whom I had not meet for the last 24 years. Brother

70. This elegant hotel was located next to the train station. The block also had retail stores selling books, clothing, stationery, and toys; a hair dresser; a lithographer; and a supply store that specialized in railroad-car fixtures.

71. Jared Randall married Matilda Tanner, a sister of Lyman's first wife, in 1820. As Lyman notes below, he visits the Randalls' son Henry and daughter Maria and their families.

72. Charles Wightman converted in New York in 1835 and moved to Kirtland, where he and his family remained while others continued on to Missouri and Illinois. After immigrating to Utah, Wightman and his family settled in Payson.

Wightman had sent his family and was prepareing to folow them to Utah. That same was the case with brother Christopher Dixon[73] and family and some other old members of the Church residents of Kirtland. I received a call from Mr Stephen Carpenter[74] whom I knew when he was a boy.

June 27, 1862; Friday. Passed the early part of the day with my Sister [in-law Matilda] Randall and in the evening I visited my Nephews ^Henry's [Randall]^ family and took sup[p]er with them.

June 28, 1862; Saturday. Visited my niece Mrs [Maria] Tuttle in company with brother [Jared] Randall & wife and daughter. Had ^a^ most agreeable visit. Found Mr. [Madison C.] Tuttle and his brother [Francis] who resides with him social and genial gentlemen. Returned to Kirtland in the evening. The prospects for crops is ^very^ good in this state (^compared^ with the New England states) for fruit & grain & hay.

June 29, 1862; Sunday. Today the rain was falling during the day. In the evening I spoke to a small audience of friends in the Temple. They listened with apparent intrest. The apartment of Temple in which we met shewed in its delapidated condition evidences of neglect and abuse which was only in keping with the moral condition of the parties who have controlled and managed the House <u>who so far from being able to build lack the capacity to take care of that that has been built for them</u>.[75]

June 30, 1862; Monday. This morning I called on some of my old aquaintences Mrs [Abigail] Bump the widow of Jacob Bump and also his Mother [Lydia] who is above 90 years old.[76] I called on Luman Carter[77] and family with whom I dined and then went to the village where

73. Dixon, Mary Ann Wightman's brother, left Ohio the next month, July 1862, and settled in Payson.

74. Originally from New York, Stephen Carpenter decided to remain in Kirtland and died there in 1896. Reuben McBride said Carpenter gave him some traveling money when McBride passed through on his way to England in 1860. McBride journal, June 22, 1860.

75. Since the temple lacked a caretaker or even clear ownership, it fell into disrepair and sometimes had cattle wandering in through open doors, which gave rise to the myth that locals intentionally desecrated it. Howlett, *Kirtland Temple*, 39–46.

76. Jacob Bump was baptized in Pennsylvania in 1833 and moved to Kirtland, and although he dissented he prevented others from resorting to violence, aligning himself with James J. Strang and later William McLellin. He died ca. 1861.

77. Luman Carter was related to the Bump family through marriage. The Carters moved to Kirtland from Vermont in 1833 and Luman became the temple chorister. He eventually committed himself to spiritualism. "Missionary Jottings," *Millennial Star*, Oct. 1, 1872, 630.

brother [Christopher] Dixon was selling his farm and property prepari-tory to folowing his family [to Utah]. Here I meet ~~he~~ with several old aquaintences among them was a Mr Pot[t]er a half brother of Stephen Markham. I knew Mr. P in Call[ifornia].[78]

July 1, 1862; Tuesday. This morning I resumed my journey west-ward. My brother-in-law [Jared Randall] and his wife [Matilda] acompanied me to the depot in Willoughby where we parted and at twenty minutes past 2 o’clock I was moving on my way and reached Detroit about 11 o’clock and put up at the Wadsworth House.

July 2, 1862; Wednesday. This day traviled to Chicago and lo^d^ged at the Massasoit House.

July 3, 1862; Thursday. This morning I meet with the Superintendent of the Railway [Charles G. Hammond][79] who gave me a pass over the road to Q[u]incy. I learned at this point that my Son F[rancis] M. Lyman had passed on the day before in charge of some 800 Saints. I learned from Mr H[ammond] that a carr load of baggage had been burned be-longing to a company of Saints. The fire was supposed to have originated from the ignition of some matches that were insecurly packed. Left Chi-cago about 9 o’clock.

July 4, 1862; Friday. This morning reached Q[u]incy at 1 o’clock. Stoped at the Quincy House and slept until 6 o’clock. Took breakfast and concluded I would not go to Hanibal [Missouri] but started for St. Joseph Via Palmyra[80] where I arived at about 11 o’clock and put up at the Pacific House[81] and as I was registering my name the clerk informed me that the steamer with the company of Saints had left that evening but told me that brothers [Henry] Lawrence & [William S.] Godbe were waiting at the P House for the return of the steamer to take their freight which they could not ship with the Saints.

78. Probably Edward Potter, son of Dinah and Samuel Potter. Another Potter son, Samuel Jr., was killed at Shiloh three months previous.

79. Charles G. Hammond ran the Chicago, Burlington and Quincy Railroad. After his 1865 death, he was eulogized as “courteous” and a “high toned Christian gen-tleman.” “Colonel Charles G. Hammond,” *Chicago Tribune*, Apr. 12, 1865.

80. Palmyra, Missouri, is fifteen miles south of Quincy, Illinois, on the opposite side of the Mississippi River.

81. The Pacific House was completed two years earlier; it would be destroyed by fire in 1868 and rebuilt as the Metropole Hotel. Rutt, *History of Buchanan County and the City of St. Joseph*, 251–52.

July 5, 1862; Saturday. This morning meet broths [Henry] Lawrence & [William S.] Godbe who very kindly invited me to stay with them instead of going by land to Florence which I concluded to do in consideration of the expected late arival of teems from Utah. Did not go out today.

July 6, 1862; Sunday. I did not go out to day but wrote in my journal while brothers [Henry] Lawrence & [William S.] Godbe went to Church. The weather has been verry hot for two days.

July 7, 1862; Monday. Some clouds to day and the weather is slightly cooler than yesterday with light wind. I did not go out to day.

July 8, 1862; Tuesday. To day about 11 o'clock the steamer Omaha arived from her trip to Florence with a company of Saints of some 800 in number in [the] charge of my son F[rancis] M. Lyman. Brother C[harles] C. Rich and his son J[oseph] C. Rich were passengers. In the afternoon in company with brothers [Henry] Lawrence & [William S.] Godbe I went on board the steamer to learn the news from the party of Saints who were her passengers on her upward trip. Of them we learned that two had died during the trip one a wooman and the other an aged man.[82] On my return to our hotell I received a call from my old aquaintence and friend Allen A. Avery who told me that he intended to go with us to Utah this fall.[83]

July 9, 1862; Wednesday. This morning we settled with the gentlemanly landlord of Pacifick House and repaired on board the steamer Omaha.[84] Through the favor of Capt Ford I received a free pass to Florence. In the evening received another call from my friend [Allen] Avery who renewed his promise to acompany us to Utah this season[,] [but this apparently went unfulfilled]. About 11 o'clock we were under way altho before leaving the dust was laid [down] by a shower of rain attended with some wind.

As I steped on board of the boat I met with brother [William]

82. William Gibson was initially in charge of the 800 immigrants but fell ill at sea, so the younger Lyman took over for the railway passage from New York to Nebraska, during which four of the immigrants died: one woman in childbirth, a man due to cholera, and two children. Lyman, "My First Mission," 531–34.

83. Allen A. Avery (not to be confused with the Welsh convert of the same name) had been a seventy in Kirtland. His name was sometimes mistakenly rendered as Arvin.

84. The side-wheel steamboat *Omaha* sailed primarily between St. Louis, Missouri, and Sioux City, Iowa.

Kidman and family from London who had taken passage by themselves in consideration of their having [been] sick with the small pox at or about the time of the sailing of the Wm Tapscott.[85] Brother Kidman had lost all his money after paying his transportation from New York. Brs [Henry] Lawrence and [William S.] Godbe gave him some money to buy provisions for his family. They also gave me 10 dollars to pay my expenses.

July 10, 1862; Thursday. To day the time passed very pleasantly. The weather was very warm an[d] sultry.

July 11, 1862; Friday. To day I found among the passengers an old acquaintence in the person of Capt. Phelps late of the army but now resigned. He said he should come home next year. He said he maried the sister of Chancy G. Weeb and that one of his sons was now in Utah, his own residence was at [blank].

July 12, 1862; Saturday. To day abo^u^t noon we arived at Omaha. While here brothers J[oseph] C. Rich & David Kimball came on board and from them I learned that on Monday the 7th ult Florence was visited by a storm of rain thunder and lightning by which two men were killed. One by the name of Henry W. Whitall from England and brother [blank] Day. Several other individuals were more or less injured but recovered. Brother Whitall had for some years been engaged in the Church printing and publishing as a compositor. He leaves a wife [Ann] and three children to mourn his suden demise and feel the loss.[86]

In the afternoon about 3 o'clock we landed at Florence and were welcomed by the Saints among whom were brothers [Charles C.] Rich[,] [James] Brown and my son F[rancis] M. Lyman. We found the camps of the Saints (numbering between 4 & 5000 souls) in tolerable good health and spirits. Brother J[oseph] W. Young who was seriously injured in the storm of Monday by being crushed by some wagon botoms that were thrown upon him by the wind, he is recovering. On landing I took lodgings and board at the Willet House.[87] Received leters from home news good.

---

85. His youngest daughter will soon die, as noted in Lyman's entry for July 21.

86. Both the *Deseret News* and *Millennial Star* reported on Whitall's death. The man whose name was given only as Day was apparently traveling separately because he was not listed on the ship's manifest.

87. By then, Winter Quarters had transformed itself into the town of Florence where in 1856 "a grand ball was given in the dining room of the Florence hotel, afterwards called the Willet House. I remember this ball well, some forty couples being

July 13, 1862; Sunday. To day in company ~~and~~ with brother [Charles C.] Rich and others I attended meetings morning and evening in the camps of the Saints and besides we organized the Danish Saints in two companies for their journey under the direction of Captain[s] [Christian A.] Madsen [and Ola N.] Liljenquist and all to be and travel under the direction of brother J[ohn] Van Cott until we should overtake him on our homeward journey when he will join our party for home. Capt H[omer] Duncan in charge of 1st Church train arrived today.

July 14, 1862; Monday. To day I visited among the Saints and administered to some who were sick. We also engaged the making of some light clothing and my friend Wm Pyper gave me a fine Panama hat. ^First Church [freight] train arrived today.^ This morning received a leter from my wife in Beaver County Minersville per hand of Joseph Hyde who came with the Church teams. Brother Hyde had his leg fractured on the journey he is at present recovering. Capt [John R.] Murdock in charge of ^2nd^ Church [freight] train arrived today.

July 15, 1862; Tuesday. Today the steamer West Wind came up the river to Florence and brought some goods and wagons for the Church.[88] Second church train arrived today.

July 16, 1862; Wednesday. Today I received a letter from brother George Q. Cannon in Washington. In the afternoon some rain was falling and I did not go out. A young man died this evening by the name of [blank] Stevens. He was from England.

July 17, 1862; Thursday. The weather still rainy and dull which slightly retards the movement of the emigration. Brother Joseph ^W.^ Young is beter his wounds all healing and his strength seems returning. During the day brothers Ormas E Bates and Wm Bringhurst arived from the east and brothers Joseph Horn and Thomas Taylor and others from the west and report the last of the Church trains far back by the road. Capt. Horn ^was^ in charge of Church [freight] train number three.

July 18, 1862; Friday. Weather very warm and sultry did not move

---

present." The hotel changed hands in 1858 for $5,000, the equivalent of $150,000 today. Morton, et al, *Illustrated History of Nebraska*, 3:389.

88. The *West Wind* carried a new invention too, a steam-powered wagon that could pull several other wagons behind it. However, it lasted only a few miles and broke a crank rod, so the immigrants had to substitute oxen. Beecher, *Massacre along the Medicine Road*, 226.

about much on acount of the heat. In the evening called at the residence of brother J[oseph] W. Young ^to^ settle some difficulty. The parties ^not^ appearing the buisness was not considered and after some desultory conversation we retired to our lodgings. Today I had a conversation with bro. ^Solomon^ Mack[89] and according to his wishes advised him to return to his family in Newhampshire.

July 19, 1862; Saturday. To day I met with brother Wm Player who with his family were this far on their way to Zion after some years of waiting in Missouri. Bro. P. was master mason on the Nauvoo Temple.[90]

July 20, 1862; Sunday. To day I attended meeting in the morning at camp of the Tapscot company. Brother [Charles C.] Rich and myself addressed the audience. In the evening attended the meeting at brother [John D. T] McAllisters camp and gave the Saints instruction in regard to their duties. In the evening the steamer West Wind arived with the last of the season's emigrants. They were from Sweden under the direction of Elder Baliff. Missionaries left today by West Wind for England[:] John Smith, Patriarch[,] Thos. Taylor[,] John Holman[,] Frank Farnsworth[,] Miles Romney Junior.[91]

July 21, 1862; Monday. To day I meet with brother Zera Coal one of the members of the Zion's Camp. He is on his way to Zion [Utah] after a residence of several years in Missouri where his family still remains. To day an old gentleman died (who arived on yesterday from Switzerland) and also a young child [Barbara] belonging to brother [William] Kidman.

July 22, 1862; Tuesday. To day in the afternoon in company with brother [Charles C.] Rich I visited and spoke to the Church [freight] train under the direction of Capt Homer Duncan which was started on its ^homeward journey.^ The company appeared in good spirits in reference to their journey. General good health in the camp.

---

89. This is a nephew of Lucy Mack Smith, mother of Joseph Smith. The nephew died in New Hampshire in 1883.

90. When Player arrived in Nauvoo from the U.K. in 1842, he immediately saw that the blocks of limestone with crescent moons inscribed on them had been "much botched," so he set about correcting them. He then supervised the placement of the sunstones and star stones (McBride, *House for the Most High*, 106–07). When his family continued on to Utah in the 1850s, he stayed behind, possibly due to health.

91. These are written vertically across the July 20 entry.

July 23, 1862; Wednesday. To day in company with brother Ormas E. Bates I went to Glenwood in Iowa and called upon my old and much valued ~~friend~~ friend and brother Joseph Coolidge by whom and family I was most kindly welcomed.[92] Brother C. said that he was not saisfied with his present situation but wished to be at home with the Saints.

While here I learned of the death of Sister Lucia Whiting whom I had until now expected to visit. I also learned that Sister L[ouisa Tanner] Follet the widow of King Follet and the most of her family were living on Silver Creek some 10 miles from the residence of brother Coolidge. I learned that Father [Alpheus] Cutler and party were living some 35 miles from the same place. It was the[re] [that] my sister in law died.[93] The Cutler faction[94] is said to be wasting away. Capt [John R.] Murdock's company was addressed to day by brother [Charles C.] Rich preparetory to starting on their journey.

July 24, 1862; Thursday. To day we bid our friends in Glenwood adieu and returned to Florence where in the evening I atended a meeting of the Tapscot Camp of Saints. Brother [Charles C.] Rich, [Francis M.] Lyman, and [Reuben] McBride were with me. Some missionaries from Zion ^enroute for England^ were present ^at^ our meeting [which] was preceded by a shower that made the ground uncomfortable and wet. The Saints were addressed by brothers [Elias H.] Blackburn & [James] Brown ^myself and br. Rich.^ We then visited brother Jas Brown camp and then returned to our lodging.

July 25, 1862; Friday. To day did not go out my health not being good as usual. Brothers [Joseph W.] Young and [Charles C.] Rich organized an independent company for the road under James S. Brown as Capt. In the evening the steamer West Wind came up bringing some freight. During the forenoon of to day we had a severe shower which made the ground very unpleasant to the dwellers in tents and wagons. In the evening weather became pleasant and buisness brisk. My health beter than in the morning.

---

92. Joseph W. Coolidge was a close associate of Joseph Smith and the executor of his estate. He made it as far as Winter Quarters but not Utah, dying in Iowa in 1871.

93. Lucia Louisa Leavitt, sister of Lyman's wife Cornelia Leavitt, died in Manti, Iowa, on May 20.

94. The Cutlerites had a falling out with Brigham Young; Alpheus Cutler will die in 1864 and his followers move to Independence, Missouri, where they are today.

July 26, 1862; Saturday. Kept house most of the day. Captain [James] Brown's ^independent^ company moved a short distance.

July 27, 1862; Sunday. Today in company with bros [Charles C.] Rich and son [Joseph C.] and J[oseph] W. Young I visited and spoke to the camps of Capts Joseph Horn and James S. Brown collectively in reference to their journey and the course of conduct necessary to secure to them the blessings of God and his protection from dangers incident to their travel by praying much and watching more. Bade them God speed and returned to our lodgings.

In the evening in company with Elders Charles C. Rich, F[rancis] M. Lyman and E[lias] H. Blackburn I visited the camp of the Saints under charge of Elder J[ohn] D. T. McAllister. Spoke to a large and attentive audience of Saints upon the principles of the gospel and their nature and tendency to enlighten and elivate the human mind and thus develop in man as he acquires knowledge, the mind of Christ. Bro Rich joined in the services. On our return to our lodgings we met with Capt H[enry] W. Miller of Church train no. five who reported his train near by and in good health and condition.

July 28, 1862; Monday. We changed our lodgings from the Willet House to a house on the hill belonging to Geo Smith (which was christened Economy Hall). I was not out much today rather unwell. In the evening Capt Horton Hate [Haight] of the last Church train arived in Florence. My health is not good today.

July 29, 1862; Tuesday. Today bro [Charles C.] Rich and son [Joseph C.] and bro Joseph W. Young went to Bluff City [Council Bluffs]:[95] bro Y. on business and bro Rich to visit his friends. I stayed by the staff in Economy Hall. My health was poor and was not much abroad. In the evening Capt [Horton] Ha[igh]tes company arived with the Treasure in their charge all in safety and good order.

July 30 1862; Wednesday. Today bros. [Charles C.] Rich and [Joseph W.] Young returned from Iowa. Steamer West Wind came up the river to Omaha where she landed her freight for Florence. Bro J. W. Young

95. When Latter-day Saints overtook Council Bluffs, Iowa, in 1846–48, they renamed the town Kanesville. After the Mormons left, the locals saw to it that the name reverted back to Council Bluffs (not Bluff City).

received a letter from br H[orace] S. Eldredge in Chicago who will be here by the next boat.

July 31, 1862; Thursday. I did not leave my bed for breakfast. I was kindly offered a bed and room by bro. George Smith in his house which I accepted and when there was made as comfortable as circumstances would allow by Sisters Smith & [Lily] Walpole. I kept my room throughout the day suffering severely from pain in my back and feverish condition of my body.

August 1, 1862; Friday. No perceptible change in my health for the better. The last night was one of feverish restle[ss]ness inducing a condition of nervous dibility which caused my stomach to reject the food necessary to health. No incident of special interest affecting the emigration came to my notice today.

August 2, 1862; Saturday. I passed another sleepless night. The business of moving emigrants ^into camp^ as reported to me has been brisk through the day. During the day bro. [Charles C.] Rich was busy making provisions for our homeward journey by preparing the cover for the wagon in which we shall travel.

August 3, 1862; Sunday. Still confined to the house. In the evening brother C[harles] C. Rich and my son F[rancis] M. Lyman went and visited and instructed the company of Saints (under the charge of Capt. Henry W. Miller) preparitory to starting on the journey homeward.

August 4, 1862; Monday. To day I was up from my bed and feeling somewhat beter. In the evening the steamer War Eagle came to Florence with freight and brought as passenger from St. Joseph H[orace] S. Eldridge. Below St. Joseph the War Eagle was fired into and brought to by a party of guerillas whom she was forced to ferry across the river when she was laid under [for] a small contribution of sugar and candles and then she was allowed to pass on up the river.[96] During the night the steamer Omaha came to Florence and delivered her freight and left. To day brother [Charles C.] Rich and son went to Iowa to visit some relations.

August 5, 1862; Tuesday. To day I walked out into town in the

96. It was not uncommon during the Civil War for guerilla bands to commandeer steamers and demand passage or tribute. The demise of the *War Eagle* came in 1870 when it was transporting petroleum and caught fire, the conflagration spreading to the river port of La Crosse, Wisconsin, and destroying several buildings.

morning but found myself very weak and was forced to take my bed again with a high fever and past a most restless and uncomfortable night. During the day brother [Charles C.] Rich returned. He told me that he meet our mutual friend Alfred Bybee and family from California. They were very glad to see him.

August 6, 1862; Wednesday. To day brother [Charles C.] Rich and my son put the cover on the wagon in which we shall travil home. I was out some to day[,] my health is improving. Brothers [Joseph W.] Young and [Horace S.] Eldridge went to Omaha. This evening we heard of the requsition of the War department for three hundred thousand more troops this causing the western fever to increase with the class who are exposed to a draft.[97]

To night brother J. W. Young went to Omaha with Mr Lovland in order to be on the alert for wagons and cattle next day at the Bluffs. Brother John Young was taken sudenly ill this evening but was soon beter.

August 7, 1862; Thursday. To day my health improving. In the evening I in company with brother [Charles C.] Rich went to the camp of Capt [Horton] Ha[ight] and gave them some instructions for their journey. Returned to my lodgings very weary. Brother Wm Godbe caried us to the meeting. Brother J[oseph] W. Young did not return today but brother John Brown bought some cattle here during the day.

August 8, 1862; Friday. Today I was co[n]siderably about and feeling an increase of strength. The day was very warm and sultry. The church train under the charge of Capt Wm H. Dame made a drive of 3 miles and formed a camp with no accident save the breaking of one wagon. Brother J[oseph] W. Y[oung] returned to day and reported success in his trip to the Bluffs in the buisness that constituted its object. Made some further preperations of our wagon for the journey. Brother J. W. Y. went to Omaha in the evening and brother [Horace S.] Eldridge acompanied him.

August 9, 1862; Saturday. Today I was about all day and felt much beter in health. In the afternoon the steamer West Wind came to Omaha and brought as passenger Capt W[illiam] H. Hooper. She brought some freight for Utah which she left at Omaha. The Capt was in fine health

97. Wealthier Americans bought their way out of the draft by paying someone else to take their place. This policy boiled over in New York City's draft riots of 1863.

and spirits. Today [Francis] Marion went to the [Elk]horn [River] on some buisness with brother H[enry] W. Miller's camp. He returned in the night and brought five men with him for teamsters in the last train.

August 10, 1862; Sunday. Today the buisness of loading the residue of Church freight progressed slowly but as the work progressed a deficiency of teams and wagons became apparent which rendered further purchase necessary. In the afternoon I had a severe attack of diarhea which made me very sick through the night which was intensely hot. In the evening brothers [Joseph W.] Young[,] [William H.] Hooper[,] and [Horace S.] Eldridge went to Omaha on buisness connected with the season's emigration.

August 11, 1862; Monday. To day my health is beter than it was on yesterday. The work of loading freight is still going on. During the day brothers [Joseph W.] Young[,] [William H.] Hooper and [Horace S.] Eldridge were in Omaha on buisness and returned. in the evening made some slight repairs on our traveling wagon. Brother [Charles C.] Rich went to Omaha to see brothers [William] Bringhurst & [William S.] Godby from whom he received a fine present of preserves and oysters for our journey. Brother Bringhurst & Godby left on their homeward journey.

August 12, 1862; Tuesday. This morning adjusted a mess box on our wagon and packed my traveling bag for the journey. The work of loading freight went on slowly.

August 13, 1862; Wednesday. Was somewhat ill today. Brother J[oseph] W. Young went to Omaha and procured a wagon for the last of the season's freight. The weather was excessively hot and sultry. Brother [Charles C.] Rich went to Omaha. In the evening a merchant from Omaha came to Florence and was baptized by Elder John Brown. His name was Milton Rogers he was in the hard-ware line. He was confirmed by Elders C. C. Rich and J. Brown.[98]

August 14, 1862; Thursday. This morning the last wagon with Church freight left town. [Francis] Marion was engaged in helping to fit up the trailing wagons of brother J[oseph] W. Young while brothers Young[,] [William H.] Hooper and [Horace S.] Eldridge were in Omaha. The steamer did not arive as expected on accident she was detained. Brother

98. He nevertheless stayed in Omaha and built up his hardware business, which he expanded in 1868. Wakeley, *Omaha*, 213–14.

Young returned and made the welcome announcement that we should start on the morow. The night came on cool and pleasant for all but the poor and the musquetoes.

August 15, 1862; Friday. Today we made ready for the start and after din[n]er about 2 oclock we left Florence and at 20 minutes to 4 oclock we were camped near Omaha the rest of our party not being ready to start. In the evening the steamer West Wind came to Omaha and brought horses and wagon for [William H.] Hooper & [Horace S.] Eldridge. Procured some corn in Omaha for animals.

August 16, 1862; Saturday. This morning at 10 o'clock we received some money in charge for John R. Young and myself and brother C[harles] C. Rich. My son [Francis] Marion and a young-man by the name of John Seymour left camp to overtake brother Young and train. Traveled untill 2 o'clock and made halt on the [Elk]horn [River] for 2 hours. The flies were very bad. Meet some parties of returning freighters from Denver. At 4 o'clock were again on the road and after Raw-hide creek found on enquiry that brother Young and train had passed early in the morning. We past the town of Fremont some 9 miles and overtook the train as they were camping at 7 o'clock. They having traveled 20 miles ourselves 45 miles. After night Mrs Ogleby ^and son^ joined the camp with her wagon. Some indications of rain altho but little fell.

August 17, 1862; Sunday. About 9 o'clock we left camp. The train having started we traveled until 11 o'clock and stop^ed^ near a farm-house and turned out our team and gave them some water from the well and we remained here untill 4 o'clock and then traviled to shell creek and camped at 7 o'clock. The train was not up—.[99] We have just met an ox train returning from Denver. Just at dark Capt [John R.] Young and train came and camped by us. There were some indications of rain and a profusion of musqutoes who during the night made us to feel most sensibly their unwelcome presence. A family of the natives was near us to night.

August 18, 1862; Monday. This morning the train started at 8 o'clock and a half hour later we left the camp-ground and at half past 1 o'clock we camped 2 miles east of Collumbus. To day [Francis] Marion killed two spring chickens of the Prairie they made us a fine diner. At night we

99. Because Lyman was in charge of the overall migration and not a particular train, he will move from one train to the other, along with his few assistants.

found our camp infested with swarms of mu[s]quietoes which interfered much with the comfort of our attempted sleep.

August 19, 1862; Tuesday. This morning at 7 o'clock the train of Capt J[ohn] R. Young passed our camp having passed the night ½ mile east of us. We taried on the camp ground until 11 o'clock when we made ready to start and as we rolled away we were joined by brothers J[oseph] W. Young[,] H[orace] S. Eldridge and W[illiam] H. Hooper[,] J[ames] Brown & E[lias] H. Blackburn and J[oseph] C. Rich who constituted the residue of our traveling party. We traveled to and crossed Loup fork 2 miles from which we camped at 20 minutes past 4 o'clock to wait the coming up of Capt Young's heavy train from the Ferry. At this point I ~~was~~ ^had^ an attack of the disentary that rendered me very ill so that I had no rest during the night.

August 20, 1862; Wednesday. About 10 o'clock we left camp [with] the freight train and traveled 25 miles. My ^illness^ continued. To day we broak our wagon-tongue which detained us a half hour to splice up. At night we encountered a most terrific storm of rain & thunder and lightning which made us very uncomfortable.

August 21, 1862; Thursday. To day traveled 38 miles. My health slightly improving. In the evening brother J[oseph] W. [Young] left us and went on with the post man to overtake Capt [William H.] Dame's company. To day was the 53d birthday of brother C[harles] C. Rich. We had stewed chicken & duck on the occasion.

August 22, 1862; Friday. Today overtook brother [William H.] Dames camp and repaired the wagon tongue an[d] rolled a few miles. In the evening as we left we learned that two sisters Sarah and Emma Owens were left from brother ~~Wates~~ [Horton] Ha[igh]te's train. We called and saw and ministered to the sisters and advised them to stay until next season as Sister Emma was too sick and weak to travel. Brother J[oseph] W. Young kindly made provisions for their sustinence and we left them.[100]

---

100. This happened near enough to Columbus, the settlement next to the Loup Fork ferry and bridge, that the plan may have been to leave the girls in the care of James Mitchell's family, who were known to Lyman and others. In any case, the young women recovered enough to be able to join the next immigrant company. They arrived in Utah in September. Both were unmarried and in their twenties. "Names of Immigrants," *Deseret News*, Sep 24. 1862.

August 23, 1862; Saturday. To day crossed over to the Platt [River] traveling about 15 miles and camped about 3 oclock. Capt [William H.] Dame's train was with us and in the evening brother J[oseph] W. Young came to us he said he had bought all the cattle he wanted. We had a meeting of the camp of Capt D. for instructing them in relation to their journey.

August 24, 1862; Sunday. Today traveled and camped with Capt [Horton] Ha[igh]te's train. Passed several graves on the way. We held meeting with the people of the train who were in good health and spirits.

August 25, 1862; Monday. Made a hard travil roads sandy. Made camp with the musquetoes had hard time.

August 26, 1862; Tuesday. This morning overtook Capt H[enry] W. Miller's train. Took breakfast at their campground and then we passed on and before nooning we passed the Bates family train.[101] Camped after dark but found a plenty of musquetoes. Nooned at cold springs.

August 27, 1862; Wednesday. This morning passed the camp of D[avid] P. Kimball. All in good health and spirits. At 8 o'clock stoped for breakfast no fuel. Flies plenty. Made noon halt on north Bluff fork. Brother West came to us to go through to the Lake for his help but he did not go but returned to his co. We crossed over two sand bluffs and camped near the river not much annoyed by flies.

August 28, 1862; Thursday. This morning started at twenty minutes past 5 o'clock. Traviled until 9 o'clock and stoped for breakfast on the bluff. Made noon halt on Goose Creek then traveled until 9 o'clock when we came to the encampment of the merchant train of W[illiam] H. Godbe[102] in charge of Benj. Hampton.[103] Had a slight shower of rain as we went to our rest on the bosom of our Mother Earth.

August 29, 1862; Friday. This morning did not leave camp until 9 o'clock taking breakfast and making some repairs on brother [William

---

101. In 1860 Ormus Ephraim Bates was called to the eastern states to help with the seasonal immigration. Like Lyman, he was not bound to any particular company while returning in 1862. In Utah he owned herds of cattle and sheep in the Tooele Valley. He had seven wives and about fifty children.

102. Lyman mistakenly wrote an *H.* Godbe's middle name was Samuel.

103. Of Godbe's two freight trains, Hampton and Ebenezer Farnes oversaw this one, while Godbe and Edwin Ward were leading the other one. The Richard Treseder family of seven was also traveling with Godbe.

H.] Hooper's wagon. We had not traveled about 5 miles when we found brother Hooper's wagon with the tongue broake which we were detained some 2 hours in repairing. The repairs completed we traveled until 4 o'clock and halted on the river for din[n]er.[104] To night camped on a slue. Brother C[harles] C. Rich stood guard.

August 30, 1862; Saturday. Started at 5 o'clock and breakfasted at 9 o'clock. Stoped for diner at 2 o'clock. Traveled 33 m[ile]s and camped with Capt [Isaac A.] Canfield's train. Were kindly entertained by brother [Christopher F.] Dixon and his family.

August 31, 1862; Sunday. To day we traveled to a point oposite the Chimney Rock for din[n]er. Wind high the morning cool making thicker clothing needed. My health rather poor suffering much from spinal irritation which was much aggravated by the rough riding. Stoped at ¼ to 3 o'clock for din[n]er. In the evening rolled on to nearly oposite the Scott's Bluffs where found Capt Ansel Ha[r]monds train camped. We stoped with them at 9 o'clock were kindly entertained by Capt H. Had a meeting of the camp the Saints were addressed by brothers C[harles] C. Rich and J[oseph] W. Young. I did not attend because of my ill health. The health of the camp was reported to be good. Traviled 40 miles – had some of the natives with us tonight.

September 1, 1862; Monday. This morning went around and saw all of the camp. They were all well with some few exceptions and in good spirits with regard to their journey. Breakfasted with some of the teamsters from Utah. At half past 8 oclock left camp and traviled until ¼ to 12 oclock. Dined and were on the road again at half past 1 o'clock. Traviled until 5 o'clock stoped on the river for sup[p]er 30 miles below Fort Larimie. After super traveled until 10 o'clock. Camped without water. Grass but midling in quality and quantity. This evening had a view of Larimie's Peak.

September 2, 1862 Tuesday. Left camp at ¼ to 6 o'clock. Traviled until half past 8 o'clock and stoped for breakfast. This morning we got some Prarie chickens. Traviled 9 miles road sandy. At 11 o'clock left and after starting myself and brother [William H.] Hooper lost our spe[c]tacles.

104. This was the last entry in this journal book, and the entries from here on out are catalogued as volume 27 at the CHL, written as a rough draft in pencil and never copied from the day book into a formal journal.

Reached Fort Larimie at half past 2 o'clock. After a short stay we traviled on. While there brother Hooper received a telegram stating that his family were well. At ¼ to 5 o'clock halted on the river for sup[p]er. At 8 o'clock left camp and traviled til half past 10 o'clock. Since sup[p]er Moroni Allen left his revolver on the camp ground. At this place we saw the grave [of] Ann Firth.[105]

September 3, 1862; Wednesday. Started at half past 6 o'clock. Halted on little biter Cottenwood for breakfast. At half past 8 o'clock made some repairs on wagon. At 11 o'clock were ready to move. Traviled until twenty five minutes to 3 o'clock and halted for diner then traviled until 10 o'clock. Had some rain before and after camping.

September 4, 1862; Thursday. Left camp ¼ past 5 o'clock. The rain made the traviling heavy and unpleasant. At half past 8 o'clock halted for breakfast at the Mail station on the Labonte [Creek]. Taried here until ¼ past 1 o'clock. While here some shoeing was done and some sage hens were killed. The rain continued to fall sometime after we started at half past 4 o'clock. Halted for super at 7 o'clock. Started on and traviled until half past 9 o'clock. The rain had ceased falling.

September 5, 1862; Friday. Left camp at 6 o'clock traviled until 8 o'clock. Halted on Box Elder for breakfast. No rain this morning. At ¼ to 11 o'clock left camp traviled to deer creek station [Glenrock, Wyoming] halted at ¼ past 2 o'clock. At ¼ past 3 o'clock were on the way. Traviled until half past 4 o'clock. Halted until 6 oclock then traviled until 10 o'clock. Made dry camp.

September 6, 1862; Saturday. Left camp at half past 5 o'clock and traviled until 8 o'clock when we overtook Capt [Joseph] Horns Train between the Platt Bridges. Taried with them until 11 oclock. During our stay held meeting with the camp. The Saints were addressed by brothers C[harles] C. Rich & J[oseph] W. Young. From thence we traviled to the uper Bridge[106] where we made brief halt and then passed on and halted for diner on the river at half past 3 o'clock. Wind high and the roads

105. Ann Firth was in the Homer Duncan Company. She died en route to Utah on Aug. 24, 1862, at sixty-seven years old.

106. The two bridges at approximately the same location on the Platte River near today's Casper were the Lower Bridge, built by John Richard in 1853, and the Upper Bridge, six miles distant and built by rival Louis Guinard in 1859. Both men had trading posts and charged travelers to cross.

dusty Traviled until half past 12 o'clock and camped on Prospect Hill. One of our mules was tired out when we arived at the camp ground.

September 7, 1862; Sunday. Started at 6 o'clock traviled until 9 o'clock. Halted for breakfast on greesewood Creek killed some ducks. The weather pleasant at 11 o'clock were on the road. About 2 o'clock reached the station at Sweetwater Bridge at this place Capt [William H.] H[ooper] sent message by the Telegraph to Salt Lake City.[107] We here received some dispaches in reference to the war. After a short delay we passed up the river above Independence rock where we halted for din[n]er after which we traviled until 12 o'clock. Distance today 22 miles camped on short feed.

September 8, 1862; Monday. Were up at 6 o'clock traviled until 9 o'clock and halted for breakfast. Some a[l]kalie in the locality health of camp good. Made noon halt at a point below the 5th crossing of the river. At half past 6 o'clock were on the way and at half past 12 o'clock we reached Capt [John R.] Murdocks camp. A guard was kindly provided for our stock so we all slept. During the night a little girl aged 10 years old died.[108]

September 9, 1862; Tuesday. This morning we breakfasted with the teamsters of the train. Had a meeting and at 9 o'clock we were on the way and made ~~noon~~ halt for din[n]er at 3 o'clock at springs the south pass in sight. Wind high. At 11 o'clock at night came to Capt [James] Wareham's camp.[109] Had a shower of rain that made us rather uncomfortable.

September 10, 1862; Wednesday. This morning our party breakfasted with the Saints and at 9 o'clock were on the way except Capt [William H.] Hooper who was determined to do some shoeing. At half past 1 o'clock halted for din[n]er and at halfpast 6 oclock came to Capt [Homer]

107. The transcontinental telegraph was completed in 1861. Much like the transcontinental railroad begun the next year, crews worked from east (St. Joseph, Missouri) and west (Sacramento, California) to meet in the middle at Fort Laramie on August 5. The fort's telegraph office allowed captains of companies to send messages ahead to Salt Lake City to report on their progress. Cf., Homer Duncan telegram to Brigham Young, Aug. 24, 1862, in Brigham Young Office Files, CHL.

108. Sarah Jane Morris's parents, William and Sarah, would settle in Parowan, Utah. There were fourteen deaths during the 1862 crossing, "principally children," according to "Arrivals of Trains During the Week," *Deseret News*, Oct. 1, 1862.

109. Wareham had over 200 in his company that was traveling independent of church control. When they left early in July, they were among the first to leave that season.

Duncan's train. Halted for sup[p]er after which we traviled until halfpast 11 o'clock. Made dry camp. The night was very cool freezing some.

September 11, 1862; Thursday. Called camp at ~~6 oclo~~ halfpast 5 o'clock. Traviled until halfpast 9 o'clock. Halted for breakfast on big sandy. Traviled on and made dry camp for night.

September 12, 1862; Friday. This morning we came to the Danish camps. Halted for breakfast found the Saints in camp generally well. After breakfast we were joined by brother J[ohn] Van Cott for home. After some detention by rain we started and halted on acount of rain at the Mail and Telegraph station kept by Mr Granger.[110] We remained here until 6 o'clock and then traviled on until 1 o'clock A.M. and camped beside black's fork. Had good feed some rain and a good sleep.

September 13, 1862; Saturday. Breakfasted before leaving camp ground. Started at half past 9 o'clock traviled until ¼ to 1 o'clock P.M. Halted on Black's fork for din[n]er stoped one hour then traviled on until ~~11 oclock~~ to Bridger. Halted on creek for sup[p]er then traviled into spring creek and camped at 11 o'clock.

September 14, 1862; Sunday. This morning started at daylight. Breakfasted at the Soda spring at half past 8 o'clock then traviled to the Bear River station. Taried 3 hours during which time we had some rain. Started at 5 o'clock traviled on to Cash Cave camped at halfpast 10 o'clock heavy rain during night.

September 15, 1862; Monday. Started at 6 o'clock traviled 10 miles & halted for breakfast. While halted a company of returning miners from Salmon River passed. Halted for din[n]er on Weber [River] at 3 o'clock then traviled until 8 o'clock. Camped just below the mouth of Silver Creek. One of our mules failed this evening.

September 16, 1862; Tuesday. Started at halfpast 7 o'clock and halted for breakfast at Kimballs Ranch [outside of Park City] and halted for breakfast a 11 o'clock.[111] Breakfast over we started on and arived at home in Salt Lake City about 8 o'clock found my family there well.

---

110. Granger Station was built in 1856 as Ham's Fork Station where Ham's Fork and Black's Fork meet. It was a Pony Express stop and then a telegraph office before 1862 when it became Granger Station, named for the local rancher who purchased it.

111. Lyman breaks off here and adds a few pages of genealogy before resuming his journal on Sep. 17. Three of his traveling companions (Eldredge, Hooper, Young) had gone on ahead and arrived two days before Lyman and Rich. Journal History, Sep. 14, 1862.

September 17, 1862; Wednesday. This morning in company with brother C[harles] C. Rich I called at the Historians Office then at the Tithing Ofice then went to the Prest's where we meet with Presidents [Heber C.] Kimball & [Daniel H.] Wells who both extended to us a hearty and warm welcome to our homes. Sat for an hour or more in conversation with the brethren. Elders J[oseph] C. Rich & F[rancis] M. Lyman were with us. Feeling much wearyness and pain from my journey I went to my house to seek some rest and in the evening called on brother [George Q.] Cannon's family and while out called on the widow Richardson. In the evening my son Platte D Lyman came to town from our farm in Farmington.

September 18, 1862; Thursday. To day went [to] the farm with my son. Found my wives Caroline & Lydia [Partridge] and their children[112] well as usual. During the evening some of my friends called on me and welcomed me home to family and friends.

September 19, 1862; Friday. Today the threshers came to thresh for brother Edward Partridge who had been working my farm in my absence to England. The weather was dry and warm. On Thursday 18th [Francis] Marion went to visit his friends on Cottonwood [Creek] in company with his uncle Nathan Tanner.

September 20, 1862; Saturday. The weather stil fine and the threshing progressing. Walked out this morning to look at a part of my farm. At noon the threshing was concluded. This morning brother E[zra] T. Clark[113] started with some loads of grain for the mail station on the line east of Salt Lake City. In the evening brother Edward [Partridge] went to mill with some wheat.

September 21, 1862; Sunday. To day I preached morning & evening in the Court house in Farmington & dined with brother Thomas Smith. The Bishop [John W. Hess] was not at meeting on acount of sickness. During the evening meeting brother Wm Muir made some very appropriate & interesting remarks on the subject of agriculture. In the evening

112. Caroline and Lydia had a total of five children, and each of them would bear two more by 1866.

113. Ezra T. Clark (1823–1901) was an early settler of Farmington and frequent missionary to the eastern states. When he was arrested for cohabitation in 1886, he spent six months in prison and paid a fine of $300. "Trial of E. T. Clark," *Deseret News*, Feb. 17, 1887.

my son [Francis] Marion and his uncle Freeman Tanner came to Farmington & taried with us over night.[114]

September 22, 1862; Monday. This morning [Francis] Marion and his uncle left for the city. Concluded to rent a part of my place to brother Edward Partridge and in the evening occupied a few hours pulling sun flowers.

September 23, 1862; Tuesday. To day I went to the city with my wife Caroline [Partridge] & children and also Sister Mary Clark[115] and my son Platt. We dined with Sister Mary Rich. The two Danish companies came in today and I received my trunk with cloths & books in good order.

September 24, 1862; Wednesday. Past the morning at home and received some calls and in the evening in company with my wife Eliza [Partridge] and my son F[rancis] M. Lyman I visited a part of the family of the President [Brigham Young] in the Lion House.[116] There I met Mother Morley[117] who was in the city on a visit. Received a hearty welcome from all. This evening Capt Homer Duncan's train came in and camped in the city on the public square.

September 25, 1862; Thursday. To day in company with brother Nathan Tanner I visited the camp of the Saints who had just come in. Found them in general good health and the poor were provided with homes by the generosity of their friends. Dined with brother Tanner and then called on some of my English friends and then called on Prest Joseph Young at his home then returned to my home.

September 26, 1862; Friday. This morning I called on the Prest [Brigham Young] and received from him a warm & hearty welcome home and went with him to see the new theatre.[118] We then called on

---

114. Francis M. Lyman also spoke in the bowery about his mission to the U.K. He was growing in prominence and would be called as an apostle in 1880.

115. Mary Clark was the first wife of Ezra T. Clark.

116. Young was visiting settlements in Nephi and Provo at the time and would not return until Sep. 25.

117. This would have been one of the wives of "Father" Isaac Morley, one of the first converts to Mormonism in Kirtland, Ohio, and the founder of Manti, Utah. His fourth of ten wives, Hannah Knight Libby, was often called Mother Morley, although her eleven children were by her first husband, John Carter, whom she left in Maine over religion.

118. The Salt Lake Theatre was dedicated in March. It was designed by church architect William Folsom as a ninety-foot-high domed structure at State Street and First South. In his dedicatory speech, Brigham Young said that in choosing between comedies and tragedies, he preferred comedies because "there is enough of tragedy in

Capt [William H.] Hooper and some gentlemen from Cal and in the evening at 4 o'clock we meet Bishop [Matthew] Simpson of the Methodist Church (^enroute^ from California to the states) in Presidents Office.[119] In the evening I rode out with Elder John Taylor to his farm returned after dark. Capt [James] Warehams train arived to day.

September 27, 1862; Saturday. Today I called at the Historian's Office. Present[:] G[eorge] A S[mith], F[ranklin] D R[ichards] and C[harles] C R[ich]. ~~After which~~ Had an ac^c^ount of the southern cotton mission from brother G A S after which I visited the public square and saw Capt [John R.] Murdock who had just come in with his train all in good health and spirits. I then called on brother Richard Hopkins at his pot[t]ery.

September 28, 1862; Sunday. To day I attended meeting and was called to address the audience. Was folowed by Prest B. Young In the afternoon we were entertained with a history of the President's late visit to the south and its leading incidents by brothers G. A. Smith and J[ohn] V. Long of the party after which I attended [circle][120] with my Quorum at the Historian's house. Present W[ilford] Woodruff, C[harles] C. Rich[,] G[eorge] A. Smith and F[ranklin] D. Richards and myself. I did not dress [in temple robes] on acount of ill health.

September 29, 1862; Monday. To day called on the President [Brigham Young] and with him visited and examined his new molasses mill which was propeled by water.[121] Called on brother Crompton from Norwich England. In the evening I went to Farmington with brother F[ranklin] D. Richards found my family well. This morning I met with brother Jacob Hamblin from Santa Clara.

September 30, 1862; Tuesday. To day I called on brother F[ranklin] D. Richards and looked over the place he had purchased for the family of

---

every-day life." The theatre was razed in the 1920s. "The New Theatre," *Deseret News*, Mar. 12, 1862.

119. Matthew Simpson was a Methodist bishop in Illinois and ideological opponent of Utah: a fierce advocate for the Union, emancipation, and later Reconstruction. He eulogized Abraham Lincoln at the president's funeral in Springfield.

120. Lyman drew a circle to indicate a prayer circle meeting, as he also did on Oct. 5, 26, and Dec. 21.

121. The first molasses mill in the Salt Lake Valley was near the mouth of Millcreek Canyon, although on Oct. 10 Lyman refers to another molasses mill near Farmington, run by Henry Steed.

brother Willard Richards after which I called at the new meetinghouse the roof of which was being raised.

October 1, 1862; Wednesday. To day I passed to Salt Lake City with bishop J[ohn] Hess. Called at the [*Deseret*] News Office and heard some news then called at the Historian's Office and had an interview with the Historian [George A. Smith]. This morning I meet with brother ~~Jacob~~ Samuel Curtis from the plains. In the evening the Church train under Capt [Joseph] Horn came in. Capt J[ames] S. Brown came in leaving his company some 10 miles out.

October 2, 1862; Thursday. To day in the morning I went to the City Potery and made some purchases after which I visited the state fare with my wife Caroline [Partridge] & children.[122] I then went to the Historian's Office and brought forward my journal. Here I meet with brother Jacob Hamblin from whom I learned some of the particulars of the tragic death ^of^ G A Smith <u>junior</u>.[123] Brother H[amblin] stated to me that he was going again to visit the Moqu^i^es [Hopis][124] the present year as some of them have moved further south than formerly and can be reached without going through the country of the Navehoes.

October 3, 1862; Friday. This morning before I was up brother [John] Horspool called on me. He and family were stoping at the residence of brother [William C.] Staines. Visited the fare after which I visited the President [Brigham Young] at his office. President [Daniel H.] Wells was present. <u>Prest</u> Young said that the labors of the twelve was as much needed in Utah as any where & told me if I knew of any place that pleased me to pitch in and mak[e] provisions for my family.[125] Capt James S. Brown came in and reported himself to the President. Capt Brown had

---

122. The state fair was held in the 44,000 ft^2 Council House on South Temple and Main, where the legislature sometimes met since returning from Fillmore. The fair featured sorghum, hemp, potatoes, cabbages, grapes and watermelons, linen and silk, saddles and harnesses, and two dozen examples of prize cattle, horses, and sheep. "Affairs in Utah," *New York Times*, Oct. 4, 1862; "Report of the Annual State Fair," *Deseret News*, Oct. 8, 1862.

123. George A. Smith Jr. was part of Jacob Hamblin's expedition to explore the Colorado River and was attacked by Indians who shot him with his own gun. His father was one of the LDS twelve apostles. "Murder of George A. Smith, jun., by Indians," *Deseret News*, Dec. 5, 1860.

124. At the time, the Hopis were known as Moquis, or Mokis, as the place names Moki Dugway, Moki Stairs, Moqui Canyon, Moqui Cave, and Moqui Lake testify.

125. This was an important moment for Lyman, as Young signaled that he would

conducted a company over the plains. He was most warmly welcomed by the president.

In the evening I called on the Prest and past the evening in conversation in relation to the present and the reminesences of the past. Present[:] Presidents Young & Wells, A[lbert] Carrington[,] D[avid] O. Calder[,] J[ohn] M Higby[,] G[eorge] A. Smith[,] J[oseph] A. Young[,] T[homas] Ellerbec[k].[126]

October 4, 1862; Saturday. This morning I assorted and arranged my journal matter and laid it by until I shall have time to transcribe it into my history. Brothers [John] Horspool & Petit called to see me & brother P. promised me some [buck] shot for my gun. In the evening my brothers-in law Sidney Tanner & Jas H. Rollins came in from Beaver to attend the conference. Called on the President [Brigham Young] at his office. Present of the twelve[:] [Amasa] Lyman, [Charles C.] Rich & [Franklin D.] Richards[,] [William] Fulsom the architect, [Albert] Carrington.

October 5 1862; Sunday. To day attended meeting ^at 10 o'clock^ in the Bowery. The audience was addressed by Elders Jas S. Brown & Wm Gibson returned missionaries from England. Meeting ajourned until 2 o'clock when meeting was again in sesion and was addressed by Elders John Brown[,] J[ohn] D. T. McAllister & J[oseph] W. Young. At 5 o'clock attended our [prayer circle]. President [Daniel H.] Wells opened meeting. I was mo^u^th in prayr. President B. Young & O[rson] Hyde were present but did not dress. Present of the 12[:] Hyde, Woodruff[,] Taylor, Smith[,] Lyman[,] Rich & Richards. A portion of brother John Brown's family stoped with us to night. Brother Isaac Turley came in to stay with us.

October 6, 1862; Monday. To day at 10 o'clock I was at the Bowery and the conference was opened by singing and prayr by Elder John Taylor of the Twelve after which the audience was addressed by Prest B[righam] Young folowed by Prest H[eber] C. Kimball. Meeting was dismissed by

---

not be calling Lyman on another mission in the near future and that he should take steps to provide for his family of eight wives and twenty-seven children.

126. The remainder of the daybook Lyman was writing in documents letters Lyman wrote. The entries pick up in vol. 28 after another list of letters written, sketches for Lyman's house, and entries he crossed out and copied into his earlier journal books. He added this: "How to Make Wine. To 5 p[in]ts of currants put a gallon of boiling water. Let it stand about a week then strain off the liquor without bruising the berries and to each gallon of the liquor add 3½ lbs. of sugar. Bottle it and after it is done working cork it for use."

Elder Orson Hyde until 2 o'clock when the meeting reassembled and was addressed by Elders C[harles] C. Rich & W[illiam] H. Hooper and then ajourned until tomorow 10 o'clock.

October 7, 1862; Tuesday. To Day attended the conference. The audience was addressed first by Prest [of the Twelve] Orson Hyde after which I spoke to them for an hour and then the meeting ajourned until 2 o'clock. When meeting was called ^and opened by brother F[ranklin] D. Richards^ and adressed by Elder Wm Moody folowed by Prest B[righam] Young who was folowed by Elder John Van Cott after which meeting was dismissed by Elder W[illiam] W. Phelps. To day my son A[masa] M. Junior came to the city. He had been to Cal[ifornia] with his uncle Freeman Tanner. At half past 6 o'clock attended the meeting of the high priests Quorum in the Tabernacle.[127] The meeting was addressed by President John Young folowed by bishops E[dwin] D. Wooley and Lorenzo Young an[d] Elder G[eorge] D. Watt. Ajourned at 9 o'clock.

October 8, 1862; Wednesday. At 10 o'clock conference was in se[s]ion and opened by singing and prayr by myself. The buisness of the conference was then disposed of after which some instruction was given by Prest H[eber] C. Kimball folowed by Prest O[rson] Hyde after which the people were blessed by Prest John Young and conference ajourned to the 6th of April 1863.

In the evening at 6 o'clock I meet with the Prests B[righam] Young and D[aniel] H Wells and several of the Quorum of the twelve. Jacob Gates and John Van Cott were ordained Presidents of the first Quorum of Seventies in the places of B[enjamin] Clap and Zera Pulsifer [who were] removed and Mark Anthony Coombs was also ordained a ~~bishop~~ patriarch in his own household and to bless all such as should require it at his hands. After which I rode out with Prest Young and Wells. During our ride President Young said he wished me to sell all my real estate and settle in Fillmore and gather my family to that place and make them a home and also educate my children which I could not well do for them in their present scatered condition.[128] This evening my son Amasa M. Lyman Jr left the city for Beaver with brother Wm J. Cox.

---

127. This was the old tabernacle; the one still standing at Temple Square was not finished until 1867.

128. Contemplating how he would house over thirty people, Lyman begins

October 9, 1862; Thursday. To day I overhauled my rifles which had rusted much in my absence from home. During the forenoon brother Edward Partridge came to town from Farmington to which place I returned with him. We did not arive until after night found all well. Brother E[zra] T. Clark returned to Farmington this evening.

October 10, 1862; Friday. This morning I saw Elder E[zra] T. Benson on his way to Cache Valley. I went to see the molasses mill of brother Henry Steed[129] and he gave me a promise of 10 gallons of molasses next week. Came home and passed the residue of the day in reading of ancient history of Egypt. In the evening Uncle Edward [Partridge] killed one of my goats. I felt much wearied with my walk today.

October 11, 1862; Saturday. To day I went to G. S. L. with brother E[zra] T. Clark with whom I took a ride around the city taking note of the improvements made in my absence.

October 12, 1862; Sunday. Attended meeting in the Tabernacle. The meeting was addressed by a Mr Milton[130] folowed by brother H[orace] S Eldridge. Dined ^with^ brother Nathan Tanner & family after which I called on Capt W[illiam] H Hooper and settled some business. On parting the Capt gave me a fine brich [breech] loading gun. Called on brother John Van Cott, [blank]. Returned home and made some preperation for my journey to the south.

October 13, 1862; Monday. This morning I started in the stage at 7 o'clock A.M. and reached Provo at sun-down. Lodged with brother Myron Tanner felt myself much wearied with my travil. Was solicited to preach but did not. Dined today with brother [Evan M.] Green's family.

October 14, 1862; Tuesday. To day at an early hour we were on the road and halted for din[n]er at Payson. Dined at brother Joseph Tanner's several members of the family were there. Traviled on to Salt Creek [Nephi] and lodged with brother S[amuel] L. Adams. Was sick through the night.

---

sketching plans for a large house. After reaching Fillmore, he stays overnight before continuing south to Minersville (near Beaver), Parowan, and St. George to see his families there. He takes an interest in a new cotton factory but decides to discontinue the crop himself and has his farmland switched to grape vineyards and fruit orchards.

129. Henry Steed was an early settler in Farmington who owned large tracts of land. He opened the first saw mill and flour mill there.

130. He was apparently a Campbellite preacher. Journal History, Oct. 12, 1862.

October 15, 1862; Wednesday. Today traviled to Round Valley and dined with Bishop P^i^erson after which we traviled to Fillmore and lodged with Bishop [Thomas] Callister.

October 16, 1862; Thursday. To day traviled to Beaver where I arived about 9 o'clock P.M. found my family well.

October 17, 1862; Friday. To day passed the time at home with my family my health not good. Received some calls from my friends.

October 18, 1862; Saturday. To day Bishop Philo T. Farnsworth[131] called on me and we passed some time in conversation and in the evening I went to Minersville and found my family there in tolerable good health. My own health is rather poor.

October 19, 1862; Sunday. To day attended a meeting of the Saints and addressed them for an hour after which I was ill through the night.

October 20, 1862; Monday. To day was confined to my bed most of the day. Received some calls from my friends during the day.

October 21, 1862; Tuesday. To day my health still bad did not go out.

October 22, 1862; Wednesday. To day returned to Beaver in company with brother [James H.] Rollins and Father [Theodore] Turley. Dined with my son in law Philo Carter and family.[132]

October 23, 1862; Thursday. To day was most of the time in bed and at night I preached to the people in the meeting house after which they at the instruction of the bishop [William S. Warren] made a donation of grain and vegitables and meat for myself and [Francis] Marion and family.

October 24, 1862; Friday. To day I went to Parrowan with brother John Christian. Found my family there all well as usual after an absence of 2½ years. Found my family well.

October 25, 1862; Saturday. To day in company with Bishop [William S.] Warren and President [Calvin C.] Pendelton[133] I visited the Cotton yarn manufactory then returned home and done some writing after which with my wives Cornelia [Leavitt] & Paulina [Phelps] I called

131. They probably talked about whether the bishop had neglected Lyman's wife. She complained to Amasa that the bishop had prevented her from moving to Beaver to be near her father. *AML*, 341.

132. Philo was married to Amasa's oldest child, Matilda Lyman.

133. Calvin C. Pendleton, a physician from Maine, became aligned with Mormons in 1838 and was the clerk of the Nauvoo High Council. In Parowan he was a counselor in the stake presidency, William H. Dame president.

at the residence of Bishop Warren & then went to the Tithing Office where I was weighed. My weight was 240 lbs. Returned home and passed some time in reading in Cobbets Grammer to my boys.[134]

October 26, 1862; Sunday. To day attended meeting in the meeting-house where I addressed an attentive audience of the Saints for above an hour. In the afternoon received some calls from my friends & at 4 o'clock meet with the [prayer circle] at their place of meeting. I did not attend the evening meeting but remained at home with my family. Bishop [William S.] Warren and wives[135] called and passed the evening with me. I ~~fell~~ felt my health improving. The weather was fine and pleasant.

October 27, 1862; Monday. To day I visited the [cotton] factory and noted the improvements that were being made. Past the evening with brother John Perkins & family. Received 11½ bushels of potatoes.[136]

October 28, 1862; Tuesday. Passed the day visiting with Sister Hanks also during the day I visited the shingle mill of brother Daniel P. Clark. Felt myself much wearied with my walking.

October 29, 1862; Wednesday. Passed the day visiting Bishop [William S.] Warren & family. In the evening Henry Noy[e]s & Leroy McBride called on the bishop[,] were enroute from Cal[ifornia].

October 30, 1862; Thursday. To day visited with brother Mark Anthony Combs.[137] The ^wind^ was very high & during the day Charles and George Crismon & Wm Huntington passed enroute for Cal[ifornia]. Passed the evening with [wife] Cornelia [Leavitt] & children &

---

134. Cornelia's two boys were Lorenzo and Henry, Paulina's four boys Oscar, Mason, Charles, and William, all of them under fifteen years of age. William Cobbett's *Grammar of the English Language* was published in New York in 1818 and London the following year. Written as letters to a fourteen-year-old son, it was wildly popular among the self-educated class for making fun of pretentious "false grammar, errors, and nonsense" in lexicographer Samuel Johnson's writings and those of various politicians and royals.

135. Warren's three wives were Elizabeth Haskell, Rebecca Harris, and Maria Holmes. They would soon be joined by four more women.

136. This was the last daily entry in that volume, and all that survives of vol. 29, with its Oct. 28–Dec. 7 entries, are from loose sheets that had come out of the daybook. The writing is in faint, smudged pencil.

137. Mark Anthony Coombs was President Calvin Pendleton's father-in-law (his daughter Mary Coombs was one of the stake president's plural wives). Before he joined the Mormon Church, Coombs was a ship captain who circumnavigated the globe. Upon arriving in Utah in 1860, he was made a patriarch but would soon die of a liver ailment. "Died," *Deseret News*, Mar. 13, 1867.

received a call from Prest C[alvin] C. Pendleton. During the afternoon I called at at the cotton factory. The improvements there were progressing.

October 31, 1862 Friday. Was not much out today wind not so high as on yesterday.

November 1, 1862; Saturday. Passed the day mostly with brother Daniel P. Clark.

November 2, 1862; Sunday. Preached in the morning and dined with brother Richard Benson & family. The weather pleasant but cool.

November 3, 1862; Monday. Was not much out today my health not being very good.

November 4, 1862; Tuesday. To day visited brother [Calvin C.] Pendleton & family. The weather growing cool.

November 5, 1862; Wednesday. Passed the day at home making my accustomed visit to the factory.

November 6, 1862; Thursday. Was not much abroad to day weather cool but pleasant. To day brother Rob at read creek had his foot badly crushed in the horse-power of a thresher.

November 7, 1862; Friday. To day visited brother [Weeden V.] Hakes & family. Were entertained with sundry good things among which was a fine article of honey produced in the state of Deseret. In the evening my son F[rancis] M. Lyman and his wife [Rhoda] came in from Beaver on a visit.

November 8, 1862; Saturday. To day passed the time with my son in the town looking at the cotton factory & shingle mill.

November 9, 1862; Sunday. Attended meeting. My son [Francis] Marion addressed audience after which I spake to them for an hour & then dined with the mother [Mary][,] wife [Emma] & brother [Silas] of Elder J[esse] N. Smith. In the evening some rain was falling. I did not attend the evening service.

November 10, 1862; Monday. The morning opened bright and clear I sent my team for wood. Called brother Miles Anderson. In the evening I visited and dined with Bishop [William S.] Warren & family. [Francis] Marion and wife [Rhoda] were with me.

November 11, 1862; Tuesday. Passed the day at home makeing some preperations for our southern visit to (Dixey).

November 12, 1862; Wednesday. To day about 12 o'clock we started on our trip. Our party was composed of myself and my wives Cornelia [Leavitt] & Paulina [Phelps][,] [Francis] Marion & wife [Rhoda] and bishop [William S.] Warren & wife. At Cedar we left an apointment for our return. We passed on and put up for the night with brother John Hambleton & family.

November 13, 1862; Thursday. We traviled [to] Toker [Toquerville] where we lodged with bishop [Joshua T.] Willis. Ariving late we had no meeting. This place has improved much ^in growth of trees^ since my last visit nearly three years since.

November 14, 1862; Friday. This morning we were early on the way for Washington where we arived about 2 o'clock. We stoped and dined with Bishop [Robert] Covington. Took a hasty look at my lots and the cotton on them and made an arangement with bishop Covington to set out my lots to peach and apple trees & grapevines for what he could make from the use of the lots for 2 years.[138] This done we proceeded to the city of St. George where we arived after dark. Myself and wife and son and wife lodged with brothers [Orson] Pratt & [Erastus] Snow by whom we were warmly welcomed.

November 15, 1862; Saturday. To day attended the [stake] conference. Present of the Quorum of the 12 [were] Orson Pratt seignior ^Erastus Snow^ A[masa] M. Lyman & the local priesthood of the county. After some local buisness had [been] disposed of & the priesthood of the church was presented & sustained by the vote of the conference [we] then ajourned for one hour and when again in session I addressed the audience for an hour. When the conference ajourned until Sunday morning 10 o'clock [we] continued [to] my lodgings at the residence of brother Orson Pratt Junior.[139]

November 16, 1862; Sunday. To day at 10 oclock conference was in cession and was addressed by Elder F[rancis] M. Lyman folowed by Elder Erastus Snow. Ajourned for din[n]er after which meeting was

---

138. This area of Washington County has rich soil and spring water that makes it a good climate for fruit.

139. Orson Pratt Jr. was the son of a church apostle. A free-thinker, when he expressed his religious doubts with candor in September 1864, he was promptly excommunicated. He and his wife moved to Ogden and he taught music the rest of his life. Van Wagoner and Van Wagoner, "Orson Pratt Jr.: Gifted Son of an Apostle and an Apostate," 84–94.

again called and was addressed by Elder Orson Pratt folowed by Elder Snow with some local remarks. Conference then ajourned. At night attended a meeting for the ordaining & seting apart of high councillors and Bishops.

November 17, 1862; Monday. Traviled with our party to Washington for our breakfast which was kindly provided by brother Wm Mathews & bishop [Robert] Covington. From thence traviled to Toker [Toquerville] & had meeting. At night lodged with bishop [Joshua T.] Willis the rest of the party lodging else where.

November 18, 1862; Tuesday. Traviled to Kanara and lodged with the family of brother E[lisha] H. Groves except bishop [William S.] Warren & wife who went to Cedar. We had meeting at Kanara.

November 19, 1862; Wednesday. Traviled to Cedar City had meeting at 2 o'clock and another at night. Lodged at the residence of bishop Henry Lunt.

November 20, 1862; Thursday. Returned to Parrowan found all well at home. In the afternoon visited brother D[aniel] P. Clark and family. Heard the news this evening that brother C[harles] C. Rich was to move to Cedar Springs in Millard County.[140]

November 21, 1862; Friday. To day visited the shingle mill of brothers [Daniel P.] Clark & [Joseph R.] Morse and witnessed its operation and in the evening called on & took sup[p]er with brother [William H.] Dame and family. At night there was a dancing party I did not attend.

November 22, 1862; Saturday. Today left Parrowan at 7 o'clock and reached Beaver about 3 o'clock P.M. Found all well the day has been cool & cloudy. In the evening brothers Sydney & Joseph Tanner called to see me.

November 23, 1862; Sunday. To day attended the meeting of the Saints at their usual place of meting. In the evening my wives Dionetia [Whitney] and Priscilla [Turley] and children[141] came up from Minersville with brothers [Theodore] Turley and Franklin. The weather very cool. ~~Brothers Taners & Shepherd started to day for Cal.~~ Called on br [Marcus L.] Shepherd.

---

140. Cedar Springs, now Holden, is ten miles north of Fillmore, meaning that Lyman and Rich would again be neighbors.

141. Lyman had no children with Dionetia. He and Priscilla had two young sons. Two additional children with Priscilla died when they were a year old each.

November 24, 1862; Monday. To day remained at home with my family. During the day brothers Sidney and Joseph Tanner and M[arcus] L. Shepherd started for Cal[ifornia] to freight in goods for Mr [William] Jenings.[142]

November 25, 1862; Tuesday. To day the members of my family from Minersville returned home.

November 26, 1862; Wednesday. To day I started for Fillmore our party consisted of myself and my wife Louisa Maria and her two sons [Francis] Marion and Amasa [Jr]. We traviled as far as Corn Creek [Kanosh] and lodged with brother Peter Robinson.

November 27, 1862; Thursday. This morning arived at Fillmore and quartered with bishop [Thomas] Callister. At night preached to the people as did my son [Francis] Marion.

November 28, 1862; Friday. To day brother Thomas R. King took his team and carried myself & sons and bishop [Thomas] Callister and brother Russell to the sink[143] to look at some land for a farm. Lodged with brother Reuben MacBride's.

November 29, 1862; Saturday. To day made some examination along Chalk Creek for water-power and spent the evening at brother [Reuben] McBride's.

November 30, 1862; Sunday. Today I attended three meetings after which I felt much wearied and went to lodge with brother Joseph Robison and family.

December 1, 1862; Monday. To day visited brother Felshaw and family and staid with them over night ^&^ while here I learned that I could procure the land I wanted for a farm.

December 2, 1862; Tuesday. Was some about town looking for fruit trees. In the evening I ~~attended a family meeting at brother Kings & lodged there~~ visited at brother Trescot's & lodged at bishop [Thomas] Callisters.

December 3, 1862; Wednesday. Passed the day about town and in

142. William Jennings was a successful Salt Lake City merchant. In two years, his lavish Eagle Emporium on Main Street, a block south of Temple Square, will be the envy of all other store owners. He later becomes mayor.

143. The area is still identified on maps as "the sink," ten miles northwest of Fillmore.

the evening held a family meeting at brother [Thomas R.] Kings and lodged there.

December 4, 1862; Thursday. This morning parted with my sons [Francis] Marion and Amasa & their mother [Maria] and in the stage I started for the north and lodged at night in Nephi.

December 5, 1862; Friday. Continued my travil and lodged at night with Alfonzo Green and family.

December 6, 1862; Saturday. About 3 o'clock I arived at home in Salt Lake City found all well. Called on the Prest [Brigham Young] and also meet bros G[eorge] A. Smith and W[ilford] Woodruff.

December 7, 1862; Sunday. Was at home all day and did not attend meeting on aco[u]nt of my weariness from my journey from the south.[144]

December 8, 1862; Monday. To day attended the session of the Legislative Assembly in the Court House[145] from which we ajourned to the State House formerly known as the Council House.[146] In the evening I called on the President [Brigham Young] and accompanied him through the theater. This evening received my sack of goods which were brought to me by brother John Young.

December 9, 1862; Tuesday. Meet pursuent to ajournment in the State House, were informed by our committee that his excelency the Governor [Stephen S. Harding] would meet us tomorow at 2 o'clock. In the [afternoon I] read some of the political doctrines [of] George Washington as given by himself in his farewell address to the people of the United States of America [and on] the occasion of the expiration of the second term of his presidential service of the American people.[147]

December 10, 1862; Wednesday. To day as per previous apointment we received an official insult from his excelency [the governor] under the title of his message.[148] In the evening past some time at the Historians

144. This is the last of the loose-leaf pages, the remaining entries for 1862 and some for 1863 having been recorded in vol. 16 after the entries for 1858.

145. The 1855 County Court House was a two-story building the same size and design as the Council House, both designed by Truman O. Angell. The court was located at 268 West 200 South.

146. Lyman represented Beaver and Millard Counties in the Utah Territorial Legislature.

147. Washington's Farewell Address advocated a strong federal government and national unity, which were popular themes in the north and west during the Civil War.

148. Governor Harding's address to the legislature condemned polygamy, and it

Office[,] present several of the members of the legislature. To day read the message of the Prest.

December 11, 1862; Thursday. Today meet in the Representative Hall at 1 o'clock. No buisness apearing requiring action the House[,] ajourned until tomorow at one o'clock after which in company with brother G[eorge] A. Smith I called on president D[aniel] H. Wells whom we found to be still slowly recovering his health. Returned home and past the evening with my [family] in reading ^the^ Ancient history of the Carthaginians. Some indications of storm in the gathering clouds in the north and west.

December 12, 1862; Friday. To day meet [in the legislature] and ajourned until Monday at one ^o^clock. To night some snow fell.

December 13, 1862; Saturday. Passed the day in town some snow falling in the afternoon. To day received my watch from the [watch] cleaner Brother [Octave] Ursenbaugh [Ursenbach][149] for which I paid him 2½ dollars in money & also 2 dollars for a pair of spectacles.

December 14, 1862; Sunday. To day did not go out on acount of cold and cough which rendered me very ucomfortable. Read some history through the day.

December 15, 1862; Monday. Meet in the Hall & transacted some buisness and adjourned. I suffered very much from my cold to day. I called at the Historians Office.

December 16, 1862; Tuesday. To day meet [in the legislature]. As per ajournment some buisness was presented and refered to the appropriate Committ^i^es. The weather is still warm and pleasant. Passed the evening in reading history with my family my cough was very severe giving me much pain. Today received my mileage from the Government $69.

December 17, 1862; Wednesday. This morning transacted some buisness in town after which I meet in [legislative] session. Some business

---

outraged Brigham Young, who made it known he did not want the address published. When no one in the territory would print it, the US Senate ordered 1,000 copies printed by the Government Printing Office as pamphlets. Apostle Wilford Woodruff called it "the most insulting document ever delivered to this assembly or any Legislative Body." Kenney, *Wilford Woodruff's Journal*, 6:81–82; Church Historian's Office, "History of the Church," Dec. 10, 1862; Harding, "Message of the Governor."

149. Octave Ursenbach was a watch and clockmaker and silk importer. He returned to his native Switzerland in 1867 on a mission but fell ill and never quite recovered, dying four years later at thirty-eight.

was presented & refered [to committee]. Today sold my draft for mileage to Lawrence & Kimball for half cash & half goods. In the evening I called at the Prest Office in company Brother Orson Pratt & John Taylor. The President [Brigham Young] was not in. My health somewhat beter this evening.

December 18, 1862; Thursday. To day attended the session of the Legislature. Attended to some items of buisness. Did not see the President today altho I was some time in his office in the afternoon. Read some history at night.

December 19, 1862; Friday. To day meet [in the legislature] as per ajournment and concluded some unfinished buisness ajourned to Tuesday next at 1 o'clock. In the evening read the history of Cyrus.[150]

December 20, 1862; Saturday. To day passed the time in writing some letters to my family in the south. In the evening read history and also attended a meeting with the male members of the 14th Ward called by the Bishop to consider some maters of buisness. In the evening received a letter from my son [Francis] Marion in Beaver.

December 21, 1862; Sunday. To day I wrote a note to my son F[rancis] M. Lyman in answer to one received from him on yesterday after which I attended meeting in the Tabernacle. The audience was addressed by Elder Lorenzo Snow. Attended meeting in the afternoon when audience was addressed by President B[righam] Young. At 5 o'clock meet [in prayer circle] with the following members of our Q[u]orum[:] O[rson] Pratt[,] J[ohn] Taylor[,] W[ilford] Woodruff, G[eorge] A. Smith[,] A[masa] M. Lyman[,] Lorenzo Snow. Returned home and read some history.

December 22, 1862; Monday. Today I went at 9 o'clock to the theater after which I returned home & read history. Called on the President [Brigham Young] after which I returned home and resumed my reading. Brother Edward [Partridge] came down this evening from Farmington reported all well there.

December 23, 1862; Tuesday. Meet [with legislature]. As per ajournment some little buisness was introduced after which ajouned until tomorow a 11 o'clock. In the evening I visited the family of brother

150. That is, Cyrus the Great, the Persian king who conquered most of the Middle East and large parts of Asia in the sixth century BCE.

Charles Crismond. Rece^i^ved to day an invitation to attend the dedication of the Theater.[151]

December 24, 1862; Wednesday. Meet as per ajournment. Some little buisness was transacted after which the House ajourned until Saturday 27th at one o'clock. In the evening I with some members of my family attended the dedication of the theater and was called upon with others to address the audience which I did for about thirty minutes. The addresses were folowed by dancing which continued after the dismisal of the Assembly at which time I retired.

December 25, 1862; Thursday. To day I past the early part of the morning in drafting a plan of a house after which in the afternoon I walked out in town[152] and in the evening I read the history of the formation of the Grecian States under the legislative guidance of their political sages Licurgas [Lycurgus] & Solon. Some of our family were in attendance at the theater. The weather still is warm some clouds that indicate some change of weather. Our attendance at the theater was for its dedication and not for a play.

December 27, 1862; Saturday.[153] To day meet in the Legislature as per adjournment. The speaker being absent I occupied the Speakers Chair pro tem. Some little buisness was transacted after which the House ajourned until Monday next at 1 o'clock.

December 28, 1862; Sunday. This morning some Snow was falling. I attended meeting in the Tabernacle and addressed the audience for one hour after which ajourned for one hour. Meeting again in session the audience was addressed by Bishop E[dwin] D. Wooley followed by President Brigham Young. The snow was still falling freely attended with high wind from the north. At night read history.

December 29, 1862; Monday. To day meet as per ajournment the Hon John Taylor was chosen Speaker pro tem. After considering some items of buisness the House ajourned until Tuesday at 1 o'clock.

December 30, 1862; Tuesday. Meet as per adjournment. I occupied the Speakers Chair. The House ajourned until Tuesday next at 1 o'clock

151. This was the second dedication of the Salt Lake Theatre. The first was to celebrate completion of the exterior. Now that the interior was finished, shows could be performed. "Christmas Eve in the Theatre," *Deseret News*, Dec. 31, 1862.

152. Lyman repeated "I walked out in town" twice.

153. Lyman recorded no entry for Dec. 26.

after which I sought for an opportunity to go to Farmington but did not succeed. In the evening attended the lecture at the Seventies Hall. The lecturer was elder E[lias] L. T. Harison the subject the odities of life.

December 31, 1862; Wednesday. Today about 12 o'clock I started for Farmington with brother [Marcus L.] Shepherd. Found the members of my family there well. Weather warm wind in the South. Brother E[zra] T. Clark called to see me.

9 Reward of the Just, 1863–1864

In his 1863 diary, Amasa Lyman reflected more than once that after thirty years on the road in service of the church, he was finally settling down. Previously he had distributed his several families throughout the Mormon settlements. At the start of this diary, for instance, he is in Farmington and Salt Lake City, adjusting to seeing himself as something other than a traveling missionary. In Fillmore he brings his far-flung family together. They will live in separate houses but within walking distance, and he felt comfortable living openly as a polygamist in that remote location. Not that he was content to stay put or no longer had responsibilities elsewhere. He continued to travel throughout the territory on preaching tours, attend meetings of the Quorum of the Twelve, participate in the territorial legislature, and attend conferences in Salt Lake City and St. George. But now he at least had a home base. However, one can detect a simultaneous shift in his diaires that hints at an intellectual restlessness and tension with Brigham Young. His wife Eliza Maria Partridge later reminisced that "Br. Lyman seemed to feel uncomfortable in his mind … I did not know what was wrong with him, but I could see that he was very unhappy."[1] After years of consistent journal keeping, he stopped keeping a diary in Jan. 1864. When he resumed four years later, it was without reflection or explanation. Either he did not want to document that time period or perhaps he kept another diary that has not survived.

1. Eliza's memory may have been colored by Lyman's excommunication in 1870. Partridge, *Eliza Maria Partridge Journal*, 81.

January 1, 1863; Thursday. Did not go out to day but passed the time in reading history. Some snow falling which gave promise of some sleighing.

January 2, 1863; Friday. Remained at home. In the evening I received an invitation to a social party held at the [Farmington] Court-House which I attended with my wife Caroline. We took super with brother Thomas Smith and family.

January 3, 1863; Saturday. Remained at home. Weather warm some rain.

January 4, 1863; Sunday. To day I attended meeting with the Saints and addressed them. In the evening I attended meeting at the same place the audience was addressed by brother E[lias] L. T. Harrison. In the evening there was some rain falling which wasted the snow and rendered the traveling rather unpleasant. Dined with Joseph Robi[n]son.

January 5, 1863; Monday. Remained at home all day. In the evening brother E[zra] T Clark and wife ~~spe^n^t the evenin~~ called and spent the evening with us.

January 6, 1863; Tuesday. This morning started for the city with brother J[udson] L. Stoddard. Meet in the Legislature as <u>per</u> ajournment. Meet with President B[righam] Young[,] this morning at the barbers.

January 7, 1863; Wednesday. Meet in the Legislature some buisness before the House for consi^d^eration. At night attended the theater with brother John Taylor.

January 8, 1863; Thursday. To day meet with the representatives; and in the evening spent some time with <u>Prests</u> [Brigham] Young & [Heber C.] Kimball and brothers [Orson] Pratt & [John] Taylor. As I returned home some snow was falling. Today received the news of the repulse of the federal forces at Vicksburg, and als[o] of the terrible slaughter of the uneion forces at Frederick's Burg.[2]

January 9, 1863; Friday. Meet in the Legislature as per ajournment. Attended to some items of buisness and ajourned. Passed the evening in reading history. The weather was mild & warm some little rain was falling.

---

2. The Battle of Fredericksburg was a blow to the Union cause with more than 12,000 casualties on their side. The *Deseret News* expressed support for the north but also criticized Lincoln's handling of the war. "The Eastern Press and People on the Fredericksburg Disaster," *Deseret News*, Jan. 21, 1863.

January 10, 1863; Saturday. Meet in Legislature. Transacted some buisness and ajourned until Monday at 1 o'clock after which I went to Farmington with brother Arthur Stainer.[3] The travil was rather unpleasant as the road was rough and the late hour brought darkness.

January 11, 1863; Sunday. To day I attended a Teachers meeting in the morning after which I meet with the Saints and addressed them and was folowed by brother Charles C. Rich. In the evening myself & wife took sup[p]er with brother E[zra] T. Clark & family.

January 12, 1863; Monday. Called at the Presidents Office before going to the Representative's Hall.[4] In session to day we disposed of some buisness after which we ajourned until tomorow at 10 o'clock. The wind was northerly and some snow falling. Brother Edward Partridge and wife was with us to night passed the evening in reading history.

January 13, 1863; Tuesday. Meet in the Representatives Hall had somewhat buisy day. Did not ajourn until near night. Passed the evening in reading Ancient History. Professor [Orson] Pratt lec^t^ured in the Seventies Hall on the subject of astronomy. Weather cool. My wife Lydia [Partridge] & children went to Farmington to day with her brother [Edward].

January 14, 1863; Wednesday. Meet in the Representatives Hall as per ajournment & dispached considerable buisness of which there was somewhat of an increase as the session draws near the time of its close. At night I attended the Theater & witnessed the representation of the play entitled Virginius or the Roman Father. Mr. B[ernard] Snow appeared as Virginius.[5] Weather to night cool and pleasant.

January 15, 1863; Thursday. Meet in the Legislature. During recess

3. Arthur Stayner led the church's long-standing, initially unsuccessful attempt to produce granular sugar from sugar beets. After the $400,000 sugar factory was built in Lehi in 1891, the enterprise that was called Utah Sugar Company (later U&I Sugar) became wildly successful. Stayner would die, satisfied with his accomplishment, eight years later.

4. This was one of two rooms on the second floor of the County Court House, both devoted to the legislature, one for the Utah Legislative Assembly and the other for the Territorial Council. Squire, *The Evolution of American Legislatures*, 122–23.

5. The play was performed in London in 1820 and later to great acclaim in the United States as "the best acting tragedy of the modern stage." It involved a father in ancient Rome killing his daughter after her abduction by a politician who turned her into a slave by claiming she was someone else. Knowles, *Virginius*.

I called on Sister Emily [Dow Partridge] Young and Mrs E[liza Snow] Young.[6] In the evening I received a call from my old & valued friend William Martindale President in Too^i^le County after which I passed some hours in reading history. Today Judge [Charles B.] Wait & lady[7] were present to witness our labors.

January 16, 1863; Friday. This day closes our term of Legislative labors for the present session. The weather is warm and pleasant as spring. His Honour Judge [John F.] Kinie [Kinney] and the U. S.Marshall [Isaac L. Gibbs] were present to witness our deliberation.

January 17, 1863; Saturday. Remained in the city and in company with brother Thomas Callister I visited the residence of Mayor [Abraham O.] Smoote[8] for the purpose of examining his molasses evaporator or boiler. Dined with the Mayor's family returned home [to Salt Lake City, just west of Temple Square,] and past the evening in reading history while some of the family went to the theater.

January 18, 1863; Sunday. To day past the morning in writing some mater for history. In the afternoon I attended the meeting in the Tabernacle. The audience was addressed by Elders James W. Cummings and Joseph W. Young, who were folowed by <u>Prest</u> Brigham Young. The morning service was by Elder E[zra] T. Benson. In the [evening] I attended [prayer circle][9] at the Historian's [office] after which I attended the meeting in the 14 Ward assembly room and there addressed the people for an hour.

January 19, 1863; Monday. To day transacted some buisness in the city and called at the State House where ^the^ Legislature of the state

6. These were plural wives of Brigham Young who were previously married to Joseph Smith. Emily Dow Partridge Young was Lyman's sister-in-law. Eliza Snow Young was the sister of a future church president, Lorenzo Snow. Amasa and Cornelia named one of their sons Lorenzo Snow Lyman.

7. Catharine Waite was an attorney who championed women's rights. In 1866 she would publish *The Mormon Prophet and His Harem* and dedicate it to "the suffering women of Utah."

8. Abraham Owen Smoot famously had six wives and as many slaves. Brigham Young later sent him to Provo, where he was stake president and mayor; his son became an apostle and US senator. See "Slave Inhabitants in the County of Great Salt Lake," Schedule 2, June 1, 1860, US Census, roll 1313.

9. Lyman drew a circle here to indicate a prayer circle and did the same on Jan. 25; Mar. 1, 8, 22; and Apr. 5, 1863; in other instances he wrote out "circle" (Dec. 13, 1863; Jan. 17, 24, 1864) or "prayer circle" (Jan. 2, 3, 1864).

was in session. The message of the Governor was read while I was present.[10] In the evening myself & my wife Eliza [Partridge] visited brother Nathan Tanner and family.

January 20, 1863; Tuesday. Today the State Legislature ajourned after the transaction of some items of buisnesss one of which ^was^ the election of myself as circuit Judge for the 2nd Judicial Circuit under the organizaton of the State of Deseret. This morning the Quorum of the Apostles received a letter from Elder George Q. Cannon in Liverpool under the date of 13th of December 1862.[11] In the evening I called on brother Thomas Callister who was intending soon to return to Fillmore his residence.

January 21, 1863; Wednesday. Today past the most of the time in the historian's Office in copying in my record of letters. In the evening I attended the theater and witnessed the play of Ingomar the Barbarian.[12] My wife Eliza [Partridge] was with me. Some snow tonight giveing us another edition of Winter the small hours of morning had arived ere we retired.

January 22, 1863; Thursday. To day passed some time in the Historian's Office in journalizing. In the evening at 5 o'clock I attended a social party (at the residence of Elder John Taylor) composed of the members of the Quorum of the Twelve who were in the city an[d] Bishop [Edward] Hunter[13] and Joseph Horn. We past a few hours very pleasantly during which the party repaired to the 14th Ward school room where [we] participated for a short time in the dance that was going on with a portion

10. This was not a meeting of the territorial legislature. It was a provisional group, held in reserve for years to act as a government body if needed, going back to when the Saints first arrived in the Great Basin. Brigham Young addressed the group as if he were governor (he wasn't) and they were a state legislature (they weren't). "We are called the State Legislature," he said, referring to the non-existent State of Deseret, "but when the time comes, we shall be called the Kingdom of God." Journal History, Jan. 19, 1863.

11. Cannon's letter relayed the French Mission president's request for assistance in helping the emigrating Saints and shipping a lithographic press to Utah. Cannon to Young, Dec. 12, 1862, in Brigham Young Office Files.

12. *Ingomar the Barbarian* was adapted by Maria Lovell in 1851 from a German play, Friedrich Halm's *Der Sohn der Wildnis* ("Son of the Wilderness"). Set in ancient Marseille (Roman Massilia), a girl resists her mother's efforts to have her marry an older man; the girl falls in love instead with Ingomar, leader of a Germanic tribe.

13. Edward Hunter was Presiding Bishop from 1851 until his death in 1883. He famously laid the cornerstone of the Salt Lake Temple, although without living to see the temple finished.

of the citizens of the ward. Returned home at midnight leaveing the ward company still engaged in the dance. Weather quite cool and sharp.

January 23, 1863; Friday. To day passed some time in the Historian's Office and in the afternoon called and spent some time in the President's Office where I had some conversation with brother [Albert] Carrington who read a letter to me he had received from brother W[illiam] H. Hooper from Galena [Illinois]. After this the Prest [Brigham Young] came in and said to me that he would call and see my residence in view of ascertaining its value before he would purchase it of me.[14] Returned home and passed the evening in reading history some little snow fell to night. Brother East came in & announced some regulations had been made for a juvenile party in the ward. To day I wrote leters to Sandpete County.

January 24, 1863; Saturday. Today I wrote leter to my sister Ruth E. Goodall and family in the State of Vermont. Today payed R[ichard] R. Hopkins $18.30 in order on the firm of Kimball & Lawrence. Did not see the Prest today. Passed most of the day in the Historians Office where I attended to my writing. In the evening past some hours in reading the history of the successors of Alexander the Great.

January 25, 1863; Sunday. Passed the day mostly at home, did not attend the meeting in the Tabernacle. President O[rson] Hyde spoke in the morning and in the afternoon Prest B[righam] Young spoke to the people. In the evening I attended the [prayer circle] at the Historian's House. Prest Orson Hyde was with us and opened our meeting. I was mouth in the prayer. Brothers Taylor[,] Pratt and Woodruff[,] Snow and Smith, were present.

January 26, 1863; Monday. This morning attended to some buisness about town after which I passed the residue of the day at the Historians Office. Past the evening at home reading history.

January 27, 1863; Tuesday. Today wrote letter to my cousin Albert Mason in New Hampshire & heard the message of Governor of New York.[15] I past the evening at the Seventies Hall[16] where we were

14. They completed the sale for $3000 (see entry for Mar. 23, 1863).

15. Governor Horatio Seymour was a Democrat who opposed some of President Lincoln's initiatives but favored the Union. He would run for president against Ulysses S. Grant. "Gov. Seymour's Message," *New York Times*, Jan. 8, 1863.

16. This was a small adobe building on State Street half a block south of Brigham Young's Beehive House.

interested with a lecture on the Science of Geology by brother [Thomas B.] Broderick. Weather clear and cold.

January 28, 1863; Wednesday. Passed the most of the day in the Historians Office. At night attended the theater and witnessed the play entitled Retribution or Justice in Cuba[17] in which Mr. [Bernard] Snow appeared in the Yanky character of Mr Seth Swap.

January 29, 1863; Thursday. Today I attended the funeral of the child of Bishop Jacob Miller, who died with croop after a very brief illness. I addressed the friends present on the subject of the life beyond the grave and our reasons for a belief in its existence and hope for its enjoyment when we shall have parted with our bodies. Returned home and past the evening in reading history.

January 30, 1863; Friday. Today about 12 o'clock I started for Farmington with brother John Taylor, stayed at F. all night. Brother Taylor preached to the people I taried with my family and past the evening in reading.

January 31, 1863; Saturday. To day myself and brother Taylor traviled to Ogden City. We dined with brother Parker[18] and family after which we lodged with brother Richard Ballantyne and family. Wind from the south[,] weather turning warmer.

February 1, 1863; Sunday. To day we attended meeting in the [Ogden] Tabernacle where I addressed the Saints who were assembled for an hour after which the meeting ajourned until evening when the audience was addressed by Elder [John] Taylor, after which we returned to our lodgings at brother [Richard] B[allantyne]'s. Tonight the wounded soldiers from the north [Bear River, Idaho] arived for whom provisions had been made by the citizens of Ogden for their night's entertainent and rest [en route back to Fort Douglas in Salt Lake City]. This kind treatment was very s^e^asonable for the sufferers and seemed to be appreciated by them. There were of [soldiers] killed in the Battle some 14 and wounded 42, many of whom were mortaly wounded. Of the Indians there were 275 killed besides some women and children whose destruction was unavoidable in the fury of the combat.[19]

17. The play is better known as *Miralda: The Justice of Tacon* or *A Yankee in Cuba*. It involved a young man working in a silver mine in Mexico and, on his way home to Maine, falling for a seductive Cuban girl named Miralda. Ballou, *Miralda*.

18. Probably William K. Parker, whose son was named Amasa Lyman Parker.

19. The soldiers grossly misrepresented the battle to the Mormons. In what is

The soldiers suffered much from the freezeing of their feet occasioned by their wading through the river and thus weting their feet as they entered the battle which is said to have lasted some four hours. A large number of the wounded were shot through the chest, one of whom died after their arival here during the night. Among the wounded oficers was Lieutenant Darwin Chase, shot in the lungs. He once had belonged to the church and was imprisoned with brother P[arley] Pratt in Missouri. He was left at Box Elder being to[o] weak to travil.[20]

February 2, 1863; Monday. To day myself & brother [John] Taylor visited the wounded soldiers and officers after which in company with brothers Taylor, [Lorin] Farr,[21] [Francis A.] Hamond, [Richard] Ballantyne and some others, we went to Slater'sville where we had meeting at 11 o'clock. Brother Taylor addressed the audience after which I folowed with a short address. We dined with brother [Ebenezer C.] Richardson and family after which we went to Plain City where we stoped with brother Hanson[22] with whom we had lodgings. Had meeting at Candle Lighting. I addressed the audience & was folowed by brother Taylor and others after which we returned and lodged with brother Hansen.

February 3, 1863; Tuesday. To day our party left the City of the Plain and went to north Ogden where we had meeting at 11 o'^c^lock after which we dined with Bishop [Thomas] Dun and then returned to Ogden and lodged with Prest [Lorin] Farr. Went this evening with the President to look over his new mill which is a very fine piece of work and which reflects the good taste of its builder & owner.

February 4, 1863; Wednesday. Passed the day in the city. Called upon

---

now known as the Bear River Massacre, the US Army, under Colonel Patrick Edward Connor, murdered hundreds of Shoshonis in a brutal fashion, including women and children. After Mormons in Cache Valley and immigrants on the Oregon Trail clashed with Indians and asked for protection, Connor's men responded, although with bloodthirsty enthusiasm. Madsen, *Shoshoni Frontier*; Christensen, *Sagwitch*.

20. Darwin Chase was baptized a Mormon in 1831. He served in the Nauvoo Legion and Mormon Battalion before being excommunicated in 1851. He died of his wounds from the Bear River action on Feb. 5.

21. Lorin Farr was the mayor and stake president in Ogden, father-in-law of apostle John Henry Smith, and grandfather of Mormon president George Albert Smith.

22. Probably Hans C. Hansen, a Danish convert, one of the original pioneer company of 1847, and among the founders of Plain City. Five months earlier he had returned from a two-year mission to Denmark. His family would grow from two wives and their children to four wives.

and dined with brother [John] Horspool and family after which I called on Sister [Sarah Keyes] Stewart wife of brother David M. Stewart who is in Scotland. Found her & child well but anxious for the return of the husband & father. The residue of the troops from the north stayed here last night & left here this morning for Camp Douglas. Brother [John] Taylor who had thought of going into the Kanyon this morning did not go on acount of deep snow. Lodged at brother [Richard] B[allantyne]'s.

February 5, 1863; Thursday. This morning Capt [Jefferson] Hunt called in to see us and brighten the recollections of olden times. As I am writing brother [Richard] Ballantyne informed me that brother David Lowdon (serving man in the family of Bishop C[hauncey] W. West) had died this morning about 7 o'clock of consumption [tuberculosis].[23] After writing up my journal myself and brother Ballantyne went to the meeting in the new school house. I addressed the Saints for half an hour after which myself an[d] brother [John] Taylor dined with Sister Mary West the first wife of Bishop West and daughter of Bishop [Abraham E. L.] Hogland of S. L. City. In the evening we took tea with brother Francis A. Hammond & family. Returned to and lodged with brother Ballantyne.

February 6, 1863; Friday. To day after brother [John] Taylor had completed his buisness, we started south and came to Kay's[ville] Ward and lodged with brother Winall and family.[24] Snow fell some four inches deep. The Bishop not being at home we had no meeting. We were very kindly made comfortable by brother Winall.

February 7, 1863; Saturday. This morning the s[n]ow was falling freely & we started for Farmington at which place I parted with Brother [John] Taylor who went to S. L. City. I remained in Farmington to attend to some buisness. Found my family here usually well. Passed the evening in reading.

February 8, 1863; Sunday. To day attended the meeting and addressed the Saints upon the necessity of practical honesty with all men

23. Chauncey W. West had served a mission to Ceylon, Hong Kong, and India prior to settling in Weber County as the bishop of Farr West, a city that was named after him and Lorin Farr. He was a prominent railroad executive; he had nine wives and thirty-five children, and curiously his servant David Lowdon was buried along with the West family in the Ogden City Cemetery and is listed on the obelisk marking their graves.

24. John Weinel was a German convert and flour miller in Kaysville. He was a president of the local Seventies.

both Saints and siners as laying the foundation of ^that^ confidence necis^s^ary to hapiness. I did not attend meeting in the evening, the audience was addressed by brother Charles Penrose. Dined with brother E[zra] T. Clark & family. While there brother C[harles] C. Rich & two of his wives[25] called.

February 9, 1863; Monday. Called at the Tithing Office and learned that the parties with whom I had buisness had left town to be gone for two days. Returned home and overhauled some of my old horse harness[es] which I found much dillapidated.

February 10, 1863; Tuesday. This morning I called at the Tithing Office where I met with brother Wm. Muir with whom I had some conversation on the subject of farming in which brother M. has been practically engaged for several years in Davis County. Dined with brother Arthur Stainer. In the evening I heard a lecture on agriculture from brother Muir after which I addressed the audience for half an hour.

February 11, 1863; Wednesday. Made some ineffectual eforts to acomplish something in the way of selling my farm. Returned home and past some time in reading.

February 12, 1863; Thursday. Called at the residence of brother Henry Steade but did not see him. Weather very mild & warm.

February 13, 1863; Friday. To day visited brother [William] Budge[26] & family. The day opened with a storm of snow which ~~which~~ however subsided as the day advanced. In the afternoon President Joseph Young and others from G.S.L. City arived here to hold meeting on Saturday & Sunday.

February 14, 1863; Saturday. To day attended meeting. The Saints were addressed by <u>Prest</u> Joseph Young folowed by Presidents [Albert P.] Rockwood and [Horace S.] Eldridge and also Joseph W. Young after which the meeting ajourned until the evening when the Saints were addressed by J. W. Young after which <u>Prest</u> B[righam] Young spoke briefly

25. Rich was living with his second and third wives, Eliza Ann Graves and Sarah J. Peck, in Centerville, five miles south of Farmington, prior to his call to settle in the Bear Lake area.

26. William Budge was born in Scotland. After serving as a missionary for nine years, he emigrated in 1860 and became the bishop of Logan. He was sent back to Europe as a mission president. When he returned he was named president of the Logan temple. His son Alfred became a prominent Idaho judge.

to the people. Dined to day with brother [Thomas] Grover & family and attended a council of the seventies which was admonished & instructed by Prest J. Young.

February 15, 1863; Sunday. This morning went with brother E[zra] T. Clark to Centerville where I spoke to the Saints. Dined with Bishop [William] Smith and attended meeting in the evening when the Saints were addressed by Prest. B[righam] Young after which I returned home to Farmington. My wife Lydia [Partridge] was with me to day. We meet brother Rich & part of his family at the Bishop's.

February 16, 1863; Monday. To day attended the Court held by Justice [William] Budge for the trial of a young man for stealing. The defendent pleading guilty was fined the sum of $25.00 and costs of suit. There being several of the youth of Farmington present by request of the Court I addressed the audience in waiting for a short time upon the pernicious influence of idleness upon the youth when the habits of life are being formed. The defendent seemed humbled and ashamed of his folly and promised reformation. Went to look at some stock which brother Mark Bigler was designing to let me have in payment for land. The price and quality not suiting I did not take it. In the evening felt quite unwell from cold taken by walking in the mud. Today brother N[athaniel] V. Jones was buried in G.S.L. City. Prest B[righam] Young preached.[27]

February 17, 1863; Tuesday. Today brother Edward Partridge [Jr.] went to the city and before going he agreed to take $300 dollars for his small piece of land in the city and take it in land of me in Farmington.[28] I visited today the family of brother J[udson] L. Stoddard. Brother S. was at home. Some snow was falling as we returned home.

February 18, 1863; Wednesday. Passed the day in making some unavailing efforts to effect something in the land trade.

February 19, 1863; Thursday. To day traviled some around town in search of the Bishop with whom I dined and he loaned me some wheat.

February 20, 1863; Friday. This evening with my wife Lydia [Partridge]

27. Jones had been close to Lyman in the British mission. He caught pneumonia ("pleurisy or lung fever") and died at forty. Journal History, Feb. 15, 1863.

28. That is, they swapped land valued equally at $300, Lyman's rural property in Farmington for his brother-in-law's urban plot in Salt Lake City.

I attended a musical entertainment given in the Court House under the management of brothers [William] Budge & [Charles] Penrose.

February 21, 1863; Saturday. Today Edward [Partridge] returned from the city and was acompanied by my wife Caroline [Partridge] and two of her children who were having the whooping cough. Weather pleasant to day.

February 22, 1863; Sunday. To day I attended the meeting of the Saints in the Court-House. I dined with brother Thomas Smith and family and was promised a ride to the city by brother Lott Smith.

February 23, 1863; Monday. This morning at 7 oclock I was on the way to the city [Salt Lake] with brother [Lot] Smith where we arived about noon this evening. I received a letter from my nephew Henry S. Goodall in the State of Vermont East Brownington Orleans County dated Jan 11/63. Also one from my son [Francis] Marion in Beaver with tithing certificate and one from [wife] Cornelia [Leavitt].

February 24, 1863; Tuesday. Today I sent by brother W[illiam] J. Cox a plough to Fillmore and some parcels to Beaver. Past some time in the Historian's Office writing up my journal. In the evening read history. Felt quite unwell at night from cold, no fresh war news to day.

February 25, 1863; Wednesday. To day visited the Prest [Brigham Young] at his office and walked with him to the theater after which past some time in the H. O. [Historian's] Office. In the afternoon called on brother Nathan Tanner. While there saw brother Sidney Tanner who informed that himself & brother M. L. Shepherd had procured a bill [set] of irons & the necissary fittings for a saw-mill which they expect to procure in Cal[ifornia] and erect the mill in Fillmore. From latest dispatch from Cal brother Tanner was afraid the constant depreciation of the government paper [money] might in some degree interfere with their plans in trade.

Weather very cold this evening. Some members of our family attended a lecture delivered in the evening. Some members of our family attended a lecture delivered in the Tabernacle by Elder Jas S. Brown. The subject the Society Islands[29] & their inhabitants.[30]

29. The Society Islands are part of French Polynesia, including the island of Tahiti. James S. Brown had been a missionary to the islands and would return twice despite losing his leg to someone in Utah who mistook him for a bear and shot him. Kenney, *Wilford Woodruff's Journal*, 6:476.

30. This entry appeared under the Feb. 24 entry but was marked with a note

February 26, 1863; Thursday. Today wrote letter to Bishop [Thomas] Callister of Fillmore & called on W[illiam] I. Appleby to make some enquiry in relation to some cotton spinning gins after which with my wife Eliza [Partridge] I visited the tow widows of Dr. Darwin Richardson [Jane Cobleigh and Grace Rose Richardson]. Brother Jas Muir and his two wives [Mary Murray][31] were present and also Sister John Van Cott,[32] and Sister Richards & Sister Staples. We taried the evening when the frost sealed up the mud.

February 27, 1863; Friday. To day passed some time in the Prests Office and then attended to some writing in the H. O. [Historian's] Office. returned home and passed the residue of the day in reading. In the evening received a call from brother Nathan Tanner & wife Rachel, & also a call on business from brother E[lias] L. T. Harrison. The weather cooll & pleasant.

February 28, 1863; Saturday. This morning passed some time in the H. O. [Historian's] Office and ^then^ called at the Prests' Office where I had some conversation with brother H[orace] S. Eldridge in relation to machinery for spining wool & cotton. In the afternoon with my wife Eliza [Partridge] I visited brother John Van Cott & family. Quite mudy this evening & very unpleasant walking.

March 1, 1863; Sunday. To day attended meeting. The audience was addressed by Elder Charles C. Rich. Ajourned for one hour when the meeting was in session and was addressed by Elder John Taylor, folowed by Prest B[righam] Young. At 5 o'clock attended the [prayer circle] at the Historian's house. Prest B. Young was present and was mo[u]th in prayr and the meeting was opened by brother Lorenzo Snow. Brother Hyrum Kimball and his associate [Thomas Atkinson] were blest this evening at the H. O. [Historian's] Office and set apart for their mission to the Sandwich Isleands. At half past 6 o'clock preached at the 13th Ward Assembly Room to an attentive audience.

March 2, 1863; Monday. Passed some time with the Prest [Brigham Young] in his Office and returned home in the evening feeling much indisposed and retired early but had but barely done so when I was waited

---

indicating that it belonged under Feb. 25.

31. Muir family records list no other wives for James Muir.

32. John Van Cott had at least four wives in 1863.

upon by brother A[mos] M. Musser[33] who stated that brother John Taylor and myself were requested to prepare some resolutions to be presented to a mass-meeting of the citizens on tomorow at 1 o'clock. On acount of my indisposition I did not arise but brother [Taylor] visited the Prest on acount of the prospective meeting. I past a sleepless night.

March 3, 1863; Tuesday. This morning I called on Elder [John] Taylor and at about 9 o'clock we repaired to the office of the President [Brigham Young] & after having consumated our arangements for the meeting while we yet taried Brother Henry Lawrence came in and informed us of a meeting of the Governor [Stephen S. Harding] and Judges and some of the military officers from Camp Douglass to prepare for sending abroad some scurrilous statements in relation to our people over their signitures. All of the conclave signed save two[,] [John F.] Kin[n]ey & Marshall [Isaac L.] Gibbs[,] withdrew his name from the paper. At 2 o'clock attended the meeting in the Tabernacle, the report of which may be found in the Deseret News No. 36, Vol 12.[34] In the evening I attended a lecture in the Seventies Hall, after the lecturer (Brother B[urr] Frost)[,] I addressed the audience. Returned home feeling somewhat beter than in the mornings.

March 4, 1863; Wednesday. Passed some time in the Tithing [office] during [which] I saw the Prest. [Brigham Young]. Attend[ed] to writing my journal in the H. O. [Historian's] Office after which I returned home. Passed the evening in reading history. My son Platte De Alton came home from the town of Farmington and reported the family there enjoying usual health.

March 5, 1863; Thursday. Passed the early part of the day at the Tithing and H. O. [Historian's] Offices, and in the afternoon I visited Dr.

33. An agent of the Presiding Bishop, Amos Milton Musser later became the Assistant Church Historian, his son a fundamentalist leader. Pace, "Changing Patterns of Mormon Financial Administration," 183–86; Bradley, "Joseph W. Musser," 262–278.

34. The meeting was in response to Governor Harding's message to the territorial legislature in 1862 (see chapter 8, note 149) and produced a resolution that President Lincoln remove the governor, Justice Thomas J. Drake, and another judge from office. Harding responded by immediately resigning, and Drake left the next year. "Mass Meeting in the Tabernacle," *Deseret News*, Mar. 4, 1863; "Reply of Judge Waite to the Committee," "Reply of His Honor Judge Drake," *Congressional Record*, 2679:160; Journal History, Mar. 4, 1863.

[Jeter] Clinton[35] and family. My wife Eliza [Partridge] was with me. Returned home ~~and passed the~~ about 2 o'clock.

March 6, 1863; Friday. Called at the H. O. [Historian's] Office brought forward my journal after which I called at the Prests' Office where I was introduced to Colo Rose from Cal, enroute for Washington City. By the request of Prest [Brigham] Yo[u]ng we with Colo R. acompanied the Prest to see the theater. In the evening I was at the Seventie's Hall and addressed the audience for one hour.

March 7, 1863; Saturday. Past the day at home & at the H. O. [Historian's] Office and in the evening I with [wife] Eliza [Partridge] attended the theater and witnessed the play of Pizaro or The Death of Rolla.[36] Mr. T[homas] A. Lyne appeared as Rolla. The House was crowded.

March 8, 1863; Sunday. Attended meeting in the Tabernacle. The audience was addressed by Prest' Brigham Young and then ajourned for an hour after which the meeting was again in session and was addressed again by the Prest. At 5 o'clock. I attended the [prayer circle] at H[istorian's] O[ffice] House.[37] Brothers [Orson] Pratt[,] [Wilford] Woodruff[,] [George A.] Smith[,] [Franklin D.] Richards[,] and myselef were present. G. A. S. was mouth in prayr.

March 9, 1863; Monday. I called on the Prest [Brigham Young] who told me that he would give me three thousand dollars for my property in the city. In the afternoon I went to Farmington with brother E[zra] T. Clark. The District Court began its session Judge [John F.] Kinnie presiding.

March 10, 1863; Tuesday. Remained in town and during the day went o[u]t in town to examine some machinery. In the afternoon [my teenage son] Platte D. [Lyman] came from the city. On yesterday acording to report a writ was issued by Judge [John F.] Kinnie & served on Prest' [Brigham] Young who is reported to have given bail for his appearance at

35. Fielding Jeter Clinton will soon develop an amusement park called Lake House on the Great Salt Lake, twenty-three years before Saltair is built ten miles east of it. The park had swimming piers, bath houses, showers, and eventually a hotel and steamboat dock for the *City of Corinne*. The park closed in 1892.

36. *Pizarro,* also known as *The Spaniards in Peru,* was adapted from a German play of the late eighteenth century by August von Kotzebue.

37. George A. Smith ran the Church Historian's Office from his home on South Temple, immediately across the street from Brigham Young's office. See Jensen, "Remarks at the Dedication of the Church History Library."

the session of the U. S. Court.[38] In the afternoon brother E[zra] T. Clark called in and spent some time with me.

March 11, 1863; Wednesday. Today I visited brother J[onathan H.] Holms & family. My wives Caroline and Lydia [Partridge] and Sisters Mary Clark and Sarah Partridge were with me. The weather warm & spring-like saw some ploughing being done.

March 12, 1863; Thursday. To day I visited the mills belonging to brothers Franklin and Samuel Richards. Returned home after noon. While out I called on brother Loren Walker & family. His wife is the eldest daughter of Hyrum Smith.[39] Past the evening in reading.

March 13, 1863; Friday. Today called on and spent some time with brother Thomas Grover. Past the residue of the day at home. Brother G told me he would like to sell out his property here.

March 14, 1863; Saturday. This morning in company with brother E[zra] T. Clark went to Bountiful to meet the Presidency in order to dedicate the new meetinghouse built by the people of that ward. The First Presidency were all there and of the twelve Orson Pratt, John Taylor[,] Wilford Woodruff[,] G. A. Smith[,] A. M. Lyman[,] C. C. Rich[,] F. D. Richards. Of the First Presidency of Seventies Joseph Young[,] A. P. Rockwood[,] J. Van Cott. The dedication prayr was offered by Prest H[eber] C. Kimball after the audience was addessed by the members of the first Presidency after which the meeting ajourned until 2 o'clock and the Presidency & the Twelve and the Presidents of the Seventies present wen[t] and dined with brother Anson Call[40] & family. The ajournment over and the meeting in session the audience was addressed by Elders

---

38. In defiance of the recent Congressional legislation against polygamy, Young took a young bride to wife, twenty-four-year-old Amelia Folsom, on January 24, followed by a fiery sermon in which Young called Governor Harding a "nigger worshipper and black-hearted abolitionist." Non-Mormon judge John F. Kinney tried to diffuse the situation, interviewing Young but not arresting him. Turner, *Brigham Young*, 328; Cannon and Knapp, *Brigham Young and His Mormon Empire*, 333.

39. The daughter of Hyrum Smith and Jerusha Barden, Lovina Smith Walker was sixteen when she married twenty-one-year-old Lorin Walker just four days before her father's assassination at Carthage Jail. She and her husband lived with Emma Smith prior to moving to Utah in 1860.

40. An important settler of Fillmore and Parowan, Anson Call claimed in his autobiography that he had heard Joseph Smith prophesy that Mormons would relocate to the Rocky Mountains. Smith could hear "the crystal streams running through the Rocky Mountains" as he spoke, according to Call, Autobiography, in CHL.

Joseph Young & John Taylor after which the meeting was ajourned until tomorow at 10 o'clock. I lodged with brother Perigreen Sessions.[41]

March 15, 1863; Sunday. Meet ~~at~~ as per adjournment. The meeting was addressed by Elders G[eorge] A. Smith and Orson Pratt. Ajourned for diner. Dined with brother [Perrigrine] Sesions. Meeting again in session at 2 o'clock. I spoke to the audience ¾ of an hour [and] was folowed by Elder John Van Cott, after which Prest' B[righam] Young delivered a short address and then dismissed the meeting. He then with his party and escort returned to G. S. L. City. I returned to Farmington and in the evening attended a meeting in the Court-House held by brother Orson Pratt.

March 16, 1863; Monday. To day concluded a trade with brother E[zra] T. Clark to whom I sold a part of my property in the town of Farmington. I received in part pay a pair of horses and harnesses & carriage. At night I attended lecture on the subject of astronomy delivered by Professor Orson Pratt.

March 17, 1863; Tuesday. To day past the time in makeing some repairs on my cariage and at night attended a meeting at the Court-House. The audience was addressed by Elder Hector Hate [Haight][42] on the subject of agriculture. After I addressed the people briefly. I returned home much wearied with the labors of the day.

March 18, 1863; Wednesday. Today went to the city. My wife Lydia [Partridge] & her children were with me. We dined with sister Mary Rich & family. At night attended the theater by invitation from brother Nathan Tanner and witnessed the play of Wm Tell.

March 19, 1863; Thursday. Today I received a note from my son F[rancis] M. Lyman in Fillmore, wrote answer. Was today afflicted with severe pain in my head.

March 20, 1863; Friday. To day I visited the premises of brothers G[eorge] D. Watt[43] and T[homas] W. Ellerbeck and took note of their

---

41. Perrigrine Sessions, son of Joseph Smith's plural wife Patty Bartlett Sessions, grew up to be one of his step-father's bodyguards. Already at age twenty-three he was made a Seventy. He and his mother were the earliest settlers of Bountiful, Utah.

42. Hector C. Haight (brother of Isaac Haight, a southern Utah stake president) was an early settler of Bountiful, a county probate judge, and a mission president in Scandinavia.

43. George D. Watt was the church recorder whose notes in shorthand of sermons delivered at general conference were written out after the meetings and published in the

improvement after which I dined with brother Watt & family. Attended to some business about town, meet with Bishop John Hess, by whom I sent some word to Farmington in relation to my business there. In the evening I called on brother Nathaniel Tanner and family.

March 21, 1863; Saturday. Passed the day in town and at the H. O. [Historian's] Office. I was introduced to his excellency Ex-Governor [William] Gilpin of Colorado who was makeing a short visit to our city.[44] In the night I attended the theater with my wife Lydia [Partridge] & daughter Caroline.[45] Some snow fell this evening making the walking very unpleasant on acount of the mud.

March 22, 1863; Sunday. Attended meeting this morning in the Tabernacle the audience was addressed by Elder [William] Squires. In the afternoon the president [Brigham Young] taught the people and in the evening I attended the [prayer circle] at the prayr-room at the H[istorian's] O[ffice]. Brother [Wilford] Woodruff & myself were all who were present. This done we called on and spent some time with President Young. Governor [William] Gilpin was present but soon Prest' [Daniel H.] Wells came in and Col R[obert] T. Burton.[46] There was a squall of snow this evening reminding us that March was with us yet.

March 23, 1863; Monday. Today I called on Prest' ~~and~~ [Brigham] Young who presented to me the total of my acount with Trustee in Trust which amounted to 3720 dollars & 65 cents, thus bringing me stil in debt above the price of the property sold him 720 dollars 65 cts.[47]

March 24, 1863; Tuesday. To day went to Farmington and sold some hay to brother Winchester for molasses. Sister Elizabeth Partridge went with me to Farmington. Weather pleasant. Brother [John] Horspool called on me today on his way to the City of Great Salt Lake.

March 25, 1863; Wednesday. To day I visited brother Jas Stuart &

Deseret News and *Journal of Discourses*. Aligning himself with William Godbe in 1869, he was excommunicated in 1874. Watt, *Mormon Passage of George D. Watt*.

44. Gilpin was the first territorial governor of Colorado, 1861–62. The war exacerbated problems in the region, so Lincoln felt he needed to remove him after a year.

45. Caroline Eliza, eleven years old, was the daughter of Eliza Partridge.

46. Robert T. Burton would become a counselor in the Presiding Bishopric. He was already known for leading a territorial militia against the Morrisite sect in 1862, authorized by Judge Kinney. Bryant, "Reviving the Millennial Kingdom."

47. Lyman owed the church $3,720.65, so after selling his property to Young for $3,000, he remained in debt with very little cash.

family. My wife Caroline [Partridge] and Sister Sarah Partridge were with me. The weather was fine and warm. We had a pleasant visit which called up many reminicences of the past fixed in our memories by the hard school of experience. My brother-in law Seth B. Tanner stayed with us over night enrout for G.S.L. City. The child of Sister Lydia Robinson died this afternoon.

March 26, 1863; Thursday. To day I called on the Bishop John Hess and dined with him an[d] he made me a present of 15 bushels of wheat. Returned home and in the evening attended the funeral of Sister [Lydia] Robinson's child. I spoke to the people on the occasion.

March 27, 1863; Friday. Taried at home to day. Passed the time in reading. Weather dry & windy but slightly cool.

March 28, 1863; Saturday. Taried in town and during the day meet with O[rrin] P. Rockwell who was in town buying horses for the mail service.

March 29, 1863; Sunday. To day I attended the meeting of the Saints in the morning and in the afternoon I attended the funeral of the child of brother Thomas Grover. Weather fine & pleasant.

March 30, 1863; Monday. Today is my 50th birth-day. The weather is fine and pleasant. Dined with brother E[zra] T. Clark & family. My wife Caroline [Partridge] was with me and also Sister Mary Rich.

March 31, 1863; Tuesday. Today I went to G.S.L. City. Sister Sarah Partridge went with me. After my arival in the city I called on the President [Brigham Young] in whose office I meet with Mr Henry Kinkade[48] (of the old firm of Livingston Kinkade, &c) enroute for Washington D.C.

April 1, 1863; Wednesday. To day I received letters from my cousin Albert Mason [in] N[ew] H[ampshire] informing me of the death of my cousin Perrez Mason Methodist Preacher in Boston on the 18th of Feb aged 57 years old [on] the 25th of July last. I also received a letter from brother Ge[o]rge Q. Cannon Liverpool Feb. 19th and in the afternoon I called on Sister [Elizabeth] Cannon. Found her and children well, she also had received a letter from brother Cannon. This morning my horses strayed from brother Tanner's correll.

April 2, 1863; Thursday. Today I witnessed a surgical operation on

48. Henry Kinkead owned a dry goods store in Utah Territory before entering politics and later becoming the first territorial governor of Alaska.

Sister Jane Titcomb[49] from whose breast a cancerous tumor of near a pound weight was taken by Dr. Anderson assisted by the Hon Frank Fuller. The patient was under the influence of chloroform.[50] In the evening visited brother Orson Pratt (who was very sick) in company with brothers G[eorge] A. Smith & F[ranklin] D. Richards. At brother P's meet with my old friend & brother Zerubabel Snow. I also meet with brother [George L.] Farrell from Cache Valley.

April 3, 1863; Friday. Pased the day in the city and in the evening my son F[rancis] M. Lyman arived from Fillmore.

April 4, 1863; Saturday. Today in company with brother Nathan Tanner and wife myself & my wives Eliza & Lydia [Partridge] & my son [Francis] Marion visited the country residence of brother Nathan Tanner on [Little] Cottonwood [Creek].

April 5, 1863; Sunday. To day attended meeting in the Tabernacle. The audience was addressed by brother Orson Hyde. In the afternoon Prest' [Brigham] Young addressed the meeting and at 5 o'clock I attended the prayr [circle] in the Historian's House. Meeting was opened by brother Erastus Snow. Prest Hyde was mouth in prayr.

April 6, 1863; Monday. Today our conference was commenced and was conducted as per minutes [of the meeting] from [this] date until the afternoon of Wednesday 8th when conference was ajourned until the 6th of Oct next. I was in attendance throughout the entire conference.

April 9, 1863; Thursday.[51] To day with others of the Quorum of the Twelve I assisted in seting apart the missionaries called by the conference after which I called on the Prest. [Brigham Young]. Our meeting of today was in the Historians' office, by night the snow of last night had mostly disappeared.

April 10, 1863; Friday. To day brought forward my journal to date, after which I called on the President [Brigham Young] in whose office I was presented with a specimin of sugar made in Toq[u]erville from

---

49. Maria Lyman's niece Lydia Jane Tanner Titcomb would live another thirty-four years.

50. The first time chloroform was used medically was only sixteen years earlier in Europe, but during the Civil War it was mass-produced in small tin cans that were carried in knapsacks by battlefield surgeons. This made its appearance in Utah possible at this early date.

51. There are no entries for Apr. 7–8.

the Sorghum, it was very creditable in quality. In the evening called on brother Nathan Tanner from whom I learned that Sister [Jane] Titcomb who recently had a part of one of her breasts cut out was recovering finely.

April 11, 1863; Saturday. Today visited brother [William] Blackhurst and family. My wife Eliza [Partridge] was with me & the Presidency and the members of the Quorum of Twelve who were in the city except brother O[rson] Pratt were of the party. We had a fine time.

April 12, 1863; Sunday. Today with my son [Francis] Marion I went to Farmington. I preached in the afternoon & brother [Charles] Penrose addressed the audience in the morning.

April 13, 1863; Monday. Attended to branding some stock, and made some feed sacks for my horses. Had some company to day & commenced to load up some things for Fillmore.

April 14, 1863; Tuesday. To day I went to the city and called and dined with brother C[harles] C. Rich at Centerville.

April 15, 1863; Wednesday. To day [Francis] Marion started for Fillmore & I executed a deed for the possesion of my city property to brother [William] Folsom & made some arangements with brother W[illiam] S. Godbe to buy some glass & nails for me in the States and also with Prest' [Brigham] Young to freight the same for me.[52]

April 16, 1863; Thursday. Today I started for Fillmore and stoped at Cottenwood & had some shoes set on my horses. Had diner with brother [Nathan] Tanner & family then I past on. The wind blew strong from the south almost blinding me with the drifting sand & gravel. At the point of the Utah [Valley] Mountain I meet the troops returning to camp Douglas from their campaign against the friendly Indians whom they fought at Battle Creek [Pleasant Grove] and at Spanish Fork at which place they killed two Indians and wounded 3, and had a Lieutenant killed.[53]

At the southern end of the dugway the wind having changed down from the north very cold. About sundown I arived at Battle Creek and

52. This was the last entry in this daybook, followed by blank pages and financial notations, and the remainder of the 1863 and Jan. 1864 entries are in volume 20 after the 1860 entries.

53. Lyman's sympathy for the Indians diverged from the *Deseret News*, which reported that the Indians had prepared to attack when they were fired on. "The Indian Attack at Battle Creek," "The Battle of Spanish Fork [Canyon]," *Deseret News*, Apr. 22, 1863.

called on brother Henson Walker[54] with whom I taried over night. I was very wet and cold on my arival but through the kindness of my friends soon became comfortable. My son [Francis] Marion stayed in town with brother Benjamin Driggs.

April 17, 1863; Friday. This morning had some snow squalls. Called on Bishop John Brown who went with me to make a call on Sister Sarah Driggs widow of Sterling Driggs. This done I traviled to Provo and called on brother Myron Tanner with whom & family took diner and then went to Springville & stoped with Bishop [Aaron] Johnson and preached to the people in the evening[,] had an attentive audience. Before leaveing Battle Creek brother Lewis Robinson presented me with a pair of gloves.

April 18, 1863; Saturday. To day I went to Payson and called on brother Freeman Tanner with whom [Francis] Marion was also stoping. Last night I preached to the people in their meeting-hall, we lodged at brother Tanners. In the evening the militia were out for drill.

April 19, 1863; Sunday. To day I traviled to Salt Creek [Nephi] and preached twice to the people and lodged with Father Kizare. [Francis] Marion lodged with brother T[imothy] B. Foot.

April 20, 1863; Monday. To day I went to Round Valley [Scipio]. I preached to the people and lodged with brother Peter Boyce. Brothers Erastus Snow & Angus Cannon were with us.

April 21, 1863; Tuesday. Today I traviled to Cedar Springs where I meet Bishop Thos Callister and my son Amasa with the Fillmore teems for Florence. After dispaching the teems on their journey we dined with Sister Johnson after which the Bishop myself and sons came to Fillmore. I lodged with the Bishop[,] was very weary.

April 22, 1863; Wednesday. To day I fited a pole to my tent. The boys were working in Marion's garden. Dined with brother Reuben McBride and wrote leters to brothers N[athan] C. Tinney and Thomas Willis.

April 23, 1863; Thursday. Passed the day in town looking for a location.

April 24, 1863; Friday. Did not leave town today did not feel very well in health.

---

54. Henson Walker, former mayor of Battle Creek (Pleasant Grove), had recently presided over the Scottish Conference of the British Mission. He had four wives and twenty children. He had also previously operated a ferry for the church on the Platte River.

April 25, 1863; Saturday. To day in company with Bishop [Thomas] Callister and others I went to Round Valley to meet the President [Brigham] Young and his party but did not find them there.[55] I lodged with brother Benjamin Johnson & family.

April 26, 1863; Sunday. Today at 10 o'clock preached to the people and in the afternoon myself & Bishop [Thomas] Callister went with brother Benj, Johnson to see the lake in Round Valley [Scipio Lake]. After returning we heard some cases of difference and settled them. Lodged with brother J.

April 27, 1863; Monday. Today continued our journey to Gunison where we meet the Prest [Brigham Young] and party. Engaged in meeting after which I lodged with brother C[hristian] A. Madsen in company with G[eorge] A. Smith.

April 28, 1863; Tuesday. Returned to Round Valley and had meeting. The Saints were instructed by Prest's [Brigham] Young and [Heber C.] Kimball. Myself & brother [George A.] Smith were lodged with brother Peter Boyce.

April 29, 1863; Wednesday. Returned to Fillmore where we had meeting in the afternoon and a dance in the evening at both of which the President [Brigham Young] seemed to feel well and in the later the President explained the nature of my appointment to Fillmore and instructed the Saints to assist me in makeing a home for my family.[56]

April 30, 1863; Thursday. The President & party left this morning for Beaver. After the Prest and company had left I concluded a trade with brother [John] Bushnel for his possesions for four hundred dollars and also with brother [Furman] Mulford for his at three hundred. In the afternoon I called on brother Reuben A. McBride and family. They had a sick child to whom I administered and then returned to my lodgings at the Bishop's who went to Corn Creek [Kanosh] on some business.

May 1, 1863; Friday. ~~Friday~~ This morning I looked over my new possessions was much afflicted with a severe headache. My son [Francis]

55. Young left Salt Lake City on Apr. 20 for a short speaking tour of the southern settlements. He was delayed in Payson by talks with the Native Americans.

56. Young thought the Fillmore Saints were rebellious. Lyman had a reputation for treating people of differing views liberally, so it was thought he could be useful in helping Bishop Callister keep things in check, and for the same reason Young appointed apostle Lorenzo Snow to Brigham City and apostle Erastus Snow to St. George. *AML*, 346.

Marion went after some oak wood. Weather quite warm and dry. Dined with the Bishop's family. In the evening the Bishop returned haveing found his stock. I turned out my horses, in order to let them have a few days on the grass.

May 2, 1863; Saturday. This morning weather fine and pleasant. Passed the day in town. [Francis] Marion went for wood.

May 3, 1863; Sunday. Preached to the people in the school house. The Bishop [Thomas Callister] announced to the people my calling to reside and labor in Fillmore and spoke of their aiding me in makeing some houses for my family. I dined with Brother Henry Noyes & family. My son F[rancis] M. and family were there.[57]

During the intermission the Bishop called some of the brethren to gather to consider what kind of houses they had best build for me. Their conclusion was to build of brick and commence the work on them ~~on them~~ immediately. In the afternoon meeting a subscription was opened for the building of the houses and brother Joseph V. ~~B~~ Robinson was appointed as committee to superintend the work.[58]

May 4, 1863; Monday. To day my son [Francis] Marion commenced to labor on my new possesion and I waited on Brother [William] Felshaw made the plan & laid out the ground for two of the houses. Some wind to day. Dined with brother [Noah] Bartholomew in the evening called on brother [Joseph] Robison & informed him that he could commence the work on the houses.

May 5, 1863; Tuesday. To day brought the water on my lots prepari-tory to ploughing. In the afternoon brother Orson Pratt came to town enroute to Dixie, his health & spirits were fine. He was traviling with brother John Nebiker who resides in Toqerville of which locality as of Dixie generaly he gave a most cheering acount.

May 6, 1863; Wednesday. To day brought the water on to my building lots. Brother [John] Bushnell moved out of his house to day to Meadow

57. Lyman bought a series of lots in Fillmore. One had a house that was inhabitable, a couple had houses in disrepair, and the rest were vacant. Eventually five wives lived there: the Partridge sisters, his first wife Maria, and Priscilla Turley, while the other three wives remained in southern Utah.

58. Joseph V. was one of nine children of Joseph and Lucretia Robison, early settlers of Fillmore, all of them still living in the area.

Creek.[59] Marion was watering the land [to prepare the foundation]. In the evening I visited the residence and garden of brother [James] Stokes who had been laboring for me ^through^ the day. He gave me some carrot seed. His place is finely improved and highly productive.

May 7, 1863; Thursday. To day the hands commenced diging out for the foundation of my houses. I spent some time with brother O[rson] Pratt & wife and in the afternoon visited with them at brother Joseph Robison's. My son A[masa] M. Junior came up from Beaver this evening. Meet with brother Isaac Laney who was suffering with the ague. The weather oppressively hot today. Passed a restless night from excessive weariness.

May 8, 1863; Friday. To day the work in my house is progressing slowly and [Francis] Marion and Amasa [Jr] were working on the garden lot. Planted some and built some rude trelises for the grapevines. I wrote letter to Bishop R[obert] D. Covington of Washington. Felt poorly to day in health.

May 9, 1863; Saturday. Passed the day in town no work going on at my building lots. Brother [Isaac] Laney went south with the mail but brother [Orson] Pratt remained to go next week. Received some potatoes from the tithing [storehouse] for deposits made in Beaver Office. The wind was high from the south with indications of a storm of rain. Read telegraphic dispaches from the states and the Deseret News through which I learned of the death by steam boat explosion of Elder Hyrum Kimball and his traviling companion ^[Thomas] Atkinson^ at San Pedro enroute for the Sandwich Islands.[60]

From the news I learned of the movements of troops from Camp Douglas to diferent points on the route of Emigrant travil to the Gold mines of the northwest and the Pacifick Coast.

May 10, 1863; Sunday. This morning attended meeting at 10 oclock. The audience was addressed by brother Orson Pratt on the subject of the fulfillment of the prophecies and the return to Jackson county. Meeting

59. Lyman purchased Bushnell's house in Fillmore, so John and Elizabeth moved to Meadow Creek (Meadow), ten miles south of Fillmore. The little town had been in existence since 1857.

60. Kimball and Atkinson were on a tender, the *Ada Hancock*, underway to the *Senator* when the tender's boiler exploded, instantly killing forty of the sixty passengers. "Horrible Explosion," *Deseret News*, May 6, 1863.

ajourned until 2 oclock when it was again in cession & I spoke [to] the congregation for an ^hour.^ At 5 o'clock I attended a meeting of Priesthood & gave them some instructions in regard to their duties in their various callings in the community of the Saints at home.

In the evening I meet brother[s] Russell, Rogers, [Orange] Warner and Huntsman and relinquished to them the land I had expected to receive from them. Brother Gabriel Huntsman said I should have his as proposed and brother Russell said nothing in the premises pro or con[,] retired feeling very weary.[61]

May 11, 1863; Monday. Today the work was not move^i^ng on my house. My horses were dr^i^ven up to day looking well. The boys planted some carrots & beets. Today weather pleasant after the rain of yesterday which has much improved the condition of the land and the recently planted crops.

May 12, 1863; Tuesday. Passed the day at home. In the afternoon brother Orson Pratt came to see my garden grounds. Later in the evening in company with brother [Thomas] Callister I called upon and ministered to Sister Thomas R. [Matilda] King who was much afflicted with neuralga. During the day I called on brother [James] Starley and had a look over his garden.

May 13, 1863; Wednesday. Relinquished my purpose of visiting Corn Creek to day and turned out my horses & went to work in my garden. Joseph A. Kelting passed through town to day enroute to Provo from Cal[ifornia]. Light showers on the mountains some thunder, no work moveing on my house.

May 14, 1863; Thursday. To day the boys [Francis and Amasa Jr] were planting in my garden. The express [mail service] passed [intent on reaching] the Prest' to day. Some light mountain showers rendering ^the^ weather cool. In the evening, I visited lime-kiln in process of erection by brother [John] ~~Bowing~~ Bourne from Africa.[62] Felt very uncomfortable at night on acount of my work through the day.

May 15, 1863; Friday. Today received word that the Prest [Brigham

61. The details of the real estate negotiations are lost, but Lyman would shortly acquire other lots instead. *AML*, 347.

62. John Beeching Bourne was from England and had relocated to Cape Town in the 1850s. In 1860 he sailed to the United States and settled in Fillmore.

Young] & party would be with us to night. In the afternoon in company with Bishop [Thomas] Callister ^&^ brother Daniel Thompson I went as far as Meadow Creek to meet the Prest' whom we meet at that point. By Mother Morley I learned of the welfare of my family in Parowan. Cousin Geo. A. Smith lodged with bishop Callister the Presidency lodged with brother Gabriel Huntsman.

May 16, 1863; Saturday. This morning had meeting at 10 oclock. The audience was addressed by Prests' [Brigham] Young & [Heber C.] Kimball folowed Elder Lorenzo Snow. The President and party dined and left for Round Valley [Scipio] about 1 o'clock P.M.

May 17, 1863; Sunday. To day had meeting at 10 o'clock. The Bishop [Thomas Callister] was indisposed & did not attend. I addressed the people and ajourned the meeting until 3 o'clock when I again spoke to the people. The Bishop was present and presented some items of instruction & business. My health was rather poor & felt myself much wearied with my labor through the day.

May 18, 1863; Monday. Passed the day in town was quite ill. To day my son Amasa M. Junior left for parts unknown. Consulting with the bishop I concluded to engage my son [Francis] Marion and team on my houses until they were built.

May 19, 1863; Tuesday. To day [Francis] Marion finished puting in potatoes. Learned from Amasa [Jr.]'[s] associates that he had gone to the Northern goldmines. My health some beter this evening.

May 20, 1863; Wednesday. To day wrote letters to G. S. L. City. In the afternoon Amasa M. Junior returned with the mail having been as far north as Payson. Myself & Amasa made some pr^e^paration for going to Beaver on tomorrow. Had some rain, called at brother Reuben McBride's. The day closed with indications of rain.

May 21, 1863; Thursday. To day Amasa [Jr.] hunted for the horses but did not find them. [Francis] Marion and myself prepared the wagon, and in the afternoon he commenced hauling rock for the foundation of my houses, thus commencing the building of my home after thirty years of labor without one, thus shewing that altho the reward of the just is slow it is nevertheless sure. Amasa after his return made another unsuccessful trip after the horses. Weather clear this evening and cool. Took tea with ~~Sister~~ ^brother^ McBride and family.

May 22, 1863; Friday. This morning Amasa [Jr.] found the horses and in the afternoon I traviled as far as Corn Creek [Kanosh] and then took an excursion with Bishop [Thomas] Callister an[d] brother Peter Robison over the Meadow ground in my cariage. This done we returned to brother R's had super and then had meeting at the residence of Sister Kay. Retired about 10 o'clock, very weary. Brother Robison promised to have some hay put up for me by the settlement.

May 23, 1863; Saturday. To day traviled as far as Beaver. Dined at Cove Creek, with brother [John] Wildens. My son A[masa] M. Junior was with me. Found the family at Beaver well and myself very weary. I here meet with Uncle David Fredrick, who was working in the garden. Received some calls from friends this evening, among them was the bishop.

May 24, 1863; Sunday. To day attended meeting morning and evening in the meeting house. Found the people with their feelings much lasserated with the fatherly admonition and counsel of the Prest [Brigham Young] in his recent visit to the South because of his never-failing rememberances of the California.[63] People made donation of lumber for my use.

May 25, 1863; Monday. To day went to Minersville[64] & found my wives [Dionetia and Priscilla] there well. Called on Bishop [James H.] Rollins & family. Dined with my daughter ^Matilda Carter^ & family at Greenville. Minersville appeared rather dull and not much improved.

May 26, 1863; Tuesday. To day returned to Beaver with my wife Priscilla [Turley]. Had some repairs put on my carriage by brother Robert Keys. Made some arangements, for Lumber for my houses with brother W[illiam] W. Willis.

May 27, 1863; Wednesday. To day went to Parowan & found my family there well but my own health was poor. Meet with Clark Fabun &

---

63. Young often complained about the failed California colony of San Bernardino and popularity of the northern gold fields. His southern Utah audiences included more than a few colonists who had been part of those experiments but had faithfully returned to Utah when summoned home.

64. Minersville supported the nearby lead mine southwest of Beaver. The work was difficult, the water limited, and the location in conflict with Native Americans who every fall camped there while they gathered berries and pine nuts. The elevation produced deep snow in winter, and the rest of the year the mine attracted seasonal laborers who lived in tents and liked to "drink, gamble, and fight." Robinson, *They Answered the Call.*

Father [Weeden V.] Hakes & Daniel Clark who were j^u^st starting for Salt Lake City.

May 28, 1863; Thursday. To day remained in Parowan and visited the cotton factory and had my horses shod and dined with brother [Ebenezer] Hanks and family. My health rather poor. My shoeing was gratuitously done by brother E. Hanks who also fed my horses during my stay.

May 29, 1863; Friday. I traviled to Old Harmony but dined with bishop Henry Lunt of Cedar City and at night stoped with brother Hill from St. George who is keeping a dairy. At this point [Hill's home] we were very kindly entertained. This morning paid to bishop W[illiam] S. Warren 3 dollars for horse shoes sold to him for brother George Crismond.

May 30, 1863; Saturday. To day traviled to St. George.[65] Dined with Sister [Emily] Lewis at Cottonwood[,][66] brother [James] Lewis haveing gone to [the Southern Utah Mission] Conference [in St. George]. At night put up with brother Erastus Snow. Here I [would] meet with brother N[athan] C. Tiney at the conference. He came from home the day before.

May 31, 1863; Sunday. To day attended Conference. The audience was addressed by brother [Erastus] Snow and then ajourned for one hour. Dined with brother Orson Pratt and in the afternoon I spoke to the people. After meeting took sup[p]er & lodged with brother Snow in his log house.

June 1, 1863; Monday. Attended Conference to day and spoke again to the people. In the evening Conference ajourned without date. We took sup[p]er with brother William Perkins & family. My health some what improved this evening. Retired when the small hours of morning had come. To day (laid the corner stone of the new tabernacle)[67] in conjunction with the local priesthood of the places.

June 2, 1863; Tuesday. To day went to the [Santa] Clara settlement

---

65. This is only the third time for Lyman to visit St. George. The town was founded in 1861 as part of the cotton mission, a relative late-comer due to the fact that the road to California bypassed the Virgin River Gorge and veered off twenty miles to the west. The remoteness was a plus for polygamists, just as the mild climate convinced Brigham Young to build a winter home there.

66. Now the ghost town of Harrisburg, fifteen miles north of St. George.

67. When the St. George Tabernacle was finished thirteen years later, it served as a place of worship and where civic events were held. It remains today a national historic site. Landon, "Shrine to the Whole Church."

to visit our old friends Bishop [William] Crosby & wife [Sarah] whom we found well and at their old place which was spared by the great flood of [18]62.[68] The general aspect of the place seems much changed by the flood. The rock fort had entirely disappeared and the water of the river is now running over ground some twenty feet below where the foundation of the fort had formerly rested.

In the evening passed over field and garden of brother Crosby, the varied crops in which were looking finely and gave promise of a bounteous harvest of fruits and grain. In my ramble I visited the vineyard which was looking finely. The vines were alredy laden with luxurient clusters of fruit alredy well grown. This morning was on the ground where the atesian well is being bored its present depth is 180 ft.

June 3, 1863; Wednesday. To day returned to Washington in [the] St. George [area]. We called on brother W[alter] E. Dodge & family. Had a look at his garden and vines. Arived in Washington we lodged with bishop R[obert] D. Covington & family. Bishop Covington reports their improvements for irrigation as now perminantly made since the great flood of [18]62.

June 4, 1863; Thursday. Taried in Washington. Made some calls during the day and at 5 o'clock meet with the people and addressed them for one hour after which we took sup[p]er and lodged with brother Wm Smithson. Washington seems much improved by the growth of fruit & shade trees. Several new houses are in process of erection.

June 5, 1863; Friday. This morning left Washington & traviled to Toquerville where we ^were^ welcomed by bishop [Joshua] Willis with whom we lodged. In the evening visited the garden-grounds of the [Charles] Stapely family where we saw a fine stand of grapevines richly laden with fruit and also some peach trees laden with fruit. Beside these were shown a luxurient growth of the lucern or clover of Australia, all of which proved the fact that industry is rewarded in this rough & rocky region which a few years since was the home of a few degraded Lamanites who now have given place to white men & civilization resulting from the increase of knowledge.

68. The Great Flood of 1862 decimated Fort Harmony, Grafton, and Santa Clara. It caused equal devastation elsewhere in the west due to unseasonably warm weather and about twenty days of rain. Dettinger and Ingram, "Coming Megafloods," 65–71; "Flood in Southern Utah," *Deseret News*, Feb. 12, 1862.

June 6, 1863; Saturday. This morning in company with bishop [Joshua] Willis I took a walk to the springs that furnish the water for Toquer[ville]. The flood of last year has uncovered several large springs which add a large contribution to the former stock of water and thus largely enhance the value of the place as it will enable the citizens to bring in to use much more land than they thought could be irrigated. In our ramble we passed over the fruit grounds of brother John Nebiker who is starting a vineyard of several thousand vines. His cutings were growing finely. With the increase of water[,] manufacturies may be established here on a moderate scale. Myself & wife [Maria] dined with brother I[saac] C. Height and family.[69] Sent an apointment for meeting to Virgin City for Monday next at 5 o'clock P.M. by brother Newman. Felt very weary with my morning walk.

June 7, 1863; Sunday. To day attended meeting with the Saints morning & evening in their school house and addressed them at both meetings on the subject of the cultivation in themselves of a spirit of improvement to apply to all their labors as Saints in building their homes and in corretly training their children for lives of virtue and usefulness in ^the^ great work of the world's regeneration and redemation from the rule of sin. Dined today with brother [Charles] Stapely & family and at night found myself very weary with the labors of the day. Lodged with the Bishop [Joshua Willis].

June 8, 1863; Monday. To day in company with Bishop [Joshua] Willis I went to Virgin City[70] and dined with brother Nephi Johnson and family and met with the people in their meeting house at 5 o'clock. Elder N[athan] C. Tiney from Grafton was with us. Brother Johnson has a fine fruit orchard a part of which has come to bearing. Lodged with brother Johnson & family.

June 9, 1863; Tuesday. This morning went to Grafton & in our travil

69. Haight had been in and around Toquerville since about 1859 after he was released as stake president and his testimony was sought relating to the Mountain Meadows Massacre. He moved a wife, Elizabeth Mary Kleinman, there in 1862 and lived in and around the town until he was indicted for murder in 1874 and slipped farther south into Arizona.

70. Virgin City (not Virginia City) was settled in 1857 on the Virgin River near today's Zion National Park. The nearby town of Grafton, a village Lyman also mentions, became a ghost town after it was rebuilt following the flood of 1862.

we past the site of old Grafton that was desolated by the great flood of [18]62. New Grafton is situated some ¾ of a mile above the old town on the oposite side of the River at which place I meet the people at 10 o'clock in their school house. In the little audience I saw several of my old Nauvoo acqaintences, among whom was Albert Petty[,] Edward Dusette and brother Miles Romney. Dined with brother [Nathan C.] Tinney & family who were rendered somewhat destitute of the conveniences for ho[u]se keeping in consequence of the entire loss of all they had in their house by the flood. Sister Olive Tinney was borne from her house in the midst of her labor pains and was delivered of a fine son on ajacent mountain-side where she remained for two days without shelter. Mother & child got along finely and is now a promising boy named ^by the mother^ Marvelous Flood.[71]

In the evening returned to Virgin City. My son Amasa M. went to the herd ground of brother Tinney and [William] Maxwell direct. Lodged with brother [Nephi] Johnson, brother Tinney was with us.

June 10, 1863; Wednesday. Did not find our team until noon when with brother [Nathan C.] Tinney we started (on a somewhat more circuitous route than that taken by Amasa [Jr.] on yesterday) for the same place where we arived about 9 o'clock much wearied with our ride as much of the way we had no roads and heavy sand. Slept to night under Heavens broad and bright canopy and we rested well, after being refreshed with some goat meat prepared by Sister Grace Tinney.[72]

June 11, 1863; Thursday. Today remained at the Ranch & rested myself. During the day my son [Amasa Jr.] and Ammon Tinney and brother Wm Poll went to Grafton for some flour & stock. In the evening brothers Web & Shirtlif came after stock. The weather very warm the water here is rather strongly impregnated with sulpher but is quite cool and this we remedied with excelent buter-milk we had from the Dary-man brother Bell. Took a short walk in the Kanyon which forms a good pasture.

The ranch is well supplied with grass & timber and has on it ~~some~~ seven places of water that can all be made available for watering stock. The

71. The child went by Marv, short for Marvelous, but died of diphtheria at age three.

72. Nathan Tenney's wife Grace, his second, would leave him to become the second wife of Bateman Williams. Eventually, though, she would abandon polygamy altogether and take the children to Kansas, living there to her death in 1916.

Ranch is six by 12 miles in extent. The stock on the place are fat & fine. Of cattle & horses [there are] 700 hundred head & 660 sheep & goats.[73]

June 12, 1863; Friday. Was not very well, the brethren were engaged in gathering and dividing stock and during the day a young colt brock his leg in the carrell. It was well set by the herdman & brother Webb. This evening the party of brethren who had been to explore the watering places called Cannara and Pipe Springs returned and gave a favorable accont of the localities visited for herding and settlement and expressed a determination to settle there soon[,] some of them this season. Today counted my goats of which ^there were^ 150 & 30 sheep and the same for Brother [Charles C.] Rich, acording to the terms of settlements.

June 13, 1863; Saturday. This morning started on our return to Virgin City where we arived near the close of the day. We made a call at the ranch of brother [Anthony] Straten, whose good wife refreshed us with some fine bread, buter and milk. Found our friend Nephi [Johnson] & his family well with whom we lodged. Brother [Nathan C.] Tinney left us & went to Grafton. As we were about to retire[,] A[masa] M. Junior arived from the herd ground via Grafton.

June 14, 1863; Sunday. Held two meetings today at both of which I spoke to the people and dined with Sister Barney whose husband had gone to Florence for the poor Saints.[74] The weather very warm & sultry felt much wearied with my labor of the day.

June 15, 1863; Monday. This morning I started on my return to Toquer[ville] where I arived before noon. Took in charge from brother Nephi Johnson a hors[e] belonging [to] brother Benjamin Robison of Fillmore left here by Prest H[eber] C. Kimball. My health being poor I did not preach stoped with the Bishop. Several of the brethren called in to converse during the evening.

June 16, 1863; Tuesday. To day traviled to the residence of Father John Hambleton, with whom & family we taried all night. To day my son

73. Lyman was not a disinterested observer. He and Charles C. Rich had owned a herd of sheep and goats in San Bernardino and had offered Nathan Tenney a third interest in the flock if he would drive them to southern Utah. Cf. Tenney and Tenney, *Nathan Cram Tenney, 1817–1882*, 34.

74. Henry Barney was a teamster who was helping transport goods to and from Florence. Family records show that he had an unknown second wife, but it was probably his first wife, Marcy Lucas, who Lyman met with.

Amasa was hurt by the falling of the horse he was rideing. He came to us after dark, we drest his bruises & he went to bed.

June 17, 1863; Wednesday. ~~Tuesd~~ This morning Amasa [Jr.] is somewhat beter altho very sore from the crushing fall of the horse on him. Traviled to Cedar City and stoped with bishop [Henry] Lunt to rest and refresh myself a little and at 5 o'clock spoke to the people of Cedar. Lodged with the bishop. My son Amasa went on to Parowan, the weather quite warm.

June 18, 1863 Thursday. Went to Parowan found my family there well. Amasa had gone to Beaver. Commenced some repairs on my cariage work done by brother Balis. Light shower in the evening makeing the air some cooler.

June 19, 1863; Friday. Taried in town and completed repairs on my carriage. Light rain today to lay dust [down]. Visited machine shop of brother Ebenezer Hanks where my [teenage] son Oscar M. Lyman is learning the buisness of machinest under Master Willcox.

June 20, 1863; Saturday. Remained in town and in the afternoon with my family visited brother Wm Dame and family.[75] Sister Zelph Smith was there. Meet and had conversation to day with brother Clark L. Fabun from San Bernardino Cal[ifornia] who has come to settle in Utah. Brother Richard Benson told me that I could have lumber (on the order I had received of brother David Fredrick calling for 2700 feet) in quality as called for.

June 21, 1863; Sunday. This morning at 10^½^ o'clock I spoke to the people. The house was well filled and the people attentive. Ajourned until 2 o'clock. Meet with and spoke to the people again after which with my family I visited with brothers [Weeden V.] Hakes, [Daniel P.] Clark and [C.] Fabun and dined with them and blest the infant daughter of Daniel Porter Clark & Hariet Hakes and administered to the infant child (of Collins Rowe Hakes and Hanna Morse) who was sick.[76] Some light rain to day air cool and pleasant.

---

75. In 1874, Dame will be incarcerated for two years for his role in the Mountain Meadows Massacre but will retain his position as stake president in Parowan and as commander of the county militia. Arguing that Isaac Haight misunderstood his order to proceed against the emigrants, he will be acquitted in 1878.

76. Daniel Clark's two wives, Sarah and Harriet Hakes, were daughters of Weeden Hakes, and the sick infant belonged to his sister and brother-in-law.

June 22, 1863; Monday. To day had my horses shod and received present from brother E[benezer] Hanks of linen for a coat and some cotton hose [socks]. Gave my family an airing in my carriage. Then sent my horses to the field to get grass, they came in at dark.

June 23, 1863; Tuesday. Today went to Beaver where we arived about 4 o'clock and found the family there all well but Mrs [Maria] Lyman who was afflicted with a severe cold. This morning the wife broth^er^ Wm Baxter was delivered of [illegible] child [while?].[77]

June 24, 1863; Wednesday. Remained at home all day engaged in the examination of my papers for history. In the evening called on brother M[arcus] L. Shepherd's family and brother Sidney's Tanner's after which I went and saw and administered to brother Orin Twitchel who was sick with the flux [dysentery].

June 25, 1863; Thursday. Wrote letters one to brother C[harles] C. Rich and one to my family at the city and in the afternoon I visited brother W. W. Wandall & family. My wives Louisa Maria [Tanner] and Priscilla [Turley] were with me. During the evening brother White called in to brother W[andall]'s. In the evening mailed letters and called on the family of brother Wm Mathews who is himself in Dixey [southern Utah]. Later in the evening Father [William] Burges called himself and daughterinlaw and others ^who^ were enroute for G. S. L. City. Some Indians in town to day, some vague rumors in circulation in relation to soldiers & their movement to the south from Camp Douglas to punish the Indians.

June 26, 1863; Friday. This [morning] with my wife Priscilla [Turley] I went to Minersville and found my wife Dionitia and her mother well and also the people generaly. Received some calls in the evening from brethren residents of the place. The general aspects of ^the^ place were not much changed by the inovating hands of improvement.

June 27, 1863; Saturday. To day visited and dined with Bp. [James H.] Rollings & family. Did not feel very well in health. In the evening received a call from Father Theodore Turly who had done some work for me during the day and also I received a present of a fine trout from

77. The full entries for June 23, June 30, and July 2 are restricted at the CHL. Textual clues suggest that a female church member became pregnant by someone who was not her husband.

sister Phebe Jane Bingham by the hand of her son Florentine Bingham, brother Edwin Bingham the husband & father being absent on a mission to the states to help in bringing home the poor Saints from Florence.

Brother Jas H. Rollins & family were with me in Cal[ifornia] and shared in common with us the keen reproffs and admonitions so unsparingly poured upon us by the Presidency of the Church impressing on us the truth of the saying that "whom the Lord loveth he chastineth."

June 28, 1863; Sunday. To day attended meeting morning & evening and addressed the Saints after which I made some calls on some families of the Saints. Saw and had conversation with brother Gilburd Summie. Retired late feeling quite weary with the labors of the day.

June 29, 1863; Monday. This morning returned to Beaver stoping & dineing with my daughter Mrs [Matilda] Carter at Greenville. Arived at Beaver about 4 o'clock found the family there well.

June 30, 1863; Tuesday. [Paragraph redacted] In the evening at 5 o'clock meet with Bishop P[hilo] T. Farnsworth's family & blest three of his infant children. School Master Loud was present & also brother Frank Wooley. This evening called on brother Wm J. Cox who said he would take charge of the donation for my houses in Fillmore.

July 1, 1863; Wednesday. Left for Beaver and arived at Corn Creek [Kanosh] about 11 o'clock. Lodged with Brother Peter Robison. The day was dusty & warm. Past several teams on the way ^to^ the north loaded with people going to G. S. L. City to participate in the festival of the 16th held for the members (now remaining) of the Mormon Battalion and the pioneers of 1847 to G. S. L.

July 2, 1863; Thursday. Arived in Fillmore about 11 o'clock found [Francis] Marion & family well and the work progressing slowly on my houses. In the evening visited my garden found trees & plants looking very well. [Seventh wife] Priscilla [Turley] went to see her house which was not yet renovated. As we returned we made a call on bishop Callister, and family found them well. To day [four lines redacted]. This evening Marion planted some corn in the garden.

July 3, 1863; Friday. Today general work on the city ditch, by order of the watermaster a few responded. Called on brother [William] Felshaw who was preparing the lintles for my house. Weather warm & sultry. To day brother [W] Wandall past on his way to Provoo.

July 4, 1863; Saturday. To day the celebration of the birthday of American announced by the fireing of guns and the u[n]furling of baners attended with martial musick and a procession of citizens which marched to the [Fillmore] State House where the Declaration of Independence was read, folowed with musick and oration from Elder [Francis] Marion Lyman after which by request I spoke briefly to the people, after which the assembly ajourned until 3 o'clock when dancing commencd and continued with brief intermission until about 11 o'clock P.M.

July 5, 1863; Sunday. Attended meeting with and spoke to the Saints this morning and in the evening went with bishop [Thomas] Callister & brother Daniel Thompson to Cedar Springs [Holden] where we spoke to the people and lodged with brother R[ichard] Jhonston. The people here are makeing adobies for a school house & there indications of improvement were visible.

July 6, 1863; Monday. To day bishop [Thomas] C[allister] & brother David Thompson went to examine the Kanyon above the Radford spring for timber. I remained with the friends at the springs. About 3 o'clock the explorers returned and reported the finding of some timber. We then returned to Fillmore. Amasa [Jr] was hunting stock to day but did not come home at night to report.

July 7, 1863; Tuesday. Today Amasa [Jr] returned late with the horses. This evening moved my wife Priscilla [Turley] & children into one of my houses thus commencing the settlement of my family in Fillmore.

July 8. 1863; Wednesday. To day visited the spring south of town near the stone quarry & concluded it offered good facilities for a stock ranch on a small scale. This morning breakfasted on vegitables produced on my garden thus over thirty one years have passed since I joined the Church up to the time of my commencing to make myself a home.

July 9, 1863; Thursday. This morning visited brother [William] Felshaw on buisness connected with my house after which with my son Amasa [Jr] I started for G. S. L. City. Halted and dined at Cedar Springs with Sister Richard Johnson then passed on to Round Valley [Scipio]. We lodged with brother Benjamin Johnson & family. Had meeting at night principaly to tell the people that I was not inclined to preach when I arived late after a day's labor. To day passed a number of teams freighted with Saints makeing their way north to attend the festival given for the members of the pioneers & the Mormon Battallion.

July 10, 1863; Friday. Traviled to Salt Creek [Nephi] where we arived about 4 o'clock. Here I meet with brother G[eorge] A. S[mith] & Judge J[ohn] F. Kinney with whom I attended a meeting of the citizens, whom we addressed on the subjects of policy & religion.

July 11, 1863; Saturday. To day traviled as far as Provo. Dined at Payson with brother Joseph Tanner & engaged some teams to move my family to Fillmore. Lodged with brother Myron Tanner. One of my horses was sick tonight.

July 12, 1863; Sunday. Traviled to S. L. City where we arived about sundown. Found Mother [Lydia Clisbee] Partridge very sick the rest of the family were well. Found the Prest [Brigham Young] was absent on a visit to Ogden City.

July 13, 1863; Monday. To day went to Farmington stoped and dined with brother C[harles] C. Rich where I meet with brother E[zra] T. Benson. Found my family well, the fields were white for the harvest.

July 14, 1863; Tuesday. To day started Amasa [Jr] and Platte [Lyman] to hunt for my stock. ~~I visited and dined with br F[ranklin] D Richards & visited the new meeting House. The work on which was progressing finely.~~

July 15, 1863; Wednesday. Today visited the new meeting house where I met with brother F[ranklin] D. Richards with whom I dined and at 5 o'clock attended a meeting of the citizens of the ward to make arrangements for the comeing election & also for the furnishing of the meeting-house. Some light showers to night.

July 16, 1863; Thursday. To day went to the city. Called on and dined with brother C[harles] C. Rich. On our arival found Mother [Lydia] Partridge somewhat beter to day. The party for the members of the pioneers & the Battallion were held in the Theater. I did not attend, not haveing the needful.

July 17, 1863; Friday. To day went to Farmington and took [fourth wife] Eliza [Partridge] with me to make preperations for moveing south. The boys [Amasa Jr and Platte Lyman] returned having seen all the stock & brought all home save 3 head they missed on their return, Amasa [Jr.] did not return in the evening from G. S. L. City to which place he went with brother E[zra] T. Clark. Did not see him any more until the 24th.

July 18, 1863; Saturday. Made some repairs on my carriage in which I was assisted by brothers Leathhead [Leatham] & Broadbent.

July 19, 1863; Sunday. This morning attended meeting in Farmington & in the afternoon went to Centerville and preached. Brother C[harles] C. Rich was with me today at both meetings. We took super with bishop [William] Smith & family and returned to Farmington in the evening.

July 20, 1863; Monday. This morning mad[e] some more repairs on my carriage. In the evening called on brother Thomas Grover & also on bishop [John] Hess.

July 21, 1863; Tuesday. To day brother David Fredrick arived and joined me in making preparation for our move.[78]

July 22, 1863; Wednesday. Today were buisy in our preperations for the move. Dined with brother Joseph Robinson & family. In the afternoon the teams arived from Payson in the care of brother Joseph Tanner. We commenced loading and brother [David] Fredrick & Platt [Lyman] went & brought home the missing stock.

July 23, 1863; Thursday. This morning finished loading and started our stock and wagons for the city where they arived without accident during the day. I was kindly furnished the use of a correll for my stock by brother Rose. My health was rather poor.

July 24, 1863; Friday. This morning started our stock & then I went to the Prest's [Brigham Young] Office but did not see him. After this started with our teams, and my wives Caroline & Lydia [Partridge] and their and Sarah Alger['s] servant, leaveing Mother [Lydia Clisbee] Partridge ~~&~~ sick & Eliza remained with her childen except Platt to take care of her until she should be able to move when they will join us in our new home in the south. We arived in Lehi in the afternoon found the people engaged in Celebrating the 24th. Stoped with bishop [David] Evans here I mee[t] with my son Amasa who joined our party for the south.

July 25, 1863; Saturday. To day dined with brother Myron Tanner & family in Provo and then traviled to Payson where stoped with brother Joseph Tanner and family until Monday.

July 26, 1863; Sunday. This morning I attended meeting and spoke to the saints and in the afternoon I went to the residence of Mother

78. This is followed by some crossed-out paragraphs, repeated in the two subsequent entries except the line "~~a son of brother Ovit's whom I hired assisted in driving the stock.~~"

[Elizabeth] Tanner on the Rancho belonging to her sons. Dined to day with Freeman Tanner & family.

July 27, 1863; Monday. Traviled to Nephi and were entertained by brother T[imothy] B. Foot.

July 28, 1863; Tuesday. Traviled to Round Valley and were entertained by brother Benj. Johnson. At this point some of our group went back.

July 29, 1863; Wednesday. We arived in Fillmore and took possession of our humble dwellings. I was quite sick all day, but we have arived at the place of our home for which we thank God.

July 30, 1863; Thursday. This morning brother Joseph [Tanner] started for home and may the Lord bless him is my prayer. In the evening put up my tent, was quite sick myself. Bishop [Thomas] Callister & wife[79] called to see us this evening. Some light showers to day. Took down my tent on acount of wind.

July 31, 1863; Friday. [Francis] Marion here on the lots the most of the day and in the afternoon we put up and strengthened the tent. Was myself quite ill with fever.

August 1, 1863; Saturday. Was confined to my bed all day. Mail arived from the north but brought us no leters from the city, but said our [live] stock would be in tomorrow. No change in my health to day.

August 2, 1863; Sunday. Stil in bed. Bishop [Thomas] Callister attended meeting and adressed the people. In the evening [Francis] Marion called to see me and Uncle <u>David</u> [Frederick] & boys with stock arived having lost nothing on the way.

August 3, 1863; Monday. Uncle David Fredrick remained with us to day. To day commenced cuting our grain at home, <u>wheat</u> & <u>oats</u>. Weather very dry, my health poor, I stil keep my bed. To day brother Franklin Young from St. George called to see me & gave me a fine specimen of molasses of his make. To day the ^anual election came off for county and teritorial officers.^ J[ohn] F. Kinney was elected to Congress.[80]

---

79. Thomas Callister had two wives, Caroline Smith and Helen Clark; he would soon marry a third one, Mary Phelps, and would add Lyman's daughter Carlie to the seraglio in 1878. The families were previously linked in 1869 when Lyman's son Francis Marion married Callister's oldest daughter, Clara.

80. Future LDS apostle Orson F. Whitney wrote that Kinney, a non-Mormon, had gained the confidence of Utahns. Kinney boldly defended their honor against slurs on their morality. Whitney, *History of Utah*, 2:104.

August 4, 1863; Tuesday. Today [Francis] Marion hawled and stacked the grain, and Uncle David [Frederick] left for Beaver. I am stil in bed.

August 5, 1863; Wednesday. To day [sons] [Francis] Marion and Amasa [Jr] and Platt went to the sink field to harvest our grain there.

August 6, 1863; Thursday. No beter in health. To day Bishop [Thomas] Callister and wife called to see me.

August 7, 1863; Friday. This evening the Boys came from the sink [northwest of Fillmore].

August 8, 1863; Saturday. To day received a present of fruit from Sister [Ann] Carlin per hand of her son and in the afternoon brother [Noah] Bartholomew came in and made some prescritions for me which proved very good.

August 9, 1863; Sunday. To day received several calls from friends. My health slightly beter to night.

August 10, 1863; Monday. Some beter to day walked out. Our children commenced to attend school to day, was not much in bed to day, but selected some mater for my scrap book from Gleasons papers.[81]

August 11, 1863; Tuesday. My health continues improving weather continues very warm & dry. Read some in Virgil. In the evening tightened my cariage wheels to have them in condition for traviling. Some teams past enroute for Beaver. Receive some buter from Sister Robison.

August 12, 1863; Wednesday. To day walked out in town and dined with brother Robison and had some talk with brother Levi Steward in relation to his locating at Black-Rock Springs (in Beaver Valley with his stock), in which I encouraged him as thinking it would induce the further development of the resources of the valley. In the afternoon I called on bishop [Thomas] Callister.

August 13, 1863; Thursday. Passed the day at home helped the boys clean off the weeds from some ground in the garden. At night received a present of a surloin of beef from brother Bohen.

August 14, 1863; Friday. To day worked some in the garden. [Francis] Marion & Amasa [Jr] came home this morning from Clear Lake[82] where

81. *Gleason's Pictorial Drawing-Room Companion* was an illustrated newspaper founded in 1851 in Boston as part of the trend to include drawings and editorial cartoons in newspapers.

82. Clear Lake, twenty miles northwest of Fillmore, is about 6 percent as large as Utah Lake and is a spring stopover for migrating geese.

they had been puting up hay. Several fires are burning on the mountain ajacent to the valley. Amasa & Platt went in search of the oxen but did not find them. Ate some grapes from Marion's vines.

August 15, 1863; Saturday. Did not go out to day until evening whe[n] I called on bishop [Thomas] Callister where I meet with brother John Maiben.

August 16, 1863; Sunday. To day attended meeting in the morning and evening and taught the people. Dined with bishop [Thomas] C[allister] and family. Light showers of rain heavy showers on the mountain at night.

August 17, 1863; Monday. Passed the day at home doing some work in garden. Amasa M. Junior left for parts unknown——. [Francis] Marion hawled wheat from the [Chalk Creek] sink.

August 18, 1863; Tuesday. ~~Marion hawled wheat from the sink.~~ [Francis] Marion helped me ~~read bishops dispatches~~ to water garden.

August 19, 1863; Wednesday. This morning Marion ~~& myself watered garden~~ worked in his garden and I called on brothers [James] Starley, [James] Stoaks & [Joseph] Robison in relation to the purchase of fruit trees. In ^the evening^ received a visit from Sisters [Martha] Knight[83] and [Rizpah] Gib[b]ons wife and daughter of Vincent [Vinson] Knight.

August 20, 1863; Thursday. This morning procured some choice varieties of plum buds which [Francis] Marion set for me in peach stocks. In the evening Marion & Platt went to the sink [northwest of Fillmore] with brother [Lewis] Brunson to bring the residue of my barley & wheat. Some indications of rain.

August 21, 1863; Friday. To day I went in company with Bishop [Thomas] Callister and brother Daniel Thompson to Meadow Creek, and called on and dined with brother Hiram [B.] Ben[n]et[t] & family after which we went to the Ranch where we taried over night. In our travils we past two fine spr^i^ngs.

August 22, 1863; Saturday. To day returned home and in the afternoon selected some hundred apple trees in brother [James] Starley's nursery.[84] [Francis] Marion & Platt [Lyman] started for Beaver this morning.

83. Martha Knight's first husband died in July 1842. Shortly thereafter she became a plural wife of Joseph Smith, later marrying Heber C. Kimball.

84. James Starley had worked on Brigham Young's gardens and orchards under William Staines. Appearing in Fillmore in 1858, it was in response to Brigham Young's call for him to serve a ten-year horticultural mission there. When his time was up, he

August 23, 1863; Sunday. This morning attended the meeting of the Saints at Cedar Springs [Holden]. Dined with Prest [William] Stevens after which we returned to Fillmore and held meeting at 5 o'clock where the conduct of brother [Nicholas] Paul[85] in whiping one of his neighbors boys was considered and instruction that was pertinent to the mater in question was given to him and the assembled Saints who generaly seemed edified & blest.

August 24, 1863; Monday. To day remained at home and had brother Robison's boy hunting my horses but he did not find them. In the evening called on the Bishops family and took tea with them and & had some mellon. Selected 50 trees in brother [Joseph] Robison's Nursery.[86]

August 25, 1863; Tuesday. Purchased some peach trees of bishop [Thomas] Callister. In the afternoon pruned some trees. My horses were hunted for but not found. I dined with bishop Callister.

August 26, 1863; Wednesday. To day remained at home. In the evening my horses were brought home by brother [Thomas] King. I walked to the saw mill where some sawing was being done for my house. My health poor.

August 27, 1863; Thursday. To day in the afternoon I started south and called on brother [Ephraim] Tompkinson & then passed on to Corn Creek where I preached and lodged with brother Peter Robison.

August 28, 1863; Friday. To day traviled to Beaver where I arived about 11 o'clock P.M. Found my family in good health. Meet [Francis] Marion and Platt [Lyman] & Uncle David [Frederick] on Indian Creek with lumber and stock.

August 29, 1863; Saturday. Passed the day in Beaver attending to some buisness connected with my building.

August 30, 1863; Sunday. Preached to the people and dined with Sister Howd[87] and family.

---

decided to stay, along with his wife and two children. "Journal of James Starley," *Utah Historical Quarterly*, 169n.

85. The forty-one-year-old British convert Nicholas Paul Jr. provided another twist in the community's story by later riding into the West Desert in a buggy and disappearing, later found dead with $171 in his pocket.

86. Robison had been cultivating fruit trees in southern Utah for several years but was beginning to slow down at age sixty. He had one wife and seven children.

87. Her husband, Simeon F. Howd, was branch president. He had three wives.

August 31, 1863; Monday. Went to Parowan and my wife L[ouisa] M[aria] went with me. Found my wife Paulina [Phelps] & child both ill from cold. Both were soon beter.

September 1, 1863; Tuesday. Visited Father [Weeden V.] Hakes who was very sick, and dined with brother [Ebenezer] Hanks & family. Tasted some fresh grapes from Toquerville and also visited the cotton mill.

September 2, 1863; Wednesday. To day selected some lumber at the mill. Ate some mellons with the Bishop.

September 3, 1863; Thursday. Returned to Beaver and encountered a heavy shower as we traviled and became very wet, arived at 9 o'clock.

September 4, 1863; Friday. Remained in Beaver and attended to some business. Secured some lumber for my house.

September 5, 1863; Saturday. This morning started for Fillmore. George Sears was with me and drove my teem. At Cove Creek we encountered a severe rain storm which was attended with hail. We arived at Corn Creek after dark, lodged with brother [Peter] Robison, the night was extremely dark.

September 6, 1863; Sunday. Rose before the sun and traviled to Fillmore, found all well at home. Attended meeting morning & evening at both of which I spoke to the people.

September 7, 1863; Monday. To day [Francis] Marion found the old oxen. I taried at home through the day. Made a call on Sister [Ann] Carlin[g].[88]

September 8, 1863; Tuesday. Remained at home with my family. In the evening my wife Lydia [Partridge] was taken sick.

September 9, 1863; Wednesday. This morning at 8 o'clock Lydia [Partridge] was delivered of a fine healthy son.[89] Mother and child seemed to do verry well under the kind ministration of Sister [Ann] Carlin[g].

September 10, 1863; Thursday. Passed the day in town made some calls. Brother [David] Fredrick and Platt [Lyman] went after fencing & wood.

88. Joseph Smith set apart Ann Carling as a midwife in Nauvoo. Years later in assisting one of Lyman's adult daughters in childbirth, the grandmother would comment that only a woman could administer such comfort and compassion as she had seen the midwife offer, and only a woman "can suffer" as much as the birthing mother "and live." In fact, in this case the mother died twelve days later. Partridge, *Eliza Maria Partridge Journal*, 126–27.

89. Frank Arthur Lyman would die the next year in Ogden.

September 11, 1863; Friday. To day I visited the clear spot at the foot of the hills a walk of several miles after which I was very weary. Uncle David [Frederick] and Platt [Lyman] hunted the cows but did not find them.

September 12, 1863; Saturday. I walked some for the cows but without success.

September, 13, 1863; Sunday. Attended meeting morning & evening & taught the people the importence of awakening a spirit of enterprise & improvement.

September 14, 1863; Monday. My health was quite poor. During the day we received a call from brother J[ames] H. Rollins with his sister Mrs. [Mary Elizabeth] Lightner & his Aunt Mrs. [Elizabeth] Gilbert who have returned to the Church after an absence of 17 years.[90] They took some refreshments and past on their way to Minersville. This evening heard of our cows. Uncle David [Frederick] went to Cedar Springs but did not get them.

September 15, 1863; Tuesday. To day Uncle David [Frederick] brought home our cows from Pioneer Creek.[91] Went to the saw mill and found my lumber sawed for my gates.

September 16, 1863; Wednesday. Commenced to build the gates for my carrell [corral]. Uncle David [Frederick] commenced the fence on which we were engaged until Saturday the 19th when I received 100 strawberry plants from brother T[homas] W. Ellerbeck.

September 20, 1863; Sunday.[92] Attended meeting morning & evening.

September 21, 1863; Monday. To day received some loads of fencing and brother Fredrick set out our strawberry plants.

September 22, 1863; Tuesday. Resumed our work on the Carrell [coral] which we continued until Friday 25th on the evening of which day my son [Francis] Marion's wife [Rhoda] was delivered of a fine son [Francis M. Jr.] at half past 11 o'clock. Brother E[lias] H. Blackburn past

90. Mary Elizabeth Rollins Lightner was married civilly to Adam Lightner, a non-Mormon, in a polyandrous arrangement because she was simultaneously married to Joseph Smith. The Lightners struggled for several years before moving in 1863 to Utah, where she spoke freely about her marriage and penned a detailed account of it. Compton, *In Sacred Loneliness*, 205–27.

91. Pioneer Creek is twelve miles northeast of Fillmore in the Pahvant Range.

92. There are no entries for Sep. 17–19. Lyman begins to show impatience with his diary, skipping days and either leaving them undocumented or summarizing them all at once.

on his way to conference. I also received a note from brother Orson Pratt inviting me to attend Conference at St. George.[93]

September 26, 1863; Saturday. To day myself & brother [David] Fredrick laid out the ground for my orchard on the rocky pearch. Found myself very weary from my labor through the week.

September 27, 1863; Sunday. This morning tried to engage a nurse for my wife Caroline [Partridge] but did not succeed.[94] After which I attended meeting and preached to the people. The wind high & southerly many teams on the road for Conference. In the evening attended the meeting of the seventies whom I addressed.

September 28, 1863; Monday. This morning with my wife Cornelia & son Henry E. Lyman I started for G. S. L. City in the stage. We dined at Round Valley stoped at Nephi over night.

September 29, 1863; Tuesday. To day traviled to Provo and lodged with brother Myron Tanner. Called on the family of G[eorge] A. Smith some of whom were sick.

September 30, 1863; Wednesday. To day arived in the city found the portion of my family resident there well as usual. Called on Prest [Brigham] Young and made some other calls. This evening recovered a parcell I had sent by mail.

October 1, 1863; Thursday. To day visited Sister Elizabeth Cannon whom I found well with her children.[95] I called on brother W[illiam] C. Staines at his residence, took a look at his garden and fruit.

October 2, 1863; Friday. To day I attended the state fare and in the evening I called on the Prest [Brigham Young] and partook of some fine fruit and had pleasant conversation with the Prest and members of his family.

October 3, 1863; Saturday. This morning I obtained some strawberry plants of brother Albert Carrington and put them up for sending south by mail to my place in Fillmore.

---

93. It appears that because his wife Caroline was about to give birth (see entry for Sept. 27), he opted to stay in Fillmore rather than attend the meeting with Pratt in St. George. That is not to say he would not preach in Fillmore the day his baby was born or travel to Salt Lake City the next day.

94. Caroline would give birth to Walter Clisbee Lyman on Oct. 1.

95. Her husband, George Q. Cannon, would not return home from his British mission for another year.

October 4, 1863; Sunday. To day attended meeting in the Tabernacle Morning & evening. In the evening I talked to the people for a short time.

October 5, 1863; Monday. Passed the day in the city large numbers were gathering in to attend the Conference.

October 6, 1863; Tuesday. This morning the Conference commenced and continued until Friday the 9th on which day it was ajourned after the morning services.

October 10, 1863; Saturday. This morning had an interview with Prest [Brigham] Young and brother N[athan] C. Tinney in relation on maters relating to our selves.[96]

October 11, 1863; Sunday. This morning attended meeting in the Tabernacle and spoke to the people for half an hour following Elder G[eorge] D. Watt.

October 12, 1863; Monday. To day packed my school books for transportation to Fillmore. In the evening felt verry unwell from cold.

October 13, 1863; Tuesday. To day called on brother Wm Godbe, after which I called on br C[harles] C. Rich at his house. As I returned to my lodgings I meet Bishop [Thomas] Callister who informed me of the arival from the plains of brother [Jacob] Croft, and of his own intention to remain until the last train should come in on Thursday next. Remained in the city until Sunday the 18th when I attended meeting in the Tabernacle & preached to the people and dined with brother Robert Burton. On Thursday the 15th the last Church train arived from the plains.

We sent some goods by the returning teams to Fillmore I folowed on Monday the 19th and arived in Fillmore on Saturday the 24th and on Sunday the 25th attended the Conference which held until Monday evening the 26th and adjourned. I remained in town until Thursday the 29th when I went to Deseret[97] with brothers [Noah] Bartholomew, [Gabriel] Huntsman, [Byron] Warner, [Levi] McColough and [Thomas] King to locate the dam for turning the water of the Se[v]ier River for the use of Deseret. I lodged with brother [Jacob] Croft and family.

---

96. Leo Lyman suggests that they were rebuked for taking an interest in spiritualism. In any case, the entry suggests an unhappy meeting. *AML*, 357–58.

97. Deseret is a small town forty miles northwest of Fillmore on the edge of the West Desert. The Mormon settlers who arrived there in 1860 lived in makeshift shelters as they irrigated and tried to build a dam that never held. After the settlement was attacked by Indians, the town was abandoned. It was later inhabited by non-Mormon miners.

October 30, 1863; Friday. We attended to the buisness of our mission and in the evening held meeting with the people, and on Saturday 31st returned to Fillmore. To night had a fall of snow, weather very cool. On Wednesday 28th. Cornelia [Leavitt] & children came with brother [Ebenezer] Hanks from the city.

November 1, 1863; Sunday. Attended meeting in the afternoon weather very cool. Continued our exertions to get off the Ruby expedition until Friday the 6th when our team started.[98] Remained in Fillmore until Sunday 8th and attended meeting in the morning & in the evening I started for Parrowan with my wife Cornelia [Leavitt].

We arived in Beaver on Monday 9th and taried one day and arived in Parrowan on Wednesday 11th. Taried until Monday 16th then went to Red Creek[99] and held meeting in their new school house and on the 17th reached Beaver and meet brother G[eorge] A. Smith and had meeting at night & held meetings through Wednesday 18th and on Thursday 19th had meeting with brother O[rson] Pratt and on the 20th I went to Minersville and had meeting on the night of the 21st and on the 22nd and on the 24th and then on the 25th returned to Beaver and held meeting on Sunday the 29th and on Monday 30th started for Fillmore where I arived on the evening of the 1st of Dec.

Remained in Fillmore one week and then on Tuesday the 8th started for G. S. L. City where I arived on Saturday the 12th and put up with brother G. A. Smith. Called on the Prest' [Brigham Young] in the evening.

December 13, 1863; Sunday. To day remained in the office writing for the southern mail. In the evening attended the [prayer] circle. Brothers [Orson] Pratt[,] [Wilford] Woodruff[,] G. A. Smith[,] F. D. Richards & A. M. Lyman [present]. Some rain & snow.

December 14, 1863; Monday. To day meet in the Legislature and effected our organization and ajourned to meet at 10 oclock tomorow.

December 15, 1863; Tuesday. Meet as per ajournment and received the message of his excellency, acting-governor [Amos] Reed.[100] After at-

98. This may be a humorous comparison of the preparations to travel to Salt Lake City and the mountains of supplies and armaments the infantry at Camp Douglas packed to visit Fort Ruby in Nevada, which they periodically did as part of their assignment to protect the mail route.

99. Red Creek (now Paragonah) is five miles northeast of Parowan.

100. Lincoln appointed James D. Doty, superintendent of Indian Affairs for Utah

tending to some buisness ajourned until 1 o'clock tomorow. This evening about 10 o'clock Jedadiah son of Brigham Young & Clarrisa, died after an illness of some 5 days.

December 16, 1863; Wednesday. Meet as per adjournment. Hon Erastus Snow came in & was qualified. In the evening I attended a juvenile concert held in the Theater some 190 children participated with adults who made the number about 300 hundred. The performance was highly creditable to Conductor David O. Calder under whose direction they had been trained. The Hon's Orson Hyde & Lorenzo Snow arived this evening.

December 17, 1863; Thursday. Meet as per ajournment. In the evening I attended a lecture on the ancient history of Ireland delivered by the Hon G[eorge] A. Smith the hall was densely crowded.

December 18, 1863; Friday. Meet as per adjournment. Attended to some buisness and ajourned to Monday 21st at 1 oclock. After which I meet with the committee on Roads[,] Bridges[,] Ferries & Kanyons.

December 19, 1863; Saturday. At 10 o'clock attended the High Council. Prest [Brigham] Young was present & gave some very valuable instruction. There were a number of bishops present. In the evening went to Centerville lodged with brother C[harles] C. Rich.

December 20, 1863; Sunday. This morning attended meeting and folowed brother C[harles] C. Rich in addressing the people. Dined with Sister Levitt. Attended meeting again in the evening & addressed the people. Lodged with Bishop William Smith.

December 21, 1863; Monday. Returned to the city with Bishop [William] Smith and mee[t] at 1 o'clock and attended to some buisness assigned to [legislative] committees and ajourned.

December 22, 1863; Tuesday. Meet and ajourned so that some of the members could attend the sitting of the court to sentence [Jason] Luce (for murder)[101] to be shot on the 12th of next month which sentence was passed upon him by Judge Elias Smith of the Probate Court for Salt Lake County.

Territory, to replace Stephen Harding. Since Doty was required in Washington on other business, he was temporarily replaced by territorial secretary Amos Reed.

101. Jason R. Luce stabbed Samuel Bunton in public view on Main Street on Dec. 7, 1863. Even though Luce claimed Bunton had attacked him in Idaho, Luce was executed by firing squad on Jan. 12, 1864. "A Murder on Main Street," "The Execution of Jason R. Luce," *Deseret News*, Dec. 9, 1863, Mar. 9, 1864.

December 23, 1863; Wednesday. Meet as per ajournment and after attending to sundary items of buisness the Cou^n^sil ajourned until the 4th of Jan 1864. I remained in the city during the Holladays, during which time I attended to funerals of the infant son of brother George Q. Cannon & Elizabeth Hogland.[102] On Wednesday 30th and on the day folowing I attended the funerel of Father David Petigrew[103] the meeting was largely attended by the Bishops of the city. On the evening Thursday 30th [31st] I attend the lecture at the seve[n]ties Hall the audience was addressed by Elder E[dward] W. Tullage.

January 1, 1864; Friday. To day took diner with brother Albert Merrill and family.

January 2, 1864; Saturday. Did not go out to day[,] past the time in reading.

January 3, 1864; Sunday. ~~Monday~~ Passed the day in writing & reading and in the evening attended the prayr circle. Prest B[righam] Young was present.

January 4, 1864; Monday. Mee[t] [in the legislature] as per ajournment. Transacted some buisness and ajourned until tomorow at 1 o'clock.

January 5, 1864; Tuesday. Meet as per ajournment [in the legislature] and were in cession until sun-down when we ajourned until tomorow 1 o'clock.

January 6, 1864; Wednesday. Meet as per ajournment [in the legislature]. Dispached business as per minutes and after our ajournment I went to take sup[p]er with brother Crompton and family.

January 7, 1864; Thursday. Meet as per ajournment after transacting some buisness ajourned until 10 o'clock tomorow. I was very sick through the night. Today wrote some letters home.

January 8, 1864; Friday. Meet at 10 o'clock. Dispached some buisness after which the Council ajourned until next Monday the 11th at 1 o'clock.

January 9, 1864; Saturday. This morning felt somewhat beter and about 8 o'clock started for Farmington with brother Edward Partridge

102. Seven-month-old George H. Cannon died of pertussis and measles on Dec. 29, just as his sister Georgianna had a few months earlier, leaving their mother, Elizabeth, alone, her husband remaining in England. Bitton, *George Q. Cannon*, 134.

103. David Pettigrew was the long-time bishop of Salt Lake's 10th ward and a former member of the Mormon Battalion.

[Jr]. The morning services had commenced when we arrived. I dined with brother P, attended meeting in the afternoon and lodged with brother John S. Gleason & family.

January 10, 1864; Sunday. Attended meeting and at night lodged with brother E[zra] T. Clark.

January 11, 1864; Monday. To day returned to the city. Meet at one o'clock, and was in attendance on the Legislature daily until Saturday 16th when we meet as per ajournment and after the transactions of the day ajourned until Monday 18th at 1 o'clock.

January 17, 1864; Sunday. I preached in the Tabernacle in the afternoon and at 4 o'clock attended the circle and Prest' [Brigham] Young was present. In the evening I preached in the Assembly Room of the 13th Ward to a large & attentive audience.

January 18, 1864; Monday. Resumed our Legislative labors as per ajournment and continued from day to day until Wednesday 21th[104] on the evening of which day I received a letter from my wife Paulina [Phelps] informing me that my wife Cornelia [Leavitt] was laying at the point of death.[105] I wrote letters to my family to night.

January 21, 1864; Thursday. Meet [in legislature] as per adjournment and prosicuted our labors. This morning I sent a package of goods by brother Elias Pearson of Round Vally to be carried to his place.

January 22, 1864; Friday. Meet as per ajournment and with the day closed our labors in a Teritorial Legislative capacity, ajourned about 11 o'clock.

January 23, 1864; Saturday. To day the State Legislature meet at 10 o'clock. This morning received my per diem from the Secretary of State. The weather soft warm and pleasant. With the day closed the session and labors of the State Legislature.

January 24, 1864; Sunday. Attended meeting in the Tabernacle and dined with brother Jacob Wiler & family and at 4 o'clock meet in the circle. All of our quorum were present except brother G[eorge] Q. Cannon. Prest B[righam] Young was present. Brothers E[zra] T. Benson and

104. Lyman wrote "21th" but meant the 20th.

105. Cornelia would partially recover to experience fluctuations in her health over the next two years, dying on Dec. 14, 1865. Lyman's letters to her in Jan. 1864 are tender, as are his notes to Paulina for her attention to her sister-wife. *AML*, 360.

L[orenzo] Snow were appointed to visit the Sandwich Islands to set in order things that might be wanting. They were to be joined by other Elders in their labors. For this service brothers J[oseph] F. Smith[,] Wm Cluff[,] Alma Smith and others were named.

January 25, 1864; Monday. Went to Farmington & preached. In the evening lodged with brother E[zra] T. Clark.

January 26, 1864; Tuesday. Today concluded an arangement with brother [Ezra T.] Clark for takeing up my note in the hands of W[illiam] H. Hooper.[106] At night preached to a large and attentive audience in the meeting house & lodged with Bishop John W. Hess.

January 27, 1864; Wednesday. Returned to the city and settled with Brother [William H.] Hooper and also made arrangements for the payment of my debt to brother Rix of two hundred dollars. This make[s] me free from my heavy and pressing liabilities. This evening heard from my wife Cornelia in Parowan. She was not expected to live. To night wrote letters for the south for the morning mail. Dined with brother Orson Hyde & family.

January 28, 1864; Thursday. Passed the day in seeking an opportunity to start for home via Sandpete [Valley] but did not succeed. Dined with brother Jas Mair & family. Snow fell to night.

January 29, 1864; Friday. Passed to day as yesterday. In the evening called upon and lodged [with] the family of brother Nathan Tanner. Brother Tanner was not at home.[107]

---

106. Clark would found the first bank in Farmington, but for now he was a rancher and mill owner whose loan would have been private.

107. This entry is followed by three blank pages ending volume 20.

10 The Spirit of the Movement, 1868–1870

Lyman stopped keeping a diary for close to five years from February 1864 to the summer of 1868, during which he was traveling and speaking less often[1] and spending more time in his garden and orchard. He was also preoccupied with the gristmill he was part owner of. Even so, it was an eventful time with the death of his wife Cornelia, who passed away in December 1864 at the end of a two-year illness, and of his fourteen-year-old son, Roswell, who accidentally shot and killed himself.

Then came the overall low point of his life in 1867 when the Quorum of Twelve Apostles demanded that he explain his 1862 sermon in Dundee, Scotland, as part of Brigham Young's campaign to rid the church of unorthodoxy. After a tense and emotional hearing on January 21, the quorum required Lyman to publish a confession in the *Deseret News,* which he did. Then about two months later, Lyman reversed himself and delivered a sermon that had essentially the same message as before, that came close to denying Christ's divinity.

In response to that, the quorum expelled him, followed almost immediately by three of his wives, the Partridge sisters, all abandoning him.[2] For a while he remained on good terms with friends and associates who assumed his rebellion would be short lived and he would re-establish harmony with the church leadership.

1. One exception was his stirring eulogy of Abraham Lincoln, a man Lyman deeply admired. *AML,* 364–65.

2. They were supported in this decision by Brigham Young, who directed Bishop Thomas Callister to assist them with church funds.

> Instead, he discovered that there were other like-minded people in Utah who were organizing what came to be known as the New Movement, with alternative church services, a political party, and a newspaper promoting economic independence and a rational approach to religion. He was hooked. By accepting the presidency of the new church, he invited his excommunication from the LDS faith, which came almost immediately.

August 24, 1868; Monday. To day brother [William] Gibbs[3] took charge of our mill which he has rented for one year.

August 31, 1868; Monday.[4] The morning bright and clear and my health improveing. We begin to feel the chilly ~~admonitions of the~~ approach of Autumn. The sores that have troubled me for the last year are subsideing. ~~To day~~ Worked at the mill takeing up and changeing the smelter ~~and beside doeing some work in the Shop~~ brother [William] Gibbs helped change the smutter.

September 1, 1868; Tuesday. Weather bright and clear ~~to day~~ worked in our Shop with Oscar [Lyman][5] putting up the turning lathe. To day brother [William] Gibbs commenced work in our shop for which he agreed to allow us five dollars per month.

September 2, 1868; Wednesday. To day worked at the shop with Oscar[6] got our lathe ready for turning. To day we borrowed some turning tools of brother J[ohn] L. Smith for present use. Weather warm and pleasant.

September 3, 1868; Thursday. Worked in the shop at fiting up for work. Brother [William] Gibbs called in the afternoon and made some repairs on the mill. Said he expected some grinding soon. To day the boys Lorenzo [Lyman] and Theodore [Lyman][7] were hawling wood and

3. William Gibbs, the primary miller at Lyman's gristmill, was also a carpenter and casket maker. Family legend says he kept his hair long thinking Indians would not kill him if he braided it.

4. This entry and other portions of the diary have a red pencil mark, probably made by someone compiling the Journal History of the Church, in this case indicating economic developments in the hinterlands.

5. Oscar Morris Lyman was the son of Amasa and Paulina Phelps.

6. Because of the frequent references to family members, I will dispense with adding the family name after I have identified someone as part of the Lyman family.

7. Lorenzo Snow Lyman, son of Amasa and Cornelia Leavitt; Theodore Kimberly Lyman, son of Priscilla Turley.

broak the wagon and brother [Noah] Bartholimew promised some timber to repair my wagon.

September 4, 1868; Friday. ~~To day~~ Procured timber and repa^i^red wagon. Some grinding in the mill. Turned off the driveing pully for the lathe. Oscar was with me and Lorenzo and Theodore watering in the field under the hill. Ira [Lyman][8] was with the herd. Some indications of storm at night.

September 5, 1868; Saturday. To day had some blacksmithing done for the lathe and made and put on some fastnings to my Secretary [desk]. In the afternoon we had a fine pleasant shower had some grinding today with very satisfactory results. Oscar went with [Francis] Marion [Lyman][9] to see some hay ground for which he traded his horse. The northern mail did not come in.

September 6, 1868; Sunday. Past most of the day with brother [William] Marsden[10] who was on his way north to the city. He went and looked at my mill and workshop. Brother Marsdens residence is in the city of Parrowan, where he has been runing brother [Ebenezer] Hank's cotton factory. Some wind with indications of rain.

September 7, 1868; Monday. To day had heavy rains which made the mountain stream quite mudy. I worked makeing a c[r]amp for the shop and Oscar was turning [a banister on the lathe] for brother [William] Gibbs. The County Court was in session to day, rain continued mostly through the day no clearing up.

September 8, 1868; Tuesday. ~~To day~~ Worked in the shop makeing furniture for shop. Weather fine and pleasant Oscar was turning [the lathe] for br [William] Gibbs. Lorenzo and Theodore hawled wood.

September 9, 1868; Wednesday. Worked in the shop finishing my cramp, Oscar finished turning banister for [William] Gibbs. In the evening Lorenzo started for Parrowan with Wm West.[11] Brother Richard

8. Ira Depo Lyman, son of Amasa and Priscilla Turley.

9. Lyman's relationship with his oldest son remained close but was overshadowed by Amasa's break with Brigham Young and the church. Francis Marion would be called as an apostle in 1880.

10. William Marsden was originally from England. In Parowan he operated the cotton factory. Less than three months earlier, on June 20, his wife, Sariah Scovil Marsden, died.

11. William Moroni West was a twenty-four-year-old, born in Kentucky to LDS parents, who had gotten married four months earlier in May. His traveling companion

Benson arived in town this evening he is returning from his mission in Europe. He was quite ill.

September 10, 1868; Thursday. Called on brother [Richard] Benson whom I found quite sick after which I started in the stage for Parrowan. Traviled to Cove Creek where I was very kindly entertained for the night by brother Ira Hinckly and family.[12] During the night brother Benson arived in a lumber wagon. Weather warm and pleasant.

September 11, 1868; Friday. Traviled to Beaver in company with brother [Richard] Benson. While in Beaver called on Postmaster [Horace A.] Skiner and saw him weaveing on his new hand loom—one of Mendenhall's.[13] While there I wrote a note to Dionitia my wife at Minersville.[14] Sent it by the hand of brother Frederick Turley. Lodged with brother Wm. Barton's. Brother Wm West was there with whom I engaged my pasage to Parrowan.

September 12, 1868; Saturday. Traviled to Parrowan found my family there well. This evening brother Ebenezer Hanks called on me. Brother [Richard] Benson is reported very sick. My [sixth] wife Paulina's health improved since I last saw her. Weather still warm and pleasant.

September 13, 1868; Sunday. Past the day at ^home^. Paulina had an attack of the asthma from which she was relieved by takeing chery pectoral[15] and applying cloths wet in cold water to her chest over the uper portion of the lungs. In the evening with my wife calling on brother [Richard] Benson. To day received a call from brother D[aniel] P. Clark

---

was Lorenzo Lyman, who was seventeen. In six years William will die of exposure while tracking horse thieves mid-winter. "Died," *Deseret News*, Feb. 18, 1874.

12. The Canadian emigrant Ira Hinckley was responsible for building Cove Fort, the main way station between Salt Lake City and St. George. He was the father of apostle Alonzo Hinckley and grandfather of later LDS president Gordon B. Hinckley.

13. The hand-operated loom developed by Stephen Mendenhall in Indiana was promoted for being "simple and easily understood, Every thing is performed by Turning a Crank." *Scott's Monthly Magazine*, June 1867.

14. For now Amasa and his second wife, Dionetia, were on good terms, but after his death she had their temple marriage canceled and had herself sealed to Joseph Smith. *AML*, 400.

15. When the young Connecticut druggist James C. Ayer developed an opium-laced cherry pectoral in the 1840s, the demand grew so fast that by 1852 he had to construct a large brick building for its manufacture next to his drug store. The medicine had no curative value, but the opium deadening pain, and it was recommended by "prominent clergymen," according to *Ayer's American Almanac*, 1878, p. 14.

and wife and Sister [Elizabeth] Warren. To day Morgan Richards Junior, was cut off from the Church for unbelief in the doctrins of the Church.[16] Weather warm and pleasant, to day brother W [Ebenezer] Hanks[17] started north to meet his wife Sarah who had been on a visit to her father's in Salt Lake County.

September 14, 1868; Monday. Today met with brother S[eth] M. Blair from the Uneion Iron Works.[18] His visit was a professional one. In the evening brother [Ebenezer] Hanks returned with his wife Sarah who had been north on a visit to her father Wm Casper whose residence was on Millcreek Salt Lake County. Brother Blair returned to Cedar this evening. Had our wagon repaired and got up our oxen for hawling. Weather pleasant and warm.

September 15, 1868; Tuesday. ~~To day~~ Lorenzo and Henry [Lyman][19] went to the Kanyon for wood. I called at brother [William] West's to see the opperation of the washing machine. Wrote letter to Fillmore and took super with brother [Ebenezer] Hanks and family.

September 16, 1868; Wednesday. ~~To day~~ Started for the Union Iron Works with brother [Ebenezer] Hanks. On the road we met Sister [Eliza] Hate wife of brother Isaac Hate from Toquerville. She gave us some grapes and as we came to Cedar we met brother Wm. Martindale who treated us to some wine in its simplest form by giveing us some grapes. At dark we arived at the residence of brother Robert Ri[t]che[y] where we lodged.

September 17, 1868; Thursday. To day after waiting for brother [Ebenezer] Hanks while he went up the Kanyon to look at the prospect for coal. Then went to the iron works which are situated in the Valey of the little Pinto below Rich's ranch some 2½ miles. The settlement

16. Morgan Richards Jr., a school teacher, argued against polygamy but later reunited with the church and became the first state auditor in 1896 (Richards, Autobiography).

17. Lyman wrote a *W* but clearly intended Ebenezer Hanks and wife Sarah Casper.

18. This was name of the mining and processing company formed in 1868 near Cedar City, unrelated to the company of the same name in San Francisco known for manufacturing railroad cars, ships, and large farm machinery. The Utah company was run by Seth M. Blair, Chapman Duncan, and Ebenezer Hanks, and the furnace was run by David B. Adams of Beaver.

19. Henry Elias Lyman was the youngest son of Amasa and Cornelia Leavitt and brother to Lorenzo Snow Lyman.

is composed of 5 families, viz S[eth] M. Blair, C[hapman] Duncan[,] P[eter] Shirts[,] [Ezra] Strong & [Charles] Pinny.

September 18, 1868; Friday. ~~To day~~ The fire was increased in the [iron works] furnace. In the afternoon some ore was put in ~~the furnace which was~~ ^and^ reduced with Cedar wood. The trial resulted favorably altho the heat was to severe for the rock of the oven causing them to fly. The proprieters have concluded to make fire brick (the material for which is convenient and abundant) for lineing the works.

September 19, 1868; Saturday. Passed the day at the works. The directors and members of the company held a meeting for buisness relating to the general interests of the company.

September 20, 1868; Sunday. This morning brother [Ebenezer] Hanks started for his horses which he folowed some 12 miles before he secured them. This made his return so late that we did not start for Parrowan as we had calculated. During the day past some time with brothers [Seth M.] Blair[,] [Chapman] Duncan and others at the iron works. Dined with brother [Peter] Shirts[20] and family.

September 21, 1868; Monday. Returned to Parowan. Made noon halt at Cedar City and dined brother George Wood.[21] Arived home at dark found our families well. The boys had broken the wagon so that it was useless. My health is better than for some days past.

September 22, 1868; Tuesday. Made some ineffectual efforts to have my wagon repaired.

September 23, 1868; Wednesday. Went to the shingle machine and procured some shingles and had the boys engaged pa[t]ching the roof of the house. Dined with brother [Ebenezer] Hanks and family and aranged with brother Hanks to let him have one yoke of my oxen for wheat for my family here. Called brother [William H.] Dame and made arangements to go to Beaver on the stage.

---

20. Peter Shirts was one of the original settlers of Parowan, the original stockade being called Shirts Fort after him. He relocated to Kanab and one day in 1882 wandered off with a pack mule and was never heard from again.

21. Six years earlier, George Wood killed Olive Coombs Higbee and maimed her thirteen-year-old daughter, Emily, saying the daughter had tried to seduce his eighteen-year-old son. The community defended Wood to the governor, who pardoned him, but historians suspect the real motive was that Olive, a school teacher, had learned too much about the 1857 Mountain Meadows Massacre. Maxwell, *The Civil War Years in Utah*, 324–27.

September 24, 1868; Thursday. Taried until noon with my family then started for Beaver. Traviled as far as the Buckhorn Springs. There we staid over the night with brother Miles Anderson. There were many teams on the road going to the conference in Salt Lake City some of whom camped with us at br A's.

September 25, 1868; Friday. Arived in Beaver at 11½ o'clock. Took din[n]er with the family of br Sidney Tanner. Here I was informed of the death of Elizabeth Jane, wife of [Sidney's son] Allen Tanner she died of brain fever. Saw br. [Marcus L.] Shepherd who told me he had sold some fifty of my goats for cotton yarn some of which he had exchanged for sheep and some was still on hand. My sheep have done but poorly only yielding 2 lbs of wool per head with light increase of the stock. This evening traviled as far as Cove Creek where we arived a eight oclock. Was kindly lodged and fed by brother [Ira] Hinckly.

September 26, 1868; Saturday. Were off this morning for Fillmore. At Corn Creek saw brother Jacob Gates who was on his way to the Conference. In the afternoon arived at home found my family well. This evening brother [William] Marsden returned from the city where he had been on business. He taried with us all night.

September 27, 1868; Sunday. Past the day mostly in writing up and copying my journal. In the evening called on br [James] Stokes and family. Took sup[p]er with Marion and family, the weather still warm and pleasant.

September 28, 1868; Monday. Commenced cuting up my corn. Visited the mill and found the custom [toll] on the increase.[22] Paid some attention to drying fruit which was beginning to hury us. The road was thronged with teams going to conference. ^Called on br [Jacob] Croft who was fiting up his molasses mill.^

September 29, 1868; Tuesday. Was buisy with the fruit and corn, had a call from brother Ezra Strong, who was on his way to conference. This evening br [Marcus L.] Shepherd called and staid all night on his way to conference.

September 30, 1868; Wednesday. Marion started this morning to go

22. Lyman apparently allowed the miller, William Gibbs, to charge farmers whatever percentage of flour he wanted in exchange for grinding their grain. Lyman makes regular visits to Jacob Croft's molasses mill as well.

to conference with his wife [Rhoda] and Lelia and his son.[23] To day I brought up the horses gathered some titheing peaches from brother Andrew Henry's trees. Was buisy with the fruit. Felt much pain from a large swelling on my side.

October 1, 1868; Thursday. Today Theodore went in search of the horses that got out of the correll last night. He succeeded in finding them and in the afternoon went to the mill for feed. In the course of the day gathered some more peaches from brother [Andrew] H[enry]'s trees. Had some showers during the day closed with some indications of ^more^ rain.

October 2, 1868; Friday. The boys have gone for wood and I passed the forenoon in cuting peaches and in the afternoon I went to see the operation of brother [Jacob] Croft's mollases mill, then I returned home, some showers this evening.

October 3, 1868; Saturday. Weather rainy suspended our peach cuting. Gathered some fruit. The boys hawled some wood and went to the mill for flour but got none. In the evening received a letter from my wife Dionitia (whose residence is in Minersville). She informs me that her own and her mother's health is poor and that the^ir^ wheat is badly spoiled with the sun flower, so much so as ^not^ to be eatible. This evening was favored with the perusal of some letters from ^some of^ the family of brother Ezra T. Clark of Farmington ~~In~~ to their friends in Parrowan in relation to the death of E[zra] J. Clark who died on his return from his mission to Europe.[24]

October 4, 1868; Sunday. Wrote some letters one to Minersville and one to Beaver. Some rain during the day, read some in the book of constitutions, and some of the instruction of the great Washington to the nation at the close of his publick labors.[25]

October 5, 1868; Monday. The boys hawled wood after going the mill. I piled some manure and gathered some fruit, cut & pealed some

23. These are Francis M. Lyman's sixteen-year-old sister, Lelia Deseret Lyman, and his five-year-old son, Francis M. Lyman Jr.

24. Ezra J. Clark was the oldest son of Ezra T. and Mary Clark. On the crossing from Europe, he complained of a severe headache and died in New York on the train.

25. People liked reading Washington's Farewell Address (see entry for Dec. 9, 1862). A written document, rather than a speech, he composed it toward the end of his second term as US president in defense of the Constitution.

peaches. In the evening some indication of beter weather. In the afternoon called to see the young son of br John Pilling who had his head crushed by a wagon wheel he appeared very low altho said to be brighter than before since his hurt.[26] To me his recovery seemed quite doubtful tho his friends were encouraged this evening. ~~This evening Amon son of brother Nathan Tinney called and staid over night. He was going to Round Valley after flour.~~

October 6, 1868; Tuesday. Brother Amon Tiney son of Nathan called and staid all night. He was on his way to Round Valley after flour. ~~This morning brother Pillings son died.~~ Spent most of the day fixing some stabling for my horses. In the evening cut some corn and worked some in the fruit. ~~Brother Tinney left early this morning. To day Theodore fell from a tree and lamed his arm.~~

October 7, 1868; Wednesday. ~~To day brother Tiney return and passed on his way home. He left with me one bushel of wheat. Commenced strip[p]ing my cane. We have had frost the two last nights.~~[27] Brother [Ammon] Tiney left early this morning. Resumed work on my stable and in the course of the day went with brother [Alfred] Gull to see some of the molasses makers in relation to makeing up our cane. To day Theodore while out after wood fell from a tree and lamed his arm. For the two last nights we have had hard frost.

October 8, 1868; Thursday. Brother [Ammon] Tiney returned and passed on his way home he left with one bushel of wheat. To day commenced the strip[p]ing of my cane, and visited brother [Joseph] Prisby who promised to grind my cane whenever I could bring it in. The weather slightly warmer.

October 9, 1868; Friday. To day had some six hands at work. This morning my son Edward L. [Lyman] came and asked me if I wished him to work for me and went to work like a man.[28] May the Lord by his spirit strengthen in his mind every good and right feeling, is my prayr on his behalf. I rose this morning and worked an hour before the sun was

26. Six-year-old Jesse Pilling succumbed to the injury the next day.

27. Fillmore was far enough south that people found they could grow sugarcane as easily as wheat. The town is "humid and subtropical," even though it sits at an elevation of 5,000 feet. See, e.g., Sorenson, "Biography of Hans Olaus Sorenson," 9.

28. Eleven-year-old Edward Leo Lyman was Amasa's and Lydia's son. His parents were estranged, so this gesture was one of independence and loyalty to his father.

up and when it went down I found myself quite weary. Read in Deseret News the report of the success of the revolution in Spain.[29]

October 10, 1868; Saturday. Help same as yesterday, at noon had finished strip[p]ing cane and then went to cuting up corn. My morning's work was in cleaning up my corr[a]ll and repairing fence and then spent most of the day in gathering peaches. At night some of our neighbor's boys helped us cut peaches. Oscar was at work repairing the cain mill of brother [Jacob] Croft, had some grinding at ~~the~~ ^our^ mill this week. Our custom is increasing.

October 11, 1868; Sunday. Passed the day mostly at home. In the evening called to see a sick child of brother Jones's. Brother [William] Gibbs had my wagon and teams to take his family and some friends out for a ride.

October 12, 1868; Monday. Commenced cuting and hawling our cain but did not get through. Today saw and spoke with brother Charles [W.] Dalton and Edward Thompson they were returning from conference. Br D's son Brigham died during his absence.[30]

October 13, 1868; Tuesday. Concluded our hawling of cain. In the evening Marion returned from conference and reported brother [William] Clayton and family well.[31] Weather pleasant during conference.

October 14, 1868; Wednesday. Made some preserves and hawled our pumice [volcanic rock] an[d] covered our stable. The boys gathered the [sugar] cain leaves and tops and in the afternoon they cut some corn, took our preserves home ~~at night and~~ our molasses was made during the night.

October 15, 1868; Thursday. Hawled our cain leaves and topings and stacked them for winter feed. In the evening brought our molasses home our share was 57 gallons. At night read the minutes of the General Conference from which I learned that G[eorge] A. Smith was selected by Prest [Brigham] Young as his First Councilor and that Brigham Young Jr was appointed one of the Twelve Apostles.[32]

---

29. In the Glorious Revolution of 1868, Queen Isabella II was ousted in favor of Prince Amadeo of Italy, but soon Isabella's family was back in power through her son Alfonso.

30. Brigham W. Dalton was fourteen when he died–but no notice of this in the *Deseret News*. His father, Charles W. Dalton, had about forty children by five wives.

31. Two years earlier, Lyman's seventeen-year-old daughter Maria Louisa became the seventh wife of fifty-two-year-old William Clayton. It would have been reason for family unity except that Amasa was associating with dissidents. Maria Louisa would soon come to side with her father and divorced Clayton in 1871.

32. George A. Smith replaced Heber C. Kimball, who died in June 1868. Brigham

October 16, 1868; Friday. To day was cuting and hawling corn and stacking it up for it to ripen. During the day my son-in-law [Isaac] Philo Carter and his [nine-year-old] son Amasa M. [Carter] came from Beaver and Amasa's M. [Lyman] Jr brought me from Beaver 12 bunches of cotten yarn and Father [Timothy B.] Foot[33] from Salt Creek [Nephi] called to see me. In the evening A. M. Jr called to see me. Oscar is stil working for brother [Jacob] Croft repairing his ^molasses^ mill.

October 17, 1868; Saturday. Today cut and hawled corn. In the afternoon brother Edwin Walker and brother John Steel called on me an[d] I paid to brother Steel seven dollars and a half which I owed him for lucern[e] [alfalfa] seed. Did not quite complete cuting of my corn. Weather very fine and favorable for saveing crops. In the evening with my wife Louisa made a call on the family of brother Clarence Merrill where we meet our old much esteemed friend Bathsheba [Smith] wife of President G[eorge] A. Smith who had come to visit her daughter Mrs. [Bathsheba Smith] Merrill.[34]

October 18, 1868; Sunday. This morning meet with Father [Samuel] White returning to his residence in Beaver from the conference. Had a report from my miller of increasing custom [toll charged to farmers] to the mill. Weather stil continues warm and pleasant. In the evening Brother Lorenzo Barton and brother Heber Benson[,] Sister [Phoebe] Benson and Sister Elizabeth Grimshaw on their way to the city they stayed with us all night.[35] Miss Grimshaw brought me a letter from my

---

Young had ordained a son, Brigham Jr., as an apostle in 1864 but had not yet added him to the Quorum of the Twelve. There would later be tension between Brigham Jr. and Joseph F. Smith, who was added to the quorum in 1866, but ultimately Smith was recognized as having greater seniority.

33. Timothy B. Foote, originally from New York, was a sixty-eight-year-old veteran of the War of 1812 and among the first settlers of Nephi, where he lived until his death in 1886.

34. Bathsheba W. Bigler Smith was George A. Smith's first of seven wives. She had served in the Relief Society presidency under Eliza R. Snow and became president of the organization herself in 1901. Her son-in-law Clarence ran the Fillmore telegraph office. Heidi S. Swinton, "'Peace be with You,': Bathsheba Wilson Bigler Smith," in Turley and Chapman, *Women of Faith*, 2:349–65; Jenson, *Latter-day Saint Biographical Encyclopedia*, 2:391–92.

35. Nineteen-year-old Heber Benson was going to Salt Lake with his mother and father, Phoebe and Heber, to be sealed to eighteen-year-old Elizabeth Grimshaw in the Endowment House.

wife Paulina in Parrowan. She wrote me that she had got the wagon repaired and that Lorenzo was hawling wood, the repairing of wagon cost 27 dollars.

October 19, 1868; Monday. This morning I finished cuting my corn. The boys were engaged in hawling corn. Visited my mill paid Judge [Thomas R.] King five dollars and owe him 2½ dollars more. Lelia is weaveing to day and br Isaac Carlin came an[d] took a draft of some parts of our loom. In the evening I divided our small stock of molasses preparitory to sending some to Paulina and Dionitia in Parrowan & Minersville. Weather continues pleasant. Oscar furnished 6 gallons of molasses out of his earnings for his mother.

October 20, 1868; Tuesday. Hawled corn with the boys the weather warm and pleasant. To day I noticed the masons were at work on the new store of King and Sons.[36] In the evening visited my mill and found the custom [toll] increasing. On my return called at the molasses mill of brother [Jacob] Croft which is reported to be doing well since its repair.

October 21, 1868; Wednesday. To day finished hawling corn and commenced husking. Took my cariage wheels to the shop to have the tire set. In the afternoon wrote letter to my wife Paulina in Parrowan. In the evening worked at my corn by the light of the moon for one or two hours. To day hear of the death of Samuel White of Beaver. His death being caused by an old ailment.[37]

October 22, 1868; Thursday. Was buisy with my corn and my own thoughts as I was alone, the boys being engaged elsewhere most of the day. I worked until near midnight in the corn.

October 23, 1868; Friday. Made arangements with brother [John] Pilling to have my horses shod. In the afternoon took a load of corn to my mill for storage and on returning to my house I learned that Oscar had scalded his arm and hand as he was preparing to dress a pig for Eliza. Worked a while by the light of the moon and shortly after retiring we were notified that some passing cows had torn down the bars and were luxurating on my corn. We drove them out and tied up the gate and then

36. This is the store of Thomas R. King. Lyman's daughter Caroline was married to King's son Volney, although they would divorce three years later in 1871.

37. According to the *Deseret News*, he had been ill for years. State records indicate a liver malfunction. "Obituary," *Deseret News*, Oct. 28, 1868.

retired to rest. I found that the late planting of my crop did not afford the small pop corn time to mature.

October 24, 1868; Saturday. Was at work before the sun rose. This morning received a sac of flour from brother Stephen Franklin of Minersville by the hand of brother [William E.] Banks who reported our friends there all well. Today Canosh ^(Indian Chief!)^[38] called in to dine with us, the local conference is in session. Elder Erastus Snow of the Twelve was present at the afternoon session. In the evening there was a meeting to make preliminary arangements for the stock-drive.

October 25, 1868; Sunday. The day opened fine and pleasant Colonel [Alden A. M.] Jackson called to see me he was on his way to Salt Lake City. I had not seen him since 1857 until now. The conference closed its session with the close of the evening meeting. Some fifteen names of members that were cut off from the Church [were read].

October 26, 1868; Monday. Was early at work in my corn and the streets were enlivened by the returning Saints going to their homes. To day the masons commenced to work on [my] new house again. Was husking corn until 9 or 10 oclock. The weather is geting slightly cool. Made a call at the grist-mill, there is some indication of change of weather.

October 27, 1868; Tuesday. Met brother [William] Gibbs at the new house to determine some points in the work. To day the miller took up and sharpened the mill and cleared away the deposit of gravel at the bottom of [the] draft tube and was grinding. In the evening some clouds were hanging around was working in the corn until late bed time.

October 28, 1868; Wednesday. This morning the most of the clouds of yesterday were gone but the wind was high. At noon Theodore went out and brought in our horse and mule. About 9 oclock this evening finished husking my corn.

October 29, 1868; Thursday. Some rain falling. Marion and brother [Seymour] Brunson returned from Deseret.[39] After their arival we experienced a light snow squall. Theodore went out on the horse drive to get stock for the cattle drive. Some squalls in the afternoon with some indications of beter weather. At sunset the air [was] cool and frosty.

38. This parenthetical was added by a later editor. The Pahvant tribe lived at the western edge of the mountains between Fillmore and Cove Fort on Corn Creek. Kanosh converted to Mormonism in the 1850s.

39. Deseret is a small town about thirty miles northwest of Fillmore.

October 30, 1868; Friday. This morning clear but cool and frosty spent some time clearing manure in my corr[a]l. Caried the last of my corn to the mill spent some time with brother [William] Gibbs. Had a [weaving] reel mended for [Marion's wife] Rhoda. Spent the evening in reading.

October 31, 1868; Saturday. To day brother Alfred Gull[40] helped me stack my corn foder. Brothers [Lorenzo] Barton and [Heber] Benson called and dined with us they we[re] returning from Salt Lake City. Brother B was maried while at the city to Miss Elizabeth Gr^i^mshaw. Weather warm and pleasant. Past the evening in reading.

November 1, 1868; Sunday. ~~August~~ Weather clear & bright, attended Church to day the first time since April 1867. Bishop [Thomas] Callister invited me to speak which I did for a short time.[41] Attended the Sabbath school and in the evening attended meeting. The audience was addressed by Bishop Callister during meeting Bishop John R. Murdock & Joseph W. Young came in. The later spoke to us on the principle of a general co-operative system in trade manufacturing and mechanical labor.[42] Weather slightly warmer than in the morning.

November 2, 1868; Monday. This morning took breakfast with brother Gabriel Huntsman & family. Brother J[oseph] W. Young and family, who were on their way to city were there. Procured some acounts from br John Pilling of work done for our mill and had the ^same^ entered in our acount of investment. In the evening brother Allen Russell called to see if I would let our school district have some land on which to build a school house.[43] Read some tonight, the masons were working on the house today. The mill had work steadily for some days.

November 3, 1868; Tuesday. This morning gave order to Thomas R.

---

40. Alfred Gull was a recent British convert who settled in Fillmore in the late 1860s and became a bishop's counselor. His wife Mary went blind shortly after they arrived.

41. Lyman's return to church lasted only eighteen months, although during that time he received visits from the apostles and an invitation from Brigham Young to join the local School of the Prophets study group.

42. Brigham Young had said that those who traded with "outsiders [should] be excommunicated." In October the Council of Fifty voted to set up a church cooperative they called Zion's Cooperative Mercantile Institution (ZCMI). Campbell, *Establishing Zion*, 317–19; Rogers, *Council of Fifty*, 254–55.

43. The first settlers in Fillmore finished a schoolhouse within fifteen days of arriving. Later they appropriated the former statehouse as a school. It is unknown if Lyman donated his land. Lyman and Newell, *History of Millard County*, 46, 139.

King for one hundred lbs. of flour. Weather clear & pleasant, Past most of the day at my mill sorting my corn. Past the evening in reading the night was quite cool. My boys Ira, Fredrick & Edward[44] have been hawling wood for three days and Theodore is out in the cattle drive.

November 4, 1868; Wednesday. I passed the most of the day at the mill with my corn and as I came home I saw Homer Duncan[45] & his father John who was baptized at the same place and time that I was, in the month of April 1832. Oscar was out in the drive of stock. To day some clouds. This evening in the evening gathered out some of my stock. The drive was rather a meager one. Read in the evening.

November 5, 1868; Thursday. This morning was early in the corr[a]l gathering the residue of my stock. Father [John] Duncan called on me again this morning. Was buisy most of the day branding my stock preparitory to takeing them to Black Rock Springs. Past the evening in reading the Telegraph on volcanoes, that transpired while the editor was in Francisco.[46]

November 6, 1868; Friday. Was up before the chickens. Called and was at the mill stiring my corn to prevent it from heating after which had my breakfast and then attended to & finished our preparations of our stock for the drive to Black Rock Spring.[47] Past the evening reading. Stormed some in the afternoon.

November 7, 1868; Saturday. Was up early and after some delay we started our stock for the Ranch. I sent twenty four head and Marion sent 49 head, the weather was quite stormy. I sent Oscar and Ira with the stock and Marion had charge and the Bishop [Thomas Callister] sent two hands. After the stock left I had a beef killed. Rain and snow squalls continued through the day. Spent the evening reading Constitution of United States. During the night some light snow fell.

November 8, 1868; Sunday. Atttended church in the morning and

44. Frederick Rich Lyman was the twelve-year-old son of Lyman and Caroline Partridge.

45. Homer was Chapman's brother. "Autobiography of Chapman Duncan, 1812–1900."

46. Lyman was reading about the Great San Francisco Earthquake of 1868, actually centered in the East Bay on October 21.

47. Black Rock Springs is fifty miles southwest of Fillmore between Cove Fort and Sevier Lake, the location of Lyman's corral and pastures.

Sabbath School in the afternoon and wrote two letters one to my son Lorenzo and one to my wife Paulina in Parrowan Iron County. Attended church in the evening. The audience was addressed by Elder Hyrum Mace[48] and Bishop [Thomas] Callister. Weather quite cool received a call to day from my old and valued friend Nathan C. Tinny who was enroute for San Pete for bread. His residence is in Toquervill in dixy.

November 9, 1868; Monday. In the morning took care of my beef and then spent some time in fileing my letters and papers. Made a visit to my mill spent the morning in reading in the afternoon received a few bushels of potatoes from the Tithing [office]. Past the evening reading. The swelling in my side gives me much pain which hinders me from sleeping. Weather quite cool.

November 10, 1868; Tuesday. This morning assisted Theodore to prepare my wagon f[or] hawling wood then spent the most of the day in repairing and clearing up my horse stable. Found by examination that my stacks of corn foder were heating badly. In the afternoon went to the mill to grind my axe (not a political one).[49] Was in so much pain I could not read to night. The weather slightly moderating passed an almost sleepless night.

November 11, 1868; Wednesday. The swelling on my side gave me so much pain that I was not able to work. Visited the mill which was reported by the miller to be doing good buisness. In the evening the boys returned from Black Rock Springs, they reported the loss of one of my calves, which ran away from them at Corn Creek. Theodore hawled a load of wood.

November 12, 1868; Thursday. Attended meeting and in the afternoon baptism was administered and some of my family were baptized the confirmation was attended to in the evening.[50] Oscar & Theodore went on the range north after a mule. Some clouds around the horizon the weather somewhat warmer.

November 13, 1868; Friday. Passed most of the day at the mill grinding my axes for the boys and sawed out some lumber for finishing my

48. Hiram Mace converted in 1841 in Michigan and helped found Fillmore, dying there in 1896 shortly after being ordained a patriarch.

49. Aside from the attempt at humor, Lyman's idiom is interesting because it entered the language fairly recently in the 1790s, according to the *Oxford English Dictionary.*

50. This may have been a rebaptism, commonly practiced at the time.

cariage top. The swelling on my side was very painful. Oscar and Theodore came home this evening without the mule. I received to day 3 dollars for flour.

November 14, 1868; Saturday. Worked in the shop framed a washboard and made a singletree.[51] Proposed to sell a cow to the merchant to whom I had been paying money for goods for the last few months. He told me very coolly that he could not pay me any money on the cow. I as coolly concluded that I would keep my property and let him alone with his money. The custom [toll] increases steadily at the mill. My cousin Mr. James Day came into the town by southern stage. Brother [William] Marsden and party stayed with us on his way to the city.

November 15, 1868; Sunday. This morning meet with Cousin [James] Day who attended church with us. After meeting went with my cousin to see my mill after which ~~my~~ we went to his Hotel,[52] after we went to church when the word reached us that a highway robery had been commited about 12 miles north of our town by Willis the son of brother Noah Bartholomew ~~on~~.[53] The men rob[b]ed were traviling to Paranigat.[54] A watch was instituted when Wilis was discovered returning from the south when sheriff [Byron] Warner and party attempted his arest when several shots were exchanged between the Sheriff's party and Bartholomew resulting in the breaking of the leg of Wiliam King and the escape of the rob[b]er who left no sign of having been injured by the shooting. This evening had a proposition from the Bishop [Callister] and brother [Hiram] Mase to teach a school, I did not accept their offer.[55]

November 16, 1868; Monday. This morning meet with brother [Noah] Bartholomew who with his family were in deep trouble on acount of

51. A singletree connects a harness to a buggy.

52. This was probably the Bartholomew Inn, attached to Noah Bartholomew's home.

53. The twenty-eight-year-old highwayman hid in a ditch until the travelers appeared. Surprising them, he was able to steal $40 and a saddle and horse blankets. After eluding the posse, he came to live in California for fifty years, dying in the Central Valley in the town of Hollister. "Home Items," *Deseret News*, Dec. 2, 9, 1868; "Willis Bartholomew," Standard Certificate of Death, California State Board of Health, Oct. 1, 1917.

54. The Pahranagat Valley was accessible off of a Nevada trail that branched off of the main Mormon path to southern California.

55. Lyman would himself begin attending grammar school by the end of the month. See his entry for November 30.

the conduct of their son. I also called on brother William King. He ~~was~~ seemed to be doing well. In course of the forenoon the Sheriff and party started in pursuit of the rob[b]er. My son Marion was of the company and Oscar started for Parrowan. At the leaving of the sherifs party it was reported that blood was found which was supposed to be that of the escaped rob[b]er. The weather quite pleasant.

Brother Jehu Blackburn[56] called and took a small package of molasses to my wife Dionitia in Minersville. Loaned my wagon to George Gull to go to the city. In the evening he returned it having procured another. At night the party that went in quest of the rober returned having learned that he went to Corn Creek and there stole a horse and went on. Spent most of the day in repairing the fence around my place between me and Bishop [Thomas] Callister. In the evening brother [Nathan C.] Tinney returned and stoped at my place.

November 17, 1868; Tuesday. Past most of the day in helping my folks do some warping[57] and during the day brother [Nathan C.] Tinney went with me to see my ~~m~~ mill and then spent the evening with me and promised to carry some molasses & fruit to my wife [Paulina] in Parrowan.

November 18, 1868; Wednesday. Worked at the shop making some addition to my warping reel. Brother [Nathan C.] Tinney left for home this morning. In the evening worked on some fixtures for my loom. Read letter from my daughter Mrs. [Maria Louisa] Clayton [addressed] to Marion.

November 19, 1868; Thursday. Worked at shop preparing some lumber for my cariage. The weather continues very fine, work brisk at the mill. To day Marion began to build his kitchen.

November 20, 1868; Friday. Worked at the shop on my cariage top. The boys went to the bench [foothills] for some timber. Work was increasing at the mill.

November 21, 1868; Saturday. Worked at shop in the forenoon and attended the meeting of the Sabbath School during which two home missionaries Commissioner Campbell & Elder Edward Stephenson

56. Jehu Blackburn was one of the earliest arrivals in the Salt Lake Valley. He was also among the first in Provo, Fillmore, and Minersville. Indicating his respect for Lyman, he named one of his children Amasa Lyman Blackburn.

57. Yarn had to be cut and wound onto reels before weaving. See the next entry.

came and both addressed the meeting.[58] In the evening the school children had their dance which I attended. Some rain in the evening.

November 22, 1868; Sunday. Attended church the audience was addressed by Elders [Edward] S[tevenson] and C[ampbell]. In the afternoon attended Sabbath School. Brother Cambell addressed the school. Attended meeting at night the audience was addressed by Elders S. & C. on the subject of education and its value to the Saints in the development of the work of God in building his kingdom. The weather somewhat stormy.

November 23, 1868; Monday. Worked in the shop. To day brother [William] Gibbs made some preperation for steeming wheat as we grind. Our custom [toll] is on the increase. Our missionaries left to day for the north. Pas[s]ed the evening in reading.

November 24, 1868; Tuesday. Worked on my cariage at the shop and during the day came home to mend a break in our loom in which I succeeded and the weaveing went on and I to my work. Passed the evening reading. Weather dull and cloudy.

November 25, 1868; Wednesday. Worked on my cariage at the shop in the forenoon. In the afternoon came home and worked on the body of cariage. Received a visit from Sister Sarah Driggs[59] wife and widow of Sterling Driggs. This evening my son in law Philo Carter and wife and children called and staid all night. They were on their way to the city they left their children all but the youngest with us until their return. Priscella's babe was slightly indisposed. Theodore hawled wood.

November 26, 1868; Thursday. Went to the shop, and had my cariage top brought home and put it on and borrowed Marion's wagon cover and put over it. Priscilla's babe is beter this evening. Passed the evening in reading some scientific mat[t]er. Bought slate and pencil for the mill for which I was to pay fifty fivee cents. The weather quite warm and pleasant for the season.

November 27, 1868; Friday. Went to the mill worked some time preparing to cover the well to prevent it from freezing. Marion went to

58. Home missionaries were assigned to missions where they lived. They mostly visited lapsed members and encouraged orthodoxy among those who were regular attenders. Taysom, *Shakers, Mormons, and Religious Worlds*, 177–78.

59. Lyman knew Sarah and Sterling Driggs in San Bernardino. She would die in 1911 in Snowflake, Arizona.

Round Valley to attend muster.[60] To day received two dollars for flour, the boys brought a load of wood. Weather warm & pleasant.

November 28, 1868; Saturday. Worked at the mill most of the day. In the evening brother Joseph Tanner, from Payson called, and staid over night. He was on his way to Dixie in response to the call of the Conference of Oct last.[61]

November 29, 1868; Sunday. Morning pleasant, took a walk to my mill with brother [Joseph] Tanner after which I went to church. Attended Sabbath School in the afternoon and by request of superintendent I spoke to the school. Attended meeting in the evening. The audience was addressed by Elders [Edward] Partridge and F[rancis] M[arion] Lyman.

November 30, 1868; Monday. This morning brother [William] Marsden went on his way homeward. Sold and delivered a cow and calf to G[abriel] Huntsman & Co for forty dollars, one half cash and half in goods. Went to the mill. This morning wrote to brother [William] Clayton to buy me some Duc[k] to cover my carriage.[62] In the evening commenced attending Gramer [grammar] school. Brother [John] Kelly was our teacher, we recited two lessons. The class is to meet three times a week.

December 1, 1868; Tuesday. Worked at the mill helping to dress the burrs [deepen the millstone furrows] and making some improvements around the mill. In the evening gave lessons in gramer to some of my children. Late in the evening my son Lorenzo arived from Parrowan having left his brother Henry at Corn Creek with brother [Collins] Hakes. Lorenzo informed me that Oscar was at work for brother [Ebenezer] Hanks at the iron works.

December 2, 1868; Wednesday. Worked at the mill the most of the day. In the afternoon procured some materials for trimming my cariage. Lorenzo and Ira went to Corn Creek and brought Henry home with them. At night with Lorenzo I attended the gramer school.

---

60. Round Valley was the site of the largest skirmish in the Black Hawk War in 1866, a year into a conflict that would last another five years. Young men from throughout the region were conscripted into the territorial militia. Spencer, "The Utah Black Hawk War," 33–36.

61. Lyman's brother-in-law, Joseph S. Tanner, was called to the Muddy River settlements for two years, and he would later become the bishop of Payson.

62. As late as 1904, buggies were advertised as having waterproof "oiled duck" trim. *The Hub*, Apr. 1904, 312.

December 3, 1868; Thursday. Attended meeting the Saints were instructed principally by the bishop [Thomas Callister]. In the evening I gave lessons in gramer to my children and a les^s^on in spelling [in] which they were tolerably proficient. To day the most of the joists were laid on the new house.

December 4, 1868; Friday. I worked repairing my wagon. In the afternoon there were some indications of a storm and in the evening I attended the gramer school. At the close of the school the snow was falling fast. I procured some stationary preparitory to taking lessons in book keeping. The cold is growing more intense the masons worked on the new house to day.

December 5, 1868; Saturday. I passed the day mostly at home. Bought a pair of shoes for Henry and had a birthday din[ner] as it was Hila's[63] eleventh birthday. In the evening I gave the boys some lessons in reading & spelling. I sent nineteen lbs of spring steel[64] to Paulina in Parrowan by brother Edward Dalton. The weather is colder than it was yesterday.

December 6, 1868; Sunday. I attended meeting and also Sabbath School in the school house. In the evening attended a meeting of the brethren of the ward at which it was determined that the City Council should be sustained in enforcing the laws of the city and the teritory against gambling & and other disordily conduct. The weather still cold.

December 7, 1868; Monday. I repaired my wagon and worked some at the mill to prevent the water from running into our shop. Bought a hat for Ira. Attended the gramer school. In the evening weather very cold and freezing. Theodore & Ira commenced going to school.

December 8, 1868; Tuesday. Bought a [s]helve for my axe and hung it, and mended my harness. At night ~~attended school~~ [I] gave lessons to my class at home.

December 9, 1868; Wednesday. To day worked some in shop. In the afternoon Philo & Matilda returned from the city and brought me some duck for the covering of my cariage. I attended school. At the school

63. Agnes Hila Lyman was the daughter of Amasa and Maria Louisa.

64. The hoop skirt that was popular in the 1860s had a steel cage under the dress. Steel was not available in quantity and was used only for small domestic items such as knives, razors, clocks, and dresses. Stamper and Condra, *Clothing through American History*, 88–89.

teacher Kelly anounced the death of Prest Daniel Spencer on the morning of the 8th.[65] The weather slightly moderating.

December 10, 1868; Thursday. I worked in the shop during the forepart of the day & about noon Philo and family started for their home in Beaver & in the afternoon I wrote to br Wm Clayton and sent him ten dollars to pay for my cariage cover. The weather cloudy with indications of snow. This evening I gave lessons to my class at home as we retired the snow was falling.

December 11, 1868; Friday. I worked in the shop and in the evening attended the gramer school. There was a dancing pa[r]ty in the hall over our heads which annoyed us very much.

December 12, 1868; Saturday. I worked in the shop and during the day John L. Smith[66] moved his chest of tools preparitory to commencing work for brother [William] Gibbs. This evening received a letter from brother Wm Clayton.

December 13, 1868; Sunday. Attended church in the morning and Sabbath School in the afternoon and meeting in the evening. The meetings were addressed by Bishop [Thomas] Callister and Elders J[ohn] L. Smith[,] H[iram] Mace and F[rancis] M. Lyman. The weather very cold.

December 14, 1868; Monday. Heard the report to day that the experiment in makeing iron on Little Pinto had proved a success. Worked in the shop and attended school in the evening. Weather still very cold.

December 15, 1868; Tuesday. In the morning studied my gramer lesson and then went to the shop where I remained at work until nearly sundown then came home and attended a school meeting of the citizens of the third district called for the purpose of organizing the district, by electing a board of trustees. Thomas R. King[,] Benjamin Robison and James Owens were elected. Lorenzo gave lesson to the children for me to night.

December 16, 1868; Wednesday. I worked in the shop and in the evening attended gramer school. The weather is more mild. Custom is increasing at the mill.

---

65. The former mayor of Nauvoo and president of the Salt Lake Stake had "delicate" health, according to his obituary in the *Deseret News*, Dec. 16, 1868.

66. John Lyman Smith was the forty-year-old brother of George A. Smith. His mother, Clarissa Lyman, was a distant cousin of Amasa Lyman. Henrie, *The Edward Leo Lyman and Mary Miranda Callister Lyman Family*, 266.

December 17, 1868; Thursday. I began the building of a been [bin] for grain in my mill and in the evening gave lessons to the children.

December 18, 1868; Friday. I finished my grain bin and some other work in the shop. Some storm in the afternoon. In the evening attended school. Early in the evening the snow ~~walling~~ was falling.

December 19, 1868; Saturday. To day made some improvement on the mill-yard, and assisted brother [William] Gibbs in the mill. Found myself very weary at night passed the evening in study.

December 20, 1868; Sunday. I attended church in the morning. Before going to the meeting I received a call from brother S[eth] M. Blair, from the iron works on little Pinto in Washington County. He went to meeting with us and addressed the audience for a short time giveing us the information that the experiments in making iron were a complete success. Brother B. was in quite delicate health, he was going to Salt Lake City where a portion of his family reside some of whom were sick.

December 21, 1868; Monday. This morning brother [Seth M.] Blair resumed his journey. I worked in the shop making some stairs for my house. In the evening Elijah Maxfield[67] and a part of his family called on us and staid all night also Albert Tanner from Beaver, I attended school this evening.

December 22, 1868; Tuesday. Worked in the shop and in the afternoon made some changes with my cariage in preparing it for covering. The weather growing quite warm.

December 23, 1868; Wednesday. Cut up my pig and worked on my cariage and in the evening went to school and bought the first Deseret [Alphabet] Book,[68] in which we read several lesons before close of school. The weather softning somewhat with indications of storm.

December 24, 1868; Thursday. Passed the day mostly in reading. Some rain during the day the snow melted quite fast. In the evening gave lesons to my [children's home-school] gramer class.

December 25, 1868; Friday. Did not engage in labor to day. Visited my mill where I received a call from brothers Gabriel Huntsman & John

67. Elijah Maxfield was a ranch hand twenty miles south of San Bernardino in the 1850s, so he had probably met Lyman. In Utah he became a Pony Express rider, then a rancher. Hansen, "History of Elijah Hiett Maxfield."

68. That is, the first reader for learning the phonetic Deseret Alphabet (see note under Feb. 5, 1856).

Turner after which I went with brother [William] Gibbs to examine our mill-race which we found needing repairs in some places. In the evening went to the State hall to witness the [Christmas] dance; came home at twenty minutes past ten oclock.

December 26, 1868; Saturday. In the morning past some time with brother [John] Kelly examining some work on education and in the afternoon attended gramer school from 1 until 5 oclock.

December 27, 1868; Sunday. Attended meeting in the morning and Sabbath School in the evening. At meeting at night, when we were entertained by br Joseph V. Robison with a relation of his experience in Mormonism and spiritualism.[69] Weather slightly cooler.

December 28, 1868; Monday. Spent a portion of the day in study. Visited the mill and at night attended gramer school. There were only five pupils in attendance we had a visit from teacher Shelton. To day Lorenzo sprained his ankle so as to hinder him from working.

December 29, 1868; Tuesday. Called on the Bishop [Thomas Callister] who was in rather poor health and while there meet with brothers [Daniel P.] Clark and [Riley] Morse from Parrowan and brother [Ira] Hinckly from Cove Creek. Brothers Clark and Morse went to see my mill with which they were hi[gh]ly pleased.

December 30, 1868; Wednesday. Passed the day mostly at home with my studies. To day heard of the murder of a man in Parrowan by his felow workman.[70]

December 31, 1868; Thursday. Passed most of the day in study and some work on my cariage curtains. In the evening had a fall of a few inches of snow.

January 1, 1869; Friday. Passed the day mostly at home. At night attended the party at the hall the weather quite warm and the snow quite soft. Had no gramar school to night on acount of the dance.

January 2, 1869; Saturday. To day had a settlement with Marion when by agrement he became owner of one third of our mill in consideration

---

69. Lyman doesn't mention his own interest in spirit communication. The movement originated with sisters Margaret and Kate Fox in 1848 and spread during the Civil War to the point that even Mary Todd Lincoln participated in séances in the White House. Lyman's interest would grow over the next few months. Doyle, *History of Spiritualism*, 1:83–90; Weisburg, *Talking to the Dead*; Faust, *This Republic of Suffering*.

70. No murder was reported in the *Deseret News*.

for the property and labor he had invested. In the afternoon I went to the mill and while in conversation with brother [William] Gibbs on platform in front of the mill and leaning against the railing it gave way. I was precipitated to the ground a distance of some 11 ft, my head strikeing on a solid rock inflicting a severe contusion and at the same time breaking the thumb of my left hand at the first joint. With these injuries I was confined the most of the time to my house until Feb.

February 28, 1869; Sunday. When I started for Beaver with the mail[71] traviled to and lodged at Cove Creek.

March 1, 1869; Monday. Arived in Beaver. Call at the residence of Father [Theodore] Turley who was absent from home at the iron works. Lodged at brother [Albert] Tanners.

March 2, 1869; Tuesday. Called on brother [Horace A.] Skiner and wrote letter to my wife M[aria] L[ouisa] in Fillmore and bought some [postage] stamps and lodged with Bishop [John R.] Murdock.[72]

March 3, 1869; Wednesday. Bishop [John R.] M[urdock] let me have some farming tools. Lodged with the bishop.

March 4, 1869; Thursday. Went to Minersville found my wife Dionitia and her mother [Nancy Walker] well, whom I had not seen for one year.

March 5, 1869; Friday. Went to see the new mill house erected by Nelson Holingshead.[73] It is quite a creditable work, sufered much from my sores day and night.

March 6, 1869; Saturday. Visited John [James] H. Rollins and family. My sores were some better today.

March 7, 1869; Sunday. Visited Sister Mary Lightner and made some calls in evening.

March 8, 1869; Monday. Passed the day at home did not go out.

---

71. The mail came by freight wagon to the LDS bishop's house in Beaver, where people throughout the region dropped off and picked up their mail. Merkley, ed., *Monuments to Courage*, 110; cf. Bancroft, *History of Utah*, 769.

72. This last entry and the previous two in Lyman's journal were duplicated in his daybook, while subsequent entries through Mar. 28 were recorded in daybook 30 after the 1869 entries.

73. According to the 1870 census, Nelson Stoyell Hollinshead, 45, was a millwright who was living with his wife, Mehetable, 40, and a "helper," Mary Elizabeth, 25. In actuality, Mary Elizabeth was a plural wife. She and Nelson had already had four children together. In 1884, Nelson was impaled by a tree branch in a wagon accident and died.

March 9, 1869; Tuesday. Visited and dined with Sister Phebe Bingham.[74]

March 10, 1869; Wednesday. Visited br. [James] McNight[75] and family.

March 11, 1869; Thursday. Visited Bishop James H. Rollins and family. Saw bishop [John R.] Murdock as he was going home from the Black Rock Springs.

March 12, 1869; Friday. ~~Thursday~~ This morning I returned to Beaver where I meet with Prest G[eorge] A Smith & Elders E[rastus] Snow & J[oseph] F. Smith of the Quorum of Twelve & other Elders they greeted me cordialy. Lodged with Bishop M[arcus] L. Shepherd.

March 13, 1869; Saturday. Traviled to Parrowan with brother Thomas Taylor. Found my family well.

March 14, 1869; Sunday. Attended meeting at which the Stake of Iron County was organized in due form.

March 15, 1869; Monday. This morning the missionaries left for the south.

March 16, 1869; Tuesday. Remained at home paid some attention to the building of some machinery for drilling grain. During the day I called on father [Samuel] Gould who was in a helpless & dying condition. Richard Benson & wife dined with us today.

March 17, 1869; Wednesday. To day wrote letters to Fillmore to my family and witnessed the trial of the drilling machine.

March 18, 1869; Thursday. Remained at home.

March 19, 1869; Friday. Dined to day with brother [Ebenezer] Hank's family. In the evening Oscar came home from the Iron Works. During this week we have had some snow.

March 20, 1869; Saturday. Wrote up my journal.

March 21, 1869; Sunday. Attended meeting in the morning the audience was addressed by visiting brethren from Cedar City. Dined with brother [Daniel] Page & family, in the evening br [Ebenezer] Hanks came home from the Iron Works. Tonight had a fall of snow.

---

74. Phebe Bingham was known for selling buckskin gloves (she had the only sewing machine in town), along with her husband's shoes and buggy whips. Her husband also taught dancing and raised cattle.

75. After James McKnight and his young wife migrated from Scotland to Australia in the 1840s in search of gold, they ended up converting to Mormonism and immigrating to Utah. He became the bishop of Minersville in 1867.

March 22, 1869; Monday. Passed the day mostly with brother [Ebenezer] Hanks and family. Read some in Journal of Health.

March 25, 1869; Thursday.[76] Friday. Today Oscar & party started for Salt Lake City and I traviled with them as far as Fillmore.[77]

March 27, 1869; Saturday. Sunday. Taried all night.

March 28, 1869; Sunday. Monday. Oscar and party resumed their journey. I was engaged until Sunday the 4th of April in work about my place.

April 4, 1869; Sunday. Attended church. To day called on br [James] Stokes.

April 5, 1869; Monday. Was engaged in pruning my trees, Theodore was driving horses. Lorenzo mad[e] ready to go to Clear Lake after hay. His company failed to be ready so he did not go. Weather warm no frost at night.

April 6, 1869; Tuesday. Went to the mill and spent the remainder of the day in pruning my fruit trees. Theodore was driveing horses no frost at night Lorenzo went to clear Lake after hay.

April 7, 1869; Wednesday. Finished pruning. Marion arived this morning from the city. I dined with him, after which I exchanged some lumber with brother [Joseph] Prisby then went to the mill with br P. & caried my lumber to the shop preparitory to makeing some gates for my corr[a]l. Lorenzo arived with hay from Clear Lake, weather warm & pleasant.

April 8, 1869; Thursday. Pruned some & went to the mill and sawed my lumber for my gates Weather fine & warm.

April 9, 1869; Friday. Was at work on my place during the forenoon & in the afternoon went to the shop and plained the lumber for my gates. Weather still warm.

April 10, 1869; Saturday. Spent the day in clearing up around the place in which I was assisted by my boys Fredrick & Edward. Lorenzo and Theodore went for wood and Ira was herding horses. Peach trees are promising a rich crop.

April 11, 1869; Sunday. Attended Church in the morning and the Sabbath school in the afternoon and meeting in the evening. Weather

---

76. Lyman labeled this entry "25th Friday," then misdated the next two entries (silently corrected). The Apr. 4–May 28 entries are in a separate journal, vol. 31.

77. Amasa's twenty-one-year-old son, Oscar Morris Lyman, was on his way to the Salt Lake City Endowment House to marry sixteen-year-old Phoebe Madora Benson.

stil warm this morning received a call from brother Albert Stodard from Minersville. He brought letter from Sister [Elizabeth] Franklin.

April 12, 1869; Monday. Worked on water ditch myself & Theodore & Lorenzo harrowed some in the field. Attended a field meeting in the evening at which brother [James] Rooley [Rowley] was appointed watermaster for our ditch.

April 13, 1869; Tuesday. Worked about my place the most of the day in the afternoon went to the mill and moved my house logs down. Home in the morning. Made some 3 head gates for our field irigation, in the afternoon began a cultivator [soil tiller].

April 14, 1869; Wednesday. Was up before the sun and was at work in my garden This morning had severe wind-storm from the north which moved a large amount of dust. Worked some in shop. In the afternoon [my son] Oscar [and new] wife [Phoebe] & [her] mother and [my] wife [Paulina] arived [back from the Endowment House in Salt Lake City].

April 15, 1869; Thursday. Worked in the shop weather windy & rough. Worked some in the garden.

April 16, 1869; Friday. Worked in shop and in the garden. This evening brother E[rastus] Snow & J[ohn] R Murdock arived in town. Br M. passed on.[78]

April 17, 1869; Saturday. Worked in shop. To day heard of the arival in St. George of the body of F. B. Woolly who was murdered on the Mohave by Indians.[79] This morning Oscar & party started for home. Brought home my corall gates. In the afternoon some thunder and hail.

April 18, 1869; Sunday. Raining gently & quite warm did not attend meeting this morning. Attended Sabbath school & meeting at 6 oclock. Meeting was addressed by <u>Prest</u> [Thomas] Callister.[80]

April 19, 1869; Monday. Was engaged in puting up my corr[a]l gates & other work about my place.

April 20, 1869; Tuesday. Worked on the Street with teem & 3 hands. The Bishops and others went [to Scipio] to meet the Prest [Brigham Young]. In the afternoon some snow squalls. The storm increased and

78. The last two sentences were repeated and crossed out in the next entry.

79. Franklin B. Woolley was killed on Mar. 21, 1869, along the Mojave River while hauling merchandise to a branch of ZCMI. He had broken off to search for missing horses and was ambushed by Indians. His body was discovered the next day by a search party.

80. Callister was made president of the Millard Stake in 1869.

continued through the day which stoped our work on the street. Worked some at home in the afternoon.

April 21, 1869; Wednesday. Wind southerly some snow falling. Worked at grading my side-walk. About 12 oclock the Prest [Brigham Young] and party arrived. Snow was falling fast at the time. Had meeting in evening the meeting was addressed by Elders G[eorge] Q. Cannon[,] [Wilford] Woodruff[,] B[righam] Young Junior[,] Prest D[aniel] H. Wells & Prest B. Young. Meeting closed at 8 oclock.

April 22, 1869; Thursday. Prest & party remained on acount of the storm & held meeting. At one oclock ceased to storm. In afternoon President and his party meet at night with the school of the Prophets.[81]

April 23, 1869; Friday. Weather more pleasant. The traviling party passed on their way. I went to work on my place, the daughter of William Lay[,] Mary[,] passed on her way to the city. Continued my work thru the day on my sidewalk.

April 24, 1869; Saturday. Continued my work at home. Three of the boys went to Cedar Springs after some cows and I went to the mill and let a sister whom I owed have some 12 lbs of flour. Resumed my work and continued until ^night^ admon^i^shed me to stop. Weather somewhat warmer. This afternoon I received a ticket of admission to the school of the Prophets from Prest B[righam] Young.

April 25, 1869; Sunday. Attended church the audience was addressed by Elders R[euben] A. McBride [and] Prest [Thomas] Callister. During meeting a messinger came from Corn Creek for some help for the child of Culbert King that was badly burnt. The Bishop with others left in response but had not gone far when they met the news of the childs death and returned. I attended meeting a sabbath school in the afternoon. The [air turned] cool at night.

April 26, 1869; Monday. Worked in garden, the teem hawled wood. Stil cool at night.

April 27, 1869; Tuesday. In the morning went to the Black-smith's. During the day planted cabbages & beets and the teem hawled some

81. Joseph Smith started the School of the Prophets in Ohio so missionaries "may be perfected in their ministry for the salvation of Zion" (D&C 90:8). Brigham Young resurrected it in Utah with branches in each community.

chalk & sand for our building. Some men went south on the cattle drive to Corn Creek. Weather warmer no frost at night.

April 28, 1869; Wednesday. Warm & pleasant this morning. Spent the morning hour in hoeing up weeds in my garden. Put out some onions and forked up some ground in my garden transplanted some peach trees.

April 29, 1869; Thursday. Worked in garden this morning and mended my hoe, and in afternoon shelled some corn for seed and went to the corr[a]l to see the stock but only a portion of my stock was up. No cows with calves which makes the prospect rather dry for milk.

April 30, 1869; Friday. Morning pleasant and spent the early hour in clearing rocks off of my ground in the field then spent some time with the stock and in the evening I sold a span of mules to brother John Bourn for $180.00 in [live]stock.

May 1, 1869; Saturday. In morning attended to branding the stock from [John] Bourn. Theodore & Ira were hunting stock & Lorenzo was working in garden. In the afternoon attended school of P[rophe]ts. To day received a parcel of onion sets from br [Ebenezer] Hanks and some Pie plant [rhubarb] seed from brother D[aniel] Page per hand of br N[elson] Hollinshead sent by Paulina with a short note. Paid Alfred Gull one cow in full on his demand on me for labor up to date. Wrote letter to Paulina in the evening was very weary.

May 2, 1869; Sunday. In the morning attended church the audience was addressed Elders Allen Russel[82] & H[iram] Mace & Prest [Thomas] Callister. Attended sabbath school & meeting in afternoon.

May 3, 1869; Monday. Laid of[f] ground for my house. Had some onions set and some ground forked up and hawled some sand.

May 4, 1869; Tuesday. I worked on my cultivator & had some Pie plant seed planted. Settled with miller. [The] mill mad[e] me ^in 4 months^ 218 dollars.

May 5, 1869; Wednesday. Finished my cultivator [tilling] & exchanged some atire with brother [John] Bourn. Boys broak the wheelbarrow.

May 6. 1869; Thursday. Attended fast meeting in the morning and after meeting mad[e] some water ditch and then brought home my

82. Allen Russell joined the LDS Church in 1840. It took him twelve years to get to Utah. Brigham Young sent him to Fillmore to grow fruit there. He died in 1919. "Fillmore Pioneer Nearly 95 Years of Age Is Dead," *Deseret News*, July 17, 1919.

two cariage wheels and put up my cariage & took it to the painters. This evening received a letter from my daughter Mrs Clayton from Salt Lake City.

May 7, 1869; Friday. Raining this morning. Raked off some ground in garden before the rain. Bored some tresels [trestles] for working my house logs. In afternoon went to the shop and ground some tools some rain. The Prest [Brigham Young] & party came in before night but held no meeting.

May 8, 1869; Saturday. Cloudy but not raining I called on brothers [Wilford] Woodruff and H[orace] S. Eldridge at the residence of J[oseph] V. Robinson did not see Prest [Brigham] Young. Commenced preparing my timber for my house. Attended the school of the P[rophe]ts and spoke to the school for a few moments.

May 9, 1869; Sunday. Wrote letters to my daughter Mrs. Clayton of Salt Lake City & then went to meeting. The audience was addressed by Elder J[ohn] L. Smith & Prest [Thomas] Callister & at 2 oclock [I] attended the sabbath school and then went with brother [William] Gibbs to stop the water out of the millrace preparitory to cleaning. To day [seventeen-year-old] Lorenzo went to Cedar Springs [ten miles north of Fillmore] as a [home] missionary his first trial.

May 10, 1869; Monday. Worked on the city ditch & the boys were h^a^uling some brush for rep^a^iring the city dam. I worked some in the afternoon but had to quit on acount of my arm which gave me much pain through the night. The water was returned to the race at night. The night was cool.

May 11, 1869; Tuesday. The morning bright and pleasant. In the forenoon worked on the mill ditch that belongs to brother [Jacob] Croft. Cleared off some of our ground for planting and brought home my cultivator [tiller]. We also hauled one load of brush for the dam and in afternoon cleared some ground for harowing.

May 12, 1869; Wednesday. ~~To day we made some repair on the dam in the forenoon in the afternoon~~ Worked all day preparing my ground for planting and ~~made the arrangement with Marion that we would send for another mill. Light rain in afternoon~~ Wrote a letter to Minersville to my wife Dionitia.

May 13, 1869; Thursday. In forenoon worked on city dam and made the arangement with Marion that we would send for another mill[stone]. In afternoon worked at preparing land for planting. Light rain in afternoon.

May 14, 1869; Friday. Commenced planting cane. I procured some cane seed from Benjamin Robinson.

May 15, 1869; Saturday. Worked at clearing rock from my ^lan^d. This morning and in the afternoon attended the school of the P[rophe]ts. My wife Louisa and daughters came home from the city. A[masa] M jr was with them. Miss Louisa Burk daughter of Charles Burk was with them on her way home to Minersville.[83] Some light showers to day. Brother Sidney Tanner passed today on his way to Beaver but did not take Miss Burk as was expected. [Instead] she took stage.

May 16, 1869; Sunday. This morning Miss [Louisa] Burk left in the stage for Beaver. Attended church this morning & Sunday school & meeting in the afternoon. Elders [Edwin] Walker, [John] Powel & [John] Cooper and Bishop [Thomas] Callister & [Edward] Partridge addressed us.

May 17, 1869; Monday. This morning I borrowed one hundred and sixty dollars curency to send for another mill[stone].[84] Got bushel of corn for seed of br [Noah] Bartholomew.

May 18, 1869; Tuesday. We planted cane to day and harowed land for corn, and cleared off some for potatoes.

May 19, 1869; Wednesday. Worked in my field and had my boots rep^a^ired.

May 20, 1869; Thursday. Planted corn and raked off rock from my ground and prepared it for the watering.

May 21, 1869; Friday. To day let brother [John] Kelley have an order for 100 lbs of flour and worked in the forenoon clearing the ditches in my place on the hill.

May 22, 1869; Saturday. Worked on my place and attended the school. Some indications of rain received leters from Paulina.

May 23, 1869; Sunday. This morning meet with Homer Duncan on his way to the city. Attended meeting and sabbath school the audience

83. The youngest daughter of Charles and Lydia Burk would soon marry John Lightner, daughter of Adam and Mary Elizabeth Rollins Lightner.

84. According to a government report, millstones in 1870 cost between $138 and $220. Weeks, *Report on the Statistics of Wages in Manufacturing Industries*, 189. See also entry for June 5 below.

was addressed by Elders T[homas] R. King and S[eymour] Brunson and Bishop [Edward] Partridge[,] Prest [Thomas] Callister and F M Lyman. Went to Meadow Creek [south of Fillmore], attended meeting at 5 oclock, indications of rain at night.

May 24, 1869; Monday. Rained so we could not plant. We cut our potatoe seed and then called on Prest [Thomas] Callister. Rained during the night.

May 25, 1869; Tuesday. Raining to day moderately. we cleaned our water ditch. I then went to the mill and then returned and pulled up some weeds and brush on my lot on the hill and then dug some rocks. The ground being so softened by the rain facilitated this branch of the work. Much during the night it rained gently. This morning it snowed.

May 26, 1869; Wednesday. Received letter from Mrs M. L. Clayton of Salt Lake City. Were buisy raising rock on my lot. At noon wrote letter to Paulina no rain to day some signs of a clearing up.

May 27, 1869; Thursday. This morning sent one hundred and sixty dollars and fifteen cents to brother William Clayton to pay for our mill[stone]. Worked at raising rock. Theodore went to Corn Creek after our mare.

May 28, 1869; Friday. Snow was falling freely this morning. In the afternoon Mother [Lydia Clisbee] Partridge and my daughter Martha arived from S L City. Some rain this evening My team went out and brought in mother and Martha.[85]

May 29, 1869; Saturday. To day transplanted some cabbages and replanted some beets and in the afternoon attended the school and then visited my mill and ground my hoes preparitory [to] weeding my crops.

May 30, 1869; Sunday. Attended meetings and the sabbath school. Cooperation in raising sheep was recommended to the people by Bishop [Edward] Partridge.

May 31, 1869; Monday. To day commenced planting potatoes and pum[p]kins and squashes. The boys were hunting horses in the forenoon. The weather warm and pleasant.

June 1, 1869; Tuesday. In forenoon was planting and in afternoon

---

85. Martha was the oldest child of Amasa and Caroline Lyman. The May 28 entry was the last one in this journal book. The following few entries through June 13 were recorded in vol. 32 after some notations from 1850.

attended to the stock that was driven in. One load of lumber came to our new house weather very warm.

June 2, 1869; Wednesday. In the morning piled some lumber and then attended to marking some stock after which we finished planting potatoes. I received to day 32½ dollars for sale of steer 2 years old. I noticed as I went home the ground was surveyed for the cooperatives store on the northeast corner of the Statehouse Block.[86]

June 3, 1869; Thursday. Attended fast meeting and in the afternoon finished planting my corn. In the evening my little grand son F. M. Lyman Junior fell into the creek but was providentialy saved from drowning. His head was much hurt on the rocks.[87]

June 4, 1869; Friday. Planted pumpkins squashes and melons in my orchard. In the afternoon visited my mill which was running. Weather very warm and sultry with some signs of showers. In the evening the boys brought in a cow and calf.

June 5, 1869; Saturday. Hoed in my garden this morning and attended the school in the afternoon and hired [borrowed] of J[oseph] V. Robinson 160 dollars in money for two percent per month until Sept.

June 6, 1869; Sunday. Attended meeting and school meeting was addressed by Elders B[enjamin] Robinson and J[ohn] Kelley and F. M. Lyman. Weather hot and windy attended meeting at 5 oclock.

June 7, 1869; Monday. This morning paid thirty dollars for stock in the cooperative store. Marion and Lorenzo started for Cove Creek & Black Rock Springs to build some corr[a]l for stock. Spent the day in the field and garden hoeing weeds, in the afternoon had a pleasant shower of rain, rendering the air cool an[d] pleasant.

June 8, 1869; Tuesday. Finished hoeing my corn weather was warm and clear.

June 9, 1869; Wednesday. Passed the day hoeing cane. Went to the mill brother [John] Powel commenced turning on my lathe to day. Received letter from my wife Paulina in Parrowan. She states that the grasshoopers

86. The Fillmore branch of ZCMI was organized in Mar. 1869. Shares in the enterprise were sold for $25 each, and Bishop Callister ran the local store. The building was completed in 1871 on the corner of Center and Main Streets. Lyman and Newell, *History of Millard County*, 140–41.

87. Francis M. Lyman Jr. was the five-year-old son of Francis and Rhoda Lyman. He recovered fully.

were destroying the crops of grain. Also received the news of a successful amputation of the leg of Jas S. Brown by surgeons [Washington F.] Anderson & [Heber J.] Richards.[88]

June 10, 1869; Thursday. Passed the day in my garden. Sister Hariet Shepherd[89] and her father [Ezra Parrish] called on me on their way to the city. Brother Parish had been some years in Cal.

June 11, 1869; Friday. Worked in my garden brother M[arcus] L. Shepherd brought me two of my sheep which I [arranged to] ha[ve] butchered in the evening. They were from the herd in Beaver.

June 12, 1869; Saturday. Worked in my garden in the forenoon and attended the school in the afternoon and took super with Father [Gabriel] Huntsman and family. ^Charles Robinson was baptized today.^ Weather very warm and sultry.

June 13, 1869; Sunday. Attend morning and evening service at Church and the sabbath school. Weather very sultry in the evening called on brother Reuben Mcbride and family. The audience was addressed today by Elders [Josiah F.] Gibbs[,] [John] Pilling and Harworth folowed by Prest [Thomas] Callister. In the afternoon the speakers were Bishop [Edward] Partridge T[homas] E. King and myself for a few moments. Brothers A[lfred] Gull[,] T[homas] Henderson and wives [Mary Gull and Martha Henderson] dined with us.[90]

June 14, 1869; Monday. This morning I worked in my garden and at noon received a disp[at]ch from Beaver stateing that my wife Dionitia at Minersville was nigh unto death. I meet with brother C[ollins] Hakes with whom I went to Canosh and from there he sent his team to Beaver where I arived on the evening of the 16th Tuesday. There I meet with Dr Christian who gave me the news that my wife was beter he had opened the abcess which discharged copiously and gave her much relief. I lodged with Father [Theodore] Turley.

---

88. Brown was shot by someone who mistook him for a bear. See Feb. 25, 1863.

89. Harriet married Marcus Shepherd a few days before the two traveled to San Bernardino with the founding colonists, and they reluctantly heeded the call to return to Beaver, where Harriet became Relief Society president.

90. Alfred and Mary Gull were the son-in-law and daughter of Thomas and Martha Henderson. This is the last entry in volume 32, followed by a few blank pages and notations. The entries for June 14–Sept. 12 in vol. 30 have been reordered in their correct chronological position here.

June 16, 1869; Wednesday. This morning [I] was kindly forwarded on to Minersville by brother S[tephen] Franklin who sent his teem and cariage with me. Arived in Minersville about 11 oclock and found my wife stil beter and well attended by kind friends. May God bless them for their kindness. The weather warm and sultry.

June 17, 1869; Thursday. My wife continued better. Weather very warm.

June 18, 1869; Friday. This morning hoed some in garden and then was attacked with choleramorbus[91] was very sick all day and through the night.

June 19, 1869; Saturday. Was beter in health my wife comfortable.

June 20, 1869; Sunday. Attended a meeting morning[,] and evening weather stil warm and sultry.

June 21, 1869; Monday. Past the day mostly at home my health improving my wife stil comfortable. Some indications of showers.

June 22, 1869; Tuesday. To day visited the new mill being built by brother Nelson Hollingshead. It is a very creditable work. This evening had [a] light shower from the change of weather Dionitia took slight cold which gave her pain through the night.

June 23, 1869; Wednesday. Cloudy this morning. Dionitia wors[e] her abcess discharged bloody mater she has light fever. My wife Paulina came to day from Parrowan with brother [Edwin] Bingham and wife [Phebe].

June 24, 1869; Thursday. Visited my daughter Matilda Carter at Greenville.[92] In the evening had a shower.

June 25, 1869; Friday. Visited the new mill in the afternoon dined with C[harles] A. Burk and family. Dionitia stil beter.

June 26, 1869; Saturday. Today went to Beaver with brother [James H.] Rollins my wife Paulina went with us. I attended the school of the prophets and by request of Prest [John R.] Murdock[93] I addressed the school.

June 27, 1869; Sunday. Attended meeting in the morning and visited and dined with brother [John W.] Christian and family.

June 28, 1869; Monday. Dined with Father [Theodore] Turley and in afternoon visited brother Wm Cox and family and also called on br Jas Low who gave me a passage in the stage home and also my wife to Parrowan.

---

91. Cholera morbus was the popular term for a stomach virus. The condition was unrelated to cholera, the infectious disease.

92. Greenville is between Beaver and Minersville.

93. Murdock was made president of the new Beaver Stake a few months prior. Lyman will still sometimes call him bishop.

June 29, 1869; Tuesday. At 12 oclock my wife started for home and I started one hour later. This morning I received one hundred dollars in currency from brother J[ohn] R. Murdock to use until fall without interest. Stoped for the night at Cove Creek with my son A. M. Junior. Light shower this afternoon.

June 30, 1869; Wednesday. Cloudy with indications of rain. Arived at home about 5 oclock found my family well, the cariage breaking I walked 4 miles.

July 1, 1869; Thursday. Attended the fast meeting after which I paid J[oseph] V. Robinson one hundred dollars on my note which he held. Paid to [Thomas] Henderson 50 lbs flour.

July 2, 1869; Friday. This morning my wife Louisa and her three youngest daughters started for Beaver with Brother [Marcus] Shepherd to take care of our wool which her brother S[idney] [Tanner] had in his possession as he kept my sheep.[94] Visited the mill did not engage in labor as I had a severe head ache. The weather quite warm. Lorenzo went after hay.

July 3, 1869; Saturday. Worked in my garden in the morning and attended the school in the afternoon and visited the mill.

July 4, 1869; Sunday. Attended meeting the congregation was addressed by Elder [John] Kelley. Attended sabbath school, and also a meeting at 5 oclock. Marion arived this evening with our mill[stone] in good order.

July 5, 1869; Monday. Moved our mill[stone] to its place of work. The boys begun ploughing corn to day. Weather very warm. Paid J[oseph] V. Robison fifty five dollars on my note.

July 6, 1869; Tuesday. Worked on my mill in forenoon. In afternoon wrote letters for north and south. Weather very warm.

July 7, 1869; Wednesday. Was quite ill not able to work was about the mill the most of the day. The boys hoed corn and hauled rock for house.

July 8, 1869; Thursday. Worked at mill my health some beter. Boys hauled rock and watered corn, wind high.

July 9, 1869; Friday. Worked at mill. A[ndrew] J. Clothier began the foundation of my house but hurt his back and quit.

94. In 1858, Lyman's flocks were herded from California by Nathan Tenney (pp. 536–37 herein), who kept them in New Harmony, twenty miles south of Cedar City, before he moved 100 miles southwest to Kanab and transferred the flocks to Lyman's brother-in-law Sidney Tanner in Beaver. Tenney and Tenney, *Nathan Cram Tenney*, 21–22, 24, 34–35.

July 10, 1869; Saturday. Attended the school brother Orson Holbrook was present. Addressed the school. Worked 4 days on mill this week at 2 dollars per day.

July 11, 1869; Sunday. Attended meeting and sabbath school the audience was addressed by Elder Orson E. Holbrook and F[rancis] M. Lyman. I received from A[masa] M. Junior five dollars per hand of Joseph Prisby.

July 12, 1869; Monday. Worked at mill. The mason was working for me today.

July 13, 1869; Tuesday. Received a call at my mill from br David Cannon on his way to City. Hurt my finger so I was unable to work received two dollars from br [William] Gibbs.

July 14, 1869; Wednesday. Worked at my mill commenced making gripes for the water trunk [flume].

July 15, 1869; Thursday. Continued the work on water trunk worked until near 9 oclock.

July 16, 1869; Friday. Continued my work at mill and had [my seventeen-year-old son] Lorenzo with me.

July 17, 1869; Saturday. Worked at mill in the morning and attended the caucus and school in the afternoon and in the evening was again at the mill. Received letter from Jas Rollins from Minersville with 25 dollars inclosed for J[oseph] V. Robison. My letter informed me that my wife Dionitia was stil improveing in health. To day finished closeing in my mill[stone] belts.

July 18, 1869; Sunday. Attended meeting morning and evening and also sabbath school.

July 19, 1869; Monday. Worked some at the mill had some watering done.

July 20, 1869; Tuesday. Commenced to put up my log house on my place under the hill. Heard of the arival of the two sons of the Prophet Joseph[,] Alexander and David.[95] To day meeting with brother [Joseph] Fish from Parrowan.

---

95. Alexander and David Hyrum Smith had just arrived on the newly completed transcontinental railroad, anxious to share the message of the Reorganized Church. However, the result of their meeting with Brigham Young, in which Young verbally attacked their mother, Emma, was a months-long print war over polygamy. Avery, *From Mission to Madness*, 94–105.

July 21, 1869; Wednesday. Worked on my house and wrote letter to Dionitia.

July 22, 1869; Thursday. Worked on my ^house^ the weather was very warm & sultry. I [had] two hands and teem hauling brush for the bowery [open-air pavilion].

July 23, 1869; Friday. Worked on my house. This evening my wife Maria and her daughter came home from Beaver with Philo Carter.

July 24, 1869; Saturday. Celebrated the event of the comeing of the Pioniers into the Vallies of Utah. Dined with brother Chandler Holbrook and family. At night attended the ball in the state house.

July 25, 1869; Sunday. Attended meeting morning and evening and also sabbath school. Weather very warm Philo started for home this morning takeing Rhoda (with him) Marion's wife.

July 26, 1869; Monday. The boys hauled wood I visited the mill and worked some in my garden.

July 27, 1869; Tuesday. Worked in my field all day hoeing potatoes the weather very hot.

July 28, 1869; Wednesday. Worked at the mill making some change in machinery for cleaning grain.

July 29, 1869; Thursday. Continued my work at the mill weather hot. The boys hoed in the field.

July 30, 1869; Friday. Tried our new screne [screen] and was pleased with its work, boys watered the crops in the field.

July 31, 1869; Saturday. Was at mill in the morning and at school in the afternoon and then to the mill again. Received letters from br [William] Clayton ~~and~~ of Salt Lake City and my wife [Dionetia] in Minersville. The mill owes me for three days work this week.

August 1, 1869; Sunday. Was at meeting morning and in the evening at sabbath school, we were addressed by brother Gabriel Huntsman. Weather very warm.

August 2, 1869; Monday. Worked at the mill the boys worked in the field.

August 3, 1869; Tuesday. Completed my work at the mill for the present.

August 4, 1869; Wednesday. To day brother William Godbe and wife came to town and stoped with brother G[abriel] Huntsman. I spent the day mostly with brother G.[96] and in the evening Bishop Wm Warren called he was on his way home to Parrowan.

August 5, 1869; Thursday. Attended fast meeting the audience was addressed by Elder Godbe. In the afternoon brother G. and wife started for their home in Salt Lake City and I worked on the bowry fence.

August 6, 1869; Friday. Helped complete the fence around the Bowry. In the afternoon we had a fine shower went to the mill. Amasa Junior and wife came home this morning from cove creek. Professors Thomas and [Edward] Tulledge were in town to hold some concerts.

August 7, 1869; Saturday. Attended the school and visited my mill.

August 8, 1869; Sunday. Attended meeting morning & evening and attend the Sabbath school, the audience was addressed by Elder Giles Frost, Cedar Springs.

August 9, 1869; Monday. Was ill did not work much.

August 10, 1869; Tuesday. Wrote letter to W[illiam] S. Godbe [and] visited the mill.

August 11, 1869; Wednesday. Did not work much to day. Marions wife came today and my wife and daughter came home. The boys hoed in the field.

August 12, 1869; Thursday. Worked in my field and visited the mill. In the evening received a Salt Lake City directory by mail thru the kindness of W[illiam] H. Hooper member of Congress.[97]

August 13, 1869; Friday. Worked in my field weather very warm.

August 14, 1869; Saturday. In the forenoon worked in my field in the afternoon attended the schooll, and in the evening received a letter from br Wm Clayton giving us the information that his wife[,] our daughter[,] had a fine son born the 12th of August.[98] Mother and child doing well, also received a letter from Paulina.

---

96. This was a turning point for Lyman. He had known Godbe in the British Mission, and his former colleague, who was now openly criticizing Brigham Young in the *Utah Magazine*, would soon be excommunicated. After corresponding, Lyman's involvement in the New Movement would grow to the point that he too would be excommunicated, as would Edward Tullidge, who is mentioned on August 6. Walker, *Wayward Saints*; *AML*, 410–11.

97. Hooper was a territorial delegate to Congress until 1873, and as such, he served on committees and was allowed to speak in favor of legislation affecting the territory without being a voting member of Congress.

98. The baby was Amasa M. (the M did not stand for anything), who would grow

August 15, 1869; Sunday. Attended meeting in morning and wrote letter to Wm Clayton.

August 16, 1869; Monday. Worked in my field hoeing weeds.

August 17, 1869; Tuesday. Worked in the field and visited the mill.

August 18, 1869; Wednesday. Worked on the dam at head of the ditch. Wrote letter to Paulina and worked in my field.

August 19, 1869; Thursday. Worked on my place.

August 20, 1869; Friday. Was engaged on my place in work.

August 21, 1869; Saturday. Worked on my place and in the afternoon attended the school. In the evening meet with Cunningham Mathews who was on his way to the city.

August 22, 1869; Sunday. Attended meeting in morning and sabbath school in the evening and visited my place under the hill.

August 23, 1869; Monday. Borrowed 10 bushels of wheat of T[homas] R. King to make flour to carry south.

August 24, 1869; Tuesday. This morning made ready for the journey south and started at 2 oclock p.m. I traviled to Corn Creek and lodged brother [Collins] Hakes and family. Elizabeth Franklin came to day from Minersville.

August 25, 1869; Wednesday. Traviled to Cove Creek and made noon halt and then went to Beaver and lodged with brother [Theodore] Turley. Left with him some flour and fruit to be sent to my wife in Minersville.

August 26, 1869; Thursday. Traviled to Parowan found my family there all well.

August 27, 1869; Friday: Made some buisness calls around town. Brother Sidney Tanner & wife and Wm Martindale were with us tonight.

August 28, 1869; Saturday. To day dined with brother Clarks family and in afternoon attended the school of the prophets and by the request of Prest [William H.] Dame addressed the school.

August 29, 1869; Sunday. Attended meeting and by request of the President I addressed the Saints. Dined with Sister Croft[99] and in the evening called on brother [Daniel] Page.

---

up to marry a niece of apostle Moses Thatcher.

99. Jacob Croft had three living wives, but this is probably a daughter of John Powell (not John Wesley Powell), Mary Ann.

August 30, 1869; Monday. Finished my preperations for returning home.

August 31, 1869; Tuesday. Traviled to Beaver and lodged with Prest. [John R.] Murdock.

September 1, 1869; Wednesday. Traviled to Cove Creek and stoped for the night.

September 2, 1869; Thursday. Traviled to Fillmore were we arived at 3 oclock. Found our family well[,] read letter from [son-in-law] [William] Clayton.

September 3, 1869; Friday. Visited my mill. The boys hauled some wood.

September 4, 1869; Saturday. Wrote note to Paulina. Attended the school at which the death of E. T. Benson was announced. He died on Friday 3rd of Sept at Ogden of apoplexy at 7 oclock P.M.[100]

September 5, 1869; Sunday. Attended meeting the audience was addressed by Elder Nathan Baldwin with Prest [Thomas] Callister. Wrote letters to Wm Clayton and Dr Ellis of N. H.

September 6, 1869; Monday. Pulled Sun flowers in my field and Lorenzo & Theodore in the can[y]on for Lumber for my house.

September 7, 1869; Tuesday. Worked on my house Lorenzo worked with me.

September 8, 1869; Wednesday. Worked on my cariage and Lorenzo went to the can[y]on and brought the jois[t]s for my house.

September 9, 1869; Thursday. Worked on my house. My son Charles[101] started for his home today in Parowan.

September 10, 1869; Friday. Worked on my house work progressed slowly, received some presents from M[aria] L[ouisa] Clayton [of] Salt Lake City.

September 11, 1869; Saturday. Finished the body of my house. Attended school.

September 12, 1869; Sunday. Attended meeting, The audience was addressed by Bishops [Edward] Partridge & [Thomas] Callister. Started for Black Rock Springs. Traviled to and camped at the Bp place at Meadow Creek.[102]

100. Benson "dropped down suddenly" at fifty-eight, probably of a heart attack. "Sudden Death of Elder Ezra T. Benson," *Deseret News*, Sep. 8, 1869.

101. Twelve-year-old Charles was the son of Paulina Phelps.

102. The day's entry is split across two diary books, the first sentence in vol. 30 and

September 13, 1869; Monday. Reached Black Rock before night and fixed our carrell [corral] for receiving the stock.

September 14, 1869; Tuesday. Marion and Thomas Callister hauled wood. Myself and Theodore and Ira worked about the corr[a]l.

September 15, 1869; Wednesday. The boys all started south to drive in stock, in the forenoon Bishop [John R.] Murdock arived and in the afternoon the stock began to come in and by sundown was all in. Br Isaac Turley came in from Beaver, and also Philo Carter and his son Lyman and Henry Tanner.

September 16, 1869; Thursday. Sorted our stock and sold six steers and one cow and calf to Bishop [John R.] Murdock for $255.

September 17, 1869; Friday. Returned home where we arived before sundown. Found the folks all well as usual.

September 18, 1869; Saturday. Worked about my place and attended the school. Paid entry money on my city land to J[ohn] Kelly.

September 19, 1869; Sunday. Attended meeting. We were addressed by Elder N[athan] Baldwin and T[homas] R. King and Bp [Edward] Partridge. In the afternoon received a call from br J[ohn] W. Christian and wife on their way home from the city. Weather cool but pleasant. This morning br. [William] Gibbs started a teem to the city for his son J[osiah] F. a returning missionary.[103]

September 20, 1869; Monday. Worked on my house tied up some corn.

September 21, 1869; Tuesday. Continued work on my house.

September 22, 1869; Wednesday. Finished sheeting my house and had my cariage seat mended and received letter from Bishop [John R.] Murdock with $105 dollars in curency.

September 23, 1869; Thursday. Commenced shingling my house. In the evening Platt D. A[l]ton came home from his mission.[104]

September 24, 1869; Friday. Finished shingling my house and fited seats in my carriage. Weather cool and pleasant.

---

the last two sentences in vol. 33. The Sep. 13–Nov. 4 entries are also in vol. 33.

103. When Josiah F. Gibbs became a journalist after his mission, he began to write critically of Mormon leaders, resulting in his 1908 excommunication. Two years later he published *Mountain Meadows Massacre*, a balanced account of the event that had haunted him since he first heard of it. Bagley, *Blood of the Prophets*, 337–38.

104. Platte married Adelia Robison in May 1867, before his departure for England. He returned with Josiah Gibbs on a steamship from Liverpool, then by rail from New York to Utah.

September 25, 1869; Saturday. Fited my cariage for the journey and in the afternoon attended the school and then gathered some minister appels.[105]

September 26, 1869; Sunday. Attended meeting. The audience was addressed by Elders P[latte] D. Lyman[,] Orson Holbrook, and Prest. [Thomas] Callister.

September 27, 1869; Monday. Started with my son Marion for Salt Lake City. Traviled to Round Valey and I put up with brother Jesse Martin. Visited the mill in process of erection by brother Jacob Croft.

September 28, 1869; Tuesday. Traviled to Salt Creek and put up with brother T[imothy] B. Foot.

September 29, 1869; Wednesday. Traviled to Payson and put up with brother Joseph Tanner with [whom] I visited the county fair which was quite creditable. To night had some rain which layed the dust.

September 30, 1869; Thursday. Traviled to Provo and put up with brother Myron Tanner and then went to Battle Creek [Pleasant Grove] and lodged with Bishop John Brown.

October 1, 1869; Friday. Traviled to the city and put up with my daughter Mrs Wm Clayton.

October 2, 1869; Saturday. Called on Sister Emily Young and family whom I found well. In the afternoon attended school and was very warmly greeted by my old friends. The city is much changed.

October 3, 1869; Sunday. Attended meeting in old Tabernacle [on Temple Square].[106] The audience was addressed by my son Platt D. Alton [Platte DeAlton Lyman] and brother Olsen, just returned from Europe. In afternoon attended meeting at the Independence Hall[107] and heard discourse from Alexander Smith son of Joseph. After meeting they introduced themselves. In the evening was introduced to Vice President Colfax.[108]

---

105. Probably Newtown–Pippin apples, promoted at Buckingham Palace by the US minister to England.

106. The new tabernacle was completed in 1867 and hosted general conference sessions that year, while the old tabernacle continued to serve for another decade for overflow crowds, where one or two church leaders were given assignments to speak each session.

107. The Congregationalists constructed Independence Hall in 1866 (300 South, near Main Street) for worship services and as a place to hear speakers of other faiths and political views who were shut out of the LDS and LDS-controlled buildings in town.

108. Schuyler Colfax claimed to be traveling in a private capacity rather than as Ulysses S. Grant's vice president. He would serve only one term because of his

October 4, 1869; Monday. Attended the ~~county~~ Teritorial fa[i]r with Prest [Brigham] Young and then dined with him.

October 5, 1869; Tuesday. Was suffering from cold was not much around.

October 6, 1869; Wednesday. Attended conference. Brother [William] Godbe came home at night from Bear Lake.

October 7, 1869; Thursday. Attended the conference. Lodged at brother G[eorge] A. Smiths was quite ill.

October 8, 1869; Friday. Attended meeting and lodged with brother [William] Godbe.

October 9, 1869; Saturday. Meet with brothers [Elias L. T.] Harison & [William] Godbe at brother Gs.

October 10, 1869; Sunday. Conference closed and I dined with Brother T[homas] B. H. Stenhouse.

October 11, 1869; Monday. Started home and we traviled to Provo and lodged with brother Myron Tanner.

October 12, 1869; Tuesday. Traviled to Nephi and lodged with brother T[imothy] B. Foot.

October 13, 1869; Wednesday. Traviled to Scipio. I lodged with brother J[esse] Martin.

October 14, 1869; Thursday. Arived home at 2 oclock found my family well.

October 15, 1869; Friday. Taried at home and weighed my dried fruit of which I had 386 lbs. Visited my mill.

October 16, 1869; Saturday. Attended school in the afternoon and was invited to speak.

October 17, 1869; Sunday. Attended meeting in morning and evening when the audience was addressed by Elders John Kelley and P[latte] D. Lyman and bishop [Edward] Partridge [Jr.] and in morning by Elders [Thomas E.] King[,] [Seymour] Brunson[,] Lyman[,] and Bp Partridge.

October 18, 1869; Monday. Made some rep[a]irs on my loom and worked some on my house. Wind high with indications of storm.

October 19, 1869; Tuesday. I worked on my house and the boys went to the muster and Ira and Edward went for wood.

October 20, 1869; Wednesday. Worked stil on my house weather pleasant.

---

involvement in the Crédit Mobilier scandal. "Arrival of Vice-President Colfax," *Deseret News*, Oct. 6, 1869.

October 21, 1869; Thursday. Worked on my house indications of rain at night, some light rain during the night.

October 22, 1869; Friday. Completed cuting out the windows of my house. Weather pleasant the militia came in from the muster ground on Pioneer Creek.[109]

October 23, 1869; Saturday. Attended [stake] conference. The audience was addressed by Prest [Thomas] Callister and Elders [Joseph V.] Robinson[,] [Thomas E.] King and Bp [Edward] Partridge [Jr]. in the forenoon and by Elders Culbert King and Bp Callister. In the evening Elder Erastus Snow came in. The audience was addressed by Elders J[osiah] F. Gibbs and P[latte] D. Lyman folowed by Elder Snow.

October 24, 1869; Sunday. Attended conference which closed on the evening of to day. Weather quite cool.

October 25, 1869; Monday. Brothers [Thomas E.] King[,] [J. B.] Robinson and [Hiram] Mace started on their mission to the states. I commenced husking my corn. Ball at the State House in the evening.

October 26, 1869; Tuesday. Worked in my corn Lorenzo h[a]uled wood weather cool and pleasant.

October 27, 1869; Wednesday. Secured materials for building my chimney. Theodore hauled wood.

October 28, 1869; Thursday. Worked with my corn wrote to brother [Elias L. T.] Harison.[110]

October 29, 1869; Friday. Sent 178 lbs of flour and 39 lbs dried peaches to Paulina by brother [Ebenezer] Hanks[,] teem in care of Indian Jo. The mason worked on my chimney in the afternoon I shucked some corn.

October 30, 1869; Saturday. In forenoon worked on my chimney. In afternoon attended the school. Some rain at night got up one load of corn.

October 31, 1869; Sunday. Attended church the audience was addressed by Elder F[rancis] M. Lyman and Prest Levi Hancock.[111]

---

109. Pioneer Creek is in the Pahvant Mountains southeast of Holden.

110. Harrison and William Godbe had been excommunicated only three days earlier by the Salt Lake High Council. *Deseret News*, Oct. 26, 1869.

111. Levi Hancock was an early convert whose life covered the major events and developments in Mormonism: Zion's Camp, president of the Seventies, Nauvoo Legion, Council of Fifty, and the Utah Territorial Legislature. He was part of the cotton mission at the moment.

November 1, 1869; Monday. Finished my chimney. In the evening attended the meeting of the seventies who were addressed by Prest [Levi] Hancock after which I by request of Prest C[handler] Holbrook spoke them briefly.

November 2, 1869; Tuesday.[112] Worked at my corn. Tonight Judge [Cyrus M.] Hawly[113] called on me to get my cariage to go to St. George which I hired [out to] him at 1½ dollars per day.

November 3, 1869; Wednesday. Finished shucking my corn brother Edwin Bingham and wife stayed with us.

November 4, 1869; Thursday. Attended fast meeting and spoke to the people by request of Prest [Thomas] Callister.[114]

November 5, 1869; Friday. Worked on my house. In the evening attended meeting the audience was addressed by Elder Orson Pratt.

November 6, 1869; Saturday. Worked on my house in the forenoon then attended the School which was addressed by Elders Orson Hyde an[d] [Orson] Pratt. ^Brother Joseph Tanner & family were with us.^

November 7, 1869; Sunday. Attended meeting the audience was addressed by Elders [Orson] Hyde and [Orson] Pratt morning and evening.

November 8, 1869; Monday. Worked on my house in the morning and in the evening I was gathering material for m[y] wagon bed. Elder [Orson] Hyde started for home.

November 9, 1869; Tuesday. Commenced makeing my wagon bed.

November 10, 1869; Wednesday. Worked on my wagon.

November 11, 1869; Thursday. Wrote letter to my wife Dionitia in Minersville and sent her some medicine. Worked in my shop.

November 12, 1869; Friday. ~~Thursday~~ Worked in my shop on my wagon bed.

November 13, 1869; Saturday. Attended School and subscribed 80 shares to the sheep growing association. Worked some in the shop received letters from Dionitia.

November 14, 1869; Sunday. My cariage was returned and the hire paid 16 dollars and a ½. Attended meeting morning and evening.

---

112. A note at the top of the page above this entry reads, "Continued in book A."

113. Hawley was a federal appointee on the Utah Territorial Supreme Court.

114. This ends vol. 33. The Nov. 5–Dec. 31, 1869, entries are located out of order at the front of vol. 30.

November 15, 1869; Monday. Worked on my wagon and spent some time fixing my loom.

November 16, 1869; Tuesday. Worked at the shop. Received letters from Dionitia bought some shoes for the children.

November 17, 1869; Wednesday. Worked in shop.[115]

November 19, 1869; Friday. Worked in shop weather pleasant.

November 20, 1869; Saturday. Attended the school and worked in the shop.

November 21, 1869; Sunday. Attended Church morning and also in evening.

November 22, 1869; Monday. Worked in the shop and on my house ~~and~~.

November 23, 1869; Tuesday. Brought my wagon bed home and my tools from the shop. Snow fell at ^night.^

November 24, 1869; Wednesday. Worked on my house.[116]

November 27, 1869; Saturday. Worked on my house and attended school and bought a barell of molasses of brother Benjamin Robinson.

November 28, 1869; Sunday. Attended meeting morning and evening. Snow fell at night.

November 29, 1869; Monday. To day meet with my cousin James Day on his way to Hico. Snow fell last night.

November 30, 1869; Tuesday. Weather cold worked on my house.

December 1, 1869; Wednesday. Visited my mill and worked on my house. Lorenzo went to Clear Lake for brother [John] Bourn.

December 2, 1869; Thursday. Attended fast meeting. In the evening worked on my house.

December 3, 1869; Friday. Worked at home.

December 4, 1869; Saturday. Attended school. In evening worked on my house. Lorenzo went to the mill in the can[y]on.

December 5, 1869; Sunday. Attended meeting and dined with brother Orson C. Holbrook and family.

December 6, 1869; Monday. Procured lumber for my floors and brought it home and commenced laying floors.

December 7, 1869; Tuesday. Continued work on my house. Ira went

---

115. He repeats the same entry the next day, Nov. 18.

116. He repeats the same entry for Nov. 25 and Nov. 26, deleted here.

on the cattle drive. Lorenzo helped me on my house, Theodore was helping brother Robinson.

December 8, 1869; Wednesday. Worked on my house. Stock came in to day.

December 9, 1869; Thursday. Attended to the stock and worked on my house.

December 10, 1869; Friday. Sent off south of Corn Creek [Kanosh] 9 calves and 2 year olds past. Ira went with them. Worked on my house.

December 11, 1869; Saturday. Attended school and worked on house.

December 12, 1869; Sunday. Attended meeting the audience was addressed by Elder P[erry] Liston.[117] In afternoon wrote letter to Mr. J. L. Richardson.

December 13, 1869; Monday. Worked on my house. The boys Lorenzo and Theodore[,] Ira[,] Frederick[,] Joseph and Edward commenced going to school to brother [Edward] Web[b].[118]

December 14, 1869; Tuesday. Worked on house.

December 15, 1869; Wednesday. Worked on my house weather very cold.

December 16, 1869; Thursday. Worked on house in the forenoon and in afternoon attended meeting held by Prest. Orson Hyde.

December 17, 1869; Friday. Worked on house. Br [Orson] Hyde went home.

December 18, 1869; Saturday. Worked on house and attended school.[119]

December 19, 1869; Sunday. Attended meeting. In the afternoon called on brother [Noah] Bartholomew and family. Remained at home during the week until Saturday 25th attended school. Some snow fell at night.

December 26, 1869. Sunday. Attended meeting. The audience was addressed by the Chief Black Hawk and brother [blank]. Dined

---

117. Commodore Perry Liston (Commodore was his given name) said in his autobiography (Utah State Historical Society) that he was an observer during the Mountain Meadows Massacre, having refused to participate. He served a mission from 1866 to 1868, prior to moving his family to St. George.

118. Edward ("Eddie") Milo Webb Jr. was twenty-two years old. Bishop Callister had sent him to Salt Lake City to study at Deseret University, but a few years after returning he was pursued by federal marshals for marrying plural wives and was forced to move to Arizona, then to Mexico. Merrill, "Biography of Edward Milo Webb."

119. A note reads, "Continued on page 78," followed by several lists of hardware for Lyman's house, data on livestock, and three sporadic entries for Dec. 19, 26, and 31 to end vol. 30.

with brother G[abriel] Huntsman and family and friends. Attended meeting in the evening the speakers were Elder P[latte] D. Lyman & J[osiah] F. Gibbs and C[ollins] Hakes folowed by Bishop [Edward] Partridge [Jr].

December 31, 1869; Friday. Worked on my house this afternoon brother Stephen Franklin and wife came from Minersville to visit us and spend New Year with us.

January 1, 1870; Saturday.[120] Attended school with brother [Stephen] Franklin and in the evening attended the Session of the high councel for the trial of parties who disturbed a social party at Meadow Creek.

January 2, 1870; Sunday. Attended meeting we were addressed by Bps [Thomas] Callister and [Edward] Partridge. Took diner with brother Nathan Baldwin and family and brother [Stephen] Franklin and wife. Was at meeting in the evening.

January 3, 1870; Monday. Commenced w[o]rking on the roof of my house preparing for shingling. Brothers Mead and Boice were helping. Assisted my folks in warping a web for weaveing.

January 4, 1870; Tuesday. P[r]osicuted the work on the house. Procured the shingles[,] some indications of storm.

January 5, 1870; Wednesday. Commenced shingling. Amasa Junior helped us.

January 6, 1870; Thursday. Attended fast meeting and shingled in the evening after dining with Marion and family.

January 7, 1870; Friday. Had 7 hands shingling. The weather very cold the air full of frost.

January 8, 1870; Saturday. So cold we could not shingle. Attended school my son Henry came home.

January 9, 1870; Sunday. Attended meeting in the morning. [We] were addressed by Elders [Nathan] Baldwin and [Platte D.] Lyman. Attended the sabbath school and read in the class in the Book of Mormon, teacher Elder P. D. Lyman.

January 10, 1870; Monday. Finished shingling my house, the weather

---

120. The Jan. 1–Dec. 31, 1870 entries are in vol. 34, a small book with "Daily Pocket Diary for the Year 1865" printed on the first page. Lyman crossed out the date and inked in his own.

is stil cold. Amasa [Jr.] found my horses which were supposed to be stolen. To day was celebrated of the completion of the Utah Central Railroad.[121]

January 11, 1870; Tuesday. Made some fixtures for my wagon. Weather warm and pleasant.

January 12, 1870; Wednesday. Worked at shop weather stil warm and pleasant wind in the south.

January 13, 1870; Thursday. Worked on ge[a]ring for spooling wheel at brother I[saac] Carlns [Carling]. Gave him order on mill for seventy five cents.

January 14, 1870; Friday. Worked on spooling machine.

January 15, 1870; Saturday. Attended school, received some lumber from John Alvice.

January 16, 1870; Sunday. Attended Church morning and evening and also Sabbath ~~sch~~ school.

January 17, 1870; Monday. Gave order to Hender^son^ for one dollar on mill. Worked in shop. Brother Mead commenced work on my house. Weather very cold.

January 18, 1870; Tuesday. Worked at shopwork and night had a sleigh ride through the kindness of brother [Noah] Bartholimew.

January 19, 1870; Wednesday. Wrote letters to Paulina and Dionitia, worked in shop. Weather warmer to day.

January 20, 1870; Thursday. Worked at shop work weather stil warm.[122]

January 22, 1870; Saturday. This morning brother John Pilling Died of Dropsy in the chest [pneumonia]. Attended school, worked at shop.

January 23, 1870; Sunday. Attended meeting in the morning and evening and also attended the funerals of brother John Pilling and the child of brother [William] Dugins.[123] There was no Sabbath school, the weather warm.

January 24, 1870; Monday. Worked at clearing out the lower part of my house weather quite warm.

January 25, 1870; Tuesday. Worked on house. To day the sisters held

---

121. In spite of the name, the Utah Central Railroad connected Ogden to Salt Lake City. The main purpose was to bring transcontinental travelers to the territorial capital.

122. The content of this entry was repeated for Jan. 21.

123. Nine-year-old Alice Duggins died of tuberculosis.

an indignation meeting to consider the Cragin Colum and co. bill.[124] Had snow squall in afternoon.

January 26, 1870; Wednesday. At shop-work[,] weather warm and pleasant.[125]

January 29, 1870; Saturday. Attended school had a large attendence. In morning worked on my wagon. At night read in Book of Mormon.

January 30, 1870; Sunday. Attended meeting in the morning and evening and attended Sabbath School. Dined with G[abriel] Huntsman and family. Weather warm and spring like.

January 31, 1870; Monday. Worked at an out building for my place on the hill. Weather pleasant.

February 1, 1870; Tuesday. Continued my house building.

February 2, 1870; Wednesday. Worked at shop work weather stil pleasant.

February 3, 1870; Thursday. Spent the day with brother Nathan Tiney who was on his way to San Pete after wheat. To day was fast day.

February 4, 1870; Friday. Prosicuted my work on my building. This morning brother Thomas Turner began to dig a well on the publick square. Brother [William] Gibbs made bill of lumber for house.

February 5, 1870; Saturday. Attended school to day. Brother J[osiah] F. Gibbs got my cariage to go to Salt Lake City to take [marry] a wife.[126] [Marie Hundera Walker]. Wrote letter to brother Wm Clayton.

February 6, 1870; Sunday. Attended meeting in morning and evening and attended sabbath school. Weather pleasant and warm. ~~Received letter~~

February 7, 1870; Monday. Worked at the improvements on my place.

February 8, 1870; Tuesday. Stil working at my improvements. The weather stil warm and pleasant.

February 9, 1870; Wednesday. Worked on my loghous[e]. Wind high from the south.

---

124. The bill sponsored by Senator Aaron Cragin of New Hampshire and Congressman Shelby Cullom of Illinois would have stripped polygamists of US citizenship, but it failed in the Senate. Gordon, *Mormon Question*, 273–74n6. Mormon women met in the Salt Lake Tabernacle to compose a protest to Congress. Derr, et al, *First Fifty Years*, 311–32.

125. The entries for Jan. 27 and Jan. 28 have the same content as for Jan. 26.

126. Amasa's millwright, Josiah Gibbs, was a young man of twenty-four; his bride, Marie Hundera Walker, eighteen.

February 10, 1870; Thursday. Made arangements for painting my log house.

February 11, 1870; Friday. Brother Speaksman and brother [Alfred] Gull worked for me on my house. Weather very warm.

February 12, 1870; Saturday. In morning worked on my house and attended school and then returned to my work on my house. Worked until dark in evening read paper some rain fell during the nig^ht.^

February 13, 1870; Sunday. This morning some snow very wet under foot and quite warm. Attended meeting morning and evening and also the sabbath School. Dined with Sister [Eunice] Huntsman.

February 14, 1870; Monday. Worked on my house under the hill.

February 15, 1870; Tuesday. Worked at my house.

February 16, 1870; Wednesday. Went to the mill and got some timber for a wagon rack. Weather cooler, wrote letter to Paulina.

February 17, 1870; Thursday. Brother [Nathan C.] Tinney returned from Sanpete with an axel broken which he repaired at my place. Weather cold but pleasant. Wrote letters for northern mail.

February 18, 1870; Friday. This morning lent bro^th^er [Nathan C.] Tiney 66 lbs of wheat. Worked at shop-work.

February 19, 1870; Saturday. Worked at shop work in morning. Attended school and ground some tools in evening after school. At night spent some time reading.

February 20, 1870; Sunday. Attended meeting morning and evening and Sabath school at mid day. Took diner with brother [John] Kelley and family. Spoke to the people in the evening for a short time. Weather quite warm. Brother [Josiah F.] Gibbs returned with [my] cariage broken.

February 21, 1870; Monday. Worked in my orchard pruneing the trees gave promise of a good fruit crop. Bought of brother [John] Bourne 55 rods of fencing for which I am to pay him corn and flour.

February 22, 1870; Tuesday. Visited the mill and had some talk with brother [William] Gibbs in regard to starting our furniture factory.

February 23, 1870; Wednesday. Worked in my orchard.

February 24, 1870; Thursday. Had some pruning tools mad[e] [and] repaired and at night I attended the meeting of the Elders Quorum. Brother Phineas Young stayed over night with us. He was on his way to Minersville.

February 25, 1870; Friday. Worked in my orchard some snow fell the last night.

February 26, 1870; Saturday. The snow mostly gone worked on my trees in the morning. Attended school in the afternoon. received letter from Paulina dated 22nd.

February 27, 1870; Sunday. Attended meeting morning and evening and also the Sabbath school. The weather warm and pleasant some mud in streets.

February 28, 1870; Monday. Visited my mill and shelled some corn and pruned some in afternoon.

March 1, 1870; Tuesday. Shelled some corn and pruned in the evening.

March 2, 1870; Wednesday. Pruned some trees. At night snow fell.

March 3, 1870; Thursday. Passed the day in town did not engage in labor to day. In afternoon the Prest [Brigham Young] and party came in I received a call [visit] from cousin G[eorge] A. Smith and attended meetings in the evening.

March 4, 1870; Friday. Visited brother Andrew Henry.

March 5, 1870; Saturday. Attended the school and in the evening attended the Lyceum [study group]. The weather turning cold.

March 6, 1870; Sunday. Attended meeting in the morning and evening and also sabbath school. Albert Tanner stayed over night with us on his way to the city. Weather cold.

March 7, 1870; Monday. Shelled some corn and in the evening pruned some trees.

March 8, 1870; Tuesday. Shelled corn some indications of change in weather.

March 9, 1870; Wednesday. Missionaries returned today.

March 10, 1870; Thursday. Shelled corn in morning. In afternoon repaired my fire places. This evening brothers Marfat and Tanner with their families called on us. Snow fell tonight.[127]

March 11, 1870; Friday. Visited brother [Edward] Web's school in company with brother [John] Kelley and F[rancis] M. Lyman. In the afternoon called on brother G[abriel] Huntsman. Past the evening at Marions.

---

127. Lyman initially put this entry under Mar. 9.

March 12, 1870; Saturday. Brother Tanner left us to day. In afternoon attended the school.

March 13, 1870; Sunday. Attended meeting morning and evening and the sabbath school.

March 14, 1870; Monday. ~~Shelled corn and~~ The boys hauled wood weather quite cold pruned some trees.

March 15, 1870; Tuesday. We shelled corn the weather somewhat milder than yesterday.

March 16, 1870; Wednesday. Had the horses shod and shelled some corn. At night attended the Seventies meeting.

March 17, 1870; Thursday. The boys hauled wood. We shelled some corn and at evening went to meeting to consider subject of our stock.

March 18, 1870; Friday. Worked on the dam the boys pruned the trees and hauled wood.

March 19, 1870; Saturday. Attended the school. In the evening met with the Lyceum.

March 20, 1870; Sunday. Attended meeting morning and evening and also the Sabbath school.

March 21, 1870; Monday. Worked on the dam and Theodore hunted stock and Lorenzo pruned trees.

March 22, 1870; Tuesday. Made some new fence and reset some old.

March 23, 1870; Wednesday. Worked at setting fence. In evening raised some apples we had buried. They were well preserved. Engaged passage in stage to Beaver. Rain falling at night.

March 24, 1870; Thursday. Started for Parowan and traviled to and lodged at Cove Creek with brother I[ra] Hinkly.

March 25, 1870; Friday. Traviled to Paragona and lodged with brother Miles Anderson.

March 26, 1870; Saturday. Traviled to Parowan and found my family well. In the afternoon attended the school [and] was invited to address the school.

March 27, 1870; Sunday. Attended meeting was invited to address the congregation by Bishop [Samuel] Rogers.[128] Dined with brother [Daniel]

128. Parowan had grown significantly. There were now two wards led by Bishops Herman Bayles and Samuel Rogers.

Page and family. In the evening Prest [William H.] Dame denounced my teachings to the people.

March 28, 1870; Monday. Remained at home with my family. During the day called on some friends.

March 29, 1870; Tuesday. Visited brother Richard Bensons family.

March 30, 1870; Wednesday. Visited brother Thomas Durham's family. Saw Prest [William H.] Dame and had some talk with him. He declared his inocence of any wrong intentions in what he said of me on Sunday. Was 51 to day.

March 31, 1870; Thursday. Remained at home.

April 1, 1870; Friday. Attended the funeral of brother John Perkins.[129]

April 2, 1870; Saturday. Visited brother [William] Warren's family at his ranch in company with brother Daniel Clark and wife.

April 3, 1870; Sunday. Returned to Parowan.

April 4, 1870; Monday. Went to Beaver with brother Thomas Richards. Stoped with brother Sidney Tanner.

April 5, 1870; Tuesday. Remained in Beaver. Dined with brother [Marcus L.] Shepherd and called on brother [William] Cox and brother Crouck.

April 6, 1870; Wednesday. Went to Minersville with brother Daniel Olsen, found my wife [Dionetia] well.

April 7, 1870; Thursday. Remained at home.

April 8, 1870; Friday. Made some calls in town. Dined with br [Edwin] Bingham and family.

April 9, 1870; Saturday. The Prest [Brigham Young] and party were here and held meeting. Dined with brother [John] Osborn and family. Friends called in the evening.

April 10, 1870 Sunday. Attended meeting and was requested to speak by Bishop [James] McNight. Dined with brother Frederick Turley & family, in evening called on Sister Nancy Rollins.

April 11, 1870; Monday. Went to Beaver with brother Edwin Bingham. Dined with my daughter Matilda and family at Greenville at the residence of brother Albert Goodwin. Meet my wife Paulina in Beaver.

---

129. John Perkins was an old friend from San Bernardino. He collapsed at forty-eight years of age while searching for a lost cow and calf.

April 12, 1870; Tuesday. Traviled to Cove Creek and was entertained by brother [Ira] Hinkley, at this place meet my sons Platt and Theodore.

April 13, 1870; Wednesday. Had a severe snow storm in which I traviled to Fillmore with the mail where we arived at dark.[130]

April 14, 1870; Thursday. Remained at home and passed the time in reading and writing for the mail east.

April 15, 1870; Friday. Assisted in working for weaveing. Weather some warmer than yesterday.

April 16, 1870; Saturday. Finished working. The weather warm and pleasant. Attended the school.

April 17, 1870; Sunday. Very pleasant in the morning. Attended meeting in the morning. Spent the evening with brother [Noah] Bartholimew. Took supper with brother [John] Kelley and family.

April 18, 1870; Monday. Worked on my place under the hill. Weather warm.

April 19, 1870; Tuesday. Continued my work on my place.

April 20, 1870; Wednesday. This evening attended to business for brothers [Gabriel and Levi] Huntsman's.

April 21, 1870; Thursday. Worked in my garden. At night received a call from brother Decker a returning missionary he staid over night. To day meet the mail agent Mr [John H.] Wickizer.[131]

April 22, 1870; Friday. Past the day at home.

April 23, 1870; Saturday. Attended School and in the evening sat in arbitration on the case of Gabriel Huntsman and the estate of Levi Huntsman. Received letter from [Brigham Young's counselor] G[eorge] A. Smith.

April 24, 1870; Sunday. Attended meeting in morning and evening. Wrote letter to Miss Sophronia Lyman of Rhode Island.

April 25, 1870; Monday. Worked on my place picking up rocks and cleaning the ditches.

April 26, 1870; Tuesday. Worked as on Monday.

April 27, 1870; Wednesday. Brother [Frederick] Turley called on us and staid all night.

---

130. Notice that he traveled to Beaver to post letters and is returning with incoming mail.

131. Wickizer was the non-Mormon federal appointee.

April 28, 1870; Thursday. Several teems passed on their way to conference.

April 29, 1870; Friday. Brother W[illiam] S. Warren called on us from the city. Made some preperations for journey to the [Salt Lake] city.

April 30, 1870; Saturday. Started for the city with brother [Gabriel] Huntsman and wife [Eunice]. Traviled to Scipio lodged with brother [Jesse] Martin's family.

May 1, 1870; Sunday. Traviled to Salt Creek. Lodged with brother Hague.

May 2, 1870; Monday. Traviled to Provo and lodged with Brother R[ichard] R. Hopkins.

May 3, 1870; Tuesday. Traviled to Salt Lake City. Put up with my daughter Mrs Clayton.

May 4, 1870; Wednesday. Called on Prest [Brigham] Young and also meet brother [Charles C.] Rich.

May 5, 1870; Thursday. Attended Conference dined with brother [William] Godbe.

May 6, 1870; Friday. Attended meeting.

May 7, 1870; Saturday. Attended meeting. Dined with brother [Frederick T.] Peris.

May 8, 1870; Sunday. Attended meeting in the morning and dined with brother C[harles] C. Rich. In the evening announced to brother [William] Clayton and my son Marion my intention to resume ^the^ preaching of the [Godbe] gospel. It gave them much pain.[132]

May 9, 1870; Monday. Parted ^with^ Marion and Lelia who returned home. I remained and stoped with [Godbe-sympathizer] br H[enry] W. Lawrence. To day meet with br Nathan Tanner who expressed himself in sympathy with the [New] Move[ment]. Attended meeting [of the New Movement] at night.

May 10, 1870; Tuesday. Passed the day in town.

May 11, 1870; Wednesday. Passed the day as yesterday. Attended meeting at night spoke for a short time.

132. Lyman had accepted the presidency of the New Movement, implying leadership of the New Zion Church as well, for which he was excommunicated within days by the Salt Lake Stake High Council. A notice of this appeared in the *Deseret News* and later in the *Millennial Star*. See Journal History, May 11, 1870.

May 12, 1870; Thursday. Visited Brother Joseph Silver and while at his place I was waited on by a deputation from the high counsil of the city composed of Elders [Joseph L.] Barfoot[,] [William] Thorne[,] [John L.] Blythe & [Emanuel M.] Murphy, on whose report to the counsil I was cut off from the Church for apostacy as per statement in Deseret News.[133]

May 13, 1870; Friday. Attended to selecting some goods to send to my family. Dined with [Godbeite] brother [William] Shirman [Shearman]. Attended meeting at night.

May 14, 1870; Saturday. Visited my cousin Mr James Day and family.

May 15, 1870; Sunday. Preached at 11 oclock at Music hall[134] and at 7 at same place had some strangers and an attentive audience. Dined with brother [John] Maning and family. Mr P T Barnum was at [New Movement] meeting.[135]

May 16, 1870; Monday. Called on brother [Elias] Harison and spent some time in [the] Tribune office[136] had an interview with Judge Bolt of Nevada who was much pleased with our sentiments.

May 17, 1870; Tuesday. Visited brother [Elias] Harison in the morning and then called on br [William] Sherman with whom I dined. While there I met with Sister Sarah Pratt[137] wife of Orson Pratt. She meet me kindly.

May 18, 1870; Wednesday. To day meet with W[illiam] H. Kimball. Dined with brother Joseph Silver and took super with my cousin James

133. The "To Whom it May Concern" notice was brief: "Amasa M. Lyman was cut off from the Church … for apostasy." *Deseret Evening News*, May 13, 1870.

134. The small Music Hall was built in 1855 for brass-band rehearsals and concerts, and it should not be confused with the larger two-story music hall that was constructed in 1884.

135. Phineas T. Barnum was the owner of Barnum's American Museum (not yet of the circus) and was in Salt Lake City on a lecture tour. The *Deseret News* thought the $1 entrance was "one of the best investments" anyone could make. "Barnum's Lecture," *Deseret News*, May 25, 1870.

136. The *Salt Lake Tribune* was founded by William Godbe, Elias L. T. Harrison, and Edward Tullidge as an organ of the New Movement, originally under the name *Mormon Tribune*. After struggling for years, it was purchased in 1901 by mining speculator and future US Senator Thomas Kearns.

137. Sarah Pratt left her apostle-husband in 1868 when she founded the Salt Lake Anti-Polygamy Society, and it resulted in her excommunication in 1874. Twelve years later she confirmed that Joseph Smith had asked her to be his wife while her husband, Orson, was away on a mission. Van Wagoner, "Sarah M. Pratt."

Day and family. Attended meeting in the evening. Had a pleasant time. Some indications of rain.

May 19, 1870; Thursday. To day visited Sister Lavina Johnson and dined with her. Some indications of rain. Called on br [Elias] Harison. Had an interview with him and br [Thomas] Stenhouse.

May 20, 1870; Friday. Dined with brother [Joseph] Silver. At evening attended the priesthood meeting and spoke for a short time.

May 21, 1870; Saturday. Meet Bayard Taylor. In the evening had an interview with Mr Taylor whom we found very genial and liberal minded gentleman.

May 22, 1870; Sunday. Attended meeting in the morning and preached. Dined with brother [John] Whiting and then went to meeting and preached in the evening had good audiences. Judge [William I.] Appleby was buried to day.[138]

May 23, 1870; Monday. Dined with brother J[oseph] Silver. Meet with brother Holyoake from Parowan. At night meet with brothers William [Godbe] and Elias [Harrison].

May 24, 1870; Tuesday. Went to Tooille in the company of brothers [William] Godbe[,] [Elias] Harison and [William] Shirman. Stopped with [Godbeite] brother [Eli] Kelsey whom we found with slightly improved health.

May 25, 1870; Wednesday. Visited the town of Stockton in Rush Valley. Returned and held meeting in Tooille had a small but attentive audience here meet with my old acquaintence Harison Sagers.

May 26, 1870; Thursday. Returned to Salt Lake City. Found [Henry Lawrence's wife,] Sister [Jennette] Lawrence quite sick. Mad[e] myself ready for my journey south. Revisited my discourse reported by Mr Anderson.

May 27, 1870; Friday. Started for home in stage. Traviled to Provo then continued my travil all night.

May 28, 1870; Saturday. Arrived home found my family mostly well.

May 29, 1870; Sunday. Attended Church in the morning and Dined with Brother Lambson and family. Some rain fell tonight.

May 30, 1870; Monday. Passed the day mostly at home, the weather was stormy. My freight arived from the city this evening.

---

138. Appleby was clerk of the territorial Supreme Court.

May 31, 1870; Tuesday. Set up my stove it worked well. Dined with brother [Noah] Bartholimew. Weather quite cool, received leter from Mr George Dickson Cahaes Albany N. Y.

June 1, 1870; Wednesday. Passed the day in making preperations for my journey to the south. Some indications of storm.

June 2, 1870; Thursday. Started for the south and traviled to Beaver and put up with Father [Theodore] Turley.

June 3, 1870; Friday. Went to Minersville found my family well and the spirit of the new movement working in the minds of the people for which some have already been cut off from the Church.

June 4, 1870; Saturday. Dined with brother Fredrick Turley and family. Called on [the bishop's wife] Sister Hanah Rollins and family. Weather some warmer.

June 5, 1870; Sunday. Held meeting at brother John Bradshaw's at 10 oclock and dined with sister Phebe Bingham and went to Beaver in the afternoon with Brother [Stephen] Franklin lodged with Father [Theodore] Turley.

June 6, 1870; Monday. Had talk with brother [Marcus L.] Shepherd about my stock. Dined with brother [Stephen] Franklin had meeting at night at the residence of br [Charles C.] Woodhouse.[139] Lodged with brother [Frederick] Turley called on br Sidney Tanner.

June 7, 1870; Tuesday. Traviled to Reed Creek and then went to Parowan on foot. Found my family well.

June 8, 1870; Wednesday. Myself and wife went to Waren's Ranch with br [William] W[arren].

June 9, 1870; Thursday. Wrote to brothers [Elias] Harison and [William] Godbe. In the evening returned to Parowan. Weather very pleasant.

June 10, 1870; Friday. Received a call from brother Miles Anderson. ~~In evening called on on Sister Ann Warren.~~ In the evening called on brother Daniel Clark and family.

June 11, 1870; Saturday. Passed the day at home in the evening called on Sister [Ann] Warren.

June 12, 1870; Sunday. Attended the orthodox meeting in morning

139. Woodhouse was an English emigrant. His son, Charles C. Woodhouse Jr., would become Beaver's postmaster and architectural designer of the Odd Fellows Hall and other historical landmarks.

and had a [Godbe] meeting at the residence of br Wm Warren. It was well attended by enquirers. Received a call from br S[eth] M. Blair.

June 13, 1870; Monday. Traviled to Beaver with ~~with~~ brother Thomas Lafeve stoped with br [Frederick] Turley. In the evening several of the brethren called on me to receive instruction in regard to the new movement.

June 14, 1870; Tuesday. Remained in Beaver and preached at night at the residence of br [Charles C.] Woodhouse. Today called on brother [John W.] Christian and dined with Sister [Mary Elizabeth] Lightner.

June 15, 1870; Wednesday. Dined with Sister Sarah Franklin. At night some of the brethren came in and I taught them the nature of the new movement.

June 16, 1870; Thursday. Started for home with br George Adair. Traviled to and camped in Bakers Kanyon [between Cove Creek and Corn Creek/Kanosh]. Had good sleep.

June 17, 1870; Friday. Came to Canosh and took breakfast with br C[ollins] Hakes and then reached home at 1 oclock where I meet my daughter Mrs Clayton from the city and visited my mill which was doing very well. Weather warm.

June 18, 1870; Saturday. Settled with mill and in afternoon called upon brother [Noah] Bartholimew from whom I received 3 dollars for the [Salt Lake] Tribune. Weather very wearm.

June 19, 1870; Sunday. Attended meeting in the morning and in the evening called on br Andrew Henry.

June 20, 1870; Monday. Started for Salt Lake traviled to Provo.

June 21, 1870; Tuesday. Traviled to the city found my friends there well.

June 22, 1870; Wednesday. Made some business calls around the city and took super with br J[oseph] Silver.

June 23, 1870; Thursday. Spent most of the day with brother [Elias] Harison also met with [Methodist] Rev. Mr [George M.] Pierce, had talk with brother Denis.

June 24, 1870; Friday. Spend the day in town with brother Elias [Harrison]. Attended the lecture of Dr [Charles] Pinkham in the evening.[140]

June 25, 1870; Saturday. Dined with br. J[oseph] Silver.

---

140. The *Salt Lake Herald* groused that the lecture on phrenology and spiritualism was lightly attended and unimpressive. "Sold," *Salt Lake Herald*, June 24, 1870.

June 26, 1870; Sunday. Preaching in morning at the Music Hall on the priesthood and in the evening on the atonement. Weather rather warm.

June 27, 1870; Monday. Wrote some letters to my family and in the afternoon called on Sister Rachel Tanner and then in company with Brother [Elias] Harison dined with br Stephens and family.

June 28, 1870; Tuesday. Wrote ~~and dispatched~~ letter to my sister Lucy.

June 29, 1870; Wednesday. Concluded letter and dispached the same with papers to my sister. At night attended meeting had a pleasant time.

June 30, 1870; Thursday. Was engaged in writing for the press [*Salt Lake Tribune*]. At night attended lecture by Dr [Charles] Pinckham on spiritualistic maters.

July 1, 1870; Friday. Past forenoon in reading report of my Sunday morning discourse but it [was] so faulty as rendered it useless. Commenced article on priesthood for publication.

July 2, 1870; Saturday. Finished article for the press. This evening meet br Richard Benson from Parowan who told me my family there were well at date of his leaveing.

July 3, 1870; Sunday. Attended meeting in the morning and preached in the evening. Attended meeting Elder [Elias] Harison spoke.

July 4, 1870; Monday. I[n] morning called on Mr [George] Cronin and in the evening attended a party on the grounds of the Walker Brothers [mercantile business].[141] [I] made [a] short speach [and we] had fire-works.

July 5, 1870; Tuesday. Received 6 or 7 letters and answered some of them. In the evening visited br Elias [Harrison] and called on br [William] Godbes sick children.

July 6. 1870; Wednesday. Wrote letter to [my son] Lorenzo. At night attended meeting. Weather very warm.

July 7, 1870; Thursday. Wrote to br [Stephen] Franklin in Beaver in regard to my stock there and wrote other letters in course of the day.

July 8, 1870; Friday. Passed most of the day in the Tribune office. To day Sister [Jennette] Lawrence went to Provo.

141. A major shopping attraction in Salt Lake City was the Walker Brothers dry goods store on Main Street, with goods imported from St. Louis and San Francisco. After butting heads with Brigham Young, the four brothers (Samuel, Joseph, David, and Mathew) resigned their church memberships and supported the New Movement.

July 9, 1870; Saturday. Today meet with brother [William] Shirman and B[ernard] Snow.

July 10, 1870; Sunday. Attended meeting in the morning. The audience was addressed by br [William] Godbe. In evening I spoke to the people had full house.

July 11, 1870; Monday. Wrote in the office. Dined with br [Joseph] Silver and in the evening meet with the brethren in council.

July 12, 1870; Tuesday. Wrote letters for the southern mail.

July 13, 1870; Wednesday. Wrote for press at night [and] attended meeting.

July 14, 1870; Thursday. Spent the day in writing an[d] reading.

July 15, 1870; Friday. Passed the day in town read some and attended the funeral of the [infant] child of Mr [Fielding] and Mrs [Melissa] Clinton. Spoke on the occasion, light shower in evening.

July 16, 1870; Saturday. Visited br Elias [Harrison] to day.

July 17, 1870; Sunday. Attended meeting and spoke morning and evening. Dined with my friend George Cronin and his daughter Mrs Wilson.

July 18, 1870; Monday. Wrote for the paper weather warm and sultry. At night attended the [New Movement] council meeting at br [Henry] Lawrences house.

July 19, 1870; Tuesday. Passed the morning in writing received a call from a Mr Hutchins who comes to advocate the claims of Sidney Rigdon to the leadership of the Church.[142] Meet uncle Sidney Tanner.

July 20, 1870; Wednesday. Gave br [Sidney] Tanner due bill on store for lumber. Received leters from home, commenced letters for home, attended our meeting in the evening.

July 21, 1870; Thursday. Finished writing and posted my mail matter.

July 22, 1870; Friday. Learned Mr [George] Cronin was missing and joined in the search for him.

July 23, 1870; Saturday. Mr [George] Cronin was found dead from the effects of morphene. He died in a store room of Mr F[rederick] T. Parises house.

---

142. Rigdon oversaw a congregation in Pittsburgh after Joseph Smith's death. When Rigdon's leadership collapsed, it was picked up by one of his followers, William Bickerton, whose church continues today with about 20,000 members in Monongahela, Pennsylvania.

July 24, 1870; Sunday. Attended and spoke at the funeral of Mr [George] Cronin and then preached at the Music Hall at 11 oclock. Attended meeting in evening brs [Elias] Harison and [William] Godbe spoke to the people.

July 25, 1870; Monday. Passed the day with my friends in town.

July 26, 1870; Tuesday. Visited his Excelency the governor [of Utah Territory and] had a very pleasant interview.[143]

July 27, 1870; Wednesday. Meet with a traviling party from the east among them Mr [Joseph B.] Lyman[144] and his wife [Laura]. Mr L is Editor of the Agricultural department of the N. Y. Tribune, in evening attended the festival.

July 28, 1870; Thursday. Passed the day at home weather very warm.

July 29, 1870; Friday. Visited brs [Elias] Harison and passed the most of the day in reading. Meet with brother W[illiam] H. Hooper.

July 30, 1870; Saturday. Attended Council at br [William] Shirmans. Dined with br J[oseph] Silver.

July 31, 1870; Sunday. Attended meeting in morning and evening[,] spoke in morning. In evening br [William] Shirman and [William] Godbe and [Elias] Harison spoke to the people.

August 1, 1870; Monday. Attended meeting for council in morning[,] passed afternoon at home.

August 2, 1870; Tuesday. Wrote to brother J[ames] H. Rollins [in] Minersville. Made arangements for our journey south for missionary purposes.

August 3, 1870; Wednesday. Wrote to Paulina. Received draft of one hundred dollars on the firm of Kimball & Lawrence.[145] Attended meeting at night.

August 4, 1870; Thursday. Wrote to Eliza & Caroline and to Marion sending him a draft of one hundred dollars.

August 5, 1870; Friday. Started south in stage with brs [Elias]

---

143. John Wilson Shaffer and his wife suffered precarious health when he was appointed governor in early 1870 by US President Grant. Shaffer's wife died before they reached Utah, and he passed away within the year on October 31.

144. No relation to Amasa.

145. Like the Walker Brothers' store, the Kimball & Lawrence (John B. Kimball and Henry W. Lawrence) merchandise company competed with ZCMI and catered to the New Movement.

Harison and [William] Godbe. Traviled to Springville and held meeting and lodged with br [Hugh M.] Dougall. Were treated with kindness.

August 6, 1870; Saturday. Called upon br William Bringhurst and family. Br. G[eorge] Garner sent his team from Payson and caried us there to where we held one meeting at night, well attended. Lodged at br Joseph Tanners.

August 7, 1870; Sunday. Br [George] G[arner] sent his team with us to Springville where we found br [Edward] Peay from Provo who took us to his home in Provo where we held one meeting to a good turnout. Lodged with Mr Cuningham who keep mail station and post office.

August 8, 1870; Monday. We returned to the city where we arived about 4 oclock found all well.

August 9, 1870; Tuesday. Received letters from home from Lorenzo and Agnes and answered the same and at 3 oclock meet the Rev Drs [John Philip] Newman and Sunderland.

August 10, 1870; Wednesday. Wrote letter to Bishop A[braham] O. Smoot. Called on my old friends Joseph Cooledge and wife. Attended meeting at night.

August 11, 1870; Thursday. Wrote letter to brother John Kelley.

August 12, 1870; Friday. Meet brother [Frederick T.] Perris and dined with him. The great debate commenced today.[146]

August 13, 1870; Saturday. Received call from br Thomas Stainer from Ogden. Wrote to Marion.

August 14, 1870; Sunday. Attended meeting morning and evening. Br [Elias] Harison spoke in morning[,] myself in the evening. A light shower in afternoon. The great debate closed this afternoon.

August 15, 1870; Monday. ~~Wrote letter to Marion.~~ Received letter from Marion with curency inclosed. ~~Attended counsil in evening.~~ Called on M[aria] L. C[layton]. Attended counsil in evening.

August 16, 1870; Tuesday. Wrote letter to Marion.

August 17, 1870; Wednesday. Made myself ready for my missionary trip south.

---

146. The debate was between the Rev. John Philip Newman, an Episcopal priest and US Senate chaplain, and Mormon apostle Orson Pratt on the topic of plural marriage. "Does the Bible Sanction Polygamy?" *Deseret News*, Aug. 17, 1870.

August 18, 1870; Thursday. Went to Provo lodged with Mr Cuningham. Aranged for meetings on the folowing Sabbath. Some rain at night.

August 19, 1870; Friday. Called on br Edward Mecham and bishop [Myron] Tanner. In the evening called on brother J[ames] H. Smith and family and was entertained with musick by his sons.

August 20, 1870; Saturday. Visited brs Mechams[,] Moses [Mecham] and Lewis [Mecham][,] and brother Mo[o]re.

August 21, 1870; Sunday. Had meeting morning as per appointment. A fine shower in the afternoon. Dined with br Willson and lodged with br Moores family.

August 22, 1870; Monday. In evening went to Springville in the stage and lodged with Cister [Emmeline] McCurdy.

August 23, 1870; Tuesday. Visited br Jesse Steel and family.[147] Failed to make any arangements for meeting. Sister H Jacobs and her mother called on me in the evening.

August 24, 1870; Wednesday. Called on br [Hugh M.] Dougal and also on brother [John] Browns family. Dined with br Dougal concluded to go to Payson in the evening stage. Had talk with Solomon Chase.[148] Went to Payson.

August 25, 1870; Thursday. Remained with br [George] Garner's and at night heard lecture by Dr [Charles] Pinkham on Phrenology. Weather somewhat cool. I wrote to br Ried in the city. Dined with Dr [Gustavus] Simonds. Attended the lecture at night delivered by Dr Pinkham.

August 26, 1870; Friday. Dined with br Joseph Tanner and family, attended the lecture at night.

August 27, 1870; Saturday. Dined at br [George] Garners and attended the lectures at night.

August 28, 1870; Sunday. Attended meeting at 4 oclock and spoke to the people.

August 29, 1870; Monday. Took breakfast with Br Freeman Tanner

147. Jesse P. Steele was captain of the Minutemen during the Black Hawk War. Strangely enough, he was also superintendent of the Springville Sunday school. He was later assigned to colonize La Plata, New Mexico, in the Four Corners area. Esshom, *Pioneers and Prominent Men of Utah*, 1182–83.

148. Solomon Chase was constructing a lumber mill in Wadsworth Canyon near Alpine. His Uncle Isaac Chase built the lumber mill in Salt Lake City at what is now a protected historical site within Liberty Park.

and family. Remained with br [George] Garners. In the evening I received some letters from the City by br Andrew Garner. Started for home at 12 oclock night.

August 30, 1870; Tuesday. Reached home [the next day] in the evening,[149] found all well, passed the Prest [Brigham Young's] party at Nephi.

August 31, 1870; Wednesday. Remained at home with my family. The Prests party arived and held meeting. In the evening [I] called on Amasa [Jr.] and family.

September 1, 1870; Thursday. Fast day the family went to meeting. Made some arangements for my journey to the south.

September 2, 1870; Friday. The workmen came to work on [seventh wife] Priscilla's house.

September 3, 1870; Saturday. Dined with Marion and family and started in the afternoon for the south. Traviled to Corn Creek [Kanosh] and lodged with br [Collins] Hakes.

September 4, 1870; Sunday. Traviled to and lodged with son inlaw Philo Carter and family near Greenville in Beaver County.

September 5, 1870; Monday. ~~Traviled to Parowan and found my family there in good health.~~ Traviled to Beaver and lodged with Uncle [brother-in-law] Sydney Tanner.

September 6, 1870; Tuesday. Traviled to Parowan found my family there well[,] as wer all my friends as far as heard from.

September 7, 1870; Wednesday. ~~Took breakfast with brother Daniel Page and family. And took supper with Sister Benson.~~ Called on some of my friends through the day.

September 8, 1870; Thursday. Took breakfast with brother [Daniel] Page and took supper with Sister [Phoebe] Benson.

September 9, 1870; Friday. Passed the day in reading. Received telegram from Salt Lake City from br H[enry] W. Lawrence which hastened my return.[150]

September 10, 1870; Saturday. In evening called on br D[aniel] P. Clarks family.

---

149. Having traveled 90 miles from Payson, the trip probably took over 23 hours in a carriage moving about 4 miles per hour, pulled by horses that needed to be periodically rested. By the time he arrived in Fillmore, it would have been Wednesday morning.

150. Lyman was summoned to meet with John Spear, a spiritualist visiting from California.

September 11, 1870; Sunday. Had meeting at the house of br W[illiam] S. Warren at 4 oclock good attendence.

September 12, 1870; Monday. Returned to Beaver and lodged with br [Marcus L.] Shepherd.

September 13, 1870; Tuesday. Traviled to Canosh and put up with br [Collins] Hakes and family.

September 14, 1870; Wednesday. Arived at home found all well. Attended to some business in the afternoon.

September 15, 1870; Thursday. Started for the city in the stage ~~tr~~ [and] arived at Chicken Creek [south of Nephi] at night.

September 16, 1870; Friday. Arived at the city this evening found my friends well.

September 17, 1870; Saturday. Passed the day in makeing some calls on my friends. To day meet with Mr J[ohn] M. Spear a spiritualist from Cal[ifornia].[151]

September 18, 1870; Sunday. Attended [meetings] morning and evening both of which times I spoke to the people.

September 19, 1870; Monday. In the morning called on my daughter Mrs. Clayton. This evening called on br [Henry] Brooks and family. Br B[ernard] Snow was present.

September 20, 1870; Tuesday. Passed the day in reading. Visited the ground of the [future] meeting house.[152]

September 21, 1870; Wednesday. Had an interview with Mr [John M.] Spear br [Elias] Harison was present.

September 22, 1870; Thursday. Received some words purporting to come from Joseph Smith through Mr [John M.] Spear.[153] Wrote letter to Dionitia filled up the time in reading.

September 23, 1870; Friday. Passed the day in reading at night attended a seance at br [Frederick T.] Peris.

---

151. There were rumors that John Murray Spear had allowed "sexual experimentation" at his commune in Chautauqua, New York. He nevertheless appealed to mainstream Christians by linking spiritualism to traditional beliefs. Walker, *Wayward Saints*, 253–54.

152. The contemplated "meeting house" would be called the Liberal Institute, or Liberal Hall, with seating for up to 1,000 people. That made it the second-largest hall in the city after the Tabernacle, which accommodated 7,000 people. Walker, "The Liberal Institute," 76.

153. In other words, Spear acted as a medium to channel the spirit of Joseph Smith. See the next three entries for further clarification.

September 24, 1870; Saturday. Passed the day in reading at night called on Mr [John M.] Spear with br [William] Shirman.

September 25, 1870; Sunday. Attended meeting. [Our] friend [John M.] Spear spoke to us br [Elias] Harison spoke and I made some close-ing remarks. Mr Spear is a spiritual medium.

September 26, 1870; Monday. I[n] morning visited the ground of the new meeting house. Passed the day mostly in reading. In company with br [John M.] Spear called on Sister Mary Godbe.

September 27, 1870; Tuesday. Passed the day mostly in reading in the afternoon called on Sister Mary Godbe whose child was blessed and named by brother [John M.] Spear. I[n] the evening attended a meeting at residence of br [Thomas C.] Armstrong.

September 28, 1870; Wednesday. Commenced writing to my sister and in after noon finished my letter and called on the governor [John Shaffer]. In evening attended a buisness meeting at br [Frederick T.] Perrise's.

September 29, 1870; Thursday. Attended the funeral of br [Samuel S.] Walkers child and in the afternoon wrote to my wife in Fillmore. In evening attended meeting at br. [Henry] Kendalls. Today a barn was burned which b[e]longed to Homer Brown. 2 children burn to death.[154]

September 30, 1870; Friday. Wrote leter to Lorenzo. Call on Sister Mary Godbe. Passed residue of day in reading. Mrs Brown the mother of the children that were burned yesterday died today.[155]

October 1, 1870; Saturday. Meet with br Nathan Tanner. Dined with him. Passed residue of day in reading. Received letter from br M. H. Tanner [and] N. Perry.

October 2, 1870; Sunday. Attended meeting in the morning spoke to the people. In the evening br [Elias] Harison preached. Dined with br and sister [Thomas and Fanny] Stenhouse. Weather warm and dry.

October 3, 1870; Monday. Met my wife Paulina from Parrowan. Attended a meeting at br. [Frederick T.] Parises. Lodged at br George Crismon's was taken sick in the night.

---

154. The two children were half-sisters Harriet and Celestia Brown, their father Homer Brown, whose two wives, Sarah and Bertha, had given birth in December 1863, just twenty-eight days apart. When Bertha died in 1866, Sarah began raising Celestia. The girls were six years old.

155. Lyman is mistaken because Sarah survived her grief to petition for divorce in 1882, thereafter remarrying and moving to Colorado.

October 4, 1870; Tuesday. Continued sick through the day. My wife went to Farmington to meet her friends.

October 5, 1870; Wednesday. Meet with br George Crouch and walked out with him. Took my bed in afternoon.

October 6, 1870; Thursday. Laid the corner stone of the New Meeting House and attended meeting in the evening at Music Hall. Lodged at G[eorge] Crismonds.

October 7, 1870; Friday. Spent some time with brs [William] Godbe and [Eli] Kelsey and [William] Shirman. Passed some time with br [George] Crouch.

October 8, 1870; Saturday. Spent early part of the day with br [John] Kelley. In evening married a couple Mr [Ephraim J.] Crossley and Miss [Keziah] All~~a~~en [Hall][156] and attended meeting lodged at [George] Crismonds.

October 9, 1870; Sunday. Wrote letter to Lorenzo. Attended meeting which was addressed by br [John M.] Spear. Dined with br [William] Godbe and attended meeting in the evening spoke for a short time to the people had a full house.

October 10, 1870; Monday. Passed [day] in assisting my wife to prepare for the return to Parrowan. She started in the evening. At night visited br [Elias] Harison.

October 11, 1870; Tuesday. Wrote letters East and South. Attended meeting in evening at br [Thomas C.] Armstrongs.

October 12, 1870; Wednesday. Wrote letter to Oscar and in the evening attended a business meeting at the house of br. [Frederick T.] Peris.

October 13, 1870; Thursday. Made some enquiries for house to rent. During day had an interview with Colonel [Peter] Saxie from Troy N.Y.[157] He was homeward bound. In the evening called on br [Elias] Harison.

October 14, 1870; Friday. Attended the funeral of the child of br John Tullidge and spoke on the occasion to the friends present.[158] Had a severe dust storm in the afternoon.

---

156. Lyman was unsure of the name Keziah Hall (not Keziah Allen), but she is the woman who married Ephraim Crossley.

157. Peter Saxe had relocated to California as a sheep rancher and had brought some stock to market in Salt Lake City and Ogden.

158. One-year-old William was one of ten children under the age of nine whom John and Mary Ann Tullidge would lose. John was the brother of Edward Tullidge.

October 15, 1870; Saturday. Confered with Mrs Kay in regard to the rent of her house. Wrote to Lorenzo in answer to his of the 12th.

October 16, 1870; Sunday. Attended meeting. In the [afternoon] spoke after br [William] Godbe. In evening brs [Bernard] Snow[,] [Eli] Kelsey and [Elias] Harison spoke. Dined with br [William S.] Warren.

October 17, 1870; Monday. Passed some time in makeing arangements for fiting up my house. In evening attended a meeting in the [music] hall to consider the mater of the raising funds for the movement.

October 18, 1870; Tuesday. Bought bedstead of br Brand for 10 dollars in the evening attended a meeting at br [Thomas C.] Armstrongs.

October 19, 1870; Wednesday. Borowed 10 dollars of br Wm Pitts to be paid when [I am flush] in funds. At night had interview with br [John M.] Spear at his room. Br [William] Godbe went to east Can[y]on.

October 20, 1870; Thursday. Br [Frederick T.] Paris let me have a bedstead and two pairs of shoes for wife and child. At night attended meeting at br [John] Maning's.

October 21, 1870; Friday. Was engaged in working on my rooms. Br Carlile was helping me. Called on br [Joseph] Salsbury at noon. Passed the evening in reading.

October 22, 1870; Saturday. Wrote letter to Lorenzo had an interview with Mr [John M.] Spear and Mr [James] Cob, at Tribune Office. At evening called on brother [Frederick T.] Peris and family.

October 23, 1870; Sunday. Attended meeting morning and evening spoke each time. Dined with br [Henry] Kendal and family and in afternoon married Br E[lias] L. T. Harison and Sister Rebeka Jones.[159]

October 24, 1870; Monday. Meet and passed some time with br [James] Henry Rollins. Failed to get any work on house.

October 25, 1870; Tuesday. Wrote letters to Priscilla in the evening attended meeting at br [Thomas C.] Armstrongs. Had some rain to day. Bought some things for my family.

October 26, 1870; Wednesday. Passed some time in reading. Obtained some lumber for furniture in evening [and] attended a meeting at br [Thomas C.] Armstrongs. As I was returning home the rain was falling quite copiously.

---

159. Two of Harrison's previous wives had passed away: Jemima Camp on the Mormon trail and Margaret in childbirth. Another wife, Jennie, would die in 1881.

October 27, 1870; Thursday. Secured some promises of help on my rooms and met with br [Eli] Kelsey. In the evening attended a meeting at the residence of br [John] Maning.

October 28, 1870; Friday. Made some advance in preparation for my family. At night dreamed of meeting my mother she seemed to be journeying.[160] Sent an apointment to Ogdden for the comeing sabbath.

October 29, 1870; Saturday. Went to Ogden and lodged with br T[homas C.] Stainer. Was very kindly received by them.

October 30, 1870; Sunday. Passed part of the day with my old friend Dr. [William] McIntire. In the evening held a meeting which was well attended. Stayed with br [Thomas C.] Staner.

October 31, 1870; Monday. Returned to the city. While waiting on the train I was informed of the death of the goviner [John W. Shaffer].

November 1, 1870; Tuesday. Called my daughter Mrs Clayton and in the afternoon attended the funeral of the governor. At night attended a meeting at br [Thomas C.] Armstrongs.

November 2, 1870; Wednesday. Had some work done on my rooms in the evening attended meeting at the residence of br [Thomas C.] Armstrong. Some indications of rain.

November 3, 1870; Thursday. Wrote letters home had some work on my house and in the evening meet with Mr Redfield at br [John] Manings. He was from California.

November 4, 1870; Friday. Called on [the] br [Frederick T.] Paris family and in evening had buisness meeting at br [Elias] Harisons. Brothers [William] Godbe[,] [Henry] Lawrence and [Frederick] Peris returned from East canyon and were present.

November 5, 1870; Saturday. To day meet with my old friend Mrs Morint from California. Received letter from br. [William] Shirman in east canyon.

November 6, 1870; Sunday. Attended meeting in morning and evening[,] spoke in evening. Br [William] Godbe spoke in morning dined with br [John] Maning. Attended seance[161] at br [James P.] Keates.

160. His mother was Martha Mason Emerson, now eighty-three years old. Lyman must have harbored some concern for her health. She would only live another four years.

161. This is the second time Lyman has explicitly referred to a séance, as he did on September 23.

November 7, 1870; Monday. Made some little advance in work on my house. At night attended meeting at br [Elias] Harisons. Snow fell to night.

November 8, 1870; Tuesday. Had stoves put in my house at night attended meeting at br [Thomas C.] Armstrongs.

November 9, 1870; Wednesday. Called at the office of the U. S. Marshall, he was not at home, At night attended a Counsil meeting at br [Elias] Harisons.

November 10, 1870; Thursday. Secured the building of my cupboard and made other preperations for my journey to my family. Called on Mrs Clayton. At night attended meeting at the [music] hall when the subject of organization was considered.[162]

November 11, 1870; Friday. Started for Fillmore weather rather cool. Had for traviling partner Sister Huldah Kimball as far as Springville.

November 12, 1870; Saturday. Arived home in evening found all well.

November 13, 1870; Sunday. Through the cou[r]tesy of <u>Prest</u> [Thomas] Callister we were favored with the use of the State House hall in which myself and brother John Kelley had meeting at 3 oclock with good attendence.

November 14, 1870; Monday. Passed day in makeing arangements for my removal to the city of Salt Lake with my family.

November 15, 1870; Tuesday. This evening my son arived home and he engaged to help me in my move to the city. Weather very fine.

November 16, 1870; Wednesday. Concluded my preperations for moveing.

November 17, 1870; Thursday. Started on our journey[,] traviled to Round Valley and camped.

November 18, 1870; Friday. Traviled to Chicken Creek. Put up with br Raymond Elmore.

November 19, 1870; Saturday. Traviled to Willow Creek. Put up with brother John Green. Nooned with Father [Timothy B.] Foot.

November 20, 1870; Sunday. Traviled to Payson and put up with br Joseph Tanners family.

---

162. He probably had reference to the Church of New Zion, of which he was president. Godbe and his cohorts had also founded a political party and a newspaper, so any number of things may have needed organizing or re-organizing.

November 21, 1870; Monday. Traviled to Provo and lodged with Bishop M[yron] Tanner.

November 22, 1870; Tuesday. Traviled to and put [up] at the Andrus place at point of mountain.

November 23, 1870; Wednesday. Reached the city about 3 oclock P.M. and camped in our house and made some demonstrations towards liveing.

November 24, 1870; Thursday. Worked at prepareing house, Amasa and Ira started for home to day.

November 25, 1870; Friday. Purchased some things for the House.

November 26, 1870; Saturday. Bought some furniture for the house.

November 27, 1870; Sunday. Attended meeting in the morning and spoke for an hour. In the afternoon went to Ogden preached in the evening had good audience. Lodged with br [Thomas C.] Stayner.

November 28, 1870; Monday. Returned to Salt lake City weather pleasant. At night visited br [Thomas C.] Armstrongs family. Received letters from the north and south of Utah and Montana.

November 29, 1870; Tuesday. Wrote letter to Paulina and made some purchases for her. At night attended a meeting at br. [Thomas C.] Armstrongs.

November 30, 1870; Wednesday. Delivered Paulina's parcel to br D[aniel] P. Clark to deliver to her. Received leter from Paulina.

December 1, 1870; Thursday. Passed the day in arangeing my papers. At night called on br [John] Maning and family.

December 2, 1870; Friday. Wrote letter to L. B. Lyman [in] Montana and spent some time in arangeing my papers.

December 3, 1870; Saturday. Passed the day as yesterday.

December 4, 1870; Sunday. Gave the use of our hall to Father Mespie a Catholick who held service morning and evening.[163] After evening services I spoke for half an hour. Br [Elias] Harison spoke at Ogden.

December 5, 1870; Monday. Passed the day in writeing and arangeing my papers. At night attended a Council at brother [Elias] Harisons.

December 6, 1870; Tuesday. Continued the arangement of my papers and finished letter to Cousin Sophronia Lyman and at night attended meeting at br [Thomas C.] Armstrong's.

---

163. The Liberal Hall would not be completed until July 1871. The church was renting the Music Hall (see entries for May 15, June 26, July 24, Oct. 6).

December 7, 1870; Wednesday. Wrote letters to Paulina and also to Father [Theodore] Turley. At night attended meeting for buisness in the [music] hall. Ajourned until next Tuesday night at same place.

December 8, 1870; Thursday. Wrote letter to br. [Theodore] Turley. At night attended a meeting at br [John] Manings. Weather cool and clear.

December 9, 1870; Friday. Wrote letter to br Hanks[,] Ebenezer. At night visited br [John] Maning's.

December 10, 1870; Saturday. Prepared to go to Ogden. Visited the new meeting-house[164] and in the evening went to Ogden. Lodged with brother [Thomas C.] Stayner and family.

December 11, 1870; Sunday. Passed the day at br [Thomas C.] Stayner's. At evening I preached at Cordons Hall[165] had attentive hearers.

December 12, 1870; Monday. Taried with br [Thomas C.] Stayner until evening then I came to Salt Lake City and meet with the Executive Committie.

December 13, 1870; Tuesday. Visited the meeting house at night[,] attended a meeting at the Hall.

December 14, 1870; Wednesday. Visited the meeting house. Passed the evening at the home.

December 15, 1870; Thursday. Past sometime in writing. Visited the meeting house attended meeting at br [John] Maning's, posted letter to Richie and received letter from Daniel Page.

December 16, 1870; Friday. Wrote letters to Br [Daniel] Page and my wife Paulina. Visited meeting house.

December 17, 1870; Saturday. Passed some time in reading. In afternoon visited meeting house and also called at [Frederick T.] Perises to return his book.

December 18, 1870; Sunday. Attended meeting morning and evening. Br [Joseph] Salsbury addressed the audience and I spoke in the evening. In afternoon visited Br R[ichard] R. Hopkins and his family.

December 19, 1870; Monday. Received leter from Father [Theodore]

---

164. Lyman seems to distinguish between the unfinished Liberal Institute and the music hall by calling the former a "meeting house."

165. Cordon's Hall in Ogden was an adobe building at 25th and Main (Washington Boulevard). The old railroad station was a mile to the west on the bank of the Weber River, accessible only by boardwalk across the intervening mud flats.

Turley and answered the same. Visited the meeting house attended council meeting. Weather very cool.

December 20, 1870; Tuesday. In the morning visited brother Dow who was sick and then visited the meeting house. Received l[e]tter from Marion [and] answered the same. In evening attended a meeting at br [Thomas C.] Armstrong's.

December 21, 1870; Wednesday. Received letter from brother John Kelley of Fillmore. Visited the mailing house and in the evening attended meeting for buisness in the hall.

December 22, 1870; Thursday. Wrote for the press and visited the meeting house and in the evening attended meeting at Br [John] Manings. Weather very cold.

December 23, 1870; Friday. Wrote letters to brothers J[ohn] Kelly and W[illiam] H. She[a]rman. Called on Mrs Shearman. Visited the meeting house. In evening attended a concert at Fausts Hall.[166] Weather very cold.

December 24, 1870; Saturday. Passed some time reading. Philo Carter son in law called to day reported his family well when he left them. Weather slightly more mild. Made my visit to the meeting house.

December 25, 1870; Sunday. In morning called at the [Godbe–Pitts] Drug Store [at 100 South Main Street]. Received from br [William H.] Pitts five dollars and a bottle of Sherry. Called on br [William] Godbe and Dined with brother [John] Maning and attend[ed] Cushmans lecture at Fausts Hall. The weather more mild.

December 26, 1870; Monday. In the morning called on Mr Cushman at the White House[167] and went with him to call on br [William] Godbe and to see our new Meeting House then spent several hours with Mr C. in his room. In the evening attended meeting at br [Thomas C.] Armstrongs.

December 27, 1870; Tuesday. Visited the Meeting House and spent some time with Mr Cushman and dined with him and in evening attended meeting at br [Thomas C.] Armstrong's. Masons working on the church [building] to day.

---

166. Faust's Hall on Second South was actually a 30' x 100' hay loft above a livery stable.

167. The White House on Main Street charged visitors and tenants $2.00 per day and fifty cents for a day's meals.

December 28, 1870; Wednesday. Wrote letter to Oscar and wife. Visited the Meeting House spent some time with Mr Cushman and in evening attended his concert in 13 Ward Hall.[168] Weather mild, called on the Dr Roberts.

December 29, 1870; Thursday. Received and answered a letter from George Garner of Payson. Spent some time in visiting the sick visited the new Church and spent some time in reading. In evening called on br [Elias] Harison and attended the concert.

December 30, 1870; Friday. Received and answered letter from Marion. Visited the new Meeting House spent some time with Mr Burk at Br [Elias] Harisons. Called on Sister [Jennette] Lawrence spent evening with brother [Elias] Harison and family & friends.

December 31, 1870; Saturday. Received letter from Father [Theodore] Turley. Visited the Meeting House passed some time in reading at night attended Cushmans concert, thus closed with me the eventful year 1870.

168. Cushman had a troupe of musical and dance performers that offered "chaste entertainments," according to a Salt Lake newspaper. "Cushman Troupe," *Salt Lake Herald*, Dec. 29, 1870.

11 "Attended Séance," 1871–1872

As Lyman begins the new year, he seems to be himself again, his schedule filled with church meetings and speaking engagements, writing that he "attended Council at Br. Harrison's," for instance. It is a different church and different council, but the routine is more or less the same as before. He checks daily on the construction of the New Zion chapel in downtown Salt Lake City. The church of which he is now president is meeting temporarily in the city's Music Hall. Instead of charismatic spiritual experiences of the Mormon type, Lyman is now speaking with the dead through séances held as part of the New Movement's devotional services. They entertain famous mediums from the East Coast, present exhibitions for the public in theaters and hold "private séances" in members' homes, sometimes two or more times a day. Then he becomes alarmed about perceived threats from the "orthodox [LDS] church" and organizes a vigilance league of liberals prepared to defend themselves if needed.

January 1, 1871; Sunday. The morning was bright and fair. Attended meeting morning and evening[,] spoke to the people in the evening. Dined with br [John] Maning and family.

January 2, 1871; Monday. Passed some time with Brother H[enry] W. Lawrence and with him and br [Frederick T.] Peris went to the new meeting house.[1] Called on <u>Mr</u>. Cushman. In the evening attended the

1. The Church of New Zion meetinghouse was at 200 East between 100 and 200 South. It was a half-shell, "half-octagonal" shape. Prior to its completion in June 1871,

party at Baloys [Ballo's] Hall.[2] Stayed until eleven then went home. The party cleared some fifty dollars for the widow Wray.

January 3, 1871; Tuesday. Wrote letter to Father [Theodore] Turley. Visited the Meeting House and saw the first tin laid on the roof. At night attended meeting at br ~~Manings~~ [Thomas C.] Armstrongs. Quite well to night.

January 4, 1871; Wednesday. Visited Mr Cushman in the morning found him slightly better in health. Received and answered letters from Paulina and Oscar. Called on br [William S.] Godbe and paid [Henry] Kimble and [Henry] Lawrence forty five dollers on acount. In evening called on Mrs. Lovina Johnson.

January 5, 1871; Thursday. Received a letter from Marion on land maters and answered. Visited the Meeting House and in the afternoon visited br [John] Manings with br [Elias] Harrison and family and Mrs Lyman. In the evening attended meeting at the same place. Weather warm.

January 6, 1871; Friday. Borowed book of br [Frederick T.] Peris entitled Strange Visitors.[3] Visited meeting House and met with br T[homas J.] Staynor from the City of Ogden. At night attended seance at the residence of br [John] Maning.

January 7, 1871; Saturday. In the morning visited the Meeting House and called on br [Elias] Harison and spent some time in reading. Father [Theodore] Turley arived here to day in the stage from Beaver he came to be treated for a cancer on his lower lip. He engaged the services of Dr Roberts Magnetic Physician who agreed to treat his case for fifty dollars.[4] Passed evening in reading. Weather slightly colder.

January 8, 1871; Sunday. Attended meeting morning and evening.

---

the church rented a hall in Salt Lake City and other private buildings in Ogden and elsewhere. *AML*, 448–49.

2. The music hall was nicknamed, after Domenico Ballo, the leader of the city's brass band. Lindsay, *Mormons and the Theatre*, 12.

3. Edited by Henry J. Horn, *Strange Visitors: A Series of Original Papers* (NY: Carleton, 1869), was a collection of essays purported to have been dictated through a clairvoyant from authors "now dwelling in the spirit world," including Lord Byron, Nathaniel Hawthorne, and Washington Irving.

4. Roberts began advertising in 1870 for his "animal magnetism" (hypnosis), saying he would only be available for thirty days, although he was still advertising years later. He claimed he could cure anything with mesmerism. *Salt Lake Herald*, Sept. 24, 1870.

The first was addressed by brother [James] Brooks[,] Carlile[,] [Frederick] Peris and [Joseph] Salsbury. the later by brothers [William] Sherman and [William] Godbe. Dined with br [John] Maning and attended seance at the residence of br John Whiteing with whom we took tea. Father [Theodore] Turley some beter this evening. Weather somewhat frosty. Received letter from Marion in regar[d] to selling our mill.

January 9, 1871; Monday. Answered letter from Marion. Visited the Meeting House the work on which is progressing finely. Called on brother [Elias] Harison who reported a good meeting at Ogden Sunday evening. Received letter from cousin Sophronia Lyman in Rhode Island and in evening attended Executive Council at the office of br [William S.] Godbe. Weather warm.

January 10, 1871; Tuesday. In morning wrote letter to cousin Sophronia Lyman. Visited Meeting House and in the evening attended meeting at Br [Thomas C.] Armstrongs. Had a fall of snow this evening makeing the walking slop[p]y and uncomfortable. Father [Theodore] Turley no beter.

January 11, 1871; Wednesday. In the morning visited the meeting house. Called on br. [John] Maning and then went to the Tribune Office. Received and answered a letter from brother John Kelly of Fillmore. Passed the evening in reading. Father [Theodore] Turley stil improveing in health. Weather colder.

January 12, 1871; Thursday. Passed most of the day in reading. Called on Mrs [Mary] Peris and borowed a book. Visited the Meeting House and received letter from brother Ebenezer Hanks of Parowan and at night attended meeting at brother [John] Manings. Weather very cold.

January 13, 1871; Friday. Passed the most of the day in reading weather pleasant but cool. Work progressing on the Meeting House, At evening attended a seance at the residence of br [John] Maning with a liberal attendance.

January 14, 1871; Saturday. Visited the Meeting House and spent some time in reading and in the evening went to Ogden and lodged with brother [John] Jost.[5]

5. John and Mary Ann Jost were second-generation German emigrants who met in Halifax, Nova Scotia, where John owned a confectioner's shop. In Ogden he was a candy maker on Main Street (Washington Blvd.). He was excommunicated for participating in the New Movement, but he later rejoined the LDS Church.

January 15, 1871; Sunday. Passed the day in reading and in the evening preached at the hall had an attentive audience.

January 16, 1871; Monday. Called on and dined with Sister [Sophia] Ross wife of brother Alexander Ross. In the afternoon called on brother Wm McIntire and family. At night attended the social party at Woodmansee Hall[6] and during the night made a short speech to the party. Staid until morning.

January 17, 1871; Tuesday. Spent the day with the family of Brother [Thomas J.] Stayner and in the evening returned to the City. Weather cold.

January 18, 1871; Wednesday. Visited the Meeting House and called on br [William S.] Godbe and received of him ten dollars in cash then went to Br [Frederick T.] Peris and procured a book from him. Passed the residue of the day in reading. Received a call from the Rev Mr. Nichols and Lady.[7]

January 19, 1871; Thursday. Visited the Meeting House. Passed most of the day in reading. Meet with brother J[ames] H. Rollins from Minersville. At night attended meeting at brother [John] Manings.

January 20, 1871; Friday. Visited the Meeting House and then called on and dined with Sister Lovina Johnson. Received letter from Branch Lyman of Montana. At night attended a seance at br [John] Manings at which my Aunt and daughter made communication the first that have reached us from them.

January 21, 1871; Saturday. Visited the Meeting House on which the work is moveing finely. At Tribune Office meet Mr Gunison a kinsman of Capt [John] Gunison who was murdered by the Indians in Utah some years ago.[8] Passed the residue of the day in reading.

January 22, 1871; Sunday. In the morning attended the lecture by Dr Roberts on animal magnitism as it is applied to the healing of diseases, and some few thoughts on spiritualism. Dined with Br [John] Maning and family and held a private seance at my house where Father

6. In 1870, Charles Woodmansee, a merchant with a store on Ogden's Main Street, purchased a former Wells Fargo station and converted it into a theater, which is where the event was held.

7. C. C. Nichols was a Methodist minister and a railroad agent who arrived in Utah with the transcontinental train. Tullidge, *Tullidge's Histories*, 185.

8. Captain John Gunnison and several others with the Army Corps of Topographical Engineers were massacred while exploring Sevier Lake in 1853.

[Theodore] Turleys daughter meet us and gave her father some directions in regard to treating the cancer with which he is afflicted. At night I preached at the hall.

January 23, 1871; Monday. Passed the day mostly in reading visited the new Church House. At night held private seance at which we received some encouraging manifestation some of ^which^ were addressed to Father [Theodore] Turley.

January 24, 1871; Tuesday. This morning called on the family of br Richard Hopkins. They had two sick children. In after noon called on br [Thomas C.] Armstrong and dined with him. To day meet with br W[illiam] S. Warren who brought me news of my family in Parowan. Prest [Brigham] Young reported to be in bad health. At night attended Council at br [Elias] Harison's. Visited the church[,] the work on which is going on finely. Weather soft and mild.

January 25, 1871; Wednesday. Received from brother [David] Williams[9] seven dollars in curency. Visited new Church and at night held private seance under the direction of br Carlile as medium. My two daughters [sixteen-year-old] Josephine and [thirteen-year-old] Hila were entranced. Received letters from my wife Paulina and my son Oscar in Parowan. Weather warm.

January 26, 1871; Thursday. In morning meet with Collins Hakes and br [William S.] Warren. Passed some time in reading received and answered letter from my wife Paulina. Received of Brother [David] Williams on behalf of some friends $48.00 in orders on stores. In after noon visited the new church Building and in the evening attended district meeting at br [John] Manings.

January 27, 1871; Friday. Passed the most of the day in reading. Received a call from my cousins James and Holland Day. At night attended meeting at br [John] Manings.

January 28, 1871; Saturday. Visited the new Church house and passed some time in reading and in the evening went to Ogden. Rece^i^ved of br [William S.] Godbe 2½ dollars. On my way encountered

9. William David Williams, a Welsh convert, came to Utah in 1854. He went by David (Lyman sometimes confused his name) and was the music director at the Church of Zion and Liberal Institute.

a very severe snow squall at Kaysville. The ground was covered with snow when I arived in Ogden. Lodged with br [Thomas J.] Stayner.

January 29, 1871; Sunday. In the morning called on br [John] Jost and in company with him to hear a discourse by Elder [William W.] Blair[10] of the Reorganized Church of Saints and in the evening preached in Cordon's Hall. Had an attentive audience. Lodged with br Horicks.

January 30, 1871; Monday. In the morning went by rail to Morgan city called on the family of br [David] Williams was kindly received by them. When br W. came home we went and called on brother [George W.] Crouch whom[,] and one of his children[,] we found sick in bed. Taried with them a while and then returned to br W[illiam']s and in evening addressed a small assembly of enquirers who had come to gather in a hall belonging to br Williams.

January 31, 1871; Tuesday. Visited and past the day with Brother [George W.] Crouch and family. The sick ones were beter and in the evening Brother Edholm and wife called and spent the evening. Held private seance at which we received some pleasant communications from Br Joseph Smith and a deceased wife of br Edholm after which I returned to br [David] Williams.

Received the folowing from Brother Joseph through Mrs Elizabeth Crouch[:][11]

Brother Lyman, I am most hapy to meet you here; I have been list[e]ning to you all the evening. It does my Soul good to hear you advance the principles that I would have taught had I been permitted to stay on Earth. But it is all right; the truth will spread outward. Humanity will be lifted up from their narrowmindedness; and many Souls will be elevated through your instrumentality.

Keep on in the good work; follow out your own councel. Give my kindest love to Brothers [Elias] Harison and [William] Godbe and accept the same yourself. Altho I have passed away from your midst stil I retain all the good feeling I had for my felow men. I heard you speak

10. Blair was on a preaching tour in California, Montana, Nevada, and Utah. He became a member of the Reorganized Church's First Presidency in 1873.

11. Lyman recorded a series of messages from séances in vol. 25 of his diary, following entries from 1862. Most likely, the messages were recorded on loose sheets and later copied into his diary. In any case, I have put them in their proper order here.

to night about ^the^ avenging of my blood. No! I answer it a thousand times no! I almost spoke through the medium and told you so but could not quite controll her. Farewell my Brethren and Sisters have courage, from your friend and brother Joseph Smith.

February 1, 1871; Wednesday. This morning returned to Ogden and spent an hour with my old friend Doctor [William] Mcintire and dined with br [Thomas J.] Stayner and in the evening returned home. Found all well as usual save Father [Theodore] Turley who was not quite so well. Weather very pleasant.

February 2, 1871; Thursday. Visited the Meeting House and called on br [John] Maning. Passed some time in reading. In the afternoon received of Br [David] Williams 17 dollars in store orders and in evening attended meeting at Manings.

February 3, 1871; Friday. Called on br [John] Maning and then visited the meeting house. Passed some time in reading. In the afternoon called on Br William Hunt and family. At night attended Council. After comeing home had a siting of an hour.

February 4, 1871; Saturday. Passed most of the day in reading. In the afternoon wrote a letter to Brother James H. Rollins. In the evening held a private seance at home. The Hunts [William and Margaret] were the mediums. Results were satisfactory.

February 5, 1871; Sunday. Attended meeting brothers [Elias] Harison and ~~Godbe~~ [Joseph] Salsbury addressed the people. After meeting dined with brother Richard Hopkins and family and in the evening attended meeting and spoke to the people. Weather warm snow fell in the night freely.

February 6, 1871; Monday. This morning meet with brother W[illiam] S. Warren and with him visited the Meetinghouse. Wrote letters to Priscilla and Stephen Franklin. In the evening held private seance with very hapy results. Weather very warm.

February 7, 1871; Tuesday.[12] Passed some time with brother [John] Jost of Ogden, called on brother J[ohn] Maning. Very slop[p]y under foot. Our Nephiew Albert Tanner called on us from Cotten Wood Can[y]on. In the evening visited brother John Tulledge and family.

12. Lyman scratched out the date ~~7th~~ and left the day as Tuesday, so it is unclear if he intended it to be a different date or that he wrote it later.

February 8, 1871; Wednesday. Received letter from my [step] Broth[er] David Emerson from Colebrook N. H. At night held private seance.

February 9, 1871; Thursday. Called on Dr [Washington F.] Anderson for Father [Theodore] Turley. Called at the Meeting House. Wrote letter to my Brother David Emerson and at night held private seance with gratifying results. Some little snow fell during the night.

February 10, 1871; Friday. This morning called on Sister [Elizabeth] Crouch she was ill with cold. At 11 oclock Drs [Washington F.] Anderson and [Joseph M.] Benidict called and removed the cancer from the lip of Father [Theodore] Turley the operation was performed with the patient in his normal state. ^Prest [Brigham] Young returned to day from the south.^

February 11, 1871; Saturday. Weather very mild. Called on Mr. Cushman who leaves to day for Ogden and from thense east to his home. At night held private seance with some satisfactory results. Br [William S.] Warren was with us and Br [Eli] Kelsey and wife [Sarah][13] and br Hyrum Combs[14] and Mrs. Kay and Mrs. [Sarah] Crosby and Mr [Eli] Kelsey Junior.

February 12, 1871; Sunday. Attended meeting and spoke to the people and then dined with Brother [James] Brooks and family. Attended meeting in the evening th[at] was addressed by Br [William S.] Godbe after which I spoke a short time. Weather warm and pleasant.

February 13, 1871; Monday. Passed the day in writeing. In the afternoon received a letter from Paulina giveing the information that she was out of bread. I borrowed ten dollars to send to her of Br [Frederick T.] Peris. At night held private seance. Br Joseph [Smith] and Father [John] Tanner and my son Roswell came and talked with us by entrancement and the table.[15]

February 14, 1871; Tuesday. Wrote letter to Paulina and remited ten dollars in curency. Passed some time with brothers [Elias] Harison and

13. Eli B. Kelsey had several living wives in 1871, but Lyman recorded only Sarah as being with the New Movement.

14. Hyrum and his brother John Coombs were Utah spiritualists. Lyman had converted their family to Mormonism in Illinois, and Hyrum would marry Lyman's daughter Love Josephine in 1872.

15. That is, the entranced person who acted as the medium between the spiritual and physical worlds knocked on the table in response to questions.

[Frederick T.] Peris in the Editors Room [of the *Tribune*]. In the afternoon visited the New Church called on brother [John] Maning for a short time. And in the evening had a private seance had some communications through table. Lelia was the medium. My father was with us for the first time also Mother [Laura] Phelps and Mother [Ruth] Turley and sister [Agnes] Flake,[16] all of whom brought us words of kindly greeting.

February 15, 1871; Wednesday. Borrowed book of br [Frederick T.] Paris called on Sister [Elizabeth] Crouch with whom I had some conversation in regard to the spiritual philosophy. At night held private seance with hapy results. Brother [Charles C.] Woodhouse arived from Beaver with his family.

February 16, 1871; Thursday. In the morning called on Br [George W.] Crouch and ther[e] meet with Br [Charles C.] Woodhouse family. In the evening held a seance with hapy results.

February 17, 1871; Friday. In morning call on brother [George W.] Crouches family and at 11 oclock attended the buriel of brother [William S.] Godbe's child,[17] then visited the New Church. At night held private seance at home.

February 18, 1871; Saturday. Received of Brother Wm Pitts ten dollers in curency. In the evening went to Ogden. Lodged with br [Thomas J.] Stayners family.

February 19, 1871; Sunday. Passed the day mostly with Br [Thomas J.] S[tayner] [and] family. In the evening preached in the hall.

February 20, 1871; Monday. Went to Morgan City and preached in William's Hall at night. Weather warm and pleasant.

February 21, 1871; Tuesday. Returned to Ogden and Mrs [Elizabeth] Crouch came with me. I lodged with br [John] Jost. Snow fell at night.

February 22, 1871; Wednesday. Returned home on the evening Train. Storming when I arived.

February 23, 1871; Thursday. Received letter from br W[illiam] H. Shirman in N.Y. Wrote letter to Daniel Williams in Morgan City[,] Morgan County. Stormed some during the day.

February 24, 1871; Friday. Called brother [John] Maning and began

16. These people, in other words, were the spirits that visited the séance.

17. A stillborn child, Lawrence Godbe.

writing to my sister Ruth. Called on Brother [Elias] Harison and agreed to go to Ogden on Saturday.

February 25, 1871; Saturday. Morning finished my letter to my Sister. In the evening went to Ogden lodged with brother [John] Jost. Weather mild and warm.

February 26, 1871; Sunday. Called on and dined with brother Alexander Ross and family. In eveing preached in Cordon's Hall had a very attentive audience. Lodged with brother Ross.

February 27, 1871; Monday. Passed the day ^in reading^ from the Stellar Key to The Sum[m]erland one of A[ndrew] J. Davis['s] works.[18] In evening returned home found all well.

February 28, 1871; Tuesday. Passed the most of the day in reading. Visited Meeting House weather warm and pleasant.

March 1, 1871; Wednesday. Passed most of the day in reading. Called on Brother [Elias] Harison visited the Meeting House called on Brother [John] Maning held private seance at night, weather somewhat cooler.

Communication through C[harles] H. Foster, N. Y.[19] In answer to questions sent him from Salt Lake City by A. M. Lyman[:][20]

I [Ruth Adelia Lyman, died 1848] am here this morning to assure that I live and I have seen John Tanner in the spirit world. He wishes to bear a message of love to his daughter Louisa. He is near her much of the time. [Grandpa] Roswell Lyman has a word for his son Amasa. He is with me dear Father. My blessed grandfather lives and is very hapy. We are all together. Martha Mason[,] Perez Mason[,] and Parley Mason would each be remembered to you. They would have you know that they are near to help you and you will be prospered. Your much loved daughter, Ruth Adelia Lyman.

From [Mason] Roswell [Lyman, died 1866][,] through Mrs [Elizabeth] Crouch[:]

My dear Father I am most hapy to see [you], Roswell. Q[u]estion[:]

---

18. In Andrew Jackson Davis's *A Stellar Key to the Summer Land*, he advanced "scientific and philosophical evidences of the existence of" a spirit world (v).

19. Foster's biographer commented that he "created quite a sensation in Salt Lake City" when he sent written responses to questions. Bartlett, *The Salem Seer*, 84–85; cf. Bitton, "Mormonism's Encounter with Spiritualism," 43. When Foster communicated with a spirit, its name would appear on his forearm, according to Doyle, *History of Spiritualism*.

20. This séance was labeled "March" in vol. 25.

Can you speak[?] [Answer:] Not at present. [Q:] I have waited for you. Can you speak through the medium[?] Answer plain yes or no. [A:] NO.

The following from my wife Cornelia [Eliza Leavitt Lyman, died 1865] through the same[:]

My dear Husband I am glad you enquired for me. I am waiting for you to come before [the veil]. I am perfectly hapy.

From br Joseph [Smith] through the same[:]

Brother Amasa I am hapy to meet you this morning in the capacity of a [spirit] circle. You are doing just what a good many others ought to do at the present time. Remember what I have told you before concerning your own council all will come out right. Your ^children will be all you wish them to be.^ Now a little word of caution. Patience Patience Patience, is the grand secret of all perfection nothing was ever discovered and investigated and done well in a hurry. We are around you and will try to help evrybody who try to help ~~evry~~ humanity. Our kindest love to those engaged in the same cause as yourself. Joseph and Heber [C. Kimball][,] Hyrum [Smith], and many friends. Holy Angels are around you, Br. Amasa.

March 2, 1871; Thursday. Passed the most of the day in reading at night held private seance. Brother [Henry W.] Lawrence and wife were present. Received 28 dollars of br [David] Williams.

March 3, 1871; Friday. This morning Father [Theodore] Turley started for his home in Beaver in the stage. Visited the Meeting House. Held seance at night. Brother H[yrum] Comb was present.

March 4, 1871; Saturday. Received letter from Paulina she spoke of brother [Nathan C.] Tiney being there on his way to the city with his wife and son. Held private seance at night. Brother [John] Low and wife [Fanny] were present and were well pleased.

March 5, 1871; Sunday. Attended Methodist meeting at Fausts Hall. Passed the afternoon with Brother [Frederick T.] Peris and family. Held seance. Brother [David] Williams was controlled [by the spirits] and wrote some. Weather warm and pleasant.

March 6, 1871; Monday. Visited New Meeting House passed some time in reading. At night held private seance at which we had some physical demonstration of spirit presence and power in the movement of the Table around the room and its suspension in the air with the light touch of the mediums. The move[ments] were attended with evidences of purpose and design.

March 7, 1871; Tuesday. Received of Brother David Williams on behalf of himself and friends 49 dollars in store orders and cash of the latter five dollers. At night held private seance with good results. Weather cooler.

March 8, 1871; Wednesday. Visited the meeting house and called at Brother [Henry W.] Lawrences. And in the evening went to Brother [Frederick T.] Perises, held a seance with good results. [Nineteen-year-old] Lorenzo [Lyman] and [thirteen-year-old] Hila [Lyman] mediums.

J[ohn] V. Long[21] Controlling Miss Hila L[yman] Medium[:] Your son Roswell is here and he wishes to write to you to night. Would you like to hear from him?

Dear Father I have been to Philidelphia with the medium who was here today she has been to Mr Foster's and tried to communicate with him but she could not make [it] out. I am acquainted with her and her son-in law. She came here to tell you of her Death and she thought that you did not believe her. She wishes to know about it whether you believe her or not. If you do will you please write on a piece of paper your answer and hand it to the medium[,] and the lady will write her thanks to you.

The following was the[n] writen and placed before the medium[:] I accept your statement as true. Amasa M. Lyman.

The following was then writen[:] Dear friend I thank you a thousand times for your kind acceptance of my statement of my death. From: Sarah Jane Ashton.

The following was then writen From Roswell my Son[:]

Dear Father and Aunt Maria[,] Adelia[22] wishes you to excuse her for not coming tonight. She has just past the last quarter of her school and has taken a new class. That is the reason she came today but she is sorry to have bothered you to day good night.

March 9, 1871; Thursday. Visited the Meeting House and made some

21. John V. Long, an LDS church recorder before he was excommunicated in 1866, was an associate of Lyman's and Godbe's. Deceased since 1869, he was the spirit controlling Hila Lyman when she was acting as a medium.

22. Adelia was Maria's deceased daughter. Roswell was the deceased son of a different wife, making him Maria's stepson. In the vernacular of plural marriage, the sister-wife of someone's father was referred to as aunt.

other calls. Received call from Sister Lovina Johnson, had for her some kind words from her spirit friends. At night visited Sister Sarah Pratt and family [and] held seance with them. Lorenzo was controlled for writing for the first time.

The folowing from Brother Joseph. Through Hila controlled by J[ohn] V. Long[:]

I know your Father [presumably Roswell Lyman]. He wishes me to tell you he would like to have you make an inquiry about that N[athan] Tanner lot and see if there will be any chance to get that paper.

March 10, 1871; Friday. Passed the day at home. Received a call from brother [Thomas J.] Stayner from Ogden and in evening held seance. Brother Cannon and Lady were present also Brothers Stayner and [Elias] Harison. We had the deaf and dumb visitor again and also br Joseph and Hyrum.

March 11, 1871; Saturday. Called on brother [Richard R.] Hopkins and family. He was confined to the bed with rheumatism. Called on the Sisters Godbes. In the evening visited brother [William] Hunt and family. Had this evening a gentle rain. Retired to night with a sore throat which gave me much uneasiness through the night.

March 12, 1871; Sunday. Passed the forenoon at home and in the afternoon visited Mrs [Harriet] Halifax and family. While there held a Seance with very gratifying results. Weather warm and pleasant.

March 13, 1871; Monday. Visited the meeting house and made some other call[s]. In the evening visited the Sisters Godbes' where we meet with brother's [Eli] Kelsey and [Henry W.] Lawrence and their wives. Returned brother [Frederick T.] Peris['s] book and drew one from the ~~Libry~~ Library.

March 14, 1871; Tuesday. Passed the day in reading. At night received a call from Sister Lovina Johnson [and] her son and niece Miss Rhoda Johnson. Weather cooler. Meeting today with brother George D. Watt.

March 15, 1871; Wednesday. Visited the meetinghouse in the morning then called on brother [Elias] Harison where I meet the Stayners [family] from the north. Passed residue of time in reading. Spent evening at home.

March 16, 1871; Thursday. Visited meeting house and passed most of the day in reading. At night held private seance. Brother [George W.]

and sister [Elizabeth] Crouch were present with their little daughter who gave indications of being in some degree mediumistic.

March 17, 1871; Friday. Visited the Meetinghouse and in the afternoon received a call from Aunts E[liza] R. Snow[23] and Basheby [Bathsheba] Smith. Had private seance at night with hapy results.

Me big Cheif American. Me Walker,[24] ~~shine~~ me much shine in spirit life on big hunting ground. Me write big lots in spirit life, Me Walker sure. Me no fool you. No! Me good. Me big cheif in Spirit. Me much shine in Spirit. Me good. Me medicine Cheif. Me [OK][25] Cheif.

From Mother Laura Phelps through Hila[:]

My Dear Son Amasa, tell my dear daughter that I am hapy in ^my^ spirit ~~life~~ home and have no sickness here. Her children are with me and join with me in sending our love to her, tell her to take care of Laura and keep her in sight, take care that she dos not get in the fire. I would like to see her at a table and see if I could not control her. Goodnight.

March 18, 1871; Saturday. Called on br [Elias] Harison and visited the meeting house and then wrote letter to Paulina. Received a call from brother R[ichard] R. Hopkins who left some papers with me to read. Weather warm and pleasant. Prepeared to receive brother [Hyrum] Combs to board [with us].

[From Chief Wakara:][26] I am here, me [OK] Chief[,] me medicine man. Me come to introduce Kit Karson.

You[27] are easier to control than a man so I come here to let you know that a feller could live arter he left here. I am here[,] me[,] name Kit. Me like you all. I ^am^ kind of a rough feller but I don't mean any harm to the medium. I guess I'll have to be arter biding you good night, take care of yourself Miss Lyman. From Kit your friend.

Writen by Hila while entranced[:]

23. Eliza R. Snow had been a plural wife of Joseph Smith, making her a sister-wife of Eliza Maria Partridge, Lyman's own onetime wife. Snow was now married to Brigham Young and was president of the Relief Society. Bathsheba Smith was her counselor.

24. For more on Wakara, see April 7, 1851, entry and note.

25. Lyman's orthography for OK is "old cay," and according to the *Oxford English Dictionary* it reflects the idiom's origin in the 1840 presidential campaign of Martin Van Buren. His nickname, "Old Kinderhook," was shortened to "Old K" and then "OK" over time. Lyman also spells it that way on March 18, changed here for comprehension.

26. There is no mention of a séance in Lyman's daily entry, but he included it for the 18th in his record of spirit communications at the back of his diary.

27. Apparently Hila Lyman was acting as the medium again.

Dear Amasa, this ^is^ the second time I have been here but could not get the chance to talk to you before. I am so glad that you let me talk to night I am hapy in Spirit Life. I have a nice home and garden I am indeed hapy. I cannot control the medium long enough to tell you about your friends but I will come again good night. From, Mason['s] spirit.

My Dear Grand Son I am hapy in being able to come and tell you that there is a life after we leave this Earth. I am acquainted with your wife and children that is in Spirit Life. And I thank our Father that you have left the Mormon Church. May he bless you and your family is my wish and show you the way to another life. Goodnight. From your Grandfather Henry Lyman.

March 19, 1871; Sunday. Passed the morning in reading. In the afternoon called on Br [Elias] Harison and family. Spent the evening with them held private seance with good results. Weather fine and warm.

Cousin Amasa I am hapy to think you remembered me. Grandpa has wanted me to come with him often but I thought you would not wish to hear from me. I am a teacher I have ten children in my class I generaly take them to my home one hour in each day. Nature is our grand teacher, that is all we study we all love it. Perez Mason.

March 20, 1871; Monday. Made some calls around town visited the Meeting House and at night held private seance with pleasant results. Weather warm and pleasant.

Received the folowing[:]

Dear Sister [Mary] Louisa I have been trying to write since I was here the other day. I am hapy in my spirit home with father and mother [word erased]. Father has a large farm and a house and is better off than he was here. Adelia is here and wishes to write. From your dear brother Elisha.[28]

My dear pa and ma I [Adelia] have come to tell you about my home in Spirit Life. ~~I have~~ I live ^with^ grandpa and grandma part of the time. When I am not with them I live with Richard in a prety little cottage with a beautiful garden and fruit trees. There are vines runing up the sides of the house. I have rose bushes in my flower garden. I call them my own. There are other rose trees there but those are[n't] mine. I have birds but I don't keep them in cages. I let them go free and when they are tired of

28. Elisha Bentley Tanner, Maria Louisa's half-brother—born to John Tanner and his first wife, Tabitha—died in 1858.

being on the wing they come to their trees and flowers and rest. I have Coley [Collie?] with me. Good night. Ruth Adelia Lyman.

March 21, 1871; Tuesday. Some little storm rain and snow. Visited Meeting house. I[n] afternoon br George Garner called from Payson stayed all night. At night held seance with good results.

Received the folowing[:]

Dear Brother Amasa. I [Joseph] have come to see you in particular. I am hapy in my Spirit Home I am with you and your brethren in the new movement. May God bless you and them in your work. I am glad to see you at the table I think it is the best way to improve your time. I am here often. Do not ^sit too long^ at one time. I think you have held most of your meetings about right and may you be prospered in trying to get the people interested in Spiritualism. Good Night. Joseph Smith.

Brother Amasa. I [Hyrum] came with Joseph and thought I could not go away without leting you know I was here although the medium knew I was here. I join with Br Joseph in what he has said I will come again I have not time to talk longer now good night. H[yrum] S[mith]

March 22, 1871; Wednesday. Visited the Meetinghouse and passed most of the day in reading and in the evening held private seance and had communications from several members of Brother [George] Garners family, writen through Hila. Weather somewhat cooler. Received a due bill of ten dollars on Elephant store[29] by [Alexander] Rogers clerk.

March 23, 1871; Thursday. Passed the day mostly in reading; and at night went to brother [Frederick T.] Perises to hold a seance. Weather mild and pleasant. Received letter from Brother Moris Phelps in Bear Lake Valley.

March 24, 1871; Friday. Spent some time with br [Elias] Harison and during the day meet with br Benjamin Winchester. Passed some time in reading. At night received call from brother Couch and wife and daughter. Held seance in the evening.

[Séance communication:] I am glad to come again and see you Amasa. I have been to see a good many of my relitives since I was here. I will answer questions if you wish me to. Your Grand Father, [Perez] Mason.

29. The Elephant Store was owned by John Cunnington and Alexander Rogers. It specialized in "fancy groceries, provisions, miners' supplies, and general heavy and shelf hardware." *Leading Industries of the West*, Feb. 1884, 74.

March 25, 1871; Saturday. Made some calls through the day and in the evening went to Ogden and lodged with brother Restall and family. Weather warm and pleasant.

March 26, 1871; Sunday. In the morning in company with br R[estall] made a call on brother [Thomas J.] Stayner and family. At night preached at the Hall had an attentive audience. Lodged with brother R. and after meeting made call on brother Stayner.

March 27, 1871; Monday. Returned home from Ogden. Visited the Meeting house in afternoon it stormed some. In the evening had seance.

Good evening Brother Amasa, try to do all the good you can while you live on the Earth and you will be rewarded for it in time. Do everything in your power to elevate humanity higher and bring them to a knowledge of the truth. I cannot write more now. Joseph Smith.[30]

March 28, 1871; Tuesday. Wrote letters to Marion and Priscilla in Fillmore and received and answered a [letter] from my brother David Emerson in N. H. Visited the Meetinghouse, weather cooler at night. At night held seance, Mrs. Kay and Mrs. [Sarah] Crosby ~~is~~ were present and received some communication from their friends through the mediums Lorenzo and Hila.

March 29, 1871; Wednesday. Pass[ed] the day mostly in reading and at night held seance. Some friends present[,] results good. Visited Meetinghouse during the day. Weather warmer.

March 30, 1871; Thursday. Passed morning in reading. Visited Meetinghouse and in the afternoon visited Mr. [John] Cunington and family. Spent the evening with our friends held seance with them.

March 31, 1871; Friday. Visited the Meetinghouse and passed most of the day in reading at night held a seance with happy results. Weather growing warmer. [Several blank lines follow.]

April 1, 1871; Saturday. Passed the most of the time in reading. Visited the M[eeting] House and in the evening held a seance. Br Grieg and wife were present.

April 2, 1871; Sunday. I[n] morning received a call from Brother Barns who had just arived from Nebraska, after which I made a call with

30. This was the last time Lyman recorded the content of his séances. The remainder of vol. 25, where the 1871 dialogues were recorded, is devoted to daily summaries of activities from late 1872.

Mr Brown on Mr Cowls the medium. Saw some of his spirit drawings. And then dined with Mr B. and family and past the evening with them. Mr Cowls and wife were present we held seance with pleasant results.

April 3, 1871; Monday. Visited Meetinghouse past some time with brother Barns and his friend. At night held seance. Brother B. and wife and daughter were present.

April 4, 1871; Tuesday. Passed most of the day in reading. Sister Frances Turley came and indicated that she was present by rapping on table clearly and distinctly. In the afternoon in company with some friends of the liberal cause[31] visited our Meetinghouse. In the evening held a private seance with pleasant results.

April 5, 1871; Wednesday. Passed most of the day in reading. In the morning called on br [William S.] Godbe and with him visited the new Meetinghouse. In the evening [the spirit of the deceased] Newel K. Whitney spoke to us of his son Orson.[32] Bishop Myron Tanners wife called on us for the night.[33] My son Marion called on us during the day.

April 6, 1871; Thursday. The orthodox [LDS] conference commenced its Cission today. Passed most of the day in reading. Brother Freeman Tanner called to day. At night held seance at [John] Manings. Some rain this morning but it ceased before meeting.

April 7, 1871; Friday. Passed most of the day in reading. Some light storm to day. Paid Allen on Stoves 15 dollars. Received Brother [David] Williams sixty one dollars in cash and store pay.

April 8, 1871; Saturday. Passed the day mostly in reading. Visited Meetinghouse held seance in evening.

April 9, 1871; Sunday. The orthodox [LDS] conference ajourned to day. Passed the day in reading in the evening visited brother Stephens

31. The New Movement used the "liberal" label for its political organization, the Liberal Party, begun in 1870 to counter Mormon political dominance. Mormons countered with the People's Party, the more successful of the two. Walker, *Wayward Saints*, 225–27.

32. Newel K. Whitney had been dead since 1850, and the son the spirit seemed worried about was Orson K., an outdoorsman, forty-one years old, who was more at home in the mountains than in the city and who had distinguished himself during the Indian wars. Orson was a coffin maker by trade. His nephew, Orson F. Whitney (Newel's grandson), would become an LDS apostle in 1906.

33. Both of Myron's wives, Mary Jane and Ann, were still alive, so they would have appeared in the flesh. Ann was no longer a practicing Mormon. See Harline, *The Polygamous Wives Writing Club*, 57.

and family. Our visit was not agreeable conditions not being good. Br Barns and family started for Minersville this morning.

April 10, 1871; Monday. This morning Brother N[oah] Bartholomew and brother [John] Kelley from Fillmore called on us and with them I visited the Meetinghouse. In our walk we meet brother [William] Sherman who has just returned from N.Y. Past some time in reading. Brother [Thomas J.] Stayner['s] wife [Rebecca], and daughter [Rosa] called and we had a short seance. Marion was present for a short time. In the evening held a seance. Brs B[artholemew] and K[elley] were present. Their friends came with kindly greetings, from their bright homes in the Better Life.

April 11, 1871; Tuesday. Passed most of the day in reading and makeing some calls. In the evening brother [William] Sherman called for a half hour and gave us some of his N. York experience with the mediums.

April 12, 1871; Wednesday. Passed most of the day in reading. Brothers [Noah] Bartholimew and [John] Kelley started for their home in Fillmore to day. Visited meetinghouse and made some calls. Had some conversation with brother [James] McNaughton from Heber City Wasatch County.

April 13, 1871; Thursday. Visited the meetinghouse. Passed some time with brother [Henry W.] Lawrence. In the afternoon visited with Brother [Thomas C.] Armstrong's family. Spent the evening with them.

April 14, 1871; Friday. Called by the Meetinghouse no work was going on there. Made call with Mrs Lyman on Mrs Horace Eldridge. In the evening Mrs Kay sat with us had a pleasant time with our friends from the beyond.

April 15, 1871; Saturday. Made some calls about the city. Passed some time with brother [Elias] Harison. In the evening had a private sitting and had my Aunt experience and brother Willard Snow to speak to us thru Hila. Sister [Agnes] Flake wrote thru the same her thanks for our care of their children.[34]

April 16, 1871; Sunday. Passed the day with brother R[ichard] R. Hopkins and family. Held seance with them with good results. Mrs Knowls was present.

April 17, 1871; Monday. Passed the day in makeing some calls around

34. See 187n132.

town. In the afternoon went to the New Church to hear our new organ played by Professor [Orson] Pratt [Jr].[35] Brother John Combs and family were with us to day. Received letter from my sister Ruth in V.T. and one from my wife Paulina in Parowan.

April 18, 1871; Tuesday. Wrote letter to my sister in Vermont. Dined with brother [Henry W.] Lawrence in afternoon. Called on Mrs. [Sarah] Kelsey. At night held seance brother John Combs and wife were present. Results were very satisfactory to the friends present.

April 19, 1871; Wednesday. Made a call at the Meetinghouse. At night held seance with pleasant results.

April 20, 1871; Thursday. Passed most of the day with Brother Robert Riche[y] from Little Pinto Iron County [now Washington County]. At night held seance with pleasant results some friends were present.

April 21, 1871; Friday. Passed the day in making preperations for my southern journey at night held a seance with good results.

April 22, 1871; Saturday. Started for the south in the stage. My daughter Hila was with me. Dined at Mr Greens and took super at Mr G[eorge] Garners [in] Payson.

April 23, 1871; Sunday. This morning reached ~~Cove~~ Chicken Creek where we took breakfast and then we passed on to ~~Parowan~~ ^Fillmore^ where we arived about ~~12 oclock at night~~ in afternoon.

April 24, 1871; Monday. This morning after we had traviled all night reached Cove Creek and took breakfast and then passed on to Parowan where we arived at 12 oclock. Found the family and friends well.

April 25, 1871; Tuesday. Passed the day with my family received some calls.

April 26, 1871; Wednesday. Passed the morning in reading and Dined with Brother [Daniel] Page and family.

April 27, 1871; Thursday. Visited and Dined with Brother [Ebenezer] Hanks and family. Received some calls at home in the evening.

April 28, 1871; Friday. Wrote letter home. Brother Wm Martindale called and took diner with us. Called on br D[aniel] P. Clarks family. Visited the Factory and shop.

---

35. The hall was not yet finished, but enough to try out the pipe organ. It was a "cabinet organ" with one keyboard, no pedals or stops, and pipes stacked on top, powered by a foot-operated bellows. Walker, "The Liberal Institute," 76.

April 29, 1871; Saturday. Visited and dined with Br D[aniel] P. Clark and family. At night held a seance with good results.

April 30, 1871; Sunday. Visited and dined with br [Daniel] Page and family. Br [Daniel P.] Clark and family were present. At 4 oclock held meeting at the same place.

May 1, 1871; Monday. Wrote letter to Beaver. Had a seance with Sister [Jane] Hanks and at night held seance at home [in Parowan with sixth wife Paulina]. Had some friends present results good and satisfactory. Retired about midnight.

May 2, 1871; Tuesday. Visited br J[ohn] Combs and family had a siting with them. In evening took super with Br R[ichard] Benson and in evening held seance at the house of br [Daniel] Page with good results. Father [Robert] Riche[y] and wife were present.

May 3, 1871; Wednesday. Parted with my family and traviled to Beaver and stoped with Father [Theodore] Turley and at night preached in the new Meeting House.[36] Had an attentive audience.

May 4, 1871; Thursday. Passed the day in waiting for brother Flake who had promised to cary me to Minersville but in the afternoon he learned that he could not go until the next morning. During the after noon called on Mrs Edward Thompson. At night had a siting with some of our friends who are inquiring after the spiritualities of life.

May 5, 1871; Friday. Went to Minersville. Found Dionitia and mother well as usual. Considerable of intrest was manifest in the mines which are promising at present.

May 6, 1871; Saturday. Made some calls on some of my friends. Myself and Hila dined with br Fredrick Turley and family. At night held a seance at br John Bradshaws with good results.

May 7, 1871; Sunday. Made some calls around town had a brief siting at the house of Mr. Carter. At night held meeting at the house of br [John] Bradshaw. Had small but attentive audience had siting for grandmother.

May 8, 1871; Monday. Made some calls in the morning and dined with brother Fred Turley and family. At night held seance at home.

36. Walker confirms that the New Movement had meeting places in "Beaver, Cottonwood, Jordan, Logan, Mount Pleasant, Park City, and Ogden." Ronald Walker, "Godbeites," in Powell, ed., *Utah History Encyclopedia*.

Brother and Sister Barns and daughter were present results were very agreeable, and impressive. Mrs [Dionetia] Lyman received of D[avid] W. Williams 39 dollars.

May 9, 1871; Tuesday. Wrote letter to Paulina. Dined with Brother Fredrick [Turley] and family. Received of Brother Barns some Railroad tickets to dispose of in the city. At night held a seance. Brother F. Turley and wife and brother John Osborn were present results were agreeable.

May 10, 1871; Wednesday. Made some calls around town and at night held a seance at home with good consequences and some favorable indications in reference to the mediumistic qualities of some who were present.

May 11, 1871; Thursday. Called upon and dined with br Edwin Bingham and family. At night held seance with good results brs [John] Osborn and [Frederick] Turley were present.

May 12, 1871; Friday. Was disappointed in ^not^ geting a chance to go to Beaver. Held seance at night with good results at home.

May 13, 1871; Saturday. Came to [son-in-law] Philo [Carter]'s with brother Omner Turley. Found [daughter] Matilda [Lyman Carter] and children well[,] taried all night.

May 14, 1871; Sunday. Came to Beaver. Stoped with br Turley. Held a seance at Sister White's residence.

May 15, 1871; Monday. Visited and dined with Brother S[tephen] Franklin and family. At home after held a family seance. Miss Franklin was developed as a medium.

May 16, 1871; Tuesday. Visited and dined with br Robert Kershaw and family after which we held seance with pleasant results. At night preached at the new meeting house had a very attentive audience.

May 17, 1871; Wednesday. Parted with our friends in Beaver and traviled to Fillmore found Priscilla and children well.

May 18, 1871; Thursday. Passed the day in makeing some buisness calls. Went to the mill with brother [William] Gibbs.

May 19, 1871; Friday. Made some calls after which myself and Hila dined with Sister Kelley after which I called on br [Noah] Bartholimew who is now recovering slowly from his recent severe sickness. Received of Marion 50.00 fifty dollars for stock sold.

May 20, 1871; Saturday. Called on br Alfred Gull who promised to deliver the fencing he was owing after which I exicuted some transfers of landed property, to my wives Eliza [Partridge], Caroline [Leavitt], and Lydia [Partridge] whose peculiar views religious would not allow them to continue to live with me. I then went to the mill with br [William] Gibbs to agree on some changes to be made. As I returned meet with br [John] Kelley and at night held seance at home with good results. Br Kelly was with us.

May 21, 1871; Sunday. Remained at home the forenoon and at 3 oclock preached ~~at~~ ^in^ the school room belonging to [Reuben] McBride.

May 22, 1871; Monday. Made some calls about town and in the afternoon called at the County Clerks office and exicuted some transfers of land to the Church and the School District No. 3. Wind very high to day.

May 23, 1871; Tuesday. Made some calls in the morning. Dined with Marion and family and at 11 oclock P.M. started in the stage for Payson.

May 24, 1871; Wednesday. Was on the road arived at Payson at 6 oclock. All comfortably quartered at br George Garners.

May 25, 1871; Thursday. Weather bright and clear. Dined and lodged with brother Augustus Simons and family held seance with them and a few friends at night.

May 26, 1871; Friday. Made some calls. Dined with brother [George] Garner and family had some talk with brother Long who seems growing in free thought.

May 27, 1871; Saturday. Took stage at 6 oclock for home[37] where we arived about 6 oclock p.m. and found the family well as usual. The weather very warm today.

May 28, 1871; Sunday. Visited the Meetinghouse and then called on brother [John] Maning and family dined with them. Held seance Mr [Frederick] Knowls was present.

May 29, 1871; Monday. Settled my rent and paid for my stoves. Made some calls in town, felt some rheumatism in my knee. Some little rain to day.

May 30, 1871; Tuesday. Rained during the entire day. I did not go out past the day in reading.

May 31, 1871; Wednesday. Made some calls about town wrote to

---

37. This was a temporary residence that Lyman rented from a Mrs. Kay in Salt Lake City. See Oct. 15, 1870.

Marion by [Henry] McClough, called on br [William] Sherman who is slowly recovering from his sickness.

June 1, 1871; Thursday. Made some calls about town. Saw the steem wagon and President Young who was to day seventy years old, weather very pleasant.[38]

June 2, 1871; Friday. Moved some lumber from my old residence in the afternoon was not very well. Visited the meetinghouse.

June 3, 1871; Saturday. Passed most of the day in reading and makeing some improvements at home. Weather slightly cool.

June 4, 1871; Sunday. Visited and dined with brother [James] Brooks and family and with them made some calls on the sick and in the evening attended meeting at Fausts Hall held by the M[ethodist] E[piscopal] Ministers. Some friends from Fillmore called to day.

June 5, 1871; Monday. Passed some time in reading, called on Dr [Washington F.] Anderson and procured and sent some medicine to Father [Theodore] Turley. In the evening we attended meting at the residence of brother [Thomas C.] Armstrong held seance with his family and other friends.

June 6, 1871; Tuesday. Passed most of the day in reading. Br F[rederick] T. Peris returned to day from Francisco Cal. Br W[illiam] H. Shirman rode out to day his health slightly improveing. At night some friends called in.

June 7, 1871; Wednesday. Passed the day in reading and makeing some calls and in the evening called on Mrs [Hannah] Steward[39] and saw Mr Jones who was cr^i^peled by a hurt of his leg by a falling rock in Bingham.

June 8, 1871; Thursday. Mad[e] calls on buisness and assisted in adjusting the shendilier [chandelier] in the meeting house. Received a call from an episcopal lady by the name of Newbold. We had a brief siting with her. Hila was entranced and gave her satisfaction in regard to the subject of her inquiry. At night visited Mrs [Hannah] Stewart and family held pleasant seance. Had seeing entrancement and healing ministrations.

---

38. Since the transcontinental railroad bypassed Salt Lake City, a "road locamotive" was designed to carry forty tons of ore from the Oquirrh Mountains to a steamboat docked at the north end of Rush Valley, and from there to the railroad in Corinne, north of Ogden. "The Steam Wagon," *Daily Corinne Reporter*, June 9, 1871, 8.

39. After Hannah's first husband died, she married Matthew D. Stewart, who reportedly died at Andersonville Prison in South Carolina during the Civil War.

June 9, 1871; Friday. Received call from Brother T[homas J.] Stayner from Ogden. Received ten dollars from br [David] Williams on Kimball & Lawrence [store credit]. Called on br [John] Maning.

June 10, 1871; Saturday. Meet with Brother J[ohn] M. Spear and wife who had just arived from Cal. Received of [David] Williams ten dollars and of [Hyrum] Coombs 5½. Wrote letter to T[homas] B. H. Stenhouse N.Y. City.

June 11, 1871; Sunday. Attended the opening of the camp meeting[40] and in the afternoon meet some of our friends at Brother [William S.] Godbe's residence and in the evening was again at the camp meeting.

June 12, 1871; Monday. Made some calls in the morning and attended the camp meeting services then passed some time with Brother [John M.] and Sister [Caroline] Spear. Received a call from Mrs Mason from the State of Illinois.

June 13, 1871; Tuesday. Passed most of the day in reading attended meeting at the tent. Received of br [David] Williams thirty three dollars and thirty cents cash. At night held seance at the residence of brother [William S.] Godbe brother [John M.] and Sister [Caroline] Spear were present.

June 14, 1871; Wednesday. Attended at the tent this morning. I was introduced to the clergymen by br [C. C.] Nichols, one of the resident Methodists. Made some calls.

June 15, 1871; Thursday. Made some calls on buisness spent some time with br [John M.] Spear. Called on Mr [John] Cunington at store, at night attended the camp meeting.

June 16, 1871; Friday. Made some calls in the morning. Meet with br Daniel Page from Parowan he stoped with us. The first of a series of meetings was held by the woomen under the direction of Mrs C[aroline] Spear at the residence of Mrs Mary Godbe, on the subject of Wooman Sufferage.

June 17, 1871; Saturday. Made some calls about town passed some time in reading. In the evening received a call from br Henry McCullough and wife and Miss M[ary] Bartholimew who stoped with us.

June 18, 1871; Sunday. Attend a meeting at brother [William S.]

40. The week-long revival was sponsored by the Methodist Episcopal Church. Many members of the Church of Zion were defecting, and the Methodists shared the same meeting space.

Godbe's. Mr [John M.] and Mrs [Caroline] Spear were present. In the evening visited the Cuningtons and had a seance. Mrs [Elizabeth] Couch was the medium Mr. Fred Walker was present. The camp meeting closed this evening.

June 19, 1871; Monday. Spent the morning with Mr [John M.] and Mrs [Caroline] Spear at brother [William S.] Godbe's with whom I dined after which I parted with the Spears who started for California. Passed the evening at home.

June 20, 1871; Tuesday. Made some calls in town wrote some letters to my friends in the south. Bought some goods to send to Paulina in Parowan by brother Hyrum Coombs.

June 21, 1871; Wednesday. Visited the meetinghouse with brother [Elias] Harison and meet with several friends from the country. Brother [Daniel] Page started for home to day also br [Hyrum] Combs started south this morning. Passed residue of time in reading made a call on Dr. Roberts.

June 22, 1871; Thursday. Made some calls in the morning. Called on Mrs. Warren of the 7th Ward. At night attended a meeting of the executive Committee at residence of br [William S.] Godbe. Weather very warm.

June 23, 1871; Friday. After makeing some calls[,] past most of the day with Mr. [Benjamin] Tod the spiritualistic lecturer from California.

June 24, 1871; Saturday. Made some calls in morning[,] worked at meetinghouse. In evening attended the lecture at Indipendence Hall by Mr Benjamin Tod a spiritualist. Weather warm.

June 25, 1871; Sunday. Attended lecture at Indipendence Hall by Mrs Tod. And in [the evening] attended lecture at same place by Mr [Benjamin] Tod. Dr Roberts took tea with us. The lectures were on the subject of spiritualism.

June 26, 1871; Monday. Called at the Meetinghouse to day br Richard Benson and wife from Parowan arived and brought with them my wife Paulina our daughter Laura, both well and left those at home well. At night attended the lecture by Mrs Tod, subject Spiritualism. It was well spoken in evry way interesting.

June 27, 1871; Tuesday. Worked at the meetinghouse in evening attended lecture by Mr [Benjamin] Tod, the attendence was good.

June 28, 1871; Wednesday. Called on the Tods, at br [Frederick T.] Perises residence. At evening met with the Executive Committee.

June 29, 1871; Thursday. Made some calls on business in the city and at night attended lecture by Mrs [Susan B.] Anthony on the subject of Woman's suferage.[41] Br George Garner and wife stayed with us.

June 30, 1871; Friday. Made some calls in the city and at night meet the Executive Committee at br [Elias] Harison's.

July 1, 1871; Saturday. Worked on the meetinghouse until midnight and stil were not ready for the meeting of tomorow.

July 2, 1871; Sunday. This morning held our opening service in the new hall which was then dedicated to the principles of truth and the cause of human freedom and the universal fraternity of Man. In the evening at 8 oclock Mrs Elizabeth C. Stanton delivered her great lecture [on] the true republic. The Hall was named the Liberal Institute.[42]

July 3, 1871; Monday. Was engaged most of the day in prepareing the Institute for the services of the fourth.

July 4, 1871; Tuesday. Attended the celebration which passed off very pleasantly closeing with exhibition of fireworks in evening thus past the fourth.[43]

July 5, 1871; Wednesday. To day Paulina started for her home and my son He[n]ry came from his home in Fillmore with Philo Carter my son in law. At night attended the Circus.

July 6, 1871; Thursday. Made some calls on buisness. Settled my taxes with brother [John] Kelley who started home today. In the evening meet br Edward Tullege who had just returned from N. Y.[44] Philo and his brothers called to night.

---

41. Susan Anthony and Elizabeth Cady Stanton wanted to thank Utah and Wyoming for approving female suffrage over the past two years, ahead of any state. "Woman Suffrage," *Salt Lake Tribune*, July 1, 1871.

42. Stanton and Anthony both spoke in the newly completed Liberal Institute, which was overflowing. But when Anthony spoke of plural wives as "slaves," she lost her audience. "Dedication of the Liberal Institute," *Salt Lake Tribune*, July 3, 1871; *AML*, 454–55.

43. There was also a joyous Fourth of July parade and celebration sponsored by the LDS Church. The *Deseret News* poked fun at the somber religious tone the Godbeites chose for the celebration which the *News* said resembled a funeral. "The Opposition," *Deseret News*, July 5, 1871.

44. Tullidge resigned from the Church of Zion over its embrace of spiritualism. He left Utah, proclaiming he was "done with damned religion of every kind," but

July 7, 1871; Friday. To day Philo started for home. Received of [David] Williams in cash five dollars and 18 [cents] in order on store. Past most of the time in reading.

July 8, 1871; Saturday. Passed most of the day in reading and makeing some calls in town. At night called on brother [Henry] Kendall and family. A light fall of rain last night air some cooler to day.

July 9, 1871; Sunday. In morning called on br [Thomas C.] Armstrong's family and held seance with them then called on cousin James Day and wife and called on br [John] Maning and took tea with them. Attended meeting in the Institute and addressed the audience for an hour they were very attentive.

July 10, 1871; Monday. Received a letter from Marion in relation to the sale of mill and answered. At night attended the circus.

July 11, 1871; Tuesday. Passed most of the day in reading and at night meet with executive committe.

July 12, 1871; Wednesday. Passed most of the day in reading and in the afternoon visited brother [Henry] Kendall and family.

July 13, 1871; Thursday. Visited brother Wm Shirman who was blind with inflamed eyes. Bought load of wood for ten dollers.

July 14, 1871; Friday. Passed most of the day in reading. Today meet with [James] Bro[o]k family.

July 15, 1871; Saturday. To day Hyrum Coombs left us for another place of lodging on the street. I meet with brother Nathan Tanner and son.

July 16, 1871; Sunday. Called on brother [James] Brooks family for a book passed day at home. At night attended the meeting at the Institute[,] Speakers [William H.] Slocum[,] [Edward] Tulege and [Elias] Harison subject <u>God</u>.

July 17, 1871; Monday. Made some calls in town and past most of the day in reading.

July 18, 1871; Tuesday. Passed the day in reading weather very warm.

July 19, 1871; Wednesday. Made one trip up town. [Son] Henry started for Fillmore to day with Orange Warner.

July 20, 1871; Thursday. Passed the day in reading Professor [William]

---

became reconnected with the New Movement and delivered speeches in the east against Brigham Young. Walker, *Wayward Saints*, 307–08.

Hosington lectured in liberal institute on Egypt. I did not attend the lecture on acount of the sickness of Mrs Lyman.

July 21, 1871; Friday. Passed the day in reading. Mrs Lyman was beter in evening received a call from Uncle Nathan Tanner and wife. Attended lecture at the Institute. Light rain.

July 22, 1871; Saturday. Was engagged in reading in the afternoon had a shower of dust folowed by rain. The sick are beter.

July 23, 1871; Sunday. Attended the Lecture at the Institute and in the afternoon attended a seance at the residence of Mr John Whiteing, and in the evening attended a lecture at the Institute. Audience fair.

July 24, 1871; Monday. In afternoon attended the Funereal of the little son of Edward W. Tull^e^dge. In the evening attended a parlor lecture by Profesor [William] Hosington at residence of Mrs A[nnie] Godbe ~~residence~~. Subject the discovery of the hyroglificks [hieroglyphics] and the relation the Egyptian bore to the Hebrew and also the Sanscrit. The professor leaves tomorow.

July 25, 1871; Tuesday. Wrote letter to cousin Sophronia Lyman in Rhode Island. At night had a committe meeting at which it was agreed that I should take charge of the publick meetings.

July 26, 1871; Wednesday. Visited brother [William] Shirman. Brother S. is geting beter tho not able to see but little. Dined with his family. Meet committe at night at br [Elias] Harisons.

July 27, 1871; Thursday. Brother [Noah] Bartholimew and his daughter came from Fillmore and stoped with us.

July 28, 1871; Friday. Brother [Noah] Bartholimew and his daughters started for their home in Fillmore. My daughter Lelia went with them. Weather very warm.

July 29, 1871; Saturday. Passed most of the day in reading and delivered Barns Railroad Tickets to Mr Hickland.

July 30, 1871; Sunday. Visited Brother [James] Brooks and family and at night attended meeting at the Institute. As we were closeing services a fire occured on adjoining premices which burned a small out building and quantity of hay.

July 31, 1871; Monday. Visited the locality of the fire of last night which I think was accidental. Received a letter from Paulina reporting those at home well. Dureing the day had an interview with a Mr

[Joseph] Warner who was participater in the Moris delusion and its bloody finale.[45]

August 1, 1871; Tuesday. Passed the day in reading. At night held seance at br [Elias] Harison's with good results. Weather cooler.

August 2, 1871; Wednesday. Made some calls in city passed most of the day in reading. Weather cooler.

August 3, 1871; Thursday. Borowed ten dollars to pay rent passed the day in reading. Had news from Fillmore of the death of one of my horses, peace to his dust he was a good servent and friend.

August 4, 1871; Friday. Meet with br Nathan Tinney and wife who had come to the city to secure surgical treatment for their son who had a hair lip. The lad is 16 years old,[46] operation takes place tomorow by Drs [Washington F.] Anderson and [Heber J.] Richards.

August 5, 1871; Saturday. Witnessed the operation on young Tinney. Bryant Stringham[47] was buried today. Commenced reading Man and His Relations by Mr S[amuel] B. Brittan.[48]

August 6, 1871; Sunday. Did not go out today in evening attended a meeting at the Institute and preached to the people.

August 7, 1871; Monday. Visited br [William] Shirman whom I found improveing in health. Myself and wife went to the polls and voted the liberals ticket then called on and took tea with br E[dward] Tulledge and family. Called on Mrs [Olive] Tiney. Aunt Jane Tanner from Provo stayed with us tonight.

August 8, 1871; Tuesday. Received money and order from [David] Williams. In evening attended the opening party at the Institute.

August 9, 1871; Wednesday. Passed the day mostly in reading. Attended counsil at night at br [Elias] Harisons.

---

45. The followers of Joseph Morris and his revelations were besieged by a territorial militia in May 1862 and some of the Morrisites ended up being killed. Howard, "Men, Motives, and Misunderstandings." See note under Mar. 22, 1863.

46. Actually, John Lowell Tenney was fifteen years old, the son of Nathan Tenney and first wife, Olive. Later photos indicate that the operation was successful.

47. Briant Stringham from Colesville, New York, was a member of one of the earliest Mormon congregations. Part of the pioneer company of 1847, he drove Brigham Young's wagon part of the way. His daughter married future LDS President Heber J. Grant in 1877.

48. The subtitle ("Illustrating the Influence of the Mind on the Body") hinted at hypnotism, clairvoyance, and conjuring spirits, the book's main topics.

August 10, 1871; Thursday. Wrote letters to my friends east and south. Passed residue of time in reading.

August 11, 1871; Friday. Attended funeral of br Cooks child in the 15th W[ard]. Light showers during day.

August 12, 1871; Saturday. Passed the day in reading. Weather growing cooler. Mad[e] a call on Dr [Washington F.] Anderson.

August 13, 1871; Sunday. Brother [Nathan C.] Tiney was with us held seance with very pleasant results. At night attended meeting at the Institute brother [Elias] Harison preached. Our Methodist friends entered upon their use of the Institute for their religious service which they will continue until their house is built.

August 14, 1871; Monday. Received of [David] Williams ten dollars at night held seance. Wrote letter to Priscilla.

August 15, 1871; Tuesday. Passed a portion of the day with br William Shirman at his residence.

August 16, 1871; Wednesday. Passed the day in reading and at night had a council at the house of br [Henry W.] Lawrence where a committee of four was appointed to take charge of the Progressive Lyceum or Sabbath School Dept. Names of committe were A. M. Lyman, E[lias] L. T. Harison T[homas C.] Armstrong D[avid] W. Williams.

August 17, 1871; Thursday. Passed the morning in reading. In the afternoon visited Mr [William] Shirman and Mrs [Lovina] Johnson. Held seance at night with good results at the house of Mr [Elias] Harison. During the evening br [William S.] Godbe called with Mr and Mrs Tebs from London they were spiritualists.

August 18, 1871; Friday. Passed the morning in reading and called on Mrs [Sarah Ann] Cook[49] on the subject of the Sabbath School. She gave a promise of her cooperation in the matter spoke with Mrs [Fanny] Stenhouse on the subject. In the afternoon visited br [William] Shirman and family in the evening held seance with them. ~~High~~ Hila was the medium results were good.

August 19, 1871; Saturday. Passed some time in reading. Received

49. Cooke was a British emigrant and widow who presided over the Anti-Polygamy Society. She would also help found the Ladies Library Association. Patricia Lyn Scott, "Sarah Ann Sutton Cooke, 1808–1885: 'The Respected Mrs. Cooke,'" in *Worth their Salt, Too*, 19–20.

letter from Marion in Fillmore encloseing my deed for my lots in that city and also a proposition to b[u]y my intrest in the mill. At night held seance with br [Elias] Harison, brother Joseph Smith was with us.

August 20, 1871; Sunday. Attended church with the Methodists at the Institute, were addressed by a Rev. br from N. Y. City. During the afternoon some rain fell. In the evening attended service in the Institute we were addressed by Mr W[illiam] S. Godbe. Weather cooler.

August 21, 1871; Monday. Attended the final operation by Drs [Washington F.] Anderson and [Heber J.] Richards on young [John] Tiney. At night held seance at home. Some friends were present results satisfactory.

August 22, 1871; Tuesday. Passed the day in reading in the afternoon received a letter from Beaver announcing the death of Father Theodore Turley by cancer on Friday 18th at 10 oclock A.M. In the evening held seance at which Father Turley gave us kindly greeting.

August 23, 1871; Wednesday. Made call to day on the family of br Mather received from them promise of help in the Lyceum Sabbath School.[50]

August 24, 1871; Thursday. Received news of the death of Mother [Nancy] Walker by letter from Priscilla in Fillmore. Wrote letter to J[ames] H. Rollins of Minersville. At night had buisness meeting at brother [Elias] Harisons.

August 25, 1871; Friday. Made some call about the city in the afternoon met with Mr. Brown a spiritualist since the days of the Rochester knockings.[51] Wrote letters to Dionitia[,] Paulina and Priscilla. In the evening held seance at the residence of br [Elias] Harison whose [dead] mother greeted her son. Mother [Nancy] Walker also came and spoke to us. Mr. Brown was with us[,] [his] daughter spoke to him through Hila, she was the only medium present at the siting.

August 26, 1871; Saturday. Walked around town on buisness connected with our prospective Sabbath School. Received and answered a letter from my son Marion in Fillmore at night held seance.

---

50. The Children's Progressive Lyceum was a Sunday school where children were "taught to do their own thinking" and where the arts and sciences were included as part of the religious instruction. According to Walker, "Liberal Institute," 82, it attracted about 150 children.

51. The Fox Sisters' tales of the supernatural inspired the modern spiritualist movement. Their parents sent them to live with relatives in Rochester for a cooling-down period, but the spirits pursued the girls to Rochester and the coded messages continued.

August 27, 1871; Sunday. Visited br Henry Kendall and family. Held seance with them had pleasant communications from [deceased] brs Hyrum [and] Joseph [Smith][,] Heber [C. Kimball] and Jedadiah [M Grant]. In evening attended at the Institute where I met br J[ohn] M Spear from Cal who addressed us briefly after I spoke for a half hour, had fine audience.

August 28, 1871; Monday. Called on br [William] Shirman at his residence. Gave to br [Nathan C.] Tiney a parcel which he was to carry to Theodore in Fillmore. At evening held seance. Some friends were with us the results were satisfactory.

August 29, 1871; Tuesday. Visited Mrs. Charlson who is sick. Called on Mr Raybold at Walker Brothers, on the matter of the Sunday School Library, received some promise of help. In the evening held seance br [Nathan C.] Tiney was present.

August 30, 1871; Wednesday. Attended the conference of the Josephites [Missouri-based Reorganized LDS Church] in the Institute. At night attended a small meeting at br [John] Manings to consider the organization of [séance] circles.

August 31, 1871; Thursday. Attended the conference the attendance was very small. In afternoon attended conference by request spoke for a short time. In the evening held seance with good results.

September 1, 1871; Friday. Called on the families of brother James Brooks and F[rederick] T. ~~Paris~~ Peris. Mrs P. gave me a basket of plumbs. At night held seance with pleasant results. Weather cooler.

September 2, 1871; Saturday. Passed the day in reading at night attended executive counsil at the residence of br [William S.] Godbe.

September 3, 1871; Sunday. Passed morning at home in the evening called on Aunt Rachel Tanner and at night attended meeting in the Institute. Br [Eli] Kelsey preached an address [explaining a letter] to the National Convention of Spiritualists[,][52] [which] was read by Mr [Elias] Harison and signed by many of the friends present.

52. For the eighth annual convention of the American Association of Spiritualists, Sept. 12–14, in Troy, New York, William and Mary Godbe sent an invitation to "mediums and speakers" to visit Utah, promising them an eager audience. The letter was entered into the minutes, and the mediums responded favorably. John Buescher, "Listings of Nineteenth-Century Spiritualists," *International Association for the Preservation of Spiritualist and Occult Periodicals*, spirithistory.iapsop.com.

September 4, 1871; Monday. Was enaged in procureing Signitures to the address to the Spiritualistic National Convention to be held in Troy, N.Y. In the evening attended a select party of Spiritualistic friends at the residence of br T[homas] C. Armstrong, the meeting was in celebration of the establishment at his house of a spiritual circle just twelve months previous to date. Br J[ohn] M. Spear was present and addressed us in the entranced condition.

September 5, 1871; Tuesday. Made some calls in the city in the evening aided in prepareing the papers to send to convention with brs [Elias] Harison and [Thomas C.] Armstrong.

September 6, 1871; Wednesday. Visited Mr W. D[avid] Williams family an[d] saw their sick child. I then called on Mrs R. R[uth] Hopkins and then called on Mr. W[illiam] H. Shearman with whom and family I dined. In the afternoon assisted br [Elias] Harison in prepareing for the mail the address and other papers for the National Convention to be held in Troy New York on the 12th of this month. To day Mrs Mary wife of Mr Mark Croxhall and daughter of Prest [Brigham] Young was buried her death folowing soon after the birth of her child.

September 7, 1871; Thursday. Made some calls in forenoon. In the afternoon held seance with Mrs [Emily] Teasdale.[53] Was present the results were gratifying. The committe failed to meet as per ajournment. Brs [Eli] Kelsey and [Thomas C.] Armstrong called in and past the hour with brother [Elias] Harison and myself.

September 8, 1871; Friday. Made some calls on buisness. At night attended a meeting for the organization of the Utah Spiritual movement.[54] Meeting ajourned for the completion of its buisness on Tuesday next. In the afternoon of to day called on Br H[enry] W. Lawrence and family.

September 9, 1871; Saturday. Repaired to the residence of br C[harles] F. Jones to attend his funeral but finding the Prest Joseph Young was

53. This was the wife of future LDS apostle George Teasdale, who had an article in the Godbeite *Utah Magazine* in October 1869, an article a few years earlier in an October 1858 issue of the *Millennial Star*, and one in the *Phrenological Journal* in May 1872, all under her full name, Emily E. Teasdale. See Walker, *Wayward Saints*, 179.

54. The pro-Mormon *Salt Lake Herald* noted the new direction with satire: "Died, at the Church of Zion, on Friday evening, Sept. 8, … the New Movement," adding that "business will be continued … under the name of the Utah Spiritual Movement." *Salt Lake Herald*, Sept. 9, 1871.

there for that purpose did not remain. In the afternoon called on Mrs Lavina Johnson.

September 10, 1871; Sunday. In the morning attended the funeral of Mr Cooks child 15th W[ard]. Spoke for a short time to the friends present. At night attended the meeting at the Institute. Br [Elias] Harison preached.

September 11, 1871; Monday. To day meet with Dr Dudley and other gentlemen at the residence of Mr [William S.] Godbe. In the morning past some time in conversation with br [John M.] Spear. Past residue of day in reading.

September 12, 1871; Tuesday. This morning settled school bill with Mr Stien Principal of School. At night attended meeting for the election of Execkutive Council for the Utah Spiritual Movement which resulted in the election of as per report of judges of the election, 30 members of Concel, twenty one men and nine women.

September 13, 1871; Wednesday. To day had a cancer cut from my lower lip by Dr [Washington F.] Anderson suffered considerable pain through the day and early part of the night, when it subsided and I had some sleep.

September 14, 1871; Thursday. In the [morning] called on the Dr passed the day without much pain in my face and at night attended lecture in the Institute.

September 15, 1871; Friday. This morning visited the Dr. In the evening attended the last of Mr [Charles G.] Ameses very interesting course of lectures[55] some pain in my face.

September 16, 1871; Saturday. Called on the Dr who thought I had beter keep the stiches in my face another day. In the evening attended a [séance] circle for a short time but had to leave on acount of the pain in my head. Medium on the occasion br Edward Holder.

September 17, 1871; Sunday. In morning attended at the Institute to hear a lecture by the Rev T. S. Burnell missionary from India. In the evening attended service in the Institute we were addressed by Mr [John M.] and Mrs [Caroline] Spear, and Mr Harison of Cal.

55. The Unitarian minister, best known for composing hymns, spoke on "Man and Woman," "Marriage," and "Domestic Life." He would later gain attention for opposing US expansion into Cuba, Guam, the Philippines, and Puerto Rico.

September 18, 1871; Monday. In the morning walked out in town. In the evening My face was very painful in consequence, At night attended a meeting as per apointment of the Executive Counsil in the institute. The members present 13 in number organized for the buisness of the evening by calling Mr A. M. Lyman to the chair and Mr. Walter Mansfield to act as clerk. The only buisness transacted folowing some general suggestions from the members present was the choice by the meeting of a committe of five to draft bylaws and also suggest the working committees necissary to meet the present wants of the movement and report the same to the nest meeting. Ajourned to next week Monday night at Institute 7½ oclock P.M.

September 19, 1871; Tuesday. Did not go out to day past the time in reading.

September 20, 1871; Wednesday. Wrote letters for Fillmore. Called on the Dr and went to the store for some medicine for my face.

September 21, 1871; Thursday. Passed the day at home did not go out ~~du~~. Passed the time in reading.

September 22, 1871; Friday. Called on br [John] Maning he let me have the Baner[56] to read. Passed residue of the day at home in reading.

September 23, 1871; Saturday. To day Mrs Theodore Turley and her son Omner called on us they intend locating in this city. Made some calls in town.

September 24, 1871; Sunday. Visited Mr Jas Brooks and family and at night was at meeting in the Institute. In morning attended the funerel of the child of H[enry] W. and [Isa]bel Lawrence.

September 25, 1871; Monday. Visited Mrs S[arah] A. Cook. In evening was at Institute as per ajournment of Council but there was not enough in attendance to do buisness but parted with promise that we would meet again on Tuesday night of next week.

September 26, 1871; Tuesday. Called on Mrs Turley at the residence of Mr [George] Crouch she suffering some from haveing her teeth extracted. Called on Mrs [Hannah] Stewart passed residue of time in reading.

September 27, 1871; Wednesday. Passed morning in reading called on Mr [George] Crouch and family and also on Mr D[avid] W. Williams

56. *The Banner of Light* was a Boston-based spiritualist publication.

whose wife was sick and his child was dieing. In afternoon called on Sister Lavina Johnson. Wind very high to day with much dust. At night held seance with brother [Elias] Harison with good results.

September 28, 1871; Thursday. Received a few bushels of peaches from Sister Lovina Johnson. To day received letter from Lorenzo in Fillmore. Less stormy than yesterday in the evening some rain falling.

September 29, 1871; Friday. Made some calls in town wrote letters to Lorenzo at Fillmore and Paulina in Parowan. Passed residue of time in reading. Some rain during the day.

September 30, 1871; Saturday. Made some calls in town received letter from Prest Thomas Callister of Fillmore. Meet Rev Charles E. Rich Temperence Lecturer.[57]

October 1, 1871; Sunday. This morning Dr Anderson cut a small canceral tumor from the face of my daughter Mrs. M[aria] L[ouisa] Clayton ~~in afternoon~~. In afternoon myself and Mrs. L[yman] visited our friends the [John] Manings. In the evening attended meeting in the Institute and heard lecture from Bro [William H.] Holmes on the origin and destiny of man.

October 2, 1871; Monday. Passed the day in reading. At night attended lecture at the Institute by Mr Charles E. Rich on the subject of Temperence. The speaker presented his thoughts in a very clear and eloquent maner.

October 3, 1871; Tuesday. Received and answered a letter from my son Oscar in Parowan. In the evening attended council at the residence of br [Elias] Harison.

October 4, 1871; Wednesday. Received per hand of D[avid] W. Williams seventeen dollars in orders on store. Passed some time in reading in the afternoon called on Mrs [Elizabeth] Armstrong. Weather cool but pleasant.

October 5, 1871; Thursday. Received a call from my son Marion and Bishops Myron and Joseph Tanner. They were in attendence on the [General] Conference.

October 6, 1871; Friday. Received of [David] Williams 36 dollers in cash. Received letter from Priscilla reporting all well at date of writeing.

---

57. Rich was in town from California lecturing throughout the territory in behalf of the Independent Order of Good Templars. "Temperance Lectures," *Salt Lake Herald*, Sep. 24, 1871.

October 7, 1871; Saturday. Made some calls in town passed most of the day in reading.

October 8, 1871; Sunday. Received a call from Wm Flake, past the day at home at night preached at the Institute. Some rain and snow fell to day and during the night weather cool.

October 9, 1871; Monday. Attended and spoke at the funeral ^of the daughter^ [elven-year-old Clara] of Mr Wm and Mrs Ann Godbe at her mother's residence.[58] Rev Mr Pierce was present and by invitation participated in the services. Received call from my son Marion aranged to sell my intrest in our mill for $2000.

October 10, 1871; Tuesday. Received from [David] Wm's 8 dollers. Passed most of the day in town. In evening had Council meeting at brother [Elias] Harisons.

October 11, 1871; Wednesday. Wrote letter to L. B. Lyman of Montana. At night held seance with the Kendall's at their residence. Dispaches from the east state the fire in Chicago was extinguished by heavy fall of rain last night.[59]

October 12, 1871; Thursday. Passed the day in reading. At night the wind blew a gale damageing slightly certain frail classes of property [such] as fences awnings and shade trees. Wrote letter to cousin Sophronia Lyman in Rhode Isleand and sent her papers.

October 13, 1871; Friday. Made several calls in the city. At night meet at home with Executive Council. Weather cool but pleasant.

October 14, 1871; Saturday. Made some calls around town. Called on Mr Barber and family also called on <u>Mrs</u> [Lavina] Johnson.

October 15, 1871; Sunday. Visited and spent the day with <u>br</u> R[ichard] R. Hopkins and family. At night attended meeting at the Institute.

October 16, 1871; Monday. To day called on Mrs Stowe at Salt Lake House.[60] Left my coat with br Henry Kendall to be cleaned and repared. At night held seance with brother [Elias] Harison for the benefit of

58. Godbe was in the process of leaving his wives Mary and Rosina in favor of his first wife, Annie. He had designed a two-story octagonal house with three apartments for his family but never moved into it. Walker, *Wayward Saints*, 326–29; Roberts, *Salt Lake City's Historic Architecture*, 107.

59. The Great Chicago Fire of Oct. 8–10 destroyed over three square miles of the city and killed hundreds of people.

60. The Salt Lake House hotel at 150 South Main Street was the first hotel in the territory, built in 1854 by James and Elizabeth Townsend and sold in 1864 to Feramorz

Sister Anna Godbe. Her daughter Clara came through Hila and most affectionately greeted her mother and friends.

October 17, 1871; Tuesday. Passed the day in reading. At night some members of the council meet but not a Quorum. No buisness was done.

October 18, 1871; Wednesday. Called on Mrs Charlson and then meet with Mr [William H.] Slocum and wife. And in the afternoon called Mr [Henry] Kendall and his family and spent the evening with them and other friends.

October 19, 1871; Thursday. Made some calls in the city passed most of the day in reading. I[n] the evening called at Tribune Office[61] with br [Elias] Harison. On our return called at the Institute where Mr [David] Williams was holding choir practice. Rain falling to night.

October 20, 1871; Friday. Passed the day in reading at night had an informal meeting with some of the members of the council.

October 21, 1871; Saturday. Passed the day in reading at night went to the Institute with [Elias] Harison.

October 22, 1871; Sunday. Passed the day at home in reading. Received letters from Marion and Lorenzo and wrote to Lelia in Fillmore. In evening attended a lecture in the Institute by Mrs Stowe after lecture went with her to her Hotell.

October 23, 1871; Monday. Passed the day in reading in the evening visited brother [Henry] Kendall. To day wrote letters to my sons Marion and Lorenzo and also Brother Wm Gibbs.

October 24, 1871; Tuesday. Passed the day mostly in reading at night held council at my House. To day Mr [William H.] Holms returned from Ogden br [John] Broom was with him.[62]

October 25, 1871; Wednesday. Called on Mr Linzy [Lindsey] and Mrs Mather on the matter of monthly donations. In the evening received a call from Professor [William H.] Holms.

Little and Brigham Young. It was the site of the future Ezra Thompson/Salt Lake Tribune Building.

61. The *Tribune* was run out of the three-story Godbe–Pitts Drug Store, half a block north of the Salt Lake House.

62. John Broom was an English convert who settled in Ogden in 1851 and bought lots in the downtown area in anticipation of the railroad. He would soon leave the LDS Church but retain what he called "feelings of kindness and great respect for the people." Tullidge, *Tullidge's Histories*, 253.

October 26, 1871; Thursday. Obtained the record book of the Movement from Mr. [Frederick T.] Peris. Passed some time in makeing transcripts of many [items]. In evening attended the choir practice of the Institute under Professor [David] Williams.

October 27, 1871; Friday. Called on Mr [James] Brooks and family. Passed most of the day in reading; and at night held seance with Br [Elias] Harison. Mr Holms was present.

October 28, 1871; Saturday. Today [LDS] Pres[idential] [counselor] D[aniel] H. Wells was arrested on the charge of murder and imprisoned at Camp Douglas. Some rain today. Hosea Stout and Wm Kimball wer[e] arrested on the same charge as Wells.[63] Recived letter from Lorenzo.

October 29, 1871; Sunday. Visited and passed the day with brother Hyrum Coombs and Sister and Mrs Turley. In the evening attended lecture at the Institute by Professor Holms. Good house.

October 30, 1871; Monday. Engaged the makeing of some clothes by Mrs [Elizabeth] Maning past some time in reading and wrote letter to Lorenzo and in the evening held seance.

October 31, 1871; Tuesday. Purchased some shoes and sent to Paulina for the children by Thomas Richards and Lorenzo Burton. At night attended Council.

November 1, 1871; Wednesday. Made some calls in town passed most of the day in reading. In the afternoon the stoves were put in their places in the Institute.

November 2, 1871; Thursday. Passed most of the day in reading in the evening attended the choir practice at the Institute.

November 3, 1871; Friday. Passed most of the day in reading wrote letter to my wife Paulina. Agreed to rent two of our rooms to E[li] B. Kelsey for ten dollars per month.

November 4, 1871; Saturday. Received per hand of [David] Williams fortynine dollers. In afternoon went to Ogden called upon brother Thomas Stainer and family with whom I stayed over night.

November 5, 1871; Sunday. Afternoon held seance with Mrs [Elizabeth]

---

63. When Mormon renegade William Hickman confessed to murdering Richard Yeates, he tried to implicate Brigham Young and other church leaders. Chief Justice James McKean accepted his testimony as credible, but the other justices thought it was contrived. Turner, *Brigham Young*, 364–71.

Crouch in the Meeting Hall took supper with Mrs Crouch and then Preached at the hall which was crowded with an attentive audience.

November 6, 1871; Monday. Returned to the City on the morning train. Some snow falling during the day[,] rendering the walking unpleasant.

November 7, 1871; Tuesday. Made some changes in the furniture of our rooms by way of prepareing for our renters tomorow. At night three members of the committe meet and ajourned. General [Christopher C.] Auger and family arived yesterday.[64]

November 8, 1871; Wednesday. Passed the day mostly at home in labor and reading. In afternoon was out in the city.

November 9, 1871; Thursday. Made some calls in the city. Received letters from Lorenzo and Priscilla. In evening attended the choir practice at the Institute. Called on Mr Holms who was sick he is geting beter.

November 10, 1871; Friday. Wrote letters to Lorenzo and Priscilla in Fillmore. In the afternoon called on Mrs Lavina Johnson. At 12 oclock last at night Mr John Kimball passed over to the other life. He is kindly remembered by many who knew him.[65]

November 11, 1871; Saturday. Made some calls ine the city and passt some time in reading. Some rain was falling in the afternoon ^was not^ well as usual today.

November 12, 1871; Sunday. Attended and spoke at the funereal of Mr John Kimball. Professor Stine was present and participated in the services. In the evening I spoke at the Institute had a very attentive audience.

November 13, 1871; Monday. Wrote letters to Stephen Franklin in Beaver in relation to my dues from the Factory in that place.

November 14, 1871; Tuesday. Wrote letter to Lorenzo in Fillmore and made some calls in the City. Past sometime in reading. Past the evening in company of brothers [Elias] Harison[,] [Alfred] Ward[,] and [Thomas C.] Armstrong.

November 15, 1871; Wednesday. Made some calls in the city[,] past the day in reading. At night called on Mr J[ohn] Maning and family and passed an hour withom [with them] and a few friends. Some indications of rain.

---

64. Auger was an officer during the Civil War, promoted by President Lincoln to the rank of major general. Afterward he was stationed in the western territories.

65. John B. Kimball, co-owner with Henry Lawrence of the Kimball & Lawrence mercantile firm, had been active in the Godbeite community.

November 16, 1871; Thursday. Passed the day at home rain and snow were falling during the day. At night went to the Institute to the choir practice the attendance was small.

November 17, 1871; Friday. Made some calls in Town and passed most of the day in reading. At night spent an hour with Mr [Thomas C.] Armstrong and other friends at formers residence.

November 18, 1871; Saturday. Made some calls in town but past most of the day and evening at home.

November 19, 1871; Sunday. In the afternoon called on Mr J[ohn] Maning and family. In evening attended meeting at the Institute. Weather cool and windy.

November 20, 1871; Monday. Called on and dined with Mrs [Mary] Perris. Some of our friends of the Tanners from Payson stayed with us over night. At night called on the Armstrongs and past a social hour with Mr Holms.

November 21, 1871; Tuesday. Received letter from my cousin Sophronia Lyman in Rhode Island. At night attended the party at the Institute. Rain fell during the night. Heard while at the party of the Death ^to day^ of Mrs Daniel Grant by apoplexy.

November 22, 1871; Wednesday. Wrote letter to my cousin in Rhode Island. To day received an acount of the reunion of the Lyman Family at Mount Tom in Mass. Sent me by my cousin Sophronia Lyman. Rain was falling most of the day.

November 23, 1871; Thursday. Made some calls in the city and past most of the day at home. In the afternoon received a call from Mr Gideon Carter with whom I had a pleasant conversation. In the evening I attended the choir practice.

November 24, 1871; Friday. On riseing this morning felt diziness in my head and sickness at my stomach. During the day feeling some better I walked to the 11th Ward.

November 25, 1871; Saturday. Made a call in town and bought some medicine. My illness abating.

November 26, 1871; Sunday. Visited and spent the day with Mr John Low and family at night attended at the Institute. Had a very interesting lecture from Mr Holmes on Then and Now. The ground is covered with snow.

November 27, 1871; Monday. Made call in the city passed the day at home. Meet on the street Mr Robert Miller from Parowan who reported all well there on the 20th of the month.

November 28, 1871; Tuesday. Made sevral calls in the city after which I read William Dentons Radical Rhymes.[66] In the evening attended to some buisness with brothers [Thomas C.] Armstrong and [Alfred] Ward who called on me. Br [Elias] Harison was ill and did not attend.

November 29, 1871; Wednesday. Passed the day mostly at home received letter from Lorenzo.

November 30, 1871; Thursday. Made one or two calls in the city passed residue of the day at home. Weather very cold. Day of Thanksgiveing and buisness mostly suspended.

December 1, 1871; Friday. Wrote letter to Lorenzo in Fillmore. Passed most of the day in reading; in the evening called with Mrs Lyman on Mrs Mary Godbe and spent an hour with her and children in their new residence. Paid five dollers on stoves in Institute.

December 2, 1871; Saturday. Passed most of the day in the City. Paid Mr. Holmes 4 dollers on school bill.

December 3, 1871; Sunday. Passed the day at home. In the evening attended at the Institute had Lecture by Dr [Orville H.] Conger on the progressive developement of the Sciences; and the human mind. Had good and attentive audience.

December 4, 1871; Monday. Made some calls in the city passed some time in reading. Weather quite warm streets very mudy.

December 5, 1871; Tuesday. Received of W. D[avid] Williams 60 dollers. Mrs Lyman suffering from neuralgia in her head. Received and read the [US] Prests message.[67] Held council at night.

December 6, 1871; Wednesday. Passed the day mostly in reading. Weather mild and pleasant.

December 7, 1871; Thursday. Spent the day mostly in readin[g] and

66. The poems were dedicated "to the friends of human progress." Denton, *Radical Rhymes*.

67. Ulysses S. Grant's "Third Annual Message," the State of Union report, was delivered to Congress in writing, as was the custom. "In Utah there still remains a remnant of barbarism, repugnant to civilization, to decency, and to the laws of the United States," he wrote, recommending charity toward the offspring but not to the parents in polygamous families.

during the day meet with Mr John Jost from Ogden. At evening attended the choir practice at the Institute.

December 8, 1871; Friday. Spent the day in reading [and] in the evening called on Mr Holms the teacher at Mr [Thomas C.] Armstrongs.

December 9, 1871; Saturday. Passed the day in reading. Received a letter from my brother David Emerson stateing that my mother had been sick some two months and that he thought she could not long survive.

December 10, 1871; Sunday. Attended Council at br [John] Manings and at night preached at the Institute. Had good attendance.

December 11, 1871; Monday. Meet with Dr Joslin an[d] wife at Tribune Office. Passed the day mostly away from home.

December 12, 1871; Tuesday. Past the day mostly at home. Called on Mrs Hudson and Mrs [Elizabeth] Crouch. In evening br [Noah] Bartholimew called on and stayed with us all night.

December 13, 1871; Wednesday. Made some calls in town with Br [Noah] B[artholomew] and meet with Brother John Kelley and J[ohn] Cavanah. During the day three men were arested on charge of the murder of Dr Robinson.[68] Brs Kelley and Cavanah called and spent the evening with me.

December 14, 1871; Thursday. Made some calls in the city. The examination of the witnesses in the Robinson Murder case was commenced. Received letter from Paulina.

December 15, 1871; Friday. Attended the Examination of Witnesses in the Robinson case at the Institute before Judge [James] McKean.[69] Received favourable word from the north and concluded to start in that direction tomorow.[70] Wrote letter to Paulina.

---

68. This was an old case dating back to October 22, 1866, when John King Robinson, a physician who had been the Assistant Surgeon at Camp Douglas, was murdered over his intent to build a hospital at the warm springs near the downtown area. People suspected Orrin Porter Rockwell. See Stenhouse, *Tell It All*, 338–39; Turner, *Brigham Young*, 350.

69. That McKean would hold court at the Liberal Institute was reflective of his position as a firm and somewhat cantankerous opponent of polygamy and Mormonism. He came to Utah after serving two terms in the US Congress and having fought in the Civil War. Alexander, "Federal Authority Versus Polygamic Theocracy."

70. The "favourable word" was that someone was interested in the Godbeite message. The New Movement was starting to fade in some areas, but membership in the Liberal Party was growing.

December 16, 1871; Saturday. Myself and Mrs Lyman dined with Mrs G[eorge] W. [Elizabeth] Crouch after which I went to Ogden and lodged with my old friend Dr [William] McIntire and family.

December 17, 1871; Sunday. Passed the day mostly with Brother [John] Broom and family and at night I spoke in Cordon's Hall had fair attendence. In afternoon had a seance in hall. Lodged with br B, at night met with br [Anne W.] Vanderwood from Malad City in Idaho who had brought butter to market but found no sale.[71]

December 18, 1871; Monday. Passed the day with Mr [John] Broom and family and in the evening went to Corrine. Called Mrs Painter and lodged at the Bear River House.

December 19, 1871; Tuesday. Left in stage for ~~Cor^i^ne~~ Malad where we arived at night. I was very kindly welcomed by Davies and was lodged at the residence of Brother [Anne W.] Vanderwood.

December 20, 1871; Wednesday. Wrote letter to Mr [Aaron] Dewit in Logan Cache Valley and at night I preached in the School House Controlled by the Josephites had a very attentive audience. The weather warm and rainy. The snow is fast going off makeing the traviling very unpleasant.

December 21, 1871; Thursday. Wrote letter to my wife in Salt Lake City passed the residue of the day in reading. Some snow in evening.

December 22, 1871; Friday. Weather cooler freezing some. Passed the day mostly in reading during the day meet with Dr [Joseph W.] Morgan.[72]

December 23, 1871; Saturday. Weather stormy past most of the day in reading.

December 24, 1871; Sunday. Did not go out to day the state of the weather hindered the people from haveing any meetings to day. Brother John Nelson called and past the day with me and in the evening we had a private seance with good results.

December 25, 1871; Monday. With Mrs [Siebregtje] Vanderwoot I visited and dined and past the day with Mr J[ohn] Nelson and family in the evening held seance. As we returned home some snow was falling.

---

71. Anne W. Vanderwood was the first settler of Malad Valley in the 1860s. He was from the Netherlands, and after converting to Mormonism in Wales in 1853, he was sent back to Holland on a mission in 1861–63. Sheers, "From Dikes to Desert," 116–18.

72. Joseph W. Morgan established a drug store and medical office in Malad in 1866. Soon he would testify that he witnessed Mormons tampering with the election by stuffing ballots. *Fenn Vs. Bennett*, "Deposition of Joseph W. Morgan," H.R., 169–72.

December 26, 1871; Tuesday. Passed most of the day in reading at night preached in the school House had an attentive audience. Snow fell at night.

December 27, 1871; Wednesday. Did not go out to day the snow was falling all day. Past the time in reading.

December 28, 1871; Thursday. Passed the day in reading and at night I preached at the Josephite House[73] had a very attentive audience. Some rain to day which makes it very slopy underfoot.

December 29, 1871; Friday. Passed the morning in reading and then went with br John Nelson to visit his children with whom we dined and in the evening held seance with good results. Snow falling at night.

December 30, 1871; Saturday. Passed the day in reading no storm to day. Wrote letter to Lorenzo in Fillmore.

December 31, 1871; Sunday. Brother [Anne W.] Vanderwood came home to day. In afternoon attended the Josephite Meeting. In evening attended a seance at Br V's.

January 1, 1872; Monday. Past the day with brother John Nelson and family at night preached in the Josephite House to a very attentive audience.

January 2, 1872; Tuesday. Meet with Dr [Joseph W.] Morgan and concluded an arangement for another lecture on Thursday night at the Josephite House. Called on Mr and Mrs [Newton and Angie] Shilling. Mr S is Telegraph Operator at this office.

January 3, 1872; Wednesday. Visited with br [John] Nelson and family had seance at night with good results.

January 4, 1872; Thursday. Passed the day in reading. Received eleven dollars from br E[phraim] Mantle makeing in all I had received in Malad City thirty six dollars. Preached at night.

January 5, 1872; Friday. Traviled by stage to Corine and lodgeed at Bear River House. Weather cold and freezing.

January 6, 1872; Saturday. Traviled by Rail to Ogden. Called on <u>br</u> [John] Broom and family dined with them and lodged with <u>br</u> [Thomas J.] Stayner and family.

---

73. The Malad branch of the RLDS Church thrived, perhaps because it was close enough to Salt Lake City to be relevant and far enough away to avoid conflict. Avery, *From Mission to Madness*, 109.

January 7, 1872; Sunday. Passed the day with brother [John] Broom. During the day called on Mrs Duncan and at night Lectured at Cordon's Hall. Lodged with Dr. [William] McIntire.

January 8, 1872; Monday. Returned home found all well. Received 36 dollers of [David] Williams. Brother J[ohn] J. Tanner[74] and wife called on us and staid all night. The Legislature meet today. Received letter from my cousin Sophronia Lyman also a book.

January 9, 1872; Tuesday. Called on Mr. Holms at his school. Paid [John] Maning 7 dollars. At night had seance with pleasant results.

January 10, 1872; Wednesday. Made some calls in the city read some. Paid Mrs [Sarah] Crosby eight dollars for chairs. At night attended seance at br [Henry] Kendalls. Signs of storm mostly disappeared.

January 11, 1872; Thursday. Wrote letters to my friends in the East. Made some calls in town at night attended seance at the residence of br J[ohn] S. Linsey. To day meet my old friend S[eth] M. Blair.

January 12, 1872; Friday. Made some calls in the city and at night attended a seance at the residence of Mr [Frederick] Knowles.

January 13, 1872; Saturday. Called on Mrs [Mary] Peris passed most of the day in reading at night had a private seance at home.

January 14, 1872; Sunday. In the morning attended Council at br [John] Manings and then called and dined with br Jas Brooks and family. At night spoke at the Institute large attendence.

January 15, 1872; Monday. Called on several friends in the City. Passed some time in reading. To day meet Wm Flake from Beaver.

January 16, 1872; Tuesday. Received of W. D[avid] Williams 15 dollars in curency. At night attended seance at the residence of Mr [William] Nowell.

January 17, 1872; Wednesday. Passed the day in reading at night attended Lecture at the Institute by Mr ~~Holems~~ Holmes subject <u>Sciencies</u>.

January 18, 1872; Thursday. Made some calls in town and attended Musick practice at the Institute.

January 19, 1872; Friday. Made some calls in the city at night attended a seance at <u>Mr [William] Nowells</u>.

74. Lyman's brother-in-law. John had a brother Nathan who was sympathetic to the New Movement (see entry for May 9, 1870).

January 20, 1872; Saturday. Passed the day mostly at home in the evening held a seance with our home circle with very good results.

January 21, 1872; Sunday. Made a call at Mr [John] Mannings. At night attended a meeting in the Institute where the admission and non-admission of Utah as a state was discussed by several speakers as per report in Tribune. Br John Coombs was with us tonight had a pleasant seance.

January 22, 1872; Monday. Meet with W[illiam] S. Godbe this morning who has just returned from London. Had a sitting at night.

January 23, 1872; Tuesday. Made some calls in town and dined with br W[illiam] S. Godbe. Held seance at night. Br [John] Coombs was with us.

January 24, 1872; Wednesday. Made some calls in town and past the day at home the weather very cold.

January 25, 1872; Thursday. Made some calls in town. Mrs [Ann] Whiteing was buried to day the wife of brother John Whiteing. Attended music practice at the Institute.

January 26, 1872; Friday. Passed some time with John Coombs who was very sick with pneumonia. At night attended seance at Mr [William] Nowells.

January 27, 1872; Saturday. Settled with br [Stephen] Franklin my wool acount to date. Visited br J[ohn] Coombs who was sick dined with br H[yrum] Coombs. Held seance at home.

January 28, 1872; Sunday. Attended council at br [John] Manings dined with him. Attended meeting at Institute.

January 29, 1872; Monday. Called on Mrs [Elizabeth] Crouch. Br [Stephen] Franklin and family Dined with us. In the evening attended the lecture of Mr. [Orson S.] Fowler[75] in Institute on phrenology and health.

January 30, 1872; Tuesday. Made some calles in town parted with br [Stephen] Franklin and family who started for their home in Beaver. At night attended lecture at Institute.

January 31, 1872; Wednesday. To day received from Mr Gilmer a free pass over the road in his stage to Pioche[76] and return. At night attended lecture at Institute by Mr [Orson S.] Fowler.

75. Orson Squire Fowler was from a family of famous phrenologists and a close associate of Henry Ward Beecher. He and his brother Lorenzo gave readings for Charles Dickens, Edgar Allen Poe, and Brigham Young. "Noted Phrenologist Dead," *New York Times*, Sep. 4, 1896.

76. Pioche is across the border from Utah in Nevada, west of Parowan.

February 1, 1872; Thursday. Made some calls in the city at night visited Mrs Anna Godbe with some frieands held seance with them.

February 2, 1872; Friday. Made some calls in city. At night held seance at home br J[ohn] Coombs was with us. Wrote letters to Paulina and Lorenzo.

February 3, 1872; Saturday. Called on Mrs [Ruth] Turley and her son Omner who has been sick but is recovering. Received my monthly dues from brother [David] Williams at night held seance.[77]

February 4, 1872; Sunday. Visited and passed the day with Brother [John] Coombs at night attended the lecture at the Institute by Mr [Orson S.] Fowler on the immortality of the soul.

February 5, 1872; Monday. Started on my journey south traviled to and lodged in Provo at the Rail Road-House.[78]

February 6, 1872; Tuesday. Called on some of my friends. Dined with W. Wilson and family in afternoon traviled to Payson and lodged at the Cal House.

February 7, 1872; Wednesday. Made appointment for Lecture in the evening at Longs Hall. Dined with Mother [Elizabeth] Tanner and at night lectured at the Hall had an attentive audience. Lodged with the Bishop Joseph Tanner.

February 8, 1872; Thursday. Made some calls on my friends. Received four dollers for traviling money took stage south in the evening to Nephi.

February 9, 1872; Friday. Called on and passed the day with brother Schofield and family.

February 10, 1872; Saturday. Took stage in the morning for Fillmore and arived about 10, oclock and found my family all well except Lelia Bartholomew.[79]

February 11, 1872; Sunday. Visited and spent the day with the Bartholomews held seance in evening Lelia was quite sick.

---

77. This is the final entry in vol. 23, which continues with entries from 1861. The material for Feb. 4–Aug. 31, 1872, is in a smaller notebook cataloged as vol. 35, with correspondingly shorter entries.

78. This was a hotel that was opened in American Fork by Benjamin F. Whittemore, who anticipated the rail line being built from Salt Lake City to Provo. "Benjamin F. Whittemore," *Salt Lake Tribune*, Oct. 10, 1897.

79. Lelia married Noah Bartholomew's son Edwin in Dec. 1871 while Lyman was traveling in Idaho.

February 12, 1872; Monday. Made some calls and visited my mill, held seance at night at br [Noah] Bartholimews.

February 13, 1872; Tuesday. Made some calls and dined with br [Noah] Bartholimew's. At night lectured at State House Hall had a very attentive audience.

February 14, 1872; Wednesday. Remained mostly at home Edwin Bartholimew came home today.

February 15, 1872; Thursday. Reached Beaver by stage lodged with Edward Thompson.

February 16, 1872; Friday. Called on and dined with br R[obert] Kershaw and family called on the family of br W[illiam] J Cox and in the evening met and conversed with Major Galiger[80] while waiting for the stage to go to Parrowan.

February 17, 1872; Saturday. Arived about daylight found my family well. Called on Mr Daniel Page and family and dined with them in the afternoon meet with Mrs. [Jane] Hanks.[81]

February 18, 1872; Sunday. Passed the day mostly with Mrs. [Jane] Hanks and the Pages. Called on the Bensons.

February 19, 1872; Monday. Some snow fell during the night but disappeared soon this morning. Received calls from some of my friends in the evening. Called on Mrs Anna Warren.

February 20, 1872; Tuesday. Passed some time in writeing called on and dined with br [Daniel] Page at night called on Mrs [Jane] Hanks.

February 21, 1872; Wednesday. Visited and dined with Brother [Daniel] Page and family.

February 22, 1872; Thursday. Wrote letter to Lorenzo, the wind very high to day. At night attended a private seance at the residence of Mrs Jane Hanks. Some snow falling tonight.

February 23, 1872; Friday. Wrote letter to my wife [Maria] in Salt Lake City and past the residue of the time in reading. The weather

80. Maj. John P. Gallagher was a partner with General Patrick E. Connor, of Fort Douglas, in the North Star mines near Beaver and Milford. Gallagher was wounded at the Bear River Massacre but survived.

81. Jane Cooper Hanks was a cook for the Mormon Battalion. She and her husband, Ebenezer, later mined gold in California. In Parowan she founded the Mother Eve Mining Company and became involved in séances. Ebenezer was less interested in the supernatural and began paying more attention to his other wives. Bate, "Jane Hanks."

pleasant and warm. D[aniel] Page junior returned from Little Pinto and brought the [word] that Father [Robert] Richey was not comeing at present so I have to find some other way of going south.

February 24, 1872; Saturday. Passed the day in reading weather pleasant.

February 25, 1872; Sunday. Visited and Dined with D[aniel] P. Clark and family and called on P. Fouts and past the evening at home.

February 26, 1872; Monday. Started on my journey to Iron City with Brother Richard Benson and wife. Traviled to Cedar and lodged with Br George Woods and family.

February 27, 1872; Tuesday. Traviled to little Pinto to the residence of Father Robert Richey where we received a most hearty welcome found the Richeys all well.

February 28, 1872; Wednesday. Snow was falling did not go out to day held seance in the afternoon with pleasant results. Snow ceased falling in the afternoon.

February 29, 1872; Thursday. This morning Ms Warren and brother [Daniel] Page and children started for Cedar and myself and wife and br [Richard] Benson and wife visited the Ironworks. Stoped with Sister [Jane] Hanks. Brother [Ebenezer] Hanks was absent on buisness to Pioche.

March 1, 1872; Friday. Visited Mrs Blair dined with her and family and in the evening returned to Brother [Robert] Richey's with whom and family we past the night and held a very pleasant seance.

March 2, 1872; Saturday. Parted with our friends the Richeys and traviled to Cedar and put up with our friend Geo Woods and family also called ~~ours~~ our friend Homar Duncan whose father was very low and feeble.

March 3, 1872; Sunday. Started for Parowan and on our way we called of Mrs [Mary] Fish at Warrens Ranch[82] with whom we dined after which we came home finding the children well except Solon who was some what afflicted with ear ache.[83]

March 4, 1872; Monday. Remained at home through the day and passed the time in reading. [Son] Charles went to hunt stock.

---

82. William S. Warren was the onetime mayor, postmaster, and bishop of Parowan and a business partner with Ebenezer Hanks. Mary and Joseph Fish were Irish emigrants. Joseph had one plural wife, and over the next decade he would acquire two more, one of whom was six years old in 1872.

83. Solon Ezra was the eight-year-old son of Amasa and Paulina Phelps.

March 5, 1872; Tuesday. Remained at home through the day and at night held private seance with Mrs [Jane] Hanks and some friends.

March 6, 1872; Wednesday. Passed the day at home in reading. Called on br [Daniel] Page in afternoon. In evening received call [visit] from br Benson who read the Tribune to me.

March 7, 1872; Thursday. Passed forenoon at br [Daniel] Page's and then visited and dined with Mrs Jane Hanks. In the evening br's Burton and Benson called and spent the hours with us in social chat. Light snow to night. To day a number of the citizens asked Prest [William H.] Dame for the meeting house for me to lecture in but he refused them stateing that any other could have it.

March 8, 1872; Friday. Passed the day at home in reading and at night had seance at the house of Mrs [Jane] Hanks the Browns were present.

March 9, 1872; Saturday. Passed the day at home.

March 10, 1872; Sunday. Visited and dined with br [Daniel] Page and his family. At evening lectured at Webbs Hall. Had seance after meeting at home. Received five dollers of W[illiam] S. Warren.

March 11, 1872; Monday. Made several calls in town with Mrs Lyman. The wind was very high to day makeing it very unpleasant being out. In evening held seance with Mrs [Jane] Hanks and friends.

March 12, 1872; Tuesday. Passed the day in reading heard from Oscar. In evening held private seance br Sidney Burton was with us and Mrs [Jane] Hanks.

March 13, 1872; Wednesday. Visited and dined with Heber Benson and family. In the evening held seance at Mrs [Jane] Hanks.

March 14, 1872; Thursday. Visited and past the day with Richard Benson family and friends. At night received calls from friends at home.

March 15, 1872; Friday. Traviled to Beaver lodged with E[zra] Thomp^s^on held seance at the residence of R[obert] Kershaw br [John] Coombs was there.

March 16, 1872; Saturday. Made some calls in town and at night held seance with the Franklins. Weather cold meet with Philo [Carter] to day. Brother E[zra] Thompson returned from Parrowan.

March 17, 1872; Sunday. Passed the day and dined with br [Stephen] Franklin and family. In the afternoon had meeting at Thompsons Hall and then went home with my daughter Mrs [Matilda] Carter.

March 18, 1872; Monday. Traviled to Minersville and lodged with my brother in law F[rederick] Turley and family.

March 19, 1872; Tuesday. Made some calls on my friends and at night attended seance at the residence of br [John] Bradshaw. To day sent an apointment to North Star [mines].

March 20, 1872; Wednesday. Traviled to North Star mineing camp and put up with Mr Adam Lightner. Here meet with some old friends engaged in mineing.

March 21, 1872; Thursday. Passed the day in the camp and preached at night at residence of Mr [Adam] Lightner.

March 22, 1872; Friday. Returned to Minersville and started for Pioche traviling in the night.

March 23, 1872; Saturday. Reached Panaka[84] about 4 oclock. Stoped with Mrs [Melissa] Lee and had diner at Mr John [Nelson] Lees.[85] Meet with Dionitia lodged at the House of Mr L[ee].

March 24, 1872; Sunday. Visited Bullion City and some of its mills. Called on and dined with C[harles] W. Wandol and family. Meet with Mr Riley Morse and family. Mr M visited the mills with me, took super with Mr [Robert] Kershaw after which I returned to Mr J[ohn] Lees.

March 25, 1872; Monday. Passed the day at Mr [John] Lees and in the evening went to Pioche. Lodged at the Grand Hotell did not find my Boys there.

March 26, 1872; Tuesday. Returned to Bullion visited Panacka and called on Mrs Hultz. Lodged with brother Rily Morse and family. Some friends called to see me.

March 27, 1872; Wednesday. Visited the mills in company with brother Smith and in the afternoon called on Mr [John Nelson] Lees family in Panacka. Lodged with br Smith. Brother [Riley] Morse and family started for Parrowan to day meet with A[bsalom] P. Dowdle.

March 28, 1872; Thursday. Passed the day with my friends in Bullionville. Dined at Mr [Robert] Kershaw's[,] lodged at brother K. Smiths. Meet with Mr Catlin and family formerly from Fillmore.

---

84. Panaca is south of Pioche. Dionetia was in Nevada visiting her niece Melissa.

85. John Nelson Lee had just married Melissa Rollins, daughter of James Henry Rollins, and was working in Bullionville, a mile north of Panaca, in the silver-purifying industry.

March 29, 1872; Friday. This day made my arangements to start homeward tomorow. Passed the day mostly in Panaka, lodged at J[ohn] [Nelson] Lees.

March 30, 1872; Saturday. To day I am fifty nine years old in good health. And traviled to the Sulpher-spring, and put up with the Warrens much exausted and sick.

March 31, 1872; Sunday. Suffering from my cold.

April 1, 1872; Monday. Henry started to the Rancho for the teem and wagon. My cold no better received letter from Lorenzo in Parowan. Charley Dalton was a passenger on the stage for Panaka.

April 2, 1872; Tuesday. Remained at the station. Had fine rain to day made the station very damp.

April 3, 1872; Wednesday. Wind very high to day my health not good.

April 4, 1872; Thursday. My health somewhat better to day. This morning saw C[harles] Dalton on his return to Beaver.

April 5, 1872; Friday. My health somewhat improved some. Snow fell to day concluded to start homeward tomorow on stage. R[ichard] R. Hopkins was on the ^stage.^

April 6, 1872; Saturday. Traviled to Minersville lodged with br [Frederick] Turley. Snow fell this evening.

April 7, 1872; Sunday. Passed the day with friends at night held seance at John Bradshaw's.

April 8, 1872; Monday. Remained in town called on and dined with the Barnses from whom I received some samples of ore to be tested for their value at Salt Lake City.

April 9, 1872; Tuesday. Came to Beaver with the Twitchels. As I came into town they were burying brother W[illiam] Willis who died from the effects of the gravel.[86] At night held seance with br [John] Coombs at the residence of brother R[obert] Kershaw.

April 10, 1872; Wednesday. Made some calls on my friends the Coxes and Franklins. Snow fell to day makeing the travil tedious.

April 11, 1872; Thursday. Called on and dined with Br [Stephen] Franklin and family as yet no chance has offered for going to Parowan.

April 12, 1872; Friday. Wrote letter home called on Mrs [Mary Ann] Kershaw, held seance at night at [Ezra] Thompsons.

86. Kidney or bladder stones.

April 13, 1872; Saturday. Called on and dined [with] Mrs White. Storm this evening high wind and snow.

April 14, 1872; Sunday. Traviled to Parowan found all well.

April 15, 1872; Monday. Made some calls on my friends in the evening received a call from Brs [Richard] Benson and [Sidney] Burton. Weather pleasant.

April 16, 1872; Tuesday. Called on and dined with Mrs [Jane] Hanks. Br [Richard] Benson was with us tonight.

April 17, 1872; Wednesday. ~~Thursday~~ Visited D[aniel] P. Clark and family. The boys returned from the cann[y]on, brs [Richard] Benson & [William S.] Waren were with us also Mrs [Jane] Hanks. ~~Boys returned today.~~

April 18, 1872; Thursday. Remained at home and past the time in reading.

April 19, 1872; Friday. Visited Riley Morse and friends and at night held seance with Mrs [Jane] Hanks and friends with pleasant results.

April 20, 1872; Saturday. Passed the day in reading did not go out held seance in evening at Mrs [Jane] Hanks. Conditions rather poor with results corisponding.

April 21, 1872; Sunday. Passed the day mostly at home. In the afternoon called on Mrs Page and in the evening held seance with Mrs [Jane] Hanks, with Mrs L. as medium, with good results.

April 22, 1872; Monday. Passed the day at home in reading. Br [Richard] Benson called in the evening.

April 23, 1872; Tuesday. Wrote letter to Mr Hazen Aldrich [in] Cal[ifornia] and visited Mr [Richard] Benson's shingle mill and made some calls in town.

April 24, 1872; Wednesday. Wrote letter to my wife in the Salt Lake City. Passed most of the day in reading. Br [Ebenezer] Hanks came home this evening. Lorenzo started to meet Oscar with some horses to help him home.

April 25, 1872; Thursday. Called on Brother [Ebenezer] Hanks passed most of the day at home. This evening Oscar came home all well.

April 26, 1872; Friday. Meet with Brother R[obert] Richey in ~~made~~ the afternoon. Made call on the Richeys at Mr [Daniel] Pages. Received calls from some friends at home in the evening.

April 27, 1872; Saturday. Dined with brother [Ebenezer] Hanks past most of the day at home.

April 28, 1872; Sunday. In the morning started for Beaver arived about one oclock. Made some calls and at 12 oclock started for Minersville on my way home.

April 29, 1872; Monday. Breakfasted [with James Henry] Rollins from thence went to the Martin station where we waited some time for the coaches, dined at Shepherds.

April 30, 1872; Tuesday. Arived home ^in Fillmore^ and found all well. Paid Marion 50 doollars for Thomas Bryant. Dined with the Bartholimews.

May 1, 1872; Wednesday. Visited and took super with Brother [John] Kelley. Made other calls during the day.

May 2, 1872; Thursday. Visited the mill and made some calls and in the afternoon went to the [mill] race. In the evening Mr Benjamin Robinson came to see me and promised to buy my interest in the mill.

May 3, 1872; Friday. Today concluded the sale and transfer of my intrest in the mill to Benjamin H. Robinson and F. M. Lyman for the sum of $2000 in cash. Dined with Marion and friends. Br Fredrick Turley staid with us tonight.

May 4, 1872; Saturday. Started home on the stage dined at Scipio suppered at Nephi. Reached Payson in the night put up at [George] Garners.

May 5, 1872; Sunday. Left Payson in the morning arived at home in the evening found my family well in their new home in the 12th Ward in the House of Abraham Taylor.

May 6, 1872; Monday. Read some letters from the east and north and made some calls in town. Weather warm and pleasant.

May 7, 1872; Tuesday. Made some calls in town and at night attended a meeting of the Executive Counsil at Mrs [Ann] Godbe's place where I meet with Mrs H[annah] F. Brown[87] and Miss [Abbie W.] Baker from Chicago.

May 8, 1872; Wednesday. Made some calls on some of my friends dined with Mrs Brooks. In the evening attended a parlor entertainment given at Mrs [Ann] Godbe's residence by Mrs H[annah] F. M. Brown

87. That Hannah Brown, president of the American Association of Spiritualists, and so many other spiritualists, such as James Martin Peebles (see below) would pass through Salt Lake City and stay for weeks points to the vitality of the Utah movement.

and Mrs [Paulina] Stephens from Sacrimento. We were much interested by the ladies mentioned, by naritive and inspirational teachings.

May 9, 1872; Thursday. Made some calls in the town and received of [David] Williams $57 dollers. Some rain to day flooding some of the street ways. At night attended lecture at the Institute by Lolier.

May 10, 1872; Friday. Called on Mr [William H.] Holms wh[o] was sick at the residence of Mr [Thomas C.] Armstrong. Visited the Tribune Office passed the residue of the time in reading.

May 11, 1872; Saturday. Called on Mr J[ohn] Whiting, passed the day in reading. Had private seance at night. Received a call from Mr T. A. Line.

May 12, 1872; Sunday. Attended seance in the Institute. Mrs [Paulina] Stephens and Mrs [Hannah] Brown were present as mediums. At 3 oclock heard lecture from Miss [Abbie W.] Baker on the subject of education as applied to children. She warmly recommended the Childrens Progressive Lyceum as instituted by A[ndrew] J. Davis[88] as the best system known at present a light reflected from the Summer Lands [heaven] through the mediumship of Mr D. In the evening were addressed by Mrs H[annah] F. M. Brown relating her experience at [a farm in] Moravia [New York].

May 13, 1872; Monday. Went to Draperville with the County School excursion had a very unpleasant day.

May 14, 1872; Tuesday. Called on and dined with Mr Treseder and there meet with Mrs John Kelley from Fillmore. Received letter from Mr E. S. Barnes with specimens for assay from the new district called the Riseing Sun of which Mr B. is the recorder.[89]

May 15, 1872; Wednesday. Called on the assayer and left som specimens with him for Assay. Called on Mrs [Paulina] Stephens the medium at the [William] Sherman house after which in company with Mrs. Lyman called on Mr [John] Kelley at Mr. Treseders. In this evening it rained very freely.

May 16, 1872; Thursday. Made some calls and an interview with Judge

88. Andrew Jackson Davis was the psychic who coined the term "harmonial philosophy" in reference to a unifying power in the universe that "unites atoms and planets" and "endows the Divine Mind with eternal power and loveliness." Davis, *Great Harmonia*, 42.

89. This was part of the Tintic Mining District southwest of Utah Lake.

[William] Haydon. Called at the Tribune Office and ordered the Weekly sent for a half year to Cousin Sophronia in Woonsocket Rhode Island. At night attended the seance given at the Institute by Mrs [Paulina] Stevens.

May 17, 1872; Friday. Received and answered a letter from Hazen Aldrich. Called on the assayer and learned the result of his assay of the rock I left with him. In the evening received a call from Mr T. A. Line.

May 18, 1872; Saturday. Wrote letter to Mr Barnes on mineing matters. Past residue of the day in reading made brief call on Mrs [Paulina] Stephens the medium.

May 19, 1872; Sunday. Past the morning in reading in afternoon attended the Lyceum and then had seance with Mrs [Paulina] Stephens at the [William] Sherman House. Attended lecture in the evening at Institute.

May 20, 1872; Monday. Made some calls in the city and passed the day mostly in reading. In the evening took tea with M E[lias] L. T. Harison where I meet Mr Crandal and Mr McKay[,] the former from the west the latter from the east. Weather warm and pleasant.

May 21, 1872; Tuesday. Made call on Mr Gideon Gibbs and family by them heard from my old friend David Frederick who lives in the town of Bountiful. In the evening indications of rain, It fell freely during the night. Wrote letter to Priscilla and sent her the Deed to her home in Fillmore. Passed the residue of time in reading.

May 22, 1872; Wednesday. ~~Thursday~~ Called at the residence of Mrs [Sarah Ann] Cook where I meet Mrs Anderson from Leith near Edinburgh Scotland. Dined with her and her son Wm. At night attended the Executive Council at the residence of Mrs Mary Godbe.

May 23, 1872; Thursday. ~~Friday~~ Called on Mr Wm J. Patch general agent for the California Mutual Life Insurance Co, who made some proposition for me to take an Agency for the company, and gave me some books to read.[90] At night attended Mrs [Paulina] Stephen's seance at the Institute.

May 24, 1872; Friday. Called on Mr. [William] Patch and received some instruction in regard to insurance, called on some parties in relation to the same matter. In evening received call from T. A. Line and Lady. In afternoon called on <u>Mr</u> E[lias] L. T. Harison.

---

90. Lyman's career as an insurance salesman was short-lived. He nevertheless liked the idea of earning a steady income independent of farming and milling.

May 25, 1872; Saturday. Made some calls the early morning and while at diner Mr. Levi brought to our place [sixteen-year-old] Alvin Turley who was sick here. His mother met him. In the afternoon I meet with Mrs [Paulina] Stephens had some pleasant and interesting manifestations from my Spirit friends.

May 26, 1872; Sunday. Went to the Institute and listened to an interesting discourse by Rev. [Norman] McLeod.[91] At 2 oclock attended seance held by Mrs [Paulina] Stephens. Dined with Mr [Elias] Harison and family. Mrs [Harriet] Halifax was with us. At 7 oclock attended council at the residence of Mrs Mary Godbe and at 8 oclock was in Institute where Mrs Stephens lectured in the transe state on subjects furnished by the audience At 3 oclock attended the Lyceum at Institute [Building].

May 27, 1872; Monday. Made some calls in the morning. In the afternoon called on Mr W[illiam] S. Godbe in relation to Buisness and then called on Mr. [William] Patch in relation to the agency for the Co. for [California Mutual] Life Assurence.

May 28, 1872; Tuesday. Made several calls on parties in regard to the matter of Assurance [insurance,] received some encouragement. Meet Mr H[enry] W. Lawrence.[92]

May 29, 1872; Wednesday. Made some calls for medicine for [teenager] Alvin [Turley]. Returned and remained with him until he died which occured at half-past 3 oclock P.M. As I was going to the Telegraph Office to let Mr Franklin of Beaver know of Alvin's death I received from Marion a telegram imforming me of the death at 3 oclock of the wife of my son A[masa] M. Junior. Her name was Olive Felshaw. I wrote a letter to Omner Turley in Star district to let him know the condition of his brother. At night attended the meeting of the Executive Committee at Mr [William S.] Godbe's. Mrs [Margaret] Hunt and Mrs Loyd were appointed collecters of dues for the Movement. Alvin H. Turley was 16 years and 6 months old at the time he passed away.[93]

91. Congregationalist minister Norman McLeod was sent to Utah by the American Home Missionary Society to convert Mormons. He liked to preach against polygamy. General Connor employed him to be the Ft. Douglas chaplain.

92. Lawrence had just been released from jail after a sweep of polygamists that Judge McKean had initiated. Lawrence was no longer a practicing Mormon but was still a practicing polygamist.

93. This long entry shows signs of being written later and with some care. It was a bad day for Lyman. First he heard that a young man he had known in San Bernardino

May 30, 1872; Thursday. Engaged in making provisions for burying Alvin [Turley]. Wrote notice of his death for the paper. I[n] after noon attended to the Buriel ~~of~~ ^for^ Alvin. At night attended the seance held by Mrs [Paulina] Stephens at Institute. Some indications of rain.

May 31, 1872; Friday. Called on and settled with the Sexton for the Burial of Mrs [Ruth] Turleys son. Made a brief call on Mrs [Paulina] Stephens had an interesting conversation on the principles of the harmonial philosophy.[94]

June 1, 1872; Saturday. Called on Mr [David] Williams who had been kept from his buisness for some days by the sickness of his child. Wrote letters one to the Editor of the Religio–Philosophical journal[95] and one to my wife Priscilla in Fillmore. In the evening called on and suped with Mr Wm Pitts and family. He thought he would insure [invest] in our company.

June 2, 1872; Sunday. Attended meeting at the [roller] Skateing Rink[96] and heard an interesting discourse from Mr [Norman] McLeod. Dined with Mrs [Mary] Kelley. Attended the seance at the Institute and after[ward] the Lyceum and then past some time with Mrs [Paulina] Stephens. To day meet Mr Borin from Sanbernidino an Elder and missionary of the Reorganized Church. At night I spoke in the Institute Subject[:] The God Idea and its influence on the human mind. Omner Turley arived this evening.

June 3, 1872; Monday. This morning settled my rent made some calls in town received and answered letters from my family in the South. Called at the residence of <u>Mr</u> [William] Patch but he was absent from home visiting the country.

(b. 1855) had died, and then he learned that his daughter-in-law expired after a difficult child birth. Her baby would die less than two weeks later.

94. The following telegram was inserted after this page: "Olive died at three today. Boy born on the Twelfth 12 he is alive and well. F M Lyman."

95. Founded in 1865 in Chicago by Stephen S. Jones, the *Religio-Philosophical Journal* survived Jones's murder in 1877 by a man who said he "shot him according to phrenological reasoning in the offending part," meaning the head. Jones's son-in-law turned the journal into a vehicle for debunking fake clairvoyants, and a third editor tilted toward psychology. The journal closed in 1905.

96. Roller skating had become a national fad, even in Salt Lake City, where a rink opened in 1871 on Second South. The building was rented on Sundays by Presbyterians and others for worship services and lectures.

June 4, 1872; Tuesday. Made some calls in the city. Bought some sumer coats. In the afternoon called on Mr [Norman] McLeod had a very pleasant and interesting interview. At night attended the meeting of the Executive Com^mittee at [William S.] Godbe's.^

June 5, 1872; Wednesday. Made some calls in the city. Called on Mr [William] Patch and received from him a commission as an Agent Special for the California Mutual Life Insurance Company. At night had a very pleasant seance at home with Mrs [Paulina] Stephens.

June 6, 1872; Thursday. Received of [David] Williams $16.00. In the afternoon called on Mr E[lias] L. T. Harison. In the evening took tea with Mr T. D. Brown and family. Meet Uncle ~~Sye~~ Sidney Tanner on the street.

June 7, 1872; Friday. Made some calls in the city. Called to see Mr [William] Shearman but did not meet him. Meet with Judge Brown.

June 8, 1872; Saturday. Made out an application for Life policy for H[yrum] S. Coombs. Received of W. D[avid] Williams forty dollers.

June 9, 1872; Sunday. In the morning went to hear [Norman] McLeod and after Dined with Mr [James] Brooks and family and then was in attendence at Lyceum and at Lecture in evening.

June 10, 1872; Monday. Received and answered from Priscilla. Called on the Manings. In the afternoon received a letter from my cousin Mrs Triphenia Morrill of Providence Rhode Island. Past residue of time in reading.

June 11, 1872; Tuesday. Made some calls in the city. Received 4 numbers of the Religio Philosophical Journal and 2 Ly[c]eum Baner.[97]

June 12, 1872; Wednesday. Made some inquiry in regard to the purchase of some land on which to build a home [in Salt Lake City]. Called on and dined with Mr. H[enry] W. Lawrence. In the evening went with Mrs Lyman to see some property that we thought of buying. Light shower this evening.

June 13, 1872; Thursday. Wrote letter to my cousin Tryphena Morrill. Done some copying received the Journal made some calls in town.

June 14, 1872; Friday. Called on Mr Nicholes and other parties on the matter of assurence [insurance]. In the after noon Philo and Lelia

97. The *Lyceum Banner* was a children's publication with spiritualist content. Its offices were in Chicago.

arived from the south. In the evening went with Mr [Elias] Harison to see some land on the hill which was for sale but was not pleased with it.

June 15, 1872; Saturday. Received answers adverse to geting the money with which to b[u]y me a place on which to make me a home. To day they recovered the body of young Broughton and intered ~~it last~~ in the night on acount of the condition of the body.[98]

June 16, 1872; Sunday. Attended meeting at the Rink at 11 oclock and then attended at the same place Gov [George L.] Woods[99] Bible Class and then attended the Lyceum at the Institute and in the evening attended the lecture at Institute by Dr [Orville H.] Conger.

June 17, 1872; Monday. Called on Mr [William] Patch. In the afternoon Philo and Mar[i]a Louisa[,] her son[,] and Lelia started the first to Beaver [and] the last to Fillmore. In evening called on Mr W[illiam] S. Godbe where we meet Mr J[ohn] Lindsey.

June 18, 1872; Tuesday. Made some calls in town [and] meet my old friend J[acob] Croft of Fillmore and Lorenzo Burton from Parowan. Wrote letter to L. B. Lyman Helena Montana in answer to his of Jan. 30th 1872.

June 19, 1872; Wednesday. Made some calls in town past the day mostly in reading. Meet on the street Mr John Jaques[100] just home from England where he had been on a mission for a time. Meet with Mr E[dward] W. Tull[i]dge who had been sick. Called on Dr J[ohn] P. Taggart[101] at his office. Br Robert Kershaw from Beaver arived to day with his sister Ms Woo^d^house. Meet my old time friend Andrew Moffat of Manti.

June 20, 1872; Thursday. Called on Mr [William] Patch in regard to

---

98. The twenty-one-year-old Arthur Broughton drowned in the Jordan River. "Local and Other Matters," *Deseret News*, June 19, 1872.

99. Territorial governor George Lemuel Woods, a devout Christian and inspirational speaker, was described by one eastern reporter as nevertheless having "little mental heft." If so, he had experience serving as governor of Oregon and was on Idaho Territory's supreme court before being appointed to Utah. He came to the position familiar with Brigham Young and the issues at play in Utah Territory.

100. Jaques was an English convert and hymn-writer ("Oh Say, What Is Truth?"). While serving a mission in England, he helped edit the *Millennial Star*, and in Utah he was hired by the *Deseret News* and the Church Historian's Office.

101. Taggart had been the Assistant Surgeon of the Union Army during the Civil War. He was afterward appointed US Tax Assessor in Salt Lake City, 1870–74.

insurance. Past some time in reading. In the evening with Mrs Lyman called on the Harisons and Shearmans and also Mrs W[illiam] G. Mills.[102]

June 21, 1872; Friday. Made some e^x^amination of land in town and in the afternoon called on Mrs Hickland. Had seance at night at which young [Arthur] Brouton manifested himself.

June 22, 1872; Saturday. Made some calls in town received and answered a letter from Mr John Kelly of Fillmore. Past residue of the time in reading. Weather very warm and sultry.

June 23, 1872; Sunday. This morning at the office Mr S[amuel] W. Richards Magistrate. My daughter Love Josephine was married to Mr Hyrum S. Coombs. We then attended service at the Rink heard from Mr [Norman] McLeod after which attended the Lyceum at the Institute in the evening [and] at the same place listened to a most eloquent discourse by Mr McLeod on the subject of the truth-ennobled Wooman. Weather hot and sultry.

June 24, 1872; Monday. Made some calls in the city. Mee[t] and conversed with br Andrew Cahoon who after 18 years of service in the position was recently drped from his office of Bishop. Any word of explanation or reason assigned for the sumary treatment [was not given]. In the afternoon had a gentle shower and in the evening with Mrs Lyman called on Mr and Mrs Stine and then attended the lecture of the Rev. Mr. Onion [Charles Onions] on the history and character of Napoleon the 3rd. The lecture was interesting and instructive.

June 25, 1872; Tuesday. Made some calls in town passed some time in reading and in the afternoon called on Mrs Compton whom we found very sick. At 8 oclock this evening a man was shot and killed at the Post Office.[103]

June 26, 1872; Wednesday. Commenced writing to my Sister in V.T. but before I got through I was called to go to Ogden to attend the funeral of Mrs Elizabeth Duncan. We held the services in the Tabernacle by the

102. Louisa Sleater Mills and her husband were English converts. He wrote hymns ("We'll Sing the Songs of Zion") and they served a mission together in England, where he was excommunicated. They returned to the U.S. and lived in Nevada and California but had recently decided to return to Utah.

103. Charles Dawson was shot by Oliver Obey after Dawson circulated a handbill saying Obey had tried to break into his safe in Virginia City and asserting that Obey's wife was a prostitute. "Murder in Salt Lake City," *Daily Alta California*, June 26, 1872.

kind permission of [stake] Prest [Franklin D.] Richards. Lodged with Mr [John] Joist.

June 27, 1872; Thursday. Called on br [Thomas J.] Stayner in the morning an[d] then called on Mr [George] Brown and family and dined and lodged with Mr Stayner and family.

June 28, 1872; Friday. Called on Mr [George] Brown and family and passed the day mostly with them and lodged with them.

June 29, 1872; Saturday. Called on Mrs Ross and then Mrs Brown. Dined with her and then called on my old friend Dr [William] McIntire and lodged with Mr [John] Joist.

June 30, 1872; Sunday. Passed the day with the Joists it rained all the day. Lectured at Cordons Hall, and lodged at Mr [George] Browns.

July 1, 1872; Monday. Left my friends the Browns and returned to my home found all well. Meet with Mr [Noah] Bartholimew who was buying goods for the free trade uneion in Fillmore. Received letters from my wife Dionitia in Beaver and one from Mr Edwin Bingham of Minersville in regard to my sheep.

July 2, 1872; Tuesday. Wrote letter to Dionitia. Made some calls in town at night attended the meeting of the Council at the residence of Mr [William S.] Godbe's. Paid $18 dollers rent. Mr [Abraham] Taylor reduced rent 2 dollers per month.

July 3, 1872; Wednesday. Made some calls in town. Received a call from Mr [William] Patch, finished and sent my letters to my sister Mrs [Ruth] Goodall. To day met with William Mathews and James Pace old friends also John Higby. With some of them the tide of friendship seemed chilled and restrained in its flow.

July 4, 1872; Thursday. At halfpast 10 oclock met at the Institute where we had music by the new National Band[104] and several Speaches and Recitations and Songs all in peace and quietude and sobriety. In the evening with the family went to the residence of Mr E[lias] L. T. Harison and held a seance had some communications. David Smith Son of Joseph ^arived to day.^

July 5, 1872; Friday. Received of [David] Williams $5.00 called on

104. The band was local. It took on a national identification because it was the Fourth of July.

Mr [William] Patch who was in feeble health. Meet with Mr George Woods from Cedar City.

July 6, 1872; Saturday. Received and answered a letter from Paulina in Parowan. Secured Assay of rock sent me by Barnes it turned out $3.39 per ton silver. Went to hear Mrs A. J. Duniway lecture in Institute.

July 7, 1872; Sunday. In the morning heard Mr [Norman] McLeod at Independence Hall at 2 oclock meet with and heard discourse from Mr. David H. Smith. In evening attended the lecture at Institute.

July 8, 1872; Monday. Made some calls in town wrote letters to Barnes of Minersville and Jones of Chicago. Called on Mrs [Margaret] Hunt and family. At night attended the lecture of D[avid] H. Smith at ^the^ Institute which was filled with an attentive auditory, many of whom appreciated the truths that were expressed.

July 9, 1872; Tuesday. Meet with Mr [William] Marsden from Parowan who brought good news from that place. In the evening with Mrs Lyman and Hila called on Mr T. A. Line and family.

July 10, 1872; Wednesday. Made some calls in the city paid four dollers and fifty cents for Daily Tribune. In afternoon called on brother D[avid] H. Smith at the residence of Mr George Bostwick. In evening attended meeting at the Institute which was well filled and were addressed by Judge [Alley D.] Boren from [San Bernardino,] Cal[ifornia].

July 11, 1872; Thursday. Received a coppy of the new work [by James Thacher Hodge] entitled First Century of National Existence. In the evening called on Mr Ashman and family and Mr Loyd and family in the 10th ward. Weather very warm.

July 12, 1872; Friday. Attended court held in the Institute by Judge McKean in case of the Illinois Co and the proprietors of the Emy [Emma] Mine.[105]

July 13, 1872; Saturday. Heard the Emma Mineing case at the Institute. The Mormons held political meeting at City Hall. I saw by the ticket as published that Mr. G[eorge] Q. Cannon was the candidate for Congressional honours as delegate from Utah. At night held seance at home.

July 14, 1872; Sunday. Attended service at Mr [Norman] McLeod's

105. The Emma Silver Mine in Little Cottonwood Canyon was established by US Senator William Stewart of Nevada and others. It made most of its income by fraudulently selling shares in England after the ore had been depleted.

Hall. In afternoon attended Lyceum of the Institute. Called on Mr William Godbe and family took supper with them then attended lecture by D[avid] H. Smith in the Institute house. Crowded.

July 15, 1872; Monday. Made some calls in town [and] past some time in reading. In the afternoon Visited and took supper with Mrs White and family.

July 16, 1872; Tuesday. Made call in town and left my watch to be cleaned at Danes place of buisness. Passed residue of time in reading.

July 17, 1872; Wednesday. Passed the morning in reading after which I made some calls in town. To day fires occured in this City and in Ogden extent of Loss not known.

July 18, 1872; Thursday. Made some calls in town. Received papers and a letter from Chicago and also a letter from Paulina. In the evening attended the lecture of Judge [Alley] Boren at the Institute on the Relative claims of the Josephites and Brighamites to the Presidency of the Church of Latterday Saints, under the law and rule of a Priesthood that is only mythical in its existence. Hence in the lecture itself I had no deep intrest beyond the hope that it might agitate thought and thus conduce to more freedom from error.

July 19, 1872; Friday. Mad[e] buisness call in the city. Past residue of the day in reading and at night held private seance at home with good results. Some spirit touches were felt[,] some spirits were seen[,] and a small hand with some flowers [was visible]. Mediums were Misses Maria Coombs and [illegible] Lyman and Mrs L[ove] J. Coombs.

July 20, 1872; Saturday. Made transfer of some property in Parowan to [estranged wife] Paulina E. Phelps. Wrote letter to her and posted with Transfer inclosed. Received letter from Mrs Jane Hanks in parowan in regard to mining matters in Iron County from which point she was sending some Ore for sale in the disposition of which she wished me to act as agent for their Co. Received letter from Lorenzo stating that himself and Henry were well.

July 21, 1872; Sunday. Attended service at Independence Hall and in the afternoon attended at the Institute. D[avid] H. Smith lectured. At night held private seance at home with pleasant results. The weather very warm.

July 22, 1872; Monday. Called on Mr T. F. Fuller at mineing Beaureau and asertained from him that the Ore that had been sent up from the Mother Eve was not valuable to them haveing nothing but copper and they had so instructed the party who had the specimens that were assayed. At night attended at the institute where we were addressed by the Hon John A. Logan, Senator from Illinois and a General in the Last war for the Salvation of our nation. He spoke of [Horace] Greely and of [Ulysses S.] Grant.[106]

July 23, 1872; Tuesday. I made call in the Town then wrote letters to Mrs [Jane] Hanks and to my son Lorenzo. Past the residue of time in reading. In evening meet with Wm Burrows who had brought a ton of Ore from the Mother Eve Mine in Iron County. I made an appointment to meet him at 12 oclock tomorow.

July 24, 1872; Wednesday. Received some Ore from the Mother Eve Co by William Burrows and stored the same with the Keeper of the Cal Corrall[107] for a few days. Meet with William Hickman on the street at night heard report that William Kimball was brought into town dead.[108] At night held a private seance at home.

July 25, 1872; Thursday. Took some Ore to the Assayers for trial of its qualities after which I called on Mrs Lavina Johnson whom we found in very poor health. Passed residue of time in reading. Received letter from Oscar M. Lyman from [illegible] Meadow Mill[,] Iron County. He reported all well.

July 26, 1872; Friday. ~~Musical Department Sarah Ann Cooke Wm D. Williams assistant.~~ Received from Mr [John] McVic[k]er report of Assay rock proveing worthless. Weather very warm.

July 27, 1872; Saturday. Made one call up town. Passed residue of day in reading[,] weather very warm. At night went to the Institute the meeting was ajourned until Tuesday night next.

106. John A. Logan was the Union general who defeated the Confederate Army of Tennessee and after whom Logan Circle in Washington D.C. is named. As commander of the GAR veterans' group, he successfully proposed a national memorial day, and now he was campaigning for President Grant's re-election against the New York journalist and US Congressman Horace Greeley.

107. The California Corral was a livery at the corner of West Temple and 200 South. Liveries were stables for city dwellers to have their horses taken care of for a monthly fee or to rent horses when needed.

108. Hickman apparently thought William H. Kimball, someone Hickman had pointed the finger at for the murder of Richard Yeates, had been killed. But Kimball, proprietor of the hotel at Kimball Junction, would live thirty-five years longer.

July 28, 1872; Sunday. Attended meeting at the Methodist house heard Dr Burns from London then called on and dined with Mr. F[rederick] T. Peris and family. Attended Institute in evening heard Mrs F[anny] T. Young from Boston. Transe speaker had full house. Weather very warm.

July 29, 1872; Monday. Wrote letters to Paulina and Oscar in Parowan. Called on Mr E[lias] L. T. Harison in the evening called on Mr John Low and family. Spent most of the day in reading.

July 30, 1872; Tuesday. Passed the day in reading did not go out until night then went to the Institute to the ratification meeting.[109] Colonel [John H.] Wickizer was called to the chair. Gould to be clerk. The meeting was addressed by Colonel Joslyn and Mr [Robert N.] Baskin. Lack of time prevented other speakers.

July 31, 1872; Wednesday. To day Mr [William] Burrows called on me and said he would remove the Ore we had stored and pay the storage. Passed the day in reading Spiritual Pilgrim biography of Mr J[ames] M. Peebles.[110]

August 1, 1872; Thursday. Called on brother David Smith at br Brownings. Dined with these friends after which called on Mrs F[anny] T. Young at the Clift place[111] had a very pleasant conversation on the subject of the Spiritual Philosophy. Called on brother [Elias] Harison and also on the Shearmans and the Crosbies, Received letter from Mr. Hazen Aldrich in California.

August 2, 1872; Friday. Answered [Hazen] Aldrich's letter. made some calls in town. D[avid] H. Smith and [Alley] Boren & J[oseph] Silver went north to day.

August 3, 1872; Saturday. Made some calls in town. Wrote letter to Orson Johnson in Trivoli Peoria County Illinois and in the evening attended a seance at Mr [Elias] Harisons. Mr Peter West and Mrs F[anny]

---

109. The territory had recently ratified a proposed state constitution after the US Congress rejected it. During the debate, the Liberal Party had sent Henry Lawrence to Washington D.C. to argue against adoption, saying it would enhance Brigham Young's political power. The party was planning its next move. Walker, *Wayward Saints*, 348.

110. James Martin Peebles was a leader in the National Spiritualist Association. He had been a Universalist minister, educator, and diplomat. He died in 1922, a month short of 100 years of age.

111. The Clift House was a three-story tenement hotel at 300 South Main Street.

T. Young were present as mediums[,] had the slate writing[112] phenomenon and other fine tests.

August 4, 1872; Sunday. Attended service at the Methodist chappel and then at 2 oclock attended seance at Mr [Frederick] Knowles and at night attended at the Institute and heard from Mr Parker Univeralist a discourse liberal in spirit and well delivered.

August 5, 1872; Monday. Attended the election and called on Mrs Lavina Johnson who had broken her arm the day before. Had an interview with Dr [Peter] West received from him some proofs of his Mediumistic powers.

August 6, 1872; Tuesday. Received of [David] Williams fifty-seven dollers. At night attended monthly meeting of the Executive Council at Mrs Godbes residence.

August 7, 1872; Wednesday. Sold 77 head of sheep to Cornelius Williams for $154.00 in curency. Received and answered letter from E. C. Dunn and in the evening attended a seance at residence of E[lias] L. T. Harison. Had the phenomena of the slate writing and the answering of unseen questions and some transe speaking. The Tests were very good, and satisfactory to the parties to whom given.

August 8, 1872; Thursday. Paid $5 for Weekly Tribune. Called on Mrs Lavina Johnson. She is geting along well with her broaken arm. Called on the Mathers at Home. ^Wrote letter to Priscilla.^

August 9, 1872; Friday. Made some calls in town received letter from Dr Poulson from Council Bluffs. At night called on and took supper br [William] Shearman. Weather somewhat cooler. ~~Wrote letter to Priscilla.~~

August 10, 1872; Saturday. Made some calls in town and call at Mr [Elias] Harisons where I meet with Mrs Emily Teasdale. Had s[eance] at home with good results. Weather cooler and pleasant. Learned by the papers that in the election Beaver County gave majority of votes for the Liberal cause.[113]

August 11, 1872; Sunday. I heard [Norman] McLeod at his hall and in the afternoon meet with Mr Ells a Josephite minister. In the evening

112. Writing would appear on a chalk board held under the table.

113. There was a state-wide election for a territorial Congressional delegate and for local municipal officers.

was at the Institute the audience was addressed by Dr. [Peter] West the discourse was good, some indications of rain.

August 12, 1872; Monday. Made calls in town and in the evening I received a call from Cousin G[eorge] A. Smith and Dr Coalman from the state of Pensylvania a kinsman of ours.

August 13, 1872; Tuesday. Made some calls in town. In the afternoon was presented with the first number of the Western Star[114] by Mr E[lias] L. T. Harison. Also borowed History of the Lyman family of G[eorge] A. Smith.[115]

August 14, 1872; Wednesday. Made some calls in town past an hour with Mrs Fany Young at her rooms. Past residue of Time in reading. Weather cooler today.

August 15, 1872; Thursday. Made some calls in town at night held seance at home.

August 16, 1872; Friday. Passed most of the day in reading. Received a letter from Cousin Orson Johnson in Illinois and also letters from Priscilla and Lorenzo.

August 17, 1872; Saturday. Received letter from Oscar M. with Gold check calling for $594.00 which I sold for $671.22. Bought Bill of Exchange for the amt of $502.30 and forwarded the same east as per his order for machine leaveing in my hands after paying for Exchange $65.92 of Oscars money. Wrote letter to Oscar, in the evening held seance at home. J[ames] M. Peebles in town to day.

August 18, 1872; Sunday. I[n] morning attended service at I[n]dipendence Hall with Mr [Norman] McLeod and at 2 oclock attended a meeting of Reorganized Saints at the residence of Father Abraham Taylor. In the evening heard Mr J[ames] M. Peebles in the Institute had a good house he was very eloquent and clear in his discourse. Weather very warm with some thunder and other indications of rain.

August 19, 1872; Monday. Was in bed most of the day on acount of ill health, at night went to the Institute to hear Mr [James M.] Peebles.

August 20, 1872; Tuesday. Called on Mr. [James M.] Peebles at

114. The *Western Star* emerged in Boston in July 1872 and lasted six months.

115. Genealogy of the Richard Lyman Family, Jan. 1870, 3 handwritten pages, in George A. Smith Papers.

residence of Mr Thomas Fitch[116] and went with him to the Depot. Before parting with him he gave me a fine photograph of himself. Wishing him the kind protection of good angels[,] we parted. I then called on Mrs Lavina Johnson who is recovering finely from the breaking of her arm. Then called on the Brookses who start in a day or two for the Teritory of Washington to make for themselves a new home in that new land peace go with them. ^Received letter from Mrs [Paulina] Stephens Sacrimento.^

August 21, 1872; Wednesday. Made some calls in town. In the evening called on Mr [Peter] West at his rooms. At night attended at the Institute to hear Dr Brenan, the Hall was well filled, and the lecture was interesting and instructive.

August 22, 1872; Thursday. Made a call on Dr [Peter] West and in the evening with other friends called on the Dr and he organized out of the persons present 3 developeing [séance] circles, one of which was composed of myself and Mr and Mrs Keats and Mrs Coombs and Mrs Jones, to hold their seances at my residence. Weather very warm and sultry.

August 23, 1872; Friday. Received letter from Mr John Clemison in Cal[ifornia]. Wrote letter to Mrs [Paulina] W. Stephens of Sacrimento. Called on Dr. [Peter] West and in ^the evening^ attended private seance with the Dr and a few friends [at] Mrs Mary Godbe's residence had some fine tests in Slate writing. Mr [Thomas J.] Stayner and wife [Rebecca] were present.

August 24, 1872; Saturday. Made some calls in town. At night had seance at home.

August 25, 1872; Sunday. Attended seance held at the residence of br William Hunt. Dr [Peter] West was present. Dined with the Hunts after which we attended the lecture at the Institute[,] lecture by Dr West. Some pleasant showers to day with thunder and lightning. My health not good to day.

August 26, 1872; Monday. Did not go out to day on acount of my health. At night held seance with pleasant results. Br [Elias] and sister [Rebecca] Harison called this evening.

116. Thomas Fitch was a Virginia City attorney who defended Brigham Young and others, 1871–72, and later defended Wyatt Earp and Doc Holliday.

August 27, 1872; Tuesday. Did not go out to day my health poor.[117]

August 28, 1872; Wednesday. My health improveing Called on br [Elias] Harison received some calls to day.

August 29, 1872; Thursday. Made some calls visited Dr [Peter] West and in the evening attended seance at Hunts.

August 30, 1872; Friday. Passed the day in reading. Some rain to day. Received letter from Maria reporting herself and friends well.

August 31, 1872; Saturday. Called on Mr [Peter] West and also on Mr [Elias] Harison. In the evening held a seance at home some rain falling at night.[118]

September 1, 1872; Sunday. In morning attended Church at [Norman] McCleod's. Called on E[lias] L. T. Harison also on R[ichard] R. Hopkins and took super with Harison. At night attended at the Institute, speaker Mr W[illiam] H. Holms. Some rain this evening weather cooler.

September 2, 1872; Monday. Made some calls in town my health not good had siting [séance] at home at night.

September 3, 1872; Tuesday. Was ill all day did with some dificulty call on br [Elias] Harison at his residence. Some little rain to day rendering the weather cooler.

September 4, 1872; Wednesday. Made some calls in town did not feel well, my feet considerably swollen.

September 5, 1872; Thursday. Kept my room all day and in the evening called on Mr. [William] Hunt. Some rain fell during the night. Weather is much cooler.

September 6, 1872; Friday. Wrote letter to Orson Johnson Altona Knox County Ill[inois]. Received of [David] Williams fifty seven dollars. Called on Mr Stien and aranged with him to take my daughter in his school. Held sitting with good results was some unwell in the night.

September 7, 1872; Saturday. Walked out in the city to day my health improving at night held seance at home. Br. [Elias] Harison and [Richard R.] Hopkins were with us and Mrs. [Ruth] Turley. Received letter from L. B. Cushman vocalist in Port Huron Mich[igan].

117. Above this entry is a note that we "must hate our friends, Luke," and "must love [our enemies], 1st John."

118. This is the last entry in vol. 35. The Sep. 1–22 entries are on the last pages of vol. 25.

September 8, 1872; Sunday. Attended at Indipendence Hall then called on and passed the day with Brother [William] Shearman and family. At night was in the Institute. Dr [Orville H.] Conger was speaker.

September 9, 1872; Monday. Called on Mr [Norman] McCleod and had an interesting interview with him in regard to the intrests and freedom of the Peoples of Utah.

September 10, 1872; Tuesday. Wrote letters to California and Michigan and in the evening attended the meeting of the executive council at Mrs Godbes. Dr [Orville H.] Conger and Lady [Louisa] were present.

September 11, 1872; Wednesday. Wrote letter to my old friend John Clemison in Cal. Called on Mrs Lavina Johnson who is stil suffering with her Broken arm and then called on Mrs Robson in 19 Ward and her friends.

September 12, 1872; Thursday. Called on Mr [William] Shearman waited for Mr [William S.] Godbe at his office but did not see him in. Called on Mrs [Mary] Kelly and Mr Treseder's.

September 13, 1872; Friday. Received letter from Paulina news good, all well buisness lively. At night had siting at home with good results.

September 14, 1872; Saturday. Wrote letter to Paulina made some enquiries for place to rent. In the evening had seance at home with our family with good results.

September 15, 1872; Sunday. In morning heard [Norman] McCleod and at night spoke at the Institute. Mrs. John Kelley was with us today and went to the Institute.

September 16, 1872; Monday. Wrote letter to Orson Johnson [in] Altona Knox County Ill[inoi]s. Visited and dined with Mrs Lavina Johnson. Had an interview with Mr McCleod at Mr [William] Shermans.

September 17, 1872; Tuesday. Called on Mr [Elias] Harison at his place on the Kimball bench.[119] Called on Mrs Rosina Godbe. Called on Mr William Godbe and dined with him. At night attended a meeting at Indipendence Hall held in the intrests of freedom of the peoples.

September 18, 1872; Wednesday. Made an early call on ~~Mrs~~ [William] Shearman where I had a brief interview with Mr [Norman] McCleod. At night had a siting at home.

119. Usually called "Heber's Bench" after Heber C. Kimball, one of the early residents of the area, the area is now called Capitol Hill.

September 19, 1872; Thursday. Wrote letters to Priscilla and Marie in Fillmore in the evening called on Mr [William] Shearman.

September 20, 1872; Friday. Made some calls in town purchased an Organ of Mr [John] Da[y]ne[120] to be delivered on tomorow. Attended committe meeting at Mr Shearmans had a Qorum present.

September 21, 1872; Saturday. Received my Organ from Mr Dane had an interview with Mr ~~G~~ [William S.] Godbe at evening had [séance] sitting at home with very pleasant results.

September 22, 1872; Sunday. In morning heard [Norman] McCleod then called on the Manings and dined with them and spent residue of the day. Went to the Institute at night heard Mr. W[illiam] S. Godbe, and Dr. [Orville H.] Conger.

September 23, 1872; Monday.[121] Bought gold pen of Dwier for four dollers and 50/100. Called on Mr [Norman] McCleod. And in the evening with Mrs Lyman called on Mrs Mary Godbe. Some rain falling which changed to snow before morning.

September 24, 1872; Tuesday. Started on my tour north traviled to Ogden and put up with br [George] Brown weather cool.

September 25, 1872; Wednesday. Made some calls in town. Dined with Mr [Thomas J.] Stayner then put out some posters for lectures on Friday & Sunday. Lodged with Dr [William] McIntire and family.

September 26, 1872; Thursday. Called on Mrs Ross who had a sick child after which dined with Mr George Brown and went with him to the Depot. At night had a conversation with some friends on the subject of the Liberating Leag[u]e of Utah.[122] Lodged with br Brown. Weather growing warmer the friends present all promised to labor for the League.

120. John Daynes arrived in Salt Lake City from England in 1862 to open a clock-repair and music store and saw his son Joseph become, at age sixteen, the first organist for the Tabernacle Choir. Lyman was probably buying a small organ like the one he had previously procured for the Liberal Institute.

121. The remaining 1872 entries come from the last sixty pages of vol. 15, following the entries for 1856.

122. According to Orson F. Whitney, the league formed because the city council seemed prepared to ban a *Tribune* reporter from its chambers, at which the liberals said they would have 100 armed men on hand to defend the reporter's presence at the next meeting. Although that did not happen, Lyman organized people into a vigilance committee, ready at a moment's notice if non-Mormons were harassed. Whitney, *History of Utah*, 724–25.

September 27, 1872; Friday. Called on and passed the day mostly with the Browns. At night lectured at Cordon's Hall. Received three dollars in currency. Lodged with Br Brown.

September 28, 1872; Saturday. Called on and dined with Mr [Thomas J.] Stayner after which called on Dr [William] McIntire then bought some tracts [on] spiritual [topics] of the news dealers McGregor and Joist.

September 29, 1872; Sunday. Passed morning with the Browns then called on Mr [John] Broom and family and also Dr [William] McIntire and spoke in Cordon's Hall in the evening received six dollars at the close of lecture.

September 30, 1872; Monday. Started for Logan at 7 oclock. Mr Campbell franked my ride to the Switch [at] Brigham [City] [and] from thence went by stage to Logan where we arived about 2 oclock and called on Mrs C[harles] C. Goodwin and then meet with brother Aaron Dewitt.

October 1, 1872; Tuesday. Commenced writing for home. In course of the day meet with the widow Benson at Dr. Wiseman's. In the evening had a pleasant conversationall meeting with a few friends at residence of br C[harles] C. Goodwin.

October 2, 1872; Wednesday. Wrote letters to my wife and to Brother [William] ^Shearman^ walked onto the hill by the park had a fine view of the town. Had another conversational meeting at Mrs [Alice] Goodwins. Meet my old and valued friend Josiah Hendricks.

October 3, 1872; Thursday. Called on Dr Wiseman passed the morning with him and wife and dined with them after which I called on Mr Bertelsen and family. Some friends called to see me in the evening.

October 4, 1872; Friday. Went to Hyde Park with my friend Wiseman called on and dined ^with^ Mr [Anthony] Me^d^caff after which we returned to Logan with the promise that we should see Br M[etcalfe] on folowing Sunday.

October 5, 1872; Saturday. Called on br ^Bertelsen^ and family then called on and dined with Dr Wiseman. In the evening took tea with Mrs [Alice] Goodwin and at night attended seance at Dr Wiseman's with but indiferent results.

October 6, 1872; Sunday. Went with br [Anthony] Medcaff to Providence where I by their permission addressed the audience apparently to their satisfaction. I read to them the circular in relation to the League which was well received by the majority. It was warmly endorsed by Br Medcalf. At night attended a seance at the residence of br Davis with happy results.

October 7, 1872; Monday. Called on and passed most of the day with Dr Wiseman and sold him some books. In the afternoon received a letter and circulars from Br W[illiam] H. Shearman of Salt Lake City.

October 8, 1872; Tuesday. Wrote letter to Br [William] Shearman dined with brother Bertelsen and family then called on br C[harles] C. Goodwin who had just returned from Salt Lake City.

October 9, 1872; Wednesday. Passed most of the day with br [Charles C.] Goodwin and in the evening held seance with him and other friends at his residence.

October 10, 1872; Thursday. Dined with Dr W[iseman] and passed the afternoon with br [Charles C.] Goodwin and attended seance at Mr. Davis residence with pleasant results. Spent some time in reading called on Bertelsen.

October 11, 1872; Friday. Passed the day mostly in reading dined with Wiseman spent afternoon with the Goodwins took supper there.

October 12, 1872; Saturday. Meet with br David H. Smith had some talk with him on the subject of the Liberating League he gave his sympathies to the work. At night held seance with him at the residence of C[harles] C. Goodwin, he lodged with me at br [Aaron] Dewitts.

October 13, 1872; Sunday. Dined with the Dr [Wiseman] and at 2 oclock heard D[avid] H. Smith speak at Mr. Bertelsen's. At night I spoke at the residence of C[harles] C. Goodwin's had an attentive and an appreciative audience.

October 14, 1872; Monday. Went with Br D[avid] H. Smith to Franklin [Idaho] by the kindness of br [Anthony] Medcalf from Hyde Park. We lodged with Mr John Johnson at night had a conversational meeting with the friends who called to see us. They seemed much interested.

October 15, 1872; Tuesday. In the morning went with br [David Hyrum] Smith to the residence of Mr Howworth whose child was blest by br S[mith]. Br H. gave us five dollers and we then started [back] for Hyd[e] Park. At Richmond we stoped and dined with Mr Robinson. Lodged with Br [Anthony] Metcalf in Hyde park.

October 16, 1872; Wednesday. Returned to Logan found the friends well and the town wearing somewhat of a Sabbath appearance in consequence of the Militia drill or muster that was going on. At night had meeting at Mr [Charles C.] Goodwins for the friends of the League of which we organized one [of] ten. Lodged with Mrs. Larsen.

October 17, 1872; Thursday. Dined with the Wisemans. Called Mrs Dewitt. Mr. [Aaron] D[ewitt] was not at home. In the evening had conversational party with br David [Hyrum Smith] and his friends at br [Charles C.] Goodwins. Lodged at Larsens.

October 18, 1872; Friday. Went to Providence and attended the meeting of the Reorganized Church. The audience was addressed by br D[avid] H. Smith. I spoke to them in the interest of the L[iberating] League and lodged with brother Chaplow and family.

October 19, 1872; Saturday. Left my friends in Logan and started with brothers [Anthony] Medcalf and Bake and traviled to Box Elder and put up with Br Ashael Thorne and wife. Our reception was most warm and cordial.

October 20, 1872; Sunday. Attended the Orthodox [LDS] meeting in the morning and at night brother David H. Smith held meeting at br [Asahel] Thorne's. Had an attentive audience. Folowing br S[mith] I addressed the meeting. Bishop [Reverend] Nichols was there and several Mormons.

October 21, 1872; Monday. Came home by the morning train found my family well and Father [Noah] Bartholimew and children were with us from Fillmore. Received letter from Cousin Sophronia in Woonsocket R.I. Took supper with Br Coombs and family. Mrs Lyman reported to me the receipt of $120.00 from the Walkers and other friends.

October 22, 1872; Tuesday. Made some calls in town. The Bartholimews started homeward this morning. At night attended the Cerimonial services held by Mr [Norman] McCleod at Indipendence Hall in commemoration of the tragic Death of Dr Robinson.[123]

October 23, 1872; Wednesday. Had interview with Mr [Norman] McCleod and at night attended council at the Indipendence Hall on business connected with the Liberating League of Utah. The meeting was composed of the Executive Committie.

123. See note 68.

October 24, 1872; Thursday. Called at Mr [Norman] McCleod office [but] he was not there. At night attended the social at Independence Hall, rain freely this evening for which reason the company was small. Meet Mr Brown of Parowan. He reported all well in that place. He came for goods for Page.

October 25, 1872; Friday. Called on Mr. [Norman] McCleod and afterwards dined with Mr [William H.] Holmes and family. At night had Mr C[harles] C. Goodwin with us who entertained us with musick after which we had a pleasant seance.

October 26, 1872; Saturday. Called on Mrs [Mary] Kelly and Mrs [Margaret] Hunt who was very ill. At night held seance at home. Mrss Kelly and [Ruth] Turley were present.

October 27, 1872; Sunday. In morning heard Mr [Norman] McCleod then called on and dined with Mr E[lias] L. T. Harison and family. No meeting at Institute on account of storm.

October 28, 1872; Monday. Made some calls in town meet Mr W[illiam] H. Shearman. The snowy indications of winter remain with us with slight increase.

October 29, 1872; Tuesday. Called on br D[avid] H. Smith in afternoon called on Mr. [Norman] McCleod.

October 30, 1872; Wednesday. Called on Mr [William] Shearmon and with him called on Mr [Norman] McCleod and Mr [William H.] Holms on buisness connected with the League. Past balance of the day in reading.

October 31, 1872; Thursday. Made some calls in town and past the day in reading. At night visited Dr [Orville H.] Conger and family. Past a pleasant evening. Indications of returning mild weather.

November 1, 1872; Friday. Made some calls in town passed the day in reading at night[,] had seance and the company of D[avid] H. Smith. Had a very pleasant time.

November 2, 1872; Saturday. Made some calls in town and past the day in reading had seance at night and forgot my meeting at Indipendence Hall.

November 3, 1872; Sunday. In morning heard Mr. [Norman] McCleod in evening spoke at Institute. In the afternoon heard David H. Smith at the Institute.

November 4, 1872; Monday. Made some calls on buisness and then called on Mrs Lavina Johnson and in the evening received a visit from Spratt and Mr. [James] Brookes enquiring after the truths of the Harmonial philosophy. Received letter from Mr. Joseph Smith [III] from Plano, Ill[inoi]s.[124]

November 5, 1872; Tuesday. Meet with Mr. [William] Marsden from Parowan, at night attended lecture of Mr. [Charles E.] Jones[125] at the Liberal Institute.

November 6, 1872; Wednesday. Meet with Mr [Charles E.] Jones had some conversation with him and at night attended his lecture on Pulpits and Preachers. Received of [David] Williams fifty seven dollers, on dues.

November 7, 1872; Thursday. Made some calls and then wrote letter to Joseph Smith [III]. Dined with Mr. Tavy and family at night attended the social gathering at the Indipendence Hall.

November 8, 1872; Friday. Called on Mr T. H. Brown and Mr. [William H.] Holms and in the evening attended the lecture of Mr. [Norman] McCleod in the Institute. Snow fell to night.

November 9, 1872; Saturday. Made some calls and past the day in reading. At night went to an appointment at Ind. Hall.

November 10, 1872; Sunday. Morning went to Indipendence Hall, dined with Mr Coombs and family and at night attended Mr [Charles E.] Jones lecture at the institute. In the afternoon attended monthly meeting of committee at Mrs Godbes.

November 11, 1872; Monday. Made some calls and passed most of the day in reading at night attended Lecture at the Institute.

November 12, 1872; Tuesday. Made some calls in town at night attended a meeting of congratulation on the Reelection of Prest. [Ulysses S.] Grant the meeting was large and enthusiastic but orderly. Judge [William] Haydon presiding.

November 13, 1872; Wednesday. Made some calls in the city and at night attended lecture at the Institute by [Norman] McCleod it was Masonick.

November 14, 1872; Thursday. Had an interview with D[avid] H.

124. "Friend of my father," the letter begins. He had heard from his brother David that Lyman wanted to correspond. He replied that Lyman should feel free to write. See Joseph Smith of Reorganized Church to Mr. Amasa Lyman, Oct. 30, 1872, Lyman Collection.

125. Charles Jones was an Australian who toured with his wife and delivered lectures on humorous themes. "About Fools," *Salt Lake Herald*, Nov. 6, 1872.

Smith. Received of Mr [Norman] McCleod fifty dollers on behalf of the League. Past the evening with Mr [Elias] Harison and family. Mr ^C. E.^ and Mrs Jones were with us.

November 15, 1872; Friday. Made some calls on buisness. At night my son Lorenzo came to us from Parowan. Reported all well there.

November 16, 1872; Saturday. Called on and dined [with] Mr Browning and family on occasion of his thirty ninth birthday. Mesers Ells and [David Hyrum] Smith were with us. In the evening attended the free Lecture of Mr [Charles E.] Jones in the Institute. Lorenzo was with us.

November 17, 1872; Sunday. Was at Indipendence Hall in morning in the afternoon was at the Institute. Took super with Mr Pierce and family. D[avid] H. Smith was there. At night heard Mr [Charles E.] Jones at Institute.

November 18, 1872; Monday. Started on my mission south traviled to Provo meet and conversed with some of my liberal friends. Put up at Bullocks Hotel.[126] Introduced the subject of the League to some of my friends who spoke favorably of the matter.

November 19, 1872; Tuesday. Called on Capt Leatham and also on Mrs Jane Tanner with whom I dined. Lodged at the Provo House.[127]

November 20, 1872; Wednesday. Made some calls on my old friends. Dined with Joseph Hyde and family at night had meeting with a few friends at the residence of Mr. Letham in the interests of the Liberating League of Utah. Organized circle No. 1 of Utah County.

November 21, 1872; Thursday. Called on and dined with Moses Mecham and family. At night lectured in the school house of 3rd Ward had an attentive audience.

November 22, 1872; Friday. Traviled to Springville and lodged with the family of br Bernard Snow. In the afternoon wrote some letters. Was most kindly entertained by Mrs [Anne] Snow and her interesting ^family^.[128]

---

126. This was Isaac Bullock's inn at 500 West Center Street. Said to be "the first hotel south of Salt Lake City," the two-story adobe structure had only two guest rooms, although it also had a comfortable sitting room and spacious dining area on the first floor. On the upper floor, each of the two bedrooms had four windows and a separate fireplace. Carter, *Our Pioneer Heritage*, 16:148–50.

127. This was an alternate name for the Bullock Hotel.

128. Actually, Bernard and his four wives and fourteen children were all crowded

November 23, 1872; Saturday. Made some calls on my friends and in the afternoon went to Payson and called on Mr [George] Garner and then Lodged with Bishop Joseph Tanner and family. Snow fell at night.

November 24, 1872; Sunday. Passed the day with the Garners and a conference with Mr M. C. Engberg who promised to interest himself in the League organization. Lodged with br Freeman Tanner and family. Weather very cold here. Meet with the wife and widow of my old friend Seymour Brunson.

November 25, 1872; Monday. Traviled to [Eureka in the] Tintick [Mining District] by stage put up with Dr [Adolphus] Noon, weather very cold but pleasan[t].

November 26, 1872; Tuesday. Had interview with Mr M. D. Harmon who said he would interest himself in and for the League. In evening went to Diamon[d].[129] Lodged with Mr Painter.

November 27, 1872; Wednesday. Passed the day in the camp. Dined with Mr. Brooks and family. At night held meeting at the residence of Mr John Brimhall and commenced the organization of the League at Painter's.

November 28, 1872; Thursday. Dined with Mr. Reese and friends and at night lectured at the residence of [John] Brimhall had good attendance. Lodged as before.

November 29, 1872; Friday. Went to Ureka, lodged at the Robins House. Traviled with Mr Leetham.

November 30, 1872; Saturday. Traviled to Payson and lodged with Garners.

December 1, 1872; Sunday. Passed the day with the Garners received some calls from my friends. Stage was so full that I could not pass on so I stayed at Freeman Tanners.

December 2, 1872; Monday. Passed the day with my friends calling on the Tanners. In the evening took stage to Nephi. Arived at half past 10 oclock. Lodged at Goldsbrough.

December 3, 1872; Tuesday. passed the day with the Schofields at night took the stage for Fillmore.

---

together in the same house, according to the 1870 census, so it would have been an "interesting family" situation.

129. Now a ghost town four miles south of Eureka, it was founded in 1870 when someone thought he had discovered diamonds. They proved to be quartz.

December 4, 1872; Wednesday. Arived at home at 10 oclock found all well. Received call from W[illiam] J. Cox.

December 5, 1872; Thursday. Dined with my Daughters Matilda[,] Maria and Lelia. Mr P[hilo] H. Carter was with us.

December 6, 1872; Friday. Received letter from D[avid] H. Smith. Made some calls on my friends. In the evening had Mr & Mrs Kelley[130] with us and Br N[athan] C. Tiney.

December 7, 1872; Saturday. Wrote letter to D[avid] H. Smith. Called on and dined with Mr. [John] Alves and family. Priscilla was with us.

December 8, 1872; Sunday. Passed the morning at home in afternoon meet some friends at the residence of Mr. John Alves and commenced the organization of the U[tah] L[iberating] L[eague] Circle No. 1. Mr. J Alves takeing the charge of Circle and Mr. J[ohn] Kelley for county. I spent evening with Mr K and family.

December 9, 1872; Monday. Dined with Marion and family. In the evening called at the Store.

December 10, 1872; Tuesday. Took the stage for Beaver arived in Minersville about 4 oclock. In morning stoped with br [James H.] Rollins where I found my wife Dionitia quite sick tho feeling some better than for some time past.

December 11, 1872; Wednesday. Dined with br [Frederick] Turley and family and in the evening called on br John Bradshaw and wife.

December 12, 1872; Thursday. Dined [with] Mr. [Philo] Carter and friends. At night held seance at the residence of Mr John Bradshaw, br [Frederick] Turley and wife were present.

December 13, 1872; Friday. Traviled and lodged with my son in law Mr Philo Carter and family. Traviled with Mr William Carter of Minersville. Mr C went to Beaver.

December 14, 1872; Saturday. Remained with my children throughout the day.[131]

December 15, 1872; Sunday. Came to Beaver and stoped with Mrs

130. Of John Kelley's two wives, Mary and Margaret, Mary would die in a year of breast cancer. She and John had lost three of her four children to diphtheria over the previous decade.

131. Lyman enjoys visiting his offspring, but he rarely mentions visiting the children he had with the Partridge sisters, and then only the older children such as Eliza's son Platte.

Thompson. In the evening called on the Kershaws then lodged with Mr C. Mathews and family.

December 16, 1872; Monday. Passed the day in town dined with Mrs Franklin and children. Lodged with Mathews had interview with Mr Hawley.

December 17, 1872; Tuesday. Traviled to Parowan found all well except Paulina. Br Samuel Thompson and Sister Sarah Phelps were there. Walked from Reed Creek.

December 18, 1872; Wednesday. Passed the day at home. At night had seance at Mrs [Jane] Hanks.

December 19, 1872; Thursday. Passed most of the day and dined with Mr [Daniel] Page and family.

December 20, 1872; Friday. Passed the day at home in reading. Prest [Brigham] Young and party were in town tonight enroute to St George. General T[homas] L. Kane was with him.

December 21, 1872; Saturday. Passed some time and dined with Mr. Richard Benson and family. At night held seance at the residence of Mrs [Jane] Hanks.

December 22, 1872; Sunday. Passed the day at home at night held seance at residence of Mrs [Jane] Hanks with gratifying results.

December 23, 1872; Monday. Called on Mr [Daniel] Page and in the evening called on Clarks[,] Marsdens and Fishes. Made some small purchases for Christmas.

December 24, 1872; Tuesday. Passed the day at home some indications of storm. Boys come home from the mill to spend Christmas at home.

December 25, 1872; Wednesday. Some light storm in the morning while the Christmas greetings went freely around. Called on Mrs Hakes who was here on a visit. Dined with Mrs [Jane] Hanks. Oscar and wife was with us. Exchanged gold pen with Oscar.

December 26, 1872; Thursday. Visited and passed the day with br Richard Benson and family in the evening received calls from some friends.

December 27, 1872; Friday. Wrote letters to my wife Louisa and Mr W[illiam] H. Holmes in Salt Lake City. Past evening with Mrs [Jane] Hanks. Dined with Mr [Daniel] Page. Light rain during the day. Oscar's mule died this morning.

December 28, 1872; Saturday. Rema^i^ned at home most of the day.

Wrote letter to my cousin Sophronia in Rhode Isleand. Called on the Clarkes. Weather cloudy with some rain during the day.

December 29, 1872; Sunday. Remained at home through the day. In the evening received calls from the Mrs Hakes and Clark. Br [Collins] Hakes came in from Pioche. Received call from br Christian Rasmussen.

December 30, 1872; Monday. Passed the day mostly at home Dined with Mrs [Jane] Hanks and in the evening had an interview with br Decker, a semi orthodox Mormon.

December 31, 1872; Tuesday. Passed most of the day at home. In the afternoon called on br [Daniel] Page and in evening called on Mrs [Jane] Hanks.

12 "False Religion," 1873–1874

As Lyman became more involved in spiritualism, he began to speak its language, even in his diary, and became critical of those who did not share his views. On the death of two grandchildren, he wrote that they had "passed away to Nature under the kindly and humane institutions of the bright land of Summer in the happy beyond." Mormons, he concluded, while accepting "the beauties of the Christian gospel, … yet are under the stronger influence of a blinding fanaticism, still clinging to the absurd dogmas and dead forms of an effete Theology." When his son, the future LDS apostle Francis M. Lyman, departed on a mission to Europe, Amasa wrote that he was headed "to the field of his labor, and folly." Remaining mostly at home but sometimes traveling to see family in Parowan and friends in Salt Lake City, he settled into a routine of building his new house and cultivating his apple orchard, while in the evenings he would read the east-coast magazines he came to love, filled with compelling short stories, radical political views, spiritualism, and feminism.

January 1, 1873; Wednesday. Stayed the day at home.[1] Mrs. [Jane] Hanks dined with us and Oscar and wife. Made an evening call on Mrs. Hanks, held a Seance. Some snow on the ground. Weather dark ~~and~~ and cloudy.

The comeing ^of^ this the first day of the new year greets us as a liveing assurence of the Deathless Love and Changeless truth of our Father

1. Lyman is visiting his wife Paulina and friends in Parowan, Utah.

God and Mother Nature, Through whose Infinite power we are and on whose munificent bounties we subsist, while Ages Eternal ^shall^ add their stores of Soul developement and hapiness; and ever increasing joy.

January 2, 1873; Thursday. Weather clear and pleasant. Dined and past a portion of the ^day^ with Mr. D[aniel] Page and family. Read news from the Weekly Tribune. At night received a call from Mr. Sidney Burton and wife. I called the attention of Mr. B. to the subject of the Liberating League of Utah, Into which he seemed to enter with the sympathies of his warm and genial Nature[,] ever awake to the intrests of Humanity whose exaltation is God's greatest Glory and the most noble object of religious sentiment and effort.

January 3, 1873; Friday. Remained at home during the day [and] passed the time re[a]ding. In the evening had the company of Mr. Richard Benson. Weather becomeing more settled, and pleasant for buisness. The men are away to their Lumber mills. G[eorge] Q. Cannon passed through, enroute for Dixie. The object of his journey, not anounced, but supposed to be in some way connected with the interests of his ideal Kingdom of God. May the Heavens speed the enlightenment of the people to the breaking of their chains of Ignorance.

January 4, 1873; Saturday. Made call on Mr. [Daniel] Page and past most of the day in reading a Work on the various forms of Insanity by A[ndrew] J. Davis[2] which in the light of a divinely true philosophy he shows have their origin in the violation of natures harmonious Laws & Knowledge of these laws and their true application to the regulation of all human action constituteing the great secret of a happy present and a future of Eternally increasing hapiness and joy. While the Soul travels on in the ceaseless unfolding of the divine qualities of its own Deific Nature.

January 5, 1873; Sunday. Passed the day at home. Brother W. Decker came in and with him had several hours ^of^ conversational, kind and social interchange of sentiment and thought. His is a case in which the Soul is strugling (through the aid of the foregleams of light that are faintly shineing through the rifts in the clouds of ignorence on to its goal of more enlarged freedom. His strongest enimy is the belief he cherishes in the Divinity of the Bible. The light of truth will melt away this cloud.

2. Davis, the author of *Mental Disorders*, was a clairvoyant and hypnotist.

Br [Sidney] Burton was with ^us^ in the evening. Had pleasant interchange of thought from his freed mind.

January 6, 1873; Monday. Passed the most of the day in reading and makeing a few calls. At night past an hour or two with br Daniel Allen and wife whom I found in the limited light of truth. They enjoy [and are] sensible of some of the beauties of the Christ[ian] gospel, and yet under the ^stronger^ influence ^with them^ of a blinding fanaticism stil clinging to the absurd dogmas and dead forms of an effete Theology. The march of truth is slow, but sure to reach its culminating point in the immancipations of Earth's Children from error the Ofspring of ignorence.

January 7, 1873; Tuesday. Passed the day at home in reading. Charles started for Pioche with Lumber this morning. The weather clear and warm. What constitutes the intrinsic value of all religious ideas? Their harmony with the truth, which is determined by its agreement with Natures Eternal Laws of cause and effects. Thus the enlightened reason and the Minds best and most extended comprehension of the principles thus learned to be true must ever be for progressive humanity the standerd of right by which truth in all matters will be determined forever.

January 8, 1873; Wednesday. Remained at home reading. Weather pleasant and warm. In the evening called on Mrs. [Jane] Hanks. Heard that Lorenzo was sick which might delay his return home.

What constitutes the virtue and goodness of all human ~~action~~ actions? Their intrinsic qualities which can only be truly known by their effects on their author and also their influence on all to whom they extend. Thus that alone is good in itself which brings good to its author and evil to none, thus is a standard of Righeousness furnished for the gu^i^dence of all in the nature of their own actions when ~~their~~ they are properly weighed before performence.

January 9, 1873; Thursday. Weather is fine and sumerlike. Called on Mr. [William] Marsden from whom I learned of Lorenzo's sickness and also of that of my Daughter Frances. Wrote letter to Priscilla giveing her advise in regard to the treatment of Frances for her sickness, after which I called on Mr. [Daniel] Page and past some time with him discussing some prospective Commercial enterprises.

What great idea Rules the world to day? As we notice the universal scramble for wealth we cannot fail to see that the commercial idea Rules for the present. One of the results will be a better and truer Education of the Masses.

January 10, 1873; Friday. Weather pleasant. Called in evening on Mrs. [Jane] Hanks. Mr. John Coombs and wife were with us and Mr. [Richard] Benson. Mr. Coombs was maried on New years day to Miss Ellen Pratt. We look for Lorenzo tomorow. Read Tribune today.

What constitutes the original foundation of hapiness in humanity? The constituent qualities of its nature in ~~I~~ a germinal state, in which they receive in the springtime of Life their earliest lessons of development under the influence of which they become decked in the floral beauty and buding promises of Summers fruitage to ripen into ^a^ golden harvest to enrich the Laboring Soul.

January 11, 1873; Saturday. Weather pleasant and warm. Passed the morning in reading. A little after noon Lorenzo and Henry came home from the north where they had been for freight for Mr. William Marsden Merchant. At night Oscar came down from the Mill and reported it haveing been doing well for the last few days; sawing some six thousand ft. per day. The Boys from the north report stormy weather and bad conditions of the roads makeing it hard times for the freighters consumeing the profites of their labors in increased expences.

January 12, 1873; Sunday. With Mrs. [Paulina] Lyman spent the day with Mr. Daniel Page and family. Mr. and Mrs. Richard [and Phoebe] Benson were with us. Mr. and Mrs. [William and Mary] Marsden were expected but they were called away to the Warren Ranch to bring home their daughter who was sick with Brain fever.[3] Our party all save Mrs. ~~pag~~ [Mary] Page visited the sick Girl in the evening at the residence of her Father. The pain in her head from the inflamation of the Brain was most excruciatein. She was relieved slightly by nursing.

January 13, 1873; Monday. This morning received and answered a letter from Mrs. W[illiam] H. Holmes of Salt Lake City. Weather clear and warm in the evening. Indications of storm. [Son] Charles returned not being able to get through to Pioche. He left his load in the Desert where some fifty others we[re] left for the same reasons. A hard leson in

3. This was probably scarlet fever, or perhaps Rocky Mountain spotted fever, which had overlapping symptoms. Twenty-two-year-old Cornelia Marsden showed signs of recovery, then died on Mar. 2, 1873.

winter freighting, one from which valuable commercial moral might be gleaned by those whose eyes are open to see that the winter is not the profitable season for that Branch of industry.

January 14, 1873; Tuesday. Called [rest of sentence illegible]. Called on Mrs. [Jane] Hanks. Past some time reading in the afternoon. Called on Mr. [Daniel] Page. Charles went after some fence posts to the Mills. Heard again from Cornelia [Marsden] that she continues to improve. We cherish hopes of her recovery. Lorenzo and Henry have concluded to return [to] Fillmore immediately.

January 15, 1873; Wednesday. In the morning prepared some posts for seting in the fence after which visited and spent the day with br [Riley] Morse and family and in the evening called on br D[aniel] P. Clarks family[,] some of whom were ill.

Oscar came home from the Mill. His wife was sick in the night. Lorenzo and Henry started for Fillmore with their teems and Wagons. The weather cool and pleasant. Miss [Cornelia] Marsden is said to be geting better continuosly. Some teems started for Pioche with lumber this morning.

January 16, 1873; Thursday. Commenced prepareing timber and siting fence. Called at br R[ichard] Benson. Madora was sick and Oscar was gone with br Benson to [William] Warren's Mill to purchase a new saw for his mill. In the evening called on the Benson's and also on Mrs. [Jane] Hanks. Commenced reading the works of Prof O[rson] S. Fowl[er] which is both interesting and richly instructive in its treatment of the glorious Science of Life and health [and] its promises and perversions in its treatment of Mankind.[4]

January 17, 1873; Friday. Received letters H[yrum] S. Coombs S. L. City and from Priscilla [in] Fillmore. Passed the Morning in reading after which called Mr. [Richard] Benson with whom I dined after which Oscar and his men started to the Mill to hang up their new saw in their Mill. After which I called on Mr. Horace Thornton and family. Mr. H. was at one time in my employ as miller in my Mill in Fillmore. Had a look at some new machinery in his mill for cleaning. Its action appeared to be good and efficient [for] scouring and thouroughly cleaning the wheat. This [is] a great consideration here.

4. Fowler's *Science of Life* was published in 1870. It had a phrenological slant.

January 18, 1873; Saturday. Wrote letters[,] one [to] Hila in Salt Lake City and one to Priscilla in Fillmore. Weather fine and pleasant. Received a call from Mr. Daniel Page. In the evening held seance with Mrs. [Jane] Hanks and Mrs. Lyman with rather pleasant results, all serving to impress us with ^the^ necessity of the proper conditions to insure good results in the way of communications. Some clouds hang around the horizon presenting a rather gloomy aspect tho all was bright beyond the present cloud[,] [a] fit emblem of Man's fitful and changing Life.

January 19, 1873; Sunday. Morning bright and pleasant. Missionaries Sheets[,] Muser[,] and Woodruff reported in town enrout south.[5] Past morning hours in reading historical ^and scientific^ works. In the afternoon called on Mr. George Grimshaw and family. Took super with them. Mr. Wilson and wife were with us.

On our return home we called on Mrs. Anna Warren and children. We heard that Miss [Cornelia] Marsden was dieing but after we came home Mr. [Richard] Benson called and said there ^were^ some favorable indications in her case.

January 20, 1873; Monday. Worked at setting my fence and at night found myself very much overdone and my Back very lame. Miss [Cornelia] Marsden stil lingers. Mr. Bryant was hunting for his Mules but did not find them. He fears they are stolen. Weather fine and almost springlike. It is so warm.

The teems are moveing Lumber[,] some for market some for Building. It seems that in the zeal of the people to get money for their Lumber and others for hawling it to market that none of it finds a lodgement in home improvements. Money rules.

January 21, 1873; Tuesday. Weather pleasant and sumerlike. Passed the morning hours in working on my fence. The Pioneer Mill car had an accident which stoped their work until they can make repairs.[6] Had a Methodist Minister here he preached in the meeting house through the gracious permision of the <u>holy</u> <u>Priesthood.</u> His ignorence of certain things secured his pass to the Sanctuary which is most scroup^u^lously

5. The traveling bishops, Elijah F. Sheets and Amos M. Musser, were probably accompanied by Wilford Woodruff Jr. or some other son of apostle Wilford Woodruff.

6. About 150 miles north of Fillmore in the Oquirrh Mountains, the Pioneer Mill was founded by the Godbeite Walker Brothers, whose activities would have interested Lyman despite the distance.

closed against ~~I~~ honest men who know the truth of Mormonism as to what it is that is good and what not good.

January 22, 1873; Wednesday. Weather warm and pleasant. Borrowed some lumber of br Richard Benson to make my gate frames and caried it to Mr. [Nathaniel P.] Worden's who agreed to frame them for me tomorow. After this I sawed to length; and pointed some pickets for the fence in which I was assisted by William. In the evening held a Seance at the residence of Mrs. [Jane] Hanks. Mr. Coombs[—]John and his Sister[—][and] Mrs. Taylor and her husband were with us. Results were satisfactory.

January 23, 1873; Thursday. Weather stil pleasant. In the forenoon worked on my fence and got another piece of timber of Mr. [Richard] Benson for my gate and caried it to Mr. [Nathaniel P.] Worden who promised to do the job to day. In the afternoon called on Mr. W. but he had not commenced the work for me, [but] renewed his promise for tomorow.

After my days work was done I called on Mrs. [Jane] Hanks. There was convened at her residence ~~an~~ a meeting of the members of the Mother Eve Company organized to work the Mother Eve Mine.

January 24, 1873; Friday. Passed the morning hours in workeing on my fence until near noon when br. [Nathan] Tiney came along on his way to his home in Dixie. Mrs. Tiney was so ill we had to lift her from the wagon and assist her to the house. A cousin of Mrs. Tineys was with them from the states. This man I saw in 1841 and when he arived in Salt Lake City [in 1848] and inquired for me and where I could be found he was told that he should look for me in the lowest drinking Dens as I had become a low down druncard.

January 25, 1873; Saturday. Cloudy with indications. Passed the Morning hours in work on my fence while William was buisy prepareing for his trip to Pioche. Wrote letter to Lorenzo in Fillmore.

Called at Thomas Yardly's to get some Blacksmithing but he had not returned from the canyon. Charles came down from the Mill and John Coombs also. They report the mill to be doing well.

Oscar did not come down. Madora is sick this evening. Held Seance at Mrs. [Jane] Hanks [and] had communication from J. Neely Johnson[7]

7. After serving as governor of California and then Nevada, J. Neely Johnson died in Salt Lake City in August 1872 from a "sunstroke." The symptoms, "delirium and

giveing an acount of his death and its causes, all of which the medium was ignorent. He mentioned his wife came to see him.

January 26, 1873; Sunday. This morning William got ready to start for Pioch[e] but because of delays did not start until afternoon. Wind was high when he started. Passed the afternoon and dined with Mrs. Almeria Barton. Mrs. [Jane] Hanks and Mrs. Burnham were with us when we came home. Some rain was falling. After the children retired I sat by the stand ~~when s~~ with Mrs. Lyman. She was controlled [by a spirit] and wrote some communications from Roswell our Son and Miss Page wife of Mr. Daniel Page.

January 27, 1873; Monday. Weather cloudy and cool. Called on the Blacksmith and got some hangings made for my gates[,] some of which I fited and hung during the day. Some light snow squalls which lasted but a short time leaveing the Horizon clear and free from storm-clouds.

In the evning had a call from Mr. Sidney Burton and wife and also Mr. W[illiam] S. Warren who was in town for a day or two. During the day called on Mr. [Daniel] Page. Mr. [Thomas] Yardly's child died this morning of croup.[8]

January 28, 1873; Tuesday. Passed the morning in working on my fence. Mrs. Lyman went to sew for Mrs. Henderson. Dined with Mrs. H. and Mrs. [Jane] Hanks. Overlooked a Sewing Machine and help[ed] repair it.

Continued my work on my fence until night. The mill froze up and the Men came down to town. At night held seance at the residence of Mrs. Hanks. Weather very cold. Much ice in the streets. Several teems started for Pioche with Lumber.

January 29, 1873; Wednesday. Weather clear and pleasant. In the forenoon worked on my gates and Dined with Bishop Warren and wife Anna. After this[,] continued my work until night. In evening received call from Heber Benson and my Son Oscar and Mr. Richard Benson.

Some parties had their trial to day before Justice Rogers for their riotous conduct on last Sunday. The parties were Brown and Worden. Mrs.

---

physical prostration, from which he never had hopes of recovery," indicated a cerebrovascular stroke rather than heat exhaustion. "Death of J. Neely Johnson," *Sacramento Daily Union*, Sept. 2, 1872.

8. A childhood infection of the windpipe.

Brown was fined some 16. dollers. [A] rather costly Sabbath devotion for Saints the Light of the World.

January 30, 1873; Thursday. Weather cool but pleasant. Buysied myself about my fence[,] completing the hangings and fitings of the large gatte. Passed the afternoon in reading. The ^wind^ was very high[,] blowing from the South some indication of storm. Mrs. [Jane] Hanks was with us today assisting Mrs. Lyman in her sewing; Received from the P. O. some papers that were over due by nearly two weeks. Oscar was with us some portion of to day. Passed the evening at home[,] the wind blowing almost a Tornado. Toward morning it subsided.

January 31, 1873; Friday. Morning opened right and clear and beautiful. Called at Mr. Richard Bensons. Mrs. B. spoke to me about a chance to go to Beaver next week with Mr. [Sidney] Burton. I promised and did secure [from] her a chance [for] us [to travel with them] through the kindness of Mr. Burton.

Called on and dined with Mr. [Daniel] Page and later in the day called on Mr. [William] Warren and discussed the prospects of trade in Parowan for some years to come until Pioche should have a Railroad communication with Salt Lake and the great commercial centers East and west. Until then it would be good[,] after that not so good. We spent the evening with the Burtons verily interesting.[9]

February 1, 1873; Saturday. Did not engage in work to day. In forenoon called on the Marsd[e]ns. Found the sick Daughter improving slowly. She is stil very weak and stil suffering much in Brain and spine.

Weather rather pleasant. High wind a portion of the time moveing the dust makeing it di[s]agreeable out of doors. Past the afternoon and evening at home reading Gleasons Monthly home companion.[10] This took up my time until I retired. During the night the wind was high.

February 2, 1873; Sunday. Light snow squalls this ^morning.^ Mrs. Lyman was called to some sick children in the family of Mr. Riley Morse[,] after which we called on and passed the day with Mr. Richard Benson and family. In the afternoon Mr. Thomas Bryan came down from the mill and brought the word that Mr. Edgar Clark had his ancle badly

9. A note down the side of the page reads: "Prepared floor in the morning."

10. *Gleason's Monthly Companion* contained short stories and articles accompanied by drawings.

crushed in the Mill. It will render him a cripple for some time to come. At night the Snow began to fall quietly and by the morning had falling a foot in depth and stil snowing.

February 3, 1873; Monday. [Philo] Dibble's [art] show was here exhibited in the Church.[11] Snow one foot deep and stil falling. Was in doors all day but few people astir in town on acount of the Storm. Past the day mostly in reading the Christian Union[,] the [weekly] [news]paper edited by H[enry] W[ard] Beecher. I found ^it^ very good[,] reflecting clearly the generous sentiments and cosmopolitan principles of its great-minded conductor.

Would that our poor and unenlightened World was blest with many more like him as torch bearers of the Sublime principles of the Nazerine that lift the soul of waiting and expectant Man above the plain of hatred and strife to that of Love & charity.

February 4, 1873; Tuesday. Weather suny and fair not much doeing in town. Mountain and Valley have doned their wintry Robes. Called on Mrs. Hanks and ~~an~~ borowed some reading mater of her with which I interested myself during the day and evening.

Workmen came down from the mill to arange some buisness in regard to the mill. In the evening George Bryan returned from Pioche. He reported the disease prevailing alarmingly among the Horses producing much derangements in ^the^ carrying buisness [with] Freight and Maills.

February 5, 1873; Wednesday. The morning opened in all the glory of a bright clear winter day, one ^or two^ solitary sleighs visible on the streets useing the snow of which there was sufficient to make Sleighing pleasant.

Past the day in reading. Did not go out at all. Mrs. [Jane] Hankes called during the day and gave me twenty dollars in gold to be paid to Mr. William C. Burows at or near Salt Lake City for the freighting of Ore from Iron County to that point for the Mother Eve Mineing Co. I gave receipt for the money. Mr. Richard Benson called and passed the evening with us.

February 6, 1873; Thursday. There was an increase in the number of

11. Philo Dibble was a pioneer impresario whose improbable art show in 1848 in the log tabernacle at Council Bluffs, Iowa, featured scenes from church history. Dibble commissioned Robert Campbell and other artists to paint the murals. In Utah, he was the first to imagine an art museum in Springville.

Sleighs on the Street improveing the opportunity afforded by the present fall of snow for pleasant recreation. Called to see Mr. [Sidney] Burton. He was not at home. Passed some hour in reading.

Called upon and dined with Mrs. [Jane] Hanks after which called on Mr. [Nathaniel P.] Worden for some promised work as on other occasions it was not completed. Obtained in its stead another promise. Mrs. Lyman passed the afternoon with Mrs. Hanks [and] suggested some thought to R[ichard] Benson and O[scar] M. Lyman in regard to a mercantile enterprise.

February 7, 1873; Friday. Weather pleasant. Called this morning to see Mr. Riley Morse and his sick children[,] two of whom were very sick[,] the other three haveing to some extent recovered. Returned home and hung up the small gate in my fence in doing which I cut my hand. In the evening in company with Mrs. Lyman I again called on Mr. Morse and his sick children. The babe was very bad [but] the other one thought to be a little beter. Returned home[,] read for a couple of hours[,] took a Bathe and went to bed. Weather clear and bright moonlight.

February 8, 1873; Saturday. Passed an early hour in reading then went to work on my gate and completed it and found myself very weary at night. Had an evening call from Mr. Richard Benson and Oscar My Son. Mr. [Riley] Morse to day reported his sick children improveing somewhat in their condition. Mrs. Burnham was reported in a dieing condition; and Miss Marsden stil lingers. Paid fifteen dollars to John Tiney for Mr. George Bryan for a strayed horse recovered for him in Toquer. Weather softning steadily. Had an hour of reading before retireing.

February 9, 1873; Sunday. Weather pleasant and warm. Passed the time in makeing preparation for my journey. Called on and held a Seance with Mrs. [Jane] Hanks. Mr. John Coombs Medium was present. Mr. George Bryan and wife started for Fillmore. Mr. Richard Benson an[d] Sidney Burton called after I had gone to bed. Mr. Benson came and brought me a letter from Lorenzo in Fillmore reporting sickness with the people there. He reported no fatal cases.

February 10, 1873; Monday. This morning said goodby to the children and friends in Parowan and with Mrs. Lyman started for Beaver with Mr. Sidney Burton and wife and children and Mrs. Richard Benson. At noon found ourselves at our friend Andersons where we took our

Lunch and then traviled on to Beaver where we arived about 7. oclock evening and stoped with our friend Edward Thompson where we were welcomed by his good lady. The traviling has been heavy to day[,] near one half of the way. Weather cool.

February 11, 1873; Tuesday. Called on Mr. Brown a Lawyer who had his Office in the house formerly ocupied by Father Turley. Called on and dined with Uncle Sidney Tanner and family. Called on br Franklin family, found Aunt Sarah much cripeled with Rheumatism. Returned to and Lodged at br Edward Thompson. Some snow falling. No opening for Lectureing. Freedom for this is reserved for the Bumers[12] who infest the Country and prey on people.

February 12, 1873; Wednesday. Snow was falling fast this morning. Called at Billiard Hall[13] after which called on Mr. [Charles] Woodhouse. Borowed his Tribune and read the bill indtroduced to the Senate by Mr. [John A.] Logan from Ill[inoi]s in relation to Utah affairs; providing for it and other Teritories.[14] After this called on and dined with Bishop M[arcus] L. Shepherd and family. While there my Son-in-law Philo Carter came up to town and after diner we went with him to his home. Found the family in good health and spirits. Some snow falling in the evening.

February 13, 1873; Thursday. The [day] was stormy and the snow several inches deep. Snow continued to fall until moon [noon]. After diner Philo went to Be[a]ver to carry Paulina my wife who will go to her home in Parowan with Mr. Sidney Burton and his wife and Mrs. Benson tomorow. The wind was moveing the snow somewhat in the afternoon[,] much to the anoyence of the group of grandchildren returning from school some half a Mile away. They were meet by their Father and brought home.

February 14, 1873; Friday. The weather is bright and clear. No rude breeze in ~~in~~ its wild frenzy is disturbing Earth's Robe of Fleecy white in the graceful folds of which the cherished form of our fond Mother, is so

---

12. The *Oxford English Dictionary* defines a *bummer* as "an idler, a loafer." The *Millennial Star,* Dec. 16, 1873, p. 791, uses the word similarly in reference to "a bummer or second-rate pettifogger."

13. Billiards was becoming popular in the 1870s but was different than today's game, often played with twenty-two balls of different colors. The balls ricocheted against round obstacles on the table, pinball-like, and stopped in depressions in side cushions. This particular establishment was owned by William Berry on a road called Montana Street.

14. Logan's bill proposed to grandfather existing practices in some areas, such as polygamy, but would prevent future marital arrangements of that type.

genererously enfolded. Thus her kindly providence preserves her treasured Germs of comeing Life. So we can in reason enligh[t]ened by experience see in the wintry storm the smile ^of^ Benificence and its dreary ^howl^ is changed to the voice of love and mercy as she treasures blessings for her children to enrich the comeing spring. Passed the day in reading.

February 15, 1873; Saturday. The weather was warm clean and pleasant. Some light cloud in the Horizon indicated a comeing change of the weather. As yet I have no news from Minersville or from [North] Star [Mining][,] only from the latter that the Snow is deep and a susp[e]nsion of work generaly in the distr[i]ct. This has lead me to give up the thought of my visit to [North] Star at present. Past the time to day in reading some historical matter and some Romantic.

February 16, 1873; Sunday. The morning opened clear and pleasant. Mr. and Mrs. [Philo and Matilda] Carter went to Beaver [and] procured some papers and letters from the P. O. but none for me. They returned shortly after Noon. Did not attend church. Passed the day in reading Historical works in magazine form, the subject our own Country and its wars, and the great Rebelion ^with^ our last National struggle for life and the perpetuity of our free Institutions the sacred Legacy from our Patriot Fathers. In the evening Snow falling.

February 17, 1873; Monday. Weather cool but little snow fell during last night. Have concluded to go to Minersville <u>tomorow</u> if the weather moderates sufficiently. Passed the day in reading Historical matter, was but little out during the day. Felt some Rheumatic pains ~~in lis a~~ in my limbs and body resulting from colds recently contracted. They may depart with the comeing of warmer weather. Ours will not be a painful parting.

February 18, 1873; Tuesday. The weather bright & warm. With Philo [Carter] and wife [Matilda] I started for Minersville. On my way home Stoped with br. [James H.] Rollins [and] found Aunt D. enjoying her usual health. Brother's [Frederick] Turley and [John] Bradshaw called and reported all well at home with them some snow falling but light in quantity. Times reported dull generaly on acount of wintry weather and the prevailing sickness among the horses. I have no assurence as to how long I may have to wait on the stage to pass on my journey. My only chance is to wait patiently.

February 19, 1873; Wednesday. Weather pleasant this morning. Made call on Uncle Adam Lightner at his place of buisness after which called on and dined with brother Fredrick Turley and family and also Mr. John Osborne and family. Mr. O. was in poor health. ~~in~~ In the evening Mr. Edwin Bingham called and we settled our matter of deal in Sheep by his agreeing to pay me ninety dollers for the lost sheep out of my flock.

February 20, 1873; Thursday. Remained in Town and made some calls. Dined with Mrs. ~~Anna~~ Hanah Rollins and friends. After diner learned that the Stage would go to Riverside to night so I waited on its uncertainties as to time until near 9 oclock when I bid my friends in Minersville Adieu and made another start in the cold homeward. The wind did not blow so we did not suffer with cold during our ride. We arived at the Station about 2. oclock A.M. and learned from passingers in waiting that we would not start until 6 oclock A.M.

February 21, 1873; Friday. The morning opened with promise of a good day for travil. The sick condition of the stock made ^it^ unpleasant to contemplate them with an appreciation of the Languor and pain in which they submited to the pressing arguments forced upon them by the Jehu who kept them and us moveing stedily altho not swiftly to our destiny for the day in Fillmore where we arived in Safety about 8. Oclock. Found Priscilla and the Children all well.

February 22, 1873; Saturday. The day opened warm and pleasant. Called on Marion at his office and received from him five hundred and forty dollers for B[enjamin] H. Robinson on his Note which Matured on the first of November 1872. After this in company with Marion went to his Mill about which they have been makeing some improvements internal and external then called~~n~~ and looked at Bishop [William Warren]'s Mill.

After this called on my Daughter Lelia at her home. Found her and babe well. Her husband was not at home. At night attened a meeting of some of the stockholders of the Freetrade union.[15] Received of Benjamin H. Robinson $53 33/100.

February 23, 1873; Sunday. The south wind was high and continued

15. The Free-trade Union was an alternative to the ZCMI co-operative chain of stores that were owned by the LDS Church. Lyman's wife, Maria Louisa, suggested to Jane Hanks on Feb. 6 that her son Oscar might be considered for a position at the store. Instead, Oscar continued to work as a machinist at the lumber mills around Parowan. The board of directors hired John Kelley as its clerk. Amasa visits the store for the first time on Feb. 25, then regularly thereafter.

so through the day melting the snow very fast. Prest Brigham Young and party left here this morning on his way to Salt Lake City. Called on and dined with Mr. [Noah] Bartholimew and his family. Had with him a treat of apples which has been very rare with me this winter. To day meet with Mr. William Gilmer[,] brother of Jack, the Stage[coach] Man.[16] In the evening had a call from Mr. John Kelley who spent the evening with us.

February 24, 1873; Monday. Weather pleasant and warm. Wind stil blowing from the South. Called on Mr. [John] Kelley and paid him on acount of stock in the [Free-trade] Union three hundred and fortyfive dollers[,] makeing my total stock in the Union $400 four hundred dollars.

Let Lorenzo have $112 one hundred and twelve dollers for which he gave me his note payable in May next with Interest at the three percent per month until paid, which by our agreement he can do in labor and furnishing material for fencing. Dined to day [with] R[euben] A. McBride.

February 25, 1873; Tuesday. Wrote letters to Paulina and Oscar M. in Parowan. Called at the store for a time then Called on Mr. [Noah] Bartholimew with whom and family I took diner. After this came down the hills and passed residue of the day reading. The weather clear and pleasant[;] somewhat more cool towards evening.

The cou[n]try generally is wearing a very wintery aspect[,] snow to[o] deep to admit of much common Labor beyond makeing the best plans for the accomplishment of labor in the spring. Winter planing to[o] good for spring.

February 26, 1873; Wednesday. Past the morning at home after which I called at the store. Had chat with br [John] Kelley after which I called on Rhoda and children. There I meet Mrs. Sarah Clayton Partridge.[17] She told me of the Death recently of her brother Joseph S Clayton[,] After which I returned home and spent the rest of the day in reading.

Purchased a third Reader for my little Son Alonzo Stephen.[18] The

16. Jack Gilmer and Monroe Salisbury of Ogden ran a stagecoach line from Wyoming to the gold-rush town of Deadwood in South Dakota. The Deadwood road was one of the most treacherous in the country. Showman William Cody purchased an iconic Deadwood-line stagecoach for his Wild West show.

17. Sarah was a daughter of William Clayton and Ruth Moon, Clayton's first of ten wives. She married Edward Partridge Jr., who was Fillmore's LDS bishop—a son of the onetime Presiding Bishop of the Church. William Clayton had been one of Joseph Smith's principal scribes.

18. Alonzo's name was actually Stephen Alonzo, in reverse order from how Amasa

weather is begining to moderate. The snow is melting considerably with indications of a breakup for the present.

February 27, 1873; Thursday. Weather pleasant and warm. The Boy[s] have gone hunting Deer in the hills. The snow is settleing fast some water in the Streets. Called at the Store. While there read the Charter of Zions Cooperative M[ercantile] Institution [ZCMI]. Bought some Gloves and Pruning Knife and an Ax and handle. Made some measurments on the front of my Lots in view of puting up fence [for] the coming spring. The hunt of the Boy's was fruitless except in the weariness it induced and the leson it added to the chapter of experience.

February 28, 1873; Friday. Some snow falling. Made some estimates of building materials and past some time at the Store. The [weather] so warm that the snow settled some. Some mud in the Streets. Made rough plan of house so as to get some Idea of the Material I should have to buy.

March 1, 1873; Saturday. The weather was warm and pleasant. In the morning went to Mr. Jackson, Blacksmith[,] to get my Apple cuter repared for which he charged fifty cents. Called on Mr. Wm Gibbs. He was gone from home. Called by where [they] were at work on the celler of the new store. Looked in where some men were building an Oven for the purpose of starting a Bakery. Mr. Gibbs called on me and we had some talk about Building My dwelling house.

March 2, 1873; Sunday. Passed the morning hours at home coning over my plans for building. At 11. oclock myself and Priscilla and [four-year-old] Frances were caried by the kindness of Lorenzo in his wagon to the residence of my Son-in-law Mr. Edwin Bartholimew with whom and his family we spent the residue of the day.

At night the teem came and took us home. Mr. [Peter] Silda gave us a call and entertained us with musick on his Flutina. Mr. [John] Kelley and wife spent the evening with us. Weather Cold an[d] freezeing. Subscribed for the Starspangled Baner[19] for which Mr. S[ilda] was canvassing.

March 3, 1873; Monday. The morning opened bright and clear[,] the mud drying in the streetts. Called on the county clerk in reference to

---

gave it, but he could hardly be expected to keep track of that kind of detail since he had nearly forty children. The boy was an eight-year-old son of Amasa's seventh wife, Priscilla Turley.

19. This was a monthly literary publication out of New Hampshire that began in 1863.

some lots included in the city Survey abuting on the Lots for which I have the Deed from the city of Fillmore. Ascertained the Lots were for sale by the city at four dollers each and the price of the deed. Called on Mr. Gabriel Huntsman and family. Afterwards called on Mr. [John] Kelley at store and read the congressional news.

March 4, 1873; Tuesday. Called on Mr. [Nicholas] Paul for estimate of the Brick needed to build my House, then spent the forenoon in makeing a plan of the House from which for him to form his estimate. Spent the afternoon and evening at home. As yet no news reaches me from Parowan. I heard it remarked this morning that probably the stage would go north ~~in the~~ daytime[,] day after tomorow. Shall try to go then for Salt Lake if I can hear from the South in time to be ready. Weather is moderating.

March 5, 1873; Wednesday. The~~y~~ morning was clear. Call[ed] Mr. [Nicholas] Paul and got his estimate of the Brick for my house which in agregate amounted to 31.000, thirty one thousand. I concluded to make the House two Stories in height with an additional expence of forty dollers in Brick.

In evening called on Mr. John Kelley jr and family at their residence. There meet with Mrs. Kelley his mother [Mary], after which I called on the Seignor Mr. Kelley at his residence. Took super with him. Remained until near 9. oclock.

March 6, 1873; Thursday. Made myself ready for starting Home [to Salt Lake City] this morning but the Stage being over loaded[,] I did not go. The weather continued warm and pleasant, drying the mud in the streets. Called on and spent an hour with the county clerk in his office while there asertained the state of my Stock in the Stock an[d] Mercantile Institutions. Stock in store, sixy eight [d]ollers and ninety seven cts; and in cattle herd four hundred dollers. So the investments pay from 21 to 30 percent per anum.

March 7, 1873; Friday. Made a call at the residence of Mr. Henry McBride to see Mr. Normon Taylor who had been there sick for some weeks but I found his health had somuch improved that he had gone out to visit a friend. Returned home and after diner found Mr. Taylor and friend at Mr. Henry. Spent some time with them. After which I spent some time with the widow Robinson. Had some of her winter Apples. The Rambo and Pairmain, they were well preserved.

March 8, 1873; Saturday. Made myself ready for starting homeward on the Stage but it was so loaded from the South that I could not get a seat so I had to wait for a[n]other chance. I saw Mr. Alfred Gull who was soon going to Salt Lake City to bring His Father-in-law home. I concluded to take my chances with him or Edwin Bartholimew. Called on Mr. John Cavanah; and looked through his Orchard and his Picture Gallery[,] then took diner with him. Attended buisiness meeting of the directors of Trade Union.

March 9, 1873; Sunday. Meet at the residence of Mr. John Alves whith Board of Directors to mak[e] out our agreement by way of preperation for our incorporation under the General Statute in such cases made and provided. After completeing our buisness we ajourned and Myself and Mr. [John] Kelley were invited To dine with Mr. [Noah] Bartholimew. After which I went to see Mr. Alfred Gull To learn when he was going to the city. Found he was not going immediately.

March 10, 1873; Monday. Morning opened bright and clear and at about ten oclock started in the stage the traviling very heavy. About 2 oclock reached [Cedar] Springs [Holden]. Here we took diner. After some other delay started on and about Sundown reached the [Scipio] Sumit and passed down into Round Valley in [which] we found the mud so extensive and deep that we had to Leave the Coach and made our way into Scip^i^o three of our party on foot and myself after until I was kindly assisted into town by a ride on one of the Stage Horses. Put up at Mr. Benjamin Johnson's.

March 11, 1873; Tuesday. This morning sent three yoke of oxen to bring in the Stage and we started on our way about 9 or 10 oclock. Some portion of the road as we neared Chicken Creek was fearfuly bad[,] the passengers all but myself walking. Took super at chicken creek then started on to find the Road al~~j~~most impassible. About 4 miles from Nephi the last of the passingers left the Stage and walked in to Town and put up at the Nephi House. The Stage was brought in about 5 oclock Morning. Called on Mr. Richard Ivy whose Son Amasa who shot himself accidentaly on yesterday while cleaning his gun.

March 12, 1873; Wednesday. At which we commenced making preperation for further traviling. To do this we substituted a dead axel^t^ree wagon for the coach left in the Mud and about 9. oclock we started on and after a very rough ride having no seats in wagon but such as were made of the Mail Sacks piled one on the other, but the day's wearisome travil like all other Sublimary trials ended and we landed at the California House ^in Payson^ where we took super and then entered on our night of travil during the most of which some of the passengers wer[e] on foot.

March 13, 1873; Thursday. The morning found us at the northern foot of the Provo Bench from which point our road had a decending grade to the terminus, where we arived in time for the Train for the city where we arived about noon, very much wearied with our rough travil. We had no sleep after we left Fillmore exc[e]pting a few hours at Scipio until last night. Had the pleasure of finding all well at home. From my weariness did not go out in the city. Towards evening there were some indications of rain which began to fall during the night gently.

March 14, 1873; Friday. The rain was falling gently until about 10 oclock after which the weather became clear and bright. I made some calls in the City. Called at the Bank and cashed some checks which Mrs. L[yman] received in my absence. After which I wrote a letter to Paulina in Parowan in answer to one received from her as I was leaving Fillmore. Made a call at the Tribune office where I meet with Mr. W[illiam] H. Shearmon and the Editors of the paper. Returned home quite weary.

March 15, 1873; Saturday. Worked om [on] m[y] House plan during the morning hours after which called K[imball] and L[awrence] Store and sold a small amount of Gold for curency. Made some inquiry for a Mr. Wm. C. Burrows for whom I had some money from the Mother Eve Mining Co in the County of Iron.

After I returned home Mr. B. called and received his money and ~~reciped~~ receited for the same. Called on and past an hour with Mr. D[avid] H[yrum] Smith at Mr. Brownings. Mr. [Henry W.] L[awrence] called on us in the afternoon & played the Organ. Meet Mr. E[li] B. Kelsey who gave me some good news.

March 16, 1873; Sunday. In the morning attended at Indipendence Hall after which we called on and dined with Mr. H[yrum] S. Coombs and wife. After diner we went to the Institute to hear Mr. D[avid] H[yrum] Smith preach. After this we returned and past the residue of the afternoon with Mr. C. and wife. At half past seven oclock we were at the Institute where we were addressed by his Honour Judge C[yrus] M. Hawley, on the deeply interesting subject ~~of~~ or question what and whence is Life. Some rain fell during meeting.

March 17, 1873; Monday. Morning opened brightly after the gentle night rain. My first call was at the drugstore for some medicine after which I called on Mrs. [Ruth] Turley whom I found very low and feeble from the effects of her protracted Illness which had extended over several months.

After this call I walked with more labor than speed up the hill to the Bench to the residence of Elias [Harrison] who first was a Mormon and then a freeman through the growth of free thought and the expansion of mind resulting therefrom.

March 18, 1873; Tuesday. Weather bright clear and springlike. Passed the morning hours at home introducing some changes into the plan of my House. After this I took a walk up the hill to the residence of Mr. [Elias L. T.] Harison who was not at home. Called on Mrs. Rosina Godbe at her residence on the Bench. As I returned I meet Mr. H. on the Street. At night attended a meeting of the Executive committee at the residence of Mrs. Mary Godbe. The attendence was slim. Mr. Harison was not there. The evening clear and starlight.

March 19, 1873; Wednesday. The weather opened this morning clear and a slight chill was perceptible in the aire. Passed most of the day in studying the plan of my House and working in some change in the arangement of the parts to increase their utility and enhance the general convenience of the whole as a home. In the afternoon walked onto the Bench when and where I meet Mr. [Elias L. T.] Harison and submited to him my changes in the plan of the House. Returning home called on Mr. [Hyrum S.] Coombs. There meet Mrs. Lyman and returned home.

March 20, 1873; Thursday. Morning was pleasant. Passed some hours at home after which I went out in Town and found in ^the^ Tribune Office a copy ^of^ Religio[-Philosophical] Journal awaiting me and also a letter from Mr. John Kelley of Fillmore, inclosed was an Official Bond (for myself as a Director in and for the Freetraders Union.) sent for my si^g^-nature. I signed and returned it immediately. Bought of K[imball] and L[awrence] some goods for some Sumer Cloths for country ware. Found myself much wearied with my walking. Worked some on my House plan.

March 21, 1873; Friday. Made some calls in Town after which I returned and wrote some letters[:] one to Mr. Benjamin Grourd of Farmington Fulton County Illinois[,] And one to Mr. John Kelley of Fillmore. As I went to post my Letters I found a letter from Lorenzo stateing that they had ~~some~~ some rain since I left which increased the mudy condition of the ground where they cut their Posts so they could not hawl them at present. Spent the evening with Mrs. [Love Josephine] Coombs at her residence.

March 22, 1873; Saturday. In the morning wrote two letters[,] one to Lorenzo and one to Mr. Bartholimew. Made some calls in the City. Bought some Pruning Sheeres and got my dividers repaired. Mr. David H. Smith called on us and spint the evening. He informed us that the smallpox was in the 7th Ward and on that acount the family with whom he had been staying had left their residence and for the present gone to the country. Mr. S. gave us musick on our Organ.

March 23, 1873; Sunday. Some indications of a change in the weather. Attended the Methodist Church [and] heard the Rev Straten in the morning services. Had Mr. and Mrs. [Hyrum and Josephine] Coombs with us to Diner.

Passed the afternoon in reading. Increasing indications of Storm with high wind from the north west. At night I spoke at the [Liberal] Institute on the subject of Goodness and Godliness as judged by the actions of peoples, and their results or fruits as the effects of causes.

March 24, 1873; Monday. The morning opened bright and Clear. I called on Mr. [William] Shearman and family and with Mr. S. went to the Tribune Office. Called at the Store of K[imball] and L[awrence] and called on Mrs. Lavina Johnson with whom[,] and her son Andrew[,] I dined after which I went and took a look at the New Gassworks which are being pushed on to completion.[20] In connection with this I noticed some pip[e]laying in the Streets aproximating Main Street. Slight chill in the air to day.

March 25, 1873; Tuesday. Mad[e] a pilgrimage to the bench [now

20. The Salt Lake City Gas Company was formed in 1872, with the gas-production and storage areas located on the west end (500 W.) of North Temple Street. The gas was a by-product of burning coal. It was transported in pipes under the streets and into the buildings and houses. Prior to this time, the only sources of illumination were kerosene lamps and candles.

Capitol Hill] to see Mr. [Elias] Harison but did not meet with him. Called at Tribune office where I meet Mr. W[illiam] H. Shearman from whom I received a Ticket to the Anaversary Concert and Ball on the 31st. Came home and went [to] bed for an hour after which I took another run up Town doing some errands connected with the makeing of a Tool to cut and core Apples. On my return home I meet Mr. C[laudius] V. Spencer. Had some talk with him and Father [Abraham] Taylor.

March 26, 1873; Wednesday. Some indications of storm. Passed some hours in reading after which I made some calls in Town extending my walk onto the Bench to the residence of Mr. Harison where I met with Mr. Edward Tull[e]dge. Remained until after diner then with him[,] Mr. H.[,] and wife had a look at their new residence in process of erection. Then returned home and at night attended a meeting of Committies engaged in makeing preperations for comeing Aniversary of the 31st.[21] Made some changes in the plan of operations from that first adopted. To day meet with Roberts and Watson from Parowan. They report much sickness there.

March 27, 1873; Thursday. Some snow this morning. Some thunder and lightning during the night folowed with the snow. Passed the day in work on my House plan and some other drawings. The storm with its clouds subsided towards noon. The weather becoming quite pleasant in the afternoon. In the afternoon in company with Mrs. L[yman] and Hila went to and spent the evening with Mr. Coombs and had a look at the news as published in the papers Local and Foreign. Indications of rain as we returned home.

March 28, 1873; Friday. Weather growing more warm and spring-like. Spent the morning and forenoon at home working on the plan of my house. After diner made some calls in town. Called at Tribune Office and found a letter of invitation to a Tea Sociable at the Methodist Church. It was Anonymous, so of course I did not respond.

Meet again with Mr. Roberts and Mr. Watson. They were purcaceing a Bill of goods at the House of Kimball and Lawrence [and] will return next week.

March 29, 1873; Saturday. Weather pleasant an[d] clear. Spent the morning and forenoon at home makeing some drawings of Machinery

21. This was the date of the Fox sisters' first experience in upstate New York in 1848.

and other work, in afternoon made some calls in town. Called on and dined with Mr. H[enry] W. Lawrence. Received letter from Paulina in which she informed of the Death by sickness of our old friend Mr. William Martindale resident of Kane County and old Grafton or Duncans retreat. At night held private Seance at home. Mr. Coombs and wife were with us. Had good manifestations.

March 30, 1873; Sunday. As we were prepareing to go to Church this morning my Son Marion from the South in Fillmore came in; and notwithstanding his Orthodoxy he went with us to hear Mr. [Norman] McLeod. After the service returned and had diner. Mr. Coombs and wife were with us. After diner our company went out; and, Myself and Mrs. Lyman called on Dr [Orville H.] Conger and family and with him and wife went [to] the ajourned meeting of Executive committee at the residence of Mrs. Mary Godbe. Attended service in [Liberal] Institute. Some indications of storm. Was sixty years old to day.

March 31, 1873; Monday. Passed the Morning hours in makeing some preperations for going south to Fillmore, by packing my chest of tools to which I made some addition by purchase. At night attended the concert and Ball held in the Institute in the interests of the childrens progressive Lyceum which a few of the friends of freedom are laboring to establish.[22] The festival was also held in commemoration of the advent of modern Spiritualism. The sup[p]er was furnished by the host of the American House Col. J[esse] C. Little a thorough orthodox Mormon.

April 1, 1873; Tuesday. Weather bright and clear. Spent a morning hour in reading, after which I mad[e] some calls in the city and waited on the Parowan freighters to get them to take 2 or 3 hundred pounds for me to Fillmore but they would not do it for me. Returned home and rested for a short time then went out to see the turnout of the Fire Brigade that was out in its full strength. They succeded in raising the water to a fair height at the distance of one hundred and ten rods from the Steem Engine. At this di^s^tance the Hose failed in strength and burst.

April 2, 1873; Wednesday. Weather warm and pleasant. Spent the morning hours in reading after which I made some calls in town and bought me a Gru[b]bing Hoe, and on my return called on D<u>r</u> [Orville]

22. The lyceum was the alternative Sunday school Lyman had previously mentioned. From the entry of Jan. 25, 1874, it seems to have prospered once it got off the ground.

Conger who informed me he was going East to be gone some forty days to place some Mining property in the Market and to deliver a course of Lectures on Utah and its resources. Marion was with us to diner after which he went North on Rail Road. I meet Robert Henry. He could not freight for me.

April 3, 1873; Thursday. Past the morning hours in reading after which I visited Mr. [Elias] Harison on the hill. He had been ill for a day or two but about from him I learned that Mr. T. D. Brown had been sick for some five months and was just able to be about. Made some buisness calls on Main Street after which I called on Mr. Brown and family with whom I dined[,] and after passing a pleasant hour with them I came home [and] spent the residue of the day in reading the Christian Union.

April 4, 1873; Friday. Weather rather dull and as I was doing my morning writing, the wildfire alarm rang o^u^t on the silence of the moment. Its warning that the Firey Friend was at its destructive work, but the Firemen were out in force and soon the fire under controll. The damage was limited to the destruction of the half story of a House belonging to Mr. Grosbeck, the property or goods in the house were all saved.[23] There was at the time of the fire no wind blowing to which circumstance and the efforts of the first troop we owe the easy extinguishment of the fire.

April 5, 1873; Saturday. This morning Mrs. Lyman and Hila went to help Mrs. Coombs about their moveing. I read some in the Morning after which I made a call at the Tribune Office and then called on Mrs. [Mary] Perris at her residence. She and Children were well. I then called on Mr. Mather and family who seemed to be very comfortably situated in their home considering that they were striped of evrything through their participation in the suferings of the Morisite Tragedy. To day bought me an Apple pealer, for one doller and a quarter.

April 6, 1873; Sunday. Attended at [Norman] McLeods. The service was an address to the Sabbath School. This over[,] I went with Mrs. Lyman and spent the residue of the day with Mr. John Low and family. While there we sat around the Table which moved by spirit force makeing some interesting revelations through the mediumship of Mrs. Low. At night in company with Mr. Low we went to the Institute where I

23. Nicholas Groesbeck's Wasatch Building at 200 South was still under construction. It was destined to become the largest commercial building west of the Missouri River.

spoke for a short time. After which Mr. [Elias L. T.] Harison delivered a short address to the attentive audience.

April 7, 1873; Monday. Morning opened pleasant. Walked onto the Kimball Bench to see Mr. [Elias] Harison in regard to the plan of my house. He made an apointment for attending to ^it^ in a day or two. On my return home I bought at the co-op a Garden fork for which I paid two dollers. After returning home I received a call from my old friend Andrew Cahoon with whom I had a pleasant conversation on the great principles of applied [science] to the thought and actions of humanity. My Son Marion and Bishop Joseph Tanner of Payson dined with us. In the evening called on [the landlady] Mrs. Kay and family. Mrs. Lyman and Hila were with me.

April 8, 1873; Tuesday. The weather pleasant but cool. Made several calls in Town and in my stroll meet Mr. [Elias L. T.] Harison who promised to complet my Ho[u]se plan by tomorow. Heard that Dr. Stephens was in the city but was unable to find him. With to day the Conference closed its labors among which that of receiving from Prest. Young the resignation of the Trustieship for the ~~chur~~ church, which office was devolved upon G[eorge] A. Smith. At night with Mrs. Lyman and Hila had Seance with Mr. [John] Low and friends.

April 9, 1873; Wednesday. Was early at the store of K[imball] and L[awrence] waiting for the parties who had promised to freight for me. This waiting detained me until 12 oclock, after which I went to Mr. [Elias] Harisons who promised to finish my drawing and send them to me by mail[,] after which meet Dr Stephens at Dr [Orville] Congers where we dined and enjoyed a pleasant hour, bade them adieu[,] and then went to the residence of Mr. Coombs where I meet Mrs. Lyman and Hila and spent the evening then returned home.

April 10, 1873; Thursday. Rose early and started to meet the street cars to go ^to^ the Depot, but was to[o] late. I then returned to await the afternoon Trains. While waiting Miss Laura Bartholimew [son-in-law's sister] from Fillmore arived to go to school. She brought me a letter from Lorenzo. I started on the 2.40 Train South. Reached the Terminus. Before [I] left [I retrieved] my baggage and went down to Lehigh and stoped all night with Mrs. Charlotte Bushman. Mr. B. was not at home[,] he was in Tintick.

April 11, 1873; Friday. This morning after our Breakfast left our friends the Bushmans, and went on the Stage[coach] to the South. Near night arived at Payson where we took super at the California-House[,] then traviled on. The night was pleasant and lighted by the moon. Arived a[t] the Chicken Creek Station half past 2 oclock. Here I was very kindly invited to take a bed during our stay at this point[,] which extended to some hours during which time the Southern Stage arived and departed, ~~we mad[e] Fillmore about 2. Oclock.~~

April 12, 1873; Saturday. We arived in Fillmore about 2 oclock. Found all well. After takeing some refreshment I made some calls in the Town. Called on the Bartholimews an[d] left some parcells that I had brought for them from the city Salt Lake. Called on Mr. [John] Kelley at the Store after which had a look at the cellar of the new Store now being built. Mr. William Marsden and his Daughter called and staid all night[,] they on their way from Salt Lake City [to their] home in Parowan.

April 13, 1873; Sunday. Passed the forenoon at home. Slept some from the weariness of my journey and after diner with Priscilla spent the afternoon with Edwin and Lelia [Bartholomew]. The weather cool[,] wind from the North. I find on examination that the earliest fruit blosms were killed by frost but enough are yet alive to make a crop if the season turns warm and favurable. Very few of my Peach trees have put out fruit bloomes this spring but they are promising well for fruit.

April 14, 1873; Monday. Rose early this morning and commenced work on my building ground[,] pulling the old roller. Lorenzo worked with me. After our d[a]y's work was done[,] made a call at the Store and bought a new hoe. Received letter from Paulina reporting all well but no sale for flour. Weather cool[,] wind from the north. Last night the frost killed some more of the fruit Buds[,] stil there are som[e] left that will make fruit if the season becomes warm in time.

April 15, 1873; Tuesday. Weather warm and spring like. Worked on my building lot and in my orchard clearing up the ground by exterminating some of natures production that were noxious to us because they were in our way. In the afternoon called at the Store and visited the new cellar[,] and while there was told that my freight from the city had come. I went to the coop to receive it. The freight came in good order. Had the favor of Bishop [Thomas] Callister's Wagon and teem to cary my goods home.

April 16, 1873; Wednesday. In the morning put up my wheelbarrow, and then made a handle to my grub[b]ing hoe, after which Mr. Joseph Turley and wife called on us and staid all night. Wrote letters to Paulina and Dionitia to whom I sent some Medicine by Mrs. Turley. Did not work in the orchard to day, my broaken ~~time~~ work and writing took up my time. My old plough came home to day minus the Beem which I left in it. Replaced with a stick.

April 17, 1873; Thursday. Worked in the orchard with Lorenzo until noon. After diner I wrote a letter to L. M. [Maria Louisa] Lyman in the City. About three oclock went to work until nearly Sundown when the weather became pleasant and cool. Mr. [Joseph] Turley and wife started for their home takeing with them the horse of Omner [Turley], for which they came. I sent by them some medicine to Dionitia. Weather warm and springlike. Peach blosoms opening very fast.

April 18, 1873; Friday. Was out early among the trees before the morning meal. After Breakfast worked for a short time and then tried to get some sleep of which I failed to get any the night before on acount of a severe cold in my head. Not succeeding in the Sleeping buisness I resumed my pruning labor in the afternoon until near night. When I left off work I found myself much oppressed with the cold in my head. I took some Barbary Snuff[24] which releived me.

April 19, 1873; Saturday. Was early at work before the sun appeared above the Hills, or the young men about the place had risen. To day the local Conference was in cession which caused a general gathering from all the settlements in the county. In the afternoon I went to see Mr. Thomas Henderson to get him to do some shoe work for me. As I went I meet Brother David Savage who greeted me very kindly and invited me to call at his residence in Cedar Springs. Meet Father [Weeden V.] Hakes. He is fast declining.

April 20, 1873; Sunday. To day [was] the Conference. I remained at home all day. Did not leave the place during the day. Some time during the day a boy[,] the Son of Mr. George Wage[,] was run over by a horse that was riden by another boy. The injured boy lived until the next morning 3 oclock. Weather warm with high and drying wind. Two of my son

24. Barbary Snuff was a moist, pungent tobacco product that worked like a decongestant. It was manufactured in Spain.

Marion's children came to see me. In the evening Mr. John Kelley called in. Past a social hour with interchange of thought on the signs of the times.

April 21, 1873; Monday. Wind high from the southwest. [Son] Henry commenced work for me this morning. During the forenoon I called at the Office of the County Clerk. He was away attending the session of the High Council, while there meet with Bishop [Edward] Partridge with [whom I] had [a] pleasant hours conversation.

Returned home and worked the residue of the day with the Boys. [In] the course of [the] afternoon the winds sudenly changed to the north and was folowed by frost at night. Found myself very tired at night. Loaned Theodore seven dollers in money.

April 22, 1873; Tuesday. Rose at five and went to work in the Orchard. Lorenzo and Henry were with me in the forenoon. Lorenzo was taken sick and quit work. Henry and myself continued work through the day. Some indications of storm. At night Mr. Erwin Stodard called on us. He was on his way to his old home in Farmington from his present residence on the Beaver. Theodore payed me the money I loaned him on yesterday.

April 23, 1873; Wednesday. Snow was falling gently when I rose and ^went^ to the Orchard, and worked for an hour when the storm increased in severity so that I had to quit work out doors; and after a while I went to Mr. [William Henry] Bishop the Gunsmith[25] to get to him to do some work on my Apple cuter on which he worked for an hour or so then quit work to rest. The storm ceased in the afternoon. I worked in the Orchard at pruning, at night the Horizon was clear and Starlight.

April 24, 1873; Thursday. Spent the Morning hours before Breakfast pruning my trees. After breakfast went with Theodore to pruning Priscilla's trees. Worked at this until afternoon then I went to Mr. [William] Bishop who done some wok on my apple cutter for [blank]. Called on brother Isaac Carlin[g] to have some soldering done which he said he would do in the morning.[26] Weather stil mild and warm. The Creek some swoollen.

---

25. Bishop did precision metal work. He made awls for Indians for sewing their moccasins and put sights on the Indians' guns. He was originally from New York but had been with Lyman in California. He had two wives.

26. Isaac Van Wagoner Carling had worked in his father's gun shop in Ogden, so

April 25, 1873; Friday. Passed morning hours in my Orchard at work. Called on [Isaac] Carlin for my work, for which I paid him fifty cents. In the afternoon worked at pruning until night. This evening Priscilla and the Boys went to a dance to Mr. J. Alexanders. I stayed with the children. Did not sleep much but the night past all the same as tho it had brought rest from my weariness and vigor for another day of toil and struggle.

April 26, 1873; Saturday. This morning I finished the pruning of my Orchard and engaged in puting some of my Tools in order for work. The Boys were working this morning in the Orchard ground. After noon I called on Mr. [Isaac] Carlin for some tinning which he done for me. I paid him twenty five cents then called on Mr. [Thomas] Henderson for my boots. They were not done. At night I attended [a Free Traders Union] Director's meeting. John Cavanah was added to building committee.

April 27, 1873; Sunday. Remained at home all day. Past the time in reading the Ban[n]er of Light [magazine]. In the afternoon I received a call from my Son Marion who offered some suggestions in regard to my building and promised to asist me in acomplishing the same. While looking over my Orchard with Marion my Daughter Lydia May[27] came to see me thus evinceing the gratifying truth that the child's affection for her Father had not died under the withering influence of fanaticism that alienated her Mother.

April 28, 1873; Monday. In the morning worked fiting up my work bench. Made Bill of Lumber to send to the Mill. At noon Called on Marion in his Office gave my Bill of Lumber to Bishop [Edward] Partridge wh[o] is to forward it to the Mill immediately. After this dined with Marion and Rhoda. Marion made me a present of a pair of Boots worth $16. Some snow falling but quite warm so it melted as fast as it fell. Worked some on my Bench.

April 29, 1873; Tuesday. Snowing gently this morning. Spent the early hours in working on my bench, in the afternoon called on Mr. [William] Gibbs and engaged a Door, and Window for my shop. Meet with Platt[e] at the co-op Store. He told me that he was going to the city

---

he had experience in what Lyman calls "tinning," soldering (see entry for Apr. 26), even though his main business was carpentry. He had two wives.

27. Lydia May was the six-year-old daughter of Amasa and eighth wife Lydia Partridge.

before he should return to Oak Creek. In the afternoon it stormed freely tho the weather was quite mild[,] the snow melting as fast as it fell[,] moistining the ground finely.

April 30, 1873; Wednesday. Pleasant this morning. To day the Boys Lorenzo and Henry finished diging my Orchard and Cleaned up the current trees along Street fence. Mr. William Marsden from Parowan on his way to Salt Lake city called on us and informed us that Dr Calvin C. Pendleton had recently died in Parowan. He says trade is very dull. At night attended a meeting of the Board of directors of the free traders Union at their Store. Quorum present.

May 1, 1873; Thursday. To day my son Amasa [Jr.]'s ^wife^ [Cynthia] was prematurely delivered of a p[a]ir of twin Daughters. They survived their birth but an hour and passed away to Nature under the kindly and humane institutions of the bright land of Sumer in the hap[p]y beyond.

Bought ^Lumber^ and fitied up some conveniences about the house. Henry and Ira went [to the] woods to commence the cuting of wood for the Brickmakers. Called in evening on Mr. [Edwin] Barthalimew who had been to see the rock and the road to them. Found both prety good[,] the road needing some repairs.

May 2, 1873; Friday. Worked on my Apple cuter, the most of the day. Theodore commenced plowing for puting in some corn on his Mother's Lot. The ground from the recent storm is in a very good condition for working. Made a call on Mr. [John] Kelley at the Store. Trade rather dull. Cloudy at night with some indications of storm altho no rain fell in the Valley on acount of the strong attraction of the Mountain for the storm clouds.

May 3, 1873; Saturday. Thick clouds were around the Horizon and the Atmosphere was quite humid. Worked on my Apple cuter until the rain began to fall when I retired to the house in good order to continue my work. Called at the store as per ajournment to meet the Directors, but none were there. Waited an hour then returned home. Received a letter from Parowan from Paulina dated May 1st, reporting a May walk and a funerel of Mr. Hill. No sale for flour.

May 4, 1873; Sunday. Weather bright and fair. After Breakfast I took a walk around our place studying the improvements that are practicable. After this I returned and wrote a letter to Paulina in Parowan in answer to one received from her bearing date of May 1st. After the writing went to the Post Office with my letter. On my return I called on Mr. Bartholimew and past an hour with him in sociable interchange of thought. Some light hails an[d] rain before night came on.

May 5, 1873; Monday. Weather fine and warm. Past the forenoon working on my Apple cuter. In afternoon went to post Office and called at the courthouse from the roof of which I enjoyed a fine view of the town and the sorounding country. Returned home quite weary. This morning called on Lelia who with her husband returned last night from Salt Lake and reported all the family well. At time of leaveing they reported the Burning of Vicker's flouring mill at Nephi.

May 6, 1873; Tuesday. The weather gradually becoming warmer. After Breakfast I went to Mr. [Peter] Silda's and procured of him a piece of Lumber with which to finish my Apple cuter on which I worked the most of the day. After which I called on Mr. [John] Kelley for some papers he had promised me to read but he had failed to bring them from home when he came. I left with him some of my Ban[n]ers of Light [magazine] to peruse.

May 7, 1873; Wednesday. Weather warm and pleasant. Worked at the Bench most of the day finishing my fruit cuter. Received another piece of rock from Mr. Barns of Beaver County with a request that I should have it Asayed to asertain its value. The Rock was ~~ha^n^d~~ handed me by Mr. Rogers of this place who was in Beaver on buisness. After my days work was done I called at the store and got from Mr. [John] Kelley some papers to read.

May 8, 1873; Thursday. Morning pleasant. Past the forenoon in makeing the plan of a House with a single story, after which I called on Mr. [William] Gibbs the Builder for some estimates of the cost of Building. After which I called at County Clerks Office and settled my taxes for 1872. After this went to the Lumberyard and selected 790 ft of Lumber fo[r] building my work shop; and Lorenzo took his teem and hauled it home, the first material on the ground for buildings.

May 9, 1873; Friday. The nights continue to be very cool. Made a call this morning after Breakfast at the Coop Lumber yard selected from the old stock some pieces to use in building my shop which Lorenzo hauled down for me in the afternoon. To day meet with Mr. [Erwin] Stodard and Mr. Clemens from Beaver County. They were returning from Salt Lake City. Made draft of House to day for my residence which I intend to build next year if prospered. Mrs. Eva Robinson wife of Mr. Almond Robinson died to day.

May 10, 1873; Saturday. Weather slightly warmer. Passed the forenoon at home in work on the plan of my house. Called at the store and loaned Mr. [John] Kelley forty dollers for a week. Selected some more Lumber at the yard for my Shop.

Mrs. Robinson was buried this afternoon. A discourse was delivered by Elder Nephi Pratt. Called on Mr. [William] Gibbs but he was e[n]gaged making the coffin for Mrs. [Eva] R[obinson] so I did not do any business with him. Meet with Platt[e] this morning.

May 11, 1873; Sunday. Morning opened warm and pleasant. The Creek swelling from the melting of the snow in the hills. This morning I wrote a letter to Mrs. Lyman in the city. In the afternoon I went with Mrs. Lyman to visit Mr. [John] Kelley and wife. During the afternoon took a look over the lots on which Mr. K. has his residences. His fruit trees are all growing timely and are giveing promise of a fine crop this year. Mrs. Hariet Shepherd and daughter stoped with us over night.

May 12, 1873; Monday. This morning received a note from my daughter Agness in Salt Lake City and with it a letter from Mr. L. B. Lyman of Helena Montana of a buisness character. To the ab^ov^e mentioned letters I gave immediate attention. After Mailing my letters called on the Widow[er] [Almond] Robinson at whose place I meet Adelia[,] my son Platts wife and her Son Alton[,] a fine Boy whom I now saw for the first time. His age nine months. Made some tresels for work in building. Some rain fell to day.

May 13, 1873; Tuesday. Weather cloudy with indications of rain. I made ^a^ call at the Freetrade [store] and received of Mr. [John] Kelley twenty dollers and Bought of [him] some nails. I then went to the Lumberyard and selected some Lumber for my Shop frame. Soon after I returned home[,] it commenced to rain. Made up a nail box. In the afternoon Mr. [William] Marsden called for the night on his way home from the city. Rain fell freely this evening.

May 14, 1873; Wednesday. Some clouds this morning and the rain had fallen freely during the night much to the good of the crops and the joy of the farmers and gardners. Commenced working on the Timbers for the frame of my shop. The day past without any rain to interupt work. Lorenzo and Theodore grub[b]ed up the Brush in front of their lots so as to grade the side walk. Called at the Store and the Lumber yard but did not get any Lumber to day.

May 15, 1873; Thursday. It stil continues to rain so the Boys did not come in with the Horses until after noon. Measured the ground for my house and worked some in my Orchard between the Showers. At 6 oclock P. M. attended a director's Meeting at the store, during which a letter was read from Mr. [John] Kelley[,] the Clerk in the Store asking the board to consider the matter of some Slanderous and as he avered fals[e] statements expressed in regard to himself by Director John Cavanah. Hearing will be tomorrow night.

May 16, 1873; Friday. This morning the rain ceased to fall for a short time so that Lorenzo hiched his teem to the wagon and we hauled off from my Orchard the Brush that had accumulated from the pruning. We worked until ten oclock when we were interrupted by the rain that fell freely. I passed the residue of the day between showers in raking up brush in the Orchard. Called at the Lumber yard and selected some Lumber, then I attended meeting of the Directors at 7 oclock.

May 17, 1873; Saturday. This morning the rain is stil falling but after Breakfast Lorenzo brought home the residue of my Lumber from the Lumberyeard. We then finished hauling the brush out of my Orchard. Called on Mr. [John] Kelley and bought of him an oil can for a trough to my grindstone. Came home and a[d]justed the same in its place.[28] Called on Mr. [George] Crane the painter at Mr. McNeals and gave him some bill posters of the Blanchard church. Edwin and Lelia [Bartholomew] called this evening.

May 18, 1873; Sunday. Weather pleasant and warm. No rain to day. Received Letter from Paulina bearing date of the 13th and some papers from the States. In the afternoon walked out for a short time. In the morning I wrote letter to Paulina and sent it by Charles wh[o] started for

28. A five-gallon can made for kerosene made a perfect bowl for holding a grindstone. With each rotation, the stone wheel picked up a little lubricant from the bottom. The stone was mounted vertically, the axle running through it resting in notches in the rim of the can. The stone was about two feet in diameter and about half of it showed above the top of the can.

home this morning with his horses. Called on Mr. Bartholimew and past with him an hour or two and then returned home after which received call from Mr. Kelley.

May 19, 1873; Monday. Cloudy this morning. Rain gently falling. Wrote letter to Paulina in answer to hers of the 13th after which between the Showers I framed and laid the sills of my shop and that were Broken off from work by the rain which fell in a series of cap[ac]ious showers all through the day until night when the rain ceased and it cleared up in the night. To day the men and Boys of the Town began a Stock drive which was made very unpleasant by the rain.

May 20, 1873; Tuesday. Weather clear and warm. Worked at frameing the timbers of my shop. They boys were mostly engaged on the Cattle drive. No rain fell to day to interupt work. In the afternoon went to the Lumberyard and procured more Lumber with which [to] go on with my work. Cynthia called on us today. I caried my Black cloths to Lelia to be cleaned. Received Leffels Mechanical papers.[29]

May 21, 1873; Wednesday. The weather clear and pleasant. I was early at work and finished frameing my Shop. The heards of stock began to come in. Lorenzo and Henry went after wood which the[y] Sold for feed to the miller. In the afternoon I went to Mr. [William] Gibbs shop for my Door and window but did not get them as Mr. G. was not at home. Returned and with the help of the Boys put up my frame. My Son-in-law P[hilo] H Carter called on me from Beaver.

May 22, 1873; Thursday. Weather pleasant. No storm. Was early at work on my frame[,] the Rafters of which completed. It was ready to receive the roof which Lorenzo assisted me to put up. This done [before] the time had arived for our ajourned meeting of Directors. I went to the store where I met Mr. Nelson Lawrence who had been to Cedar City on buisness and with Mr. Sharp Walker was returning home to Salt Lak[e] City. We had no meeting [as] no quorum [at] present.

May 23, 1873; Friday. Weather pleasant in the morning but clouds soon arose which gave out rain and Hail much to the anoyence and discomfirture of a large party of our Town's people who had gone out for a

29. James Leffel was publisher of *Mechanical News*, the semi-monthly magazine out of New York devoted to "manufacturing, engineering, milling, and mining," as its masthead explained.

May party and Picknick up near the Foot hills. After the rain Lorenzo and myself continued our work on the Shop and in the afternoon we went to the Lumberyard an[d] got five hundred ft. of Lumber. Received letter from L. M. [Lyman] in the City.

May 24, 1873; Saturday. Weather pleasant. Laid the floor in my shop and worked some on the roof[,] after which before diner I went up in Town. Called on Bishop [Edward] Partridge and learned from him that my Lumber Bill amounted to something over fifty dollers. Procured door and window from Mr. [William] Gibbs for $4.60. The Boys brought them home. About five oclock, it commenced to rain freely and continued through the night.

May 25, 1873; Sunday. Some rain fell today. Wrote Letter to Mrs. Lyman in Salt Lake City after which I called and spent an hour or two with Mr. [John] Kelley and read his last [issue of the] paper the [Religio-Philosophical] Journal. While there Mr. [Noah] Bartholimew called. From him I learned that he had succeeded in paying Phelps for the Land on which the new store is being built. Received of Mr. B. seventeen dollers on acount of Laura [Bartholomew]'s board. After this called on Edwin and Lelia [Bartholomew]. Found L[elia] somewhat better than when I called before.

May 26, 1873; Monday. Was early at work to day fixing the Door and window. The day and the Labor was interupted by a Shower of rain in the Midst of which Mr. Stott from the Meadow Creek [Meadow] Settlement called in and borowed a Wagon cover for a day. Lorenzo went in the morning after his horses but did not find them. My Colonel horse came up to day looking very well. Lorenzo and Henry found some stock in the evening.

May 27, 1873; Tuesday. Weather pleasant and warm. After our Breakfast went up in Town and waited at free Trade [store] some time for Mr. [John] Kelley and bought of him some hangings for my Door and Window. After this called at the co-op and settled my Lumber account of over fifty dollers. Bought of them a Lock for my Door and bought some Lumber for a work bench. Returned and hung up my Door and window shuter. Found myself very tired and weary with my days Labors.

May 28, 1873; Wednesday. Some cloudy indications of more storm. Was early at work in my shop. Wind from the Southwest very high in which some of the trees lost some of their fruit. This morning Lorenzo brought home my lumber from the yard for the Bench on which I worked through the day. Moved my chest of Tools into the Shop to day.[30] Lorenzo hauled a load of wood for Marion. Towards evening the wind subsided. Weather cool.

May 29, 1873; Thursday. Worked in my Shop dressing Lumber for my new Bench. Some clouds indicating more storm. The Boys some of them were hunting stock but had no success. Lorenzo went with his teem and caried Marion and Bishop [Edward] Partridge out to their Ranch. Called on Mr. Andrew Henry wh[o] has been ill for some weeks with affection [infection] of the Liver. He thinks himself to be slowly recovering. Borowed Pla[ne] of brother Gibbs. Some rain was falling as I returned home.

May 30, 1873; Friday. Some clouds with rain interupting my work on account of the open condition of my shop. Between Showers I went up in town and paid Mr. [William] Gibbs for my Door and window. Bought Oil Stone [whetstone] of Mr. McRay. And while out I made an arangement with Mr. [Christian] Anderson of the cooperative Meat Market[31] for Beef to Pay in Oct next. Weather Cleared up in the afternoon and [I] worked until night in the Shop.

May 31, 1873; Saturday. Weather bright clear and warmer than yesterday. Passed the day in the shop working on my Bench. Chalk Creek is at this time more swolin with Melting snow from the Mountain than at any time before the present spring. Indications are in favor of dry weather at present. The vegitables and fruit come forward rather slowly. The weather is generally so cold.

June 1, 1873; Sunday. June opens on us rather cool. Past a portion of the morning hours in the Shop writing in my Diary. In the afternoon went with Priscilla to call on Lelia whom we found ill [and] not able to do her work. She was sufering som[e] from an attack of Rheumatism for which they were useing the Gargling Oil.[32] After returning home I

30. In the past when Lyman said he was at shop, he might have meant at his or someone else's barn or temporary shed. Now he would have a permanent place for his tools, his own workbench, and a lock on the door.

31. This was an LDS Church-run institution like ZCMI.

32. Gargling oil was not a mouthwash. Why it was not is, according to one commentator, one of the world's great mysteries. It was actually a salve that was rubbed onto

wrote a letter and mailed it to Agness[']s [house] in the City. The weather growing warmer.

June 2, 1873; Monday. The morning was quite pleasant. The Boys were preparing to go their several ways. Lorenzo to the Mountain to get fencing for Marion[;] Theodore to hunting a horse[;] Ira to go to Oak Creek,[33] to receive my dues from the horseherd. Some startling signs of more storm were to be seen in dark and skowling Clouds that floated above the Mountains for a time. The first and lower of the timbers were placed on the new store. The cloud[s] were scattered at night.

June 3, 1873; Tuesday. This morning all the indications of more rain had passed away and the indications are now rather of drouth than of rain. With Henry to help me I put some large boards on my Shop. The Sun [s]hone on us with intense heat and labor was very hard and fatiguing. After its completion I [was] quite overdone and remained at home did not go out. Theodore returned from hunting Stock having found the horse he was searching for. Lost and found my gold pen.

June 4, 1873; Wednesday. The weather is becoming warm and sumerlike. This morning made calls on buisness. Saw Mr. [Dodd] Davies the Sawyer of the Co-op Mill. He promised to saw some square pickets for me. Went with Bishop [Edward] Partridge and counted some nine hundred fence pickets which I design to use in ~~in~~ fencing my Orchard. On my return homeward I met Assesor Giles and past the Ordeal of Assessment. Did no special labor to day. Read some.

June 5, 1873; Thursday. Did not enter upon any regular work today with doing some little jobs about the place. Past the day in reading. In the afternoon received a letter from Mr. Elias Harison of Salt Lake City and Religio[-Philosophical] Journal from [Richard R.] Hopkins. Late in the afternoon Marion Called to say to me that he was going to start on the morrow for Beaver and Parowan. Our Minersville friends the Turleys called for the night. They were on their way to Salt Lake City. Received word from Paulina in Parowan.

June 6, 1873; Friday. Did not rise quite so early this morning as usual.

---

the skin, containing such ingredients as "petroleum, soap, ammonia water, oil of amber, iodine tincture, benzine, and water." Piepenbring, "For Man and Beast."

33. The Oak Creek/Oak City area thirty miles north of Fillmore was at the edge of the Canyon Mountains, about fifteen miles east of what is now Delta.

Our traviling friends haveing to wait for the ~~rair~~ ^repair^ of brother Turleys Wagon wheel. Weather increasingly warm. Not feeling well I did not engage in work to day. About noon Joseph Turley and Wife left. Fredrick [Turley] waited until 4.oclock when he started. I called at the Store where the secretary and his helpers were engaged in takeing an acount of Stock. Indications of rain this evening. Ira returned from Oak creek without stock.

June 7, 1873; Saturday. Weather warm this morning. The Boys branded the colts [and two adults][,] one a bay mare with right hind foot white and a white spot in her forehead[,] the other was a horse [with] his right hip slightly depressed. I commenced the labor of making the water ditches to my Apple trees. The heat and Labor were rather to[o] much for my endurence. I was at night uncommonly weary and not feeling [as] well as comon.

June 8, 1873; Sunday. Weather stil growing warm attended with a steady rise of the creek as the snow is fast melting in the Hill. Made call at [Noah] Bartholimew. Remained at home the most part of the day. In the afternoon went to see Mr. [John] Kelley but did not find him. The school meeting appointed for to day [a Sunday] turned out to be a failure as the dull heads who moved it concluded that buisness transacted on Sunday would ^not^ have the quality of Legality.

June 9, 1873; Monday. Weather very warm to day. I commenced making water ways to my Apple trees but found that the heat and labor were more than I could endure. This morning Lorenzo brought home for me from the Lumber yard nine hundred pickets. We piled them by the shop, not feeling well. Did not work until after noon. Theodore started this morning for Willow Creek in Juab county to get a horse of Mine that had been gone for 3 or 4 years.

June 10, 1873; Tuesday. Was engaged in the ditching and watering of my Orchard and while thus engaged I received a friendly call from Mr. Charles Smith Son of G[eorge] A. Smith. He told me that he expected his Father home[,] this [w]as [because] when last heard from he had left England homeward bound. Mr. S. invited me very warmly to call on him at his home in Provo assureing me of a hearty welcome there. He had been to Pioche.

June 11, 1873; Wednesday. I arose feeling very weary from my labors of yesterday from which I failed to rest last night. Found myself to[o] much wearied to make [a] ditch in the intense heat. Lorenzo Broak his [wagon's] doubletree and I went into the Shop and made him a new one while he made ditch[es] for me. Received of Mr. Borwin an order of Twenty dollers for Wheelbarrow which they recieved at the co-op and credited me with [the] amount on [my] Lumber acount. Meet my daughter Caroline in store.

June 12, 1873; Thursday. Was early in the orchard. The Boys at home were most of the day engaged in watching a Horse race. In the afternoon Theodore came home without the Horse whi^c^h he went after but Minus thre[e] dollers expences. I called at Mr. [Noah] Bartholimew to day and waited some time to see Mr. Pierce but he had gone out in Town [and] I did not see him. With much pain I worked out one long ditch through my Orchard and put in the water near night.

June 13, 1873; Friday. Worked in my orchard to day and completed the arangements for watering my trees. Did not go up in Town. To day Henrys Horse D$\underline{r}$ was drove up.[34] He was looking verry well [but] did not feel verry well in health. A constant weariness caused by labor is the cause. Weather verry warm with Thunder and some cloudy indications of rain which were folowed by a fine gentle rain at night.

June 14, 1873; Saturday. The air slightly cooler since the rain but becomeing hot as the day advanced. Lorenzo was trying to water his Lot where the old truth was again demonstrated that it is a difficult matter to run water up hill. Finished watering and plucking Suc^c^ers from my Fruit trees. Repaired plough and cleared out some water ditch for Priscilla. Passed some time in reading the Tribune. Weather hot and Sultry. Did not go out in town to day.

June 15, 1873; Sunday. Weather very warm and sultry. Mad[e] an early call on Mr. [John] Kelley to return his [copy of the] Tribune. Was more than usual troubled with bodily pains and a great sense of weariness. Spent the day at home[,] [my] principle company my own thoughts hap[p]y companions if of a pleasant and an agreeable character. They may beguile us of present care[,] and [they may] also open up to our minds stores of wisdom when they are the kindly sugge[s]tions of enlightened minds past away.

---

34. Veterinarians were rare. The horse doctor is mentioned again on July 24, 1873.

June 16, 1873; Monday. Was early with the trees and run the water over my own and Priscilla's Orchards during the day. About noon received a call from Marion who reported the friends generaly well in Parowan and Beaver where he and Rhoda had been visiting for the last 8 or ten days. He reported haveing meet in Beaver with our old friend Montgomery Button from California. Weather continues dry throwing almost evry day tokens of rain but they soon are disapated and the drowth continues. Marion reported the Mariage of my Daughter Maria Louisa to Mr. [John Smith] Stre[d]der and living at Meadow Creek.[35]

June 17, 1873; Tuesday. Weather very warm and sultry. Commenced prepareing some cedar fencing. Called on Mr. Bartholimew and procured from him some corn to plant to raise foder. In the afternoon I had the water on a part of my Orchard that was not included in the watering of Monday. Lorenzo was watering his ground preparitory to planting. I was much overcome with the heat and past much of the [day] in the House reading.

June 18, 1873; Wednesday. Did not ^feel^ sufficiently well this Morning to engage in Labor but Made call at Lumberyard from which most of the Lumber had been sold during the high stage of Chalk Creek which is now subsiding and there will soon be a supply of Lumber. As I we[n]t up Town I meet Uncle Sydney Farmer enroute to Salt Lake City. He reported all well in Beaver. In afternoon our friends The Turley's called on us on their way home from the City. Called on Mrs. Belinda Pratt.[36]

June 19, 1873; Thursday. Did not feel well this morning. Past the early hours in reading. Lorenzo was planting corn and the oth[e]r Boys were engaged in hunting Horses and cows but found none. I made one call in town and in afternoon looked over my Orchard and Cleared the Sukers from my trees to promote the growth of the Fruit. The work on the new Store is progressing steadily. Two masons at work to day. The other one was drunk.

June 20, 1873; Friday. This morning I saw My Son Platt[e] and wife [Adelia] just starting for Oak Creek. Joseph was with them. The Weather

35. Maria Louisa was only twenty-four when she left William Clayton. Her new husband, John Smith Stredder, was even younger at nineteen. Why Lyman did not attend their wedding is unknown.

36. Belinda was one of apostle Parley P. Pratt's widows.

was very warm. Saw some parties going to Oak Creek to a dance. Some d[r]oves of Horses passed to day from California. Called on Mr. [William] Gibbs to make bill of Lumber for my House so that I can make arangements for it when I go to Parowan next week. Received a letter from Paulina dated 17th.

June 21, 1873; Saturday. During the morning hours I wrote a letter to Paulina in Answer to one from her of date of the 17th. Made call at P. O. The Stone Lintels were placed on the new store to day. The wind high which with the influence of Liquor drank by them prevented the masons from working in the afternoon. Mr. [George] Crane called in the evening and Drunken [Andrew] Jackson Clothier anoyed us with a call.

June 22, 1873; Sunday. Was early astir as the young Men of our family with their Lady associates wer[e] going on a ride for pleasure and a picknick to the cold spring in the cinder Banks or Lava Bed of our County. I past the day in reading. Did not go out in town. Was in expectation of a call from Mr. [William] Gibbs but he did not come. Late in after noon Mr. [John] Kelley called.

June 23, 1873; Monday. Started early with Henry for Parowan. The weather was warm and pleasant all day. I was interested in noteing[,] as we ~~past~~ passed along[,] the movements and labors of the people under the influence of the diferent incentives moveing them. While some of the Settlers at Corn Creek had moved to Kanosh to build up the Kingdom of God[,] another portion remained on the old location to secure to and for themselves the few and limited advantages resulting from the others moveing away, both serving God.

June 24, 1873; Tuesday. From our camp on cove creek we started at the riseing of the Sun and traviled to Pine Creek where we halted and fed and Breakfasted after which we traviled on. The wind rising with the Sun became very anoying and very distressing all the day. We camped for the Night some two miles south of the summit south of Beaver on the road to Parowan. After Sundown and we had camped[,] we were joined by Mr. Wm Adams of Parowan on his way home from Beaver. Night pleasant.

June 25, 1873; Wednesday. Left camp while the Stars were yet sh^i^neing and traviled to Buckhorn Springs. Here we stoped and fed and I took my Breakfast with my old friend Mr. Miles Anderson. Wind not so high as yesterday. Arived in Parowan about 1.oclock. Found

Paulina some better of her attack of Quinzy [inflammation of tonsils] but not entirely recovered, tho children were well as usual. I found myself very tired from my ride of 3 days. Found the sick improveing

June 26, 1873; Thursday. Foun[d] on riseing that the weariness of the journey was but partially relieved. After Breakfast called on my old friend Daniel Page esq. and wrote up my Diary to date from the time of leaveing Fillmore. Borowed of Mr. P. the Religio-Philosophical Journal which I read during the day. Received call from Mr. John Coombs who is at present engaged in Shingle makeing with Mr. George Taylor. In the afternoon with Mrs. Lyman I called on Mrs. Jane Hanks and gave her [William] Burrow's recipt and received mine from her.

June 27, 1873; Friday. Made a morning call on Mr. [Daniel] Page and there wrote up my Diary. Procured some copies of the Weekly Tribune wh[ich] I read during the day. I[n] the afternoon Oscar came down from the Shingle Mill to get some Blacksmithing done and as he was about to start up to the mill he hurt his Thumb so he staid down all night but got no sleep for the pain of his injured Thumb. Weather very warm. Paulina's health slowly~~g~~ improveing.

June 28, 1873; Saturday. Weather stil growing warmer. Did not go out to day until late in the afternoon when I made a brief call on Mr. Riley Morses family. Received a call from Mrs. Sarah Clark and her Sister Hariet. In the evening Mr. Richard Benson came in for an hour. He had not learned until to day that I was in Town. Mrs. Jane Hanks called with the contribution of Roses for the Fare, the Specimins were very fine and beautiful.

June 29, 1873; Sunday. Weather warm and rather sultry. Passed the morning hours at home in reading. About noon went in company with Mrs. Lyman and Mrs. [Jane] Hanks to visit Mr. John Coombs and family with whom we spent the residue of the day. After Diner we received a passing call from Mrs. Joseph Fish and Mrs. J. West. After they left we had a seance. Mr. G[eorge] Taylor and wife were with us before going home. I with Mrs. L[yman] called on Mr. H. Mortisen and family. Mrs. M. ^was^ not well.

June 30, 1873; Monday. Made a morning call on Mr. [Daniel] Page and borowed of him a Religio[-Philosophical] Journal which I read during the day and helped the Boys [Paulina's sons] about the watering of the lot. Borowed and read Dr. [John C.] Gun[n]'s ~~W~~ Work on Dropsy and its treatment.[37] In the afternoon I was solicited to deliver an Oration on the 4th of July which I declined doing as I considered the contemplated demonstration to[o] Par^t^isan in its character to promote the good feelings of the people generaly, as citizens of our comon Country.

July 1, 1873; Tuesday. Weather stil very warm. Made Morning call on friend [Daniel] Page and of him borowed some reading mater for the day. Passed the day at home reading some Magazines I procured from Mrs. J[ane] Hanks. In the afternoon Wm went to the Can[y]on to the Shingle Mill. The Boys have not yet commenced cuting Shingles. Henry came down from the Mill this evening and stayed over Night. Received no calls to day. Have as yet no word from Fillmore.

July 2, 1873; Wednesday. Nothing transpired with us this morning to vary the monotinous ongoing of time. Passed the Morning hours in reading some Magazine and other Litrature. Mrs. [Jane] Hanks invited myself and Mrs. Lyman to diner. A little after noon we went and spent the residue of the day with Mrs. H. The Boys all came home from the mill this evening. They cut some [shingles] to day but their knife failed and they quit and came home.

July 3, 1873; Thursday. Weather pleasant and warm. Passed the morning hours in reading. Did not go out in Town to day. William went stockhunting but ~~w~~ met with no success. The other Boys were about Town. General quiet pervaded Town and no active demonstrations were being made for the celebration of the Nations Natal day on the morow. A dull apathy seemed brooding over the people varied only by the talk of prospective dances and horse racings. This indiference is born of false religion and devotion to its Dogmas.[38]

July 4, 1873; Friday. Arose from a night of broaken slumber as the quiet of the night had been interupted by the clang of the Bell of the Meetinghouse which was by some of youths of Town made to pour out

37. He consulted the 1868 publication, *Gunn's New Family Physician: Or Home Book of Health*, 307–14.

38. Lyman missed life in the city. In Salt Lake there were various celebrations, including a procession of the fire brigade and a band, a concert in the tabernacle, and fireworks. The *Deseret News* announced that businesses would be closed and that the daily paper would not be available because printers were taking the day off. "The Glorious Fourth"; "The Fourth," *Deseret News*, July 9, 1873.

its discordent musick on the otherwise quiet night much to the anoyence of those who wished for quiet sleep. At length the morning of the 4th dawned up on us bright and beautiful. Troops of the young men were in the streets all mounted on horses whose comfort was not increased by the Labor.

July 5, 1873; Saturday. Passed the morning hours in reading. Returned Mrs. [Jane] H[anks]'s paper [and] after this went to the Store of Watsons an[d] Roberts and bought some cloth for some shirts, and after returning home I was attacked with an obstruction in my respiration which made me very uncomfortable for several hours until the cool of evening when I found relief. My feet and ancles were much swollen. Attended with a burning sensation which partially subsided at evening. Mrs. Sarah Hakes called on us to day.

July 6, 1873; Sunday. Have passed a rather restless night and find myself much oppressed for breath feeling an almost constant sense of sufocation, and a sense of general weariness. Passed most of the day at home in reading ~~alowed~~ aloud which I found very dificult on acount of the dificulty in respiration. In the afternoon received a call from Mr. John Coombs and wife. At evening made a brief call on our old friend Daniel P. Clark and family and also on Richard Benson and family.

July 7, 1873; Monday. Did not go out to day was much troubled in my breathing during the early portion of the day. After we procured some Cactus and made of it some Drafts [extracts] and applied them to my feet, they soon eased the pain in my limbs and reduced the swelling in my feet and my breathing became easy and Natural. This morning I wrote two letters[,] one to Lorenzo and one to Mrs. Lyman in Salt Lake City. In the evening I received a friendly call from my Neighbor br Decker.

July 8, 1873; Tuesday. Rose this morning feeling some better than yesterday. My respiration was more free and my limbs less swollen than yesterday altho in the middle of the day I had some fever. The runigaway of the Horses prevented us from going up to the mill. The Boys went after the Horses and drove the cows up the canon. In the afternoon Mrs. [Jane] Hanks gave us a call and later in the evening Mr. Decker Came in and passed an hour or two in talk on various subjects.

July 9, 1873; Wednesday. This morning William came down from the Mill and brought the Teems to take us to the can[y]on. We were buisy with our preparations for the move. In the afternoon we started for the Mill where we arived a little before Sundown. On our way up we met brother Collins [Hakes] Who was on his return to Corn Creek. Further on we passed Bensons ranche. Mrs. B. greeted us kindily as we passed.

July 10, 1873; Thursday. Assisted the Boys in improveing the corrall so as to secure the cows. Late in the afternoon Oscar and Edgar Clark arived an[d] Oscar commenced puting the [mill-saw] Machine in order for work.[39] This morning Henry Started for Fillmore tired of waiting for his Load, but on his way he Met Oscar who induced him to return an[d] wait until he could give him his load. Mid day quite warm but eve and morn cool.

July 11, 1873; Friday. This morning we were awakened by a call from brother Richard Benson who came to get some help[,] for his Son Heber was suffering from an atack of pl[e]ur[isy]. Myself and Mr. B. went to see Heber whom we found in great pain. We recommended steeming with boiled pine Blocks. He was soon sweating freely which in the course of the day gave slight relief. Had the [mill-saw] Machine nearly ready to Run.

July 12, 1873; Saturday. This morning after some delay in making preperations we then commenced cuting out the shingles for Henry. By the diner hour we were fairly under way. In the afternoon I relieved Solon in making [shingles] into the night. We only lacked about two thousand of the quality Henry wanted. Heber Benson was reported to be some what better. Read some this evening.

July 13, 1873; Sunday. Passed the morning in cuting out the residue of Shingles for Henry after which we went in the afternoon to Yankee Meadow[40] to see the Clarks. We received a call to day from parties from the Coop Mill. Oscar went hunting but got no game. Heber [Benson] is reported to be worse this evening. Oscar and wife went to see him. Assisted Henry to finish loading his Shingles, for a start in early Morning.

July 14, 1873; Monday. Passed the day in helping Oscar in m[a]king some repairs on the [sawing] machine after the water failed, so that we

39. The main piece of machinery at the time was a guillotine with a large blade that dropped down to chop the wood. It was common to have a gang saw, too, with vertical blades that were moved in an up-and-down motion and made uniform widths of cuts as the logs passed through them.

40. Yankee Meadows is fifty miles southeast of Parowan near Cedar Breaks on the Markagunt Pleateau.

could not saw. Henry started for Fillmore with His load of shingles. I[n] the afternoon I went with Oscar and Edgar Clark to look for a chance to get in some more watter and we found a chance to turn another stream into Yanke Meadow so as to save what water runs during the night above the Meadow Dams[,] thus increasing our store of water.

July 15, 1873; Tuesday. To day Oscar [Lyman][,] Edgar [Clark][,] and Charley [Lyman] commenced makeing the ditch to turn the water. Worked all day on the ditch but did not get through. Heber [Benson] wa[s] very sick to day.

July 16, 1873; Wednesday. To day continued our work on the ditch which we completed in the afternoon much to our satisfaction. After we came home brother [Daniel] Clark came up from Town. And shortly after his arrival the Boys William and Porter [Clark] came with some stock which they went [with] after[ward] to Town[,] a part of which belonged to Paulina. As we were in bed Richard Benson called. He had just come from town.

July 17, 1873; Thursday. This morning Oscar and his Mother went to Town for provisions and goods. I worked with Charles and William Sawing and filling the Steemer.[41] About noon the water failed but we had nearly enough sawed to fill up [the steam box] with. After I quit work I went to call on the Bensons. Heber I found some better, while a party that had been to Fish Lake[42] returned[,] among whom was Mr. Sidney Burton. Mr. George Grimshaw and wife came up from town to see Heber.

July 18, 1873; Friday. To day finished filling the Steemer and sawed until noon and then shut off the water. In the afternoon we made some improvement in our sawing department and fited up the runway to the mill. Received a call from Mr. George Grimshaw who was up from Town to visit his Son-in-law Heber Benson. Later in afternoon we gave poison to the Squirels a goodly number of whom with some of the mouse family ate and went to sleep. E[dgar] Clark and wife went to Town to day.

July 19, 1873; Saturday. This morning we commenced cuting out [shingles] with a fair supply of water. Received an early call from Messers

---

41. After cutting, they would lash the shingles together into blocks and steam them to acquire a uniform curvature.

42. Fish Lake is more than 100 miles northeast of Parowan near what is now Capitol Reef.

Wilcox and Ward who later in the Day came with their wives and dined with us. We cut out ten thousand [shingles]. Some Thunder and lightning with showers around on the Mountains but no rain fall in our immediate vicinity. In ~~our~~ the afternoon our visitors from the Town returned home. Oscar and wife went to stay with Heber [Benson] tonight.

July 20, 1873; Sunday. This morning we finished cuting out [shingles] after which the Boys went diferent ways to spend the residue of the day in the afternoon. I went with Mrs. Lyman to call on the Bensons, found Heber able to leave his Room and go out doors. Late in the afternoon as we were returning home Mr. [Richard] Benson arived from Parowan and brought some letters and a paper. Weather cloudy with Thunder and rain in the distence around us but we were not wet.

July 21, 1873; Monday. To day we sawed and filled up [the steamer]. We had a good run of water and were filled up by noon. Some rain fell to day. Edgar Clark came up from Town to day. William put up five thousand Shingles today. Heber [Benson] is reported to be stil gaining strength. During the night some rain fell and the air became much cooler.

July 22, 1873; Tuesday. To day we cut out [shingles] by securing the help of Mr. William Benson. Charles went to Town. The Clarks brought in two Logs to day. We had the water about eight hours. The work of today proves that we can get out a cuting evry two days of about twelve thousand [pieces]. In the evening D[aniel] P. Clark and wife came along in their Wagon and invited us to go with them to call on the Bensons. We accepted the invitation and at B<u>s</u> we meet with Charles Adams & Morgan Richards from town.

July 23, 1873; Wednesday. To day commenced to fill up for another cuting. William hunted up the Teem and went to Town [to buy] some shingle racks and some other necissarys for our buisness.

Some time before noon Charles quit work which left the labor filling the Steem Box to be completed by Oscar myself and Solon. We continued Sawing until noon when we had enough in the Box for eight or ten thousand [shingles]. [The] Clarks hawled two logs. Madora went to Town with her Mother and Heber [Benson] to celebrate the 24<u>th</u>. Received letter from Lorenzo.

July 24, 1873; Thursday. To day we cut out shingles to the amount of eight or nine thousand by one <u>oclock</u>. After which Oscar and Myself made up a press to tighten up the Bunches of Shingles. Charles to the Horse Doctor and left for Town much against the wishes of his Mother. After our days work was done William and Solon and Po[r]ter Clark went to the woods and gathered some Goosberys but the[y] were much like the Indians gun costing more than they come to when cleaned sweetened and cooked.

July 25, 1873; Friday. To day we Sawed and fill[ed] up [the box] for steem~~d~~^in^g. To day our friends from Yanke Meadow Mrs. Clark and Mrs. [Sarah] Hakes with their children came to our place as their Men folks were away in Parowan. The water failed about noon. While filling the Steemer I droped a large heavy Shingle Block and crushed my foot[,] bursting it on the side of the joint of the little toe. In the afternoon Oscar went to Town. Charles came home to day.

July 26, 1873; Saturday. To day cut out the fill of [shingles] yesterday with light head of water. Finished cuting a little after noon. While at diner Brother [Daniel] Clark came from Town and after takeing diner he with the women and children returned to their home at Yanke Meadow. Some parties came to the Machine for Shingles. Oscar concluded he would try and run the Machine to make the Shingles he is oweing and some for me. As we returned to bed there was some thunder with some rain.

July 27, 1873; Sunday. This morning we sawed and bolted timber until near noon when the water failed us and we went to Yanke Meadow and called on the Clarks. After Diner Oscar and D[aniel] P. Clark went into the Mountains to see some small Lakelets and see whether their water could be made available to increase the water that propells our Shingle mill, but they found this impracticable, But we agreed to enlarge the outlet of the Meadow water so as to enlarge our supply from that water.

July 28, 1873; Monday. This morning finished sawing and filling up [the machine house] for our next cuting. Mr. D[aniel] P. Clark went to Town to day and W<u>m</u> went with him to do some [shopping] for Oscar and his Mother and get some things she wanted. My foot was so badly swollen as to keep me to the house all the afternoon during which time I kept it in cold wet clothes. Charles went to the mountain to find a chance to get some stove wood. He found a chance for poles.

July 29, 1873; Tuesday. We cut out two thirds of what we had in the Box[,] Mrs. Lyman takeing the blocks [of shingles] from the Steem Box.

After this I wrote two letters[,] one to Fillmore and one to Salt Lake City. Oscar went to the Coop Mill and after I had closed my letters William came up from Parowan and he brought me a letter from My folks in Salt Lake City. My lame foot is getting better slowly. Charles brought two loads of poles to the place to day preparitory to takeing them to town. Some indications of rain.

July 30, 1873; Wednesday. This morning we cut out the residue of the shingle Blocks left in the [steam] Box from yesterdays cuting which we completed about eleven oclock. The Benson family came and dined with us on the occasion of ~~Rl~~ Madora's twenty first Birthday. Charles went to Town with a load of poles. The proprietors of the mill have suspended work on the machine in favor of the farmers haveing the water. In the evening we went with the Benson's to Yanke Meadow and called on the Clarks and Mrs. [Sarah] Hakes. Sent letters to the Office by Oscar for the Northern Mail.

July 31, 1873; Thursday. Charles came up from Town. He brought me a letter from Lorenzo and some Magazines from Mrs. [Jane] Hanks for my reading. I passed the day in reading Leslie's paper. This evening as we were milking Oscar came home with his cow from Town. He tells me that he will move to town tomorow. The Clarks made a call on the Bensons in the afternoon and returned as we were finishing our milking. Madora went with them to her Mothers. Weather cool and pleasant.

August 1, 1873; Friday. Some indication of rain this morning. Oscar was buisy makeing preperations to move himself to Town while [he] secures his hay. In the afternoon we had some fine showers after the first of which Oscar and wife and William started for town. Some rain fell after they left attended with heavy thunder and lightning which cooled the air nicely makeing the weather fine and pleasant. I passed the day in reading, My injured foot improveing finely.

August 2, 1873; Saturday. This morning the weather was cool and fresh from yesterdays rain with its attendent thunder and lightning. Passed the morning hours in reading. Received an early call from Mr. [Edward] Willcox who is Moveing his Steem Lumber Mill from its present to a more feasible locality in the Bowery Meadow. After diner assisted Mr. Clark in rep^a^iring some damage he had done to the floor of the Machine in breaking down some of its supports which we restored with an hours anxious and hard labor. Then we resumed work with the machine.

August 3, 1873; Sunday. In the morning Mrs. Benson and family called as they were on their way to Yanke M[eadow] to spend the day with the~~y~~ Clarks. They passed on and Myself ^and Mrs. L[yman]^ folowed them when our morning labors were don[e].

As we were nearing the Meadow we were kindly meet with a Wagon by Mr. C[ollins] Hakes and caried to Mr. C[lark's] residence where we passed a pleasant day. After diner Mr. Clark and wife and Mrs. Benson went to the coop Mill; and as we returned home we wer[e] thoroughly drenched by a driveing rain storm.

August 4, 1873; Monday. This morning the water was flush from yesterdays rain and commended our cuting [at the sawmill] with a full head, which our use of the water through the day did not reduce and at the Meadow the head increased considerable. Some considerable rain fell during the early pa[r]t of the day. In the afternoon it cl[e]ared up with promise of fair weather. Received a call from Mrs. Sarah Clark who was attacked with severe head ache so she could not go to town.

August 5, 1873; Tuesday. This morning sawing and bunching. C[ollins] Hakes came up this Morning and Mr. H. took Mrs. Sarah Clark to town. She was partially recovered from her attack of illness of yesterday. We bunched four thousand shingles and filled up [the machine house] for another cuting. This Morning made maul for spliting Blocks. My lame foot gave me considerable pain today. Weather is very cold since the rain. Some light fall of rain this morning. Mrs. Lyman assisted in bunching to day.

August 6, 1873; Wednesday. This morning weather quite cool with frost. Commenced cuting with rather a meager supply of help for the work. Br [Daniel P.] Clark called on us as he was on his way to town to attend to some Official buysness as Sheriff of the County. Mrs. C. and children came down to stop with us until her husband returns. Bunched two thousand [shingles] after we stoped cuting. I wheeled away to the pile all of my shingles that were put up <u>10,000</u>.

August 7, 1873; Thursday. This morning commenced cuting [shingles]. The water stil holds up very well. Mrs. ~~Hakes~~ Clark and children left us this morning and to Mr. [Richard] Benson's place. We finished our cuting a little past two oclock after which I bunched some shingles and the Boys Charles and William cleared up the Mill yard and Burned the Bark and split some Blocks that were sawed before. Our daughter Laura has been ill from a cold and the effects of an u[l]cerated tooth attended with high fever.

August 8, 1873; Friday. I commenced the day with bunching Shingles before Breakfast after which Charles was ingaged with Sawing [and] spliting for filling up [the steamer]. I continued Bunching through the day with some interuption with my lame foot which was very painful at times so that I had to cease working for a time but with the close of the day I had the satisfaction of seeing the last of my shingles in the Bunch ready for transportation. Had some rain to day. The water is falling slowly. The weather cool.

August 9, 1873; Saturday. Comenced to cut out [shingles] about 9 oclock, and finished about 2 oclock after which Charles started for town and I with Paulina started to see the Pony Mill in Bowery Meadow. When we arived at the Mill they were sawing. While there we meet Mr. and Mrs. Harvey. Mrs. H. said Hila went to school where she taught in the city. Oscar and wife returned from town this evening all well.

August 10, 1873; Sunday. Clouds with some light rain during the day. Brother Woolley called during the shower and dined with us after which he went to the Yanke Meadow with Oscar. He was hunting stock, and left a cow with us to Milk while we stay in the can[y]on. Considerable speculation was indulged in by some of the proprietors of the Shingle Mill and some talk of sale and purchase. Oscar left this evening for Johnson's Mill where he is engaged for a month. John Coombs called on his way to the same Mill.

August 11, 1873; Monday. Made a rather late start at work at the [sawing] machine. Charles employed Joseph Brown to help on the Machine. Mr. [Richard] Benson and [Daniel] Clark made some improvement in the working of the machinery. I buisied my self bunching shingles. Rain fell almost incesently through the day. William hunted the horses but did not find them. At night rain stil falling freely.

August 12, 1873; Tuesday. Was early at work clearing up the [sawmill] machine ready for work. Light rain falling. Water was flush in our stream. We finished cuting at two ~~ocol~~ oclock, after which we continued to saw and fill up [the machine house] for tomorow. William took the teem and Wagon and went to the coop Mill for some rack timber. Mrs. Lyman and Oscar's wife went with him. I remained at the Machine bunching. Heavy rain this evening and just at dark the parties from the Mill returned wet and cold.

August 13, 1873; Wednesday. Were early at work in the [sawing] machine during the [time the] Bensons came up and spent the day with us. Mr. Clark hawled in some logs to day. We Closed out our cuting a little after 3. Oclock. Mr. Clark and wife from Yanke Meadow took supper with us. We had no rain to day. Bunched some shingles Besides cuting [them] out. From the signs it seems that [Richard] Benson is working to get the entire controll of the machine in his own intrests evincing the most supreme selfishness

August 14, 1873; Thursday. This morning we were late in beginining to cut out [shingles] but we were through a little before noon. We spent the residue of the day in bunching. We completed the puting up of Oscar's Shingles and repileing some of the racks that fell down. No rain to day. The weatherly cool. I have concluded that with the close of this week I shall close my stay in this part of the country and return to Fillmore to look after my intrest there and the fruit.

August 15, 1873; Friday. Made another cuting [at the lumber mill][,] some what less than yesterday. Did feel as well as usual. After the cuting was out I bunched some shingles the residue of the day. To day closes my engagement with Oscar to remain in the work with the Boys until the present date. At night the grand children Oscar and George were sick through the night. The weather cool and pleasant. D[aniel] P. Clark went to town to day and is going to Iron city before his return.

August 16, 1873; Saturday. Commenced to cut out [shingles] rather late in the morning. D[aniel] P. Clark came back from Town and called as he went. Oscar came home from the Mill where he had been working through the week. The children were better of their ~~flour~~ sickness. Mr. [Richard] Benson called this evening. He was sufering some from the hur[t] of his arm which he received while working with the circ[u]lar saw in Mr. Wordens Shop.

August 17, 1873; Sunday. Charles went to town yesterday and we are expecting Lorenzo from Fillmore shortly with a load of fruit. Near noon we started for Town. Joseph Brown had charge of the teem, as we were geting ready to start[,] Mr. [Richard] Benson very kindly profered us the use of his Wagon with spring seat and Brake. When we arived in town we found Lorenzo there haveing arived the night before with a few bushels of apples.

August 18, 1873; Monday. Weather very warm. The Boys Lorenzo and Charles went to the can[y]on after shingles. Called on Mr. Calhoon of the Cal[ifornia] store. He did wish to buy apples. Afterwards I with Mrs. Lyman called on Mr. [Daniel] Page and family with whom we dined. In the afternoon called at Mr. Watsons store and bought me a hat for which I paid apples, and also sold some apples to Mr. Page. The Boys returned with part of their shingles.

August 19, 1873; Tuesday. ~~In~~ In the morning were early astir geting ready for our return to the [sawmill] machine to bunch the residue of shingles there cut by Charles and remaining in the machine house. Meeting with some delays we did not start up the can[y]on until afternoon. It was very hot at first of our trip[,] but as we proceeded fart[h]er up the Mountain way we rose unto a cooler atmosphere. Mrs. Jane Hanks was with us. We found all well. Mrs. Hariet Clark was with us at night.

August 20, 1873; Wednesday. The Bensons commenced cuting shingles to day. I was buisy through the day bunching shingles. Charles went in the woods for poles with his shadow Joseph Brown.[43] Lorenzo went to Johnsons Mill to see Oscar. I was releived for an hour or two in~~ny~~ ^my^ labor by William and Po[r]ter Clark in the after part of the day and evening. Rain fell freely attended with Thunder and Lightning. In the evening Lorenzo and Oscar came from the Mill and reported Mr. J geting better.

August 21, 1873; Thursday. I was to[o] much distressed for breath to engage in work this morning. We engaged William in the bunching and Lorenzo and Charles went to town with poles and shingles. The Bensons were sawing and filling up [the machine room]. The Boys William and [son-in-law] Porter used up all of the lock Irons that were on hand. [There were] some indications of rain that were verified during the night

43. Charles was sixteen, and Joseph Lowe, who was seventeen (his step-father's name was Brown), must have been a close friend. See the entries for Aug. 11, 24.

by a heavy rain. The Boys did not return from Town as we hoped they would to bring some Iron from some of the Mills below.

August 22, 1873; Friday. My respiration was so dificult that I could not engage in any labor this morning. The Benson-boys were runing the Machine to day. For want of racks we could not do any Bunching. Our friends Mrs. Hanks and Mrs. Clark and Oscar['s] wife we[n]t to visit Mrs. Benson. About Sundown the Boys returned from town but brought no Iron for racks so our dificulty in that respect stil remains. Some rain fell during the night.

August 23, 1873; Saturday. My health did not alow me to work to day. Mrs. Clark went to her home this morning and M[a]dora went with her. Mr. Richard Benson[,] to evince his Ruling p[a]ssion of greed[,] hauled two loads of our unbunched shingles away from the Machine as we could not Bunch them for want of Iron. Mrs. Hanks went to town with Mr. B. In the evening Oscar and John Coombs came from Johnsons whom they report dieing. Mr. C. lodged with us and Oscar stoped at the Meadow.

August 24, 1873; Sunday. This Sunday passed very quietly by. The Boys were hunting horses until noon when Charles and Joseph Brown started for town. The latter takeing a load of poles[,] Oscar and John Coombs starting down on foot. D[aniel] P. Clark called on us this afternoon. He brought a log to the Machine. While he was with us it rained lightly. After we had ret[i]red to bed Oscar and the other Boys returned from town.

August 25, 1873; Monday. This morning we were early astir geting ready to move back to Parowan [from Yankee Meadows]. During [which] we were ap^p^arently closely wached by Mr. R[ichard] Benson to see that we did not carry off any thing that did not belong to us. Oscar's Wife moved with us to day. We arived home [in Parowan] about 3. oclock without accident. Late this evening Charles returned to the Machine to get some shingles to freight to [North] Star for Mr. Edward Wilcock for which he was to recieve $4. dollers per thousand and one doller and seventy five sents freight per 1000.

August 26, 1873; Tuesday. Passed the day at home mostly in reading. In the afternoon Charles came down from the machine with his load of shingles. The Boys were buisy geting ready for the Morning start. Lorenzo for Fillmore and Charles for [the North] Star District. Received call from Mr. Coombs and wife. At night spent an hour with the Coombses at their residence. Had a siting but no marked results. Weather warm and pleasant.

August 27, 1873; Wednesday. This morning we started about 9 oclock and we traviled to and stoped at Buckhorn springs and made a noon halt for refreshment and at that place we meet the Son of Mr. ~~Orson~~ H[orace] K. Whitney who informed me that his Aunt Mrs. Sarah A[nn] Whitney was laying at the point of Death in Salt Lake City.[44] Were meet here Mr. Jackson Stewart, Surveyor who remarked to me propheticaly that in 3 years we should have a Railroad starting from the Iron Works south and meeting the extension of the Utah Southern.[45]

August 28, 1873; Thursday. Left camp early on the South side of the Beaver Ridge and as we passed throug[h] Beaver I saw and spoke with Charles Wood House and Mr. G[eorge] W. Crouch. Made Noon halt at Indian Creek and as we passed up Wild Cat [Creek] we found a Well that had Been recently Made which was 105 fts deep with five feet of water. We camped near the foot of the Hill north of Cove Creek Fort. Found teems there for Pioche.

August 29, 1873; Friday. Left camp early and traviling on we stoped in Dog Valley, and got water for our teem. Mr. John Webb and some other parties are diging for water. They are down about 60 feet. No water yet. They have the word of a water witch that they will find abundant water. They calculate to push their experiment. We dined at Canosh with our friends the Hakeses. The Old man went with us to Fillmore. I paid him three dollers for shoemaking. He stayed with us all night. Arived home at 9 oclock all well.

August 30, 1873; Saturday. Called on Mr. [John] Kelley at the free-trade store and asertained the state of my account with the Store, after which I called on Marion at his Office and then took a look through the Lumber in the yard and found varieties suiting my wants for my house, and mad[e] an arangement with [him] to draw the Lumber on what he

---

44. Sarah Ann Whitney had been a plural wife to both Joseph Smith and Heber C. Kimball and was still only forty-eight years old when she died on September 4, 1873.

45. There was excitement when the Utah Southern Railroad reached Provo in late 1873. Three years later, it had still not made it as far as the southern part of the state, falling fifteen miles short of Nephi and about 200 miles away from the iron furnaces. An 1881 extension took it to the boom town of Frisco, west of Milford, still 100 miles from Cedar City.

was owing me, after which I called at the Post Office and then called on Marions wife Clarisa, where I meet her Mother.

August 31, 1873; Sunday. I passed the morning hours in reading during which time My Son-in-law Edwin Bartholimew called on me with his daughter Gay, who is just recovering from sickness. About Noon I went to dine with my daughters Maria Louisa and Lelia at the residence of Mrs. Bartholimew. Before and while at diner we had a shower of rain making mud in the street. Diner over I returned home and wrote and posted a letter to Mrs. L[yman] in the City, telling her of Lorenzo's comeing for her.

September 1, 1873; Monday. Commenced my labor to day by procureing a bill of the finishing lumber needed for my House, which I dispached by Mail to Parowan to be filled by my Son Oscar who is working in one of the Steem mills there. This done I went to the lumber yard and bought some lumber for battons [battens] which Lorenzo hauled home for me. Theodore laid a part of the shingles on his Mother's Kitchen. Weather very warm. In the evening went to Mr. Robinson's House to see some [of] the finishing work of [William] Gibbs.

September 2, 1873; Tuesday. This morning Lorenzo started for Salt Lake. Priscilla's boys finished puting ~~on~~ the shingles on her Kitchen, during the forenoon. In which time I made some calls around town after which I commenced to clear up about my shop and in the afternoon commenced with the help of Henry to lay the shingles on my shop but I found myself unable to continue at that work so I gave up the job to Henry who about half completed it during the afternoon. Will be able to finish it tomorrow.

September 3, 1873; Wednesday. To day I continued fiting up things in my shop and Henry continued and with some help from the other Boys finished the shingleing early in the afternoon. Today I began to gather the windfall Appels from my Orchard saveing the best for drying and the others for Pig feed. Late in the afternoon I called on the Gibb's for some information in regard to m[y] House but found them engaged in makeing [a] Coffin for a stranger who died this morning at the residence of Mr. Bartholimew, of consum[p]tion.

September 4, 1873; Thursday. This morning I gathered up apples from a portion of my Orchard and in the afternoon prepared some for drying and put them out. Henry commenced cuting the weeds in the orchard. Ira was hauling rock for Mr. Barrows and his Partner. Theodore was working for Mr. McNeal. Late in the afternoon I called on Mr. [John] Kelley at the store where I learned by reading the Religio-Philosophical Journal that my old friend W[alter] E. Dodge was cut off the [LDS] Church.[46]

September 5, 1873; Friday. Passed the morning in gathering apples and found that some reckless cow not haveing the fear of the Dog sufficiently before her eyes had destroyed a portion of my appels prepared with so much labor the day before. Found my revolver minus the loading rod shot away by a double discharge caused by being loaded~~g~~ with imperfect bullets which dificulty can be avoided by puting some talow on top of the charge when loaded. This will prevent the double discharge.

September 6, 1873; Saturday. This morning was at work with my fruit. Ira started for Clear Lake after hay. Expects to return tomorow. Received some circulars by mail advertseing a large gift enterprise of 1½ Million dollers. Commenced to cut my peaches to day. After I had cut and put out my Peaches I paired and cut some appels after which I went up town and meet Marion and the Assessor and aranged the settlement of my Taxes for this year. John Kelley returned from the city to day with goods.

September 7, 1873; Sunday. Rose early as usual and took a walk in my orchard. And after breakfast I wrote a letter to Mr. S[tephen] S. Jones remiting him five dollers in curency in pay for his paper but when I called at the Post Office I was told I could not have my letters registered until tomorow. This will keep brother Jones out of his money a day longer. Ira returned to day all right with his hay. After leaving the P.O. I called on Mr. [John] Kelley at his residence. Then I returned home and pared and cut some Appels and put them to dry.

September 8, 1873; Monday. Rose early and cut some Appels after writing my Journal, then I called on Marion at his office and with him made some estimates of the lumber for my house and while there I meet ~~m~~ Mr. Giles the Assessor and settled my Taxes for this year. After which I came home and Cut some App^e^ls and then I went to the Lumber

46. Walter Dodge, who was sent by Brigham Young to southern Utah to make wine, informed the publication that he had been "cut off from the church for reading your paper, and for not knowing that Christ died for me." He affirmed that he would not exchange "all [the] other papers in the world" for his subscription to their periodical. "Voices from the People," *Religio-Philosophical Journal*, Sept. 4, 1873, 6.

yard and commenced selecting my Lumber for my house and fence. Weather very warm.

September 9, 1873; Tuesday. ~~Rose early as usual an[d] took a walk in my Orchard. After Breakfast I wrote a letter to S. S. Jones of Chicago remiting to him five dollers in curency in pay for his paper but as I called on the Post Master he told me he could not register my letter until~~

Past the morning hours in helping Ira to load his appels for Sandpete market. And in the afternoon with the help of Henry and Ira selected and piled some of the Joists and Rafters for my house. Mr. Gibbs promised to select lumber for the frames.

September 10, 1873; Wednesday. Gathered and pared some Apples. Henry began to clear off the weeds from the ground where I desig~~h~~n building my House. These labors engaged us until Noon. In the afternoon I went with Henry to the Lumber yard, and selected some more lumber for my House. While there Mr. William Gibbs came and made a selection of the lumber for the Door and Window frames. Sent Bill to Saw Mill for the residue of the Joists for my House.

September 11, 1873; Thursday. Was engaged most of the day in the work of clearing off the ground on which I de[s]ign to build next spring. Heard to day that Lorenzo and Mrs. [Mary] Kelley and Mrs. Lyman would arive here on Saturday from the City. The weather is very warm and sultry. The fruit is ripening very fast and will crowd us to take care of it so as to save it from wasting.

September 12, 1873; Friday. Was early at work with my fruit called on Mrs. Richmond to see her Peach parer. She said it did not work very well but I came to the conclusion that principal trouble was in their not knowing how to use it and the improper state of the fruit its being to[o] ripe and soft. I called at Mr. John Cavanah and his lady. Used their pairer while I was there. It p[a]red the peaches well.

September 13, 1873; Saturday. Brushed up my shop and put some fruit out to dry. Were in expectation of Mrs. Lyman comeing to day but time passed and disapated the Illusion. Just at night I received a letter from Lorenzo dated the 9th. He said he should start that afternoon at 2 oclock. This delay will prevent his arival to day. In the afternoon we cut some Peaches for Priscilla. While we were thus engaged the Widow [Ruth] Turley and her Son Omner came from Beaver.

September 14, 1873; Sunday. Rose from my first sleep in my shop feeling refreshed. Called on Mr. [Noah] Bartholimew and with him went to have a look at the Free trade store in reference to some features in its finish. We found the work aproximating readiness for the plastering. This morning I read ~~tow~~ two Numbers of the Tribune of Salt Lake from which it appears that the great reactionary and regenerative work is going on in the city and country. Mrs. Lyman arrived to night.

September 15, 1873; Monday. Commenced Moveing my Lumber home from the yard but did not bring it all. Commenced with Mrs. L[yman] to work on the fruit which [is] now ripening very fast. I was attacked with Diareah which made me quite sick for a night and a day. Lelia mad[e] a call and stayed with us during the day. Edwin called in the afternoon. Marion and children called this morning.

September 16, 1873 Tuesday. Was out early gathering fruit on which we worked during the day. To day Henry brought home with his teem the residue of the Lumber which I had selected. In the afternoon I began to feel somewhat relieved from my attack of illness. Did not leave home during the day. In the evening we went to Marion's. On the way we made a momentary call ~~of~~ on Mrs. Kelley who said she was feeling slightly better than on yesterday.

September 17, 1873; Wednesday. Was early among the fruit and my health was slightly improved since last night. Worked until 4 oclock when we went to call on Edwin and Lelia. When we arived there we met Mr. ^Mc^Neal and Miss Matilda Bartholimew. Mrs. M. and Miss B. went home before night. We took Super and then returned home near nine oclock. I had during the night another attack of the Disentary tho not so severe as before.

September 18, 1873; Thursday. Arose this morning feeling rather ill but went about work with the fruit and so p[a]ssed the day feeling better as the day advanced. Late in the afternoon we received a call from Mrs. Struder and Mrs. Bartholimew and also Mrs. Turley. Some indications of rain which were verified by a gentle rain through the night. This hurried us in covering our fruit we had put out. In the evening we cut and prepared some Apples for drying.

September 19, 1873; Friday. Was early among [the apple trees] my health not yet returned to its usual tone. After morning hours I went to the Store and to the P. O. And while I was out I Bought two chairs of Gabriel Huntsman for which I paid three dollers and fifty cents. On my return to my shop I felt much weak and weary from my walk. Our Little grand Son M[arion] Clayton was with us through the day. Mrs. [Ruth] Turley called in the evening.

September 20, 1873; Saturday. Worked at my fruit during the day but did not feel well in health. Rhoda Visited us today. Had her youngest daughter with her. Marion called late in the afternoon. I received a letter to day from Paulina in Parowan reporting all well there. Lorenzo to day secured the chance of a load of freight from the city for Johnson & Barows. He starts north Monday or next week if all is well. Put some batons [battens] on the shop.

September 21, 1873; Sunday. Rose early this morning[,] the weather stil fine and pleasant. Passed the day mostly with the Bartholimews and Mrs. Gillmer. While there I wrote a letter to Paulina in Parowan in relation to the Lumber I had previously ordered at that place. I went to the Office with my letter and then returned home. Mrs. [Ruth] Turley called on us this morning. We had some talk in relation to the purchase by her of a home in Fillmore.

September 22, 1873; Monday. This morning Lorenzo started for S. Lake City for goods for Johnson and Barows. John Kelley went with him We were busy at home with our fruit of which we sent a small package of green and dried [fruit] to our children in the city. Mrs. Lelia Bartholimew was with us until late in the afternoon. After this we gathered our Apples for the evening's cuting which finished about 9. oclock and then retired weary to rest which was undisturbed by care and blest with pleasant dreams.

September 23, 1873; Tuesday. Was early at work with my fruit. Turned out a pretty good lot of Apples and Peaches and during the day Omner Turley came in and talked about buying some fruit to take with him to Beaver for which place he said he should start tomorow in the morning. At night made a good evenings work with the Apples, and then retired weary. The night was quite cool and dry for the fruit.

September 24, 1873; Wednesday. Worked at my fruit until Breakfast after which I went up town and called on Mr. [John] Kelley at the Store an[d] bought some sugar and some domestic [cloth] for sacks for my fruit.[47] Called at P. O. and found a letter for [daughter-in-law] Synth[i]a from Cal[ifornia]. Sold some Peaches and Apples to Omner Turley who started for the South this Morning. While here he Bought Mr. Paul's place for his Mother, a home they [will] have in a month. Marsden and Mrs. Benson called for the night.

September 25, 1873; Thursday. Rose early and was at work until breakfast after which I went to the Store and the P. O. Received a letter from the Religio Philosophical Publishing House in Chicago, to which I wrote an answer. Mr. Struder and wife were with us to day.[48] In the afternoon Mrs. Lelia Bartholimew called on us and also Mrs. Synthia L[yman] called. Cut Apples in the evening. The wind blew some to night but brought no rain.

September 26, 1873; Friday. Gathered and cut a lot of peaches this mroning and after Breakfast I went to the P. O. and bought some Stationary. Bought me a pocket knife. Returned home not feeling very well. After geting the fruit on hand pared[,] I laid down for a short time, had a little sleep. Called on some parties in regard to Adobi makeing but did not make any arangements with any of them. I[n] the afternoon Mr. and Mrs. Struder called and spent the evening.

September 27, 1873; Saturday. I Worke[d] in the fruit through the day. About mid day I called at the Cal[ifornia] Store and bought some Sard^i^nes and some suspenders. Returned to the Free Trade and waited some time for Mr. [John] Kelley to return from di[n]ner. I bought of him some candles, and then returned home and continued my work with the fruit. Late in the afternoon My Son Theodore and his Uncle Stephen Franklin and wife with Mrs. Phebe Bingham arived from [North] Star.

September 28, 1873; Sunday. The night was very cold but the morning opened bright and fair. After Breakfast Mrs. L[yman] and myself took a walk around my Lots on the Bench and while out we found the corner stake at the Northeast Corner of my Block of six lots. After our Ramble we went to and spent the day with the Kelleys. Had a very pleasant visit. After our return home we received some evening calls from some of our friends. The evening was quite cool.

47. Domestic cloth was unbleached cotton, sometimes called muslin ("calico" in England), used for backing quilts, straining cheese, and making inexpensive clothing.

48. Lyman consistently misspells the name of his son-in-law, John Stredder, who married Lyman's daughter Maria Louisa, rendering the name "Struder."

September 29, 1873; Monday. Began the week's work with the fruit. The weather growing slightly warmer. Mr. [Stephen] Franklin started fore Gunison in Sandpete County for grain. Mrs. [Ruth] Turley called this morning. She was not feeling very well. Did not go up town to day.

Mr. Ayres from Parowan enroute for Salt Lake called and Bought some fruit for eating. In the evening we continued our work with the fruit. We felt the weather was growing warmer.

September 30, 1873; Tuesday. Weather mild this morning. Mr. Isaac Turley enroute for Sandpete called and passed on his way. Mr. John Struder to day grubed up the Greesewood along the Street side of my Orchard, fence, and commenced removeing the sand drift that had accumulated since the seting of the fence. Received one load of Lumber from the yard. Hawled home by Henry[,] the Bill but partially filled, will have another load tomorow. Weather stil mild and warm.

October 1, 1873; Wednesday. Dit [Did] not work in the fruit to day. Mrs. Lyman washed and I received some Lumber from the yard. Marion started for Conference, before going he settled my Lumber Bill with the coop on acount of what he was owing me. Later in the afternoon I made some measurements to determine the front line of my house I expect to build next spring. Mrs. Lelia Bartholimew was with us through the day. Mrs. Struder called in the evening. Received letter from Paulina in Parowan.

October 2, 1873; Thursday. Wrote letter to Paulina and as I went to the P. O. I meet Edwin Web and engaged him to make my Adobies for the Partitions in my house. He agreed to make them for $4.50/100 per thousand. Past the residue of the day working with the fruit. Mrs. Struder was with us to day makeing presrves. I[n] the evening Mrs. Franklin called. Weather stil mild and good for drying fruit. My legs and feet are swelling badly evry day. They give me no pain as yet.

October 3, 1873; Friday. Cleared off the s[u]c[k]ers from a couple of rows of fruit trees before Breakfast after which I worked at the fruit until near night when I mad[e] a call up town an[d] bought me a long handled round pointed steel shovel for which I paid one doller and fifty cents. Returned home and gathered and cut out a lot of peaches. Received a call from Mr. [Stephen] Franklin who [ha]d just returned from Gunison with a load of wheat for which he paid.65 cents per Bushel.

October 4, 1873; Saturday. Was working in the fruit all the day through. Called on Mr. [Peter] Silda in view of engageing him to do some work for me in prepareing my fenceing which he promised to do for me as I wanted. Received a passing call from Mr. James Thompson of Canara,[49] enroute to the City of Salt Lake. Late in the afternoon Mr. Franklin and wife called for a short time. Some indications of rain which induced us to cover our fruit after which the clouds dispersed. Had pleasant night.

October 5, 1873; Sunday. This morning received a call from Mr. Edwin Bingham and wife. Mr. Bingham paid me twenty dollers in curency on his due bill which I held of ninety dollers leaveing the balence of seventy dollers yet due me.

After breakfast myself and Mrs. Lyman started out to make some calls[,] the first at Mr. Bartholomews. From there we went to Marion's and dined with Rhoda. From the^re^ went to Mr. [John] Struders and then to Amasa [Jr.]'s then to Lelia's. Found Edwin gone to Sandpete.

October 6, 1873; Monday. Was early at work with the fruit. The weather was very warm with Thunder and lightning folowed later in the day by light showers of rain which made it necissary to take in and cover our fruit to prevent [it] from being injured by the rain. Our friends Bingham and Franklin started for home to day. In the afternoon I called at the store where I received a copy of the Religio[-Philosophical] Journal. Weather much cooler after the rain.

October 7, 1873; Tuesday. Passed the morning in working with the ^fruit^. After Breakfast wrote a letter to my old friend Richard R. Hopkins in Salt Lake City. Went with it to the P. O. On my return called at the Free trade [store][,] bought some things and then came home and was engaged with the fruit through the afternoon and evening. Weather much cooler since the Thunder and Lightning. Mr. [John] Struder worked on my side walk. To day I spent an hour clearing up on the inside of the Street fence.

October 8, 1873; Wednesday. Before Breakfast I worked for an hour on the Sidewalk. Past an hour prepareing fruit for preserveing. Mrs. L[elia] Bartholimew was with us to day. In the afternoon my Sons Marion and Amasa [Jr.] called on us the former haveing been called on a mission to Europe by the Late General Conference. He starts from Fillmore on

49. Kanarra (later renamed Kanarraville) lies south of Cedar City. Its residents were refugees from the flood of 1862 that washed away Fort Harmony.

Sunday morning next for Salt Lake City from whence he goes immediately to the field of his Labor, and folly.

October 9, 1873; Thursday. Worked an hour or two on the Sidewalk then took Breakfast after which I went to the Lumber yard until after noon during which time I selected the rails that were lacking for my fence. While on the yard meet with my old time friend Appleton Ha^m^mon~~d~~. Meet Marion for a few moments in his Office and learned the state of my accounts with the co-op. Returned home and moved my fence pickets into the shop.

October 10, 1873; Friday. Worked an hour or two on the sidewalk and after Breakfast called on Marion at his Office. Aranged for the purchase of four City lots which join the lots that belong to the Boys on the east. Found some Butter at the freetrade [store]. In the afternoon went to the Lumberyard with Lorenzo and commenced selecting the Boards for the Base of my fence but owing to the maner in which the Lumber was piled we only got a part of what we wanted. The clerk promised to select the residue as it came in.

October 11, 1873; Saturday. Was early at work on the Street before the Sun was up and after the Breakfast hour I went to the Lumber yard and selected some thin Lumber for Bat[te]ning[50] my shop some two hundred an[d] nineteen feet. The Boys all gone for wood to day [and] will return tomorow. After Sundown received a call [visit] from Mr. [Peter] Silda. In the evening cut some Apples and put them out to dry. Received a brief call from Mr. John Cavanah who was hunting Landmarks.

October 12, 1873; Sunday. Weather very warm to day. Passed the morning at home and afternoon ^went^ with Mrs. Lym[an] and made a call at the residence of Mr. Edwin Bartholimew but found they were from home. We returned home feeling much wearied with the walk and the heat. After resting at home for a short time we went to Mr. [John] Kelleys where we took tea and remained in the evening until half past seven Oclock when we returned home weary but feeling better in health than in the morning.

October 13, 1873; Monday. This morning Henry hauled home the

50. Board-and-batten siding involved a row of vertical planks, the seams covered over by narrow strips of wood, and sometimes a second layer of planks arranged horizontally.

Bat[te]ning from the Lumber yard. Received a call from Marion in relation to a [financial] settlement. In the afternoon with Lorenzo's help I put the Bat[te]ning on the shop. This kept us very buisy until Sundown. Lelia was with us to day. Mrs. Lyman was makeing preperations for her return to the City of the Saints. The weather growing constantly cooler with some indication of storm.

October 14, 1873; Tuesday. This morning after Breakfast I called on and settled with Marion after settleing my account for Lumber with the co-op. There remained due on his Note to me a Balence of one hundred and twenty nine ^dollers^ and forty cents to be paid the first day of Jan 1874. I received of him twenty-one [sacks of flour weighing] one-hundred lb[s]. and sixteen fifty lb. sacks of Flour, at three an[d] a half dollers per hundred. To night some snow fell[,] loading heavily the fruit trees. The fruit was not injured.

October 15, 1873; Wednesday. This morning called on Mr. [William] Gibbs at the Tithing House for some advice in regard to my Lumber for my house. In the afternoon with Henry's help I sorted and repiled my thin Lumber preparitory for winter. Worked some with the fruit. Mrs. Lyman makeing ready for her return to the City. The weather cool and frosty since the fall of snow. Made trench for burying my Apples.

October 16, 1873; Thursday. Were early astir in expectation that Mrs. Lyman would start on her return to the city this morning but some hindrences occuring. Mr. Bartholimew did not start until about 2. Oclock in the afternoon when I was left to the enjoyment of a Bachelor's Bliss and all that was pleasant in the cold weather. Repiled some more of my Lumber. This afternoon Henry brought home the last of my Lumber from the yard.

October 17, 1873; Friday. Was early at work on the sidewalk and after Breakfast I went to the Lumber yard and bought some planks to put on the wagons for hawling Rock for my House. The ^first^ two loads of which they, Ira and Henry[,] hawled on to the ground to day. In the afternoon I gathered some of my winter Apples into the trench for burying. The weather is slightly warmer than yesterday. Saw Mr. [Nicholas] Paul he said he would work here next week.

October 18, 1873; Saturday. Worked on the sidewalk this morning after which went up town for an hour after which I came home and repiled some of my Lumber to clear the way to my building ground. After noon I made some measurements and set some stakes indicating the locality of my house. The Boys hawled 4 loads of rock to day[,] two from the canon and two from Pine Creek. Weather still growing mild and warm.

October 19, 1873; Sunday. Weather warm and pleasant. The local Conference of the Saints is in Session since Saturday morning. Wrote a letter to my friend Richard R. Hopkins Salt Lake City, from whom I received the R[eligio-] P[hilosophical] Journal and Ban[n]er of Light, in reading which I passed a portion of the day. As I went to the P. O. I mee[t] Mr. Brown the Lawyer from Beaver. He is stoping a few days on buisness of his profesion.

October 20, 1873; Monday. Spent an hour or two on the Sidewalk before Breakfast. Worked some part of forenoon in takeing care of and sorting the Appels that were in the Shop and moveing them to the Loft so as to make room for work in the Shop below. I gathered my Paimains [pearmains] for winter and put them in the ground to the amount of five Bushels, with some others, [and] took in the last of my dried fruit.

October 21, 1873; Tuesday. Worked on the sidewalk before Breakfast after ^which^ repiled some of my Lumber to make room for the rock the Boys ar[e] to hawl for the House. After this spent some time in sawing fence pickets. After diner I went to the Brick yard to learn the state of the Adobie makeing and found that none had been made since last week when I visited the yard before. [I] came home and gathered some appl[e]s and buried them. Weather cold.

October 22, 1873; Wednesday. Worked some hours on the sidewalk and the Boys hawled wood from Cedar Mountain. After breakfast I went to gathering the residue of the Apples in my Orchard some of which were touched with the frost of last night altho not very seriously injured. After secureing the apples I sawed pickets for an hour and after night rep[a]ired some breakage on Priscilla's Lamp. The weather somewhat milder than yesterday. Boys returned at dark with wood.

October 23, 1873; Thursday. Worked on the Sidewalk. Called on the Widow Robinson and filled my under bed from her stack of ^straw^. Returned home and sawed pickets for a while and after diner with Henry's help I gathered some of the apples from the last of the trees in my

Orchard but the wind was so high we did not get them all. Mr. Isaac Turley called for the night during which the snow began to fall. He is enroute for home.

October 24, 1873; Friday. Performed my morning tour of work on the Street. After Breakfast went up in town. The snow was falling freely giving to evry thing around a wintry aspect. Bro. Turley went on his way home. Returned home after purchaseing some hardware for fiting up my work bench. Sorted my winter Apples that were not buried and moved them so as to have room to work at the Bench, and late in the afternoon commenced dressing fence pickets.

October 25, 1873; Saturday. Rose early this morning and dressed fence pickets until B[r]eakfast call. Weather cold but pleasant. ~~I there~~ In the afternoon there were some indications of storm in the North which subsided after an abortive attempt to give more snow. The cold was to[o] intense for this, night came on increasingly cold and frosty. Received a letter of adieu from my Son F[rancis] M. Lyman from Salt Lak[e]. His address is 42 Islington Liverpool.

October 26, 1873; Sunday. Weather bright and pleasant. While some of the children went to meeting, I wrote a letter to Mrs. Lyman in Salt Lake City and as I went to the P. O. to post my letter I received a letter from R[ichard] R. Hopkins Salt Lake City; and also two papers the R[eligio-] P[hilosophical] journal and Ban[n]er of Light. The snow was melting some to day altho towards evening the air was chilly sufficient to freeze. The night was cool and frosty.

October 27, 1873; Monday. Worked until Breakfast call, after which I worked at the picketts until after diner when I went up in town and called on the clerk of the co-op in reference to the dividend on the Stock herd, he told me the dividend would be declared on the second Monday in Nov next. The weather continues warm and the snow is disappearing quite fast. I called on Mr. [William] Gibbs for a bill of the timber needed in my house for lintl[e]s and went to the Lumber yar^d^ and bought it. 100 feet.

October 28, 1873; Tuesday. Was early at the Bench and at Breakfast call had dressed 50 pickets. After breakfast worked at the bench until Noon. After diner I sorted and Buried for the winter the residue of my apples. This done I went to the Street and cleared off some 30 feet of the

Sidewalk. The Melting snow had much softened the ground. While on the Street Mr. [Nicholas] Paul pased with Lime. He told me he should come in again tomorow to work.

October 29, 1873; Wednesday. Was early at work at the Bench, at which I continued until noon. After diner I completed my work on the sidewalk after which I sawed the residue of my square pickiting. The weather quite warm in the afternoon. There was a stock drive at Cedar springs to day. Mesers Bartholimew and [John] Kelley returned to day from Salt Lake City where they had been to buy goods and attend to other buisness. Received Star Spangled Ban[n]er [magazine] to day.

October 30, 1873; Thursday. Made my Morning tour of work at the Bench. After Breakast Made some calls in town and received My Watch from Mr. [John] Kelley and some Notes on hand [of payments due me], on B[enjamin] H. Robins[on] and F[rancis] M. Lyman. Called on Mrs. Rhoda Lyman and Made an indorsement of what Marion had paid on his Note leaveing a Balence due Me of 129 dollers 40/100 to be paid the firs[t] of Jan. 1874.

October 31, 1873; Friday. Was early at work and kept to the Bench until the Middle of the Afternoon when I had dressed 150 pickets and left the same number to dress on tomorow to finish the flat pickets. In the afternoon went to the Store and helped to put away the goods which were freighted by Mr. [Henry] Noyes from the City. Received my Auger bit which I sent for by Mr. [John] Kelley. Lorenzo received his tools.

November 1, 1873; Saturday. Before breakfast this morning Mr. [Nicholas] Paul called on me for the purpose of laying out the foundation of my house. This done I spent the residue of the day in dressing the residue of my flat pickets to the number of 150, which work I completed by a little after Sundown. The weather continues warm and pleasant. Received the papers the R[eligio-] P[hilosophical] Journal and Ban[n]er of Light. They wer[e] specialy rich this week with contributions from Bradlaw & [James M.] Peebles.

November 2, 1873; Sunday. Wrote a letter to my friend [Richard] Hopkins in Salt Lake City after which I went to Mr. [John] Struders with whom and Lady [Maria Louisa] I taried a few hours and took diner after which I called on Mr. [John] Kelley at his residence. Then by his request I went with Him to call on Mr. [Peter] Silda but he was not at home. We returned and stoped some time with Priscilla. I then went to Mr. Ks residence and stayed until evening and took super.

November 3, 1873; Monday. This morning I was early at work diging for the foundation of my house. The Boys Henry and Ira were hawling ^cobble^ rock for the under part of the foundation, I dug the trench 2 x 2 feet across one end, and found myself very weary at night. After finishing my days work I went to the free Trade Store and bought me a coat for which I paid $13. dollers and also bought a knit Jumper for 2.50.

November 4, 1873; Tuesday. Was early on the trench. Joh[n] Struder worked for me to day. We dug out two lines of the large trench the length and the width of the House. The Boys Henry and Ira were hawling Cobbles. In the afternoon I went up in town to find a chance of geting some cobbles to finish the work of the foundation. Obtained leave to hawl from the public square and also from Mr. Andersons Lot.

November 5, 1873; Wednesday. Was early at work on the foundation and John Struder was with me. Henry and Ira were hauling rock in the morning and in the after noon Ira started for Clear Lake with John Borin for hay. I repiled some of my Lumber so as to make way for the Wagons around the House; and also repiled some of the rock on the Ground to make ~~room~~ for more. In evening called at the Store.

November 6, 1873; Thursday. Was early at work. The indications of storm of yesterday have all subsided and the prospects are good for continued fair weather. Henry was hawling Cobbles to day. He secured the chance of a large pile of Cobbles on the place of Mr. Jensen. After quiting work I called on Edwin and Lelia and took super with them. When I returned home [I] found Mr. Kershaw there enroute for Salt Lake City.

November 7, 1873; Friday. Worked in ^the^ trenches before Breakfast. In the forenoon I called on Mrs. Rhoda Lyman and borowed a Wheel barrow for moveing the dirt from the foundation of my House. In the afternoon made some preparation for finishing up my pickets for my fence. This evening Omner [Turley] and Theodore [Lyman] came home. Ira also came home with hay from Clear Lake and Henry hawled Rock.

November 8, 1873; Saturday. Was out to work while the Stars were yet on their watch for the comeing day. The Boys hawled no rock to day. I made a begining of the division fence between my lots and Priscilla's. Late in the afternoon it was anounced that General [George R.]

Maxwell[51] and Mr. [Cyrus M.] Hawley from Beaver would speak to the people, which they did in the State House. Their talk had the effect to somewhat riffle[52] the tide of Mormon feeling.[53]

November 9, 1873; Sunday. This morning I wrote a letter to Paulina After which made a brief call at Mr. Bartholimew's. After 12. oclock went to the P. O. and droped my letter in the Box. The office not being open I did not receive my Mail mater as I expe^c^ted. General Maxwell left town on the Stage for Salt Lake City. He was acompanied by Mr. Duncan, U. S. Deputy Marshall. The news of J[ohn] D. Lee's arest is to day confirmed he is in Irons at Camp in Beaver.[54]

November 10, 1873; Monday. Worked until the Breakfast call moveing the earth from my house ground [yard]. I then worked at boreing pickets until 2. oclock, when I went to the P. O. and got the R[eligio-] P[hilosophical] Journal and from there I went to the Meeting of the Stockholders of the Cooperative Mercantile Institution. They declared a Dividend of 12. per cent for the last half year. Came home and worked until night and then read the Journal.

November 11, 1873; Tuesday. Worked at boreing my pickets for fence. John Struder finished wheeling out the dirt from the House ground [yard] after which he was engaged the residue of the day in clearing up the ground on the inside of the Street fence by the Orchard. In the afternoon I called on the Sec of the Co-op Store and got a due bil for the last

---

51. Maxwell was the thirty-one-year-old US Marshal for Utah Territory, originally from Michigan, a veteran of the Michigan Cavalry Brigade under George Armstrong Custer. During the Civil War, he lost a leg and several fingers at the Battle of Five Forks and Gettysburg. His traveling companion was a territorial supreme court judge, originally from Illinois. When a discovery reached the newspapers that Hawley had a second wife and children back in Illinois, Utah polygamists were delighted to see the anti-polygamy judge squirm.

52. "Riffle" meant to "channel," in this case to mollify (the opposite of "ruffle"), according to Webster's 1828 dictionary.

53. The US Army had recently constructed Camp Beaver (later renamed Fort Cameron) to quarter about 250 troops at the end of the Black Hawk War and to provide security during the anticipated trial of those responsible for the Mountain Meadows Massacre. However, the trial would not begin for another two years. It would end in a hung jury.

54. Lee was in northeastern Arizona at this time, Perhaps he was deposed and released. In any case, he was re-arrested a year later to stand trial. See the entry below for Nov. 14, 1874.

two dividends due me. Worked in the shop until night on my fencing. No rock hawled to day.

November 12, 1873; Wednesday. Was early at work pointing pickets. Henry was hawling wood. Theodore went to Cedar Spring after a cow. Ira started for Sandpete. Omner went with him. They were after some Wheat. Ira caried some Apples to sell. In the afternoon I received a letter from Paulina saying she was expecting to come soon to Fillmore with Mr. E[dward] Dalton.

November 13, 1873; Thursday. In the morning worked at boreing pickets, during the day bored some 272. To day Mrs. Sarah Clark and Mrs. Hellen Collister came to visit us. In the evening as I had quit work Paulina arived from Parowan. She came with Mr. Nelson Holingshead. She brought Laura with her who had been ill for some time in hopes that the traviling and change would benifit her health.

November 14, 1873; Friday. Some indications of rain this morning which were folowed by gentle showers through the day. Worked at pointing pickets all the day and after I had finished my day's work I called at Rhoda's for Paulina and took super with them and then we came home. The Stars were shineing brightly. The night was cool and frosty. No work on my house to day.

November 15, 1873; Saturday. I was early at work boreing the last lot of my flat pickets which I completed about 4 oclock in the afternoon, after which I called on Mr. [Peter] Silda where he was with his hands building fence for Mr. John Cavanah. Paulina spent the day with Rhoda. The weather cool but pleasant. Mr. Cavanah is agitating the mater of building a Liberal Social Hall for the Benifit of the Liberal party in Fillmore.

November 16, 1873; Sunday. Weather growing warmer. Taried at home until after diner. The Boys Lorenzo and Theodore had their photographs taken by Mr. Cavanah. In the afternoon went with Paulina and Priscilla to visit Amasa [Jr.] and his wife and took super with them, after which I went with Paulina to call on Lelia whose Baby wa[s] very sick. Stayed in the evening a while and then returned home.

November 17, 1873; Monday. Was early at work on the last lot of my flat pickets which I finished up before night. The weather growing milder and less frost at night. No work on my House this week. Have not seen Mr. [Nicholas] Paul for a week or more. After my days' work was done I called around to Mr. Cavanah to see his new fence just being built by Mr. [Peter] Sylda. On my way home I saw Edwin and Lelia [Bartholomew]. Their baby was beter.

November 18, 1873; Tuesday. Commenced plaining my Square pickets. This morning the Boys Theodore Henry and Alonzo went on the Stock drive. The weather is growing cooler. The nights are quite frosty. During the afternoon Omner [Turley] and Ira [Lyman] returned from the Seveir [Valley][55] where they had been to buy grain, in which however they did not succeed as well as they expected when they left home. Wheat had risen to two dollers.

November 19, 1873; Wednesday. Worked at the Bench through the forenoon when I received an invitation to dine with Bishop [Thomas] Callister and family with whom I spent the afternoon. Before comeing home I called on Rhoda who reported herself and children well. On my return home I got a [kerosene] Oil can for Paulina to put preserves in, which she is to make before she returns home to Parowan. The weather is warm and pleasant.

November 20, 1873; Thursday.[56] Worked at the Bench during the forenoon and after diner until Rhoda sent for me to take super. My daughter Lydia May came to see me. Mr. [William] Marsden and Son called for the night. They were on their way to Salt Lake. During the evening I received a Telegram from Hyrum Coombs anounceing the arival of [Charles] Foster the Medium. He remains in the City two weeks, and then he goes to California.

November 21, 1873; Friday. Worked at the Bench until noon. During the Morning hours Mr. [Nicholas] Paul called to see me in regard to my House. After hearing his estimates of the relative costs of the two kinds of work[,] the Stone and Brick[,] [was] when I concluded to give up the idea of the rock and take the chance of geting Brick in the spring. Rain fell freely through the day and at sundown I went to Rhoda's, took super with her and Paulina who staid there all night.

November 22, 1873; Saturday. Worked at finishing my square pickets.

55. This would be the area on the other side of the Pavant Mountains from Fillmore, including the town of Richfield.

56. When Lyman realized he had entered this and the next three entries out of order, he over-rode the pre-printed dates with, "This belongs on the 20th," etc.

Some snow fell thorugh the day. During the day Mr. [Peter] Silda called and had some talk about makeing my fence when he has finished the work on the Free Trade Store and the weather clears up. Paulina and Laura c[ame] back to night. To day they visited Lydia [Partridge], L[elia] [Bartholomew][,] and Eliza [Partridge], at their residences and renewed their acquaintence with their children. She [Laura] saw while there Mother [Lydia Clisbee] Partridge who is over eighty years old.

November 23, 1873; Sunday. Passed the day at home in reading. The weather growing slightly warmer. In the afternoon Paulina and Priscilla went to visit Mr. Horace Rusels family. In the afternoon I made a call on Mr. Bartholimew after which I returned home. Heard the report of the Death of our old acquaintance and friend Mrs. Jane Grover Stewart of Farmington Davis County. Heard first report of the Seances of [Charles] Foster in the city by the Tribune.[57]

November 24, 1873; Monday. Was early at the Bench and worked at the fencing until afternoon when I went to Mrs. Caroline Callister's where I visited during the afternoon. Paulina was there and Priscilla. Mother Partridge was with us. While there Lydia [Partridge] Lyman brought her Daughter Ida to see me. We had not meet for several years.[58] The weather stil growing warmer tho much drying in the streets. Came home at dark, Dock Piersons called on me

November 25, 1873; Tuesday. Worked at the Bench during the forenoon in which time the frost of the night before mostly left the ground. After diner with Henry's help I layed down a morter Bed [be]fore makeing the morter for my House, the material for the foundation of which are mostly on hand waiting for the mason. Finished up the day working on my fence. The weather is growing steadily warmer, no frost to night. My cough was severe.

November 26, 1873; Wednesday. Worked at the Bench during the day. Henry hawled one load of sand[,] the first for the mortar for my House. In the evening Mr. Rowly came in to make some inquiry of Omner Turley about where his son Walter got the whiskey on which he got drunk

57. "The great Foster" is how the newspaper referred to the clairvoyant Charles H. Foster when he announced his intent to visit. "Foster," *Salt Lake Tribune*, Nov. 18, 1873.

58. Notice that he refers to Ida Evelyn as Lydia's girl. She was also Amasa's daughter.

at Meadow Creek, in which condition he came home to a kind Father & fond Mother to blast their hopes in him.

November 27, 1873; Thursday. Was early at the Bench until the Breakfast call. After Breakfast I ground my plan[er]s, Paulina helping me. Worked at my fencing until near night when I called on Mrs. Turley and took super with her, Paulina[,] and Priscilla who had been sewing through the day for Mrs. Turley. Shortly after we returned home Charles arived from Parowan which place he left on Tuesday last. He reported all well at home.

November 28, 1873; Friday. Was early at the Bench and during the day plained 44 pickets and finished up all the square pickets but 44. After finishing my days work I went up in Town and called at the New [Free Trade] store where Mr. [Nicholas] Paul was finishing the plastering of the Building. On my return I called at Mr. Bartholimew where I meet Maria and Lelia. The former had received a letter from H[yrum] S. Coombs which stated that his wife had a young daughter.

November 29, 1873; Saturday. Was early at the Bench plaining the last of my fence pickets which I completed just as the call was made for diner. After diner I finished my pickets and piled them snugly away and while doing this Charley unloaded some six thousand and a half of my Shingles at my Shop. After my day's work was done I called at the Free Trade [store] and bought some cloth for some under clothes.[59]

November 30, 1873; Sunday. To day Paulina and Charles and Laura Started for their home in Parowan takeing with them three hundred pounds of Flour which I sold them at four dollers per hundred.[60] I also let them have 68 lbs of dried fruit. The indications of storm are stil around. In the afternoon late I went to and called at Mr. E[dwin] Bartholimew's with whom I took super. To day read Medium and Day break.[61]

---

59. Lyman probably wanted a flannel union suit, which his wife would sew for him to keep him warm in winter. In summer men preferred to wear linen nightshirts under their clothing, and beginning mid-century they began purchasing off-the-rack, knee-length linen drawers that had ties at the waist and at the knee.

60. Interesting that Lyman would charge his children and former wife $4.00 per hundredweight for flour. His diary entries for Oct. 13–14, 30, 1873, belie an equally strong fixation with his son's debt prior to his son leaving on a mission. Amasa agreed to let Marion's wife Rhoda absorb the debt and make periodic payments while her husband was away, documented herein on Jan. 15, 17, 1874.

61. *The Medium and Daybreak* was a London spiritualist weekly.

December 1, 1873; Monday. Did not work in the shop to day heavy clouds hangin around indicating a coming storm. After the Breakfast hour I went to the Lumber yar[d] and selected some lumber for my Kitchen room, which I am going to build immediately if the weather will permit. The Sun went down bright and clear. Bought [daughter] Frances some dresses for winter, Henry hauled home my Lumber.

December 2, 1873; Tuesday. Some snow fell this morning. This morning the Stove was put up in the New Store and a fire mad[e] in it which made the room very comfortable and warm and very inviting to the idlers who have no time or disposition to work. In the afternoon I framed the Lower timbers of my Kitchen but could not do much[,] for the cold was to[o] intence to allow me to stand in the snow at the work.

December 3, 1873; Wednesday. During the last night some snow had fallen. I passed the day in reading. During the day I called at the Free Trade store and bought a pair of over shoes. And while in Town I procured some Theater tickets for the play to night. Past some time in the New Store. Then returned home haveing bought a pair of Rubers for Priscilla. At night went to the Theater. Took Priscilla with me, returned about 10. Oclock, snow was falling.

December 4, 1873; Thursday. In the morning the weather was somewhat mild and the snow began aga[i]n to fall and continued to do so through the day. During the forenoon my Sons Amasa jr, Theodore and Henry went to the Mountains for a Deer Hunt. The weather continues mild and the snow falls freely all day. At night it had attained a depth of from a foot to eighteen inches snow was falling when we retired to bed about half past 8 oclock.

December 5, 1873; Friday. Weather warm this morning almost springlike. Passed most of the day in reading [about] the wonders of the world, and the Ban[n]er of Light [magazine]. In the afternoon made a ten <u>foot</u> Measure. Some snow fell to day. The Boys hunted and killed some Rabits. From the Deer Hunters in the Mountains we have as yet no news. Some Wagons on the road to day. The snow is settling quite fast makeing it slopy under foot[,] a good time for snowballing which is improved by the Boys.

December 6, 1873; Saturday. Worked at the Bench half of the day. The residue of the day I passed in reading. Late in the afternoon I received a letter from my friend Elias L. T. Harison and a copy of the Salt Lake Leader[62] giveing the reasons for its discontinuence. In looking over its pages I saw the notice of the Death of Alfred Cumings of Georgia[,] Ex Governor of Utah, with comments on the same from the City Journals.

December 7, 1873; Sunday. Weather mild to day. Some clouds hanging around the Horizon. Passed the day mostly in reading until late in the afternoon when I called on the Bartholimews. The work has progressed rather slowly during the past week on the new Store. It is not yet ready to receive its stock of goods[,] the carpenters work not being finished nor the Painting. The snow is not melting to day and the clouds indicate the comeing of more altho the present supply seems sufficient.

December 8, 1873; Monday. To day concluded to change my plan of building and build with wood in stead of Brick. Calculated the amount of timber I should need and the Lath. In the morning I wrote a letter to Mrs. Lyman in Salt Lake City. After posting the same I called on Mr. [William] Gibbs carpenter and advised with him in regard to my house. He said the change was a good one and would be less expensive. Wind high from the South[,] a light fall of snow though the night.

December 9, 1873; Tuesday. Weather cool and crispy this morning. I was engaged in writing a letter to my friend Mr. E[lias] L. T. Harison of Salt Lake City. Called on Mr. [William] Gibbs and advised with him in regard to My building. After posting my letter I returned home and passed residue of the day in makeing some estimates and specifications of materials ^and^ cost of my house. Received from Postmaster [Andrew] Henry two copies of the Saturday Night[,] a [weekly] paper [with] literary [content] published in the City of Philadelphia.

December 10, 1873; Wednesday. Passed the Morning hours in calculating the Lumber needid for my House and makeing Bill for the same. Then called at the residence of Mr. [Doreas] Warner to give him the Bill to fill but he was in the Can[y]on at his Mill and would not be in town until Saturday. Made a call on Mrs. Struder and then called at the

62. In 1871 the *Salt Lake Tribune* went daily under a new editor, Oscar Sawyer, who had been with the *New York Herald* and wanted the *Tribune* to be more secular. Godbe and Harrison retained what they called the *Weekly Tribune* to discuss religious issues, but when they hired additional outside journalists in 1873, they decided to change the weekly's name to the *Salt Lake Leader* to avoid confusion, then discontinued it altogether. Heller, *Study of the Utah Newspaper War*, 32–36.

New Store where Mr. [George] Crane and Mr. Wade werre painting. Returned home and in the evening called on Mrs. [Mary] Kelley who is sick and very low.

December 11, 1873; Thursday. Weather growing cooler. Spent the forenoon on the plan of my [blank]. As we were about to dine we received the news of the Death of Mrs. Mary Kelley this Morning at 3 oclock. After diner I called on Mr. [John] Kelley for an hour, and learned from him that the funerel [of his wife] would take place tomorow at ten oclock. I was told she requested that I should speak at the funeral. I returned home and cleared off the ground on which I shall build my room.

December 12, 1873; Friday. Weather crispy and cold. At ten oclock we attended the funeral and Burial of Sister Mary Kelley, on which occasion I spoke briefly to the people in attendence. Mrs. K. before her Death came to be[l]ieve in the truths of the communeion of the risen Immortals with those stil in the [human] form. The Earth clad in its wintry robe of Virgin snow seemed [a] fiting emblem of the bright pure and hapy home to which our Sister had gone to meet her children gone before.

December 13, 1873; Saturday. Passed the morning hours in reading the Baner of Light [magazine]. After diner hour I went up in town and called at the Free Trade store and from thence I went to the residence of Mrs. Eliza Lym[an] where I meet my Daughters Martha and Caroline and Mrs. Lydia [Partridge] and her children[,] with Platt and Wife. It was Joseph's birth day and by the invitation of the Children I took diner with them, what I had not done for some years before[,] and on biding them goo[d]by[e] I received a warm and appare[n]tly earnest invitation to call again. Mother Partridge was there.

December 14, 1873; Sunday. The weather is becoming slighly warmer this morning. During the forenoon I wrote a letter to Mr. Hyrum S. Coombs of Salt Lake City. After sending my letter to the P. O. I went to Mr. Edwin Bartholimew's and dined with them and passed the residue of the day there. This evening there is a marked change in the weather. Mr. B. was ill and had been so for some days past. The other members of the family were well.

December 15, 1873; Monday. The weather more mild and warm this morning, rendering it more or less slopy in the Streets. During the forenoon I read the [fifth annual] Presidents Message [of Ulysses S. Grant] and other mater in the N. Y. Sun. After diner I called on the family of my son Marion, all of whom I found well. From them I learned that Marion ^was^ laboring in Notingham England. Returned home and laid the sills of my new room.

December 16, 1873; Tuesday. After the morning hours I engaged in the work of puting up my Kitchen. The frame of which I mostly completed during the day. In course of the day called at the Meat market and the Store. Returned home and continued my work until night when I attended a Meeting of the [Free Trade Union] Board of Directors[,] at the conclusion of which the Board ajourned until the next night at 6. oclock, at the new Store. Some indications of storm when I came home at 8 oclock.

December 17, 1873; Wednesday. In the morning made a call on Mr. Edwin Bartholimew. After continued the work on my building[,] the weather being mild through the day. Last night some snow fell. During the day I received letters from the North and the south; and some papers. The Boys returned from their Deer hunt but they brought no venison. At six oclock was at the New Store as per appointment of the night before. At bedtime it was freezeing hard.

December 18, 1873; Thursday. Weather pleasant and warm, makeing it somewhat Mudy. Worked on my building. Henry helped me in the afternoon. We got up the rafters and then put on some of the sideing and made it ready for the sheeting. Towards night the weather turned much colder and froze hard. To night Lorenzo went to a primary meeting held by the young Men for the purpose of organizeing an improvement society on a mutual principle.

December 19, 1873; Friday. Theodore and Henry went after wood to day which left me without any help on my building on which I prosicuted my work alone through the day. After my days work was done I called at the free trade store for some nails with which to carry on my building but not finding the varieties I wanted I had to go to the Co-op. On my way I called at our New Store on which Mr. [George] Crane the painter was at work, and said by Christmas we could come in.

December 20, 1873; Saturday. This morning the weather was unfavorable for working on the roof of my building, and [so I] quit and went up in town. I went into the shop and made and put into the building a

Door frame. In the afternoon it ceased storming; and I put on the sheeting on my roof and made it ready for shingling. The Saints are holding a two day's meeting. In the evening the [store's] Board of Directors was in Session to prepare for the coming general meeting.

December 21, 1873; Sunday. In the morning wrote a letter to Paulina and after posting my letter I went to Mr. Bartholimews. Spent some hours with him and dined. After diner returned home and past the evening in reading.

December 22, 1873; Monday. This morning the weather was cool but after breakfast Ira commenced to put the shingles on the roof of my building. The other Boys were engaged in Butchering a hog and Henry hawled me a load of wood, the first brought to the place of my home. In the evening I went to the ajourned meeting of the [Free Trade Union] Board of Directors at which Mr. [John] Cavanah most grossly insulted the Board and abruptly left but we secured Mr. Alvice and done some work.

December 23, 1873; Tuesday. A heavy fog this morning through which the Sun shone but feebly after the cold became a little modified. Ira put on the residue of the shingle[s] on my building and while he was doing this I called on Mr. [William] Gibbs and engaged a Door and lock and bolts to hang it for which I am to pay him four dollers and eighty five cents. Returned and helped Ira to put on the last courses of shingles. After diner Henry went ~~went~~ with me to Mr. Gibbs and brought the door to the new store to be painted.

December 24, 1873; Wednesday. Did not engage in work on acount of the cold. Assisted in receiveing the goods from Mr. Noys, of which we had to open some at the old stand as the new Store was not yet ready to receive goods. Bought some presents for the children. Late in the afternoon I put some Baton on my Building. Henry brought my door home from the painter's. Made an evening call on Mr. Bar^t^holimew.

December 25, 1873; Thursday. This Christmas morning opened as usual in a semi civilized way[,] it being attended with the burning of an indefinite amount of Powder and a noisy demand for presents ^by the juviniles^ (not being content with the liberal gratuities of Santi Claus) much to the anoyence of the older members of the community. I with Priscilla spent the evening and dined with the Kelleys and other friends. Called on Rhoda [and] found her and children well.

December 26, 1873; Friday.[63] Called on Edwin Bartholimew and family. Took Breakfast with them after which I done some work on my building finishing up the roof. Cleaned out the frozen Appels from my Shop.

December 27, 1873; Saturday. This morning I received two hundred dollers from Benjamin Robinson on his note. After this assisted in Moveing into our New Store. I worked at this until 3 oclock. Then went to diner. We put up a part only of our goods to day. After the day's work was over we held a general meeting of the Stockholders of the [Free Trade] Union, at the conclusion of which held an election of Officers. Mr. J. Alves President.

December 28, 1873; Sunday. This morning wrote a letter to Hyrum and the family at Salt Lake while the Boys were geting ready to start on our journey to Parowan. After diner we started for the south. We found the road very rough and the traviling very hard and heavy, but our slow travil brought us to Canosh at the close of the day and to the Hospitable Home of Mr. John Black by whose kind Lady we were made very welcome, in the absence of her husband until he came home.

December 29, 1873; Monday. We were early on the road and traviling slow. We reached Pine Creek at night and camped at the residence of Mr. Isaac Riddle. He gave me a chance to sleep in his House. Through the night the wind was high from the South altho it froze some in the night.

December 30, 1873; Tuesday. We were early on the way and made a short halt at Mr. Edward Thompson's who let us have some hay for our Teem. We traviled to and camped on the ridge south of Beaver. North of Beaver we passed Uncle Sydney Tanner with his freight Teems.

December 31, 1873; Wednesday. Early this morning we were on the move and when we reached Buckhorn Springs we made a short halt and fed our teem and took a cold Lunch, and then were again on the road. We reached Parowan in the afternoon and found Paulina and the children well. In the evening Oscar and Madora were with us. Some of the Boys were at the party. During the evening some of our neighbors called to see us, and express[ed] good wishes for our hapiness.

---

63. This entry was written on a predated page for Dec. 27, with Lyman's note that it "belongs on page 26th." The next entry was written on a page printed as Dec. 26, with Lyman's similar correction.

January 1, 1874; Thursday. Morning opened bright and pleasant, attended with the unusual amount of good wishes for our peace and hapiness from our friends who called on us. Remained at home until afternoon when we went to Oscar's and spent the afternoon. Mr. and Mrs. Benson were with us. In the evening Mr J[ohn] W. Young preached to the people on the subject of the Railway from Iron City northward.

January 2, 1874; Friday. Passed the morning hours at home. Mr. Wm Roberts called and in his conversation made allusions to some dark and bloody incidents in the past history of Parowan. I called at the Shop of my old friend Dr [Calvin C.] Pendleton, the place with is old appointments was familiar but the genial kindly face [of] its old Master was not there. Called on Mr. [George] Grimshaw and Lady for an hour and the[n] called on Mrs [Jane] Hanks.

January 3, 1874; Saturday. Passed the morning hours in reading after which I called on Mr Calhoun merchant, and then called at the Co-op to enquire after the Troop Dramatick from Beaver but they had not arived. On my return I called on Mrs. Taylor.

In the afternoon I had with Paulina and the little children a sleigh ride around Town. At night received the news that the Actors had broak down on the road and did not arive in time to perform. The play was defered until Monday night.

January 4, 1874; Sunday. Weather cool but pleasant. Passed the day at home. In the after noon Mr. and Mrs. Croff came in and dined with us and then they spent the evening with us. Lorenzo attended meeting, others of the Boys remained at home. The Actors from Beaver arived during the day. I did not go out today.

January 5, 1874; Monday. Passed the morning at home after doing my writing I went [to] Mr. [William] Marsdens Store. He gave me some Door fastnings for Priscilla. I bought some Tea returned home after which I called on Mrs. [Jane] Hanks and borowed some magazines to read in the afernoon. Brother [Ebenezer] Hanks came up with others from the Iron works. Oscar went up ^to^ the Mill to day for some Lumber.

January 6, 1874; Tuesday. This morning called on br. [Ebenezer] Hanks but found a buisness meeting in session so I had no opportunity for conversation with him. I returned home and passed the residue of the day in reading the Magazines. Another Theatrical performence was had in the Basement of the Church House to night at half the full price of the first.

January 7, 1874; Wednesday. Passed the day at home during which I received a call from Mr. [Ebenezer] Hanks who was expecting to return immediately to Iron city. Oscar returned to day with half of the Wagon. He broak down in the Can[y]on where he left his load and part of the wagon. I[n] the evening went to Mr Mc Guffies and past a social hour. Mrs. Newman was with us. The weather continues mild.

January 8, 1874; Thursday. Passed the morning hours at home. About 11, oclock we went to Mr. Richard Benson's and spent the day with them. Oscar and wife were with us. Mr. B. was absent on buisness until evening, when with us and others of the neighbors we attended a surprise Party at Mr Sidney Burton's on the occasion of his 36th Birth day.

January 9, 1874; Friday. Passed the hours at home reading[,] after which I went to Mr [William] Marsden's and on my way called at Mr Calhouns, but failed to find the Shirt Bosoms[64] which I wanted. Returned home and past the residue of the day reading History. Oscar gave me his Brass mounted Rule for my plan[e][,] one which I bought at the Co-op for 85/100.

January 10, 1874; Saturday. Passed the morning hours in reading the Herald of Health[65] after which I called on Rily Morse at his residence and bargained with him for some Shingles for which I was to pay him in dried fruits. Bought me a Lantern at the Co-op Store. Passed the residue of the day at home. Mrs. Fish and Mrs. Burton called for Mariage Certificates.

January 11, 1874; Sunday. Passed the day mostly at home engaged in reading. Received some calls through the day. Mrs. [Jane] Hanks, and in the afternoon Mr. D[aniel] P. Clark. Made a call, Social of an hour or two. Some of our time was taken up in prepareing for our return to Fillmore for which place we expect to start in the morning of tomorow.

January 12, 1874; Monday. A little before 7 oclock this morning we said our adi[e]us and were on the way. The frost had sealed up the Mud

---

64. For formal wear, a shirt bosom was a four-ply area of cloth in the front that resisted wrinkling or shifting when wearing a coat. It was the portion one could see between the tie and coat. It was sometimes detachable.

65. This was a popular monthly magazine that published word-of-mouth remedies for illness and warned of consequences for violating what it considered to be natural moral laws.

but our teem being very smo[o]th in the condition of their shoes their travil was vey hard and wearisom. Made noon halt at Buckhorn Springs where I called on my old friend Mr. Miles Anderson. Staye[d] with Mrs Julia Tanner in Beaver all night.

January 13, 1874; Tuesday. Were on the road but not so early as yesterday. The traviling was very slipery and toilsome. At dark we were at the Fort at Cove Creek and watered our Animals and passed on to the Timber near the foot of the hill and there under the sheltering Boughs of the Cedars we made our night Camp with a fair degree of comfort, surounded as we were by the snowy evidences of Winter.

January 14, 1874; Wednesday. Before the friendly Stars were drowned in the light of the returning day we were on the road, and in passing down Bakers Can[y]on, we Meet Mr. Wm Bishop and wife who were enroute to Beaver. Made Noon halt and took diner with Mrs. Jane Black and started on our way. We took on board Mrs Hellen Callister and brought her to Fillmore where we arived at night. Found all well. Found letter awaiting me from Marion, in England.

January 15, 1874; Thursday. After the morning writing I went up in town and called at the Store where I meet Mr. [George] Crane the Painter who promised to make for me a Bill of Painting Materials needed for the Painting of my House and Fence. Called on Rhod[a] who paid me $105.00 on Marions Note, After which I was invited by Platt to call at his Mothers and see his wife and young Daughter. Dined with them. Fredrick was there. Crane gave me promised Bill.

January 16, 1874; Friday. Wrote letter to Paulina and also inclosed to her the Mariage certificates of parties in Parowan Maried by me in March 1859. After the writing went to work on my new room and laid some floor and then with Lorenzo's help hung the door. Let Lorenzo have five dollers to shoe his horses for the trip to Salt Lake City next week.

January 17, 1874; Saturday. After the morning hour I went up town and called on Rhoda and received of ^her^ the Balence of money due on Marions Note and left the note with Rhoda. From this place I went to Mr [William] Gibbs Shop and advised with him about my House[,] then I went home and put a pair of rockers on a chair after which I went to Edwins [and] found them all well. I returned home the mud was very deep on the street and some ~~of~~ rain was falling.

January 18, 1874; Sunday. This morning the Snow was about one foot in depth and did not melt much. During the day we concluded to defer our starting to the city for a day for the road to improve in condition. I past the day at home and was not out [of doors] but passed the time in reading the [Religio-Philosophical] Journal and the Banner of Light and the Fireside Friend. Weather cooler at evening.

January 19, 1874; Monday. After morning hour went to the shop and Made a frame and put in the window of my new room and finished up the boarding. At the close of my days work called at the Store and bought some provisions for our journey to the City. Returned home and went with Lorenzo to see the Danish Athlete and trickster.[66] When we returned home weather was clear and cool altho it snowed before morning.

January 20, 1874; Tuesday. This morning Started for Salt Lake and traviled to Scipeo and put up with Mrs. Wm Robins. The night was cold. To day the Man who was lost from the Stage was found. His feet were badly frozen, otherwise he was not injured. He was evidently insane. He was taken to the Mail Station and cared for by the people there.

January 21, 1874; Wednesday. Wednesday Morning the weather very cold. Traviled to Chicken-creek and put up with Dr Palmer and family. At night the weather was very cold. Found the Dr. and family well. He extended his good offices to us gratuitously.

January 22, 1874; Thursday. This morning the Snow was falling very fast attended with Southerly wind which circumstance caused us to delay our Starting until the Storm abated which occured about 11 oclock when we started for Salt Creek. The travil was slow and wearisome as the tracks were all filled with drifting snow. Near Sundown we put up with Father Foot, who entertained us with kindness as in other times.

January 23, 1874; Friday. Early in the morning we left our friends of Nephi and traviled to Payson and put up with Bishop Joseph S. Tanner and family whom we found well with the exception of the children some of whom had the Hooping cough. While here meet with Mother [Elizabeth] Tanner and her Sister Polly Cook. The old Ladies[,] the one 76, the other 70 years of age were in their usual health, going down Life's declivity to their rest in the bright Sumerland of the Immortals.

66. This was most likely a vaudeville act with feats of strength and magic tricks.

January 24, 1874; Saturday. Early this morning got aboard of a light Wagon, with my nephew Mark Tanner who kindly whirled me over the road to the R. R. Depot, at Provo where we arived at half past 11 oclock. The wind blew very kene and cold as we crossed the Bench between Spanish fork and Springville. At half past 12 oclock [we] were on the way to the City where we arived about 4. Oclock. Found all well at home.

January 25, 1874; Sunday. This morning went to the Methodist Church and heard the Rev. [Charles C.] Straten. He spoke as an Apologist for Moses, and his acts as narated in the Bible, this and more like it. The old story needs to preserve its hold on the credulity of the people. Attended the Children's Lyceum at the Institute after which took tea with the Shearman's. In the evening heard Barnum at Institute.

January 26, 1874; Monday. After the morning hour I went and made some purchases [in Salt Lake City] of the Paints and Oils for my house and fence [in Fillmore]. Then I went and called on Mr Latimer and was very kindly shown his asortment of Doors and Windows. Paid Godbe & Co. $50.40. Paid K. & L. $13.95. Lorenzo arived to day all right, the weather more mild and warm. Some Mud on S[tree]ts. In my walk in the City I called on my old friend and his Lady T. A. Line. Returned home and passed the evening ~~at~~ with family.

January 27, 1874; Tuesday. Traviled about Town and made some purchases of fitings for my house. During the forenoon went home to Diner after which I continued my buisness in the City, and at night found myself very weary.

January 28, 1874; Wednesday. Traviled about Town and collected our purchases preparatory for our return journey. Some Mud on the Streets so we did not load any goods to day. At night held a family Seance with very gratifying results. [My deceased wife] Cornelia[,] [deceased daughter] Adelia[,] and Mrs. Mary Kelley were with us, and gave us renewed assurances of their hapiness in their bright homes in the Sumer Land of the blest Immortals. To day meet several of my old acquaintences who greeted me very warmly as of Yore.

January 29, 1874; Thursday. During the morning hours I made some preperation for the loading of our goods for our move to the south. Mad[e] some small purchaces and then Called on the Photographer and had my Negative taken for some pictures which he promised to have for me in a day or two. Was suffering from an atack of Diarea induced by cold.

January 30, 1874; Friday. Was rather ill this morning but after morning hour feeling some better I walked up in the city and called [at] Godbe & Co. [drug store] and had some medicine prepared after takeing which I felt better. Called at Tribune Office was introduced to the Editors, after which I called and had a look at a variety of Pumps both force & lifting. I also saw some Water Rams. Called on and Dined with Mr J[ohn] Maning and wife. Returned home and had a siting [séance] with Mrs. Lyman and Hila.

January 31, 1874; Saturday. Spent the morning hour in Loading some of our goods for the Journey, after which I made some calls in the City, and in my rambles I meet Uncle E[zra] T. Clark, and James Stewart, whose wife had died since I last saw them last Spring. After this I called on my old and valued friend R[ichard] R. Hopkins and family at their residence. Mr. H. had been suffering from illness, for the last week. He is slowly recovering. While there Mrs. Kimball their eldest Daughter came home from Provo, on a visit to her parents.

February 1, 1874; Sunday. Passed the morning in ajusting some of our loading for the journey after which we called the Manings and spent the day with them. At night attended a Lecture at the Institute by Mrs. Dr. Perkins, a Trance speaker. Weather rather warm.

February 2, 1874; Monday. Were early astir and between 7 and 8 oclock were on the road. It was tolerable good as far as it had been worked. At night we found our selves safely at the Andrus House, the home and property of Mr. Milo Andrus. Weather cooler than yesterday. Mr A. was absent in Dixie.

February 3, 1874; Tuesday. ^Were^ moveing early we found the road heavy. We nooned at Lehi. While there we meet Mr Jacob Bushman who told of the Death of his Daughter on the 26th of Jan. At night found ourselves at Battle Creek [Pleasant Grove], kindly taken in by Bishop John Brown who with his family we have known for many years, and their value as friends has not diminished with passing years. It has its growth in truth and is Immortal.

February 4, 1874; Wednesday. In the morning we were early astir and myself and Mrs. L[yman] took [railroad] Carrs, while Lorenzo crossed the Bench with the Wagon. Arived in Provo we called on Bishop Myron Tanner and family, the Bishop was home at night.

February 5, 1874; Thursday. Started on the road and reached Spanish Fork at night. We made our Noon halt at Mr Treats. We were very kindly pulled out of the mud by Mr Crandall whose Grand parents I baptized into the Church near 40. years ago. Put up with my old and valued friend Mr. Samuel Thompson.

February 6, 1874; Friday. In the morning we started for Payson where we arived a little after noon. Put up with Bishop Joseph S. Tanner. We have concluded to remain here until the road is in better condition for travil.

February 7, 1874; Saturday. Remained at the Bishops through the day only makeing a brief call at the res[i]dence of Mr George Garner. The condition of the road stil is forbiding to travil.

February 8, 1874; Sunday. Called on and spent the day with the Garners and in the evening Called on brother D[avid] D. Tanner and family. Roads stil bad.

February 9, 1874; Monday. Called on Dr. [Gustavus] Simonds Family. The Dr. was not at home. Mrs S. Loaned me a Book. At night attended an entertainment given in the Church by Mr. Hood Alston. Heard to day that brother Freeman [Tanner] had returned home. The entertainment consisted of Poetick readings by Mr. Hood Alston. To some [hearers] he was interesting to others rather <u>light</u> and Vapory.

February 10, 1874; Tuesday. Passed the morning hours at the Bishops [Joseph S. Tanner's] after which I called on brother Freeman Tanner with whom I passed a few hours pleasantly, his wife being absent in Tintick [Eureka]. After Diner I called at the residence of Mr. Christopher Dixon. Found Mrs. D. at home but Mr. D. was not at home. At night attended meeting at the Church. Heard addresses from [traveling] bishop [Elijah F.] Sheets and [Brother] Taylor from Salt Lake. Weather stil warm.

February 11, 1874; Wednesday. Passed the morning hours at the Bishops[,] after which with Mrs Lyman I went to Mr Christopher Dixons, with whom and family we spent the day very pleasantly. In the afternoon the Snow fell freely to the depth of 4 or 5 inches. The weather was quite mild and warm. Freemans wife returned home to day from Tintick.

February 12, 1874; Thursday. Some snow fell during last night. Remained with the Dixons during the morning hours After which we called on Mr. Marquis Tanner and family with whom we passed some hours and took Diner, after which we returned to the Bishops [Joseph S. Tanner's]. The weather was warm and pleasant[,] some indications of chang[e] of the weather.

February 13, 1874; Friday. Passed the morning hours at the Bishops after which we went to the residence of Mr. Freeman Tanners with whom and family and friends we spent the day. At night went to the residence of Mrs. Leatha Tanner with whom we taried through the night. The wind was high through the night from the South West.

February 14, 1874; Saturday. We were early astir[,] the wind stil high from the Southwest. We passed the morning hours and Breakfasted with Mrs. [Leatha] Tanner and her [four-month-old] son George A. [Tanner]. After Breakfast with Mrs Lyman went to the residence of Dr. Gustavus Simonds with whom and family we taried a portion of the day. We dined with them, the snow was falling freely the most of the day. In the afternoon we returned to Bishop Tanner's. At night the snow ceased falling[,] the weather still warm.

February 15, 1874; Sunday. Passed the day with the Bishop [Joseph S. Tanner] and family and party of invited friends on the occasion of the Birth day of one of the Bishops Son's, [five-year-old] Henry. A frienly and social feeling was one of the richest features of the occasion. The weather was very warm and pleasant. We parted our friends of the party with the expresion of the warmest of friendship and kindness.

February 16, 1874; Monday. This morning I called on Mr J. Finlayson in regard to the price for which he would furnish the Lath for my House. He proposed to make them for 65 cents per Hundred; this was five cents more than I was asked in the City. Passed the day with the Bishop and family. They the Bishop and ~~family~~ [first] wife [Elizabeth] had been maried some 15 years.

February 17, 1874; Tuesday. This morning we bid our fri[e]nds good by and started on our homeward journey. We found the roads very heavy. At 11. oclock we were at Santaquin where I meet our old friend John D. Holady whom and wife I Maried in Camp in 1851. We dined with our friends. Mother Holliday called to see us and brother Thomas Holliday also called. We traviled to and stoped for the night with Mr George Johnson of Willow Creek or Mona, [as] is the Name of the ~~wil~~ Post Office.

February 18, 1874; Wednesday. Traviled to Nephi and called on our old friend Father [Timothy B.] Foot with whom we dined after which we traviled to Chicken-Creek, and put up with Dr. [Luther M.] Palmer who keeps the Post office and Mail station. We traviled until after dark as the road was heavy before retireing. The wind changed into the North, the ground where bare froze very hard, thus helping the traviling some. Our friends received us very kindly and made us comfortable.

February 19, 1874; Thursday. On riseing this morning we meet Bishop John Sharp and Mr. Feramorz Little, who were enroute for Dixie and came in the night in the Stage.[67] In the morning after Breakfast we started on the road but we had not traviled far when we found our wagon fast in the mud beyond the ability of our Teem to pull it out. We hired a man with teem to pull us out, traviled to the Sevier [River] and camped. Meet Mr. John Lawson.

February 20, 1874; Friday. Traviled to Scipio and made our noon halt and Telegraphed to Henry to meet us with some fresh horses. After our diner it began to Storm so furiously from the North that we could not travil, so we stayed all night with Mr. Thomas Gollop and family. While here a Mr. Philips called and spent the Afternoon with us, he as well as the Gollops seemed somewhat in the fog of uncertainly in regard to the Mormon Problem.

February 21, 1874; Saturday. Left the Gollops and had traviled but a short distance when the Bottom seemed to leave the sod and we were fast in the mud. From this dificulty we were able to extricate our selves by the help of a fence pole which we presed into service. Out of the Mud we traviled on to Goose Creek, where we made our Noon halt, and as we started on we meet Henry with some horses, that helped us to wade alone through the Mud. We arived at home about 8 oclock. Found all well.

February 22, 1874; Sunday. Passed the day at home. Shoveled some snow paths about the place, and made the floor tight in our new room so as to get our stove up. The snow was falling fast some part of the day. In the evening Mr. Albert Tanner and Mr. Bird called. They were

---

67. Little and Sharp were officers in the Utah Southern Railroad company. Little was also a nephew of Brigham Young and a future mayor of Salt Lake City, and Sharp was chair of the LDS-sponsored People's Party.

freighting Bullion from [North] Star to Provo. They concluded to relinquish the trip for the present on acount of the state of the roads. Some snow falling to night.

February 23, 1874; Monday. Snow falling very fast this forenoon. After the snowing abated, I spent some hours moveing the snow from the ground on the south side of our new room. In the afternoon the Boys moved the wagon with its load down near our house. Mrs. Lyman and myself unloaded a portion of our goods which we found had come safely over the rough traviling. Weather very cold this evening.

February 24, 1874; Tuesday. Unloaded our goods from the wagon and moved them into the House and put up the Stove and sawed some wood. Weather cold but pleasant.

At evening we received a call from Mrs. [Maria Louisa] Struder and Mrs. [Lelia] Bartholimew. They spent the evening with us. To night some indications of more storm in the hazy condition of the Atmosphere. Some freight teems passing to day.

February 25, 1874; Wednesday. To day continued our work around the house. Moved our Bed and made it up in our House. The weather quite warm and pleasant. In the afternoon went up in Town and called on Rhoda and gave her a parc[e]l that Marion Left with our folks in the city when he left for Europe last fall. Found his family all well. Made some purchases in the Market for the House of provisions and Gr[o]ceries. Found brother [John] Kelley in [blank] health.

February 26, 1874; Thursday. Continued work on my house through the early part of the day. The weather is growing more mild and warm. The Boys were hawling wood. In the afternoon I called at the residence of Prest. [Thomas] Callister but did not see him.

Called on Mr. [John] Kelley at the Store and got from him his Journal to read. Came home very tired. The weather pleasant but cool at night freezing hard.

February 27, 1874; Friday. To day finished the Batoning of my room and made some improvements in side of the house. The weather is warm and pleasant. In the afternoon I called on Mr. [John] Kelley at the store and bought some butter. I found in the store Mr. Wm Bishop reading some liberal papers which is an indication of an extension of thought in the direction of man's improvement.

February 28, 1874; Saturday. Continued my improvements in the House and on the outside; and shoveled away the snow from the east end of the House. In the afternoon I went up in town and meet with Mr. [John] Alves and Mr. B[enjamin] Robison who promised me some Money to morow. At night through the kindness of Lorenzo Mrs L[yman] and myself attended the Theater. This afternoon I received my first installment of Lumber on my Bill in Mr. [Dorus] Warners hand to Saw.

March 1, 1874; Sunday. Passed the morning hours at home. The weather warm and pleasant. The Streets were very mudy. After the morning work I went with Mr[s]. Lyman to call on Mr. [Edwin] Bartholimew and family and Mrs. [Maria Louisa Lyman] Struder and Son [Amasa M. Clayton]. While there we read a letter from H[yrum] S. Coombs in Salt Lake City reporting all well there at date of writing. Visited Father [Noah] Bartholimew and family in evening. Weather stil warm.

March 2, 1874; Monday. After the morning hour I went up town and bought some things for the House. Bought 2 chairs of G[abriel] Huntsman, some Lard [from] Mrs. Pratt, and some Soap of the Free Trade. Returned home and continued my work about the House. This morning received a call from Benjamin Robison who paid me fifty dollers in curency on his Note and promised me more next Month. Weather Cloudy and dark[,] snow falling. The evening weighed out fruit for [Riley] Morse.

March 3, 1874; Tuesday. Passed the morning hours in work about the House. Made some changes in the shop after which wrote letter to Paulina in Parowan. Passed some time in reading and in looking over My goods that I brought from the city. All right and safe haveing received no damage in transit. In afternoon meet the County Judge [Edward] Partridge [Jr.] and the other members of Board of Directors and Presidents of the Fre[e] Traders Uneion and [found they] were qualified. [John] Cavanah would not qualify.

March 4, 1874; Wednesday. Passed the morning hours in snow from the ground ajacent to my House. The snow was some 4 inches deep that fell last night. I made some changes about the shop. After this made a call on Mr. [John] Kelley at the Store and bought some Potatoes of him. At 6. oclock meet the New Board of Directors at the Store. Our first buisness was to fill a vacancy in the board of Directors by the appointment of Mr. Kelley as director and Treasurer.

March 5, 1874; Thursday. Passed the morning in reading and then I moved the snow from and around some of the piles of my Lumber; and after diner I called on Mr. Horace Rusel and had some talk with him about puting in my Foundation for my House. He promised to see me tomorow at my place and give the matter further consideration. After this I called at the Store and read the Tribune. Weather pleasant and cool.

March 6, 1874; Friday. Passed the mor[n]^i^ng hours in work at the House puting up some of my timber out of the way of the Snow. After which Mr. [Horace] Rusel, called as per promise of the day before, and had a look at the ground on which my House is to be built and made some proposition for doing the work of puting in the foundation. He took the dimentions of the work so as to make an estimate of the quantity of wall to be built. I cleared off some snow from the Lumber piles.

March 7, 1874; Saturday. To day Lorenzo came down and helped me to saw and point some 200 fence pickets for my division fence between my Lots and Priscilla's. To day John Struder came with Philo [Carter]'s teem and Wagon to move his family to Carters Ranch near Greenville in Beaver County.[68] He brought us some potatoes, which Philo sent us by him. We sent them some dried fruit in return. In afternoon went to Edwin [Bartholomew]'s and returned about 10. oclock, in Wagon.

March 8, 1874; Sunday. Passed the day at home and had to dine with us John Struder and wife [Maria Louisa] who were on their way to their home for the present at Carters Ranch in Beaver County. Mrs. Lelia Bartholimew and Mrs. Synthia Lyman were also with [us] through the day. Late in the evening we had a call from Mrs. McKay and Miss Laura Bartholimew and Mr. Edwin Bartholimew. The weather stil warm and pleasant.

March 9, 1874; Monday. To day Lorenzo commenced to dress the Base boards for my fence. I made a call up town in quest of a Molding plain but did not obtain any. Returned and called on the Butcher for some meat. In the after Noon worked some in the Shop and also made some changes in the Lumber to secure its drying so that we could continue working it.

March 10, 1874; Tuesday. To day Lorenzo was [not] working in shop on acount of the cold he had recently taken. I made some change[s] in

68. Greenville lies west of Beaver on the road to Minersville.

my work bench. To day Rhoda and Alice came and passed the day with us. In the afternoon we changed the residue of the plank that we shall use in our fence so as to give it a beter chance to dry than in the close pile in which it had lain through the winter. The weather was Suny and Warm hastening the going off of the snow.

March 11, 1874; Wednesday. Passed the morning hours in reading Goo[d]rich's Universal History of all Nations.[69] The weather bright and pleasant. The conditions of the Streets improveing. Did not do much in the Shop to day. We opened the cach[e] of Appels and found them in a good~~s~~ state of preservation and retaining perfectly all their Native qualities and flavor. This experiment satisfies me that to preserve the Appel in its best state it should be kept cool and from the air.

March 12, 1874; Thursday. Cleared off the snow from some of the ground around the Hous[e] to give the ground a chance to dry. Worked for a short time in the Shop, makeing up some conveniences for the House. Made a call on Mr. Bartholimew who promised to get me some fence posts [as] soon as the state of the ground would ~~admit~~ permit them to go to the mountain for them. Some indications of storm this evening, streets are drying finely.

March 13, 1874; Friday. This morning the snow was falling fast and continued through most of the day. I spent some time in sweeping the snow from my piles of Lumber thus securing to a greater extent the benifit of the Sun when it did shine between the squalls of snow. I did not go uptown to day. The weather is warm the snow melting almost as fast as it fell. At night the ground was freezing, slightly.

March 14, 1874; Saturday. The ground slightly frozen this morning. I spent some hours in reading History after which I called on Mr. [William] Gibbs for some information in regard to some of the work on my house. On my return I called at the P. O. and from the Post Master I received a Copy of the Omaha Herald sent by Marion to his wife Rhoda which I delivered to her and she not wishing to read it she gave it to me. I also caried a letter to my daughter Ida.

March 15, 1874; Sunday. Passed morning in reading History until

---

69. Samuel G. Goodrich's book, *History of All Nations*, was written for young adults in simple language with over 700 illustrations and maps. It was a large book, however, with over 1200 pages. It covered every known present or past country.

about 11 oclock when with Mrs. Lyman I went to the residence of my Son Marion and passed the residue of the day with his wife Rhoda and her children. Edwin B. [Bartholomew] and wife [Lelia] and children wer[e] with us. Frequent squalls of snow and some rain yielded their contributions to make up any lack [that] might exist in our winter. A[t] evening returned home. The ground was covered with snow.

March 16, 1874; Monday. Passed the morning in reading and in movein[g] snow around my building place. During the day I went up town and called at the co-op, and while there I meet with Prest. [Thomas] Callister. Had some talk with him in regard to lath which he said they should be makeing so soon as they should put up and start the Mill, to cut them. Called at the Free Trade [store] and bought some [canned] salmon. In the afternoon the snow fell freely to the depth of about 6 in.

March 17, 1874; Tuesday. Passed the morning hours in reading History, after which I spent some time in removeing the snow that fell during the last night, from the ground contiguous to my house and the Lumber piles. Through the day we had frequent squalls of snow. Towards night the weather became cooler, freezeing the ground at night. Did not go out to day but done some light work about the House. The residue of my time I spent in reading.

March 18, 1874; Wednesday. Winter stil lingers in the Lap of spring and defiantly shakes her snowy tres[s]es in the face of the Verdent Q[u]een of the Se[a]sons. Passed the morning hours in reading. After this I worked some time in the plaining some of the boards for the Base of my fence. The residue of the day and evening were past in reading. I to day received R[eligio-]P[hilosophical] Journal with its treasures of free thoughts clothed in ^its^ usual hapy an[d] lucid style of expression. Weather cool at night.

March 19, 1874; Thursday. The weather stil cool[,] and boaken [broken] storm clouds are floating around the Horizon as evidence that winter is stil lo[a]th[e] to relinquish his reign in favor of spring. To day received some fence posts from Mr. Bartholimew which we trimed and prepared for setting, 8 in number Obtained [these] from Mr. Bartholimew [and] some fresh pork. The residue of the day I passed in reading History. Lorenzo worked a part of the day.

March 20, 1874; Friday. Passed the day in reading History and the

News of the day from the papers. The weather was hazy and not clear[,] some light snow flying in the aire, the [weather] growing milder at night, freezing but lightly through the night. Did not go [o]ut to day the streets were very mudy, and the traviling very heavy for the freighters with heavy teems and loads.

March 21, 1874; Saturday. Passed the day in reading History. I was suffering very much to day from the effects of a severe cold in my head attended with slight soarness of my throat, and Neuralgia through my head. Amasa and Lorenzo went out for Deer but theirs was hunters luck[,] they came home without game. The weather is now becomeing gradualy warmer the snow is melting and grass is starting finely on the Benches. Samuel McBride was buried today.

March 22, 1874; Sunday. I was feeling quite Ill from the effects of cold in my head attended with fever. We made ready for our friends the Kelley's who came in about 12. Oclock. Mr. K. wife and children and Shortly after Mr. E[dwin] Bartholimew and wife and Children came in and spent the day with us very pleasantly. The weather is to day warm and springlike. The [United] Order of Enoch[70] was ventilated by the Church folks preparitory to drawing more ties around the people.

March 23, 1874; Monday. Passed the morning hours in reading. Went up town and made some inquiries about Nails for my fence, after I had my spade mended that was broaken by the Boys. Received a call from br [Charles] Andersen. He wished to borow some fence Rails from me. Made an examination to be certain that I had Lumber to meet my wants.

March 24, 1874; Tuesday. To day was not able to work much. Passed the forenoon about the house. Mrs. Turley called this morning and also Cynthia and Children. In the afternoon I overlooked some fence lines and engaged Henry to dig my Post holes for ten cents each. He dug out 10. in the afternoon. These I filled with their posts. As night aproached there were some indications of rain. We received some letters from Marion.

March 25, 1874; Wednesday. After some reading during the Morning I [was] buisy with some light work about the shop after which I set some posts. My head was very painful to day. Lorenzo was working on the Base

70. In February 1874, Brigham Young advised the residents of some 200 rural settlements that they should organize communes he called the United Order of Enoch. Most efforts lasted only a few months before they failed.

Boards for my fence. Mrs. Lelia Bartholimew and Children wer[e] with us through the day. The weather stil becomeing more warm and spring-like. The snow is melting very fast.

March 26, 1874; Thursday. My health not very good to day. Worked some at my fence, and made a call on brother [William] Gibbs for a tool but did not get it as it was lent out. Lorenzo finished Moulding the Base-Boards for the fence. Edwin brought me 11. more posts to day. The weather stil warm and pleasant. My cold in my head gives me much pain and almost disqualifies me for labor.

March 27, 1874; Friday. Tried to work some this morning but the pain was so severe in my head I had to quit and go to bed an[d] made some applications of cold water to my head which after a while afforded me relief from the intense pain and a free discharge of Bloody matter since which I have had ease in my head. In the afternoon I called on Clarra[,] Marions wife, and from there call[ed] at the residence of Mr Hansen, and got a plain.

March 28, 1874; Saturday. Tried to work a little but had to quit a[nd] go to bed for a short time, after which went up in Town and called on Rhoda and then went to Mr Hansens and returned his plain. Received Tickets to go to the Theater from Lorenzo. I did not acomplish much work as my health was poor. At night attended the Theater and was very well entertained. Returned home about 12. oclock.

March 29, 1874; Sunday. Passed the morning hours at home after [which] I went with Mrs. L[yman] to visit Mrs Clara Lyman[,] with whom we pased the residue of the day. Bishop [Edward] Partridge [Jr.] and wife Sarah, called. Mrs. P. remained but the Bishop passed on. Mrs Rhoda L[y-man][,] came in and vis^i^ted with us. The weather was showery through the day [but] the rain abated towards evening. We called at Amasa's as we returned home where we meet Edwin and Lelia and children.

March 30, 1874; Monday. The snow was falling all day. My health was not good. I did not go out to day but was in bed part of the day, the diziness in my head prevented me from going around much. During the day snow fell to the depth of one foot.

March 31, 1874; Tuesday. Snow was falling this morning. My health did not allow me to go out to day. In the forenoon wrote letter to Paulina. The snow was melting considerable through the day, frezeing very lightly at night. I had to keep [to] my bed a portion of the day on acount of the pain in my head, which became easy near night and is I think geting better altho the diziness in my [head] has not ~~altho~~ altogether subsided but is gradualy becomeing less.

April 1, 1874; Wednesday. This morning we cut up the timbers for our Gates which Lorenzo dressed up in part. I made a call in town and saw Mr. Russel about Burning Lime. He promised to get about it soon. He afterwards came to see me at my house about the same matter of preliminaries to the Work.

April 2, 1874; Thursday. To day we began to put ^up^ our gate frames and put up the large frames and fited the pickets. Mrs. Turley was with us to day. I made ^a^ call up town and procured a due bill on our Store of seven dollers and made some purch[a]ces for the House. After which I returned and helped Lorenzo on the Gate frames until night. The weather stil warm and pleasant, not freezeing any at night. My head geting better. Dr. [Gustavus] Simonds called to day enroute for Payson.

April 3, 1874; Friday. This morning we moved a large Plumb Tree onto my place from near Priscilla's house. My self and Lorenzo wer[e] engaged on the Gates of which we completed one ready for painting. I made a call up town for some screws which I found at the Co-op. Weather warm and springlike.

April 4, 1874; Saturday. To day Lorenzo an[d] I worked on the Gates which we completed[,] after which I pruned some of my Trees which had been neglected in this respect formerly. At early candlelight I with Lorenzo attended a meeting of the Directors of the Free Traders Union at the Store, the Board were all in attendence. On my return home I called at the residence of my Son Amasa for Mr[s]. Lyman.

April 5, 1874; Sunday. During the morning hours I wrote a letter to Hila at Salt Lake City after which I went with Mrs. Lyman to visit Edwin and Lelia with whom we dined after which I went to the P. O. and posted my letter and returned to Edwin's and came home near Sundown. Some indications of more storm through the day but was quite clear at night and no storm until the Morning. During the evening read History.

April 6, 1874; Monday. To day worked in the Shop ajusting the fastnings to my Large Gates. During the afternoon received a call from Mr Wm Bishop. Some snow fell today.

April 7, 1874; Tuesday. In the morning I finis^h^ed the fastenings to my large gates after which I went up town and made an arangement with the C<u>o-o</u>p for Beef, to the amount of twenty five dollers. Returned home and with Lorenzo to help me I pruned about ~~I~~ half of my Orchard but when I had got thorugh I found I had worked to[o] hard. I was very restless the night through from over weariness. Did not rest much. Made [en]dorsement on Lorenzo's not[e] of $64.75.

April 8, 1874; Wednesday. To day was engaged in removeing and reseting some of my fruit trees. Lorenzo was geting out the lumber for the top molding for my fence. In the afternoon I called on Rhoda and engaged her Wheelbarow to do some moveing of dirt on my place. After which I called on my friend brother Hansen to borow a plain with which he accomodated me, on my return home I called on Eliza [Partridge], and saw Hariet.

April 9, 1874; Thursday. This morning was engaged for a time in seting some fence posts in my division fence after which I was engaged the balence of the day in looking out a chance to bring the water to my orchard and Grubing out the brush for the same. Received letter from M[a]rie my daughter Mrs Struder. To day Cynthia Amasa [Jr.]'s wife had a fine boy Baby.

April 10, 1874; Friday. This morning commenced to take down my old fence in front so as to commence puting up my new fence[,] the material for which is mostly prepared for use. Called on Mr [Peter] Silda, and engaged him to help us next week on our fence. At dark Paulina and Laura arived enroute to the home of her friends in Idaho Teritory. They were traviling with a Mr. Lemons as far as Salt Lake City. Weather cooler with high wind.

April 11, 1874; Saturday. In the morning went up to town and bought some Nails of the Co-op for my fence. No Meat in Market to day. Returned home and done some dikenig [diking] for the Water ditch. Paulina and Laura left early this morning on their journey North. Wind high to day[,] Weather cool. In the afternoon Saw Mr. Thomas Turner. He promised to work for me next week.

April 12, 1874; Sunday. Remained at home all day and had Lelia with us through the day. Wind high with indications of storm. Some light sprinkle of Rain through the Night. Mr [Peter] Silde called to day and said he would help me during the week to put up my fence.

April 13, 1874; Monday. This morning we commenced the days work by takeing down the old fence in the front of the Orchard to make place for the new. Mr Peter Silde worked for me to day on the fence, of which we put up the Posts and rails for 11 Rods [60½ yards]. Henry was diging the post holes in front of the Orchard. Mr. Ja[me]s Razor called on me to day. Rhoda called in the afternoon for a short time. To day my Son Theodore was 21. years old. Some indications of storm.

April 14, 1874; Tuesday. Weather rather squally so we did not work on our fence. Lorenzo went to Mountain to hunt Deer, but killed none. I worked in the Shop puting some braces in my Gates. Made a call up Town to buy some screws for my work. Mr. [Peter] Silde called during the day, but not to work on acount of the weather. The Pres[iden]ts Party arived from the south this evening. Weather cool with indications of storms.

April 15, 1874; Wednesday. I was engaged in puting Pickets on my fence and in the morning I pruned some trees. In the afternoon Mr. Silda helped me on my fence and we put on all of the Square pickets. The Prest [Brigham Young] and his party held meetings to day to Enochize the people.[71] Lorenzo attended the meeting, they had meeting at night to organize. Weather quite cool.

April 16, 1874; Thursday. I was early at work cleaning off my fence posts. The weather was quite cool. The President and party left this morning for the No[r]th enroute for Salt Lake. Mr. [Peter] Silda and Lor[e]nzo [Lyman] were working with me to day. The horse race came off to day between Mac Neil an[d] King the horse of the former win[n]ing.[72] The weather quite cool. Paid Turner three dollers, and Silda one.

April 17, 1874; Friday. I was early at work on my fence and finished cleaning the posts after which we placed the bot[t]om Rail and I commenced puting on the pickets. In the afternoon Mr. [Peter] Silda and Lorenzo Nailed pickets and I waited on them. Wind was very high to day and troublesome and cooll. Indications are for fair weather. Turner worked on the water d^i^tch. At close of days work found myself very weary and tired.

71. As mentioned in note 70, this was President Young's attempt to establish a communal society as the United Order of Enoch.

72. The likely loser was Bishop Culbert King's horse. King was breeding stallions in Kanosh.

April 18, 1874; Saturday. Weather warm and springlike, but no work on my fence but what I done myself. Turner was working on the Levee, and ditch. I went up in town to look for some lumber to make the cap to my fenceposts but did not find any. Returned home and found some pieces that would answer the purpose. Paid [Thomas] Turner in flour three dollers and a half. Weather becoming gradually more warm.

April 19, 1874; Sunday. The weather was warm and pleasant. In the morning wrote a letter to my daughter Mrs. [Maria Louisa] Struder in Beaver County. Remained at home during the day. In the afternoon took a short walk with Mrs. L. on the Bench on the eastern portion of our place. At night there were thick clouds with indications of storm which came in snow during the night.

April 20, 1874; Monday. This morning the snow was falling and continued to do so through the day. Done some errends in town. Lorenzo was not with us to day. I done some work in the Shop sawing out some caps for my fence posts. Spent some hours in reading. Indications of storm at night. The aire was quite warm.

April 21, 1874; Tuesday. Snow stil falling pr[o]fusely. I made a call on Mr. [Peter] Silde in relation to the Caps for my posts. I returned and then I commenced to dress up the caps which kept me buisy for the residue of the day. At night it ceased snowing for a short time, freezeing lightly during the night. Not much travil on the Streets to day. A large increase of mud from the melting of the snow, makeing the travil diagreable [disagreeable] and heavy, hard on the freighters and the travilers.

April 22, 1874; Wednesday. Awoke this morning to find it had not stormed during the night but ~~had froze lightly~~ it stormed some in the morning. I finished up my Caps for the fence, and then went up in town to buy a ~~fen~~ bench Screw but did not find one. I then called on Isaac Carlin and had him turn me a head to put on my Iron screw, for which he charged me half a doller.[73] Weather fair at night.

April 23, 1874; Thursday.[74] This day was engaged cuting lumber for caseings for my posts.

73. In the 1840s when cast-iron screws replaced wooden ones, manufacturers were unable to keep up with demand. In 1873, Christopher Spencer of Connecticut invented the camshaft lathe, leading to mass-production, so the market supply would soon improve.

74. This and the next entry were mistakenly written out of order. Lyman wrote

April 24, 1874; Friday. This day was early at ^work^ and saw the Sun rise. Mr [Peter] Silde worked for me to day caseing my posts in my fence seven in number. Lorenzo worked at the Bench all day, and I made one call up town to get some Nails. The residue of the day I worked with Mr. Selde. Mr S worked for me four days and a half.

April 25, 1874; Saturday. This morning with Lorenzo [I] finished puting the pickets on my fence. Made a call in Town for Nails and screws[,] after which I with Lorenzo hung the Gates in my fence. The wind was very high and troublesom[e]. Called on G[abriel] Huntsman and bought of him a Paint Brush, for painting my fence. After this with Mr[s]. Lyman made a call on Edwin and Lelia at their residence. Some indication of storm.

April 26, 1874; Sunday. Went to day with Mrs. Lyman and spent the day with Mr. John Kelley and family. Mrs. John Kelley jr. was with [them]. As we started home we Meet Lorenzo who informed us that Mr. Daniel Page and family had called at our place to stop for the Night. Mr. P. and family were on ther[e] way home from the North.

April 27, 1874; Monday. Called at ^the^ Drugist and bought some Alcohol for noting. Returned and worked until noon on the Water Ditch under the direction of Master Rowley. After Noon Went to the County Clerks Office and exicuted two Deeds[,] one to Lorenzo and one to Theodore, of Lots of land included in and covered by my Deed. After which I prepared some paint and done some painting. The Pages left this morning for home.

April 28, 1874; Tuesday. Was engaged in painting my gates. The weather quite warm and the Fruit Trees are now comeing out. The Apricots are in Bloom and the Apple leaves are like Squirels ears, the prospects for the fruit are good at present. To day I received the first Number of a New Reformatory Paper just started in N. Y. It is Called the Champion of Humanity. Its Editors are Lessie G[oodell] Steamitze and J[ohn] B[rown] Smith.[75]

April 29, 1874; Wednesday. Was early at work on my fence and fixed

---

at the bottom of the page pre-printed as Thursday, "This belongs to Friday," and at the bottom of the Friday page, "This belongs to Thursday."

75. Lyman would have seen an ad for the *Champion of Humanity* in the *Herald of Health* or *Banner of Light* and subscribed. The newspaper folded within the year. Braude, "News from the Spirit World," 414.

up my Morter Bench. The weather was Increasingly warm. To day I received a letter from Mrs. [Maria Louisa] Stredder informing me that Mrs. Matilda [Carter] had a Daughter born on the 20th. Mother and child doing well. Mrs. Lyman made [a call] on Edwin and Lelia [Bartholomew and] found all well. Some indications of storm as night aproached.

April 30, 1874; Thursday. I was engaged on my fence to day. Lorenzo was dressing Moldings for the fence. The wind was very high to day from the Southwest, with indications of a Storm. As night aproached I found myself very weary from my days labor. At night read the Ban[n]er [of Light] before going to Bed. The wind still Blowing briskly as we retired to rest.

May 1, 1874; Friday. ~~Was early at work on the fence~~ During the forenoon the weather was warm and pleasant. In the afternoon had some Storm. In early Morning the Snow was falling but it soon melted so that I could pursue my work. The Sun went down in a bank of dark clouds.

May 2, 1874; Saturday. The day opened bright and pleasant after the last storm. I was engaged for a short time on my fence, after which I spent some time in cl[e]aning up in side of the fence in fron[t] of the House. Lorenzo and Henry were engaged in the work of reseting some old fence around their lots. Late in the afternoon I received an instalment of Lumber from [Dorus] Warner on his Bill. To day took some Appels from the ground. They were well saved.

May 3, 1874; Sunday. This morning the weather [was] warm and pleasant. I wrote a Letter to Mr. Richard R. Hopkins of S. L. City. I^n^ the afternoon with Mrs. Lyman [went] to Edwin's residence but finding no one at home we went to their farm, where they were puting in Barley. We taried in the field for an hour or two after which we returned and took Super with Edwin and Lelia, and then returned home. The night warm.

May 4, 1874; Monday. This morning I set some Posts to secure my large Gate, after which I with Lorenzo finished pruning my Orchard. In the afternoon I commenced the Painting of my fence. In forenoon [I] made a call up town and bought some soap. At night went to store to meet the Directors but concluded to defer the Meeting until next Saturday evening in view of a full Board.

May 5, 1874; Tuesday. Today continued my painting and the Boys Lorenzo and Henry Cleaned up the Orchard and commenced ploughing and hawled the fencing onto the ground for my fence below my Orchard between my Lots and those of the Boys.

May 6, 1874; Wednesday. To day I was painting and the Boys were ploughing and in the forenoon Lorenzo comenced to put up my division fence of which he put up about one half. Mrs. Turley was with us to day and also Lelia and her children. Edwin called in the evening. Late in the afternoon Mr. [Dorus] Warner brought another Load of Lumber on his Bill and said he would have the balence in two day[s]. Some clouds at night. Weather quite warm.

May 7, 1874; Thursday. Was early at work on my fence. Went up in town to the Co-op Meat market. The wind was so high that I had to quit painting And in the afternoon I looked over my Appels and took out those that were not sound and left the residue in the ground. This afternoon I received two letters one[,] from Agness in the City and one from [ex-wife] Paulina in Farmington where she will stay until after Conference.

May 8, 1874; Friday. I was early at work and after Breakfast I wrote a letter to Paulina in Farmington. This morning I received from Mr. [Dorus] Warner the residue of my Bill of Lumber and paid him $83. dollers in curency. At noon received a call from Mr. Stredder who brought me some potatoes from Mr. Philo Carters Ranch near Greenville[,] Beaver County. Mr Stredder was enroute for Salt Lake City for goods for Mr. Woodhouse of Beaver City. Some indications of storm.

May 9, 1874; Saturday. Past a portion of the day in painting until broaken off by the rain. When I went up town and made a call on Mr. [William] Gibbs, in relation to my house[,] after which I called at the Lumberyard and bought some plank to put on the top of my foundation on which to rest the walls of the building. Called at the Store and made some small purc[h]ases for the house. Returned home and spent residue of day in painting; and in evening attended a meeting of the Board of Directors, the weather turning pleasant.

May 10, 1874; Sunday. Passed the day at home. Had Amasa [Jr.] and ^wife^[,] Edwin and wife[,] with us through the day. Received a call from Mr. William Bishop who freely expressed his own sceptical views and in an indirect way inquired for the works of Thomas Paine.[76]

---

76. Thomas Paine's 1794 criticism of the Bible, *The Age of Reason*, was nearly as

May 11, 1874; Monday. Was early at work, after Breakfast had a call from Mr. H[orace] Rusell, who had Burned lime for me during the past week. He said that in two or three [days] the Lime could be handled. I advanced him some seven dollers and eighty five cents on the Lime. After this I went out in Town to engage a Man to tend Mason[ry] but did not find any that would engage. Returned home and past the residue of the day in painting. Paid [Peter] Selde two dollers.

May 12, 1874; Tuesday. In the morning I was early at work on my fence and continued to work uninter^r^upted until in the afternoon when I was sped from my work by a shower of rain attended with thunder and Lightning and some Hail. After the rain subsided I then finished painting my [fence] the first coat. Weather pleasant and warm after the shower. Lorenzo ploughed some ground and planted some corn for Priscilla before the shower.

May 13, 1874; Wednesday. Was early at Break of day at work, until Breakfast call, after which I made a call up town and paid Mr [Horace] Russel three dollers and ninety cents on the Meat Market. Returned to my work but was soon caused to stop by the Rain. We received a call from our old friends Robert Riche and wife who were enroute for Salt Lake City. Mrs. R. was just recovering from severe indisposition.[77] Mr. Johnson was with them. Late in the evening had a call from Mr. [William] Marsden from Parowan enroute for Salt Lake City.

May 14, 1874; Thursday. Was engaged in cleaning up my cur[ra]nt trees. Lorenzo and Henry were planting Corn. Mr [Horace] Rus[s]ell found his Lime Kiln to[o] hot to ~~l~~ allow him to handle the Lime. In the afternoon had a call from Mr Robert Walters whose Saintly qualities were recently evinced by turning his wife with her babe out of Doors in the Night and Snow storm. Such we[re] fruits of his Righteousness which he did not fail to tell me was faultless in his practical Life.

May 15, 1874; Friday. I was engaged~~d~~ to day in working my ground among my cur[ra]nts. During the day made a call up town, after which

---

influential as his previous work, *Common Sense*, one of the sparks that ignited the American Revolution.

77. *Indisposition* could imply a physical illness, lack of appetite, or lack of interest, according to Noah Wester's 1828 dictionary. It hinted at a possible psychological depression, but that was not its exclusive meaning.

I finished my diging. In the evening with Mrs. Lyman I called [on] Mr. [John] Kelley and returned his History, which I [had] been reading. It was Goodriches Universal History of all Nations. The weather was quite warm through the day. Some juvinile May parties were out today[,] mostly Sunday school scholars. Mrs. Rhod[a] L[yman] called to day.

May 16, 1874; Saturday. Weather very warm to day. Done some diging to day and made one call up Town and bought some Nails, after which I with Lorenzo commenced to put on the Moldings to the fence and in the afternoon we put on some of the Base Boards. Weather warm at night. During the day I mad[e] a water way to b[r]ing the water we shall need at our Mason work next week in puting in our Foundation. The Houds passed to day enrout for Beaver.

May 17, 1874; Sunday. In the morning I wrote a letter to Hyrum Coombs in Salt Lake City, After which with Mrs. Lyman I went to and spent the day with the Bartholimews. On our way there we meet with brothers George Woods and Homer Duncan, the former enroute for England[,] the latter for Salt Lake City. At Mr. B's we meet Mrs. Willis[,] Widow of [William] Wesley Willis. She was enroute for the City of the Saints. Late in the afternoon Mr. Joh[n] Vance and wife called on Mr. B.

May 18, 1874; Monday. Commenced the painting of the Base on my fence. After Breakfast went to the Store and bought some Ɨ Oil and after finishing my Primeing I then Rip[p]ed some plank to get some bed[-timber] pieces for my House. Received some sixteen bushels of Lime from Mr. [Horace] Russell. Allen & Henry Tanner called. They were freighting for the Post at Beaver. Some Thunder to day.

May 19, 1874; Tuesday. I was early at work clearing the trenches for puting in the Foundation. Henry worked with me to day, and after completing the dirt heaving we let in the water and watered the Orchard. This finished our days work. During the day Mr. [Horace] Rusell delivered five bushels of Lime, making twenty one in all that I have received from him. Mrs. Lyman went in the afternoon to Edwins. Priscilla and children and Mrs. [Francis] Turley started [for] Minersville to day.

May 20, 1874; Wednesday. This morning I commenced to frame the timber for My House. Mr. [Horace] Russell went after Lime this forenoon and Lorenzo was Harowing and Henry was helping him. In the afternoon Mr. Russell came and commenced laying the foundation for my House. The weather was quite warm all day. [Teenage sons] Ira and Henry were both helping in the afternoon.

May 21, 1874; Thursday. I was early at work first filling Earth around the Mason work put in yesterday. I had to regulate the water which was neglected by the Boys when they quit work at evening. Mr. [Horace] Russell was on his work to day and progressed very well. In the evening I Turned in the water and watered the residue of my Orchard. After[ward] Mrs. Lyman sorted some Appels[,] while doing which John Stredder called. He was enroute for home at Carters Ranch Near Greenville[,] Beaver [County]. We gave him fruit for family.

May 22, 1874; Friday. I was early at work filling in dirt around the wall that had been built the day before. After Breakfast I continued my work on my timbers for the House. Henry ploughed and Lorenzo helped Ira to tend [the] Mason[ry]. The weather was very hot so that I took my work into the shop and ~~shop~~ shade.

May 23, 1874; Saturday. I was early at work filling dirt around my Mason work. [Horace] Russell an[d] [Ralph] Rowley were working to day. I finished up some of the timbers and in the afternoon I tended [the] Mason[ry] and filled in dirt around the Mason work. Weather warm and sultry. Mad[e] call up town [and] procured order for [Peter] Silda on Meat Market.

May 24, 1874; Sunday. This morning I wrote letter to Misses Latimer & Taylor. I call[ed] on Mr. [William] Gibbs for some directions about my Doors & Windows for my Hous[e] which I am to get from the City. He promised to make my French Windows for me at City cost. Called on Mr [John] Kelley who said he could let me have a Box in which I could slack my lime for my Mason work. Called with Mrs. Lyman on Edwin & Lelia.

May 25, 1874; Monday. I was early at work and after Breakfast I made a call on Mr. Henry Noyes in view of geting him to freight some goods for me from the City, which he agreed to do on the same terms he was freig^h^ting for the Store. Had the news this week of the Killing by Indians of 28 Miners at Circleville on the Sevier River.[78] Lorenzo hawled

78. Lyman got this report from the *Salt Lake Tribune*, which wrote that soldiers returning from Beaver found the bodies. It was, however, a rumor. Circleville was the site of the 1866 massacre of twenty-five Paiutes by Mormon settlers. "Fight on the Sevier," *Salt Lake Tribune*, May 22, 1874.

some sand and tended Mason[ry] a part of the afternoon. Laid the first timbers on the foundation. Hired one extra hand in the afternoon.

May 26, 1874; Tuesday. This [morning] was early at work. Both masons were on hand to day. I made two calls in town to day and paid [William] Gibbs for Door and [John] Kelley for the Boots for Ira. John Mills worked to day Makeing up Mortar. Lorenzo and Henry waited on the Masons. The ~~M~~ wind was very high to day with some indication of rain. Had a call to day from Mr. John Coombs enrout for the City.

May 27, 1874; Wednesday. I was early at work clearing up the ground around the house before the Mason[s] came to their work. During the forenoon the wind was not high, the workmen progressed very well with there work.

In the after[noon] they closed the walls of the foundation ready for the Floor Joists. During the afternoon the wind was very high and [there was] some light fall of rain not enough to inter^r^upt the work. [William] Marsden called to day.

May 28, 1874; Thursday. Passed the morning hour makeing some measurements about my building. In the afternoon it rained so that the Masons quit work. I^n the^ afternoon I cleared up some of the ground around the House. Father Robert Richie and wife called and dined. They were enroute for their Home in Iron Conty. Rain commenced falling soon after they started.

May 29, 1874; Friday. I was early out this morning and remeasured my house for the ajustment of the residue of the Timbers. About 8 oclock the Masons came to work and by a little after Noon they completed the work on the foundation and I then settled with and paid them for the work fifty eight dollars and fifty cents. After this made a call up town and after my return filled in some dirt around the House. Some rain and some Hail to day.

May 30, 1874; Saturday. Passed most of the day in leveling the ground around my house, had some showers with hail thorugh the day. Lorenzo and Henry finished ploughing and planting the Orchard. The friends of Enoch [Mormons][79] held conference to day and will continue tomorow. Henry planted some mellons to day.

---

79. See March 22, 1874.

May 31, 1874; Sunday. Passed the day at home makeing such preperations for our journey as the circumstances allowed. Therre were some showers on the mountains. Edwin and Lelia came up and spent the afternoon with us and they went home. Edwin showed me a specimen of fine sand for plastering, in the Street. The Conference is to continue another day.

June 1, 1874; Monday. This morning I called on Bishop [Edward] Partridge [Jr.] and gave him a bill of my lath which he promised to bring to the notice of the Sawyer at the earliest practicable moment. After this about 8 or 9 oclock I started with Lorenzo [to] S. L. City. We traviled to and camped on the Seveir Hill. The roads were some mudy when we started but became drier as we traviled North. Weather Clear and pleasant at night.

June 2, 1874; Tuesday. This morning we were early on the road and traviled Past Salt Creek and Camped. There were indications of Storm but no rain fell.

June 3, 1874; Wednesday. Started early and arived in Payson after noon and dined at Bishop Joseph Tanners, and then we passed on to Spanish Fork and stoped for the Night at the residence of Mr. Samuel Thompson. Some rain fell while we were passing from Payson to Spanish Fork. We were kindly received by our friends the Thompsons.

June 4, 1874; Thursday. Were early on the road to Provo where we arived about 9. <u>oclock</u>. Here I parted with Lorenzo to take the [railroad] carrs for the City. I was kindly invited to Breakfast with Dr. Roberts. Reached the City about one oclock and found the folks all well. I made several Buisness calls in order to hasten our return, Meet with friendly gre[e]tings from old friends.

June 5, 1874; Friday. Called ^on^ Mr. William Godbe at his residence, after which I called on Mr. Stien and paid Hila's school bill after which I bought a smal bill of Goods at Kimbles & Lawrence. Lorenzo arived to day. In the afternoon left my Organ at the store of Mr. Danes & Son to be cased and packed for transportation to Fillmore. I Paid for my Doors & Windows sixty one dollers and 90 cents.

June 6, 1874; Saturday. Commenced loading our Wagon for the return journey and made a few purchases in the City. By night had the most of our goods in the wagon. Meet with several old friends to day whose greetings were warm and cordial, at evening found myself weary from my day's labor. The huried nature of my visit to the city has prevented me from calling on my friends as I would like to have done.

June 7, 1874; Sunday. Was engaged the most of the day in loading the Wagon for the journey. Did not go to church to day.

June 8, 1874; Monday. This morning we were early on the road, and traviled to and mad[e] Noon halt at Smith's place near Drapersville. In the afternoon traviled to and camped for the night at Green's place. Some Daneish men from Sandpete were camped there. Their Horses left them during the Night. They had not recovered them when we started.

June 9, 1874; Tuesday. Started early this morning and made noon halt at [Jesse] Steele's place near Springville during which the wind blew very hard. Reached Payson at night and put up with Bishop Joseph Tanner. Here we meet with Father T[imothy] B. Foot ^and^ Brother Freeman Tanner who had broaken his arm a day or two before. His wife we learned had left him and had gone to her relations in Tintick [Eureka].

June 10, 1874; Wednesday. We were early on the road and made our Noon halt hear Mona in Juab Valley Then traviled to and camped for the night near 4 mile Creek in sight of Levan without wood or water. Weather very warm.

June 11, 1874; Thursday. Started early this morning and made our Noon at Sevier, at Brigs place after which we traviled to the can[y]on south [of] Scipio, where we arived and camped after dark. The night was quite cool.

June 12, 1874; Friday. In the morning started for home where we arived at 1. oclock and found all well. Rhoda and Clarry [Clara] were there and they reported all well at home.

June 13, 1874; Saturday. Passed the day mostly at Home. Lorenzo & Henry were Hoeing their Corn. Weather warm and dry. During the day I saw the Mare for which Theodore traded my Horse. She and colt were together. Took some Apples from the ground to day [and] found them very well preserved. Some of the Grand children called to day also Mrs. McKay and Her sister Miss Laura Bartholimew.

June 14, 1874; Sunday. This morning I wrote two letters[,] one to Hyrum and Josephine [Coombs] in Salt Lake and one to Marie at Beaver. We then went to Edwins and spent the most of the day; and as we came home in the afternoon Mr. [John] Kelley and wife [Margaret] called on us and also Mr. McKay and wife and Miss Laura Bartholimew. Weather warm and pleasant. The grand children were some of them around to day, some oposition to Enoch in the meeting to day as reported by those present.

June 15, 1874; Monday. To day I commenced to fit the timbers for my house body. Mad[e] two calls up town during the day, in the afternoon received a letter from Paul[i]na who is with her friends in Idaho.

June 16, 1874; Tuesday. I was buisy on the House timbers. The weather was very warm. Mrs. Lelia Bartholimew spent the afternoon with us with her children. In the evening I had some talk with Mr. [Peter] Silda about working for me on my House. He said he would com[e] to work in a few days.

June 17, 1874; Wednesday. I was early at work puting my timbers in the water to soften them so that I could adjust them in their places. In the evening John Stredder and Lyman Carter called on us from Beaver, and they reported all well when they left home. Later in the evening received call from Mr. Henry Tanner of Beaver and Miss Alice Lyman and Marion Jr.

June 18, 1874; Thursday. I was early at work puting the Bed timbers on the foundation and frameing some of the wall timbers. John Stredder and Lyman Carter started for home in the afternoon. Synthia and children were with us to day. Lorenzo and Henry finished hoeing their first planting of corn to day, the crop is looking fine.

June 19, 1874; Friday. I was early at work puting on the remaining bed timbers on my Foundation. I made a call on Mr. [William] Gibbs for some information in reference to puting on the Cornice. Past the residue of the day in framing the timbers for my house. The weather was very warm. Lorenzo and Henry went to the Mountain in the afternoon to get some timber for shed and Corall. Bought some Fish of Uncle Moses Benet.

June 20, 1874; Saturday. I passed the early morning in working on my timbers, after which I watered the Orchard runing the water over it twice. ~~A~~ The Boys returned about 9. oclock, with their load of Timber. I spent the residue of the day in hoeing up the weeds on the lots. I worked at this until after the s[u]n went down. The weather very hot. A light sprinkle of rain fell in the afternoon.

June 21, 1874; Sunday. Remained at home during the forenoon. Passed the most of the time in reading. Received a call from Mother Huntsman and her little Grand Daughter. After Diner with Mrs. Lyman and Hila[,] called on and spent the afternoon with the Bartholimews. Weather very sultry. Some little rain fell during the afternoon. Took supper with our friends and then came home. Some indications of rain.

June 22, 1874; Monday. Was early at work. Called on Mr. [Peter] Silda in regard to his coming to help this week. He promised to come on Wednesday. Made a call up Town. Returned and made a commencement to frameing the Rafters for the front Section of my House. Lorenzo & Henry were to day seting the Posts for their Shed and Stable. In the afternoon I had a call from Mr. Davis & Son who are runing the Lumber Mill at Cave Creek.

June 23, 1874; Tuesday. I was early at work on my timbers and about noon I went to the Meat Market, but I got no meat as the shop was Closed. I called at the Store and bought a can of Fish. Lelia and Children were with us to day. Had a call from Mr [Peter] Silda, who said he could not come to work on to morow, but would come next day and bring a hand with him.

June 24, 1874; Wednesday. Was engaged with Lorenzo in Sawing and fiting Lumber for the House. Omner Turley and his Mother returned from Beaver to day.

June 25, 1874; Thursday. To day Mr. [Peter] Silda and Charles Andersen worked for me and we put up the front section of my House. Bought nails twice to day. In the afternoon I attended the meeting of the Directors. We ajourned the general meeting until the 11th of July.

June 26, 1874; Friday. To day was early at work and with the help of Mr. Silda and Anderson we put up the residue of my house, which we completed without accident to any of the hands. In the afternoon the wind was some troublesom[e]. We put up the House in two days, its length was 40 ft & three inches and its width 30 ft, and six inches, and height 14 ft to the square.

June 27, 1874; Saturday. This morning I turned the water on to my Orchard, after which Henry took charge of the water and completed the watering of the Fruit trees. During the forenoon I called on Mr. [William] Gibbs for some information in regard to my House.

I then called on Mr. Henry Noyes. After this done some work about my House then worked a while clearing the ground near my House of the grass and weeds on it. Then mad[e] call on Edwin's family. Received letter from Paulina.

June 28, 1874; Sunday. In the morning I wrote two letters[,] one to Paulina in Farmington and one to Richard Hopkins in Salt Lake City. After diner with Mrs. Lyman & Hila we went to Mr [John] Kelleys and made an evening call. Here we meet Mrs. Dudson & a daughter of brother Lovell from Oak Creek.

June 29, 1874; Monday. Today made some preparation and commenced to lay my floors. During the day I hurt my foot by the fall of a Board. I[t] gave me much pain. Lelia and children were here in the after part of the day. To day Lorenzo and Henry began to plough their Corn, preparitory to wattering. In the evening cleaned the grass off some of my ground ajacent to my House.

June 30, 1874; Tuesday. Continued the work on my floor. In the morning made a call on Mr. [William] Gibbs and then called at the store and bought some nails. Received from Mr. [John] Kelley the first number of The Spiritualist at Work, published in New York by D. M. Ben[n]et[t] & E. V. Wilson at three dollers per year. The paper represented by this number is very good in Matter and its arangement. In the evening I cleaned off some more of the ground ajacent to the House. The boys finished ploughing their corn.

July 1, 1874; Wednesday. Worked on my [floor] until the Nails were exhausted. After this I went to Mr. Coalgroves and borowed of him fifteen and ¼ lbs of nails. After my return I slept for a time on acount of the heat & weariness. The Boys were engaged in the watering of their corn the[n] gave me some help during the day on my floor. Weather was very hot all day. Bought of Bartholimew 35½ lbs. of Pork.

July 2, 1874; Thursday. I was engaged to day on my flooring and nearly completed the central section of the same. Weather excessively hot to day. The boys were watering their corn to day. Late in afternoon I received a letter and some specimens of Rock fore Assay from Mr. E. S. Barns at Rocky Ford on the Beaver in Beaver County. In the evening received a call from Mr. [William] Gibbs the Builder. He came to look at my House which he said was good.

July 3, 1874; Friday. I was early at work on my floor and the Boys continued the watering of their corn which they completed in the afternoon. The weather to day very hot and sultry. In the afternoon we received the news of the Death of Mrs. Mary Brunson Bryant, Wife of George Bryant & Daughter of Mr. Lewis Brunson. She left a young Babe to take its chances in Life through the kindness and care of other friends.

July 4, 1874; Saturday. There was not in our Town any special notice by Celebration of the Nations Natal day. This shows to some extent how weak the Tie of sympathy between the Mormon heart and our Nation and Government. To day Mrs Bryant was buried. We had some fine showers in the afternoon which continued into the night. Finished laying the floor in the front section of my House.

July 5, 1874; Sunday. This morning I wrote letter to Mr. E. S. Barnes at Rocky Ford on the Beaver. Dined at Home and after Diner with Mrs. Lyman and Hila made a call on Lelia with whom Hila stoped for the night as Edwin was gone to Clear Lake to cut hay. Some very light sprinkle of rain in the afternoon. Some Troops were moveing by to day for the Post at Be[a]ver. I[n] the evening called on Mrs. [Ruth] Turley at her residence.

July 6, 1874; Monday. Began we[e]ding out my Orchard. The Boys started after Diner for Clear Lake to make hay. Made call at the Store and bought some [dry] goods, for pants. Lelia and her children were with us to day. The weather very Warm all day. Mr. James Decker from Parowan passed here to day enrout for Salt Lake City to get maried. Rather to[o] expensive for poor men of little means.

July 7, 1874; Tuesday. I was buisy in my Orchard to day. The weather was very warm and Sultry. Mrs Bartholimew and Children were with us to day ^And^ also Mrs [Ruth] Turley passed a part of the day with us. I had my Apple pearer repaired by Mr. McKay. Some Troops were passing on to the Station at Beaver. The Comet shone to night with unusual splend[o]r in contrast with some dark clouds around the Horizon.[80]

July 8, 1874; Wednesday. I ^was^ engaged to day in hoeing in the Orchard, but did [not] feel very well and the heat was very opressive. Some Troops were passing on to the Post at Beaver. My work in the Orchard

80. This was one of the most visible comets of the nineteenth century. The so-called Great Comet of 1874 was visible for seventy days.

was very slow and Toilsome as the ground was some Rocky and dry. No Lath yet for my House and no prospect at present.

July 9, 1874; Thursday. Passed the early morning in work about home after which I went up Town and bought Nails and paid those I borowed of Mr. Coalgrove. Inquired about Lath at the Co-op but got no encouragement. Weather very hot. Did not feel well to day. Done some hoeing in the evening. Heard from Sand Pete [Sanpete Valley] that the Danes did not see the [United] Order so Clearly as its friends wished them to. Time tells Truth.[81]

July 10, 1874; Friday. Passed the morning in choiring [doing chores] about the place after which I made a call up Town and bought som[e] dry goods [fabric] and a churn. While out I received of Mr. [John] Kelley twenty dollers of the curency I had loaned him. After my return I fitted up the Churn with dasher [plunger] and then put in some hours makeing some water ditch at the head of my Orchard which would be a way to take off the waste water from Priscilla's Orchard.

July 11, 1874; Saturday. I was engaged to day in watering my Orchard, in the morning[,] after which I went up Town and called on The Gibbses' at the Courthouse. I then called on Rhoda and examined my flour of which there was some 1,750 lbs. stil on hand. At 6. oclock attended the ajourned meeting of the Stockholders of the free Traders Union. The attendence was to[o] small to do any buisness. Weather very warm. Received letter from Hyrum [Coombs].

July 12, 1874; Sunday. This morning I wrote a letter to Oscar in Parowan inquireing after the chance to get some Lath for my House. After this I went with Mrs Lyman and Hila to Marions and passed the residue of the day during which I went to the P. O. and bought some stamps. The Boys Lorenzo & Henry returned to day from Clear Lake, where they had put up hay during the week. Weather very hot and sultry.

July 13, 1874; Monday. I was early at work hoeing in my Orchard at which I worked until the heat became to[o] intense to endure when I ceased my labor for a time until afternoon when Henry joined me in the hoeing. Late in the afterno[o]n we had some thunder attended with light showers of rain. At dusk the party that went to the Can[y]on for Beries

81. If Lyman is referring to the United Order of Enoch, it was already failing in some areas of Sanpete Valley. Allen Roberts, "Fairview," in *Utah History Encyclopedia*.

returned all well except some wet feet by skiping in the Creek. No rain through the night.

July 14, 1874; Tuesday. I was engaged in hoeing in the Orchard through the early part of the day after which I was on the Bed for some ~~the~~ time. Mrs. Lelia Bartholimew and children were with us in the afternoon. Weather very sultry & warm. In the afternoon the Boys were watering their Corn. Made some change in the floor of the shop by puting supports under the Joists. Past a few hours in reading history of our Countrymen.

July 15, 1874; Wednesday. In the morning finished hoeing out the lower part of my Orchard. After this I went to see Mr. Coalgrove to get some information in regard to the Steel Mill which he had visited for Lumber recently. Did not feel very well to day. Past some hours in bed. Late in the afternoon had some thunder and Light sprinkle of rain. Hoed some weeds in front of the House Lot. The Boys were not at work to day. I read some during the day.

July 16, 1874; Thursday. I feel well to day but I did some work on the ground ajacent to my house. The heat was very opressive to day but it was ^s^lightly relieved in the afternoon by a fine pleasant rain of a half hours duration after which I kept to my work while there was light. Henry found his horse. At night almost the entire Horizon was clothed with dark leaden Clouds which seemed to promise more rain, but the stillness of Death was in the atmosphere. Not a leaf was stired by the evening's zephyr's gentle breath.

July 17, 1874; Friday. I was poorly in health to day and did but little work in the forenoon, except some light work about the House. In the afternoon made some new diches for watering the Shade trees. To day, I ate green appels of ~~two years~~ the growth of two years[,] seventy three and four. This proves that we need not be without the Luxury of fruit in its green state through the entire year, by haveing a proper asorted varieties of Appels.

July 18, 1874; Saturday. I had the water runing on my Orchard to day. I made a call up Town an[d] gave [Peter] Silda an order on our Store for Two dollers and one on the Beef Market for nine dollers, which paid him in full for his work on my House. Called at the P. O. but received nothing. In the afternoon had a fine rain. This morning some Troops on their way to Arizona left our Town where they camped last night.

July 19, 1874; Sunday. In the morning I wrote two letters[,] one to H[yrum] S. Coombs Salt Lake City and one to Mrs Matilda Carter My Daughter in Beaver Co[u]nty. The weather was very warm to day. Amasa [Jr.][,] Lorenzo[,] & Henry with Cynthia and children went to the Can[y]on for beries. In their trip encountered some Rattlesnakes but received no harm beyond the fright. After posting my letters I went with Mrs Lyman and Hila and dined with Edwin [Bartholomew] and family.

July 20, 1874; Monday. During the morning I was engaged in hoeing up the weeds on the ground in front of the House After diner I made a call on Mr. [William] Gibbs in regard to the arangement of the Stairs in my house. While I was out I called on Mr. Thomas Turner in regard to diging a well but failing to secure the necissary impliments for the work I was forced to relinqish the undertakeing for the present. After my return home we had a fine shower of rain.

July 21, 1874; Tuesday. In the morning I worked at hoeing on the front ground. After this I commenced shifting the dirt and rock in front of my house so that I could put down the timbers of the Coridor [hallway]. This work engaged me until some tine in the afternoon. When this was completed I commenced to prepare the timbers for the cross partitions in the house and also commenced to set them up. Indications of rain but none fell until night.

July 22, 1874; Wednesday. I was engaged in clearing up the ground around my House. Lorenzo & Henry made a begining to move the surplus rock that was around the House so that we could lay the botom timbers of the coridor to my House. I worked on the partitions and in the afternoon commenced puting in the Lintels over the Doors & Windows & made a call on Mr. [William] Gibbs at the Court House. After continued my work on my Lintels until night. Some rain to day.

July 23, 1874; Thursday. Worked at hoeing in the mor[ni]ng. Afterwards I went to work on my house and fell and sprained my wrist so I had to quit work. Received letter from Oscar.

July 24, 1874; Friday. Wrote letter to Oscar and with one hand managed to water the Orchard. The Mormons were Celebrating the day [Pioneer Day]. Heavy showers in the afternoon.

July 25, 1874; Saturday. My wrist kept me from work to day. Received letter from H[yrum] S. Coombs. Rain fell profusely at Northern terminus of Main Street. They had two considerable floods during the day from the Bench east of the Street. Amasa [Jr.] brought me a stick from the Can[y]on to put in front of my gate to hi[t]ch horses to.

July 26, 1874; Sunday. Passed this day mostly at home. We had rains in and during the forenoon. In the afternoon it clear[e]d up and the Sun shone out Brightly. In evening called on Mr. [John] Kelley for some outfits for our journey to Parowan for the Lath for the House. The weather prospects are good. Heard to day of the drowning in Nevada of John Turner of Cedar Springs[82] and also of accident by Lightning at Salt Creek.

July 27, 1874; Monday. This morning Started with Henry for Parowan. Nooned at Canosh with our friends the Blacks, and Camped for the night at Cove Creek. Weather warm and the Roads good.

July 28, 1874; Tuesday. Were on the road before the Sun shone on us. Nooned at Beaver with Our friends the Tanners and called on Mr. Crouch and then traviled to and camped at Buckhorn springs with the Anderson's.

July 29, 1874; Wednesday. This morning traviled to Parowan and stoped with Oscar's family whom we found well.[83] He was at the Co-op Mill. Called on some of my old friends in Town. Weather warm with indications of rain.

July 30, 1874; Thursday. Remained in Town through the day. Called on Mrs [Jane] Hanks. Dined with the Pages.

July 31, 1874; Friday. Stil waiting for Paulina's return. Dined with Mrs. Hanks. In evening had Seance[,] Mr. J[ohn] Coombs Medium present.

August 1, 1874; Saturday. To day Mrs. Lyman returned from her Northern friends. She returned in good Health.

August 2, 1874; Sunday. Remained at home most of the day. Dined with Mrs [Jane] Hanks. We Breakfasted with Oscar.

August 3, 1874; Monday. To day the Boys Henry and Charles went to the co-op Mill for Lath. To day was elections.

---

82. There was a flash flood in Eureka, Nevada, located in the middle of the state, west of Ely and south of Elko. The flood destroyed the main theater, a commercial building, a stable, and about thirty houses and killed fifteen people, including Turner. "Eureka Flooded," *Nevada State Journal*, July 25, 1874, plus "second dispatch," July 26. .

83. Oscar Lyman was now twenty-six, and he and his wife, Phoebe Madora Benson, who would turn twenty-two the next day, had two children, one and three years old. Oscar's mother, Paulina, who lived nearby, had children by Amasa who were as young as eight and ten.

August 4, 1874; Tuesday. To day the Boys returned with a portion of the Lath.

August 5, 1874; Wednesday. To day Henry and William went and brought the balence of the Lath. I remained at home [and] passed the time in reading.

August 6, 1874; Thursday. We were buisy in preparing for our return home. In the evening had some talk with Mr. William Hollyyoke in regard to Plastering for me.

August 7, 1874; Friday. This morning we started for home. William was with us to take back the horse of Charleys which we had to work in place of ours that had a soar neck which rendered him unfit to work on our return. We traviled to and camped at Beaver with Mr. John Coombs.

August 8, 1874; Saturday. After Breakfasting with our friends we traviled to and camped at Cove Creek Fort and put our Horses in the Barn.

August 9, 1874; Sunday. To day traviled to Fillmore and found all well at home where we arived at about 9 oclock P. M.

August 10, 1874; Monday. To day in the afternoon commenced puting the Lath on the Body of the House. Mrs. George Taylor called to day. She was enroute for Salt Lake City.

August 11, 1874; Tuesday. I worked at Lathing through the day and in the afternoon Lorenzo and Henry with William began to Load the Wagon with Apples to take to Market in the South where he was going for the residue of the Lath and Shingles. Mrs. Lelia Bartholimew was with us to day with Children. Received a letter from Marion in England. He was well at date.

August 12, 1874; Wednesday. To day Lorenzo Started with his load of Apples and William went with him. I sent by them three hundred lbs. of Flour to Paulina. I worked at the lathing and Henry helped me after the Boys left. Made Call in town. Synthia and Lelia were here with their children.

August 13, 1874; Thursday. I [was] buisy on my house but during the day Made a call up towwn and saw Mr. [William] Gibbs at the Courthouse. Henry was irigating in the afternoon. Weather warm and dry.

August 14, 1874; Friday. Was engaged in Lathing and Henry was watering his corn. Weather warm and not much wind.

August 15, 1874; Saturday. I was at work on my House all the day and Henry was with me. Mr. [Peter] Silda was at work for me to day puting on the Base on my fence. Made call up town for some nails.

August 16, 1874; Sunday. To day remained at home all day but found on attempting to write that my hand was to[o] lame to allow me to write the long letter to Marion in answer to his last to me. Rhoda and her small Children were with us in the afternoon. Lelia and children were also with us. Edwin called and gave me a drink of new cider.

August 17, 1874; Monday. Worked on my House, and made one call up town. In the afternoon had some light showers. Laid down the lower timbers of my Coridor in front of my House. Pared some apples during the rain.

August 18, 1874; Tuesday. Called on Mr. [William] Gibbs who came down and looked over my House and gave me advise about the work. Heard that [Henry] Noyes would be in to day or tomorrow. Some showers of rain to day. Paired some Apples while it was raining. Little or no rain through the night.

August 19, 1874; Wednesday. Was working on my house; and Mr. [Peter] Silda came to work in the afternoon. Mrs. Lyman was quite sick to day. Mrs. Lelia B[artholomew] and her children were with us to day. In the afternoon Mr. [Henry] Noyes came from the City and brought my Doors and Windows and Organ[,] all of which came in good order without damage. Some showers during the day but we had all our goods in <u>doors</u> without being wet.

August 20, 1874; Thursday. Was at work on the timbers for my coridor roof. Mr. Silde was working on my fence and Henry was Lathing an[d] in the afternoon was watering. Mrs Lyman was so far recovered as to be able to work. Made up some scaffolding for drying fruit. Some showers during the day. At night the weather was pleasant and cool but no rain fell.

August 21, 1874; Friday. To day Mr. [Peter] Silda finished ^the Base^ [of] my fence after which we put up the timbers of the Coridor to the square. The weather was very warm and during the day we had one shower. Henry was watering. Called at the store for Nails. Progressed so far with our work that we put up the first rafter on the coridor. Night cool and pleasant.

August 22, 1874; Saturday. To day put the roof on my Porch also bought some lumber for and put in the collar beams in my House roof.

I[n] the forenoon Lorenzo came home from his southern trip and brought some shingles and some Lath. On acount of mud he left 4,000 shingles at Beaver. Weather very warm. Made two calls up town.

August 23, 1874; Sunday. Remained at home through the day.

August 24, 1874; Monday. Worked on my house until noon when I fell from the uper to the lower[,] Breaking my left leg through the [k]nee joint. I was caried to my bed from which I walked away with wooden helps after a detention of 35 days of pain and suffering.[84]

September 28, 1874; Monday. This morning I made my first walk into the ajoining apartment and wrote letter to Mr. E[lias] L. T. Harison. Alice Lyman my Grand Daughter called on us with Synthia's babe which its Aunts Clara and Rhoda were taking care of during its Mother's Illness.

September 29, 1874; Tuesday. Passed the last night with the most ease of any since the Break. Weather pleasant. Pared some two bushels of apples and wrote letter to Mrs. L[yman]. Amasa [Jr.]'s wife is reported to be beter to day. Edwin started for Sand Pete with a load of fruit. His wife and children stoped with us at night.

September 30, 1874; Wednesday. Pared one bushel of Apples. My sick limb geting along much as usual. At evening Mr. Andersen called and promised to make me some shoes when he returned from Conference. Finished out another lot of Apples and in the evening cut them. During the day cut a lot of Peaches.[85]

October 1, 1874; Thursday. Pared one bushel of Apples. Some rain to day attended with heavy thunder and lightning. In evening cut the Apples, after which had a very painful and sick Night.

October 2, 1874; Friday. My leg much as usual. I pared some Apples and cut them in the evening. Mr. Bartholimew called to day and looked at my leg and thought it to be doing very well.

October 3, 1874; Saturday. To day pared some Apples. Lorenzo Started to the South with part of a load of peaches. Received a letter from Paulina reporting all well an[d] said she would star[t] the Lumber as soon as they could get the horses shod. Mrs. Richard Benson called. She

84. There are no journal entries from Aug. 25 through Sept. 27. Lyman suffered pain in his knee for the rest of his life after this fall.

85. He wrote these last two sentences on the predated page for Thursday, adding, "This work belongs to Wednesday 30th," separating that portion with a line.

was inroute to the City to attend Conference, and to marry her daughter to Mr. Horace Smith. Edwin B[artholomew] returned from Sandpete.

October 4, 1874; Sunday. Sunday some rain to day. Mr. [Peter] Silda called to day. In the evening Mr. [William] Gibbs called and chated me for a short time. My Leg steadily improveing. [C]ynthia, no better.

October 5, 1874; Monday. To day Mr. [Peter] Silda helped to move and fit up our stove in the House. Henry done some Batning on the room we ar[e] to [s]tay in this coming winter. In the evening pared and cut a bushel of Ap[p]les. My leg slowly geting better. Weather cool. Mr. John Mills called and promised to do some work for me in course of this week. Synthia no better. Our grand daughter Ethel Lyman came from Cedar springs this Morning and stoped with us.

October 6, 1874; Tuesday. To day Mr Stephen Franklin and wife Came to Priscilla's. They reported all well at [t]heir home on the Beaver [River] near the Star [mines]. Synthia stil low. To day Mr. [Peter] Silda brought me my new Crutches on which I walked out of the house into the open air for the first time after a confinement of 43 days.

October 7, 1874; Wednesday. This morning Mr. [Stephen] Franklin called on me and spent a little time with me. During the day Mrs. Franklin and her Sister called. To day walked out around my house deriving as I think benifit from the exercise. Some indications of rain.

October 8, 1874; Thursday. To day wrote letter to Paulina and pared and cut some Ap[p]les. Walked out some, My leg swelling considerably. Synthia is reported to be Better. Mr. [Stephen] Franklin started for home in the afternoon. Weather clear and pleasant.

October 9, 1874; Friday. Today Mr. [John] Mills banked the dirt around my house after which with Mrs. Lyman, he gathered and put in the ground the first of my winter Appels. Received a letter from Mr. E[lias] L T Harison of Salt Lake City. Synthia stil better. Amasa & Henry started for Oak Creek this morning. Weather stil warm & pleasant.

October 10, 1874; Saturday. Passed the morning hours in reading. In the afternoon I pared and cut some Apples. In the evening cut Peaches. Lorenzo came home to day. He could not sell his fruits.

October 11, 1874; Sunday. To day I was for the most of the day engaged in writing a letter to Marion in England. Mr. [William] Gibbs called and spent an hour with me. Edwin returned from Cove Creek Mill with his Lumber. Him and wife Dined with us. Mr. [John] Kelley called [and] spent the evening with us. Slight indications of storm.

October 12, 1874; Monday. Passed most of the day in writing[;] did not work with the Fruit. Some l[i]ght rain during the day with indications of more.

October 13, 1874; Tuesday. Finished copying letter to Marion. In the evening cut peaches. My leg much as usual.

October 14, 1874; Wednesday. Passed the day in reading and in working with the fruit. My leg improveing. Weather warm and pleasant.

October 15, 1874; Thursday. Passed the day in reading an[d] cuting fruit. Weather warm & pleasant. Synthia is reported worse to day.

October 16, 1874; Friday. To day cut peaches and read History. During the day Benjamin Robinson called and paid me $50.00 dollers on his Note. Weather stil warm and pleasant. Synthia stil lingers.

October 17, 1874; Saturday. Wrote letter to Josephine and made up a package of fruit to send to her by Lorenzo. Late in afternoon some light rain. Synthia stil lingers.

October 18, 1874; Sunday. This Morning Mr. [John] Kelley called as he was starting for Salt Lake, and I let him have $135.00 dollers in curency part on account and part to be repaid to me on his return. In afternoon Mr. Ja[me]s Thompson called and bought a Bushel of Apples. Mrs. Turley called to day. Some light rain to day.

October 19, 1874; Monday. To day Mr. [John] Mills wa[s] helping to gather and bury my Winter Apples. Some light rain during the day. Amasa [Jr.']s wife Died about 8 oclock P.M. Her age was 23 years in August. Her Illness was of some seven weeks duration.[86]

October 20, 1874; Tuesday. To day Mr. [John] Mills was helping us and we finished gathering and buriying my Apples for Winter. At 4. oclock C[y]nth[i]a was buryed. Weather fair and pleasant. Mr. [Peter] Silda called. Mrs. Lelia Bartholimew and children were with us to day.

October 21, 1874; Wednesday. Amasa called this morning and we agreed to keep the two oldest children Ethel and Mason[87] & the babe

86. After Amasa Jr.'s first wife, Olive, died in early 1872, he married Cynthia Wright. She had just given birth to a son in April before dying in October 1874 of typhoid fever, a disease caused by drinking contaminated water.

87. Ethel and Mason were the six- and four-year-old children of Amasa Jr.'s deceased first wife. Amasa Jr. would not marry again for another three years.

was taken by the Widow Fisher at Scipio. Wrote letter to Marie Streder in Beaver County. To day finished gathering the Apples. I passed most of the day in reading.

October 22, 1874; Thursday. Passed the day in reading. The Weather stil warm and pleasant. At night received as we were retireing to rest, a Message by Telegraph[88] bringing to us the Sad News of the Death of my Son Oscar, who [was] killed at 4. oclock P. M. by the explosion of the Boiler of the Steem Mill of Fish & Warren in Red Creek Kan[y]on in Iron County. Others were wounded but no particulars were given to me in regard to the accident fatal to Oscar in the prime of Life. Wife & children must feel his departure a loss.[89]

October 23, 1874; Friday. Passed the day mostly in reading History. Some indications or rain in Afternoon but not much fell.

October 24, 1874; Saturday. This morning I received a call from stake president [Thomas] Callister who gave me some particulars of the sad accident at the Mill where Oscar was killed.[90] One of the Men wounded at the time Died the folowing Night. Passed the day in reading. Sent some Apples to the Mill, to be made into cider at Mr. Bartholimews.

October 25, 1874; Sunday. ~~This morning had a call from President Callister~~ To day wrote Letters to Paulina and Madora in Parowan. Late in the afternoon we received a call from Mr. Stephen Dugins and Wife. No rain ~~to~~ after the morning.

October 26, 1874; Monday. Passed the day in reading. Our peopple were buisy in puting away Amasa [Jr.]'s Household goods. Amasa went to the Can[y]on to day. Some rain to day.

October 27, 1874; Tuesday. To day Mrs Lyman [was] engaged in puting away some apples for use this fall. Some rain in the early morning folowed by wind through the day.

October 28, 1874; Wednesday. To day Mrs. Lyman was engaged as on yesterday with the Apples. In the evening had a call from Mr. Jacob

88. The curt telegraph read "Your son Oscar was killed this afternoon at four oclock by the blowing up of Warren & Fishe's Saw Mill in Red Creek Canon." William H. Dame to Amasa M. Lyman, Oct. 22, 1874, Amasa M. Lyman collection, CHL.

89. For more, see Oct. 28 and annotation for Oct. 30. Lyman's injury prevented him from attending his son's funeral.

90. Lyman was told that Oscar had shouted at the other men to run before the explosion and had thereby saved many lives, which offered some comfort to the family.

Bushman from Lehi enroute for Beaver with his family to see their friends there. Also had a call from Mr. Dewit Tyler who was at Parowan the day that Oscar was killed and saw his Mutilated form when brought home from the scene of the sad catastrophe.

October 29, 1874; Thursday. To day passed the day in reading. During the day I received a letter from Mrs. M[aria] L[ouisa] Stredder, in Beaver County. She reported the Death of Mr. John Rease on Friday the 23rd by accidentaly shooting himself while on the range hunting stock. Several Wagons of imigrants going South passed here today. Weather clear and cool.

October 30, 1874; Friday. To day passed the time in reading. During the day I received a letter from Paulina giving some of the particulars of the circumstances connected with Oscars Death, and that of [Frank] Westbrook who lived two hours after the explosion. She recited the scene of the disaster before the Dead and injured were removed to Parowan, a distance of some 15 miles. The Locality was in Red Creek Can[y]on.[91] Mr. Bartholimew returned to day from Salt Lake City.

October 31, 1874; Saturday. Passed the most of the day in reading. In the afternoon Mr. Wesley Dame returned from Salt Lake and he brought some goods for our Store. At night Amasa [Jr.] brought u[s] a ham of ven[i]son.

November 1, 1874; Sunday. Mrs. Lelia B[artholomew] and her chi[l]dren were with us to day.

---

91. "With a broken heart I sit down to write you what I can of our grief," Paulina explained. "Last Thursday just at dark, Mrs. Halterman came to the back door and screamed 'The mill had blown up and all the men killed.' I hoped but only to get to the front door when I met Brother Benson, crying, and said our Oscar was gone. With the children crying and screaming I started to see Madora who was at her Father's. Her mother had just come. I found her fainting … We got up there about twelve o'clock. There lay the two men up on some boards outdoors. You can gauge my feelings when I saw our boy scalded from head to foot. His right arm and shoulder all broke to pieces, his right leg tore nearly off just above the knee, … the foot and ankle [detached] … And there I was. I had not you, nor Marion, nor Lorenzo, no father, brother, no strong arm to lean on, and there lay my dear Oscar who had watched like a husband or father over the family, had been the dutiful child and pride of his parents and loved by all who knew him … The supposed cause—for the want of a lead fuse in the crown sheet … [that] melt[s] out [to prevent an explosion] … When I think how them boys was cried into the wourld to be shot out so suden, … I am almost crazy and then I try to reason that I will try to do the best that I can by those I have left … Oh, I cannot write more this time." Paulina E. Lyman to Amasa M. Lyman, Oct. 27, 1874, Amasa M. Lyman Collection, CHL.

November 2, 1874; Monday. To day Mr. [John] Kelley and Lorenzo [Lyman] returned from Salt Lake and by the latter I received a package from Mrs. Coombs. During ~~my~~ the day my old friend Mr. Allen Taylor passed enrout for Salt Lake City.

November 3, 1874; Tuesday. To day Mr. [Ralph] Rowly called to get some seasoned Lumber for Brother Croft but I had none such as he wanted. While he was here his little dog was caught in a trap the Boys had set for Wolves. Weather Cloudy but mild.

November 4, 1874; Wednesday. To day Edwin brought us some Cider which we Commenced to boil and made some Apple sauce. Assorted my papers, the Weekly published by Woodhull & Claflin of New York.[92]

November 5, 1874; Thursday. Passed most of the day in reading. Cut some Apples for sauce. My Kne[e] improving. Received a copy of the Christian Union by Mail.

November 6, 1874; Friday. To day the Boys went on the Cattle drive. Amasa [Jr.] found a yearling of mine that somebody had ear marked. Theodore drove home some stock he was to del[i]ver to me in pay for the Mare I soldd him. At night we had a fall of snow some 4. inches.

November 7, 1874; Saturday. Snow fell last night. Passed the day in reading. Theodore delivered two steers to me today[,] one two year old and one yearling which was branded and turned out.

November 8, 1874; Sunday. Remained at home to day and Received calls from friends during the day beginning with Mr. [William] Gibbs in the Morning and in the Afternoon Mr. McKay and wife and later in the evening Mr. [John] Kelley and wife. Mr K. payed me $20. /100 in curency. Weather growing more Mild.

November 9, 1874; Monday. To day walked on My wooden helpers as far as Mr. Bartholimew's. I dined with them. This was quite a relief after a Confinement of 78 days. During my out[ing] saw Mr. [Nathan] Baldwin in regard to Lime for puting up my Chimneys. He could not spare me any but Mr. [Ralph] Rowley said he would let me have what I might Need.

November 10, 1874; Tuesday. To day was at home during the forenoon. In the afternoon I went to Mr. Huntsmans store and the Co-op.

92. *Woodhull & Claflin's Weekly* was edited by Channing Woodhull and his wife, Victoria Claflin Woodhull, on radical politics, spiritualism, and women's rights.

November 11, 1874; Wednesday. Did not walk out from home to day during the day. Received two papers from my old friend [Richard] Hopkins in S. L. Passed the day in reading.

November 12, 1874; Thursday. To day called on the widow [Francis] Turley. Wrote letter to Mr. Richard Hopkins in Salt Lake City. Weather pleasant and warm.

November 13, 1874; Friday. This morning walked up in town. Called on my Daughter Carley [Caroline Eliza], who was very sick. Here meet with Mrs Caroline [Partridge] Lyman. I then called on Mrs Lydia [Partridge] Lyman whom I found very Low with Dropsy. Here I meet Mr. Peter Weimer and family enrout for their home in Parowon. Called Rhoda's place. She was gone to Corn Creek. Received five dollers from Mr. [John] Kelley.

November 14, 1874; Saturday. Today walked as far [as] Neighbor [Stephen] Dugins new House. Passed the day in reading History. During the day the report of the arrest and Imprisonment at the Beaver Post of John D Lee.[93]

November 15, 1874; Sunday. Remained at home and Mrs. Lyman went to Church, and in the afternoon Mrs. Lelia Bartholimew was with us with her children.

November 16, 1874; Monday. To day worked more on my Organ. Mr. Olson promised to come and look at it.

November 17, 1874; Tuesday. To day Mr. Olsen assisted us in overhauling and refiting our Organ which we found not so much injured by the Mice as we had anticipated. Weather cloudy with indications of Storm.

November 18, 1874; Wednesday. To day walked up to the Store and after my return home worked some at repairing my Organ which had been injured by the Mice. I received a letter from Mr. Hopkins in Salt Lake City. Recived a call to day from Messers. Mortisen and Durham from Parowan enroute for Provo with wool for the Factory. They reported all well at home when they left, the wounded at the time of Oscar's Death have all of them recovered but Mr. Halterman.

November 19, 1874; Thursday. To day received Calls from brothers

93. Lee's trial, where Lyman would be summoned as a witness but ultimately not testify, would not begin until July 1875.

Reuben McBride and Volney King[,] the latter haveing recently returned from his Mission in England. We were all invited to attend the weding on Saturday.

November 20, 1874; Friday. To day Nathan Baldwin commenced hawling sand to plaster my House. He hauled 6 Loads. Weather pleasant. Mad[e] call at Store.

November 21, 1874; Saturday. To day paid Nathan Baldwin six dollers for 12 loads of Sand. A[t] 4. oclock P. M. we attended the wedding of Mr. Lorenzo Snow Lyman and Miss Zuriah Rowley, at the residence of Mrs. Priscilla Lyman. Judge Edward Partridge [Jr.] officiating. The Weding was folowed by Diner and dancing which continued until 12. oclock. This evening W[Illiam] H. Dame past [by] in the Stage as pr^i^soner for participation in the Mountain Meadows Murders.

November 22, 1874; Sunday. I remained at home all day and passed the time in reading. In the evening received a Call from Mr. Kelley and wife. Also had a call from Mr. Clothier who promised to put up my chimney tops for me soon as his present engagements were filled. Weather cloudy indicating rain.

November 23, 1874; Monday. To day Mr. [Nathan] Baldwin hawled 7 loads of Sand for which I paid him 3½ dollers in the Store. During the day I made a call at the Store on my return [and] got my Apple parer from Mr. D. McKay's Shop. Some little rain fell to day, but the Sunset was bright and clear.

November 24, 1874; Tuesday. To day went to Mr. Bartholimews and past the day with them. Called at the Store. Mr. Kelley was away, promised Mr. Olsen the use of my small Plough to plow among his trees. Weather cloudy but little rain fell to day.

November 25, 1874; Wednesday. To day called on Mrs. Rhoda Lyman. Dined with her. Wrote letters to H[yrum] S. Coombs, Salt Lake City and one to Mrs. P[aulina] E. Lyman Parowan. Weather Cloudy and warm. As I returned home I meet my Son Platt, at the co-op. Received from the Secretary a Certificate of Dividend on the Store $6.89/100.

November 26, 1874; Thursday. This morning made some calls in Town on buisness after which I went to Mr. Bartholimews with whom and family myself and Mrs. Lyman spent the day. Mr. [John] Kelley and his wife [Margaret] were with us and Mr. Edwin Bartholimew and family were with us. Asertained my Credit with the Stock herd to be $313 /100.

November 27, 1874; Friday. To day Lorenzo hawled from the Lumberyard my Pickets and Rails for my Division fence betwe[e]n my lots and Priscillas. Weather Cooler than yesterday. Called at the Freetrade [store] and read the Tribune. My knee is gaining strength very slowly. Bought Shoes for [daughter] Hila at the Coop.

November 28, 1874; Saturday. To day Lorenzo hawled the residue of my Lumber from the yard. I paid for all the Lumber received and bought one Bunch of Shingles for which I am to pay Mr. Tyler when he returns from the city. Weather stil pleasant.

November 29, 1874; Sunday. To day remained at home through the day and passed the time in reading. In the afternoon received a call from Mr. [Peter] Silda and later in the evening had a call from [fifteen-year-old] Miss Allice Lyman and [eight-year-old] Miss Hariett Pa[r]tridge.

November 30, 1874; Monday. To day remained at home all day. In the afternoon received a letter from Marion in England. Mrs. Lelia Bartholimew and children were with us to day. In the evening received a call from Messers [Stephen] Franklin and [Jacob] Bushman and their wives. Amasa [Jr.] & Henry returned from the can[y]on and reported finding the Oxen and killing of 4 Deer.

December 1, 1874; Tuesday. This morning our winter opens on us almost like Sumer save the sombre hue, of shrub and tree. I called to day on Mr. Bartholimew and settled some buisness with him. Lelia and Children were with us to day. Lorenzo Started to day for Sandpete to get pay for fruit sold there in the fall. Messers Durham and Mortisen past today enrout for home in Parowan. Peter Huntsman to day took from my place three thousand shingles, on Bartholimews acount.

December 2, 1874; Wednesday. Remained at home all day. Passed the Time in reading. Mrs. Lelia Bartholimew and children were with us to day. Received letter from H[yrum] S. Coombs Salt Lake City. Weather mild and Sumerlike.

December 3, 1874; Thursday. To day wrote letter to H[yrum] S. Coombs Salt Lake City. Made call on Mr. Bartholimew and then at the Store and read the Tribune in which there was the statement of the ~~report~~ corispondent of the Sacrimento Record of the condition of Prest

Young as he Meet him on his way to St. George, in the Town of Parowan Iron County.[94]

December 4, 1874; Friday. To day went to Rhod[a]s and dined with her and as I returned home I received a letter from Mrs. M[yron] J. Tanner of Provo. Today heard of the Death of Prest Youngs Daughter in St. George. She was the wife of H[iram] B. Clawson.[95] Orson Hyde was in Town to day.

December 5, 1874; Saturday. To day [John] Mills made Morter for Chimneys. Henry helped him. Wrote letter to Mrs. M[yron] J. Tanner Provo. Had 4 bush[e]ls of Lime from Ralf Rowley.

December 6, 1874; Sunday. Made call at the residence of Mr. [John] Kelley but the family were not at home. We returned home and past the residue of the day in reading. During the day I received a call from Mr. John Eldridge.

December 7, 1874; Monday. Clothier put up my chimney tops in ^the^ front of my house. Buried 17 bushels of potatoes, which I received from Lorenzo for Apples. Beside these I took 2 bushels into the house. To day I received from Lorenzo a Receipt for six bushels and 16 lbs of wheat from the Miller at Lyman's and Robinsons Mill. Weather warm and pleasant. John Henry Rollins passed here to day.

December 8, 1874; Tuesday. To day Mr. Clothier finished my Chimney Tops for which he charged me five dollers. Weather stil warm and pleasant.

December 9, 1874; Wednesday. Made ready for my journey to the South to Parowan.

December 10, 1874; Thursday. Started on our journey and traviled to and camped at Cove Creek. Lorenzo and wife in the Wagon and myself in the Fort.

December 11, 1874; Friday. Traviled to and stoped for the night with My Daughters Mrs. [Matilda] Carter and [Maria Louisa] Stredd[er] at Carter's Ranch.

---

94. The reporter confessed that he had forgotten the church president's advanced age and was "unprepared for the sight of this weak … invalid." "A Trembling Old Dotard," *Salt Lake Tribune*, Dec. 2, 1874.

95. Alice Young Clawson was thirty-five years of age, with four living children and three deceased. Complications with the final birth ultimately caused her death. Her husband was the general superintendent of ZCMI.

December 12, 1874; Saturday. To day traviled to Parowan [and] found the Family well. Mrs. Mary Fish died this Morning about 6. oclock A. M.

December 13, 1874; Sunday. Attended the Buriel of Mrs. Fish. Weather cool.

December 14, 1874; Monday. Spent the day with Mr. Daniel Page and family. Mr Robert Riche and wife were with us.

December 15, 1874; Tuesday. Remained at home and past the time in reading. Today Lorenzo and wife started on their return home to Fillmore. Paid Jesse N Smith $29.80/100 for Lath.

December 16, 1874; Wednesday. Remained at home and in the Morning I received a call from my old friend Mr. E[benezer] Hanks. In the evening received a letter from Mr. John Kelley of Fillmore.

December 17, 1874; Thursday. Remained at home during the day and past the time in reading. Wrote letter to Mr. [John] Kelley.

December 18, 1874; Friday. With Mrs. Lyman I spent the day with the Hankse's. In the evening received letters from Lorenzo and Philo, from Beaver informing me that Lath could not be obtained there. Received a call from Mr. Riley Morse and wife this evening.

December 19, 1874; Saturday. Answered my letters of yesterday from Philo & Lorenzo. Bought 8 thousand Lath of the Co-op for which I promised to pay 48 doll[a]rs in Curency on or before the first of June next. In the evening had a call from Dr. John Christian who looked at my broaken knee but gave no encouragement as to the chances of recovering the use of the knee Joint. Mr. D[aniel] P. Clark called this evening.

December 20, 1874; Sunday. Remained at home and wrote letter to [nine-year-old] Miss L[ydia] M[ay] Lyman in Fillmore. Mr. E[benezer] Hanks called this morning.

December 21, 1874; Monday. Passed the day in writing letter to Marion in England.

December 22, 1874; Tuesday. Passed the day in reading; and in the afternoon went to the Co-op Lumber yard and found some Lumber which Oscar had furnished on My Bill, for the finishing of my House.

December 23, 1874; Wednesday. Finished and Copied and posted my letter to Marion in England. Called on Mr. Worden and engaged him to do some plaining for me. Weather cold and pleasant.

December 24, 1874; Thursday. To day Selected some three hundred feet of inch Lumber at the Lumberyard, which increased my debt at the Co-op to $57.0/100 dollers. Called on Mr. Worden, and he promised to plain my Lumber. Weather becoming more mild.

December 25, 1874; Friday. Passed the day with the Benson's. Returned home at evening. Orson Hyde preached at night.

December 26, 1874; Saturday. Remained at home through the day. In the afternoon William hawled my Lumber from the Lumberyard to Mr. Worden's shop to be plained and brought home that which was plained.

December 27, 1874; Sunday. With Mrs. Lyman spent the day with Mrs. Jane Hanks. In evening received calls from Mr. Benson and Rily Morse and wife. Weather cool and pleasant. John L Smith was in town to day and preached.

December 28, 1874; Monday. To day remained at home and did not go out. Had my Boots half soled by Father Hakes, for which I paid him 1.85/100. In evening had a call from Richard Benson.

December 29, 1874; Tuesday. Wrote letter to Philo Carter. Made a call on Mr. Warden. He had not plained my Lumber.

December 30, 1874; Wednesday. Remained at home and in the evening received a call from D[aniel] P. Clark and ^his^ wife Sarah. Weather growing more mild.

December 31, 1874; Thursday. Made call on Worden. Passed the day at home. Made call on Mrs. Hanks. And thus went out the old year 1874 with fine and pleasant weather.

13 Free from Pain, 1875–1877

During his last two years, Lyman's life revolved around the house he was constructing and time spent with his first wife, Maria Louisa. In most of his diary entries, he mentioned getting lumber for the house, working with carpenters, and irrigating his fruit orchard, followed by quiet nights at home. His leg caused him considerable discomfort. He complained about having to hobble on crutches across town only to find that someone was not at home or that his carriage was not ready.

He began attending church with his family, although he could not resist adding critical remarks in his diary about the content of the services. Gradually he began referring to his sons-in-law by their first names, and he was pleased to be invited to dinner at Eliza's house when their son Platte returned from his mission. This trajectory of good feelings was to be short-lived, however, because as he mentioned on January 28, 1877, he became ill, followed by a short period when he was "free from pain" but "very weak," and then passed away on February 4, less than a week after falling ill. A heartbroken son, Francis Marion, wrote that his father's death elicited the "largest funeral procession ever seen in Fillmore."

January 1, 1875; Friday. Spent the day [in Parowan] with the families of Messers D[aniel] P. Clark and Rily Morse and other of their friends who were invited guests. Passed the time agreeably. Returned home before dark.

January 2, 1875; Saturday. In morning paid [Nathaniel P.] Warden $3.00 for the plaining of my Lumber. During the day he sent it home. Spent most of the day with Mrs Zilpha Smith and her Daughter Mrs Peter Weimer.[1] [Former sixth wife] Mrs [Paulina] L[yman] and [son Oscar's widow] Madora [Benson Lyman] were there. In the evening had a call from Mr Benj[amin] Croft and wife.

January 3, 1875; Sunday. In the morning called at the residence of Mr Daniel Page. The family wer not at home. I then called on Mrs [Jane] Hanks and spent the day there. Mrs Lyman was with us. In the evening Mr [Nathaniel P.] Warden called on me and paid me the change due me in settlement for plaining Lumber. Weather growing more mild.

January 4, 1875; Monday. In the morning called on Mr [Daniel] Page and passed the time with him until late in the afternoon. Weather warm and pleasant. In the evening received a call from Mr Richard Benson. My knee gives me considerable pain through the day.

January 5, 1875; Tuesday. Passed the day with [son-in-law] Mr Edgar Clark and family and a few invited friends. Had a pleasant visit. Some light snow fell during the day. Mrs Lyman and Madora spent the day with us.

January 6, 1875; Wednesday. Passed the day in visiting D[aniel] P. Clark and family and invited friends. At night received a letter from [son-in-law] Philo Carter with the news of [grandson] Lyman's broaken arm[,] and setting the time he would come to Parowan for my Lumber.

January 7, 1875; Thursday. Remained at home all day passed the time in reading after writeing letter to Philo Carter in answer to his received last night. Weather stil becoming more mild and warm.

January 8, 1875; Friday. To day visited and spent the day with Mr Watson and family and Mrs Lyman and Madora and Mr Collins Hakes and wife were with us.

January 9, 1875; Saturday. Passed the most of the day with Mrs Jane Hanks. In the evening received calls from Mr Sidney Burton and Mr Richard Benson. In the morning I received a call from Mr Timothy

---

1. Zilpha Stark Smith was a plural wife of George A. Smith. Her only surviving child was Mary Amelia, who was thirteen years old when she married Peter Wimmer. Family histories emphasize that she "matured early." Ash, "Peter Wimmer, Mary Amelia Smith, and Sarah Ann Hulet Family of Parowan."

Adams from Cedar City which called up some reminesences of bygone years that seemed fresh in his memory tho not so fresh in mine.

January 10, 1875; Sunday. Passed the day at home had Mr Richard Benson and wife were with us to day. Had a brief call from Mr [Daniel] Allen. In evening Mr Benson called in after the meeting. Weather stil pleasant.

January 11, 1875; Monday. Remained at home passed the day in reading. At night received a call from Mr Richard Benson. Wind very high all day with other indications of a coming storm.

January 12, 1875; Tuesday. Remained at home all day and in the evening received calls from Mr E[benezer] Hanks from Iron City and also from Mr Richard Benson. The weather is not warm enough to melt the snow wich stil covers the ground.

January 13, 1875; Wednesday. Remained at home and passed the time in reading Wrote letter to Mrs L. M. [Maria Louisa] Lyman[2] in Fillmore.

January 14, 1875; Thursday. Passed the day at the residence of Mrs Jane Hanks. After diner Mr E[benezer] Hanks started for Iron City where he is employed as general superentendent of the Iron works. Weather pleasant.

January 15, 1875; Friday. Visited Mr Geo Taylor and family and the widow Mary Pendleton. In the afternoon Mr Pope came with the teems for my lumber and lath, we loaded the lumber ready for the road. Some slight rain was falling this evening folowed by light snow. Philo sent two teems and Wagons.

January 16, 1875; Saturday. This morning we loaded our lath and completed our preperations for the road, and about 12 oclock the teems started on their way. Last night we had a light fall of snow. Late in the afternoon my daughter Mrs Martha Roper called on us she was returning to Fillmore from St. Geo where her husband is working on the temple when he ought to be at work makeing himself a home.[3]

January 17, 1875; Sunday. Remained at home through the day and

2. Lyman sometimes transposed his wife's full name, and to this day family histories refer to her as both Maria Louisa and Louisa Maria.

3. Martha Lydia Lyman was the oldest daughter of Amasa and Caroline Partridge. Relations with the Partridges had improved, but Amasa let Martha's marriage to Alvin Roper in October 1874 and Lydia Partridge's death on Jan. 16, 1875, pass without comment. In addition, he clearly objected to his new son-in-law's choice of employment.

Mrs [Jane] Hanks was with us. This morning my Daughter [Martha] left us with her friends McCullock and Lovell on her way home [from Parowan] to her mothers [house] in Fillmore.

January 18, 1875; Monday. Buised myself in prepareing patterns for my apple cutter some parts of which Mr [Benjamin] Croft promised to make tomorow. Weather pleasant no storm to day.

January 19, 1875; Tuesday. Wrote letter to Mrs Lyman in Fillmore after which I went to see Mr D[aniel] P. Clark who promised to go and take us to Philo's on next Friday. I then went to the shop of Mr B[enjamin] Croft who made me a feril [ferrule] of steel for my Apple cutter for which he would have me pay. Weather pleasant with considerable wind which had the effect to dry the roads.

January 20, 1875; Wednesday. passed the forenoon in makeing bill of Lumber for my Barn. In afternoon called on Mrs Mort[en]sen. In the evening finished my bills of Lumber.[4] Some snow fell late in the afternoon weather somewhat cooler.

January 21, 1875; Thursday. Remained at home most of the day. Made call on Mrs [Jane] Hanks.

January 22, 1875; Friday. Were to day disappointed about starting on our visit to the Beaver by the suden illness of Mrs [Sarah] Clark. Remained at home through the day.

January 23, 1875; Saturday. Started homeward with brother D[aniel] P. Clark and his wife Sarah and my wife Paulina. We made noon halt at the Buckhorn Springs with our old friend Miles Anderson, the traviling was heavy. We arived in Beaver about 10 oclock at night and put up with Uncle Sidney Tanner and his wife Julia.

January 24, 1875; Sunday. This morning we traviled to and called on my Daughter Matilda Carter. [Her husband] Philo and my son Charles started for Fillmore with my Lumber. They expect to be back on Thursday. Weather pleasant. Mr [son-in-law] John Stredder and wife [Maria] were with us today.

January 25, 1875; Monday. To day went to Minersville and called on our old friend Henry Rollins and family whom we found well. Here we

4. Throughout the diaries, when Lyman refers to a bill, he means a bill of goods, or list of items to be purchased—an order—not an invoice.

meet my wife Dionitia.[5] A very light fall of snow this evening. During the afternoon Mr John Bradshaw called in for an hour.

January 26, 1875; Tuesday. Remained through the day at brother [James H.] Rollins. During the day received several calls. Mrs Mary Lightner and widow Gilbert and a Mr Weeden. Mr Rollins went to Beaver to day. Weather pleasant.

January 27, 1875; Wednesday. To day Mr [Daniel P.] Clark and wife [Sarah] and Paulina started for Beaver enroute for Parowan. In course of the day I made a call on Mrs [Frances] Turley. Mr [James H.] Rollins came home about noon.

January 28, 1875; Thursday. To day bade my friends in Minersville Farewell and went with Mr [James H.] Rollins to the residence of my son-in-law Philo Carter near Greenville on Beaver. This evening Mr Carter and the Boys Lyman Carter and Charles Lyman came home from Fillmore where they had been with my Lumber.

January 29, 1875; Friday. Remained at Mr Carters all the day during which my Daughter Mrs [Maria Louisa] Stredder called. Passed my time in reading.

January 30, 1875; Saturday. Remained at home all day. To day Mr [Philo] Carter went on Buisiness to Lincon and Star [Mining] Districts on Horseback.[6]

January 31, 1875; Sunday. To day called on and dined [with] Mrs Maria Stredder and friends. Mrs [Matilda] Carter was of the party. Just at night Mr [Philo] Carter returned from his trip to Lincoln and Star.

February 1, 1875; Monday. Went to Beaver with Mr [Philo] Carter and wife [Matilda] and called on B[isho]p [John R.] Murdock and family with whom we dined. Here we meet Judge [Enos P.] Hoge. In the evening returned to Mr. C[arter's] [residence].

February 2, 1875; Tuesday. to day started for home with Mr [Philo] Carter. We made our noon halt at Mr [Edward] Daltons Ranch in Wildcat Can[y]on where I meet my son Ira with Mr Omner Turley. We stoped for the night with Mr Miner Prisb[r]e[y] at Pine Creek.

---

5. Lyman continued to periodically visit his wives, sometimes in a formal and duty-bound manner. However, he remained genuinely close to Paulina, who lived in Parowan.

6. The mines were west of Beaver near Milford. The Lincoln Mine was south of Milford and the North Star Mine was to the north.

February 3, 1875; Wednesday. Were on the road early and made noon halt with our friend George at Corn Creek. From thence we arived home in Fillmore about sundown and found all well at home, myself very weary with the ride.

February 4, 1875; Thursday. To day Philo started on his return home. Weather cool and pleasant. Mrs Lelia Bartholimew called to day and in the evening her husband [Edwin] called to say he would start in the morning for Salt Lake City.

February 5, 1875; Friday. Remained at home during the day and passed the time in reading. Received a call from Mr Gibbs.[7] He thought he would commence my work the first of April. Weather still pleasant but cool. To day suffered some from neuralga in my face.

February 6, 1875; Saturday. Remained at home all day. Mrs Lyman opened one of the apple deposits and found the fruit in a good state of preservation. Amasa Jr came home to day. Weather pleasant.

February 7, 1875; Sunday. Remained at home today. Mr Edwin Bartholimew and family were with us to day. Some of Marion's children were here to day. In the afternoon Mr [John] Kelley made a call. The weather cool and pleasant.

February 8, 1875; Monday. Wrote letter to Paulina in Parowan. To day [son] Henry began to put on lath. Opened the other cache of apples found them very well preserved. Passed some time in reading.

February 9, 1875; Tuesday. Remained at home passed the most of the day in looking after our apples. Henry done a little to day in lathing. Had a call to day from one of Apostle John Taylor's sons who was canvassing the country in the intrests of the Juvin[i]le Instructor [magazine]. He was the son of Elizabeth.[8]

February 10, 1875; Wednesday. Made a call in town at the Store and on my way home called on and dined with Mr Bartholimew then called on Mr Wm Bishop.

---

7. Lyman was now relying on both William Gibbs and his son Josiah for help with construction.

8. This was probably Arthur Taylor. The *Juvenile Instructor* was founded in 1866 by George Q. Cannon, with children as the intended audience. Later it was acquired by the LDS Church for Sunday school teachers, with supplementary lesson material and sophisticated pedagogical instruction. "Prospectus," *Juvenile Instructor* 35, no. 24 (Dec. 15, 1900).

February 11, 1875; Thursday. Passed a part of the day with Mr [William] Bishop who was doing some work on my Apple Cutter. Made a call on Mrs [Ann] Ashman to borow some tressels belonging to Mr A who was absent in Beaver.

February 12, 1875; Friday. This morning called on [daughter-in-law] Rhoda and let her have some of Marions Letters to copy for him. Dined with her before leaveing. On my return home I called on Mr [William] Bishop who was doing some work on my apple cuter. Weather becomeing more warm and Springlike.

February 13, 1875; Saturday. Passed the forenoon with the blacksmith at work on my apple cuter. In the afternoon prosicuted my work at home. Light in evening had call from Mr [John] Mills who had been reading my Spiritual Papers in which he has become interested. Received from Mr [John] Kelley 1 sack of flour 100 lbs.

February 14, 1875; Sunday. With Mrs Lyman passed the day with Mr John Kelley and family and other invited friends. Mr Dewit Tyler was with us a short time in the afternoon. Weather stil mild.

February 15, 1875; Monday. Made a call at the home of Mr Isaac Carlin he not being home I failed to get my work done which was the object of my call. After this I made calls at the co-op and free trade stores before returning home. Weather mild with indications of storm. To day spake with Mr Joseph Barton of Read Creek Iron County enroute to Salt Lake City. Received letter from Marion.

February 16, 1875; Tuesday. Made another bootless [worthless] trip to Mr [Isaac] Carlins as he was not home. After returning home passed the remainder of the day in working on my apple machine. Made a call on Mr Henry Noy[e]s who has recently bought a place in our vicinity which he is improveing finely by his labor. Some indications of stormy weather. Mrs Lelia Bartholimew and children were with us to day.

February 17, 1875; Wednesday. Remained at home all day and worked on my apple cuter. During the last night there was a light fall of Snow which me[l]ted soon this morning. Weather cloudy in afternoon indications of more storm. Prest [Brigham] Young and his party left Fillmore this morning enroute for Salt Lake City.

February 18, 1875; Thursday. Remained at home all day and worked on my [apple] machine. Light fall of snow last night. Sun shone some during the day which was warm melting the snow that fell the night before.

February 19, 1875; Friday. Remained at home and buisi^e^d myself at work indoors all the day. Some snow fell last night but it all disappeared soon when the Sun arose. Gave nor received calls to day.

February 20, 1875; Saturday. Did not leave home to day. Walked on the street north as far as [son] Lorenzo's place where he was engaged in working on his house timbers. While here meet with Mr John Eldridge. Today the local conference of the Saints was in cession. Received call from Mr Bartholimew in regard to some buisness connected with the Store.

February 21, 1875; Sunday. Wrote letter to Marion in England. To day Amasa [Jr] started for [the town of] Deseret with four loads of Timber and Lumber for the new dam.[9] The snow was falling fast as he started with a warm gentle wind from the South. Snow ceased falling about noon and the weather became cool and frosty.

February 22, 1875; Monday. Commenced pointing my pickets for my division fence. The weather was Suny and pleasant. At night found myself very weary from my days work.

February 23, 1875; Tuesday. This morning the ground was covered with snow which fell during last night. Passed the day in reading. Some little snow fell during the day.

February 24, 1875; Wednesday. To day made call on Mr [Isaac] Carlin to get him to do some work for me which he promised to do for me tomorow. Worked some on my fencing. Six months ago to day I broak my knee and am stil on my crutches.

February 25, 1875; Thursday. Passed the morning hours in reading then went to work on my fencing. To day the Boys were hawling wood after their return. Henry called on Mr [Isaac] Carlin for my work[,] which was not done[,] Mr Carlin haveing been sick. He then brought me a large box from the store for a Hencoup. Weather clear and bright to day.

February 26, 1875; Friday. Passed the day in makeing coup for the poultry which was a generous gift from our friends. Weather bright and warm. Received my work from Mr [Isaac] Carlin for which he charged me 65/100 cents. Was at night quite w[e]ary with my days labor.

9. The dam provided a small diversion of water from the Sevier River for irrigation at Deseret.

February 27, 1875; Saturday. In the forenoon finished my apple cutter. In the afternoon worked at pointing fence pickets. Weather warm and pleasant until near night when there some cloudy indications of comeing storm.

February 28, 1875; Sunday. Passed the day at home in reading and received some calls. Mrs Fisher called on us with Amasa's child Willard.[10] He appeared in good health and growing finely. Some snow fell during the day. Miss Sarah Benet called on [my daughter] Hila. Winter has retired and we have no regrets at parting with the hoary King of the frosty season. Wrote letter to [son-in-law] Hyrum an[d] [daughter] Jos[ephine] [Coombs] ^in Salt Lake City.^

March 1, 1875; Monday. Finished pointing my pickets. Snow falling during the day. Weather turned colder which gave me cold which induced an atack of neuralga from which I suffered through the night. The cold increasing steadily in intensity.

March 2, 1875; Tuesday. Remained at home all day and sufered some from neuralga in my face and head. Mrs Lelia Bartholimew and children were with us to day. To day heard of the Death of Mr Frederick Turley of Minersville which transpired on the 17th of February. Disease consumption. Some snow fell last night.

March 3, 1875; Wednesday. Remained at home and did not leave the house during the day. In course of the day received letters from Mr W[illiam] H. Shearman of NY City and Mr E[lias] L. T. Harison of Salt Lake City. I was measurably free from the neuralgic pain in my face and head.

March 4, 1875; Thursday. Remained at home and passed the time in reading. Weather blustering and cold.

March 5, 1875; Friday. Remained at home and passed the day in reading. There were some indications of returning pleasant weather. Received no calls to day.

March 6, 1875; Saturday. Remained indoors all day and passed the time in reading. Weather bright and pleaseant.

March 7, 1875; Sunday. Remained at home to day and past the time in reading. Mr Edwin Bartholimew and family wer[e] with us to day. In the afternoon I received a letter from Paulina in Parowan reporting

10. Amasa Jr. married Cynthia Wright shortly after his first wife died. Cynthia herself died two years later in 1874, leaving Willard behind as her only surviving child.

her self and family well at date altho Madora['s] eldest[,] [four-year-old] Oscar had ben sick since my last visit to them.

March 8, 1875; Monday. Remained at home and passed the time in reading and in the afternoon. Amused myself in makeing a picture frame.

March 9, 1875; Tuesday. Remained at home. In the forenoon I received a call from Mr Stephen Dugins who came to borow some of my tools as his were at Deseret. In the afternoon Mr Gibbs called in relation to commencing work on my house for which I agreed to pay him in flour one half and the other half in stock herd.

March 10, 1875; Wednesday. Remained at home and did not go out. Passed the time in reading. Had no calls to day. Weather mor[e] moderate. Mr [William] Marsden from Parowan passed to day enroute for Salt Lake City.

March 11, 1875; Thursday. Passed the time today mostly in reading and did not go out. The weather is becoming more mild and springlike. Loaned my Henry rifle[11] to Mr E[dwin] Bartholimew for Hunting Deer in the mountains.

March 12, 1875; Friday. Passed most of the day in working about my bench but found it very tiresome haveing to stand mostly on one leg. To day Mrs Lelia Bartholimew and children were with us. The weather continues warm. To day the Body of L. N. [J. S.] Scoville was caried through Town enroute for Provo for interment. He died in Dixie.[12]

March 13, 1875; Saturday. Remained at home and passed the day in reading. The wind blew from the North makeing us very uncomfortable with the smoke.

March 14, 1875; Sunday. Passed the day with the Bartholimew's [and] with Mrs Lyman.[13]

March 15, 1875; Monday. Remained at home and worked in the shop.

---

11. The Henry repeating rifle's lever-and-spring mechanism automatically expelled spent cartridges and loaded new ones from a magazine that held fifteen cartridges. The shooter could load the chamber by simply rotating a sleeve on the muzzle. The gunsmiths behind the invention were Horace Smith (Smith & Wesson), Daniel Wesson, Benjamin Henry, and Oliver Winchester (Winchester rifle).

12. Joseph Smith Scofield (see Mar. 15 entry) was sixty-five when he passed away in Bellevue (Pintura). He was interred in Salt Lake City.

13. This is the last entry in vol. 37. He resumes in vol. 39 to continue through the entry for June 20, 1875.

Mrs Rhoda Lyman called on us to day. The Scoville of whose Death we learned some few d[a]ys since was Joseph and not L. N.

March 16, 1875; Tuesday. Passed the day in work about the shop. Henry done some lathing to day. Had a call from Miss Ellen Lee from Beaver Daughter of Mr John D. Lee. At night Miss Lee and her associate gave a theatrical entertainment at the State House. Weather mild.

March 17, 1875; Wednesday. Made some calls up Town in quest of some cans to put in [and line the inside of] my chimney. Called on Mr McKay for some Blacksmithing. The wind blew from the North very cold. Borowed an Elbow of Stovepipe to put on top of ours from Mrs Rhoda Lyman which stoped the smokeing in the house. The weather milder at evening.

March 18, 1875; Thursday. Passed the day in prepareing a pole for hiching horses to in front of the house in the street. Henry and Lorenzo were lathing part of the day. Received a part of my work from the Blacksmith. Weather cool towards evening.

March 19, 1875; Friday. Put up my hi[t]ching pole on the street. Mr [John] Mills helped me to day in the forenoon. In afternoon I walked out and made a call at the residence of Mr [Peter] Silda and then extended my walk to the residence of Mr Edwin Bartholimew. Weather growing more mild with indications of snow.

March 20, 1875; Saturday. We rose this morning to find the earth manteled in snow of the last night's falling on account of which our work was suspended. I remained in doors through the day and passed the time in ~~the~~ reading.

March 21, 1875; Sunday. Remained at home through the day. Weather warm and pleasant. Mrs Lelia Bartholimew and children were with us to day. Wrote letter to Mr H[yrum] S. Coombs of Salt Lake City. Calculated my stairs for my new House.

March 22, 1875; Monday. Mr. [Peter] Silda worked for me to day ^and^ with Henry put in the bridging in my house. I commenced to build an out house. Weather warm and springlike. Had a call from Mr [John] Ashman.

March 23, 1875; Tuesday. I worked on my out building the weather warm and pleasant. Henry was lathing.

March 24, 1875; Wednesday. Passed the day in work on my house. The weather was warm. Henry was lathing. Travil quite brisk on the Road. Amasa [Jr] went to Deseret to work on the dam.

March 25, 1875; Thursday. Worked on my house through the day put on all the shingles. Had a brief call from neighbor Stephen Dugins. Weather warm and pleasant. Henry was lathing.

March 26, 1875; Friday. Was at work on my house and Henry was lathing. The weather was fine and springlike.

March 27, 1875; Saturday. To day I worked on my house and Henry was lathing. Weather fine and pleasant. In the afternoon we received two Hens sent to us by Mrs Rhoda Lyman by two of her little girls.

March 28, 1875; Sunday. With Mrs Lyman I passed the day with our neighbor Stephen Dugins and family.

March 29, 1875; Monday. This morning we moved our outhouse to its position over the vault and as this was done the Snow began to fall and continued through the day. In course of the day with Hila overhauled the organ which had received some slight damage from the mice.

March 30, 1875; Tuesday. To day is my 62nd birthday. I buisied my self in makeing a shutter for the front of my organ to prevent the mice from geting into it. Passed the residue of the day in reading.

March 31, 1875; Wednesday. Weather cold in the morning with Mr [John] Mills I put some pol^e^s on my stockade fence near the street with some rawhide. Worked some at the bench. Passed the residue of the day in reading.

April 1, 1875; Thursday. Made a call at the Blacksmiths and then at the Store. As I left home I meet Apostle Erastus Snow enroute to Salt Lake City to attend Conference. The mice made another attack on our organ which rendered some further precautions necessary to prevent their depredations. Weather becoming more mild and warm.

April 2, 1875; Friday. Worked on my house most of the day and prepared some tin pipes to put through the ceiling into chimneys. Received a letter from Paulina in Parowan reporting all well there but mentioned the illness at [the] residence on Little Pinto of Mr Robert Riche[y] from [whom] rec[o]very was considered to be doubtful.

April 3, 1875; Saturday. Passed the day in work on my house makeing and hanging a door. Wind high from the South, drying the mud considerably.

April 4, 1875; Sunday. I[n] morning wrote letter to Paulina in Parowan[,] after this with Mrs Lyman spent the day with Mrs Rhoda Lyman. Here we meet Mr Henry Tanner of Beaver and Miss Haris of the same place. We also here meet our old time friend Mrs Chandler Holbrook.

April 5, 1875; Monday. To day made some calls in town on buisness. Called on Mr [Josiah] Gibbs who was makeing my cornise [ornamental molding] for my house. Called on Mr Conk and had some heeling [a new heel] put on my boot. In the evening had a call from Mr Doreas Warner with whom I bargained for some flooring.

April 6, 1875; Tuesday. This morning the ground was covered with snow that had fallen during the night before. Passed the day at work in the house reparing some of my tools. Sold some apples to Mr [William] Pulsipher who was enroute for Salt Lake City from which point he was to start for the Sandwich Islands on a mission to save the heathen from one error by involveing them in another.

April 7, 1875; Wednesday. Snow was falling through the forenoon our missionary friend passed on in afternoon when the snow ceased to fall. I passed the day in reading History of the Franco-Prusian war. Weather very cold as night came on.

April 8, 1875; Thursday. Passed the day in reading and received no calls did not go out from home during the day.

April 9, 1875; Friday. Remained at home and received a call from Mr Peter Silda with [whom] I concluded an arangement for doing a portion of the finishing work on my house which he proposed to begin as soon as the weather becomes settled and warm.

April 10, 1875; Saturday. Remained at home and passed the time in reading. Walked out in afternoon and made a call upon neighbor [Henry] Noy[e]s. Weather warm and mud drying some. Received letter from Marion in England.

April 11, 1875; Sunday. With Mrs Lyman passed the day with Mr Edwin Bartholimew and family. The mud drying through the day some prospects of continued pleasant weather. Ira returned from Sandpete on his way to Minersville with grain for Mr Omner Turley.

April 12, 1875; Monday. Called on Mr [Peter] Silda who promised to come to work in a few days. I the[n] called on Mr Gibbs who also said he would be ready to work this week if the weather continued pleasant. I then called on Mrs Rhoda Lyman with whom I dined. Called at the co-op and engaged some timbers for my fruit celler. Henry was lathing.

April 13, 1875; Tuesday. Remained at home through the day and passed the most of the time in reading. Henry was lathing sold some Apples. Weather fine and pleasantly warm.

April 14, 1875; Wednesday. Remained at home and pased the time in reading. Henry ~~was~~ ^is^ lathing. Weather stil warm and pleasant.

April 15, 1875; Thursday. Called on Mr [Peter] Silda this morning and received another of his promises that he would come tomorow to beign work at my house. After returning home I hobeled out to the orchard and hoed some among my currant bushes. Henry was lathing.

April 16, 1875; Friday. Remained at home and during the day ajusted som tin shields in my chimneys. Passed the residue of the time in reading. Henry was lathing.

April 17, 1875; Saturday. Made a call on Wm King at the co-op Store and bought of him some timbers for which I paid him six dollers on [credit against the] stock herd. After returning home received a call from Mr Freeman Tanner who was enroute for Beaver with his neices Mrs [Mary Louise] Crismond and Mrs [Elsie] Chase. Henry worked ½ day.

April 18, 1875; Sunday. Remained at home and had the compnay of Mr Stephen Dugins and wife through the day. The weather warm and pleasant.

April 19, 1875; Monday. Remained at home through the day and had some cleaning up done about the place. Passed some hours in reading. Weather warm and pleasant Henry was lathing.

April 20, 1875; Tuesday. To day Mr Gibbs called and made a commencement of his work on my house. I paid him 25 dollers by order on [Benjamin H.] Robison [account]. Henry was lathing.

April 21, 1875; Wednesday. Made a call uptown and had my plough pointed and sharpened. Amasa [Jr] brought home my timbers from the Lumber yard which I bought for my fruit cellar. Henry was lathing. Weather warm and pleasant. Mr [Noah] Bartholimew promised me some seed corn.

April 22, 1875; Thursday. To day Mr [Peter] Silda commenced work on my house[,] himself and hired man. In the afternoon Mr [Josiah]

Gibbs brought the cornice boards for the house and said he should soon be on hand to work. Hemry was lathing in [the] chamber [bedroom].

April 23, 1875; Friday. Was working on my coridor with the carpenters and commenced laying the floor. Henry was lathing ½ a day.

April 24, 1875; Saturday. The carpenters were at work and finished laying what lumber I had for my coridor floor for the completion of which I lacked some 58 ft. Mr [William] Pulsipher called and got his sack of feed which he left when [he] went up to [general] conference.[14] Some light sprinkle of rain during the day. Walked through the orchard and observed the indications of the same frost at night.[15] The local conference in cession.

April 25, 1875; Sunday. Wrote letters one to Marion in England and one to H[yrum] S. Coombs Salt Lake City. Mr Edwin Bartholimew and family were with us to day.

April 26, 1875; Monday. The carpenters were at work to day on the window frames. Uncle Freeman Tanner returned with his party from the South to day and in the afternoon made a call with Mrs Lyman and children on Mrs Rhoda Lyman and our neices Mrs [Mary Louise] Crismon and Mrs [Elsie] Chases. Before we returned home we with uncle Freeman made a call on Mr Edwin Bartholimew and family.

April 27, 1875; Tuesday. To day the carpenters set the window frames. This occupied the most of the forenoon after which they commenced geting out the caseing for Windows. This morning Uncle Freeman and party past on their way homeward. Hobled out and cleaned up one row of trees through my orchard.

April 28, 1875; Wednesday. In the morning made several calls on buisness up town and after returning I went to the residence of Mr [Peter] Silda to note some of his improvements about his cellar. In the afternoon Mr S put on the caseing to one [window] of the house. Henry done some lathing in forenoon some of my stock came up in the drive north & south.

April 29, 1875; Thursday. Worked about the House. Mrs Caroline

---

14. Pulsipher was set apart for his mission to the Sandwich Islands on Apr. 11 and left on June 8. In the islands he was constantly sick, resulting in his return to Utah in Feb. 1876.

15. Cf. May 7, 1875.

Callister and daughter Clarra Lyman were with us through the day. In the evening Prest [Thomas] Callister came for his wife and daughter.

April 30, 1875; Friday. To day went with Amasa [Jr] to the mill of Hamon and Stringham on Pioneer Creek where I purchased one thousand feet of Lumber for which I paid by Order on Robison. Amasa brought home the Lumber with his teem. Arived at home before Sundown. Some indications of rain.

May 1, 1875; Saturday. Put up my lumber for seasoning. The carpenters were at work in the forenoon and finished the caseing of the windows. In the morning I worked some on my trees in the orchard. Some indications of rain.

May 2, 1875; Sunday. Remained at home [during] the day [and] wrote letter to Paulina in Parowan. Weather clear and warm.

May 3, 1875; Monday. In the morning made call at the co-op Store and as I returned home I called at the residence of Mr Bartholimew. Mr Gibbs called and done a little work to day. Mr [Peter] Silda and man were at work to day. I worked some in my Orchard. Weather warm and dry.

May 4, 1875; Tuesday. The carpenters were at work an[d] I worked in my orchard. Mr [Benjamin] Stringham called and got his order in pay for the Lumber from his mill on Pioneer Creek. Weather warm & pleasant.

May 5, 1875; Wednesday. Worked in my orchard. The carpenters were working on the House. Mr Gibbs was here a part of the day. To day mad[e] orders for [Peter] Silda. Gibbs Promised to put up the cornice next week. Henry was lathing in the chamber.

May 6, 1875; Thursday. In the morning worked in my orchard. The carpenters were at work to day wind high all the day. This morning heard of the death of the daughter of Prest [Thomas] Callister and also the death of the wife of Miles Anderson.[16]

May 7, 1875; Friday. Finished cleaning up my Apple trees. The carpenters were at their work to day. They commenced puting down the base. The clouds of last night mostly passed away during the day no frost as yet with the change of the weather. Miss Callister was buried to day. She was in her seventeenth year. She passed away in the Springtime of her life.

May 8, 1875; Saturday. Done some hoeing about the premises and

---

16. Sixteen-year-old Margaret Jane Callister died of "inflammation of the bowels." Seventy-four-year-old Nancy Pace Anderson had died two weeks earlier.

removed and repiled [re-stacked] my pickets to make room for the carpenters to go on with their work puting down the Base. Mr [Peter] Silda only was at work a part of the day. Had a neighborly call from Mr George Walters. Some light rain during the day.

May 9, 1875; Sunday. With Mrs Lyman passed the day with Mr Edwin Bartholimew and family. Weather warm and pleasant.

May 10, 1875; Monday. This morning called on Mr Isaac Carlin who promised to come down and put some tin around my chimney to stop the water from the roof. After this I called at the co-op shoe shop. Mr Anderson promised to mend my boot tomorow. Put up the stringers [side boards] for my Stairs. In the morning done some hoeing and some in evening.

May 11, 1875; Tuesday. Called at the co-op sh[o]e shop to get my boot repired and while waiting for this I called on Prest [Thomas] Callister with whom and his wives and son I went to the Brickyard where Brick were being made for him with which to build his house which he began last year. Dined with Mrs Rhoda Lyman. [Peter] Silda made the stairs.

May 12, 1875; Wednesday. Worked about the house made some steps for my back door. Done some lathing. Mr [Peter] Silda & man were on the range for stock. Mr Gibbs called and renewed his promise to come to work tomorow. Amasa [Jr] & Ira started to day for Shauntie[17] for Bullion to freight to the Terminus of the railway. Gave order to Silda.

May 13, 1875; Thursday. Made Coop for chickens and past the day in work about the place Hoeing and cleaning up the ground near the house. A light sprinkle of rain in forenoon but the afternoon was dry and breezy. No work on the house to day.

May 14, 1875; Friday. The carpenters were at work. Mr Gibbs was here part of the day [and Peter] Silda worked on the stairs. In the morning hours I done some hoeing in my grounds. We looked for rain but none fell to day.

May 15, 1875; Saturday. Passed the morning hours in hoeing in my grounds. The carpenters were at work to day three in the forenoon and one in the afternoon. Some light rain during the day. My lame knee gave

17. Shauntie was the main settlement in the Star Mining District, "the hub of freighting and smelting activities." Bradley, *History of Beaver County*, 110.

me much pain during the day. In the afternoon one of the carpenters Charles Christof[f]e[r]sen got his thumb broaken by Ball playing.

May 16, 1875; Sunday. With Mrs Lyman and the grand children visited Mrs [cousin] Clarisa Lyman and passed the [d]ay with her. Some light showers in the afternoon the Rain mostly falling on the mountain. Weather cooler in the evening to day Marion was attending conference in London.

May 17, 1875; Monday. Passed the day in hoeing in my ground. Mr [Josiah] Gibbs worked for a short time in the morning and then went home. He put on the first board of the cornice. Weather pleasantly cool. [Peter] Silda was away on search for stock.

May 18, 1875; Tuesday. Made a call up town to see Mr [Benjamin H.] Robison but he was not at home. Mr [Josiah] Gibbs put up some of the cornice. Lorenzo and Henry done some ploughing and planting of corn on the Orchard. Received a letter from Mrs [Maria Louisa] Stredder from Greenville reporting all well at date ^May^ 16th.

May 19, 1875; Wednesday. Worked in my Orchard. Mr [Josiah] Gibbs put on some cornice. Mr Stephen Dugins promised to do some work for me in cleaning up my Orchard. In afternoon received a letter from Mr A. B. Benson of Cal Sanbernardino, with a deed for a lot of which he wished me to sign and acknowledge in proper form and return to him. He sent $5.00 for expenses.

May 20, 1875; Thursday. To day signed and acknowledged a deed for a lot of land in San Bernardino Cal, before Judge Edward Partridge [Jr.] and sent the same on its way back to its owner. Mr [Josiah] Gibbs was on the work to day part of the day. Mr Stephen Dugins was at work hoeing the weeds in my rows of Apple Trees. he agreed to do the whole for $12.00.

May 21, 1875; Friday. To day Mr [Josiah] Gibbs finished the cornice on the South end of the House. Henry finished up the lathing inside and then done some shingling over the new cornice. Mr [Benjamin H.] Robison called on me in the afternoon and promised me to settle my debt in Parowan during next week. Mr [Stephen] Dugins was at ~~was~~ to day. Mr [George] Greenway promised to help me tomorow to bring the water on my lots.

May 22, 1875; Saturday. During last night & this morning we were favored with a fine rain which was much needed. Mr [Josiah] Gibbs put up a stage for puting up the residue of the cornice. I gave Order of five dollers on [Benjamin H.] Robison to [Peter] Silda. Done some work at the [shop] bench. In afternoon the storm cleared up warm and bright. ^Had a call from Mrs Rhoda Lyman to day.^

May 23, 1875; Sunday. Wrote letters one to Mr L. B. Lyman Montana and one to Miss Sophronia Lyman Wo[o]nsocket ~~RI~~ Rhode Isleand. Passed the residue of the day in reading. The night cool and the day warm. In afternoon had a call from Mrs Lelia D. Bartholimew and her children. She was in feeble Health.

May 24, 1875; Monday. To day Mr [George] Greenway worked for me on Mr [John] Mills account and we brought the water in on the Dike I put in its place last year. The water came in pleasantly and well suited to the watering of my entire Orchard. Mr [Stephen] Dugins completed the hoeing of the Orchard which he commenced one week ago.

May 25, 1875; Tuesday. Finished watering my Orchard after which I made a call on Mr [John] Kelley [at the] Free Trade Store. Mr Josiah Gibbs came down and put on a part of the cornise. The the wind rose and blew so hard that he could nto complete the work. Charles Cristofesen was at work on the chamber flooring. Some light spr^i^nkling of rain near night. Edwin Bartholimew ^and family started this morning for Sand Pete.^

May 26, 1875; Wednesday. Mr J[osiah] Gibbs completed the cornice on the front section of the House. Charls Christofisen was at work preparing flooring. We had some rain[,] he did not work in the afternoon. I made a call at the Free Store for Nails. The residue of the time I passed in improveing my water ways in my Orchard. At evening received a call from Mr [William] Marsden of Parowan enroute to S.L. ^He gave us the news of the Death of our friend Mr Robert Richie at Little Pinto [at] his residence.^

May 27, 1875; Thursday. This morning began the watering of my orchard. Charley finished the porch floor. Henry and Lorenzo done some lathing in the top of the porch. Weather bright and warm. Henry Tanner son of Sidney passed through Town enroute for home in Beaver. Miss Alice Lyman Daughter of Marion went with him to Beaver. ^Paid Tremble for makeing cloths $4.00 on Robison [account].^

May 28, 1875; Friday. Passed the morning in work in my orchard. The carpenters were at work to day. Charley commenced to lay the chamber floor. Mr [Peter] Silda was at other parts of the work. Henry done a little lathing in the early part of the day. My lame knee was very painful to day and feeling very tender to the touch.

May 29, 1875; Saturday. In the morning I worked in the Orchard. The carpenters were on the work to day. Henry finished up the Lathing to day. In the evening had a call from my son-in-law John Stredder from Greenville Beaver County. He was enroute for Santaquin with a load of Bullion from Shauntie in Star District. He reported all well at his leaveing home his own and Philo's family.

May 30, 1875; Sunday. Passed the day at home in reading. Mrs Lyman and Hila went out during the afternoon. Weather dry and cool. News was received by telegraph to day announcing the dangerous illness of G[eorge] A. Smith.

May 31, 1875; Monday. In the morning I worked in the orchard. The carpenters were at work[,] Charley in the forenoon Mr [Peter] Silda in the afternoon. During the afternoon Mr Nicholos Paul called on me and He agreed to do my plastering for fifteen cents per yd and take for pay one third in the Store & one third in flour one third on the stock herd.

June 1, 1875; Tuesday. In the morning worked in my ground around my house. After the breakfast hour I made a call at the store and had a talk with mister [John] Kelley about takeing flour of me and paying for it in goods. I called on Mr Charles Lavy at Mrs Merills. He promised to make the morter and tend the mason who was to do my plastering for lime and charged me 10 cents per yard. ^I called on Mr Gibbs who came to my place and made some plans for work with [Peter] Silda.^

June 2, 1875; Wednesday. In the morning worked in orchard. [Peter] Silda worked in the forenoon and in the afternoon he went to drive Stock. Charles was in the Drive since yesterday. Finished watering my Orchard this afternooon. My lame leg gave me much pain through the day. I noticed to day that the Apple Trees were makeing a great growth of wood this season.

June 3, 1875; Thursday. Passed the morning hours in working in my orchard. Passed the residue of the day in reading. In the afternoon received a passing call from my old time friend G[eorge] P. Dikes who was with his family enroute for Toquerville in Kane County w[h]ere he thinks of makeing himself a home. Wind high moveing large amounts of dust.

June 4, 1875; Friday. Made some calls in Town after the morning hours of work in my Orchard.

June 5, 1875; Saturday. Worked in my orchard through the morning hours and passed the residue of the day in reading. Mrs Lelia Bartholimew and children came to stop a few [days] with us Mrs B. being indisposed [ill]. During the day with Henry's help laid out and commenced diging my fruit celler. The carpenters put in no appearance today. ^Father [Noah] Bartholimew was taken sudenly ill last night. We slept in new house for first time.^

June 6, 1875; Sunday. Made calls on Mr Lorenzo Lyman and Mr [Peter] Silda. Passed the residue of the day at home. In the afternoon Mrs [Leilia] Bartholimew and children rode out for an airing. Sold some Apples the last of the season. Weather very warm.

June 7, 1875; Monday. This morning I received a call from Mr B[enjamin] H. Robison who brought me a voucher for haveing settled my account at the co-op Store in Parowan which I indorsed on his note.[18] I received a passing call from Mr Curtis who was enroute for Salt Lake by Stage. Mr [John] Stredder also called on his return from the North sent by him some dried apples to the [Lyman] children in Beaver County. ^Mr [Peter] Silda was on the work to day.^

June 8, 1875; Tuesday. Mr [Peter] Silda was on the work to day. I watered my orchard. My knee was very painful to day. Amasa [Jr] called on his way to Shauntie he said that while he was in Salt Lake he made some search for his sister Mrs [Josephine] Coombs but did not find her residence so failed to see her. Wind high some part of the day moveing heavy clouds of dust. More stock drives.

June 9, 1875; Wednesday. The wind was very high from the south covering the whole country with clouds of dust. I made some calls in town and in my [time] out I meet with Mr B[enjamin] H. Robison and mad[e] arangements with him for a q[u]antity of flour on what he was

18. Goods and services were sometimes purchased with I.O.U.s: promissory notes, in other words. When the debtor made a partial payment, it was written and initialed on the back of the note, which might then be passed from one person to the next and used as currency at stores until someone collected the balance due from the debtor.

owing me. He paid me ten dollers in curency. No carpenters on the work to day. Meet Mr Smith the miner and musician from N.Y.

June 10, 1875; Thursday. Passed the morning hours in the orchard after called on Mr Bartholimew who is just recovering from a severe attack of illness. Returned home and worked some hours makeing repares, and rehanging my gate on the street which had been broaken by the wind and the school children. No carpenters on the work to day. Called on Mr Rogers about hair for plastering.[19]

June 11, 1875; Friday. Passed the morning hours in my Orchard after this I wen[t] to the Tanery and procured some hair for my plastering. After this past some time in Livingstone Lost and Found. In the afternoon I went to Mr Bartholimew [and] to see [the blacksmith] Mr McKay. While there I read the Tribune which contained the news of Governor [Samuel] Axtell's removal an[d] the appointment of his successor ^of Mr [George] Emory.[20]

June 12, 1875; Saturday. After the morning hours work in the Orchard, I called at the Store and made some purchases for the House[,] and from the Store I was favored with a ride to the mill by Mr Nathan Baldwin. I secured the promise of the miller that he would grind my wheat next Monday. I saw the carpenters who promised that they would work all of next week on the House.

June 13, 1875; Sunday. Remained at home all day and read Livingstone Lost and Found.[21] During the day had some very high wind. In the afternoon received a call from Mrs Rhoda Lyman.

June 14, 1875; Monday. Passed the morning hours in the Orchard. [Peter] Silda and man were on the work to day the former but half the day. I received a letter to day from Mrs Triphena Morill of Providence Rhode Isleand which informed me of the Death of my cousin Sophronia

19. Horse hair was commonly used in lime plaster to bind it together.

20. Samuel Axtell, like many of his predecessors, did not last long as Utah's governor–only six months. President Grant put George W. Emery in his place. Emery had just spent four years overseeing the Internal Revenue Service in the South. That may have prepared him for Utah, where he stayed five years.

21. Rev. Josiah Tyler's *Livingstone Lost and Found: Or Africa and Its Explorers* told of missionary David Livingstone's disappearance in 1865 and discovery by *New York Herald* reporter Henry Stanley in 1871. If Tyler had waited a little longer, he could have reported the equally surprising news of Livingstone's death of malaria in 1873.

Lyman in Wo[o]nsocket R.I. some two years since.[22] Went to the mill with [son] Theodore the miller was not there. ^Meet with Board of Directors of the Free Traders Union.^

June 15, 1875; Tuesday. Worked out the morning hours in the orchard. The carpenters were on the work to day. Charley finished laying the chamber floor and Mr [Peter] Silda hung several doors and one of the transons. Lorenzo worked part of the day on the cellar. Received flour from the mill for wheat on deposit. High wind part of the day.

June 16, 1875; Wednesday. Worked in Orchard in the morning. Mr [Peter] Silda was on the work to day. I loaned him a sack of flour. In the afternoon I went up town to get some work done by the Blacksmith. Mr McKay promised me my work in the morning. Some wind to day. Called on Mr [Clarence] Meril at the Telegraph Office he let me have some wier.

June 17, 1875; Thursday. After the morning hours of work in the Orchard I made some calls up town for some sash [window] locks of which I found some of a new kind at the Free Trade [store] which we concluded to use and found them to answer the purpose very well. Mr [Peter] Silda was fiting the windows all of the square ones he put in and attached the fastnings.

June 18, 1875; Friday. After doeing my usual morning's [work] in the Orchard I received thirty two and a half bushels of Lime at fifty cents per bu[shel]. Mr [Peter] Silda finished up the Windows and Charley put down the last of the Base in the chamber. Weather warm. In afternoon I was supboened to attend the court at Beaver on the 12th of July at the trials ^of [William H.] Dame & [John D.] Lee.^[23]

June 19, 1875; Saturday. Worked my morning hours in the orchard. To day Mr [Peter] Silda and man finished the work they had engaged to do on my House. Some wind to day. Passed some hours in reading Livingston Lost & Found.

June 20, 1875; Sunday. Wrote letters to Mrs Triphena Morill of

---

22. Sophronia died unmarried in 1873 at age sixty-nine, having lived with her sister Tryphena and brother-in-law Nathaniel Morrill through her later life.

23. The Mountain Meadows trial was about to begin. Even though the prosecutors thought Lyman might be an asset, they decided, after meeting with him, that they would not call him to the stand. The trial ended without convictions, and only Lee would be re-tried again and found guilty. See Lyman's visit with John D. Lee the next year on Oct. 18, 1876; *AML*, 476–77.

Providence Rhode Island and one to my Brother David Emerson of Coalbrook N.H. Pas[s]ed residue time in reading Livingstone Lost and found[,] [how he was found] by Stanley[,] published [written by] J[osiah] Tyler.[24]

June 21, 1875; Monday. Worked the morning hours in the Orchard after this I settled with Mr [Peter] Silda for the work he had done which in the agragate amounted ^to^ one hundred seventy eight dollers and fifty eight cents. After this I made a call at the co-op store and secured an order on the Stock Herd for what I was to pay Silda in that way. Received a letter from Paulina in Parowan. Weather very warm.

June 22, 1875; Tuesday. Worked the morning hours in the orchard. Mr [Charles] Lavy commenced his preparations for makeing morter for plastering my house. [Peter] Silda and man were at work on the house and made and set the frames in the front of the House. Weather hot with some thunder and other indications of rain. Received a call from Mr [Stephen] Dugins and paid him for his work in the Orchard. Paid Silda $7.

June 23, 1875; Wednesday. After my usual work in the morning I made some calls up Town in quest of a Box in which to run off the Lime for plastering my House but did not find one and when I returned Mr [Charles] Lavy had fited up the old one so as to answer the purpose. [Peter] Silda and man were on the work to day. Weather warm and dry. Rabits are reported destroying the crops ^here and at [the town of] Deseret.^

June 24, 1875; Thursday. After my morning work made a call up town and saw Mr Smith the teacher of music who came home with me and had a look at my organ and made an arangement to give Hila a course of lesons on the organ. Mr [Peter] Silda and Man were on the work to day as also was Mr [Charles] Lavy makeing morter for plastering. Weather very warm.

June 25, 1875; Friday. Visited Mr [Isaac] Carlin who promised that he would come and fix my chimney. After this I called on Dor[r]us [Berzee] Warner and bought of him a piece of timber for my Banisters then I called on Mr Gibbs who selected some lumber for finishing the coridor which [I] bought and brought home. Mr [Peter] Silda left to day to make hay for a week or more.

---

24. This is the last entry in vol. 39. Entries for June 21–Dec. 13, 1875, pick up in vol. 40.

June 26, 1875; Saturday. My workmen on the house left to day to engage for a time in hay makeing. I made a call on Prest [Thomas] Callister who kind[ly] promised me a ride with him to Corn Creek on tomorow. Mr [George] Walters worked on my partition fence on which he has been engaged for two day[s]. Weather very warm.

June 27, 1875; Sunday. Rose early and made ready to ride with the Prest [Thomas Callister] to Canosh as he promised me on yesterday but when I had hobeled up to his place he told me he was not going as promised on yesterday, but would go in the afternoon. I then went to Rhoda's to await his starting in the afternoon when his messenger informed me that his wagon was full so I did not go ^but wrote Letter to Mr [George] Crowe [Crane] Painter at Canosh to come and see me.^

June 28, 1875; Monday. To day after my mornings work I was invited by Brother [Nephi] Pratt to a seat in the Prest [Thomas] Callisters wagon and with them meeting of Canosh and his Indians on Dry Creek where some eighty of the Indians were baptized, Mr Culbert King of Canosh officiating. This over we went to Canosh and had some refreshments with Mr King then called at the residence of Mr [George] Crane the Painter ^he was not at home. Mr C thought he would respond to my wish to come to see me. Mr Gibbs moved Lumber to his shop.^

June 29, 1875; Tuesday. Remained at home through the day no workmen on the house to day. Mr [Nicholas] Paul has not yet put in an apearence to commence plastering. In the afternoon Mr [George] Crane called and agreed to prime my house for twenty five dollers and I gave him five dollers in Curency. He said he would be here as soon as the fifth of next month.

June 30, 1875; Wednesday. Mr [Josiah] Gibbs called on me this morning and took some measurements for the cornice of the porch. After his call I went up Town and paid him twenty dollers in Order on Stock Head. Returned home after calling on Mr Gibbs at his shop where he was working on my work. ~~I re~~ Feeling very weary and full of pain in my limbs. Weather warm and dry.

July 1, 1875; Thursday. To day was engaged in watering my orchard and late in the afternoon made a ditch to some of my trees that had not been watered this season. Mr Ralph Rowley very kindly assisted me in making the ditch. My leg gave me much pain all through the day.

Weather warm with Thunder and light showers of rain on the mountains we only had light sprinkles in the valley.

July 2, 1875; Friday. After the morning hour I made some calls in Town first at Mr [William] Bishop's where I had an Iron fitted for hanging my gate. I then called at the P.O. and then at Mr Gibbs shop he was engaged on my work. I gave Mr G. an order on B[enjamin] H. R[obison's account] for fifteen dollers in flour. Returned home and prepared some posts for hanging my gate.

July 3, 1875; Saturday. In the morning made some calls up town and settled with Bishop [Edward] Partridge [Jr.] for the lumber I got in his absence from home by giving him an Order on B[enjamin] H. R[obison's account] for flour. I then called on the Gibbs and let them have an order of fifteen dollers for flour. Received card from Mr [Nicholas] Paul saying he would be on hand in a day or two. Called on Mrs Lelia Bartholimew late in afternoon.

July 4, 1875; Sunday. Passed the morning in reading Natural ~~History~~ Philosophy[25] after which I went and passed the residue of the day with Mr [Noah] Bartholimew and family. Mr Edwin Bartholimew and family were there. After returning home I received a call from Mr [Nicholas] Paul who said he would commence plastering in the morning. Weather cool and pleasant.

July 5, 1875; Monday. Mr [Nicholas] Paul came to commence plastering and made some preparations for begining the work. The master ma[son] did not put in an appearance to day. Paid Mr [Peter] Silda in full for his first job of work in the finishing of the House. In course of the day received a letter from Marion who is in London Prest over that conference.

July 6, 1875; Tuesday. Today the plasterers commenced their work puting on plaster on the house in the afternoon and covered in the north end. I[n] the afternoon Mr [George] Crane came and commenced his work of primeing the cornice. Some indications of rain the most of which fell on the mountains and but a light sprinkle in the valley. Mr [Isaac] Carlin fixed my chimney.

July 7, 1875; Wednesday. The mason and the painter were at work to day and the carpenter in the afternoon. I made a call on Mr Henry at the

25. This may have been the primer on physics by David Ames Wells, *Natural Philosophy*, with chapters on architecture, fluid flow, sound, combustion, light, and electricity.

P.O. and there I called on Mr Gibbs who said he would be ready to put up my work on my coridor on next Monday. As I inquired for a chance to go to Beaver [to the Mountain Meadows trial][,] Theodore said he would take me if he could get a wagon. Had a fine shower of rain.

July 8, 1875; Thursday. Men on the work as yesterday in its diferent branches. I made a call up town in quest of Lumber which I found at Mr R[euben] McBrides of whom I purchased what I wanted for present use. The painting and plastering progressed very well to day. Weather very hot and dry.

July 9, 1875; Friday. I made some calls in Town and while out meet with Mrs Emily Young and her son from S.L. City wife and son of Brigham Young. Made payments to my workmen in view of leaveing for a time to attend the court at Beaver in the cases of [William H.] Dame and [John D.] Lee on the Mountain Meadows Massacre. Weather very warm we progressed finely to day. Received lumber ^from [Reuben] McBride.^

July 10, 1875; Saturday. To day started for Beaver with Mr Dewit Tyler we traviled to and camped for the night in Baker's Can[y]on. We left Fillmore about noon. I left the pa[i]nter and the plasterer and carpenter at work on my House. The weather was very warm with some light sprinkling of rain in the evening. Meet some loads of Lumber from the mill on Cove Creek.

July 11, 1875; Sunday. We were early on the Road and we traviled to and made our noon halt on Pine Creek near the residence of Mr Miner Prisb[re]y. From this point we traviled to a point near Dalton Ranch in Wild Cat [Creek] where we meet with Mr Curtis E. Bolton and Son enroute for Beaver. Some light rain in the evening while here the Stage with W[illiam] H. Dame past on to Beaver.

July 12, 1875; Monday. This morning we arived in Beaver in time for the session of the court. The town presented quite a lively appearence as we aproached it on acount of the numbers who had come in from the country to attend the court through the trials of [William H.] Dame and [John D.] Lee.[26] Philo[,] Matilda[,] and Amasa [Jr] came to see me and

26. The trial was reported in newspapers from Oregon to New York. See "Trial of John D. Lee and Others," *State Rights Democrat* (Oregon), July 30, 1875; "The Mountain Meadows Massacre," *New York Herald*, July 21, 1875.

with them I dined with Mr Albert Goodwin and Family then went to Mr Sidney Tanner's to lodge.

July 13, 1875; Tuesday. The court was in session to day and was engaged in other maters beside the cases of [William H.] Dame and [John D.] Lee which were set for Wednesday. The weather was very hot to day. Passed most of the time at the place of my lodgings. During the day two of the wives of J[ohn] D. Lee called on me to learn my feelings towards their husband which they had been informed ^^were pr^e^judicial to him.^^

July 14, 1875; Wednesday. Court in session and the cases of [William H.] Dame and [John D.] Lee were set for next Monday. To day haad a long and pleasant talk with Uncle Sidney [Tanner] which seemed to bring him back to the spirit of olden times. Uncle William Mathews called in for a short talk about the Mountain Meadows Butchery. The old man seemed quite feeble in health his articulation was ^faint and to[o] low to be herd distinctly.^

July 15, 1875; Thursday. This morning went down town and had an interview with Judge [William] Cary, the Prosicuting Atorney, in regard to the Mountain Meadows Masacre. The atorney seemed hopeful that the investigation would result in bringing out the facts in regard to that bloody tragidy. As I left the judge I meet Amasa [Jr.] and went with him to Philo's. Amasa [Jr.] then started for Fillmore. ^Learned that Mrs [Matilda] Carter was hurt by the tiping over of the wagon as they were returning home from Beaver on Monday evening. Some indications of rain to day.^

July 16, 1875; Friday. Passed the day mostly in reading in the evening. Mr Richard Benson and wife and son and Mrs Paulina E. Lyman arived from Parowan.

July 17, 1875; Saturday. To day went to Beaver while there had an interview with Mr [William] Cary and Mr Clinkin Smith [Philip Klingensmith] in regard to the Mountain Meadows affair. Dined with Mrs Rachel Tanner after which I went down Town and had an interview with Mr Cary and Mr W[illiam] Hickman. While here meet with Mr Daniel Page of Parowan.

July 18, 1875; Sunday. Remained at home. Mr John Stredder and family were with us through the day we had some light rain. This morning

Mr Richard Benson wife and son Heber started for Parowan via Beaver. Weather very warm.

July 19, 1875; Monday. This morning went to Beaver and at ten oclock the court was in Session and the Roll of Witnesses called and the Defence not being ready, the court dismissed the Witnesses until tomorow at ten oclock. After diner I went to the office of the prosicuting at^t^orney Judge [William] Cary and while there I meet Mr Jacob Hamlin.

July 20, 1875; Tuesday. Court was in Session transacted some buisness preliminary to the trial of [John D.] Lee & [William H.] Dame. In the afternoon had an interview with Attorney [William] Cary and others. Lee and his family were in court to day.

July 21, 1875; Wednesday. To day meet on the street my son Amasa [Jr.] who had returned from Fillmore bringing Hila with him. Attended court to day. [John D.] Lee and family were present there was some buisness done. In the afternoon meet with Henry Rollins from Minersville also meet with Mr George V. Dieterich of Galesburg Ill[inois]. From him I learned of my cousins children [in] Galesburg.

July 22, 1875; Thursday. The labors of the Court to day resulted in geting Jury to try the case of J[ohn] D. Lee. The Jury was given into the charge of the Marshals with the Court's instructions as to their treatment during the trial. Court ajourned until tomorow 10 oclock. In evening called on the Watchmaker at the residence of Mr Wm Thompson to get a [winding] key for my watch.

July 23, 1875; Friday. Court in session. The preliminaries being settled the witnesses present for the prosicution were sworn and received instructions from the Court to remain within call of the Court. They were then all excluded from the Court Room to be called as wanted. I called on the Watchmaker and procured a key for my watch. ^Dined at E[dward] Thompsons.^

July 24, 1875; Saturday. Court in session P[hilip] K[lingen] Smith stil in the witness stand. Wrote letter to Mrs L. M. Lyman in Fillmore. Passed some time in reading Alexander Popes Essay on Man.[27] I[n] the afternoon my daughters Matilda and Hila called to see me at Mr Edward Thompson's.

27. Alexander Pope's 1734 work, *An Essay on Man*, was reprinted in New York in 1875 with illustrations and notes by Samuel Wells.

July 25, 1875; Sunday. Remained at my lodgings all day did not go out during the day but passed the time in reading Kidd's Elocution.[28] To day Mr Hamond from St George who was here as a witness [and] haveing been excused started on his return home. During the afternoon some rain fell attended with high wind rendering the air much cooler at evening.

July 26, 1875; Monday. To day the Court closed the examination of [Philip Klingen]Smith and [Joel] White and others for the prosicution. During the day through the kindness of Mr [William] Cary I read a Unitarian Discourse on the Divinity of Christ by Mr Powel. In evening had a long talk with Mr Edward Dalton of Parowan. Rain fell freely to night. I was to day ^released from a longer stay as a witness my dues was $31.50.^

July 27, 1875; Tuesday. This morning made arangements with some parties to go with them. In the afternoon Paulina started for Parowan with Mr Edward Dalton and Sidney Burton of that place. When my party came to start they had no seat nor cover to their wagon so I declined going with them and waited for another chance. ^Freeman Tanner came in as a witness in the [John D.] Lee case this evening.^

July 28, 1875; Wednesday. Did not start for home to day. In the afternoon I was supboned for the defence as the prosecution had introduced the most of their evidence and turned the case over to the defence. To day a search of the prisoner's room in the prison resulted in the discovery of sundary implements with which the prisoner it is supposed intended to liberate himself ^from confinement. A hatchet a file a butcher knife two case knives one made into a saw and a pair of compasses, a rope.^[29]

July 29, 1875; Thursday. Court was in session some witnesses were introduced for the defence whose cross examination in several points did coroborate the evidence for the prosecution.

July 30, 1875; Friday. Court in session and some witnesses were introduced on the part of the defence but nothing that changed the aspect of the case.

July 31, 1875; Saturday. This morning made ready for the journey home and about noon started. Our party consisted of Uncle Freeman

28. Kidd's *Vocal Culture and Elocution* was published in 1857.

29. After Lee was moved from Fort Cameron to the Beaver County jail, authorities discovered his plan to escape and were compelled to place him in restraints. Whitney, *History of Utah*, 2:786.

Tanner and myself and two young Ladies by the name of Smithson of Sumer Creek Utah County. We traviled to and put up at Cove Creek where we were kindly entertained by Mr [Ira] Hinkly. Weather very warm. Nooned at Dalton's Ranch in Wild Cat [Creek].

August 1, 1875; Sunday. About 5 oclock we were on the road and about 11 oclock we called at Mr Peter Robison's at Corn Creek where we had diner. From [there] we traviled to Fillmore where we arived about sundown found all well at home. Uncle Freeman [Tanner] stayed with us over night and the young ladies staid with Mrs S[tephen] Dugins [Leminder Clementine] with whom they were acquainted. Weather sultry and close [muggy].

August 2, 1875; Monday. Mr [Nicholas] Paul was at work to day. I made a call at the Drugists and bought some Chery Pectoral for my cough, it gave me relief. In the afternoon I went to the Election where they were runing two candidates for the mayoralty of the City. The candidates were J[oseph] V[ickery] Robison & Gilbert Web. Weather very warm.

August 3, 1875; Tuesday. Remained home all day the plasterer was at work to day. Paid Lavy six dollers on the Store. Passed the most of the day in reading.

August 4, 1875; Wednesday. Remained at home and passed most of the time in reading. Mr [Nicholas] Paul was at work during the forenoon but Mr Lavy not being able to serve him in the afternoon [so] the work stoped for the rest of the day. Gave Mr Paul an order on the store for fifteen dollers. Weather very warm some indications of rain in evening.

August 5, 1875; Thursday. Called on Mr [Josiah] Gibs who said he would be down tomorow to do some work. Called at the store and bought some glass for the sidelights to my front door. Weather very warm. In the evening Mr [Peter] Silda gave in his bill for the last work he had done on the house. To day Joseph A. Young died at Manti Sandpete County.[30]

August 6, 1875; Friday. To day settled with and paid Mr [Peter] Silda for his work on my house. I also settled with Mr Gibbs and found that when he should have made the Sash for my French windows I should

30. Forty-year-old Joseph A. Young, the oldest son of Brigham Young, was the stake president in Richfield. His father had ordained him an apostle but never placed him in the Quorum of the Twelve. He died of malaria ("congestive chills"). "Death of Elder Joseph A. Young," *Deseret News*, Aug. 11, 1875.

owe him a little over seventy dollers haveing paid him over seventy dollers. [Benjamin] Robison returned from the North with wheat to day. Weather very warm.

August 7, 1875; Saturday. Made a call at the Free Trade Store and while there received a letter from my cousin [in] Providence Rhode Isle- and by name Triphenia Moril with her photo. Henry started for Shauntie for Bullion. Received a letter from Mr C[harles] C. Rich in Idaho with a deed sent to him and me from Cal which I signed as he had done and sent it to Mr Hanks Iron City.

August 8, 1875; Sunday. Called on Mr McKay at the residence of Mr Bartholimew to get him to rear the spring to the belows of the Organ. Dined with the Bartholimews after returning home passed the evening in reading. Paid Mr Gibbs thirty dollers on [Benjamin H.] Robisons [account] leaveing a balence of $42.25 still due him to be paid on stockherd. Weather very warm.

August 9, 1875; Monday. Made a long walk up Town made calls on Mr Petersen and then on Mr McKay from there I went to the store and there read the Tribune giving the latest news of the Lee trial and the disagreement of the jury. The press of the country speaks out its sentiments of condemnation at the bloddy tragidy so long tried to be hid from public view.

August 10, 1875; Tuesday. Remained at home during the day. [Andrew J.] Clothier worked on the celler [Nicholas] Paul came but did not work. In the afternoon received letters one from Brother David Emerson and one from my sister Mrs Lucy Pilbro both of which contained the news of the death of my mother which occured on the 11th of Dec 1874. She passed away without suffering and finds her rest with the just where we hope to meet her when we have done our labors here and life's lamp ^burns only for us on the bright shore of the hapy immortals where the weary rest and the good are hapy.^

August 11, 1875; Wednesday. Wrote letters to my Brother and Sister in N.H. and one to Marion in ^London^ England and one to Paulina in Parowan Iron Co. Called on Mrs Rhoda Lyman with whom I dined. Called at the residence of Mrs [daughter-in-law] Clara Lyman to see her boy Richard who had been biten by a dog in the arm. The wound was severe as the limb was severely las[c]erated but it appear[ed] to be doing well and healing. Got four bushels of lime of Mr Baldwin. Mr [Nicholas] Paul brought it home for me with his teem.

August 12, 1875; Thursday. In the morning went over my Orchard. Mr [Nicholas] Paul was at work in the afternoon on the last room in the house. In the afternoon I called on the Gibbs. They had made a beginning on my work [for the house] tho small. G[eorge] A. Smith reported to be very Low his friends seem to have given up all hopes of his recovery. Mr [Andrew J.] Clothier was not on the work to day his clerk being sick. Weather geting slightly cooler, some clouds.

August 13, 1875; Friday. Passed the morning in reading the report of the Lee Trial in the Tribune. In the afternoon went up Town and called at the Free Trade Store while there read the Opinions of the press East and west as published in our local papers.

August 14, 1875; Saturday. To day Mr [Nicholas] Paul made a finish of the plastering of my house. Mr [Andrew J.] Clothier and man were at work on the celler. [Benjamin H.] Robison paid me twenty five dollers in curency on his note to me. In the evening Mrs Lyman was called to go and sit up with Mrs Bartholimew to whi[ch] [she] responded and returned home about 3 oclock in Morning. Weather cooler.

August 15, 1875; Sunday. Passed the morning hours in reading. To day Henry returned with a load of Bullion from Troy [near Milford]. Reported our friends well at Carters Ranch near Greenville. Henry has to lay over here one day to repare wagon before he can proceed on his way to York the present terminus of the Utah Southern [railroad]. Mr John Ashman's child died last night. Called on Mr [Noah] Bartholimew and ^found Mrs B somewhat better than last night. Weather cooler.^

August 16, 1875; Monday. This morning called on Mr John Ashman at his residence he promised to cary the Spring seat belonging to Bishop [Marcus L.] Shepherd of Beaver to him when he went to Beaver. Called on Mr [John] Kelley at the Store. Mr K had received on yesterday a severe hurt on his face from the kick of a Horse. In evening I settled with Mr Lavy for his work. Mr [Nicholas] Paul measured the work he had done and found ^it to be 798 yds and ½ and counting to $119.30.

August 17, 1875; Tuesday. Made ready to start on our Northern journey but failing to secure all the stock we did not start. I called on Mr Gibbs and on my way there I called on the Widow Fisher an saw my

Grand Son in her care. He was appearning well and hearty. Mr G was engaged on my work. Gave Mr [Andrew J.] Clothier some Orders in payment on his work also paid Mr Day. Received a call from ^Mr [John] Kelley his face was badly swollen from his recent hurt.^

August 18, 1875; Wednesday. This morning started for Salt Lake City our traviling party was composed of self and Lorenzo and Henry & Mr Jas Petersen. We traviled to near the Sumit between Cedar Springs and Scipio where we camped[,] where we were joined by Mr Adams from Parowan and Borough from Cotten Wood. Roads very dry and dusty. Weather very warm.

August 19, 1875; Thursday. We traviled to the cedar ridge on the road to Levan whe[re] [we] camped in the night after the moon rose. Tolerable good grass. We were by ourselves as our southern friend had passed on ahead. Weather stil hot and the roads very dusty. As we passed the Sevier. There were some natives having their noon rest at that point from which they left as we did to pursue their journey further south.

August 20, 1875; Friday. Traviled to Four Mile Creek[31] and passed it a short distence and camped with good grass for stock.

August 21, 1875; Saturday. Traviled to the [railroad] Terminus nooned near the spring south of Mona. As we left our noon halt the teem on Mr Petersen's wagon took fright and in their attempt to run they broak the wagons but so bad as to stop our travil only so long as it took us to tie up the broaken parts. We reached the terminus about sundown. Camped in the dirt at this point.

August 22, 1875; Sunday. This morning the boys unloaded their Bullion which was received and paid for. After this as I walked up the track to the House of rest I found it in charge of my old time friend Mr Charles Decker with whom I past an hour in calling up the reminiscences of the past in our experiences of the past of our lives as thrown together in the history of the church. ^At noon took the carrs and reached the city [Salt Lake City] near night and found my children well in evening went to Institute to hear Mrs Alyn speak.^

August 23, 1875; Monday. In morning passed some time in writing

31. Fourmile Creek is six miles south of Nephi. As Lyman mentioned on Aug. 15, their immediate destination was the southernmost stop on the Utah Southern Railroad, fifteen miles north of Nephi in York.

after which I made some calls in the city. While out had an interview with Mr Jason Briggs an Apostle of the Josephite Church. I meet him at the U. S. Marshalls Office. Dined with my old friend H[enry] W. Lawrence and family. After diner with Mr L[awrence][,] I went through the Methodist Church Building which is one of the best in the city.[32] Called on Mr J[oseph] M. ^Allen who promised to furnish the tin spouting I wanted for my house as soon as wanted.^

August 24, 1875; Tuesday. After the morning hour made some calls in Town first at K[imball] & L[awrence]'s where I found some goods that I wanted. I called on J[oseph] M. Allen and gave him my Order for my Tin work which he said he would put up for me immediately. I then called on the Tribune folks for a few moments and then called on my old friend Mr John Maning and lunched with him and family.

August 25, 1875; Wednesday. Lorenzo arived last night and went up Town this morning to dispose of his load of hides. I called at the residence of Dr [Washington F.] Anderson but he was away on the Cottenwood. I then called on Mr W[illiam] H. Shearman's family at his residence where I meet with the Widow Kay and her daughters Mrs [Sarah] Hawkins and Mrs [Ellen] Robinson. Made some purchase of goods at the store of Walker Brothers ^and also at Kimble & Lawrence. Dined with Mr [Henry W.] Lawrence after which I returned to my lodgings very weary from being so long on my feet.^

August 26, 1875; Thursday. Made some purchases of carpet and window blinds and also a hundred lbs of sugar. Called on Mr [Joseph M.] Allen and settled for my guter and water pipes which were delivered to Lorenzo in the afternoon. Returned to my lodgings very weary. Weather much cooler meet on the street Mr [George M.] Pierce and Mr Lyford ministers in the Methodist Church.

August 27, 1875; Friday. To day loaded our goods prepareatory to starting them for Fillmore tomorow. This ocupied myself and Lorenzo all the day. We had some help from Mrs [Josephine] Coombs. Weather cool but pleasant.

August 28, 1875; Saturday. This morning Lorenzo put on the wagon

---

32. The First Methodist Episcopal Church at Third South was still under construction at the time. The Episcopal cathedral on First South and the Presbyterian church at Second South had both been consecrated in 1874.

the last of the goods we were to cary and started for Fillmore. This done I called on Dr. [Washington F.] Anderson and he examined my broaken knee but gave but very little encouragement that it could be any much better. I then called on Mrs Kay at Mr [William] Shearmans with whom I dined. Called at Mr [Joseph M.] Allen's for the straps to hang my guter. Called at K[imball] & L[awrence] and got some nails. ^On the street meet my old friend Andrew Cahoon from Cottenwood.^

August 29, 1875; Sunday. Remained at home did not go out during the day but passed the time in reading. Weather cool and clear mad[e] ready for the journey tomorow to Fillmore in company with Mr [Hyrum] Coombs and wife [Josephine] and child.

August 30, 1875; Monday. This morning at half past 6 oclock took the St carrs[33] for the depot, where we took the train for the terminus of the Utah Southern R[ail] R[oad]. At one of the Utah settlements we were joined [by] Mr Joseph Kelting and wife from Sanbernardino Cal up on a visit after an absence of some 15 years from Utah. At the terminus we met & took the stage ^and reached Fillmore the next morning at daylight [and] found all well. Mr [Hyrum] Combs remained with Lorenzo with the goods to come with him.^

August 31, 1875; Tuesday. Found all well on our arival home this morning. After breakfast I took a short sleep which I failed to get last night in the stage. In the afternooon I called on Mr [Noah] Bartholimew at his residence. He told me that on yesterday a whirlwind took out the end of his millhouse a brick structure. Very fortunately no damage was done but that to the building. While here Mr Edward Thompson of Beaver called he was ^his way home from Salt Lake City where he had been to see his son on his way to Ill[inoi]s to enter college to complete his e[d]ucation.^

September 1, 1875; Wednesday. Passed the day in pareing and cuting apples did not go out today. The weather was warm and pleasant through the day. In the evening as we were enjoying our Musick before retireing for the night Mr [Hyrum] Coombs came in on foot as one of the horses

33. Salt Lake City had two streetcars. Since 1872 the mule-drawn cars ran from Third West and South Temple, a short block from the juncture of the Utah Central and Utah Southern Railroads, east to Main Street, then south three blocks to the heart of the non-Mormon business district. Bennett and Woolley, "Mass Transit in the Salt Lake Valley."

in the teem with which Lorenzo was bringing our goods gave out some fifteen ^miles back on the road and they left the wagon and goods and came in on foot.^

September 2, 1875; Thursday. Passed the forenoon [the same] as yesterday in pareing and cuting apples and in the afternoon I made some change in my cuting machine. Did not go out today found myself very weary at night and retired earlier than usual and soon after I retired Lorenzo came with the goods from Salt Lake in good order, considering the length [of the trip] and the rough condition of the roads. ^Prest [Thomas] Callister and others started for Salt Lake this morning to attend the Funerel of G[eorge] A. Smith who died on the first.

September 3, 1875; Friday. Passed the morning hours in takeing care of some of the goods brought from the city after which I called at the Free Trade [store] and at the co-op and then went to Mr Gibbs he told my work was nearly ready to put up and he would bring it home tomorow. I returned home much wearied with the for me long walk. Theodore was geting ready for his southern trip with fruit. ^Pared and cut some apples in the afternoon. Received letter from Mrs [Maria Louisa] Stredder asking us to send [her ten-year-old son] Marion to her by the first good chance [see next entry].

September 4, 1875; Saturday. Cut some apples in the morning after which I made some repares on some of the furniture that was damaged with moveing. To day Theodore and Mr [Hyrum] Coombs started for Beaver and took with them o[u]r grandson Marion Clayton who had been some weeks on a visit with us. In the afternoon Mr Gibbs brought the work he promised me on yesterday.

September 5, 1875; Sunday. In company with Mrs Lyman and Mrs [Josephine] Coombs called on and passed the day with Mr Edwin Bartholimew and family. Weather very warm some light rain on he mountains. On returning home found Mr [John] Kelley and family at our place. Mrs Lyman and Mrs Coombs this evening called on Mrs Clara Lyman ~~who~~ wife of Marion ^who was reported to us to be very ill with Tiphoid fever, she was in a helpless condition.^

September 6, 1875; Monday. ~~Tuesday~~ Passed the morning in paring and cuting apples. Mr Gibbs came and commenced puting in the French windows. After diner I made some calls in town for some screws and while out I called to see Clara my sons wife and weak with apparently small chances of recovery. Had a call to day from Mr Savery of St aquin [Santaquin] let him have some apples.

September 7, 1875; Tuesday. ~~Wednesday~~ Passed the morning cuting apples and in cleaning the cuter I cut the thumb of my right hand severly which prevented me from continuing my work. Mr Gibbs was on the work to day. Mr [Nicholas] Paul called and I paid him ten dollars on account. He agreed to Whitewash my house next week on the outside going over it twice for ten dollers. Some indications of rain.

September 8, 1875; Wednesday. With much dificulty cut some apples. Mr [Nicholas] Paul done some work plastering under the watertable. In ther afternoon Mr Gibbs called he was not on the work to day. He reported the sick at his place as being beterer and also told me that Mr Merrill told him that Clarra [Lyman] was also better.[34]

September 9, 1875; Thursday. In morning pared some apples, and passed some hours in reading the news of the day. Mr Gibbs came and closed up his work which completed the joiner work on my house after which I paid in full for his work which in all amounted to the sum of one hundred and forty four dollers and fifty cents. In the evening asisted the women to cut apples. Weather stil warm.

September 10, 1875; Friday. I made some calls in town at the Freetrade [store] where I looked over the endorsements on the note of [Benjamin H.] Robison and found that in July it was worth over eight hundred dollers. [A Singer] sewing machine exibition was advertised to day to come off tomorow at Olson's Hall free to all. The machine Wheelers & Wilsons improved.[35]

September 11, 1875; Saturday. Passed the day mostly in working with the fruit. In the afternoon Uncle Henry Rollins called for a few minutes. He was enroute to Salt Lake City on buisness. He reported all well at home in Minersville except his wife Evaline and Aunt Dionitia. Later in the afternoon [Andrew] Jackson Clothier called and I paid him four

---

34. Clara Callister Lyman recovered and would live another seventeen years, although with stomach ulcers.

35. Sewing machines were uncommon until the 1850s when Isaac Singer invented an improved model, followed by subsequent improvements by Nathaniel Wheeler and Allen Wilson in the following decade. Singer soon purchased Wheeler and Wilson's company. See Mar. 25, 1876.

dollers on account by order on [the] [Benjamin H.] Robison [account]. Weather remains warm.

September 12, 1875; Sunday. In company with Mrs Lyman Mrs Coombs and Mrs Bartholimew I went to and passed the day with Mrs Rhoda Lyman. After noon Mrs L. went to Mr Callisters to see Mrs Clara Lyman who is sick with the Tipoid fever she found her very low and weak. Heard to day that Mr Gibbs buried his wife that was Mrs Pilling on yesterday.[36] When I returned home I met Mr Eldridge who is teaching school in one of ^our districts. I found him a young man of more than usual thought for a Utah raised boy. He has been raised by Mr Hoyt formerly of this place Fillmore.^

September 13, 1875; Monday. Passed the entire day in cuting and working with the fruit. Mrs L[elia] Bartholimew and children were with us to day. Mrs [Josephine] Coombs and her sister Hila passed the day with Mr John Kelley and family. My reading to day was brief. I waited all day for but had no word from men whom I was expecting to work on my house. [Nicholas] Paul to white wash [George] Crane to paint.

September 14, 1875; Tuesday. Passed the morning hours in work with the fruit and in reading. I then went in company with Mrs Lyman and Mrs [Josephine] Coombs and Mrs Lelia Bartholimew and passed the residue of the day with Mr N[oah] Bartholimew and family. Weather warm and sultry with some clouds in the afternoon. Mr [Hyrum] Coombs returned this evening from his visit to his friends in the south. Mrs Amelia Widow of Mr Frederick Turley[37] arived in Town this evening. Her son was with her. Their home is in Minersville Beaver County.

September 15, 1875; Wednesday. Passed the day at home working with the fruit. In the afternoon had some showers of rain attended with Thunder. In this evening Mr [Hyrum] Coombs made me a proposition to buy one of my lots he at present thinks of comeing here to make a home next Spring.

September 16, 1875; Thursday. This morning walked over my place with Mr [Hyrum] Coobs who thinks of maeking a home here. After this I made a call on Bishop [Edward] Partridge [Jr.] and procured an order

---

36. Mary Jane had married William Gibbs in about 1870, after the death of her first husband, John Pilling.

37. The surname is written in pencil in a different hand.

on the stock herd for twenty six dollers and thirty cents it being all that I had in the herd except the real estate intrest which is twenty dollers. No rain to day. The Widow Turley called this evening. It was ^the widow of Frederick Turley. To day meet Mr Berick from California.^

September 17, 1875; Friday. Remained at home the entire day and was engaged in working up peaches. Mr and Mrs Coombs dined out to day. In the evening I pared and cut a lot of apples. Mrs Lyman worked up some of her plumbs to day into Jelly and some she scalded for drying. We find our peaches are coming on very fast requiring immediate attention. Weather pleasant.

September 18, 1875; Saturday. Passed the principal part of the day in makeing some change[s] in my apple cutter. In the afternoon I cut peaches and so on into evening. O^ur^ visitors from the South have again disappointed us and have not come. The weather remains fine for our fruit. Theodore drove up some of my stock from the Range to day.

September 19, 1875; Sunday. Passed the day at home and had the pleasure of the company of Mrs Mary Bartholimew and Mrs Matilda McKay and Mrs Lelia Bartholimew with their children. They passed the day with us and Miss Laura B was with us Mr and Mrs Coombs and daughter were of our party. Weather was pleasant.

September 20, 1875; Monday. Some light rain falling this morning. After breakfast I commenced pareing apple, after pareing a bushel or two my parer gave out and we turned our attention to the peaches for the balance of the day. In the evening our visitors from the south Mrs Matilda Carter and children arived from their home near Greenville Beaver County. We had with us tonight four children and ^thirteen grandchildren.^

September 21, 1875; Tuesday. To day we gathered and loaded in the wagon some twenty two bushels of fruit seventeen of apples and five of peaches. Lyman will start tomorrow with his load of fruit for home. Mr [Hyrum] Coombs and wife expect to start for their home in the City of Salt Lake to remain there until next spring when they expect to return to Fillmore to reside. ^Received a letter from Mr George Crane of Canosh he will be her[e] next Monday.^

September 22, 1875; Wednesday. This morning I made some calls in Town on buisness and Started Lyman with his load of fruit after geting some small repares on his wagon. After this called on Mr McKay and had some work done on my Apple cutter which improved its working. Hyrum and Josephine started for their home in Salt Lake City. The[y] went with Mr John Kelley.

September 23, 1875; Thursday. I remained at home all day and worked in the apples and peaches. The weather stil is very pleasant and favorable for drying our fruit.

September 24, 1875; Friday. Was engaged in cutting apples after getting my parer repared. Henry brought me a load of wood to day from Clear Lake. In the afternoon I received a letter from Marion in London England stateing that he would start for home on the thirteenth of Oct and arive about the 10th of Nov. Mr [Omner] Turley and party from Star left to day for home.

September 25, 1875; Saturday. Finished up a lot of apples after which I made a call up Town and where I meet with a copy of the R[eligio–] P[hilosophical] Journal which Mr [John] Kelley very kindly loaned me to read. After returning home I let Mr McKay have some peaches on account. Received a call from Uncle Sidney Tanner and Bishop M[arcus] L. Shepherd they were enrout for Salt Lake City to sell sheep. In the evening I received a letter from my Sister Ruth Goodall in North Derby Vermonth.

September 26, 1875; Sunday. This morning commenced writing letter to my sister Mrs Ruth E. Goodall in North Derby V.T. The morning hours passed I then in the company of Mrs Lyman and Mrs Carter went to the residence of Mr Edwin Bartholimew with whom and family we spent the day until late in the afternoon when we returned home where we found Mr [John] Kelley awaiting our return. [My daughter] Hila gave us musick on the organ.

September 27, 1875; Monday. To day finished writing and copied my letter to my Sister Ruth in Vermont North Derby. This done I passed some hours in cutting peaches for drying. Late in the afternoon the monotony of our work was enlivened by the arival of Mrs Philo Carter from his Ranch near Greenville in ~~Beav~~ Beaver County. As I was concluding my letter a telegram [was] put into my hand stateing that Marion would be in Salt Lake City on the 2 Oct. ^Mrs Rhod[a] Lyman and her daughter called this evening. Mr [Nicholas] Paul called to day and renewed his promise to do my work.^

September 28, 1875; Tuesday. Wrote letter to my cousin Mrs. Tryphena L. Morrill of Providence Rhode Isleand after which I worked in the fruit helping cut a lot of peaches after which I pared and cut out a lot of apples. In the afternoon Mr [George] Crane called and we concluded a bargain for painting for which I was to pay him seventy five dollers in such pay as I could get from B[enjamin] H. Robison. Philo and family were makeing ready to start ^home tomorow. Mrs Lelia Bartholimew was with us to day with her children.^

September 29, 1875; Wednesday. In the morning pared and cut a lot of apples. After which I mad[e] a call at the Free Trade [store]. The painters were at their work to day which made some change in the appearance of the front of the house. The weather quite warm through the day but the night is quite cool. Cut fruit in the evening.

September 30, 1875; Thursday. The painters were at work to day. I was engaged in working in the fruit. In the afternoon I shucked out some corn. Did not go out to day. Mr Coal Grove mad[e] calls to see the painter. The Lamanites gathered some peaches to day.[38] The weather continues very fine and pleasant in the day but cool at night.

October 1, 1875; Friday. I remained at home and buisy with the fruit cuting. The painters were at work to day and seem to be progressing well with their work. To day the word reached us that we were to have the honor of an Apostolick visit on the next Sunday from Apostles [Daniel H.] Wells and Lorenzo Snow. Weather warm and pleasant, very favorable for our fruit drying.

October 2, 1875; Saturday. This morning took a walk through my orchard to ascertain the condition of my peaches and found them in condition to hurry us in the cuting and drying department of our labor. I passed the forenoon in pairing and cuting peaches. After made a call at store for some glass to replace some. The glazier broak in the side lights to my front entrance. Some clouds indicating a change of weather.

October 3, 1875; Sunday.[39] I remained at home all the day and passed the most of the time in reading. In the afternoon I received a call from a

38. One could pass off Lyman's use of "Lamanite" for Indians as an old habit, but coupled with other clues, it suggests that he continued to believe in the Book of Mormon.

39. On this date, Lyman received a letter from Nathan Tanner containing a spirit communication from Joseph Smith. Headed "Celestial Sphear," it quoted the spirit saying that Brigham Young was wrong in "meny things," including being "to[o] fond of

couple of Swedish friends one of whom assumed the roll of teacher and seemed very certain the much talked of good time was now near at hand and the Saints would soon return to build up the waste places of Zion and in his blind zeal said that I should go with them. ^I requested him [when] they comfortably settled [in Zion] to drop me a note of information.^

October 4, 1875; Monday. Passed the most of the day with the fruit. I made a call at the Free Trade [store]. The painters were at their work a part of the day. Found and bought some butter to day. Late in the afternoon Uncle Sidney Tanner called and stoped with us over night. I stabled and fed his Horses at the tavern. The Apostolick party left for their more northern home I did not see them.

October 5, 1875; Tuesday. Remained at home and worked in[doors]. The painters were on their work a part of the day. Mr Jas Wolsey called as he was passing on his way to the Sand Pete for grain. Late in the afternoon Mr John Coombs called he was on his way to the Terminus of the Rail Road takeing some parties who were going to Salt Lake on buisness and to attend the conference.

October 6, 1875; Wednesday. This morning I with Mrs Lyman gathered a lot of peaches for cutting and drying. The painters were on the work to day. Mr [John] Coombs and party were early on the road calling on us as they passed. I made a call at the Free Trade [store] and Henry brought me a sack of flour from the mill. Weather quite cool at night.

October 7, 1875; Thursday. Remained at home and was buisy with the fruit during the day. I had a call from Mr [Nicholas] Paul to whom I had written a letter in the morning. He promised to be here to do his work next Monday. Mr [George] Crane was away most of the day at work else where. Cut out a lot of peaches in the evening all we had gathered in.

October 8, 1875; Friday. The painters were at the work to day. Gathered and cut some fruit in course of the day. Mrs Lelia Bartholimew and children were with us to day. Weather growing cooler at night but pleasant through the day.

October 9, 1875; Saturday. Mr [George] Crane went away this morning after working a short time to do some work for other parties. Mr [John] Mills remained on my [house] until after diner when he also left.

---

money" and "neglect[ing] His duty to His true & tried followers." Nathan Tanner to Amasa Lyman, Oct. 3, 1875, in Lyman Collection.

Mr Crane's son Owen came with a teem from Canosh to take his Father and Mr [John] Mills to their homes so the residue of my painting must await their return. Weather still pleasant and favorable for drying fruit.

October 10, 1875; Sunday. Remained at home all the day. Lelia and children were with us to day. Weather warm and pleasant.

October 11, 1875; Monday. Passed the morning hours in pareing apples. After this was done I made a call up town to get some tacks with which to hang our window blinds. I found them at the Co-op. Returned home and [w]hile there was told that Clara[,] Marions wife[,] was very ill. Returned home and with Hila hung up some of the blinds. In the evening kored apples and after we had retired Marion called as he was on his way home [from his British mission].

October 12, 1875; Tuesday. In the morning pared peaches and after Breakfast I went up Town and called at the store and then at the co-op. From here I went to Marion's residence and remained with him and family until after diner. Called on his sick wife Clarra. While with Marion he presented me with a verry neat walking stick which was presented to him in London. Came home and husked out some corn cut peaches in evening.

October 13, 1875; Wednesday. In the morning we prepared for storeing our apples ~~tempral~~ for the present in the new house (until I can complete my new celler.) This done I went to Mr Conks shop and he repared my boot, after my return home we commenced to gather some of our winter varieties of apples into the House. Mr [Nicholas] Paul came and made ready for work[,] t[he] effect [of] which [was that] I had to make another trip up town for Lamp Black.[40]

October 14, 1875; Thursday. I was slightly sick the effects of cold. Mr [Nicholas] Paul was on the work to day. Ira returned hom[e] to day. In the evening we had a call from Marion and Rhoda. They gave us an invitation to dine with them on next Sunday. Passed some hours in reading and did not engage in work to day. Mrs Lelia Bartholimew and children were with us to day.

October 15, 1875; Friday. Gathered some apples this morning after which I went to the shop of Mr McKay with my ax to have it repared.

---

40. A fine soot produced as a byproduct of burning oil in lamps and used as a pigment.

Called at his residence and read the Tribune. Mr [Nicholas] Paul was on the work until late in the afternoon when he left with the promise that he would return and finish on Monday morning next. Mr John Coombs called in the evening and had a short seance with us.

October 16, 1875; Saturday. Passed some hours in preparing peaches for preserveing after which I fixed some fastnings on some of my windows. During the afternoon had a call from our nephew Mr Allen Tanner and party who were enroute for the Terminus with Bullion from the Mamoth mine. Before returnign they were going out to Sandpete. Took in some of our fruit that was ~~dry~~ dried.

October 17, 1875; Sunday. Remained at home all the morning hours and then with Mrs Lyman went to Marion's where we dined and passed the residue of the day and while there Marion presented me with a fine overcoat and his mother with a fine shawl. Mr Collins Hakes called on us at Marion's and gave us a jarr of butter sent to us from Parowan by Paulina. I wrote to Nathan Tanner this morning in answer ^to his of the 3d of this month from Cottenwood.^

October 18, 1875; Monday. To day Mr [Nicholas] Paul finished work on the out side of the house and went home. In the morning I work^ed^ at the fruit and in the afternoon I went to the Co-op and bought some fastnings for my French windows. In the evening I pared a lot of apples and cored some of them. Hila and Henry were at the ball given by a troop of Italian musicians in the State House.

October 19, 1875; Tuesday. Remained at home working in and in gathering fruit and while we were at diner Mr Philo Carter and Mr William Barton called on us and remained with us all night. They were enroute for Salt Lake City to [s]ecure their claims on their Homesteads. This morning Mr [John] Kelley started for Salt Lake City with two teems loaded with dried fruit for his son John[,] and my son Henry went with [one of] the teams.

October 20, 1875; Wednesday. This morning Messers Carter and Barton were early on the road to their destination. After their departure I cut out a lot of apples and after diner went up town and done some errands and returned to my work with the fruit at home. This afternoon commenced to assort my letters and file them away for preservation. Marion called this evening to look at the house and Orchard[,] with both of which he was pleased. ^Received a note from Mr [George] Crane the painter from Canosh.^

October 21, 1875; Thursday. Remained at home all day buisy with the apples and ajusting some of the fixtures about the house. To day received a parting call from my son Platt DeAlton and Prest [Thomas] Callister who were just starting on their mission to Europe to be for an indefinite time absent from their families and deprived of the chance of ministering to their wants, to carry out an Illusory idea that God requires of them the care ^that should be given to the comfort of their families who might be benefited by their efforts but God can not [benefit][,] he lives beyond want.^

October 22, 1875; Friday. Worked in the fruit all day and found myself very weary at night and much pain in my broaken limb. In the morning gathered Apples and also in the afternoon. The residue of the day I pared and cut apples. Past an hour at my desk asorting and arangeing my papers. Before retireing we had some musick from Hila on the organ this with some reading. Closed the day and we retired to rest. ^Mrs Lelia Bartholimew and children were with us to day. Mr [Edwin] B. dined with us.^

October 23, 1875; Saturday. Was gathering fruit in the forenoon and in the afternoon sat down to pareing apples and my machine failed. Went up town to get it r[e]pared. Failing in this I borowed one from Mr [Noah] Bartholimew with which I pared out my apples for the evenings work. Some clouds hanging around indicating a change of weather soon.

October 24, 1875; Sunday. Remaned at home all the day gathered some fruit in the forenoon after which I passed the residue of the day in assorting and arangeing my papers. In the evening had some reading a part of which was a lecture on Babylon by Mr Martin delivered in London. This afternoon the clouds scatered giving indications of a cool change of weather. The air is quite chilly.

October 25, 1875; Monday. Gathered Apples and put in the ground 12 bushels of Virginia Greenings. Pased some time with my papers. Moved our large stove into our new kitchen and had our diner in our new dineing room and had the company of Mrs Agness Henry to diner we also put up the parlor stove. In the evening we had reading.

October 26, 1875; Tuesday. Finished gathering my Winesap apples and put them in the ground. Mr [Peter] Silda prepared my timbers for my cellar on which Mr [Andrew J.] Clothier was at work to day. Mr [Joseph] Bradfield hauled me a load of chalk and waited on the mason. In the forenoon Mr [Philo] Carter and Mr [William] Barton returned from their visit to Salt Lake City and stoped with us for diner. Sold Mr some apples to take to his children. After diner they passed ^on[,] Mr C[arter] takeing his daughter with him who had been staying with us for a short time.^

October 27, 1875; Wednesday. To day gathered apples. Mr [Andrew J.] Clother nearly completed the rock work of my cellar. To day heard the news of Mr [John] Borne accident by which he badly fractured his right leg below the knee and received other serious injuries in body and limbs. He was in the Clear Lake neighborhood when hurt. He was brought home last night I with Mrs Lyman was present when he arived.

October 28, 1875; Thursday. Some storm of rain and snow last night and to day during the day between the showers made up the ridge pole [ridge beam] for the roof of my cellar. Settled with [Andrew J.] Clothier for his work on the cellar which amonted to $35 of [which] I paid him all but eight. In the evening Prest [Noah] Bartholimew and two of the directors meet at my place and agreed to settle with and to discharge Mr [John] Kelley.[41]

October 29, 1875; Friday. This morning Mr Edwin Bartholimew with teem hauled my large timbers around for my cellar[,] and Marion and Lorenzo put them in their places and Mr [Andrew J.] Clothier finished up the mason work. In the afternoon with Mrs Lyman gathered in some of our winter Apples. Mrs Lelia Bartholimew and children were with us to day. In the evening had a call from Mr Charles McBride an[d] Miss Alice Lyman.[42] ^To day loaned my Henry Rifle to Mr Nephi Pratt for ex Bishop [Seymour] Brunson who perched himself on a box by the roadside [outside the house] while the other done his borowing[,] [since it was being borrowed] from the apostate who was unworthy to receive a personal call from him.^

October 30, 1875; Saturday. Gathered some apples in the forenoon

41. The nature of the dispute is unknown. In any case, Kelly continued on as the store clerk and a presence within the Free Trade Union.

42. Rhoda Alice Lyman was the oldest daughter of Francis M. and Rhoda Lyman. She will marry Charles McBride in three weeks on Nov. 20.

cleaned up and made some calculations about my cellar. In the afternoon had together a party of some half dozen of our grand children who belonged to our sons[:] four to Marion and two to Amasa M. Jr. They came together on the occasion of the eighth Birthday of Miss Ethel [Lyman] [,] only daughter of A[masa] M. Jr. The day has been quite warm and pleasant. Miss [Leminder Melissa] Dugins called this evening.

October 31, 1875; Sunday. Remained at home most of the day. In the morning called on Mr [Peter] Silda at his residence after which I gathered some Apples. During the day our nephew Mr Allen Tanner [and] son and daughter call on us. Sold 1 bushe[l] of apples to Mr Keys and a ½ to Mr Allen Tanner. Wrote letter to Mr Wm. Barton in Beaver County. Miss Laura Bartholimew ^called^ in the evening. ^Paid Lorenzo twenty dollers for his trip to the city and bringing my goods from there to this place while he owed me $117.18.^

November 1, 1875; Monday. In the morning helped gather apples and in the afternoon began making my stairs for the cellar and Mrs Lyman and the children brought in from the orchard the last of our apple crop. This evening received a friendly call from Brother [James] Starley. Miss Alice Lyman called this evening.

November 2, 1875; Tuesday. Finished up my cellar stairs and commenced cleaning up the ground around my house. Weather warm with indications of comeing storm. Lorenzo called and told me that Mr [Henry] Noy[e]s was engaged to tend the store. Heard the report to day that some half dozen carpenters had been called from Fillmore to work on the temple at St. George. Henry arived after night.

November 3, 1875; Wednesday. The report of yesterday that Henry had returned proved to be fals[e] as he did not arive until last night. Rain falling most of the day[,] did not go out. In the evening Mr [John] Kelley and son John called with Lorenzo.

November 4, 1875; Thursday. This morning early to the store where I meet the Board of dire[c]tors and transacted some buisness with them after which I helped to open and mark and put up the new goods which Mr [John] Kelley had bought when he was last at the city. Weather pleasant but cool. As I returned home I called on Mr [John] Bourne who was suffering much with his broaken leg. ^Today received fifty dollers from Benjamin Robison on his note.^

November 5, 1875; Friday. This morning sett[l]ed with and paid [Andrew J.] Clothier the $8 dollers due him for work and paid Andersen the like amount. In the afternoon bought two Boxes of the Store for which I paid one doller. Wrote letter to [George] Crane at Canosh. Had the children with us to diner Lorenzo and wife and Henry. Called on Mr [James] Starley and examined his cedar mill and tasted his cider.

November 6, 1875; Saturday. Was engaged in work on my place cleareing up around the house and in makeing some coops for our hens. This morning at about 8 oclock Lorenzo and Henry with their party started to find their new home on the peaceful shores of the Pacific in or near Sta Barbara.[43] Dense clouds around the Horizon indicating rain soon. Considerable travil on the road to the South. ^Mr Robert Miller from Parowan past to day on his way to Salt Lake [and] reported all well when he left home.^

November 7, 1875; Sunday. Remained at home all day. Passed the time in reading. Some rain fell last night, the weather is becomeing cold and like winter minus the snow.

November 8, 1875; Monday. Passed the morning in cuting wood and after breakfast made preparation for and moved some our winter apples into the house to prevent them from freezeing after which spent some time in prepareing my stove pipe for puting up in my parlor. Hila went to Edwin's and staid all night with Lelia. Weather cold frezeing quite hard at night.

November 9, 1875; Tuesday. In the forenoon went to see Mr Reuben McBride but he was gone from home. Looed at his lumber and returned home. In comeing home I called on Mrs Adelia Lyman my son Platt's wife. Her children were suffering with whoping cough. At home I passed the residue of the day in work about the House and place. Called at the P.O. and received papers from Boston and letter from Paulina in Parowan.

November 10, 1875; Wednesday. This morning repeated my call on Mr [Reuben] McBride of whom I bought some five hundred feet of lumber for covering my cellar for which I paid him twenty five dollers out of the Store [credit]. He delivered it at my place. In the evening I called on Mr

43. Henry stayed in California the rest of his life. Lorenzo and Zulia traveled to the coast hoping to find a spot "where a man can be treated decent whether a Mormon or otherwise," but could not get situated and soon returned. *AML*, 478.

Stephen Dugins in relation to some slabs for batening my celler. Weather somewhat warmer with indications of Storm.

November 11, 1875; Thursday. In the morning I went up Town to find some slabs to baten my celler and succeeded in geting a load from Mr Nathan Baldwin. Dined with Marion and his wife Clarra and after returning home I cleaned out the bottom of my celler while a light mist of rain was falling from which I took some cold. In the evening Mr [William] Marsden from Parowan came in and took my parcel of dried fruit to Paulina. ^To day wrote letter to Paulina.^

November 12, 1875; Friday. Was buisy prepareing for covering my celler and for this work received a load of slabs from Mr Nathan Baldwin for which I paid him seven dollers. Some indications of a comeing storm. Mad[e] a wearisome trip to the residence of Mr Jas Rowly in quest of Mr [George] Walters to help me on my celler which he promised to do on the morow.

November 13, 1875; Saturday. To day Mr [George] Wal[t]ers came and helped me to put the covering on my celler wh[ich] job we completed before night for which I paid him two dollers. Some snow falling on the mountains but none to hinder our work. The Autumn winds are fast denuding the trees of their sumer dress as its sighs through their leafless branches tells of the aproach of Winter to wrap Mother Earth in its cold embrace. ^Priscilla returned to day from her visit to Beaver. She failed to see the Franklins as they started before she arived. Her broth Isaac came with her but did not call on me.^

November 14, 1875; Sunday. In the morning called on Mr [Peter] Silda after which I called on Mr Joseph Bradfield who agreed to haul wood for me this week the weather permiting. Some indications of a storm.

November 15, 1875; Monday. Last night snow fell for the first time this fall to cover the ground in the valley. I worked on my celler through the day. The last night's storm prevented Mr [Joseph] Bradfield from hauling wood for me to day.

November 16, 1875; Tuesday. Some snow fell last night. Passed the day as yesterday. Mrs Lelia Bartholimew and children were with us to day. No rain fell to day altho the weather was quite mild melting the snow of the last night. Quite pleasant working but for the mud under foot. Ajusted some fastnings on some of my front Windows.

November 17, 1875; Wednesday. Worked on my house over my celler stairway. Weather warm and pleasant with the clouds but did not storm. In the afternoon Mr [Joseph] Bradfield brought me a load of wood for which he cha[r]ged me three dollers and promised to get me enough for the winter at the same rate. Passed the evening in reading. Received posta[l] card from Mr [George] Crane of Canosh saying he would make ^an effort to come and assist me in puting up my water pipes to my house.^

November 18, 1875; Thursday. Work all the day on my cellar. During the day Mr Wm Bradfield[44] called to see me and I engaged him to work for me at 1½ dollrs per day and weather being favorable he would commence tomorow. Stil indication of a storm.

November 19, 1875; Friday. Worked about my celler and during the day gave Mr Joseph Bradfield an order of five dollers on B[enjamin] R[obison] account of wood hawling. Wm Bradford worked half a day puting the earth covering on my celler. In the afternoon delivered my dried peaches 125 lbs on Mr [John] Kelleys order to Mr Safford. A gentle rain was falling most of the forenoon after which it cleared up. ^Mrs Lelia Bartholimew and children were with us through the day.^

November 20, 1875; Saturday. Worked on my celler to day. [William] Bradfield was with me and made a day [of it]. Joseph [Bradfield] hauled me another load of wood. About noon we received an invitation to attend the weding of Miss Rhoda Alice Lyman and Mr Charles R. McBride at the Father of the Bride['s] Mr F[rancis] M. Lyman. The ceremony was performed by Judge Edward Partridge [Jr.].[45] Returned hom about 9 oclock some clouds in the west.

November 21, 1875; Sunday. A light rain was falling this morning. I remained at home until after the diner hour after which with Mrs Lyman I mad[e] a call on Mr [John] Bourne whom we found in better condition and spirits than when we visited him before. He said his fractured limb was doing very well. Weather slightly cooler. Mrs [Lelia] Bartholimew and children were with us last night and to day.

---

44. William Bradfield was the teenage brother (16 years old) of Joseph (25 years old), both of whom were helping Lyman haul and chop wood and do carpentry work. They arrived from England in 1868, with their parents and eight siblings.

45. Without a functioning temple in the territory, couples married civilly and then traveled to the Endowment House in Salt Lake City to be sealed.

November 22, 1875; Monday. Worked on my celler and in the afternoon Mr [George] Crane and [John] Mills came to put up my Water Gutters and pipes. They commenced the job and went to Mrs Forties to lodge. William Bradfield did not work to day.

November 23, 1875; Tuesday. This morning finish^ed^ up the roof of my celler and house ready for the Earth covering which William put on to day. Mr [George] Crane and man finished their job before night for whi^ch^ I paid $6.50 ~~fif~~. Paid Mr Crane the balence due him for painting $32.50 by Order on B[enjamin] R[obison] for flour. To day received postal card from Lorenzo in Nevada all well.

November 24, 1875; Wednesday. Hung the door to my celler, and commenced makeing some walks in the rear of my house. Marion and Rhoda were with us to day to diner[,] their daughter Mary was with them. Late in the afternoon it commenced to rain. In the morning I went to the Store and got some things on account [in return for] peaches[,] [which] we let them have to the amount of $22.66. When we retired it was raining.

November 25, 1875; Thursday. Worked on the celler and put in the grating to the windows. In the afternoon William Bradfield called and received his pay for his work.

November 26, 1875; Friday. In the morning continued the work on my celler and made a call at the Store. Some indications of a storm. Much trav[e]l on the Road South. Received a letter from Mr W. T. Williams of San Beneventura Cal[ifornia] containing questions he wished me to answer.

November 27, 1875; Saturday. This morning wrote a letter to Mr W. T. Williams in Cal[ifornia]. During the day done some work about the House and in the afternoon shifted some of the dirt around my celler. Some indications of fairer weather.

November 28, 1875; Sunday. Remained at home to day and did not go out passed the time in reading the [backlog of] Daily Tribunes. In the afternoon Mr Philo Carter called on us with a load of wheat and potatoes to exchange for Apples. He reported all well at home. In the evening had a call from Mr Charles McBride and wife. Had musick during the evening from Hila and Mrs M.

November 29, 1875; Monday. Went to the mill with my wheat to be floured and on the way called on Marion at his office when he told me that there was a balance due me of some $104 of dividend on the stock herd. After returning home I worked some on my celler. Philo brought me from the mill some twelve hundred lbs of flour from thirty ½ bushels of wheat and the bran and shorts.[46] Weather fine.

November 30, 1875; Tuesday. This morning delivered to Philo his Appls for the wheat and potatoes. He let me have some thirty and ½ bushels of wheat and twenty bushels of potatoes. He started for home this forenoon. After returning home ^from the store^ passed the residue of the day in work on the ground about my celler and house. The weather was very fine and pleasant. Madam Lelia and her children were with us.

December 1, 1875; Wednesday. To day let Mr Silas Smith have twenty-one bushels of apples which he was to trade for wheat in Sandpete of which he was to give me one half in Fillmore. Passed the day in work on my cellar and during the day I engaged a man to cut my wood for $1.75 per load. Some indications of coming storms.

December 2, 1875; Thursday. This morning the man who had engaged to chop my wood came and gave up the job as being to hard to perform at his own proposition so after cuting a little he left. I finished closeing up the north end of my celler after which I went up town and called at the residence of Mr [James] Starley but he was not at home so I failed to see him. Called at the store and bought some oil.

December 3, 1875; Friday. I was engaged through the day in takeing care of my apples and in work on my celler. And in the evening I finished shelling some corn which I commenced two nights since. Some indications of storm. In the afternoon moved some dirt in the rear of my house.

December 4, 1875; Saturday. Remained at home all day at work about the place and sorting and moveing some of our apples makeing ready for winter. Weather becomeing much cooler with frost at night. Did not go out from home to day. Had a call from Mr Huntly who wished to get a load of apples to carry away to the Sevier to exchange for wheat.

December 5, 1875; Sunday. To day visited Mr John Kelley and family. Mr Bartholimew and wife were there. As we returned home we called on Mr [John] Bourne whom we found stil improveing and indulging

46. Wheat shorts were used as animal feed. It was a medium-fine flour, sometimes called middlings. Bran was used as chicken feed (see the entry below for Aug. 25, 1876).

in the hope to be able to get about in a few more days of waiting on his sick limb. The cold is growing more intense. At home we meet with Marion and Rhoda.

December 6, 1875; Monday. Worked some in the morning moveing earth on my walks. After breakfast I went up in Town and called at the home of Mr [James] Starley to see his cider mill after which I called on Mr S. at the Titheing Office. After returning home I had a call from Mr Joseph Bradfield with whom I agre^e^d for the cuting of my wood. ^With Mrs L[yman] spent the evening with Mr John Cavanah and family.^

December 7, 1875; Tuesday. Remained at home the most of the day at work about my place and in takeing care of my apples. Late in the afternoon I called on Marion at his Office and ordered a deed for the Lots of land sold by Henry to Theodore. I also procured an order on stockherd for fifteen dollers which [I] turned [in] to [Timothy] Scotern [Scottorn] the Bucher on which I received one quarter of beef weight 100 lbs for $7. He balenced my account and gave me credit for the balence.

December 8, 1875; Wednesday. Remained at home and passed the day in work about the place and finished movening my Apples to the celler. After which I graded the walk ^and moved the rocks^ at the south end of my House. This morning received my Beef from the Butchers. [Joseph] Bradfield brought his fifth load of wood to day. Weather cool and clear[,] considerable travil to the south[,] some religious some commercial. So the world goes.

December 9, 1875; Thursday. Remained at home all day buisy with my work on the ground in rear of the House. Mr [Joseph] Bradfield brought the sixth load of wood on account of wood he delivered to me. I paid him $18 dollers in flour at Lymans and Robisons mill.

December 10, 1875; Friday. Worked about place during the forenoon called on Mr [William] Bishop at his shop and had some irons prepared for securing my celler door. Moved some gravel onto the walks in the rear of my house. Weather somewhat milder which people are improveing in traviling freighting and their labor.

December 11, 1875; Saturday. Worked at home through the forenoon after which I went to see Marion with whom and his wife Rhoda I dined after which I called on Mr Theodore Rogers to get some information in regard to Mr Samuel Rogers of Parowan who is up north and is to be back soon with him. I hop[e] to go South when he returns. On my way home I was informed of the Death of my old friend Rogers on last Monday.

December 12, 1875; Sunday. Remained at home through the day. Passed most of the time in reading. In the evening had a call from Mr Noah Bartholimew and the Misses Bartholimew[,] [and] Pew and Brown. Later in the evening Mr [John] Kelley called we had during the evening songs accompanied by the Organ by Miss Agne and Miss Pew and Brown. This morning Mr [Silas] Smith called and told me that ^for the apples he had from me there was comeing to me some 9 bushels of wheat five of which he pays me now and 4 by and by when he has made another trip.^

December 13, 1875; Monday. I[n] morning before breakfast [I] wheeled some gravel to the rear of my House after which I went up Town and learned that Theodore was to start for Beaver in the morning. I saw him and engaged a passage with him he caried me to the mill and brought home my mail. Authorized Mr John Kelley to represent me in the meeting of the share holders of the Free Traders Union.[47]

December 14, 1875; Tuesday. This morning I started for Beaver with Theodore and Mr Peter Silda. Made noon halt at Corn Creek [Kanosh] and camped for the night in Bakers Can[y]on. The night was very cold.

December 15, 1875; Wednesday. We were early on the road and made halt at Cove Creek for Breakfast. We reached Beaver at night and put up with Mr Isaac Turley with whom we found comfort and a hearty welcome. The night was very cool.

December 16, 1875; Thursday. This morning made some calls in town after which Theodore went to Adamsville and I went with him to Philo's who with his family we found well.

December 17, 1875; Friday. To day with Philo and wife went to Minersville and put up with Mr Ervin Stoddard and family in the evening I made calls on several of my old friends about town. The night was very cold.

December 18, 1875; Saturday. This morning Mr [Philo] Carter started for Lincoln Mining camp where [we] called on and dined with my daughter Mrs [Maria Louisa] Stredder. My son Amasa Jr was not

47. This is the last entry in vol. 40. The Dec. 14, 1875–Mar. 4, 1876, entries are in vol. 41.

in camp so we did not see him. After diner we returned to Mr Carter's residence some indications of storm.

December 19, 1875; Sunday. Passed most of the day in reading. Snow began to fall on the mountains.

December 20, 1875; Monday. This morning snow was falling and we concluded not to start for Parowan until tomorow. In the afternoon the snow ceased falling and the weather became very cold. Passed the day in reading.

December 21, 1875; Tuesday. This morning with Philo were early on the way for Parowan when we arived at the [Buckhorn] Springs. We meet Mr John Coombs and family on their way to Beaver and Mrs [Mary] Page and [Mary] Marsden bound for the same place in quest of some surgical help for the child of Mrs P, which had a button in its nose. The night was very cold, freezing very hard.

December 22, 1875; Wednesday. This morning made a call on Mr Horoun at his shop. Called ^on^ Mrs Jane Hanks.

December 23, 1875; Thursday. To day called on Mr George Grimshaw at the P.O. Passed the day in reading The Innocents Abroad.[48]

December 24, 1875; Friday. Passed the morning in reading after which I called on Mr Richard Benson with whom and his family I dined. After which I called on my old friend D[aniel] P. Clark and famly. Mr Benson promised me a piece of timber for the cilinder to my cider mill.[49] In the evening had a call from my old friend Mr. W. Decker.

December 25, 1875; Saturday. Did not go out to day the day passed very quietly. Weather pleasant but cool. Was treated to a song from the [Christmas] Serenading Troup.

December 26, 1875; Sunday. Passed the morning at home in reading after which [I] visited Mrs Jane Hanks with whom myself and Mrs. Lyman dined and at the close of the day we returned home.

December 27, 1875; Monday. Remained at home through the day and passed the time in reading Innocents Abroad. Weather mild and warm. Had an evening call from my friend Decker.

---

48. Mark Twain's best-selling humor and travel book, published in 1869.

49. A cider mill typically had a crusher consisting of two wooden cylinders, one with teeth and the other with corresponding depressions, through which the apples passed, and a screw press to extract any remaining juice. See Nov. 5, Dec. 6, 1875; Jan. 3–4, 1876.

December 28, 1875; Tuesday. Passed the morning hours at home in reading after which with Mrs L[yman] went [to] the residence of Mr Daniel Page and passed the residue of the day with his family. After returning home received a call from my old friend Mr E[benezer] Hanks from Iron City. Wind high from the South. Mr Page returned home this evening from his northern visit.

December 29, 1875; Wednesday. The last night snow fell to the depth of nearly one foot and to day the young men of the town were hunting rabits some hundreds were killed. Weather slightly cool at night. Had calls to day from friend McAty from Sumit Creek who has been cut off from the Church for dareing to think for himself and express his thoughts.

December 30, 1875; Thursday. After the morning hours passed the residue of the day with the Hankses. In the evening had a call from Mr [Edward] Dalton Mayor of Parowan.

December 31, 1875; Friday. After the morning hour I called on Mr [Daniel] Page with whom and family I dined and returned home and passed the residue of the day in reading. Had a lengthy talk with Mr Decker.

January 1, 1876; Saturday. Remained at home through the day which passed very quietly. No noisey demonstration attended comeing of the New Year.

January 2, 1876; Sunday. Passed the forenoon at home and wrote a letter to Mrs L. M. Lyman in Fillmore. In afternoon we went to the residence of Mr D[aniel] P. Clark and family with whom we passed the residue of the day, and as we came home in the evening we called on Mr Richard Benson and family. Weather growing more mild with indications of storm.

January 3, 1876; Monday. To day I procured some iron for my celinder for my cider mill. The weather warm and pleasant the snow melting fast.

January 4, 1876; Tuesday. To day had my Irons fited and my cilinder turned by Mr [Nathaniel P.] Worden. A rough snow squall this morning after which it became fair and pleasant. Dined with Mr Horoun and family. The rioters Dalton and Whitney were tried to day and the former was fined and the latter was aquited. Mrs Sarah Driggs and daughter called on us to day.

January 5, 1876; Wednesday. This morning made call on Mr [William]

Marsden at his residence after which called on Mrs Elizabeth Benson at her residence. On returning home I called on and dined with Mrs Zilpha Smith. In evening had a call from Mr McNelly and Mr R[ichard] Benson. Mr N. gave seance. The rabit hunt commenced to day [for adults]. ^Madora [Lyman] and [her] Father [Richard Benson] returned from Beaver to day.^

January 6, 1876; Thursday. This morning received a call from Mr Be[n]son and McNelly who is going to St. George. Some indications of storm. Received to day a call from Mr Decker. The rabit hunt was continued to day.

January 7, 1876; Friday. Remained at home through the day and passed most of the time in reading. Mr Decker passed some time with me during the day and evening. Had a call from Mr Daniel Page. Weather cool and pleasant.

January 8, 1876; Saturday. Remained at home did not go out to day. Some snow fell last night. Had a call from Mr [William] Marsden. In the evening I received a call from Mr Richard Benson. The dancing party for the school came off to day.

January 9, 1876; Sunday. Passed the morning at home after which called on and passed the day and evening with Mrs Jane Hanks. Mrs Henderson was with us and Mrs Barton and Mr Mayor[,] [Edward] Dalton[,] was with us during the evening. Mr ~~Christian~~ ^Hans^ Hansen[50] was brought here a raving maniack from St. George wher[e] he had been working. His home is in Fillmore to which he is being ^taken by the Bishops.^

January 10, 1876; Monday. Remained at home through the day and in the evening attended a social party in the meeting house. Had sup[p]er at the residence of Mr Wm Hollyoke and came home about one oclock in morning.

January 11, 1876; Tuesday. Passed the morning hours at home after which with Mrs L[yman] went to the residence of Mr Peter Heiner with whom and family we passed the day. Mr Decker and wife were with us. In the evening had a call from Mr Edward Dalton and Mr Richard Benson.

---

50. The name is struck through in different ink and the substituted name is in a different hand. If it was Hans Hansen, he was a carpenter who worked on the St. George temple and later the Manti temple.

January 12, 1876; Wednesday. Passed the day with Mr Daniel Page and family and in the evening we attended meeting in the meeting house where service was held by Mr [George M.] Pierce from Beaver he was of the Methodist denomination.

January 13, 1876; Thursday. Remained at home and read Lectures by Mr Robert G. Ingersol.[51] During the day made call on Mrs Jane Hanks. As we were retiring had a call from Mr Richard Benson.

January 14, 1876; Friday. After the morning hour with Mr Richard Benson and wife[,] Madora and her children and Mrs Jane Hanks and Mrs Lyman and Laura went to the residence of Mr Niels [Otto] Mort[en]sen with whom and family we passed the day very pleasantly. After returning home passed evening in reading.

January 15, 1876; Saturday. Remained at home through the forenoon and passed the time in reading. In afternoon with Mrs Lyman and Laura went to the residence of Mr D[aniel] P. Clark's with whom and family we passed the residue of the day. Mrs Sarah Driggs and daughter Olivia called in the afternoon at Mr Clarks.

January 16, 1876; Sunday. To day attended meeting.[52] In the morning we went to the residence of Mr Thomas Durham with whom and family we dined after which we attended meeting together and then returned with Mr [Durham] and passed the residue of the day with them.

January 17, 1876; Monday. Remained at home and passed the time in reading. In the evening had a call from Mr R[ichard] Benson.

January 18, 1876; Tuesday. Passed the morning hours at home after which with Mrs L[yman] I went to the residence of Richard Benson with whom and family we dined after which we were informed that Father [Morris C.] Phelps and wife had returned from their visit in Dixie. The old man is very feeble in health.[53] Had calls from Mr R[ichard] Benson and also Mr Edward Dalton.

January 19, 1876; Wednesday. We attended meeting to listen to the what was to us idle twaddle of the propogandists of a credal faith which

51. Ingersoll was a Civil War veteran and attorney who delivered popular speeches on politics, family life, and religion. Over time he came to be known as "the Great Agnostic."

52. Lyman attended both the Methodist and Mormon meetings in order to be supportive of his wives and children. See Jan. 19, Feb. 20, Mar. 5, 12, Sept. 10, 1876.

53. Paulina's father, Morris Phelps, would die on May 22. In the space of a little over two years, Paulina would lose her son, Oscar; her father, Morris; and her husband, Amasa.

is narow in its charities to meet the wants of humanity and to[o] poor in adaptation to bear a practicable application to the wants of humanity. In the evening I recived a letter from my grand daughter Miss A[delia] Carter in Greenville.[54]

January 20, 1876; Thursday. Attended meeting which passed off much as yesterday. In evening had calls from neighbors Decker[,] [Edward] Dalton and [Richard] Benson. Father [Morris C.] Phelps is feeble in health and so also his wife. Wind Southerly to day and snow melting quite fast. At night the weather turned cooler freezing considerably.

January 21, 1876; Friday. In morning wrote letter to my Grand Daughter Miss A.M.L. Carter in Greenville after which I called on Mr Daniel Page with whom I dined. In evening with Mrs Lyman and our Daughter Laura we attended the theatrical exhibition which entertainment was given in the intrest of and in behalf of the Sabbath School children.

January 22, 1876; Saturday. Remained at home all day and did not go out. In the evening passed a few hours with Mrs Jane Hanks and a few other friends. To day [grandson] William killed his first deer. Weather cool but pleasant.

January 23, 1876; Sunday. Remained at home through the day and passed the time in reading ancient history.

January 24, 1876; Monday. In the morning after breakfast made a call at the residence of Mr [William] Marsden but he gave me no promise of takeing me to Fillmore when he starts for Salt Lake in a few days.

January 25, 1876; Tuesday. Passed the day at the residence of Mr [William E.] Banks and family where Mrs Lyman was engaged in makeing coat and pants. In the afternoon Mr W[illiam] H. Dame returned home (after over a years imprisonment) in custody of the U.S. Marshall, not yet having had his trial.[55]

January 26, 1876; Wednesday. Passed the day as yesterday with the Bankses. When we returned home in the evening we learned that Mr Hendricksen had shot himself accidentally in the leg below the knee.

---

54. He writes "Miss A.M.L. Carter" (also on Jan. 21) but means Adelia, which he spells out explicitly on Feb. 23. as "Adelia M. Carter" even though her name was Ida Ruth Adelia. She was nineteen years old. Her seventeen-year-old brother's initials were A.M.L., but he is apparently not intended.

55. Dame was indicted, held in prison for over a year, released on bail, and finally cleared of all charges later in 1876.

January 27, 1876; Thursday. In forenoon made call on Mrs Jane Hanks's and read the paper, the R[eligio–] P[hilosophical] Journal. President [William H.] Dame addressed his flock this evening. Snow fell freely this evening.

January 28, 1876; Friday. After the morning hours we went to the residence of Mr Watson with whom and family we passed the day. Mrs Sarah Clark was with us and Mr D[aniel] P. Clark a part of the afternoon. Mr W. presented us with tickets for the evening theater. Weather very cold.

January 29, 1876; Saturday. In the morning I called on Mr W[illiam] H. Dame at his residence and while there I was presented with Tickets (for the theatrical entertainment at night) by Mr Charles Adams. Weather very cold. William went hunting deer to day.

January 30, 1876; Sunday. Ramained at home through the day did not go out. Passed the day in reading. Mr [William H.] Dame preached to the people. Madora [Lyman] and children were with us to day.

January 31, 1875; Monday. We rose early and after a hasty breakfast Father [Morris C.] Phelps and wife started on their homeward journey. Weather more mild. In the evening had a call from Mr Richard Benson.

February 1, 1876; Tuesday. Remained at home all day and passed time in reading. In the evening had a friendly call from neighbor Decker. Weather moderating and the snow is melting rapidly. William hawled a load of wood.

February 2, 1876; Wednesday. After the morning hour called on Mrs Jane Hanks with whom myself and Mrs Lyman dined. Passed the time in reading. This morning we heard the news of the death of Father [George] Taylor who died last night. Funeral will take place tomorow. Weather stil mild.

February 3, 1876; Thursday. To day attended fast meeting and the funeral of Father [George] Taylor after which we dined with Richard Benson and family. In evening had a call from Mr Richard Benson.

February 4, 1876; Friday. Did not go out today Mrs Lym[an] was very sick all day with an atack of cramp colick [appendicitis]. Our neighbors Mrs Decker and Mrs [Jane] Hanks were in attendence with their offices of kindness. In the evening had calls from Mr [Edward] Dalton and Mr [Richard] Benson. William went on a deer hunt. Mrs Sarah Ward called in evening.

February 5, 1876; Saturday. Mrs Lym[an] is better to day than yesterday. After the morning hour I called on Mr [Daniel] Page and passed with him a few hours. Weather stil mild. In the evening mad[e] a call on Mr R[ichard] Benson.

February 6, 1876; Sunday. Remained at home all the day and passed the time in reading Ancient History of the Pers^i^ans and Grecians.

February 7, 1876; Monday. To day called on Mrs Alice Marsden at her residence. After returning home passed the residue of the day in reading. In the evening had a call from Mr Benj[amin] Croft who had just returned from the Leeds mine of which [he] gave a good report. Mr [Richard] Benson called in.

February 8, 1876; Tuesday. Passed the morning at home after which with Mrs L[yman] called on Mrs J[ane] Hanks with whom we dined. William and others went out to drive stock to the desert where they might find feed. Mr [Benjamin] Croft called as he was [s]tarting for ^his^ home in Minersville on the Beaver [River].

February 9, 1876; Wednesday. Remained at home all day and passed the time in reading history. In the evening Elder G[eorge] M. Pierce of the M[ethodist] E[piscopal] Church held forth in Webs Hall, Received no calls to day. In forenoon some snow fell but the afternoon was fair[,] freezeing at night.

February 10, 1876; Thursday.[56] With Mrs L[yman] spent the day with Mr Richard Benson and family at night attended the lecture on Temperence by Mr Edward Dalton Seignor.

February 11, 1876; Friday. After the morning hour I called on Mr Daniel Page with whom and family I spent the day. In afternoon Mrs [Paulina] L[yman] called with Mrs. M[adora] Lyman. In evening had a call from friend Decker.

February 12, 1876; Saturday. In the morning called on Mr [Richard] Benson and Mr [Daniel P.] Clark and Mr [Sidney] Burton to find convaince to go to Beaver but met with no encouragement but good wishes. Visited the P.O. and then returned home and passed the day in reading.

February 13, 1876; Sunday. Remained at home all the day and had the company of <u>Mrs</u> Sarah Driggs and <u>Mrs</u> Jane Hanks. In the evening

56. Just above this entry is a list of how many "yards of plastering" Lyman had ordered for his house.

with Mrs Lyman called on Mrs [Jane] Hanks at her residence and held a seance. Mrs [Almera] Barton was present. Weather pleasant but freezeing hard at night.

February 14, 1876; Monday. In the morning made call on Mr Richard Benson. After returning home received a call by Mrs Jane Hanks with whom at her residence myself and Mrs Lyman dined. Weather mild to day.

February 15, 1876; Tuesday. After the morning hour I made a call on Mrs [Jane] Hanks and after returning home I called on Mr Geor[ge] Grimshaw at the P.O. and learned from him that Mr Ja[me]s Low was the mail contractor on the line to Beaver.[57]

February 16, 1876; Wednesday. Visited and passed the day with Mrs Almera Barton at her residence. Mrs Jane Hanks was with us and Mrs L[yman] and Laura. In evening had a call from Mr R[ichard] Benson.[58]

February 17, 1876; Thursday. This morning called on Mr [George] Grimshaw at the P.O. and after that I called on Mrs Maria Taylor at her residence where I saw a letter from her Br Hyrum Coombs of Salt Lake City reporting himself and family well and calculating to move to Fillmore in the Spring. Mrs. Lyman was sick to day.

February 18, 1876; Friday. After the morning hour I called on Mr Richard Benson with whom and family I dined, after returning home [I] passed [the] residue of the day in reading.

February 19, 1876; Saturday. This morning called on [William] Marsden at his residence [and] by him had some news from Fillmore. After returning home [I] received a call from Mr E[dward] Dalton seign [senior] and also one from Mr James Adams who presented us with tickets for the Sabbath School Exhibition in the evening. Bishop [Henry] Lunt and party ^[from] Cedar^ were present at the exhibition. Snow fell ~~las~~ to night.

February 20, 1876; Sunday. Attended meeting this forenoon and then dined with Mrs [Jane] Hanks. In the afternoon attended meeting. The meetings were interesting only in the evidences they afforded of the

57. James A. Low was a forty-seven-year-old emigrant from Scotland; his wife was from Tennessee. For a few years, the mail was dropped off at the James Low Hotel in Beaver, so he had previous contact with the freighters. When a small post office was built in 1874, Horace Skinner was named postmaster. Bradley, *History of Beaver County*, 144

58. A page of measurements for Lyman's home in Fillmore separates this entry from the next.

blindness of the dupes of Religious Fanaticism. In the evening had the company of Madora [Lyman] and children and of D[aniel] P. Clark and wife Sarah and also of Mr E[dward] Dalton.[59]

February 21, 1876; Monday. This morning called on Mr [Daniel] Page where I meet Mr [William] Marsden [and] after had a call from Mr N[icholas] Paul from Fillmore who said he would take me home on his return from Toquerville. Dined with the Pages.

February 22, 1876; Tuesday. Remained at home and passed the day in reading and in the evening called on Mrs Jane Hanks where we had a pleasant seance.

February 23, 1876; Wednesday. This morning wrote and posted a letter to Miss Adelia M. Carter[60] of Greenville. In the afternoon Mr[s] [Paulina] Lyman had a violent attack of sickness that almost rendered her life doubtful for a time, was beter in evening.

February 24, 1876; Thursday. Remained at home did not go out but passed the time in reading. In evening Mr [Edward] Dalton lectured at the meetinghouse. Weather warm and Springlike.

February 25, 1876; Friday. This morning called on Mr D[aniel] P. Clark with whom and family I dined. Mrs Lyman's health slightly improved. Wind high from the south with indications of more snow.

February 26, 1876; Saturday. To day mad[e] family record of Paulina and children.[61] Wrote note to Dr Fitch in New York. Passed residue of the day in reading. Weather turning colder.

February 27, 1876; Sunday. Passed the morning at home after which with Mrs. Lyman passed the residue of the day with Mrs Jane Hanks and in the evening held a seance. Weather not so cold as yesterday.[62]

February 29, 1876; Tuesday. In the morning called on Mr [William] Marsden and made an arangement with him for some alfalfa seeds. After I returned hom[e] Mr [Nicholas] Paul arived from the South and we

---

59. Two pages of math notations follow. The remaining entries through Mar. 3 are on smaller pages that were tipped into the diary.

60. As noted previously, the middle initial is a mistake. On Mar. 6, he writes to his grandson and adds a superfluous "L" to the name. His grandson is Amasa Mason Carter, not Lyman-Carter.

61. He wrote this on loose sheets at the back of this diary. The list has the names and birthdates of all of their children and death dates for those who had died.

62. There is no Feb. 28 entry.

made ready and started to the north in the afternoon an[d] camped for night at Read Creek. Some indications of storm.

March 1, 1876; Wednesday. Were early on the ro[a]d and reached Beaver about 9 oclock p.m. and lodged with Mr Allen Tanner and family whom we found in good health.

March 2, 1876; Thursday. Traviled to and camped at Cove Creek Fort. I had lodgings in the Fort. Weather pleasant and cool.

March 3, 1876; Friday. Traviled to Meadowcreek. Camped, I lodged at the House of Father [William] Stott.

March 4, 1876; Saturday.[63] Arived at home [in Fillmore] about noon, found all well after being absent [in Parowan for] 81 days. Remained at home all day. Passed the time in reading my letters from my eastern corispondents, and others from California which had accumulated during my visit to Parowan. In afternoon snow fell.

March 5, 1876; Sunday. Attended meeting in the forenoon, the audience was addressed by Elder F[rancis] M. Lyman with whom and family we dined and passed the residue of the day[,] and at night we attended meeting and were addressed by Elder Nephi Pratt. Weather clear and pleasant. Mrs [Maria Louisa] Lyman was with me to day.

March 6, 1876; Monday. In morning wrote letter to Mr Amasa M. L. Carter of Greenville Beaver County. After this made call at the Store and in afternoon cleaned up some ground in front of the House. In the evening with Mrs Lyman and Hila attended the Atheneum.[64]

March 7, 1876; Tuesday. In the morning pruned some of my apple trees and commenced writing to my sons in Cal[ifornia] after which [I] called on Mr [John] Kelley at the store. On my return I called on Mr William Bishop from whom I procured the book written by Mrs. Ann Eliza Young entitled Wife No. 19.[65]

March 8, 1876; Wednesday. Remained at home all day and passed the

63. This entry is split across two volumes. The first sentence is from vol. 41 and the remaining entry from vol. 13. The Mar. 5–Apr. 30, 1876, entries are at the end of vol. 13, immediately after entries from 1855.

64. The Athenaeum was founded in Fillmore in 1873 as a club for those who were interested in pursuing issues from different perspectives through "elocution, composition, and debate." It welcomed men and women, young and old, Mormon and non-Mormon and lasted four years. Parshall, "Living History: Utah's First Come-One, Come-All Social Club, *Salt Lake Tribune*, May 26, 2012.

65. Ann Eliza Denning was a former plural wife of Brigham Young who spoke out

time in reading Mrs Ann Eliza Young's Wife No. 19. Weather squally some snow. At night some indications of more snow.

March 9, 1876; Thursday. To day asorted and moved some of my [blank] in the celler and in the morning wrote letter to Paulina in Parowan and passed the residue of the day in reading. In afternoon received letter from Hyrum & Jose[phine] [Coombs] in Salt Lake City.

March 10, 1876; Friday. In the morning wrote letter to Mr H[yrum] S. Coombs of Salt Lake City after which I called at the Store and sent my letter to the P.O. On my return made a call on Mr Edward Web and family at his residence. Returned home and had some reading by Hila my hoarsness not allowing me to read.

March 11, 1876; Saturday. After the morning hour I made a call at the store and bought me some over shoes. To keep the damp from my feet returned home and passed the residue of the day in reading. Weather cool some snow fell to day.

March 12, 1876; Sunday. This morning with Mrs Lyman attended church and after service dined with Marion with whom and family we spent the afternoon and attended church in the evening. Weather warm and streets muddy. Our religious entertainment was of the old unimproved Mormon style.

March 13, 1876; Monday. After the morning hour I called at the store and then on the Widow Robison where I meet the wife of my son Platte and her children. I then called on Mrs. Julia Merrill and her sister Mrs. Lucy Wilson and then I called on Mrs Helen Coalgrove with whom and her father I dined. ^In evening with family attended Athineum.^

March 14, 1876; Tuesday. This mornin[g] received a call from Mr George Crane the painter from Canosh. Passed the day in reading. Several inches of snow fell during the day and the wind changed to the north.

March 15, 1876; Wednesday. During forenoon assorted and moved to my cellar (by help of Mrs. Lyman) 25 bushels of apples. They were pairmains. In the afternoon made a call at the store and received from Mr [John] Kelley the Rocky Mountain Saints[66] for perusal. Weather quite

---

against polygamy on the lecture circuit. She divorced Young in 1873 and then published *Wife No. 19* in 1875.

66. *Rocky Mountain Saints* was written by Lyman's former Godbeite associate, Thomas B. H. Stenhouse, whose wife, Fanny Stenhouse, wrote her own book, *Tell It All,* adding to the national literature on polygamy and Mormon society.

warm and pleasant. Mud in the streets from the melting of the snow. Hila went to Mr Bartholimews to stay with her Sister [Lelia] in absence of her husband.

March 16, 1876; Thursday. This morning let Mr George Crane have 100 lbs of flour and delivered some dried Apples to the Store. In the evening had a call from Mr William Bishop and Mr John Kelley. Snow melting fast to day.

March 17, 1876; Friday. This morning made some calls up town and dined with Marion an[d] Clara. Returned home much wearied walking through the mud. Weather warm and springlike. On my way home called on Mr [Noah] Bartholimew whom and wife were quite ill. Gave order to Joseph Bradfield of $9.00 for cuting wood.

March 18, 1876; Saturday. Remained at home all day. Some snow fell during the day[,] in early morning there was some rain. Wind changed to the north and brought some snow which was mostly melted by night. Passed the day in reading.

March 19, 1876; Sunday. Attended Church this morning with Mrs Lyman. The audience was addressed by Elders [Reuben] McBride and [Seymour] Brunson. Mrs Lelia Bartholimew and children were with us to day. In the evening again we [were] at Church. The audience was addressed by Elders Gibbs and Watts the latter from Canosh City [on] Corncreek.

March 20, 1876; Monday. This morning received letters[,] one from Parowan[,] one from San Francisco Cal[,] both of which I answered. At night attended the Atheneum which was ajourned Sinadie.

March 21, 1876; Tuesday. In the morning called on Mr [John] Kelley at the store and sent my letters to the P.O. Procured some reading matter from Mr K and returned home. I was this morning presented with some raspberry sets[67] for puting out by Brother Alfred Gull. To day we received a call from Mrs Edward Web. Passed most of the time in reading ^the^ history of the Carthaginians.

March 22, 1876; Wednesday. During forenoon had light fall of rain. Between the showers I set out some twenty eight raspberry trees [trellises]. In the afternoon made a call at the store and returned some reading matter he [John Kelly] had loaned to me on yesterday.

67. In the next entry, Lyman refers to raspberry trees, which would have been trellises for the vines to grow on, the "sets" he refers to here.

March 23, 1876; Thursday. This morning made a call at Lyman's and Robison's Mill[68] where I learned that Mr Silas Smith had not deposited the wheat he owed me at the mill as he agreed to. As I returned hom I called at the residence of Mr [John] Kelley whom I found in his orchard. I dined with him and family. Returning home had a call from Mr [Peter] Silda. ^Received letter from Hyrum [Coombs] stateing he could not come down this year.^

March 24, 1876; Friday. Made a call up town in quest of some carpet nails of which there were none in town so from necesity we had to substitute the Hungarian nails.[69] After returning home I passed some time in reading and late in the afternoon done some pruning.

March 25, 1876; Saturday. To day Mr. [Horace] Thornton called and engaged board for himself and two others and the use of so much of our house and premices as was needed for the exposeure of their wares as agents for the Singer Sewing Machine. At night with Hila attended the meeting of the Theological Class.

March 26, 1876; Sunday. In the morning with Hila attended Church the audience was addressed by Elders Jackson and Russell. Dined and passed the residue of the day with the Bartholimews. Late in the afternoon Mr William Godbe called on me and staid all night.

March 27, 1876; Monday. Made two calls up town during the day and passed most of my time in reading finished the first volume of Rollins Ancient History. In the evening with Hila attended the lecture on Travils on the Continent of Europe by Mr. F[rancis] M. Lyman Missionary and Tourist.

March 28, 1876; Tuesday. To day had a long walk through town in search of some one to work for me but did not find any. Returned home and passed residue of the day in reading History of the Persians and Greeks.

---

68. Lyman is apparently still part owner of the grist mill with Benjamin H. Robison (Lyman often spells it Robinson), despite Robison's intent to buy Lyman's share. See May 2, 1872; Dec. 27, 1873; May 2, Oct. 16, 1874; Aug. 14, Sept. 10, Nov. 4, 1875. Originally from New York, Robison had two wives and twelve children and was a son of the late Joseph Robison, mentioned in the diaries through mid-1868.

69. Hungarian nails (hobnails) were used in boots, hammered into the sole from the outside and leaving the thick heads of the nail exposed to give the wearer traction when hiking off-trail.

March 29, 1876; Wednesday. Remained at home during the day and in the morning I pruned some of my apple trees, after which I passed the residue of the day in reading the History of the Persians and Greeks. Mrs Lelia Bartholimew and children were with us to day. Weather warm with some indications of storm. To day received of Mr. Stokes nine goosebery trees for which I paid $1 80/100 cts.

March 30, 1876; Thursday. To day is my sixty third birthday passed the day at home as a brisk snow storm was raging out side. Received from Mrs Lyman a present of one of Lymans Historical Charts and the key to the same. Passed the day in historical studies.

March 31, 1876; Friday. Snow ceased falling this morning. Remained at home through the day and passed the time in reading Historical matter. Mr Bulger left us this morning to go to his home at Nephi on acount of ill health.

April 1, 1876; Saturday. This morning mad[e] a call on Mr William Bishop and made some rep[air]s on the Handle of my front door. After returning home passed residue of the day in read[ing] and study of [the] History of Ancient Greece.

April 2, 1876; Sunday. Remained at home through the day and passed the time in reading history. Snow melting quite fast in the afternoon had a call from Mr John Kelley and son John.

April 3, 1876; Monday. To day had [son] Walter and Wade helping me to prune my orchard. Weather quite warm the snow mostly disappearing from the Valley. In afternoon some clouds in the northwest indicative of a comeing storm. Wrote letter to my Daughter Mrs [Maria Louisa] Stredder in Lincoln Districk in answer to one received from her this morning.

April 4, 1876; Tuesday. Some light snow fell last night. The men finished the pruning of my orchard to day. The snow of last night mostly disappeared to day. Passed the time in reading.

April 5, 1876; Wednesday. This morning settled [with] Mr [Horace] Thornton and Pratt who left for the north. After their departure I made a call at the store and paid one of the men ^Wade^ for pruneing. After [that I] called at Marions place and then returned home and was buisy about the place the residue of the day.

April 6, 1876; Thursday. This morning took some dried apples to the store [and] after my return buised my self at some work in my shop and while there had a call from Mr [Nicholas] Paul who agreed to take my apples in payment of what I was oweing him. Called Mr [John] Bourne and Mr [John] Cavanah.

April 7, 1876; Friday. Was engaged most of the day in changeing my front gate. In afternoon made a call up town to get some blacksmithing. To day received a call from Mr [John] Cavanah. Also received two letters from Parowan one from my son Charles R. and one from Mrs Madora Lyman.

April 8, 1876; Saturday. Passed the morning in the house during which time it was storming out of doors. In afternoon it cleared up and I made some more improvements on my gate passed some time in reading.

April 9, 1876; Sunday. To day with Mrs Lyman and Hila passed the day with Mrs [Helen V.] Colegrove and her father [Reuben McBride] and mother [Mary] and her brother Reuben A and wives [Harriet and Sarah] and also Mr T[homas] C. Callister and wife [Alice]. The day cool and toward the evening indications of a storm.

April 10, 1876; Monday. Made some paths through the snow after which I wrote letters one to Mrs Madora [Lyman] and one to Mr Charles R. Lyman in Parowan. Passed the residue of the day in reading history. Weather pleasant and thawing some at midday but geting cooler towards night. Snow settling some[,] clear starlight at night.

April 11, 1876; Tuesday. This morning went to the P.O. found the walking very unpleasant on acount of the melting of the snow. Returned home and done some work in the shop and then passed the residue of the day in reading.

April 12, 1876; Wednesday. Passed the morning at home in reading after [which] I made my way through the mud to the residence of Mr [Peter] Silda with whom I had some buisness. Returned home and passe^d^ the residue of the day in reading.

April 13, 1876; Thursday. In the morning called at [t]he Free Trader Store. On my way called on Mr Isaac Carlin for some work of his line after which on my way met with Mr Veale and at the store meet with Mr Gilbert Web who gave me an invitation to dine with him and friends. After which called on Mr [William] Beeston and gave money for the musical visitor.

April 14, 1876; Friday. Made a call at the store and from thence to the mill. On my way called on Mr Reuben McBride with whom I dined. I missed seeing Mr [Silas] Smith at the mill. Called at Marions residence.

April 15, 1876; Saturday. To day had Mr. Ralf Rowley to lay some rock for my walk in front of my house. During the day received a letter from my Daughter Mrs [Maria Louisa] Stredder at Sulpher Springs Iron County.

April 16, 1876; Sunday. This morning with Mrs. Lyman attended Church the audience was addressed by Elder F[rancis] M. Lyman. After services were over we called on and passed the residue of the day with Mr. Edward Web and family. Mrs Web entertained us with musick from her organ and with song. Weather warm and pleasant. Wrote letter to my Duaghter Mrs M[aria] L[ouisa] Stredder [in] Sulpher Springs Iron County.

April 17, 1876; Monday. To day finished laying the border rock for the walk in front of my house for which the mason charged me four dollers. In the afternoon received a passing call from my old and much esteemed friend William J. Cox and his son. They were enroute for their home in Beaver.

April 18, 1876; Tuesday. To day called at the store and extending my walk to the co-op. There I meet with Mrs Moore from Payson who gave me news from our friends in that place. Called on Marion was favored with a ride by Mr Joseph Smith [Anderson]. Passed residue of the day at home in work & reading. ^In evening had some rain and light Hail.^

April 19, 1876; Wednesday. Remained at home all day engaged in a work about my place. During the day received a call from Mr George Crane and his brother with whom in the evening we held a seance. Had a call from Mr Stephen Dugins who wished to buy some Apples.

April 20, 1876; Thursday. This morning removed the earth from the Apples that were buried and in the afternoon delivered to Mr Stephen Dugins seven bushels of Apples for which he agreed to pay me fourteen dollers on or before his return from Leedes [near St. George]. Received letter from Beaver from Daniel Tyler.

April 21, 1876; Friday. To day took the residue of my apples from the ground where they had been buried for six months they were in a good state of preservation. During the forenoon Mr. [Nephi] Pratt & Bulger came to our place from Cedar Springs on buisness of their agency for the Singer Sewing Machine Company.

April 22, 1876; Saturday. This morning made a call on Mr [John]

Kelley at the store. On my return home I called on Mr [Noah] Bartholimew whom with his wife were sick. Mr [Nephi] Pratt & Bulger left to day for Cedar Springs after which I made [a] water trunk for my front walk.[70] Some light rain this evening.

April 23, 1876; Sunday. This morning attended Church with Mrs Lyman. The audience was addressed by Mr McMillin of Presbyterian order folowed by Mr J. L. Smith. From church went to the residence of Mrs Caroline Callister with whom and family we passed the residue of the day.

April 24, 1876; Monday. After the morning hours I made a call on Mr [Peter] Silda and left my saws with him to be sharpened after which I called on Mr Edwin Bartholimew and family with whom I dined. Returned home and done some work on my walk in front of the house.

April 25, 1876; Tuesday. Passed the morning in working about my place after which I called on Marion with whom I dined and after returning home I received two letters one from my son in California and one from my Sister Ruth E. Goodall from North Derby V.T. Mr [Nicholas] Paul called this evening and said he would call in the morning for the Apples.

April 26, 1876; Wednesday. To day delivered to Mr [Nicholas] Paul 1,364 lbs [34 bushels] of apples as payment in full for all I owed him for his work on my house. In the afternoon Mr [William] Marsden brought me some 60 lbs of alfalfa seed for which I paid him fifteen dollers in cash.

April 27, 1876; Thursday. Passed the morning hours at home at work in my orchard after which I helped to clear up our apples in the celler. After diner I went to the store and after my return worked in the orchard for an hour.

April 28, 1876; Friday. Went to see Mr J[oseph] V. Robison in regard to Fruit Trees for Paulina & Madora after which I wrote the[m] a letter apprizeing them of the arangement I had made. After my return home I spent some hours on my trees. Moved some earth on my lawn ground in

---

70. He probably added an underground rocky bed to drain water and keep it from pooling on his walkway. In urban areas, people were beginning to install rudimentary plumbing that included a rooftop cistern for collecting cold water, a pipe to bring the water to the kitchen for cooking or filling a bathtub, and an exit pipe called a water trunk that emptied into an underground rock bed. Maureen Ogle, "All the Modern Conveniences: American Household Plumbing, 1840–1870," Ph.D. diss. (Ames: Iowa State University, 1992), 150.

front of my House. Heard that neighbor [Noah] Bartholimew was not expected to live until the morning.[71] ^Some indications of rain.^

April 29, 1876; Saturday. This morning finished the work of cleaning up the trees in my orchard after which I called at the store and on my way home called on Mr [Noah] Bartholimew who was better than on yesterday. In afternoon passed some hours in work on my ground in the orchard.

April 30, 1876; Sunday. Remained at home and passed the time in writing letters one to my children in Cal[ifornia] and one to my Sister in Derby V.T. and commenced to write in Answer to Mr [Daniel] Tyler's letter. Mother [Maria Louisa Lyman] and Hila were away visiting the sick all the day.[72]

July 28, 1876; Friday. Watered my lots after which I call on Mrs [Sarah] Web and her sick child and also on Mr [Noah] Bartholimew after which I called on Mr [John] Kelley at the store. The weather very warm.

July 29, 1876; Saturday. Passed the morning pulling weeds and not feeling well did no more work through the day. Weather very warm with some indications of rain.

July 30, 1876; Sunday. Attended church the audience was addressed by Elders Pratt and Andersen. Had a call from ^Mr [John] Kelley and wife [Margaret].^

July 31, 1876; Monday. Was engaged through the day in pulling weeds in the orchard. Weather cloudy with indications of rain in the evening heavy thunder and Lightning with rain. Received letters from Paulina and my son Charles. They gave me news of the death of Paulina's Father Mr Morris Phelps.

August 1, 1876; Tuesday. Wrote letters to Paulina and Charles in Parowan. Received letter from H[yrum] S. C[oombs] Salt Lake.

August 2, 1876; Wednesday. Wrote letter to H[yrum] S. Coombs of Salt Lake City and worked some about my place. ^Weather very hot.^

August 3, 1876; Thursday. To day received lumber from Mr Reuben McBride on my bill for finishing [the] pantr[y]. Worked about my place all day. To day Theodore drove up one of my young horses.

---

71. Bartholomew lived until August. Lyman's account of the funeral, eliciting more than passing mention (Aug. 15–16), probably indicates their depth of friendship.

72. This is the last entry in vol. 13, with a gap until July 28 when the entries pick up again in vol. 42, continuing through vol. 43.

August 4, 1876; Friday. Worked on my place, during the day some showers while it rained passed some hours in reading. Weather very sultry before the rain.

August 5, 1876; Saturday. Worked in the morning after which went to P.O. received letter from Philo [Carter]. Dined with Marion he gave me a ride to his field and home. Answered Philo's letter.

August 6, 1876; Sunday. Attended Church the audience was addressed by Elder Powel after the meeting I called on Mr [Noah] Bartholimew who seems to be slowly dieing. Wrote letter for Hyrum [Coombs] on the subject of Mothers [Maria Louisa's] return but did not post it but posted one to Philo [Carter].

August 7, 1876; Monday. Went to work this morning but feeling unwell had to desist and kept the house all day. Election to day did not attend.

August 8, 1876; Tuesday. Passed the morning in work and the residue of the day in reading. In afternoon had rain. Did not feel well.

August 9, 1876; Wednesday. After the morning rain ceased I called on Marion at his Office and procured on order on the me[a]t market of $5. Receied note from Marion saying his son and team would start for the [railroad] Terminus [near Beaver] tomorow.

August 10, 1876; Thursday. Worked at hoeing on my front ground. Marions team and boy started for the Terminus to day with Mr [John] Bourne. ^Wrote to Hyrum [Coombs].^

August 11, 1876; Friday. Worked morning and evening and passed the residue of the time in reading.

August 12, 1876; Saturday. Watered my orchard which made me very weary being on my feet all the day. During the day received a letter from Hyrum [Coombs] in the city of Salt Lake. He reported all well on the 9th.

August 13, 1876; Sunday. Attended Church. Elders Stokes and Hinkly spoke folowed by Bishop P[artridge]. Called on Mr [Noah] Bartholimew who seemed near his end. ^Weather quite warm again.^

August 14, 1876; Monday. Worked on my lawn ground through the entire day. Weather warm some wind in afternoon with clouds.

August 15, 1876; Tuesday. This morning at five minutes past 8 oclock Mr [Noah] Bartholimew Died. I passed the forenoon with the sorrowing family makeing arangements for the funeral services on the morrow for which the Bishop [Edward] Partridge [Jr.] tendered them the use of the meeting house wich was declined on account of the delicate health of Mrs Bartholimew who could not leave her House.[73]

August 16, 1876; Wednesday. Attended the funeral services of the late Noah Willis Bartholimew and addressed the audience. Bishop Edward Partridge and Elder Gabriel Huntsman and members of the choir also took parts in the services. The audience was attentive and evinced much sympathy and kindness of feeling for the bereaved family. We laid the body of our friend away to its final rest and bade farewell to his toil-wearied spirit as it took its airy flight to the bright sumerland of happy immortals. And we stil toil on in ^our chequred path of joy and sorrow to the same hapy land of rest and home of our dear ones departed.^

August 17, 1876; Thursday. Worked some morning & evening and passed residue of the day in reading. In afternoon received a call from Mr John Crane from Canosh he brought us a few peaches and plumbs.

August 18, 1876; Friday. Worked on my place at hoeing part of the day passed residue of time in reading. Marion's team came home to day but Mother did not come with it. Some cloudy indications of rain to day which cleared up at night.

August 19, 1876; Saturday. After a little morning work I made some calls on the sick of the neighborhood. Called on the Bartholimew's with whom I dined after which I went to the P.O. and on my return home I was sumoned by the sheriff to act as a juror in the case of assault wherein the people of the U.S. Millard County were plantif and John Alvis defendant. The assault was charged to have been perpetrated upon the person of Gabriel Riley Huntsman. The jury not agreeing were dismissed ^after siting until 9 oclock by Justice B[enjamin] H. Robison.[74]

August 20, 1876; Sunday. Attended church the audience was addressed by Elder Levi W. Hancock folowed in conclusion by Bishop [Edward] Partridge [Jr.]. Dined with Mr John Kelley and family.

August 21, 1876; Monday. Was engaged in watering through the forenoon and in the afternoon had some rain attended with thunder and

73. The funeral was held in the common area of the Bartholomew inn. The house had a total of eight rooms on the main floor, a large kitchen and modern oven in the basement, and family quarters upstairs.

74. The nature of this incident is unknown, only that Gabriel's parents owned the Huntsman Hotel on Main and Center Streets with twenty-four guest rooms, a barbershop, and stables. The incident may have involved a guest.

lightning. After my days work was done I called on Mr Edward Webb and family who had a very sick child who seems to be slowly dieing.

August 22, 1876; Tuesday. Worked about my place through the day in course of which I received a letter from Lorenzo reporting all well with him. To day sold Theodore my mare for thre[e] young cows one two years old and two three years old.

August 23, 1876; Wednesday. Worked on my place in the morning after which called on Mr [Edward] Web whose sick child was [s]til lingering. Wrote and posted letter to Lorenzo. In the afternoon the child of Mr Web died.

August 24, 1876; Thursday. Worked some during the morning hours after which I attended the funeral of the child Spencer son of Mr Edward Web.

August 25, 1876; Friday. Passed morning at work after which I went up town. Called on Marion and borowed some bran for chicken feed. Wearied with my walk did no more work to day. ^Received from Marion 100 lbs of bran.^

August 26, 1876; Saturday. Wrote letter to Hyrum [Coombs] after which called on Mrs Clara Lyman and Mrs Caroline Callister. ^Worked through morning hours.^

August 27, 1876; Sunday. Passed most of the day with Mr Edwin Bartholimew and family. Some rain on the mountains but did not reach the town. Received letter from Mrs M[aria] L[ouisa] Stredder.

August 28, 1876; Monday. In the morning watered a portion of my ground and in afternoon made some calls in town. Posted letter to Maria S[tredder].

August 29, 1876; Tuesday. Watered my ground to day[,] at night very weary. Weary and much pain in my broaken limb [knee].

August 30, 1876; Wednesday. To day received letters from Hyrum [Coombs] and wrote one to Mrs [Maria Louisa] Lyman who had left Salt Lake and come to Provo on her way home. She stoped with her brother Bishop Myron Tanner.

August 31, 1876; Thursday. In the morning finished and posted my letter to Hyrum [Coombs] and after returning home pared some apples for drying and in the afternoon gathered the Apples from one of my Porter [apple] trees.

September 1, 1876; Friday. Made a call at the store not feeling well did not work to day but in the afternoon gathered a few apples. Whil[e] up town heard of the death of the child of Mr Jas Owens by Diptheria.

September 2, 1876; Saturday. Not feeling ^well^ to day did not engage in any work but passed the most of the day in reading. In the afternoon walked up to the store. Mr Owen's child was burie^d^ this forenoon.

September 3, 1876; Sunday. Passed the day in reading history did not go out to day. In afternoon some light sprinkle of rain.

September 4, 1876; Monday. I[n] forenoon gathered the residue of my Porter Apples after which we had a heavy shower of hail covering the ground like snow. After the storm I went to the P.O. and in the evening had a call from Mr [Nephi] Pratt and Mr [Horace] Thornton Sewing Machine agents.

September 5, 1876; Tuesday. This morning pulled up the sunflowers in my orchard. Made call on Mr [Henry] Noy[e]s after which I called at the store where I meet Mr Martin from Meadow Creek to whom I sold 20 bushels of apples at $1.25 per Bushel. Delivered the Apples this evening.

September 6, 1876; Wednesday. Passed the day in watering my orchard grounds. The weather was pleasant with some high wind during the day. Suffered much pain in my broaken limb all day.

September 7, 1876; Thursday. Pared some apples for drying after which I went to the P.O. and got a letter from Paulina reporting her health improved but that Madora had fallen in her barn and seriously sprained both of her ankles and injured her back. Thinks she will recover.

September 8, 1876; Friday. Walked to the P.O. and posted my letter to P[aulina] L[yman] in Parowan. Passed residue of the day in reading.

September 9, 1876; Saturday. Passed the most of the day in reading. In the after^n^oon went to P.O. and received a postal card from Mrs M[ary] J. Tanner from Payson stateing that herself [and Maria Louisa Lyman] were on the road enroute for Fillmore.

September 10, 1876; Sunday. Attended Church the audience was addressed by Elders Fortie and Day. The addresses had the usual amount of contradictions and inconsistencies in case of Mr F. there was evidence of some thought and exercise of reason. ^Received letter from Freight agent at York the Terminus.^

September 11, 1876; Monday. To day made a call at the residence of

Mr Reuben McBride in quest of some lumber. In the afternoon made a call on Mrs Lelia Bartholimew later in the day we were pleased with the return to our cottage home of Mrs Lyman acompanied by Mrs Mary J. Tanner and eldest daughter [Bessie]. Mrs L. had been absent since the 22ond of June on a visit to our Daughter in Salt Lake City.[75]

September 12, 1876; Tuesday. With Mrs [Mary] Tanner passed the day with Mrs Rhoda Lyman and as we returned we called on Mrs Chandler Holbrook and Mrs Eunice Huntsman.

September 13, 1876; Wednesday. With Mrs Lyman and Mrs [Mary] Tanner passed the day with Mrs Lelia Bartholimew and family.

September 14, 1876; Thursday. Was engaged in watering. Mrs [Mary] Tanner concluded to defer starting home for one day.

September 15, 1876; Friday. This morning Mrs [Mary] Tanner started for home takeing our daughter Hila with her and her own daughter Bessie. Their means of conveyence was a light job wagon drawn by a somewhat large and formidable mule of rather pale complexion[,] in disposition gentle and kind[,] allowing for the fact that he was unmistakeably a mule of much experience as well as natural sagasity. For more than a score of sumers and winters had shone and snowed on him until he was white with age[,] ~~and~~ so Donkey farewell.

September 16, 1876; Saturday. During the day I visited the mill and had some lumber from [Reuben] McBride's through the kindness of Brother L[oren] E. Kinney. Received postal card from Mrs M[ary] J. Tanner from Scipio reported self and Hila well.

September 17, 1876; Sunday. Attended Church the audience was addressed by Elder Nephi Pratt and J[oseph] V. Robison. Passed the residue of the day with Marion and family. Some indications of rain this evening.

September 18, 1876; Monday. To day commenced cuting my corn. Wrote letter to Hyrum [Coombs] in S.L. City.

September 19, 1876; Tuesday. Finished cuting up my corn. Called at the P.O. and received a letter from Lorenzo reporting all well except that he had cut his foot somewhat seriously but was recovering from the hurt.

September 20, 1876; Wednesday. Wrote letter to cousin Tryphena Morrill in Rhode Island. Called at Store and P.O.

---

75. A note at the bottom of the entry says "carried forward." The entries continue after a few pages of financial notations.

September 21, 1876; Thursday. Closed an[d] posted my letter to Lorenzo. And to day had the news that the jury in the case of John D. Lee returned a verdict of guilty of murder in the first degree.[76] In the afternoon made a call with Mrs L[yman] on Mr Edwin Bartholimew and family.

September 22, 1876; Friday. Caried my lumber into the shop preparitory to the begining of work on my pantry. Made a call at the store. Weather dry and the nights cool.

September 23, 1876; Saturday. Passed the day in reading did [not] engage in work to day in the afternoon called at the P.O. but got no news.

September 24, 1876; Sunday. Attended Church the audience was addressed by Elder Erastus Snow. After services called at the P.O. and then with Elder [Wayne] Carver of the M[ethodist] E[piscopal] Church called on and dined with the widows [Miranda and Mary] Bartholomew and passed the afternoon with them. Elder Carver thinks of establishing a school in the Town.

September 25, 1876; Monday. Received a call from and passed the day with Elder [Wayne] Carver of the M[ethodist] E[piscopal] Church who proposed to open a school here as soon as a place could be procured an[d] teacher for the same.

September 26, 1876; Tuesday. Wrote [lette]rs[,] one to Mrs [Maria Louisa] Stredder and one to Rev [Wayne] Carver of Salt Lake. In afternoon Mrs Lyman was called to attend to the confinement [late pregnancy and labor] of Mrs Rhoda Lyman. Received two letters one from I[saac] P[hilo] Carter and one from J[oseph] M. Tanner of Provo.

September 27, 1876; Wednesday. Did not engage in work today. Mrs Rhoda Lyman had a Daughter born at 2 oclock p.m. of to day. Mrs L[yman] came home this evening.

September 28, 1876; Thursday. Wrote letters to Philo [Carter] in Beaver and Joseph Tanner in Provo. Called on and dined with Marion. While there meet with Mrs Lucinda Houd from Beaver.

September 29, 1876; Friday. Passed the day mostly in reading. In evening with Mrs L[yman] called on Lelia with her sick children who were suffering from canker[s].

September 30, 1876; Saturday. Gathered and cut for drying a few

76. Lee was executed at Mountain Meadows by firing squad on March 23, 1877. Cf. the entry for Oct. 12, 1876, below.

peaches after which made a call at the store and received a letter from Hila in Provo. Lelia's children reported [better] this evening.

October 1, 1876; Sunday. Attended Church. The audi^e^nce was addressed by Elders Markisen[,] Holbrook and King folowed by Bishop [Edward] Partridge. Called on and dined with Mrs Clara Lyman. Mrs L[yman] was with us and Mrs Caroline Callister.

October 2, 1876; Monday. Wrote letter to Hila in Provo and in afternoon called on Mrs Rhoda Lyman she was somewhat beter than yesterday.

October 3, 1876; Tuesday. Mr Cumton hawled my corn and I passed the residue of the day in husking corn for Mr Edwin Bartholomew. Mrs Lyman helped in the afternoon.

October 4, 1876; Wednesday. Passed the day in husking corn had no help today. Dined with Mrs Bartholimew. Weather pleasantly warm not sultry.

October 5, 1876; Thursday. Passed the day in husking corn. Weather fine and pleasant Indian sumer.

October 6, 1876; Friday. Passed the day in husking corn. Weather continues pleasant. My hands very sore from my work hardly allowing me to sleep at night.

October 7, 1876; Saturday. Husked corn to day and Mrs Lyman helped me. Some cloudy indications of falling weather.

October 8, 1876; Sunday. Attended Church the audience was addressed by Elder Powel. In afternoon had a visit from Mrs Edward Web and children. Towards evening some indications of rain. Mrs Lyman called on Mrs Rhoda Lyman in the evening. Received letter from nephew Joseph M. Tanner [in] Provo.

October 9, 1876; Monday. This morning commenced husking corn and during the day had a series of showers attended with some thunder.

October 10, 1876; Tuesday. Worked in the corn all day. Some clouds but no rain reached the Valley to day altho there was some thunder and showers in the distance.

October 11, 1876; Wednesday. Worked at the corn until the rain caused us to quit work. Hila returned to day from her visit to the city and Provo reporting haveing had a pleasant time with her friends.

October 12, 1876; Thursday. Wrote letter to J[oseph] M. Tanner in Provo and read the sentence of John D. Lee to be shot to death on the 26th of Jan 1877. Sentence was pronounced by Judge [Jacob] Boreman at Beaver.

October 13, 1876; Friday. This morning wrote letter to Mrs M[aria] L[ouisa] Stredder [in] Adamsville Beaver County. In afternoon went to the P.O. and made some improvements about the house. Considerable rain fell in the afternoon rendering the streets somewhat mudy and unpleasant for walkers and freighters.

October 14, 1876; Saturday. Made a call at the mill. In the afternoon Paulina and Wm and Laura and Madora and children came on their way to Salt Lake City. They stoped for the night. Clouds heavy with promise of more rain.

October 15, 1876; Sunday. Attended Church the audience was addressed by Elders F[rancis] M. Lyman, Stokes and Melville. Dined with Marion at Rhodas. Received letter from Rev W[ayne] Carver, Salt Lake City.

October 16, 1876; Monday. Paulina and party started on the journey north this morning. I passed the day in husking corn until broaken off by the rain which fell freely in afternoon and evening. Wrote letter to Rev W[ayne] Carver of Salt Lake City.

October 17, 1876; Tuesday. Passed the forenoon in work on my place. In the afternoon husked corn. Some indications of fair weather.

October 18, 1876; Wednesday. Worked on my place. In the evening had a call from J[ohn] D. Lee in care of the Marshall going to Salt Lake.

October 19, 1876; Thursday. Worked at home through the forenoon, and in the afternoon husked corn. At evening clouds with indications of coming storm.

October 20, 1876; Friday. During the forenoon snow was falling passed the day in work about the house.

October 21, 1876; Saturday. Made a call at the store. In the ^evening^ received a call from the Directors [of the Free Trade Union] [John] Kelley[,] [Henry] Noy[e]s and Dame to consider the state and int[e]rests of the store and the purcace of winter goods.

October 22, 1876; Sunday. Attended Church the audience was addressed by Prest [Thomas] Callister folowed by Bishop [Edward] Partridge [Jr]. In the afternoon wrote letter to Lorenzo and posted it.

October 23, 1876; Monday. Passed the day in husking corn. Received letters from W[illiam] S. Godbe and from Godbe[,] Pitts, & Co.

October 24, 1876; Tuesday. Wrote letter to W[illiam] S. Godbe. Passed the day in husking corn. Received a letter from W. S. Godbe.

October 25, 1876; Wednesday. In the morning wrote letter to W[illiam] S. Godbe. Passed the day in husking corn some indications of comeing storm.

October 26, 1876; Thursday. Passed the day in husking corn. Weather cloudy threatening storm.

October 27, 1876; Friday. Worked at the corn all day[,] weather cloudy no rain.

October 28, 1876; Saturday. Passed the day in husking corn in the evening it rained.

October 29, 1876; Sunday. Attended Church the audience was addressed Professor[,] name not remembered[,] folowed by Bishop Ross Kelley, from Cash Valley. In the afternoon called on the Widows [Miranda and Mary] Bartholimew. Weather pleasant to day.

October 30, 1876; Monday. Passed the most of the day in husking corn. Weather cloudy and cool. Received letter from the Rev Mr [Wayne] Carver.

October 31, 1876; Tuesday. Worked at the corn to day heavy frost last night. This made my work unpleasant.

November 1, 1876; Wednesday. Worked in the corn all day. Received letters from Cove Creek and from Salt Lake.

November 2, 1876; Thursday. Worked in corn. Wrote to Godbe Pitts & Co. Weather cloudy and dull some snow on the highlands.

November 3, 1876; Friday. Worked on my building prepareing it for moveing. Light snow last night. Prest [Brigham] Young and Suit[e] [entourage] arived in town to day.

November 4, 1876; Saturday. Worked at moveing my building. Received [letter] from Rev W[ayne] Carver. Weather cloudy and cool.

November 5, 1876; Sunday. Attended Church. The audience was addressed by Elder H[iram] Mace folowed by Bishop [Edward] Partridge [Jr].

November 6, 1876; Monday. Worked in the corn to day. Weather cool and clear. This day Mrs Mary Lyman wife of Theodore Lyman was delivered of a son [Guy Kimberly Lyman]. Mother and child doing well.

November 7, 1876; Tuesday. Finished the removal of my building in the morning. Attended election in the afternoon.

November 8, 1876; Wednesday. Worked at the corn [all] the day. Mr [John] Kelley arived from S. L. City with goods.

November 9, 1876; Thursday. Worked at the corn to day. To day a stock drive is in progress at Cedar Springs. Mr [John] Kelley is puting up new goods.

November 10, 1876; Friday. Finished husking corn for Edwin [Bartholomew] to day. After we returned ^home^ we had a call from Uncle Seth B. Tanner and family who were on their way to Arizona to render some assistence to the Lord who is represented as being in rather a poor condition not being able to accomplish his work with the help of the poor women and children. It is well that in the nature of things their labors and privations will in some degree help the cause of human civilization[,] and time[,] in its endless duration[,] will bring them relief from their ignorence so may they have peace and prosperity in their labors is my wish.

November 11, 1876; Saturday. As the Arizona Missionarys left us Elder W[ayne] Carver came in. With him I spent a part of the day in makeing some preperations for holding service in the State House tomorow. Some rain during the day.

November 12, 1876; Sunday. Attended Church in the morning the audience was addressed by William King folowed by Bp [Thomas] Callister. In afternoon heard Rev W[ayne] Carver at State House in evening heard him again. Received letter from W[illiam] S. Godbe [in] N. Y. City.

November 13, 1876; Monday. Worked through the early morning. Went to the meat market returned and passed the afternoon with Mr [Wayne] Carver and in the evening received a call from Mr Robert Martin. He deposited at Lyman's and Robisons mill 20 bushels of wheat to my credit the balence that was due me from him for Apples.

November 14, 1876; Tuesday. Worked on cowhouse [barn] through the early part of the day then went to the mill with sacks for my flour. The weather pleasant but cool some hazy at evening.

November 15, 1876; Wednesday. Worked on my cowhouse in the evening had a call from Mr [Wayne] Carver who was about to leave for Salt Lake to return again in Dec.

November 16, 1876; Thursday. Made a call at the store for nails worked on my cowhouse through the day. Received from Edwin [Bartholomew] my corn for husking for him. In the afternoon my son P[latte] D. Lyman arived from his mission in Europe.

November 17, 1876; Friday. Worked on the cowhouse and in the evening Platt arived. Did not come yesterday as reported. Paulina and her party returned to day.

November 18, 1876; Saturday. Worked on my cowhouse in afternoon had a call from some of my children from Oak Creek. Paulina was with us to night.

November 19, 1876; Sunday. Attended Church the audience was addressed by Elders P[latte] D. and F[rancis] M. Lyman. After the services Dined with Platt and family at the residence of his Mother.[77] In the evening had a call from Mr [John] Kelley. Received letters from Lorenzo in Cal[ifornia] one from Philo [Carter] in Beaver and one from Maria and one from J[oseph] M. Tanner [in] Provo.

November 20, 1876; Monday. Worked on my building. Weather cool but pleasant.

November 21, 1876; Tuesday. Wrote to Lorenzo. Called on the County Recorder and ordered a Deed of the city lot to Mr Henry Noy[e]s. Dined with Marion.

November 22, 1876; Wednesday. Worked on my barn and pig pen. Mrs Lelia Bartholimew and children were with us to day. Weather cool but pleasant.

November 23, 1876; Thursday. Worked on my henhouse called on Mr [Henry] Noy[e]s in evening.

November 24, 1876; Friday. Worked on my hen house all day and in the afternoon had a call from Uncle Freeman Tanner who was enroute for St. George.

November 25, 1876; Saturday. In morming made [a] call at the store. Passed the residue of the day in work on my building.

November 26, 1876; Sunday. Attended Church the audience was addressed by Elders Horn and Coombs. Called on the Bartholimew widows.

November 27, 1876; Monday. Received some goods from my friend W[illiam] S. Godbe of Salt Lake City. Made a call on Mr Gabriel Huntsman at his store. Some rain to day.

November 28, 1876; Tuesday. To day Mrs Lyman was fifty eight years old. We had Mrs Lelia Bartholimew and children with us through the day. In the evening had a call from Marion and Rhoda.

---

77. This was a remarkable development for Lyman to be invited to Eliza Partridge's home. In eleven weeks she will attend his funeral, hinting at a prior rapprochement.

November 29, 1876; Wednesday. Worked on my Barn in forenoon. In afternoon went to the publick stock corrall on returning home.

November 30, 1876; Thursday. Worked on my barn during the day and received twenty bushels of Potatoes from Philo Carter per hand of Mr Murry Fisher.

December 1, 1876; Friday. Called on the butcher and engaged him to kill my beef tomorow and passed residue of the day in work at home.

December 2, 1876; Saturday. To day had my beef killed.

December 3, 1876; Sunday. Attended church with Mrs Lyman after which Marion[,] Rhoda[,] and Mrs Alice McBride dined with us. Mr Cumpton and wife spent the evening with us. Received letter from Philo [Carter].

December 4, 1876; Monday. To day Ira brought my flour from the mill and my stove from the store. The butcher cut up my beef.

December 5, 1876; Tuesday. Made an early call up town to accomodate Mr [Murray] Fisher who was returning to Greenville and heard this morning of the Death of Mr Thomas Henderson who died last night. Passed residue of the day in prepareing to put up my stove.

December 6, 1876; Wednesday. Attended the funeral of Mr Thomas Henderson after which [we] called on and dined with the Bartholimew widows [Miranda and Mary]. Called ^on^ Mr [Joseph] Bradfield and engaged him to hawl my wood.

December 7, 1876; Thursday. Worked about my place and during the day I received a letter from H[yrum] S. Coombs. ^Wrote letter to Philo [Carter].^

December 8, 1876; Friday. Made platform for and put up our new stove in the parlor.

December 9, 1876; Saturday.[78] Called on Mr Ja[me]s Starley and engaged him to fit up my stove pipe.

December 10, 1876; Sunday. Attended Church the audience was addressed by Elders McBride and Pratt. In afternoon with Mrs Lyman called on Mrs Edward Web.

December 11, 1876; Monday. Took my stove pipe to Mr [James] Starley to have it changed in size. In the evening made a call at the store. Made my manger in my cow house.

---

78. This entry was written on a half sheet of loose paper and inserted into the diary.

December 12, 1876; Tuesday. In forenoon went up town and brought home my stove pipe passed the residue of the day in work at home. In the evening with Mrs Lyman and Hila attended the Atheneum the first of the term.

December 13, 1876; Wednesday. Passed the day in work at home. Commenced looking over my journal for matters of history.

December 14, 1876; Thursday. Passed the day in work at home.

December 15, 1876; Friday. Made a call at the store made some smal purchases for the House. Had some bolts mad[e] for bed stead.

December 16, 1876; Saturday. Worked about home most of the day made a call at the store.

December 17, 1876; Sunday. Attended church and after service[,] with Mrs Lyman dined and passed the residue of the day with Bartholimew Widows. The audience was addressed by Elder William Brand of Springville Agent for Deseret News.

December 18, 1876; Monday. Wrote letter to W[illiam] S. Godbe of Salt Lake [and] worked some in shop. [Joseph] Bradfield brought [a] load of wood.

December 19, 1876; Tuesday. Worked in the shop all the day and at night attended the Atheneum with Mrs Lyman and Hila. Mr Fortee Lectured.

December 20, 1876; Wednesday. Worked in shop through the day. Weather fair and colld.

December 21, 1876; Thursday. Worked in my shop all the day. Some indications of storm.

December 22, 1876; Friday. Worked at home all day in the shop some signs of storm.

December 23, 1876; Saturday. Worked in the shop until near night when I made a call up town. Last night we had a fall of snow of a few inches. During the day I received a letter from Mr J[ohn] R. MacBride of Salt Lake City.

December 24, 1876; Sunday. Remained at home and answered my letters[79] of yesterday and received a call from Mr Murry Fisher by whom we ^received^ a parcel of dried grapes from Philo [Carter]'s folks. Wrote letter to Philo. Some snow fell to day.

---

79. The top few lines of the next page are missing, although it is unclear if they contained anything pertaining to this entry.

December 25, 1876; Monday. Remained at home all the day and had Mr Edwin Bartholimew and family with us. In evening I called at store.

December 26, 1876; Tuesday. Was at home through the day at night attended the Atheneum. Had ^call^ in the afternoon from Mr Edward Webb and wife. ^Snow falling at night.^

December 27, 1876; Wednesday. With Mrs Lyman visited Mr E[dward] W[ebb] and family where we meet Mr G[ilbert] S. Webb our old friend. ^Snow falling all day.^

December 28, 1876; Thursday. Shelled some corn which resulted in makeing some blisters on my fingers. The snow ceased falling to day and began to melt.

December 29, 1876; Friday. Hung my beef for drying this morning and in the afternoon mad[e] [visits] at the P.O. and at the residence of the County Clerk.

December 30, 1876; Saturday. Remained at home all day at work in my shop. Weather cold but pleasant.

December 31, 1876; Sunday. Attended church the audience was addressed by Elders [William] King and [Hiram] Mace. Mrs Lelia Bartholimew and children were with us to day.

January 1, 1877; Monday. Worked at home in the shop and in the afternoon made a call at the store.

January 2, 1877; Tuesday. Worked in the shop[,] at night with Mrs Lyman and Hila attended Atheneum. Today had call from Marion.

January 3, 1877; Wednesday. Worked in the shop all day weather cold.

January 4, 1877; Thursday. In the morning made a call to the store and in the afternoon with Mrs Lyman and Hila passed the residue of the day and evening with Mr [John] Cavinah and family. Mr [John] Kelley and wife were with us.

January 5, 1877; Friday. Remained at home through the day. Worked in the shop.

January 6, 1877; Saturday. Went up town called at the P.O. and dined with Marion.

January 7, 1877; Sunday. To day had the first of what we intend to be a series of parlor or social entertainments of an intellectual nature for the benifit of the class who are denied the benifit of Church aid and help in the struggle for hapiness.

January 8, 1877; Monday. Worked at home most of the day after waiting on Mr Bishop for some of his work as blacksmith.

January 9, 1877; Tuesday. Worked in my shop in forenoon and in the afternoon visited Mr Scottorn and family. In evening attended the Atheneum.

January 10, 1877; Wednesday. Worked at home in the shop.

January 11, 1877; Thursday. Worked in shop and during the day received a call from F[rancis] M. L[yman] and N[ephi] Pratt. Received letter from H[yrum] S. C[oombs].

January 12, 1877; Friday. Had the company of Mr R[euben] McBride and Mr [Harley] Coalgrove and their wives in the afternoon. In forenoon worked in my shop. ^Had a call from F[rancis] M. Lyman and N[ephi] Pratt.

January 13, 1877; Saturday. Worked in shop through the forenoon[,] in afternoon called at the P.O. Received letter from Rev [Wayne] Carver Salt Lake City. Signed Deed for lots to Mr W[illiam] Dame.

January 14, 1877; Sunday. Snow fell last night. To Day visited and dined with Mr John Kelley family and friends. Snow falling most of the day.

January 15, 1877; Monday. Worked until late in the afternoon then I made a call at the store and passed the evening with Mrs Lyman at the Bartholomew Widows.

January 16, 1877; Tuesday. To day Mr [Peter] Silda came and commenced work. In evening attended the Atheneum. Hila sang.

January 17, 1877; Wednesday. Remained at home. Mr [Peter] Silda worked on the pantry to day. [Joseph] Bradfield brought a load of wood to day. Wind Southerly but cool.

January 18, 1877; Thursday. Made a call at the P.O. Received letter from Paulina which reported all well in Parowan.

January 19, 1877; Friday. Wrote letter to Paulina called at the P.O. Bought some paper for commencing writing my history. Weather softening down with indications of snow, which commenced falling after night.

January 20, 1877; Saturday. Received a call from Marion in quest of historical matter. Mr [Peter] Silda worked today.

January 21, 1877; Sunday. Remained at home all the day and in the afternoon held our parlor meeting to the apparent satisfaction of those present. The excercises were readings and musick ^and informal conversation.^

January 22, 1877; Monday. Wrote letter to Br Nathan Tanner [in]

Cottenwood. Visited the P.O. called on Mr [John] Kelley. In the evening attended a meeting of the stockholders of the Free Traders Union for the election of Officers of the institution. Weather very cold.

January 23, 1877; Tuesday. Made a call up town worked some at the bench. Lectured in the ^atheneum on "What We Want."^

January 24, 1877; Wednesday. Made a call at P.O. Received a chart of Lyman family from my cousin ^Tryphen L. Morrill [of] Rhode Island.^

January 25, 1877; Thursday. Remained at home all the day and worked at the bench.

January 26, 1877; Friday. Worked at home through the day.

January 27, 1877; Saturday. Worked at home in forenoon. In afternoon waited on the Probate Judge and was qualified as Prest of the Free Traders Union. F[rancis] M. Lyman and B[enjamin] H. Robison were my securities. The bond was $1000.00 ^To day my son Marion gave me a gold pen and holder and cash.^

January 28, 1877; Sunday. Wrote letter to Lorenzo. ^Was taken with a chill in evening.^

January 29, 1877; Monday. Not feeling very well went up town called on Mr Alvin Roberson of whom I borrowed some books.

January 30, 1877; Tuesday. Much worse confined to my bed.

January 31, 1877; Wednesday. Still ill.

February 1, 1877; Thursday. No better.

February 2, 1877; Friday. Free from pain but very weak.

February 3, 1877; Saturday. The same as yesterday.[80]

---

80. Francis wrote to his Aunt Ruth that "a finer corps[e] was never laid out, and yesterday at 4:30 P.M. he was placed in his last earthly house, followed there by the largest funeral procession ever seen in Fillmore." Francis M. Lyman to Ruth Goodall, Feb. 6, 1877, in Amasa M. Lyman Collection, CHL.

His estranged wife Eliza was less forgiving. "I shall not attempt to describe the feelings that I had when I saw the father of my children sleeping the sleep of death," she wrote, complaining that "instead of being buried in the robes of the priesthood, he requested to be buried in a black coat and pants. It was grievous to think of the change a few short years had brought about in his case, and how easy it is to be overcome with evil if we are not continually on our guard."

By comparison, her own brother Edward wrote, "Thus ended the earthly career of a man of more than ordinary ability, who spent the greater part of his life in preaching the doctrines of the Latter-day Saints and finally died a Spiritualist. He had many friends but few enemies. A man who always taught and practiced mortality as he understood it." Partridge, *Eliza Maria Partridge Journal*, 94–95.

A The Dundee Sermon, March 1862

What follows is the first of two sermons Lyman delivered on March 16, 1862, in Scotland, in which he suggested that Jesus's mission was primarily to teach the truth, rather than to die for sins. Although the crucifixion was foretold in the Old Testament, Lyman explained, it was not an integral part of Jesus's salvific role. Brigham Young had been similarly speculative about the identity and mission of Jesus but became concerned about eight passages he and his counselors and members of the Quorum of Twelve Apostles saw as problematic in Lyman's address. On January 21, 1867, they called Lyman to account for his views at a joint meeting of the First Presidency and Quorum of the Twelve. After listening to criticisms from fellow apostles, Lyman issue a statement to the *Deseret News* admitting his "grievous sin in teaching a doctrine which makes the death of Jesus Christ of no force." He was not looking for controversy and dearly wanted to remain in step with his brethren, but he found he could not reconcile his personal logic with that of his peers. Ultimately he decided to stand his ground, for which he was removed from the quorum and then from the church.[1]

Nature of the Mission of Jesus

I feel grateful this morning, my friends, that I enjoy another opportunity of meeting with you, and to enjoy with you the comforts of the reflection that, though time has been passing since we last met, we still survive those whom its resistless current has borne away, to meet

1. See *AML*, 327–30; Hefner, "Amasa Mason Lyman," 93–101; *Latter-day Saints Millennial Star* 24, no. 14 (Apr. 5, 1862): 209–17.

again, as we continue our labour for the attainment of that happiness, the existence of which renders sure to us the realization of our hopes, if we continue to act and live in harmony with the law and purposes of our being. We have no different work to-day to engage us than that which engaged us when we last met. We have no matter to interest us but the truth, no labour in which to be engaged but in the acquirement of a knowledge of its principles and their application; and as the fountain of truth, from its boundless extent, is exhaustless, of course we have not acquired a knowledge of it all as yet.

There remains an infinitude of knowledge yet to acquire; and if we could compare the little we know with what remains in the future to be learned, its comparative littleness, in point of extent and magnitude, would appear [obvious]. But small as the amount of knowledge may be that we possess, we know that the knowledge of the truth developed within us constitutes all of [the] ability and capacity that we possess for the acquirement of intellectual or physical happiness. To continue and extend this good work is the labour that should engage us continually, calling into exercise all of our ever-increasing powers for the development of human happiness.

I have no labour in which to engage myself, only to exert what influence I may possess to lead people to an understanding of the truth, that they may be enlightened, consistent worshippers of God, consistently religious, and honestly devoted in their religion to the love of God and the truth, which brings freedom to the soul from the bondage of ignorance, sin and death. And in order that they may be so, mankind must have knowledge; for how could we act consistently for the accomplishment of any purpose of which we were ignorant? We can only hope to act consistently by having a knowledge of the truth. There is no great difficulty in understanding that the knowledge of the truth, as unfolding to our opening minds to some extent the purposes of God in our being, is the first and most valuable blessing connected with our existence as intellectual human beings here upon the earth; for only by this knowledge so revealed can our actions be correctly and consistently regulated, and all other blessings will follow as a natural consequence of the presence of this knowledge in the soul.

We have not come here, then, to worship religion, or bow down to it with the soul's reverence and adoration, good as it may be, valuable as it may be, and dearly as we may have learned to look upon it. Our worship on the present occasion should be an honest, earnest desire to know the truth of which we are ignorant, with a fixed determination to give that truth an application to ourselves. Then our worship would be acceptable to God, the object of our worship, and our offering would be pleasing in his sight. Such a worship would render a people [who are] offering it acceptable to God, for it would be honestly, consistently, and intelligently offered by beings who understood the nature of their worship. We should remember that the blessing that is to result from our worship and devotion to God, from all our services rendered to him, is the good that it will bring to ourselves. We can render to God no happiness, offer unto him no adoration or homage that would compensate him for seeing us degraded and damned, instead of seeing us saved and exalted to everlasting life and infinite happiness.

This is the purpose for which we were made and constituted with the germ of every principle of greatness and power implanted within us, that under the enlightening and fructifying influence of the Gospel we might emerge from our condition of ignorance and nakedness to put on the habiliments of light and glory. It is the happiness resulting from a consistency and harmony of developed knowledge that makes heaven a place to be desired—a place where joy is developed without sorrow, where pleasure is unalloyed with anguish or pain, where death finds no habitation, and misery no abode; but where glory and happiness, truth, light, and life that has no sorrowing termination are continually found.

That this might be our lot, and that we might be raised to enjoy these blessings, was the purpose that induced our Father to give us a being upon the earth. Then no senseless worship, (and by senseless I mean that which is ignorantly offered, unguided by a knowledge of the truth,) no worship that is blindly and ignorantly presented, is acceptable before him; but that which is radiant in the light of truth, and that comes from a soul made free by the knowledge of God, is the only acceptable worship that can be rendered to him. That we may be enabled to become devoted to God, loving the truth because we comprehend its value and feel its emancipating influence upon the mind, awakening within us aspirations for glory and endless life, and feeling the chains that have held us in the bondage of ignorance bursting asunder, and emerging into that world of glowing light and fadeless glory to which our heavenly aspirations direct us,—to establish this upward and glorious tendency in the feelings of the soul, is the object for which religion has been revealed to us, that through the truth we acquire we may be prepared for this glory as children of God.

This view of religion should influence us, because it is right. "Well now," says one, "if I could only know that it is right! What are the evidences in support of its being so? Do the Scriptures tell us it is right?" Suppose they do not tell us anything about it at all, could we know, comprehend, or understand anything about it? Would we be capable of having developed within us a principle of truth, supposing that the record contained in the Bible had never reached us? I know we would be the same thinking beings we are now. Our minds would not be closed up, and our powers of thought and reflection rendered incapable of action, but we would think of everything we saw, everything that presented itself to our minds furnishing material for thought and reflection.

Where would we find the evidences that this view of religion and worship would be acceptable to God as a right one, calculated to elevate his children and exalt them to happiness and glory in his presence? Why, within ourselves, where reflection has its origin. We are capable of knowing that if we pursue the path of truth and travel in the ways of peace, falsehood and contention can never lie at our doors. Could we appreciate the difference between being surrounded with turmoil and strife to being surrounded by scenes of an opposite character—between the blessings of harmony and peace understood and appreciated and contention that was entirely in opposition to our feelings and desires, we would exert all our influence in favour of peace—peace continually rich in the development of happiness and blessing. There is no mind, however darkened by scepticism or unbelief, that could question this. It is truth, and a plan that commends itself to every mind that is open to conviction. This, then, is my reason, and the reason I assign to you, that the worship I have described is acceptable to God, because it makes you and me better, and saves us from the curse of strife and contention. And as it relieves you and me, so it would release from this misery and wretchedness all who would give it an application as we do.

Whether this view of the matter is consistent or not with truth and reason, many would feel a delicacy in coming to a conclusion, unless they could know it was consistent with the Scriptures? But what are the Scriptures? They are simply a record of a small portion of what God is said to have done with and for the inhabitants of the earth during a small portion of the time that the earth has been the home of humanity. The Apostle instructed the ancient Saints to "prove all things and hold fast that which is good;" and as the Scriptures form a part of *all* things, they are part of that which is to be proved, and, when found good, to be retained. But we have been taught that they are not only true and in every way sufficient for the salvation of man, but that they have been made, by a marvelous exercise of credulity, to extend over all the broad surface of human existence. There is no point so far remote in that dark and indefinite future that extends away before us, but they are made to extend there, and have their application to human beings with equal force upon all. This involves us in a great amount of difficulties, and a few of those which surround us are something like these: We are told that the Scriptures contain what is necessary and requisite for the salvation of humanity, and that the fullness of the Gospel contained in them was not revealed till Jesus came preaching the Gospel of the kingdom of God.

Considering it thus, the reflecting mind in a moment is troubled with this question—If it was necessary, when Jesus came into the world, that all the Gospel truth should be made known and sustained by the power he had, and if it required that power for the proclamation of the Gospel and its ministration, that it should become a perfect salvation to those who should believe it, what has been the condition of the many millions who have never had any understanding of it? What is to become of them? For if it was necessary at any one time to save men and women constituted as we are—if a knowledge of its principles was requisite to secure their salvation, does it not prove to us that it was and is necessary for every other person constituted as we are and sustaining the same relationship to God as we do[?] Now, from the light of the Gospel as it is revealed in the Scriptures of truth, and at the time when Jesus was its great exponent, we arrive at our conclusions that this being necessary at that time, it was always necessary,—that there never was a time when humanity did not need all that Jesus taught for the consummation of their exaltation and glory.

Another of the difficulties which surround us in our efforts to arrive at a comprehension of the truth is tha[t] we suppose, under the influence of our education, (and our suppositions are according to our education,) that the Gospel was not revealed in its fullness until the meridian of time, when Jesus came, the great herald of mercy and expositor of the Gospel to man. A little calm reflection will lead us to know that this conception is erroneous and at war with the purposes of God. "Well, if that is so," you may say, "how are we to become satisfied of it?" By looking at the mission of Jesus and the Gospel he came to preach, not from where we are, but, leaving the mists of tradition, (the fogs of error that becloud the minds of men here,) travel backward on the stream of time to the point when the purposes of man's being as the child of earth was formed by God, and the Gospel had a formation suited to his constitutional wants and requirements. We will find, when it first became a purpose in the mind of our Father that man should live on earth, the point we seek. If we possess any degree of imaginative power, let us go back to that point, that we may learn, by contemplating man as he appeared there, the nature of his constitution as it was determined by the purpose of God, what he was constituted for, and the nature of the Gospel that was there prepared to be revealed in the future for all humanity. "But were there men there?" Oh yes. If no others were there, "the man Christ Jesus" was there; and others were with him too, for it is said, "The morning stars sang together, and *all* the *sons* of *God* shouted for joy." "Well, if men were there, what kind of men were they? and how were they constituted?" Why, just as we are. I do not say they were weak and sickly as we are, nor corrupt as degenerated man has become. They were not the subjects of disease and pain, as we are; but they possessed the same constitution, with minds having the same properties as ours—possessing the same germs of greatness, influence, and power.

Thus constituted, man was there, the subject of his Father's care and provision—the leading object, the primal object that moved the mind of the Father in the great enterprise of developing intellectual humanity upon the earth—of sending out His children here upon the earth, that they might return to Him clothed in a fadeless glory and exalted to majesty and power in those abodes of celestial bliss where they might drink of the cup of felicity drawn from an exhaustless fountain. Man thus constituted was man for whom the Savior was prepared—man who had never sinned—who had never perpetrated a wrong. For man thus pure and holy, thus unstained by guilt or wrong, pure as the Father who had given him his constitution, the Savior was prepared and the Gospel was ordained.

"But was it decreed, then, that Jesus should die to save men who were thus pure and holy? No: it did not form any part of the purpose of God that he should die. "[For] what, then, was he ordained to as a Savior?" Why, to be a Prophet, Priest, and King—a preacher of the Gospel of the kingdom of God. "What! was he ordained there to officiate thus, when in the meridian of time he should travel among his brethren shrouded in mortality?" Why, yes. When he came into the world, he told the people that he came to do the will of his Father, and none other work had he to do than he had seen his Father doing. What was the work he came doing? Read the history of John the Baptist as he went preaching from place to place, and continue it down until the time when Herod shut him up in prison, so that he could not preach to the people any longer, and there you will find that Jesus followed his fore-runner in the great work of human instruction—that he came preaching the Gospel of the kingdom of God.

Was it a part of his preaching to people that he came to pour out his life's blood—that in the crimson tide the guilt of a sin-stricken world might be washed away? Did he speak of his death as the object to which their thoughts and attentions should be turned? Why, he told them to cease from sinning and turn unto righteousness—to put evil and corruption from them and live in purity and holiness before God. What did he say to the poor unfortunate woman brought before him, when her hypocritical accusers slunk in guilty silence away before the majesty of his rebuke? "He that is without sin, let him cast the first stone!" Looking up and seeing her standing with downcast eyes, he said, "Go thy way and sin no more."

That was the lesson he inculcated to all—"Cease to do evil, learn to do well." I wish you to remember this incident in the history of Jesus—to treasure up this little portion of the Scripture in your minds. It will not be unwieldy, or troublesome to carry; and when you wish to see the principle upon which God designed to save mankind, you will see there, when you look at it, a truthful reflection of the principles upon which he purposed to exalt poor sinful humanity—of how man, whom you saw so pure and holy before he became a denizen of the earth, was to return to the scenes of hallowed felicity from whence he had come; not on the crimson tide of Emmanuel's blood poured forth on Calvary's mount, but by ceasing the perpetuation of those wrongs which have brought misery, suffering, and death upon the family of man. This is the Gospel that was determined in yonder heavens before the foundations of the earth were laid. "But does not Scripture speak of Jesus as 'Lamb slain from the foundation of the world?'" "Why," says one, "I supposed that it was pre-determined before the world was[,] that Jesus must die, and that naught but his blood could bring God's children back to the home from whence they had simply gone abroad for a time." Is it said so in the Scriptures? No. This is the inference we draw from the fact that we see humanity cursed with sin till we travel back beyond that time when sin brought misery and death upon the race. We contemplate them as having the black stain of wrong fixed upon them; and seeing them thus, we conceive this to be something that had its origin in the purposes of our Father, which caused it to be predetermined that Jesus must die, or man could never return back again to the bosom of his Father. What was necessary, before man transgressed, that he should be saved? Why, simply that he should be taught.

The infant being, inhaling for the first time the free air of heaven with opening mind, simply needed to have principles of truth kept ceaselessly before it to lead from its undeveloped condition onward and upward to God. Instead of man's becoming the corrupt degraded being we now behold him [to be], he only needed healthy, truthful, and pure elements of knowledge imparted to him continuously, as his enlarging capacity prepared him to receive them, in order to become all that he was constituted to become as the child of God. Without this, he could not reach the high destiny that was made attainable for him. Was a Gospel combining the elements of this instruction prepared that it might bring happiness, blessing, and eternal life to man? Yes. But did not this Gospel have associated with it, as a necessary pre-requisite for man's salvation, the death of Jesus? No; for if so, he failed to tell the people the true nature of the Gospel he preached and his mission among men, and the means by which eternal life was to be gained. He told this to men who were constituted to learn, who could receive not one lesson, but with minds constituted to receive knowledge eternally.

This was the constitution of the human mind; and, for the benefit of men thus constituted, he said, when praying to the Father, "This is life eternal, that they might know thee the only true God, and Jesus Christ whom thou hast sent." This is what you and I need to know, that our worship may be acceptable to God as being first conducive to our happiness, enlightenment, and emancipation from the bonds of ignorance and death. Shall we, with all these reasons before our minds, arrive at any other conclusion than that man was constituted to become possessed of knowledge, and the Gospel constituted of what would lead him to the acquirement of that knowledge[?]

The Gospel is nowhere said to have been constituted of the death of Jesus. Where shall we find in the record of his teachings anything that would sustain such an idea? Nowhere. We see him as he was revealed among humanity, and read the truths he taught, so far as they have been transmitted to us through an imperfect medium; and we can see that his life was devoted to the truth, if the light of heaven has given to us any degree of understanding.

What, then, was the nature of the mission of Jesus when he came into the world? Some may be startled, doubtless, at the idea that it was not necessary, as having been predetermined and designed by the purposes of the Father, that Jesus should die. Did it ever occur to you how the death of Jesus could effect intellectual humanity? Did you ever think of it? But that we may entertain no wrong reflection on this point, I will call your attention to a parable spoken by Jesus, as recorded in Matthew xxi., 33–39, expressive of the nature of his mission. He speaks of an individual who owned a vineyard, and let it out to certain husbandmen; and when the season came round, he sent his servants to receive the fruits of it, or collect the rent, as would be said now. He had let the vineyard, and he sent his servants down to receive that which was justly his from those in whose care it was. But these men cast the servants out—beat one, killed another, and stoned a third, and would not pay the rent. Other embassies were sent and treated in the same manner as the first.

At last the master said, "I will send my son down to them. If they have abused my servants, they will not presume to abuse my son and heir." What did the master say he was sending the son down for? Simply to collect the rent—to be the same representative of the master's interests that the servants who preceded him were. How did the husbandmen receive the son? They said, This is the son and heir. If we can kill him and get him out of the way, then the inheritance will be our own, for there will be no heir to it. The result was, the son was killed the same as those who had been sent before him. If Jesus knew it was necessary that they should be killed, as a part of the mission they were sent to perform, he failed to say so. They were killed because of the wickedness and murderous designs of those to whom they were sent, and the purposes of the master in sending them were not then accomplished. If the rent had been faithfully and honestly paid, there would have been no wrong done, no murder committed. Why did they do this evil?—why commit the murders which stained their souls with guilt and crime? Because they followed after an evil thought, and, being seduced by corrupt reasoning, concluded that they would reap some advantage if they could cast out those idle pretenders, as they called those who were sent to them.

These servants and this dear son were alike killed. The same procuring causes led to the same result in the one case as in the other. I wish you to have Jesus' own interpretation of his mission into the world. Jesus has shown how the servants and the son came, and how they were treated when they did come; but he never said it was necessary that they should die. That they did die is a sad fact. The mission of Jesus to the earth not only cost him poverty and misery, but it cost him his life. Now, when we look at this parable and consider, in connection with it, that eternal life is "to know God and Jesus Christ whom He has sent," and that this knowledge alone can raise mankind from their misery and degradation to enjoy the blessings of salvation, we see clearly that the Gospel was prepared before the foundation of the world to educate men and lead them from their weakness and ignorance to knowledge, through which and by which alone they could become clothed with the habiliments of might and glory. Men were all constituted alike to receive, understand, and acquire knowledge; and the great necessity with regard to the coming of Jesus was that man could not be redeemed and exalted without knowledge, which constitutes the Gospel[,] "the power of God unto salvation," that would enable man thus enlightened to comprehend the purpose of his own existence, and the nature of his relationship to the Father.

That human action would become rightly and properly directed under its influence, the Gospel was prepared, because the moment God entertained the design to exalt humanity to glory and immortality with himself, the provision of the means that were required to accomplish his designs became a necessity. If it had not been so, Jesus would never have been put in jeopardy, nor any of the Prophets and Apostles have suffered from cruelty and persecution; but the very salvation of man depending upon his becoming enlightened rendered it imperative that that which would bring the Gospel within the reach [of man] should be done. Thus Jesus, at the time of his manifestation on the earth, became the great expositor of the Gospel. If he had declared that it was his blood that would cleanse us from sin, we would not have questioned it. "But does not the Scripture say his blood cleanses from sin?" Why, yes. John speaks of "Him that loved us and washed us from our sins in his own blood;" and if that was all we knew of John, we would be led to form our conclusions from that saying.

But there are some other things to be considered concerning him before our thought ripens into conviction. [John] was one of those to whom Jesus said, when opening his mission, as they toiled with their nets on the blue waters of Palestine, that if they would come with him, he would make them fishers of men. Did he become obedient to that call? Yes. Then, as through his future life, he rendered a ready response to the voice of him whom he learned to love so dearly. He was one of those who were baptized for the remission of sins; he was taught of Jesus and was ordained by him as his Apostle to represent him when he was gone. Under the sound of the voice of Jesus, he learned those truths which he was to proclaim to the nations as Heaven's ambassador and representative, and, in learning them, learned their worth—their priceless value, and learned to govern himself and regulate his actions by them. This is the way John became cleansed from sin—by acting consistently with the truth he had learned, and doing no wrong, and not by the blood of Jesus in any other way applied.

Do you see any connection between the shedding of the blood of Jesus and the regeneration of the great Apostle John, the friend of Jesus, who shared with him his sorrows and rejoiced under his teachings, the beloved disciple who had leaned in the fondness of his soul upon the breast of that Master he so dearly loved, and who, when he regarded his own salvation, could not take into account all it had cost and leave out the tragedy of Calvary[?] He had seen him whom he had travelled and lived with—whom he had learned to appreciate and love with the heart's fondest affections,—he had seen him in his sufferings and misery, and witnessed the excruciating agonies he endured in Gethsemane and on Calvary. Could he forget all this? No; the thoughts moved by the rising sympathy of the soul assumed consistency and form, and said, "Can I forget the cost of the proclamation that brought all that life and light to my soul which I enjoy—that said to the captive soul, 'Go forth to life and glory and freedom,' and which cost the lifeblood of my brother and my God?" This was the estimate made in the mind of the Apostle when he calculated the cost of what had brought salvation to him. Yet it was by doing just as Jesus told the poor frail woman to do—"Go thy way and sin no more." It was thus when John ceased to do sin, that he was cleansed from sin by the blood of Jesus. The last bond was severed, the last restraint thrown off, which bound him in sin. I wish you to see and understand this, because I do not wish you in the future to bear record that I ever used an influence to lead humanity to believe that they could derive salvation, or a freedom from the consequences of sin, only by ceasing from sinning. I learn this from what I have learned of the Gospel. Did Jesus go about seeking to procure his own death, that the world might benefit by it? No. Did he know that such would be his fate? Yes. Where did he learn that it would be so? Why, yonder in the heavens, before the foundation of the earth was laid, when the great scroll on which the records of humanity were written was spread out before him, and in the light of truth the history of humanity was read.

It was known then that Jesus would thus die, that the wickedness and evil passions of mankind would cause his death. Then he was known as the "Lamb slain from before the foundation of the world." He could not be known in any other character, because his mission was to [inevitably] lead him [to] where men were vile and wicked—men who could believe they could gain some advantage by slaying the Son as they had slain the servants who preceded him. What I find fault with is that when we are told the blood of Jesus will cleanse us from all sin, without any effort on our part to do right, it is virtually a proclamation to us that we can do nothing for ourselves; and then we will sit down supinely waiting for the blood of Jesus to free us from the consequences of the wrongs we are committing—for the work that God has done or will do to take effect, when we are the authors of the wrongs that exist.

It is you and I who do wrong, and from that wrong we want to be saved. How can we be saved from it but by ceasing to do the wrong? Did Jesus say the wicked who continue to do wrong shall be saved? No. With all the power he possessed as the Son of God, and with all the glory he was heir to, he could not save the sinner in his sins. He could only bless those who hearkened to the truth he taught and ceased to do wrong. Listen to his language when he looked upon the city where Prophets had raised their warning voice again and again:—"O Jerusalem! Jerusalem! how often would I have gathered you, as a hen gathereth her chickens under her wings, but ye would not!" If he had power, why did he weep over the city devoted to ruin? Why lament over its approaching desolation? Because its inhabitants would not listen to his offers of mercy. He reviewed how often Prophets had been sent to them and [were] rejected, and how last of all the darling of the Father had been sent, whom they treated with contumely and bitter persecution; and yet he could not, with all the God-like charity and ability he possessed, save the unbelievers who still persisted in their iniquities. Who were saved? Why, those and those only who laid off their iniquities. They were the recip[i]ents of his mercy, and the only ones who could receive the blessings of the Gospel.

I wish to look at this consistently, and reflect upon it. My remarks have not been made to institute any criticism upon the opinions of others, but I wish you to look upon them reasonably, because I wish to place before you an incentive to practice virtue, cultivate charity, and live lives of truthfulness. I would be as glad as any one if I could believe and understand that my salvation was sure simply because Jesus had died. What would there be to hinder me from being happy? But I cannot believe it, and I will show you a reason why. I cannot believe it, because, if I am a liar, there cannot [be] people enough in the world [to] leave off lying to constitute me a truthful man. Suppose I were to profess religion, and day after day continued lying, what would I be? Why, I should be a liar! Although numbered among a congregation of so-called believers, and consequently one of those taught to look forward to salvation as the reward of those who simply believe in Jesus, which they blindly suppose they do by adopting the false opinions of their teachers[,] if there is any one thing in the wide region of delusion more soul-destroying than another, it is this. What difference does it make to me, though I thus believe? I am a mean man, a false man, because I am a liar; consequently, an impure man. Yet by this false religion I am taught, with all that impunity and falsehood clinging around me, and without one effort to cast it off, to aspire to a seat in mansions of perfect purity, where God reigns! "But," says one, "we must forsake our wrongs in order for the blood of Jesus to cleanse us from our sins." This is all I ask you to do. When you cease from all wrongs, I do not care what you say has cleansed you from sin; but I do not want you to believe that the blood of Jesus has cleansed you from all sin, and yet see you going down to perdition because you have continued to sin.

I want you to understand that by practising purity continually, by being righteous and holy, honest with our God and with one another,—by all means we will avoid doing evil. All is embraced in that creed that calls upon us to love our neighbour as ourselves and devote our hearts to God:—"Thou shalt love the Lord thy God with all thy heart, and with all thy might, and with all thy mind, and with all thy strength; and thy neighbor as thyself." You will love your neighbor, the man and the woman with whom you associate, as you love yourself. But who are your neighbours? All those people around us. Who acted the neighbour's part to the poor, beaten, wounded, and robbed traveler who lay by the wayside? The Samaritan who relieved his wants, dressed his wounds, and cared for him with a brother's tenderness, or the Levite and Jew who passed by on the other side and left him to perish? Was not the Samaritan the best man as evinced by the discharge of the neighbor's duty to the poor sufferer? Who were the Samaritan, the Jew, and the wounded traveler? Why, simply so many of God's children, sent into the world for the same holy purpose. Why love your neighbour as well as yourself? Because he is just as good as you are, descended from the same high parentage as the Saviour who came into the world that sinners might be saved and exalted. For whom did he die? For you and me, and not for our neighbour? No; but alike for all. He did not command his Apostles to go and preach to a few for whom he died, but to go and preach to "every creature," saying, "He that believeth and is baptized shall be saved, but he that believeth not shall be damned."

What would have been the utility or wisdom of extending their mission to all, if only a part could have been benefited by it? All were alike the objects of the Father's parental care, and were alike provided for, if they would only do that which Jesus could not do for them, and which you and I would blush to ask him to do. You could not ask him to cease lying for you, to avoid corruptions for you, to become godly, pure, holy, and righteous for you—a possession of the fullness of principles which have exalted him to immortality and endless life. No. But if we practice the same principles, they will place us in a similar position of happiness and exaltation. You may ask God to help you and strengthen you; you may invoke his blessings to be ever round about you, and the genial influence of his Spirit is waiting to be with you, to bestow upon you the blessings you lack and desire to obtain. If you do not possess it, it is because you have not prepared a place for it to dwell with you. This is what I want you to see and understand; and that God may bless you and preserve you in your departure from doing wrong, in breaking off your sins by righteousness and your iniquities by turning unto God, is my prayer in the name of Jesus. Amen.

Biographical register

This register is divided into two parts. The first section shows Lyman's wives in the order he married them, according to biographer E. Leo Lyman's chronology, with children listed below each wife. The second section gives Lyman's closest associates in alphabetical order.

Maria Louisa Tanner (1818–1906). Daughter of John Tanner and Lydia Stuart. Married Lyman Feb. 4, 1837. Mother of eight children, seven of whom lived into adulthood. Lived with her husband in Ohio, Missouri, Illinois, Utah, and California. Died in Salt Lake City.

Matilda (1836–1903). Born in Kirtland, Lake County, Ohio. Married Isaac Philo Carter, 1856, at San Bernardino, and was the mother of ten children. Died at Greenville, Beaver County, Utah.

Francis Marion (1840–1916). Born at Goodhope, McDonough County, Illinois. Married Rhoda Taylor, 1857; Clara Caroline Callister, 1869; and Susan Delilah Callister, 1884. Ordained to Quorum of Twelve Apostles in 1880, became president of the quorum in 1903. Died in Salt Lake City.

Ruth Adelia (1843–1848). Born at Shokokon, Illinois. Died at age four at Mormon Winter Quarters in what became Florence, Nebraska, while Lyman was away on a mission.

Amasa Mason Jr. (1846–1937). Born at Nauvoo, Illinois. Married Hannah Olive Felshaw, 1869. After her death, married Cynthia Wright, 1872. After her death, married Roseanna Reynolds, 1877. Died in Provo.

Maria Louisa (1849–1877). Born at Little Cottonwood, Salt Lake

County, Utah. Married William Clayton as plural wife, 1866, at age seventeen when Clayton was fifty-two. Left Clayton in 1871 and married John Smith Stredder that same year. Died at Beaver, Utah, following birth of her third child.

Lelia Deseret (1852–1904). Born at San Bernardino. Married Edwin Bartholomew, 1871, and bore five children. Often acted as spiritual medium at father's séances. Died at Fillmore.

Love Josephine (1854–1940). Born at San Bernardino. Married Hyrum Coombs, 1872, and bore six children. Supported her father and spiritualism after he left the LDS Church. For the rest of her life she drifted through a variety of religions. Died at Salt Lake City.

Agnes Hila (1857–1881). Born in San Bernardino. Married George Christian Veile and had two children. Embraced spiritualism, sometimes as medium. Died at Fillmore.

Dionetia Walker Whitney (1816–1894). Born at Dayton, Ohio. Married Micah Whitney, 1830, at age fourteen. He and their four children later died. Married Lyman 1843, but bore no children with him. Had sealing to Lyman canceled in 1886 in favor of Joseph Smith. Died at Minersville, Utah.

Caroline Ely Partridge (1827–1908). Born at Painesville, Ohio, to Edward Partridge and Lydia Clisbee. Married Amasa M. Lyman, 1844, at Nauvoo and bore five children. Left Lyman after his removal from Quorum of Twelve in 1867 and maintained only infrequent contact until his death. Had sealing to Lyman canceled in 1881 in favor of Joseph Smith. Died at Oak City, Utah.

Martha Lydia (1853–1922). Born at Salt Lake City. Married Alvin Roper and bore ten children. Had little contact with father after his expulsion from Quorum of Twelve. Died at Oak City, Utah.

Frederick Rich (1856–1911). Born at Salt Lake City. Married Ann Lovell, 1875. Had little contact with father after Lyman's expulsion from Quorum of Twelve. Died at Oak City, Utah.

Annie (1860–1921). Born at Salt Lake City shortly after Lyman departed for mission to Europe. Married William Dutson, 1878. Married Anders Anderson, 1882. Had little contact with father after his expulsion from Quorum of Twelve. Died at Oak City, Utah.

Walter Clisbee (1863–1943). Born at Fillmore. Married Sylvia Lovell, 1883, fathering three children. After Sylvia's death married Elizabeth Finlinson and fathered ten children, then three children with Lucy Halls. Died at Moab.

Harriett Jane (1866–1946). Born at Fillmore. Married John Lovell, 1883, and bore twelve children, ten who lived to adulthood. Rarely saw Lyman during his lifetime. Died at Oak City, Utah.

Eliza Maria Partridge (1820–1886). Born at Painesville, Ohio, to Edward Partridge and Lydia Clisbee. Became plural wife of Joseph Smith, April 1843. After Smith's death became plural wife of Lyman, Sept. 1844. Left Lyman after his removal from Quorum of Twelve in 1867 and had only infrequent contact with him until his death. Died at Oak City, Utah.

Don Carlos (1846–1846). Born at Winter Quarters in Florence, Nebraska, and died there four and a half months later.

Platte DeAlton (1848–1901). Born on east bank of the Platte River near Laramie, Wyoming. Married Adelia Robison, 1867; married Annie Clark as plural wife, 1878. Led Mormon pioneers through the Hole-in-the-Rock expedition. Died at Bluff, Utah.

Caroline "Carlie" Eliza (1851–1879). Born at Salt Lake City. Married Thomas Callister as his fourth plural wife, 1878. Died at Oak City, Utah, two weeks after birth of first child.

Joseph Alvin (1856–1925). Born at Salt Lake City. Married Nellie Roper, 1878, and bore thirteen children. Had little contact with Lyman after his expulsion from Quorum of Twelve. Died at Mayfield, Utah.

Lucy Zina (1860–1930). Born at Salt Lake City. Married Lemuel Redd Jr., 1883, and bore four children. Died at Oak Creek, Utah.

Cornelia Eliza Leavitt (1825–1864). Born at Warren, Ohio, to Enoch Leavitt and Lenora Snow. Married Lyman Nov. 1844 and bore two children. Suffered from illness much of her life. Died at Parowan. The Partridge family canceled her sealing to Lyman in 1881 and posthumously sealed her to Joseph Smith.

Lorenzo Snow (1851–1927). Born at San Bernardino. Left LDS Church after Lyman's expulsion from Quorum of Twelve. Married

Zuriah Rowley, 1874, and fathered six children. After her death married Alpha Easton, 1892. Died at Bloomington, California.

Henry Elias (1854–1930). Born at San Bernardino. Became disenchanted with Mormonism and moved with his brother from Utah to California in 1875. There Married Ina Cadwell, 1883, fathering five children. Died at Santa Barbara.

Paulina Eliza Phelps (1827–1912). Born at Lawrence, Illinois, to Morris Phelps and Laura Clark. Married Lyman Jan. 1846 and bore seven children. After Lyman's death when she was over fifty years old, studied obstetrics under Dr. Ellis Shipp and helped deliver more than 500 babies. Died at Parowan.

Oscar Morris (1847–1874). Born at Florence, Nebraska. Married Phoebe Madora Benson, 1869, fathering two children. Died in sawmill boiler explosion at Parowan.

Mason Roswell (1851–1866). Born at Salt Lake City. Died of accidental gunshot wound at Parowan, just before fifteenth birthday.

Clark (1853–1854). Born at Salt Lake City and died there eight months later.

Charles Rich (1857–1922). Born at Farmington, Utah. Married Barbara Alice Ward, 1876, and fathered eleven children. After her death in 1919, married Evelyn Van Noy. Died at Cowley, Wyoming.

William Horn Dame (1859–1948). Born at Farmington, Utah. Married Julia McGregor, 1888, and fathered seven children. Died at Parowan.

Solon Ezra (1863–1941). Born at Parowan. Married Luella Ward, 1884, and fathered nine children. Moved to La Grande, Oregon, in early 1900s and died there.

Laura Paulina (1865–1943). Born at Parowan. Married Porter Vander Clark, 1883, and fathered seven children. Died at Cedar City, Utah.

Priscilla Rebecca Turley (1829–1904). Born in Toronto, to Theodore Turley and Frances Kimberley. Married Lyman, Jan. 1846, and bore six children. Lyman maintained strong relationships with Priscilla's parents after his excommunication. Died at Redlands, California.

Theodore Kimberly (1853–1925). Born at San Bernardino. Married Mary Duggins, 1875, and fathered four children. Sometime after her death in 1884, he married Sarah Gould. Died at San Bernardino.

Ira Depo (1855–1917). Born at San Bernardino. Married Elizabeth Rowley, 1878, and fathered seven children. Died at Randlett, Utah.

Isaac Newton (1857–1858). Born at San Berndardino and died eleven months later, after the family returned to southern Utah.

Albert Augustus (1859–1860). Born at Salt Lake City and died just over a year later at Minersville, Utah, while Lyman was on mission to England.

Stephen Alonzo (1865–1930). Born at Fillmore. Married Ellen King, 1887, and fathered six children. Died at Logandale, Nevada.

Frances Priscilla (1868–1892). Born at Fillmore. Lyman's only child conceived after expulsion from Quorum of Twelve. Married Robert Barry, 1883, and bore four children. Died at Colton, California.

Lydia Partridge (1830–1875). Born at Painesville, Ohio, to Edward Partridge and Lydia Clisbee. Married Lyman, 1853, as his last plural wife and bore four children. Lyman was often away when these children were young; after expulsion from Quorum of Twelve he rarely saw them. Lydia probably had sealing to Lyman canceled simultaneously with sisters Caroline and Eliza. Died at Fillmore.

Edward Leo (1857–1906). Born at Salt Lake City. Married Mary Callister, 1878, and fathered ten children, six that lived to adulthood. Died of pneumonia at Oak City, Utah.

Ida Evelyn (1859–1922). Born at Salt Lake City. Married Hans Nielson, 1881, and bore nine children. Died at Blanding, Utah.

Frank Arthur (1863–1864). Born at Salt Lake City and died there seven months later.

Lydia May (1865–1906). Born at Fillmore. Married Kumen Jones, 1882, and bore ten children. Burned to death after clothes caught fire from oil lamp at Bluff, Utah.

Adams, Samuel Lorenzo (1833–1910). Born at Tipton, Staffordshire, England, to John Adams and Eleanor Danks. Married Emma Jackson in England, 1852; married Mary Ann Morgan, 1863, and Almira Jackson, 1885, both in Utah. Served mission to England with Lyman from 1860–62. Died in St. George.

Andrus, Milo (1814–1893). Born at Wilmington, New York, to Ruluf Andrus and Azuba Smith. Converted to Mormonism at age seventeen and marched to Missouri as member of Zion's Camp. Served mission to Great Britain with Lyman, 1860–62. Ordained patriarch in 1884. Died at Oxford, Idaho.

Bartholomew, Noah Willis (1808–1876). Born in Dryden, New York, to Jehiel Bartholomew and Jerusha Maltbie. Married Miranda Catlin, 1828, and fathered seven children. While crossing the plains he married Miranda's sister, Mary Catlin, who bore five children. Early settler of Fillmore and close friend to Lyman in later years. Died at Fillmore.

Benson, Ezra Taft (1811–1869). Born at Mendon, Massachusetts, to John Benson and Chloe Taft. Ordained apostle in 1846 and served with Lyman in the quorum until Lyman's 1867 expulsion. Married six wives and fathered thirty-four children. Died in Ogden.

Benson, Richard (1816–1895). Born at Wrightington, England. Son of Thomas Benson and Margaret Marsden. Married Phoebe Forrester, 1844, and shortly immigrated to America, settling in St. Louis. Lyman maintained close relationship with Benson and family for fifteen years prior to his death. Died at Parowan.

Bingham, Thomas (1824–1889). Born at Grafton, New Hampshire, to Erastus Bingham and Lucinda Gates. Married Caron H. Holladay, 1849. In 1851 helped settle San Bernardino with Lyman and Charles C. Rich, where he was key founder and owner of saw mill. Later served as bishop in Uintah County. Died in Ashley Valley, Utah.

Brannan, Samuel (1819–1889). Born in Saco, Maine, to Thomas Brannan and Mary Goodridge. In 1846, under direction of church authorities, chartered the ship *Brooklyn* and sailed from New York to San Francisco. There he associated with Lyman, who was collecting tithing from California gold fields. Died at San Diego.

Bringhurst, William (1818–1883). Born at Passyunk, Pennsylvania, to Joseph Bringhurst and Elizabeth Evans. Married two wives and fathered ten children. Served special mining mission to Las Vegas during 1850s and associated with Lyman as he journeyed between San Bernardino and Utah. Bishop of Springville from 1870 to 1883, where he died.

Brown, James Stephens (1828–1902). Born in Davidson County, North Carolina, to Daniel Brown and Elizabeth Stephens. Traveled with Lyman to Great Britain in 1860 where he served mission. Married four wives and fathered thirty-one children. Died at Salt Lake City.

Brown, John (1820–1896). Born in Castalian Springs, Tennessee, to John Brown and Martha Chapman. Married three wives and fathered numerous children. Brown and Lyman crossed the plains together in 1847 and again in 1848; served in British mission together in 1860. Later served as bishop and mayor of Pleasant Grove, where he died.

Brunson, Seymour (1799–1840). Born in Orwell, Vermont, to Reuben Brunson and Sarah Clark. Veteran of War of 1812. Joined LDS Church in 1831 and associated with Lyman on first missions. Died at Nauvoo, Illinois.

Callister, Thomas (1821–1880). Born on the Isle of Man to John Callister and Catherine Murphy. Became bishop of Fillmore and later stake president of Millard Stake, where he closely associated with Lyman. Lyman's daughter Carlie became Callister's fourth and final wife. Died at Fillmore.

Cannon, George Quayle (1827–1901). Born in Liverpool to George Cannon and Ann Quayle. Called as apostle in 1860 and oversaw British mission finances while Lyman and Charles C. Rich focused on proselytizing. Served five terms in US Congress and as editor of *Deseret News*, 1867–1882. Died at Monterey.

Carter, Isaac Philo (1829–1913). Born at Benson, Vermont, to Gideon Haden Carter and Hila Burwell. Married Matilda Lyman, oldest daughter of Amasa and Maria Louisa, 1856, and fathered ten children. One of the settlers of San Bernardino. Served as stage coach driver between Southern California and Salt Lake City. Lyman maintained close relationship with this son-in-law, who died at Heyburn, Idaho.

Chorpenning, George (1785–1857). Born at Somerset County, Pennsylvania, to John Chorpenning and Anna Ankeny. First mail contractor to operate between Utah and Southern California. Visited San Bernardino in November 1853 and soon began mail delivery on regular basis.

Clark, Daniel Porter (1824–1885). Born at Fabius, New York, to Russell Kilburn Clark and Elizabeth Towne. Married sisters Sarah Hakes, 1845, and Harriett Hakes, 1858, fathering sixteen children. Remained one of Lyman's few lifelong friends; associated together for nearly thirty years in California and later in Parowan, Utah, where Clark died.

Clift, Robert (1824–1859). Born at Gloucester, England, to Robert Clift and Elizabeth Cantle. Lieutenant in Mormon Battalion and helped settle San Bernardino, where he served for a time as sheriff. Killed by Indians while carrying mail in Nevada.

Coltrin, Zebedee (1804–1887). Born at Ovid, New York, to John Coltrin and Sarah Graham. Traveled west with Lyman in 1847 and knew him during Lyman's tenure as apostle. Died at Spanish Fork, Utah.

Cox, William James (1815–1905). Born at Nashville, Tennessee, to Archibald Cox and Francis Hill. Married at least three wives and fathered several children. Part of original pioneering group to settle San Bernardino, where he served on high council, as city coroner, water master, and stake president. Lyman continued to associate with Cox in southern Utah. Died at Beaver, Utah.

Crismon, George C. (1833–1908). Born at Jacksonville, Illinois, to Charles Crismon and Mary Hill. Married Lyman's niece Mary Louise Tanner, 1856, in San Bernardino and fathered thirteen children; married Mary Ann Foster Weiler, 1871, and fathered seven children. Died at Salt Lake City.

Crosby, William (1808–1880). Born in Knox County, Indiana, to John Jeter Crosby and Elizabeth Glenn Coleman. Married Sarah Harmon and fathered two children. Among the Mississippi Mormons, associated with Lyman in colonizing San Bernardino, where he was active in lumbering and served as bishop. Died at Kanab, Utah.

Dame, William Horne (1819–1884). Born at Farmington, New Hampshire, to Jeremiah and Susan Horne. Moved to Parowan in 1856 where he was called as stake president and later associated frequently with Lyman. In 1860 began two-year mission to England with Lyman. Died at Parowan.

Davis, Edward (1807–1859). Born at Guiltsfield, Wales, to David Davis and Elizabeth Davies. Married Elizabeth Jasper, 1827, and fathered eight children. Worked with Lyman in San Bernardino as director of flour mill. Stayed in California and died at La Puente.

Driggs, Sterling Graves (1822–1860). Born in Pennsylvania to Uriel Driggs and Hannah Ford. Crossed plains with Lyman in 1847 and was prominent member of San Bernardino community. Later settled in Parowan. Married Sarah Rodgers in Salt Lake City, 1855. Died at Parowan.

Duncan, Chapman (1812–1900). Born at Bath, New Hampshire, to John Duncan and Betsy Taylor Putnam. Sailed from New York on *Brooklyn*. After working in gold fields, joined Saints at San Bernardino. Married three wives and fathered nine children. Died at Cainesville, Utah.

Egan, Howard (1815–1878). Born at Tullamore, Ireland, to Howard Egan and Ann Meade. Associated with Lyman in Illinois and while journeying across the Great Plains. Operated Salt Lake Trading Company in Merced, California. Died at Salt Lake City.

Flake, Agnes Haley (1819–1855). Born at Richmond, North Carolina, to William Love Haley and Agnes Haley. Married James Madison Flake and journeyed to Southern California where they joined Mormons at San Bernardino. Like other "Mississippi Saints," arrived in California with slaves as part of their family group. Died at San Bernardino.

Flake, James Madison (1815–1850). Born at Lilesville, North Carolina, to Flake and Faithy Elizabeth Hannah. Married Agnes Haley, 1838, and fathered eight children. After embracing Mormonism in Mississippi, moved to Nauvoo, Illinois, and to Salt Lake Valley, then after James's death joined Mormon colony in San Bernardino. Died near San Joaquin Valley, California.

Flanigan, James Henry (1822–1851). Born in Down County, Ireland, to Daniel and Nancy Flanigan. After joining LDS Church, immigrated to Nauvoo, Illinois. Served mission to South with Lyman before mission assignment to Great Britain. Presided over Birmingham Conference. Died there from small pox.

Godbe, William Samuel (1833–1902). Born at London, to John Godbe and Sarah LaRevere. Married Mary Hampton and fathered seven children.

Later took additional wives. Became leading Utah merchant, crossing Atlantic 21 times and plains over 50 times. Chaffed under leadership of Brigham Young and became leader of Godbeite movement. Died at Salt Lake City.

Granger, Lewis Cass (1819–1890). Born at Granville, Ohio, to Ralph Granger and Hannah Spelman. Married Isabella Wilson, 1843, and fathered six children. Sometime after June 1848, immigrated to California, settling in Los Angeles. Served as legal advisor to Lyman and Rich; referred to as "a Los Angeles attorney." Died at Oroville, California.

Grouard, Benjamin Franklin (1819–1894). Born at Stratham, New Hampshire, to Francis and Sophronia Grouard. Returned to US in 1852 from mission to the Pacific Islands and settled in San Bernardino. Clashed with Mormon leadership and eventually left the church and embraced spiritualism. Died at Santa Ana.

Hakes, Weeden Vander (1800–1884). Born at Stephentown, New York, to James Hakes and Martha Adams. Married Eliza Amanda Beebe and Harriet Miller and fathered seven children. Long-time friend of Lyman during trek across the plains, in San Bernardino where he owned a shoemaking and harness shop, and later in southern Utah. Died at Mesa, Arizona.

Hamblin, Jacob (1819–1886). Born at Salem, Ohio, to Isaiah Hamblin and Daphne Haynes. Established Indian mission on Santa Clara River in 1854 and in 1876 was ordained an apostle to the Indians. He was the husband of four wives and the father of twenty-four children. Associated with Lyman at various times in southern Utah during 1850s and 1860s. Died at Pleasanton, New Mexico.

Hanks, Ebenezer Joseph (1815–1884). Born at Greenwich, New York, to Joseph Hanks and Almira Kennedy. Served in Mormon Battalion alongside his wife, Jane, one of the camp cooks. In California opened boarding house on American River and later helped colonize San Bernardino. Jane Hanks was later one of Lyman's closest spiritualist associates. Ebenezer died at Hanksville, Utah.

Harrison, Elias Lacy Thomas (1838–1900). Born at Barking, England. Became leading intellectual force behind the Godbeite movement in Utah. Followed British intellectuals who were unhappy under leadership of

Brigham Young. Excommunicated from church, remained close associate of Lyman and on good terms with church leaders. Died at Salt Lake City.

Hendricks, Josiah (1824–1895). Born at Louisville, Kentucky, to Samuel Hendricks and Rebecca Dorris. Among original colony to San Bernardino, where he worked with Lyman. After return to Utah, married Sarah Potts, 1860, and fathered fourteen children. Died at Logan, Utah.

Holladay, John Davis (1798–1862). Born at Camden, South Carolina, to Daniel Holladay and Keziah Terry. Arrived in Salt Lake in 1847 with Mississippi Saints, along with wife and five children. Moved with family to California with pioneers who colonized San Bernardino, worked closely with Lyman. In 1858 resettled in Utah County. Died at Santaquin, Utah.

Hopkins, Richard Rockwell (1821–1882). Born at Edwardsville, Illinois, to William Hector Hopkins and Frances Gardner Ruffin. Married Ruth Crandell, 1848, at St. Louis, and fathered six children. Moved with Lyman to San Bernardino, served as ward and stake clerk. Returned with family to Utah, 1857, remained close friend of Lyman. Died at Salt Lake City.

Horner, John Meirs (1821–1907). Born at New Jersey to Stacy Horner and Sarah Jonson. Sailed to San Francisco on the *Brooklyn*, established farm at southern end of San Francisco Bay. Prospered and built schools, church, mills, and contributed significantly to LDS Church in 1850s, though had to back out of promise to pay off San Bernardino debt. Died at Kukuiau, Hawaii.

Hunt, Jefferson (1803–1879). Born in Bracken County, Kentucky, to John Hunt and Martha Jenkins. In California worked often with Lyman, erected first sawmill in San Bernardino County, served in state legislature. Returned to Utah 1857 during Utah War and settled in Ogden Valley, Huntsville named after him. Died at Oxford, Idaho.

Hunter, Jesse D. (1804–1882). Born at Hopkinsville, Kentucky, to Samuel Hunter and Lydia Devinney. Worked in northern California during 1850s, knew and worked with Lyman. Never came to Utah but remained in California as Indian agent at San Luis Rey. Died at Los Angeles.

Hyde, Orson (1805–1878). Born at Oxford, Connecticut, to Nathan Hyde and Sally Thorpe. Joined church 1831, served on first high council in Kirtland, an early apostle working closely with Lyman in Quorum of Twelve. Died at Spring City, Utah.

Jackson, Alden Appolos Moore (1805–1867). Born at Rensselaerville, New York, to Jeremiah Jackson and Martha Keyes. Known as Colonel Jackson after service in Mexican-American War. Prominent in San Bernardino, serving as justice of peace and city attorney. Settled with family in St. George during early 1860s. Died at Salt Lake City.

Johnson, Luke S. (1807–1861). Born in Promfret, Vermont, to John Johnson and Elsa Jacobs. Converted to Mormonism in 1831 and a successful missionary, working with Lyman. One of original apostles chosen in 1835. Left church and was removed as apostle in 1837, later returned and traveled to Utah. Died at Salt Lake City.

Jones, Nathaniel Very (1822–1863). Born at Brighton, New York, to Samuel Jones and Lucinda Kingsley. Called on mission to England in 1858, worked closely with Lyman as mission secretary. Married five wives and fathered sixteen children. Died at Salt Lake City.

Kelly, John (1824–1905). Born at Kilmarnock, Scotland, to James Kelly and Elisabeth Wallace. Married two wives and fathered ten children. Resided with families at Fillmore where, in addition to close friendship with Lyman, was member of Seventies quorum, county assessor, treasurer and collector, town clerk, school trustee, and member of city council. Died at Fillmore.

Kelsey, Eli B. (1819–1905). Born at Portsmouth, Ohio, to Eli Kelsey and Mary Oldfield. After years of activity in Mormonism, was strongly influenced by Godbeite movement and worked closely with Lyman. Died at Salt Lake City.

Kimball, Heber Chase (1801–1868). Born at Sheldon, Vermont, to Solomon Farnham Kimball and Anna Spaulding. Ordained apostle and then member of Brigham Young's First Presidency, worked with Lyman until Amasa's removal from quorum. Married seventeen wives and fathered sixty-five children. Died at Salt Lake City.

Lawrence, Henry William (1835–1924). Born at Pickering, Ontario, Canada, to Edward Lawrence and Margaret Major. Became a leading

Utah merchant, which led to excommunication and leadership in Godbeite movement. Died at Salt Lake City.

Lytle, Andrew (1812–1870). Born at Milton, Pennsylvania, to Andrew Lytle and Sarah Davidson. Married Hannah Hull and fathered seven children. Original settler of San Bernardino, elected mayor of city. Close associate of Lyman's, lost enthusiasm for Mormonism and remained in California. Died at San Bernardino.

Mathews, William (1808–1888). Born at Pendleton, South Carolina, to Thomas Mathews and Jane McDavid. One of the "Mississippi Saints" who later went to California and was part of colonizing effort at San Bernardino, prominent serving in various civic and church roles. Died at Washington, Utah.

Matthews, Joseph (1809–1886). Born at Johnston, North Carolina, to Lazarus Matthews and Dilly Howard. Married three wives and fathered numerous children. Called to California in 1851 to settle San Bernardino, remained there until settlement was abandoned in 1857. Died at Pima, Arizona.

McBride, Reuben (1803–1891). Born at Chester, New York, to Daniel McBride and Abigal Mead. Married Mary Ann Anderson and fathered nine children. Lyman met him as a missionary in early 1830s; later served mission together in Britain in early 1860s. Settled in southern Utah, continued his association with Lyman. Died at Fillmore.

McIntyre, William Ludlow (1809–1887). Born at Middlefield, New York, to Aaron McIntyre and Clarinda Lomas. Surgeon in Mormon Battalion and doctor at San Bernardino. Returned to Utah and lived in Ogden, continued friendship with Lyman and was preached to on behalf of Godbeite movement. Died at Ogden.

Morse, Justus (1809–1887). Born at Chester, Massachusetts, to Stephen Morse and Mabel Adkins Riley. Married Eleanor Earl, 1846, and fathered one child; married Elizabeth Towne, 1834, and fathered 18 children. Settled in San Bernardino, operated saw mill. Later returned to Iowa, died at Lamoni.

Murdock, John R. (1792–1871). Born at Kortright, New York, to John Murdock Sr. and Eleanor Riggs. Married several wives and fathered numerous children. After two-year mission in Australia, returned to Utah and lived in southern colonies and associated with Lyman. Died at Beaver, Utah.

Nickerson, Freeman (1778–1847). Born at South Dennis, Massachusetts, to Eleazer Nickerson and Thankful Chase. Baptized in 1833 by Zerubbabel Snow and knew Lyman in early years when Lyman was missionary. Died at the Chariton River in Iowa.

Noyes, Henry Harrison (1825–1895). Born at Minot, Minnesota, to Eliphalet Noyes and Joanna Record. Married Mary Louisa BcBride and fathered seven children. Worked with Lyman during mission to Europe in 1860 and after settling in Fillmore. Died at Fillmore.

Partridge Jr., Edward (1833–1900). Born at Independence, Missouri, to Edward Partridge and Lydia Clisbee. Married Sarah Lucretia Clayton and fathered eight children; married Elizabeth Buxton and fathered nine. Was Lyman's brother-in-law, later bishop in southern Utah, and maintained a good relationship despite Lyman's excommunication. Died at Provo.

Penrose, Charles William (1832–1925). Born at London, to Richard Penrose and Matilda Sims. Eventually married three wives and fathered twenty-eight children. Knew Lyman well in British mission, collaborating on *Millennial Star*. Immigrated to Utah in 1861 and served as Church Historian, apostle, and member of First Presidency. Died at Salt Lake City.

Perkes, William Henry (1838–1900). Born at Dudley, England, to Henry Perkes and Charlotte Catherine Lowe. Labored in business office of British Mission headquarters in Liverpool and worked closely with Lyman. Married Mathilda Johannisson, 1875, and fathered six children. Died at Salt Lake City.

Pratt, Addison (1802–1872). Born at Winchester, New Hampshire, to Henry Pratt and Rebekah Jewell. Married Louisa Barnes, 1831, and fathered four children. Frequent missionary to Tahiti and worked with Lyman in California. Stayed in California after French colonists turned away missionaries. Died at Anaheim.

Pratt, Orson (1811–1881). Born at Hartford, New York, to Jared Pratt and Charity Dickinson. Married ten wives and fathered forty-five children.

Prominent apostle and intellectual Mormon who worked with Lyman and clashed with Brigham Young. Died at Salt Lake City.

Parley Parker Pratt (1807-1857). Born at Burlington, Otsego County, New York, to Jared Pratt and Charity Dickinson. Baptized in 1830 by Oliver Cowdery and immediately ordained elder and began service as missionary. Member of Zion's Camp and ordained apostle in 1835. Called on mission to England in 1840 to be editor and publisher of *Millennial Star*. Member of pioneer party to Great Basin, after which served mission to South Seas and South America. Was on mission to states in 1856 when murdered near Van Buren, Arkansas.

Rich, Charles C. (1809–1883). Born at Campbell, Kentucky, to Joseph Rich and Nancy O'Neal. As an apostle, Rich was Lyman's closest friend and associate. Helped colonize San Bernardino and with Lyman oversaw British mission, 1860–62. Initially called with Lyman to relocate to central Utah, but led colonizing effort to Bear Lake Region of northern Utah. Died at Paris, Idaho.

Richards, Franklin Dewey (1821–1899). Born at Richmond, Massachusetts, to Phineas Richards and Wealthy Dewey. Married ten wives and fathered twenty-four children. Called as apostle and worked with Lyman in Quorum of Twelve. Died at Ogden.

Richards, Willard (1804–1854). Born at Hopkinton, Massachusetts, to Joseph Richards and Rhoda Howe. Cousin of Brigham Young, member of Quorum of Twelve Apostles, counselor in First Presidency. Died in Salt Lake City.

Rubidoux, Louis (1796–1868). Born at St. Louis, Missouri, to Joseph Rubidoux and Catherine Rolet. Married Guadalupe Garcia and fathered nine children. Settled in California, bought Rancho de Jurupa for $1,500, combined it with the Rancho Jacinto. Worked closely with Mormons establishing San Bernardino, withdrew support after they asserted political control. Died at Riverside.

Robison, Joseph Vickory (1832–1914). Born at Clay, New York, to Joseph Robison and Lucretia Hancock. Family settled at Fillmore, planted fruit orchards. Married Martha Jane Olmstead, 1868, and fathered ten children. Served in various civic offices and was close to Lyman, 1860s–70s. Died at Fillmore.

Rockwell, Orrin Porter (1813–1878). Born at Belcher, Massachusetts, to Orin Rockwell and Sarah Witt. Married several wives and fathered numerous children. Famous as rugged frontiersman, rumored to have killed several men. Associated with Lyman on trek west and Lyman's first overland journey to California. Died at Salt Lake City.

Rollins, James Henry (1816–1899). Born at Lima, New York, to James Porter Rollins and Keziah Keturah Van Benthuysen. Married Eveline Walker, 1838, and fathered nine children; later married Hannah Hulme and fathered fourteen children. Moved family to San Bernardino and later to Minersville in Beaver County, continuing association with Lyman. Died at Lyman, Wyoming.

Savage, David Leonard (1812–1886). Born in Leeds, Ontario, Canada, to Roger Savage and Phoebe Stevens. Married four wives and fathered numerous children. Freighted between Salt Lake City and California, also carried mail. Died at Snowflake, Arizona.

Seeley, David (1819–1892). Born at Pickering, Ontario, Canada, to Justus Seelye and Mehittabil Bennett. One of original colonizers called to settle San Bernardino. Married Mary Pettit and fathered ten children. First president of San Bernardino Stake. Returned to Utah in 1858, later returned to San Bernardino, where he died.

Shearman, William Henry (1831–1892). Born in England, converted by Lyman in 1849 while traveling to California. Served mission in England, 1862, becoming president of Liverpool Conference. Prominent merchant, became unhappy with LDS Church, became leading member of Godbeite movement. Died at Salt Lake City.

Shepherd, Marcus Lafayette (1824–1904). Born in Willoughby, Ohio, to Samuel Shepherd and Roxie Lane. Married two wives and fathered seventeen children. Settled in San Bernardino in 1851 and in 1858 settled in Beaver County. Bishop and member of Beaver stake presidency. Died at Beaver, Utah.

Sirrine, George Warren (1820–1902). Born at Phillip, New York, to Isaac Sirrine and Sarah Garrison. Married Emeline Amanda Lane; after her death married Esther Ann Crismon. Sailed to California on *Brooklyn* and later assisted Lyman in milling in San Bernardino. Died at Mesa, Arizona.

Smith, George Albert (1817–1875). Born at Potsdam, New York, to John Smith and Clarissa Lyman, as Lyman's second cousin. Served with him in Quorum of Twelve Apostles. Added to Brigham Young's First Presidency in 1868. Died at Salt Lake City.

Snow, Erastus (1818–1888). Born at St. Johnsbury, Vermont, to Levi Snow and Lucina Streeter. Married several wives and fathered over two-dozen children. Traveled with Lyman across plains twice, became apostle in 1849, serving with Lyman in Quorum of Twelve. Died at Salt Lake City.

Snow, William (1806–1879). Born at St. Johnsbury, Vermont, to Levi Snow and Lucina Streeter. Married several wives and fathered numerous children. Called to "Dixie" mission in southern Utah in 1861 and associated with Lyman. Served as member of territorial legislature as probate judge and bishop of Pine Valley Ward in Washington County. Died at Pine Valley, Utah.

Snow, Zerubbabel (1809–1888). Born at St. Johnsbury, Vermont, to Levi Snow and Lucina Streeter. Lyman's first missionary companion, worked often with Lyman. Elected attorney general of Utah in 1869. Died at Salt Lake City.

Sparks, Quartus Strong (1820–1891). Born at Northampton, Massachusetts, to David Sparks and Mercy Thayer. Married Mary Holland Hamilton, 1844, and fathered five children. Family traveled to California on *Brooklyn*, worked closely with Lyman in San Bernardino. Wives left him, perhaps because he refused to return to Utah. Died at San Bernardino.

Stark, Daniel (1820–1907). Born at Windsor, Nova Scotia, Canada, to John Stark and Sarah Mann. Sailed on *Brooklyn* with wife Ann Cook and daughter, was among the Mormons who discovered gold. Joined Mormon colony in San Bernardino as successful farmer and member of city council. Died at Payson, Utah.

Stenhouse, Thomas Brown Holmes (1824–1882). Born in Dalkieth, Scotland, to George Stenhouse and Elizabeth Armstrong. Married Fanny Warn, 1850, and fathered ten children. After immigration to Utah, events led to exit from church and involvement with Godbeites. Both authored popular books on Mormons, *Rocky Mountain Saints* and *Tell It All*. Died at San Francisco.

Summe, Gilbard (1802–1867). Born in Randolph County, North Carolina, to John and Caroline Summe. Married Sarah Jackson and later pioneered in San Bernardino and Nevada. Called to Muddy Mission in 1857. Died at Harrisburg, Utah.

Swarthout, Truman Thurmon (1826–1898). Born at Huron, Ohio, to Philip Swarthout and Charity Bates. Married Mary Brain and fathered three children. Early settler of San Bernardino. Returned to Provo, in 1859, where he lived the rest of his life.

Tanner, Myron (1826–1903). Born at Bolton, New York, to John Tanner and Elizabeth Beswick. Married Mary Jane Mount, 1837, and fathered nine children; married Ann Crosby, 1866, and fathered eight children. Was Lyman's half-brother-in-law, maintained good relationship despite Lyman's removal from church. Bishop in Provo. Died at Salt Lake City.

Tanner, Nathan (1815–1910). Born in Greenwich, New York, to John Tanner and Lydia Stewart. Ordained a seventy in 1835 and filled mission to eastern states in company with Lyman, his future brother-in-law. Died at Granger, Utah.

Tanner, Sidney (1809–1895). Born at Bolton, New York to John Tanner and Lydia Stewart. Brother-in-law to Lyman. Married three wives and fathered twenty children. Participated in San Bernardino colonization 1849–57. Moved family to Beaver, Utah, served in bishopric. Died at Beaver.

Tenney, Nathan Cram (1817–1882). Born at Ontario, New York, to Meshach Tenney and Phebe Cram. Married Olive Strong, 1841, and fathered ten children. Later married two additional wives. Part of original pioneer group to settle San Bernardino. Returned to southern, continued to associate with Lyman. Died at St. Johns, Arizona.

Thomas, Preston F. (1814–1877). Born at Rockingham, North Carolina, to Daniel Thomas and Nancy Ann Morehead. Missionary with Lyman to southern states in 1848. Married four wives and fathered twenty-four children. Immigrated to Utah in 1850 and settled in Lehi. Died at Franklin, Idaho.

Tullidge, Edward William (1829–1894). Born in Weymouth, England, to John Tullidge and Elizabeth Daw. Baptized in 1848. Immigrated to Utah, clashed with orthodox practices and joined Godbeite movement. Family records list various wives and unknown number of children. Prolific author and playwright. Died at Salt Lake City.

Turley, Theodore (1801–1871). Born at Birmingham, England, to William Turley and Elizabeth Yates. Married five wives and fathered twenty-two children. Was close to son-in-law Lyman. Part of colonizing party to southern California in 1851, senior member of San Bernardino high council. In Utah settled in Beaver. Died at Beaver.

Van Cott, John (1814–1883). Born in Canaan, New York, to Losee Van Cott and Lovinia Pratt. Married Lucy Sackett and fathered several children. Oversaw Scandinavian Mission, 1859–62, corresponded often with Lyman. Died at Salt Lake City.

Wakara (d. 1855). One of the most important Indian leaders during the years of Mormon settlement in Utah Territory. Became famous as trader of stolen horses and slaves. Initially friendly, grew angry over settlers' monopolization of territory. Lyman said Wakara visited him after his death during a séance.

Wells, Daniel Hamner (1814–1891). Born at Trenton Falls, New York, to Daniel Wells and Catherine Chapin. Married several wives and fathered numerous children. Second counselor to Brigham Young 1857–77, associated with Lyman in hierarchy. Died at Salt Lake City.

Williams, Isaac Don (1799–1856). Former mountain man, traveled to Southern California under Mexico, obtained land for Chino Ranch. Offered to sell to Mormon settlers at bargain price, changed mind. Maintained cordial relations with Lyman and Rich. Married Maria Lugo, died at Chino, California.

Winner, George King (1807–1877). Born at Toms River, New Jersey, to Isaac Winner and Naomi Johnson. Married woman named Hannah, traveled together to California on *Brooklyn*. Worked with Lyman during California mission and in San Bernardino. Objected to Mormon political power. Died at La Honda, California.

Woodruff, Wilford (1807–1898). Born at Farmington, Connecticut, to Aphek Woodruff and Beulah Thompson. Married several wives and fathered many children. Ordained apostle in 1839, worked with Lyman in Quorum of Twelve. President of LDS Church from 1887. Died at San Francisco.

Young, Brigham (1801–1877). Born at Whittingham, Vermont, to John Young and Abigail Howe. Married dozens of wives, fathered some sixty children. One of original apostles of 1835, later LDS Church president. Worked closely with Lyman, whom he distrusted after San Bernardino incurred too much debt. Died at Salt Lake City.

Bibliography

Abbreviations for frequently cited sources (see full citations below)

AML	*Amasa Mason Lyman, Mormon Apostle and Apostate* by Edward Leo Lyman
CHL	Church History Library of the Church of Jesus Christ of Latter-day Saints (LDS)
D&C	Doctrine and Covenants of the LDS Church, 2013 edition
Journal History	Journal History of the Church of Jesus Christ of Latter-day Saints

Alder, Douglas D., Paula J. Goodfellow, and Ronald G. Watt. "Creating a New Alphabet for Zion: The Origin of the Deseret Alphabet." *Utah Historical Quarterly* 52, no. 3 (Summer 1984): 275–86.

Alexander, Thomas G. "Federal Authority versus Polygamic Theocracy: James B. McKean and the Mormons." *Dialogue: A Journal of Mormon Thought* 1, no. 3 (Autumn 1966): 85–100.

———. *Things in Heaven and Earth: The Life and Times of Wilford Woodruff, a Mormon Prophet*. Salt Lake City: Signature Books, 1991.

Alford, Kenneth L., ed. *Civil War Saints*. Provo: BYU Religious Studies Center, 2012.

Allen, James B., and Glen M. Leonard. *The Story of the Latter-day Saints*. Salt Lake City: Deseret Book, 1976.

Anderson, Devery S., ed. *The Development of LDS Temple Worship, 1846–2000: A Documentary History*. Salt Lake City: Signature Books, 2011.

Anderson, Devery S., and Gary James Bergera, eds. *The Nauvoo Endowment Companies, 1845–1846: A Documentary History*. Salt Lake City: Signature Books, 2005.

Anderson, Lavina Fielding, ed. *Lucy's Book: A Critical Edition of Lucy Mack Smith's Family Memoir*. Salt Lake City: Signature Books, 2001.

Arrington, Leonard J. *Brigham Young: American Moses*. New York: Alfred A. Knopf, 1985.

———. *Charles C. Rich*. Provo: Brigham Young University Press, 1974.

———. *Great Basin Kingdom: An Economic History of the Latter-day Saints, 1830–1900*. 2nd ed. Urbana: University of Illinois Press, 2005.

———. "Mississippi Mormons." *Ensign*, June 1977.

Arrington, Leonard J., and Davis Bitton. *The Mormon Experience: A History of the Latter-day Saints*. 2nd. ed. Urbana: University of Illinois Press, 1992.

Ash, Peggy Parker Throckmorton. "The Peter Wimmer, Mary Amelia Smith, and Sarah Ann Hulet Family of Parowan, Utah." Online at *Family Search*.

Atchley, Tom. "Program Will Trace History of Mission School." *Redlands Daily Facts*, Sept. 8, 2012.

Avery, Valeen Tippetts. *From Mission to Madness: Last Son of the Mormon Prophet*. Urbana: University of Illinois Press, 1998.

Ayer's American Almanac. Lowell, MA: J. C. Ayer, 1888.

Bagley, Will. *Blood of the Prophets: Brigham Young and the Massacre at Mountain Meadows*. Norman: University of Oklahoma Press, 2002.

———, ed. *The Pioneer Camp of the Saints: The 1846 and 1847 Mormon Trail Journals of Thomas Bullock*. Spokane: Arthur H. Clark, 2001.

Ballou, M. M., Esq. *Miralda: Or the Justice of Tacon. A Drama in Three Acts*. Boston: William V. Spencer, 1858.

Bancroft, Hubert Howe. *History of Utah, 1540–1886*. San Francisco: History Company, 1889.

Banks, G. Linnaeus. *Blondin: His Life and Performances*. London: Routledge, 1862.

Banner of Light. Boston, 1857–1907.

Bartlett, George C. *The Salem Seer: Reminiscences of Charles H. Foster*. New York: John W. Lovell, 1891.

Baskin, R. N. *Reminiscences of Early Utah*. Salt Lake City: By the author, 1914.

Bate, Kerry William. "Jane Hanks: Businesswoman, Spiritualist." Unpublished manuscript, MSS A798, Utah State Historical Society Library, Salt Lake City.

Bates, A. W. "Dr Kahn's Museum: Obscene Anatomy in Victorian London." *Journal of the Royal Society of Medicine* 99, no. 12 (Dec. 1999): 618–24.

———. "'Indecent and Demoralizing Representations': Public Anatomy Museums in Mid-Victorian England." *Medical History* 52, no. 1 (2008): 1–22.

Beattie, George William, and Helen Pruitt Beattie. *Heritage of the Valley: San Bernardino's First Century*. Oakland: Bio Books, 1951.

Beecher, Ronald. *Massacre along the Medicine Road: A Social History of the Indian War of 1864 in Nebraska Territory*. Caldwell, ID: Caxton Press, 1999.

Bennett, Douglas F., and James W. Woolley. "Mass Transit in the Salt Lake Valley, 1872–1960." *Utah Economic and Business Review* 37, no. 9 (Sept. 1977).

Bennett, Richard E. "Mormon Renegade: James Emmett at the Vermillion, 1846." *South Dakota History* 15 (Fall 1985): 217–33.

———. *Mormons at the Missouri: Winter Quarters, 1846–1852*. Norman: University of Oklahoma Press, 2004.

Bergera, Gary James. "'The Commencement of Great Things': The Origins, Scope, and Achievement of the Journal History of the Church." *Mormon Historical Studies* 4, no. 1 (Spring 2003): 23–39.

———. *Conflict in the Quorum: Orson Pratt, Brigham Young, Joseph Smith*. Salt Lake City: Signature Books, 2002.

Bigler, David L. *Forgotten Kingdom: The Mormon Theocracy in the American West, 1847–1896*. Spokane: Arthur H. Clark, 1998.

Bigler, David L., and Will Bagley. *Army of Israel: Mormon Battalion Narratives*. Spokane: Arthur H. Clark, 2000.

Bitton, Davis. *George Q. Cannon: A Biography*. Salt Lake City: Deseret Book, 1999.

———. "Mormonism's Encounter with Spiritualism." *Journal of Mormon History* 1 (1974): 39–50.

Bloxham, V. Ben, James R. Moss, and Larry C. Porter, eds. *Truth Will Prevail: The Rise of the Church of Jesus Christ of Latter-day Saints in the British Isles, 1837–1987*. Solihull, Engl.: LDS Church, 1987.

Bowman, Matthew. *The Mormon People: The Making of an American Faith*. New York: Random House, 2012.

Bradley, Martha Sonntag. *A History of Beaver County*. Salt Lake City: Utah State Historical Society, 1999.

———. "Joseph W. Musser: Dissenter or Fearless Crusader for Truth?" in *Differing Visions: Dissenters in Mormon History*, edited by Roger

D. Launius and Linda Thatcher. Urbana: University of Illinois Press, 1994.

Bradley, Martha Sonntag, and Mary Brown Firmage Woodward. *Four Zinas: A Story of Mothers and Daughters on the Mormon Frontier.* Salt Lake City: Signature Books, 2000.

Braude, Ann. "News from the Spirit World: A Checklist of American Spiritualist Periodicals, 1847–1900." *Proceedings of the American Antiquarian Society* 99, part 2 (Oct. 1989): 399–462.

Brewster, Rhoda Larkin, and D. Colleen Coult Perry. "A History of the Life of Elijah Larkin." Online at *Family Search.*

Brittan, Samuel B. *Man and His Relations: Illustrating the Influence of the Mind on the Body*. New York: W. A. Townsend, 1864.

Brooks, Juanita. "The Cotton Mission." *Utah Historical Quarterly* 29, no. 3 (July 1961): 201–21.

———. *The Mountain Meadows Massacre.* Norman: University of Oklahoma Press, 1962.

Brown, John. "Report, Company of 10." June 1848. Camp of Israel Schedules and Reports, 1845–1849. MS 14290, CHL.

Brown, John Jr., and James Boyd. *History of San Bernardino and Riverside Counties.* Chicago: Western Historical Association, 1922.

Brown, Lisle G. *Nauvoo Sealings, Adoptions, and Anointings: A Comprehensive Register of Persons Receiving LDS Temple Ordinances, 1841–1846.* Salt Lake City: Smith-Pettit Foundation, 2006.

Bryant, Seth L. "Reviving the Millennial Kingdom: Mormons, Morrisites, and Massacre." *John Whitmer Historical Journal* 29 (2009): 115–39.

Buchanan, James. "Proclamation—Rebellion in the Territory of Utah," Apr. 6, 1858. Online at Gerhard Peters and John T. Woolley, *American Presidency Project.*

Buchanan, Thomas C. *Black Life on the Mississippi: Slaves, Free Blacks, and the Western Steamboat World.* Chapel Hill: University of North Carolina Press, 2004.

Buerger, David John. *The Mysteries of Godliness: A History of Mormon Temple Worship.* San Francisco: Smith Research Associates, 1994.

Burrows, Edwin G., and Mike Wallace. *Gotham: A History of New York City to 1898.* New York: Oxford University Press, 1999.

Burton, Richard F. *The City of the Saints and Across the Rocky Mountains to California.* Edited by Fawn M. Brodie. New York: Alfred A. Knopf, 1963.

Bushman, Claudia L. "Edward W. Tullidge and the Women of Mormondom." *Dialogue: A Journal of Mormon Thought* 33, no. 4 (Winter 2000): 15–26.

Bushman, Richard L., with Jed Woodworth. *Joseph Smith: Rough Stone Rolling. A Cultural Biography of Mormonism's Founder*. New York: Alfred A. Knopf, 2005.

Call, Anson. Autobiography, undated reminiscence. MS 313, CHL.

Campbell, Eugene E. *Establishing Zion: The Mormon Church in the American West, 1847–1869*. Salt Lake City: Signature Books, 1988.

Cannon, Donald Q. "George Q. Cannon and the British Mission." *Brigham Young University Studies* 27, no. 1 (Winter 1987): 97–112.

Cannon, Frank J., and George L. Knapp. *Brigham Young and His Mormon Empire*. New York: Fleming H. Revell, 1913.

Carter, Kate B. *Our Pioneer Heritage*, 20 vols. Salt Lake City: Daughters of the Utah Pioneers, 1967.

———. "Pioneers of San Bernardino: The Amasa Mason Lyman Family." *Heart Throbs of the West*, 12 vols. Salt Lake City: Daughters of the Utah Pioneers, 1939–51.

Cataldo, Nick. *Images of America: San Bernardino California*. Charleston: Arcadia, 2002.

Child, Hamilton. *Gazetteer of Grafton County, New Hampshire, 1709–1886*. Syracuse: By the author, 1886.

Christensen, Scott R. *Sagwitch: Shoshone Chieftain, Mormon Elder, 1822–1887*. Logan: Utah State University Press, 1999.

Church Historian's Office. Historian's Office Journal, 1844–1870. CR 100 1, CHL.

———. History of the Church, 1839–ca. 1882. Chronological manuscript history. CR 100 102, CHL.

———. Journal History of the Church of Jesus Christ of Latter-day Saints. Chronological scrapbook of typed entries and newspaper clippings, 1830–present. CR 100 137, CHL.

Clark, James R. *Messages of the First Presidency*, 6 vols. Salt Lake City: Bookcraft, 1965–75.

Clarke, T. E. *Guide to Merthyr-Tydfil*. Merthyr-Tydfil: H. W. White, 1848.

Cleland, Robert Glass, and Juanita Brooks, eds. *A Mormon Chronicle: The Diaries of John D. Lee, 1848–1876*. San Marino: Huntington Library Press, 2003.

Collins, A. Harvey. "At the End of the Trail: The Mormon Outpost of San Bernardino Valley." *Historical Society of Southern California Annual* 11, no. 2 (1919): 65–81.

Colvin, Don F. *Nauvoo Temple: A Story of Faith*. American Fork: UT: Covenant Communications, 2002.

Compton, Todd M. *A Frontier Life: Jacob Hamblin, Explorer and Indian Missionary*. Salt Lake City: University of Utah Press, 2013.

Congressional Record. Washington, DC: Government Printing Office.

Coulter, E. Merton. *The Confederate States of America, 1861–1865,* 7 vols. Austin: University of Texas, 1978.

Cowan, Richard O., and William E. Homer. *California Saints: A 150-Year Legacy in the Golden State*. Provo: BYU Religious Studies Center, 1996.

Cowlie, Helen. *Exhibiting Animals in Nineteenth-Century Britain*. Hampshire, Eng.: Palgrave Macmillan, 2014.

Crawley, Peter. *A Descriptive Bibliography of the Mormon Church,* 3 vols. Provo: BYU Religious Studies Center, 1997–2012.

Daily Alta California. San Francisco, 1849–91.

Dalin, David G., and Charles A. Fracchia. "Forgotten Financier, Francois L. A. Pioche." *California Historical Quarterly* 53, no. 1 (Spring 1974): 17–24.

Daughters of Utah Pioneers. *An Enduring Legacy,* 12 vols. Salt Lake City: Daughters of Utah Pioneers, 1978–89.

Davis, Andrew Jackson. *The Great Harmonia: Being a Philosophical Revelation of the Natural, Spiritual, and Celestial Universe*. Boston: Benjamin B. Mussey, 1851.

———. *Mental Disorders: Or Diseases of the Brain and Nerves*. New York: American News, 1871.

———. *A Stellar Key to the Summer Land*. Boston: Colby and Rich, 1867.

De Beck, William L. *Murder Will Out: The First Step in Crime Leads to the Gallows*. Cincinnati: 1867.

Denton, William. *Radical Rhymes*. Boston: Colby and Rich, 1875.

"Deposition of Joseph W. Morgan," *Fenn vs. Bennett*. In *Congressional Record,* H.R. 44th Cong. 82 (1876): 169–72.

Derr, Jill Mulvay, et al., eds. *The First Fifty Years of Relief Society: Key Documents in Latter-day Saint Women's History*. Salt Lake City: Church Historian's Press, 2016.

Derry, Charles. "Autobiography of Charles Derry." *Journal of History* (RLDS) 4, no. 1 (Jan. 1911): 46–47, 308.

Deseret News. Salt Lake City, June 1850–present.

Dettinger, Michael D., and B. Lynn Ingram. "The Coming Megafloods." *Scientific American*, Jan. 2013, 65–71.

Dinger, John S., ed. *The Nauvoo City and High Council Minutes*. Salt Lake City: Signature Books, 2011.

Dirkmaat, Gerrit J., et al., eds. *The Joseph Smith Papers: Documents Vol. 3, Feb. 1833–Mar. 1834,* Salt Lake City: Church Historian's Press, 2014.

Doctrine and Covenants of the Church of Jesus Christ of Latter-day Saints. Salt Lake City: LDS Church, 2013.

Doyle, Sir Arthur Conan. *The History of Spiritualism,* 2 vols. London: Cassell, 1926.

Driggs, Howard R. *Driggs Family History*. Salt Lake City: By the author, 1959.

Duncan, Chapman. "Biography, 1812–1900." In *Journal of the Southern Indian Mission,* edited by Thomas D. Brown. Provo: Brigham Young University, 1952.

Egan, Howard R. *Pioneering the West, 1846 to 1878: Major Howard Egan's Diary*. Richmond, UT: Howard R. Egan Estate, 1917.

Ellin, Phyllis Minerva. "At Home with the Range: The American Cooking Stove, 1865–1920." Master's thesis, University of Pennsylvania, 1985.

English, Rebecca. "Was Albert Killed by Crohn's Disease? Prince's Death Has Been Blamed on Typhoid until Now." *Daily Mail*, Dec. 16, 2011.

Esshom, Frank. *Pioneers and Prominent Men of Utah,* 2 vols. Salt Lake City: Utah Pioneer Book, 1913.

"The Execution of Kobler." *Columbia Democrat*, Jan. 11, 1840.

Fairclough, Oliver. *The Holtes and Their Successors at Ashton Hall, 1618–1864*. Birmingham: Birmingham Museums and Art Gallery, 1984.

FamilySearch. www.familysearch.org.

Faust, Drew Gilpin. *This Republic of Suffering: Death and the American Civil War.* New York: Vintage, 2009.

Flanders, Robert Bruce. *Nauvoo: Kingdom on the Mississippi*. Urbana: University of Illinois Press, 1965.

Fluhman, J. Spencer. *"A Peculiar People": Anti-Mormonism and the Making of Religion in Nineteenth-Century America*. Chapel Hill: University of North Carolina Press, 2012.

Fotheringham, Shirley, ed. and comp. *William Fotheringham: History of His Life and Labors*. N.p.: privately printed, 1977.

Fowler, Orson Squire. *Science of Life: Its Principles, Faculties, Organs, Temperaments*. New York: National, 1870.

Fox, Henry Clay, ed. *Memoirs of Wayne County and the City of Richmond, Indiana,* 2 vols. Madison: Western Historical Association, 2012.

Frank Leslie's Illustrated Newspaper. New York, 1852–1922.

Frazer, Robert W., ed. "Lovell's Report on the Cahuilla Indians, 1854." *Journal of San Diego History* 22, no. 1 (Winter 1976): 4–10.

Freeman, Ron. *Life and Times of William Jordan Flake, 1839–1932*. Hurricane, UT: 2011.

Geertsen, Jeff, ed. "The Journal of Peter Christian Geertsen," trans. Richard L. Jensen and Ulla Christensen. Online at *Family Genealogy Pages*.

Gentry, Leland H., and Todd M. Compton. *Fire and Sword: A History of the Latter-day Saints in Northern Missouri, 1836–39*. Salt Lake City: Greg Kofford Books, 2010.

Gibbs, Josiah F. *The Mountain Meadows Massacre*. Salt Lake City: Tribune Company, 1910.

Gilbert, Bil. *Westering Man: The Life of Joseph Walker*. Norman: University of Oklahoma Press, 1985.

Givens, Terryl L., and Matthew J. Grow. *Parley P. Pratt: The Apostle Paul of Mormonism*. New York: Oxford University Press, 2011.

Godfrey, Matthew C., et al., eds. *The Joseph Smith Papers: Documents Vol. 2, July 1831–Jan. 1833*. Salt Lake City: Church Historian's Press, 2013.

Goodrich, S. G. *History of All Nations, from the Earliest Periods to the Present Time*. Auburn, NY: Derby and Miller, 1852.

Goodridge, Paul F. *William Brockman Bankhead: Speaker of the House of Representatives, United States Congress, 1936–1940*. New York: Page Publishing, 2015.

Gordon, Sarah Barringer. *The Mormon Question: Polygamy and Constitutional Conflict in Nineteenth-Century America*. Chapel Hill: University of North Carolina Press, 2002.

Goss, Charles Frederic. *Cincinnati: The Queen City, 1788–1912,* 4 vols. Cincinnati: Clarke, 1912.

Grant, Bryan J. "The Church in the British Isles." In *Encyclopedia of Mormonism*, edited by Daniel H. Ludlow. New York: Macmillan, 1992, 228.

Grant, Ulysses S. "Third Annual Message," Dec. 4, 1871. Online at Gerhard Peters and John T. Woolley, *American Presidency Project*.

Greene, Evan M. Diaries, 1833–52. MS 1442, CHL.

Grow, Matthew J., and Ronald W. Walker. *The Prophet and the Reformer: The Letters of Brigham Young & Thomas L. Kane*. New York: Oxford University Press, 2015.

Guinn, James Miller. *A History of California and an Extended History of Los Angeles and Environs*, vol. 1. Los Angeles: Historic Record Co., 1915.

Gunn, John C. *Gunn's New Family Physician: Or Home Book of Health*, rev. and enl. New York: Moore, Wilstach and Baldwin, 1868.

Hansen, Judith W., and Norma Lundberg, comps. *Marriages in Utah Territory, 1850–1884*. Salt Lake City: Utah Genealogical Association, 1998.

Hansen, Klaus J. *Quest for Empire: The Political Kingdom of God and the Council of Fifty in Mormon History*. East Lansing: Michigan State University Press, 1967.

Hansen, Wealthy Lucile. "History of Elijah Hiett Maxfield," undated typescript. Online at *Family Search*.

Harding, Stephen S. "Message of the Governor of Utah to the Territorial Legislature." Washington, DC: Government Printing Office, 1863.

Harline, Paula Kelly. *The Polygamous Wives Writing Club: From the Diaries of Mormon Pioneer Women*. New York: Oxford University Press, 2014.

Harper, Charles A. Diary, Apr.–Aug. 1847. MS 1152, CHL.

Harrison, James T. Papers, 1770–1896. Wilson Library, University of North Carolina at Chapel Hill.

Hartley, William G. "Mormons and Early Iowa History (1838 to 1858): Eight Distinct Connections." *Annals of Iowa* 59 (Summer 2000), 217–60.

Hartshorn, Leon R. "Philip De La Mare, Pioneer Industrialist." Master's thesis, Brigham Young University, 1959.

Hatch, John P., ed. *Danish Apostle: The Diaries of Anthon H. Lund, 1890–1921*. Salt Lake City: Signature Books, 2006.

Hedges, Andrew H., et al., eds. *The Joseph Smith Papers: Journals Vol. 3, May 1843–June 1844*. Salt Lake City: Church Historian's Press, 2015.

Hefner, Loretta L. "The Apostasy of Amasa Mason Lyman." Master's thesis, University of Utah, 1977.

Heller, Luther L. "A Study of the Utah Newspaper War, 1870–1900." Master's thesis, Brigham Young University, 1966.
Hemenway, Abby Maria, ed. *Vermont Historical Gazetteer: A Magazine Embracing a History of Each Town,* 3 vols. Burlington: By the author, 1871.
Henrie, Mary Lyman. *The Edward Leo Lyman & Mary Miranda Callister Lyman Family*. Salt Lake City: Matthew J. Lyman, 1984.
Historical Record. Salt Lake City, 1890.
Historical Sketch of the Town of Boston. Boston: Edward L. Mitchell, 1861.
History of Erie County, Pennsylvania. Chicago: Warner, Beers and Co., 1884.
"History of Steam Navigation in the United States." *Report of the Agencies of Transportation*. Washington, DC: Department of the Interior, 1883.
Hogan, Mervin B., comp. and ed. "The Founding Minutes of Nauvoo Lodge." In Papers, 1833–1996. MS 0241, Special Collections, Marriott Library, University of Utah, Salt Lake City.
Holladay, Fred. "Pioneer Mail Carrier." *San Bernardino Sun*, Sept. 6, 1987.
Holliday, J. S. *The World Rushed In: The California Gold Rush Experience*. Norman: University of Oklahoma Press, 2002.
Homer, Michael W. *Joseph's Temples: The Dynamic Relationship between Mormonism and Freemasonry*. Salt Lake City: University of Utah Press, 2014.
The Hub. New York: Trade News Publishing, 1904.
Hyde, Myrtle Stevens. *Orson Hyde: The Olive Branch of Israel.* Salt Lake City: Agreka Books, 2000.
Jackson, Donald, and Mary Lee Spence, eds. *The Expeditions of John Charles Fremont,* 3 vols. Chicago: University of Illinois Press, 1970–84.
Jackson, James R. *History of Littleton, New Hampshire,* 3 vols. Cambridge, MA: University Press, 1905.
Jensen, Marlin K. "Remarks at the Dedication of the Church History Library," June 20, 2009. Online at *BYU Religious Studies Center*.
Jensen, Richard E. "The Pawnee Mission, 1834–1846." *Nebraska History* 75 (Winter 1994): 301–10.
Jensen, Richard L. "From Denmark to Manti: One Man's Experience." *Ensign*, Jan. 1980.
Jensen, Richard L., and Malcolm R. Thorp, eds. *Mormons in Early Victorian Britain*. Salt Lake City: University of Utah Press, 1989.

Jenson, Andrew. *Church Chronology: A Record of Important Events Pertaining to the History of the Church of Jesus Christ of Latter-day Saints*. Salt Lake City: Deseret News, 1914.

———. *History of the Scandinavian Mission*. Salt Lake City: Deseret News Press, 1927.

———. *Latter-day Saint Biographical Encyclopedia,* 4 vols. Salt Lake City: Jenson History, 1920.

Johnson, Benjamin F. *My Life's Review: The Autobiography of Benjamin F. Johnson*. Edited by Lyndon W. Cook. Provo: Grandin Book, 1997.

Johnson, Melvin C. *Polygamy on the Pedernales: Lyman Wight's Mormon Villages in Antebellum Texas, 1845 to 1858*. Logan: Utah State University Press, 2006.

Jorgensen, Lynne Watkins. "John Hyde, Jr., Mormon Renegade." *Journal of Mormon History* 17 (Spring 1991): 120–44.

Journal of Discourses. London and Liverpool: LDS Booksellers Depot, 1854–86.

The Juvenile Instructor. Salt Lake City, 1866–1929.

Kenney, Scott G., ed. *Wilford Woodruff's Journal,* 9 vols. Midvale, UT: Signature Books, 1983–85.

Kidd, Robert. *Vocal Culture and Elocution: With Numerous Exercises in Reading and Speaking*. Cincinnati: Sargent, Wilson & Hinkle, 1857.

Kimball, Stanley B. *Heber C. Kimball: Mormon Patriarch and Pioneer*. Urbana: University of Illinois Press, 1981.

———. *Historic Resource Study: Mormon Pioneer National Historic Trail*. Washington, DC: National Park Service, 1991.

———. *Historic Sites and Markers along the Mormon and Other Great Western Trails*. Urbana: University of Illinois Press, 1988.

Knowles, James Sheridan. *Virginius. A Tragedy in Five Acts*. New York: John Douglas, 1848.

Lancaster, Dennis R. "Dixie Wine." Master's thesis, Brigham Young University, 1972.

Landon, Michael N. "'A Shrine to the Whole Church': The History of the St. George Tabernacle." *Mormon Historical Studies* 12, no. 1 (Spring 2011): 124–46.

Lapp, Rudolph M. *Blacks in Gold Rush California*. New Haven: Yale University Press, 1995.

Larson, Andrew Karl. *Erastus Snow: The Life of a Missionary and Pioneer for the Early Mormon Church*. Salt Lake City: University of Utah Press, 1971.

Launius, Roger D. *Zion's Camp: Expedition to Missouri, 1834*. Independence, MO: Herald House, 1984.

LDS Church. "Mormon Pioneer Overland Travel, 1847–1868." Online at Church History, *Church of Jesus Christ of Latter-day Saints.*

Lech, Steve. *Pioneers of Riverside County: The Spanish, Mexican, and Early American Periods*. Charleston, SC: History Press, 2012.

Leonard, Glen M. *Nauvoo: A Place of Peace, a People of Promise*. Salt Lake City: Deseret Book, 2002.

Lindsay, John S. *The Mormons and the Theatre: Or the History of Theatricals in Utah*. Salt Lake City: By the author, 1905.

Los Angeles Star. Los Angeles, California, 1851–64.

Lovell, Maria. *Ingomar the Barbarian. A Play in Five Acts*. Boston: Walter H. Balur, 1896.

Lyman, Albert R. *Amasa Mason Lyman: Trailblazer and Pioneer from the Atlantic to the Pacific*. Delta, UT: 1957.

Lyman, Amasa M. "Autobiography, 1856." In the Historian's Office Histories of the Twelve, 1856–1861. CR 100 93, CHL.

Lyman Collection, Amasa M., 1832–1877. MS 829, CHL.

Lyman, Edward Leo. *Amasa Mason Lyman, Mormon Apostle and Apostate: A Study in Dedication*. Salt Lake City: University of Utah Press, 2009.

———. *The Overland Journey from Utah to California: Wagon Travel from the City of Saints to the City of Angels*. Las Vegas: University of Nevada Press, 2004.

———. *San Bernardino: The Rise and Fall of a California Community*. Salt Lake City: Signature Books, 1996.

Lyman, Edward Leo, and Linda King Newell. *A History of Millard County*. Salt Lake City: Utah State Historical Society, 1999.

Lyman, Edward Leo, et al., eds. *No Place to Call Home: The 1807–1857 Life Writings of Caroline Barnes Crosby, Chronicler of Outlying Mormon Communities*. Logan: Utah State University Press, 2005.

Lyman, Leo, and Larry Reese. *The Arduous Road: Salt Lake to Los Angeles, the Most Difficult Wagon Road in American History*. Victorville, CA: Lyman Historical Research, 2001.

Lyman, Francis M. "My First Mission." *The Contributor*, July 1896, 528–36.

Lyman, Melvin A. *Amasa Mason Lyman, Pioneer*. Delta, UT: 1957.

Lyman Papers, Paulina Phelps, 1839–1884. MS 22808, CHL.

Lythgoe, Dennis L. "Negro Slavery in Utah." *Utah Historical Quarterly* 39, no. 1 (Winter 1971): 40–54.

MacKinnon, William P. *At Sword's Point, Part 1: A Documentary History of the Utah War to 1858*. Norman, OK: Arthur H. Clark, 2008.

Madsen, Brigham D. *The Shoshoni Frontier and the Bear River Massacre*. Salt Lake City: University of Utah Press, 1985.

Major, Jill C. "Artworks in the Celestial Room of the First Nauvoo Temple." *Brigham Young University Studies* 41, no. 2 (2002): 47–69.

"Marine Disasters." *Seaman's Friend: The Sailor's Magazine,* New York, 1860.

Maryatt, Horace. *A Residence in Jutland, the Danish Isles, and Copenhagen*. London: John Murray, 1860.

Maxwell, John Gary. *The Civil War Years in Utah: The Kingdom of God and the Territory That Did Not Fight*. Norman: University of Oklahoma Press, 2016.

McBride, Matthew. *A House for the Most High: The Story of the Original Nauvoo Temple*. Salt Lake City: Greg Kofford Books, 2006.

McBride Journals, Reuben A., 1860–1862, 1867. MS 8198, CHL.

McPherson, James M. *Battle Cry of Freedom: The Civil War Era*. New York: Oxford University Press, 1988.

———. *Crossroads of Freedom: Antietam*. New York: Oxford University Press, 2002.

Medium and Daybreak. London, 1870–1895.

Merchants' Magazine and Commercial Review, 1850.

Merkley, Aird G., ed. *Monuments to Courage: A History of Beaver County*. Beaver: Daughters of Utah Pioneers, 1948.

Merrill, Irene Webb. "Biography of Edward Mil Webb." Territorial Statehouse Museum, Fillmore, Utah. Excerpted online at *Family Search*.

Minutes of the Apostles of the Church of Jesus Christ of Latter-day Saints, 1835–1951, 4 vols. Salt Lake City: 2013.

"Minutes of the School of the Prophets, 1870–1874," photocopy of typescript. In Leonard J. Arrington Papers, 1839–1999, USU_LJAHA 001, Special Collections and Archives, Merrill-Cazier Library, Utah State University.

Mississippi Company. "Report," May 1848. Camp of Israel Schedules and Reports, 1845–1849, in CHL.

Moore, Michael. "Felipe Alvitre is Hanged Twice and Dave Brown is Lynched Once with a Used Rope." *San Leandro Patch*, Jan. 12, 2013.

Mortimer, Dic. *Cardiff: The Biography*. Gloucester: Amberley, 2014.
Morton, Julius Sterling, et al. *Illustrated History of Nebraska,* 3 vols. Lincoln: Western Publishing and Engraving, 1913.
Nagel, Paul C. *John Quincy Adams: A Public Life, a Private Life*. Cambridge: Harvard University Press, 1997.
Neilson, Reid L., and Fred E. Woods, eds. *Go Ye into All the World: The Growth & Development of Mormon Missionary Work*. Provo: BYU Religious Studies Center, 2012.
Nevada State Journal. Reno, 1870–1983.
New York Times. New York City, 1851–present.
Ogle, Maureen. "All the Modern Conveniences: American Household Plumbing, 1840–1870." Ph.D. diss. Ames: Iowa State University, 1992.
Orton, Chad M., ed. *The Journals of George Q. Cannon: Hawaiian Mission, 1850–1854*. Salt Lake City: Deseret Book, 2014.
Owens, Kenneth N. *Gold Rush Saints: California Mormons and the Great Rush for Riches*. Spokane: Arthur H. Clark, 2004.
Pace, D. Gene. "Changing Patterns of Mormon Financial Administration: Traveling Bishops, Regional Bishops, and Bishop's Agents, 1851–88." *Brigham Young University Studies* 23, no. 2 (1983): 183–86.
Palmer, Chuck. "Historians Make Room for a Landmark Hotel." *San Bernardino County Sun*, Aug. 18, 1985.
Park, Benjamin E. "Developing a Historical Conscience: Wilford Woodruff and the Preservation of Church History." In *Preserving the History of the Latter-day Saints*, edited by Richard E. Turley Jr. and Steven C. Harper. Provo: BYU Religious Studies Center, 2010, 115–34. .
Parshall, Ardis E. "'Pursue, Retake, & Punish': The 1857 Santa Clara Ambush." *Utah Historical Quarterly* 73, no. 1 (Winter 2005): 64–86.
Partridge, Scott H., ed. *Eliza Maria Partridge Journal*. Provo: Grandin Book, 2003.
Perrin, Joseph. *Manchester Handbook: An Authentic Account of the Place and People*. Manchester: Hale and Roworth, 1857.
Peterson, John A. "Warren Stone Snow, a Man In Between: The Biography of a Mormon Defender." Master's thesis, Brigham Young University, 1985.
Peterson, Paul H. "An Historical Analysis of the Word of Wisdom." Master's thesis, Brigham Young University, 1972.

———. "The Mormon Reformation of 1856–1857: The Rhetoric and the Reality." *Journal of Mormon History* 15 (1989): 59–87.

Piepenbring, Dan. "For Man and Beast." *The Paris Review*. Blog post, May 13, 2014, online at *Paris Review*.

Pierson, George Wilson. *Tocqueville in America*. Baltimore: Johns Hopkins University Press, 1996.

Platt, Lyman D. "Early Branches of the Church of Jesus Christ of Latter-day Saints, 1830–1850," online at *Mormon Historic Sites*.

Powell, Alan Kent, ed. *Utah History Encyclopedia*. Salt Lake City: University of Utah Press, 1994.

Powell, E. J. *History of the Smithfield Club from 1798–1900*. London: Smithfield Club, 1902.

Powers, L. G. *Third Biennial Report of the Bureau of Labor Statistics of the State of Minnesota, 1891–1892*. Minneapolis: Harrison & Smith, 1893.

Pratt Family Papers, Addison, 1830–1931. USU_COLL MSS 228b, Special Collections and Archives, Merrill-Cazier Library.

Pratt, Parley P. *Autobiography of Parley Parker Pratt*. Chicago: Law, King, and Law, 1888.

———. *History of the Late Persecution Inflicted by the State of Missouri upon the Mormons*. Mexico, NY: Oswego County Democrat, 1840.

Quinn, D. Michael. "Latter-day Saint Prayer Circles." *Brigham Young University Studies* 19, no. 1 (Fall 1978): 79–105.

———. *The Mormon Hierarchy: Extensions of Power*. Salt Lake City: Signature Books, 1997.

———. *The Mormon Hierarchy: Origins of Power*. Salt Lake City: Signature Books, 1994.

Radke, Andrea G. "We Also Marched: The Women and Children of Zion's Camp, 1834." *Brigham Young University Studies* 39, no. 1 (2000): 146–65.

Raymond, Robert. "Council Bluffs, 1846–1852." Online at *RootsWeb*.

Reeve, W. Paul. *Religion of a Different Color: Race and the Mormon Struggle for Whiteness*. New York: Oxford University Press, 2015.

Reeve, W. Paul, and Ardis E. Parshall, eds. *Mormonism: A Historical Encyclopedia*. Santa Barbara: ABC–CLIO, 2010.

Reeves, Theda Grant. Reminiscences as told to Joseph Hyrum Grant Jr., typescript. Lathrop, MO, Nov. 26, 1904, copy in author's possession.

"Register of Elias H. Blackburn's LDS Records under His Bishopric, 1851–59, 1882–87." L. Tom Perry Special Collections, Brigham Young University, Provo.

Religio-Philosophical Journal. Chicago, 1865–1905.

Remy, Jules, and Julius Brenchley. *A Journey to Great Salt Lake City,* 2 vols. London: W. Jeffs, 1861.

Reports of the Inspectors of Prisons. City Document No. 49, June–July 1858. Boston: Board of Aldermen, 1858.

Rich Collection, Charles C., 1832–1908. MS 889, CHL.

Richards Family Collection, 1837–1961. MS 1215, CHL.

Richards, Morgan Jr. "Autobiography." Rpt. in Greg Christensen, *Kaysville & Kiel.* Kaysville, UT: By the author, 2011.

Richards Papers, Willard, 1821–1854. MS 1490, CHL.

Ricks, Nathaniel R., ed. *"My Candid Opinion": The Sandwich Islands Diaries of Joseph F. Smith, 1856–1857.* Salt Lake City: Smith-Pettit Foundation, 2011.

Ritner, Robert K. *The Joseph Smith Papyri: A Complete Edition.* Salt Lake City: Signature Books, 2013.

Roberts, Allen Dale. *Salt Lake City's Historic Architecture.* Charleston: Arcadia Publishing, 2012.

Robinson, Alvaretta, ed. *They Answered the Call: A History of Minersville, Utah.* Minersville: Centennial Committee, 1962.

Robinson, John W., and David Money Harris. *San Bernardino Mountain Trails,* rev. ed. Birmingham, AL: Wilderness Press, 2004.

Rogers, Jedediah S., ed. *The Council of Fifty: A Documentary History.* Salt Lake City: Signature Books, 2014.

"Royal Bank." *Bankers' Magazine and Statistical Register*, Nov. 1860.

Rutt, Christian L. *History of Buchanan County and the City of St. Joseph.* Chicago: Biographical Publishing, 1904.

Sacramento Daily Union. Sacramento, California, 1851–1994.

Salt Lake Herald. Salt Lake City, 1870–1920.

Salt Lake Tribune. Salt Lake City, 1871–present.

Sangamo Journal. Springfield, Illinois, 1831–1853.

Scherer, Mark A. *The Journey of a People,* vol. 2: The Era of Reorganization, 1844–1946. Independence, MO: Community of Christ Seminary Press, 2013.

Schindler, Harold. *Orrin Porter Rockwell: Man of God, Son of Thunder.* Salt Lake City: University of Utah Press, 1966.

Scholten, Jacqueline. "A Look into Black History in San Bernardino." *Coyote Chronicle*, Feb. 17, 2012.

Shaw, Steven. *San Bernardino*. Postcard History Series. San Francisco: Arcadia, 2007.

Sheeres, Janet Sjaarda. "From the Dikes to the Desert: The First Dutch Mormons in Utah in the Last Half of the 1800s." *Utah Historical Quarterly* 74, no. 2 (Spring 2006): 114–30.

Shepard, William, and H. Michael Marquardt. *Lost Apostles: Forgotten Members of Mormonism's Original Quorum of Twelve*. Salt Lake City: Signature Books, 2014.

Sheriff, Carol. *The Artificial River: The Erie Canal and the Paradox of Progress, 1817–1862*. New York: Hill and Wang, 1996.

Sillito, John R., ed. *History's Apprentice: The Diaries of B. H. Roberts*. Salt Lake City: Signature Books, 2004.

Sloan, Edward L., ed. *Gazeteer of Utah and Salt Lake City Directory*. Salt Lake City: Salt Lake Herald, 1874.

Smith Papers, George A., 1834–1877. MS 1322. CHL.

Smith, George D., ed. *An Intimate Chronicle: The Journals of William Clayton*. Salt Lake City: Signature Books, 1995.

———. *Nauvoo Polygamy: "... But we Called It Celestial Marriage,"* rev. ed. Salt Lake City: Signature Books, 2011.

Snow Journals, Erastus, 1835–1851, 1856–1857. MS 1329, CHL.

Somers, Amos Newton. *History of Lancaster, New Hampshire*. Concord, NH: Rumford Press, 1899.

Sonoma County Journal. Petaluma, California, 1856–1864.

Sorenson, David L. "Biography of Hans Olaus Sorenson," online at *Ancestry*.

Spearman, C. F. "The Wreck of the Yankee Blade." *Journal of San Diego History* 59, no. 2 (Apr. 1959).

Spencer, Deloy J. "The Utah Black Hawk War, 1865–1871." Master's thesis, Utah State University, 1969.

Squire, Peverill. *The Evolution of American Legislatures*. Ann Arbor: University of Michigan Press, 2012.

Staker, Mark Lyman. *Hearken, O Ye People: The Historical Setting of Joseph Smith's Ohio Revelations*. Salt Lake City: Greg Kofford Books, 2010.

Stamper, Anita A., and Jill Condra. *Clothing through American History: The Civil War through the Gilded Age*. Santa Barbara: Greenwood, 2011.

Stansbury, Howard. *Exploration and Survey of the Valley of the Great Salt Lake of Utah Including a Reconnaissance of a New Route through the Rocky Mountains*. Philadelphia: Lippincott, Grambo, 1852.

Starley, James. "Journal of James Starley." *Utah Historical Quarterly* 9, no. 3 (July 1941): 169–78.

Stenhouse, T.B.H. *Rocky Mountain Saints: A Full and Complete History of the Mormons*. New York: D. Appleton, 1873.

Stenhouse, Mrs. T.B.H. *Tell It All: The Story of a Life's Experience in Mormonism*. Hartford, CT: A. D. Worthington, 1875.

Taylor, George J. "Inventory of the George J. Taylor Papers." Accn 1454, J. Willard Marriott Digital Library, University of Utah.

Taysom, Stephen C. *Shakers, Mormons, and Religious Worlds: Conflicting Visions, Contested Boundaries*. Bloomington: Indiana University Press, 2011.

Tenney, Janice W., and Paul A. Tenney. *Nathan Cram Tenney, 1817–1882*. Apple Valley, CA: By the authors, 2007.

Thiriot, Amy Tanner. "Hark (Lay) Wales: A Slave in Zion," online at *Keepapitchinin*.

Thomas, Daniel H. "Preston Thomas: 1814–1877, a Biography." Unpublished typescript, 1970, CHL.

———. "Preston Thomas: His Life and Travels." Unpublished typescript, 1942. MS 1928, CHL.

Timbs, John. *Curiosities of London: Exhibiting the Most Rare and Remarkable Objects of Interest in the Metropolis*. London: David Bogue, 1855.

Times and Seasons. Nauvoo, Illinois, Nov. 1839–Feb. 1846.

"Translation and Historicity of the Book of Abraham." Gospel Topics, online at *Church of Jesus Christ of Latter-day Saints*, originally published 2014.

Treadwell and Pell. *Catalogue, with Full Description of Agricultural and Horticultural Implements and Machinery*. New York: 1859.

Tullidge, Edward W. *History of Salt Lake City*. Salt Lake City: Star Printing, 1886.

———. *Tullidge's Histories*. Salt Lake City: Juvenile Instructor Press, 1889.

———. *The Women of Mormondom*. New York: Tullidge and Crandall, 1877.

Tullidge's Quarterly Magazine. Salt Lake City, 1880–85.

Turley, Richard E. Jr., and Brittany A. Chapman, eds. *Women of Faith in the Latter Days*, 3 vols. Salt Lake City: Deseret Book, 2011–14.

Turner, John G. *Brigham Young: Pioneer Prophet*. Cambridge: Harvard University Press, 2012.

Twain, Mark. *Innocents Abroad, or the New Pilgrim's Progress*. Hartford: American Publishing, 1869.

Tyler, Daniel. *A Concise History of the Mormon Battalion in the Mexican War, 1846–1847*. Washington, DC: By the author, 1881.

Tyler, Josiah. *Livingstone Lost and Found, or Africa and its Explorers*. Hartford: Mutual Publishing, 1873.

Van Wagoner, Richard S., ed. *The Complete Discourses of Brigham Young*, 5 vols. Salt Lake City: Smith-Pettit Foundation, 2009.

———. "Sarah M. Pratt: The Shaping of an Apostate." *Dialogue: A Journal of Mormon Thought* 19, no. 2 (Summer 1986): 69–99.

———. *Sidney Rigdon: A Portrait of Religious Excess*. Salt Lake City: Signature Books, 1994.

Vogel, Dan, ed. *History of Joseph Smith and the Church of Jesus Christ of Latter-day Saints: A Source and Text-Critical Edition*, 8 vols. Salt Lake City: Smith-Pettit Foundation, 2015.

Vogel, Dan, and Scott C. Dunn. "The Tongue of Angels: Glossolalia among Mormonism's Founders." *Journal of Mormon History* 19, no. 2 (Fall 1993): 1–34.

Von Kotzebue, Augustus. *Pizarro: The Spaniards in Peru, or the Death of Rolla. A Tragedy in Five Acts*. London: R. Phillips, 1799.

Waite, Mrs. C. V. *The Mormon Prophet and His Harem, or an Authentic History of Brigham Young, His Numerous Wives and Children*. New York: Hurd and Houghton, 1866.

Wakeley, Arthur C., ed. *Omaha: The Gate City and Douglas County Nebraska*. Chicago: S. J. Clark, 1917.

Walker, Kyle R. *William B. Smith: In the Shadow of a Prophet*. Salt Lake City: Greg Kofford Books, 2015.

Walker, Ronald W. "The Liberal Institute: A Case Study in National Assimilation." *Dialogue: A Journal of Mormon Thought* 10, no. 4 (Autumn 1977): 74–85.

———. *Wayward Saints: The Social and Religious Protests of the Godbeites against Brigham Young*. Provo: Brigham Young University Press, 2009.

Walker, Ronald W., et al. *Massacre at Mountain Meadows*. New York: Oxford University Press, 2008.

Walters, Ronald G. *American Reformers: 1815–1860*, rev. ed. New York: Hill and Wang, 1997.

Watson, Elden J. "The Nauvoo Tabernacle." *Brigham Young University Studies* 19, no. 3 (Spring 1979): 416–21.

Watt, Ronald G. *The Mormon Passage of George D. Watt: First British Convert, Scribe for Zion*. Logan: Utah State University Press, 2009.

Webster, Noah. *American Dictionary of the English Language*. San Francisco: Foundation for American Christian Education, 1980.

Weeks, Joseph D. *Report on the Statistics of Wages in Manufacturing Industries*. Washington, DC: US Census Office, 1886.

Weisberg, Barbara. *Talking to the Dead: Kate and Maggie Fox and the Rise of Spiritualism*. New York: HarperCollins, 2004.

Wells, David Ames. *Natural Philosophy, for the use of Schools, Academies, and Private Students,* 5th ed. New York: Ivison & Phinney, 1858.

"Welsh Mormon History." Online at the Center for Family History and Genealogy, *BYU Family History Portal.*

Western Law Journal. Cincinnati, 1847.

Wheatley, Henry B. *London Past and Present: Its History, Associations, and Traditions,* 3 vols. London: John Murray, 1891.

Whitley, Colleen, ed. *Worth Their Salt, Too: More Notable but Often Unnoted Women of Utah*. Logan: Utah State University Press, 2012.

Whitney, Orson F. *History of Utah,* 4 vols. Salt Lake City: George Q. Cannon and Sons, 1892–1904.

Whitney, Orson F. *Life of Heber C. Kimball, an Apostle: The Father and Founder of the British Mission*. Salt Lake City: Kimball family, 1888.

Wimmer, Ryan Elwood. "The Walker War Reconsidered." Master's thesis, Brigham Young University, 2010.

Woods, Fred E. *A Gamble in the Desert: The Mormon Mission in Las Vegas, 1855–1857*. Salt Lake City: Mormon Historic Sites Foundation, 2005.

———. "The Palawai Pioneers on the Island of Lanai." *Mormon Historical Studies* 5, no. 2 (Fall 2004): 3–35.

Young, Ann Eliza. *Wife Number Nineteen: Or the Story of a Life in Bondage, Being a Complete Exposé of Mormonism*. Hartford: Dustin, Gilman, 1876.

Young Office files, Brigham, 1832–1878. CR 1234. CHL.

Index

About the editor

Scott H. Partridge passed away in 2015 while this book was in production. He was Professor Emeritus in Business Administration at California State University–Hayward, where he taught for thirty-two years, authoring the popular *Cases in Business and Society* textbook. His MBA was from the University of Oregon, his Ph.D. in history from Harvard University. His previous works included the *Eliza Maria Partridge Journal* and "The Failure of the Kirtland Safety Society" in *BYU Studies*. He was a descendant of Amasa Lyman through Francis M. Lyman's daughter Lucy, who married George A. Partridge, himself a nephew of three of Amasa's seven wives, the sisters Caroline, Eliza, and Lydia Partridge.

"The diaries of Amasa M. Lyman, edited by his great-grandson, provide invaluable insights into the missionary efforts of early Latter-day Saints, the LDS settlements in California and southern Utah, and the development of the Godbeite New Movement. The editor's introduction provides essential details about Lyman's life and what he included in his diaries, as well as, equally important, what he left out. The later entries remind me of Wilford Woodruff's journal, often cited as essential for LDS history although Woodruff sometimes only gave farm and weather reports. Having such a reliable transcript of Lyman's diary, the significant and the banal, combined with excellent explanatory notes, simplifies research for other scholars probing all aspects of nineteenth-century Mormon history."

—**Jessie L. Embry,** retired associate director, Charles Redd Center for Western Studies; editor, *Journal of Mormon History*; author of ten books and many articles dealing with Utah history

"These journals, as they came from Amasa Lyman's own pen, provide an irresistible window into the LDS Church in its first few decades through Joseph Smith's martyrdom, the many obstacles in settling the West, and prosecution for the embrace of polygamy. Lyman records his daily activities as a ranking church leader, then as a disaffected former member, and Scott Partridge has done a masterful job in providing context and clarification for these events through his informative footnotes. This is an essential resource for historians, family members, and anyone interested in a first-hand account by someone so closely aligned with the leading elders of the church. Here we have the good, the bad, and everything in between."

—**David D. Busath,** Professor of Physiology and Biophysics, Brigham Young University; descendant of Amasa Lyman and Maria Louisa Tanner; president of the Amasa Mason Lyman Educational and Historical Society

"In these engrossing diaries, we see Amasa Mason Lyman solving problems among the church's untrained leadership and their congregants. He served as Joseph Smith's counselor in the Quorum of the Anointed, as cofounder of San Bernardino, and as president of the British Mission, among other far-flung assignments. In the 1860s he chose to associate with dissidents who emphasized Smith's axiom to 'teach them correct principles and [let them] govern themselves' over Brigham Young's authoritarian rule. All of this is detailed in Lyman's engaging trademark style."

—**Edward Leo Lyman,** retired Professor of History, California Polytechnic University and California State University–San Bernardino; author of *Amasa Mason Lyman: Mormon Apostle and Apostate* and *Political Deliverance: The Mormon Quest for Utah Statehood*

A SPECIMEN

By WILLIAM CASLON, Letter-Founder, in Chiswell-Street, LONDON.

ABCD
ABCDE
ABCDEFG
ABCDEFGHI
ABCDEFGHIJK
ABCDEFGHIJKL
ABCDEFGHIKLMN

French Cannon.

Quousque tandem abutere, Catilina, pati-
Quousque tandem

DOUBLE PICA ROMAN.

Quousque tandem abutere, Catilina, patientia nostra? quamdiu nos etiam furor iste tuus eludet? quem ad finem sese effrenata jac-
ABCDEFGHJIKLMNOP

GREAT PRIMER ROMAN.

Quousque tandem abutere, Catilina, patientia nostra? quamdiu nos etiam furor iste tuus eludet? quem ad finem sese effrenata jactabit audacia? nihilne te nocturnum præsidium palatii, nihil urbis vigiliæ, nihil timor populi, nihil con-
ABCDEFGHIJKLMNOPQRS

ENGLISH ROMAN.

Quousque tandem abutere, Catilina, patientia nostra? quamdiu nos etiam furor iste tuus eludet? quem ad finem sese effrenata jactabit audacia? nihilne te nocturnum præsidium palatii, nihil urbis vigiliæ, nihil timor populi, nihil consensus bonorum omnium, nihil hic munitissimus
ABCDEFGHIJKLMNOPQRSTVUW

PICA ROMAN.

Melium, novis rebus studentem, manu sua occidit. Fuit, fuit ista quondam in hac repub. virtus, ut viri fortes acrioribus suppliciis civem perniciosum, quam acerbissimum hostem coërcerent. Habemus enim senatusconsultum in te, Catilina, vehemens, & grave: non deest reip. consilium, neque autoritas hujus ordinis: nos, nos, dico aperte, consules desumus. De-
ABCDEFGHIJKLMNOPQRSTVUWX

Double Pica Italick.

Quousque tandem abutere, Catilina, patientia nostra? quamdiu nos etiam furor iste tuus eludet? quem ad finem sese effrenata jac-
ABCDEFGHJIKLMNO

Great Primer Italick.

Quousque tandem abutere, Catilina, patientia nostra? quamdiu nos etiam furor iste tuus eludet? quem ad finem sese effrenata jactabit audacia? nihilne te nocturnum præsidium palatii, nihil urbis vigiliæ, nihil timor populi, nihil con-
ABCDEFGHIJKLMNOPQR

English Italick.

Quousque tandem abutere, Catilina, patientia nostra? quamdiu nos etiam furor iste tuus eludet? quem ad finem sese effrenata jactabit audacia? nihilne te nocturnum præsidium palatii, nihil urbis vigiliæ, nihil timor populi, nihil consensus bonorum omnium, nihil hic munitissimus habendi se-
ABCDEFGHIJKLMNOPQRSTVU

Pica Italick.

Melium, novis rebus studentem, manu sua occidit. Fuit, fuit ista quondam in hac repub. virtus, ut viri fortes acrioribus suppliciis civem perniciosum, quam acerbissimum hostem coërcerent. Habemus enim senatusconsultum in te, Catilina, vehemens, & grave: non deest reip. consilium, neque autoritas hujus ordinis: nos, nos, dico aperte, consules desumus. Decrevit quondam senatus
ABCDEFGHIJKLMNOPQRSTVUWXYZ

Pica Black.

And be it further enacted by the Authority aforesaid, That all and every of the said Exchequer Bills to be made forth by virtue of this Act, or so many of them as shall from

Brevier Black.

Pica Gothick.

Pica Coptick.

Pica Armenian.

English Syriack.

Pica Samaritan.

Thirteenth Apostle is set in Adobe Caslon, a revival typeface based on British gunsmith and type designer William Caslon's 1734 London design. The titles and running heads are set in Neue Helvetica, a version of Swiss designer Max Miedinger's original typeface, refined by German type foundry Stempel in 1983 for digital composition. The shaded bars throughout the book represent the timeline of the diaries.